AIRBAND RADIOS

We specialist in top quality airband radios. Usually available from stock are the SIGNAL, AOR and WIN radios, probably some of the best available today. The Signal range includes the top of the range R535 which covers the entire VHF and UHF airbands without breaks, and for the more basic market the R537S. We carry the range of Yupitery radios. The WIN-108 is also usually in stock and is one of the most popular hand-held VHF scanners in use today.

AIRLINES 92

The 10th edition available late March is the established spotters favourite for coverage of the world's airline fleet listing. Every airline in the world where aircraft from light twin to wide bodies are operated. 170 countries, 1,700 airlines, 25,000 registrations. Each aircraft is listed with registration, type, c/n, p/i, and where applicable line and fleet number and name. Available as Comb Bound (ie metal lay flat binding at just **£7.50** or in a loose leaf binder at **£10.50**.

TURBO PROP AIRLINER PRODUCTION LIST

Full production and service histories of every Western built turbo prop airliner which has entered service. Each aircraft is listed by manufacturer and type in construction number sequence. Each individual entry then lists the line number (where applicable), sub-type and first flight date where known. The entry then goes on to list every registration carried by the airframe, owners and delivery dates, leases and crash or withdrawal from service dates and any other relevant information. There is a complete cross reference of registration to c/n. The publication is available in two formats: Soft back in sewn card covers at **£8.95** or in a dark green loose leaf binder at **£10.95**.

ALSO IN STOCK AT ANY TIME

We stock AVIATION BOOKS for all aspects of aviation interest by well known and small time publishers. PLASTIC KITS for the modelling enthusiast are always in stock from around 30 different manufacturers including a range of specialist vacforms and many accessories manufactured by the growing 'cottage industries' not readily available in the average model shop. We also stock what we believe to be the widest range of AVIATION POSTCARDS available in one shop in the UK – usually around 1,300 different in stock at any time. ORIGINAL COLOUR SLIDES are also available.

JET AIRLINER PRODUCTION LIST

Full production and service histories of every Western built jet airliner which has entered service. Each aircraft is listed by manufacturer and type in construction number sequence. Each individual entry then lists the line number (where applicable), sub-type and first flight date where known. The entry then goes on to list every registration carried by the airframe, owners and delivery dates, leases, crash or withdrawal from service dates and any other relevant information. There is a complete cross reference of registration to c/n. Available in Spring '92.
Price to be advised.

PISTON ENGINE AIRLINER PRODUCTION LIST

Full production and service histories of every major Western built piston engined airliner which has entered service since the end of World War II. Each aircraft is listed by manufacturer and type in construction number sequence. Each individual entry then lists the line number (where applicable), sub-type and first flight date where known. The entry then goes on to list every registration carried by the airframe and delivery dates, leases and crash or withdrawal from service dates and any other relevant information. There is a complete cross reference of registration to c/n. The publication is available in two formats: Soft back in sewn card covers at **£8.95** or in light green loose leaf binder at **£11.95**.

MILITARY AIRCRAFT SERIALS OF EUROPE

The second edition of this standard reference book is now available. Contents include military aircraft serials of 21 European countries. The 280 pages include a selection of black and white photographs and in excess of 25,000 serials. This latest edition of **Military Aircraft Serials of Europe** is available in a grey loose leaf binder at **£10.95**.

MILITARY AIRCRAFT SERIALS OF NORTH AMERICA

The third edition of this standard reference book was published in December 1991. Contents include every serial of every operational type in USAF, USN, USMC, US Army, NASA and the Canadian Armed Forces service. Listed by type, each serial is individually listed showing full fiscal serial where applicable, type/sub type, operating unit and date last noted as such. Price **£8.95**.

FREE CATALOGUE

All our goods are listed in our catalogue which can be yours absolutely free. Just write to us or ring for your copy.

We are just 10 minutes drive from Heathrow Airport, just off the M4/M25 motorways.
Bus 223 operates between Heathrow Central and West Drayton BR station, two minutes walk from the shop. *All major credit cards accepted. 24hr 'Ansaphone' service.*

The Aviation Hobby Shop

(Dept CAM), 4 HORTON PARADE, HORTON ROAD,
WEST DRAYTON, MIDDLESEX UB7 8EA
Tel: 0895 442123   Fax: 0895 421412

TOP TITLES
FOR THE ENTHUSIAST IN 1992

WORLDAIRLINE FLEETS NEWS
Published monthly, World Airline Fleets News brings you the latest news and photographs from around the world. Available as single copies or on subscription, WAF News provides an excellent photographic record of the ever changing airliner scene. A high quality PVC binder, holding 12 issues, is also available (see order form for details).

BOEING 747 – THE FIRST 20 YEARS
Details and fleet lists of all past and present Boeing 747 operators are contained in this invaluable reference book, together with a full production list providing roll-out and first flight dates. Also included is an illustrated historical background and details of construction and the numerous variants (including the 747-400), plus 16 pages of colour photographs.
SPECIAL OFFER – NOW ONLY £7-50 (was £14-95)

BIZ JET 1992
The new completely updated edition of the world's leading executive jet listing. Biz Jet covers all the world's business jets – including for each individual aircraft, registration, type, construction number, owner/operator and all previous identities.

BUCHairPORTS
Previously known as Airports for Enthusiasts, Martin Harrison's guide is essential for anyone travelling the world in pursuit of their hobby. Viewing facilities at nearly 500 airports throughout the world are detailed, with a guide to resident/visiting aircraft and photographic opportunities. Also includes 60 airport maps and a selection of colour illustrations.

BUCHair HELICOPTERS
Published in December '91, this invaluable reference title lists more than 18,000 helicopters in the same format as sister publication – Biz Jet, by registration, type, construction number and owner etc. 300 pages (including colour).

JET AIRLINER PRODUCTION LIST (new edition)
Now the standard production reference for the enthusiast, Jet Airliner Production List contains complete production details covering all western-built jet airliners – past and present. Listed in construction number order, each individual entry includes first flight and delivery dates, model number, full service history with lease, acquisition and write-off dates and all registrations and names carried by the aircraft.

TURBOPROP AIRLINER PRODUCTION LIST
Sister volume to the Jet Airliner Production List detailed above, the turboprop edition provides complete production details of all turboprop airliners – past and present. Manufacturers include Aerospatiale/Aeritalia, Armstrong Whitworth, Avro, Beech, British Aerospace, Bristol, Canadair, CASA, Convair, de Havilland Canada, Dornier, Embraer, Fairchild, Fokker, GAF, Grumman, Handley Page, HAL, IAI, Lockheed, NAMC, Nord, Saab, Saunders, Shorts and Vickers.

PISTON AIRLINER PRODUCTION LIST
As above, but featuring production lists for piston-engined aircraft. Includes: Airspeed Ambassador, ATL.98 Carvair, Avro Tudor/York, Boeing Stratocruiser, Bristol 170, Canadair C-4 Argonaut, Convair 240/340/440, Douglas C-54 Skymaster, DC-6/DC-7, Hangley Page Hermes, Lockheed L-049/749/1049/1649, Martin 202/404 and Vickers Viking.

AIRLINES '92
Published by T.H.A.S., Airlines '92 contains fleet lists for all the world's airlines in a handy portable format with optional lay-flat opening. Each airline entry includes; head office address, flight codes, fleet – by registration, type, c/n, line number and previous identity, together with individual aircraft names and lease/order details. Available in lay-flat or bound formats, Airlines '92 comes highly recommended for anyone seeking an up to date fleet list for the summer season.

1992 JET & PROPJET CORPORATE DIRECTORY

All the world's executive jet and turboprop aircraft have been combined into one fully comprehensive directory, offering a convenient and cost-effective way of keeping track of all corporate-owned aircraft; listed in country order by registration, type, c/n, registered owner and previous identity. Also includes a useful serial/cross-reference index, offering easy access to any aircraft listed in the main body when only the serial number is known.

Please add the following for postage and packing.
UK: Add 10% to the value of your order (minimum charge £1-50)
EUROPE: Add 20% (minimum charge £2-00)
OUTSIDE EUROPE (surface): Add 20% (minimum charge £2-00)
OUTSIDE EUROPE (airmail): Add 50% (minimum charge £6-00)

ORDER FORM

Airlines '92		£7-50 ☐
Jet and Propjet Corporate Directory		£10-50 ☐
Biz Jet 1992		£6-95 ☐
BUCHairPorts		£8-95 ☐
BUCHair Helicopters		£8-95 ☐
Jet Airliner Production List		£8-95 ☐
JP Airline Fleets Intl. 1992-93		£23-50 ☐
Piston Airliner Production List		£8-95 ☐
World Airline Colours Vol. 4	NOW	£6-00 ☐
Boeing 747 – The first 20 years	NOW	£7-50 ☐
Illustrated History of British European Airways	NOW	£8-00 ☐
World Airline Fleets News (single copy)		£2-75 ☐
annual subscription 12 issues	UK	£30-00 ☐

SPECIAL OFFER – SPEND £30-00 OR MORE ON BOOKS (INCLUDING SUBSCRIPTIONS TO WORLD AIRLINE FLEETS NEWS) AND RECEIVE A SET OF 112 AIRLINER POSTCARDS – WORTH £24-50 – ABSOLUTELY FREE!

AUTUMN/WINTER CATALOGUE AVAILABLE FROM SEPTEMBER '92.

How to pay: Cheques made payable to 'The Aviation Data Centre', Access or VISA credit card, Postal Order, International Money Order, Foreign Cheque payable on a UK Bank. All payments must be in pounds sterling.

Name: _____

Address: _____

_____

_____

total enclosed: £ _____ Credit Card type: _____

Card No. _____ Exp. date: _____

Send your order to:
The Aviation Data Centre, PO Box 92, Feltham, Middlesex, TW13 4SA, England.

CIVIL
Aircraft Markings

ALAN J. WRIGHT

IAN ALLAN
1942 1992
50th ANNIVERSARY

IAN ALLAN
Publishing

Contents

This forty-third edition published 1992

ISBN 0 7110 2027 2

Published by Ian Allan Ltd, Shepperton, Surrey;
and printed by Ian Allan Printing Ltd at their works
at Coombelands in Runnymede, England.

Front cover: G-BRYI, a D.H.C.8-311 Dash Eight of Bryman Airways.   *Peter R. March (PRM)*
Rear cover, bottom: G-BTPA, a BAe ATP of British Airways.   *PRM*
Rear cover, top: G-BSTJ, a D.H.82A Tiger Moth.   *PRM*

Introduction

The 'G' prefixed four letter registration system was adopted in 1919 after a short-lived spell of about three months with serial numbers beginning at K-100. Until July 1928 the UK allocations were in the G-Exxx range, but as a result of further International agreements, this series was ended at G-EBZZ, the replacement being G-Axxx. From this point the registrations were issued in a reasonably orderly manner through to G-AZZZ, reached in July 1972. There were two exceptions. To avoid possible confusion with signal codes, the G-AQxx sequence was omitted, while G-AUxx was reserved for Australian use originally. In recent years however, an individual request for a mark in the latter range has been granted by the Authorities.

Although the next logical sequence was started at G-Bxxx, it was not long before the strictly applied rules relating to aircraft registration began to be relaxed. Permission was readily given for personalised marks to be issued incorporating virtually any four letter combination, while re-registration has also become a common feature, a practice almost unheard of in the past. In this book, where this has taken place at some time, the previous UK civil identity appears in parenthesis after the owner's/operator's name. An example of this is One-Eleven G-BBMG which originally carried G-AWEJ.

Some aircraft have also been allowed to wear military markings without displaying their civil identity. In this case the serial number actually carried is shown in parenthesis after the type's name. For example Mosquito G-ASKH flies as RR299 in RAF colours. As an aid to the identification of these machines, a military conversion list is provided.

Other factors caused a sudden acceleration in the number of registrations allocated by the Civil Aviation Authority in the early 1980s. The first surge came with the discovery that it was possible to register plastic bags and other items even less likely to fly, on payment of the standard fee. This erosion of the main register was checked in early 1982 by the issue of a special sequence for such devices commencing at G-FYAA. Powered hang-gliders provided the second glut of allocations as a result of the decision that these types should be officially registered. Although a few of the early examples penetrated the normal in-sequence register, the vast majority were given marks in other special ranges, this time G-MBxx, G-MGxx, G-MJxx, G-MMxx, G-MNxx, G-MTxx, G-MVxx, G-MWxx, G-MYxx and G-MZxx. At first it was common practice for microlights to ignore the requirement to carry their official identity. However the vast majority now display their registration somewhere on the structure, the size and position depending on the dimensions of the component to which it is applied.

Throughout the UK section of this book, there are many instances where the probable base of the aircraft has been included. This is positioned at the end of the owner/operator details preceded by an oblique stroke. It must of course be borne in mind that changes do take place and that no attempt has been made to record the residents at the many private strips. The base of airline equipment has been given as the company's headquarter's airport, although frequently aircraft are outstationed for long periods.

Non-airworthy preserved aircraft are shown with a star after the type.

The three-letter codes used by airlines to prefix flight numbers are included for those carriers appearing in the book. Radio frequencies for the larger airfields/airports are also listed.

Acknowledgements

Once again thanks are extended to the Registration Department of the Civil Aviation Authority for their assistance and allowing access to their files. The comments and amendments flowing from Wal Gandy have as always proved of considerable value, while Ian Checkley, Richard Lawsey and Kenneth Nimbley also contributed useful facts. The help given by numerous airlines or their information agencies has been much appreciated. The work of A. S. Wright and C. P. Wright during the update of this edition must not go unrecorded, since without it, deadlines would probably become impossible.   **AJW**

International Civil Aircraft Markings

A2-	Botswana	P-	Korea (North)
A3-	Tonga	P2-	Papua New Guinea
A5-	Bhutan	P4-	Aruba
A6-	United Arab Emirates	PH-	Netherlands
A7-	Qatar	PJ-	Netherlands Antilles
A9-	Bahrain	PK-	Indonesia and West Irian
A40-	Oman	PP-, PT-	Brazil
AP-	Pakistan	PZ-	Surinam
B-	China/Taiwan	RDPL-	Laos
C-F, C-G	Canada	RP-	Philippine Republic
C2-	Nauru	S2-	Bangladesh
C3	Andora	S7-	Seychelles
C5-	Gambia	S9-	São Tomé
C6-	Bahamas	SE-	Sweden
C9-	Mozambique	SP-	Poland
CC-	Chile	ST-	Sudan
CCCP-*	Soviet Union	SU-	Egypt
CN-	Morocco	SX-	Greece
CP-	Bolivia	T2	Tuvalu
CS-	Portugal	T3-	Kiribati
CU-	Cuba	T7-	San Marino
CX-	Uruguay	TC-	Turkey
D-	Germany	TF-	Iceland
D2-	Angola	TG-	Guatemala
D4	Cape Verde Islands	TI-	Costa Rica
D6-	Comores Islands	TJ-	United Republic of Cameroon
DQ-	Fiji	TL-	Central African Republic
EC-	Spain	TN-	Republic of Congo (Brazzaville)
EI-	Republic of Ireland	TR-	Gabon
EL-	Liberia	TS-	Tunisia
EP-	Iran	TT-	Chad
ET-	Ethiopia	TU-	Ivory Coast
F-	France, Colonies and Protectorates	TY-	Benin
G-	United Kingdom	TZ-	Mali
H4-	Solomon Islands	V2-	Antigua
HA-	Hungarian People's Republic	V3-	Belize
HB-	Switzerland and Liechtenstein	V5-	Namibia
HC-	Ecuador	V8-	Brunei
HH-	Haiti	VH-	Australia
HI-	Dominican Republic	VN-	Vietnam
HK-	Colombia	VP-F	Falkland Islands
HL-	Korea (South)	VP-LMA/LUZ	Montserrat
HP-	Panama	VP-LVA/LZZ	Virgin Islands
HR-	Honduras	VQ-T	Turks & Caicos Islands
HS-	Thailand	VR-B	Bermuda
HV-	The Vatican	VR-C	Cayman Islands
HZ-	Saudi Arabia	VR-G	Gibraltar
I-	Italy	VR-H	Hong Kong
J2-	Djibouti	VT-	India
J3-	Grenada	XA-, XB-,	
J5-	Guinea Bissau	XC-,	Mexico
J6-	St Lucia	XT-	Burkina Faso
J7-	Dominica	XU-	Kampuchea
J8-	St Vincent	XY-, XZ-	Burma
JA-	Japan	YA-	Afghanistan
JY-	Jordan	YI-	Iraq
LN-	Norway	YJ-	Vanuatu
LV-	Argentine Republic	YK-	Syria
LX-	Luxembourg	YN-	Nicaragua
LZ-	Bulgaria	YR-	Romania
MI-	Marshall Islands	YS-	El Salvador
N-	United States of America	YU-	Yugoslavia
OB-	Peru	YV-	Venezuela
OD-	Lebanon	Z-	Zimbabwe
OE-	Austria	ZA-	Albania
OH-	Finland	ZK-	New Zealand
OK-	Czechoslovakia	ZP-	Paraguay
OO-	Belgium	ZS-	South Africa
OY-	Denmark	3A-	Monaco

3B-	Mauritius	7O-	Democratic Yemen
3C-	Equatorial Guinea	7P-	Lesotho
3D-	Swaziland	7Q-	Malawi
3X-	Guinea	7T-	Algeria
4R-	Sri Lanka	8P-	Barbados
4U	United Nations Organisation	8Q-	Maldives
4X-	Israel	8R-	Guyana
4YB	Jordanian-Iraqi Co-op Treaty	9G-	Ghana
5A-	Libya	9H-	Malta
5B-	Cyprus	9J-	Zambia
5H-	Tanzania	9K-	Kuwait
5N-	Nigeria	9L-	Sierra Leone
5R-	Malagasy Republic (Madagascar)	9M-	Malaysia
5T-	Mauritania	9N-	Nepal
5U-	Niger	9Q-	Zaire
5V-	Togo	9U-	Burundi
5W-	Western Samoa (Polynesia)	9V-	Singapore
5X-	Uganda	9XR-	Rwanda
5Y-	Kenya	9Y-	Trinidad and Tobago
6O-	Somalia		
6V-	Senegal		
6Y-	Jamaica	* Cyrillic letters for SSSR.	

Aircraft Type Designations & Abbreviations

(eg PA-28 Piper Type 28)

A.	Beagle, Auster	GY	Gardan
AA-	American Aviation, Grumman American	H	Helio
		HM.	Henri Mignet
AB	Agusta-Bell	HP.	Handley Page
AG	American General	HR.	Robin
AS	Aérospatiale	H.S.	Hawker Siddeley
A.S.	Airspeed	IL	Ilyushin
A.W.	Armstrong Whitworth	IMCO	Intermountain Manufacturing Co
B.	Blackburn, Bristol Boeing, Beagle	J.	Auster
		L.	Lockheed
BAC	British Aircraft Corporation	L.A.	Luton
BAe	British Aerospace	M.	Miles, Mooney
BAT	British Aerial Transport	MBB	Messerschmitt-Bölkow-Blohm
B.K.	British Klemm	MJ	Jurca
BN	Britten-Norman	M.S.	Morane-Saulnier
Bo	Bolkow	NA	North American
Bu	Bucker	P.	Hunting (formerly Percival), Piaggio
CAARP	Co-operative des Ateliers Aer de la Région Parisienne	PA-	Piper
		PC.	Pilatus
CCF	Canadian Car & Foundry Co	QAC	Quickie Aircraft Co
C.H.	Chrislea	R.	Rockwell
CHABA	Cambridge Hot-Air Ballooning Association	S.	Short, Sikorsky
		SA., SE, SO.	Sud-Aviation, Aérospatiale, Scottish Aviation
CLA	Comper		
CP.	Piel	SC	Short
D.	Druine	SCD	Side Cargo Door
DC-	Douglas Commercial	Soc	Society
D.H.	de Havilland	S.R.	Saunders-Roe, Stinson
D.H.C.	de Havilland Canada	ST	SOCATA
DR.	Jodel (Robin-built)	T.	Tipsy
EMB	Embraer	TB	SOCATA
EoN	Elliotts of Newbury	Tu	Tupolev
EP	Edgar Percival	UH.	United Helicopters (Hiller)
F.	Fairchild, Fokker	UTA	Union de Transports Aérien
FFA	Flug und Fahrzeugwerke AG	V.	Vickers-Armstrongs, BAC
FH	Fairchild-Hiller	V.S.	Vickers-Supermarine
G.	Grumman	WAR	War Aircraft Replicas
GA	Gulfstream American	W.S.	Westland
G.A.L.	General Aircraft	Z.	Zlin
G.C.	Globe		

9

British Civil Aircraft Registrations

Reg.	Type (†False registration)	Owner or Operator	Notes
G-EACN	BAT BK23 Bantam (K123) ★	Shuttleworth Trust/O. Warden	
G-EAGA	Sopwith Dove	R. H. Reeves	
G-EASQ	Bristol Babe (replica) (BAPC87) ★	Bomber County Museum/Hemswell	
G-EAVX	Sopwith Pup (B1807)	K. A. M. Baker	
G-EBHX	D.H.53 Humming Bird	Shuttleworth Trust/O. Warden	
G-EBIA	S.E.5A (F904)	Shuttleworth Trust/O. Warden	
G-EBIB	S.E.5A (F939) ★	Science Museum	
G-EBIC	S.E.5A (F938) ★	RAF Museum	
G-EBIR	D.H.51	Shuttleworth Trust/O. Warden	
G-EBJE	Avro 504K (E449)★	RAF Museum	
G-EBJG	Parnall Pixie III ★	Midland Aircraft Preservation Soc	
G-EBJO	ANEC II ★	Shuttleworth Trust/O. Warden	
G-EBKY	Sopwith Pup (N5180)	Shuttleworth Trust/O. Warden	
G-EBLV	D.H.60 Cirrus Moth	British Aerospace/Hatfield	
G-EBMB	Hawker Cygnet I ★	RAF Museum	
G-EBNV	English Electric Wren	Shuttleworth Trust/O. Warden	
G-EBQP	D.H.53 Humming Bird ★	Russavia Collection	
G-EBWD	D.H.60X Hermes Moth	Shuttleworth Trust/O. Warden	
G-EBYY	Cierva C.8L ★	Musée de l'Air, Paris	
G-EBZM	Avro 594 Avian IIIA ★	Greater Manchester Museum of Science & Technology	
G-EBZN	D.H.60X Moth	I. B. Grace (G-UAAP)	
G-AAAH	D.H.60G Gipsy Moth (replica) (BAPC 168) ★	Hilton Hotel/Gatwick	
G-AAAH	D.H.60G Gipsy Moth *Jason* ★	Science Museum	
G-AACN	H.P.39 Gugnunc ★	Science Museum/Wroughton	
G-AADR	D.H.60GM Moth	H. F. Moffatt	
G-AAHY	D.H.60M Moth	M. E. Vaisey	
G-AAIN	Parnall Elf II	Shuttleworth Trust/O. Warden	
G-AAMX	D.H.60GM Moth	R. J. Parkhouse	
G-AAMY	D.H.60M Moth	R. M. Brooks	
G-AAMZ	D.H.60G Moth	C. C. & J. M. Lovell	
G-AANG	Blériot XI	Shuttleworth Trust/O. Warden	
G-AANH	Deperdussin Monoplane	Shuttleworth Trust/O. Warden	
G-AANI	Blackburn Monoplane	Shuttleworth Trust/O. Warden	
G-AANJ	L.V.G.-C VI (7198/18)	Shuttleworth Trust/O. Warden	
G-AANL	D.H.60M Moth	D. & P. Ellis	
G-AANM	Bristol 96A F.2B (D7889)	Aero Vintage Ltd	
G-AANO	D.H.60GMW Moth	A. W. & M. E. Jenkins	
G-AANV	D.H.60G Moth	R. I. Souch	
G-AAOK	Curtiss Wright Travel Air 12Q	Shipping & Airlines Ltd/Biggin Hill	
G-AAOR	D.H.60G Moth (EM-01)	J. A. Pothecary/Shoreham	
G-AAPZ	Desoutter I (mod.) ★	Shuttleworth Trust/O. Warden	
G-AAUP	Klemm L.25-1A	J. I. Cooper	
G-AAVJ	D.H.60GMW Moth	R. M. Brooks	
G-AAWO	D.H.60G Gipsy Moth	N. J. W. Reid & L. A. Fenwick	
G-AAXK	Klemm L.25-1A	C. C. Russell-Vick (*stored*)	
G-AAYX	Southern Martlet	Shuttleworth Trust/O. Warden	
G-AAZP	D.H.80A Puss Moth	R. P. Williams	
G-ABAA	Avro 504K (H2311) ★	Greater Manchester Museum of Science & Technology	
G-ABAG	D.H.60G Moth	Shuttleworth Trust/O. Warden	
G-ABDW	D.H.80A Puss Moth (VH-UQB) ★	Museum of Flight/E. Fortune	
G-ABDX	D.H.60G Moth	M. D. Souch	
G-ABEE	Avro 594 Avian IVM (Sports) ★	Aeroplane Collection Ltd	
G-ABEV	D.H.60G Moth	Wessex Aviation & Transport Ltd	
G-ABLM	Cierva C.24 ★	Mosquito Aircraft Museum	
G-ABLS	D.H.80A Puss Moth	R. C. F. Bailey	
G-ABMR	Hart 2 (J9941)★	RAF Museum	
G-ABNT	Civilian C.A.C.1 Coupe	Shipping & Airlines Ltd/Biggin Hill	
G-ABNX	Redwing 2	J. Pothecary (*stored*)	
G-ABOI	Wheeler Slymph ★	Midland Air Museum	
G-ABOX	Sopwith Pup (N5195)	Museum of Army Flying/Middle Wallop	
G-ABSD	D.H.60G Moth	M. E. Vaisey	
G-ABTC	CLA.7 Swift	P. Channon (*stored*)	
G-ABUS	CLA.7 Swift	R. C. F. Bailey	

11

Notes	Reg.	Type	Owner or Operator
	G-ABUU	CLA.7 Swift	H. B. Fox
	G-ABVE	Arrow Active 2	J. D. Penrose
	G-ABWP	Spartan Arrow	R. E. Blain/Barton
	G-ABXL	Granger Archaeopteryx ★	Shuttleworth Trust/O. Warden
	G-ABZB	D.H.60G-III Moth Major	R. E. & B. A. Ogden
	G-ACAA	Bristol 96A F.2B (F4516)	Patina Ltd/Duxford
	G-ACBH	Blackburn B.2 ★	R. Coles
	G-ACCB	D.H.83 Fox Moth	E. A. Gautrey
	G-ACDA	D.H.82A Tiger Moth	R. J. Biddle
	G-ACDC	D.H.82A Tiger Moth	Tiger Club Ltd/Headcorn
	G-ACDJ	D.H.82A Tiger Moth	P. Henley & J. K. Moorhouse
	G-ACEJ	D.H.83 Fox Moth	J. I. Cooper
	G-ACET	D.H.84 Dragon	M. C. Russell
	G-ACGT	Avro 594 Avian IIIA ★	Yorkshire Light Aircraft Ltd/Leeds
	G-ACIT	D.H.84 Dragon ★	Science Museum/Wroughton
	G-ACLL	D.H.85 Leopard Moth	D. C. M. & V. M. Stiles
	G-ACMA	D.H.85 Leopard Moth	S. J. Filhol/Sherburn
	G-ACMD	D.H.82A Tiger Moth	J. A. Pothecary/Shoreham
	G-ACMN	D.H.85 Leopard Moth	H. D. Labouchere
	G-ACOJ	D.H.85 Leopard Moth	Aviation Heritage Ltd
	G-ACOL	D.H.85 Leopard Moth	M. J. Abbott
	G-ACSP	D.H.88 Comet	Saltair Ltd/Staverton
	G-ACSS	D.H.88 Comet	Shuttleworth Trust Grosvenor House/ Hatfield
	G-ACTF	CLA.7 Swift ★	Brooklands Museum of Aviation/ Weybridge
	G-ACUS	D.H.85 Leopard Moth	T. P. A. Norman/Panshanger
	G-ACUU	Cierva C.30A (HM580)★	G. S. Baker/Duxford
	G-ACUX	S.16 Scion (VH-UUP) ★	Ulster Folk & Transport Museum
	G-ACVA	Kay Gyroplane★	Glasgow Museum of Transport
	G-ACWM	Cierva C.30A ★	International Helicopter Museum/ Weston-s-Mare
	G-ACWP	Cierva C.30A (AP507) ★	Science Museum
	G-ACXB	D.H.60G-III Moth Major	I. B. Grace
	G-ACXE	B.K.L-25C Swallow	J. C. Wakeford
	G-ACYK	Spartan Cruiser III ★	Museum of Flight (front fuselage)/ E. Fortune
	G-ACZE	D.H.89A Dragon Rapide	Wessex Aviation & Transport Ltd (G-AJGS)/Henstridge
	G-ADAH	D.H.89A Dragon Rapide ★	Greater Manchester Museum of Science & Technology
	G-ADCG	D.H.82A Tiger Moth	D. A. Lowe (stored)
	G-ADEV	Avro 504K (H5199)	Shuttleworth Trust (G-ACNB)/O. Warden
	G-ADFO	Blackburn B-2 ★	R. Cole
	G-ADFV	Blackburn B-2 ★	Humberside Aircraft Preservation Soc
	G-ADGP	M.2L Hawk Speed Six	R. I. Souch
	G-ADGT	D.H.82A Tiger Moth	D. R. & Mrs M. Wood
	G-ADGV	D.H.82A Tiger Moth	K. J. Whitehead
	G-ADHA	D.H.83 Fox Moth	Wessex Aviation & Transport Ltd
	G-ADHD	D.H.60G-III Moth Major	M. E. Vaisey
	G-ADIA	D.H.82A Tiger Moth	M. F. W. B. Maunsell/Goodwood
	G-ADJJ	D.H.82A Tiger Moth	J. M. Preston
	G-ADKC	D.H.87B Hornet Moth	L. E. Day/Carlisle
	G-ADKK	D.H.87B Hornet Moth	C. P. B. Horsley & R. G. Anniss
	G-ADKL	D.H.87B Hornet Moth	A. de Cadenet
	G-ADKM	D.H.87B Hornet Moth	L. V. Mayhead
	G-ADLY	D.H.87B Hornet Moth	R. M. Brooks
	G-ADMT	D.H.87B Hornet Moth	M. A. Livett
	G-ADMW	M.2H Hawk Major (DG590) ★	Museum of Army Flying/Middle Wallop
	G-ADND	D.H.87B Hornet Moth	Shuttleworth Trust/O. Warden
	G-ADNE	D.H.87B Hornet Moth	R. Twisleton-Wykeham Fiennes/Biggin Hill
	G-ADNL	M.5 Sparrowhawk	K. D. Dunkerley
	G-ADNZ	D.H.82A Tiger Moth	C. A. Pullan
	G-ADOT	D.H.87B Hornet Moth ★	Mosquito Aircraft Museum
	G-ADPJ	B.A.C. Drone	N. H. Ponsford
	G-ADPR	P.3 Gull	Shuttleworth Trust Jean/O. Warden
	G-ADPS	B.A. Swallow 2	Wessex Aviation & Transport Ltd
	G-ADRA	Pietenpol Air Camper	A. J. Mason & R. J. Barrett
	G-ADRC	K. & S. Jungster J-1	J. J. Penney & L. R. Williams
	G-ADRG†	Mignet HM.14 (replica) (BAPC77) ★	Stratford Aircraft Collection

Notes	Reg.	Type	Owner or Operator
	G-ADRR	Aeronca C.3	D. S. Morgan
	G-ADRY†	Mignet HM.14 (replica) (BAPC29) ★	Brooklands Museum of Aviation/ Weybridge
	G-ADUR	D.H.87B Hornet Moth	Wessex Aviation & Transport Ltd
	G-ADWJ	D.H.82A Tiger Moth	C. R. Hardiman
	G-ADWO	D.H.82A Tiger Moth (BB807)	Wessex Aviation Soc
	G-ADXS	Mignet HM.14 ★	Thameside Aviation Museum/E. Tilbury
	G-ADXT	D.H.82A Tiger Moth	R. G. Hanauer/Goodwood
	G-ADYS	Aeronca C.3	B. C. Cooper
	G-AEBB	Mignet HM.14 ★	Shuttleworth Trust/O. Warden
	G-AEBJ	Blackburn B-2	British Aerospace PLC/Brough
	G-AEDB	B.A.C. Drone 2	M. C. Russell
	G-AEDT	D.H.90 Dragonfly	Wessex Aviation & Transport Ltd
	G-AEDU	D.H.90 Dragonfly	T. Norman (on rebuild)
	G-AEEG	M.3A Falcon	Skysport Engineering Ltd
	G-AEEH	Mignet HM.14 ★	RAF Museum/St Athan
	G-AEFG	Mignet HM.14 (BAPC75) ★	N. Ponsford
	G-AEFT	Aeronca C.3	C. E. Humphreys & ptnrs/Henstridge
	G-AEGV	Mignet HM.14 ★	Midland Aircraft Preservation Soc
	G-AEHM	Mignet HM.14 ★	Science Museum/Wroughton
	G-AEJZ	Mignet HM.14 (BAPC120) ★	Bomber County Museum/Hemswell
	G-AEKR	Mignet HM.14 (BAPC121) ★	S. Yorks Aviation Soc
	G-AEKV	Kronfield Drone ★	Brooklands Museum of Aviation/ Weybridge
	G-AELO	D.H.87B Hornet Moth	D. E. Wells
	G-AEML	D.H.89 Dragon Rapide	Proteus Petroleum Ltd/Goodwood
	G-AENP	Hawker Hind (K5414) (BAPC78)	Shuttleworth Trust/O. Warden
	G-AEOA	D.H.80A Puss Moth	P. & A. Wood/O. Warden
	G-AEOF†	Mignet HM.14 (BAPC22) ★	Aviodome/Schiphol, Holland
	G-AEOF	Rearwin 8500	Shipping & Airlines Ltd/Biggin Hill
	G-AEOH	Mignet HM.14 ★	Midland Air Museum
	G-AEPH	Bristol F.2B (D8096)	Shuttleworth Trust/O. Warden
	G-AERV	M.11A Whitney Straight ★	Ulster Folk & Transport Museum
	G-AESB	Aeronca C.3	D. S. & I. M. Morgan
	G-AESE	D.H.87B Hornet Moth	J. G. Green/Redhill
	G-AESZ	Chilton D.W.1	R. E. Nerou
	G-AETA	Caudron G.3 (3066) ★	RAF Museum
	G-AEUJ	M.11A Whitney Straight	R. E. Mitchell
	G-AEVS	Aeronca 100	A. J. E. Smith
	G-AEVZ	B. A. Swallow 2	J. R. H. Ealand
	G-AEXD	Aeronca 100	Mrs M. A. & R. W. Mills
	G-AEXF	P.6 Mew Gull	J. D. Penrose/Old Warden
	G-AEXT	Dart Kitten II	A. J. Hartfield
	G-AEXZ	Piper J-2 Cub	Mrs M. & J. R. Dowson/Leicester
	G-AEYY	Martin Monoplane ★	Martin Monoplane Syndicate/Hatfield
	G-AEZF	S.16 Scion 2 ★	Southend Historic Aircraft Soc
	G-AEZJ	P.10 Vega Gull	R. A. J. Spurrell/White Waltham
	G-AEZX	Bucker Bu133C Jungmeister	A. J. E. Ditheridge
	G-AFAP†	C.A.S.A. C.352L ★	Aerospace Museum/Cosford
	G-AFAX	B. A. Eagle 2	J. G. Green
	G-AFBS	M.14A Hawk Trainer ★	G. D. Durbridge-Freeman (G-AKKU)/ Duxford
	G-AFCL	B. A. Swallow 2	A. M. Dowson/O. Warden
	G-AFDO	Piper J-3F-60 Cub	R. Wald
	G-AFDX	Hanriot HD.1 (75) ★	RAF Museum
	G-AFEL	Monocoupe 90A	M. A. Hales
	G-AFFD	Percival Q-6 ★	B. D. Greenwood
	G-AFFH	Piper J-2 Cub	M. J. Honeychurch
	G-AFFI	Mignet HM.14 (replica) (BAPC76) ★	Yorkshire Air Museum/Elvington
	G-AFGC	B. A. Swallow 2	H. Plain
	G-AFGD	B. A. Swallow 2	A. T. Williams & ptnrs/Shobdon
	G-AFGE	B. A. Swallow 2	G. R. French
	G-AFGH	Chilton D.W.1.	M. L. & G. L. Joseph
	G-AFGI	Chilton D.W.1. ★	J. E. McDonald
	G-AFGM	Piper J-4A Cub Coupé	A. J. P. Marshall/Carlisle
	G-AFGZ	D.H.82A Tiger Moth	M. R. Paul (G-AMHI)
	G-AFHA	Mosscraft M.A.1. ★	C. V. Butler
	G-AFIN	Chrislea Airguard ★	Aeroplane Collection Ltd
	G-AFIU	Parker C.A.4 Parasol (LA-3 Minor) ★	Aeroplane Collection Ltd/Warmingham

Notes	Reg.	Type	Owner or Operator
	G-AFJA	Watkinson Dingbat ★	K. Woolley
	G-AFJB	Foster-Wikner G.M.1. Wicko (DR613) ★	K. Woolley
	G-AFJR	Tipsy Trainer 1	M. E. Vaisey (*Stored*)
	G-AFJV	Mosscraft MA.2	C. V. Butler
	G-AFLW	M.17 Monarch	N. I. Dalziel/Biggin Hill
	G-AFNG	D.H.94 Moth Minor	T. E. G. Buckett/White Waltham
	G-AFNI	D.H.94 Moth Minor	B. M. Welford
	G-AFOB	D.H.94 Moth Minor	Wessex Aviation & Transport Ltd
	G-AFOJ	D.H.94 Moth Minor	Mosquito Aircraft Museum
	G-AFPN	D.H.94 Moth Minor	J. W. & A. R. Davy/Carlisle
	G-AFPR	D.H.94 Moth Minor	J. A. Livett
	G-AFRZ	M.17 Monarch	R. E. Mitchell (G-AIDE)
	G-AFSC	Tipsy Trainer 1	R. V. & M. H. Smith
	G-AFSV	Chilton D.W.1A	R. Nerou
	G-AFSW	Chilton D.W.2 ★	R. I. Souch
	G-AFTA	Hawker Tomtit (K1786)	Shuttleworth Trust/O. Warden
	G-AFTN	Taylorcraft Plus C2	Leicestershire County Council Museums
	G-AFUP	Luscombe 8A Silvaire	Trust Me Airtours
	G-AFVE	D.H.82 Tiger Moth	R. J. F. Parker/Denham
	G-AFVN	Tipsy Trainer 1	W. Callow & ptnrs
	G-AFWH	Piper J-4A Cub Coupé	J. R. Edwards & D. D. Smith
	G-AFWI	D.H.82A Tiger Moth	E. Newbigin
	G-AFWT	Tipsy Trainer 1	J. S. Barker/Redhill
	G-AFYD	Luscombe 8E Silvaire	J. D. Iliffe
	G-AFYO	Stinson H.W.75	R. N. Wright
	G-AFZA	Piper J-4A Cub Coupé	J. R. Joiner & M. L. Ryan
	G-AFZE	Heath Parasol	K. C. D. St Cyrien
	G-AFZK	Luscombe 8A Silvaire	M. G. Byrnes
	G-AFZL	Porterfield CP.50	P. G. Lucas & ptnrs/White Waltham
	G-AFZN	Luscombe 8A Silvaire	A. L. Young/Henstridge
	G-AGAT	Piper J-3F-50 Cub	Wessex Aviation & Transport Ltd
	G-AGBN	G.A.L.42 Cygnet 2 ★	Museum of Flight/E. Fortune
	G-AGEG	D.H.82A Tiger Moth	T. P. A. Norman
	G-AGFT	Avia FL.3	P. A. Smith
	G-AGHY	D.H.82A Tiger Moth	P. Groves
	G-AGIV	Piper J-3C-65 Cub	P. C. & F. M. Gill
	G-AGJG	D.H.89A Dragon Rapide	M. J. & D. J. T. Miller/Duxford
	G-AGLK	Auster 5D	W. C. E. Tazewell
	G-AGMI	Luscombe 8A Silvaire	Bluegale Ltd
	G-AGNJ	D.H.82A Tiger Moth	B. P. Borsberry & ptnrs
	G-AGNV	Avro 685 York 1 (TS798) ★	Aerospace Museum/Cosford
	G-AGOH	J/1 Autocrat	Leicestershire County Council Museums
	G-AGOS	R.S.4 Desford Trainer (VZ728)	Museum of Flight/E. Fortune
	G-AGOY	M.48 Messenger 3 (U-0247)	P. A. Brooks
	G-AGPG	Avro 19 Srs 2 ★	Brenzett Aviation Museum
	G-AGPK	D.H.82A Tiger Moth	P. D. Castle
	G-AGRU	V.498 Viking 1A ★	Brooklands Museum of Aviation/Weybridge
	G-AGSH	D.H.89A Dragon Rapide 6	Venom Jet Promotions Ltd/Bournemouth
	G-AGTM	D.H.89A Dragon Rapide 6 (NF875)	Russavia Ltd
	G-AGTO	J/1 Autocrat	M. J. Barnett & D. J. T. Miller/Duxford
	G-AGTT	J/1 Autocrat	R. Farrer
	G-AGVG	J/1 Autocrat	S. J. Riddington/Leicester
	G-AGVN	J/1 Autocrat	P. A. Fitzpatrick
	G-AGVV	Piper J-3C-65 Cub	P. R. Lewis
	G-AGWE	Avro 19 Srs 2 ★	Phoenix Aviation Museum
	G-AGXN	J/1N Alpha	I. R. Walters/Cranwell
	G-AGXT	J/1N Alpha ★	Nene Valley Aircraft Museum
	G-AGXU	J/1N Alpha	R. J. Guess/Sibson
	G-AGXV	J/1 Autocrat	B. S. Dowsett
	G-AGYH	J/1N Alpha	W. R. V. Marklew
	G-AGYK	J/1 Autocrat	D. A. Smith
	G-AGYL	J/1 Autocrat ★	Military Vehicle Conservation Group/Havant
	G-AGYT	J/1N Alpha	P. J. Barrett
	G-AGYU	DH.82A Tiger Moth (DE208)	Amalgamated Investments Ltd
	G-AGYY	Ryan ST.3KR	D. S. & I. M. Morgan
	G-AGZZ	D.H.82A Tiger Moth	G. P. L. Shea-Simonds/Netheravon
	G-AHAL	J/1N Alpha	Wickenby Flying Club Ltd
	G-AHAM	J/1 Autocrat	P. J. Stock/Goodwood

Reg.	Type	Owner or Operator	Notes
G-AHAN	D.H.82A Tiger Moth	A. J. Clarry & S. F. Bancroft/Redhill	
G-AHAP	J/1 Autocrat	V. H. Bellamy	
G-AHAU	J/1 Auto\crat	B. W. Webb	
G-AHAV	J/1 Autocrat	C. J. Freeman/Headcorn	
G-AHBL	D.H.87B Hornet Moth	Dr Ursula H. Hamilton	
G-AHBM	D.H.87B Hornet Moth	P. A. & E. P. Gliddon	
G-AHCK	J/1N Alpha	Skegness Air Taxi Service Ltd	
G-AHCR	Gould-Taylorcraft Plus D Special	D. E. H. Balmford & D. R. Shepherd/ Dunkeswell	
G-AHEC	Luscombe 8A Silvaire	Luscombe EC Group	
G-AHED	D.H.89A Dragon Rapide (RL962) ★	RAF Museum Storage & Restoration Centre/Cardington	
G-AHGD	D.H.89A Dragon Rapide	R. Jones	
G-AHGW	Taylorcraft Plus D (LB375)	C. V. Butler/Coventry	
G-AHGZ	Taylorcraft Plus D	P. N.Cooke	
G-AHHH	J/1 Autocrat	H. A. Jones/Norwich	
G-AHHP	J/1N Alpha	D. J. Hutcheson (G-SIME)	
G-AHHT	J/1N Alpha	A. C. Barber & N. J. Hudson	
G-AHHU	J/1N Alpha ★	L. Groves & I. R. F. Hammond	
G-AHIP	Piper J-3C-65 Cub	R. E. Nerou/Coventry	
G-AHIZ	D.H.82A Tiger Moth	C.F.G. Flying Ltd/Cambridge	
G-AHKX	Avro 19 Srs 2	British Aerospace PLC/Woodford	
G-AHKY	Miles M.18 Series 2	Museum of Flight/E. Fortune	
G-AHLI	Auster 3	G. A. Leathers	
G-AHLK	Auster 3	E. T. Brackenbury/Leicester	
G-AHLT	D.H.82A Tiger Moth	R. C. F. Bailey	
G-AHMJ	Cierva C.30A (K4235) ★	Shuttleworth Trust/O. Warden	
G-AHMN	D.H.82A Tiger Moth (N6985)	Museum of Army Flying/Middle Wallop	
G-AHNH	Bucker Bu181 Bestmann	R. A. Anderson	
G-AHNR	Taylorcraft BC-12D	M. L. Balding & J. M. Oakins/Biggin Hill	
G-AHOO	D.H.82A Tiger Moth	G. W. Bisshopp	
G-AHRI	D.H.104 Dove 1 ★	Newark Aviation Museum	
G-AHRO	Cessna 140	R. H. Screen/Kidlington	
G-AHSA	Avro 621 Tutor (K3215)	Shuttleworth Trust/O. Warden	
G-AHSD	Taylorcraft Plus D	A. Tucker	
G-AHSO	J/1N Alpha	W. P. Miller	
G-AHSP	J/1 Autocrat	N. J. Hudson & A. C. Barber	
G-AHSS	J/1N Alpha	P. J. Wenman/Denham	
G-AHST	J/1N Alpha	C. H. Smith	
G-AHTE	P.44 Proctor V	J. G. H. Hassell (*stored*)	
G-AHTW	A.S.40 Oxford (V3388) ★	Skyfame Collection/Duxford	
G-AHUF	D.H.82A Tiger Moth	D. S. & I. M. Morgan	
G-AHUG	Taylorcraft Plus D	D. Nieman	
G-AHUI	M.38 Messenger 2A ★	Berkshire Aviation Group	
G-AHUJ	M.14A Hawk Trainer 3 (R1914)	—	
G-AHUN	Globe GC-1B Swift	A. G. Craig	
G-AHUV	D.H.82A Tiger Moth	W. G. Gordon	
G-AHVU	D.H.82A Tiger Moth (T6313)	Foley Farm Flying Group	
G-AHVV	D.H.82A Tiger Moth	R. Jones	
G-AHWJ	Taylorcraft Plus D (LB294)	Museum of Army Flying/Middle Wallop	
G-AHXE	Taylorcraft Plus D (LB312)	J. Pothecary/Shoreham	
G-AIBE	Fulmar II (N1854) ★	F.A.A. Museum/Yeovilton	
G-AIBH	J/1N Alpha	M. J. Bonnick	
G-AIBM	J/1 Autocrat	D. G. Greatrex	
G-AIBR	J/1 Autocrat	A. A. Marshall	
G-AIBW	J/1N Alpha	W. E. Bateson/Blackpool	
G-AIBX	J/1 Autocrat	Wasp Flying Group	
G-AIBY	J/1 Autocrat	D. Morris/Sherburn	
G-AICX	Luscombe 8A Silvaire	R. V. Smith/Henstridge	
G-AIDL	D.H.89A Dragon Rapide 6	Snowdon Mountain Aviation Ltd	
G-AIDS	D.H.82A Tiger Moth	K. D. Pogmore & T. Dann	
G-AIEK	M.38 Messenger 2A (RG333)	J. Buckingham	
G-AIFZ	J/1N Alpha	C. P. Humphries	
G-AIGD	J/1 Autocrat	R. B. Webber & P. K. Pike	
G-AIGF	J/1N Alpha	A. R. C. Mathie	
G-AIGM	J/1N Alpha	Wickenby Flying Club Ltd	
G-AIGT	J/1N Alpha	P. R. & J. S. Johnson	
G-AIGU	J/1N Alpha	N. K. Geddes	
G-AIIH	Piper J-3C-65 Cub	J. A. de Salis	
G-AIJI	J/1N Alpha ★	C. J. Baker	
G-AIJM	Auster J/4	N. Huxtable	
G-AIJR	Auster J/4	B. A. Harris/Halfpenny Green	

Notes	Reg.	Type	Owner or Operator
	G-AIJS	Auster J/4 ★	stored
	G-AIJT	Auster J/4 srs 100	Aberdeen Auster Flying Group
	G-AIJZ	J/1 Autocrat	stored
	G-AIKE	Auster 5	C. J. Baker
	G-AIPR	Auster J/4	MPM Flying Group/Booker
	G-AIPV	J/1 Autocrat	W. P. Miller
	G-AIPW	J/1 Autocrat	B. Hillman
	G-AIRC	J/1 Autocrat	R. C. Tebbett
	G-AIRI	D.H.82A Tiger Moth	E. R. Goodwin (stored)
	G-AIRK	D.H.82A Tiger Moth	R. C. Teverson & ptnrs
	G-AISA	Tipsy B Srs 1	J. W. Thomson & R. P. Aston
	G-AISC	Tipsy B Srs 1	Wagtail Flying Group
	G-AISS	Piper J-3C-65 Cub	K. W. Wood & F. Watson
	G-AIST	V.S.300 Spitfire IA (AR213)	Proteus Petroleum Ltd/Goodwood
	G-AISX	Piper J-3C-65 Cub	V. Luck
	G-AITB	A.S.10 Oxford (MP425) ★	Newark Air Museum
	G-AIUA	M.14A Hawk Trainer 3	P. A. Brook
	G-AIUL	D.H.89A Dragon Rapide 6	I. Jones
	G-AIXA	Taylorcraft Plus D	A. A. & M. J. Copse
	G-AIXD	D.H.82A Tiger Moth	Sark International Airways/Guernsey
	G-AIXJ	D.H.82A Tiger Moth	D. Green
	G-AIXN	Benes-Mraz M.1c Sokol	A. J. E. Smith
	G-AIYG	SNCAN Stampe SV-4B	J. F. Hopkins/Old Sarum
	G-AIYR	D.H.89A Dragon Rapide	Clacton Aero Club (1988) Ltd
	G-AIYS	D.H.85 Leopard Moth	Wessex Aviation & Transport Ltd
	G-AIZE	F.24W Argus 2 ★	RAF Museum/Henlow
	G-AIZF	D.H.82A Tiger Moth ★	stored
	G-AIZG	V.S. Walrus 1 (L2301) ★	F.A.A. Museum/Yeovilton
	G-AIZU	J/1 Autocrat	C. J. & J. G. B. Morley
	G-AIZZ	J/1 Autocrat	M. J. Murphy
	G-AJAD	Piper J-3C-65 Cub	R. A. C. Hoppenbrouwers
	G-AJAE	J/1N Alpha	M. G. Stops
	G-AJAJ	J/1N Alpha	R. B. Lawrence
	G-AJAM	J/2 Arrow	D. A. Porter
	G-AJAO	Piper J-3C-65 Cub	P. L. Jones
	G-AJAP	Luscombe 8A Silvaire	R. J. Thomas
	G-AJAS	J/1N Alpha	C. J. Baker
	G-AJCP	D.31 Turbulent	B. R. Pearson
	G-AJDW	J/1 Autocrat	D. R. Hunt
	G-AJDY	J/1 Autocrat	Truck Panels Ltd
	G-AJEB	J/1N Alpha ★	Aeroplane Collection Ltd/Warmingham
	G-AJEE	J/1 Autocrat	A. R. C. De Albanoz/Bournemouth
	G-AJEH	J/1N Alpha	J. T. Powell-Tuck
	G-AJEI	J/1N Alpha	W. P. Miller
	G-AJEM	J/1 Autocrat	J. C. Greenslade
	G-AJES	Piper J-3C-65 Cub (330485)	P. Crawford
	G-AJGJ	Auster 5 (RT486)	S. C. Challis
	G-AJHJ	Auster 5	stored
	G-AJHS	D.H.82A Tiger Moth	S. R. N. Higgins/Holland
	G-AJHU	D.H.82A Tiger Moth	M. E. R. Coghlan
	G-AJIH	J/1 Autocrat	T. Boyd & A. H. Diver
	G-AJIS	J/1N Alpha	K. J. Slattery
	G-AJIT	J/1 Kingsland Autocrat	A. J. Kay
	G-AJIU	J/1 Autocrat	W. Greenhalgh & Son Ltd/Doncaster
	G-AJIW	J/1N Alpha	N. A. Roberts
	G-AJJP	Jet Gyrodyne (XJ389) ★	Aerospace Museum/Cosford
	G-AJJS	Cessna 120	L. G. Sharkey
	G-AJJT	Cessna 120	P. M. Hallett & J. S. Robson
	G-AJJU	Luscombe 8E Silvaire	L. C. Moon
	G-AJKB	Luscombe 8E Silvaire	A. F. Hall & P. S. Hatwell/Ipswich
	G-AJOA	D.H.82A Tiger Moth (T5424)	F. P. Le Coyte
	G-AJOC	M.38 Messenger 2A ★	Ulster Folk & Transport Museum
	G-AJOE	M.38 Messenger 2A	Cotswold Aircraft Restoration Group
	G-AJON	Aeronca 7AC Champion	A. Biggs & J. L. Broad/Booker
	G-AJOV†	Sikorsky S-51 ★	Aerospace Museum/Cosford
	G-AJOZ	F.24W Argus 2 ★	Lincolnshire Aviation Museum
	G-AJPI	F.24R-41a Argus 3 (314887)	M. R. Keen/Liverpool
	G-AJPZ	J/1 Autocrat ★	Wessex Aviation Soc
	G-AJRB	J/1 Autocrat	S. C. Luck/Sywell
	G-AJRC	J/1 Autocrat	S. W. Watkins & ptnrs
	G-AJRE	J/1 Autocrat (Lycoming)	T. A. Hodges
	G-AJRH	J/1N Alpha	Leicestershire County Council Museums

Reg.	Type	Owner or Operator	Notes
G-AJRS	M.14A Hawk Trainer 3 (P6382)	Shuttleworth Trust/O. Warden	
G-AJTW	D.H.82A Tiger Moth (N6965)	J. A. Barker	
G-AJUD	J/1 Autocrat	C. L. Sawyer	
G-AJUE	J/1 Autocrat	P. H. B. Cole	
G-AJUL	J/1N Alpha	M. J. Crees	
G-AJVE	D.H.82A Tiger Moth	P. A. Layzell	
G-AJXC	Auster 5	J. E. Graves	
G-AJXV	Auster 4 (NJ695)	P. C. J. Farries/Leicester	
G-AJXY	Auster 4	G. B. Morris	
G-AJYB	J/1N Alpha	P. J. Shotbolt	
G-AKAA	Piper J-3C-65 Cub	G. J. C. Ball	
G-AKAT	M.14A Magister (T9738)	A. J. E. Smith	
G-AKAZ	Piper J-3C-65 Cub	AKAZ Group	
G-AKBM	M.38 Messenger 2A ★	Bristol Plane Preservation Unit	
G-AKBO	M.38 Messenger 2A	B. du Cros	
G-AKDN	D.H.C. 1A Chipmunk 10	M. F. Newman	
G-AKEL	M.65 Gemini 1A ★	Ulster Folk & Transport Museum	
G-AKER	M.65 Gemini 1A ★	Berkshire Aviation Group	
G-AKEZ	M.38 Messenger 2A (RG333)	P. G. Lee	
G-AKGD	M.65 Gemini 1A ★	Berkshire Aviation Group	
G-AKGE	M.65 Gemini 3C ★	Ulster Folk & Transport Museum	
G-AKHP	M.65 Gemini 1A	P. G. Lee	
G-AKHZ	M.65 Gemini 7 ★	Berkshire Aviation Group	
G-AKIB	Piper J-3C-90 Cub (480015)	M. C. Bennett	
G-AKIF	D.H.89A Dragon Rapide	Airborne Taxi Services Ltd/Booker	
G-AKIN	M.38 Messenger 2A	R. Spiller & Sons/Sywell	
G-AKIU	P.44 Proctor V	J. N. Sharman	
G-AKKB	M.65 Gemini 1A	J. Buckingham	
G-AKKH	M.65 Gemini 1A	M. C. Russell	
G-AKKR	M.14A Magister (T9707) ★	Greater Manchester Museum of Science & Technology	
G-AKKY	M.14A Hawk Trainer 3 (L6906) (BAPC44) ★	Berkshire Aviation Group/Woodley	
G-AKLW	SA.6 Sealand 1 ★	Ulster Folk & Transport Museum	
G-AKOE	D.H.89A Dragon Rapide 4	J. E. Pierce/Chirk	
G-AKOT	Auster 5 ★	C. J. Baker	
G-AKOW	Auster 5 (TJ569) ★	Museum of Army Flying/Middle Wallop	
G-AKPF	M.14A Hawk Trainer 3 (V1075)	P. A. Brook/Shoreham	
G-AKPI	Auster 5 (NJ703)	B. H. Hargrave/Doncaster	
G-AKRA	Piper J-3C-65 Cub	W. R. Savin	
G-AKSY	Auster 5	Aerofab Flying Group	
G-AKSZ	Auster 5	A. R. C. Mathie	
G-AKTH	Piper J-3C-65 Cub	A. L. Wickens	
G-AKTI	Luscombe 8A Silvaire	N. C. W. N. Lester	
G-AKTK	Aeronca 11AC Chief	N. G. Gullis	
G-AKTM	Luscombe 8F Silvaire	D. J. Christy	
G-AKTN	Luscombe 8A Silvaire	R. G. Morris	
G-AKTO	Aeronca 7AC Champion	D. C. Murray	
G-AKTP	PA-17 Vagabond	L. A. Maynard	
G-AKTR	Aeronca 7AC Champion	C. & G. Fielder	
G-AKTS	Cessna 120	J. Greenaway	
G-AKTT	Luscombe 8A Silvaire	S. J. Charters	
G-AKUE	D.H.82A Tiger Moth	D. F. Hodgkinson	
G-AKUF	Luscombe 8A Silvaire	A. G. Palmer	
G-AKUG	Luscombe 8A Silvaire	P. & L. A. Groves	
G-AKUH	Luscombe 8E Silvaire	I. M. Bower	
G-AKUI	Luscombe 8E Silvaire	M. A. Watts	
G-AKUJ	Luscombe 8E Silvaire	D. Delaney & C. L. Cooper	
G-AKUK	Luscombe 8A Silvaire	Leckhampstead Flying Group	
G-AKUL	Luscombe 8A Silvaire	E. A. Taylor	
G-AKUM	Luscombe 8F Silvaire	R. J. Willies	
G-AKUN	Piper J-3F-65 Cub	W. A. Savin	
G-AKUO	Aeronca 11AC Chief	A. C. Cassidy/White Waltham	
G-AKUP	Luscombe 8E Silvaire	R. J. Williams	
G-AKUR	Cessna 140	P. Power & L. P. Z. Yelland	
G-AKUW	C.H.3 Super Ace	D. R. Bean	
G-AKVF	C.H.3 Super Ace	P. V. B. Longthorp/Bodmin	
G-AKVM	Cessna 120	C120 Group/Norwich	
G-AKVN	Aeronca 11AC Chief	J. S. R. Lancaster	
G-AKVO	Taylorcraft BC-12D	R. J. Whybrow & S. R. Roberts	
G-AKVP	Luscombe 8A Silvaire	R. M. Shipp	
G-AKVZ	M.38 Messenger 4B	Shipping & Airlines Ltd/Biggin Hill	

Notes	Reg.	Type	Owner or Operator
	G-AKWS	Auster 5-160	J. E. Homewood
	G-AKWT	Auster 5 ★	Loughborough & Leicester Aircraft Preservation Soc
	G-AKXS	D.H.82A Tiger Moth	P. A. Colman
	G-AKZN	P.34A Proctor 3 (Z7197) ★	RAF Museum/St Athan
	G-ALAH	M.38 Messenger 4A (RH377) ★	RAF Museum/Henlow
	G-ALAX	D.H.89A Dragon Rapide ★	Durney Aeronautical Collection/Andover
	G-ALBJ	Auster 5	P. N. Elkington
	G-ALBK	Auster 5	S. J. Wright & Co (Farmers) Ltd
	G-ALBN	Bristol 173 (XF785) ★	RAF Museum/Henlow
	G-ALCK	P.34A Proctor 3 (LZ766) ★	Skyfame Collection/Duxford
	G-ALCS	M.65 Gemini 3C ★	Stored
	G-ALCU	D.H.104 Dove 2 ★	Midland Air Museum/Coventry
	G-ALDG	HP.81 Hermes 4 ★	Duxford Aviation Soc (Fuselage only)
	G-ALEH	PA-17 Vagabond	A. D. Pearce/Redhill
	G-ALFA	Auster 5	H&B Auster Group
	G-ALFM	D.H.104 Devon C.2	C. Charalambous
	G-ALFT	D.H.104 Dove 6 ★	Snowdon Mountain Aviation Museum
	G-ALFU	D.H.104 Dove 6 ★	Duxford Aviation Soc
	G-ALGA	PA-15 Vagabond	M. J. Markey/Biggin Hill
	G-ALGT	V.S.379 Spitfire 14 (RM689)	Rolls-Royce Ltd
	G-ALIJ	PA-17 Vagabond	RFC Flying Group/Popham
	G-ALIW	D.H.82A Tiger Moth	D. I. M. Geddes & F. Curry/Booker
	G-ALJF	P.34A Proctor 3	J. F. Moore/Biggin Hill
	G-ALLF	Slingsby T.31A Kirby Prefect	N. J. Churcher
	G-ALJL	D.H.82A Tiger Moth	C. G. Clarke
	G-ALNA	D.H.82A Tiger Moth	P. D. Castle
	G-ALND	D.H.82A Tiger Moth (N9191)	J. T. Powell-Tuck
	G-ALNV	Auster 5 ★	stored
	G-ALOD	Cessna 140	J. R. Stainer
	G-ALRH	EoN Type 8 Baby (AST)	P. D. Moran/Chipping
	G-ALRI	D.H.82A Tiger Moth (T5672)	Wessex Aviation & Transport Ltd
	G-ALSP	Bristol 171 (WV783) Sycamore ★	RN Fleetlands Museum
	G-ALSS	Bristol 171 (WA576) Sycamore ★	E. Fortune
	G-ALST	Bristol 171 (WA577) Sycamore ★	N.E. Aircraft Museum/Usworth
	G-ALSW	Bristol 171 (WT933) Sycamore ★	Newark Air Museum
	G-ALSX	Bristol 171 (G-48-1) Sycamore ★	International Helicopter Museum/Weston-s-Mare
	G-ALTO	Cessna 140	J. P. Bell
	G-ALTW	D.H.82A Tiger Moth ★	A. Mangham
	G-ALUC	D.H.82A Tiger Moth	D. R. & M. Wood/Shipdham
	G-ALVP	D.H.82A Tiger Moth ★	V. & R. Wheele (stored)
	G-ALWB	D.H.C.1 Chipmunk 22A	M. L. & J. M. Soper/Perth
	G-ALWF	V.701 Viscount ★	Viscount Preservation Trust RMA Sir John Franklin/Duxford
	G-ALWS	D.H.82A Tiger Moth ★	Air Service Training Ltd/Perth
	G-ALWW	D.H.82A Tiger Moth	F. W. Fay & ptnrs
	G-ALXT	D.H.89A Dragon Rapide ★	Science Museum/Wroughton
	G-ALXZ	Auster 5-150	B. J. W. Thomas & R. A. E. Witheridge
	G-ALYB	Auster 5 (RT520)★	S. Yorks Aircraft Preservation Soc
	G-ALYG	Auster 5D	A. L. Young/Henstridge
	G-ALYW	D.H.106 Comet 1 ★	RAF Exhibition Flight (fuselage converted to Nimrod)
	G-ALZE	BN-1F ★	M. R. Short/Southampton Hall of Aviation
	G-ALZO	A.S.57 Ambassador★	Duxford Aviation Soc
	G-AMAW	Luton LA-4 Minor	R. H. Coates
	G-AMBB	D.H.82A Tiger Moth	J. Eagles
	G-AMCA	Dakota 3	Air Atlantique Ltd/Coventry
	G-AMCK	D.H.82A Tiger Moth	V. S. E. Norman
	G-AMCM	D.H.82A Tiger Moth	G. C. Masterton
	G-AMDA	Avro 652A Anson 1 (N4877)★	Skyfame Collection/Duxford
	G-AMEN	PA-18 Super Cub 95	A. Lovejoy & W. Cook
	G-AMHF	D.H.82A Tiger Moth	A. J. West
	G-AMHJ	Dakota 6	Air Atlantique Ltd/Coventry
	G-AMIU	D.H.82A Tiger Moth	R. & Mrs J. L. Jones
	G-AMKU	J/1B Aiglet	Southdown Flying Group (stored)
	G-AMLZ	P.50 Prince 6E ★	J. F. Coggins/Coventry
	G-AMMS	J/5F Aiglet Trainer	A. J. Large
	G-AMNN	D.H.82A Tiger Moth	M. Thrower/Shoreham
	G-AMOG	V.701 Viscount ★	Aerospace Museum/Cosford
	G-AMOU	D.H.82A Tiger Moth	Fortress Wastecare (Spa) Ltd

Reg.	Type	Owner or Operator	Notes
G-AMPG	PA-12 Super Cruiser	R. Simpson	
G-AMPI	SNCAN Stampe SV-4C	J. Hewett	
G-AMPO	Dakota 4	Air Atlantique Ltd/Coventry	
G-AMPP	Dakota 3 (G-AMSU) ★	Aces High Ltd/North Weald	
G-AMPY	Dakota 4	Air Atlantique Ltd/Coventry	
G-AMPZ	Dakota 4	Air Atlantique Ltd/Coventry	
G-AMRA	Dakota 6	Air Atlantique Ltd/Coventry	
G-AMRF	J/5F Aiglet Trainer	A. I. Topps/E. Midlands	
G-AMRK	G.37 Gladiator 1 (N2308)	Shuttleworth Trust/O. Warden	
G-AMSG	SIPA 903	S. W. Markham	
G-AMSV	Dakota 4	Air Atlantique Ltd/Coventry	
G-AMTA	J/5F Aiglet Trainer	H. J. Jauncey/Rochester	
G-AMTD	J/5F Aiglet Trainer	Leicestershire Aero Club Ltd	
G-AMTK	D.H.82A Tiger Moth	S. W. McKay & M. E. Vaisey	
G-AMTM	J/1 Autocrat	R. Stobo & D. Clewley	
G-AMTV	D.H.82A Tiger Moth	K. J. Slattery	
G-AMUF	D.H.C.1 Chipmunk 21	Redhill Tailwheel Flying Club Ltd	
G-AMUI	J/5F Aiglet Trainer	D. P. Copse	
G-AMVD	Auster 5	R. F. Tolhurst	
G-AMVP	Tipsy Junior	A. R. Wershat	
G-AMVS	D.H.82A Tiger Moth	J. T. Powell-Tuck	
G-AMXP	D.H.104 Sea Devon C.20	M. A. Knowles	
G-AMXT	D.H.104 Sea Devon C.20	W. Gentle & P. C. Gill	
G-AMYA	Zlin Z.381	D. M. Fenton	
G-AMYD	J/5L Aiglet Trainer	G. H. Maskell	
G-AMYJ	Dakota 6	Air Atlantique Ltd/Coventry	
G-AMYL	PA-17 Vagabond	P. J. Penn-Sayers/Shoreham	
G-AMZI	J/5F Aiglet Trainer	J. F. Moore/Biggin Hill	
G-AMZT	J/5F Aiglet Trainer	D. Hyde & J. W. Saull/Cranfield	
G-AMZU	J/5F Aiglet Trainer	J. A. Longworth & ptnrs	
G-ANAF	Dakota 3	Air Atlantique Ltd/Coventry	
G-ANAP	D.H.104 Dove 6 ★	Brunel Technical College/Lulsgate	
G-ANCF	B.175 Britannia 308 ★	—/Weybridge	
G-ANCS	D.H.82A Tiger Moth (R4907)	P. G. Wright	
G-ANCX	D.H.82A Tiger Moth	D. R. Wood/Biggin Hill	
G-ANDE	D.H.82A Tiger Moth	The Vintage Aeroplane Co Ltd	
G-ANDM	D.H.82A Tiger Moth	J. G. Green	
G-ANDP	D.H.82A Tiger Moth	A. H. Diver	
G-ANDX	D.H.104 Devon C.2	L. Richards	
G-ANEC	D.H.82A Tiger Moth ★	(stored)	
G-ANEF	D.H.82A Tiger Moth (T5493)	RAF College Flying Club Co Ltd/Cranwell	
G-ANEH	D.H.82A Tiger Moth	P. A. Shaw	
G-ANEL	D.H.82A Tiger Moth (N9238)	Chauffair Ltd	
G-ANEM	D.H.82A Tiger Moth	P. J. Benest	
G-ANEW	D.H.82A Tiger Moth	A. L. Young	
G-ANEZ	D.H.82A Tiger Moth	C. D. J. Bland & T. S. Warren/Sandown	
G-ANFC	D.H.82A Tiger Moth (DE363)	H. J. Jauncey	
G-ANFH	Westland S-55 ★	International Helicopter Museum/ Weston-s-Mare	
G-ANFI	D.H.82A Tiger Moth (DE623)	D. H. R. Jenkins	
G-ANFL	D.H.82A Tiger Moth	R. P. Whitby & ptnrs	
G-ANFM	D.H.82A Tiger Moth	S. A. Brook & ptnrs/Booker	
G-ANFP	D.H.82A Tiger Moth ★	Mosquito Aircraft Museum	
G-ANFU	Auster 5 (NJ719)★	N.E. Aircraft Museum	
G-ANFV	D.H.82A Tiger Moth (DF155)	R. A. L. Falconer	
G-ANFW	D.H.82A Tiger Moth	G. M. Fraser/Denham	
G-ANGK	Cessna 140A	D. W. Munday	
G-ANHK	D.H.82A Tiger Moth	J. D. Iliffe	
G-ANHR	Auster 5	C. G. Winch	
G-ANHS	Auster 4	Tango Uniform Group	
G-ANHU	Auster 4	D. J. Baker	
G-ANHX	Auster 5D	D. J. Baker	
G-ANHZ	Auster 5 (TW384)	D. W. Pennell	
G-ANIE	Auster 5 (TW467)	S. J. Partridge	
G-ANIJ	Auster 5D (TJ672)	M. Pocock & R. Eastmann	
G-ANIS	Auster 5	J. Clarke-Cockburn	
G-ANJA	D.H.82A Tiger Moth (N9389)	J. J. Young	
G-ANJD	D.H.82A Tiger Moth	H. J. Jauncey/(stored)	
G-ANJK	D.H.82A Tiger Moth	A. D. Williams	
G-ANJV	W.S.55 Whirlwind 3 (VR-BET)★	International Helicopter Museum/ Weston-s-Mare	
G-ANKK	D.H.82A Tiger Moth (T5854)	Halfpenny Green Tiger Group	

Notes	Reg.	Type	Owner or Operator
	G-ANKT	D.H.82A Tiger Moth (T6818)	Shuttleworth Trust/O. Warden
	G-ANKZ	D.H.82A Tiger Moth (N6466)	R. Stephens
	G-ANLD	D.H.82A Tiger Moth	K. Peters
	G-ANLH	D.H.82A Tiger Moth	The Aeroplane Co (Hamble) Ltd
	G-ANLS	D.H.82A Tiger Moth	P. A. Gliddon
	G-ANLU	Auster 5	S. C. Challis & G. Guinn
	G-ANLW	W.B.1. Widgeon (MD497) ★	Wilkie Museum Collection/Blackpool
	G-ANLX	D.H.82A Tiger Moth	B. J. Borsberry & ptnrs
	G-ANMO	D.H.82A Tiger Moth	E. Lay
	G-ANMV	D.H.82A Tiger Moth (T7404)	J. W. Davy/Cardiff
	G-ANMY	D.H.82A Tiger Moth	D. J. Elliott
	G-ANNB	D.H.82A Tiger Moth	Cormack (Aircraft Services) Ltd
	G-ANNK	D.H.82A Tiger Moth	P. J. Wilcox/Cranfield
	G-ANNN	D.H.82A Tiger Moth	T. Pate
	G-ANOA	Hiller UH-12A ★	Redhill Technical College
	G-ANOD	D.H.82A Tiger Moth	P. G. Watson
	G-ANOH	D.H.82A Tiger Moth	N. Parkhouse/White Waltham
	G-ANOK	Saab S.91C Safir ★	A. F. Galt & Co (*stored*)
	G-ANOM	D.H.82A Tiger Moth	P. A. Colman
	G-ANON	D.H.82A Tiger Moth (T7909)	A. C. Mercer/Sherburn
	G-ANOO	D.H.82A Tiger Moth	R. K. Packman
	G-ANOR	D.H.82A Tiger Moth (T6991)	C. L. Keith-Lucas & Aero Vintage Ltd
	G-ANOV	D.H.104 Dove 6 ★	Museum of Flight/E. Fortune
	G-ANPE	D.H.82A Tiger Moth	I. E. S. Huddleston (G-IESH)
	G-ANPK	D.H.82A Tiger Moth	The D. & P. Group
	G-ANPP	P.34A Proctor 3	C. P. A. & J. Jeffery
	G-ANRF	D.H.82A Tiger Moth	C. D. Cyster
	G-ANRM	D.H.82A Tiger Moth	Clacton Aero Club (1988) Ltd & A. B. Cutting
	G-ANRN	D.H.82A Tiger Moth	J. J. V. Elwes
	G-ANRP	Auster 5 (TW439)	C. T. K. Lane
	G-ANRS	V.372 Viscount ★	Wales Aircraft Museum/Cardiff
	G-ANRX	D.H.82A Tiger Moth ★	Mosquito Aircraft Museum
	G-ANSM	D.H.82A Tiger Moth	J. L. Bond
	G-ANTE	D.H.82A Tiger Moth	T. I. Sutton & B. J. Champion/Chester
	G-ANTK	Avro 685 York ★	Duxford Aviation Soc
	G-ANTS	D.H.82A Tiger Moth (N6532)	J. G. Green
	G-ANUO	D.H.114 Heron 2D	Avtech Ltd/Biggin Hill
	G-ANUW	D.H.104 Dove 6 ★	(*stored*)/Stansted
	G-ANWB	D.H.C.1 Chipmunk 21	G. Briggs/Blackpool
	G-ANWO	M.14A Hawk Trainer 3 ★	P. A. Brook
	G-ANWX	J/5L Aiglet Trainer	L. P. Mullins
	G-ANXB	D.H.114 Heron 1B ★	Newark Air Museum
	G-ANXC	J/5R Alpine	C. J. Repek & ptnrs
	G-ANXR	P.31C Proctor 4 (RM221)	L. H. Oakins/Biggin Hill
	G-ANYP	P.31C Proctor 4 (NP184)	R. A. Anderson
	G-ANZJ	P.31C Proctor 4 (NP303) ★	A. Hillyard
	G-ANZT	Thruxton Jackaroo	D. J. Neville & P. A. Dear
	G-ANZU	D.H.82A Tiger Moth	P. A. Jackson/Sibson
	G-ANZZ	D.H.82A Tiger Moth	D. L. Frankel
	G-AOAA	D.H.82A Tiger Moth	R. C. P. Brookhouse
	G-AOAR	P.31C Proctor 4 (NP181) ★	Historic Aircraft Preservation Soc
	G-AOBG	Somers-Kendall SK.1 ★	*stored*
	G-AOBH	D.H.82A Tiger Moth (T7997)	D. S. & I. M. Morgan
	G-AOBJ	D.H.82A Tiger Moth	D. H. R. Jenkins
	G-AOBO	D.H.82A Tiger Moth	P. A. Brook
	G-AOBU	P.84 Jet Provost ★	Shuttleworth Trust/Loughborough
	G-AOBV	J/5P Autocar	P. E. Champney
	G-AOBX	D.H.82A Tiger Moth	M. Gibbs/Redhill
	G-AOCP	Auster 5 ★	C. Baker (*stored*)
	G-AOCR	Auster 5D	J. M. Edis
	G-AOCU	Auster 5	S. J. Ball/Leicester
	G-AODA	Westland S-55 Srs 3	Bristow Helicopters Ltd
	G-AODT	D.H.82A Tiger Moth	A. H. Warminger
	G-AOEH	Aeronca 7AC Champion	M. Weeks & ptnrs/Eglinton
	G-AOEI	D.H.82A Tiger Moth	C.F.G. Flying Ltd/Cambridge
	G-AOEL	D.H.82A Tiger Moth (N9510) ★	Museum of Flight/E. Fortune
	G-AOES	D.H.82A Tiger Moth	A. Twemlow & G. A. Cordery
	G-AOET	D.H.82A Tiger Moth	Venom Jet Promotions Ltd/Bournemouth
	G-AOEX	Thruxton Jackaroo	A. T. Christian
	G-AOFE	D.H.C.1 Chipmunk 22A (WB702)	R. J. F. Parker/Denham
	G-AOFM	J/5P Autocar	N. P. Beaumont

Reg.	Type	Owner or Operator	Notes
G-AOFS	J/5L Aiglet Trainer	P. N. A. Whitehead	
G-AOGA	M.75 Aries ★	Irish Aviation Museum (*stored*)	
G-AOGE	P.34A Proctor 3	N. I. Dalziel/Biggin Hill	
G-AOGI	D.H.82A Tiger Moth	W. J. Taylor	
G-AOGR	D.H.82A Tiger Moth (T6099)	M. I. Edwards	
G-AOGV	J/5R Alpine	R. E. Heading	
G-AOHL	V.802 Viscount ★	British Air Ferries (Cabin Trainer)/ Southend	
G-AOHM	V.802 Viscount	British Air Ferries *Viscount Sir George Edwards*/Southend	
G-AOHT	V.802 Viscount	British Air Ferries(*withdrawn*)/Southend	
G-AOHY	D.H.82A Tiger Moth	C. R. Hardiman/Shobdon	
G-AOHZ	J/5P Autocar	P. H. Yarnold	
G-AOIL	D.H.82A Tiger Moth	T. C. Lawless	
G-AOIM	D.H.82A Tiger Moth	C. R. Hardiman/Shobdon	
G-AOIR	Thruxton Jackaroo	L. H. Smith	
G-AOIS	D.H.82A Tiger Moth	V. B. & R. G. Wheele/Shoreham	
G-AOIY	J/5G Autocar	C. N. Towers	
G-AOJC	V.802 Viscount ★	Wales Aircraft Museum/Cardiff	
G-AOJH	D.H.83C Fox Moth	R. M. Brooks	
G-AOJJ	D.H.82A Tiger Moth (DF128)	E. Lay	
G-AOJK	D.H.82A Tiger Moth	P. A. de Courcy Swoffer	
G-AOJS	D.H.C.1 Chipmunk 22A	R. H. Cooper	
G-AOJT	D.H.106 Comet 1 ★	Mosquito Aircraft Museum	
G-AOKH	P.40 Prentice 1	J. F. Moore/Biggin Hill	
G-AOKL	P.40 Prentice 1 (VS610)	D. L. Claydon	
G-AOKO	P.40 Prentice 1 ★	J. F. Coggins/Coventry	
G-AOKZ	P.40 Prentice 1 (VS623) ★	Midland Air Museum	
G-AOLK	P.40 Prentice 1	Hilton Aviation Ltd/Southend	
G-AOLU	P.40 Prentice 1 (VS356) ★	—	
G-AORB	Cessna 170B	Eaglescott Parachute Centre	
G-AORG	D.H.114 Heron 2	Duchess of Brittany (Jersey) Ltd	
G-AORW	D.H.C.1 Chipmunk 22A	V. P. Butler/Biggin Hill	
G-AOSK	D.H.C.1 Chipmunk 22	A. M. S. Cullen	
G-AOSO	D.H.C.1 Chipmunk 22	Earl of Suffolk & Berkshire & J. Hoerner	
G-AOSU	D.H.C.1 Chipmunk 22 (Lycoming)	RAFGSA/Bicester	
G-AOSY	D.H.C.1 Chipmunk 22 (WB585)	Franbrave Ltd	
G-AOTD	D.H.C.1 Chipmunk 22 (WB588)	Shuttleworth Trust/O. Warden	
G-AOTF	D.H.C.1 Chipmunk 23 (Lycoming)	RAFGSA/Bicester	
G-AOTI	D.H.114 Heron 2D	Avtech Ltd/Biggin Hill	
G-AOTK	D.53 Turbi	The T. K. Flying Group/Hatfield	
G-AOTR	D.H.C.1 Chipmunk 22	Ulster Chipmunk Club/Newtownards	
G-AOTY	D.H.C.1 Chipmunk 22A (WG472)	P. D. Harrison	
G-AOUJ	Fairey Ultra-Light ★	International Helicopter Museum/ Weston-s-Mare	
G-AOUO	D.H.C.1 Chipmunk 22 (Lycoming)	RAFGSA/Bicester	
G-AOUP	D.H.C.1 Chipmunk 22	Wessex Flying Group	
G-AOUR	D.H.82A Tiger Moth	Ulster Folk & Transport Museum	
G-AOVF	B.175 Britannia 312F ★	Aerospace Museum/Cosford	
G-AOVT	B.175 Britannia 312F ★	Duxford Aviation Soc	
G-AOVW	Auster 5	B. Marriott/Cranwell	
G-AOXG	D.H.82A Tiger Moth (XL717)	FAA Museum/Yeovilton	
G-AOXN	D.H.82A Tiger Moth	S. L. G. Darch	
G-AOYG	V.806 Viscount	British Air Ferries *Viscount Sir Peter Masefield*/Southend	
G-AOYL	V.806 Viscount	British Air Ferries *Viscount Churchill*/ Southend	
G-AOYN	V.806 Viscount	British Air Ferries/Southend	
G-AOYP	V.806 Viscount	British Air Ferries/Southend	
G-AOYR	V.806 Viscount	British Air Ferries/Southend	
G-AOZH	D.H.82A Tiger Moth (K2572)	V. B. & R. G. Wheele/Shoreham	
G-AOZL	J/5Q Alpine	E. A. Taylor/Southend	
G-AOZP	D.H.C.1 Chipmunk 22	M. Darlington	
G-AOZU	D.H.C.1 Chipmunk 22A	R. H. Cooper	
G-APAA	J/5R Alpine ★	L. A. Groves (*stored*)	
G-APAF	Auster 5 (TW511)	J. E. Allen (G-CMAL)	
G-APAH	Auster 5	D. P. Williams	
G-APAL	D.H.82A Tiger Moth (N6847)	P. S. & R. A. Chapman	
G-APAM	D.H.82A Tiger Moth	R. P. Williams	
G-APAO	D.H.82A Tiger Moth	F. J. Longe	
G-APAP	D.H.82A Tiger Moth	R. A. Slade	
G-APAS	D.H.106 Comet 1XB ★	Aerospace Museum/Cosford	

Notes	Reg.	Type	Owner or Operator
	G-APBE	Auster 5	C. W. Wilkinson/Panshanger
	G-APBI	D.H.82A Tiger Moth (EM903)	R. Devaney & ptnrs/Audley End
	G-APBO	D.53 Turbi	T. W. Harris
	G-APBW	Auster 5	N. Huxtable
	G-APCB	J/5Q Alpine	M. J. Wilson/Redhill
	G-APCC	D.H.82A Tiger Moth	L. J. Rice/Henstridge
	G-APDB	D.H.106 Comet 4 ★	Duxford Aviation Soc
	G-APEG	V.953C Merchantman	Air Bridge Carriers Ltd (*withdrawn*)/ E. Midlands
	G-APEJ	V.953C Merchantman	Air Bridge Carriers Ltd *Ajax*/E. Midlands
	G-APEK	V.953C Merchantman	Air Bridge Carriers Ltd *Dreadnought*/ E. Midlands
	G-APEM	V.953C Merchantman	Air Bridge Carriers Ltd/DHL *Agamemnon*/ E. Midlands
	G-APEP	V.953C Merchantman	Air Bridge Carriers Ltd *Superb*/E. Midlands
	G-APES	V.953C Merchantman	Air Bridge Carriers Ltd *Swiftsure*/ E. Midlands
	G-APET	V.953C Merchantman	Air Bridge Carriers Ltd *Temeraire*/ E. Midlands
	G-APEY	V.806 Viscount	British Air Ferries/Southend
	G-APFA	D.54 Turbi	A. Eastelow & F. J. Keitch/Dunkeswell
	G-APFG	Boeing 707-436 ★	*Cabin water spray tests*/Cardington
	G-APFJ	Boeing 707-436 ★	Aerospace Museum/Cosford
	G-APFU	D.H.82A Tiger Moth	Mithril Racing Ltd/Goodwood
	G-APGL	D.H.82A Tiger Moth	B. H. Strudwick
	G-APHV	Avro 19 Srs 2 (VM360) ★	Museum of Flight/E. Fortune
	G-APIE	Tipsy Belfair B	P. A. Smith
	G-APIH	D.H.82A Tiger Moth (R5086)	C. R. Kirby
	G-APIK	J/1N Alpha	N. D. Voce
	G-APIM	V.806 Viscount ★	Brooklands Museum of Aviation/ Weybridge
	G-APIT	P.40 Prentice 1 (VR192) ★	WWII Aircraft Preservation Soc/Lasham
	G-APIU	P.40 Prentice 1 ★	J. F. Coggins/Coventry
	G-APIY	P.40 Prentice 1 (VR249) ★	Newark Air Museum
	G-APIZ	D.31 Turbulent	M. J. Whatley/Booker
	G-APJB	P.40 Prentice 1 (VR259) ★	City Airways/Coventry
	G-APJJ	Fairey Ultra-light ★	Midland Aircraft Preservation Soc
	G-APJO	D.H.82A Tiger Moth	D. R. & M. Wood
	G-APJZ	J/1N Alpha	P. G. Lipman
	G-APKH	D.H.85 Leopard Moth	R. G. Grocott (G-ACGS)
	G-APKM	J/1N Alpha	D. E. A. Huggins
	G-APKN	J/1N Alpha	Felthorpe Auster Group
	G-APKY	Hiller UH-12B	D. A. George (*stored*)
	G-APLG	J/5L Aiglet Trainer	G. R. W. Brown
	G-APLK	Miles M.100 Student 2	A. S. Topen (G-MIOO)/Cranfield
	G-APLO	D.H.C.1 Chipmunk 22A (WD379)	Lindholme Aircraft Ltd/Jersey
	G-APLU	D.H.82A Tiger Moth	The Intrepid Flying Group
	G-APMB	D.H.106 Comet 4B ★	Gatwick Handling Ltd (*ground trainer*)
	G-APMH	J/1U Workmaster	R. E. Neal & E. R. Stevens/Leicester
	G-APML	Dakota 6	Air Atlantique Ltd
	G-APMM	D.H.82A Tiger Moth (K2568)	R. K. J. Hadlow
	G-APMX	D.H.82A Tiger Moth	For rebuild
	G-APMY	PA-23 Apache 160 ★	NE Wales Institute of Higher Education (*instructional airframe*)/Clwyd
	G-APNJ	Cessna 310 ★	Chelsea College/Shoreham
	G-APNS	Garland-Bianchi Linnet	Paul Penn-Sayers Model Services Ltd
	G-APNT	Currie Wot	J. W. Salter
	G-APNZ	D.31 Turbulent	Tiger Club (1990) Ltd/Headcorn
	G-APOA	J/1N Alpha	J. S. M. Norman
	G-APOD	Tipsy Belfair	L. F. Potts
	G-APOI	Saro Skeeter Srs 8 ★	Wilkie Museum Collection/Blackpool
	G-APOL	D.31 Turbulent	A. Gregori & S. Tinker
	G-APPA	D.H.C.1 Chipmunk 22	I. R. Young/Glasgow
	G-APPL	P.40 Prentice 1	S. J. Saggers/Biggin Hill
	G-APPM	D.H.C.1 Chipmunk 22	Freston Aviation Ltd
	G-APRF	Auster 5	R. Giles & ptnrs/Clacton
	G-APRJ	Avro 694 Lincoln B.2 ★	Aces High Ltd/North Weald
	G-APRL	AW.650 Argosy 101 ★	Midland Air Museum
	G-APRR	Super Aero 45	R. H. Jowett
	G-APRT	Taylor JT.1 Monoplane	G. E. Valler
	G-APSA	Douglas DC-6A	Instone Air Line Ltd/Coventry
	G-APSR	J/1U Workmaster	D. & K. Aero Services Ltd/Shobdon
	G-APTH	Agusta-Bell 47J	A. M. Parkes

Reg.	Type	Owner or Operator	Notes
G-APTP	PA-22 Tri-Pacer 150	R. J. & F. A. Fox	
G-APTR	J/1N Alpha	C. J. & D. J. Baker	
G-APTS	D.H.C.1 Chipmunk 22A	Wycombe Air Centre Ltd	
G-APTU	Auster 5	Rutland Aviation	
G-APTW	W.B.1 Widgeon ★	Cornwall Aero Park/Helston	
G-APTY	Beech G.35 Bonanza	G. E. Brennand & ptnrs	
G-APTZ	D.31 Turbulent	F. R. Hutchings	
G-APUD	Bensen B.7M (modified) ★	Greater Manchester Museum of Science & Technology	
G-APUE	L-40 Meta Sokol	S. E. & M. J. Aherne	
G-APUK	J/1 Autocrat	P. L. Morley	
G-APUP	Sopwith Pup (N5182) (replica)★	RAF Museum/Hendon	
G-APUR	PA-22 Tri-Pacer 160	P. J. Hewitt	
G-APUW	J/5V-160 Autocar	Anglia Auster Syndicate	
G-APUY	D.31 Turbulent	C. Jones & ptnrs/Barton	
G-APUZ	PA-24 Comanche 250	N. Parkinson & W. Smith	
G-APVF	Putzer Elster B (97+04)	K. P. Rusling	
G-APVG	J/5L Aiglet Trainer	C. M. Daggett/Cranfield	
G-APVN	D.31 Turbulent	R. Sherwin/Shoreham	
G-APVS	Cessna 170B	N. Simpson	
G-APVY	PA-25 Pawnee 150	KK Aviation (*stored*)	
G-APVZ	D.31 Turbulent	H. R. Oldland	
G-APWA	HPR-7 Herald 101 ★	Museum of Berkshire Aviation/Woodley	
G-APWJ	HPR-7 Herald 201 ★	Duxford Aviation Soc	
G-APWN	WS-55 Whirlwind 3 ★	Midland Air Museum	
G-APWY	Piaggio P.166 ★	Science Museum/Wroughton	
G-APWZ	EP.9 Prospector ★	Museum of Army Flying/Middle Wallop	
G-APXJ	PA-24 Comanche 250	T. Wildsmith/Netherthorpe	
G-APXM	PA-22 Tri-Pacer 160	R. J. Chinn	
G-APXR	PA-22 Tri-Pacer 160	A. Troughton	
G-APXT	PA-22 Tri-Pacer 150 (modified)	J. W. & I. Daniels	
G-APXU	PA-22 Tri-Pacer 125	Medway Aircraft Preservation Soc Ltd	
G-APXW	EP.9 Prospector ★	Museum of Army Flying/Middle Wallop	
G-APXX	D.H.A.3 Drover 2 (VH-FDT) ★	WWII Aircraft Preservation Soc/Lasham	
G-APXY	Cessna 150	Merlin Flying Club Ltd/Hucknall	
G-APYB	Tipsy T.66 Nipper 3	B. O. Smith	
G-APYD	D.H.106 Comet 4B ★	Science Museum/Wroughton	
G-APYG	D.H.C.1 Chipmunk 22	E. J. I. Musty & P. A. Colman	
G-APYI	PA-22 Tri-Pacer 135	G. K. Hare/Fenland	
G-APYN	PA-22 Tri-Pacer 160	W. D. Stephens	
G-APYT	Champion 7FC Tri-Traveller	B. J. Anning	
G-APYW	PA-22 Tri-Pacer 150	Fiddian Ltd	
G-APZJ	PA-18 Super Cub 150	Southern Sailplanes	
G-APZK	PA-18 Super Cub 95	W. T. Knapton	
G-APZL	PA-22 Tri-Pacer 160	R. T. Evans	
G-APZR	Cessna 150 ★	*Engine test-bed*/Biggin Hill	
G-APZS	Cessna 175A	G. A. Nash/Booker	
G-APZX	PA-22 Tri-Pacer 150	Applied Signs Ltd	
G-ARAM	PA-18 Super Cub 150	Clacton Aero Club (1988) Ltd	
G-ARAN	PA-18 Super Cub 150	A. P. Docherty/Redhill	
G-ARAO	PA-18 Super Cub 95 (607327)	R. T. Bennett & N. Tyler	
G-ARAS	Champion 7EC Traveller	B. W. Webb	
G-ARAT	Cessna 180C	Eaglescott Parachute Centre	
G-ARAU	Cessna 150	S. Lynn/Sibson	
G-ARAW	Cessna 182C Skylane	P. Channon	
G-ARAX	PA-22 Tri-Pacer 150	S. J. Kew/Booker	
G-ARAZ	D.H.82A Tiger Moth (R4959)	R. M. Brooks	
G-ARBE	D.H.104 Dove 8	A. Freeman & T. Howe	
G-ARBG	Tipsy T.66 Nipper 2	Felthorpe Tipsy Group	
G-ARBM	J/1B Aiglet	Aerofab Flying Group	
G-ARBN	PA-23 Apache 160	H. Norden & H. J. Liggins	
G-ARBO	PA-24 Comanche 250	D. M. Harbottle & I. S. Graham/Goodwood	
G-ARBP	Tipsy T.66 Nipper 2	F. W. Kirk	
G-ARBS	PA-22 Tri-Pacer 160 (modified to PA-20 Pacer 160)	S. D. Rowell	
G-ARBV	PA-22 Tri-Pacer 150	Piper Flyers/Biggin Hill	
G-ARBZ	D.31 Turbulent	B. I. Edgeworth/Scampton	
G-ARCC	PA-22 Tri-Pacer 150	RFC Flying Group/Popham	
G-ARCF	PA-22 Tri-Pacer 150	R. E. Ryan	
G-ARCH	Cessna 310D ★	*Instructional airframe*/Perth	
G-ARCS	Auster D6/180	E. A. Matty/Shobdon	
G-ARCT	PA-18 Super Cub 95	M. J. Kirk	

25

Notes	Reg.	Type	Owner or Operator
	G-ARCV	Cessna 175A	R. Francis & C. Campbell
	G-ARCW	PA-23 Apache 160	D. R. C. Reeves
	G-ARCX	AW Meteor 14 ★	Museum of Flight/E. Fortune
	G-ARDB	PA-24 Comanche 250	R. A. Sareen/Booker
	G-ARDD	CP.301C1 Emeraude	R. M. Shipp
	G-ARDE	D.H.104 Dove 6	R. J. H. Small/North Weald
	G-ARDG	EP.9 Prospector ★	Museum of Army Flying/Middle Wallop
	G-ARDJ	Auster D.6/180	RN Aviation (Leicester Airport) Ltd
	G-ARDO	Jodel D.112	W. R. Prescott
	G-ARDP	PA-22 Tri-Pacer 150	G. M. Jones
	G-ARDS	PA-22 Caribbean 150	D. V. Asher/Leicester
	G-ARDT	PA-22 Tri-Pacer 160	M. Henderson
	G-ARDV	PA-22 Tri-Pacer 160	B. R. Griffiths
	G-ARDY	Tipsy T.66 Nipper 2	M. J. Mann
	G-ARDZ	Jodel D.140A	M. J. Wright
	G-AREA	D.H.104 Dove 8 ★	Mosquito Aircraft Museum
	G-AREB	Cessna 175B Skylark	R. J. Postlethwaite & ptnrs/Wellesbourne
	G-AREF	PA-23 Aztec 250 ★	Southall College of Technology
	G-AREH	D.H.82A Tiger Moth	T. Pate
	G-AREI	Auster 3 (MT438)	J. A. Vetch
	G-AREL	PA-22 Caribbean 150	H. H. Cousins/Fenland
	G-AREO	PA-18 Super Cub 150	Scottish Gliding Union Ltd
	G-ARET	PA-22 Tri-Pacer 160	D. T. Daniels
	G-AREV	PA-22 Tri-Pacer 160	Spatrek Ltd/Barton
	G-AREX	Aeronca 15AC Sedan	R. J. Middleton-Turnbull & P. Lowndes
	G-AREZ	D.31 Turbulent	J. St. Clair-Quentin/Shobdon
	G-ARFB	PA-22 Caribbean 150	C. T. Woodward & ptnrs
	G-ARFD	PA-22 Tri-Pacer 160	P. C. Hambilton & G. F. Martin/Blackpool
	G-ARFG	Cessna 175A Skylark	R. J. Fray/Sibson
	G-ARFH	PA-24 Comanche 250	L. M. Walton
	G-ARFI	Cessna 150A	J. H. Fisher
	G-ARFL	Cessna 175B Skylark	D. J. Mason & E. G. Whelan
	G-ARFN	Cessna 150A ★	Instructional airframe/Perth
	G-ARFO	Cessna 150A	Moray Flying Club Ltd
	G-ARFT	Jodel DR. 1050	R. Shaw
	G-ARFV	Tipsy T.66 Nipper 2	C. G. Stone/Biggin Hill
	G-ARGB	Auster 6A ★	C. Baker (stored)
	G-ARGG	D.H.C.1 Chipmunk 22 (WD305)	Willpower Garage Ltd
	G-ARGO	PA-22 Colt 108	B. E. Goodman/Liverpool
	G-ARGV	PA-18 Super Cub 150	Deeside Gliding Club (Aberdeenshire) Ltd/
			Aboyne
	G-ARGZ	D.31 Turbulent	J. C. Mansell
	G-ARHB	Forney F-1A Aircoupe	A. V. Rash & D. R. Wickes
	G-ARHC	Forney F-1A Aircoupe	A. P. Gardner/Elstree
	G-ARHF	Forney F-1A Aircoupe	R. A. Nesbitt-Dufort
	G-ARHI	PA-24 Comanche 180	W. H. Entress/Swansea
	G-ARHL	PA-23 Aztec 250	J. J. Freeman & Co Ltd/Headcorn
	G-ARHM	Auster 6A	D. Hollowell & ptnrs/Finmere
	G-ARHN	PA-22 Caribbean 150	D. B. Furniss & A. Munro/Doncaster
	G-ARHP	PA-22 Tri-Pacer 160	W. Wardle
	G-ARHR	PA-22 Caribbean 150	J. A. Hargraves/Fairoaks
	G-ARHT	PA-22 Caribbean 150 ★	Moston Technical College
	G-ARHU	PA-22 Tri-Pacer 160	B. L. Newbold & ptnrs
	G-ARHW	D.H.104 Dove 8	R. M. Brooks
	G-ARHX	D.H.104 Dove 8*	—/Booker
	G-ARHZ	D.62 Condor	M. J. Groome & ptnrs
	G-ARID	Cessna 172B	A. Taylor
	G-ARIE	PA-24 Comanche 250	W. Radwanski (stored)/Coventry
	G-ARIF	Ord-Hume O-H.7 Minor Coupé	N. H. Ponsford
	G-ARIH	Auster 6A (TW591)	India Hotel Ltd
	G-ARIK	PA-22 Caribbean 150	C. J. Berry
	G-ARIL	PA-22 Caribbean 150	G. N. Richardson Motors/Shobdon
	G-ARIM	D.31 Turbulent	D. J. Hockings
	G-ARIV	Cessna 172B	G-ARIV Group
	G-ARIW	CP.301B Emeraude	P. J. Marsh
	G-ARJB	D.H.104 Dove 8 ★	J. C. Bamford (stored)
	G-ARJC	PA-22 Colt 108	F. W. H. Dulles
	G-ARJE	PA-22 Colt 108	C. I. Fray
	G-ARJF	PA-22 Colt 108	M. J. Collins
	G-ARJH	PA-22 Colt 108	Isabella Properties
	G-ARJR	PA-23 Apache 160G ★	Instructional airframe/Kidlington
	G-ARJS	PA-23 Apache 160G	Bencray Ltd/Blackpool
	G-ARJT	PA-23 Apache 160G	Hiveland Ltd

Reg.	Type	Owner or Operator	Notes
G-ARJU	PA-23 Apache 160G	Chantaco Ltd/Biggin Hill	
G-ARJV	PA-23 Apache 160G	Photractive Ltd	
G-ARJW	PA-23 Apache 160G	*stored*/Bristol	
G-ARJZ	D.31 Turbulent	N. H. Jones	
G-ARKG	J/5G Autocar	C. M. Milborrow	
G-ARKJ	Beech N35 Bonanza	Mouldrite Products Ltd	
G-ARKK	PA-22 Colt 108	A. T. J. Hyatt	
G-ARKM	PA-22 Colt 108	B. V. & E. A. Howes/Earls Colne	
G-ARKN	PA-22 Colt 108	R. A. & N. L. E. Dupee	
G-ARKP	PA-22 Colt 108	C. J. & J. Freeman/Headcorn	
G-ARKR	PA-22 Colt 108	J. Fell	
G-ARKS	PA-22 Colt 108	J. Dickenson	
G-ARLG	Auster D.4/108	Auster D4 Group	
G-ARLK	PA-24 Comanche 250	M. Walker & C. Robinson	
G-ARLO	A.61 Terrier 1 ★	*stored*	
G-ARLP	A.61 Terrier 1	A. P. Twort & N. A. M. Pelling	
G-ARLR	A.61 Terrier 2	W. H. Dyozinski	
G-ARLU	Cessna 172B Skyhawk ★	*Instructional airframe*/Irish AC	
G-ARLV	Cessna 172B Skyhawk	P. D. Lowdon	
G-ARLW	Cessna 172B Skyhawk	S. Lancashire Flyers Ltd/Barton	
G-ARLX	Jodel D.140B	Shipping & Airlines Ltd/Biggin Hill	
G-ARLZ	D.31A Turbulent	R. S. Hatwell & A. F. Hall	
G-ARMA	PA-23 Apache 160G ★	*Instructional airframe*/Kidlington	
G-ARMB	D.H.C.1 Chipmunk 22A (WB660)	P. A. Layzell/Goodwood	
G-ARMC	D.H.C.1 Chipmunk 22A (WB703)	West London Aero Services Ltd/ White Waltham	
G-ARMD	D.H.C.1 Chipmunk 22A ★	K. & L. Aero Services (*stored*)	
G-ARMG	D.H.C.1 Chipmunk 22A	Chipmunk Preservation Group Ltd/ Wellesbourne	
G-ARML	Cessna 175B Skylark	R. C. Convine	
G-ARMN	Cessna 175B Skylark ★	Southall College of Technology	
G-ARMO	Cessna 172B Skyhawk	G. R. E. Evans & D. J. Clark	
G-ARMR	Cessna 172B Skyhawk	Sunsaver Ltd/Barton	
G-ARMZ	D.31 Turbulent	J. E. M. B. Millns	
G-ARNB	J/5G Autocar	R. F. Tolhurst	
G-ARND	PA-22 Colt 108	A. Cambridge	
G-ARNE	PA-22 Colt 108	T. D. L. Bowden/Shipdham	
G-ARNG	PA-22 Colt 108	S. S. Delwarte/Shoreham	
G-ARNI	PA-22 Colt 108	P. R. Monk & A. C. Savage	
G-ARNJ	PA-22 Colt 108	Colt Flying Group	
G-ARNK	PA-22 Colt 108 (tailwheel)	G. K. Hare	
G-ARNL	PA-22 Colt 108	J. A. & J. A. Dodsworth/White Waltham	
G-ARNO	A.61 Terrier 1	M. B. Hill	
G-ARNP	A.109 Airedale	S. W. & M. Isbister	
G-ARNY	Jodel D.117	D. J. Lockett	
G-ARNZ	D.31 Turbulent	N. J. Mathias	
G-AROA	Cessna 172B Skyhawk	D. E. Partridge	
G-AROE	Aero 145	Panther Aviation	
G-AROF	L.40 Meta-Sokol	G. D. H. Crawford	
G-AROJ	A.109 Airedale ★	D. J. Shaw (*stored*)	
G-AROM	PA-22 Colt 108	J. R. Colthurst	
G-ARON	PA-22 Colt 108	R. W. Curtis	
G-AROO	Forney F-1A Aircoupe	W. J. McMeekan/Newtownards	
G-AROW	Jodel D.140B	Acebell Aviation Ltd/Redhill	
G-AROY	Boeing Stearman A.75N.1	W. A. Jordan	
G-ARPH	H.S.121 Trident 1C ★	Aerospace Museum, Cosford	
G-ARPK	H.S.121 Trident 1C ★	Manchester Airport Authority	
G-ARPL	H.S.121 Trident 1C ★	BAA Airport Fire Service/Edinburgh	
G-ARPN	H.S.121 Trident 1C ★	BAA Airport Fire Service/Aberdeen	
G-ARPP	H.S.121 Trident 1C ★	BAA Airport Fire Service/Glasgow	
G-ARPX	H.S.121 Trident 1C ★	Airwork Services Ltd/Perth	
G-ARPZ	H.S.121 Trident 1C ★	RFD Ltd/Dunsfold	
G-ARRD	Jodel DR.1050	C. M. Fitton	
G-ARRE	Jodel DR.1050	A. Luty & M. P. Edwards/Barton	
G-ARRF	Cessna 150A	Electrical Engineering Services	
G-ARRL	J/1N Alpha	G. N. Smith & C. Webb	
G-ARRM	Beagle B.206-X ★	Shoreham Airport Museum	
G-ARRS	CP.301A Emeraude	E. H. Booker	
G-ARRT	Wallis WA-116-1	K. H. Wallis	
G-ARRU	D.31 Turbulent	N. C. Lowes	
G-ARRW	H.S. 748 Srs 1	—	
G-ARRX	Auster 6A	J. E. D. Mackie	
G-ARRY	Jodel D.140B	R. C. Partridge & M. J. Oliver/Ipswich	

Notes	Reg.	Type	Owner or Operator
	G-ARRZ	D.31 Turbulent	C. I. Jefferson
	G-ARSB	Cessna 150A	B. T. White/Andrewsfield
	G-ARSG	Roe Triplane Type IV replica	Shuttleworth Trust/O. Warden
	G-ARSJ	CP.301-C2 Emeraude	R. J. Lewis
	G-ARSL	A.61 Terrier 2	R. A. Hutchinson & P. T. M. Hardy
	G-ARSP	L.40 Meta-Sokol	R. E. Carpenter
	G-ARSU	PA-22 Colt 108	W. H. & D. Gough
	G-ARSW	PA-22 Colt 108	Sierra Whisky Flying Group/Sibson
	G-ARSX	PA-22 Tri-Pacer 160	S. Hutchinson
	G-ARTD	PA-23 Apache 160	Dr. D. A. Jones
	G-ARTF	D.31 Turbulent	J. R. D. Bygraves
	G-ARTG	Hiller UH-12C ★	White Hart Inn/Stockbridge
	G-ARTH	PA-12 Super Cruiser	A. Horsfall/Sherburn
	G-ARTJ	Bensen B.8 ★	Museum of Flight/E. Fortune
	G-ARTL	D.H.82A Tiger Moth (T7281)	P. A. Jackson
	G-ARTT	M.S.880B Rallye Club	R. N. Scott
	G-ARTW	Cessna 150B ★	*Instructional airframe*/Perth
	G-ARTX	Cessna 150B ★	*Instructional airframe*/Perth
	G-ARTY	Cessna 150B ★	*Instructional airframe*/Perth
	G-ARTZ	McCandless M.4 Gyrocopter	W. E. Partridge (*stored*)
	G-ARUG	J/5G Autocar	D. P. H. Hulme/Biggin Hill
	G-ARUH	Jodel DR.1050	PFA Group/Denham
	G-ARUI	A.61 Terrier	A. C. Ladd
	G-ARUL	Cosmic Wind	P. G. Kynsey
	G-ARUO	PA-24 Comanche 180	Uniform Oscar Group/Elstree
	G-ARUR	PA-28 Cherokee 160	The G-ARUR Group/Redhill
	G-ARUV	CP.301A Emeraude	J. Tanswell
	G-ARUY	J/1N Alpha	D. L. Webley
	G-ARUZ	Cessna 175C Skylark	Cardiff Skylark Group
	G-ARVM	V.1101 VC10 ★	Aerospace Museum/Cosford
	G-ARVO	PA-18 Super Cub 95	Mona Aviation Ltd
	G-ARVS	PA-28 Cherokee 160	Skyscraper Ltd/Stapleford
	G-ARVT	PA-28 Cherokee 160	Roses Flying Group
	G-ARVU	PA-28 Cherokee 160	D. J. Hockings/Biggin Hill
	G-ARVV	PA-28 Cherokee 160	G. E. Hopkins
	G-ARVZ	D.62B Condor	C. Watson & W. H. Cole/Redhill
	G-ARWB	D.H.C.1 Chipmunk 22 (WK611)	L. J. Willcocks
	G-ARWH	Cessna 172C Skyhawk ★	—
	G-ARWO	Cessna 172C Skyhawk	J. R. Woolford
	G-ARWR	Cessna 172C Skyhawk	The Devanha Flying Group Ltd
	G-ARWS	Cessna 175C Skylark	E. N. Skinner
	G-ARWW	Bensen B.8M	B. McIntyre
	G-ARXD	A.109 Airedale	D. Howden
	G-ARXG	PA-24 Comanche 250	I. M. Callier
	G-ARXH	Bell 47G	A. B. Searle
	G-ARXP	Luton LA-4A Minor	W. C. Hymas
	G-ARXT	Jodel DR.1050	CJM Flying Group
	G-ARXU	Auster 6A	The A Team
	G-ARXW	M.S.885 Super Rallye	M. A. Jones
	G-ARXX	M.S.880B Rallye Club	P. S. E. Clifton
	G-ARYB	H.S.125 Srs 1 ★	British Aerospace PLC/Hatfield
	G-ARYC	H.S.125 Srs 1 ★	The Mosquito Aircraft Museum
	G-ARYD	Auster AOP.6 (WJ358) ★	Museum of Army Flying/Middle Wallop
	G-ARYF	PA-23 Aztec 250B	I. J. T. Branson/Biggin Hill
	G-ARYH	PA-22 Tri-Pacer 160	Filtration (Water Treatment Engineers) Ltd
	G-ARYI	Cessna 172C	J. Rhodes
	G-ARYK	Cessna 172C	J. H. Emery
	G-ARYR	PA-28 Cherokee 180	R. J. Gerrard & C. S. Wilkinson/Booker
	G-ARYS	Cessna 172C Skyhawk	Guildbrook Associates Ltd
	G-ARYV	PA-24 Comanche 250	Ilford Business Machines Ltd
	G-ARYZ	A.109 Airedale	J. D. Reid
	G-ARZB	Wallis WA-116 Srs 1	K. H. Wallis
	G-ARZE	Cessna 172C ★	*Parachute jump trainer*/Cockerham
	G-ARZM	D.31 Turbulent	Tiger Club (1990) Ltd/Headcorn
	G-ARZN	Beech N35 Bonanza	D. W. Mickleburgh/Leicester
	G-ARZP	A.109 Airedale	G. B. O'Neill (*stored*)/Booker
	G-ARZW	Currie Wot	J. H. Blake
	G-ARZX	Cessna 150B	Woodside Flying Group
	G-ASAA	Luton LA-4A Minor	R. J. Moore
	G-ASAI	A.109 Airedale	K. R Howden & ptnrs.
	G-ASAJ	A.61 Terrier 2 (WE569)	S. J. B. White & V. M. Howard
	G-ASAK	A.61 Terrier 2	Rochford Hundred Flying Group/Southend

Reg.	Type	Owner or Operator	Notes
G-ASAL	SAL Bulldog 120	British Aerospace PLC/Prestwick	
G-ASAM	D.31 Turbulent	Tiger Club (1990) Ltd/Headcorn	
G-ASAN	A.61 Terrier 2	D. R. Godfrey	
G-ASAT	M.S.880B Rallye Club	M. Cutovic	
G-ASAU	M.S.880B Rallye Club	T. C. & R. Edwards	
G-ASAX	A.61 Terrier 2	G. Strathdee	
G-ASAZ	Hiller UH-12E4	Wessex Air Contracts Ltd	
G-ASBA	Currie Wot	M. A. Kaye	
G-ASBB	Beech 23 Musketeer	D. Silver/Southend	
G-ASBH	A.109 Airedale	D. T. Smollett	
G-ASBY	A.109 Airedale	M. R. H. Wheatley & R. K. Wilson	
G-ASCC	Beagle E.3 AOP Mk 11	Old Training Plane Co	
G-ASCM	Isaacs Fury II (K2050)	D. S. T. Eggleton	
G-ASCU	PA-18A Super Cub 150	Farm Aviation Services Ltd	
G-ASCZ	CP.301A Emeraude	Hylton Flying Group/Newcastle	
G-ASDF	Edwards Gyrocopter ★	B. King	
G-ASDK	A.61 Terrier 2	M. L. Rose	
G-ASDL	A.61 Terrier 2	T. J. Rilley & C. E. Mason	
G-ASDO	Beech 95-A55 Baron ★	No 2498 Sqn ATC/Jersey	
G-ASDY	Wallis WA-116/F	K. H. Wallis	
G-ASEA	Luton LA-4A Minor	G. C. Jones	
G-ASEB	Luton LA-4A Minor	S. R. P. Harper	
G-ASEG	A.61 Terrier (VF548)	R .S. O. B. Evans & J. P. P. A. Midgley	
G-ASEO	PA-24 Comanche 250	Planetalk Ltd	
G-ASEP	PA-23 Apache 235	Arrowstate Ltd/Denham	
G-ASEU	D.62A Condor	W. Grant & D. McNicholl	
G-ASFA	Cessna 172D	The Dakota Flying Club/Cranfield	
G-ASFD	L-200A Morava	M. Emery/Bournemouth	
G-ASFK	J/5G Autocar	R. W. & M. Struth	
G-ASFL	PA-28 Cherokee 180	D. F. Ranger/Popham	
G-ASFR	Bo.208A1 Junior	S. T. Dauncey	
G-ASFX	D.31 Turbulent	E. F. Clapham & W. B. S. Dobie	
G-ASGC	V.1151 Super VC10 ★	Duxford Aviation Soc	
G-ASHA	Cessna F.172D	G-ASHA Flying Group	
G-ASHB	Cessna 182F	Sport Parachute Centre Ltd/Tilstock	
G-ASHD	Brantly B-2A ★	International Helicopter Museum/ 　Weston-s-Mare	
G-ASHH	PA-23 Aztec 250	Leicestershire Thread & Trimming 　Manufacturers Ltd/Sibson	
G-ASHS	SNCAN Stampe SV-4B	Three Point Flying Ltd	
G-ASHT	D.31 Turbulent	C. W. N. Huke	
G-ASHU	PA-15 Vagabond	G. J. Romanes	
G-ASHV	PA-23 Aztec 250B	R. J. Ashley & G. O'Gorman	
G-ASHX	PA-28 Cherokee 180	Sunsaver Ltd	
G-ASIB	Cessna F.172D	G-ASIB Flying Group	
G-ASII	PA-28 Cherokee 180	T. R. Hart & Natocars Ltd	
G-ASIJ	PA-28 Cherokee 180	Precision Products Ltd & D. Beadle	
G-ASIL	PA-28 Cherokee 180	N. M. Barker & ptnrs/Leicester	
G-ASIS	Jodel D.112	E. F. Hazel	
G-ASIT	Cessna 180	A. & P. A. Wood	
G-ASIY	PA-25 Pawnee 235	RAFGSA/Bicester	
G-ASJC	BAC One-Eleven 201AC	British Air Ferries Ltd/Southend	
G-ASJL	Beech H.35 Bonanza	MLP Aviation Ltd/Elstree	
G-ASJM	PA-30 Twin Comanche 160 ★	Via Nova Ltd (*stored*)	
G-ASJO	Beech B.23 Musketeer	M. Corbett & B. Hamilton	
G-ASJV	V.S.361 Spitfire IX (MH434)	Nalfire Aviation Ltd/Duxford	
G-ASJY	GY-80 Horizon 160	Horizon Flyers Ltd/Denham	
G-ASJZ	Jodel D.117A	J. M. Gough/Barton	
G-ASKC	D.H.98 Mosquito 35 (TA719) ★	Skyfame Collection/Duxford	
G-ASKH	D.H.98 Mosquito T.3 (RR299)	British Aerospace PLC/Chester	
G-ASKJ	A.61 Terrier 1 (VX926)	N. K. & M. D. Freestone	
G-ASKK	HPR-7 Herald 211 ★	Norwich Aviation Museum	
G-ASKL	Jodel D.150A	J. M. Graty	
G-ASKP	D.H.82A Tiger Moth	Tiger Club (1990) Ltd/Headcorn	
G-ASKS	Cessna 336 Skymaster	M. J. Godwin	
G-ASKT	PA-28 Cherokee 180	A. Mattacks & T. Hood	
G-ASKV	PA-25 Pawnee 235	Southdown Gliding Club Ltd	
G-ASLH	Cessna 182F	R. W. Boote	
G-ASLK	PA-25 Pawnee 235	Bristol Gliding Club (Pty) Ltd/Nympsfield	
G-ASLL	Cessna 336 ★	*stored*/Bournemouth	
G-ASLR	Agusta-Bell 47J-2	Leeds & Manchester Group Ltd	
G-ASLV	PA-28 Cherokee 235	C.S.E. Aviation Ltd/Kidlington	
G-ASLX	CP.301A Emeraude	K. C. Green/Panshanger	

Notes	Reg.	Type	Owner or Operator
	G-ASMA	PA-30 Twin Comanche 160 C/R	B. D. Glynn/Redhill
	G-ASMC	P.56 Provost T.1.	W. Walker (stored)
	G-ASME	Bensen B.8M	D. A. Farnworth
	G-ASMF	Beech D.95A Travel Air	M. J. A. Hornblower
	G-ASMJ	Cessna F.172E	J. E. Tribe & Z. W. Jakubowski/Audley End
	G-ASML	Luton LA-4A Minor	Fenland Strut Flying Group
	G-ASMM	D.31 Tubulent	G. E. Arthur
	G-ASMO	PA-23 Apache 160G ★	Aviation Enterprises/Fairoaks
	G-ASMS	Cessna 150A	K. R. & T. W. Davies
	G-ASMT	Fairtravel Linnet 2	A. F. Cashin
	G-ASMU	Cessna 150D	Telepoint Ltd/Barton
	G-ASMV	CP.1310-C3 Super Emeraude	P. F. D. Waltham/Leicester
	G-ASMW	Cessna 150D	Yorkshire Light Aircraft Ltd/Leeds
	G-ASMY	PA-23 Apache 160H	Hanseviter Aviation/Ipswich
	G-ASMZ	A.61 Terrier 2 (VF516)	R. C. Burden
	G-ASNB	Auster 6A (VX118)	M. Pocock & ptnrs
	G-ASNC	D.5/180 Husky	Peterborough & Spalding Gliding Club/ Boston
	G-ASND	PA-23 Aztec 250	Commercial Air (Woking) Ltd/Fairoaks
	G-ASNH	PA-23 Aztec 250B	J. Hoerner & The Earl of Suffolk & Berkshire
	G-ASNI	CP.1310-C3 Super Emeraude	D. Chapman
	G-ASNK	Cessna 205	Justgold Ltd
	G-ASNU	H.S.125 Srs. 1	Flintgrange Ltd
	G-ASNW	Cessna F.172E	J. A. Gibbs
	G-ASNY	Bensen B.8M	D. L. Wallis
	G-ASOC	Auster 6A	J. A. Rayment/Hinton-in-the-Hedges
	G-ASOH	Beech 95-B55A Baron	GMD Group
	G-ASOI	A.61 Terrier 2	D. I. H. Johnstone
	G-ASOK	Cessna F.172E	Okay Flying Group/Denham
	G-ASOM	A.61 Terrier 2	J. E. Tootell (G-JETS)
	G-ASON	PA-30 Twin Comanche 160	Follandbeech Ltd
	G-ASOO	PA-30 Twin Comanche 160	K. H. Acketts
	G-ASOP	Sopwith F.1 Camel (B6291)	K. C. D. St Cyrien/Middle Wallop
	G-ASOX	Cessna 205A	Border Parachute Centre
	G-ASPF	Jodel D.120	T. J. Bates
	G-ASPI	Cessna F.172E	Icarus Flying Group/Rochester
	G-ASPK	PA-28 Cherokee 140	Westward Airways (Lands End) Ltd/St Just
	G-ASPP	Bristol Boxkite replica	Shuttleworth Trust/O. Warden
	G-ASPS	Piper J-3C-90 Cub	A. J. Chalkley/Blackbushe
	G-ASPU	D.31 Turbulent	I. Maclennan
	G-ASPV	D.H.82A Tiger Moth	B. S. Charters/Shipdham
	G-ASRB	D.62B Condor	T. J. McRae & H. C. Palmer/Shoreham
	G-ASRC	D.62B Condor	J. Knight
	G-ASRF	Jenny Wren	G. W. Gowland (stored)
	G-ASRH	PA-30 Twin Comanche 160	Island Aviation & Travel Ltd
	G-ASRI	PA-23 Aztec 250B ★	Graham Collins Associates Ltd
	G-ASRK	A.109 Airedale ★	R. K. Wilson & M. R. H. Wheatley
	G-ASRO	PA-30 Twin Comanche 160	D. W. Blake
	G-ASRR	Cessna 182G	J. A. Rees
	G-ASRT	Jodel D.150	H. M. Kendall
	G-ASRW	PA-28 Cherokee 180	Astro Electrical & Heating Ltd/Shoreham
	G-ASSB	PA-30 Twin Comanche 160	J. D. Crinnan
	G-ASSE	PA-22 Colt 108	J. B. King/Goodwood
	G-ASSF	Cessna 182G Skylane	Burbage Farms Ltd/Lutterworth
	G-ASSP	PA-30 Twin Comanche 160	P. H. Tavener
	G-ASSR	PA-30 Twin Comanche 160	D. W. Smith
	G-ASSS	Cessna 172E	D. H. N. Squires & P. R. March/Bristol
	G-ASST	Cessna 150D	F. R. H. Parker
	G-ASSU	CP.301A Emeraude	R. W. Millward (stored)/Redhill
	G-ASSW	PA-28 Cherokee 140	C. J. Plummer/Biggin Hill
	G-ASTA	D.31 Turbulent	R. N. Steel
	G-ASTH	Mooney M.20C ★	E. Martin (stored)
	G-ASTI	Auster 6A	M. Pocock
	G-ASTL	Fairey Firefly 1 (Z2033) ★	Skyfame Collection/Duxford
	G-ASTP	Hiller UH-12C ★	International Helicopter Museum/ Weston-s-Mare
	G-ASTV	Cessna 150D (tailwheel) ★	stored
	G-ASUB	Mooney M.20E Super 21	P. K. Pemberton
	G-ASUD	PA-28 Cherokee 180	S. E. Hobbs & Co Ltd
	G-ASUE	Cessna 150D	D. Huckle/Panshanger
	G-ASUG	Beech E18S ★	Museum of Flight/E. Fortune
	G-ASUI	A.61 Terrier 2	K. W. Chigwell & D. R. Lee
	G-ASUL	Cessna 182G Skylane	Blackpool & Fylde Aero Club Ltd

Reg.	Type	Owner or Operator	Notes
G-ASUP	Cessna F.172E	GASUP Air/Cardiff	
G-ASUR	Dornier Do 28A-1	Sheffair Ltd	
G-ASUS	Jurca MJ.2B Tempete	D. G. Jones/Coventry	
G-ASVG	CP.301B Emeraude	K. R. Jackson	
G-ASVM	Cessna F.172E	A. P. D. Hynes & ptnrs/Cambridge	
G-ASVN	Cessna U.206 Super Skywagon	British Skysports/Sibson	
G-ASVO	HPR-7 Herald 214	British Air Ferries Ltd/Southend	
G-ASVP	PA-25 Pawnee 235	Aquila Gliding Club Ltd	
G-ASVZ	PA-28 Cherokee 140	Taylor Aircraft Services/Sywell	
G-ASWB	A.109 Airedale	C. Gene & G. Taylor/Teesside	
G-ASWH	Luton LA-5A Major	J. T. Powell-Tuck	
G-ASWJ	Beagle 206 Srs 1 (8449M) ★	RAF Halton	
G-ASWL	Cessna F.172F	Bagby Aviation Flying Group	
G-ASWN	Bensen B.8M	D. R. Shepherd	
G-ASWP	Beech A.23 Musketeer	H. Mendelssohn & M. H. Rennie/Edinburgh	
G-ASWW	PA-30 Twin Comanche 160	D. M. White	
G-ASWX	PA-28 Cherokee 180	A. F. Dadds	
G-ASXC	SIPA 901	M. K. Dartford	
G-ASXD	Brantly B.2B	Lousada PLC	
G-ASXI	Tipsy T.66 Nipper 3	P. F. J. Wells	
G-ASXJ	Luton LA-4A Minor	J. S. Allison/Halton	
G-ASXR	Cessna 210	A. Schofield	
G-ASXS	Jodel DR.1050	R. A. Hunter	
G-ASXU	Jodel D.120A	G. W. Worley	
G-ASXX	Avro 683 Lancaster 7 (NX611) ★	Lincolnshire Aviation Heritage Centre/ E. Kirkby	
G-ASXY	Jodel D.117A	P. A. Davies & ptnrs/Cardiff	
G-ASXZ	Cessna 182G Skylane	P. M. Robertson/Perth	
G-ASYD	BAC One-Eleven 670	British Aerospace	
G-ASYG	A.61 Terrier 2 ★	stored/Hinton-in-the-Hedges	
G-ASYJ	Beech D.95A Travel Air	Crosby Aviation (Jersey) Ltd	
G-ASYK	PA-30 Twin Comanche 160	M. S. Harvell	
G-ASYP	Cessna 150E	Henlow Flying Group	
G-ASYW	Bell 47G-2	Bristow Helicopters Ltd	
G-ASYZ	Victa Airtourer 100	N. C. Grayson	
G-ASZB	Cessna 150E	W. A. Smale/Exeter	
G-ASZD	Bo 208A2 Junior	A. J. Watson & ptnrs/O. Warden	
G-ASZE	A.61 Terrier 2	P. J. Moore	
G-ASZJ	S.C.7 Skyvan 3A-100	GEC Marconi Ltd/Luton	
G-ASZR	Fairtravel Linnet	H. C. D. & F. J. Garner	
G-ASZS	GY.80 Horizon 160	J. M. B. Duncan	
G-ASZU	Cessna 150E	T. H. Milburn	
G-ASZV	Tipsy T.66 Nipper 2	R. L. Mitcham/Elstree	
G-ASZX	A.61 Terrier 1	C. A. Bailey	
G-ATAF	Cessna F.172F	S. Lancashire Flyers Ltd	
G-ATAG	Jodel DR. 1050	T. M. Dawes-Gamble	
G-ATAI	D.H.104 Dove 8	L. A. Wootton/France	
G-ATAS	PA-28 Cherokee 180	E. J. Titterrell	
G-ATAT	Cessna 150E	The Derek Pointon Group (stored)	
G-ATAU	D.62B Condor	M. A. Peare/Redhill	
G-ATAV	D.62C Condor	The Condor Syndicate	
G-ATBF	F-86E Sabre 4 (XB733) ★	T. Bracewell (stored)	
G-ATBG	Nord 1002 (NJ-C11)	L. M. Walton	
G-ATBH	Aero 145	P. D. Aberbach	
G-ATBI	Beech A.23 Musketeer	R. F. G. Dent/Staverton	
G-ATBJ	Sikorsky S-61N	British International Helicopters Ltd	
G-ATBL	D.H.60G Moth	J. J. V. Elwes	
G-ATBP	Fournier RF-3	Dishforth Flying Group	
G-ATBS	D.31 Turbulent	D. R. Keene & J. A. Lear	
G-ATBU	A.61 Terrier 2	P. R. Anderson	
G-ATBW	Tipsy T.66 Nipper 2	Stapleford Nipper Group	
G-ATBX	PA-20 Pacer 135	G. D. & P. M. Thomson	
G-ATBZ	W.S.58 Wessex 60 ★	International Helicopter Museum/ Weston-s-Mare	
G-ATCC	A.109 Airedale	J. F. Moore & ptnrs/Biggin Hill	
G-ATCD	D.5/180 Husky	Oxford Flying & Gliding Group/Enstone	
G-ATCE	Cessna U.206	J. Fletcher & D. Hickling/Langar	
G-ATCJ	Luton LA-4A Minor	R. M. Sharphouse	
G-ATCL	Victa Airtourer 100	A. D. Goodall	
G-ATCN	Luton LA-4A Minor	J. C. Gates & C. Neilson	
G-ATCR	Cessna 310 ★	ITD Aviation Ltd/Denham	
G-ATCU	Cessna 337	University of Cambridge	

Notes	Reg.	Type	Owner or Operator
	G-ATCX	Cessna 182H Skylane	K. J. Fisher/Bodmin
	G-ATDA	PA-28 Cherokee 160	Global Aircraft Services Ltd
	G-ATDN	A.61 Terrier 2 (TW641)	S. J. Saggers/Biggin Hill
	G-ATDO	Bo 208C Junior	H. Swift
	G-ATEF	Cessna 150E	Swans Aviation
	G-ATEG	Cessna 150E	A. W. Woodward/Biggin Hill
	G-ATEK	H.S. 748 Srs 2B	STH Sales Ltd
	G-ATEM	PA-28 Cherokee 180	Chiltern Valley Aviation Ltd
	G-ATEP	EAA Biplane ★	E. L. Martin (*stored*)/Guernsey
	G-ATES	PA-32 Cherokee Six 260 ★	*Parachute jump trainer*/Ipswich
	G-ATET	PA-30 Twin Comanche 160	P. W. Bayliss
	G-ATEV	Jodel DR. 1050	R. A. Smith
	G-ATEW	PA-30 Twin Comanche 160	Air Northumbria Group/Newcastle
	G-ATEX	Victa Airtourer 100	Medway Victa Group
	G-ATEZ	PA-28 Cherokee 140	J. A. Burton/E. Midlands
	G-ATFD	Jodel DR. 1050	V. Usher
	G-ATFF	PA-23 Aztec 250C	Neatspin Ltd
	G-ATFG	Brantly B.2B ★	Museum of Flight/E. Fortune
	G-ATFK	PA-30 Twin Comanche 160	D. J. Crinnon/White Waltham
	G-ATFM	Sikorsky S-61N	British International Helicopters Ltd/ Aberdeen
	G-ATFR	PA-25 Pawnee 150	R. R. Harris
	G-ATFU	D.H.85 Leopard Moth	A. H. Carrington & C. D. Duthy-James
	G-ATFV	Agusta-Bell 47J-2A	Alexander Warren & Co Ltd
	G-ATFW	Luton LA-4A Minor	C. Kirk
	G-ATFX	Cessna F.172G	Isabella Properties Ltd
	G-ATFY	Cessna F.172G	H. Bennett & P. McCabe
	G-ATGE	Jodel DR.1050	J. R. Roberts
	G-ATGH	Brantly B.2B	Helihire Ltd
	G-ATGN	Thorn Coal Gas balloon	British Balloon Museum
	G-ATGO	Cessna F.172G	J. A. & R. M. Nicol/Carlisle
	G-ATGP	Jodel DR.1050	N. J. Heaton/Sherburn
	G-ATGY	GY.80 Horizon	P. W. Gibberson/Birmingham
	G-ATGZ	Griffiths GH-4 Gyroplane	G. Griffiths
	G-ATHA	PA-23 Apache 235 ★	Brunel Technical College/Bristol
	G-ATHD	D.H.C.1 Chipmunk 22 (WP971)	Spartan Flying Group Ltd/Denham
	G-ATHF	Cessna 150F ★	Lincolnshire Aircraft Museum
	G-ATHI	PA-28 Cherokee 180 ★	*Instructional airframe*/Dublin
	G-ATHK	Aeronca 7AC Champion	N. S. Chittenden
	G-ATHM	Wallis WA-116 Srs 1	Wallis Autogyros Ltd
	G-ATHN	Nord 1101 Noralpha	E. L. Martin (*stored*)/Guernsey
	G-ATHR	PA-28 Cherokee 180	Britannia Airways Ltd/Luton
	G-ATHT	Victa Airtourer 115	H. C. G. Munroe
	G-ATHU	A.61 Terrier 1	J. A. L. Irwin
	G-ATHV	Cessna 150F	P. Cooper
	G-ATHX	Jodel DR. 100A	A. D. Massey & R. C. Hibberd
	G-ATHZ	Cessna 150F	E. & R. D. Forster
	G-ATIA	PA-24 Comanche 260	L. A. Brown
	G-ATIC	Jodel DR.1050 ★	*stored*
	G-ATID	Cessna 337	M. R. Tarrant/Bourn
	G-ATIE	Cessna 150F ★	*Parachute jump trainer*/Chetwynd
	G-ATIG	HPR-7 Herald 214	Janes Aviation Ltd/Blackpool
	G-ATIN	Jodel D.117	D. R. Upton & J. G. Kay/Barton
	G-ATIR	AIA Stampe SV-4C	N. M. Bloom
	G-ATIS	PA-28 Cherokee 160	S. Boon & P. J. Fydelor
	G-ATIZ	Jodel D.117	R. Frith & ptnrs
	G-ATJA	Jodel DR.1050	Bicester Flying Group
	G-ATJC	Victa Airtourer 100	Aviation West Ltd
	G-ATJG	PA-28 Cherokee 140	Royal Aircraft Establishment Dept/ Thurleigh
	G-ATJL	PA-24 Comanche 260	M. J. Berry & T. R. Quinn/Blackbushe
	G-ATJM	Fokker DR.1 replica (152/17)	R. Lamplough/Duxford
	G-ATJN	Jodel D.119	R. F. Bradshaw
	G-ATJR	PA-E23 Aztec 250C	W. A. G. Willbond/Bourn
	G-ATJT	GY.80 Horizon 160	N. Huxtable
	G-ATJV	PA-32 Cherokee Six 260	SMK Engineers Ltd
	G-ATKF	Cessna 150F	A. F. G. Clutterbuck
	G-ATKH	Luton LA-4A Minor	H. E. Jenner
	G-ATKI	Piper J-3C-65 Cub	J. H. Allistone/Booker
	G-ATKS	Cessna F.172G	Blois Aviation Ltd
	G-ATKT	Cessna F.172G	P. J. Megson
	G-ATKU	Cessna F.172G	Heatherlake Ltd
	G-ATKX	Jodel D.140C	A. J. White & G. A. Piper/Biggin Hill

Reg.	Type	Owner or Operator	Notes
G-ATKZ	Tipsy T.66 Nipper 2	M. W. Knights	
G-ATLA	Cessna 182J Skylane	Shefford Transport Engineers Ltd/Luton	
G-ATLB	Jodel DR.1050/M1	La Petit Oiseau Syndicate/Sherburn	
G-ATLC	PA-23 Aztec 250C ★	Alderney Air Charter Ltd (*stored*)	
G-ATLG	Hiller UH-12B	Bristow Helicopters Ltd	
G-ATLM	Cessna F.172G	Air Fotos Aviation Ltd/Newcastle	
G-ATLP	Bensen B.8M	C. D. Julian	
G-ATLT	Cessna U-206A	Army Parachute Association/Netheravon	
G-ATLV	Jodel D.120	W. H. Greenwood	
G-ATLW	PA-28 Cherokee 180	Lima Whisky Flying Group	
G-ATMC	Cessna F.150F	C. J. & E. J. Leigh	
G-ATMG	M.S.893 Rallye Commodore 180	D. R. Wilkinson & T. Coldwell	
G-ATMH	D.5/180 Husky	Devon & Somerset Gliding Club Ltd	
G-ATMI	H.S.748 Srs 2A	Dan-Air Services Ltd/Gatwick	
G-ATMJ	H.S.748 Srs 2A	Dan-Air Services Ltd/Gatwick	
G-ATML	Cessna F.150F	B. A. Pickers	
G-ATMM	Cessna F.150F	R. Jacobs & R. Felton	
G-ATMT	PA-30 Twin Comanche 160	D. H. T. Bain/Newcastle	
G-ATMU	PA-23 Apache 160G	P. K. Martin & R. W. Harris	
G-ATMW	PA-28 Cherokee 140	Bencray Ltd/Blackpool	
G-ATMX	Cessna F.150F	Homeward Flying Group	
G-ATMY	Cessna 150F	C. F. Read/Doncaster	
G-ATNB	PA-28 Cherokee 180	R. F. Hill	
G-ATNE	Cessna F.150F	J. & S. Brew	
G-ATNJ	Cessna F.150F ★	*Instructional airframe*/Perth	
G-ATNK	Cessna F.150F	Pegasus Aviation Ltd	
G-ATNL	Cessna F.150F	S. M. Kemp & ptnrs	
G-ATNV	PA-24 Comanche 260	B. S. Reynolds & P. R. Fortescue/Bourn	
G-ATNX	Cessna F.150F	P. Jenkins	
G-ATOA	PA-23 Apache 160G	K. White	
G-ATOD	Cessna F.150F	E. Watson & ptnrs/St Just	
G-ATOE	Cessna F.150F	S. Armstrong	
G-ATOF	Cessna F.150F ★	*Instructional airframe*/Perth	
G-ATOG	Cessna F-150F ★	*Instructional airframe*/Perth	
G-ATOH	D.62B Condor	L. S. Thorne	
G-ATOI	PA-28 Cherokee 140	O. & E. Flying Ltd/Stapleford	
G-ATOJ	PA-28 Cherokee 140	Firefly Aviation Ltd/Glasgow	
G-ATOK	PA-28 Cherokee 140	WLS Flying Group/Blackbushe	
G-ATOL	PA-28 Cherokee 140	L. J. Nation & G. Alford	
G-ATOM	PA-28 Cherokee 140	R. W. Mason/Kidlington	
G-ATON	PA-28 Cherokee 140	R. G. Walters	
G-ATOO	PA-28 Cherokee 140 ★	*Instructional airframe*/Moston Centre	
G-ATOP	PA-28 Cherokee 140	P. R. Coombs/Blackbushe	
G-ATOR	PA-28 Cherokee 140	D. Palmer & V. G. Whitehead	
G-ATOS	PA-28 Cherokee 140	Matthews Air Trading Services	
G-ATOT	PA-28 Cherokee 180	J. B. Waterfield & G. L. Birch	
G-ATOU	Mooney M.20E Super 21	P. R. & M. R. Parr	
G-ATOY	PA-24 Comanche 260 ★	Museum of Flight/E. Fortune	
G-ATOZ	Bensen B.8M	J. Jordan	
G-ATPD	H.S.125 Srs 1B	G. M. Kay	
G-ATPN	PA-28 Cherokee 140	M. F. Hatt & ptnrs/Southend	
G-ATPT	Cessna 182J Skylane	Western Models Ltd/Redhill	
G-ATPV	JB.01 Minicab	I. A. J. Lappin	
G-ATRA	LET L.13 Blanik	Blanik Sydincate	
G-ATRC	Beech B.95A Travel Air	P. J. Simmons	
G-ATRG	PA-18 Super Cub 150	Lasham Gliding Soc Ltd	
G-ATRI	Bo 208C Junior	Chertwood Ltd	
G-ATRK	Cessna F.150F	J. Rees & F. Doncaster	
G-ATRL	Cessna F.150F	S. S. Delwarte/Shoreham	
G-ATRO	PA-28 Cherokee 140	390th Flying Group	
G-ATRR	PA-28 Cherokee 140	Marnham Investments Ltd	
G-ATRW	PA-32 Cherokee Six 260	Pictex Ltd	
G-ATRX	PA-32 Cherokee Six 260	J. W. Stow	
G-ATSI	Bo 208C Junior	Hostworth Ltd	
G-ATSL	Cessna F.172G	D. Le Cheminant/Guernsey	
G-ATSM	Cessna 337A	Tremlett (Skicraft) Ltd	
G-ATSR	Beech M.35 Bonanza	Alstan Aviation Ltd	
G-ATSU	Jodel D.140B	B. M. O'Brien & P. J. Sellar	
G-ATSX	Bo 208C Junior	R. J. C. Campbell & M. H. Goley	
G-ATSY	Wassmer WA41 Super Baladou IV	Baladou Flying Group	
G-ATTB	Wallis WA-116-1 (XR944)	D. A. Wallis	
G-ATTD	Cessna 182J Skylane	K. M. Brennan & ptnrs	
G-ATTF	PA-28 Cherokee 140	D. H. Fear	

Notes	Reg.	Type	Owner or Operator
	G-ATTG	PA-28 Cherokee 140	Arrow Air Services Engineering Ltd/ Shipdham
	G-ATTI	PA-28 Cherokee 140	Parry & Co/Bristol
	G-ATTK	PA-28 Cherokee 140	G-ATTK Flying Group/Southend
	G-ATTM	Jodel DR.250-160	R. W. Tomkinson
	G-ATTR	Bo 208C Junior 3	S. Luck
	G-ATTU	PA-28 Cherokee 140	Lion Flying Group/Elstree
	G-ATTV	PA-28 Cherokee 140	D. R. Winder
	G-ATTX	PA-28 Cherokee 180	Ipac Aviation Flying Group
	G-ATTY	PA-32 Cherokee Six 260	F. J. Wadia
	G-ATUB	PA-28 Cherokee 140	R. H. Partington & M. J. Porter
	G-ATUD	PA-28 Cherokee 140	E. J. Clempson
	G-ATUF	Cessna F.150F	A. R. Hawes/Ipswich
	G-ATUG	D.62B Condor	HMW Aviation
	G-ATUH	Tipsy T.66 Nipper 1	D. G. Spruce
	G-ATUI	Bo 208C Junior	A. W. Wakefield
	G-ATUL	PA-28 Cherokee 180	H. M. Synge
	G-ATVF	D.H.C.1 Chipmunk 22	RAFGSA/Dishforth
	G-ATVK	PA-28 Cherokee 140	JRB Aviation Ltd/Southend
	G-ATVL	PA-28 Cherokee 140	West London Aero Services Ltd/ White Waltham
	G-ATVO	PA-28 Cherokee 140	Cormack (Aircraft Services) Ltd/Glasgow
	G-ATVP	F.B.5 Gunbus (2345) ★	RAF Museum/Hendon
	G-ATVS	PA-28 Cherokee 180	Markel Aviation
	G-ATVW	D.62B Condor	J. P. Coulter & J. Chidley/Panshanger
	G-ATVX	Bo 208C Junior	G. & G. E. F. Warren
	G-ATWA	Jodel DR.1050	Jodel Syndicate
	G-ATWB	Jodel D.117	W. Bampton & ptnrs/Andrewsfield
	G-ATWE	M.S.892A Rallye Commodore	D. I. Murray
	G-ATWJ	Cessna F.172F	C. J. & J. Freeman/Headcorn
	G-ATWP	Alon A-2 Aircoupe	H. Dodd & I. Wilson
	G-ATWR	PA-30 Twin Comanche 160B	Lubair (Transport Services) Ltd/ E. Midlands
	G-ATXA	PA-22 Tri-Pacer 150	R. C. Teverson
	G-ATXD	PA-30 Twin Comanche 160B	Jet Heritage Ltd/Bournemouth
	G-ATXF	GY-80 Horizon 150	D. C. Hyde
	G-ATXJ	H.P.137 Jetstream 300 ★	British Aerospace (*display mock-up*)/ Prestwick
	G-ATXM	PA-28 Cherokee 180	J. Khan/Ipswich
	G-ATXN	Mitchell-Proctor Kittiwake	D. W. Kent
	G-ATXO	SIPA 903	M. Hillam/Sherburn
	G-ATXZ	Bo 208C Junior	L. S. Johnson/Ipswich
	G-ATYM	Cessna F.150G	J. F. Perry & Co
	G-ATYN	Cessna F.150G	Skegness Air Taxi Services Ltd
	G-ATYS	PA-28 Cherokee 180	R. V. Waite
	G-ATZA	Bo 208C Junior	Skyward Services Ltd/Jersey
	G-ATZG	AFB2 gas balloon	Flt Lt S. Cameron *Aeolis*
	G-ATZK	PA-28 Cherokee 180	R. W. Nash & J. A. Gibbs/Kidlington
	G-ATZM	Piper J-3C-65 Cub	R. W. Davison
	G-ATZS	Wassmer WA41 Super Baladou IV	G. R. Outwin & D. P. Bennett
	G-ATZY	Cessna F.150G	J. Easson/Edinburgh
	G-ATZZ	Cessna F.150G	Matthews Air Trading Services/Southend
	G-AVAA	Cessna F.150G	LAR Aviation Ltd/Shoreham
	G-AVAK	M.S.893A Rallye Commodore 180	W. K. Anderson (*stored*)/Perth
	G-AVAP	Cessna F.150G	Seawing Flying Club/Southend
	G-AVAR	Cessna F.150G	J. A. Rees & F. Doncaster
	G-AVAU	PA-30 Twin Comanche 160B	L. Batin/Fairoaks
	G-AVAW	D.62B Condor	Avato Flying Group
	G-AVAX	PA-28 Cherokee 180	J. J. Parkes
	G-AVBG	PA-28 Cherokee 180	G-AVBG Flying Group/White Waltham
	G-AVBH	PA-28 Cherokee 180	T. R. Smith (Agricultural Machinery) Ltd
	G-AVBP	PA-28 Cherokee 140	Bristol & Wessex Aeroplane Club
	G-AVBS	PA-28 Cherokee 180	G. W. Atkins/St Just
	G-AVBT	PA-28 Cherokee 180	P. O. Hire & D. J. Spicer/Denham
	G-AVBZ	Cessna F.172H	M. G. Hill
	G-AVCE	Cessna F.172H	Doncaster Aero Club Ltd
	G-AVCM	PA-24 Comanche 260	F. Smith & Sons Ltd/Stapleford
	G-AVCS	A.61 Terrier 1	A. Topen/Cranfield
	G-AVCT	Cessna F.150G	M. L. Biggs/Shobdon
	G-AVCU	Cessna F.150G	Farley Aviation Ltd
	G-AVCV	Cessna 182J Skylane	University of Manchester Institute of Science & Technology/Woodford

Reg.	Type	Owner or Operator	Notes
G-AVCX	PA-30 Twin Comanche 160B	T. Barge	
G-AVCY	PA-30 Twin Comanche 160B	R. C. Pugsley/Cardiff	
G-AVDA	Cessna 182K Skylane	J. W. Grant	
G-AVDF	Beagle Pup 100 ★	Shoreham Airport Museum	
G-AVDG	Wallis WA-116 Srs 1	K. H. Wallis	
G-AVDT	Aeronca 7AC Champion	D. Cheney & J. G. Woods	
G-AVDV	PA-22 Tri-Pacer 150 (modified to Pacer)	S. C. Brooks/Slinfold	
G-AVDW	D.62B Condor	Essex Aviation/Andrewsfield	
G-AVDY	Luton LA-4A Minor	D. E. Evans & ptnrs	
G-AVEB	Morane MS 230 (157)	T. McG. Leaver	
G-AVEC	Cessna F.172H	W. H. Ekin (Engineering) Co Ltd	
G-AVEF	Jodel D.150	Tiger Club (1990) Ltd/Headcorn	
G-AVEH	SIAI-Marchetti S.205	B. Thaler/Booker	
G-AVEM	Cessna F.150G	P. Brown	
G-AVEN	Cessna F.150G	N. J. Budd/Aberdeen	
G-AVEO	Cessna F.150G	H. I. Matthews/Southend	
G-AVER	Cessna F.150G	Telair Manchester Ltd	
G-AVET	Beech 95-C55A Baron	S. P. Glover	
G-AVEU	Wassmer WA.41 Baladou IV	M. A. Hales	
G-AVEX	D.62B Condor	Cotswold Roller Hire Ltd/Long Marston	
G-AVEY	Currie Super Wot	A. Easteclow/Dunkeswell	
G-AVEZ	HPR-7 Herald 210 ★	*Rescue Trainer*/Norwich	
G-AVFB	H.S.121 Trident 2E ★	Duxford Aviation Soc	
G-AVFE	H.S.121 Trident 2E ★	Belfast Airport Authority	
G-AVFG	H.S.121 Trident 2E ★	*Ground handling trainer*/Heathrow	
G-AVFH	H.S.121 Trident 2E ★	Mosquito Aircraft Museum (Fuselage only)	
G-AVFK	H.S.121 Trident 2E ★	Metropolitan Police Training Centre/Hounslow	
G-AVFM	H.S.121 Trident 2E ★	Brunel Technical College/Bristol	
G-AVFP	PA-28 Cherokee 140	H. D. Vince Ltd/Woodvale	
G-AVFR	PA-28 Cherokee 140	VFR Flying Group/Newtownards	
G-AVFS	PA-32 Cherokee Six 300	Comed Aviation Ltd/Blackpool	
G-AVFU	PA-32 Cherokee Six 300	Ashley Gardner Flying Club Ltd	
G-AVFX	PA-28 Cherokee 140	D. J. Young & H. Weldon	
G-AVFZ	PA-28 Cherokee 140	R. S. Littlechild & V. B. G. Childs	
G-AVGA	PA-24 Comanche 260	Conram Aviation/Biggin Hill	
G-AVGB	PA-28 Cherokee 140	D. J. Hill/Fowlmere	
G-AVGC	PA-28 Cherokee 140	P. A. Hill	
G-AVGD	PA-28 Cherokee 140	S. & G. W. Jacobs	
G-AVGE	PA-28 Cherokee 140	H. H. T. Wolf	
G-AVGH	PA-28 Cherokee 140	Phoenix Aviation Services Ltd	
G-AVGI	PA-28 Cherokee 140	D. G. Smith & C. D. Barden	
G-AVGJ	Jodel DR.1050	S. T. Gilbert & D. J. Kirkwood	
G-AVGK	PA-28 Cherokee 180	Golf Kilo Flying Group	
G-AVGP	BAC One-Eleven 408EF	Birmingham European Airways Ltd *City of Coventry*	
G-AVGV	Cessna F.150G	Bagby Aviation Flying Group	
G-AVGY	Cessna 182K Skylane	Clifford F. Cross (Wisbech) Ltd/Fenland	
G-AVGZ	Jodel DR.1050	D. C. Webb	
G-AVHH	Cessna F.172H	M. J. Mann & J. Hickinbotom	
G-AVHL	Jodel DR.105A	G. L. Winterbourne/Redhill	
G-AVHM	Cessna F.150G	A. G. Wintle & J. Knight/Elstree	
G-AVHN	Cessna F.150F ★	Brunel Technical College/Bristol	
G-AVHT	Auster AOP.9 (WZ711)	M. Somerton-Rayner/Middle Wallop	
G-AVHY	Fournier RF.4D	R. Swinn & J. Conolly	
G-AVIA	Cessna F.150G	Cheshire Air Training School (Merseyside) Ltd/Liverpool	
G-AVIB	Cessna F.150G	Group India Bravo	
G-AVIC	Cessna F.172H	Pembrokeshire Air/Haverfordwest	
G-AVID	Cessna 182J	T. D. Boyle	
G-AVIE	Cessna F.172H	M. P. Parker	
G-AVII	AB-206A JetRanger	Bristow Helicopters Ltd	
G-AVIL	Alon A.2 Aircoupe	M. J. Close	
G-AVIN	M.S.880B Rallye Club	G. I. J. Thomson/Norwich	
G-AVIO	M.S.880B Rallye Club	H. Plain/Exeter	
G-AVIP	Brantly B.2B	P. J. Troy-Davies	
G-AVIS	Cessna F.172H	R. T. Jones/Rochester	
G-AVIT	Cessna F.150G	Shropshire Aero Club Ltd/Sleap	
G-AVIZ	Scheibe SF.25A Motorfalke	D. C. Pattison & D. A. Wilson	
G-AVJE	Cessna F.150G	G-AVJE Syndicate	
G-AVJF	Cessna F.172H	J. A. & G. M. Rees	
G-AVJG	Cessna 337B	P. R. Moss/Bournemouth	

Notes	Reg.	Type	Owner or Operator
	G-AVJI	Cessna F.172H	M. A. Kempson
	G-AVJJ	PA-30 Twin Comanche 160B	A. H. Manser
	G-AVJK	Jodel DR.1050/M1	G. Wylde
	G-AVJO	Fokker E.III Replica (422-15)	Bianchi Aviation Film Services Ltd
	G-AVJV	Wallis WA-117 Srs 1	K. H. Wallis (G-ATCV)
	G-AVJW	Wallis WA-118 Srs 2	K. H. Wallis (G-ATPW)
	G-AVKB	MB.50 Pipistrelle	B. H. Pickard
	G-AVKD	Fournier RF-4D	Lasham RF4 Group
	G-AVKE	Gadfly HDW.1 ★	International Helicopter Museum/ Weston-s-Mare
	G-AVKG	Cessna F.172H	P. E. P. Sheppard
	G-AVKI	Slingsby T.66 Nipper 3	J. Fisher
	G-AVKJ	Slingsby T.66 Nipper 3	J. M. Greenway
	G-AVKK	Slingsby T.66 Nipper 3	C. Watson
	G-AVKN	Cessna 401	Law Leasing Ltd
	G-AVKP	A.109 Airedale	D. R. Williams
	G-AVKR	Bo 208C Junior	C. W. Grant
	G-AVKY	Hiller UH-12E	Agricopters Ltd/Chilbolton
	G-AVKZ	PA-23 Aztec 250C	Tindon Ltd/Little Snoring
	G-AVLB	PA-28 Cherokee 140	J. A. Overton Ltd/Andrewsfield
	G-AVLC	PA-28 Cherokee 140	F. C. V. Hopkins/Swansea
	G-AVLD	PA-28 Cherokee 140	WLS Flying Group/White Waltham
	G-AVLE	PA-28 Cherokee 140	Video Security Services/Tollerton
	G-AVLF	PA-28 Cherokee 140	G. H. Hughesdon
	G-AVLG	PA-28 Cherokee 140	R. Friedlander & D. C. Raymond
	G-AVLH	PA-28 Cherokee 140	P. Preece/Goodwood
	G-AVLI	PA-28 Cherokee 140	J. V. White
	G-AVLJ	PA-28 Cherokee 140	E. Berks Boat Company Ltd
	G-AVLN	B.121 Pup 2	C. A. Thorpe
	G-AVLO	Bo 208C Junior	J. A. Webb & K. F. Barnard/Popham
	G-AVLR	PA-28 Cherokee 140	Group 140/Panshanger
	G-AVLT	PA-28 Cherokee 140	R. W. Harris & ptnrs/Southend
	G-AVLU	PA-28 Cherokee 140	London Transport (CRS) Sports Association Flying Club/Fairoaks
	G-AVLW	Fournier RF-4D	F. Mumford
	G-AVLY	Jodel D.120A	G-AVLY Flying Group
	G-AVMA	GY-80 Horizon 180	B. R. Hildick
	G-AVMB	D.62B Condor	J. C. Mansell
	G-AVMD	Cessna 150G	Bagby Aviation Flying Group
	G-AVMF	Cessna F. 150G	J. F. Marsh & M. J. Oliver
	G-AVMH	BAC One-Eleven 510ED	British Airways *County of Cheshire*
	G-AVMI	BAC One-Eleven 510ED	British Airways *County of Merseyside*
	G-AVMJ	BAC One-Eleven 510ED	British Airways *Strathclyde Region*
	G-AVMK	BAC One-Eleven 510ED	British Airways *County of Kent*
	G-AVML	BAC One-Eleven 510ED	British Airways *County of Surrey*
	G-AVMM	BAC One-Eleven 510ED	British Airways *County of Antrim*
	G-AVMN	BAC One-Eleven 510ED	British Airways *County of Essex*
	G-AVMO	BAC One-Eleven 510ED	British Airways *Lothian Region*
	G-AVMP	BAC One-Eleven 510ED	British Airways *Bailiwick of Jersey*
	G-AVMR	BAC One-Eleven 510ED	British Airways *County of Tyne & Wear*
	G-AVMS	BAC One-Eleven 510ED	British Airways *County of West Sussex*
	G-AVMT	BAC One-Eleven 510ED	British Airways *County of Berkshire*
	G-AVMU	BAC One-Eleven 510ED	British Airways *County of Dorset*
	G-AVMV	BAC One-Eleven 510ED	British Airways *Greater Manchester County*
	G-AVMW	BAC One-Eleven 510ED	British Airways *Grampian Region*
	G-AVMX	BAC One-Eleven 510ED	British Airways *County of East Sussex*
	G-AVMY	BAC One-Eleven 510ED	British Airways *County of Derbyshire*
	G-AVNC	Cessna F.150G	J. Turner
	G-AVNE	W.S.58 Wessex Mk 60 Srs 1 ★	International Helicopter Museum/ Weston-s-Mare
	G-AVNN	PA-28 Cherokee 180	B. Andrews & C. S. Mitchell
	G-AVNO	PA-28 Cherokee 180	Allister Flight Ltd/Stapleford
	G-AVNP	PA-28 Cherokee 180	R. W. Harris & ptnrs
	G-AVNR	PA-28 Cherokee 180	W. A. Webb & Co Ltd/Biggin Hill
	G-AVNS	PA-28 Cherokee 180	November Sierra Flying Group
	G-AVNU	PA-28 Cherokee 180	O. Durrani
	G-AVNW	PA-28 Cherokee 180	Len Smith's School & Sports Ltd
	G-AVNX	Fournier RF-4D	Nymphsfield RF-4 Group
	G-AVNY	Fournier RF-4D	V. S. E. Norman/Staverton
	G-AVNZ	Fournier RF-4D	Aviation Special Developments (ASD) Ltd/ Biggin Hill
	G-AVOA	Jodel DR.1050	D. A. Willies/Cranwell

Reg.	Type	Owner or Operator	Notes
G-AVOD	D.5/180 Husky	M. E. Taylor	
G-AVOH	D.62B Condor	D. F. Ranger/Popham	
G-AVOM	Jodel DR.221	M. A. Mountford/Headcorn	
G-AVOO	PA-18 Super Cub 150	London Gliding Club Ltd/ Dunstable	
G-AVOZ	PA-28 Cherokee 180	J. R. Winning/Booker	
G-AVPC	D.31 Turbulent	J. Sharp (stored)	
G-AVPD	D.9 Bebe	S. W. McKay (stored)	
G-AVPH	Cessna F.150G	W. Lancashire Aero Club/Woodvale	
G-AVPI	Cessna F.172H	R. W. Cope	
G-AVPJ	D.H.82A Tiger Moth	C. C. Silk	
G-AVPK	M.S.892A Rallye Commodore	B. A. Bridgewater/Halfpenny Green	
G-AVPM	Jodel D.117	J. Houghton/Breighton	
G-AVPN	HPR-7 Herald 213	British Air Ferries Ltd/Southend	
G-AVPO	Hindustan HAL-26 Pushpak	J. C. Rimell	
G-AVPR	PA-30 Twin Comanche 160B	Cold Storage (Jersey) Ltd	
G-AVPS	PA-30 Twin Comanche 160B	J. M. Bisco/Staverton	
G-AVPT	PA-18 Super Cub 150	Tiger Club (1990) Ltd/Headcorn	
G-AVPV	PA-28 Cherokee 180	MLP Aviation Ltd/Elstree	
G-AVRK	PA-28 Cherokee 180	J. Gama	
G-AVRN	Boeing 737-204	Britannia Airways Ltd Capt James Cook/ Luton	
G-AVRP	PA-28 Cherokee 140	T. Hiscox	
G-AVRS	GY-80 Horizon 180	Air Venturas Ltd	
G-AVRT	PA-28 Cherokee 140	R. S. Stopp	
G-AVRU	PA-28 Cherokee 180	G-AVRU Partnership/Clacton	
G-AVRW	GY-20 Minicab	Kestrel Flying Group/Tollerton	
G-AVRY	PA-28 Cherokee 180	Brigfast Ltd/Blackbushe	
G-AVRZ	PA-28 Cherokee 180	Mantavia Group Ltd	
G-AVSA	PA-28 Cherokee 180	G-AVSA Flying Group	
G-AVSB	PA-28 Cherokee 180	White House Garage Ashford Ltd	
G-AVSC	PA-28 Cherokee 180	Medidata Ltd	
G-AVSD	PA-28 Cherokee 180	Landmate Ltd	
G-AVSE	PA-28 Cherokee 180	Yorkshire Aeroplane Club Ltd/Leeds	
G-AVSF	PA-28 Cherokee 180	Monday Club	
G-AVSI	PA-28 Cherokee 140	CR Aviation Ltd	
G-AVSP	PA-28 Cherokee 180	Devon School of Flying/Dunkeswell	
G-AVSR	D.5/180 Husky	A. L. Young	
G-AVTC	Slingsby T.66 Nipper 3	M. K. Field	
G-AVTJ	PA-32 Cherokee Six 260	Fly By Night Corporation Ltd	
G-AVTK	PA-32 Cherokee Six 260	Malu Aviation Ltd/Alderney	
G-AVTP	Cessna F.172H	W. Murphy	
G-AVTT	Ercoupe 415D	Wright's Farm Eggs Ltd/Andrewsfield	
G-AVTV	M.S.893A Rallye Commodore	D. B. Meeks	
G-AVUD	PA-30 Twin Comanche 160B	F. M. Aviation/Biggin Hill	
G-AVUG	Cessna F.150H	Skyways Flying Group/Netherthorpe	
G-AVUH	Cessna F.150H	G-AVUH Group	
G-AVUL	Cessna F.172H	R. Bilson & R. D. Turner	
G-AVUS	PA-28 Cherokee 140	R. Groat/Glasgow	
G-AVUT	PA-28 Cherokee 140	Bencray Ltd/Blackpool	
G-AVUU	PA-28 Cherokee 140	A. Jahanfar & ptnrs/Southend	
G-AVUZ	PA-32 Cherokee Six 300	Ceesix Ltd/Jersey	
G-AVVC	Cessna F.172H	J. S. M. Cattle	
G-AVVE	Cessna F.150H ★	R. Windley (stored)	
G-AVVI	PA-30 Twin Comanche 160B	H. E. Boulter & D. G. Bligh	
G-AVVJ	M.S.893A Rallye Commodore	Herefordshire Gliding Club Ltd/ Shobdon	
G-AVVL	Cessna F.150H	N. E. Sams/Cranfield	
G-AVVO	Avro 652A Anson 19 (VL348) ★	Newark Air Museum	
G-AVVV	PA-28 Cherokee 180	A. H. Lavender & D. M. Smith	
G-AVVX	Cessna F.150H	Hatfield Flying Club	
G-AVWA	PA-28 Cherokee 140	Incipient Stall Co/Elstree	
G-AVWD	PA-28 Cherokee 140	M. P. Briggs	
G-AVWE	PA-28 Cherokee 140	W. C. C. Meyer (stored)/Biggin Hill	
G-AVWG	PA-28 Cherokee 140	Bencray Ltd/Blackpool	
G-AVWH	PA-28 Cherokee 140	G-OHOG Flying Ltd	
G-AVWI	PA-28 Cherokee 140	L. M. Veitch	
G-AVWJ	PA-28 Cherokee 140	M. J. Steer/Biggin Hill	
G-AVWL	PA-28 Cherokee 140	P. J. Pratt/Dunkeswell	
G-AVWM	PA-28 Cherokee 140	P. E. Preston & ptnrs/Southend	
G-AVWN	PA-28R Cherokee Arrow 180	Vawn Air Ltd/Jersey	
G-AVWO	PA-28R Cherokee Arrow 180	P. D. Cahill/Biggin Hill	
G-AVWR	PA-28R Cherokee Arrow 180	D. A. Howe	
G-AVWT	PA-28R Cherokee Arrow 180	Cloud Base Aviation Group	
G-AVWU	PA-28R Cherokee Arrow 180	Arrow Flyers Ltd	

Notes	Reg.	Type	Owner or Operator
	G-AVWV	PA-28R Cherokee Arrow 180	Strathtay Flying Group
	G-AVWY	Fournier RF-4D	ASD Formaero Ltd/Biggin Hill
	G-AVXA	PA-25 Pawnee 235	S. Wales Gliding Club Ltd
	G-AVXC	Slingsby T.66 Nipper 3	S. D. Todd
	G-AVXD	Slingsby T.66 Nipper 3	D. A. Davidson
	G-AVXF	PA-28R Cherokee Arrow 180	JDR Arrow Group
	G-AVXI	H.S.748 Srs 2A	Civil Aviation Authority/Stansted
	G-AVXJ	H.S.748 Srs 2A	Civil Aviation Authority/Stansted
	G-AVXV	Bleriot XI (BAPC 104) ★	Bleriot Aeronautique Ltd
	G-AVXW	D.62B Condor	A. J. Cooper/Rochester
	G-AVXX	Cessna FR.172E	Goldensimple Ltd
	G-AVXY	Auster AOP.9 (XK417) ★	R. Windley (on rebuild)/Leicester
	G-AVXZ	PA-28 Cherokee 140 ★	ATC Hayle (instructional airframe)
	G-AVYB	H.S.121 Trident 1E-140 ★	SAS training airframe/Hereford
	G-AVYE	H.S.121 Trident 1E-140 ★	Test airframe/Hatfield
	G-AVYK	A.61 Terrier 3	A. R. Wright/Booker
	G-AVYL	PA-28 Cherokee 180	Cherokee G-AVYL Flying Group
	G-AVYM	PA-28 Cherokee 180	Carlisle Aviation (1985) Ltd/Crosby
	G-AVYP	PA-28 Cherokee 140	T. D. Reid (Braids) Ltd/Newtownards
	G-AVYR	PA-28 Cherokee 140	D.R. Flying Club Ltd/Staverton
	G-AVYS	PA-28R Cherokee Arrow 180	D. H. Saunders/Ipswich
	G-AVYT	PA-28R Cherokee Arrow 180	Blackpool & Fylde Aero Club
	G-AVYV	Jodel D.120	A. J. Sephton
	G-AVZB	Aero Z-37 Cmelak ★	Science Museum/Wroughton
	G-AVZI	Bo 208C Junior	C. F. Rogers
	G-AVZM	B.121 Pup 1	ARAZ Group/Elstree
	G-AVZN	B.121 Pup 1	V. B. Wheele/Shoreham
	G-AVZO	B.121 Pup 1 ★	Thameside Aviation Museum/E. Tilbury
	G-AVZP	B.121 Pup 1	T. A. White
	G-AVZR	PA-28 Cherokee 180	W. E. Lowe/Halfpenny Green
	G-AVZU	Cessna F.150H	R. D. & E. Forster/Swanton Morley
	G-AVZV	Cessna F.172H	B. Schreiber
	G-AVZW	EAA Biplane Model P	R. G. Maidment & G. R. Edmundson/ Goodwood
	G-AVZX	M.S.880B Rallye Club	H & H Aviation Group
	G-AWAA	M.S.880B Rallye Club	P. A. Cairns/Dunkeswell
	G-AWAC	GY-80 Horizon 180	R. D. Harper
	G-AWAD	Beech 95-D55 Baron	Aero Lease Ltd/Bournemouth
	G-AWAH	Beech 95-D55 Baron	B. J. S. Grey
	G-AWAI	Beech 95-D55 Baron	Alibear Ltd/Booker
	G-AWAJ	Beech 95-D55 Baron	Standard Hose Ltd/Leeds
	G-AWAT	D.62B Condor	Tarwood Ltd/Redhill
	G-AWAU	Vickers F.B.27A Vimy (replica) (F8614) ★	Bomber Command Museum/Hendon
	G-AWAW	Cessna F.150F	P. Brown
	G-AWAZ	PA-28R Cherokee Arrow 180	A. & A. A. Buckley
	G-AWBA	PA-28R Cherokee Arrow 180	March Flying Group/Stapleford
	G-AWBB	PA-28R Cherokee Arrow 180	M. D. Parker & J. Lowe
	G-AWBC	PA-28R Cherokee Arrow 180	M. J. Blanchard
	G-AWBE	PA-28 Cherokee 140	B. E. Boyle
	G-AWBG	PA-28 Cherokee 140	Westward Airways (Lands End) Ltd
	G-AWBH	PA-28 Cherokee 140	R. C. A. Mackworth
	G-AWBJ	Fournier RF-4D	J. M. Adams
	G-AWBL	BAC One-Eleven 416EK	Birmingham European Airways Ltd City of Birmingham
	G-AWBM	D.31 Turbulent	A. D. Pratt
	G-AWBN	PA-30 Twin Comanche 160B	Stourfield Investments Ltd/Jersey
	G-AWBP	Cessna 182L Skylane	Bournemouth Aviation
	G-AWBS	PA-28 Cherokee 140	W. London Aero Services Ltd/ White Waltham
	G-AWBT	PA-30 Twin Comanche 160B ★	Instructional airframe/Cranfield
	G-AWBU	Morane-Saulnier N (replica) (M.S.50)	Personal Plane Services Ltd/ Booker
	G-AWBV	Cessna 182L Skylane	Aerofilms Ltd/Elstree
	G-AWBW	Cessna F.172H ★	Brunel Technical College/Bristol
	G-AWBX	Cessna F.150H	D. F. Ranger
	G-AWCM	Cessna F.150H	Cheshire Air Training School (Merseyside) Ltd/Liverpool
	G-AWCN	Cessna FR.172E	LEC Refrigeration Ltd
	G-AWCP	Cessna F.150H (tailwheel)	C. E. Mason/Shobdon
	G-AWCW	Beech E.95 Travel Air	H. W. Astor/White Waltham
	G-AWDA	Slingsby T.66 Nipper 3	J. A. Cheesebrough

Reg.	Type	Owner or Operator	Notes
G-AWDD	Slingsby T.66 Nipper 3	T. D. G. Roberts/Inverness	
G-AWDI	PA-23 Aztec 250C	(stored)	
G-AWDO	D.31 Turbulent	R. N. Crosland	
G-AWDP	PA-28 Cherokee 180	B. H. & P. M. Illston/Shipdham	
G-AWDR	Cessna FR.172E	B. A. Wallace	
G-AWDU	Brantly B.2B	G. E. J. Redwood	
G-AWEF	SNCAN Stampe SV-4B	Tiger Club (1990) Ltd/Headcorn	
G-AWEI	D.62B Condor	Snowhit Ltd	
G-AWEL	Fournier RF-4D	A. B. Clymo/Halfpenny Green	
G-AWEM	Fournier RF-4D	B. J. Griffin/Wickenby	
G-AWEN	Jodel DR.1050	L. G. Earnshaw & ptnrs	
G-AWEP	Ord-Hume JB-01 Minicab	J. A. Stewart & S. N. Askey	
G-AWER	PA-23 Aztec 250C	H. McC. Clarke/Ronaldsway	
G-AWET	PA-28 Cherokee 180	Broadland Flying Group Ltd/ Shipdham	
G-AWEV	PA-28 Cherokee 140	Broxbow Ltd	
G-AWEX	PA-28 Cherokee 140	R. Badham	
G-AWEZ	PA-28R Cherokee Arrow 180	C. H. Elliott	
G-AWFB	PA-28R Cherokee Arrow 180	Luke Aviation Ltd/Bristol	
G-AWFC	PA-28R Cherokee Arrow 180	K. A. Goodchild/Southend	
G-AWFD	PA-28R Cherokee Arrow 180	A. L. Irwin	
G-AWFF	Cessna F.150H	Shobdon Aircraft Maintenance	
G-AWFJ	PA-28R Cherokee Arrow 180	D. C. E. Davies	
G-AWFK	PA-28R Cherokee Arrow 180	Steepletone Products Ltd	
G-AWFN	D.62B Condor	R. James	
G-AWFO	D.62B Condor	T. A. Major	
G-AWFP	D.62B Condor	Blackbushe Flying Club	
G-AWFR	D.31 Turbulent	L. W. Usherwood	
G-AWFT	Jodel D.9 Bebe	W. H. Cole	
G-AWFW	Jodel D.117	F. H. Greenwell	
G-AWFZ	Beech A23 Musketeer	R. Sweet & B D. Corbett	
G-AWGA	A.109 Airedale ★	stored/Sevenoaks	
G-AWGD	Cessna F.172H	Aero Marine Technology Ltd	
G-AWGJ	Cessna F.172H	J. & C. J. Freeman/Headcorn	
G-AWGK	Cessna F.150H	G. R. Brown/Shoreham	
G-AWGM	Arkle Kittiwake 2	M. K. Field	
G-AWGN	Fournier RF-4D	R. H. Ashforth/Staverton	
G-AWGP	Cessna T.210H	S. Harcourt/Elstree	
G-AWGR	Cessna F.172H	P. A. Hallam	
G-AWGZ	Taylor JT.1 Monoplane	A. Hill	
G-AWHB	C.A.S.A. 2-111D (6J+PR) ★	Aces High Ltd/North Weald	
G-AWHV	Rollason Beta B.2A	D. M. J. Jones	
G-AWHX	Rollason Beta B.2	S. G. Jones	
G-AWHY	Falconar F.11-3	J. R. Riley-Gale (G-BDPB)	
G-AWIF	Brookland Mosquito 2	—/Husbands Bosworth	
G-AWII	V.S.349 Spitfire VC (AR501)	Shuttleworth Trust/Duxford	
G-AWIP	Luton LA-4A Minor	J. Houghton	
G-AWIR	Midget Mustang	K. E. Sword/Leicester	
G-AWIT	PA-28 Cherokee 180	Manco Ltd	
G-AWIV	Airmark TSR.3	D. J. & F. M. Nunn	
G-AWIW	SNCAN Stampe SV-4B	R. E. Mitchell	
G-AWIY	PA-23 Aztec 250C	B. Anderson/Belfast	
G-AWJE	Slingsby T.66 Nipper 3	T. Mosedale	
G-AWJF	Slingsby T.66 Nipper 3	R. Wilcock/Shoreham	
G-AWJI	M.S.880B Rallye Club	D. V. Tyler/Southend	
G-AWJV	D.H.98 Mosquito TT Mk 35 (TA634) ★	Mosquito Aircraft Museum	
G-AWJX	Zlin Z.526 Akrobat	Aerobatics International Ltd	
G-AWJY	Zlin Z.526 Akrobat	Elco Manufacturing Co	
G-AWKB	M.J.5 Sirocco F2/39	G. D. Claxton	
G-AWKD	PA-17 Vagabond	A. T. & M. R. Dowie/ White Waltham	
G-AWKM	B.121 Pup 1	D. M. G. Jenkins/Swansea	
G-AWKO	B.121 Pup 1	P. A. Brook/Redhill	
G-AWKP	Jodel DR.253	D. A. Hood	
G-AWKT	M.S.880B Rallye Club	D. C. Strain	
G-AWKX	Beech A65 Queen Air ★	(Instructional airframe)/Shoreham	
G-AWLA	Cessna F.150H	Royal Artillery Aero Club Ltd/Middle Wallop	
G-AWLE	Cessna F.172H	H. Mendelssohn & H. I. Shott	
G-AWLF	Cessna F.172H	Gannet Aviation Ltd	
G-AWLG	SIPA 903	S. W. Markham	
G-AWLI	PA-22 Tri-Pacer 150	J. S. Lewery/Shoreham	
G-AWLL	AB-206B JetRanger 2	Base Helicopters Ltd	
G-AWLO	Boeing Stearman E.75	N. D. Pickard/Shoreham	
G-AWLP	Mooney M.20F	Petratek Ltd	

Notes	Reg.	Type	Owner or Operator
	G-AWLR	Slingsby T.66 Nipper 3	C. F. O'Neill
	G-AWLS	Slingsby T.66 Nipper 3	Stapleford Nipper Group
	G-AWLZ	Fournier RF-4D	E. V. Goodwin & C. R. Williamson
	G-AWMD	Jodel D.11	N. R. Windley & P. G. Haines
	G-AWMF	PA-18 Super Cub 150 (modified)	Booker Gliding Club Ltd
	G-AWMI	Glos-Airtourer 115	Airtourer Group 86/Cardiff
	G-AWMK	AB-206B JetRanger	Bristow Helicopters Ltd
	G-AWMM	M.S.893A Rallye Commodore 180	D. P. & S. White
	G-AWMN	Luton LA-4A Minor	R. E. R. Wilks
	G-AWMP	Cessna F.172H	Blois Aviation Ltd
	G-AWMR	D.31 Turbulent	C. F. Kennedy
	G-AWMT	Cessna F.150H	R. V. Grocott/Sleap
	G-AWMZ	Cessna F.172H ★	Parachute jump trainer/Cark
	G-AWNA	Boeing 747-136	British Airways Colliford Lake
	G-AWNB	Boeing 747-136	British Airways Llangorse Lake
	G-AWNC	Boeing 747-136	British Airways Lake Windermere
	G-AWNE	Boeing 747-136	British Airways Derwent Water
	G-AWNF	Boeing 747-136	British Airways Blagdon Water
	G-AWNG	Boeing 747-136	British Airways Rutland Water
	G-AWNH	Boeing 747-136	British Airways Devoke Water
	G-AWNJ	Boeing 747-136	British Airways Bassenthwaite Lake
	G-AWNL	Boeing 747-136	British Airways Ennerdale Water
	G-AWNM	Boeing 747-136	British Airways Ullswater
	G-AWNN	Boeing 747-136	British Airways Lowes Water
	G-AWNO	Boeing 747-136	British Airways Grafham Water
	G-AWNP	Boeing 747-136	British Airways Hanningfield Water
	G-AWNT	BN-2A Islander	Aerofilms Ltd/Elstree
	G-AWOA	M.S.880B Rallye Club	M. Craven & ptnrs/Barton
	G-AWOE	Aero Commander 680E	J. M. Houlder/Elstree
	G-AWOF	PA-15 Vagabond	K. Hassall
	G-AWOH	PA-17 Vagabond	The High Flats Flying Group
	G-AWOT	Cessna F.150H	J. M. Montgomerie & J. Ferguson
	G-AWOU	Cessna 170B	S. Billington/Denham
	G-AWOX	W.S.58 Wessex 60 ★	International Helicopters Museum/ Weston-s-Mare
	G-AWPH	P.56 Provost T.1	J. A. D. Bradshaw
	G-AWPJ	Cessna F.150H	W. J. Greenfield
	G-AWPN	Shield Xyla	M. J. Herlihy
	G-AWPP	Cessna F.150H	R. W. Brown/Denham
	G-AWPS	PA-28 Cherokee 140	K. J. Steele & D. J. Hewitt
	G-AWPU	Cessna F.150J	Telair Manchester Ltd
	G-AWPW	PA-12 Super Cruiser	J. E. Davies/Sandown
	G-AWPY	Bensen B.8M	J. Jordan
	G-AWPZ	Andreasson BA-4B	J. M. Vening
	G-AWRK	Cessna F.150J	Southern Strut Flying Group/Shoreham
	G-AWRL	Cessna F.172H	B. Welsh
	G-AWRS	Avro 19 Srs. 2 ★	N. E. Aircraft Museum
	G-AWRY	P.56 Provost T.1 (XF836)	Slymar Aviation & Services Ltd
	G-AWRZ	Bell 47G-5	Hammond Aerial Spraying Ltd
	G-AWSA	Avro 652A Anson 19 (VL349) ★	Norfolk & Suffolk Aviation Museum
	G-AWSD	Cessna F.150J	British Skysports
	G-AWSL	PA-28 Cherokee 180D	Fascia Ltd/Southend
	G-AWSM	PA-28 Cherokee 235	S. J. Green
	G-AWSN	D.62B Condor	J. Leader
	G-AWSP	D.62B Condor	R. Q. & A. S. Bond/Wellesbourne
	G-AWSS	D.62C Condor	G. Bruce/Inverness
	G-AWST	D.62B Condor	Humberside Aviation/Doncaster
	G-AWSV	Skeeter 12 (XM553)	Maj. M. Somerton-Rayner/Middle Wallop
	G-AWSW	D.5/180 Husky (XW635)	RAF College Flying Club/Cranwell
	G-AWSY	Boeing 737-204	Britannia Airways Ltd General James Wolfe/ Luton
	G-AWTA	Cessna E.310N	Heliscott Ltd
	G-AWTJ	Cessna F.150J	Metropolitan Police Flying Club/Biggin Hill
	G-AWTL	PA-28 Cherokee 180D	D. M. Bailey
	G-AWTS	Beech A.23 Musketeer	M. Corbett & ptnrs
	G-AWTV	Beech A.23 Musketeer	A. Johnston/Blackbushe
	G-AWTW	Beech 95-B55 Baron	R. W. Davies/Staverton
	G-AWTX	Cessna F.150J	R. D. & E. Forster
	G-AWUB	GY-201 Minicab	H. P. Burrill
	G-AWUE	Jodel DR.1050	S. Bichan
	G-AWUG	Cessna F.150H	J. Easson/Edinburgh
	G-AWUH	Cessna F.150H	Airtime (Hampshire) Ltd
	G-AWUJ	Cessna F.150H	W. Lawton/Doncaster

Reg.	Type	Owner or Operator	Notes
G-AWUL	Cessna F.150H	Alderquest Ltd	
G-AWUN	Cessna F.150H	Northamptonshire School of Flying Ltd/Sywell	
G-AWUO	Cessna F.150H	Air Fenland Ltd	
G-AWUS	Cessna F.150J	Recreational Flying Centre (Popham) Ltd	
G-AWUT	Cessna F.150J	E. Phillips & P. Reddy	
G-AWUU	Cessna F.150J	D. G. Burden	
G-AWUW	Cessna F.172H	B. Stewart/Panshanger	
G-AWUX	Cessna F.172H	D. K. Brian & ptrs	
G-AWUZ	Cessna F.172H	G. F. Burling	
G-AWVA	Cessna F.172H	Barton Air Ltd	
G-AWVB	Jodel D.117	D. J. R. Chapple	
G-AWVC	B.121 Pup 1	J. H. Marshall & J. J. West	
G-AWVE	Jodel DR.1050/M1	E. A. Taylor/Southend	
G-AWVF	P.56 Provost T.1 (XF877)	Jet Heritage Ltd/Bournemouth	
G-AWVG	AESL Airtourer T.2	C. J. Schofield	
G-AWVN	Aeronca 7AC Champion	Bowker Air Services Ltd/Rush Green	
G-AWVZ	Jodel D.112	D. C. Stokes	
G-AWWE	B.121 Pup 2	J. M. Randle/Coventry	
G-AWWF	B.121 Pup 1	N. M. Morris/Denham	
G-AWWI	Jodel D.117	J. C. Hatton	
G-AWWM	GY-201 Minicab	J. S. Brayshaw	
G-AWWN	Jodel DR.1051	T. W. M. Beck & ptnrs	
G-AWWO	Jodel DR.1050	Whiskey Oscar Group/Barton	
G-AWWP	Aerosport Woody Pusher III	M. S. Bird & R. D. Bird	
G-AWWT	D.31 Turbulent	P. J. Simpson	
G-AWWU	Cessna FR.172F	Westward Airways (Lands End) Ltd	
G-AWWW	Cessna 401	Air Charter & Travel Ltd	
G-AWWX	BAC One-Eleven 509EW	Dan-Air Services Ltd/Gatwick	
G-AWXA	Cessna 182M	P. Cannon	
G-AWXO	H.S.125 Srs. 400B	Twinjet Aircraft Sales Ltd/Luton	
G-AWXR	PA-28 Cherokee 180D	J. D. Williams	
G-AWXS	PA-28 Cherokee 180D	Rayhenro Flying Group/Shobdon	
G-AWXU	Cessna F.150J	Howe Aviation Group	
G-AWXY	M.S.885 Super Rallye	Sussex Spraying Services Ltd/Shoreham	
G-AWXZ	SNCAN Stampe SV-4C	Personal Plane Services Ltd/Booker	
G-AWYB	Cessna FR.172F	C. W. Larkin/Southend	
G-AWYF	G.159 Gulfstream 1	Ford Motor Co Ltd/Stansted	
G-AWYJ	B.121 Pup 2	H. C. Taylor	
G-AWYL	Jodel DR.253B	M. J. McRobert	
G-AWYO	B.121 Pup 1	B. R. C. Wild/Popham	
G-AWYR	BAC One-Eleven 501EX	British Airways *County of Suffolk*	
G-AWYS	BAC One-Eleven 501EX	British Airways *County of Norfolk*	
G-AWYT	BAC One-Eleven 501EX	British Airways *County of Gwynedd*	
G-AWYU	BAC One-Eleven 501EX	British Airways *County of Avon*	
G-AWYV	BAC One-Eleven 501EX	British Airways *County of Powys*	
G-AWYX	M.S.880B Rallye Club	J. M. L. Edwards/Exeter	
G-AWYY	T.57 Camel replica (B6401)	FAA Museum/Yeovilton	
G-AWZE	H.S.121 Trident 3B ★	*Instructional airframe*/Heathrow	
G-AWZI	H.S.121 Trident 3B ★	Surrey Fire Brigade (*instructional airframe*)/Reigate	
G-AWZJ	H.S.121 Trident 3B ★	British Airports Authority/Prestwick	
G-AWZK	H.S.121 Trident 3B ★	*Ground trainer*/Heathrow	
G-AWZM	H.S.121 Trident 3B ★	Science Museum/Wroughton	
G-AWZN	H.S.121 Trident 3B ★	Cranfield	
G-AWZO	H.S.121 Trident 3B ★	British Aerospace PLC/Hatfield	
G-AWZP	H.S.121 Trident 3B ★	Greater Manchester Museum of Science & Technology (*nose only*)	
G-AWZR	H.S.121 Trident 3B ★	CAA Fire School/Teesside	
G-AWZU	H.S.121 Trident 3B ★	BAA Airport Fire Service/Stansted	
G-AWZX	H.S.121 Trident 3B ★	BAA Airport Fire Services/Gatwick	
G-AWZZ	H.S.121 Trident 3B ★	Airport Fire Services/Birmingham	
G-AXAB	PA-28 Cherokee 140	Bencray Ltd/Blackpool	
G-AXAK	M.S.880B Rallye Club	R. L. & C. Stewart	
G-AXAN	D.H.82A Tiger Moth (EM720)	M. E. Carrell	
G-AXAO	Omega 56 balloon	P. D. Furlong	
G-AXAS	Wallis WA-116T	K. H. Wallis (G-AVDH)	
G-AXAT	Jodel D.117A	P. S. Wilkinson	
G-AXAU	PA-30 Twin Comanche 160C	Bartcourt Ltd (*derelict*)/Bournemouth	
G-AXAX	PA-23 Aztec 250D	Woodvale Aviation Co Ltd	
G-AXBF	D.5/180 Husky	C. H. Barnes	
G-AXBH	Cessna F.172H	Photoair Ltd/Sibson	

Notes	Reg.	Type	Owner or Operator
	G-AXBJ	Cessna F.172H	Bravo Juliet Group/Leicester
	G-AXBW	D.H.82A Tiger Moth (T5879)	R. Venning
	G-AXBZ	D.H.82A Tiger Moth	D. H. McWhir
	G-AXCA	PA-28R Cherokee Arrow 200	D. T. Wright
	G-AXCG	Jodel D.117	Charlie Golf Group/Andrewsfield
	G-AXCI	Bensen B.8M ★	Loughborough & Leicester Aircraft Museum
	G-AXCL	M.S.880B Rallye Club	L. A. Christie & D. P. Barclay
	G-AXCM	M.S.880B Rallye Club	Avcom Developments Ltd/Denham
	G-AXCN	M.S.880B Rallye Club	J. E. Compton
	G-AXCX	B.121 Pup 2	L. A. Pink
	G-AXCY	Jodel D.117	R. Thwaites & P. G. Bumpus/Shoreham
	G-AXDB	Piper J-3C-65 Cub	J. R. Wraight
	G-AXDC	PA-23 Aztec 250D	N. J. Lilley/Bodmin
	G-AXDI	Cessna F.172H	M. F. & J. R. Leusby/Conington
	G-AXDK	Jodel DR.315	Delta Kilo Flying Group/Sywell
	G-AXDM	H.S.125 Srs 400B	GEC Ferranti Defence Systems Ltd/ Edinburgh
	G-AXDN	BAC-Sud Concorde 01 ★	Duxford Aviation Soc
	G-AXDU	B.121 Pup 2	J. R. Clegg
	G-AXDV	B.121 Pup 1	C. N. G. Hobbs & J. J. Teagle
	G-AXDW	B.121 Pup 1	Cranfield Institute of Technology
	G-AXDY	Falconar F-II	J. Nunn
	G-AXDZ	Cassutt Racer Srs IIIM	A. Chadwick/Little Staughton
	G-AXEB	Cassutt Racer Srs IIIM	G. E. Horder/Redhill
	G-AXEC	Cessna 182K	H. S. Mulligan & E. R. Wilson
	G-AXED	PA-25 Pawnee 235	Wolds Gliding Club Ltd/Pocklington
	G-AXEH	B.121 Pup ★	Museum of Flight/E. Fortune
	G-AXEI	Ward Gnome ★	Lincolnshire Aviation Museum
	G-AXEO	Scheibe SF.25B Falke	Newcastle & Tees-side Gliding Club Ltd
	G-AXES	B.121 Pup 2	P. A. G. Field/Nairobi
	G-AXEV	B.121 Pup 2	D. S. Russell
	G-AXFG	Cessna 337D	Oston Airfinance Ltd
	G-AXFH	D.H.114 Heron 1B/C	(stored)/Southend
	G-AXFN	Jodel D.119	D. J. Williams & H. R. Leafe
	G-AXGC	M.S.880B Rallye Club	Ian Richard Transport Services Ltd
	G-AXGE	M.S.880B Rallye Club	R. P. Loxton
	G-AXGG	Cessna F.150J	A. R. Nicholls
	G-AXGP	Piper J-3C-65 Cub	W. K. Butler
	G-AXGR	Luton LA-4A Minor	B. Thomas
	G-AXGS	D.62B Condor	R. J. Hirst
	G-AXGT	D.62B Condor	P. A. Wensak & D. Wilson
	G-AXGV	D.62B Condor	R. J. Wrixon
	G-AXGZ	D.62B Condor	Lincoln Condor Group/Sturgate
	G-AXHA	Cessna 337A	G. Evans
	G-AXHC	SNCAN Stampe SV-4C	D. L. Webley
	G-AXHE	BN-2A Islander	NW Parachute Centre Ltd/Cark
	G-AXHI	M.S.880B Rallye Club	J. M. Whittard (stored)/Sandown
	G-AXHO	B.121 Pup 2	L. W. Grundy/Stapleford
	G-AXHP	Piper J-3C-65 Cub	T. Coote
	G-AXHR	Piper J-3C-65 Cub (329601)	G-AXHR Cub Group
	G-AXHS	M.S.880B Rallye Club	B. & A. Swales
	G-AXHT	M.S.880B Rallye Club	D. Sharpe
	G-AXHV	Jodel D.117A	D. M. Cashmore
	G-AXHX	M.S.892A Rallye Commodore	D. W. Weever
	G-AXIA	B.121 Pup 1	Cranfield Institute of Technology
	G-AXIE	B.121 Pup 2	G. A. Ponsford/Goodwood
	G-AXIF	B.121 Pup 2	T. G. Hiscock & R. G. Knapp
	G-AXIG	B.125 Bulldog 104	George House (Holdings) Ltd
	G-AXIO	PA-28 Cherokee 140B	W. London Aero Services Ltd/ White Waltham
	G-AXIR	PA-28 Cherokee 140B	M. F. L. Purse/Weston Zoyland
	G-AXIT	M.S.893A Rallye Commodore 180	T. J. Price
	G-AXIW	Scheibe SF.25B Falke	Sailplane Services/Nympsfield
	G-AXIX	Glos-Airtourer 150	J. C. Wood
	G-AXIY	Bird Gyrocopter ★	Motor Museum/Chudleigh
	G-AXJB	Omega 84 balloon	Southern Balloon Group
	G-AXJH	B.121 Pup 2	J. S. Chillingworth
	G-AXJI	B.121 Pup 2	Cole Aviation Ltd/Southend
	G-AXJJ	B.121 Pup 2	J. H. Askew & B. Ward
	G-AXJK	BAC One-Eleven 501EX	British Airways County of Hereford
	G-AXJM	BAC One-Eleven 501EX	British Airways County Durham
	G-AXJN	B.121 Pup 2	D. M. Jenkins & D. F. Jenvey/Shoreham

Reg.	Type	Owner or Operator	Notes
G-AXJO	B.121 Pup 2	J. A. D. Bradshaw	
G-AXJR	Scheibe SF.25B Falke	D. R. Chatterton	
G-AXJV	PA-28 Cherokee 140B	Mona Aviation Ltd	
G-AXJX	PA-28 Cherokee 140B	Patrolwatch Ltd	
G-AXJY	Cessna U-206D	B. W. Wells	
G-AXKD	PA-23 Aztec 250D	Levenmere Ltd/Norwich	
G-AXKH	Luton LA-4A Minor	M. E. Vaisey	
G-AXKI	Jodel D.9 Bebe	M. R. M. Welch	
G-AXKJ	Jodel D.9 Bebe	C. C. Gordon	
G-AXKK	Westland Bell 47G-4A	Alan Mann Helicopters Ltd/Fairoaks	
G-AXKO	Westland-Bell 47G-4A	Alan Mann Helicopters Ltd/Fairoaks	
G-AXKR	Westland Bell 47G-4A	F. C. Owen	
G-AXKS	Westland Bell 47G-4A ★	Museum of Army Flying/Middle Wallop	
G-AXKW	Westland-Bell 47G-4A	Atlas Aviation Ltd/Bournemouth	
G-AXKX	Westland-Bell 47G-4A	Alan Mann Helicopters Ltd/Fairoaks	
G-AXKY	Westland Bell 47G-4A	L. Goddard	
G-AXLG	Cessna 310K	Smiths (Outdrives) Ltd	
G-AXLI	Slingsby T.66 Nipper 3	N. J. Arthur/Finmere	
G-AXLL	BAC One-Eleven 523FJ	British Airways *County of Yorkshire*	
G-AXLS	Jodel DR.105A	E. Gee/Southampton	
G-AXLZ	PA-18 Super Cub 95	J. C. Quantrell/Shipdham	
G-AXMA	PA-24 Comanche 180	Tegrel Products Ltd/Newcastle	
G-AXMB	Slingsby T.7 Motor Cadet 2	I. G. Smith/Langar	
G-AXMD	Omega O-56 balloon ★	British Balloon Museum	
G-AXMN	J/5B Autocar	A. Phillips	
G-AXMP	PA-28 Cherokee 180	B. Stewart	
G-AXMS	PA-30 Twin Comanche 160C	G. J. Mendes	
G-AXMW	B.121 Pup 1	DJP Engineering (Knebworth) Ltd	
G-AXMX	B.121 Pup 2	Susan A. Jones/Cannes	
G-AXNC	Boeing 737-204	Britannia Airways Ltd *Isambard Kingdom Brunel*/Luton	
G-AXNJ	Wassmer Jodel D.120	Clive Flying Group/Sleap	
G-AXNK	Cessna F.150J	Fowler Aviation Ltd/Leavesden	
G-AXNL	B.121 Pup 1	Northamptonshire School of Flying Ltd/ Sywell	
G-AXNM	B.121 Pup 1	J. & F. E. Green	
G-AXNN	B.121 Pup 2	Gabrielle Aviation Ltd/Shoreham	
G-AXNP	B.121 Pup 2	J. W. Ellis	
G-AXNR	B.121 Pup 2	S. T. Raby & ptnrs	
G-AXNS	B.121 Pup 2	Derwent Aero/Netherthorpe	
G-AXNW	SNCAN Stampe SV-4C	C. S. Grace	
G-AXNX	Cessna 182M	Cast High Ltd	
G-AXNZ	Pitts S.1C Special	W. A. Jordan	
G-AXOG	PA-E23 Aztec 250D	R. W. Diggens/Denham	
G-AXOH	M.S.894 Rallye Minerva	Bristol Cars Ltd/White Waltham	
G-AXOI	Jodel D.9 Bebe	D. G. Garner	
G-AXOJ	B.121 Pup 2	Pup Flying Group	
G-AXOL	Currie Wot	R. G. Boyes	
G-AXOR	PA-28 Cherokee 180D	Oscar Romeo Aviation	
G-AXOS	M.S.894A Rallye Minerva	D. R. C. Bell	
G-AXOT	M.S.893 Rallye Commodore 180	P. Evans & J. C. Graves	
G-AXOV	Beech 95-B55A Baron	S. Brod/Elstree	
G-AXOZ	B.121 Pup 1	Touchdown Aviation Ltd	
G-AXPB	B.121 Pup 1	M. J. K. Seary	
G-AXPF	Cessna F.150K	D. R. Marks/Denham	
G-AXPG	Mignet HM-293	W. H. Cole (*stored*)	
G-AXPM	B.121 Pup 1	M. J. Coton	
G-AXPN	B.121 Pup 2	D. J. Elbourn & ptnrs	
G-AXPZ	Campbell Cricket	W. R. Partridge	
G-AXRC	Campbell Cricket	K. W. Hayr (*stored*)	
G-AXRL	PA-28 Cherokee 160	T. W. Clark/Headcorn	
G-AXRO	PA-30 Twin Comanche 160C	S. M. Bogdiukiewicz/Staverton	
G-AXRP	SNCAN Stampe SV-4C	C. C. Manning	
G-AXRR	Auster AOP.9 (XR241)	The Aircraft Restoration Co/Duxford	
G-AXRT	Cessna FA.150K (tailwheel)	W. R. Pickett/Southampton	
G-AXRU	Cessna FA.150K	Arrival Enterprises Ltd/Denham	
G-AXSC	B.121 Pup 1	T. R. Golding & C. Spencer	
G-AXSD	B.121 Pup 1	A. C. Townend	
G-AXSF	Nash Petrel	Nash Aircraft Ltd/Lasham	
G-AXSG	PA-28 Cherokee 180	Shropshire Aero Club Ltd/Sleap	
G-AXSI	Cessna F.172H	S. M. Burrows & R. I. Chantrey (G-SNIP)	
G-AXSM	Jodel DR.1051	C. Cousten/White Waltham	
G-AXSV	Jodel DR.340	Leonard F. Jollye Ltd/Panshanger	

Notes	Reg.	Type	Owner or Operator
	G-AXSW	Cessna FA.150K	Furness Aviation Ltd/Walney Island
	G-AXSZ	PA-28 Cherokee 140B	Kilo Foxtrot Group/Sandown
	G-AXTA	PA-28 Cherokee 140B	G-AXTA Syndicate
	G-AXTC	PA-28 Cherokee 140B	B. Mellor & J. Hutchinson
	G-AXTD	PA-28 Cherokee 140B	G. R. Walker/Southend
	G-AXTH	PA-28 Cherokee 140B	W. London Aero Services Ltd/ White Waltham
	G-AXTI	PA-28 Cherokee 140B	London Transport (CRS) Sports Association Flying Club/Fairoaks
	G-AXTJ	PA-28 Cherokee 140B	A. P. Merrifield/Stapleford
	G-AXTL	PA-28 Cherokee 140B	Jenrick Flying Group
	G-AXTO	PA-24 Comanche 260	J. L. Wright
	G-AXTP	PA-28 Cherokee 180	E. R. Moore/Elstree
	G-AXTX	Jodel D.112	J. J. Penney
	G-AXUA	B.121 Pup 1	F. R. Blennerhassett & ptnrs
	G-AXUB	BN-2A Islander	Headcorn Parachute Club
	G-AXUC	PA-12 Super Cruiser	J. J. Bunton
	G-AXUE	Jodel DR.105A	L. Lewis
	G-AXUF	Cessna FA.150K	A. D. McLeod
	G-AXUI	H.P.137 Jetstream 1	Cranfield Institute of Technology
	G-AXUJ	J/1 Autocrat	R. G. Earp & J. W. H. Lee/Sibson
	G-AXUK	Jodel DR.1050	D. MacCallum
	G-AXUM	H.P.137 Jetstream 1	Cranfield Institute of Technology
	G-AXUW	Cessna FA.150K	Coventry Air Training School
	G-AXVB	Cessna F.172H	C. Gabbitas/Staverton
	G-AXVC	Cessna FA.150K	V. F. Lynn/Sibson
	G-AXVK	Campbell Cricket	L. W. Harding
	G-AXVM	Campbell Cricket	D. M. Organ
	G-AXVN	McCandless M.4	W. R. Partridge
	G-AXVS	Jodel DR.1050	D. T. J. Harwood
	G-AXVV	Piper J-3C-65 Cub	J. MacCarthy
	G-AXVW	Cessna F.150K	J. M. R. Layton
	G-AXWA	Auster AOP.9 (XN437)	M. L. & C. M. Edwards/Biggin Hill
	G-AXWB	Omega 65 balloon	A. Robinson & M. J. Moore *Ezekiel*
	G-AXWH	BN-2A Islander	Midland Parachute Centre Ltd
	G-AXWP	BN-2A Islander	Isles of Scilly Skybus Ltd/St Just
	G-AXWR	BN-2A Islander	Isles of Scilly Skybus Ltd/St Just
	G-AXWT	Jodel D.11	R. C. Owen
	G-AXWV	Jodel DR.253	J. R. D. Bygraves/O. Warden
	G-AXWZ	PA-28R Cherokee Arrow 200	E. J. M. Kroes
	G-AXXV	D.H.82A Tiger Moth (DE992)	R. Jones
	G-AXXW	Jodel D.117	A. Szep/Netherthorpe
	G-AXYD	BAC One-Eleven 509EW	Dan-Air Services Ltd/Gatwick
	G-AXYK	Taylor JT.1 Monoplane	T. W. M. Beck & M. J. Smith
	G-AXYY	WHE Airbuggy	R. A. A. Chiles
	G-AXYZ	WHE Airbuggy	W. B. Lumb
	G-AXZA	WHE Airbuggy	B. Gunn
	G-AXZB	WHE Airbuggy	D. R. C. Pugh
	G-AXZD	PA-28 Cherokee 180E	M. D. & V. A. Callaghan
	G-AXZF	PA-28 Cherokee 180E	E. P. C. & W. R. Rabson/Southampton
	G-AXZK	BN-2A Islander	M. E. Mortlock/Pampisford
	G-AXZM	Slingsby T.66 Nipper 3	G. R. Harlow
	G-AXZO	Cessna 180	G. James
	G-AXZP	PA-E23 Aztec 250D	J. Durkin
	G-AXZT	Jodel D.117	N. Batty
	G-AXZU	Cessna 182N	The Biplane Co Ltd
	G-AYAA	PA-28 Cherokee 180E	Alpha-Alpha Ltd
	G-AYAB	PA-28 Cherokee 180E	J. A. & J. C. Cunningham
	G-AYAC	PA-28R Cherokee Arrow 200	Fersfield Flying Group
	G-AYAJ	Cameron O-84 balloon	E. T. Hall
	G-AYAL	Omega 56 balloon ★	British Balloon Museum
	G-AYAR	PA-28 Cherokee 180E	D. M. Markscheffel/Stapleford
	G-AYAT	PA-28 Cherokee 180E	AYAT Flying Group
	G-AYAU	PA-28 Cherokee 180E	Tiarco Ltd
	G-AYAV	PA-28 Cherokee 180E	Tee Tee Aviation Ltd/Biggin Hill
	G-AYAW	PA-28 Cherokee 180E	Wizard Air Services Ltd/Coventry
	G-AYBD	Cessna F.150K	F. A. Fox/Southampton
	G-AYBG	Scheibe SF.25B Falke	D. J. Rickman
	G-AYBO	PA-23 Aztec 250D	Twinguard Aviation Ltd/Elstree
	G-AYBP	Jodel D.112	G-AYBP Group
	G-AYBR	Jodel D.112	D. H. Nourish
	G-AYBU	Western 84 balloon	D. R. Gibbons

Reg.	Type	Owner or Operator	Notes
G-AYBV	Chasle YC-12 Tourbillon	B. A. Mills	
G-AYCC	Campbell Cricket	D. J. M. Charity	
G-AYCE	CP.301C Emeraude	R. A. Austin/Bodmin	
G-AYCF	Cessna FA.150K	E. J. Atkins/Popham	
G-AYCG	SNCAN Stampe SV-4C	N. Bignall/Booker	
G-AYCJ	Cessna TP.206D	H. O. Holm/Bournemouth	
G-AYCN	Piper J-3C-65 Cub	W. R. & B. M. Young	
G-AYCO	CEA DR.360	G. T. Birks & T. M. Curry/Booker	
G-AYCP	Jodel D.112	D. J. Nunn	
G-AYCT	Cessna F.172H	Charlie Tango Flying Group	
G-AYDG	M.S.894A Rallye Minerva	D. L. Rhoades & R. C. Taylor	
G-AYDI	D.H.82A Tiger Moth	R. B. Woods & ptnrs	
G-AYDR	SNCAN Stampe SV-4C	A. J. Mcluskie	
G-AYDV	Coates SA.II-1 Swalesong	J. R. Coates/Rush Green	
G-AYDW	A.61 Terrier 2	A. Topen/Cranfield	
G-AYDX	A.61 Terrier 2	G. W. & M. M. Bisshopp	
G-AYDY	Luton LA-4A Minor	T. Littlefair & N. Clark	
G-AYDZ	Jodel DR.200	F. M. Ward/Sherburn	
G-AYEB	Jodel D.112	M. A. Watts	
G-AYEC	CP.301A Emeraude	R. S. Needham	
G-AYED	PA-24 Comanche 260	G. N. Snell	
G-AYEE	PA-28 Cherokee 180E	D. J. Beale	
G-AYEF	PA-28 Cherokee 180E	S. R. J. Attwood	
G-AYEG	Falconar F-9	T. J. Wilkinson	
G-AYEH	Jodel DR.1050	S. Penson	
G-AYEI	PA-31 Turbo Navajo	Stewart McDonald & Co	
G-AYEJ	Jodel DR.1050	J. M. Newbold	
G-AYEN	Piper J-3C-65 Cub	P. Warde & C. F. Morris	
G-AYET	M.S.892A Rallye Commodore 150	R. N. Jones	
G-AYEU	Brookland Hornet	M. G. Reilly	
G-AYEV	Jodel DR.1050	L. G. Evans/Headcorn	
G-AYEW	Jodel DR.1051	Taildragger Group/Halfpenny Green	
G-AYEY	Cessna F.150K	W. J. Moyse	
G-AYFA	SA Twin Pioneer 3	Flight One Ltd/Shobdon	
G-AYFC	D.62B Condor	P. A. Wensak & D. J. Wilson	
G-AYFD	D.62B Condor	B. G. Manning	
G-AYFE	D.62C Condor	J. Abbess/Andrewsfield	
G-AYFF	D.62B Condor	A. F. S. Caldecourt	
G-AYFG	D.62C Condor	W. A. Braim	
G-AYFJ	M.S.880B Rallye Club	Rallye FJ Group	
G-AYFP	Jodel D.140	S. K. Minocha/Sherburn	
G-AYFT	PA-39 Twin Comanche 160 C/R	Subtec Aviation Ltd/Shoreham	
G-AYFV	Crosby BA-4B	A. R. C. Mathie/Norwich	
G-AYGA	Jodel D.117	R. L. E. Horrell	
G-AYGB	Cessna 310Q ★	*Instructional airframe*/Perth	
G-AYGC	Cessna F.150K	Alpha Aviation Group/Barton	
G-AYGD	Jodel DR.1051	B. A. James	
G-AYGE	SNCAN Stampe SV-4C	The Hon A. M. J. Rothschild/Booker	
G-AYGG	Jodel D.120	G-AYGG Group	
G-AYGK	BN-2A Islander	Pathcircle Ltd/Langar	
G-AYGX	Cessna FR.172G	A. Douglas & J. K. Brockley	
G-AYHA	AA-1 Yankee	Elstree Emus Flying Group	
G-AYHI	Campbell Cricket	J. F. MacKay/Inverness	
G-AYHX	Jodel D.117A	L. J. E. Goldfinch	
G-AYHY	Fournier RF-4D	P. M. & S. M. Wells	
G-AYIA	Hughes 369HS ★	G. D. E. Bilton/Sywell	
G-AYIF	PA-28 Cherokee 140C	The Hare Flying Group/Elstree	
G-AYIG	PA-28 Cherokee 140C	Snowdon Mountain Aviation Ltd	
G-AYII	PA-28R Cherokee Arrow 200	Devon Growers Ltd & A. L. Bacon/Exeter	
G-AYIJ	SNCAN Stampe SV-4B	K. B. Palmer/Headcorn	
G-AYIO	PA-28 Cherokee 140C	Teesside Flight Centre Ltd	
G-AYIT	D.H.82A Tiger Moth	Ulster Tiger Group/Newtownards	
G-AYJA	Jodel DR.1050	G. I. Doake	
G-AYJB	SNCAN Stampe SV-4C	F. J. M. & J. P. Esson/Middle Wallop	
G-AYJD	Alpavia-Fournier RF-3	E. Shouler	
G-AYJP	PA-28 Cherokee 140C	RAF Brize Norton Flying Club Ltd	
G-AYJR	PA-28 Cherokee 140C	RAF Brize Norton Flying Club Ltd	
G-AYJU	Cessna TP-206A	P. W. & A. Yates	
G-AYJW	Cessna FR.172G	R. T. Burton	
G-AYJY	Isaacs Fury II	A. V. Francis	
G-AYKA	Beech 95-B55A Baron	Walsh Bros (Tunnelling) Ltd/Elstree	
G-AYKD	Jodel DR.1050	B. P. Irish	
G-AYKF	M.S.880B Rallye Club	R. N. Preston/Cranfield	

Notes	Reg.	Type	Owner or Operator
	G-AYKJ	Jodel D.117A	Juliet Group/Shoreham
	G-AYKK	Jodel D.117	D. M. Whitham
	G-AYKL	Cessna F.150L	M. A. Judge
	G-AYKS	Leopoldoff L-7	C. E. & W. B. Cooper
	G-AYKT	Jodel D.117	G. Wright/Sherburn
	G-AYKW	PA-28 Cherokee 140C	A. G. Hopwood
	G-AYKX	PA-28 Cherokee 140C	M. J. Garland & ptnrs/Woodford
	G-AYKZ	SAI KZ-8	R. E. Mitchell/Coventry
	G-AYLA	Glos-Airtourer 115	R. E. Parker
	G-AYLB	PA-39 Twin Comanche 160 C/R	Penny (Mechanical Services) Ltd
	G-AYLE	M.S.880B Rallye Club	G-AYLE Syndicate
	G-AYLF	Jodel DR.1051	Sicile Group
	G-AYLL	Jodel DR.1050	B. R. Cornes
	G-AYLP	AA-1 Yankee	D. Nairn & E. Y. Hawkins
	G-AYLV	Jodel D.120	M. R. Henham
	G-AYLX	Hughes 269C	J. Lloyd
	G-AYLY	PA-23 Aztec 250C	—/Shoreham
	G-AYME	Fournier RF-5	R. D. Goodger/Biggin Hill
	G-AYMG	HPR-7 Herald 213	Channel Express PLC/Bournemouth
	G-AYMK	PA-28 Cherokee 140C	The Piper Flying Group
	G-AYMO	PA-23 Aztec 250C	Supreme Windows
	G-AYMP	Currie Wot Special	H. F. Moffatt
	G-AYMR	Lederlin 380L Ladybug	J. S. Brayshaw
	G-AYMT	Jodel DR.1050	Merlin Flying Club Ltd/Hucknall
	G-AYMU	Jodel D.112	M. R. Baker
	G-AYMV	Western 20 balloon	G. F. Turnbull
	G-AYMW	Bell 206A JetRanger 2	Dollar Air Services Ltd/Coventry
	G-AYMZ	PA-28 Cherokee 140C	T. H. & M. G. Weetman/Prestwick
	G-AYNA	Currie Wot	J. M. Lister
	G-AYNC	W.S. 58 Wessex 60 Srs 1 ★	International Helicopter Museum/ Weston-s-Mare
	G-AYND	Cessna 310Q	Source Premium & Promotional Consultants Ltd/Fairoaks
	G-AYNF	PA-28 Cherokee 140C	W. S. Bath
	G-AYNJ	PA-28 Cherokee 140C	Lion Flying Group Ltd/Elstree
	G-AYNN	Cessna 185B Skywagon	Bencray Ltd/Blackpool
	G-AYNP	W.S.55 Whirlwind Srs 3	Bristow Helicopters Ltd
	G-AYOD	Cessna 172	E. N. Simmons
	G-AYOM	Sikorsky S-61N Mk 2	British International Helicopters Ltd/ Aberdeen
	G-AYOP	BAC One-Eleven 530FX	British Airways *County of Humberside*
	G-AYOW	Cessna 182N Skylane	A. T. Jay
	G-AYOY	Sikorsky S-61N Mk 2	British International Helicopters Ltd/ Aberdeen
	G-AYOZ	Cessna FA.150L	Exeter Flying Club Ltd
	G-AYPD	Beech 95-B55A Baron	F. Sherwood & Sons (Transport) Ltd
	G-AYPE	Bo 209 Monsun	Papa Echo Ltd/Biggin Hill
	G-AYPF	Cessna F.177RG	S. J. Westley
	G-AYPG	Cessna F.177RG	D. Davies
	G-AYPH	Cessna F.177RG	W. J. D. Tollett
	G-AYPI	Cessna F.177RG	Cardinal Aviation Ltd/Guernsey
	G-AYPJ	PA-28 Cherokee 180	Mona Aviation Ltd
	G-AYPM	PA-18 Super Cub 95	N. H. Chapman
	G-AYPO	PA-18 Super Cub 95	A. W. Knowles
	G-AYPR	PA-18 Super Cub 95	J. W. Hollingsworth/Blackpool
	G-AYPS	PA-18 Super Cub 95	Tony Dyer Television
	G-AYPT	PA-18 Super Cub 95	P. Shires
	G-AYPU	PA-28R Cherokee Arrow 200	Alpine Ltd/Jersey
	G-AYPV	PA-28 Cherokee 140D	R. J. & J. M. Charlton
	G-AYPZ	Campbell Cricket	A. Melody
	G-AYRF	Cessna F.150L	D. T. A. Rees
	G-AYRG	Cessna F.172K	W. I. Robinson
	G-AYRH	M.S.892A Rallye Commodore 150	J. D. Watt
	G-AYRI	PA-28R Cherokee Arrow 200	E. P. Van Mechelen & Delta Motor Co (Windsor) Sales Ltd/White Waltham
	G-AYRM	PA-28 Cherokee 140D	E. S. Dignam/Biggin Hill
	G-AYRN	Schleicher ASK.14	T. M. Austin/Lasham
	G-AYRO	Cessna FA.150L Aerobat	Thruxton Flight Centre
	G-AYRR	H.S.125 Srs 403B	Duke of Westminster
	G-AYRS	Jodel D.120A	K. Heeley
	G-AYRT	Cessna F.172K	K. W. J. & A. B. L. Hayward
	G-AYRU	BN-2A-6 Islander	Joint Service Parachute Centre/ Netheravon

Reg.	Type	Owner or Operator	Notes
G-AYSA	PA-23 Aztec 250C	N. Parkinson & W. Smith	
G-AYSB	PA-30 Twin Comanche 160C	R. K. Buckle/Booker	
G-AYSD	Slingsby T.61A Falke	G-AYSD Flying Group	
G-AYSH	Taylor JT.1 Monoplane	C. J. Lodge	
G-AYSJ	Bucker Bu133 Jungmeister (LG+O1)	Patina Ltd/Duxford	
G-AYSK	Luton LA-4A Minor	M. P. Lobb	
G-AYSX	Cessna F.177RG	C. P. Heptonstall	
G-AYSY	Cessna F.177RG	Horizon Flyers Ltd/Denham	
G-AYSZ	Cessna FA.150L	E. J. Miller/Dubai	
G-AYTA	M.S.880B Rallye Club	Kemps Corrosion Services Ltd	
G-AYTJ	Cessna 207 Super Skywagon	Foxair/Perth	
G-AYTN	Cameron O-65 balloon	P. G. Hall & R. F. Jessett Prometheus	
G-AYTR	CP.301A Emeraude	P. J. Hall	
G-AYTT	Phoenix PM-3 Duet	H. E. Jenner	
G-AYTV	MJ.2A Tempete	Tempete Group/Barton	
G-AYTY	Bensen B.8	J. H. Wood & J. S. Knight	
G-AYUB	CEA DR.253B	D. J. Brook	
G-AYUH	PA-28 Cherokee 180F	G-AYUH Group	
G-AYUI	PA-28 Cherokee 180	Semloh Aviation Services/Andrewsfield	
G-AYUJ	Evans VP-1 Volksplane	S. W. Cross & M. A. Farrelly	
G-AYUM	Slingsby T.61A Falke	Hereward Flying Group/Sibson	
G-AYUN	Slingsby T.61A Falke	C. W. Vigar & R. J. Watts	
G-AYUP	Slingsby T.61A Falke	Cranwell Gliding Club	
G-AYUR	Slingsby T.61A Falke	W. A Urwin	
G-AYUS	Taylor JT.1 Monoplane	R. R. McKinnon	
G-AYUT	Jodel DR.1050	R. Norris	
G-AYUV	Cessna F.172H	Snowdon Mountain Aviation Ltd/ Caernarfon	
G-AYUW	BAC One-Eleven 476FM★	AIM Aviation Ltd (cabin water spray tests)/ Bournemouth	
G-AYVA	Cameron O-84 balloon	A. Kirk April Fool	
G-AYVO	Wallis WA120 Srs 1	K. H. Wallis	
G-AYVP	Woody Pusher	J. R. Wraight	
G-AYVT	Brochet MB.84 ★	Dunelm Flying Group (stored)	
G-AYVU	Cameron O-56 balloon	Shell-Mex & B.P. Ltd Hot Potato	
G-AYWA	Avro 19 Srs 2 ★	Strathallan Aircraft Collection	
G-AYWD	Cessna 182N	Trans Para Aviation Ltd	
G-AYWE	PA-28 Cherokee 140	N. Roberson	
G-AYWH	Jodel D.117A	D. Kynaston & J. Deakin	
G-AYWM	Glos-Airtourer Super 150	The Star Flying Group/Staverton	
G-AYWT	AIA Stampe SV-4C	B. K. Lecomber/Denham	
G-AYXP	Jodel D.117A	G. N. Davies	
G-AYXS	SIAI-Marchetti S205-18R	J. J. Barnett/Old Sarum	
G-AYXT	W.S. 55 Whirlwind Srs 2 (XK940)	Wilkie Museum Collection/Blackpool	
G-AYXU	Champion 7KCAB Citabria	Norfolk Gliding Club Ltd/Tibenham	
G-AYXV	Cessna FA.150L	Wreck/Popham	
G-AYXW	Evans VP-1	J. S. Penny/Doncaster	
G-AYYF	Cessna F.150L	D. T. A. Rees	
G-AYYK	Slingsby T.61A Falke	Cornish Gliding & Flying Club Ltd/ Perranporth	
G-AYYL	Slingsby T.61A Falke	C. Wood	
G-AYYO	Jodel DR.1050/M1	Bustard Flying Club Ltd/Old Sarum	
G-AYYT	Jodel DR.1050/M1	Sicile Flying Group/Sandown	
G-AYYU	Beech C23 Musketeer	P. Peck	
G-AYYW	BN-2A Islander	RN & R. Marines Sport Parachute Association/Dunkeswell	
G-AYYX	M.S.880B Rallye Club	J. Turnbull & P. W. Robinson	
G-AYYY	M.S.880B Rallye Club	T. W. Heffer/Elstree	
G-AYZE	PA-39 Twin Comanche 160 C/R	J. E. Palmer/Staverton	
G-AYZH	Taylor JT.2 Titch	P. J. G. Goddard	
G-AYZI	SNCAN Stampe SV-4C	W. H. Smout & C. W. A. Simmons	
G-AYZJ	W.S. 55 Whirlwind Srs 2 (XM685) ★	Newark Air Museum	
G-AYZK	Jodel DR.1050/M1	D. G. Hesketh & D. Lees	
G-AYZN	PA-23 Aztec 250D	D. J. Sewell/Nigeria	
G-AYZS	D.62B Condor	P. E. J. Huntley & M. N. Thrush	
G-AYZU	Slingsby T.61A Falke	The Falcon Gliding Group/Enstone	
G-AYZW	Slingsby T.61A Falke	J. A. Dandie & R. J. M. Clement	
G-AZAB	PA-30 Twin Comanche 160B	T. W. P. Sheffield/Humberside	
G-AZAD	Jodel DR.1051	Cawdor Flying Group/Inverness	
G-AZAJ	PA-28R Cherokee Arrow 200B	J. McHugh & ptnrs/Stapleford	

Notes	Reg.	Type	Owner or Operator
	G-AZAV	Cessna 337F	J. R. Surbey
	G-AZAW	GY-80 Horizon 160	E. P. Sadler
	G-AZAZ	Bensen B.8M ★	FAA Museum/Yeovilton
	G-AZBA	T.66 Nipper 3	Nipper Aerobatic Flying Group
	G-AZBB	MBB Bo 209 Monsun 160FV	G. N. Richardson/Staverton
	G-AZBC	PA-39 Twin Comanche 160 C/R	H. G. Orchin
	G-AZBE	Glos-Airtourer Super 150	F. B. Miles
	G-AZBH	Cameron O-84 balloon	—
	G-AZBI	Jodel D.150	T. A. Rawson & W. H. Milner
	G-AZBK	PA-23 Aztec 250E	ATS Aircharter Ltd/Blackbushe
	G-AZBL	Jodel D.9 Bebe	West Midlands Flying Group
	G-AZBN	AT-16 Harvard IIB (FT391)	Swaygate Ltd/Shoreham
	G-AZBT	Western O-65 balloon	D. J. Harris *Hermes*
	G-AZBU	Auster AOP.9	K. H. Wallis
	G-AZBY	W.S.58 Wessex 60 Srs 1 ★	International Helicopter Museum/ Weston-s-Mare
	G-AZBZ	W.S.58 Wessex 60 Srs 1 ★	International Helicopter Museum/ Weston-s-Mare
	G-AZCB	SNCAN Stampe SV-4C	M. J. Cowburn/Redhill
	G-AZCI	Cessna 320A Skyknight	Landsurcon (Air Survey) Ltd
	G-AZCK	B.121 Pup 2	G. C. B. Weir
	G-AZCL	B.121 Pup 2	E. G. A. Prance
	G-AZCP	B.121 Pup 1	Pup Group 87/Elstree
	G-AZCT	B.121 Pup 1	N. J. Hall
	G-AZCU	B.121 Pup 1	A. A. Harris
	G-AZCV	B.121 Pup 2	N. R. W. Long/Elstree
	G-AZCZ	B.121 Pup 2	P. R. Moorehead
	G-AZDA	B.121 Pup 1	G. H. G. Bishop/Shoreham
	G-AZDD	MBB Bo 209 Monsun 150FF	Double Delta Flying Group/Biggin Hill
	G-AZDE	PA-28R Cherokee Arrow 200B	Electro-Motion UK (Export) Ltd/ E. Midlands
	G-AZDF	Cameron O-84 balloon	K. L. C. M. Busemeyer
	G-AZDG	B.121 Pup 2	D. J. Sage/Coventry
	G-AZDK	Beech 95-B55 Baron	C. C. Forrester
	G-AZDX	PA-28 Cherokee 180F	M. Cowan
	G-AZDY	D.H.82A Tiger Moth	J. B. Mills
	G-AZEE	M.S.880B Rallye Club	P. L. Clements
	G-AZEF	Jodel D.120	J. R. Legge
	G-AZEG	PA-28 Cherokee 140D	Ashley Gardner Flying Club Ltd
	G-AZER	Cameron O-42 balloon	M. P. Dokk-Olsen & P. L. Jaye
	G-AZEU	B.121 Pup 2	P. Tonkin & R. S. Kinman
	G-AZEV	B.121 Pup 2	G. P. Martin/Shoreham
	G-AZEW	B.121 Pup 2	K. Cameron
	G-AZEY	B.121 Pup 2	B. F. Hill
	G-AZFA	B.121 Pup 2	K. F. Plummer
	G-AZFC	PA-28 Cherokee 140D	M. L. Hannah/Blackbushe
	G-AZFF	Jodel D.112	C. R. Greenaway
	G-AZFI	PA-28R Cherokee Arrow 200B	G-AZFI Ltd/Sherburn
	G-AZFM	PA-28R Cherokee Arrow 200B	Linco (Holdings) Ltd
	G-AZFP	Cessna F.177RG	Allen Aviation Ltd/Goodwood
	G-AZFR	Cessna 401B	Westair Flying Services Ltd/Blackpool
	G-AZFZ	Cessna 414	Redapple Ltd/Fairoaks
	G-AZGA	Jodel D.120	D. H. Pattison
	G-AZGC	SNCAN Stampe SV-4C (No 120)	V. Lindsay
	G-AZGE	SNCAN Stampe SV-4A	M. R. L. Astor/Booker
	G-AZGF	B.121 Pup 2	K. Singh
	G-AZGI	M.S.880B Rallye Club	J. & S. Cattle/Newcastle
	G-AZGJ	M.S.880B Rallye Club	P. Rose
	G-AZGL	M.S.894A Rallye Minerva	The Cambridge Aero Club Ltd
	G-AZGY	CP.301B Emeraude	J. R. Riley-Gale
	G-AZGZ	D.H.82A Tiger Moth (NM181)	F. R. Manning
	G-AZHB	Robin HR.100-200	C. & P. P. Scarlett/Sywell
	G-AZHC	Jodel D.112	J. A. Summer & A. Burton/Netherthorpe
	G-AZHD	Slingsby T.61A Falke	J. Sentance
	G-AZHH	SA 102.5 Cavalier	D. W. Buckle
	G-AZHI	Glos-Airtourer Super 150	H. J. Douglas/Biggin Hill
	G-AZHJ	S.A. Twin Pioneer Srs 3	Prestwick Pioneer Preservation Soc Ltd
	G-AZHK	Robin HR.100/200B	D. J. Sage (G-ILEG)
	G-AZHR	Piccard Ax6 balloon	G. Fisher
	G-AZHT	Glos-Airtourer T.3	Aviation West Ltd/Glasgow
	G-AZHU	Luton LA-4A Minor	W. Cawrey/Netherthorpe
	G-AZIB	ST-10 Diplomate	Diplomate Group
	G-AZID	Cessna FA.150L	Exeter Flying Club Ltd

Reg.	Type	Owner or Operator	Notes
G-AZII	Jodel D.117A	J. S. Brayshaw	
G-AZIJ	Jodel DR.360	Rob Airway Ltd/Guernsey	
G-AZIK	PA-34-200 Seneca II	C.S.E. Aviation Ltd/Kidlington	
G-AZIL	Slingsby T.61A Falke	D. W. Savage	
G-AZIO	SNCAN Stampe SV-4C (Lycoming) ★	/Booker	
G-AZIP	Cameron O-65 balloon	Dante Balloon Group *Dante*	
G-AZJC	Fournier RF-5	J. J. Butler/Biggin Hill	
G-AZJE	Ord-Hume JB-01 Minicab	J. B. Evans/Sandown	
G-AZJI	Western O-65 balloon	W. Davison *Peek-a-Boo*	
G-AZJN	Robin DR.300/140	Wright Farm Eggs Ltd	
G-AZJV	Cessna F.172L	J. A. & A. J. Boyd/Cardiff	
G-AZJY	Cessna FRA.150L	G. Firbank	
G-AZJZ	PA-23 Aztec 250E	Encee Services Ltd/Cardiff	
G-AZKC	M.S.880B Rallye Club	L. J. Martin/Redhill	
G-AZKD	M.S.880B Rallye Club	P. Feeney/Kidlington	
G-AZKE	M.S.880B Rallye Club	B. S. Rowden & W. L. Rogers	
G-AZKK	Cameron O-56 balloon	Gemini Balloon Group *Gemini*	
G-AZKN	Robin HR.100/200	Sussex Flying Group/Goodwood	
G-AZKO	Cessna F.337F	Crispair Aviation Services Ltd	
G-AZKP	Jodel D.117	J. Lowe	
G-AZKR	PA-24 Comanche 180	P. I. Kempsey & S. McGovern	
G-AZKS	AA-1A Trainer	M. D. Henson	
G-AZKW	Cessna F.172L	J. C. C. Wright	
G-AZKZ	Cessna F.172L	R. D. & E. Forster/Swanton Morley	
G-AZLE	Boeing N2S-5 Kaydet	Parker Airways Ltd/Denham	
G-AZLF	Jodel D.120	M. S. C. Ball	
G-AZLH	Cessna F.150L	Skegness Air Taxi Service Ltd/Boston	
G-AZLL	Cessna FRA.150L	Air Service Training Ltd/Perth	
G-AZLN	PA-28 Cherokee 180F	Liteflite Ltd/Kidlington	
G-AZLO	Cessna F.337F	*Stored*/Bourn	
G-AZLV	Cessna 172K	B. L. F. Karthaus	
G-AZLY	Cessna F.150L	Cleveland Flying School Ltd/Tees-side	
G-AZLZ	Cessna F.150L	Exeter Flying Club Ltd	
G-AZMB	Bell 47G-3B	Helitech (Luton) Ltd	
G-AZMC	Slingsby T.61A Falke	Essex Gliding Club Ltd	
G-AZMD	Slingsby T.61C Falke	R. A. Rice	
G-AZMF	BAC One-Eleven 530FX	British Airways *County of Northumberland*	
G-AZMH	Morane-Saulnier M.S.500 (ZA+WN)	Wessex Aviation & Transport Ltd	
G-AZMJ	AA-5 Traveler	R. T. Love/Bodmin	
G-AZMN	Glos-Airtourer T.5	W. Crozier & I. Young/Glasgow	
G-AZMX	PA-28 Cherokee 140 ★	NE Wales Institute of Higher Education (Instructional airframe)/Clwyd	
G-AZMZ	M.S.893A Rallye Commodore 150	P. J. Wilcox/Cranfield	
G-AZNA	V.813 Viscount	British Air Ferries Ltd/Southend	
G-AZNF	AIA Stampe SV-4C	H. J. Smith/Shoreham	
G-AZNK	SNCAN Stampe SV-4A	P. D. Jackson	
G-AZNL	PA-28R Cherokee Arrow 200D	P. L. Buckley Ltd	
G-AZNO	Cessna 182P	M&D Aviation/Bournemouth	
G-AZNT	Cameron O-84 balloon	N. Tasker	
G-AZOA	MBB Bo 209 Monsun 150FF	R. P. Wilson	
G-AZOB	MBB Bo 209 Monsun 150FF	G. N. Richardson/Staverton	
G-AZOE	Glos-Airtourer 115	R. J. Zukowski	
G-AZOF	Glos-Airtourer Super 150	D. C. Macdonald	
G-AZOG	PA-28R Cherokee Arrow 200D	J. G. Collins/Cambridge	
G-AZOH	Beech 65-B90 Queen Air	Genoex UK Ltd	
G-AZOL	PA-34-200 Seneca II	St Bridgets Aviation Ltd & MTV Designs Ltd	
G-AZON	PA-34-200 Seneca II	Willowvale Electronics Ltd/Elstree	
G-AZOO	Western O-65 balloon	Southern Balloon Group *Carousel*	
G-AZOR	MBB Bo 105D	Bond Helicopters Ltd/Bourn	
G-AZOS	Jurca MJ.5-F1 Sirocco	O. R. B. Dixon/Barton	
G-AZOT	PA-34-200 Seneca II	G. S. Jenkins & M. R. C. Smerald	
G-AZOU	Jodel DR.1051	Horsham Flying Group/Slinfold	
G-AZOZ	Cessna FRA.150L	Seawing Flying Club Ltd/Southend	
G-AZPA	PA-25 Pawnee 235	Black Mountain Gliding Co Ltd	
G-AZPC	Slingsby T.61C Falke	B. C. Dixon	
G-AZPF	Fournier RF-5	R. Pye/Blackpool	
G-AZPH	Craft-Pitts S-1S Special ★	Science Museum/London	
G-AZPV	Luton LA-4A Minor	J. Scott/(*Stored*)	
G-AZPX	Western O-31 balloon	Eugena Rex Balloon Group	
G-AZPZ	BAC One-Eleven 515FB	British Airways *Dumfries and Galloway Region*	
G-AZRA	MBB Bo 209 Monsun 150FF	Alpha Flying Ltd/Denham	

Notes	Reg.	Type	Owner or Operator
	G-AZRD	Cessna 401B	Morbaine Ltd
	G-AZRG	PA-23 Aztec 250D	Woodgate Aviation (IOM) Ltd/Ronaldsway
	G-AZRH	PA-28 Cherokee 140D	Newcastle-upon-Tyne Aero Club Ltd
	G-AZRI	Payne balloon	G. F. Payne Shoestring
	G-AZRK	Fournier RF-5	Thurleigh Flying Group
	G-AZRL	PA-18 Super Cub 95	B. J. Stead
	G-AZRM	Fournier RF-5	A. R. Dearden & R. Speer/Shoreham
	G-AZRN	Cameron O-84 balloon	C. A. Butter & J. J. T. Cooke
	G-AZRP	Glos-Airtourer 115	B. F. Strawford
	G-AZRR	Cessna 310Q	Routarrow Ltd/Norwich
	G-AZRS	PA-22 Tri-Pacer 150	T. W. R. Case
	G-AZRV	PA-28R Cherokee Arrow 200B	Designed for Sound Ltd
	G-AZRW	Cessna T.337C	R. C. Frazle/Southend
	G-AZRX	GY-80 Horizon 160	Horizon Flying Group
	G-AZRZ	Cessna U.206F	Cyprus Combined Services Parachute Club/Akrotiri
	G-AZSA	Stampe SV-4B	J. K. Faulkner/Biggin Hill
	G-AZSC	AT-16 Harvard IIB	Machine Music Ltd/Fairoaks
	G-AZSD	Slingsby T.29B Motor Tutor	R. G. Boynton
	G-AZSF	PA-28R Cherokee Arrow 200D	W. T. Northorpe & R. J. Mills/Coventry
	G-AZSG	PA-28 Cherokee 180E	Aero Group 78/Netherthorpe
	G-AZSH	PA-28R Cherokee Arrow 180	C. R. Hayward
	G-AZSN	PA-28R Cherokee Arrow 200	Jetstream Air Couriers Ltd/Bristol
	G-AZSU	H.S.748 Srs 2A	Aberdeen Airways Ltd
	G-AZSW	B.121 Pup 1	Northamptonshire School of Flying Ltd/ Sywell
	G-AZSZ	PA-23 Aztec 250D	Strata Surveys Ltd
	G-AZTA	MBB Bo 209 Monsun 150FF	M. E. F. Reynolds/Goodwood
	G-AZTD	PA-32 Cherokee Six 300D	Presshouse Publications Ltd/Enstone
	G-AZTF	Cessna F.177RG	J. Bolson & Son Ltd/Bournemouth
	G-AZTI	MBB Bo 105D	Bond Helicopters Ltd
	G-AZTK	Cessna F.172F	C. O. Simpson
	G-AZTO	PA-34-200 Seneca II	Bulldog Aviation Ltd
	G-AZTR	SNCAN Stampe SV-4C	P. G. Palumbo/Booker
	G-AZTS	Cessna F.172L	J. F. Morgan/Humberside
	G-AZTV	Stolp SA.500 Starlet	G. R. Rowland
	G-AZTW	Cessna F.177RG	R. M. Clarke/Leicester
	G-AZUK	BAC One-Eleven 476FM	British Air Ferries Ltd/Southend
	G-AZUM	Cessna F.172L	Fowlmere Fliers
	G-AZUO	Cessna F.177RG	C. W. Hall
	G-AZUP	Cameron O-65 balloon	R. S. Bailey & ptnrs
	G-AZUT	M.S.893A Rallye Commodore 180	Rallye Flying Group
	G-AZUV	Cameron O-65 balloon ★	British Balloon Museum
	G-AZUX	Western O-56 balloon	M. W. H. Henton
	G-AZUY	Cessna E.310L	Drawline Transport Group PLC
	G-AZUZ	Cessna FRA.150L	D. J. Parker/Netherthorpe
	G-AZVA	MBB Bo 209 Monsun 150FF	K. H. Wallis
	G-AZVB	MBB Bo 209 Monsun 150FF	P. C. Logsdon/Dunkeswell
	G-AZVE	AA-5 Traveler	G-AZVE Flying Group/Rochester
	G-AZVF	M.S.894A Rallye Minerva	P. D. Lloyd
	G-AZVG	AA-5 Traveler	G. Phillips
	G-AZVH	M.S.894A Rallye Minerva	Bristol Cars Ltd/White Waltham
	G-AZVI	M.S.892A Rallye Commodore	Shobdon Flying Group
	G-AZVJ	PA-34-200 Seneca II	Skyfotos Ltd/Lydd
	G-AZVL	Jodel D.119	Forest Flying Group/Stapleford
	G-AZVM	Hughes 369HS	Diagnostic Reagents Ltd
	G-AZVP	Cessna F.177RG	Horizon Flyers Ltd
	G-AZVT	Cameron O-84 balloon	Sky Soarer Ltd *Jules Verne*
	G-AZWB	PA-28 Cherokee 140	Skyscraper Ltd
	G-AZWD	PA-28 Cherokee 140	BM Aviation (Winchester)
	G-AZWE	PA-28 Cherokee 140	Devon School of Flying/Dunkeswell
	G-AZWF	SAN Jodel DR.1050	J. S. Hill
	G-AZWS	PA-28R Cherokee Arrow 180	J. E. Shepherd & C. A. Douglas
	G-AZWT	Westland Lysander IIIA (V9441)	Strathallan Aircraft Collection
	G-AZWW	PA-23 Aztec 250E	Phoenix Aviation (Bedford) Ltd/Cranfield
	G-AZWY	PA-24 Comanche 260	Keymer Son & Co Ltd/Biggin Hill
	G-AZXA	Beech 95-C55 Baron	F.R. Aviation Ltd/Bournemouth
	G-AZXB	Cameron O-65 balloon	R. J. Mitchener & P. F.Smart
	G-AZXC	Cessna F.150L	S. Redfearn/Netherthorpe
	G-AZXD	Cessna F.172L	Birdlake Ltd/Wellesbourne
	G-AZXG	PA-23 Aztec 250D	N. J. Le Fevre & M. J. Leeder/Norwich
	G-AZXR	BN-2A-9 Islander	Fenchurch Leasing Ltd
	G-AZYA	GY-80 Horizon 160	T. Poole & ptnrs/Sywell

Reg.	Type	Owner or Operator	Notes
G-AZYB	Bell 47H-1 ★	International Helicopter Museum/ Weston-s-Mare	
G-AZYD	M.S.893A Rallye Commodore	Buckminster Gliding Club Ltd/Saltby	
G-AZYF	PA-28 Cherokee 180	J. C. Glynn/E. Midlands	
G-AZYM	Cessna E.310Q	Kingswinford Engineering Co Ltd	
G-AZYS	CP.301C-1 Emeraude	F. P. L. Clauson	
G-AZYU	PA-23 Aztec 250E	L. J. Martin/Biggin Hill	
G-AZYV	Burns O-77 balloon	B. F. G. Ribbans Contrary Mary	
G-AZYY	Slingsby T.61A Falke	J. A. Towers	
G-AZYZ	WA.51A Pacific	Yankee Zulu Ltd/Biggin Hill	
G-AZZG	Cessna 188 Agwagon	N. C. Kensington	
G-AZZH	Practavia Pilot Sprite 115	K. G. Stewart	
G-AZZK	Cessna 414	D. O. McIntyre	
G-AZZO	PA-28 Cherokee 140	R. J. Hind/Elstree	
G-AZZP	Cessna F.172H	M. Bell & ptnrs/Exeter	
G-AZZR	Cessna F.150L	J. B. Small/Swansea	
G-AZZS	PA-34-200 Seneca II	Robin Cook Aviation/Shoreham	
G-AZZT	PA-28 Cherokee 180 ★	Ground instruction airframe/Cranfield	
G-AZZV	Cessna F.172L	Century Composites Ltd	
G-AZZW	Fournier RF-5	Aviation Special Developments	
G-AZZX	Cessna FRA.150L	J. E. Uprichard & ptnrs/Newtownards	
G-AZZZ	D.H.82A Tiger Moth	S. W. McKay	
G-BAAD	Evans Super VP-1	R. A. Martin	
G-BAAF	Manning-Flanders MF1 replica	Aviation Film Services Ltd/Booker	
G-BAAI	M.S.893A Rallye Commodore	R. D. Taylor/Thruxton	
G-BAAK	Cessna 207	B. W. Wells	
G-BAAL	Cessna 172A	Rochester Aviation Ltd	
G-BAAP	PA-28R Cherokee Arrow 200	Shirley A. Shelley/Biggin Hill	
G-BAAT	Cessna 182P Skylane	A. H. Hunt/St Just	
G-BAAU	Enstrom F-28C-UK	M. Upton	
G-BAAW	Jodel D.119	K. J. Cockrill/Ipswich	
G-BAAX	Cameron O-84 balloon	The New Holker Estate Co Ltd Holker Hall	
G-BAAZ	PA-28R Cherokee Arrow 200D	A. W. Rix/Guernsey	
G-BABB	Cessna F.150L	Seawing Flying Club Ltd/Southend	
G-BABC	Cessna F.150L	Suffolk Aero Club Ltd/Ipswich	
G-BABD	Cessna FRA.150L	C. J. Hopewell	
G-BABE	Taylor JT.2 Titch	P. D. G. Grist/Sibson	
G-BABG	PA-28 Cherokee 180	Mendip Flying Group/Bristol	
G-BABK	PA-34-200 Seneca II	D. F. J. & N. R. Flashman/Biggin Hill	
G-BABY	Taylor JT.2 Titch	R. E. Finlay	
G-BACB	PA-34-200 Seneca II	London Flight Centre (Stansted) Ltd	
G-BACC	Cessna FRA.150L	C. M. & J. H. Cooper/Cranfield	
G-BACE	Fournier RF-5	R. W. K. Stead/Perranporth	
G-BACH	Enstrom F-28A	M. & P. Food Products Ltd	
G-BACJ	Jodel D.120	Wearside Flying Association/Newcastle	
G-BACL	Jodel D.150	M. L. Sargeant/Biggin Hill	
G-BACN	Cessna FRA.150L	Air Service Training Ltd/Perth	
G-BACO	Cessna FRA.150L	W. R. Burgess & ptnrs/Sibson	
G-BACP	Cessna FRA.150L	B. A. Mills	
G-BADC	Luton Beta B.2A	H. M. Mackenzie	
G-BADH	Slingsby T.61A Falke	Falke Flying Group	
G-BADI	PA-23 Aztec 250D	W. London Aero Services Ltd/ White Waltham	
G-BADJ	PA-E23 Aztec 250E	CKS Air Ltd/Southend	
G-BADL	PA-34-200 Seneca II	Cartographical Services (Southampton) Ltd/ Birmingham	
G-BADM	D.62B Condor	K. P. Wordsworth	
G-BADO	PA-32 Cherokee Six 300E	B. J. Haylor & ptnrs/Southampton	
G-BADP	Boeing 737-204	Britannia Airways Ltd Sir Arthur Whitten Brown/Luton	
G-BADR	Boeing 737-204	Britannia Airways Ltd Capt Robert Falconer Scott/Luton	
G-BADU	Cameron O-56 balloon	J. Philp Dream Machine	
G-BADV	Brochet MB-50	P. A. Cairns/Dunkeswell	
G-BADW	Pitts S-2A Special	R. E. Mitchell/Coventry	
G-BADZ	Pitts S-2A Special	Tiger Club (1990) Ltd/Headcorn	
G-BAEB	Robin DR.400/160	P. D. W. King	
G-BAEC	Robin HR.100/210	Robin Travel	
G-BAED	PA-23 Aztec 250C	Advanced Airship Corp. Ltd/Jurby	
G-BAEE	Jodel DR.1050/M1	R. Little	
G-BAEF	Boeing 727-46	Dan-Air Services Ltd/Gatwick	
G-BAEM	Robin DR.400/125	M. A. Webb/Booker	

Notes	Reg.	Type	Owner or Operator
	G-BAEN	Robin DR.400/180	B. T. & L. M. Spreckley/Shoreham
	G-BAEP	Cessna FRA.150L (modified)	A. M. Lynn
	G-BAER	Cosmic Wind	R. S. Voice/Redhill
	G-BAET	Piper J-3C-65 Cub	C. J. Rees
	G-BAEU	Cessna F.150L	Skyviews & General Ltd
	G-BAEV	Cessna FRA.150L	N. J. Wiszowaty/Blackbushe
	G-BAEW	Cessna F.172M	Northamptonshire School of Flying Ltd/Sywell
	G-BAEY	Cessna F.172M	R. Fursman/Southampton
	G-BAEZ	Cessna FRA.150L	E. Bannister
	G-BAFA	AA-5 Traveler	C. F. Mackley/Stapleford
	G-BAFD	MBB Bo 105D	Bond Helicopters Ltd/Aberdeen
	G-BAFG	D.H.82A Tiger Moth	J. E. & P. J. Shaw
	G-BAFH	Evans VP-1	C. M. Gibson
	G-BAFI	Cessna F.177RG	M. P. Clery
	G-BAFL	Cessna 182P	Threshold Ltd
	G-BAFM	AT-16 Harvard IIB (FS728)	Parker Airways Ltd/Denham
	G-BAFP	Robin DR.400/160	A. S. Langdale & J. Bevis-Lawson/Shoreham
	G-BAFS	PA-18 Super Cub 150	M. D. Morris/Sandown
	G-BAFT	PA-18 Super Cub 150	T. Watson
	G-BAFU	PA-28 Cherokee 140	R. C. Saunders/Gamston
	G-BAFV	PA-18 Super Cub 95	P. Elliott
	G-BAFW	PA-28 Cherokee 140	Foxtrot Whisky Aviation
	G-BAFX	Robin DR.400/140	Nicholas Advertising Ltd
	G-BAGB	SIAI-Marchetti SF.260	British Midland Airways Ltd/E. Midlands
	G-BAGC	Robin DR.400/140	Hempalm Ltd/Headcorn
	G-BAGF	Jodel D.92 Bebe	E. Evans
	G-BAGG	PA-32 Cherokee Six 300E	Hornair Ltd
	G-BAGI	Cameron O-31 balloon	D. C. & S. J. Boxall
	G-BAGL	SA.341G Gazelle Srs 1	Autokraft Ltd
	G-BAGN	Cessna F.177RG	R. W. J. Andrews
	G-BAGO	Cessna 421B	Jadealto (Sales & Marketing) Ltd
	G-BAGR	Robin DR.400/140	F. C. Aris & J. D. Last/Mona
	G-BAGS	Robin DR.400/180 2+2	Headcorn Flying School Ltd
	G-BAGT	Helio H.295 Courier	B. J. C. Woodall Ltd
	G-BAGV	Cessna U.206F	Scottish Parachute Club/Strathallan
	G-BAGX	PA-28 Cherokee 140	Klingair Ltd/Conington
	G-BAGY	Cameron O-84 balloon	P. G. Dunnington *Beatrice*
	G-BAHD	Cessna 182P Skylane	G. G. Ferriman
	G-BAHE	PA-28 Cherokee 140	A. H. Evans & A. O. Jones/Sleap
	G-BAHF	PA-28 Cherokee 140	S. J. Green/Halfpenny Green
	G-BAHG	PA-24 Comanche 260	Friendly Aviation (Jersey) Ltd
	G-BAHH	Wallis WA-121	K. H. Wallis
	G-BAHI	Cessna F.150H	A. G. Brindle/Blackpool
	G-BAHJ	PA-24 Comanche 250	K. Cooper
	G-BAHL	Robin DR.400/160	R. E. Thorns & G. W. Dimmer/Old Sarum
	G-BAHN	Beech 95-58TC Baron	AM Aviation Ltd
	G-BAHO	Beech C.23 Sundowner	G-ATJG Private Aircraft Syndicate Ltd
	G-BAHP	Volmer VJ.22 Sportsman	J. F. Morris
	G-BAHS	PA-28R Cherokee Arrow 200-II	A. A. Wild & ptnrs
	G-BAHX	Cessna 182P	PP Dupost Group
	G-BAHZ	PA-28R Cherokee Arrow 200-II	J. H. Reynolds
	G-BAIA	PA-32 Cherokee Six 300E	Langham International (Aircraft) Ltd/Southend
	G-BAIB	Enstrom F-28A	Farmax Helicopters
	G-BAIH	PA-28R Cherokee Arrow 200-II	G. J. Williamson
	G-BAII	Cessna FRA.150L	Air Service Training Ltd/Perth
	G-BAIK	Cessna F.150L	Wickenby Aviation Ltd
	G-BAIL	Cessna FR.172J	G. Greenall
	G-BAIM	Cessna 310Q	Air Service Training Ltd/Perth
	G-BAIN	Cessna FRA.150L	Air Service Training Ltd/Perth
	G-BAIP	Cessna F.150L	W. D. Cliffe & J. F. Platt/Wellesbourne
	G-BAIR	Thunder Ax7-77 balloon	P. A. & Mrs M. Hutchins
	G-BAIS	Cessna F.177RG	A. J. Everex & T. W. Goodall
	G-BAIW	Cessna F.172M	Humber Aviation Ltd
	G-BAIX	Cessna F.172M	R. A. Nichols/Elstree
	G-BAIY	Cameron O-65 balloon	Budget Rent A Car (UK) Ltd
	G-BAIZ	Slingsby T.61A Falke	Falke Syndicate
	G-BAJA	Cessna F.177RG	Don Ward Productions Ltd/Biggin Hill
	G-BAJB	Cessna F.177RG	G. J. Banfield
	G-BAJC	Evans VP-1	R. A. Hazelton
	G-BAJE	Cessna 177 Cardinal	N. C. Butcher

Reg.	Type	Owner or Operator	Notes
G-BAJN	AA-5 Traveler	Janacrew Flying Group	
G-BAJO	AA-5 Traveler	J. R. Howard/Blackpool	
G-BAJR	PA-28 Cherokee 180	Chosen Few Flying Group/Newtownards	
G-BAJY	Robin DR.400/180	F. Birch & K. J. Pike/Sturgate	
G-BAJZ	Robin DR.400/125	Rochester Aviation Ltd	
G-BAKD	PA-34-200 Seneca II	Andrews Professional Colour Laboratories/ Elstree	
G-BAKH	PA-28 Cherokee 140	Woodgate Air Services (IoM) Ltd/ Ronaldsway	
G-BAKJ	PA-30 Twin Comanche 160B	M. F. Fisher & W. R. Lawes/Biggin Hill	
G-BAKK	Cessna F.172H ★	Parachute jump trainer/Coventry	
G-BAKL	F.27 Friendship Mk 200	Air UK Ltd/Norwich	
G-BAKM	Robin DR.400/140	MKS Syndicate	
G-BAKN	SNCAN Stampe SV-4C	M. Holloway	
G-BAKO	Cameron O-84 balloon	D. C. Dokk-Olsen Pied Piper	
G-BAKR	Jodel D.117	A. B. Bailey/White Waltham	
G-BAKS	AB-206B JetRanger 2	Dollar Air Services Ltd/Coventry	
G-BAKV	PA-18 Super Cub 150	Pounds Marine Shipping Ltd/Goodwood	
G-BAKW	B.121 Pup 2	Oakley Motor Units Ltd & J. P. Baudrier	
G-BAKY	Slingsby T.61C Falke	G. A. Schulz & A. Jones/Leicester	
G-BALF	Robin DR.400/140	F. A. Spear/Panshanger	
G-BALG	Robin DR.400/180	R. Jones	
G-BALH	Robin DR.400/140B	J. D. Copsey	
G-BALI	Robin DR.400 2+2	Robin Flying Group	
G-BALJ	Robin DR.400/180	D. A. Bett & D. de Lacey-Rowe	
G-BALK	SNCAN Stampe SV-4C	L. J. Rice	
G-BALM	Cessna 340	KK Demel Ltd	
G-BALN	Cessna T.310Q	O'Brien Properties Ltd/Shoreham	
G-BALT	Enstrom F-28A	Codnor Pet-Aquatics	
G-BALX	D.H.82A Tiger Moth (N6848)	Toadair	
G-BALY	Practavia Pilot Sprite 150	A. L. Young	
G-BALZ	Bell 212	B.E.A.S. Ltd/Redhill	
G-BAMB	Slingsby T.61C Falke	Bambi Aircraft Club	
G-BAMC	Cessna F.150L	D. F. Smith	
G-BAME	Volmer VJ-22 Sportsman	A. McLeod	
G-BAMF	MBB Bo 105D	Bond Helicopters Ltd/Bourn	
G-BAMJ	Cessna 182P	A. E. Kedros	
G-BAMK	Cameron D-96 airship	D. W. Liddiard	
G-BAML	Bell 206B JetRanger 2	Heliscott Ltd	
G-BAMM	PA-28 Cherokee 235	G-BAMM Group	
G-BAMR	PA-16 Clipper	H. Royce	
G-BAMS	Robin DR.400/160	G-BAMS Ltd/Headcorn	
G-BAMU	Robin DR.400/160	The Alternative Flying Group/Sywell	
G-BAMV	Robin DR.400/180	Rochester Aviation Ltd	
G-BAMY	PA-28R Cherokee Arrow 200-II	G-BAMY Group/Birmingham	
G-BANA	Robin DR.221	G. T. Pryor	
G-BANB	Robin DR.400/180	Time Electronics Ltd/Biggin Hill	
G-BANC	GY-201 Minicab	J. T. S. Lewis & J. E. Williams	
G-BAND	Cameron O-84 balloon	Mid-Bucks Farmers Balloon Group Clover	
G-BANE	Cessna FRA.150L	Spectrum Flying Group/Newtownards	
G-BANF	Luton LA-4A Minor	W. J. McCollum	
G-BANG	Cameron O-84 balloon	R. F. Harrower	
G-BANK	PA-34-200 Seneca II	Cleveland Flying School Ltd/Teesside	
G-BANT	Cameron O-65 balloon	M. A. Dworski & R. M. Bishop	
G-BANU	Wassmer Jodel D.120	C. E. McKinney	
G-BANV	Phoenix Currie Wot	K. Knight	
G-BANW	CP.1330 Super Emeraude	P. S. Milner	
G-BANX	Cessna F.172M	J. F. Davis/Badminton	
G-BAOB	Cessna F.172M	Bulldog Aviation Ltd/Earls Colne	
G-BAOG	M.S.880B Rallye Club	G. W. Simpson	
G-BAOH	M.S.880B Rallye Club	A. Devery	
G-BAOJ	M.S.880B Rallye Club	BAOJ Ltd	
G-BAOM	M.S.880B Rallye Club	D. H. Tonkin	
G-BAOP	Cessna FRA.150L	M. K. Field	
G-BAOS	Cessna F.172M	F. W. Ellis & ptnrs	
G-BAOU	AA-5 Traveler	C. J. Earle & I. S. Hacon	
G-BAOV	AA-5A Cheetah	A. Kerridge	
G-BAOW	Cameron O-65 balloon	P. I. White Winslow Boy	
G-BAOY	Cameron S-31 balloon	Shell-Mex BP Ltd New Potato	
G-BAPA	Fournier RF-5B Sperber	Nuthampstead G-BAPA Group	
G-BAPB	D.H.C.1 Chipmunk 22	R. C. P. Brookhouse/Redhill	
G-BAPC	Luton LA-4A Minor ★	Midland Aircraft Preservation Soc	
G-BAPF	V.814 Viscount	British Air Ferries/Southend	

Notes	Reg.	Type	Owner or Operator
	G-BAPG	V.814 Viscount	Ali Finance Ltd/Southend
	G-BAPI	Cessna FRA.150L	Industrial Supplies (Peterborough) Ltd/ Sibson
	G-BAPJ	Cessna FRA.150L	M. D. Page/Manston
	G-BAPK	Cessna F.150L	Andrewsfield Flying Club Ltd
	G-BAPL	PA-23 Turbo Aztec 250E	Medici Spa Marine & Exploration Ltd
	G-BAPM	Fuji FA.200-160	R. P. Munday/Biggin Hill
	G-BAPP	Evans VP-1	N. H. Eastwood
	G-BAPR	Jodel D.11	R. G. Marshall
	G-BAPS	Campbell Cougar ★	International Helicopter Museum/ Weston-s-Mare
	G-BAPV	Robin DR.400/160	J. D. & M. Millne
	G-BAPW	PA-28R Cherokee Arrow 180	Papa Whisky Flying Group
	G-BAPX	Robin DR.400/160	M. A. Musselwhite
	G-BAPY	Robin HR.100/210	Gloria Baby Aviation Ltd
	G-BARB	PA-34-200 Seneca II	S. Wood
	G-BARC	Cessna FR.172J	G. N. Hopcraft
	G-BARD	Cessna 337C	D. W. Horton
	G-BARF	Jodel D.112 Club	P. G. Rose
	G-BARG	Cessna E.310Q	Sally Marine Ltd
	G-BARH	Beech C.23 Sundowner	MLP Aviation Ltd/Elstree
	G-BARJ	Bell 212	Autair International Ltd/Panshanger
	G-BARN	Taylor JT.2 Titch	R. G. W. Newton
	G-BARP	Bell 206B JetRanger 2	S.W. Electricity Board/Bristol
	G-BARS	D.H.C.1 Chipmunk 22	T. I. Sutton/Chester
	G-BARV	Cessna 310Q	Old England Watches Ltd/Elstree
	G-BARZ	Scheibe SF.28A Tandem Falke	J. A. Fox & ptnrs/Dishforth
	G-BASB	Enstrom F-28A	GTS Engineering (Coventry) Ltd
	G-BASD	B.121 Pup 2	C. C. Brown/Leicester
	G-BASG	AA-5 Traveler	ASG Aviation/Glenrothes
	G-BASH	AA-5 Traveler	J. J. Woodhouse
	G-BASJ	PA-28 Cherokee 180	ABS Group (UK) Ltd & W. Brown
	G-BASL	PA-28 Cherokee 140	Air Navigation & Trading Ltd/Blackpool
	G-BASM	PA-34-200 Seneca II	Poplar Aviation/Ipswich
	G-BASN	Beech C.23 Sundowner	M. F. Fisher
	G-BASO	Lake LA-4 Amphibian	R. J. Willies
	G-BASP	B.121 Pup 1	Northamptonshire School of Flying Ltd/ Sywell
	G-BASX	PA-34-200 Seneca II	J. W. Anstee & Anstee & Ware Ltd
	G-BATC	MBB Bo 105D	Bond Helicopters Ltd/Swansea
	G-BATJ	Jodel D.119	E. G. Waite/Shobdon
	G-BATM	PA-32 Cherokee Six 300E	Patgrove Ltd/Bolney
	G-BATN	PA-23 Aztec 250E	Marshall of Cambridge Ltd
	G-BATR	PA-34-200 Seneca II	Aerohire Ltd/Halfpenny Green
	G-BATT	Hughes 269C	Fairglobe Ltd
	G-BATV	PA-28 Cherokee 180D	J. N. Rudsdale
	G-BATW	PA-28 Cherokee 140	C. R. Lambert/Earls Colne
	G-BATX	PA-23 Aztec 250E	Tayside Aviation Ltd/Dundee
	G-BAUA	PA-23 Aztec 250D	David Parr & Associates Ltd/Shobdon
	G-BAUC	PA-25 Pawnee 235	Southdown Gliding Club Ltd
	G-BAUD	Robin DR.400/160	E. J. A. Woolnough
	G-BAUE	Cessna 310Q	A. J. Dyer/Elstree
	G-BAUH	Jodel D.112	G. A. & D. Shepherd
	G-BAUI	PA-23 Aztec 250D	SFT Aviation Ltd/Bournemouth
	G-BAUJ	PA-23 Aztec 250E	S. J. & C. J. Westley/Cranfield
	G-BAUK	Hughes 269C	Curtis Engineering (Frome) Ltd
	G-BAUR	F.27 Friendship Mk 200	Air UK Ltd *Robert Louis Stevenson*/ Norwich
	G-BAUV	Cessna F.150L	Skyviews & General Ltd
	G-BAUW	PA-23 Aztec 250E	R. E. Myson
	G-BAUY	Cessna FRA.150L	The PMM Group/Glenrothes
	G-BAUZ	SNCAN NC.854S	W. A. Ashley & D. Horne
	G-BAVB	Cessna F.172M	T. J. Nokes & T. V. Phillips
	G-BAVC	Cessna F.150L	Butler Associates (Aviation) Ltd
	G-BAVH	D.H.C.1 Chipmunk 22	Portsmouth Naval Gliding Club/ Lee-on-Solent
	G-BAVL	PA-23 Aztec 250E	D. M. Charrington/Teesside
	G-BAVO	Boeing Stearman N2S (26)	V. A. Holliday & T. E. W. Terrell
	G-BAVR	AA-5 Traveler	E. R. Pyatt
	G-BAVS	AA-5 Traveler	V. J. Peake/Headcorn
	G-BAVU	Cameron A-105 balloon	J. D. Michaelis
	G-BAVZ	PA-23 Aztec 250E	Ravenair/Manchester
	G-BAWB	PA-23 Aztec 250C	Emberden Ltd/Biggin Hill

Reg.	Type	Owner or Operator	Notes
G-BAWG	PA-28R Cherokee Arrow 200-II	Solent Air Ltd	
G-BAWI	Enstrom F-28A-UK	M. & P. Food Products Ltd	
G-BAWK	PA-28 Cherokee 140	Newcastle-upon-Tyne Aero Club Ltd	
G-BAWN	PA-30 Twin Comanche 160C	P. A. Greenhalgh	
G-BAWR	Robin HR.100/210	Yarmouth Marine Service/Sandown	
G-BAWU	PA-30 Twin Comanche 160B	CCH Aviation Ltd	
G-BAWW	Thunder Ax7-77 balloon	M. L. C. Hutchins *Taurus*/Holland	
G-BAXD	BN-2A Mk III Trislander	Aurigny Air Services/Guernsey	
G-BAXE	Hughes 269A	Reethorpe Engineering Ltd	
G-BAXF	Cameron O-77 balloon	R. D. Sargeant & M. F. Lasson	
G-BAXH	Cessna 310Q	D. A. Williamson	
G-BAXJ	PA-32 Cherokee Six 300B	UK Parachute Services/Ipswich	
G-BAXK	Thunder Ax7-77 balloon	T. J. Orchard & A. R. Snook	
G-BAXP	PA-23 Aztec 250E	Ashcombe Ltd	
G-BAXS	Bell 47G-5	Helicopter Supplies & Engineering Ltd/Bournemouth	
G-BAXT	PA-28R Cherokee Arrow 200-II	P. R. Phealon/Old Sarum	
G-BAXU	Cessna F.150L	W. Lancs Aero Club Ltd/Woodvale	
G-BAXY	Cessna F.172M	N. A. Ali	
G-BAXZ	PA-28 Cherokee 140	H. Martin & D. Norris/Halton	
G-BAYC	Cameron O-65 balloon	D. Whitlock & R. T. F. Mitchell	
G-BAYL	Nord 1203/III Norecrin	D. M. Fincham	
G-BAYO	Cessna 150L	Cheshire Air Training School (Merseyside) Ltd/Liverpool	
G-BAYP	Cessna 150L	Three Counties Aero Engineering Ltd/Lasham	
G-BAYR	Robin HR.100/210	Gilbey Warren Co Ltd/Stapleford	
G-BAYV	SNCAN 1101 Noralpha (1480)★	Booker Aircraft Museum	
G-BAYZ	Bellanca 7GCBC Citabria	Cambridge University Gliding Trust Ltd/Gransdon	
G-BAZB	H.S.125 Srs 400B	Short Bros PLC/Sydenham	
G-BAZC	Robin DR.400/160	Southern Sailplanes	
G-BAZH	Boeing 737-204	Britannia Airways Ltd *Sir Frederick Handley Page*/Luton	
G-BAZJ	HPR-7 Herald 209 ★	Guernsey Airport Fire Services	
G-BAZM	Jodel D.11	Bingley Flying Group/Leeds	
G-BAZS	Cessna F.150L	Sherburn Aero Club Ltd	
G-BAZT	Cessna F.172M	M. Fraser/Exeter	
G-BAZU	PA-28R Cherokee Arrow 200	S. C. Simmons/White Waltham	
G-BBAE	L.1011-385 TriStar 100	Caledonian Airways *Loch Earn*/Gatwick	
G-BBAF	L.1011-385 TriStar 100	Caledonian Airways/Gatwick	
G-BBAG	L.1011-385 TriStar 1	British Airways *Bridgwater Bay*/Heathrow	
G-BBAH	L.1011-385 TriStar 100	Caledonian Airways/Gatwick	
G-BBAI	L.1011-385 TriStar 1	Caledonian Airways *Loch Inver*/Gatwick	
G-BBAJ	L.1011-385 TriStar 100	Caledonian Airways *Loch Rannoch*/Gatwick	
G-BBAK	M.S.894A Rallye Minerva	R. B. Hemsworth & C. L. Hill/Exeter	
G-BBAW	Robin HR.100/210	Scoba Ltd/Goodwood	
G-BBAX	Robin DR.400/140	S. R. Young	
G-BBAY	Robin DR.400/140	Rothwell Group	
G-BBAZ	Hiller UH-12E	Copley Farms Ltd	
G-BBBC	Cessna F.150L	W. J. Greenfield	
G-BBBI	AA-5 Traveler	J. Tomkins	
G-BBBK	PA-28 Cherokee 140	Bencray Ltd/Blackpool	
G-BBBM	Bell 206B JetRanger 2	Express Newspapers PLC	
G-BBBN	PA-28 Cherokee 180	BT Flying Group	
G-BBBO	SIPA 903	J. S. Hemmings & C. R. Steer	
G-BBBW	FRED Series 2	C. Briggs	
G-BBBX	Cessna E310L	Atlantic Air Transport Ltd/Coventry	
G-BBBY	PA-28 Cherokee 140	J. L. Yourell/Luton	
G-BBCA	Bell 206B JetRanger 2	E. Wootton	
G-BBCB	Western O-65 balloon	G. M. Bulmer	
G-BBCC	PA-23 Aztec 250D	Dorglen Ltd/Coventry	
G-BBCD	Beech 95-B55 Baron	L. M. Tulloch	
G-BBCH	Robin DR.400/2+2	Headcorn Flying School Ltd	
G-BBCI	Cessna 150H	N. R. Windley	
G-BBCK	Cameron O-77 balloon	R. J. Leathart *The Mary Gloster*	
G-BBCN	Robin HR.100/210	K. T. G. Atkins/Teesside	
G-BBCP	Thunder Ax6-56 balloon	J. M. Robinson *Jack Frost*	
G-BBCS	Robin DR.400/140	A. R. G. Besler	
G-BBCW	PA-23 Aztec 250E	JDT Holdings Ltd/Sturgate	
G-BBCY	Luton LA-4A Minor	D. C. Stokes	

Notes	Reg.	Type	Owner or Operator
	G-BBCZ	AA-5 Traveler	P. J. Kember
	G-BBDB	PA-28 Cherokee 180	T. D. Strange/Newtownards
	G-BBDC	PA-28 Cherokee 140	C. Doggett & A. Dunk
	G-BBDD	PA-28 Cherokee 140	Midland Air Training School
	G-BBDE	PA-28R Cherokee Arrow 200-II	R. L. Coleman & A. E. Stevens
	G-BBDG	Concorde 100 ★	British Aerospace PLC/Filton
	G-BBDH	Cessna F.172M	P. S. C. & B. J. Comina
	G-BBDJ	Thunder Ax6-56 balloon	S. W. D. & H. B. Ashby Jack Tar
	G-BBDK	V.808C Viscount Freightmaster	British Air Ferries Viscount Linley/ Southend
	G-BBDL	AA-5 Traveler	D. S. Hopkins & W. Woods/Coventry
	G-BBDM	AA-5 Traveler	D. J. & P. L. Hazell
	G-BBDN	Taylor JT.1 Monoplane	T. Barnes
	G-BBDO	PA-23 Turbo Aztec 250E	R. Long/Bristol
	G-BBDP	Robin DR.400/160	Robin Lance Aviation Associates Ltd
	G-BBDT	Cessna 150H	U. K. Mercer & J. K. Sibbald
	G-BBDV	SIPA S.903	W. McAndrew
	G-BBEA	Luton LA-4A Minor	W. E. R. Jenkins
	G-BBEB	PA-28R Cherokee Arrow 200-II	R. D. Rippingale/Thruxton
	G-BBEC	PA-28 Cherokee 180	C. F. Bishop/Clacton
	G-BBED	M.S.894A Rallye Minerva 220	Sky-Ad Ltd/Birmingham
	G-BBEF	PA-28 Cherokee 140	Air Navigation & Trading Co Ltd/Blackpool
	G-BBEI	PA-31 Turbo Navajo	BKS Surveys Ltd/Exeter
	G-BBEL	PA-28R Cherokee Arrow 180	G. R. Cole & A. Grimshaw/Ronaldsway
	G-BBEN	Bellanca 7GCBC Citabria	C. A. G. Schofield
	G-BBEO	Cessna FRA.150L	R. H. Ford
	G-BBEV	PA-28 Cherokee 140	Comed Aviation Ltd/Blackpool
	G-BBEX	Cessna 185A Skywagon	Westward Airways (Lands End) Ltd
	G-BBEY	PA-23 Aztec 250E	Cormack (Aircraft Services) Ltd/Glasgow
	G-BBFC	AA-1B Trainer	T. F. Shorter/Lydd
	G-BBFD	PA-28R Cherokee Arrow 200-II	CR Aviation Ltd
	G-BBFL	GY-201 Minicab	D. B. Busfield
	G-BBFS	Van Den Bemden gas balloon	A. J. F. Smith Le Tomate
	G-BBFV	PA-32 Cherokee Six 260	C. J. Janson
	G-BBGB	PA-E23 Aztec 250E	Ravenair/Manchester
	G-BBGC	M.S.893E Rallye 180GT	Mark Thorpe & ptnrs
	G-BBGE	PA-23 Aztec 250D	B. Jones
	G-BBGH	AA-5 Traveler	L. W. Mitchell & D. Abbiss
	G-BBGI	Fuji FA.200-160	D. T. C. Pollock
	G-BBGJ	Cessna 180	B. W. Wells & Burbage Farms Ltd
	G-BBGL	Baby Great Lakes	F. Ball
	G-BBGR	Cameron O-65 balloon	M. L. & L. P. Willoughby
	G-BBGX	Cessna 182P Skylane	WOC Hire Ltd
	G-BBGZ	CHABA 42 balloon	G. Laslett & ptnrs
	G-BBHB	PA-31 Turbo Navajo	Photomap (Jersey) Ltd
	G-BBHC	Enstrom F-28A	Blades Helicopters Ltd/Goodwood
	G-BBHD	Enstrom F-28A	R. E. Harvey
	G-BBHF	PA-23 Aztec 250E	Bevan Lynch Aviation Ltd/Birmingham
	G-BBHG	Cessna E310Q	G. P. Williams
	G-BBHI	Cessna 177RG	T. G. W. Bunce
	G-BBHJ	Piper J-3C-65 Cub	R. V. Miller & J. Stanbridge
	G-BBHK	AT-16 Harvard IIB (FH153)	Bob Warner Aviation/Exeter
	G-BBHL	Sikorsky S-61N Mk II	Bristow Helicopters Ltd Glamis
	G-BBHM	Sikorsky S-61N Mk II	Bristow Helicopters Ltd Braemar
	G-BBHX	M.S.893E Rallye Commodore	JKP Aviation
	G-BBHY	PA-28 Cherokee 180	Air Operations Ltd/Guernsey
	G-BBIA	PA-28R Cherokee Arrow 200-II	A. G. (Commodities) Ltd/Stapleford
	G-BBIC	Cessna 310Q	H. Bollmann Manufacturers Ltd
	G-BBID	PA-28 Cherokee 140	M. & J. M. McCormac
	G-BBIF	PA-23 Aztec 250E	Northern Executive Aviation Ltd/ Manchester
	G-BBIH	Enstrom F-28A-UK	Pyramid Precision Engineering Ltd
	G-BBII	Fiat G-46-3B	A. L. Lindsay & ptnrs/Booker
	G-BBIL	PA-28 Cherokee 140	D. Arlette/Stapleford
	G-BBIN	Enstrom F-28A	Southern Air Ltd/Shoreham
	G-BBIO	Robin HR.100/210	R. A. King/Headcorn
	G-BBIT	Hughes 269B	Contract Development & Projects (Leeds) Ltd (stored)
	G-BBIV	Hughes 269C	Pyramid Precision Engineering Ltd
	G-BBIX	PA-28 Cherokee 140	Sterling Contract Hire Ltd
	G-BBJB	Thunder Ax7-77 balloon	St Crispin Balloon Group Dick Darby
	G-BBJI	Isaacs Spitfire (RN218)	A. N. R. Houghton & ptnrs
	G-BBJU	Robin DR.400/140	J. C. Lister

Reg.	Type	Owner or Operator	Notes
G-BBJV	Cessna F.177RG	Pilot Magazine/Biggin Hill	
G-BBJX	Cessna F.150L	Yorkshire Flying Services Ltd/Leeds	
G-BBJY	Cessna F.172M	J. Lucketti/Barton	
G-BBJZ	Cessna F.172M	Burks, Green & ptnrs	
G-BBKA	Cessna F.150L	R. Hall & L. W. Scattergood	
G-BBKB	Cessna F.150L	Justgtold Ltd/Blackpool	
G-BBKC	Cessna F.172M	W. F. Hall	
G-BBKE	Cessna F.150L	Wickenby Aviation Ltd	
G-BBKF	Cessna FRA.150L	Compton Abbas Airfield Ltd	
G-BBKG	Cessna FR.172J	Sech Services Ltd	
G-BBKI	Cessna F.172M	C. W. & S.A . Burman	
G-BBKL	CP.301A Emeraude	R. Wells & H. V. Hunter	
G-BBKR	Scheibe SF.24A Motorspatz	P. I. Morgans	
G-BBKU	Cessna FRA.150L	LAR Aviation Ltd/Shoreham	
G-BBKX	PA-28 Cherokee 180	RAE Flying Club Ltd/Farnborough	
G-BBKY	Cessna F.150L	Telair Manchester Ltd	
G-BBKZ	Cessna 172M	Exeter Flying Club Ltd	
G-BBLA	PA-28 Cherokee 140	Woodgate Aviation Co Ltd/Woodvale	
G-BBLE	Hiller UH-12E	Agricopters Ltd/Chilbolton	
G-BBLH	Piper J-3C-65 Cub	Shipping & Airlines Ltd/Biggin Hill	
G-BBLL	Cameron O-84 balloon	University of East Anglia Hot-Air Ballooning Club *Boadicea*	
G-BBLM	SOCATA Rallye 100S	M. & J. Grafton	
G-BBLP	PA-23 Aztec 250D	Donington Aviation Ltd/E. Midlands	
G-BBLS	AA-5 Traveler	D. A. Reid/Prestwick	
G-BBLU	PA-34-200 Seneca II	F. Tranter/Manchester	
G-BBMB	Robin DR.400/180	J. T. M. Ball/Biggin Hill	
G-BBME	BAC One-Eleven 401AK	Birmingham European Airways Ltd (G-AZMI)/*City of Nottingham*	
G-BBMG	BAC One-Eleven 408EF	Birmingham European Airways Ltd (G-AWEJ)/*Stratford upon Avon*	
G-BBMH	EAA. Sports Biplane Model P.1	K. Dawson	
G-BBMJ	PA-23 Aztec 250E	Tindon Ltd/Little Snoring	
G-BBMK	PA-31 Turbo Navajo	Steer Aviation Ltd/Biggin Hill	
G-BBMN	D.H.C.1 Chipmunk 22	R. Steiner/Panshanger	
G-BBMO	D.H.C.1 Chipmunk 22	Holland Aerobatics Ltd	
G-BBMR	D.H.C.1 Chipmunk T.10 (WB763) ★	Southall Technical College	
G-BBMT	D.H.C.1 Chipmunk 22	V. F. J. Falconer & W. A. Lee/Dunstable	
G-BBMV	D.H.C.1 Chipmunk 22 (WG348)	P. J. Morgan (Aviation) Ltd	
G-BBMW	D.H.C.1 Chipmunk 22 (WK628)	Mike Whisky Group/Shoreham	
G-BBMX	D.H.C.1 Chipmunk 22	A. L. Brown & P. S. Murchison	
G-BBMZ	D.H.C.1 Chipmunk 22	Wycombe Gliding School Syndicate/ Booker	
G-BBNA	D.H.C.1 Chipmunk 22 (Lycoming)	Coventry Gliding Club Ltd/ Husbands Bosworth	
G-BBNC	D.H.C.1 Chipmunk T.10 (WP790) ★	Mosquito Aircraft Museum	
G-BBND	D.H.C.1 Chipmunk 22 (WD286)	A. J. Organ/Bourn	
G-BBNG	Bell 206B JetRanger 2	Helicopter Crop Spraying Ltd	
G-BBNH	PA-34-200 Seneca II	Lawrence Goodwin Machine Tools Ltd/ Coventry	
G-BBNI	PA-34-200 Seneca II	Channel Aviation (UK) Ltd	
G-BBNJ	Cessna F.150L	Sherburn Aero Club Ltd	
G-BBNN	PA-23 Aztec 250D	J. W. B. Wimble	
G-BBNO	PA-23 Aztec 250E	Hedley & Ellis Ltd/Conington	
G-BBNT	PA-31-350 Navajo Chieftain	Northern Executive Aviation Ltd/ Manchester	
G-BBNV	Fuji FA.200-160	G. C. Thomas/Kidlington	
G-BBNX	Cessna FRA.150L	General Airline Ltd	
G-BBNY	Cessna FRA.150L	Air Tows Ltd/Lasham	
G-BBNZ	Cessna F.172M	Anchor Plastics (UK) Ltd	
G-BBOA	Cessna F.172M	J. W. J. Adkins/Southend	
G-BBOC	Cameron O-77 balloon	J. A. B. Gray	
G-BBOD	Thunder O-45 balloon	B. R. & M. Boyle	
G-BBOE	Robin HR.200/100	Aberdeen Flying Group	
G-BBOH	Pitts S-1S Special	Venom Jet Promotions Ltd/Bournemouth	
G-BBOJ	PA-23 Aztec 250E ★	*Instructional airframe*/Cranfield	
G-BBOL	PA-18 Super Cub 150	Lakes Gliding Club Ltd	
G-BBOO	Thunder Ax6-56 balloon	K. Meehan *Tigerjack*	
G-BBOR	Bell 206B JetRanger 2	Autair Ltd	
G-BBOX	Thunder Ax7-77 balloon	R. C. Weyda *Rocinante*	
G-BBOY	Thunder Ax6-56A balloon	N. C. Faithull *Eric of Titchfield*	

Notes	Reg.	Type	Owner or Operator
	G-BBPJ	Cessna F.172M	B. W. Aviation Ltd/Cardiff
	G-BBPK	Evans VP-1	G. D. E. Macdonald
	G-BBPM	Enstrom F-28A	D. Newman
	G-BBPN	Enstrom F-28A	Selecting Ltd
	G-BBPO	Enstrom F-28A	Southern Air Ltd/Shoreham
	G-BBPS	Jodel D.117	A. Appleby/Redhill
	G-BBPU	Boeing 747-136	British Airways *Virginia Water*
	G-BBPW	Robin HR.100/210	D. H. Smith
	G-BBPX	PA-34-200 Seneca II	Richel Investments Ltd/Guernsey
	G-BBPY	PA-28 Cherokee 180	T. Ogden
	G-BBRA	PA-23 Aztec 250D	Mainable Ltd/White Waltham
	G-BBRB	D.H.82A Tiger Moth (DF198)	R. Barham/Biggin Hill
	G-BBRC	Fuji FA.200-180	BBRC Ltd
	G-BBRH	Bell 47G-5A	Helicopter Supplies & Engineering Ltd
	G-BBRI	Bell 47G-5A	Camlet Helicopters Ltd/Fairoaks
	G-BBRN	Procter Kittiwake (XW784)	Vari-Prop (GB) Ltd/Exeter
	G-BBRV	D.H.C.1 Chipmunk 22	HSA (Chester) Sports & Social Club
	G-BBRX	SIAI-Marchetti S.205-18F	A. L. Cogswell & R. C. West
	G-BBRZ	AA-5 Traveler	C. P. Osbourne
	G-BBSA	AA-5 Traveler	K. Lynn
	G-BBSB	Beech C23 Sundowner	Sundowner Group/Manchester
	G-BBSC	Beech B24R Sierra	Beechcombers Flying Group
	G-BBSM	PA-32 Cherokee Six 300E	Wardle/Smith Group
	G-BBSS	D.H.C.1A Chipmunk 22	Coventry Gliding Club Ltd/ Husbands Bosworth
	G-BBSU	Cessna 421B	Holding & Barnes PLC/Southend
	G-BBSV	Cessna 421B	R. & M. International Helicopters Ltd
	G-BBSW	Pietenpol Air Camper	J. K. S. Wills
	G-BBTB	Cessna FRA.150L	Compton Abbas Airfield Ltd
	G-BBTG	Cessna F.172M	D. H. Laws
	G-BBTH	Cessna F.172M	S. Gilmore/Newtownards
	G-BBTJ	PA-23 Aztec 250E	Geonex Ltd
	G-BBTK	Cessna FRA.150L	Air Service Training Ltd/Perth
	G-BBTL	PA-23 Aztec 250C	Air Navigation & Trading Co Ltd/Blackpool
	G-BBTS	Beech V35B Bonanza	P. S. Bubbear & J. M. Glanville
	G-BBTU	ST-10 Diplomate	P. Campion/Stapleford
	G-BBTX	Beech C23 Sundowner	K. Harding/Blackbushe
	G-BBTY	Beech C23 Sundowner	TY Club/Biggin Hill
	G-BBTZ	Cessna F.150L	Woodgate Air Services Ltd
	G-BBUD	Sikorsky S-61N Mk II	British International Helicopters Ltd/ Aberdeen
	G-BBUE	AA-5 Traveler	S. D. Cole
	G-BBUF	AA-5 Traveler	W. McLaren
	G-BBUG	PA-16 Clipper	J. Dolan
	G-BBUJ	Cessna 421B	Merlin Marine Aviation (Jersey) Ltd
	G-BBUL	Mitchell-Procter Kittiwake 1	R. Bull
	G-BBUT	Western O-65 balloon	G. F. Turnbull
	G-BBUU	Piper J-3C-65 Cub	O. J. J. Rogers
	G-BBVA	Sikorsky S-61N Mk II	Bristow Helicopters Ltd *Vega*
	G-BBVE	Cessna 340	Beechair Ltd/Biggin Hill
	G-BBVF	SA Twin Pioneer III ★	Museum of Flight/E. Fortune
	G-BBVG	PA-23 Aztec 250C	R. F. Wanbon & P. G. Warmerdan/ Panshanger
	G-BBVI	Enstrom F-28A ★	*Ground trainer*/Kidlington
	G-BBVJ	Beech B24R Sierra	A. R. Mead
	G-BBVM	Beech A.100 King Air	Northern Executive Aviation Ltd/ Manchester
	G-BBVO	Isaacs Fury II (S1579)	C. M. Barnes
	G-BBVP	Westland-Bell 47G-3B1	CKS Air Ltd/Southend
	G-BBWM	PA-E23 Aztec 250E	Guernsey Air Search Ltd
	G-BBWN	D.H.C.1 Chipmunk 22 (WZ876)	D. C. Budd
	G-BBXB	Cessna FRA.150L	M. L. Swain (*stored*)/Bourn
	G-BBXG	PA-34-200 Seneca II	London Flight Centre (Stansted) Ltd
	G-BBXH	Cessna FR.172F	H. H. Metal Finishing (Wales) Ltd
	G-BBXK	PA-34-200 Seneca II	Mona Travel Ltd
	G-BBXL	Cessna E310Q	Chatsworth Studios Ltd/Newcastle
	G-BBXO	Enstrom F-28A	Southern Air Ltd/Shoreham
	G-BBXS	Piper J-3C-65 Cub	M. J. Butler (G-ALMA)/Langham
	G-BBXU	Beech B24R Sierra	B. M. Russell/Coventry
	G-BBXW	PA-28-151 Warrior	Shropshire Aero Club Ltd
	G-BBXX	PA-31-350 Navajo Chieftain	Natural Environment Research Council
	G-BBXY	Bellanca 7GCBC Citabria	J. Turner/Shoreham
	G-BBXZ	Evans VP-1	M. J. Herlihy

Reg.	Type	Owner or Operator	Notes
G-BBYB	PA-18 Super Cub 95	Tiger Club (1990) Ltd/Headcorn	
G-BBYE	Cessna 195	Profile Productions Ltd & TAC Productions Ltd	
G-BBYH	Cessna 182P	Croftmarsh Ltd	
G-BBYK	PA-23 Aztec 250E	Kraken Air/Cardiff	
G-BBYL	Cameron O-77 balloon	Buckingham Balloon Club *Jammy*	
G-BBYM	H.P.137 Jetstream 200	British Aerospace PLC (G-AYWR)/Warton	
G-BBYO	BN-2A Mk III Trislander	Aurigny Air Services (G-BBWR)/Guernsey	
G-BBYP	PA-28 Cherokee 140	R. A. Wakefield	
G-BBYS	Cessna 182P Skylane	I. M. Jones	
G-BBZF	PA-28 Cherokee 140	J. A. Havers & M. G. West/Elstree	
G-BBZH	PA-28R Cherokee Arrow 200-II	Zulu Hotel Club	
G-BBZI	PA-31-310 Turbo Navajo	Air Care (South West) Ltd	
G-BBZJ	PA-34-200 Seneca II	Sentry Courier Ltd/Blackbushe	
G-BBZN	Fuji FA.200-180	J. Westwood & P. D. Wedd	
G-BBZO	Fuji FA.200-160	Melton Concrete Floors Ltd	
G-BBZS	Enstrom F-28A	Southern Air Ltd/Shoreham	
G-BBZV	PA-28R Cherokee Arrow 200-II	Unicol Engineering/Kidlington	
G-BCAC	M.S.894A Rallye Minerva 220	R. S. Rogers/Cardiff	
G-BCAH	D.H.C.1 Chipmunk 22 (WG316)	V. B. Wheele/Shoreham	
G-BCAN	Thunder Ax7-77 balloon	Wessex Hot-Air Team	
G-BCAP	Cameron O-56 balloon	S. R. Seager	
G-BCAR	Thunder Ax7-77 balloon	T. J. Woodbridge/Australia	
G-BCAT	PA-31-310 Turbo Navajo	Hubbardair Ltd	
G-BCAZ	PA-12 Super Cruiser	A. D. Williams	
G-BCBD	Bede BD-5B	Brockmore-Bede Aircraft (UK) Ltd/ Shobdon	
G-BCBG	PA-23 Aztec 250E	M. J. L. Batt/Booker	
G-BCBH	Fairchild 24R-46A Argus III	Bluegale Ltd/Biggin Hill	
G-BCBJ	PA-25 Pawnee 235	Deeside Gliding Club (Aberdeenshire) Ltd	
G-BCBK	Cessna 421B	Robinson Publications Ltd	
G-BCBL	Fairchild 24R-46A Argus III (HB751)	F. J. Cox	
G-BCBM	PA-23 Aztec 250C	S. Lightbrown & M. Kavanagh	
G-BCBR	AJEP/Wittman W.8 Tailwind	D. A. Hood	
G-BCBW	Cessna 182P	Teesside Aero Club Ltd	
G-BCBX	Cessna F.150L	J. Kelly/Newtownards	
G-BCBY	Cessna F.150L	Scottish Airways Flyers (Prestwick) Ltd	
G-BCBZ	Cessna 337C	J. J. Zwetsloot	
G-BCCB	Robin HR.200/100	M. J. Ellis	
G-BCCC	Cessna F.150L	Donington Aviation Ltd/E. Midlands	
G-BCCD	Cessna F.172M	Austin Aviation Ltd	
G-BCCE	PA-23 Aztec 250E	Falcon Flying Services/Biggin Hill	
G-BCCF	PA-28 Cherokee 180	J. T. Friskney Ltd/Skegness	
G-BCCG	Thunder Ax7-65 balloon	N. H. Ponsford	
G-BCCJ	AA-5 Traveler	T. Needham/Manchester	
G-BCCK	AA-5 Traveler	Prospect Air Ltd/Barton	
G-BCCR	CP.301A Emeraude (modified)	I. G. & M. Glenn	
G-BCCX	D.H.C.1 Chipmunk 22 (Lycoming)	RAFGSA/Dishforth	
G-BCCY	Robin HR.200/100	Bristol Strut Flying Group	
G-BCDA	Boeing 727-46	Dan-Air Services Ltd/Gatwick	
G-BCDB	PA-34-200 Seneca II	A. & G. Aviation Ltd/Bournemouth	
G-BCDC	PA-18 Super Cub 95	Cotswold Aero Club Ltd/Staverton	
G-BCDJ	PA-28 Cherokee 140	C. Wren/Southend	
G-BCDK	Partenavia P.68B	Truman Aviation Ltd/Tollerton	
G-BCDL	Cameron O-42 balloon	D. P. & Mrs B. O. Turner *Chums*	
G-BCDN	F.27 Friendship Mk 200	Air UK/Norwich	
G-BCDO	F.27 Friendship Mk 200	Air UK *Lord Butler*/Norwich	
G-BCDR	Thunder Ax7-77 balloon	W. G. Johnston & ptnrs *Obelix*	
G-BCDY	Cessna FRA.150L	Air Service Training Ltd/Perth	
G-BCEA	Sikorsky S-61N Mk II	British International Helicopters Ltd/ Aberdeen	
G-BCEB	Sikorsky S-61N Mk II	British International Helicopters Ltd/ Penzance	
G-BCEC	Cessna F.172M	United Propedent Ltd/Manchester	
G-BCEE	AA-5 Traveler	Echo Echo Ltd/Bournemouth	
G-BCEF	AA-5 Traveler	Forest Aviation Ltd/Guernsey	
G-BCEN	BN-2A Islander	Atlantic Air Transport Ltd/Coventry	
G-BCEO	AA-5 Traveler	G-BCEO Flying Group/Shoreham	
G-BCEP	AA-5 Traveler	D. V. Reynolds	
G-BCER	GY-201 Minicab	D. Beaumont/Sherburn	
G-BCEU	Cameron O-42 balloon	Entertainment Services Ltd *Harlequin*	

Notes	Reg.	Type	Owner or Operator
	G-BCEX	PA-23 Aztec 250E	Weekes Bros (Welling) Ltd/Biggin Hill
	G-BCEY	D.H.C.1 Chipmunk 22	Gopher Flying Group
	G-BCEZ	Cameron O-84 balloon	Anglia Aeronauts Ascension Association *Stars and Bars*
	G-BCFB	Cameron O-77 balloon	J. J. Harris & P. Pryce-Jones *Teutonic Turkey*
	G-BCFC	Cameron O-65 balloon	B. H. Mead *Candy Twist*
	G-BCFD	West balloon ★	British Balloon Museum *Hellfire*
	G-BCFF	Fuji FA-200-160	G. W. Brown & M. R. Gibbons
	G-BCFN	Cameron O-65 balloon	W. G. Johnson & H. M. Savage
	G-BCFO	PA-18 Super Cub 150	Portsmouth Naval Gliding Club/ Lee-on-Solent
	G-BCFR	Cessna FRA.150L	J. J. Baumhardt/Southend
	G-BCFW	Saab 91D Safir	D. R. Williams
	G-BCFY	Luton LA-4A Minor	J. Knight
	G-BCGB	Bensen B.8	A. Melody
	G-BCGC	D.H.C.1 Chipmunk 22 (WP903)	Culdrose Gliding Club
	G-BCGG	Jodel DR.250 Srs 160	C. G. Gray (G-ATZL)
	G-BCGH	SNCAN NC.854S	Nord Flying Group
	G-BCGI	PA-28 Cherokee 140	A. Dodd/Redhill
	G-BCGJ	PA-28 Cherokee 140	J. Miller & J. L. Hunter/Edinburgh
	G-BCGL	Jodel D.112	J. Harris
	G-BCGM	Jodel D.120	D. N. K. & M. A. Symon
	G-BCGN	PA-28 Cherokee 140	Oxford Flyers Ltd/Kidlington
	G-BCGS	PA-28R Cherokee Arrow 200	Arrow Aviation
	G-BCGT	PA-28 Cherokee 140	T. D. Bugg
	G-BCGW	Jodel D.11	G. H. & M. D. Chittenden
	G-BCGX	Bede BD-5A/B	R. Hodgson
	G-BCHK	Cessna F.172H	E. Yorks Aviation Ltd
	G-BCHL	D.H.C.1 Chipmunk 22A (WP788)	Shropshire Soaring Ltd
	G-BCHM	SA.341G Gazelle 1	Bristol Helicopters Ltd/Yeovil
	G-BCHP	CP.1310-C3 Super Emeraude	R. F. Sothcott (G-JOSI)
	G-BCHT	Schleicher ASK.16	D. E. Cadisch & K. A. Lillywhite/Dunstable
	G-BCHV	D.H.C.1 Chipmunk 22	N. F. Charles/Sywell
	G-BCHX	SF.23A Sperling	R. L. McClean/Rufforth
	G-BCID	PA-34-200 Seneca II	C. J. Freeman/Headcorn
	G-BCIE	PA-28-151 Warrior	J. A. & J. V. Bridger/Exeter
	G-BCIF	PA-28 Cherokee 140	Fryer-Robins Aviation Ltd/E. Midlands
	G-BCIH	D.H.C.1 Chipmunk 22 (WD363)	J. M. Hosey/Stansted
	G-BCIJ	AA-5 Traveler	I. J. Bond & D. J. McCooke
	G-BCIK	AA-5 Traveler	S. F. Lister/Tollerton
	G-BCIN	Thunder Ax7-77 balloon	P. G & R. A. Vale
	G-BCIO	PA-39 Twin Comanche 160 C/R	F. Duckworth
	G-BCIR	PA-28-151 Warrior	Alfred Graham Ltd
	G-BCIT	CIT/A1 Srs 1	Cranfield Institute of Technology
	G-BCIW	D.H.C.1 Chipmunk 22 (WZ868)	Chipmunk G-BCIW Syndicate/Duxford
	G-BCJF	Beagle B.206 Srs 1	A. A. Mattacks/Biggin Hill
	G-BCJH	Mooney M.20F	P. B. Bossard
	G-BCJM	PA-28 Cherokee 140	Top Cat Aviation Ltd
	G-BCJN	PA-28 Cherokee 140	A. J. Steed/Goodwood
	G-BCJO	PA-28R Cherokee Arrow 200	Tomcat Aviation/Norwich
	G-BCJP	PA-28 Cherokee 140	K. E. Tolliday & ptnrs
	G-BCJS	PA-23 Aztec 250C ★	derelict/Ronaldsway
	G-BCKN	D.H.C.1A Chipmunk 22	RAFGSA/Cranwell
	G-BCKO	PA-23 Aztec 250E	Planning & Mapping Ltd
	G-BCKP	Luton LA-5A Major	J. Horovitz & ptnrs
	G-BCKS	Fuji FA.200-180	J. T. Hicks/Goodwood
	G-BCKT	Fuji FA.200-180	Littlewick Green Service Station Ltd/ Booker
	G-BCKU	Cessna FRA.150L	Air Service Training Ltd/Perth
	G-BCKV	Cessna FRA.150L	Air Service Training Ltd/Perth
	G-BCLC	Sikorsky S-61N	Bristow Helicopters/HM Coastguard
	G-BCLD	Sikorsky S-61N	Bristow Helicopters Ltd
	G-BCLI	AA-5 Traveler	Albemotive Ltd
	G-BCLJ	AA-5 Traveler	E. A. A. A. Wiltens
	G-BCLL	PA-28 Cherokee 180	K. J. Scamp
	G-BCLS	Cessna 170B	Teesside Flight Centre Ltd
	G-BCLT	M.S.894A Rallye Minerva 220	S. Clough
	G-BCLU	Jodel D.117	N. A. Wallace
	G-BCLW	AA-1B Trainer	E. J. McMillan
	G-BCMD	PA-18 Super Cub 95	R. G. Brooks/Dunkeswell
	G-BCMJ	SA.102.5 Cavalier (tailwheel)	R. G. Sykes/Shoreham
	G-BCMT	Isaacs Fury II	M. H. Turner

Reg.	Type	Owner or Operator	Notes
G-BCNC	GY.201 Minicab	J. R. Wraight	
G-BCNP	Cameron O-77 balloon	M. L. J. Ritchie	
G-BCNR	Thunder Ax7-77A balloon	S. J. Miliken & ptnrs	
G-BCNT	Partenavia P.68B	Welsh Airways Ltd	
G-BCNX	Piper J-3C-65 Cub	K. J. Lord/Ipswich	
G-BCNZ	Fuji FA.200-160	J. Bruton & A. Lincoln/Manchester	
G-BCOB	Piper J-3C-65 Cub	R. W. & Mrs J. W. Marjoram	
G-BCOE	H.S.748 Srs 2B	British Airways *Glen Livet*/Glasgow	
G-BCOF	H.S.748 Srs 2B	British Airways *Glen Fiddich*/Glasgow	
G-BCOG	Jodel D.112	C. Hughes & W. K. Rose/Kidlington	
G-BCOH	Avro 683 Lancaster 10 (KB976)	Bitteswell Ltd/Biggin Hill	
G-BCOI	D.H.C.1 Chipmunk 22	D. S. McGregor & A. T. Letham	
G-BCOJ	Cameron O-56 balloon	T. J. Knott & M. J. Webber	
G-BCOL	Cessna F.172M	Calros Ltd	
G-BCOM	Piper J-3C-65 Cub	Dougal Flying Group/Shoreham	
G-BCOO	D.H.C.1 Chipmunk 22	T. G. Fielding & M. S. Morton/Blackpool	
G-BCOP	PA-28R Cherokee Arrow 200-II	E. A. Saunders/Halfpenny Green	
G-BCOR	SOCATA Rallye 100ST	D. Wright & R. J. Doughton	
G-BCOU	D.H.C.1 Chipmunk 22 (WK522)	P. J. Loweth	
G-BCOX	Bede BD-5A	H. J. Cox	
G-BCOY	D.H.C.1 Chipmunk 22	Coventry Gliding Club Ltd/Husbands Bosworth	
G-BCPB	Howes radio-controlled model free balloon	R. B. & Mrs C. Howes *Posbee 1*	
G-BCPD	GY-201 Minicab	A. H. K. Denniss/Halfpenny Green	
G-BCPE	Cessna F.150M	Semloh Aviation Services/Andrewsfield	
G-BCPF	PA-23 Aztec 250D	Chapman Commercials Ltd	
G-BCPG	PA-28R Cherokee Arrow 200-II	Roses Flying Group/Liverpool	
G-BCPH	Piper J-3C-65 Cub (329934)	M. J. Janaway	
G-BCPJ	Piper J-3C-65 Cub	P. Turton	
G-BCPK	Cessna F.172M	Air & General Services Ltd	
G-BCPN	AA-5 Traveler	B.W. Agricultural Equipments Ltd	
G-BCPO	Partenavia P.68B	H. Russell	
G-BCPU	D.H.C.1 Chipmunk T.10	P. Waller/Booker	
G-BCPX	Szep HFC.125	A. Szep/Netherthorpe	
G-BCRB	Cessna F.172M	Specialised Laboratory Equipment Ltd	
G-BCRE	Cameron O-77 balloon	A. R. Langton	
G-BCRH	Alaparma Baldo B.75	A. L. Scadding/(stored)	
G-BCRI	Cameron O-65 balloon	V. J. Thorne *Joseph*	
G-BCRJ	Taylor JT.1 Monoplane	S. Wolstenholme	
G-BCRK	SA.102.5 Cavalier	D. E. Freeman	
G-BCRL	PA-28-151 Warrior	F. N. Garland/Biggin Hill	
G-BCRN	Cessna FRA.150L	Air Service Training Ltd/Perth	
G-BCRP	PA-E23 Aztec 250E	ReFair/Sibson	
G-BCRR	AA-5B Tiger	Capulet Flying Group/Elstree	
G-BCRT	Cessna F.150M	Suffolk Aero Club Ltd/Ipswich	
G-BCRX	D.H.C.1 Chipmunk 22 (WD292)	J. R. Chapman & ptnrs	
G-BCSA	D.H.C.1 Chipmunk 22	RAFGSA/Kinloss	
G-BCSB	D.H.C.1 Chipmunk 22 (Lycoming)	RAFGSA/Cosford	
G-BCSL	D.H.C.1 Chipmunk 22	Jalawain Ltd/Barton	
G-BCSM	Bellanca 8GCBC Scout	B. T. Spreckley/Southampton	
G-BCST	M.S.893A Rallye Commodore 180	P. J. Wilcox/Cranfield	
G-BCSX	Thunder Ax7-77 balloon	A. T. Wood *Whoopski*	
G-BCSY	Taylor JT.2 Titch	T. Hartwell & D. Wilkinson	
G-BCTA	PA-28-151 Warrior	T. G. Aviation Ltd/Manston	
G-BCTF	PA-28-151 Warrior	Premier Plane Leasing Co Ltd	
G-BCTI	Schleicher ASK.16	Tango India Syndicate/Cranfield	
G-BCTJ	Cessna 310Q	S. E. Clark/Biggin Hill	
G-BCTK	Cessna FR.172J	C. Wellington & M. Slattery/Blackbushe	
G-BCTT	Evans VP-1	B. J. Boughton	
G-BCTU	Cessna FRA.150M	J. H. Fisher & N. D. Hall	
G-BCUB	Piper J-3C-65 Cub	A. L. Brown & G. Attwell/Bourn	
G-BCUF	Cessna F.172M	G. H. Kirke Ltd	
G-BCUH	Cessna F.150M	M. G. Montgomerie	
G-BCUI	Cessna F.172M	Hillhouse Estates Ltd	
G-BCUJ	Cessna F.150M	Sandtoft Air Services (1985) Ltd	
G-BCUL	SOCATA Rallye 100ST	C. A. Ussher & Fountain Estates Ltd	
G-BCUW	Cessna F.177RG	S. J. Westley	
G-BCUY	Cessna FRA.150M	S. R. Cameron	
G-BCVA	Cameron O-65 balloon	J. C. Bass & ptnrs *Crepe Suzette*	
G-BCVB	PA-17 Vagabond	A. T. Nowak/Popham	
G-BCVC	SOCATA Rallye 100ST	J. L. & T. A. Hodges	
G-BCVE	Evans VP-2	D. Masterson & D. B. Winstanley	

Notes	Reg.	Type	Owner or Operator
	G-BCVF	Practavia Pilot Sprite	D. G. Hammersley
	G-BCVG	Cessna FRA.150L	Air Service Training Ltd/Perth
	G-BCVH	Cessna FRA.150L	Yorkshire Light Aircraft Ltd/Leeds
	G-BCVI	Cessna FR.172J	R. M. Savage
	G-BCVJ	Cessna F.172M	Rothland Ltd
	G-BCVW	GY-80 Horizon 180	P. M. A. Parrett/Dunkeswell
	G-BCVY	PA-34-200T Seneca II	C.S.E. Aviation Ltd/Kidlington
	G-BCWA	BAC One-Eleven 518 FG	Dan-Air Services Ltd (G-AXMK)/Gatwick
	G-BCWB	Cessna 182P	G. McCabe
	G-BCWF	S.A. Twin Pioneer 1	Flight One Ltd (G-APRS)/Staverton
	G-BCWH	Practavia Pilot Sprite	R. Tasker/Blackpool
	G-BCWK	Alpavia Fournier RF-3	D. I. Nickolls & ptnrs
	G-BCWL	Westland Lysander III (V9281)	Wessex Aviation & Transport Ltd
	G-BCWR	BN-2A-21 Islander	Pilatus BN Ltd/Bembridge
	G-BCXB	SOCATA Rallye 100ST	A. Smails
	G-BCXE	Robin DR.400/2+2	C. J. Freeman
	G-BCXF	H.S.125 Srs 600B	Aravco Ltd/Heathrow
	G-BCXJ	Piper J-3C-65 Cub (413048)	W. F. Stockdale/Compton Abbas
	G-BCXN	D.H.C.1 Chipmunk 22 (WP800)	G. M. Turner/Duxford
	G-BCXO	MBB Bo 105D	Bond Helicopters Ltd
	G-BCXR	BAC One-Eleven 517FE	Dan-Air Services Ltd (G-BCCV)/Gatwick
	G-BCYH	DAW Privateer Mk. 2	D. B. Limbert
	G-BCYI	Schleicher ASK-16	J. Fox & J. Harding/Lasham
	G-BCYJ	D.H.C.1 Chipmunk 22 (WG307)	R. A. L. Falconer
	G-BCYK	Avro CF.100 Mk 4 Canuck (18393) ★	Imperial War Museum/Duxford
	G-BCYM	D.H.C.1 Chipmunk 22	C. R. R. Eagleton/Headcorn
	G-BCYR	Cessna F.172M	Donne Enterprises
	G-BCZH	D.H.C.1 Chipmunk 22 (WK622)	A. C. Byrne & D. Featherby/Norwich
	G-BCZI	Thunder Ax7-77 balloon	R. G. Griffin & R. Blackwell
	G-BCZM	Cessna F.172M	Cornwall Flying Club Ltd/Bodmin
	G-BCZN	Cessna F.150M	Mona Aviation Ltd
	G-BCZO	Cameron O-77 balloon	W. O. T. Holmes *Leo*
	G-BDAB	SA.102.5 Cavalier	A. H. Brown
	G-BDAC	Cameron O-77 balloon	D. Fowler & J. Goody *Chocolate Ripple*
	G-BDAD	Taylor JT.1 Monoplane	G-BDAD Group
	G-BDAE	BAC One-Eleven 518FG	Dan-Air Services Ltd (G-AXMI)/Gatwick
	G-BDAH	Evans VP-1	A. M. Carter
	G-BDAI	Cessna FRA.150M	A. Sharma
	G-BDAK	R. Commander 112A	S. E. Boyles
	G-BDAL	R. 500S Shrike Commander	Quantel Ltd
	G-BDAM	AT-16 Harvard IIB (FE992)	N. A. Lees & E. C. English
	G-BDAO	SIPA S.91	A. L. Rose
	G-BDAP	AJEP Tailwind	J. Whiting
	G-BDAR	Evans VP-1	R. B. Valler
	G-BDAS	BAC One-Eleven 518FG	Dan-Air Services Ltd (G-AXMH)/Gatwick
	G-BDAT	BAC One-Eleven 518FG	Dan-Air Services Ltd (G-AYOR)/Gatwick
	G-BDAV	PA-23 Aztec 250C	Acketts Ltd
	G-BDAX	PA-23 Aztec 250C	P. G. Lawrence
	G-BDAY	Thunder Ax5-42A balloon	T. M. Donnelly *Meconium*
	G-BDBD	Wittman W.8 Tailwind	E. D. Bond
	G-BDBF	FRED Srs 2	R. G. Boyton
	G-BDBH	Bellanca 7GCBC Citabria	Inkpen Gliding Club Ltd/Thruxton
	G-BDBI	Cameron O-77 balloon	C. A. Butter & J. J. Cook
	G-BDBJ	Cessna 182P	H. C. Wilson
	G-BDBL	D.H.C.1 Chipmunk 22	R. J. Fox
	G-BDBP	D.H.C.1 Chipmunk 22	R. M. Brooks
	G-BDBS	Short SD3-30	Short Bros PLC/Belfast City
	G-BDBU	Cessna F.150M	Andrewsfield Flying Club Ltd
	G-BDBV	Jodel D.11A	Seething Jodel Group
	G-BDBZ	W.S.55 Whirlwind Srs 2 ★	*Ground instruction airframe*/Kidlington
	G-BDCB	D.H.C.1 Chipmunk 22 (WP835)	R. F. Tolhurst
	G-BDCC	D.H.C.1 Chipmunk 22	Coventry Gliding Club Ltd/ Husbands Bosworth
	G-BDCD	Piper J-3C-85 Cub (480133)	Suzanne C. Brooks/Slinfold
	G-BDCE	Cessna F.172H	Lord Valentine William Cecil
	G-BDCI	CP.301A Emeraude	D. L. Sentance
	G-BDCK	AA-5 Traveler	Northfield Garage Ltd
	G-BDCL	AA-5 Traveler	J. Crowe
	G-BDCM	Cessna F.177RG	P. R. Gunnel/Gamston
	G-BDCO	B.121 Pup 1	K. R. Knapp
	G-BDCS	Cessna 421B	British Aerospace PLC/Warton

Reg.	Type	Owner or Operator	Notes
G-BDCU	Cameron O-77 balloon	H. P. Carlton	
G-BDDD	D.H.C.1 Chipmunk 22	RAE Aero Club Ltd/Farnborough	
G-BDDF	Jodel D.120	Sywell Skyriders Flying Group	
G-BDDG	Jodel D.112	J. W. Cudby	
G-BDDS	PA-25 Pawnee 235	Vale of Neath Gliding Club	
G-BDDT	PA-25 Pawnee 235	Boston Aviation Services	
G-BDDX	Whittaker MW.2B Excalibur ★	Cornwall Aero Park/Helston	
G-BDDZ	CP.301A Emeraude	V. W. Smith & E. C. Mort	
G-BDEA	Boeing 707-338C	Anglo Cargo Airlines Ltd/Gatwick	
G-BDEC	SOCATA Rallye 100ST	L. J. R. C. Bolingbroke	
G-BDEF	PA-34-200T Seneca II	Haylock Son & Hunter	
G-BDEH	Jodel D.120A	EH Flying Group/Bristol	
G-BDEI	Jodel D.9 Bebe	P. M. Bowden/Barton	
G-BDEN	SIAI-Marchetti SF.260	I. Best-Devereux	
G-BDET	D.H.C.1 Chipmunk 22	R. T. Heinen/Shoreham	
G-BDEU	D.H.C.1 Chipmunk 22 (WP808)	A. Taylor	
G-BDEV	Taylor JT.1 Monoplane	D. A. Bass	
G-BDEW	Cessna FRA.150M	Compton Abbas Airfield Ltd	
G-BDEX	Cessna FRA.150M	Compton Abbas Airfield Ltd	
G-BDEY	Piper J-3C-65 Cub	Ducksworth Flying Club	
G-BDEZ	Piper J-3C-65 Cub	R. J. K. Spurrell	
G-BDFB	Currie Wot	J. Jennings	
G-BDFC	R. Commander 112A	R. Fletcher	
G-BDFG	Cameron O-65 balloon	N. A. Robertson *Golly II*	
G-BDFH	Auster AOP.9 (XR240)	R. O. Holden/Booker	
G-BDFI	Cessna F.150M	LAR Aviation Ltd/Shoreham	
G-BDFJ	Cessna F.150M	T. J. Lynn/Sibson	
G-BDFM	Caudron C.270 Luciole	G. V. Gower	
G-BDFR	Fuji FA.200-160	A. Wright	
G-BDFS	Fuji FA.200-160	R. W. Struth & A. H. Biggs	
G-BDFU	Dragonfly MPA Mk 1 ★	Museum of Flight/E. Fortune	
G-BDFW	R. Commander 112A	W. P. Simpson	
G-BDFX	Auster 5 (TW517)	G.R. Mills & C. Fielder	
G-BDFY	AA-5 Traveler	Edinburgh Flying Club Ltd	
G-BDFZ	Cessna F.150M	Skyviews & General Ltd	
G-BDGA	Bushby-Long Midget Mustang	J. R. Owen	
G-BDGB	GY-20 Minicab	D. G. Burden	
G-BDGH	Thunder Ax7-77 balloon	R. J. Mitchener & P. F. Smart	
G-BDGM	PA-28-151 Warrior	B. Whiting	
G-BDGN	AA-5B Tiger	R. Stone	
G-BDGO	Thunder Ax7-77 balloon	International Distillers & Vintners Ltd	
G-BDGP	Cameron V-65 balloon	Warwick Balloons Ltd	
G-BDGY	PA-28 Cherokee 140	R. E. Woolridge/Staverton	
G-BDHJ	Pazmany PL.1	C. T. Millner	
G-BDHK	Piper J-3C-65 Cub (329417)	A. Liddiard	
G-BDHL	PA-23 Aztec 250E	Cheshire Flying Services Ltd/Manchester	
G-BDIC	D.H.C.1 Chipmunk 22 (WD388)	Woodvale Aviation Co Ltd	
G-BDIE	R. Commander 112A	C. A. Ringrose & H. J. Bendiksen	
G-BDIG	Cessna 182P	D. P. Cranston & Bob Crowe Aircraft Sales Ltd/Cranfield	
G-BDIH	Jodel D.117	N. D. H. Stokes	
G-BDIJ	Sikorsky S-61N	Bristow Helicopters Ltd	
G-BDIM	D.H.C.1 Chipmunk 22	Historic Flying Ltd/Cambridge	
G-BDIX	D.H.106 Comet 4C ★	Museum of Flight/E. Fortune	
G-BDJB	Taylor JT.1 Monoplane	J. F. Barber	
G-BDJC	AJEP W.8 Tailwind	J. H. Medforth	
G-BDJD	Jodel D.112	Drem Sport Aviation Group	
G-BDJF	Bensen B.8MV	R. P. White	
G-BDJG	Luton LA-4A Minor	A. W. Anderson & A. J. Short	
G-BDJN	Robin HR.200/100	Northampton School of Flying Ltd/Sywell	
G-BDJP	Piper J-3C-90 Cub	J. M. Pothecary (*stored*)/Shoreham	
G-BDJR	SNCAN NC.858	R. F. M. Marson & P. M. Harmer	
G-BDKB	SOCATA Rallye 150ST	N. C. Anderson	
G-BDKC	Cessna A185F	Bridge of Tilt Co Ltd	
G-BDKD	Enstrom F-28A	TR Bitz	
G-BDKH	CP.301A Emeraude	P. G. & F. M. Morris	
G-BDKI	Sikorsky S-61N	British International Helicopters Ltd	
G-BDKJ	SA.102.5 Cavalier	H. B. Yardley	
G-BDKK	Bede BD-5B	A. W. Odell (*stored*)/Headcorn	
G-BDKM	SIPA 903	S. W. Markham	
G-BDKU	Taylor JT.1 Monoplane	C. M. Harding & J. Ball	
G-BDKV	PA-28R Cherokee Arrow 200-II	B. Carter	
G-BDKW	R. Commander 112A	Denny Bros Printing Ltd	

Notes	Reg.	Type	Owner or Operator
	G-BDLO	AA-5A Cheetah	S. & J. Dolan/Denham
	G-BDLR	AA-5B Tiger	MAGEC Aviation Ltd/Luton
	G-BDLS	AA-1B Trainer	P. W. Vaughan & M. D. Harling/ Andrewsfield
	G-BDLT	R. Commander 112A	Wintergrain Ltd/Exeter
	G-BDLY	SA.102.5 Cavalier	P. R. Stevens/Southampton
	G-BDMB	Robin HR.100/210	R. J. Hitchman & Son
	G-BDMM	Jodel D.11	P. N. Marshall
	G-BDMO	Thunder Ax7-77A balloon	G. C. Elson
	G-BDMS	Piper J-3C-65 Cub	A. T. H. Martin & K. G. Harris
	G-BDMW	Jodel DR.100	R. O. F. Harper
	G-BDNC	Taylor JT.1 Monoplane	G. A. Stanley
	G-BDNG	Taylor JT.1 Monoplane	J. M. Fforde
	G-BDNO	Taylor JT.1 Monoplane	W. R. Partridge
	G-BDNP	BN-2A Islander ★	*Ground parachute trainer*/Headcorn
	G-BDNR	Cessna FRA.150M	Cheshire Air Training School Ltd/Liverpool
	G-BDNT	Jodel D.92	R. F. Morton
	G-BDNU	Cessna F.172M	C. H. P. Bell
	G-BDNW	AA-1B Trainer	T. D. Saveker
	G-BDNX	AA-1B Trainer	R. M. North
	G-BDNZ	Cameron O-77 balloon	I. L. McHale
	G-BDOC	Sikorsky S-61N Mk II	Bristow Helicopters Ltd
	G-BDOD	Cessna F.150M	Latharp Ltd/Booker
	G-BDOE	Cessna FR.172J	Rocket Partnership
	G-BDOF	Cameron O-56 balloon	New Holker Estates Co *Fred Cavendish*
	G-BDOG	SA Bulldog Srs 200/2100	D. C. Bonsall/Netherthorpe
	G-BDOI	Hiller UH-12E	T. J. Clark
	G-BDOL	Piper J-3C-65 Cub	U. E. Allman & M. C. Jordan/Shoreham
	G-BDON	Thunder Ax7-77A balloon	J. R. Henderson & ptnrs
	G-BDOR	Thunder Ax6-56A balloon	M. S. Drinkwater & G. Fitzpatrick
	G-BDOW	Cessna FRA.150M	Scottish Airways Flyers (Prestwick) Ltd
	G-BDPA	PA-28-151 Warrior	Noon (Aircraft Leasing) Ltd/Shoreham
	G-BDPF	Cessna F.172M	Semloh Aviation Services/Andrewsfield
	G-BDPK	Cameron O-56 balloon	Rango Balloon & Kite Co
	G-BDPV	Boeing 747-136	British Airways *Blea Water*
	G-BDRB	AA-5B Tiger	Dorset Air Ltd
	G-BDRC	V.724 Viscount ★	Fire School/Manston
	G-BDRD	Cessna FRA.150M	Air Service Training Ltd/Perth
	G-BDRF	Taylor JT.1 Monoplane	B. R. Ratcliffe
	G-BDRG	Taylor JT.2 Titch	D. R. Gray
	G-BDRJ	D.H.C.1 Chipmunk 22 (WP857)	J. C. Schooling
	G-BDRK	Cameron O-65 balloon	D. L. Smith *Smirk*
	G-BDSB	PA-28-181 Archer II	Testair Ltd/Blackbushe
	G-BDSE	Cameron O-77 balloon	British Airways *Concorde*
	G-BDSF	Cameron O-56 balloon	A. R. Greensides & B. H. Osbourne
	G-BDSH	PA-28 Cherokee 140	BCF Roofing Ltd
	G-BDSK	Cameron O-65 balloon	Southern Balloon Group *Carousel II*
	G-BDSL	Cessna F.150M	Cleveland Flying School Ltd/Tees-side
	G-BDSM	Slingsby T.31B Cadet III	J. A. L. Parton
	G-BDSN	Wassmer WA.52 Europa	Sierra November Group (G-BADN)
	G-BDSO	Cameron O-31 balloon	Budget Rent-a-Car *Baby Budget*
	G-BDTB	Evans VP-1	S. Pearl
	G-BDTL	Evans VP-1	A. K. Lang
	G-BDTN	BN-2A Mk III-2 Trislander	Aurigny Air Services Ltd/Guernsey
	G-BDTU	Omega III gas balloon	G. F. Turnbull
	G-BDTV	Mooney M.20F	A. L. Burton & A. J. Daley
	G-BDTW	Cassutt Racer	B. E. Smith & C. S. Thompson/Redhill
	G-BDTX	Cessna F.150M	A. A. & R. N. Croxford/Southend
	G-BDUI	Cameron V-56 balloon	D. C. Johnson
	G-BDUJ	PA-31-310 Turbo Navajo	Club Air (Europe) Ltd
	G-BDUL	Evans VP-1	J. T. Taylor
	G-BDUM	Cessna F.150M	SFG Ltd/Shipdham
	G-BDUN	PA-34-200T Seneca II	Air Medical Ltd
	G-BDUO	Cessna F.150M	Sandown Aero Club
	G-BDUX	Slingsby T.31B Cadet III	J. C. Anderson/Cranfield
	G-BDUY	Robin DR.400/140B	J. M. Dean & A. L. Jubb
	G-BDUZ	Cameron V-56 balloon	Zebedee Balloon Service
	G-BDVA	PA-17 Vagabond	I. M. Callier
	G-BDVB	PA-15 (PA-17) Vagabond	B. P. Gardner
	G-BDVC	PA-17 Vagabond	A. R. Caveen
	G-BDVG	Thunder Ax6-56A balloon	R. F. Pollard *Argonaut*
	G-BDVS	F.27 Friendship Mk 200	Air UK *Eric Gandar Dower*/Norwich
	G-BDVU	Mooney M.20F	Digital Duplication Ltd/Stapleford

Reg.	Type	Owner or Operator	Notes
G-BDWA	SOCATA Rallye 150ST	J. T. Wilson/Newtownards	
G-BDWE	Flaglor Scooter	D. W. Evernden	
G-BDWG	BN-2A Islander	Wilsons Transport Ltd	
G-BDWH	SOCATA Rallye 150ST	M. A. Jones	
G-BDWJ	SE-5A replica (F8010)	S. M. Smith/Booker	
G-BDWK	Beech 95-58 Baron	Cammac Coal Ltd	
G-BDWL	PA-25 Pawnee 235	Peterborough & Spalding Gliding Club	
G-BDWM	Mustang 2/3 scale replica	D. C. Bonsall	
G-BDWO	Howes Ax6 balloon	R. B. & Mrs C. Howes *Griffin*	
G-BDWP	PA-32R Cherokee Lance 300	W. M. Brown & B. J. Wood/Birmingham	
G-BDWV	BN-2A Mk III-2 Trislander	Aurigny Air Services Ltd/Guernsey	
G-BDWX	Jodel D.120A	J. P. Lassey	
G-BDWY	PA-28 Cherokee 140	Comed Aviation Ltd/Blackpool	
G-BDXA	Boeing 747-236B	British Airways *City of Peterborough*	
G-BDXB	Boeing 747-236B	British Airways *City of Liverpool*	
G-BDXC	Boeing 747-236B	British Airways *City of Manchester*	
G-BDXD	Boeing 747-236B	British Airways *City of Plymouth*	
G-BDXE	Boeing 747-236B	British Airways *City of Glasgow*	
G-BDXF	Boeing 747-236B	British Airways *City of York*	
G-BDXG	Boeing 747-236B	British Airways *City of Oxford*	
G-BDXH	Boeing 747-236B	British Airways *City of Elgin*	
G-BDXI	Boeing 747-236B	British Airways *City of Cambridge*	
G-BDXJ	Boeing 747-236B	British Airways *City of Birmingham*	
G-BDXK	Boeing 747-236B	British Airways *City of Canterbury*	
G-BDXL	Boeing 747-236B	British Airways *City of Winchester*	
G-BDXM	Boeing 747-236B	British Airways *City of Derby*	
G-BDXN	Boeing 747-236B	British Airways *City of Stoke-on-Trent*	
G-BDXO	Boeing 747-236B	British Airways *City of Bath*	
G-BDXP	Boeing 747-236B (SCD)	British Airways *City of Salisbury*	
G-BDXX	SNCAN NC.858S	J. R. Rowell & J. E. Hobbs/Sandown	
G-BDYC	AA-1B Trainer	N. F. Whisler	
G-BDYD	R. Commander 114	SRS Aviation	
G-BDYF	Cessna 421C	Simco 408 Ltd	
G-BDYG	P.56 Provost T.1 (WV493) ★	Museum of Flight/E. Fortune	
G-BDYH	Cameron V-56 balloon	B. J. Godding	
G-BDYM	Skysales S-31 balloon	Miss A. I. Smith & M. J. Moore *Cheeky Devil*	
G-BDYZ	MBB Bo 105D	Bond Helicopters Ltd/Bourn	
G-BDZA	Scheibe SF.25E Super Falke	Norfolk Gliding Club Ltd/Tibenham	
G-BDZB	Cameron S-31 balloon	Kenning Motor Group Ltd *Kenning*	
G-BDZD	Cessna F.172M	Three Counties Aero Engineering Ltd/Lasham	
G-BDZF	G.164 Ag-Cat B	CKS Air Ltd	
G-BDZS	Scheibe SF.25E Super Falke	A. D. Gubbay/Panshanger	
G-BDZU	Cessna 421C	Calmcraft Ltd	
G-BDZX	PA-28-151 Warrior	Catalina Seaplanes Ltd	
G-BEAB	Jodel DR.1051	C. Fitton	
G-BEAC	PA-28 Cherokee 140	D. J. Hockings/Biggin Hill	
G-BEAD	WG.13 Lynx ★	*Instructional airframe*/Middle Wallop	
G-BEAG	PA-34-200T Seneca II	C.S.E. Aviation Ltd/Kidlington	
G-BEAH	J/2 Arrow	W. J. & Mrs M. D. Horler	
G-BEAK	L-1011-385 TriStar 50	British Airways *Carmarthen Bay*	
G-BEAL	L-1011-385 TriStar 50	British Airways *Cardigan Bay*	
G-BEAM	L-1011-385 TriStar 50	British Airways *Swansea Bay*	
G-BEBC	W.S.55 Whirlwind 3 (XP355) ★	Norwich Aviation Museum	
G-BEBE	AA-5A Cheetah	Denham School of Flying Ltd	
G-BEBF	Auster AOP.9	M. D. N. & Mrs A. C. Fisher	
G-BEBG	WSK-PZL SDZ-45A Ogar	The Ogar Syndicate	
G-BEBI	Cessna F.172M	Calder Equipment Ltd/Hatfield	
G-BEBL	Douglas DC-10-30	British Airways *Forest of Dean*/Gatwick	
G-BEBM	Douglas DC-10-30	British Airways *Sherwood Forest*/Gatwick	
G-BEBN	Cessna 177B	Franchi Aviation Ltd & Lynair Aviation	
G-BEBO	Turner TSW-2 Wot	The Turner Special Flying Group	
G-BEBR	GY-201 Minicab	A. S. Jones & D. R. Upton	
G-BEBS	Andreasson BA-4B	J. S. Mortimer	
G-BEBT	Andreasson BA-4B	A. Horsfall	
G-BEBU	R. Commander 112A	M. Rowland & J. K. Woodford	
G-BEBZ	PA-28-151 Warrior	Goodwood Terrena Ltd/Goodwood	
G-BECA	SOCATA Rallye 100ST	Bredon Flying Group	
G-BECB	SOCATA Rallye 100ST	A. J. Trible	
G-BECC	SOCATA Rallye 150ST	Golf Charlie Group/Booker	
G-BECD	SOCATA Rallye 150ST	A. J. Liddle	

Notes	Reg.	Type	Owner or Operator
	G-BECF	Scheibe SF.25A Falke	D. A. Wilson & ptnrs
	G-BECG	Boeing 737-204ADV	Britannia Airways Ltd *Amy Johnson*/Luton
	G-BECH	Boeing 737-204ADV	Britannia Airways Ltd *Viscount Montgomery of Alamein*/Luton
	G-BECJ	Partenavia P.68B	Covex PLC
	G-BECK	Cameron V-56 balloon	D. W. & P. Allum
	G-BECN	Piper J-3C-65 Cub (480480)	R. C. Partridge & M. Oliver
	G-BECO	Beech A.36 Bonanza	Euro Aviation Ltd/ Conington
	G-BECT	C.A.S.A.1.131 Jungmann	Shoreham 131 Group
	G-BECW	C.A.S.A.1.131 Jungmann	N. C. Jensen/Redhill
	G-BECZ	CAARP CAP.10B	Aerobatic Associates Ltd
	G-BEDA	C.A.S.A.1.131 Jungmann	M. G. Kates & D. J. Berry
	G-BEDB	Nord 1203 Norecrin	B. F. G. Lister
	G-BEDD	Jodel D.117A	A. T. Croy/Kirkwall
	G-BEDF	Boeing B-17G-105-VE (485784)	B-17 Preservation Ltd/Duxford
	G-BEDG	R. Commander 112A	L. E. Blackburn
	G-BEDI	Sikorsky S-61N	British International Helicopters Ltd
	G-BEDJ	Piper J-3C-65 Cub (44-80594)	D. J. Elliott
	G-BEDK	Hiller UH-12E	Agricopters Ltd/Chilbolton
	G-BEDL	Cessna T.337D	T. J. Brammer & R. Masterman
	G-BEDV	V.668 Varsity T.1 (WJ945) ★	D. S. Selway/Duxford
	G-BEDZ	BN-2A Islander	Loganair Ltd/Glasgow
	G-BEEE	Thunder Ax6-56A balloon	I. R. M. Jacobs *Avia*
	G-BEEG	BN-2A Islander	Telair Manchester Ltd/Barton
	G-BEEH	Cameron V-56 balloon	B. & N. V. Moreton
	G-BEEI	Cameron N-77 balloon	P. S. & G. G. Rankin
	G-BEEJ	Cameron O-77 balloon	DAL (Builders Merchants) Ltd *Dal's Pal*
	G-BEEO	Short SD3-30	Shorts Aircraft Leasing Ltd
	G-BEEP	Thunder Ax5-42 balloon	Mrs B. C. Faithful/Holland
	G-BEER	Isaacs Fury II	Baycol Aviation
	G-BEEU	PA-28 Cherokee 140E	Berkshire Aviation Services Ltd
	G-BEEW	Taylor JT.1 Monoplane	K. Wigglesworth/Breighton
	G-BEFA	PA-28-151 Warrior	Firmbeam Ltd/Booker
	G-BEFC	AA-5B Tiger	Portway Aviation/Shobdon
	G-BEFF	PA-28 Cherokee 140	C. Haymes & G. M. Thurlow/Shipdham
	G-BEFO	BN-2A Mk III-3 Trislander	Oston Air Finance Ltd (G-SARN)
	G-BEFP	BN-2A Mk III-2 Trislander	Air & General Services Ltd/Biggin Hill
	G-BEFR	Fokker DR.1/(replica) (2009)	R. A. Bowes & P. A. Crawford
	G-BEFT	Cessna 421C	Michael A. Lenihan & Associates Ltd
	G-BEFV	Evans VP-2	D. A. Cotton
	G-BEFY	Hiller UH-12E	Copley Farms Ltd
	G-BEGA	Westland-Bell 47G-3B1	Flight 47 Ltd
	G-BEGG	Scheibe SF.25E Super Falke	G-BEGG Flying Group
	G-BEGV	PA-23 Aztec 250F	Flamex Ltd
	G-BEHH	PA-32R Cherokee Lance 300	SMK Engineering Ltd/Leeds
	G-BEHS	PA-25 Pawnee 260C	S. L. Robinson
	G-BEHV	Cessna F.172N	P. P. D. Howard-Johnston/Edinburgh
	G-BEHW	Cessna F.150M	W. Lancashire Aero Club Ltd/Woodvale
	G-BEHX	Evans VP-2	G. S. Adams
	G-BEIA	Cessna FRA.150M	Air Service Training Ltd/Perth
	G-BEIB	Cessna F.172N	Sheltons of Wollaston (Garages) Ltd
	G-BEIC	Sikorsky S-61N	British International Helicopters Ltd/ Aberdeen
	G-BEIF	Cameron O-65 balloon	C. Vening
	G-BEIG	Cessna F.150M	Herefordshire Aero Club Ltd/Shobdon
	G-BEII	PA-25 Pawnee 235D	Burn Gliding Club Ltd
	G-BEIL	SOCATA Rallye 150T	The Rallye Flying Group
	G-BEIP	PA-28-181 Archer II	M. Ferguson Ltd/Newtownards
	G-BEIS	Evans VP-1	P. J. Hunt
	G-BEJA	Thunder Ax6-56A balloon	P. A. Hutchins *Jackson*
	G-BEJB	Thunder Ax6-56A balloon	International Distillers & Vinters Ltd
	G-BEJD	H.S.748 Srs 1	Dan-Air Services Ltd/Gatwick
	G-BEJE	H.S.748 Srs 1	Dan-Air Services Ltd/Gatwick
	G-BEJK	Cameron S-31 balloon	Rango Balloon & Kite Co
	G-BEJL	Sikorsky S-61N	British International Helicopters Ltd/ Aberdeen
	G-BEJM	BAC One-Eleven 423ET	Ford Motor Co Ltd/Stansted
	G-BEJP	D.H.C.6 Twin Otter 310	Loganair Ltd/Glasgow
	G-BEJV	PA-34-200T Seneca II	C.S.E. Aviation Ltd/Kidlington
	G-BEJW	BAC One-Eleven 423ET	Ford Motor Co Ltd/Stansted
	G-BEKA	BAC One-Eleven 520FN	Dan-Air Services Ltd/Gatwick
	G-BEKC	H.S.748 Srs 1 ★	Airport Fire Service/Manchester
	G-BEKE	H.S.748 Srs 1	Dan-Air Services Ltd/Gatwick

Reg.	Type	Owner or Operator	Notes
G-BEKG	H.S.748 Srs 1	—/(G-VAJK)	
G-BEKL	Bede BD-4E	H. B. Carter	
G-BEKM	Evans VP-1	G. J. McDill/Glenrothes	
G-BEKN	Cessna FRA.150M	RFC (Bourn) Ltd	
G-BEKO	Cessna F.182Q	Tyler International	
G-BEKR	Rand KR-2	A. N. Purchase	
G-BELF	BN-2A Islander	Flying Tigers Ltd/Goodwood	
G-BELR	PA-28 Cherokee 140	H. M. Clarke	
G-BELT	Cessna F.150J	Yorkshire Light Aircraft Ltd (G-AWUV)/ Leeds	
G-BELX	Cameron V-56 balloon	P. A. & N. J. Foot	
G-BEMB	Cessna F.172M	Stocklaunch Ltd	
G-BEMD	Beech 95-B55 Baron	A. G. Perkins	
G-BEMM	Slingsby T.31B Motor Cadet	M. N. Martin	
G-BEMU	Thunder Ax5-42 balloon	I. J. Liddiard & A. Merritt	
G-BEMW	PA-28-181 Archer II	Charta Furniture Ltd/Goodwood	
G-BEMY	Cessna FRA.150M	L. G. Sawyer/Blackbushe	
G-BEND	Cameron V-56 balloon	Dante Balloon Group Le Billet	
G-BENJ	R. Commander 112B	R. C. Wilcox/Blackbushe	
G-BENK	Cessna F.172M	Graham Churchill Plant Ltd	
G-BENN	Cameron V-56 balloon	S. H. Budd	
G-BENT	Cameron N-77 balloon	N. Tasker	
G-BEOD	Cessna 180	Avionics Research Ltd/Cranfield	
G-BEOE	Cessna FRA.150M	J. R. Nicholls/Sibson	
G-BEOH	PA-28R-201T Turbo Arrow III	Larkshill Ltd	
G-BEOI	PA-18 Super Cub 150	Southdown Gliding Club Ltd	
G-BEOK	Cessna F.150M	Stardial Ltd/Southend	
G-BEOO	Sikorsky S-61N Mk. II	British International Helicopters Ltd	
G-BEOX	L-414 Hudson IV (A16-199) ★	RAF Museum/Hendon	
G-BEOY	Cessna FRA.150L	R. W. Denny	
G-BEOZ	A.W.650 Argosy 101 ★	Aeropark/E. Midlands	
G-BEPB	Pereira Osprey II	J. J. & A. J. C. Zwetsloot/Bourn	
G-BEPC	SNCAN Stampe SV-4C	J. A. Bridger & A. J. Foan	
G-BEPE	SC.5 Belfast	HeavyLift Cargo Airlines Ltd (G-ASKE) (withdrawn)/Southend	
G-BEPF	SNCAN Stampe SV-4A	L. J. Rice	
G-BEPH	BN-2A Mk III-2 Trislander	Aurigny Air Services Ltd/Guernsey	
G-BEPI	BN-2A Mk III-2 Trislander	Aurigny Air Services Ltd/Guernsey	
G-BEPO	Cameron N-77 balloon	G. Camplin & V. Aitken	
G-BEPS	SC.5 Belfast	HeavyLift Cargo Airlines Ltd/Stansted	
G-BEPV	Fokker S.11-1 Instructor	L. C. MacKnight	
G-BEPY	R. Commander 112B	Emin Aviation Ltd/Biggin Hill	
G-BEPZ	Cameron D-96 hot-air airship	D. W. Liddiard	
G-BERA	SOCATA Rallye 150ST	Air Touring Services Ltd/Biggin Hill	
G-BERC	SOCATA Rallye 150ST	Severn Valley Aero Group	
G-BERD	Thunder Ax6-56A balloon	P. M. Gaines	
G-BERI	R. Commander 114	K. B. Harper/Blackbushe	
G-BERN	Saffrey S-330 balloon	B. Martin Beeze	
G-BERT	Cameron V-56 balloon	Southern Balloon Group Bert	
G-BERW	R. Commander 114	C. D. Allison	
G-BERY	AA-1B Trainer	R. H. J. Levi	
G-BESO	BN-2A Islander	Isles of Scilly Skybus Ltd/St Just	
G-BESP	H.S. 125 Srs 700B	British Aerospace PLC (G-PRMC)	
G-BETD	Robin HR.200/100	R. A. Parsons/Bourn	
G-BETE	Rollason B.2A Beta	T. M. Jones/Tatenhill	
G-BETF	Cameron 'Champion' balloon	Balloon Stable Ltd Champion	
G-BETG	Cessna 180K Skywagon	T. P. A. Norman/Panshanger	
G-BETI	Pitts S-1D Special	P. Metcalfe/Tees-side	
G-BETL	PA-25 Pawnee 235D	Boston Aviation Services	
G-BETM	PA-25 Pawnee 235D	Yorkshire Gliding Club (Pty) Ltd	
G-BETO	M.S.885 Super Rallye	BETO Group	
G-BETP	Cameron O-65 balloon	J. R. Rix & Sons Ltd	
G-BETT	PA-34-200 Seneca II	Andrews Professional Colour Laboratories Ltd/Headcorn	
G-BETV	HS.125 Srs 600B	Rolls-Royce PLC/Filton	
G-BEUA	PA-18 Super Cub 150	London Gliding Club (Pty) Ltd/Dunstable	
G-BEUD	Robin HR.100/285R	E. A. & L. M. C. Payton/Cranfield	
G-BEUI	Piper J-3C-65 Cub	M. J. Whatley	
G-BEUK	Fuji FA.200-160	Euro Marine Group Ltd	
G-BEUL	Beech 95-58 Baron	Foyle Flyers Ltd/Eglinton	
G-BEUM	Taylor JT.1 Monoplane	M. T. Taylor	
G-BEUN	Cassutt Racer IIIm	R. S. Voice/Redhill	
G-BEUP	Robin DR.400/180	A. V. Pound & Co Ltd	

Notes	Reg.	Type	Owner or Operator
	G-BEUR	Cessna F.172M	M. E. Moore/Compton Abbas
	G-BEUS	AIA Stampe SV-4C	G-BEUS Flying Group
	G-BEUU	PA-18 Super Cub 95	F. Sharples/Sandown
	G-BEUV	Thunder Ax6-56A balloon	Silhouette Balloon Group
	G-BEUX	Cessna F.172N	Ladel Ltd
	G-BEUY	Cameron N-31 balloon	M. W. A. Shemilt
	G-BEVA	SOCATA Rallye 150ST	The Rallye Group
	G-BEVB	SOCATA Rallye 150ST	R. B. Tope & C. M. Blanchard
	G-BEVC	SOCATA Rallye 150ST	B. W. Walpole
	G-BEVG	PA-34-200T-2 Seneca	Pullploy Ltd/Bournemouth
	G-BEVI	Thunder Ax7-77A balloon	The Painted Clouds Balloon Co Ltd
	G-BEVO	Sportavia-Pützer RF-5	T. Barlow
	G-BEVP	Evans VP-2	C. M. Gooch
	G-BEVS	Taylor JT.1 Monoplane	D. Hunter
	G-BEVT	BN-2A Mk III-2 Trislander	Aurigny Air Services Ltd/Guernsey
	G-BEVW	SOCATA Rallye 150ST	P. C. Goodwin
	G-BEWJ	Westland-Bell 47G-3B1	Ropeleyville Ltd
	G-BEWM	Sikorsky S-61N Mk II	British International Helicopters Ltd
	G-BEWN	D.H.82A Tiger Moth	H. D. Labouchere
	G-BEWO	Zlin Z.326 Trener Master	Nimrod Group Ltd/Staverton
	G-BEWR	Cessna F.172N	Cheshire Air Training School Ltd/Liverpool
	G-BEWX	PA-28R-201 Arrow III	A. Vickers
	G-BEXK	PA-25 Pawnee 235D	Howard Avis (Aviation) Ltd
	G-BEXN	AA-1C Lynx	Scotia Safari Ltd/Prestwick
	G-BEXO	PA-23 Apache 160	Man-Air
	G-BEXR	Mudry/CAARP CAP-10B	Man-Air
	G-BEXS	Cessna F.150M	Firecrest Aviation Ltd
	G-BEXW	PA-28-181 Archer II	R. P. Crozier
	G-BEXX	Cameron V-56 balloon	K. A. Schlussler
	G-BEXY	PA-28 Cherokee 140	G. J. Jenkins & D. L. James
	G-BEXZ	Cameron N-56 balloon	D. C. Eager & G. C. Clark
	G-BEYA	Enstrom 280C Shark	Aspleys Antiques Ltd
	G-BEYB	Fairey Flycatcher (replica) (S1287)	John S. Fairey/Duxford
	G-BEYD	HPR-7 Herald 401	*Stored*/Southend
	G-BEYF	HPR-7 Herald 401	Channel Express (Air Services) PLC/ Bournemouth
	G-BEYK	HPR-7 Herald 401	Janes Aviation Ltd/Blackpool
	G-BEYL	PA-28 Cherokee 180	B. G. & G. Airlines Ltd/Jersey
	G-BEYO	PA-28 Cherokee 140	Mersey Control Systems Ltd
	G-BEYT	PA-28 Cherokee 140	H. Foulds
	G-BEYV	Cessna T.210M	Forth Engineering Ltd
	G-BEYW	Taylor JT.1 Monoplane	R. A. Abrahams/Barton
	G-BEYY	PA-31 Turbo Navajo	Salon Aviation Ltd
	G-BEYZ	Jodel DR.1051/M1	M. J. McCarthy & S. Aarons/Biggin Hill
	G-BEZA	Zlin Z.226T Trener	L. Bezak
	G-BEZC	AA-5 Traveler	P. N. & S. E. Field
	G-BEZE	Rutan Vari-Eze	H. C. Mackinnon
	G-BEZF	AA-5 Traveler	G. A. Randall/Exeter
	G-BEZG	AA-5 Traveler	B. A. & P. G. Osburn/Biggin Hill
	G-BEZH	AA-5 Traveler	H. & L. Sims Ltd
	G-BEZI	AA-5 Traveler	BEZI Flying Group/Cranfield
	G-BEZJ	MBB Bo 105D	Bond Helicopters Ltd/Bourn
	G-BEZK	Cessna F.172H	Zulu Kilo Flying Group
	G-BEZL	PA-31-310 Turbo Navajo C	Filemart Ltd
	G-BEZM	Cessna F.182Q	E. Smith (G-WALK)/Leeds
	G-BEZO	Cessna F.172M	Staverton Flying Services Ltd
	G-BEZP	PA-32 Cherokee Six 300D	Falcon Styles Ltd/Booker
	G-BEZR	Cessna F.172M	Kirmington Aviation Ltd
	G-BEZS	Cessna FR.172J	R. E. Beeton & M. R. Cavinder
	G-BEZV	Cessna F.172M	Insch Flying Group/Aberdeen
	G-BEZY	Rutan Vari-Eze	R. J. Jones
	G-BEZZ	Jodel D.112	G-BEZZ Jodel Group
	G-BFAA	GY-80 Horizon 160	Mary Poppins Ltd
	G-BFAB	Cameron N-56 balloon	Phonogram Ltd *Phonogram*
	G-BFAC	Cessna F.177RG	J. J. Baumhardt/Southend
	G-BFAF	Aeronca 7BCM (7797)	D. C. W. Harper/Finmere
	G-BFAH	Phoenix Currie Wot	N. Hamlin-Wright
	G-BFAI	R. Commander 114	D. S. Innes/Guernsey
	G-BFAK	M.S.892A Rallye Commodore 150	P. G. Wells & J. D. Hensby
	G-BFAM	PA-31P Pressurised Navajo	Ashcombe Ltd
	G-BFAN	H.S.125 Srs 600F	British Aerospace (G-AZHS)/Hatfield
	G-BFAO	PA-20 Pacer 135	J. Day & ptnrs/Goodwood

Reg.	Type	Owner or Operator	Notes
G-BFAP	SIAI-Marchetti S.205-20R	A. O. Broin	
G-BFAR	Cessna 500-1 Citation	Club Air (Europe) Ltd	
G-BFAS	Evans VP-1	A. I. Sutherland	
G-BFAW	D.H.C.1 Chipmunk 22	R. V. Bowles	
G-BFAX	D.H.C.1 Chipmunk 22 (WG422)	B. Earl/Biggin Hill	
G-BFBA	Jodel DR.100A	A. Brown & R. Wood	
G-BFBB	PA-23 Aztec 250E	Dollar Air Services Ltd/Coventry	
G-BFBC	Taylor JT.1 Monoplane	D. Oxenham	
G-BFBD	Partenavia P.68B	Calmsafe Ltd	
G-BFBE	Robin HR.200/100	T. Keeley	
G-BFBF	PA-28 Cherokee 140	Marnham Investments Ltd	
G-BFBM	Saffery S.330 balloon	B. Martin *Beeze II*	
G-BFBR	PA-28-161 Warrior II	Lowery Holdings Ltd/Fairoaks	
G-BFBU	Partenavia P.68B	W. Holmes & Son Ltd	
G-BFBY	Piper J-3C-65 Cub	L. W. Usherwood	
G-BFCT	Cessna TU.206F	Cecil Aviation Ltd/Cambridge	
G-BFCZ	Sopwith Camel (B7270) ★	Brooklands Museum Trust Ltd/Weybridge	
G-BFDC	D.H.C.1 Chipmunk 22	N. F. O'Neill/Newtownards	
G-BFDE	Sopwith Tabloid (replica) (168) ★	RAF Museum Storage & Restoration Centre/Cardington	
G-BFDF	SOCATA Rallye 235E	J. H. Atkinson/Skegness	
G-BFDG	PA-28R-201T Turbo-Arrow III	Richard Pearson Ltd	
G-BFDI	PA-28-181 Archer II	Truman Aviation Ltd/Tollerton	
G-BFDK	PA-28-161 Warrior II	C.S.E. Aviation Ltd/Kidlington	
G-BFDL	Piper J-3C-65 Cub (454537)	P. B. Rice & A. White	
G-BFDM	Jodel D.120	Worcestershire Gliding Ltd	
G-BFDN	PA-31-350 Navajo Chieftain	Genoex Ltd	
G-BFDO	PA-28R-201T Turbo Arrow III	M. I. & D. G. Goss	
G-BFDZ	Taylor JT.1 Monoplane	H. R. Leefe	
G-BFEB	Jodel D.150	S. Russell	
G-BFEC	PA-23 Aztec 250F	P. V. Naylor-Leyland	
G-BFEE	Beech 95-E55 Baron	Interair (Aviation) Ltd/Bournemouth	
G-BFEF	Agusta-Bell 47G-3B1	R. I. C. Huxtable/Exeter	
G-BFEH	Jodel D.117A	C. V. & S. J. Philcott	
G-BFEI	Westland-Bell 47G-3B1	Trent Air Services Ltd/Cranfield	
G-BFEK	Cessna F.152	Staverton Flying Services Ltd	
G-BFER	Bell 212	Bristow Helicopters Ltd	
G-BFEV	PA-25 Pawnee 235	T. Miller	
G-BFEW	PA-25 Pawnee 235	B. Walker & Co (Dursley) Ltd	
G-BFEY	PA-25 Pawnee 235	Howard Avis Aviation Ltd	
G-BFFC	Cessna F.152-II	Yorkshire Flying Services Ltd/Leeds	
G-BFFE	Cessna F.152-II	Doncaster Aero Club	
G-BFFG	Beech 95-B55 Baron	B. Walker & Co (Dursley) Ltd	
G-BFFJ	Sikorsky S-61N Mk II	British International Helicopters Ltd/ Aberdeen	
G-BFFK	Sikorsky S-61N Mk II	British International Helicopters Ltd/ Aberdeen	
G-BFFP	PA-18 Super Cub 150 (modified)	Booker Gliding Club Ltd	
G-BFFT	Cameron V-56 balloon	R. I. M. Kerr & D. C. Boxall	
G-BFFW	Cessna F.152	Tayside Aviation Ltd/Dundee	
G-BFFY	Cessna F.150M	Northside Aviation Ltd/Liverpool	
G-BFFZ	Cessna FR.172 Hawk XP	H. H. Elder	
G-BFGD	Cessna F.172N-II	Falcon Flying Services/Biggin Hill	
G-BFGF	Cessna F.177RG	Victree (V.M.) Ltd/Birmingham	
G-BFGG	Cessna FRA.150M	Air Service Training Ltd/Perth	
G-BFGH	Cessna F.337G	T. Perkins/Sherburn	
G-BFGK	Jodel D.117	B. F. J. Hope	
G-BFGL	Cessna FA.152	Yorkshire Flying Services Ltd/Leeds	
G-BFGO	Fuji FA.200-160	Gt Consall Copper Mine Co Ltd	
G-BFGS	M.S.893E Rallye 180GT	K. M. & H. Bowen	
G-BFGW	Cessna F.150H	J. F. Morgan	
G-BFGX	Cessna FRA.150M	Air Service Training Ltd/Perth	
G-BFGZ	Cessna FRA.150M	Air Service Training Ltd/Perth	
G-BFHG	C.A.S.A. C.352L (VK+AZ)	Aces High Ltd/North Weald	
G-BFHH	D.H.82A Tiger Moth	P. Harrison & M. J. Gambrell/Redhill	
G-BFHI	Piper J-3C-65 Cub	J. M. Robinson	
G-BFHP	Champion 7GCAA Citabria	T. A. Holding	
G-BFHR	Jodel DR.220/2+2	R. J. Fray	
G-BFHT	Cessna F.152-II	Riger Ltd/Luton	
G-BFHU	Cessna F.152-II	Deltair Ltd/Chester	
G-BFHV	Cessna F.152-II	Aerohire Ltd	
G-BFHX	Evans VP-1	P. Johnson	
G-BFIB	PA-31 Turbo Navajo	Mann Aviation Ltd/Fairoaks	

Notes	Reg.	Type	Owner or Operator
	G-BFID	Taylor JT.2 Titch Mk III	G. Hunter
	G-BFIE	Cessna FRA.150M	RFC (Bourn) Ltd
	G-BFIF	Cessna FR.172K XPII	Falcon Flight Training Ltd/Eglinton
	G-BFIG	Cessna FR.172K XPII	Tenair Ltd
	G-BFIJ	AA-5A Cheetah	J. H. Wise/Redhill
	G-BFIN	AA-5A Cheetah	G-BFIN Group
	G-BFIP	Wallbro Monoplane 1909 replica	K. H. Wallis/Swanton Morley
	G-BFIR	Avro 652A Anson 21 (WD413)	G. M. K. Fraser (*stored*)/Arbroath
	G-BFIT	Thunder Ax6-56Z balloon	J. A. G. Tyson
	G-BFIU	Cessna FR.172K XP	B. M. Jobling
	G-BFIV	Cessna F.177RG	Kingfishair Ltd/Blackbushe
	G-BFIX	Thunder Ax7-77A balloon	E. Sowden Ltd
	G-BFJA	AA-5B Tiger	Sentry Courier Ltd/Blackbushe
	G-BFJH	SA.102-5 Cavalier	B. F. J. Hope
	G-BFJI	Robin HR.100/250	M. A. Egerton
	G-BFJJ	Evans VP-1	M. J. Collins
	G-BFJK	PA-23 Aztec 250F	R. Marsden & P. E. T. Price
	G-BFJN	Westland-Bell 47G-3B1	Howden Helicopters
	G-BFJR	Cessna F.337G	Mannix Aviation/E. Midlands
	G-BFJV	Cessna F.172H	Southport & Merseyside Aero Club Ltd
	G-BFJW	AB-206B JetRanger	European Aviation Ltd
	G-BFJZ	Robin DR.400/140B	Forge House Restaurant Ltd/Biggin Hill
	G-BFKA	Cessna F.172N	D. J. A. Seagram
	G-BFKB	Cessna F.172N	R. E. Speigel
	G-BFKC	Rand KR.2	L. H. S. Stephens & I. S. Hewitt
	G-BFKD	R. Commander 114B	M. D. Faiers
	G-BFKF	Cessna FA.152	Klingair Ltd/Conington
	G-BFKG	Cessna F.152	Luton Flight Training Ltd
	G-BFKH	Cessna F.152	T. G. Aviation Ltd/Manston
	G-BFKL	Cameron N-56 balloon	Merrythought Toys Ltd *Merrythought*
	G-BFKY	PA-34-200 Seneca II	S.L.H. Construction Ltd/Biggin Hill
	G-BFLH	PA-34-200T Seneca II	C.S.E. Aviation Ltd/Kidlington
	G-BFLI	PA-28R-201T Turbo Arrow III	Cowley (Recruitment) Ltd
	G-BFLK	Cessna F.152	N. A. Ali
	G-BFLL	H.S.748 Srs 2A	Aberdeen Airways Ltd
	G-BFLM	Cessna 150M	Cornwall Flying Club Ltd/Bodmin
	G-BFLN	Cessna 150M	Sherburn Aero Club Ltd
	G-BFLP	Amethyst Ax6 balloon	K. J. Hendry *Amethyst*
	G-BFLU	Cessna F.152	Inverness Flying Services Ltd
	G-BFLV	Cessna F.172N	Cheshire Air Training School (Merseyside) Ltd/Liverpool
	G-BFLX	AA-5A Cheetah	Abraxas Aviation Ltd/Denham
	G-BFLZ	Beech 95-A55 Baron	W. G. Thompson
	G-BFMC	BAC One-Eleven 414FG	Ford Motor Co Ltd/Stansted
	G-BFME	Cameron V-56 balloon	Warwick Balloons Ltd
	G-BFMF	Cassutt Racer Mk IIIM	P. H. Lewis
	G-BFMG	PA-28-161 Warrior II	Bailey Aviation Ltd
	G-BFMH	Cessna 177B	Span Aviation Ltd/Newcastle
	G-BFMK	Cessna FA.152	RAF Halton Aeroplane Club Ltd
	G-BFMM	PA-28-181 Archer II	Bristol & Wessex Aeroplane Club Ltd
	G-BFMR	PA-20 Pacer 125	J. E. Cummings
	G-BFMX	Cessna F.172N	Colton Aviation Aero Spraying Ltd
	G-BFMY	Sikorsky S-61N	Bristow Helicopters Ltd
	G-BFMZ	Payne Ax6 balloon	G. F. Payne
	G-BFNC	AS.350B Ecureuil	Dollar Air Services Ltd/Coventry
	G-BFNG	Jodel D.112	M. Lomax/Booker
	G-BFNI	PA-28-161 Warrior II	P. Elliott/Biggin Hill
	G-BFNJ	PA-28-161 Warrior II	C.S.E. Aviation Ltd/Kidlington
	G-BFNK	PA-28-161 Warrior II	C.S.E. Aviation Ltd/Kidlington
	G-BFNM	Globe GC.1 Swift	Nottingham Flying Group/Tatenhill
	G-BFNU	BN-2B Islander	Isle of Scilly Sky Bus Ltd/St Just
	G-BFOD	Cessna F.182Q	G. N. Clarke
	G-BFOE	Cessna F.152	B. W. Wells & Burbage Farms Ltd
	G-BFOF	Cessna F.152	Staverton Flying School Ltd
	G-BFOG	Cessna 150M	W. J. Pinches & M. D. Bayliss
	G-BFOJ	AA-1 Yankee	A. J. Morton/Bournemouth
	G-BFOL	Beech 200 Super King Air	Bristow Helicopters Ltd
	G-BFOM	PA-31-325 Turbo Navajo C	Herbison Air Services Ltd
	G-BFOP	Jodel D.120	R. J. Wesley & G. D. Western/Ipswich
	G-BFOS	Thunder Ax6-56A balloon	N. T. Petty
	G-BFOU	Taylor JT.1 Monoplane	G. Bee
	G-BFOV	Cessna F.172N	D. J. Walker
	G-BFOZ	Thunder Ax6-56 balloon	R. L. Harbord

Reg.	Type	Owner or Operator	Notes
G-BFPA	Scheibe SF.25B Super Falke	Yorkshire Gliding Club (Pty) Ltd/ Sutton Bank	
G-BFPB	AA-5B Tiger	Guernsey Aero Club	
G-BFPH	Cessna F.172K	J. M. Reid	
G-BFPL	Fokker D.VII (replica) (4253/18)	A. E. Hutton/North Weald	
G-BFPM	Cessna F.172M	N. R. Havercroft	
G-BFPO	R. Commander 112B	J. G. Hale Ltd	
G-BFPP	Bell 47J-2	J. F. Kelly	
G-BFPS	PA-25 Pawnee 235D	Kent Gliding Club Ltd/Challock	
G-BFPZ	Cessna F.177RG	R. P. Nash/Norwich	
G-BFRA	R. Commander 114	Sabre Engines Ltd/Bournemouth	
G-BFRD	Bowers Flybaby 1A	F. R. Donaldson	
G-BFRF	Taylor JT.1 Monoplane	E. R. Bailey	
G-BFRI	Sikorsky S-61N	Bristow Helicopters Ltd	
G-BFRL	Cessna F.152	J. J. Baumhardt/Southend	
G-BFRM	Cessna 550 Citation II	Marshall of Cambridge (Engineering) Ltd	
G-BFRO	Cessna F.150M	Skyviews & General Ltd/Carlisle	
G-BFRR	Cessna FRA.150M	Interair Aviation Ltd/Bournemouth	
G-BFRS	Cessna F.172N	Poplar Toys Ltd	
G-BFRV	Cessna FA.152	Rogers Aviation Ltd/Cranfield	
G-BFRX	PA-25 Pawnee 260	Yorkshire Gliding Club (Pty) Ltd/ Sutton Bank	
G-BFRY	PA-25 Pawnee 260	B. Walker & Co (Dursley) Ltd	
G-BFSA	Cessna F.182Q	Clark Masts Ltd/Sandown	
G-BFSB	Cessna F.152	Seal Executive Aircraft Ltd/E. Midlands	
G-BFSC	PA-25 Pawnee 235D	Farm Aviation Services Ltd/Enstone	
G-BFSD	PA-25 Pawnee 235D	Deeside Gliding Club Ltd/Aboyne	
G-BFSK	PA-23 Apache 160 ★	Oxford Air Training School/Kidlington	
G-BFSR	Cessna F.150J	Air Fenland Ltd	
G-BFSS	Cessna FR.172G	Minerva Services	
G-BFSY	PA-28-181 Archer II	Downland Aviation/Goodwood	
G-BFTC	PA-28R-201T Turbo Arrow III	D. Hughes/Sherburn	
G-BFTF	AA-5B Tiger	F. C. Burrow Ltd/Leeds	
G-BFTG	AA-5B Tiger	D. Hepburn & G. R. Montgomery	
G-BFTH	Cessna F.172N	Bath Stone Co Ltd	
G-BFTT	Cessna 421C	P&B Metal Components Ltd/Manston	
G-BFTX	Cessna F.172N	E. Kent Flying Group	
G-BFTY	Cameron V-77 balloon	Regal Motors (Bilston) Ltd Regal Motors	
G-BFTZ	MS.880B Rallye Club	R. & B. Legge Ltd	
G-BFUB	PA-32RT-300 Lance II	Jolida Holdings Ltd	
G-BFUD	Scheibe SF.25E Super Falke	S. H. Hart	
G-BFUG	Cameron N-77 balloon	Headland Services Ltd	
G-BFUZ	Cameron V-77 balloon	Skysales Ltd	
G-BFVB	Boeing 737-204ADV	Britannia Airways Ltd Sir Thomas Sopwith/ Luton	
G-BFVF	PA-38-112 Tomahawk	Ipswich School of Flying Ltd	
G-BFVG	PA-28-181 Archer II	G-BFVG Flying Group/Blackpool	
G-BFVH	D.H.2 Replica (5894)	Wessex Aviation & Transport Ltd	
G-BFVI	H.S.125 Srs 700B	Bristow Helicopters Ltd	
G-BFVM	Westland-Bell 47G-3B1	K. R. Dossett	
G-BFVO	Partenavia P.68B	Travelair UK Ltd	
G-BFVP	PA-23 Aztec 250F	R. H. Bicker	
G-BFVS	AA-5B Tiger	S. W. Biroth & T. Chapman/Denham	
G-BFVU	Cessna 150L	Thruxton Flight Centre Ltd	
G-BFVV	SA.365C-3 Dauphin 2	Bond Helicopters Ltd	
G-BFVW	SA.365C-3 Dauphin 2	Bond Helicopters Ltd	
G-BFWB	PA-28-161 Warrior II	C.S.E. Aviation Ltd/Kidlington	
G-BFWD	Currie Wot	F. E. Nuthall	
G-BFWE	PA-23 Aztec 250E	Air Navigation & Trading Co Ltd/Blackpool	
G-BFWK	PA-28-161 Warrior II	Woodgate Air Services (IoM) Ltd	
G-BFWL	Cessna F.150L	Telair Manchester Ltd	
G-BFWW	Robin HR.100/210	Willingair Ltd	
G-BFXC	Mooney M.20C	Kent Engraving Ltd	
G-BFXD	PA-28-161 Warrior II	C.S.E. Aviation Ltd/Kidlington	
G-BFXE	PA-28-161 Warrior II	C.S.E. Aviation Ltd/Kidlington	
G-BFXF	Andreasson BA.4B	A. Brown/Sherburn	
G-BFXH	Cessna F.152	Aerohire Ltd/Halfpenny Green	
G-BFXI	Cessna F.172M	Thanet Electronics/Manston	
G-BFXK	PA-28 Cherokee 140	G. S. & Mrs M. T. Pritchard/Southend	
G-BFXL	Albatross D.5A (D5397/17)	FAA Museum/Yeovilton	
G-BFXR	Jodel D.112	G. Barthorpe	
G-BFXS	R. Commander 114	Keats Printing Ltd	
G-BFXW	AA-5B Tiger	Crosswind Aviation Ltd/Leeds	

Notes	Reg.	Type	Owner or Operator
	G-BFXX	AA-5B Tiger	M. J. Porter
	G-BFYA	MBB Bo 105D	Veritair Ltd
	G-BFYB	PA-28-161 Warrior II	C.S.E. Aviation Ltd/Kidlington
	G-BFYC	PA-32RT-300 Lance II	A. A. Barnes
	G-BFYE	Robin HR.100/285 ★	stored/Sywell
	G-BFYI	Westland-Bell 47G-3B1	B. Walker & Co (Dursley) Ltd
	G-BFYJ	Hughes 369HE	Krystle Aviation
	G-BFYL	Evans VP-2	A. G. Wilford
	G-BFYM	PA-28-161 Warrior II	C.S.E. Aviation Ltd/Kidlington
	G-BFYN	Cessna FA.152	Phoenix Flying Services Ltd/Glasgow
	G-BFYO	Spad XIII (replica) (3398) ★	FAA Museum/Yeovilton
	G-BFYP	Bensen B.7	A. J. Philpotts
	G-BFYU	SC.5 Belfast	HeavyLift Cargo Airlines Ltd/Stansted
	G-BFZB	Piper J-3C-85 Cub	Zebedee Flying Group/Shoreham
	G-BFZD	Cessna FR.182RG	R. B. Lewis & Co/Sleap
	G-BFZG	PA-28-161 Warrior II	C.S.E. Aviation Ltd/Kidlington
	G-BFZH	PA-28R Cherokee Arrow 200	K. E. Miles
	G-BFZL	V.836 Viscount	British Air Ferries Ltd/Southend
	G-BFZM	R. Commander 112TC	Rolls-Royce Ltd/Filton
	G-BFZN	Cessna FA.152	Falcon Flying Services/Biggin Hill
	G-BFZO	AA-5A Cheetah	Heald Air Ltd/Manchester
	G-BFZT	Cessna FA.152	One Zero One Three Ltd/Guernsey
	G-BFZU	Cessna FA.152	R. T. Love
	G-BFZV	Cessna F.172M	R. Thomas
	G-BGAA	Cessna 152 II	PJC Leasing Ltd
	G-BGAB	Cessna F.152 II	TG Aviation Ltd/Manston
	G-BGAD	Cessna F.152 II	J. G. Bell
	G-BGAE	Cessna F.152 II	Klingair Ltd/Conington
	G-BGAF	Cessna FA.152	Suffolk Aero Club Ltd/Ipswich
	G-BGAG	Cessna F.172N	Semloh Aviation Services/Andrewsfield
	G-BGAJ	Cessna F.182Q II	Ground Airport Services Ltd/Guernsey
	G-BGAK	Cessna F.182Q II	Safari World Services Ltd
	G-BGAU	Rearwin 9000L	T. G. Ratsey-Woodroffe/Sandown
	G-BGAX	PA-28 Cherokee 140	Devon School of Flying/Dunkeswell
	G-BGAY	Cameron O-77 balloon	S. W. C. & P. C. A. Hall
	G-BGAZ	Cameron V-77 balloon	Cameron Balloons Ltd Silicon Chip
	G-BGBA	Robin R.2100A	D. Faulkner/Redhill
	G-BGBC	L.1011-385 TriStar 200	British Airways St Andrews Bay
	G-BGBE	Jodel DR.1050	J. A. & B. Mawby
	G-BGBF	D.31A Turbulent	S. P. Wakeham
	G-BGBG	PA-28-181 Archer II	Harlow Printing Ltd/Newcastle
	G-BGBI	Cessna F.150L	Bugby Flying Group
	G-BGBK	PA-38-112 Tomahawk	F. Marshall & R. C. Priest/Netherthorpe
	G-BGBN	PA-38-112 Tomahawk	Leavesden Flight Centre Ltd
	G-BGBP	Cessna F.152	Stapleford Flying Club Ltd
	G-BGBR	Cessna F.172N	Falcon Flying Services/Biggin Hill
	G-BGBU	Auster AOP.9 (XN435)	P. Neilson
	G-BGBW	PA-38-112 Tomahawk	Truman Aviation Ltd/Tollerton
	G-BGBX	PA-38-112 Tomahawk	Ipswich School of Flying Ltd
	G-BGBY	PA-38-112 Tomahawk	Ravenair Ltd/Manchester
	G-BGBZ	R. Commander 114	R. S. Fenwick/Biggin Hill
	G-BGCG	Douglas C-47A	on rebuild
	G-BGCL	AA-5A Cheetah	AIG Air Services Ltd
	G-BGCM	AA-5A Cheetah	M. Swanborough
	G-BGCO	PA-44-180 Seminole	J. R. Henderson
	G-BGCX	Taylor JT.1 Monoplane	G. M. R. Walters
	G-BGCY	Taylor JT.1 Monoplane	M. T. Taylor
	G-BGDA	Boeing 737-236	British Airways River Tamar
	G-BGDB	Boeing 737-236	British Airways River Tweed
	G-BGDC	Boeing 737-236	British Airways River Humber
	G-BGDD	Boeing 737-236	British Airways River Tees
	G-BGDE	Boeing 737-236	British Airways River Avon
	G-BGDF	Boeing 737-236	British Airways River Thames
	G-BGDG	Boeing 737-236	British Airways River Medway
	G-BGDH	Boeing 737-236	British Airways River Clyde
	G-BGDI	Boeing 737-236	British Airways River Ouse
	G-BGDJ	Boeing 737-236	British Airways River Trent
	G-BGDK	Boeing 737-236	British Airways River Mersey
	G-BGDL	Boeing 737-236	British Airways River Don
	G-BGDN	Boeing 737-236	British Airways River Tyne
	G-BGDO	Boeing 737-236	British Airways River Usk
	G-BGDP	Boeing 737-236	British Airways River Taff

Reg.	Type	Owner or Operator	Notes
G-BGDR	Boeing 737-236	British Airways *River Bann*	
G-BGDS	Boeing 737-236	British Airways *River Severn*	
G-BGDT	Boeing 737-236	British Airways *River Forth*	
G-BGDU	Boeing 737-236	British Airways *River Dee*	
G-BGEA	Cessna F.150M	Agricultural & General Aviation Ltd	
G-BGED	Cessna U.206F	Peterborough Parachute Centre Ltd/ Sibson	
G-BGEE	Evans VP-1	D. P. Byatt	
G-BGEF	Jodel D.112	G. G. Johnson & S. J. Davies	
G-BGEH	Monnet Sonerai II	A. Dodd	
G-BGEI	Baby Great Lakes	K. A. Davies	
G-BGEK	PA-38-112 Tomahawk	Cheshire Flying Services Ltd/Manchester	
G-BGEL	PA-38-112 Tomahawk	Ravenair Ltd/Manchester	
G-BGEM	Partenavia P.68B	Meridian Air Services Ltd/Staverton	
G-BGEN	D.H.C.6 Twin Otter 310	Loganair Ltd/Glasgow	
G-BGEP	Cameron D-38 balloon	Cameron Balloons Ltd	
G-BGEW	SNCAN NC.854S	R. A. Yates	
G-BGEX	Brookland Mosquito 2	R. T. Gough	
G-BGFC	Evans VP-2	N. G. Abbott	
G-BGFF	FRED Srs 2	F. Bolton/Blackpool	
G-BGFG	AA-5A Cheetah	Fletcher Aviation Ltd/Biggin Hill	
G-BGFH	Cessna F.182Q	Sunseeker Leisure PLC	
G-BGFI	AA-5A Cheetah	I. J. Hay & A. Nayyar/Biggin Hill	
G-BGFJ	Jodel D.9 Bebe	C. M. Fitton	
G-BGFT	PA-34-200T Seneca II	C.S.E. Aviation Ltd/Kidlington	
G-BGFX	Cessna F.152	A. W. Fay/Cranfield	
G-BGGA	Bellanca 7GCBC Citabria	I. N. Jennison	
G-BGGB	Bellanca 7GCBC Citabria	M. D. Cowburn	
G-BGGC	Bellanca 7GCBC Citabria	R. P. Ashfield & J. P. Stone	
G-BGGD	Bellanca 8GCBC Scout	Bristol & Gloucestershire Gliding Club/ Nympsfield	
G-BGGE	PA-38-112 Tomahawk	Truman Aviation Ltd/Tollerton	
G-BGGF	PA-38-112 Tomahawk	Truman Aviation Ltd/Tollerton	
G-BGGG	PA-38-112 Tomahawk	Teesside Flight Centre Ltd	
G-BGGI	PA-38-112 Tomahawk	Truman Aviation Ltd/Tollerton	
G-BGGL	PA-38-112 Tomahawk	Pan-Air Ltd/Leavesden	
G-BGGM	PA-38-112 Tomahawk	Pan-Air Ltd/Leavesden	
G-BGGN	PA-38-112 Tomahawk	Domeastral Ltd/Elstree	
G-BGGO	Cessna F.152	E. Midlands Flying School Ltd	
G-BGGP	Cessna F.152	E. Midlands Flying School Ltd	
G-BGGT	Zenith CH.200	P. R. M. Nind	
G-BGGU	Wallis WA-116R-R	K. H. Wallis	
G-BGGV	Wallis WA-120 Srs 2	K. H. Wallis	
G-BGGW	Wallis WA-112	K. H. Wallis	
G-BGGY	AB-206B Jet Ranger ★	*Instructional airframe*/Cranfield	
G-BGHE	Convair L-13A	J. Davis/USA	
G-BGHF	Westland WG.30 ★	International Helicopter Museum/ Weston-s-Mare	
G-BGHI	Cessna F.152	Taxon Ltd/Shoreham	
G-BGHM	Robin R.1180T	H. Price	
G-BGHP	Beech 76 Duchess	Net Supply Co Ltd	
G-BGHS	Cameron N-31 balloon	W. R. Teasdale	
G-BGHT	Falconar F-12	C. R. Coates	
G-BGHU	NA T-6G Texan (115042)	C. E. Bellhouse	
G-BGHV	Cameron V-77 balloon	E. Davies	
G-BGHW	Thunder Ax8-90 balloon	Edinburgh University Balloon Group	
G-BGHY	Taylor JT.1 Monoplane	R. A. Hand	
G-BGHZ	FRED Srs 2	A. Smith	
G-BGIB	Cessna 152 II	Mona Aviation Ltd	
G-BGIC	Cessna 172N	T. R. Sinclair	
G-BGID	Westland-Bell 47G-3B1	M. J. Cuttell	
G-BGIG	PA-38-112 Tomahawk	Scotia Safari Ltd/Prestwick	
G-BGII	PA-32 Cherokee Six 300E	D. L. P. Milligan	
G-BGIO	Bensen B.8M	C. G. Johns	
G-BGIP	Colt 56A balloon	J. G. N. Perfect	
G-BGIU	Cessna F.172H	Metro Equipment (Chesham) Ltd/ Panshanger	
G-BGIV	Bell 47G-5	Abraxas Aviation Ltd	
G-BGIX	H.295 Super Courier	C. M. Lee/Andrewsfield	
G-BGIY	Cessna F.172N	G. Gormack/Glasgow	
G-BGIZ	Cessna F.152	Creaton Aviation Services Ltd	
G-BGJB	PA-44-180 Seminole	Oxford Management Ltd	
G-BGJE	Boeing 737-236	British Airways *River Wear*/Gatwick	

Notes	Reg.	Type	Owner or Operator
	G-BGJF	Boeing 737-236	British Airways *River Axe*/Gatwick
	G-BGJG	Boeing 737-236	British Airways *River Arun*/Gatwick
	G-BGJH	Boeing 737-236	British Airways *River Lyne*/Gatwick
	G-BGJI	Boeing 737-236	British Airways *River Wey*/Gatwick
	G-BGJJ	Boeing 737-236	British Airways *River Swale*/Gatwick
	G-BGJK	Boeing 737-236	British Airways *River Cherwell*/Gatwick
	G-BGJM	Boeing 737-236	British Airways *River Ribble*/Gatwick
	G-BGJU	Cameron V-65 Balloon	S. B. Sperring
	G-BGJW	GA-7 Cougar	Lambill Ltd
	G-BGKC	SOCATA Rallye 110ST	J. H. Cranmer & T. A. Timms
	G-BGKD	SOCATA Rallye 110ST	W. G. Dunn & A. G. Cameron
	G-BGKE	BAC One-Eleven 539GL	GEC Ferranti Defence Systems Ltd
	G-BGKJ	MBB Bo 105C	Bond Helicopters Ltd
	G-BGKM	SA.365C-3 Dauphin 2	Bond Helicopters Ltd
	G-BGKO	GY-20 Minicab	R. B. Webber
	G-BGKS	PA-28-161 Warrior II	Marnham Investments Ltd
	G-BGKT	Auster AOP.9 (XN441)	K. H. Wallis
	G-BGKU	PA-28R-201 Arrow III	Caplane Ltd
	G-BGKV	PA-28R-201 Arrow III	R. Haverson & R. G. Watson
	G-BGKY	PA-38-112 Tomahawk	Prospect Air Ltd
	G-BGKZ	J/5F Aiglet Trainer	J. K. Cook
	G-BGLA	PA-38-112 Tomahawk	Norwich School of Flying
	G-BGLB	Bede BD-5B	W. Sawney
	G-BGLE	Saffrey S.330 balloon	C. J. Dodd & ptnrs
	G-BGLF	Evans VP-1 Srs 2	M. Hartigan/Fenland
	G-BGLG	Cessna 152	Skyviews & General Ltd/Bourn
	G-BGLH	Cessna 152	Deltair Ltd/Chester
	G-BGLI	Cessna 152	Luton Flying Club (*stored*)
	G-BGLK	Monnet Sonerai II	N. M. Smorthit
	G-BGLN	Cessna FA.152	Bournemouth Flying Club
	G-BGLO	Cessna F.172N	A. H. Slaughter/Southend
	G-BGLS	Super Baby Great Lakes	J. F. Dowe
	G-BGLW	PA-34-200 Seneca	Stapleford Flying Club Ltd
	G-BGLX	Cameron N-56 balloon	Sara A. G. Williams
	G-BGLZ	Stits SA-3A Playboy	B. G. Ell
	G-BGMA	D.31 Turbulent	G. C. Masterton
	G-BGME	SIPA S.903	M. Emery (G-BCML)/Redhill
	G-BGMJ	GY-201 Minicab	S. L. Wakefield & ptnrs
	G-BGMN	H.S.748 Srs 2A	—
	G-BGMO	H.S.748 Srs 2A	—
	G-BGMP	Cessna F.172G	D. Rowe
	G-BGMR	GY-201 Minicab	T. J. D. Hodge & ptnrs
	G-BGMS	Taylor JT.2 Titch	M. A. J. Spice
	G-BGMT	MS.894E Rallye 235GT	M. E. Taylor
	G-BGMU	Westland-Bell 47G-3B1	V. L. J. & V. English
	G-BGMV	Scheibe SF.25B Falke	Mendip Falke Flying Group
	G-BGNB	Short SD3-30 Variant 100	Celtic Airways Ltd *Celtic Warrior*
	G-BGND	Cessna F.172N	Stansted Fluid Power (Products) Ltd
	G-BGNG	Short SD3-30	Gill Aviation Ltd/Newcastle
	G-BGNH	Short SD3-30	Gill Aviation Ltd/Newcastle
	G-BGNM	SA.365C-3 Dauphin 2	Bond Helicopters Ltd
	G-BGNR	Cessna F.172N	Picturama Group Ltd
	G-BGNT	Cessna F.152	Klingair Ltd/Conington
	G-BGNV	GA-7 Cougar	E. C. & C. E. E. Craven Walker
	G-BGNZ	Cessna FRA.150L	G. P. Grant-Suttie
	G-BGOD	Colt 77A balloon	C. Allen & M. D. Steuer
	G-BGOG	PA-28-161 Warrior II	W. D. Moore
	G-BGOI	Cameron O-56 balloon	S. H. Budd
	G-BGOL	PA-28R-201T Turbo Arrow III	Clark Aviation Services Ltd
	G-BGOM	PA-31-310 Turbo Navajo	Oxford Aero Charter Ltd/Kidlington
	G-BGON	GA-7 Cougar	BLS Aviation Ltd/Elstree
	G-BGOO	Colt 56 SS balloon	British Gas Corporation
	G-BGOP	Dassault Falcon 20F	Nissan (UK) Ltd/Heathrow
	G-BGOR	AT-6D Harvard III (14863)	M. L. Sargeant
	G-BGOX	PA-31-350 Navajo Chieftain	Woodgate Aviation (IoM) Ltd
	G-BGPA	Cessna 182Q	Guildcroft Enterprises Ltd
	G-BGPB	CCF T-6J Texan (20385)	Aircraft Restorations Ltd/Duxford
	G-BGPD	Piper J-3C-65 Cub	P. D. Whiteman
	G-BGPH	AA-5B Tiger	A. J. Dales
	G-BGPI	Plumb BGP-1	B. G. Plumb
	G-BGPJ	PA-28-161 Warrior II	W. Lancs Warrior Co Ltd
	G-BGPK	AA-5B Tiger	Ann Green Manufacturing Co Ltd/Elstree
	G-BGPL	PA-28-161 Warrior II	T. G. Aviation Ltd/Manston

Reg.	Type	Owner or Operator	Notes
G-BGPM	Evans VP-2	M. G. Reilly	
G-BGPN	PA-18 Super Cub 150	Clacton Aero Club (1988) Ltd	
G-BGPU	PA-28 Cherokee 140	Air Navigation & Trading Co Ltd/Blackpool	
G-BGPZ	M.S.890A Rallye Commodore	Popham Flying Group	
G-BGRC	PA-28 Cherokee 140	Arrow Air Centre Ltd/Shipdham	
G-BGRE	Beech A200 Super King Air	Martin-Baker (Engineering) Ltd/Chalgrove	
G-BGRG	Beech 76 Duchess	Arrows Aviation Co Ltd/Manchester	
G-BGRH	Robin DR.400/22	Rochester Aviation Ltd	
G-BGRI	Jodel DR.1051	B. Gunn & K. L. Burnett	
G-BGRK	PA-38-112 Tomahawk	Goodwood Terrena Ltd	
G-BGRL	PA-38-112 Tomahawk	Goodwood Terrena Ltd	
G-BGRM	PA-38-112 Tomahawk	Goodwood Terrena Ltd	
G-BGRN	PA-38-112 Tomahawk	Goodwood Terrena Ltd	
G-BGRO	Cessna F.172M	Northfield Garage Ltd/Prestwick	
G-BGRR	PA-38-112 Tomahawk	Prospect Air Ltd	
G-BGRS	Thunder Ax7-77Z balloon	W. & J. Evans	
G-BGRT	Steen Skybolt	R. C. Nichols & ptnrs/Stapleford	
G-BGRX	PA-38-112 Tomahawk	Leavesden Flight Centre Ltd	
G-BGSA	M.S.892E Rallye 150GT	Colin Draycott Group Ltd/Leicester	
G-BGSG	PA-44-180 Seminole	D. J. McSorley	
G-BGSH	PA-38-112 Tomahawk	Scotia Safari Ltd/Prestwick	
G-BGSI	PA-38-112 Tomahawk	Cheshire Flying Services Ltd/Manchester	
G-BGSJ	Piper J-3C-65 Cub	W. J. Higgins/Dunkeswell	
G-BGSM	M.S.892E Rallye 150GT	D. H. Rider & P. Curley	
G-BGSO	PA-31-310 Turbo Navajo	Everts Balloon Co Ltd	
G-BGST	Thunder Ax7-65 balloon	J. L. Bond	
G-BGSV	Cessna F.172N	Southwell Air Services Ltd	
G-BGSW	Beech F33 Debonair	Marketprior Ltd/Swansea	
G-BGSX	Cessna F.152	B. W. Wells & Burbage Farms Ltd	
G-BGSY	GA-7 Cougar	Van Allen Ltd/Guernsey	
G-BGTB	SOCATA TB.10 Tobago ★	D. Pope (stored)	
G-BGTC	Auster AOP.9 (XP282)	P. T. Bolton/Tollerton	
G-BGTF	PA-44-180 Seminole	New Guarantee Trust Properties Ltd	
G-BGTG	PA-23 Aztec 250F	R. J. Howard/Sherburn	
G-BGTI	Piper J-3C-65 Cub	A. P. Broad	
G-BGTJ	PA-28 Cherokee 180	Serendipity Aviation/Staverton	
G-BGTK	Cessna FR.182RG	Barmoor Aviation	
G-BGTP	Robin HR.100/210	J. C. Parker	
G-BGTR	PA-28 Cherokee 140	Liverpool Flying School Ltd	
G-BGTT	Cessna 310R	Aviation Beauport Ltd/Jersey	
G-BGTU	BAC One-Eleven 409AY	Turbo Union Ltd/Filton	
G-BGTX	Jodel D.117	Madley Flying Group/Shobdon	
G-BGUA	PA-38-112 Tomahawk	Rhodair Maintenance Ltd/Cardiff	
G-BGUB	PA-32 Cherokee Six 300E	R. Howton	
G-BGUY	Cameron V-56 balloon	J. L. Guy	
G-BGVB	Robin DR.315	Victor Bravo Group	
G-BGVE	CP.1310-C3 Super Emeraude	Victor Echo Group	
G-BGVH	Beech 76 Duchess	Velco Marketing	
G-BGVK	PA-28-161 Warrior II	D. S. Wells	
G-BGVL	PA-38-112 Tomahawk	R. A. Crook/Norwich	
G-BGVN	PA-28RT-201 Arrow IV	Essex Aviation Ltd/Stapleford	
G-BGVR	Thunder Ax6-56Z balloon	A. N. G. Howie	
G-BGVS	Cessna F.172M	P. D. A. Aviation Ltd/Tollerton	
G-BGVT	Cessna R.182RG	D. C. Massey	
G-BGVU	PA-28 Cherokee 180	P. E. Toleman	
G-BGVV	AA-5A Cheetah	A. H. McVicar	
G-BGVW	AA-5A Cheetah	Jetbonus Ltd/Biggin Hill	
G-BGVY	AA-5B Tiger	Porter Bell Ltd/Goodwood	
G-BGVZ	PA-28-181 Archer II	MS 124 Ltd	
G-BGWA	GA-7 Cougar	Lough Erne Aviation Ltd	
G-BGWC	Robin DR.400/180	E. F. Braddon & D. C. Shepherd/ Rochester	
G-BGWF	PA-18 Super Cub 150	D. B. Meeks	
G-BGWH	PA-18 Super Cub 150	Clacton Aero Club (1988) Ltd	
G-BGWI	Cameron V-65 balloon	Army Balloon Club/Germany	
G-BGWJ	Sikorsky S-61N	British Executive Air Services Ltd	
G-BGWK	Sikorsky S-61N	Bristow Helicopters Ltd	
G-BGWM	PA-28-181 Archer II	Thames Valley Flying Club Ltd	
G-BGWN	PA-38-112 Tomahawk	Teesside Flight Centre Ltd	
G-BGWO	Jodel D.112	K. McBride	
G-BGWS	Enstrom 280C Shark	I. J. & G. J. Wooldridge	
G-BGWU	PA-38-112 Tomahawk	R. J. Howard	
G-BGWV	Aeronca 7AC Champion	RFC Flying Group/Popham	

Notes	Reg.	Type	Owner or Operator
	G-BGWW	PA-23 Turbo Aztec 250E	L. B. Pegg
	G-BGWY	Thunder Ax6-56Z balloon	J. G. O'Connel
	G-BGWZ	Eclipse Super Eagle ★	FAA Museum/Yeovilton
	G-BGXA	Piper J-3C-65 Cub (329471)	K. Nicholls
	G-BGXB	PA-38-112 Tomahawk	AT Aviation Ltd/Cardiff
	G-BGXC	SOCATA TB.10 Tobago	N. N. Tullah/Cranfield
	G-BGXD	SOCATA TB.10 Tobago	Selles Dispensing Chemists Ltd
	G-BGXJ	Partenavia P.68B	Cecil Aviation Ltd/Cambridge
	G-BGXK	Cessna 310R	Air Service Training Ltd/Perth
	G-BGXL	Bensen B.8MV	B. P. Triefus
	G-BGXN	PA-38-112 Tomahawk	Panshanger School of Flying Ltd
	G-BGXO	PA-38-112 Tomahawk	Goodwood Terrena Ltd
	G-BGXP	Westland-Bell 47G-3B1	Ace Motor Salvage (Norfolk)
	G-BGXR	Robin HR.200/100	J. P. Kistner & E. G. Cleobury
	G-BGXS	PA-28-236 Dakota	Bawtry Road Service Station Ltd
	G-BGXT	SOCATA TB.10 Tobago	County Aviation Ltd/Halfpenny Green
	G-BGXU	WMB-1 balloon	C. J. Dodd & ptnrs
	G-BGXZ	Cessna FA.152	Alouette Flying Club Ltd/Biggin Hill
	G-BGYG	PA-28-161 Warrior II	C.S.E. Aviation Ltd/Kidlington
	G-BGYH	PA-28-161 Warrior II	C.S.E. Aviation Ltd/Kidlington
	G-BGYJ	Boeing 737-204	Britannia Airways Ltd *Sir Barnes Wallis*/Luton
	G-BGYK	Boeing 737-204	Britannia Airways Ltd *R. J. Mitchell*/Luton
	G-BGYL	Boeing 737-204	Britannia Airways Ltd *Jean Batten*/Luton
	G-BGYN	PA-18 Super Cub 150	A. G. Walker
	G-BGYR	H.S.125 Srs 600B	British Aerospace/Warton
	G-BGYT	EMB-110P1 Bandeirante	Business Air Travel
	G-BGYV	EMB-110P1 Bandeirante	Business Air Travel
	G-BGZF	PA-38-112 Tomahawk	Cambrian Flying Club/Swansea
	G-BGZJ	PA-38-112 Tomahawk	W. R. C. M. Foyle
	G-BGZK	Westland-Bell 47G-3B1	Dawnville Ltd
	G-BGZL	Eiri PIK-20E	G-BGZL Flying Group/Enstone
	G-BGZN	WMB.2 Windtracker balloon	S. R. Woolfries
	G-BGZO	M.S.880B Rallye Club	G-BGZO Flying Group
	G-BGZR	Meagher Model balloon Mk.1	S. C. Meagher
	G-BGZS	Keirs Heated Air Tube	M. N. J. Kirby
	G-BGZW	PA-38-112 Tomahawk	Ravenair Ltd/Manchester
	G-BGZY	Jodel D.120	M. Hale
	G-BGZZ	Thunder Ax6-56 balloon	J. M. Robinson
	G-BHAA	Cessna 152	Herefordshire Aero Club Ltd/Shobdon
	G-BHAC	Cessna A.152	Herefordshire Aero Club Ltd/Shobdon
	G-BHAD	Cessna A.152	Shropshire Aero Club Ltd/Sleap
	G-BHAF	PA-38-112 Tomahawk	Notelevel Ltd
	G-BHAI	Cessna F.152	P. P. D. Howard-Johnston/Edinburgh
	G-BHAJ	Robin DR.400/160	Rowantask Ltd
	G-BHAL	Rango Saffery S.200 SS	A. M. Lindsay *Anneky Panky*
	G-BHAM	Thunder Ax6-56 balloon	D. Sampson
	G-BHAR	Westland-Bell 47G-3B1	E. A. L. Sturmer
	G-BHAT	Thunder Ax7-77 balloon	C. P. Witter Ltd *Witter*
	G-BHAV	Cessna F.152	Iceni Leasing
	G-BHAW	Cessna F.172N	Jet Support Flying Centre/Manston
	G-BHAX	Enstrom F-28C-UK-2	PVS (Barnsley) Ltd
	G-BHAY	PA-28RT-201 Arrow IV	Alpha Yankee Group/Newcastle
	G-BHBA	Campbell Cricket	S. M. Irwin
	G-BHBB	Colt 77A balloon	S. D. Bellew/USA
	G-BHBE	Westland-Bell 47G-3B1 (Soloy)	T. R. Smith (Agricultural Machinery) Ltd
	G-BHBF	Sikorsky S-76A	Bristow Helicopters Ltd
	G-BHBG	PA-32R Cherokee Lance 300	R. W. F. Warner
	G-BHBI	Mooney M.20J	B. K. Arthur/Exeter
	G-BHBL	L.1011-385 TriStar 200	British Airways *Largs Bay*
	G-BHBM	L.1011-385 TriStar 200	British Airways *Poole Bay*
	G-BHBN	L.1011-385 TriStar 200	British Airways *Bideford Bay*
	G-BHBO	L.1011-385 TriStar 200	British Airways *St Magnus Bay*
	G-BHBR	L.1011-385 TriStar 200	British Airways *Bude Bay*
	G-BHBS	PA-28RT-201T Turbo Arrow IV	B. C. Oates/Barton
	G-BHBT	Marquart MA.5 Charger	R. G. & C. J. Maidment/Shoreham
	G-BHBZ	Partenavia P.68B	T. Hayselden (Doncaster) Ltd
	G-BHCC	Cessna 172M	T. Howard
	G-BHCE	Jodel D.112	D. M. Parsons
	G-BHCF	WMB.2 Windtracker balloon	C. J. Dodd & ptnrs
	G-BHCM	Cessna F.172H	The English Connection Ltd/Panshanger
	G-BHCP	Cessna F.152	Sherburn Aero Club Ltd

Reg.	Type	Owner or Operator	Notes
G-BHCW	PA-22 Tri-Pacer 150	B. Brooks	
G-BHCX	Cessna F.152	A. S. Bamrah/Biggin Hill	
G-BHCZ	PA-38-112 Tomahawk	J. E. Abbott	
G-BHDD	V.668 Varsity T.1 (WL626) ★	Aeropark/E. Midlands	
G-BHDE	SOCATA TB.10 Tobago	A. A. Dooley/Popham	
G-BHDH	Douglas DC-10-30	British Airways Benmore Forest/Gatwick	
G-BHDI	Douglas DC-10-30	British Airways Forest of Ae/Gatwick	
G-BHDJ	Douglas DC-10-30	British Airways Glen Cap Forest/Gatwick	
G-BHDK	Boeing B-29A-BN (461748) ★	Imperial War Museum/Duxford	
G-BHDM	Cessna F.152 II	Tayside Aviation Ltd/Dundee	
G-BHDP	Cessna F.182Q II	R. J. D. Rimmer/Elstree	
G-BHDR	Cessna F.152 II	Tayside Aviation Ltd/Dundee	
G-BHDS	Cessna F.152 II	Tayside Aviation Ltd/Dundee	
G-BHDT	SOCATA TB.10 Tobago	R. D. Hill	
G-BHDU	Cessna F.152 II	Falcon Flying Services/Biggin Hill	
G-BHDV	Cameron V-77 balloon	P. Glydon	
G-BHDW	Cessna F.152	Tayside Aviation Ltd/Dundee	
G-BHDX	Cessna F.172N	Skyhawk DX Group	
G-BHDZ	Cessna F.172N	J. B. Roberts	
G-BHEC	Cessna F.152	W. R. C. Foyle	
G-BHED	Cessna FA.152	TG Aviation Ltd/Manston	
G-BHEG	Jodel D.150	P. R. Underhill	
G-BHEH	Cessna 310G	Thorney Machinery Co Ltd/Conington	
G-BHEK	CP.1315-C3 Super Emeraude	D. B. Winstanley/Barton	
G-BHEL	Jodel D.117	J. F. Dowe	
G-BHEM	Bensen B.8M	A. M. Sands	
G-BHEN	Cessna FA.152	Leicestershire Aero Club Ltd	
G-BHEO	Cessna FR.182RG	M. C. Costin	
G-BHEP	Cessna 172 RG Cutlass	Full Sutton Flying Centre Ltd	
G-BHER	SOCATA TB.10 Tobago	Vale Aviation Ltd	
G-BHET	SOCATA TB.10 Tobago	Claude Hooper Ltd	
G-BHEU	Thunder Ax7-65 balloon	M. H. R. Govett	
G-BHEV	PA-28R Cherokee Arrow 200	E. & G. H. Kelk	
G-BHEX	Colt 56A balloon	A. S. Dear & ptnrs Super Wasp	
G-BHEZ	Jodel D.150	D. R. Elpick/O. Warden	
G-BHFC	Cessna F.152	T. G. Aviation Ltd/Manston	
G-BHFE	PA-44-180 Seminole	Grunwick Ltd/Elstree	
G-BHFF	Jodel D.112	P. J. Swain	
G-BHFG	SNCAN Stampe SV-4C (45)	Stormswift Ltd	
G-BHFH	PA-34-200T Seneca II	Hendefern Ltd/Goodwood	
G-BHFI	Cessna F.152	BAe (Warton) Flying Group/Blackpool	
G-BHFJ	PA-28RT-201T Turbo Arrow IV	T. L. P. Delaney	
G-BHFK	PA-28-151 Warrior	Ilkeston Car Sales Ltd	
G-BHFM	Murphy S.200 balloon	M. Murphy	
G-BHFR	Eiri PIK-20E-1	J. MacWilliam & T. Dalrymple-Smith	
G-BHFS	Robin DR.400/180	Flair (Soft Drinks) Ltd/Shoreham	
G-BHGA	PA-31-310 Turbo Navajo	Heltor Ltd	
G-BHGC	PA-18 Super Cub 150	D. E. Schofield	
G-BHGF	Cameron V-56 balloon	P. J. Smart	
G-BHGJ	Jodel D.120	Q. M. B. Oswell	
G-BHGK	Sikorsky S-76A	Bond Helicopters Ltd	
G-BHGM	Beech 76 Duchess	T. Hayselden	
G-BHGO	PA-32 Cherokee Six 260	Sydney House Communities/Manston	
G-BHGP	SOCATA TB.10 Tobago	C. Flanagan	
G-BHGX	Colt 56B balloon	M. N. Dixon	
G-BHGY	PA-28R Cherokee Arrow 200	V. Humphries/Gamston	
G-BHHB	Cameron V-77 balloon	R. Powell & K. G. Betts	
G-BHHE	Jodel DR.1051/M1	P. Bridges	
G-BHHG	Cessna F.152	Northamptonshire School of Flying Ltd/ Sywell	
G-BHHH	Thunder Ax7-65 balloon	C. A. Hendley (Essex) Ltd	
G-BHHI	Cessna F.152	Semloh Aviation Services/Andrewsfield	
G-BHHK	Cameron N-77 balloon	S. Bridge & ptnrs	
G-BHHN	Cameron V-77 balloon	Itchen Valley Balloon Group	
G-BHHU	Short SD3-30	Celtic Airways Ltd	
G-BHHX	Jodel D.112	C. F. Walter	
G-BHHZ	Rotorway Scorpion 133	L. W. & O. Usherwood	
G-BHIA	Cessna F.152	W. H. Wilkins/Stapleford	
G-BHIB	Cessna F.182Q	Gogood Ltd	
G-BHIC	Cessna F.182Q	General Building Services Ltd/Leeds	
G-BHIH	Cessna F.172N	Merlin Marine Aviation (Jersey) Ltd	
G-BHII	Cameron V-77 balloon	R. V. Brown	
G-BHIJ	Eiri PIK-20E-1	R. W. Hall & ptnrs/Swanton Morley	

Notes	Reg.	Type	Owner or Operator
	G-BHIK	Adam RA-14 Loisirs	L. Lewis
	G-BHIN	Cessna F.152	P. Skinner/Netherthorpe
	G-BHIR	PA-28R Cherokee Arrow 200	Cheshire Flying Services Ltd/Manchester
	G-BHIS	Thunder Ax7-65 balloon	Hedgehoppers Balloon Group
	G-BHIT	SOCATA TB.9 Tampico	Air Touring Services Ltd/Biggin Hill
	G-BHIY	Cessna F.150K	Westfield Flying Group
	G-BHJA	Cessna A.152	Cornwall Flying Club Ltd/Bodmin
	G-BHJB	Cessna A.152	Thruxton Flight Centre Ltd
	G-BHJF	SOCATA TB.10 Tobago	D. G. Dedman/Leavesden
	G-BHJI	Mooney M.20J	Christian Newman Aviation
	G-BHJK	Maule M5-235C Lunar Rocket	P. F. Hall & R. L. Sambell/Coventry
	G-BHJN	Fournier RF-4D	R. G. Trute
	G-BHJO	PA-28-161 Warrior II	Nairn Flying Services Ltd/Inverness
	G-BHJS	Partenavia P.68B	Sound Technology PLC
	G-BHJU	Robin DR.400/2+2	Harlow Transport Services Ltd/Headcorn
	G-BHJZ	EMB-110P2 Bandeirante	Streamline Aviation/E. Midlands
	G-BHKA	Evans VP-1	M. L. Perry
	G-BHKH	Cameron O-65 balloon	D. G. Body
	G-BHKJ	Cessna 421C	Crosslee PLC
	G-BHKR	Colt 12A balloon ★	British Balloon Museum
	G-BHKT	Jodel D.112	M. L. & P. J. Moore
	G-BHKV	AA-5A Cheetah	Alouette Flying Club Ltd/Biggin Hill
	G-BHKX	Beech 76 Duchess	Jetstream Air Couriers Ltd
	G-BHKY	Cessna 310R II	Air Service Training Ltd/Perth
	G-BHLE	Robin DR.400/180	L. H. Mayall
	G-BHLF	H.S.125 Srs 700B	MAGEC Aviation Ltd/Luton
	G-BHLH	Robin DR.400/180	Trinecare Ltd/Southend
	G-BHLJ	Saffery-Rigg S.200 balloon	I. A. Rigg
	G-BHLK	GA-7 Cougar	Autair Ltd
	G-BHLT	D.H.82A Tiger Moth	P. J. & A. J. Borsberry
	G-BHLU	Fournier RF-3	M. C. Roper
	G-BHLW	Cessna 120	R. E. & E. P. Nerou
	G-BHLX	AA-5B Tiger	Tiger Aviation (Jersey) Ltd
	G-BHLY	Sikorsky S-76A	Bristow Helicopters Ltd
	G-BHMA	SIPA 903	H. J. Taggart
	G-BHMC	M.S.880B Rallye Club	The G-BHMC Group
	G-BHME	WMB.2 Windtracker balloon	I. R. Bell & ptnrs
	G-BHMG	Cessna FA.152	R. D. Smith
	G-BHMI	Cessna F.172N	W. Lancashire Aero Club Ltd (G-WADE)/ Blackpool
	G-BHMJ	Avenger T.200-2112 balloon	R. Light *Lord Anthony 1*
	G-BHMK	Avenger T.200-2112 balloon	P. Kinder *Lord Anthony 2*
	G-BHML	Avenger T.200-2112 balloon	L. Caulfield *Lord Anthony 3*
	G-BHMM	Avenger T.200-2112 balloon	M. Murphy *Lord Anthony 4*
	G-BHMO	PA-20M Cerpa Special (Pacer)	A. B. Holloway & ptnrs
	G-BHMT	Evans VP-1	P. E. J. Sturgeon
	G-BHMU	Colt 21A balloon	J. R. Parkington & Co Ltd
	G-BHMW	F.27 Friendship Mk 200	Air UK *Amy Johnson*/Norwich
	G-BHMX	F.27 Friendship Mk 200	Air UK *Fred Truman*/Norwich
	G-BHMY	F.27 Friendship Mk 200	Air UK/Norwich
	G-BHMZ	F.27 Friendship Mk 200	Air UK *R. J. Mitchell*/Norwich
	G-BHNA	Cessna F.152	Sheffield Aero Club Ltd/Netherthorpe
	G-BHNC	Cameron O-65 balloon	D. & C. Bareford
	G-BHND	Cameron N-65 balloon	Hunter & Sons (Wells) Ltd
	G-BHNL	Jodel D.112	G. van der Gaag
	G-BHNM	PA-44-180 Seminole	Standby One Flight Services Ltd
	G-BHNO	PA-28-181 Archer II	Davison Plant Hire Co/Compton Abbas
	G-BHNP	Eiri PIK-20E-1	J. T. Morgan
	G-BHNU	Cessna F.172N	B. Swindell (Haulage) Ltd/Barton
	G-BHNV	Westland-Bell 47G-3B1	Leyline Helicopters Ltd
	G-BHNX	Jodel D.117	R. V. Rendall
	G-BHOA	Robin DR.400/160	Ferguson Aviation Ltd
	G-BHOF	Sikorsky S-61N	Bristow Helicopters Ltd
	G-BHOG	Sikorsky S-61N	Bristow Helicopters Ltd
	G-BHOH	Sikorsky S-61N	Bristow Helicopters Ltd
	G-BHOL	Jodel DR.1050	D. G. Hart
	G-BHOM	PA-18 Super Cub 95	C. H. A. Bott
	G-BHOO	Thunder Ax7-65 balloon	D. Livesey & J. M. Purves *Scraps*
	G-BHOP	Thunder Ax3 balloon	B. Meeson
	G-BHOR	PA-28-161 Warrior II.	Oscar Romeo Flying Group/Biggin Hill
	G-BHOT	Cameron V-65 balloon	Dante Balloon Group
	G-BHOU	Cameron V-65 balloon	F. W. Barnes
	G-BHOW	Beech 95-58PA Baron	Anglo-African Machinery Ltd/Coventry

Reg.	Type	Owner or Operator	Notes
G-BHOZ	SOCATA TB.9 Tampico	M. Brown	
G-BHPJ	Eagle Microlite	G. Breen/Enstone	
G-BHPK	Piper J-3C-65 Cub (236800)	H. W. Sage/Sywell	
G-BHPL	C.A.S.A. 1.131E Jungmann	M. G. Jeffries	
G-BHPM	PA-18 Super Cub 95	P. I. Morgans	
G-BHPO	Colt 14A balloon	C. J. Boxall	
G-BHPS	Jodel D.120A	C. J. Francis/Swansea	
G-BHPT	Piper J-3C-65 Cub	D. I. Cooke	
G-BHPX	Cessna 152	J. A. Pothecary/Shoreham	
G-BHPY	Cessna 152	Christopher Lunn & Co	
G-BHPZ	Cessna 172N	O'Brian Properties Ltd/Redhill	
G-BHRA	R. Commander 114A	P. A. Warner	
G-BHRB	Cessna F.152	Telair Manchester Ltd	
G-BHRC	PA-28-161 Warrior II	Sherwood Flying Club Ltd/Tollerton	
G-BHRD	D.H.C.1 Chipmunk 22 (WP977)	A. J. Dunstan & P. R. Joshua/Kidlington	
G-BHRH	Merlin Flying Club Ltd/Hucknall		
G-BHRI	Saffery S.200 balloon	N. J. & H. L. Dunnington	
G-BHRM	Cessna F.152	Aerohire Ltd/Halfpenny Green	
G-BHRN	Cessna F.152	J. Easson/Edinburgh	
G-BHRO	R. Commander 112A	John Raymond Transport Ltd/Cardiff	
G-BHRP	PA-44-180 Seminole	BLS Aviation Ltd/Elstree	
G-BHRR	CP.301A Emeraude	T. W. Offen	
G-BHRW	Jodel DR.221	J. D. Hunter & M. A. Britton	
G-BHRY	Colt 56A balloon	A. S. Davidson	
G-BHSA	Cessna 152	Skyviews & General Ltd/Sherburn	
G-BHSB	Cessna 172N	Saunders Caravans Ltd	
G-BHSD	Scheibe SF.25E Super Falke	Lasham Gliding Soc Ltd	
G-BHSE	R. Commander 114	604 Sqdn Flying Group Ltd	
G-BHSL	C.A.S.A. 1.131 Jungmann	Cotswold Flying Group/Badminton	
G-BHSN	Cameron N-56 balloon	I. Bentley	
G-BHSP	Thunder Ax7-77Z balloon	Out-Of-The-Blue	
G-BHSS	Pitts S-1C Special	C. I. Fray	
G-BHST	Hughes 369D	Acme Jewellery Ltd	
G-BHSU	H.S.125 Srs 700B	Shell Aircraft Ltd/Heathrow	
G-BHSV	H.S.125 Srs 700B	Shell Aircraft Ltd/Heathrow	
G-BHSW	H.S.125 Srs 700B	Shell Aircraft Ltd/Heathrow	
G-BHSY	Jodel DR.1050	S. R. Orwin & T. R. Allebone	
G-BHTA	PA-28-236 Dakota	Stenloss Ltd/Sywell	
G-BHTC	Jodel DR.1050/M1	D. Masterson & ptnrs/Blackpool	
G-BHTD	Cessna T.188C AgHusky	ADS (Aerial) Ltd/Southend	
G-BHTG	Thunder Ax6-56 balloon	F. R. & Mrs S. H. MacDonald	
G-BHTH	T-6G Texan (2807)	A. Reynard/Kidlington	
G-BHTJ	H.S.125 Srs 700B	British Aerospace PLC (G-BRDI/ G-HHOI)	
G-BHTM	Cameron 80 Can SS balloon	BP Oil Ltd	
G-BHTR	Bell 206B JetRanger 3	Huktra (UK) Ltd	
G-BHTT	Cessna 500 Citation	Paycourt Ltd	
G-BHTV	Cessna 310R	Brenair Ltd/Cardiff	
G-BHUB	Douglas C-47A (315509) ★	Imperial War Museum/Duxford	
G-BHUE	Jodel DR.1050	M. J. Harris	
G-BHUG	Cessna 172N	Property Maintenance File	
G-BHUI	Cessna 152	Cheshire Air Training School Ltd	
G-BHUJ	Cessna 172N	Three Counties Aero Engineering Ltd/ Lasham	
G-BHUM	D.H.82A Tiger Moth	S. G. Towers	
G-BHUO	Evans VP-2	D. Harker	
G-BHUP	Cessna F.152	Stapleford Flying Club Ltd	
G-BHUR	Thunder Ax3 balloon	B. F. G. Ribbons	
G-BHUU	PA-25 Pawnee 235	Pawnee Aviation/Boston	
G-BHVB	PA-28-161 Warrior II	Bobbington Air Training School Ltd/ Halfpenny Green	
G-BHVC	Cessna 172RG Cutlass	I. B. Willis/Panshanger	
G-BHVE	Saffery S.330 balloon	P. M. Randles	
G-BHVF	Jodel D.150A	C. A. Parker & ptnrs/Sywell	
G-BHVN	Cessna 152	Three Counties Aero Engineering Ltd/ Lasham	
G-BHVP	Cessna 182Q	Air Tows/Lasham	
G-BHVR	Cessna 172N	Three Counties Aero Engineering Ltd/ Lasham	
G-BHVV	Piper J-3C-65 Cub	W. A. N. Jenkins	
G-BHVZ	Cessna 180	R. Moore/Blackpool	
G-BHWA	Cessna F.152	Wickenby Aviation Ltd	
G-BHWB	Cessna F.152	Wickenby Aviation Ltd	

Notes	Reg.	Type	Owner or Operator
	G-BHWE	Boeing 737-204ADV	Britannia Airways Ltd/*Sir Sidney Camm*/ Luton
	G-BHWF	Boeing 737-204ADV	Britannia Airways Ltd/*Lord Brabazon of Tara*/ Luton
	G-BHWG	Mahatma S.200SR balloon	H. W. Gandy *Spectrum*
	G-BHWH	Weedhopper JC-24A	G. A. Clephane
	G-BHWK	M.S.880B Rallye Club	Arrow Flying Group
	G-BHWN	WMB.3 Windtracker 200 balloon	C. J. Dodd & G. J. Luckett
	G-BHWS	Cessna F.152	Turnhouse Flying Club
	G-BHWW	Cessna U.206G	Fife Airport Management Ltd
	G-BHWY	PA-28R Cherokee Arrow 200-II	Piper Arrow Group
	G-BHWZ	PA-28-181 Archer II	I. R. McCue
	G-BHXA	SA Bulldog Srs 120/1210	AW Aviation Ltd
	G-BHXB	SA Bulldog Srs 120/1210	AW Aviation Ltd
	G-BHXD	Jodel D.120	K. B. Sutton & D. R. Taylor/Cranfield
	G-BHXK	PA-28 Cherokee 140	GXK Flying Group
	G-BHXL	Evans VP-2	R. S. Wharton
	G-BHXS	Jodel D.120	I. R. Willis
	G-BHXT	Thunder Ax6-56Z balloon	Ocean Traffic Services Ltd
	G-BHXU	AB-206B JetRanger 3	Castle Air Charters Ltd
	G-BHXV	AB-206B JetRanger 3	Compass Aviation Ltd (G-OWJM)
	G-BHXY	Piper J-3C-65 Cub (44-79609)	Grasshopper Flyers
	G-BHYA	Cessna R.182RG II	Stainless Steel Profile Cutters Ltd
	G-BHYB	Sikorsky S-76A	British International Helicopters Ltd/ Beccles
	G-BHYC	Cessna 172RG Cutlass	J. D. B. Hamilton & J. McW. Henderson
	G-BHYD	Cessna R.172K XP II	Sylmar Aviation Services Ltd
	G-BHYE	PA-34-200T Seneca II	C.S.E. Aviation Ltd/Kidlington
	G-BHYF	PA-34-200T Seneca II	C.S.E. Aviation Ltd/Kidlington
	G-BHYG	PA-34-200T Seneca II	C.S.E. Aviation Ltd/Kidlington
	G-BHYI	SNCAN Stampe SV-4A	P. A. Irwin
	G-BHYN	Evans VP-2	D. Cromie
	G-BHYO	Cameron N-77 balloon	C. Sisson
	G-BHYP	Cessna F.172M	G-BHYP Flying Group/Blackpool
	G-BHYR	Cessna F.172M	Alumvale Ltd/Stapleford
	G-BHYV	Evans VP-1	L. Chiappi/Blackpool
	G-BHYW	AB-206B JetRanger	Lakeside Helicopters Ltd
	G-BHYX	Cessna 152 II	Stapleford Flying Club Ltd
	G-BHZE	PA-28-181 Archer II	Northfield Garage Ltd
	G-BHZF	Evans VP-2	P. Jenkins
	G-BHZH	Cessna F.152	Havelet Leasing Ltd
	G-BHZK	AA-5B Tiger	N. K. Margolis/Elstree
	G-BHZM	Jodel DR.1050	G. H. Wylde/Manchester
	G-BHZO	AA-5A Cheetah	Scotia Safari Ltd/Prestwick
	G-BHZR	SA Bulldog Srs 120/1210	AW Aviation Ltd
	G-BHZS	SA Bulldog Srs 120/1210	AW Aviation Ltd
	G-BHZT	SA Bulldog Srs 120/1210	AW Aviation Ltd
	G-BHZU	Piper J-3C-65 Cub	J. K. Tomkinson
	G-BHZV	Jodel D.120A	J. G. Munro/Perth
	G-BHZX	Thunder Ax7-65A balloon	R. J. & H. M. Beattie
	G-BIAA	SOCATA TB.9 Tampico	T. Smith
	G-BIAB	SOCATA TB.9 Tampico	H. W. A. Thirlway
	G-BIAC	SOCATA Rallye 235E	Anpal Finance Ltd & Aerial Facilities Ltd/ Biggin Hill
	G-BIAH	Jodel D.112	D. Mitchell
	G-BIAI	WMB.2 Windtracker balloon	I. Chadwick
	G-BIAK	SOCATA TB.10 Tobago	Trent Combustion Components Ltd/ Tollerton
	G-BIAL	Rango NA.8 balloon	A. M. Lindsay
	G-BIAO	Evans VP-2	P. J. Hall
	G-BIAP	PA-16 Clipper	I. M. Callier & P. J. Bish/White Waltham
	G-BIAR	Rigg Skyliner II balloon	I. A. Rigg
	G-BIAU	Sopwith Pup Replica (N6452)	FAA Museum/Yeovilton
	G-BIAV	Sikorsky S-76A	British International Helicopters Ltd
	G-BIAW	Sikorsky S-76A	British International Helicopters Ltd
	G-BIAX	Taylor JT.2 Titch	G. F. Rowley
	G-BIAY	AA-5 Traveler	M. D. Dupay & ptnrs
	G-BIBA	SOCATA TB.9 Tampico	TB Aviation Ltd
	G-BIBB	Mooney M.20C	J. R. Gardiner
	G-BIBC	Cessna 310R	Air Service Training Ltd/Perth
	G-BIBD	Rotec Rally 2B	A. Clarke
	G-BIBG	Sikorsky S-76A	Bristow Helicopters Ltd

Reg.	Type	Owner or Operator	Notes
G-BIBJ	Enstrom 280C-UK-2 Shark	Tindon Ltd/Little Snoring	
G-BIBK	Taylor JT.2 Titch	J. G. McTaggart	
G-BIBN	Cessna FA.150K	P. H. Lewis	
G-BIBO	Cameron V-65 balloon	I. Harris	
G-BIBP	AA-5A Cheetah	Scotia Safari Ltd/Prestwick	
G-BIBS	Cameron P-20 balloon	Cameron Balloons Ltd	
G-BIBT	AA-5B Tiger	Fergusons (Blyth) Ltd/Newcastle	
G-BIBU	Morris Ax7-77 balloon	K. Morris	
G-BIBV	WMB.3 Windtracker balloon	P. B. Street	
G-BIBW	Cessna F.172N	Deltair Ltd/Chester	
G-BIBX	WMB.2 Windtracker balloon	I. A. Rigg	
G-BIBY	Beech F33A Bonanza	Baythorne Ltd/Fairoaks	
G-BIBZ	Thunder Ax3 balloon	F. W. Barnes	
G-BICB	Rotec Rally 2B	J. D. Lye & A. P. Jones	
G-BICC	Vulture Tx3 balloon	C. P. Clitheroe	
G-BICD	Auster 5	R. T. Parsons	
G-BICE	AT-6C Harvard IIA (41-33275)	C. M. L. Edwards/Ipswich	
G-BICG	Cessna F.152	Falcon Flying Services/Biggin Hill	
G-BICJ	Monnet Sonerai II	D. J. Marks	
G-BICM	Colt 56A balloon	Avon Advertiser Balloon Club	
G-BICN	F.8L Falco	R. J. Barber	
G-BICP	Robin DR.360	Bravo India Flying Group/Woodvale	
G-BICR	Jodel D.120A	Beehive Flying Group/White Waltham	
G-BICS	Robin R.2100A	G-BICS Group/Sibson	
G-BICT	Evans VP-1	A. S. Coombe & D. L. Tribe	
G-BICU	Cameron V-56 balloon	K. C. Tanner	
G-BICW	PA-28-161 Warrior II	T. W. Aisthorpe/Exeter	
G-BICX	Maule M5-235C Lunar Rocket	A. T. Jeans & I. Best-Devereux/Old Sarum	
G-BICY	PA-23 Apache 160	A. M. Lynn/Sibson	
G-BIDD	Evans VP-1	J. E. Wedgbury	
G-BIDE	CP.301A Emeraude	D. Elliott	
G-BIDF	Cessna F.172P	J. J. Baumhardt/Southend	
G-BIDG	Jodel D.150A	D. R. Gray/Barton	
G-BIDI	PA-28R-201 Arrow III	LBE Contract Tooling Ltd	
G-BIDJ	PA-18A Super Cub 150	AB Plant (Bristol) Ltd	
G-BIDK	PA-18 Super Cub 150	Scottish Gliding Union Ltd	
G-BIDM	Cessna F.172H	D. A. Mortimore/Humberside	
G-BIDO	CP.301A Emeraude	A. R. Plumb	
G-BIDP	PA-28-181 Archer II	H. S. Elkins/Bristol	
G-BIDU	Cameron V-77 balloon	E. Eleazor	
G-BIDV	Colt 14A balloon	International Distillers & Vintners (House Trade) Ltd	
G-BIDW	Sopwith 11/2 Strutter replica (A8226) ★	RAF Museum/Hendon	
G-BIDX	Jodel D.112	H. N. Nuttall & R. P. Walley	
G-BIDY	WMB.2 Windtracker balloon	D. M. Campion	
G-BIEC	AB-206A JetRanger 2	Autair Helicopters Ltd	
G-BIEF	Cameron V-77 balloon	D. S. Bush	
G-BIEH	Sikorsky S-76A	Bond Helicopters Ltd/Bourn	
G-BIEJ	Sikorsky S-76A	Bristow Helicopters Ltd	
G-BIEK	WMB.4 Windtracker balloon	P. B. Street	
G-BIEN	Jodel D.120A	Echo November Flight/Bristol	
G-BIEO	Jodel D.112	Woodside Flying Group	
G-BIEP	PA-28-181 Archer II	Bickerton Aerodromes Ltd	
G-BIES	Maule M5-235C Lunar Rocket	William Proctor Farms	
G-BIET	Cameron O-77 balloon	G. M. Westley	
G-BIEY	PA-28-151 Warrior	J. A. Pothecary/Shoreham	
G-BIFA	Cessna 310R-II	E. A. Pitcher	
G-BIFB	PA-28 Cherokee 150	C. J. Reed/Elstree	
G-BIFD	R. Commander 114	D. F. Soul	
G-BIFH	Short SD3-30	Gill Air Ltd/Newcastle	
G-BIFK	Short SD3-30	Gill Aviation Ltd/Newcastle	
G-BIFN	Bensen B.8M	B. Gunn	
G-BIFO	Evans VP-1	D. J. Rees	
G-BIFP	Colt 56C balloon	J. Philp	
G-BIFT	Cessna F.150L	Colton Aviation Ltd	
G-BIFV	Jodel D.150	J. H. Kirkham/Barton	
G-BIFY	Cessna F.150L	Colton Aviation Ltd	
G-BIFZ	Partenavia P.68C	ALY Aviation Ltd/Henstridge	
G-BIGD	Cameron V-77 balloon	D. L. Clark Frog	
G-BIGF	Thunder Ax7-77 balloon	M. D. Stever & C. A. Allen	
G-BIGH	Piper J-3C-65 Cub	W. McNally	
G-BIGJ	Cessna F.172M	Clacton Aero Club (1988) Ltd	
G-BIGK	Taylorcraft BC-12D	H. L. M. & G. R. Williams	

Notes	Reg.	Type	Owner or Operator
	G-BIGL	Cameron O-65 balloon	P. L. Mossman
	G-BIGM	Avenger T.200-2112 balloon	M. Murphy
	G-BIGN	Attic Srs 1 balloon	G. P. Nettleship
	G-BIGP	Bensen B.8M	R. H. S. Cooper
	G-BIGR	Avenger T.200-2112 balloon	R. Light
	G-BIGX	Bensen B.8M	P. R. Moore & M. B. Stone
	G-BIGY	Cameron V-65 balloon	Dante Balloon Group
	G-BIGZ	Scheibe SF.25B Falke	K. Ballington
	G-BIHD	Robin DR.400/160	Alexander Howden Group Sports & Social Club/Biggin Hill
	G-BIHE	Cessna FA.152	Inverness Flying Services Ltd
	G-BIHF	SE-5A (replica) (F943)	K. J. Garrett Lady Di/Booker
	G-BIHG	PA-28 Cherokee 140	T. M. Plewman
	G-BIHI	Cessna 172M	J. H. Ashley-Rogers
	G-BIHN	Skyship 500 airship	Airship Industries Ltd/Cardington
	G-BIHO	D.H.C.6 Twin Otter 310	Aeronautical Services Ltd
	G-BIHP	Van Den Bemden gas balloon	J. J. Harris
	G-BIHT	PA-17 Vagabond	G. H. Cork/Burnaston
	G-BIHU	Saffery S.200 balloon	B. L. King
	G-BIHW	Aeronca A65TAC Defender	T. J. Ingrouille
	G-BIHY	Isaacs Fury	P. C. Butler
	G-BIIA	Fournier RF-3	T. M. W. Webster
	G-BIIB	Cessna F.172M	Civil Service Flying Club (Biggin Hill) Ltd
	G-BIID	PA-18 Super Cub 95	875 (Westhill) Squadron ATC/Aberdeen
	G-BIIE	Cessna F.172P	Shoreham Flight Simulation Ltd/Bournemouth
	G-BIIF	Fournier RF-4D	J. A. Bridges & J. A. Taylor (G-BVET)/Biggin Hill
	G-BIIG	Thunder Ax-6-56Z balloon	Chiltern Flyers Ltd
	G-BIIJ	Cessna F.152 II	Leicestershire Aero Club Ltd
	G-BIIK	M.S.883 Rallye 115	Chiltern Flyers Ltd
	G-BIIL	Thunder Ax6-56 balloon	G. W. Reader
	G-BIIT	PA-28-161 Warrior II	Tayside Aviation Ltd/Dundee
	G-BIIV	PA-28-181 Archer II	Stratton Motor Co Ltd
	G-BIIX	Rango NA.12 balloon	Rango Kite Co
	G-BIIZ	Great Lakes 2T-1A Sport Trainer	J. R. Lindsay/Booker
	G-BIJB	PA-18 Super Cub 150	Essex Gliding Club/North Weald
	G-BIJD	Bo 208C Junior	K. Cameron
	G-BIJE	Piper J-3C-65 Cub	R. L. Hayward & A. G. Scott
	G-BIJS	Luton LA-4A Minor	I. J. Smith
	G-BIJT	AA-5A Cheetah	Mid-Sussex Timber Co Ltd
	G-BIJU	CP.301A Emeraude	Eastern Taildraggers Flying Group (G-BHTX)
	G-BIJV	Cessna F.152 II	Falcon Flying Services/Biggin Hill
	G-BIJW	Cessna F.152 II	Falcon Flying Services/Biggin Hill
	G-BIJX	Cessna F.152 II	Civil Service Flying Club (Biggin Hill) Ltd
	G-BIKA	Boeing 757-236	British Airways Dover Castle
	G-BIKB	Boeing 757-236	British Airways Windsor Castle
	G-BIKC	Boeing 757-236	British Airways Edinburgh Castle
	G-BIKD	Boeing 757-236	British Airways Caernarfon Castle
	G-BIKE	PA-28R Cherokee Arrow 200	R. V. Webb Ltd/Elstree
	G-BIKF	Boeing 757-236	British Airways Carrickfergus Castle
	G-BIKG	Boeing 757-236	British Airways Stirling Castle
	G-BIKH	Boeing 757-236	British Airways Richmond Castle
	G-BIKI	Boeing 757-236	British Airways Tintagel Castle
	G-BIKJ	Boeing 757-236	British Airways Conwy Castle
	G-BIKK	Boeing 757-236	British Airways Eilean Donan Castle
	G-BIKL	Boeing 757-236	British Airways Nottingham Castle
	G-BIKM	Boeing 757-236	British Airways Glamis Castle
	G-BIKN	Boeing 757-236	British Airways Bodiam Castle/
	G-BIKO	Boeing 757-236	British Airways Harlech Castle
	G-BIKP	Boeing 757-236	British Airways Enniskillen Castle
	G-BIKR	Boeing 757-236	British Airways Bamburgh Castle
	G-BIKS	Boeing 757-236	British Airways Corfe Castle
	G-BIKT	Boeing 757-236	British Airways Carisbrooke Castle
	G-BIKU	Boeing 757-236	British Airways Inverary Castle
	G-BIKV	Boeing 757-236	British Airways Raglan Castle
	G-BIKW	Boeing 757-236	British Airways Belvoir Castle
	G-BIKX	Boeing 757-236	British Airways Warwick Castle
	G-BIKY	Boeing 757-236	British Airways Leeds Castle
	G-BIKZ	Boeing 757-236	British Airways Kenilworth Castle
	G-BILA	Daletol DM.165L Viking	R. Lamplough (stored)
	G-BILB	WMB.2 Windtracker balloon	B. L. King
	G-BILE	Scruggs BL.2B balloon	P. D. Ridout

Reg.	Type	Owner or Operator	Notes
G-BILF	Practavia Sprite 125	G. Harfield	
G-BILG	Scruggs BL.2B balloon	P. D. Ridout	
G-BILI	Piper J-3C-65 Cub (454467)	G-BILI Flying Group	
G-BILJ	Cessna FA.152	Shoreham Flight Simulation Ltd/ Bournemouth	
G-BILK	Cessna FA.152	Exeter Flying Club Ltd	
G-BILL	PA-25 Pawnee 235	Pawnee Aviation	
G-BILR	Cessna 152	Skyviews & General Ltd	
G-BILS	Cessna 152	Skyviews & General Ltd	
G-BILU	Cessna 172RG	Full Sutton Flying Centre Ltd	
G-BILZ	Taylor JT.1 Monoplane	A. Petherbridge	
G-BIMK	Tiger T.200 Srs 1 balloon	M. K. Baron	
G-BIMM	PA-18 Super Cub 150	Clacton Aero Club (1988) Ltd	
G-BIMN	Steen Skybolt	C. R. Williamson	
G-BIMO	SNCAN Stampe SV-4C	R. A. Roberts	
G-BIMT	Cessna FA.152	Staverton Flying Services Ltd	
G-BIMU	Sikorsky S-61N	Bristow Helicopters Ltd	
G-BIMX	Rutan Vari-Eze	A. S. Knowles	
G-BIMZ	Beech 76 Duchess	Barrein Engineers Ltd/Lulsgate	
G-BINA	Saffery S.9 balloon	A. P. Bashford	
G-BINB	WMB.2A Windtracker balloon	S. R. Woolfries	
G-BINF	Saffery S.200 balloon	T. Lewis	
G-BING	Cessna F.172P	J. E. M. Patrick	
G-BINI	Scruggs BL.2C balloon	S. R. Woolfries	
G-BINL	Scruggs BL.2B balloon	P. D. Ridout	
G-BINM	Scruggs BL.2B balloon	P. D. Ridout	
G-BINO	Evans VP-1	A. M. S. Liggat	
G-BINR	Unicorn UE.1A balloon	Unicorn Group	
G-BINS	Unicorn UE.2A balloon	Unicorn Group	
G-BINT	Unicorn UE.1A balloon	Unicorn Group	
G-BINU	Saffery S.200 balloon	T. Lewis	
G-BINX	Scruggs BL.2B balloon	P. D. Ridout	
G-BINY	Oriental balloon	J. L. Morton	
G-BINZ	Rango NA.8 balloon	T. J. Sweeting & M. O. Davies	
G-BIOB	Cessna F.172P	Aerofilms Ltd/Elstree	
G-BIOC	Cessna F.150L	Seawing Flying Club/Southend	
G-BIOE	Short SD3-30	Fairflight/Gill Air/Newcastle	
G-BIOI	Jodel DR.1051/M	H. F. Hambling	
G-BIOJ	R. Commander 112TCA	A. T. Dalby	
G-BIOK	Cessna F.152	Tayside Aviation/Dundee	
G-BIOM	Cessna F.152	Falcon Flying Services/Biggin Hill	
G-BION	Cameron V-77 balloon	Elliott's Pharmacy Ltd	
G-BIOO	Unicorn UE.2B balloon	Unicorn Group	
G-BIOP	Scruggs BL.2D balloon	J. P. S. Donnellan	
G-BIOR	M.S.880B Rallye Club	Aircraft Dept. Royal Aircraft Establishment/ Farnborough	
G-BIOU	Jodel D.117A	M. S. Printing & Graphics Machinery Ltd/ Booker	
G-BIOW	Slingsby T.67A	A. B. Slinger/Sherburn	
G-BIOX	Potter Crompton PRO.1 balloon	G. M. Potter	
G-BIPA	AA-5B Tiger	J. Campbell/Barrow	
G-BIPH	Scruggs BL.2B balloon	C. M. Dewsnap	
G-BIPI	Everett Blackbird Mk 1	R. Spall	
G-BIPJ	PA-36-375 Brave	G. B. Pearce/Shoreham	
G-BIPK	Saffery S.200 balloon	P. J. Kelsey	
G-BIPM	Flamboyant Ax7-65 balloon	Pepsi Cola International Ltd/S. Africa	
G-BIPN	Fournier RF-3	S. N. Lawrence	
G-BIPO	Mudry/CAARP CAP.20LS-200	W. Brady/Booker	
G-BIPS	SOCATA Rallye 100ST	McAully Flying Group/Little Snoring	
G-BIPT	Jodel D.112	C. R. Davies	
G-BIPV	AA-5B Tiger	Solent Flight	
G-BIPW	Avenger T.200-2112 balloon	B. L. King	
G-BIPY	Bensen B.8	W. J. Pope	
G-BIRA	SOCATA TB.9 Tampico	Goldangel Ltd/Swansea	
G-BIRB	M.S.880B Rallye 100T	E. Smith	
G-BIRD	Pitts S-1C Special	Pitts Artists Flying Group	
G-BIRE	Colt 56 Bottle balloon	K. R. Gafney	
G-BIRH	PA-18 Super Cub 135 (R-163)	I. R. F. Hammond/Lee-on-Solent	
G-BIRI	C.A.S.A. 1.131E Jungmann	M. G. & J. R. Jeffries	
G-BIRK	Avenger T.200-2112 balloon	D. Harland	
G-BIRL	Avenger T.200-2112 balloon	R. Light	
G-BIRM	Avenger T.200-2112 balloon	P. Higgins	
G-BIRO	Cessna 172P	M. C. Grant	

Notes	Reg.	Type	Owner or Operator
	G-BIRP	Arena Mk 17 Skyship balloon	A. S. Viel
	G-BIRS	Cessna 182P	John E. Birks & Associates Ltd (G-BBBS)
	G-BIRT	Robin R.1180TD	W. D'A. Hall/Booker
	G-BIRW	M.S.505 Criquet (F+IS) ★	Museum of Flight/E. Fortune
	G-BIRY	Cameron V-77 balloon	J. J. Winter
	G-BIRZ	Zenair CH.250	A. W. F. Richards
	G-BISB	Cessna F.152 II	Sheffield Aero Club Ltd/Netherthorpe
	G-BISF	Robinson R-22	C. R. James
	G-BISG	FRED Srs 3	R. A. Coombe
	G-BISH	Cameron O-42 balloon	Zebedee Balloon Service
	G-BISJ	Cessna 340A	Bobbington Air Training School Ltd
	G-BISK	R. Commander 112B ★	P. A. Warner
	G-BISL	Scruggs BL.2B balloon	P. D. Ridout
	G-BISM	Scruggs BL.2B balloon	P. D. Ridout
	G-BISS	Scruggs BL.2C balloon	P. D. Ridout
	G-BIST	Scruggs BL.2C balloon	P. D. Ridout
	G-BISV	Cameron O-65 balloon	Hylyne Rabbits Ltd
	G-BISW	Cameron O-65 balloon	Rango Balloon & Kite Co
	G-BISX	Colt 56A balloon	J. R. Gore
	G-BISZ	Sikorsky S-76A	Bristow Helicopters Ltd
	G-BITA	PA-18 Super Cub 150	J. & S. A. S. McCullough
	G-BITE	SOCATA TB.10 Tobago	M. A. Smith & R. J. Bristow/Fairoaks
	G-BITF	Cessna F.152	Tayside Aviation Ltd/Dundee
	G-BITH	Cessna F.152	Tayside Aviation Ltd/Dundee
	G-BITK	FRED Srs 2	D. J. Wood
	G-BITL	Horncastle LL-901 balloon	M. J. Worsdell
	G-BITM	Cessna F.172P	D. G. Crabtree/Barton
	G-BITO	Jodel D.112D	A. Dunbar/Barton
	G-BITR	Sikorsky S-76A	Bristow Helicopters Ltd
	G-BITS	Drayton B-56 balloon	M. J. Betts
	G-BITW	Short SD3-30	Shorts Aircraft Financing Ltd (G-EASI)
	G-BITY	FD.31T balloon	A. J. Bell
	G-BIUL	Cameron 60 SS balloon	D. C. Patrick-Brown
	G-BIUM	Cessna F.152	Sheffield Aero Club Ltd/Netherthorpe
	G-BIUP	SNCAN NC.854S	C. M. Mogg
	G-BIUU	PA-23 Aztec 250D ★	G. Cormack/Glasgow
	G-BIUV	H.S.748 Srs 2A	Dan-Air Services Ltd (G-AYYH)/Gatwick
	G-BIUW	PA-28-161 Warrior II	D. R. Staley
	G-BIUY	PA-28-181 Archer II	Maidenhead Electrical Services Ltd/ White Waltham
	G-BIVA	Robin R.2112	Cotswold Aero Club Ltd/Staverton
	G-BIVB	Jodel D.112	D. H. Anderson
	G-BIVC	Jodel D.112	M. J. Barmby/Cardiff
	G-BIVK	Bensen B.8	J. G. Toy
	G-BIVL	Bensen B.8	R. Gardiner
	G-BIVT	Saffery S.80 balloon	L. F. Guyot
	G-BIVU	AA-5A Cheetah	Lowlog Ltd
	G-BIVV	AA-5A Cheetah	W. Dass
	G-BIVY	Cessna 172N	Goodwood Aircraft Management Services Ltd
	G-BIVZ	D.31A Turbulent	I. Maclennan
	G-BIWB	Scruggs RS.5000 balloon	P. D. Ridout
	G-BIWC	Scruggs RS.5000 balloon	P. D. Ridout
	G-BIWD	Scruggs RS.5000 balloon	D. Eaves
	G-BIWF	Warren balloon	P. D. Ridout
	G-BIWG	Zelenski Mk 2 balloon	P. D. Ridout
	G-BIWJ	Unicorn UE.1A balloon	B. L. King
	G-BIWK	Cameron V-65 balloon	I. R. Williams & R. G. Bickerdike
	G-BIWL	PA-32-301 Saratoga	Harwoods of Essex Ltd
	G-BIWN	Jodel D.112	C. R. Coates
	G-BIWP	Mooney M.20J	J. K. McWhinney
	G-BIWR	Mooney M.20F	A. C. Brink
	G-BIWU	Cameron V-65 balloon	J. T. Whicker & J. W. Unwin
	G-BIWW	AA-5 Traveler	B&K Aviation/Cranfield
	G-BIWX	AT-16 Harvard IV (FT239)	A. E. Hutton/North Weald
	G-BIWY	Westland WG.30 ★	*Instructional airframe*/Sherborne
	G-BIXA	SOCATA TB.9 Tampico	Lord de Saumarez
	G-BIXB	SOCATA TB.9 Tampico	Kitchen Bros/Little Snoring
	G-BIXH	Cessna F.152	Cambridge Aero Club Ltd
	G-BIXI	Cessna 172RG Cutlass	J. F. P. Lewis/Sandown
	G-BIXJ	Saffery S.40 balloon	T. M. Pates
	G-BIXL	P-51D Mustang (472216)	R. Lamplough/North Weald
	G-BIXN	Boeing A.75N1 Stearman	I. L. Craig-Wood & ptnrs

Reg.	Type	Owner or Operator	Notes
G-BIXR	Cameron A-140 balloon	Skysales Ltd	
G-BIXS	Avenger T.200-2112 balloon	M. Stuart	
G-BIXV	Bell 212	Bristow Helicopters Ltd	
G-BIXW	Colt 56B balloon	J. R. Birkenhead	
G-BIXX	Pearson Srs 2 balloon	D. Pearson	
G-BIXZ	Grob G-109	V. J. R. Day	
G-BIYG	Short SD3-30	Gill Aviation Ltd/Newcastle	
G-BIYH	Short SD3-30	Celtic Airways Ltd	
G-BIYI	Cameron V-65 balloon	Sarnia Balloon Group	
G-BIYJ	PA-18 Super Cub 95	S. Russell	
G-BIYK	Isaacs Fury	R. S. Martin/Dunkeswell	
G-BIYM	PA-32R-301 Saratoga SP	Pinta Investments Ltd	
G-BIYO	PA-31-310 Turbo Navajo	Northern Executive Aviation Ltd/ Manchester	
G-BIYP	PA-20 Pacer 135	R. J. Whitcombe	
G-BIYR	PA-18 Super Cub 135	Delta Foxtrot Flying Group/Dunkeswell	
G-BIYT	Colt 17A balloon	A. F. Selby	
G-BIYU	Fokker S.11.1 Instructor (E-15)	H. R. Smallwood & A. J. Lee/Denham	
G-BIYW	Jodel D.112	J. D. Bysh & P. Franzini	
G-BIYX	PA-28 Cherokee 140	A. Gowlett/Blackpool	
G-BIYY	PA-18 Super Cub 95	A. E. & W. J. Taylor/Ingoldmells	
G-BIZF	Cessna F.172P	R. S. Bentley/Bourn	
G-BIZG	Cessna F.152	M. A. Judge	
G-BIZI	Robin DR.400/120	Headcorn Flying School Ltd	
G-BIZK	Nord 3202	A. I. Milne/Swanton Morley	
G-BIZM	Nord 3202	Magnificent Obsessions Ltd	
G-BIZN	Slingsby T.67A	Condor Aeroplane Co	
G-BIZO	PA-28R Cherokee Arrow 200	Bowlish Roofing Supplies Ltd	
G-BIZR	SOCATA TB.9 Tampico	R. M. Shears (G-BSEC)	
G-BIZT	Bensen B.8M	J. Ferguson	
G-BIZU	Thunder Ax6-56Z balloon	S. L. Leigh	
G-BIZV	PA-18 Super Cub 95 (18-2001)	S. J. Pugh & M. Risdale	
G-BIZW	Champion 7GCBC Citabria	G. Read & Son	
G-BIZY	Jodel D.112	Wayland Tunley & Associates	
G-BJAD	FRED Srs 2	C. Allison	
G-BJAE	Lavadoux Starck AS.80	D. J. & S. A. E. Phillips/Coventry	
G-BJAF	Piper J-3C-65 Cub	P. J. Cottle	
G-BJAG	PA-28-181 Archer II	K. F. Hudson & D. J. Casson/Sherburn	
G-BJAJ	AA-5B Tiger	A. H. McVicar/Prestwick	
G-BJAL	C.A.S.A. 1.131E Jungmann	W. J. Perrins & E. A. C. Elliott	
G-BJAN	SA.102-5 Cavalier	J. Powlesland	
G-BJAO	Bensen B.8M	G. L. Stockdale	
G-BJAP	D.H.82A Tiger Moth	J. A. Pothecary	
G-BJAR	Unicorn UE.3A balloon	Unicorn Group	
G-BJAS	Rango NA.9 balloon	A. Lindsay	
G-BJAV	GY-80 Horizon 160	T. T. Parr	
G-BJAW	Cameron V-65 balloon	G. W. McCarthy	
G-BJAX	Pilatus P2-05 (U-108)	Pilatus Partnership/Goodwood	
G-BJAY	Piper J-3C-65 Cub	K. L. Clarke/Ingoldmells	
G-BJBI	Cessna 414A	Borfin Ltd/Manchester	
G-BJBK	PA-18 Super Cub 95	M. S. Bird/Old Sarum	
G-BJBM	Monnet Sonerai II	J. Pickerell & B. L. Sims/Southend	
G-BJBO	Jodel DR.250/160	C. C. Gordon	
G-BJBP	Beech A200 Super King Air	All Charter Ltd (G-HLUB)/Bournemouth	
G-BJBS	Robinson R-22	R. L. G. Vine	
G-BJBV	PA-28-161 Warrior II	C.S.E. Aviation Ltd/Kidlington	
G-BJBW	PA-28-161 Warrior II	C.S.E. Aviation Ltd/Kidlington	
G-BJBX	PA-28-161 Warrior II	C.S.E. Aviation Ltd/Kidlington	
G-BJBY	PA-28-161 Warrior II	C.S.E. Aviation Ltd/Kidlington	
G-BJBZ	Rotorway Executive 133	P. J. D. Kerr	
G-BJCA	PA-28-161 Warrior II	D. M. & J. E. Smith	
G-BJCD	Bede BD-5BH	Brockmoor-Bede Aircraft (UK) Ltd	
G-BJCF	CP.1310-C3 Super Emeraude	K. M. Hodson & C. G. H. Gurney	
G-BJCI	PA-18 Super Cub 150 (modified)	The Borders (Milfield) Aero-Tour Club Ltd	
G-BJCP	Unicorn UE.2B balloon	Unicorn Group	
G-BJCR	Partenavia P.68C	Nullifire Ltd/Coventry	
G-BJCT	Boeing 737-204ADV	Britannia Airways Ltd *The Hon C. S. Rolls*/ Luton	
G-BJCU	Boeing 737-204ADV	Britannia Airways Ltd *Sir Henry Royce*/ Luton	
G-BJCV	Boeing 737-204ADV	Britannia Airways Ltd *Viscount Trenchard*/ Luton	

Notes	Reg.	Type	Owner or Operator
	G-BJCW	PA-32R-301 Saratoga SP	Viscount Chelsea/Kidlington
	G-BJDE	Cessna F.172M	H. P. K. Ferdinand/Denham
	G-BJDF	M.S.880B Rallye 100T	W. R. Savin & ptnrs
	G-BJDI	Cessna FR.182RG	Sunningdale Aviation Services Ltd/ Blackpool
	G-BJDJ	H.S.125 Srs 700B	British Aerospace PLC
	G-BJDK	European E.14 balloon	Aeroprint Tours
	G-BJDO	AA-5A Cheetah	Solent Flight
	G-BJDT	SOCATA TB.9 Tampico	Tampico Group/Old Sarum
	G-BJDW	Cessna F.172M	J. Rae/Ipswich
	G-BJEI	PA-18 Super Cub 95	H. J. Cox
	G-BJEL	SNCAN NC.854	N. F. & S. G. Hunter
	G-BJEN	Scruggs RS.5000 balloon	N. J. Richardson
	G-BJEO	PA-34-220T Seneca III	D. W. Clark Land Drainage Ltd (G-TOMF)
	G-BJES	Scruggs RS.5000 balloon	J. E. Christopher
	G-BJEU	Scruggs BL.2D-2 balloon	G. G. Kneller
	G-BJEV	Aeronca 11AC Chief (897)	R. F. Willcox
	G-BJEX	Bo 208C Junior	G. D. H. Crawford/Thruxton
	G-BJFB	Mk 1A balloon	Aeroprint Tours
	G-BJFC	European E.8 balloon	P. D. Ridout
	G-BJFE	PA-18 Super Cub 95	J. H. Allistone
	G-BJFI	Bell 47G-2A1	Helicopter Supplies & Engineering Ltd/ Bournemouth
	G-BJFL	Sikorsky S-76A	Bristow Helicopters Ltd
	G-BJFM	Jodel D.120	J. V. George & P. A. Smith/Popham
	G-BJGC	Mk IV balloon	Windsor Balloon Group
	G-BJGD	Mk IV balloon	Windsor Balloon Group
	G-BJGE	Thunder Ax3 balloon	K. A. Williams
	G-BJGF	Mk 1 balloon	D. & D. Eaves
	G-BJGG	Mk 2 balloon	D. & D. Eaves
	G-BJGK	Cameron V-77 balloon	A. Simpson & R. Bailey
	G-BJGL	Cremer balloon	G. Lowther
	G-BJGM	Unicorn UE.1A balloon	D. Eaves & P. D. Ridout
	G-BJGO	Cessna 172N	Stratair Ltd/Wellesbourne
	G-BJGX	Sikorsky S-76A	Bristow Helicopters Ltd
	G-BJGY	Cessna F.172P	Lucca Wines Ltd
	G-BJHA	Cremer balloon	G. Cape
	G-BJHB	Mooney M.20J	Zitair Flying Club Ltd/Redhill
	G-BJHC	Swan 1 balloon	C. A. Swan
	G-BJHD	Mk 3B balloon	S. Meagher
	G-BJHK	EAA Acro Sport	D. Calabritto
	G-BJHL	Osprey 1C balloon	E. Bartlett
	G-BJHN	Osprey 1B balloon	J. E. Christopher
	G-BJHO	Osprey 1C balloon	G. G. Kneller
	G-BJHP	Osprey 1C balloon	N. J. Richardson
	G-BJHS	S.25 Sunderland V	Sunderland Ltd
	G-BJHT	Thunder Ax7-65 balloon	A. H. & L. Symonds
	G-BJHU	Osprey 1C balloon	G. G. Kneller
	G-BJHV	Voisin Replica ★	Brooklands Museum of Aviation/Weybridge
	G-BJHW	Osprey 1C balloon	N. J. Richardson
	G-BJIA	Allport balloon	D. J. Allport
	G-BJIB	D.31 Turbulent	N. H. Lemon
	G-BJIC	Dodo 1A balloon	P. D. Ridout
	G-BJID	Osprey 1B balloon	P. D. Ridout
	G-BJIF	Bensen B.8M	H. Redwin
	G-BJIG	Slingsby T.67A	Acebell G-BJIG Syndicate/Redhill
	G-BJIR	Cessna 550 Citation II	Gator Aviation Ltd
	G-BJIV	PA-18 Super Cub 150 (modified)	Yorkshire Gliding Club (Pty) Ltd/ Sutton Bank
	G-BJJE	Dodo Mk 3 balloon	D. Eaves
	G-BJJN	Cessna F.172M	Ospreystar Ltd (stored)/Stapleford
	G-BJJO	Bell 212	British Executive Air Services Ltd
	G-BJJP	Bell 212	British Executive Air Services Ltd
	G-BJJW	Mk B balloon	S. Meagher
	G-BJJX	Mk B balloon	S. Meagher
	G-BJJY	Mk B balloon	S. Meagher
	G-BJKB	SA.365C-3 Dauphin 2	Bond Helicopters Ltd
	G-BJKF	SOCATA TB.9 Tampico	Manor Promotion Services Ltd/Booker
	G-BJKW	Wills Aera II	J. K. S. Wills
	G-BJKY	Cessna F.152	Air Charter & Travel Ltd/Ronaldsway
	G-BJLB	SNCAN NC.854S	M. J. Barnaby
	G-BJLC	Monnet Sonerai IIL	P. J. Robins & R. King/Sywell
	G-BJLE	Osprey 1B balloon	I. Chadwick

Reg.	Type	Owner or Operator	Notes
G-BJLF	Unicorn UE.1C balloon	I. Chadwick	
G-BJLG	Unicorn UE.1B balloon	I. Chadwick	
G-BJLH	PA-18 Super Cub 95 (K-33)	D. S. Kirkham	
G-BJLK	Short SD3-30	Shorts Aircraft Financing Ltd	
G-BJLO	PA-31-310 Turbo Navajo	Linco (Holdings) Ltd	
G-BJLU	Featherlight Mk 3 balloon	T. J. Sweeting & N. P. Kemp	
G-BJLV	Sphinx balloon	L. F. Guyot	
G-BJLX	Cremer balloon	P. W. May	
G-BJLY	Cremer balloon	P. Cannon	
G-BJMG	European E.26C balloon	D. Eaves & A. P. Chown	
G-BJMI	European E.84 balloon	D. Eaves	
G-BJMJ	Bensen B.8M	J. I. Hewlett	
G-BJML	Cessna 120	D. F. Lawlor/Inverness	
G-BJMO	Taylor JT.1 Monoplane	R. C. Mark	
G-BJMR	Cessna 310R	J. McL. Robinson/Sherburn	
G-BJMU	European E.157 balloon	A. C. Mitchell	
G-BJMV	BAC One-Eleven 531FS	Dan-Air Services Ltd/Gatwick	
G-BJMW	Thunder Ax8-105 balloon	G. M. Westley	
G-BJMX	Jarre JR.3 balloon	P. D. Ridout	
G-BJMZ	European EA.8A balloon	P. D. Ridout	
G-BJNA	Arena Mk 117P balloon	P. D. Ridout	
G-BJND	Osprey Mk 1E balloon	A. Billington & D. Whitmore	
G-BJNF	Cessna F.152	Exeter Flying Club Ltd	
G-BJNG	Slingsby T.67A	D. F. Ranger	
G-BJNN	PA-38-112 Tomahawk	Scotia Safari Ltd/Prestwick	
G-BJNP	Rango NA.32 balloon	N. H. Ponsford	
G-BJNX	Cameron O-65 balloon	B. J. Petteford	
G-BJNY	Aeronca 11CC Super Chief	P. I. & D. M. Morgans	
G-BJNZ	PA-23 Aztec 250F	Leavesden Flight Centre Ltd (G-FANZ)	
G-BJOA	PA-28-181 Archer II	Channel Islands Aero Holdings (Jersey) Ltd	
G-BJOB	Jodel D.140C	T. W. M. Beck & M. J. Smith	
G-BJOE	Jodel D.120A	Forth Flying Group	
G-BJOI	Isaacs Special	J. O. Isaacs	
G-BJOP	BN-2B Islander	Loganair Ltd/Glasgow	
G-BJOT	Jodel D.117	E. Davies	
G-BJOV	Cessna F.150K	W. H. Webb & P. F. N. Burrow	
G-BJOZ	Scheibe SF.25B Falke	P. W. Hextall	
G-BJPB	Osprey Mk 4A balloon	C. B. Rundle	
G-BJPI	Bede BD-5G	M. D. McQueen	
G-BJPJ	Osprey Mk 3A	K. R. Bundy	
G-BJPL	Osprey Mk 4A balloon	M. Vincent	
G-BJPM	Bursell PW.1 balloon	I. M. Holdsworth	
G-BJPV	Haigh balloon	M. J. Haigh	
G-BJPW	Osprey Mk 1C balloon	P. J. Cooper & M. Draper	
G-BJRA	Osprey Mk 4B balloon	E. Osborn	
G-BJRB	European E.254 balloon	D. Eaves	
G-BJRC	European E.84R balloon	D. Eaves	
G-BJRD	European E.84R balloon	D. Eaves	
G-BJRF	Saffery S.80 balloon	C. F. Chipping	
G-BJRG	Osprey Mk 4B balloon	A. de Gruchy	
G-BJRH	Rango NA.36 balloon	N. H. Ponsford	
G-BJRI	Osprey Mk 4D balloon	G. G. Kneller	
G-BJRJ	Osprey Mk 4D balloon	G. G. Kneller	
G-BJRK	Osprey Mk 1E balloon	G. G. Kneller	
G-BJRL	Osprey Mk 4B balloon	G. G. Kneller	
G-BJRP	Cremer balloon	M. Williams	
G-BJRS	Cremer balloon	P. Wallbank	
G-BJRT	BAC One-Eleven 528FL	British Airways County of South Glamorgan	
G-BJRU	BAC One-Eleven 528FL	British Airways County of West Glamorgan	
G-BJRV	Cremer balloon	M. D. Williams	
G-BJRW	Cessna U.206G	A. I. Walgate & Son Ltd	
G-BJRY	PA-28-151 Warrior	Routair Aviation Services Ltd/Southend	
G-BJRZ	Partenavia P.68C	Air Kilroe Ltd/Manchester	
G-BJSA	BN-2A Islander	Foxair/Glasgow	
G-BJSC	Osprey Mk 4D balloon	N. J. Richardson	
G-BJSD	Osprey Mk 4D balloon	N. J. Richardson	
G-BJSE	Osprey Mk 1E balloon	J. E. Christopher	
G-BJSF	Osprey Mk 4B balloon	N. J. Richardson	
G-BJSG	V.S.361 Spitfire LF.IXE (ML417)	Patina Ltd/Duxford	
G-BJSI	Osprey Mk 1E balloon	N. J. Richardson	
G-BJSK	Osprey Mk 4B balloon	J. E. Christopher	
G-BJSL	Flamboyant Ax7-65 balloon	Pepsi Cola International Ltd	
G-BJSP	Guido 1A Srs 61 balloon	G. A. Newsome	

Notes	Reg.	Type	Owner or Operator
	G-BJSR	Osprey Mk 4B balloon	C. F. Chipping
	G-BJSS	Allport balloon	D. J. Allport
	G-BJST	CCF Harvard 4	V. Norman & M. Lawrence
	G-BJSU	Bensen B.8M	J. D. Newlyn
	G-BJSV	PA-28-161 Warrior II	R. Gilbert & J. Cole
	G-BJSW	Thunder Ax7-65 balloon	Sandicliffe Garage Ltd
	G-BJSX	Unicorn UE-1C balloon	N. J. Richardson
	G-BJSZ	Piper J-3C-65 Cub	H. Gilbert
	G-BJTA	Osprey Mk 4B balloon	C. F. Chipping
	G-BJTB	Cessna A.150M	Clacton Aero Club (1988) Ltd
	G-BJTG	Osprey Mk 4B balloon	M. Millen
	G-BJTH	Kestrel AC Mk 1 balloon	R. P. Waller
	G-BJTK	Taylor JT.1 Monoplane	E. N. Simmons (G-BEUM)
	G-BJTN	Osprey Mk 4B balloon	M. Vincent
	G-BJTO	Piper J-3C-65 Cub	K. R. Nunn
	G-BJTP	PA-18 Super Cub 95 (115302)	J. T. Parkins
	G-BJTV	M.S.880B Rallye Club	E. C. Hender
	G-BJTW	European E.107 balloon	C. J. Brealey
	G-BJTY	Osprey Mk 4B balloon	A. E. de Gruchy
	G-BJUB	BVS Special 01 balloon	P. G. Wild
	G-BJUC	Robinson R-22	The Helicentre/Blackpool
	G-BJUD	Robin DR.400/180R	Lasham Gliding Soc Ltd
	G-BJUE	Osprey Mk 4B balloon	M. Vincent
	G-BJUG	SOCATA TB.9 Tampico	R. A. Stockdale
	G-BJUI	Osprey Mk 4B balloon	B. A. de Gruchy
	G-BJUK	Short SD3-30	Shorts Aircraft Leasing Ltd (G-OCAS)
	G-BJUR	PA-38-112 Tomahawk	Truman Aviation Ltd/Tollerton
	G-BJUS	PA-38-112 Tomahawk	Panshanger School of Flying
	G-BJUU	Osprey Mk 4B balloon	M. Vincent
	G-BJUV	Cameron V-20 balloon	Cameron Balloons Ltd
	G-BJUW	Osprey Mk 4B balloon	C. F. Chipping
	G-BJUX	Bursell balloon	I. M. Holdsworth
	G-BJUZ	BAT Mk II balloon	A. R. Thompson
	G-BJVA	BAT Mk I balloon	B. L. Thompson
	G-BJVC	Evans VP-2	W. E. King
	G-BJVF	Thunder Ax3 balloon	A. G. R. Calder
	G-BJVH	Cessna F.182Q	A. R. G. Brooker Engineering Ltd/ Wellesbourne
	G-BJVJ	Cessna F.152	Cambridge Aero Club Ltd
	G-BJVK	Grob G-109	B. Kimberley/Enstone
	G-BJVM	Cessna 172M	Mercia Aircraft Leasing & Sales Ltd
	G-BJVS	CP.1310-C3 Super Emeraude	A. E. Futter/Norwich
	G-BJVT	Cessna F.152	Cambridge Aero Club Ltd
	G-BJVU	Thunder Ax6-56 balloon	G. V. Beckwith
	G-BJVV	Robin R.1180	Medway Flying Group Ltd/Rochester
	G-BJVX	Sikorsky S-76A	Bristow Helicopters Ltd
	G-BJVZ	Sikorsky S-76A	Bristow Helicopters Ltd
	G-BJWC	Saro Skeeter AOP.12 (XK 482)★	Wilkie Museum Collection/Blackpool
	G-BJWH	Cessna F.152	Biggin Hill School of Flying
	G-BJWI	Cessna F.172P	Agricultural & General Aviation Ltd/ Bournemouth
	G-BJWJ	Cameron V-65 balloon	R. G. Turnbull & S. G. Forse
	G-BJWO	BN-2A-8 Islander	Chapman Aviation Ltd (G-BAXC)/Biggin Hill
	G-BJWT	Wittman W.10 Tailwind	J. F. Bakewell & R. A. Shelley
	G-BJWV	Colt 17A balloon	D. T. Meyes
	G-BJWW	Cessna F.172N	Shireburn Carpets Ltd
	G-BJWX	PA-18 Super Cub 95	A. Haig-Thomas
	G-BJWY	S-55 Whirlwind HAR.21 (WV198)	Wilkie Museum Collection/Blackpool
	G-BJWZ	PA-18 Super Cub 95	G. V. Harfield/Thruxton
	G-BJXA	Slingsby T.67A	Comed Aviation Ltd/Blackpool
	G-BJXB	Slingsby T.67A	Light Planes (Lancs) Ltd/Barton
	G-BJXJ	Boeing 737-219	Britannia Airways Ltd *The O'Neill Hereditary King of Ulster*/Luton
	G-BJXK	Fournier RF-5	G-BJXK Syndicate/Cardiff
	G-BJXP	Colt 56B balloon	Birmingham Broadcasting Ltd
	G-BJXR	Auster AOP.9 (XR267)	Cotswold Aircraft Restoration Group
	G-BJXU	Thunder Ax7-77 balloon	S. M. Vardey
	G-BJXX	PA-23 Aztec 250E	V. Bojovic
	G-BJXZ	Cessna 172N	T. M. Jones
	G-BJYC	Cessna 425	Carters Aviation Ltd/E. Midlands
	G-BJYD	Cessna F.152 II	Cleveland Flying School Ltd/Teesside
	G-BJYF	Colt 56A balloon	Hot Air Balloon Co Ltd
	G-BJYG	PA-28-161 Warrior II	Browns of Stoke Ltd

Reg.	Type	Owner or Operator	Notes
G-BJYK	Jodel D.120A	T. Fox & D. A. Thorpe	
G-BJYL	BAC One-Eleven 515FB	Dan-Air Services Ltd (G-AZPE)/Gatwick	
G-BJYM	BAC One-Eleven 531FS	Dan-Air Services Ltd/Gatwick	
G-BJYN	PA-38-112 Tomahawk	Panshanger School of Flying Ltd (G-BJTE)	
G-BJZA	Cameron N-65 balloon	A. D. Pinner	
G-BJZB	Evans VP-2	J. A. Macleod	
G-BJZC	Thunder Ax7-65Z balloon	Greenpeace (UK) Ltd/S. Africa	
G-BJZD	Douglas DC-10-10	— (G-GFAL)	
G-BJZE	Douglas DC-10-10	— (G-GSKY)	
G-BJZF	D.H.82A Tiger Moth	R. Blast	
G-BJZK	Cessna T.303	Landlink Ltd	
G-BJZL	Cameron V-65 balloon	S. L. G. Williams	
G-BJZN	Slingsby T.67A	D. M. Upfield	
G-BJZR	Colt 42A balloon	C. F. Sisson	
G-BJZT	Cessna FA.152	Biggin Hill School of Flying	
G-BJZX	Grob G.109	Oxfordshire Sport Flying Ltd/Enstone	
G-BJZY	Bensen B.8MV	D. E. & M. A. Cooke	
G-BKAC	Cessna F.150L	Seawing Flying Club Ltd/Southend	
G-BKAE	Jodel D.120	M. P. Wakem	
G-BKAF	FRED Srs 2	L. G. Millen	
G-BKAM	Slingsby T.67M Firefly	A. J. Daley & R. K. Warren	
G-BKAN	Cessna 340A	Arrows Aviation Co Ltd/Manchester	
G-BKAO	Jodel D.112	R. Broadhead	
G-BKAR	PA-38-112 Tomahawk	R. Thomas	
G-BKAS	PA-38-112 Tomahawk	Falcon Flying Services/Biggin Hill	
G-BKAY	R. Commander 114	The Rockwell Group	
G-BKAZ	Cessna 152	Skyviews & General Ltd	
G-BKBD	Thunder Ax3 balloon	G. A. McCarthy	
G-BKBF	M.S.894A Rallye Minerva 220	M. S. Wright	
G-BKBH	H.S.125 Srs 600B	Westminster Aviation Ltd (G-BDJE)	
G-BKBK	SNCAN Stampe SV-4A	Freshname No77 Ltd	
G-BKBN	SOCATA TB.10 Tobago	RFA Flying Club Ltd	
G-BKBO	Colt 17A balloon	J. Armstrong & ptnrs	
G-BKBP	Bellanca 7GCBC Scout	H. G. Jefferies & Son	
G-BKBR	Cameron Chateau 84 SS balloon	Forbes Europe Ltd/France	
G-BKBS	Bensen B.8MV	Construction & Site Administration Ltd	
G-BKBV	SOCATA TB.10 Tobago	R. M. Messenger	
G-BKBW	SOCATA TB.10 Tobago	Merlin Aviation	
G-BKCB	PA-28R Cherokee Arrow 200	Bristol & Wessex Aeroplane Club Ltd	
G-BKCC	PA-28 Cherokee 180	Cowie Aviation Ltd/Staverton	
G-BKCE	Cessna F.172PII	M. Askanoglu	
G-BKCF	Rutan LongEz	I. C. Fallows	
G-BKCH	Thompson Cassutt	S. C. Thompson/Redhill	
G-BKCI	Brügger MB.2 Colibri	E. R. Newall	
G-BKCJ	Oldfield Baby Great Lakes	S. V. Roberts/Sleap	
G-BKCK	CCF Harvard IV (P5865)	E. T. Webster/North Weald	
G-BKCL	PA-30 Twin Comanche 160C	T-Comm Aviation Ltd/Leeds	
G-BKCN	Currie Wot	S. E. Tomlinson	
G-BKCR	SOCATA TB.9 Tampico	Surrey & Kent Flying Club (1982) Ltd/ Biggin Hill	
G-BKCT	Cameron V-77 balloon	Quality Products General Engineering (Wickwat) Ltd	
G-BKCV	EAA Acro Sport II	M. J. Clark	
G-BKCW	Jodel D.120A	A. Greene & G. Kerr/Dundee	
G-BKCX	Mudry CAARP CAP.10	Mahon & Associates/Booker	
G-BKCY	PA-38-112 Tomahawk II	Wellesbourne Aviation Ltd	
G-BKCZ	Jodel D.120A	M. R. Baker/Shoreham	
G-BKDC	Monnet Sonerai II	K. McBride	
G-BKDD	Bell 206B JetRanger	Dollar Air Services Ltd/Coventry	
G-BKDH	Robin DR.400/120	Wiltshire Aeroplane Club/Old Sarum	
G-BKDI	Robin DR.400/120	Cotswold Aero Club Ltd/Staverton	
G-BKDJ	Robin DR.400/120	Wiltshire Aeroplane Club/Old Sarum	
G-BKDK	Thunder Ax7-77Z balloon	A. J. Byrne	
G-BKDP	FRED Srs 3	M. Whittaker	
G-BKDR	Pitts S.1S Special	N. A. Bloom	
G-BKDX	Jodel DR.1050	T. G. Collins	
G-BKEK	PA-32 Cherokee Six 300	Flyfast Ltd	
G-BKEM	SOCATA TB.9 Tampico	C. J. Burt/Biggin Hill	
G-BKEP	Cessna F.172M	R. Green/Glasgow	
G-BKER	SE-5A replica (F5447)	N. K. Geddes	
G-BKET	PA-18 Super Cub 95	H. M. Mackenzie	
G-BKEU	Taylor JT.1 Monoplane	R. J. Whybrow & J. M. Springham	

Notes	Reg.	Type	Owner or Operator
	G-BKEV	Cessna F.172M	One Zero One Three Ltd
	G-BKEW	Bell 206B JetRanger 3	N. R. Foster
	G-BKEX	Rich Prototype glider	D. B. Rich
	G-BKEY	FRED Srs 3	G. S. Taylor
	G-BKEZ	PA-18 Super Cub 95	G. V. Harfield
	G-BKFA	Monnet Sonerai IIL	R. F. Bridge
	G-BKFC	Cessna F.152 II	Sulby Aerial Surveys Ltd
	G-BKFG	Thunder Ax3 balloon	P. Ray
	G-BKFI	Evans VP-1	F. A. R. de Lavergne
	G-BKFK	Isaacs Fury II	G. C. Jones
	G-BKFM	QAC Quickie	R. Scroby
	G-BKFP	Bell 214ST	Bristow Helicopters Ltd
	G-BKFR	CP.301C Emeraude	C. R. Beard
	G-BKFV	Rand KR-2	F. H. French/Swansea
	G-BKFW	P.56 Provost T.1 (XF597)	Slymar Aviation & Services Ltd
	G-BKFZ	PA-28R Cherokee Arrow 200	Shacklewell Flying Group/Leicester
	G-BKGA	M.S.892E Rallye 150GT	B. F. Hill
	G-BKGB	Jodel D.120	R. W. Greenwood
	G-BKGC	Maule M.6-235	Stol-Air Ltd/Sibson
	G-BKGD	Westland WG.30 Srs 100	British International Helicopters Ltd (G-BKBJ)/Aberdeen
	G-BKGL	Beech 18 (1164)	The Aircraft Restoration Co/Duxford
	G-BKGR	Cameron O-65 balloon	S. R. Bridge
	G-BKGT	SOCATA Rallye 110ST	Long Marston Flying Group
	G-BKGW	Cessna F.152-II	Leicestershire Aero Club Ltd
	G-BKHA	W.S.55 Whirlwind HAR.10 (XJ763)	C. J. Evans
	G-BKHC	W.S.55 Whirlwind HAR.10 (XP328)	Flight C Helicopters Ltd
	G-BKHD	Oldfield Baby Great Lakes	P. J. Tanulak
	G-BKHE	Boeing 737-204	Britannia Airways Ltd *Sir Francis Chichester*/Luton
	G-BKHG	Piper J-3C-65 Cub (479766)	K. G. Wakefield
	G-BKHL	Thunder Ax9-140 balloon	R. Carr/France
	G-BKHP	P.56 Provost T.1 (WW397)	M. J. Crymble/Lyneham
	G-BKHR	Luton LA-4 Minor	A. C. P. de Labat
	G-BKHT	BAe 146-100	Dan-Air Services Ltd/Gatwick
	G-BKHW	Stoddard-Hamilton Glasair SH.2RG	N. Clayton
	G-BKHX	Bensen B.8M	D. H. Greenwood
	G-BKHY	Taylor JT.1 Monoplane	M. C. Holmes & A. Shuttleworth
	G-BKHZ	Cessna F.172P	Warwickshire Flying Training Centre Ltd
	G-BKIA	SOCATA TB.10 Tobago	D. H. Barton/Redhill
	G-BKIB	SOCATA TB.9 Tampico	A. J. Baggerley & F. D. J. Simmons/Goodwood
	G-BKIC	Cameron V-77 balloon	C. A. Butler
	G-BKIF	Fournier RF-6B	G. G. Milton
	G-BKII	Cessna F.172M	M. S. Knight/Goodwood
	G-BKIJ	Cessna F.172M	V. Speck
	G-BKIK	Cameron DG-10 airship	Airspace Outdoor Advertising Ltd
	G-BKIM	Unicorn UE.5A balloon	I. Chadwick & K. H. Turner
	G-BKIN	Alon A.2A Aircoupe	P. A. Williams/Blackbushe
	G-BKIR	Jodel D.117	R. Shaw & D. M. Hardaker/Sherburn
	G-BKIS	SOCATA TB.10 Tobago	Ospreystar Ltd
	G-BKIT	SOCATA TB.9 Tampico	D. G. Bligh/Ipswich
	G-BKIU	Colt 17A balloon	Robert Pooley Ltd
	G-BKIV	Colt 21A balloon	Colt Balloons Ltd
	G-BKIX	Cameron V-31 balloon	G. Stevens
	G-BKIY	Thunder Ax3 balloon	A. Hornak
	G-BKIZ	Cameron V-31 balloon	A. P. Greathead
	G-BKJB	PA-18 Super Cub 135	Cormack (Aircraft Services) Ltd/Glasgow
	G-BKJD	Bell 214ST	Bristow Helicopters Ltd
	G-BKJE	Cessna 172N	The G-BKJE Group
	G-BKJF	M.S.880B Rallye 100T	Nova Flying Group
	G-BKJG	BN-2B-21 Islander	Pilatus BN Ltd/Bembridge
	G-BKJH	BN-2B-21 Islander	Medical Aviation Services Ltd
	G-BKJR	Hughes 269C	March Helicopters Ltd/Sywell
	G-BKJS	Jodel D.120A	S. Walmsley
	G-BKJT	Cameron O-65 balloon	K. A. Ward
	G-BKJW	PA-23 Aztec 250E	Alan Williams Entertainments Ltd
	G-BKKN	Cessna 182R	R A. Marven/Elstree
	G-BKKO	Cessna 182R	B. & G. Jebson Ltd/Crosland Moor
	G-BKKP	Cessna 182R	ISF Aviation Ltd/Leicester
	G-BKKR	Rand KR-2	D. Beale & S. P. Gardner
	G-BKKZ	Pitts S-1D Special	G. C. Masterton

Reg.	Type	Owner or Operator	Notes
G-BKLB	R. S2R Thrush Commander	Ag-Air	
G-BKLC	Cameron V-56 balloon	M. A. & J. R. H. Ashworth	
G-BKLJ	Westland Scout AH.1 ★	Wilkie Museum Collection/Blackpool	
G-BKLM	Thunder Ax9-140 balloon	Aerial Promotions Balloon Club	
G-BKLO	Cessna F.172M	Stapleford Flying Club Ltd	
G-BKLP	Cessna F.172N	Hana Aviation Ltd	
G-BKLS	SA.341G Gazelle 1	J. W. Davy (G-TURP)	
G-BKLT	SA.341G Gazelle 1	Specialist Flying Training Ltd/Carlisle	
G-BKMA	Mooney M.20J Srs 201	P. M. Breton	
G-BKMB	Mooney M.20J Srs 201	W. A. Cook & ptnrs/Sherburn	
G-BKMD	SC.7 Skyvan Srs 3	London Skydiving Centre Ltd/Cranfield	
G-BKMH	Flamboyant Ax7-65 balloon	Pepsi-Cola International Ltd/S. Africa	
G-BKMI	V.S.359 Spitfire HF VIII (MV154)	Aerial Museum (North Weald) Ltd	
G-BKMK	PA-38-112 Tomahawk	D. W. Higgins/Glasgow	
G-BKMM	Cessna 180K	M. Kirk	
G-BKMN	BAe 146-100	Dan-Air Services Ltd (G-ODAN)/Gatwick	
G-BKMR	Thunder Ax3 balloon	B. F. G. Ribbons	
G-BKMT	PA-32R-301 Saratoga SP	Severn Valley Aviation Group	
G-BKMU	Short SD3-30 Variant 100	Shorts Aircraft Financing Ltd	
G-BKMX	Short SD3-60	Manx Airlines Ltd/Ronaldsway	
G-BKNA	Cessna 421	Young Investments Ltd	
G-BKNB	Cameron V-42 balloon	S. A. Burnett	
G-BKND	Colt 56A balloon	Flying Colours Balloon Group	
G-BKNH	Boeing 737-210	Dan-Air Services Ltd/Gatwick	
G-BKNI	GY-80 Horizon 160D	A. Hartigan & ptnrs/Fenland	
G-BKNL	Cameron D-96 airship	Drawarm Ltd	
G-BKNN	Cameron Minar E Pakistan balloon	Forbes Europe Ltd/France	
G-BKNO	Monnet Sonerai IIL	E. J. Lloyd	
G-BKNY	Bensen B.8MPV	D. A. C. MacCormack	
G-BKNZ	CP.301A Emeraude	R. Evernden/Barton	
G-BKOA	SOCATA M.S.893E Rallye 180GT	B. Conway & P. J. Clegg	
G-BKOB	Z.326 Trener Master	W. G. V. Hall	
G-BKOR	Barnes 77 balloon	Robert Pooley Ltd	
G-BKOT	Wassmer WA.81 Piranha	B. D. Deubelbeiss	
G-BKOU	P.84 Jet Provost T.3 (XN637)	A. Topen/Cranfield	
G-BKOV	Jodel DR.220A	Merlin Flying Club Ltd/Hucknall	
G-BKOW	Cameron 77A balloon	Hot Air Ballon Co Ltd	
G-BKPA	Hoffman H-36 Dimona	A. Mayhew	
G-BKPB	Aerosport Scamp	E. D. Burke	
G-BKPC	Cessna A.185F	Black Knights Parachute Centre	
G-BKPD	Viking Dragonfly	E. P. Browne & G. J. Sargent	
G-BKPE	Jodel DR.250/160	J. S. & J. D. Lewer	
G-BKPG	Luscombe Rattler Strike	Luscombe Aircraft Ltd	
G-BKPK	John McHugh Gyrocopter	J. C. McHugh	
G-BKPM	Schempp-Hirth HS.5 Nimbus 2	J. L. Rolls	
G-BKPN	Cameron N-77 balloon	R. H. Sanderson	
G-BKPS	AA-5B Tiger	Earthline Ltd	
G-BKPT	M.H.1521M Broussard (192)	R. M. Johnston	
G-BKPV	Stevex 250.1	A. F. Stevens	
G-BKPW	Boeing 767-204	Britannia Airways Ltd *The Earl Mountbatten of Burma*/Luton	
G-BKPX	Jodel D.120A	N. H. Martin	
G-BKPY	Saab 91B/2 Safir (56321)★	Newark Air Museum Ltd	
G-BKPZ	Pitts S-1T Special	P. R. Rutterford/Redhill	
G-BKRA	NA T-6G Texan (51-15227)	Pulsegrove Ltd/Shoreham	
G-BKRB	Cessna 172N	Saunders Caravans Ltd	
G-BKRD	Cessna 320E	Jadealto Ltd	
G-BKRF	PA-18 Super Cub 95	K. M. Bishop	
G-BKRG	Beechcraft C-45G	Aces High Ltd/North Weald	
G-BKRH	Brügger MB.2 Colibri	M. R. Benwell	
G-BKRI	Cameron V-77 balloon	J. R. Lowe & R. J. Fuller	
G-BKRJ	Colt 105A balloon	Owners Abroad Group PLC	
G-BKRK	SNCAN Stampe SV-4C	J. M. Alexander & ptnrs/Aberdeen	
G-BKRL	Chichester-Miles Leopard	Chichester-Miles Consultants Ltd	
G-BKRM	Boeing 757-236	Air 2000 Ltd/Manchester	
G-BKRN	Beechcraft D.18S ★	S. Topen/Cranfield	
G-BKRR	Cameron N-56 balloon	S. L. G. Williams	
G-BKRS	Cameron V-56 balloon	D. N. & L. J. Close	
G-BKRT	PA-34-220T Seneca III	Paucristar Ltd	
G-BKRU	Ensign Crossley Racer	M. Crossley	
G-BKRV	Hovey Beta Bird	A. V. Francis	
G-BKRW	Cameron O-160 balloon	Bondbaste Ltd	
G-BKRX	Cameron O-160 balloon	Bondbaste Ltd	

Notes	Reg.	Type	Owner or Operator
	G-BKRZ	Dragon 77 balloon	J. R. Barber
	G-BKSC	Saro Skeeter AOP.12 (XN351)	R. A. L. Falconer
	G-BKSD	Colt 56A balloon	M. J. & G. C. Casson
	G-BKSE	QAC Quickie Q.2	M. D. Burns
	G-BKSH	Colt 21A balloon	Smith Smart Partnership
	G-BKSJ	Cameron N-108 balloon	Cameron Balloons Ltd
	G-BKSP	Schleicher ASK.14	J. H. Bryson & E. A. H. Boyle
	G-BKSR	Cessna 550 Citation II	Moseley Group (PSV) Ltd/E. Midlands
	G-BKSS	Jodel D.150	D. H. Wilson-Spratt/Ronaldsway
	G-BKST	Rutan Vari-Eze	R. Towle
	G-BKSX	SNCAN Stampe SV-4C	C. A. Bailey & J. A. Carr
	G-BKSZ	Cessna P.210N	Blessvale Ltd
	G-BKTA	PA-18 Super Cub 95	K. E. Chapman/Southend
	G-BKTH	CCF Hawker Sea Hurricane IB (Z7015)	Shuttleworth Trust/Duxford
	G-BKTM	PZL SZD-45A Ogar	Ogar Syndicate
	G-BKTR	Cameron V-77 balloon	R. W. Keron
	G-BKTS	Cameron O-65 balloon	C. H. Pearce & Sons (Contractors) Ltd
	G-BKTT	Cessna F.152	Stapleford Flying Club Ltd
	G-BKTU	Colt 56A balloon	E. Ten Houten
	G-BKTV	Cessna F.152	London Flight Centre Ltd/Stansted
	G-BKTY	SOCATA TB.10 Tobago	B. M. & G. M. McClelland
	G-BKTZ	Slingsby T.67M Firefly	E. Hopper (G-SFTV)
	G-BKUE	SOCATA TB.9 Tampico	W. J. Moore/Kirkbride
	G-BKUJ	Thunder Ax6-56 balloon	R. J. Bent
	G-BKUR	CP.301A Emeraude	R. Wells & H. V. Hunter
	G-BKUS	Bensen B.8M	G. F. Gardener
	G-BKUT	M.S.880B Rallye Club	Rallye Aircraft Flyers
	G-BKUU	Thunder Ax7-77-1 balloon	City of London Balloon Group
	G-BKUY	BAe Jetstream 3102	British Aerospace PLC/Prestwick
	G-BKVA	SOCATA Rallye 180T	Buckminster Gliding Club Syndicate
	G-BKVB	SOCATA Rallye 110ST	Martin Ltd/Biggin Hill
	G-BKVC	SOCATA TB.9 Tampico	Martin Ltd/Biggin Hill
	G-BKVE	Rutan Vari-Eze	R. M. Smith (G-EZLT)
	G-BKVF	FRED Srs 3	D. Coging
	G-BKVG	Scheibe SF.25E Super Falke	G-BKVG Ltd
	G-BKVK	Auster AOP.9 (WZ662)	J. D. Butcher
	G-BKVL	Robin DR.400/160	The Cotswold Aero Club Ltd/Staverton
	G-BKVM	PA-18 Super Cub 150	D. G. Caffrey
	G-BKVN	PA-23 Aztec 250F	B. A. Eastwell/Shoreham
	G-BKVO	Pietenpol Air Camper	G. H. & M. G. A. Phillipson
	G-BKVP	Pitts S-1D Special	P. J. Leggo
	G-BKVR	PA-28 Cherokee 140	D. P. Alexander
	G-BKVS	Bensen B.8M	V. Scott
	G-BKVT	PA-23 Aztec 250E	Express Bond Ltd (G-HARV)
	G-BKVV	Beech 95-B55 Baron	L. Mc. G. Tulloch
	G-BKVW	Airtour 56 balloon	L. D. & H. Vaughan
	G-BKVX	Airtour 56 balloon	E. G. Woolnough
	G-BKVY	Airtour 31 balloon	Airtour Balloon Co Ltd
	G-BKVZ	Boeing 767-204	Britannia Airways Ltd *Sir Winston Churchill*/ Luton
	G-BKWB	EMB-110P2 Bandeirante	Alexandra Aviation Ltd (G-CHEV)
	G-BKWD	Taylor JT.2 Titch	E. Shouler
	G-BKWE	Colt 17A balloon	Hot-Air Balloon Co Ltd
	G-BKWG	PZL-104 Wilga 35A	Machinery International Ltd
	G-BKWI	Pitts S-2A	R. A. Seeley/Denham
	G-BKWP	Thunder Ax7-77 balloon	G. V. Beckwith
	G-BKWR	Cameron V-65 balloon	D. H. Usill
	G-BKWW	Cameron O-77 balloon	A. M. Marten
	G-BKWY	Cessna F.152	Cambridge Aero Club
	G-BKXA	Robin R.2100	G. J. Anderson & ptnrs
	G-BKXC	Cameron V-77 balloon	P. Sarretti
	G-BKXD	SA.365N Dauphin 2	Bond Helicopters Ltd
	G-BKXE	SA.365N Dauphin 2	Bond Helicopters Ltd
	G-BKXF	PA-28R Cherokee Arrow 200	P. L. Brunton
	G-BKXG	Cessna T.303	Wilton Construction Ltd
	G-BKXL	Cameron Bottle 70 balloon	Cameron Balloons Ltd
	G-BKXM	Colt 17A balloon	R. G. Turnbull
	G-BKXN	ICA IS-28M2A	British Aerospace PLC/Filton
	G-BKXO	Rutan LongEz	P. J. Wareham
	G-BKXP	Auster AOP.6	B. J. & W. J. Ellis
	G-BKXR	D.31A Turbulent	M. B. Hill
	G-BKXT	Cameron D-50 airship	Cameron Balloons Ltd

Reg.	Type	Owner or Operator	Notes
G-BKXX	Cameron V-65 balloon	J. D. Pilkington	
G-BKYA	Boeing 737-236	British Airways *River Derwent*	
G-BKYB	Boeing 737-236	British Airways *River Stour*	
G-BKYC	Boeing 737-236	British Airways *River Wye*	
G-BKYD	Boeing 737-236	British Airways *River Conwy*	
G-BKYE	Boeing 737-236	British Airways *River Lagan*	
G-BKYF	Boeing 737-236	British Airways *River Spey*	
G-BKYG	Boeing 737-236	British Airways *River Exe*	
G-BKYH	Boeing 737-236	British Airways *River Dart*	
G-BKYI	Boeing 737-236	British Airways *River Waveney*	
G-BKYJ	Boeing 737-236	British Airways *River Neath*	
G-BKYK	Boeing 737-236	British Airways *River Foyle*	
G-BKYL	Boeing 737-236	British Airways *River Isis*	
G-BKYM	Boeing 737-236	British Airways *River Cam*	
G-BKYN	Boeing 737-236	British Airways *River Ayr*	
G-BKYO	Boeing 737-236	British Airways *River Kennet*	
G-BKYP	Boeing 737-236	British Airways *River Ystwyth*	
G-BKZA	Cameron N-77 balloon	University of Bath Students Union	
G-BKZB	Cameron V-77 balloon	A. J. Montgomery	
G-BKZE	AS.332L Super Puma	British International Helicopters/Aberdeen	
G-BKZF	Cameron V-56 balloon	G. M. Hobster	
G-BKZG	AS.332L Super Puma	British International Helicopters/Aberdeen	
G-BKZH	AS.332L Super Puma	British International Helicopters/Aberdeen	
G-BKZI	Bell 206B JetRanger 2	Heliwork Services Ltd/Thruxton	
G-BKZJ	Bensen B.8MV	J. C. Birdsall	
G-BKZR	Short SD3-60 Variant 100	Euroworld Airways Ltd (G-OAEX/G-SALU/ Gatwick	
G-BKZT	FRED Srs 2	M. G. Rusby	
G-BKZV	Bede BD-4A	A. L. Bergamasco/Headcorn	
G-BKZY	Cameron N-77 balloon	W. Counties Automobile Co Ltd	
G-BLAA	Fournier RF-5	A. D. Wren/Southend	
G-BLAC	Cessna FA.152	Telair Manchester Ltd	
G-BLAD	Thunder Ax7-77-1 balloon	Somerset Balloon Safaris Ltd	
G-BLAF	Stolp SA.900 V-Star	P. R. Skeels	
G-BLAG	Pitts S-1D Special	R. G. Gee & E. H. Williams	
G-BLAH	Thunder Ax7-77-1 balloon	T. Donnelly	
G-BLAI	Monnet Sonerai IIL	T. Simpson	
G-BLAM	Jodel DR.360	B. F. Baldock	
G-BLAT	Jodel D.150	D. J. Dulborough & A. J. Court	
G-BLAW	PA-28-181 Archer II	Luton Flight Training Ltd	
G-BLAX	Cessna FA.152	Shoreham Flight Simulation Ltd/ Bournemouth	
G-BLAY	Robin HR.100/200B	B. A. Mills	
G-BLCA	Bell 206B JetRanger 3	R.M.H. Stainless Ltd	
G-BLCC	Thunder Ax7-77Z balloon	P. Hassell Ltd	
G-BLCF	EAA Acro Sport 2	M. J. Watkins & ptnrs	
G-BLCG	SOCATA TB.10 Tobago	Charlie Golf Flying Group (G-BHES)/ Shoreham	
G-BLCH	Colt 56D balloon	Balloon Flights Club Ltd	
G-BLCI	EAA Acro Sport	M. R. Holden	
G-BLCK	V.S.361 Spitfire F.IX (TE566)	Historic Aircraft Collection Ltd	
G-BLCM	SOCATA TB.9 Tampico	Repclif Aviation Ltd/Liverpool	
G-BLCT	Jodel DR.220 2+2	H. W. Jemmett	
G-BLCU	Scheibe SF.25B Falke	B. Lumb/Rufforth	
G-BLCV	Hoffman H-36 Dimona	Charlie Victor Motor Glider Group	
G-BLCW	Evans VP-1	K. D. Pearce	
G-BLCY	Thunder Ax7-65Z balloon	Thunder Balloons Ltd	
G-BLDB	Taylor JT.1 Monoplane	C. J. Bush	
G-BLDC	K&S Jungster 1	A. W. Brown	
G-BLDD	WAG-Aero CUBy AcroTrainer	C. A. Laycock	
G-BLDE	Boeing 737-2E7	Dan-Air Services Ltd/Gatwick	
G-BLDG	PA-25 Pawnee 260C	Ouse Gliding Club Ltd/Rufforth	
G-BLDH	BAC One-Eleven 475EZ	McAlpine Aviation Ltd/Luton	
G-BLDK	Robinson R-22	R. H. Cleare & Co Ltd	
G-BLDL	Cameron Truck 56 balloon	Cameron Balloons Ltd	
G-BLDN	Rand KR-2	R. Y. Kendal	
G-BLDP	Slingsby T.67M Firefly	Sherburn Aero Club Ltd	
G-BLDY	Bell 212	Bristow Helicopters Ltd	
G-BLEB	Colt 69A balloon	I. R. M. Jacobs	
G-BLEC	BN-2B-27 Islander	LEC Refrigeration PLC (G-BJBG)	
G-BLEJ	PA-28-161 Warrior II	Eglinton Flying Club Ltd	
G-BLEL	Price Ax7-77-245 balloon	T. S. Price	

Notes	Reg.	Type	Owner or Operator
	G-BLEP	Cameron V-65 balloon	D. Chapman
	G-BLES	Stolp SA.750 Acroduster Too	T. W. Harris
	G-BLET	Thunder Ax7-77-1 balloon	Servatruc Ltd
	G-BLEW	Cessna F.182Q	Interair Aviation Ltd/Bournemouth
	G-BLEY	SA.365N Dauphin 2	Bond Helicopters Ltd
	G-BLEZ	SA.365N Dauphin 2	Bond Helicopters Ltd
	G-BLFE	Cameron Sphinx SS balloon	Forbes Europe Inc
	G-BLFF	Cessna F.172M	Air Advertising UK Ltd
	G-BLFJ	F.27 Friendship Mk 100	Air UK Ltd (G-OMAN/G-SPUD)/Norwich
	G-BLFT	P.56 Provost T.1 (WV686)	B. W. H. Parkhouse
	G-BLFW	AA-5 Traveler	Grumman Club
	G-BLFY	Cameron V-77 balloon	A. N. F. Pertwee
	G-BLFZ	PA-31-310 Turbo Navajo C	Huktra UK Ltd
	G-BLGB	Short SD3-60	Loganair Ltd/Glasgow
	G-BLGH	Robin DR.300/180R	Booker Gliding Club Ltd
	G-BLGM	Cessna 425	UST Ltd
	G-BLGO	Bensen B.8M	F. Vernon
	G-BLGR	Bell 47G-4A	Autair Ltd
	G-BLGS	SOCATA Rallye 180T	Lasham Gliding Society Ltd
	G-BLGT	PA-18 Super Cub 95	T. A. Reed/Dunkeswell
	G-BLGV	Bell 206B JetRanger	Base Helicopters Ltd
	G-BLGW	F.27 Friendship Mk 200	Air UK Ltd *Louis Marchesi*/Norwich
	G-BLGX	Thunder Ax7-65 balloon	Harper & Co (Glasgow) Ltd
	G-BLHA	Thunder Ax10-160 balloon	Thunder Balloons Ltd
	G-BLHB	Thunder Ax10-160 balloon	Thunder Balloons Ltd
	G-BLHF	Nott-Cameron ULD-2 balloon	J. R. P. Nott
	G-BLHH	Jodel DR.315	G. G. Milton
	G-BLHI	Colt 17A balloon	Thunder & Colt Ltd
	G-BLHJ	Cessna F.172P	P. P. D. Howard-Johnston/Edinburgh
	G-BLHK	Colt 105A balloon	Hale Hot-Air Balloon Club
	G-BLHM	PA-18 Super Cub 95	N. M. Bloom
	G-BLHN	Robin HR.100/285	H. M. Bouquiere/Biggin Hill
	G-BLHR	GA-7 Cougar	Fotex Aviation Ltd
	G-BLHS	Bellanca 7ECA Citabria	J. W. Platten & E. J. Timmins
	G-BLHW	Varga 2150A Kachina	D. M. Jagger
	G-BLHZ	Varga 2150A Kachina	MLP Aviation Ltd/Elstree
	G-BLID	D.H.112 Venom FB.50 (J-1605) ★	P. G. Vallance Ltd/Charlwood
	G-BLIE	D.H.112 Venom FB.50	R. J. Everett
	G-BLIG	Cameron V-65 balloon	W. Davison
	G-BLIH	PA-18 Super Cub 135	I. R. F. Hammond
	G-BLIK	Wallis WA-116/F/S	K. H. Wallis
	G-BLIP	Cameron N-77 balloon	L. A. Beardall & G. R. Hunt
	G-BLIT	Thorp T-18 CW	A. J. Waller
	G-BLIV	Cameron O-105 balloon	A. M. Thompson
	G-BLIW	P.56 Provost T.51 (177)	Pulsegrove Ltd (*stored*)/Shoreham
	G-BLIX	Saro Skeeter Mk 12 (XL809)	A. P. Nowicki
	G-BLIY	M.S.892A Rallye Commodore	A. J. Brasher & K. R. Haynes
	G-BLJD	Glaser-Dirks DG.400	G. G. Hearne & M. I. Gee
	G-BLJE	AB-206B JetRanger	Nexgen Ltd
	G-BLJF	Cameron O-65 balloon	C. Dupernex & L. Kindley
	G-BLJG	Cameron N-105 balloon	J. W. Cato
	G-BLJH	Cameron N-77 balloon	Phillair
	G-BLJI	Colt 105A balloon	Tempowish Ltd
	G-BLJJ	Cessna 305 Bird Dog	P. Dawe
	G-BLJM	Beech 95-B55 Baron	Elstree Aircraft Hire Ltd
	G-BLJN	Nott-Cameron ULD-1 balloon	J. R. P. Nott
	G-BLJO	Cessna F.152	Redhill School of Flying Ltd
	G-BLJP	Cessna F.150L	Three Counties Aero Engineering Ltd/ Lasham
	G-BLKA	D.H.112 Venom FB.54 (WR410)	A. Topen/Cranfield
	G-BLKB	Boeing 737-3T5	Britannia Airways Ltd/Luton
	G-BLKC	Boeing 737-3T5	Britannia Airways Ltd/Luton
	G-BLKD	Boeing 737-3T5	Britannia Airways Ltd/Luton
	G-BLKE	Boeing 737-3T5	Britannia Airways Ltd/Luton
	G-BLKF	Thunder Ax10-160 balloon	Thunder Balloons Ltd
	G-BLKG	Thunder Ax10-160 balloon	Thunder Balloons Ltd
	G-BLKH	Thunder Ax10-160 balloon	Thunder Balloons Ltd
	G-BLKI	Thunder Ax10-160 balloon	Thunder Balloons Ltd
	G-BLKJ	Thunder Ax7-65 balloon	D. T. Watkins
	G-BLKK	Evans VP-1	R. W. Burrows
	G-BLKL	D.31 Turbulent	D. L. Ripley
	G-BLKM	Jodel DR.1051	T. C. Humphreys
	G-BLKP	BAe Jetstream 3102	British Aerospace PLC/Warton

Reg.	Type	Owner or Operator	Notes
G-BLKU	Colt 56 SS balloon	Hot-Air Balloon Co Ltd	
G-BLKY	Beech 95-58 Baron	Kebbell Holdings Ltd/Leavesden	
G-BLKZ	Pilatus P2-05	Autokraft Ltd	
G-BLLA	Bensen B.8M	K. T. Donaghey	
G-BLLB	Bensen B.8M	D. H. Moss	
G-BLLD	Cameron O-77 balloon	I. O. Gracie	
G-BLLE	Cameron 60 Burger King SS balloon	Burger King UK Ltd	
G-BLLH	Jodel DR.220A 2+2	D. R. Scott-Longhurst & V. D. Stotter	
G-BLLM	PA-23 Aztec 250E	C. & M. Thomas (G-BBNM)/Cardiff	
G-BLLN	PA-18 Super Cub 95	A. L. Hall-Carpenter	
G-BLLO	PA-18 Super Cub 95	D. G. & M. G. Marketts	
G-BLLP	Slingsby T.67B	Devon School of Flying/Dunkeswell	
G-BLLR	Slingsby T.67B	Trent Air Services Ltd/Cranfield	
G-BLLS	Slingsby T.67B	Trent Air Services Ltd/Cranfield	
G-BLLT	AA-5B Tiger	Alpha Welding & Engineering Ltd	
G-BLLU	Cessna 421C	Bumbles Ltd	
G-BLLV	Slingsby T.67B	R. L. Brinklow	
G-BLLW	Colt 56B balloon	J. C. Stupples	
G-BLLY	Cessna 340A	Thunder & Colt Ltd	
G-BLLZ	Rutan LongEz	G. E. Relf & ptnrs	
G-BLMA	Zlin 326 Trener Master	G. P. Northcott/Shoreham	
G-BLMC	Avro 698 Vulcan B.2A (XM575) ★	Aeropark/E. Midlands	
G-BLME	Robinson R-22	Skyline Helicopters Ltd	
G-BLMG	Grob G.109B	K. & A. Barton	
G-BLMI	PA-18 Super Cub 95	B. J. Borsberry	
G-BLMN	Rutan LongEz	G-BLMN Flying Group	
G-BLMP	PA-17 Vagabond	M. Austin/Popham	
G-BLMR	PA-18 Super Cub 150	W. J. J. Kamper	
G-BLMT	PA-18 Super Cub 135	I. S. Runnalls	
G-BLMV	Jodel DR.1051	S. Windsor	
G-BLMW	T.66 Nipper 3	S. L. Millar	
G-BLMX	Cessna FR.172H	A. J. Fuller & ptnrs/Felthorpe	
G-BLMZ	Colt 105A balloon	M. J. Hutchins	
G-BLNB	V.802 Viscount	British Air Ferries (G-AOHV)/Southend	
G-BLNJ	BN-2B-26 Islander	Loganair Ltd/Glasgow	
G-BLNO	FRED Srs 3	L. W. Smith	
G-BLNW	BN-2B-26 Islander	Loganair Ltd/Glasgow	
G-BLOA	V.806 Viscount Freightmaster II	British Air Ferries Ltd (G-AOYJ) *Viscount Jock Bryce OBE*/Southend	
G-BLOB	Colt 31A balloon	Jacques W. Soukup Ltd	
G-BLOE	PA-31-350 Navajo Chieftain	PW Cleaning Services Ltd (G-NITE)	
G-BLOJ	Thunder Ax7-77 Srs 1 balloon	J. W. Cato	
G-BLOK	Colt 77A balloon	D. L. Clark *Spritsa*	
G-BLOL	SNCAN Stampe SV-4A	Skysport Engineering Ltd	
G-BLOO	Sopwith Dove Replica	Skysport Engineering Ltd	
G-BLOR	PA-30 Twin Comanche 160	J. A. Burton	
G-BLOS	Cessna 185A (also flown with floats)	E. Brun	
G-BLOT	Colt Ax6-56B balloon	H. J. Anderson	
G-BLOU	Rand KR-2	D. Cole	
G-BLOV	Colt Ax5-42 Srs 1 balloon	Thunder & Colt Ltd	
G-BLPA	Piper J-3C-65 Cub	G. A. Card	
G-BLPB	Turner TSW Hot Two Wot	J. R. Woolford	
G-BLPE	PA-18 Super Cub 95	A. Haig-Thomas	
G-BLPF	Cessna FR.172G	A. C. McKay & A. H. McVicar	
G-BLPG	J/1N Alpha (16693)	Q. J. Ball (G-AZIH)	
G-BLPH	Cessna FRA.150L	New Aerobat Group/Shoreham	
G-BLPI	Slingsby T.67B	W. F. Hall	
G-BLPK	Cameron V-65 balloon	A. J. & C. P. Nicholls	
G-BLPM	AS.332L Super Puma	Bristow Helicopters Ltd	
G-BLPP	Cameron V-77 balloon	L. P. Purfield	
G-BLPV	Short SD3-60 Variant 100	Shorts Aircraft Financing Ltd	
G-BLRC	PA-18 Super Cub 135	Grays (Pakefield) Ltd	
G-BLRD	MBB Bo.209 Monsun 150FV	M. D. Ward	
G-BLRF	Slingsby T.67C	Bristow Helicopters Ltd/Redhill	
G-BLRG	Slingsby T.67B	Devon School of Flying/Dunkeswell	
G-BLRH	Rutan LongEz	G. L. Thompson	
G-BLRJ	Jodel DR.1051	M. P. Hallam	
G-BLRL	CP.301C-1 Emeraude	M. Howells/Barton	
G-BLRM	Glaser-Dirks DG.400	D. J. Barke	
G-BLRN	D.H.104 Dove 8 (WB531)	C.W. Simpson/Exeter	
G-BLRP	FMA IA.58A Pucará	R. J. H. Butterfield	

Notes	Reg.	Type	Owner or Operator
	G-BLRW	Cameron 77 Elephant SS balloon	Forbes Europe Inc
	G-BLRX	SOCATA TB.9 Tampico	Wiselock Ltd/Elstree
	G-BLRY	AS.332L Super Puma	Bristow Helicopters Ltd
	G-BLRZ	SOCATA TB.9 Tampico	Aldred Associates Ltd
	G-BLSC	Consolidated PBY-5A Catalina (JV928)	J. P. Warren Wilson/Duxford
	G-BLSD	D.H.112 Venom FB.55 (J-1758)	Aces High Ltd/North Weald
	G-BLSF	AA-5A Cheetah	J. P. E. Walsh (G-BGCK)
	G-BLSH	Cameron V-77 balloon	C. N. Luffingham
	G-BLSJ	Thunder Ax8-90 balloon	Thunder Balloons Ltd
	G-BLSK	Colt 77A balloon	Solarmoor Ltd
	G-BLSM	H.S.125 Srs 700B	Dravidian Air Services Ltd/Heathrow
	G-BLSN	Colt AS-56 airship	Flying Pictures (Balloons) Ltd
	G-BLSO	Colt AS-42 airship	Huntair Ltd
	G-BLST	Cessna 421C	Cecil Aviation Ltd/Cambridge
	G-BLSU	Cameron A-210 balloon	Skysales Ltd
	G-BLSX	Cameron O-105 balloon	B. J. Petteford
	G-BLTA	Thunder Ax7-77A	K. A. Schlussler
	G-BLTC	D.31 Turbulent	G. P. Smith & A. W. Burton
	G-BLTF	Robinson R-22A	J. Holt
	G-BLTG	WAR Sea Fury (WJ237)	A. N. R. Houghton & D. H. Nourish
	G-BLTK	R. Commander 112TC	B. Rogalewski/Denham
	G-BLTM	Robin HR.200/100	B. D. Balcanquall
	G-BLTN	Thunder Ax7-65 balloon	J. A. Liddle
	G-BLTP	H.S.125 Srs 700B	Dravidian Air Services Ltd/Heathrow
	G-BLTR	Scheibe SF.25B Falke	V. Mallon/Germany
	G-BLTS	Rutan LongEz	R. W. Cutler
	G-BLTT	Slingsby T.67B	Devon School of Flying/Dunkeswell
	G-BLTU	Slingsby T.67B	The Neiderhein Powered Flying Club/Germany
	G-BLTV	Slingsby T.67B	Trent Air Services Ltd/Cranfield
	G-BLTW	Slingsby T.67B	Devon School of Flying/Dunkeswell
	G-BLTZ	SOCATA TB.10 Tobago	Martin Ltd/Biggin Hill
	G-BLUA	Robinson R-22	J. R. Budgen
	G-BLUE	Colting Ax7-77A balloon	M. R. & C. Cumpston
	G-BLUI	Thunder Ax7-65 balloon	S. Johnson
	G-BLUJ	Cameron V-56 balloon	J. N. W. West
	G-BLUK	Bond Sky Dancer	J. Owen
	G-BLUL	Jodel DR.1051/M1	J. Owen
	G-BLUM	SA.365N Dauphin 2	Bond Helicopters Ltd
	G-BLUN	SA.365N Dauphin 2	Bond Helicopters Ltd
	G-BLUO	SA.365N Dauphin 2	Bond Helicopters Ltd
	G-BLUP	SA.365N Dauphin 2	Bond Helicopters Ltd
	G-BLUV	Grob G.109B	Go-Grob Ltd
	G-BLUX	Slingsby T.67M	Slingsby Aviation Ltd/Kirkbymoorside
	G-BLUY	Colt 69A balloon	The Balloon Goes Up Ltd
	G-BLUZ	D.H.82B Queen Bee (LF858)	B. Bayes
	G-BLVA	Airtour AH-56 balloon	Airtour Balloon Co Ltd
	G-BLVB	Airtour AH-56 balloon	Airtour Balloon Co Ltd
	G-BLVC	Airtour AH-31 balloon	Airtour Balloon Co Ltd
	G-BLVG	EMB-110P1 Bandeirante	Alexandra Aviation Ltd (G-RLAY)
	G-BLVI	Slingsby T.67M	Slingsby Aviation Ltd/Kirkbymoorside
	G-BLVK	CAARP CAP-10B	E. K. Coventry/Earls Colne
	G-BLVL	PA-28-161 Warrior II	C.S.E. Aviation Ltd/Kidlington
	G-BLVN	Cameron N-77 balloon	B. Hodge
	G-BLVS	Cessna 150M	W. Lancashire Aero Club Ltd/Woodvale
	G-BLVU	Pitts S-2A	A. J. E. Ditheridge
	G-BLVV	Bell 206B JetRanger	Bristow Helicopters Ltd
	G-BLVW	Cessna F.172H	R. & D. Holloway Ltd
	G-BLWB	Thunder Ax6-56 balloon	S. A. Simington
	G-BLWD	PA-34-200T Seneca	C.S.E. Aviation Ltd/Kidlington
	G-BLWE	Colt 90A balloon	Huntair Ltd
	G-BLWF	Robin HR.100/210	K. J. Weston
	G-BLWH	Fournier RF-6B-100	Gloster Aero Club Ltd/Staverton
	G-BLWM	Bristol M.1C replica (C4994) ★	RAF Museum/Hendon
	G-BLWP	PA-38-112 Tomahawk	A. Dodd/Booker
	G-BLWR	Currie Wot	H. Moffat
	G-BLWT	Evans VP-1	C. J. Bellworthy
	G-BLWV	Cessna F.152	Redhill Flying Club
	G-BLWW	Taylor Mini Imp Model C	M. K. Field
	G-BLWX	Cameron N-56 balloon	W. Evans
	G-BLWY	Robin 2161D	A. Spencer & D. A. Rolfe
	G-BLWZ	M.S.883 Rallye 115	J. H. Betton

Reg.	Type	Owner or Operator	Notes
G-BLXA	SOCATA TB.20 Trinidad	R. A. McCarthy	
G-BLXF	Cameron V-77 balloon	G. McFarland	
G-BLXG	Colt 21A balloon	Balloon & Airship Co Ltd	
G-BLXH	Fournier RF-3	A. Rawicz-Szczerbo	
G-BLXI	CP.1310-C3 Super Emeraude	RAE Bedford Flying Club	
G-BLXK	Agusta-Bell 205	Autair Helicopters Ltd	
G-BLXO	Jodel D.150	P. R. Powell	
G-BLXP	PA-28R Cherokee Arrow 200	A. M. Bailey & T. A. Shears	
G-BLXR	AS.332L Super Puma	Bristow Helicopters Ltd	
G-BLXS	AS.332L Super Puma	Bristow Helicopters Ltd	
G-BLXT	RAF SE-5A (B4873)	Museum of Army Flying/Middle Wallop	
G-BLXX	PA-23 Aztec 250F	ABR Aviation Ltd (G-PIED)	
G-BLXY	Cameron V-65 balloon	Gone With The Wind Ltd	
G-BLYB	Beech B200 Super King Air	Alfred McAlpine Aviation Ltd	
G-BLYC	PA-38-112 Tomahawk	Liverpool Flying School Ltd	
G-BLYD	SOCATA TB.20 Trinidad	CB Helicopters	
G-BLYE	SOCATA TB.10 Tobago	R. C. Watts	
G-BLYJ	Cameron V-77 balloon	E. E. Clark & J. A. Lomas	
G-BLYK	PA-34-220T Seneca III	P. G. Somers	
G-BLYM	B.121 Pup 2	D. J. Sage	
G-BLYP	Robin 3000/120	Lydd Air Training Centre Ltd	
G-BLYR	Airtour AH-77B balloon	Airtour Balloon Co Ltd	
G-BLYT	Airtour AH-77 balloon	Airtour Balloon Co Ltd	
G-BLYU	Airtour AH-31 balloon	Airtour Balloon Co Ltd	
G-BLYV	Airtour AH-56 balloon	Airtour Balloon Co Ltd	
G-BLYY	PA-28-181 Archer II	A. C. Clarke	
G-BLZA	Scheibe SF.25B Falke	P. Downes & D. Gardner	
G-BLZB	Cameron N-65 balloon	D. Bareford	
G-BLZD	Robin R.1180T	J. R. Howard & P. D. Wheatland	
G-BLZE	Cessna F.152	Flairhire Ltd (G-CSSC)/Redhill	
G-BLZF	Thunder Ax7-77 balloon	H. M. Savage	
G-BLZH	Cessna F.152	Biggin Hill School of Flying	
G-BLZM	Rutan LongEz	Zulu Mike Group	
G-BLZN	Bell 206B JetRanger	Helicopter Services	
G-BLZP	Cessna F.152	E. Midlands Flying School Ltd	
G-BLZR	Cameron A-140 balloon	Clipper Worldwide Trading Ltd	
G-BLZS	Cameron O-77 balloon	M. M. Cobbold	
G-BLZT	Short SD3-60	Air UK Ltd/Norwich	
G-BMAA	Douglas DC-9-15	British Midland Airways Ltd *The Shah Diamond*/(G-BFIH)/E. Midlands	
G-BMAB	Douglas DC-9-15	British Midland Airways Ltd *The Great Mogul Diamond*/E. Midlands	
G-BMAC	Douglas DC-9-15	British Midland Airways Ltd *The Eugenie Diamond*/E. Midlands	
G-BMAD	Cameron V-77 balloon	F. J. J. Fielder	
G-BMAF	Cessna 180F	P. Channon	
G-BMAG	Douglas DC-9-15	British Midland Airways Ltd *The Nassak Diamond*/E. Midlands	
G-BMAH	Douglas DC-9-14	British Midland Airways Ltd *The Florentine Diamond*/E. Midlands	
G-BMAI	Douglas DC-9-14	British Midland Airways Ltd *The Star of Este Diamond*/E. Midlands	
G-BMAK	Douglas DC-9-30	British Midland Airways Ltd *The Stewart Diamond*/E. Midlands	
G-BMAL	Sikorsky S-76A	Bond Helicopters Ltd	
G-BMAM	Douglas DC-9-30	British Midland Airways Ltd *The Cullinan Diamond*/E. Midlands	
G-BMAO	Taylor JT.1 Monoplane	V. A. Wordsworth	
G-BMAR	Short SD3-60	Loganair Ltd (G-BLCR)/Glasgow	
G-BMAV	AS.350B Ecureuil	Southern Trust Co Ltd/Jersey	
G-BMAX	FRED Srs 2	D. A. Arkley	
G-BMAY	PA-18 Super Cub 135	Target Technology Ltd	
G-BMBB	Cessna F.150L	Dacebow Aviation	
G-BMBC	PA-31-350 Navajo Chieftain	Air & General Services Ltd	
G-BMBE	PA-46-310P Malibu	Barfax Distributing Co Ltd & Glasdon Group Ltd/Blackpool	
G-BMBF	Nord 3202B	F. & H. Aircraft Ltd/Breighton	
G-BMBI	PA-31-350 Navajo Chieftain	Ennemix Holdings Ltd/E. Midlands	
G-BMBJ	Schempp-Hirth Janus CM	RAF Germany Gliding Assoc	
G-BMBS	Colt 105A balloon	H. G. Davies	
G-BMBT	Thunder Ax8-90 balloon	Capital Balloon Club Ltd	
G-BMBW	Bensen B.80	M. Vahdat	

Notes	Reg.	Type	Owner or Operator
	G-BMBY	Beech A36 Bonanza	Arthur Webb Engineers Ltd/Birmingham
	G-BMBZ	Scheibe SF.25E Super Falke	Buckminster Super Falke Syndicate
	G-BMCC	Thunder Ax7-77 balloon	H. N. Harben Ltd
	G-BMCD	Cameron V-65 balloon	M. C. Drye
	G-BMCG	Grob G.109B	Lagerholm Finnimport Ltd/Booker
	G-BMCH	AB-206B JetRanger 3	Autair Helicopters Ltd/Luton
	G-BMCI	Cessna F.172H	A. B. Davis/Edinburgh
	G-BMCJ	PA-31-350 Navajo Chieftain	Chelsea Land (Finance) Ltd
	G-BMCK	Cameron O-77 balloon	D. L. Smith
	G-BMCM	Grob G.109B	C. J. Partridge/Blackbushe
	G-BMCN	Cessna F.152	Lincoln Aero Club Ltd/Sturgate
	G-BMCO	Colomban MC.15 Cri-Cri	G. P. Clarke/Enstone
	G-BMCS	PA-22 Tri-Pacer 135	C. J. Weaver
	G-BMCV	Cessna F.152	Leicestershire Aero Club Ltd
	G-BMCW	AS.332L Super Puma	Bristow Helicopters Ltd
	G-BMCX	AS.332L Super Puma	Bristow Helicopters Ltd
	G-BMCZ	Colt 69A balloon	Thunder & Colt Ltd
	G-BMDB	SE-5A replica (F235)	D. Biggs
	G-BMDC	PA-32-301 Saratoga	Maclaren Aviation/Newcastle
	G-BMDD	Slingsby T.29	A. R. Worters
	G-BMDE	Pientenpol Air Camper	D. Silsbury
	G-BMDF	Boeing 737-2E7	Dan-Air Services Ltd/Gatwick
	G-BMDG	Cameron O-105 balloon	Buddy Bombard Balloons Ltd
	G-BMDH	Cameron O-105 balloon	Buddy Bombard Balloons Ltd
	G-BMDI	Thunder Ax8-105Z balloon	Buddy Bombard Balloons Ltd
	G-BMDJ	Price Ax7-77S balloon	T. S. Price
	G-BMDK	PA-34-220T Seneca III	Triple Oak Ltd
	G-BMDO	ARV Super 2	R. Lloyd
	G-BMDP	Partenavia P.64B Oscar 200	D. Foey
	G-BMDS	Jodel D.120	D. Stansfield
	G-BMDW	Bell 47G-5	Trent Air Services Ltd/Cranfield
	G-BMDW	Dangerous Sports Club/Colt Hoppalong 1 balloon	D. A. C. Kirke
	G-BMDY	GA-7 Cougar	P. J. Bristow
	G-BMEA	PA-18 Super Cub 95	C. L. Towell
	G-BMEB	Rotorway Scorpion 145	I. M. Bartlett
	G-BMEE	Cameron O-105 balloon	A. G. R. Calder
	G-BMEG	SOCATA TB.10 Tobago	G. H. N. & R. V. Chamberlain
	G-BMEH	Jodel Special Super Mascaret	W. Coupar Ltd
	G-BMEJ	PA-28R Cherokee Arrow 200	London Flight Centre (Stansted) Ltd
	G-BMEK	Mooney M.20K	Atlantic Film Investments Ltd/USA
	G-BMET	Taylor JT.1 Monoplane	M. K. A. Blyth
	G-BMEU	Isaacs Fury II	A. W. Austin
	G-BMEX	Cessna A.150K	S. G. Eldred & N. A. M. Brain
	G-BMFD	PA-23 Aztec 250F	Rangemile Ltd (G-BGYY)/Coventry
	G-BMFG	Dornier Do.27A-4 (3460)	R. F. Warner
	G-BMFI	PZL SZD-45A Ogar	Marrix Ltd/Redhill
	G-BMFL	Rand KR-2	E. W. B. Comber & M. F. Leusby
	G-BMFN	QAC Quickie Tri-Q.200	A. W. Webster
	G-BMFP	PA-28-161 Warrior II	Bravo-Mike-Fox-Papa Group
	G-BMFT	H.S.748 Srs 2A	—
	G-BMFU	Cameron N-90 balloon	J. J. Rudoni
	G-BMFW	Hughes 369E	Ford Helicopters Ltd
	G-BMFY	Grob G.109B	P. J. Shearer
	G-BMFZ	Cessna F.152	Cornwall Flying Club Ltd
	G-BMGB	PA-28R Cherokee Arrow 200	Malmesbury Specialist Cars
	G-BMGC	Fairey Swordfish Mk II (W5856)	FAA Museum/Yeovilton
	G-BMGD	Colt 17A balloon	Airbureau Ltd
	G-BMGG	Cessna 152	Falcon Flying Services/Biggin Hill
	G-BMGH	PA-31-325 Turbo Navajo C/R	Jet West Ltd/Exeter
	G-BMGP	Hughes 269C	Orion Atlantic Ltd
	G-BMGR	Grob G.109B	M. Clarke & D. S. Hawes
	G-BMGT	Cessna 310R	Air Service Training Ltd/Perth
	G-BMGV	Robinson R-22	D. L. Weldon
	G-BMGY	Lake LA-4-200 Buccaneer	M. A. Ashmole (G-BWKS/G-BDDI)
	G-BMHA	Rutan LongEz	S. F. Elvins
	G-BMHC	Cessna U.206G	Clacton Aero Club (1988) Ltd
	G-BMHJ	Thunder Ax7-65 balloon	M. G. Robinson
	G-BMHK	Cameron V-77 balloon	B. J. Workman
	G-BMHL	Wittman W.8 Tailwind	T. G. Hoult
	G-BMHN	Robinson R-22A	Fulford Builders (York) Ltd
	G-BMHR	Grob G.109B	HRN Aviation Ltd
	G-BMHS	Cessna F.172M	C. H. Ludar-Smith

Reg.	Type	Owner or Operator	Notes
G-BMHT	PA-28RT-201T Turbo Arrow IV	Relay Services Ltd	
G-BMHX	Short SD3-60	Loganair Ltd/Glasgow	
G-BMHZ	PA-28RT-201T Turbo Arrow IV	M. A. Grayburn	
G-BMIA	Thunder Ax8-90 balloon	A. G. R. Calder	
G-BMIB	Bell 206B JetRanger	Lee Aviation Ltd/Booker	
G-BMID	Jodel D.120	P. D. Smoothy	
G-BMIF	AS.350B Ecureuil	Colt Car Co Ltd/Staverton	
G-BMIG	Cessna 172N	J. R. Nicholls/Conington	
G-BMIM	Rutan LongEz	R. M. Smith	
G-BMIO	Stoddard-Hamilton Glasair RG	A. H. Carrington	
G-BMIP	Jodel D.112	M. T. Kinch	
G-BMIR	Westland Wasp HAS.1 (XT788)	R. Windley	
G-BMIS	Monnet Sonerai II	B. A. Bower/Thruxton	
G-BMIV	PA-28R-201T Turbo Arrow III	Maurice Mason Ltd	
G-BMIW	PA-28-181 Archer II	Oldbus Ltd	
G-BMIY	Oldfield Baby Great Lakes	J. B. Scott (G-NOME)	
G-BMJA	PA-32R-301 Saratoga SP	Continental Cars (Stansted) Ltd	
G-BMJB	Cessna 152	Bobbington Air Training School Ltd/ Halfpenny Green	
G-BMJC	Cessna 152	Cambridge Aero Club Ltd	
G-BMJD	Cessna 152	Fife Airport Management Ltd	
G-BMJG	PA-28R Cherokee Arrow 200	D. J. D. Ritchie & ptnrs/Elstree	
G-BMJL	R. Commander 114	H. Snelson	
G-BMJM	Evans VP-1	K. D. Smith	
G-BMJN	Cameron O-65 balloon	E. J. A. Machole	
G-BMJO	PA-34-220T Seneca III	B. Walker & Co (Dursley) Ltd & John Ward (Holdings) Ltd	
G-BMJR	Cessna T.337H	John Roberts Services Ltd (G-NOVA)	
G-BMJS	Thunder Ax7-77 balloon	Foulger Transport Ltd	
G-BMJT	Beech 76 Duchess	Mike Osborne Properties Ltd	
G-BMJW	NA AT-6D Harvard III (EZ259)	J. Woods	
G-BMJX	Wallis WA-116X	K. H. Wallis	
G-BMJY	Yakolev C18M	R. Lamplough/North Weald	
G-BMJZ	Cameron N-90 balloon	Windsor Pharmaceuticals Ltd	
G-BMKB	PA-18 Super Cub 135	C. Marsh	
G-BMKC	Piper J-3C-65 Cub (329854)	R. J. H. Springall	
G-BMKD	Beech C90A King Air	A. E. Bristow	
G-BMKE	PA-28RT-201 Arrow IV	AT Aviation Ltd/Cardiff	
G-BMKF	Jodel DR.221	B. M. R. Clavel & J. M. A. Lassauze	
G-BMKG	PA-38-112 Tomahawk	R. J. Hickson	
G-BMKH	Colt 105A balloon	Scotia Balloons Ltd	
G-BMKI	Colt 21A balloon	Thunder & Colt Ltd	
G-BMKJ	Cameron V-77 balloon	R. C. Thursby	
G-BMKK	PA-28R Cherokee Arrow 200	J. H. Hutchinson	
G-BMKM	AB-206B JetRanger 3	Fizzle Ltd	
G-BMKO	PA-28-181 Archer II	Northfield Garage (Cowdenbeath) Ltd	
G-BMKP	Cameron V-77 balloon	Jacques W. Soukup Enterprises Ltd	
G-BMKR	PA-28-161 Warrior II	Field Flying Group (G-BGKR)/Goodwood	
G-BMKV	Thunder Ax7-77 balloon	A. Hornak & M. J. Nadel	
G-BMKW	Cameron V-77 balloon	A. C. Garnett	
G-BMKX	Cameron 77 Elephant SS balloon	Cameron Balloons Ltd	
G-BMKY	Cameron O-65 balloon	K. M. Taylor	
G-BMLA	Bell UH-1H ★	Grampian Helicopters International Ltd	
G-BMLB	Jodel D.120A	W. O. Brown	
G-BMLC	Short SD3-60 Variant 100	Loganair Ltd/Glasgow	
G-BMLH	Mooney M.20C	G. D. Bowd	
G-BMLJ	Cameron N-77 balloon	C. J. Dunkley	
G-BMLK	Grob G.109B	A. Batters/Rufforth	
G-BMLL	Grob G.109B	A. H. R. Stansfield	
G-BMLP	Boeing 727-264	Dan-Air Services Ltd/Gatwick	
G-BMLS	PA-28R-201 Arrow III	Faukland Flyers Ltd	
G-BMLT	Pietenpol Air Camper	W. E. R. Jenkins	
G-BMLU	Colt 90A balloon	Danish Catering Services Ltd	
G-BMLV	Robinson R-22A	Skyline Helicopters Ltd/Booker	
G-BMLW	Cameron V-65 balloon	M. L. & L. P. Willoughby	
G-BMLX	Cessna F.150L	S. G. P. Foster/Headcorn	
G-BMLY	Grob G.109B	P. H. Yarrow & D. G. Margetts	
G-BMLZ	Cessna 421C	Jet West Ltd (G-OTAD/G-BEVL)/Exeter	
G-BMMC	Cessna T310Q	Cooper Clegg Ltd	
G-BMMD	Rand KR-2	K. R. Wheatley & R. S. Stoddart-Jones	
G-BMMF	FRED Srs 2	J. M. Jones	
G-BMMG	Thunder Ax 7-77 balloon	G. V. Beckwith	
G-BMMI	Pazmany PL.4	M. L. Martin	

Notes	Reg.	Type	Owner or Operator
	G-BMMJ	Siren PIK-30	J. P. Greig
	G-BMMK	Cessna 182P	M. S. Knight/Goodwood
	G-BMML	PA-38-112 Tomahawk	Cumbernauld Aviation Ltd
	G-BMMM	Cessna 152	Luton Flight Training Ltd
	G-BMMN	Thunder Ax8-105 balloon	R. C. Weyda
	G-BMMP	Grob G.109B	B. F. Fraser-Smith & B. F. Pearson
	G-BMMR	Dornier Do.228-200	Suckling Airways Ltd/Cambridge
	G-BMMU	Thunder Ax8-105 balloon	H. C. Wright
	G-BMMV	ICA-Brasov IS-28M2A	T. Cust
	G-BMMW	Thunder Ax7-77 balloon	P. A. Georges
	G-BMMX	ICA-Brasov IS-28M2A	G-BMMX Syndicate
	G-BMMY	Thunder Ax7-77 balloon	D. A. Lawson
	G-BMNF	Beech B200 Super King Air	Bernard Matthews PLC/Norwich
	G-BMNL	PA-28R Cherokee Arrow 200	I. H. Nettleton
	G-BMNP	PA-38-112 Tomahawk	APB Leasing Ltd/Welshpool
	G-BMNT	PA-34-220T Seneca III	Airpart Supply Ltd
	G-BMNU	Cameron V-77 balloon	B. K. & G. S. Palmer
	G-BMNV	SNCAN Stampe SV-4D	Wessex Aviation & Transport Ltd
	G-BMNW	PA-31-350 Navajo Chieftain	Crosswind Consultants
	G-BMNX	Colt 56A balloon	J. H. Dryden
	G-BMNY	Everett gyroplane	G. Jenkis-Lover
	G-BMNZ	Cessna U206F	Macpara Ltd/Shobdon
	G-BMOE	PA-28R Cherokee Arrow 200	B. J. Mason/Shoreham
	G-BMOF	Cessna U206G	Integrated Hydraulics Ltd
	G-BMOG	Thunder Ax7-77A balloon	P. J. Burn
	G-BMOH	Cameron N-77 balloon	P. J. Marshall & M. A. Clarke
	G-BMOI	Partenavia P.68B	Simmette Ltd
	G-BMOJ	Cameron V-56 balloon	S. R. Bridge
	G-BMOK	ARV Super 2	P. E. Barker
	G-BMOL	PA-23 Aztec 250D	LDL Enterprises (G-BBSR)/Elstree
	G-BMOM	ICA-Brasov IS-28M2A	Brasov Flying Group
	G-BMOO	FRED Srs 2	N. Purllant
	G-BMOP	PA-28R-201T Turbo Arrow III	Coleridge Self Service/Cardiff
	G-BMOT	Bensen B.8M	R. S. W. Jones
	G-BMOV	Cameron O-105 balloon	C. Gillott
	G-BMOW	G.159 Gulfstream 1	Birmingham European Airways Ltd
	G-BMOX	Hovey Beta Bird	A. K. Jones
	G-BMPA	G.159 Gulfstream 1	Aberdeen Airways Ltd
	G-BMPC	PA-28-181 Archer II	Trent Securities Ltd
	G-BMPD	Cameron V-65 balloon	G. J. Barton
	G-BMPL	OA.7 Optica	Lovaux Ltd/Bournemouth
	G-BMPP	Cameron N-77 balloon	Sarnia Balloon Group
	G-BMPR	PA-28R-201 Arrow III	AH Flight Services Ltd
	G-BMPS	Strojnik S-2A	G. J. Green
	G-BMPY	D.H.82A Tiger Moth	S. M. F. Eisenstein
	G-BMRA	Boeing 757-236	British Airways *Beaumaris Castle*
	G-BMRB	Boeing 757-236	British Airways *Colchester Castle*
	G-BMRC	Boeing 757-236	British Airways *Rochester Castle*
	G-BMRD	Boeing 757-236	British Airways *Bothwell Castle*
	G-BMRE	Boeing 757-236	British Airways *Killyleagh Castle*
	G-BMRF	Boeing 757-236	British Airways *Hever Castle*
	G-BMRG	Boeing 757-236	British Airways *Caerphilly Castle*
	G-BMRH	Boeing 757-236	British Airways *Norwich Castle*
	G-BMRI	Boeing 757-236	British Airways *Tonbridge Castle*
	G-BMRJ	Boeing 757-236	British Airways *Old Wardour Castle/ Loch Tummel*
	G-BMSA	Stinson HW.75 Voyager	M. A. Thomas (G-BCUM)/Barton
	G-BMSB	V.S.509 Spitfire IX (MJ627)	M. S. Bayliss (G-ASOZ)
	G-BMSC	Evans VP-2	F. R. Donaldson
	G-BMSD	PA-28-181 Archer II	Courtridge Ltd
	G-BMSE	Valentin Taifun 17E	K. P. O'Sullivan & G. T. Birks/Booker
	G-BMSF	PA-38-112 Tomahawk	N. Bradley/Leeds
	G-BMSG	Saab 32A Lansen ★	Aces High Ltd/Cranfield
	G-BMSI	Cameron N-105 balloon	Direction Air Conditioning Ltd
	G-BMSK	Hoffman H-36 Dimona	J. P. Kovacs
	G-BMSL	FRED Srs 3	A. C. Coombe
	G-BMSR	G.159 Gulfstream 1	Aberdeen Airways Ltd
	G-BMST	Cameron N-31 balloon	Hot Air Balloon Co Ltd
	G-BMSU	Cessna 152	M. T. Tidswell
	G-BMSW	Cessna T.210M	Foxgrove Construction Ltd
	G-BMSX	PA-30 Twin Comanche 160	M. Sparks/Bristol
	G-BMSY	Cameron A-140 balloon	GT Flying Clubs Ltd
	G-BMSZ	Cessna 152	Aerohire Ltd

Reg.	Type	Owner or Operator	Notes
G-BMTA	Cessna 152	Turnhouse Flying Club	
G-BMTB	Cessna 152	J. A. Pothecary/Shoreham	
G-BMTJ	Cessna 152	Creaton Aviation Services Ltd	
G-BMTK	Cessna 152	N. A. Ali	
G-BMTL	Cessna 152	Agricultural & General Aviation/ Bournemouth	
G-BMTN	Cameron O-77 balloon	Industrial Services (MH) Ltd	
G-BMTO	PA-38-112 Tomahawk	N. A. Ali	
G-BMTP	PA-38-112 Tomahawk	R. A. Wakefield	
G-BMTR	PA-28-161 Warrior II	London Flight Centre (Stansted) Ltd	
G-BMTS	Cessna 172N	Luton Flight Training Ltd	
G-BMTU	Pitts S-1E Special	O. R. Howe	
G-BMTW	PA-31-350 Navajo Chieftain	Air Northwest Ltd	
G-BMTX	Cameron V-77 balloon	J. A. Langley	
G-BMTY	Colt 77A balloon	L. D. Ormerod	
G-BMUD	Cessna 182P	M. A. Hocking	
G-BMUG	Rutan LongEz	P. Richardson & J. Shanley	
G-BMUH	Bensen B.8MR	A. Shuttleworth	
G-BMUI	Brügger MB.2 Colibri	Carlton Flying Group/Netherthorpe	
G-BMUJ	Colt Drachenfisch balloon	Air 2 Air Ltd	
G-BMUK	Colt UFO balloon	Air 2 Air Ltd	
G-BMUL	Colt Kindermond balloon	Air 2 Air Ltd	
G-BMUN	Cameron Harley 78 balloon	Forbes Europe Inc/France	
G-BMUO	Cessna A.152	Redhill Flying Club	
G-BMUR	Cameron gas airship	Cameron Balloons Ltd	
G-BMUT	PA-34-200T Seneca II	G. G. Long	
G-BMUU	Thunder Ax7-77 balloon	Thunder & Colt Ltd	
G-BMUZ	PA-28-161 Warrior II	Newcastle-upon-Tyne Aero Club Ltd	
G-BMVA	Schiebe SF.25B Falke	C. A. Simmonds	
G-BMVB	Cessna 152	Telair Manchester Ltd	
G-BMVE	PA-28RT-201 Arrow IV	F. E. Gooding/Biggin Hill	
G-BMVG	QAC Quickie Q.1	P. M. Wright	
G-BMVI	Cameron O-105 balloon	Heart of England Balloons	
G-BMVJ	Cessna 172N	G & B Aviation Ltd/Coventry	
G-BMVK	PA-38-112 Tomahawk	Airways Aero Associations Ltd/Booker	
G-BMVL	PA-38-112 Tomahawk	Airways Aero Associations Ltd/Booker	
G-BMVM	PA-38-112 Tomahawk	Airways Aero Associations Ltd/Booker	
G-BMVO	Cameron O-77 balloon	Warners Motors (Leasing) Ltd	
G-BMVS	Cameron 77 SS balloon	Shellrise Ltd	
G-BMVT	Thunder Ax7-77A balloon	M. L. & L. P. Willoughby	
G-BMVU	Monnet Moni	F. S. Beckett	
G-BMVV	Rutan Vari-Viggen	G. B. Roberts	
G-BMVW	Cameron O-65 balloon	S. P. Richards	
G-BMVX	M.S.733 Alcyon Srs 1	J. D. Read	
G-BMVY	Beech B200 Super King Air	A. F. Budge (Aviation) Ltd/Gamston	
G-BMVZ	Cameron 66 Cornetto SS balloon	Gone With The Wind Ltd	
G-BMWA	Hughes 269C	JKG Air Services	
G-BMWB	Cessna 421C	Capital Trading Aviation Ltd/Cardiff	
G-BMWE	ARV Super 2	Interair (Aviation) Ltd/Bournemouth	
G-BMWF	ARV Super 2	ARV Aviation Ltd/Sandown	
G-BMWG	ARV Super 2	Falstaff Finance Ltd/Sandown	
G-BMWJ	ARV Super 2	ARV Aviation Ltd/Sandown	
G-BMWM	ARV Super 2	R. Scroby	
G-BMWN	Cameron 80 SS Temple balloon	Forbes Europe Inc/France	
G-BMWP	PA-34-200T Seneca II	R. H. Steward	
G-BMWR	R. Commander 112A	M. Edwards & B. Fields	
G-BMWU	Cameron N-42 balloon	The Hot Air Balloon Co Ltd	
G-BMWV	Putzer Elster B	E. A. J. Hibberd	
G-BMWX	Robinson R-22B	LTG Motors (Baldock)	
G-BMXA	Cessna 152	Chamberlain Leasing	
G-BMXB	Cessna 152	Semloch Aviation Services/Andrewsfield	
G-BMXC	Cessna 152	Vectair Aviation Ltd	
G-BMXD	F.27 Friendship Mk 500	Air UK Ltd *Victor Hugo*/Norwich	
G-BMXH	Robinson R-22HP	R. Towle	
G-BMXJ	Cessna F.150L	J. W. G. Ellis	
G-BMXL	PA-38-112 Tomahawk	Airways Aero Associations Ltd/Booker	
G-BMXM	Colt 180A balloon	Thunder & Colt Ltd	
G-BMXW	D.H.C.6 Twin Otter 310	Loganair Ltd/Glasgow	
G-BMXX	Cessna 152	Aerohire Ltd/Halfpenny Green	
G-BMXY	Schiebe SF.25B Falke	Marrix Ltd	
G-BMYA	Colt 56A balloon	Flying Pictures (Balloons) Ltd	
G-BMYC	SOCATA TB.10 Tobago	C. J. Crooks/Southampton	
G-BMYD	Beech A36 Bonanza	F. B. Gibbons & Sons Ltd	

Notes	Reg.	Type	Owner or Operator
	G-BMYE	BAe 146-200	British Aerospace PLC (G-WAUS/ G-WISC)/ Hatfield
	G-BMYF	Bensen B.8M	T. H. G. Russell
	G-BMYG	Cessna F.152	Rolim Ltd/Aberdeen
	G-BMYH	Rotorway Executive 133	D. W. Smith
	G-BMYI	AA-5 Traveler	W. C. & S. C. Westran
	G-BMYJ	Cameron V-65 balloon	S. M. Antony & R. J. Christopher
	G-BMYK	BAe ATP	British Midland Airways Ltd/E. Midlands
	G-BMYM	BAe ATP	British Midland Airways Ltd/E. Midlands
	G-BMYN	Colt 77A balloon	J. D. Shapland & ptnrs
	G-BMYO	Cameron V-65 balloon	N. V. Moreton
	G-BMYP	Fairey Gannet AEW.3 (XL502)	R. King
	G-BMYR	Robinson R-22	B. Warrington
	G-BMYS	Thunder Ax7-77Z balloon	J. E. Weidema
	G-BMYU	Jodel D.120	I. A. Marsh/Elstree
	G-BMYV	Bensen B.8M	R. G. Cotman
	G-BMYW	Hughes 269C	William Tomkins Ltd
	G-BMZA	Air Command 503 Commander	R. W. Husband
	G-BMZB	Cameron N-77 balloon	D. C. Eager
	G-BMZC	Cessna 421C	Gilchrist Enterprises
	G-BMZD	Beech C90 King Air	Colt Transport Ltd
	G-BMZE	SOCATA TB.9 Tampico	Air Touring Club Ltd/Biggin Hill
	G-BMZF	Mikoyan Gurevich MiG-15 (1420) ★	FAA Museum/Yeovilton
	G-BMZG	QAC Quickie Q.2	K. W. Brooker
	G-BMZH	Cameron A-140 balloon	The Balloon Stable Ltd
	G-BMZJ	Colt 400A balloon	Thunder & Colt Ltd
	G-BMZN	Everett gyroplane	R. J. Brown
	G-BMZP	Everett gyroplane	B. C. Norris
	G-BMZS	Everett gyroplane	C. W. Cload
	G-BMZV	Cessna 172P	Mid Shires Aviation Ltd
	G-BMZW	Bensen B.8	P. D. Widdicombe
	G-BMZX	Wolf W-II Boredom Fighter (146-11042)	J. J. Penney
	G-BMZZ	Stephens Akro Z	P. G. Kynsey & J. Harper/Redhill
	G-BNAA	V.806 Viscount	British Air Ferries (G-AOYH)/Southend
	G-BNAB	GA-7 Cougar	Brod Gallery (G-BGYP)/Elstree
	G-BNAD	Rand KR-2	R. A. Davis
	G-BNAG	Colt 105A balloon	R. W. Batcholer
	G-BNAH	Colt Paper Bag SS balloon	Thrustell Ltd
	G-BNAI	Wolf W-II Boredom Fighter (146-11083)	P. J. D. Gronow
	G-BNAJ	Cessna 152	G. Duncan
	G-BNAL	F.27 Friendship Mk 600	Air UK Ltd/Norwich
	G-BNAN	Cameron V-65 balloon	A. M. Lindsay
	G-BNAO	Colt AS-105 airship	Heather Flight Ltd
	G-BNAP	Colt 240A balloon	Heather Flight Ltd
	G-BNAR	Taylor JT.1 Monoplane	C. J. Smith
	G-BNAU	Cameron V-65 balloon	J. Buckle
	G-BNAW	Cameron V-65 balloon	A. Walker
	G-BNAY	Grob G.109B	Microperm Ltd
	G-BNBJ	AS.355F-1 Twin Squirrel	Coln Helicopters Ltd
	G-BNBL	Thunder Ax7-77 balloon	J. R. Henderson
	G-BNBM	Colt 90A balloon	Huntair Ltd
	G-BNBR	Cameron N-90 balloon	Morning Star Motors Ltd
	G-BNBU	Bensen B.8MV	D. T. Murchie
	G-BNBV	Thunder Ax7-77 balloon	J. M. Robinson
	G-BNBW	Thunder Ax7-77 balloon	I. S. & S. W. Watthews
	G-BNBY	Beech 95-B55A Baron	C. Wright (G-AXXR)
	G-BNBZ	LET L-200D Morava	M. Emery/Redhill
	G-BNCA	Lightning F.2A ★	P. Hoar/Cranfield
	G-BNCB	Cameron V-77 balloon	Tyred & Battered Balloon Group
	G-BNCC	Thunder Ax7-77 balloon	C. J. Burnhope
	G-BNCG	QAC Quickie Q.2	T. F. Francis
	G-BNCH	Cameron V-77 balloon	Royal Engineers Balloon Club
	G-BNCJ	Cameron V-77 balloon	I. S. Bridge
	G-BNCK	Cameron V-77 balloon	G. Randall/Germany
	G-BNCL	WG.13 Lynx HAS.2 (XX469) ★	Wilkie Museum Collection/Blackpool
	G-BNCM	Cameron N-77 balloon	S. & A. Stone Ltd
	G-BNCN	Glaser-Dirks DG.400	M. C. Costin
	G-BNCO	PA-38-112 Tomahawk	Cambrian Flying Club/Swansea
	G-BNCR	PA-28-161 Warrior II	Airways Aero Associations Ltd/Booker

Reg.	Type	Owner or Operator	Notes
G-BNCS	Cessna 180	C. Elwell Transport Ltd	
G-BNCU	Thunder Ax7-77 balloon	J. A. Lister	
G-BNCV	Bensen B.8	L. W. Cload	
G-BNCW	Boeing 767-204	Britannia Airways Ltd/Luton	
G-BNCX	Hunter T.7	Lovaux Ltd	
G-BNCY	F.27 Friendship Mk 500	Air UK Ltd *Lillie Langtry*/Norwich	
G-BNCZ	Rutan LongEz	R. M. Bainbridge/Sherburn	
G-BNDD	PA-31-310 Turbo Navajo B	Aviation & Marine Interiors Ltd	
G-BNDG	Wallis WA-201/R Srs1	K. H. Wallis	
G-BNDH	Colt 21A balloon	Hot-Air Balloon Co Ltd	
G-BNDM	Short SD3-60 Variant 100	Shorts Aircraft Financing Ltd	
G-BNDN	Cameron V-77 balloon	J. A. Smith	
G-BNDO	Cessna 152 II	V. B. Cheesewright	
G-BNDP	Brügger MB.2 Colibri	D. A. Peet	
G-BNDR	SOCATA TB.10 Tobago	Air Touring Services Ltd/Biggin Hill	
G-BNDS	PA-31-350 Navajo Chieftain	Solomon Investment Co Ltd	
G-BNDT	Brügger MB.2 Colibri	D. J. Minary	
G-BNDV	Cameron N-77 balloon	R. Jones	
G-BNDW	D.H.82A Tiger Moth	N. D. Welch	
G-BNDY	Cessna 425-1	Standard Aviation Ltd/Newcastle	
G-BNED	PA-22 Tri-Pacer 135	P. Storey	
G-BNEE	PA-28R-201 Arrow III	Britannic Management (Aviation) Ltd	
G-BNEF	PA-31-310 Turbo Navajo B	Seraph Aviation/Shoreham	
G-BNEH	BAe 125 Srs 800B	British Aerospace PLC	
G-BNEI	PA-34-200T Seneca II	A. Bucknole	
G-BNEJ	PA-38-112 Tomahawk	V. C. & S. G. Swindell	
G-BNEK	PA-38-112 Tomahawk	Pool Aviation Ltd/Welshpool	
G-BNEL	PA-28-161 Warrior II	J. A. Pothecary/Shoreham	
G-BNEN	PA-34-200T Seneca II	Willall Ltd	
G-BNEO	Cameron V-77 balloon	J. G. O'Connell	
G-BNEP	PA-34-220T Seneca III	Handhorn Ltd/Blackpool	
G-BNER	PA-34-200T Seneca II	Compass Peripherial Systems Ltd	
G-BNES	Cameron V-77 balloon	G. Wells	
G-BNET	Cameron O-84 balloon	J. Bennett & Son (Insurance Brokers) Ltd	
G-BNEU	Colt 105A balloon	I. Lilja	
G-BNEV	Viking Dragonfly	N. W. Eyre	
G-BNEX	Cameron O-120 balloon	The Balloon Club Ltd	
G-BNEZ	Cessna 421C	Air & General Servcies Ltd/Biggin Hill	
G-BNFG	Cameron O-77 balloon	Capital Balloon Club Ltd	
G-BNFI	Cessna 150J	M. Jackson	
G-BNFK	Cameron 89 Egg SS balloon	Forbes Europe Inc/France	
G-BNFL	WHE Airbuggy	Roger Savage (Photography) (G-AXXN)	
G-BNFM	Colt 21A balloon	M. E. Dworksi	
G-BNFN	Cameron N-105 balloon	Air 2 Air Ltd	
G-BNFO	Cameron V-77 balloon	D. C. Patrick-Brown	
G-BNFP	Cameron O-84 balloon	A. J. & E. J. Clarke	
G-BNFR	Cessna 152 II	London Flight Centre (Stansted) Ltd	
G-BNFS	Cessna 152 II	London Flight Centre (Stansted) Ltd	
G-BNFV	Robin DR.400/120	FTI Aviation Ltd/Biggin Hill	
G-BNFW	H.S.125 Srs 700B	British Aerospace PLC	
G-BNFY	Cameron N-77 balloon	Holker Estates Ltd	
G-BNGC	Robinson R-22	T. J. Clark	
G-BNGD	Cessna 152	AV Aviation Ltd	
G-BNGE	Auster AOP.6 (TW536)	R. W. W. Eastman	
G-BNGH	Boeing 707-321C	Sovereign Air Ltd (G-BFZF)	
G-BNGJ	Cameron V-77 balloon	Latham Timber Centres (Holdings) Ltd	
G-BNGL	Boeing 737-3Y0	Inter European Airways Ltd/Cardiff	
G-BNGM	Boeing 737-3Y0	Inter European Airways Ltd/Cardiff	
G-BNGN	Cameron V-77 balloon	A. R. & L. J. McGregor	
G-BNGO	Thunder Ax7-77 balloon	J. S. Finlan	
G-BNGP	Colt 77A balloon	Headland Services Ltd	
G-BNGR	PA-38-112 Tomahawk	Teesside Flight Centre Ltd	
G-BNGS	PA-38-112 Tomahawk	Frontline Aviation Ltd/Teesside	
G-BNGT	PA-28-181 Archer II	Aviation Development & Management Ltd	
G-BNGV	ARV Super 2	Super Two Group	
G-BNGW	ARV Super 2	Southern Gas Turbines Ltd	
G-BNGX	ARV Super 2	Southern Gas Turbines Ltd	
G-BNGY	ARV Super 2	N. R. F. McNally (G-BMWL)	
G-BNHB	ARV Super 2	Engine Developments Ltd	
G-BNHC	ARV Super 2	M. J. Snelling	
G-BNHD	ARV Super 2	Falstaff Finance Ltd/Sandown	
G-BNHE	ARV Super 2	Falstaff Finance Ltd/Sandown	
G-BNHF	Cameron N-31 balloon	P. G. Dunnington	

Notes	Reg.	Type	Owner or Operator
	G-BNHG	PA-38-112 Tomahawk	W. J. Lumby & M. R. Walker
	G-BNHH	Thunder Ax7-77 balloon	Gee-Tee Signs Ltd
	G-BNHI	Cameron V-77 balloon	Phillair
	G-BNHJ	Cessna 152	Ladel Ltd
	G-BNHK	Cessna 152	Osprey Flying Club/Cranfield
	G-BNHL	Colt 90 Beer Glass SS balloon	G. V. Beckwith
	G-BNHM	Thunder Ax8-105 balloon	Thunder & Colt Ltd
	G-BNHN	Colt Aerial Bottle SS balloon	The Balloon Stable Ltd
	G-BNHO	Thunder Ax7-77 balloon	M. J. Forster
	G-BNHP	Saffrey S.330 balloon	N. H. Ponsford *Alpha II*
	G-BNHR	Cameron V-77 balloon	R. L. Rummery
	G-BNHS	Thunder Ax7-77 balloon	M. V. Farrant
	G-BNHT	Fournier RF-3	D. Harker
	G-BNHV	Thunder Ax10-180 balloon	Thunder & Colt Ltd
	G-BNIB	Cameron A-105 balloon	A. G. E. Faulkner
	G-BNID	Cessna 152	Mercia Aircraft Leasing & Sales Ltd/ Coventry
	G-BNIE	Cameron O-160 balloon	Bristol Balloons
	G-BNIF	Cameron O-56 balloon	D. V. Fowler
	G-BNII	Cameron N-90 balloon	DW (Direct Wholesale) PLC
	G-BNIJ	SOCATA TB.10 Tobago	Alandi Investments Ltd
	G-BNIK	Robin HR.200/120	W. C. Smeaton/Popham
	G-BNIM	PA-38-112 Tomahawk	T. Miller & F. R. H. Parker
	G-BNIN	Cameron V-77 balloon	Cloud Nine Balloon Group
	G-BNIO	Luscombe 8A Silvaire	P. T. Szluha
	G-BNIP	Luscombe 8A Silvaire	D. R. C. Hunter & S. Maric
	G-BNIT	Bell 206B JetRanger	Black Isle Helicopters Ltd
	G-BNIU	Cameron O-77 balloon	A. J. Matthews & D. S. Dunlop
	G-BNIV	Cessna 152	Aerohire Ltd/Halfpenny Green
	G-BNIW	Boeing Stearman PT-17	Lintally Ltd/E. Midlands
	G-BNIX	EMB-110P1 Bandeirante	Aeroservices (E. Midlands) Ltd
	G-BNJA	WAG-Aero Wag-a-Bond	J. A. Hutchings
	G-BNJB	Cessna 152	Klingair Ltd/Conington
	G-BNJC	Cessna 152	Stapleford Flying Club Ltd
	G-BNJD	Cessna 152	J. A Pothecary/Shoreham
	G-BNJE	Cessna A.152	Seawing Flying Club Ltd/Southend
	G-BNJF	PA-32RT-300 Lance II	T. D. C. Lloyd & B. F. Brown
	G-BNJG	Cameron O-77 balloon	A. M. Figiel
	G-BNJH	Cessna 152	Turnhouse Flying Club
	G-BNJJ	Cessna 152	Merrett Aviation Ltd
	G-BNJK	Macavia BAe 748 Turbine Tanker	Macavia International Ltd
	G-BNJL	Bensen B.8	T. G. Ogilvie
	G-BNJM	PA-28-161 Warrior II	Teesside Flight Centre Ltd
	G-BNJO	QAC Quickie Q.2	J. D. McKay
	G-BNJR	PA-28RT-201T Turbo Arrow IV	D. F. Grey & DVF Electrical Ltd
	G-BNJT	PA-28-161 Warrior II	Airways Aero Associations Ltd/Booker
	G-BNJU	Cameron 80 Bust SS balloon	Forbes Europe Inc/France
	G-BNJV	Cessna 152	Alouette Flying Club Ltd/Biggin Hill
	G-BNJX	Cameron N-90 balloon	Mars UK Ltd
	G-BNKC	Cessna 152	Herefordshire Aero Club Ltd/Shobdon
	G-BNKD	Cessna 172N	Bristol Flying Centre Ltd
	G-BNKE	Cessna 172N	Jacques Hall & Co Ltd
	G-BNKF	Colt AS-56 airship	Formtrack Ltd
	G-BNKG	Alexander Todd Steen Skybolt	Cavendish Aviation Ltd (G-RATS/G-RHFI)
	G-BNKH	PA-38-112 Tomahawk	Goodwood Terrena Ltd
	G-BNKI	Cessna 152	RAF Halton Aeroplane Club Ltd
	G-BNKL	Beech 95-58PA Baron	E. L. Klinge/Fairoaks
	G-BNKN	G.159 Gulfstream 1	Birmingham European Airways Ltd
	G-BNKP	Cessna 152	Clacton Aero Club (1988) Ltd
	G-BNKR	Cessna 152	Fife Airport Management Ltd
	G-BNKS	Cessna 152	Shropshire Aero Club Ltd/Shobdon
	G-BNKT	Cameron O-77 balloon	British Airways PLC
	G-BNKV	Cessna 152	I. C. Adams & Vectair Aviation Ltd
	G-BNKW	PA-38-112 Tomahawk	D. M. Maclean
	G-BNKX	Robinson R-22	A. G. Macmillan
	G-BNKZ	Hughes 369HS	Reeds Motor Co/Sywell
	G-BNLA	Boeing 747-436	British Airways *City of London*
	G-BNLB	Boeing 747-436	British Airways *City of Edinburgh*
	G-BNLC	Boeing 747-436	British Airways *City of Cardiff*
	G-BNLD	Boeing 747-436	British Airways *City of Belfast*
	G-BNLE	Boeing 747-436	British Airways *City of Newcastle*
	G-BNLF	Boeing 747-436	British Airways *City of Leeds*
	G-BNLG	Boeing 747-436	British Airways *City of Southampton*

Reg.	Type	Owner or Operator	Notes
G-BNLH	Boeing 747-436	British Airways *City of Westminster*	
G-BNLI	Boeing 747-436	British Airways *City of Sheffield*	
G-BNLJ	Boeing 747-436	British Airways *City of Nottingham*	
G-BNLK	Boeing 747-436	British Airways *City of Bristol*	
G-BNLL	Boeing 747-436	British Airways *City of Leicester*	
G-BNLM	Boeing 747-436	British Airways *City of Durham*	
G-BNLN	Boeing 747-436	British Airways *City of Portsmouth*	
G-BNLO	Boeing 747-436	British Airways *City of Dundee*	
G-BNLP	Boeing 747-436	British Airways *City of Aberdeen*	
G-BNLR	Boeing 747-436	British Airways *City of Hull*	
G-BNLS	Boeing 747-436	British Airways *City of Chester*	
G-BNLT	Boeing 747-436	British Airways	
G-BNLU	Boeing 747-436	British Airways *City of Bangor*	
G-BNLV	Boeing 747-436	British Airways *City of Exeter*	
G-BNLW	Boeing 747-436	British Airways *City of Norwich*	
G-BNLX	Boeing 747-436	British Airways *City of Worcester*	
G-BNLY	Boeing 747-436	British Airways	
G-BNLZ	Boeing 747-436	British Airways	
G-BNMA	Cameron O-77 balloon	Flying Colours Balloon Group	
G-BNMB	PA-28-151 Warrior	Angelchain Ltd/Manchester	
G-BNMC	Cessna 152	M. L. Jones	
G-BNMD	Cessna 152	T. M. Jones	
G-BNME	Cessna 152	L. V. Atkinson	
G-BNMF	Cessna 152	Aerohire Ltd	
G-BNMG	Cameron V-77 balloon	Windsor Life Assurance Co Ltd	
G-BNMH	Pietenpol Air Camper	N. M. Hitchman	
G-BNMI	Colt Flying Fantasy SS balloon	Air 2 Air Ltd	
G-BNMK	Dornier Do.27A-1	G. Machie	
G-BNML	Rand KR-2	R. J. Smyth	
G-BNMM	Bell 206B JetRanger	Veritair Ltd	
G-BNMN	PA-28R-201 Arrow III	Sandford Aviation Ltd	
G-BNMO	Cessna TR.182RG	G-BNMO Flying Group	
G-BNMP	Cessna R.182RG	American Aviation Technologies Ltd	
G-BNMX	Thunder Ax7-77 balloon	S. A. D. Beard	
G-BNNA	Stolp SA.300 Starduster Too	D. F. Simpson	
G-BNNB	PA-34-200 Seneca II	Shoreham Flight Simulation/Bournemouth	
G-BNNC	Cameron N-77 balloon	West Country Business Machines Ltd	
G-BNNE	Cameron N-77 balloon	The Balloon Stable Ltd	
G-BNNF	SA.315B Alouette III Lama	Dollar Air Services Ltd/Coventry	
G-BNNG	Cessna T.337D	Somet Ltd (G-COLD)	
G-BNNI	Boeing 727-276	Dan-Air Services Ltd/Gatwick	
G-BNNJ	Boeing 737-3Q8	Dan-Air Services Ltd/Gatwick	
G-BNNK	Boeing 737-4Q8	Dan-Air Services Ltd/Gatwick	
G-BNNL	Boeing 737-4Q8	Dan-Air Services Ltd/Gatwick	
G-BNNO	PA-28-161 Warrior II	W. Lancs Aero Club Ltd/Woodvale	
G-BNNR	Cessna 152	Interair (Aviation) Ltd/Bournemouth	
G-BNNS	PA-28-161 Warrior II	P. A. Lancaster	
G-BNNT	PA-28-151 Warrior	S. W. Clark & ptnrs/Booker	
G-BNNU	PA-38-112 Tomahawk	APB Leasing Ltd/Welshpool	
G-BNNX	PA-28R-201T Turbo Arrow III	C. Dugard Ltd/Shoreham	
G-BNNY	PA-28-161 Warrior II	Falcon Flying Services/Biggin Hill	
G-BNNZ	PA-28-161 Warrior II	D. Heater/Fairoaks	
G-BNOA	PA-38-112 Tomahawk	Aerohire Ltd/Halfpenny Green	
G-BNOB	Wittman W.8 Tailwind	M. Robson-Robinson	
G-BNOD	PA-28-161 Warrior II	BAe Flying College/Prestwick	
G-BNOE	PA-28-161 Warrior II	BAe Flying College/Prestwick	
G-BNOF	PA-28-161 Warrior II	BAe Flying College/Prestwick	
G-BNOG	PA-28-161 Warrior II	BAe Flying College/Prestwick	
G-BNOH	PA-28-161 Warrior II	BAe Flying College/Prestwick	
G-BNOI	PA-28-161 Warrior II	BAe Flying College/Prestwick	
G-BNOJ	PA-28-161 Warrior II	BAe Flying College/Prestwick	
G-BNOK	PA-28-161 Warrior II	BAe Flying College/Prestwick	
G-BNOL	PA-28-161 Warrior II	BAe Flying College/Prestwick	
G-BNOM	PA-28-161 Warrior II	BAe Flying College/Prestwick	
G-BNON	PA-28-161 Warrior II	BAe Flying College/Prestwick	
G-BNOO	PA-28-161 Warrior II	BAe Flying College/Prestwick	
G-BNOP	PA-28-161 Warrior II	BAe Flying College/Prestwick	
G-BNOR	PA-28-161 Warrior II	BAe Flying College/Prestwick	
G-BNOS	PA-28-161 Warrior II	BAe Flying College/Prestwick	
G-BNOT	PA-28-161 Warrior II	BAe Flying College/Prestwick	
G-BNOU	PA-28-161 Warrior II	BAe Flying College/Prestwick	
G-BNOV	PA-28-161 Warrior II	BAe Flying College/Prestwick	
G-BNOW	PA-28-161 Warrior II	BAe Flying College/Prestwick	

Notes	Reg.	Type	Owner or Operator
	G-BNOX	Cessna R.182	R. Evans/Swansea
	G-BNOY	Colt 90A balloon	Huntair Ltd
	G-BNPD	PA-23 Aztec 250E	Cormack (Aircraft Services) Ltd/Glasgow
	G-BNPE	Cameron N-77 balloon	Kent Garden Centres Ltd
	G-BNPF	Slingsby T.31M	S. Luck & ptnrs
	G-BNPH	P.66 Pembroke C.1 (WV740)	R. J. F. Parker/Denham
	G-BNPI	Colt 21A balloon	Airship & Balloon Co ltd
	G-BNPK	Cameron DP-70 airship	Cameron Balloons Ltd
	G-BNPL	PA-38-112 Tomahawk	Tomahawk Aviation Ltd/Leavesden
	G-BNPM	PA-38-112 Tomahawk	Papa Mike Aviation Ltd/Leavesden
	G-BNPN	PA-28-181 Archer II	Sherani Aviation/Elstree
	G-BNPO	PA-28-181 Archer II	Leavesden Flight Centre Ltd
	G-BNPP	Colt 90A balloon	Huntair Ltd
	G-BNPT	PA-38-112 Tomahawk II	Cumbernauld Aviation Ltd
	G-BNPU	P.66 Pembroke C.1 (XL929) ★	Chelsea College/Shoreham
	G-BNPV	Bowers Flybaby 1A	J. G. Day
	G-BNPY	Cessna 152	Doncaster Aero Club Ltd
	G-BNPZ	Cessna 152	Bristol Flying Centre Ltd
	G-BNRA	SOCATA TB.10 Tobago	D. & G. P. Marriott
	G-BNRC	AB-206A JetRanger	M. & P. Food Products Ltd
	G-BNRD	AB-206A JetRanger	M. & P. Food Products Ltd
	G-BNRE	AB-206A JetRanger	Tindon Ltd/Little Snoring
	G-BNRF	PA-28-181 Archer II	G-Air Ltd/Goodwood
	G-BNRG	PA-28-161 Warrior II	RAF Brize Norton Flying Club Ltd
	G-BNRH	Beech 95-E55 Baron	K. L. Hawes/Elstree
	G-BNRI	Cessna U.206G	MLP Aviation Ltd/Elstree
	G-BNRK	Cessna 152	Redhill Flying Club
	G-BNRL	Cessna 152	J. R. Nicholls/Sibson
	G-BNRP	PA-28-181 Archer II	Atomchoice Ltd/Goodwood
	G-BNRR	Cessna 172P	Skyhawk Group
	G-BNRT	Boeing 737-3T5	Britannia Airways/Luton
	G-BNRU	Cameron V-77 balloon	M. A. Mueller
	G-BNRW	Colt 69A balloon	Callers Pegasus Travel Service Ltd
	G-BNRX	PA-34-200T Seneca II	Futurama Signs Ltd
	G-BNRY	Cessna 182Q	Reefly Ltd
	G-BNRZ	Robinson R-22B	W. Jorden-Millers Ltd
	G-BNSD	Boeing 757-236	Entrepot Aircraft Ltd
	G-BNSE	Boeing 757-236	Entrepot Aircraft Ltd
	G-BNSG	PA-28R-201 Arrow III	Transair (UK) Ltd/Fairoaks
	G-BNSH	Sikorsky S-76A	Bond Helicopters Ltd
	G-BNSI	Cessna 152	Interair (Aviation) Ltd
	G-BNSL	PA-38-112 Tomahawk II	M. H. Kleiser
	G-BNSM	Cessna 152	Cornwall Flying Club Ltd/Bodmin
	G-BNSN	Cessna 152	M. K. Barnes & G. N. Olson/Bristol
	G-BNSO	Slingsby T.67M Mk II	Trent Air Services Ltd/Cranfield
	G-BNSP	Slingsby T.67M	Trent Air Services Ltd/Cranfield
	G-BNSR	Slingsby T.67M	Trent Air Services Ltd/Cranfield
	G-BNSS	Cessna 150M	Interair (Aviation) Ltd
	G-BNST	Cessna 172N	E. J. H. Morgan
	G-BNSU	Cessna 152	Channel Aviation Ltd/Bourn
	G-BNSV	Cessna 152	Channel Aviation Ltd/Bourn
	G-BNSW	Cessna 152	One Zero One Three Ltd
	G-BNSY	PA-28-161 Warrior II	Carill Aviation Ltd/Southampton
	G-BNSZ	PA-28-161 Warrior II	Carill Aviation Ltd/Southampton
	G-BNTC	PA-28RT-201T Turbo Arrow IV	Techspan Aviation Ltd/Booker
	G-BNTD	PA-28-161 Warrior II	S. S. Copsey/Ipswich
	G-BNTE	FFA AS.202/184A Wren	BAe Flying College Ltd/Prestwick
	G-BNTF	FFA AS.202/184A Wren	BAe Flying College Ltd/Prestwick
	G-BNTG	FFA AS.202/184A Wren	BAe Flying College Ltd/Prestwick
	G-BNTH	FFA AS.202/184A Wren	BAe Flying College Ltd/Prestwick
	G-BNTI	FFA AS.202/184A Wren	BAe Flying College Ltd/Prestwick
	G-BNTJ	FFA AS.202/184A Wren	BAe Flying College Ltd/Prestwick
	G-BNTK	FFA AS.202/184A Wren	BAe Flying College Ltd/Prestwick
	G-BNTL	FFA AS.202/184A Wren	BAe Flying College Ltd/Prestwick
	G-BNTM	FFA AS.202/184A Wren	BAe Flying College Ltd/Prestwick
	G-BNTN	FFA AS.202/184A Wren	BAe Flying College Ltd/Prestwick
	G-BNTO	FFA AS.202/184A Wren	BAe Flying College Ltd/Prestwick
	G-BNTP	Cessna 172N	Telair Manchester Ltd/Barton
	G-BNTS	PA-28RT-201T Turbo Arrow IV	Nasire Ltd
	G-BNTT	Beech 76 Duchess	L. & J. Donne
	G-BNTU	Cessna 152	APB Leasing Ltd/Welshpool
	G-BNTV	Cessna 172N	Brandon Aviation/Biggin Hill
	G-BNTW	Cameron V-77 balloon	I. R. Comley

Reg.	Type	Owner or Operator	Notes
G-BNTX	Short SD3-30 Variant 100	Shorts Aircraft Leasing Ltd (G-BKDN)	
G-BNTY	Short SD3-30 Variant 100	Shorts Aircraft Leasing Ltd (G-BKDO)	
G-BNTZ	Cameron N-77 balloon	Balloon Team	
G-BNUC	Cameron O-77 balloon	T. J. Bucknall	
G-BNUG	Cameron O-105 balloon	Thunder & Colt Ltd	
G-BNUH	Cameron O-105 balloon	Thunder & Colt Ltd	
G-BNUI	Rutan Vari-Eze	T. N. F. Skead	
G-BNUK	Cameron O-84 balloon	Thunder & Colt Ltd	
G-BNUL	Cessna 152	Osprey Air Services Ltd	
G-BNUN	Beech 95-58PA Baron	British Midland Airways Ltd/E. Midlands	
G-BNUO	Beech 76 Duchess	B. & W. Aircraft Ltd	
G-BNUR	Cessna 172E	Newland Ltd	
G-BNUS	Cessna 152	Stapleford Flying Club Ltd	
G-BNUT	Cessna 152 Turbo	Stapleford Flying Club Ltd	
G-BNUU	PA-44-180T Turbo Seminole	TEL (IOM) Ltd/Ronaldsway	
G-BNUV	PA-23 Aztec 250F	L. J. Martin	
G-BNUX	Hoffmann H-36 Dimona	K. H. Abel	
G-BNUY	PA-38-112 Tomahawk II	AT Aviation Ltd/Cardiff	
G-BNUZ	Robinson R-22B	J. C. Reid	
G-BNVB	AA-5A Cheetah	W. J. Siertsema & A. M. Glazer	
G-BNVD	PA-38-112 Tomahawk	Channel Aviation Ltd	
G-BNVE	PA-28-181 Archer II	Tewin Aviation/Panshanger	
G-BNVF	Robinson R-22B	Jetbury Ltd	
G-BNVG	ARV Super 2	ARV Aviation Ltd/Sandown	
G-BNVH	ARV Super 2	ARV Aviation Ltd/Sandown	
G-BNVI	ARV Super 2	Adrianair Ltd	
G-BNVJ	ARV Super 2	ARV Aviation Ltd/Sandown	
G-BNVT	PA-28R-201T Turbo Arrow III	Victor Tango Group	
G-BNVV	Cameron DG-19 gas airship	US Skyship (UK) Ltd	
G-BNVZ	Beech 95-B55 Baron	C. A. Breeze/Barton	
G-BNWA	Boeing 767-336	British Airways *City of Brussels*	
G-BNWB	Boeing 767-336	British Airways *City of Paris*	
G-BNWC	Boeing 767-336	British Airways *City of Frankfurt/*	
G-BNWD	Boeing 767-336	British Airways *City of Copenhagen*	
G-BNWE	Boeing 767-336	British Airways *City of Lisbon*	
G-BNWF	Boeing 767-336ER	British Airways *City of Milan*	
G-BNWG	Boeing 767-336ER	British Airways *City of Strasbourg/*	
G-BNWH	Boeing 767-336ER	British Airways *City of Rome*	
G-BNWI	Boeing 767-336ER	British Airways *City of Madrid*	
G-BNWJ	Boeing 767-336	British Airways *City of Athens*	
G-BNWK	Boeing 767-336	British Airways *City of Amsterdam*	
G-BNWL	Boeing 767-336	British Airways *City of Luxembourg*	
G-BNWM	Boeing 767-336ER	British Airways *City of Toulouse*	
G-BNWN	Boeing 767-336ER	British Airways *City of Berlin*	
G-BNWO	Boeing 767-336ER	British Airways *City of Barcelona*	
G-BNWP	Boeing 767-336ER	British Airways *City of Dublin*	
G-BNWR	Boeing 767-336ER	British Airways *City of Hamburg*	
G-BNWS	Boeing 767-336ER	British Airways	
G-BNWT	Boeing 767-336ER	British Airways	
G-BNWU	Boeing 767-336ER	British Airways	
G-BNWV	Boeing 767-336ER	British Airways	
G-BNWW	Boeing 767-336ER	British Airways	
G-BNWX	—	—	
G-BNWY	—	—	
G-BNWZ	—	—	
G-BNXA	BN-2A Islander	Atlantic Air Transport Ltd/Coventry	
G-BNXC	Cessna 152	Sir W. G. Armstrong-Whitworth Flying Group/Coventry	
G-BNXD	Cessna 172N	Interair (Aviation) Ltd/Bournemouth	
G-BNXE	PA-28-161 Warrior II	Rugby Autobody Repairs	
G-BNXF	Bell 206B JetRanger	P. Pilkington & K. M. Armitage	
G-BNXG	Cameron DP-70 airship	Rexstyle Ltd	
G-BNXH	Cessna T.210N	Wilson Feeds Ltd	
G-BNXI	Robin DR.400/180R	London Gliding Club Ltd/Dunstable	
G-BNXK	Nott-Cameron ULD-3 balloon	J. R. P. Nott	
G-BNXL	Glaser-Dirks DG.400	B. A. Eastwell	
G-BNXM	PA-18 Super Cub 95	G-BNXM Group	
G-BNXN	Partenavia P.68B	N. P. W. G. Edmiston	
G-BNXO	Colt 21A balloon	Thunder & Colt Ltd	
G-BNXR	Cameron O-84 balloon	J. A. & N. J. Ballard Gray	
G-BNXS	Cessna 404	Turnbull Associates	
G-BNXT	PA-28-161 Warrior II	Falcon Flying Services/Biggin Hill	
G-BNXU	PA-28-161 Warrior II	V. J. Rutherford & P. D. Donoghue	

Notes	Reg.	Type	Owner or Operator
	G-BNXV	PA-38-112 Tomahawk	Falcon Flying Services/Biggin Hill
	G-BNXX	SOCATA TB.20 Trinidad	EAC Components Ltd
	G-BNXZ	Thunder Ax7-77 balloon	Hale Hot Air Balloon Group
	G-BNYA	Short SD3-30	Shorts Aircraft Leasing Ltd (G-BKSU)
	G-BNYB	PA-28-201T Turbo Dakota	Blackpool Air Centre
	G-BNYD	Bell 206B JetRanger	Sterling Helicopters Ltd
	G-BNYJ	Cessna 421B	Charles Robertson (Developments) Ltd
	G-BNYK	PA-38-112 Tomahawk	Seal Executive Aircraft Ltd
	G-BNYL	Cessna 152	APB Leasing Ltd/Welshpool
	G-BNYM	Cessna 172N	G. Manning/Coventry
	G-BNYN	Cessna 152	Redhill Flying Club
	G-BNYO	Beech 76 Duchess	Skyhawk Ltd
	G-BNYP	PA-28-181 Archer II	R. D. Cooper/Cranfield
	G-BNYS	Boeing 767-204	Britannia Airways Ltd/Luton
	G-BNYU	Faithfull Ax7-61A balloon	M. L. Faithfull
	G-BNYV	PA-38-112 Tomahawk	Channel Aviation Ltd
	G-BNYX	Denney Aerocraft Kitfox	R. W. Husband
	G-BNYY	PA-28RT-201T Turbo Arrow IV	Kendrick Construction Ltd
	G-BNYZ	SNCAN Stampe SV-4E	Tapestry Colour Ltd
	G-BNZB	PA-28-161 Warrior II	Hillvine Ltd
	G-BNZC	D.H.C.1 Chipmunk 22 (671)	The Aircraft Restoration Co (G-ROYS)/ Duxford
	G-BNZF	Grob G.109B	N. Adam
	G-BNZG	PA-28RT-201T Turbo Arrow IV	Trinity Garage (Gainsborough) Ltd
	G-BNZJ	Colt 21A balloon	Willowbest Ltd
	G-BNZK	Thunder Ax7-77 balloon	P. M. Davies & D. R .Groves
	G-BNZL	Rotorway Scorpion 133	J. R. Wraight
	G-BNZM	Cessna T.210N	Stansted Fluid Power (Products) Ltd
	G-BNZO	Rotorway Executive	M. G. Wiltshire
	G-BNZR	FRED Srs 2	R. M. Waugh
	G-BNZS	Mooney M.20K	P. E. Sandy
	G-BNZV	PA-25 Pawnee 235	Northumbria Soaring Co Ltd
	G-BNZX	—	—
	G-BNZZ	PA-28-161 Warrior II	J. P. Alexander/Denham
	G-BOAA	Concorde 102	British Airways (G-N94AA)
	G-BOAB	Concorde 102	British Airways (G-N94AB)
	G-BOAC	Concorde 102	British Airways (G-N81AC)
	G-BOAD	Concorde 102	British Airways (G-N94AD)
	G-BOAE	Concorde 102	British Airways (G-N94AE)
	G-BOAF	Concorde 102	British Airways (G-N94AF/G-BFKX)
	G-BOAG	Concorde 102	British Airways (G-BFKW)
	G-BOAH	PA-28-161 Warrior II	Denham School of Flying Ltd
	G-BOAI	Cessna 152	G. Duncan
	G-BOAK	PA-22 Caribbean 150	I. B. Grace & ptnrs
	G-BOAL	Cameron V-65 balloon	A. M. Lindsay
	G-BOAM	Robinson R-22B	Bristow Helicopters Ltd/Redhill
	G-BOAN	PA-30 Twin Comanche 160B	R. L. C. Appleton
	G-BOAO	Thunder Ax7-77 balloon	D. V. Fowler
	G-BOAS	Air Command 503 Commander	R. Robinson
	G-BOAU	Cameron V-77 balloon	J. Smallwood
	G-BOAW	D.H.C.7-110 Dash Seven	British Midland Airways
	G-BOAY	D.H.C.7-110 Dash Seven	British Midland Airways
	G-BOAZ	D.H.C.7-102 Dash Seven	British Midland Airways
	G-BOBA	PA-28R-201 Arrow III	GNJ Engineering Ltd
	G-BOBB	Cameron O-120 balloon	J. M. Albury
	G-BOBC	BN-2T Islander	Rhine Army Parachute Association (G-BJYZ)
	G-BOBD	Cameron O-160 balloon	A. C. K. Rawson & J. J. Rudoni
	G-BOBE	Cameron O-160 balloon	Heart of England Balloon Club
	G-BOBF	Brügger MB.2 Colibri	R. Bennett
	G-BOBG	Jodel D.150	C. A. Laycock
	G-BOBH	Airtour AH-77 balloon	Airtour Balloon Co Ltd
	G-BOBJ	PA-38-112 Tomahawk	Air Touring Services Ltd/Biggin Hill
	G-BOBK	PA-38-112 Tomahawk	Air Touring Services Ltd/Biggin Hill
	G-BOBL	PA-38-112 Tomahawk	Dayrell Air Ltd
	G-BOBN	Cessna 310R	Edinburgh Air Charter Ltd
	G-BOBR	Cameron N-77 balloon	C. Bradley
	G-BOBS	Quickie Q.2	R. R. Stevens/Denham
	G-BOBT	Stolp SA.300 Starduster Too	A. M. Bailey & T. A. Shears
	G-BOBU	Colt 90A balloon	Thunder & Colt Ltd
	G-BOBV	Cessna F.150M	T. M. & A. Poppleton/Doncaster
	G-BOBX	G.159 Gulfstream 1 ★	Airport Fire Section/Birmingham

Reg.	Type	Owner or Operator	Notes
G-BOBY	Monnet Sonerai II	R. G. Hallam (*stored*)/Sleap	
G-BOBZ	PA-28-181 Archer II	Trustcomms International Ltd	
G-BOCB	H.S.125 Srs 1B/522	MAGEC Aviation Ltd (G-OMCA/ G-DJMJ/G-AWUF)/Luton	
G-BOCC	PA-38-112 Tomahawk	Goodwood Terrena Ltd	
G-BOCD	Grob G.115	Landlink PLC	
G-BOCF	Colt 77A balloon	P. S. J. Mason	
G-BOCG	PA-34-200T Seneca II	Airways Flight Training (Exeter) Ltd	
G-BOCH	PA-32 Cherokee Six 300	Basic Vale Ltd	
G-BOCI	Cessna 140A	D. Nieman	
G-BOCK	Sopwith Triplane (replica) (N6290)	Shuttleworth Trust/O. Warden	
G-BOCL	Slingsby T.67C	C.S.E. Aviation Ltd/Kidlington	
G-BOCM	Slingsby T.67C	C.S.E. Aviation Ltd/Kidlington	
G-BOCN	Robinson R-22B	J. Bignall	
G-BOCP	PA-34-220T Seneca III	BAe Flying College Ltd/Prestwick	
G-BOCR	PA-34-220T Seneca III	BAe Flying College Ltd/Prestwick	
G-BOCS	PA-34-220T Seneca III	BAe Flying College Ltd/Prestwick	
G-BOCT	PA-34-220T Seneca III	BAe Flying College Ltd/Prestwick	
G-BOCU	PA-34-220T Seneca III	BAe Flying College Ltd/Prestwick	
G-BOCV	PA-34-220T Seneca III	BAe Flying College Ltd/Prestwick	
G-BOCW	PA-34-220T Seneca III	BAe Flying College Ltd/Prestwick	
G-BOCX	PA-34-220T Seneca III	BAe Flying College Ltd/Prestwick	
G-BOCY	PA-34-220T Seneca III	BAe Flying College Ltd/Prestwick	
G-BOCZ	PA-34-220T Seneca III	BAe Flying College Ltd/Prestwick	
G-BODA	PA-28-161 Warrior II	C.S.E. Aviation Ltd/Kidlington	
G-BODB	PA-28-161 Warrior II	C.S.E. Aviation Ltd/Kidlington	
G-BODC	PA-28-161 Warrior II	C.S.E. Aviation Ltd/Kidlington	
G-BODD	PA-28-161 Warrior II	C.S.E. Aviation Ltd/Kidlington	
G-BODE	PA-28-161 Warrior II	C.S.E. Aviation Ltd/Kidlington	
G-BODF	PA-28-161 Warrior II	C.S.E. Aviation Ltd/Kidlington	
G-BODG	Slingsby T.31 Motor Cadet III	H. P. Vox	
G-BODH	Slingsby T.31 Motor Cadet III	H. P. Vox	
G-BODI	Stoddard-Hamilton Glasair III	Jackson Barr Ltd	
G-BODK	Rotorway Scorpion 133	J. Brannigan	
G-BODL	Steen Skybolt	K. E. Armstrong	
G-BODM	PA-28 Cherokee 180	Bristol & Wessex Aeroplane Club Ltd	
G-BODN	PA-28R-201 Arrow III	N. M. G. Pearson/Bristol	
G-BODO	Cessna 152	A. R. Sarson	
G-BODP	PA-38-112 Tomahawk	N. C. Gray	
G-BODR	PA-28-161 Warrior II	Airways Aero Associations Ltd/Booker	
G-BODS	PA-38-112 Tomahawk	Ipswich School of Flying Ltd	
G-BODT	Jodel D.18	R. A. Jarvis	
G-BODU	Scheibe SF.25C	Monica English Memorial Trust	
G-BODW	Bell 206B JetRanger	Wood Hall Helicopters Ltd	
G-BODX	Beech 76 Duchess	Neric Ltd	
G-BODY	Cessna 310R	Atlantic Air Transport Ltd/Coventry	
G-BODZ	Robinson R-22B	Langley Construction Ltd	
G-BOEC	PA-38-112 Tomahawk	R. A. Wakefield	
G-BOED	Cameron Opera House SS balloon	Cameron Balloons Ltd	
G-BOEE	PA-28-181 Archer II	T. B. Parmenter	
G-BOEH	Jodel DR.340	E. J. & P. E. Horsfall/Blackpool	
G-BOEK	Cameron V-77 balloon	A. J. E. Jones	
G-BOEM	Aerotek-Pitts S-2A	Walsh Bros (Tunneling) Ltd	
G-BOEN	Cessna 172M	P. N. Herold	
G-BOER	PA-28-161 Warrior II	Ridgway Aviation Services Ltd/Booker	
G-BOES	Cessna FA.152	J. R. Nicholls (G-FLIP)	
G-BOET	PA-28RT-201 Arrow IV	IBEC (Holdings) Ltd (G-IBEC)/Liverpool	
G-BOEW	Robinson R-22B	Bristow Helicopters Ltd	
G-BOEX	Robinson R-22B	Bristow Helicopters Ltd	
G-BOEY	Robinson R-22B	Bristow Helicopters Ltd	
G-BOEZ	Robinson R-22B	Bristow Helicopters Ltd	
G-BOFA	Robinson R-22	Panair Ltd	
G-BOFB	Sikorsky S-76A	Bond Helicopters Ltd/Bourn	
G-BOFC	Beech 76 Duchess	Wickenby Aviation Ltd	
G-BOFD	Cessna U.206G	D. M. Penny	
G-BOFE	PA-34-200T Seneca II	E. C. English	
G-BOFF	Cameron N-77 balloon	Systems-80 Double Glazing Ltd & N. M. Gabriel	
G-BOFL	Cessna 152	Coventry (Civil) Aviation Ltd	
G-BOFM	Cessna 152	Coventry (Civil) Aviation Ltd	
G-BOFV	PA-44-180 Seminole	Stapleford Flying Club Ltd	

Notes	Reg.	Type	Owner or Operator
	G-BOFW	Cessna A.150M	Three Counties Aero Engineering Ltd/ Lasham
	G-BOFX	Cessna A.150M	Shropshire Aero Club Ltd/Sleap
	G-BOFY	PA-28 Cherokee 140	Bristol & Wessex Aeroplane Club Ltd
	G-BOFZ	PA-28-161 Warrior II	Bristol & Wessex Aeroplane Club Ltd
	G-BOGB	Hawker Tempest II replica	D. L. Riley
	G-BOGC	Cessna 152	Skyviews & General Ltd/Leeds
	G-BOGG	Cessna 152	J. S. & S. Peplow
	G-BOGI	Robin DR.400/180	Shepair Ltd
	G-BOGK	ARV Super 2	D. R. Trouse
	G-BOGL	Thunder Ax7-77 balloon	Thunder & Colt Ltd
	G-BOGM	PA-28RT-201T Turbo Arrow IV	RJP Aviation
	G-BOGO	PA-32R-301T Saratoga SP	S. D. Cole
	G-BOGP	Cameron V-77 balloon	The Wealden Balloon Group
	G-BOGR	Colt 180A balloon	The Balloon Club of Great Britain Ltd
	G-BOGT	Colt 77A balloon	The Hot Air Balloon Co Ltd
	G-BOGV	Air Command 532 Elite	G. M. Hobman
	G-BOGW	Air Command 532 Elite	K. Ashford
	G-BOGY	Cameron V-77 balloon	Dante Balloon Group
	G-BOHA	PA-28-161 Warrior II	London Flight Centre (Stansted) Ltd
	G-BOHB	Cessna 152	London Flight Centre (Stansted) Ltd
	G-BOHC	Boeing 757-236	Entrepot Aircraft Ltd
	G-BOHD	Colt 77A balloon	County Garage Ltd
	G-BOHE	Cameron O-120 balloon	Border Balloon Co
	G-BOHF	Thunder Ax8-84 balloon	Slater Hogg & Howison Ltd
	G-BOHG	Air Command 532 Elite	T. E. McDonald
	G-BOHH	Cessna 172N	J. S. Baxter
	G-BOHI	Cessna 152	Clacton Aero Club (1988) Ltd
	G-BOHJ	Cessna 152	F. E. P. Holmes
	G-BOHL	Cameron A-120 balloon	The Balloon Stable Ltd
	G-BOHM	PA-28 Cherokee 180	M. J. Anthony & B. Keogh
	G-BOHN	PA-38-112 Tomahawk	AT Aviation Ltd
	G-BOHO	PA-28-161 Warrior II	Egressus Flying Club
	G-BOHR	PA-28-151 Warrior	L. T. Evans
	G-BOHS	PA-38-112 Tomahawk	Falcon Flying Services/Biggin Hill
	G-BOHT	PA-38-112 Tomahawk	Falcon Flying Services/Biggin Hill
	G-BOHU	PA-38-112 Tomahawk	Falcon Flying Services/Biggin Hill
	G-BOHV	Wittman W.8 Tailwind	R. A. Povall
	G-BOHW	Van's RV-4	R. W. H. Cole
	G-BOHX	PA-44-180 Seminole	K. D. & D. C. Horton
	G-BOIA	Cessna 180K	R. E. Styles & ptnrs
	G-BOIB	Wittman W.10 Tailwind	P. H. Lewis
	G-BOIC	PA-28R-201T Turbo Arrow III	M. J. Pearson
	G-BOID	Bellanca 7ECA Citabria	Sherwood Flying Club Ltd
	G-BOIF	Beech 95-B55 Baron	Seal Executive Aircraft Ltd
	G-BOIG	PA-28-161 Warrior II	D. Vallence-Pell/Jersey
	G-BOIH	Pitts S-1E Special	S. L. Goldspink
	G-BOII	Cessna 172N	Trevair Group/Bournemouth
	G-BOIJ	Thunder Ax7-77 balloon	Shropshire Lad Original Ballooning
	G-BOIK	Air Command 503 Commander	D. W. Smith
	G-BOIL	Cessna 172N	Upperstack Ltd
	G-BOIM	Cessna 150M	E. Alexander
	G-BOIN	Bellanca 7ECA Citabria	J. P. Bell
	G-BOIO	Cessna 152	AV Aviation Ltd
	G-BOIP	Cessna 152	Stapleford Flying Club Ltd
	G-BOIR	Cessna 152	Shropshire Aero Club Ltd/Sleap
	G-BOIS	PA-31 Turbo Navajo	Compass Aviation Ltd (G-AYNB)
	G-BOIT	SOCATA TB.10 Tobago	Air Touring Services Ltd/Biggin Hill
	G-BOIU	SOCATA TB.10 Tobago	Portman Welbeck Ltd
	G-BOIV	Cessna 150M	Andrewsfield Pension Scheme
	G-BOIW	Cessna 152	London Flight Centre (Stansted) Ltd
	G-BOIX	Cessna 172N	JR Flying Ltd
	G-BOIY	Cessna 172N	London Flight Centre (Stansted) Ltd
	G-BOIZ	PA-34-200T Seneca II	Northumbria Aviation Ltd
	G-BOJB	Cameron V-77 balloon	K. L. Heron & R. M. Trotter
	G-BOJD	Cameron V-77 balloon	The Independent Balloon Co Ltd
	G-BOJE	PA-28-236 Dakota	M. J. Martin
	G-BOJF	Air Command 532 Elite	P. J. Davies
	G-BOJH	PA-28R Cherokee Arrow 200	P. S. Kirby
	G-BOJI	PA-28RT-201 Arrow IV	Market Penetration Services Ltd
	G-BOJJ	BAe 146-300	British Aerospace PLC/Hatfield
	G-BOJK	PA-34-220T Seneca III	Redhill Flying Club (G-BRUF)
	G-BOJL	M.S.885 Super Rallye	J. Rees

Reg.	Type	Owner or Operator	Notes
G-BOJM	PA-28-181 Archer II	H. Skelton	
G-BOJO	Colt 120A balloon	Airbureau Ltd	
G-BOJR	Cessna 172P	Exeter Flying Club Ltd	
G-BOJS	Cessna 172P	J. D. Beckett/Exeter	
G-BOJT	Beech 76 Duchess	Bobbington Air Training School Ltd	
G-BOJU	Cameron N-77 balloon	The Hot Air Balloon Co Ltd	
G-BOJW	PA-28-161 Warrior II	Piper Warrior G-BJOW Flying Group	
G-BOJX	PA-28-181 Archer II	Southern Air Ltd/Shoreham	
G-BOJY	PA-28-161 Warrior II	Southern Air Ltd/Shoreham	
G-BOJZ	PA-28-161 Warrior II	Southern Air Ltd/Shoreham	
G-BOKA	PA-28-201T Turbo Dakota	CBG Aviation Ltd/Biggin Hill	
G-BOKB	PA-28-161 Warrior II	Southern Air Ltd/Shoreham	
G-BOKE	PA-34-200T Seneca II	Gwent Plant Sales	
G-BOKF	Air Command 532 Elite	P. T. Waldron	
G-BOKG	Slingsby T.31 Motor Cadet III	A. M. Witt	
G-BOKH	Whittaker MW.7	M. W. J. Whittaker	
G-BOKI	Whittaker MW.7	R. K. Willcox	
G-BOKJ	Whittaker MW.7	M. N. Gauntlett	
G-BOKK	PA-28-161 Warrior II	C. J. Freeman/Headcorn	
G-BOKL	PA-28-161 Warrior II	BAe Flying College Ltd/Prestwick	
G-BOKM	PA-28-161 Warrior II	BAe Flying College Ltd/Prestwick	
G-BOKN	PA-28-161 Warrior II	BAe Flying College Ltd/Prestwick	
G-BOKO	PA-28-161 Warrior II	BAe Flying College Ltd/Prestwick	
G-BOKP	PA-28-161 Warrior II	BAe Flying College Ltd/Prestwick	
G-BOKR	PA-28-161 Warrior II	BAe Flying College Ltd/Prestwick	
G-BOKS	PA-28-161 Warrior II	BAe Flying College Ltd/Prestwick	
G-BOKT	PA-28-161 Warrior II	BAe Flying College Ltd/Prestwick	
G-BOKU	PA-28-161 Warrior II	BAe Flying College Ltd/Prestwick	
G-BOKW	Bo 208C Junior	R. A. Farrington (G-BITT)	
G-BOKX	PA-28-161 Warrior II	W. P. J. Jackson	
G-BOKY	Cessna 152	London Flight Centre (Stansted) Ltd	
G-BOLB	Taylorcraft BC-12-65	G-BOLB Flying Group	
G-BOLC	Fournier RF-6B-100	I. Perry	
G-BOLD	PA-38-112 Tomahawk	B. R. Pearson & B. F. Fraser-Smith/ Eaglescott	
G-BOLE	PA-38-112 Tomahawk	M. W. Kibble & E. A. Minard	
G-BOLF	PA-38-112 Tomahawk	Teesside Flight Centre Ltd	
G-BOLG	Bellanca 7KCAB Citabria	B. R. Pearson/Eaglescott	
G-BOLI	Cessna 172P	Boli Flying Club	
G-BOLJ	GA-7 Cougar	Hastemark Ltd	
G-BOLL	Lake LA-4 Skimmer	S. D. Foster	
G-BOLN	Colt 21A balloon	Airship & Balloon Co Ltd	
G-BOLO	Bell 206B JetRanger	Hargreaves Construction Co Ltd/ Shoreham	
G-BOLP	Colt 21A balloon	Airship & Balloon Co Ltd	
G-BOLR	Colt 21A balloon	Airship & Balloon Co Ltd	
G-BOLS	FRED Srs 2	R. G. Goodburn	
G-BOLT	R. Commander 114	R. D. Rooke/Elstree	
G-BOLU	Robin R.3000/120	Lydair Ltd/Lydd	
G-BOLV	Cessna 152	London Flight Centre (Stansted) Ltd	
G-BOLW	Cessna 152	Seawing Flying Club Ltd/Southend	
G-BOLX	Cessna 172N	London Flight Centre (Stansted) Ltd	
G-BOLY	Cessna 172N	London Flight Centre (Headcorn) Ltd	
G-BOLZ	Rand KR-2	B. Normington	
G-BOMB	Cussutt Racer	P. P. Chapman/Biggin Hill	
G-BOML	Hispano HA.1112MIL (—)	R. G. Hanna/Duxford	
G-BOMN	Cessna 150F	D. G. Williams	
G-BOMO	PA-38-112 Tomahawk	Aerohire Ltd/Halfpenny Green	
G-BOMP	PA-28-181 Archer II	Falcon Flying Services/Biggin Hill	
G-BOMS	Cessna 172N	Osprey Air Services Ltd/Cranfield	
G-BOMT	Cessna 172N	Herefordshire Aero Club Ltd/Shobdon	
G-BOMU	PA-28-181 Archer II	RJ Aviation/Blackbushe	
G-BOMY	PA-28-161 Warrior II	Carill Aviation Ltd/Southampton	
G-BOMZ	PA-38-112 Tomahawk	BOMZ Aviation/White Waltham	
G-BONC	PA-28RT-201 Arrow IV	Modern Air	
G-BOND	Sikorsky S-76A	Manchester Helicopter Centre/Barton	
G-BONE	Pilatus P2-06 (U-142)	D. C. R. Writer	
G-BONG	Enstrom F-28A	Run Length Ltd	
G-BONH	Enstrom F-28A	Blades Helicopters Ltd	
G-BONK	Colt 180A balloon	Wye Valley Aviation Ltd	
G-BONO	Cessna 172N	M. Rowe/Sywell	
G-BONP	CFM Streak Shadow	CFM Metal-Fax Ltd	
G-BONR	Cessna 172N	Atlaslocal Ltd/Biggin Hill	

Notes	Reg.	Type	Owner or Operator
	G-BONS	Cessna 172N	BONS Group/Leavesden
	G-BONT	Slingsby T.67M Mk II	Slingsby Aviation Ltd/Kirkbymoorside
	G-BONU	Slingsby T.67B	Slingsby Aviation Ltd/Kirkbymoorside
	G-BONV	Colt 17A balloon	Bryant Group PLC
	G-BONW	Cessna 152	Lincoln Aero Club Ltd/Sturgate
	G-BONY	Denney Aerocraft Kitfox	Penny Hydraulics Ltd
	G-BONZ	Beech V35B Bonanza	P. M. Coulten
	G-BOOB	Cameron N-65 balloon	I. J. Sadler
	G-BOOC	PA-18 Super Cub 150	R. R. & S. A. Marriott
	G-BOOD	Slingsby T.31M Motor Tutor	G. F. M. Garner
	G-BOOE	GA-7 Cougar	G. L. Cailes
	G-BOOF	PA-28-181 Archer II	Golf Boof Group
	G-BOOG	PA-28RT-201T Turbo Arrow IV	A. W. D. Perkins & J. C. Walton
	G-BOOH	Jodel D.112	D. F. Madams
	G-BOOI	Cessna 152	Stapleford Flying Club Ltd
	G-BOOJ	Air Command 532 Elite	G. Snook
	G-BOOK	Pitts S-1S Special	A. N. R. Houghton
	G-BOOL	Cessna 172N	AVA Flyers/Biggin Hill
	G-BOOM	Hunter T.7	Hunter Wing Ltd/Bournemouth
	G-BOON	PA-32RT-300 Lance II	G-BOON Ltd/Luton
	G-BOOO	Brügger MB .2 Colibri	D. G. Cole
	G-BOOP	Cameron N-90 balloon	The Hot Air Balloon Co Ltd (G-BOMX)
	G-BOOS	Colt 240A balloon	Thunder & Colt Ltd
	G-BOOT	Colt 240A balloon	Thunder & Colt Ltd
	G-BOOU	Cameron N-77 balloon	Aqualisa Products Ltd
	G-BOOV	AS.355F-2 Twin Squirrel	Merseyside Police Authority
	G-BOOW	Aerosport Scamp	B. I. Turner
	G-BOOX	Rutan LongEz	I. R. Thomas & I. R. Wilde
	G-BOOZ	Cameron N-77 balloon	J. E. F. Kettley
	G-BOPA	PA-28-181 Archer II	J. E. Strutt Ltd
	G-BOPB	Boeing 767-204ER	Britannia Airways Ltd *Captain Sir Ross Smith*/Luton
	G-BOPC	PA-28-161 Warrior II	Channel Aviation Ltd
	G-BOPD	Bede BD-4	S. T. Dauncey
	G-BOPG	Cessna 182Q	Rajmech Ltd & Charles Hawkins Ltd
	G-BOPH	Cessna TR.182RG	E. A. L. Sturmer
	G-BOPL	PA-28-161 Warrior II	Cambrian Flying Club/Swansea
	G-BOPN	Brooklands OA.7 Optica	Lovaux Ltd/Bournemouth
	G-BOPT	Grob G.115	Telair Manchester Ltd/Barton
	G-BOPU	Grob G.115	Telair Manchester Ltd/Barton
	G-BOPV	PA-34-200T Seneca II	Tewin Aviation
	G-BOPW	Cessna A.152	Northamptonshire School of Flying Ltd/ Sywell
	G-BOPX	Cessna A.152	Osprey Air Services Ltd/Cranfield
	G-BOPZ	Cameron DP-70 airship	The Hot Air Balloon Co Ltd (G-BOMW)
	G-BORA	Colt 77A balloon	Cala Homes (Southern) Ltd
	G-BORB	Cameron V-77 balloon	M. H. Wolff
	G-BORC	Colt 180A balloon	Airship & Balloon Co Ltd
	G-BORD	Thunder Ax7-77 balloon	D. D. Owen
	G-BORE	Colt 77A balloon	Little Secret Hot-Air Balloon Group
	G-BORG	Campbell Cricket	N. G. Bailey
	G-BORH	PA-34-200T Seneca II	C. Dugard Ltd & SCA Ltd
	G-BORI	Cessna 152	R. D. Ward
	G-BORJ	Cessna 152	Antler Enterprises Ltd
	G-BORK	PA-28-161 Warrior II	J. A. Hilton/Coventry
	G-BORL	PA-28-161 Warrior II	D. C. Harry
	G-BORM	H.S.748 Srs 2B	Sean T. Hully (Sales) Ltd
	G-BORN	Cameron N-77 balloon	Laing Homes Ltd
	G-BORO	Cessna 152	Seal Executive Aircraft Ltd
	G-BORP	PA-46-310P Malibu	SMC Aviation Ltd/Southend
	G-BORR	Thunder Ax8-90 balloon	W. J. Harris
	G-BORS	PA-28-181 Archer II	Modern Air/Panshanger
	G-BORT	Colt 77A balloon	I. E. A. Joslyn/Germany
	G-BORV	Bell 206B JetRanger 2	P. V. Doman
	G-BORW	Cessna 172P	Briter Aviation Ltd/Coventry
	G-BORY	Cessna 150L	Airspeed Aviation Ltd
	G-BOSA	Boeing 737-204ADV	Santa Fe Aviation Leasing Ltd (G-BAZI)
	G-BOSB	Thunder Ax7-77 balloon	M. Gallagher
	G-BOSC	Cessna U.206G	A. J. Buczkowski/Cranfield
	G-BOSD	PA-34-200T Seneca II	Barnes Olson Aeroleasing Ltd
	G-BOSE	PA-28-181 Archer II	M. A. Bath
	G-BOSF	Colt 69A balloon	Airship & Balloon Co Ltd
	G-BOSG	Colt 17A balloon	Airship & Balloon Co Ltd

Reg.	Type	Owner or Operator
G-BOSH	Thunder Ax8-84 balloon	Ace Balloons (Bath) Ltd
G-BOSJ	Nord 3400	M. F. W. Boyd-Maunsell
G-BOSK	AS.355F-1 Twin Squirrel	McAlpine Helicopters Ltd/Hayes
G-BOSM	Jodel DR.253B	J. Cantellow
G-BOSO	Cessna A.152	Redhill Flying Club
G-BOSP	PA-28-151 Warrior	M. E. Williams/Andrewsfield
G-BOSR	PA-28 Cherokee 140	R. D. Cornish
G-BOSU	PA-28 Cherokee 140	M. A. Roberts
G-BOSV	Cameron V-77 balloon	K. H. Greenaway
G-BOSW	Bell 206B JetRanger	Walsh Aviation
G-BOTB	Cessna 152	Stapleford Flying Club Ltd
G-BOTC	Cessna 152	Stapleford Flying Club Ltd
G-BOTD	Cameron O-105 balloon	P. J. Beglan
G-BOTE	Thunder Ax8-90 balloon	R. S. Hunjan
G-BOTF	PA-28-151 Warrior	G-BOTF Group/Southend
G-BOTG	Cessna 152	Donington Aviation Ltd/E. Midlands
G-BOTH	Cessna 182Q	R. H. Durston
G-BOTI	PA-28-151 Warrior	Tango India Flying Group/Biggin Hill
G-BOTK	Cameron O-105 balloon	S. J. Fensome
G-BOTM	Bell 206B JetRanger 2	R. J. & E. M. Frost
G-BOTN	PA-28-161 Warrior II	W. Lancashire Aero Club Ltd/Woodvale
G-BOTO	Bellanca 7ECA Citabria	G-BOTO Group
G-BOTP	Cessna 150J	R. E. Thorne
G-BOTS	Hughes 269C	Horizon Helicopters
G-BOTT	Rand KR-2	M. D. Ott & M. R. Hutchins
G-BOTU	Piper J-3C-65 Cub	T. L. Giles
G-BOTV	PA-32RT-300 Lance II	Robin Lance Aviation Association Ltd
G-BOTW	Cameron V-77 balloon	D. N. Malcolm
G-BOTY	Cessna 150J	T. J. C. Darby & G. Webster
G-BOTZ	Bensen B.80R	C. Jones
G-BOUD	PA-38-112 Tomahawk	K. & C. J. Powell/Southend
G-BOUE	Cessna 172N	E. Alexander
G-BOUF	Cessna 172N	Zycomm Electronics Ltd/Burnaston
G-BOUH	Cessna 172RG	M. G. Fountain
G-BOUI	PA-28-236 Dakota	Solvit Software
G-BOUJ	Cessna 150M	J. B. Mills
G-BOUK	PA-34-200T Seneca II	Airtime (Hampshire) Ltd
G-BOUL	PA-34-200T Seneca II	C.S.E. Aviation Ltd/Kidlington
G-BOUM	PA-34-200T Seneca II	C.S.E. Aviation Ltd/Kidlington
G-BOUN	Rand KR-2	W. J. Allen
G-BOUO	Thunder Ax8-105 balloon	Border Balloon Co
G-BOUP	PA-28-161 Warrior II	C.S.E. Aviation Ltd/Kidlington
G-BOUR	PA-28-161 Warrior II	C.S.E. Aviation Ltd/Kidlington
G-BOUS	PA-28RT-201 Arrow IV	Hamilton Compass Aviation Ltd
G-BOUT	Colomban MC.12 Cri-Cri	C. K. Farley
G-BOUV	Bensen B.8R	P. Wilkinson
G-BOUZ	Cessna 150G	G. Webster & T. J. C. Darby
G-BOVA	PA-31-310 Turbo Navajo C	Birmingham Aviation Ltd (G-BECP)
G-BOVB	PA-15 Vagabond	Oscar Flying Group/Shoreham
G-BOVC	Everett gyroplane	J. W. Highton
G-BOVG	Cessna F.172H	The G-BOVG Group
G-BOVH	PA-28-161 Warrior II	R. W. Tebby
G-BOVK	PA-28-161 Warrior II	Hamilton Compass Aviation Ltd
G-BOVL	SNCAN Stampe SV-4C	T. A. Reed
G-BOVP	Air Command 532 Elite	C. K. Park
G-BOVR	Robinson R-22	P. J. Homan
G-BOVS	Cessna 150M	V. B. Cheesewright
G-BOVT	Cessna 150M	R. G. Moss
G-BOVU	Stoddard-Hamilton Glasair III	W. N. Blair-Hickman
G-BOVV	Cameron V-77 balloon	J. P. Clifford
G-BOVW	Colt 69A balloon	V. Hyland
G-BOVX	Hughes 269C	McIntyre Aviation Ltd/Staverton
G-BOVY	Hughes 269C	R. C. Button
G-BOVZ	Hughes 269C	March Helicopters Ltd/Sywell
G-BOWA	Thunder Ax8-90 balloon	G. & L. Fitzpatrick
G-BOWB	Cameron V-77 balloon	R. C. Stone
G-BOWC	Cessna 150J	G-BOWC Flying Group/Southend
G-BOWD	Cessna F.337G	Rising Dry Ltd (G-BLSB)
G-BOWE	PA-34-200T Seneca II	C.S.E. Aviation Ltd/Kidlington
G-BOWK	Cameron N-90 balloon	S. R. Bridge
G-BOWL	Cameron V-77 balloon	Matrix Computers Ltd
G-BOWM	Cameron V-56 balloon	C. G. Caldecott & G. Pitt
G-BOWN	PA-12 Super Cruiser	F. E. P. Holmes/Andrewsfield

Notes	Reg.	Type	Owner or Operator
	G-BOWO	Cessna R.182	Kenbal Properties Ltd
	G-BOWP	Jodel D.120A	A. G. Gedney & ptnrs/Sibson
	G-BOWR	Boeing 737-3Q8	Dan-Air Services Ltd/Gatwick
	G-BOWS	Cessna 150M	Semloh Aviation Services/Andrewsfield
	G-BOWT	Stolp SA.300 Starduster Too	F. E. P. Holmes/Andrewsfield
	G-BOWU	Cameron O-84 balloon	Raybrake & Co Ltd
	G-BOWV	Cameron V-65 balloon	C. P. R. & S. J. Baxter
	G-BOWY	PA-28RT-201T Turbo Arrow IV	Littlebird (UK) Ltd/Elstree
	G-BOWZ	Benson B.80V	W. M. Day
	G-BOXA	PA-28-161 Warrior II	CI Aero Holdings Ltd
	G-BOXB	PA-28-161 Warrior II	CI Aero Holdings Ltd
	G-BOXC	PA-28-161 Warrior II	CI Aero Holdings Ltd
	G-BOXG	Cameron O-77 balloon	S. J. Butler
	G-BOXH	Pitts S-1S Special	S. Fenwick
	G-BOXJ	Piper J-3C-65 Cub	J. L. Quick & A. J. P. Jackson/Biggin Hill
	G-BOXK	Slingsby T.67C	Slingsby Aviation Ltd/Kirkbymoorside
	G-BOXN	Robinson R-22B	Conguess Aviation Ltd
	G-BOXR	GA-7 Cougar	Campbell Air Services Ltd/Booker
	G-BOXS	Hughes 269C	Ford Helicopters Ltd
	G-BOXT	Hughes 269C	Elite Helicopters Ltd
	G-BOXU	AA-5B Tiger	J. J. Woodhouse
	G-BOXV	Pitts S-1S Special	G. R. Clark
	G-BOXW	Cassutt Racer Srs IIIM	D. I. Johnson
	G-BOXX	Robinson R-22B	Doncaster Helicopter Services
	G-BOXY	PA-28-181 Archer II	Sheffield Aero Club Ltd/Netherthorpe
	G-BOYB	Cessna A.152	Northamptonshire School of Flying Ltd/Sywell
	G-BOYC	Robinson R-22B	Northern Helicopters (Leeds) Ltd
	G-BOYE	Cessna TR.182RG	S. K. & W. J. Boettcher
	G-BOYF	Sikorsky S-76B	Darley Steel Management Co Ltd
	G-BOYH	PA-28-151 Warrior	Superpause Ltd/Booker
	G-BOYI	PA-28-161 Warrior II	Rankart Ltd/Kidlington
	G-BOYK	Montgomerie-Benson B.8	H. P. Latham
	G-BOYL	Cessna 152	Sandtoft Air Services (1985) Ltd
	G-BOYM	Cameron O-84 balloon	Frontline Distribution Ltd
	G-BOYO	Cameron V-20 balloon	Cameron Balloons Ltd
	G-BOYP	Cessna 172N	S. J. Randle & T. W. Crow
	G-BOYR	Cessna F.337G	Bournewood Aviation
	G-BOYS	Cameron N-77 balloon	The Independent Balloon Co Ltd
	G-BOYT	PA-38-112 Tomahawk	APB Leasing Ltd/Welshpool
	G-BOYU	Cessna A.150L	Flightweel Ltd
	G-BOYV	PA-28R-201T Turbo Arrow III	P. R. Goldsworthy
	G-BOYX	Robinson R-22B	R. Towle
	G-BOYY	Cameron A-105 balloon	Hoyers (UK) Ltd
	G-BOYZ	Laser Z.200	M. G. Jefferies
	G-BOZA	Boeing 737-3L9	British Airways *River Lossie*
	G-BOZB	Boeing 737-3L9	British Airways *River Wyre*
	G-BOZI	PA-28-161 Warrior II	Klingair Ltd/Conington
	G-BOZJ	Thunder Ax8-105 balloon	G. V. Beckwith
	G-BOZK	AS.332L Super Puma	British International Helicopters Ltd
	G-BOZL	Bell 206B JetRanger	Ernest George Aviation Ltd
	G-BOZM	PA-38-112 Tomahawk	S. J. Green
	G-BOZN	Cameron N-77 balloon	Calarel Developments Ltd
	G-BOZO	AA-5B Tiger	Becketts Honda Car Centre Ltd
	G-BOZP	Beech 76 Duchess	Millhouse Developments Ltd
	G-BOZR	Cessna 152	Interair (Aviation) Ltd/Bournemouth
	G-BOZS	Pitts S-1C Special	R. J. & M. B. Trickey
	G-BOZT	PA-28-181 Archer II	Andrews Aviation Ltd
	G-BOZU	Sparrow Hawk Mk II	R. V. Phillimore
	G-BOZV	CEA DR.340 Major	E. H. Ellis
	G-BOZW	Benson B.8M	M. E. Wills
	G-BOZX	Robinson R-22B	M. J. Burgess
	G-BOZY	Cameron RTW-120 balloon	G. C. Ludlow
	G-BOZZ	AA-5B Tiger	P. R. Draper
	G-BPAA	Acro Advanced	Acro Engines & Airframes Ltd
	G-BPAB	Cessna 150M	A. & B. Aviation/Earls Colne
	G-BPAC	PA-28-161 Warror II	G. G. Pratt
	G-BPAD	PA-34-200T Seneca II	Liverpool Flying School Ltd
	G-BPAE	Cameron V-77 balloon	A. R. Peart & J. E. Astall
	G-BPAF	PA-28-161 Warrior II	Hendafern Ltd
	G-BPAG	Bellanca 8KCAB Decathlon	Deltaflight Ltd
	G-BPAH	Colt 69A balloon	International Distillers & Vintners Ltd

Reg.	Type	Owner or Operator	Notes
G-BPAI	Bell 47F-2A1	Fizzle Ltd	
G-BPAJ	D.H.82A Tiger Moth	P. A. Jackson (G-AOIX)	
G-BPAL	D.H.C.1 Chipmunk 22 (WG350)	D. F. Ranger (G-BCYE)	
G-BPAM	Jodel D.150A	A. J. Symes-Bullen	
G-BPAO	Air Command 503 Commander	D. J. Sagar	
G-BPAS	SOCATA TB.20 Trinidad	J. Miskelly	
G-BPAU	PA-28-161 Warrior II	Lapwing Flying Group Ltd/Denham	
G-BPAV	FRED Srs 2	P. A. Valentine	
G-BPAW	Cessna 150M	Skegness Air Taxi Service Ltd	
G-BPAX	Cessna 150M	Barry Aviation Ltd	
G-BPAY	PA-28-181 Archer II	Quest Consultants Ltd	
G-BPBA	Benson B.8	M. E. Green	
G-BPBC	Bell 206B JetRanger	Delfino Maritime Ltd	
G-BPBG	Cessna 152	Atlantic Air Transport Ltd/Coventry	
G-BPBI	Cessna 152	B. W. Wells & Burbage Farms Ltd	
G-BPBJ	Cessna 152	A. Windley/Tattershall	
G-BPBK	Cessna 152	B. W. Wells & Burbage Farms Ltd	
G-BPBL	Cessna 152	B. W. Wells & Burbage Farms Ltd	
G-BPBM	PA-28-161 Warrior II	Sandtoft Air Services (1985) Ltd	
G-BPBO	PA-28RT-201T Turbo Arrow IV	Arrow Associates/Bournemouth	
G-BPBR	PA-38-112 Tomahawk	A.T. Aviation Ltd/Cardiff	
G-BPBU	Cameron V-77 balloon	G. Illing	
G-BPBV	Cameron V-77 balloon	J. E. Smith	
G-BPBW	Cameron O-105 balloon	R. J. Mansfield	
G-BPBX	Cameron V-77 balloon	A. R. M. Hill & C. J. Bell (G-BPCU)	
G-BPBY	Cameron V-77 balloon	T. J. & K. A. Brewster (G-BPCS)	
G-BPBZ	Thunder Ax7-77 balloon	Wye Valley Aviation Ltd	
G-BPCA	BN-2B Islander	Loganair Ltd (G-BLNX)/Glasgow	
G-BPCE	Stolp SA.300 Starduster Too	R. E. Todd	
G-BPCF	Piper J-3C-65 Cub	A. J. Cook	
G-BPCG	Colt AS-80 airship	Willowbest Ltd	
G-BPCI	Cessna R.172K	B. E. Simpson	
G-BPCJ	Cessna 150J	C. R. Hughes & B. E. Simpson	
G-BPCK	PA-28-161 Warrior II	C. R. Hughes & B. E. Simpson	
G-BPCL	SA Bulldog Srs 120/128	Isohigh Ltd/Denham	
G-BPCM	Rotorway Executive	Normans (Burton-on-Trent) Ltd	
G-BPCN	Cameron A-160 balloon	Chard Balloon Co Ltd	
G-BPCR	Mooney M.20K	T. & R. Harris	
G-BPCT	Bell 206L-1 LongRanger	Trillionair Ltd	
G-BPCV	Montgomerie Bensen MB.8R	J. Fisher	
G-BPCW	Slingsby T.31 Motor Cadet III	P. C. Williams	
G-BPCX	PA-28-236 Dakota	P. Hartley	
G-BPCY	PA-34-200T Seneca	Compton Abbas Airfield Ltd	
G-BPDA	H.S.748 Srs 2A	Janes Aviation Ltd (G-GLAS)/Blackpool	
G-BPDC	PA-46-310P Malibu	D. W. Clark	
G-BPDD	Colt 240A balloon	Heather Flight Ltd	
G-BPDE	Colt 56A balloon	J. W. Weidema	
G-BPDF	Cameron V-77 balloon	Boyson Construction Ltd	
G-BPDG	Cameron V-77 balloon	A. & M. A. Dunning	
G-BPDJ	Chris Tena Mini Coupe	Air Time Acquisition Ltd	
G-BPDK	Sorrell SNS-7 Hyperbipe	A. J. Cable/Barton	
G-BPDL	EMB-110P1 Bandeirante	Titan Airways Ltd/Stansted	
G-BPDM	C.A.S.A. 1.131E Jungmann (E3B-369)	Spanish Acquisition/Shoreham	
G-BPDN	PA-28R-201 Arrow III	J. M. C. Crompton	
G-BPDS	PA-28-161 Warrior II	Hendafern Ltd	
G-BPDT	PA-28-161 Warrior II	Hendafern Ltd	
G-BPDU	PA-28-161 Warrior II	Hendafern Ltd	
G-BPDV	Pitts S-1S Special	D. Clarke	
G-BPDY	Westland-Bell 47G-3B1	Fairglobe Ltd	
G-BPDZ	Cessna 340A	J. G. Kelwick	
G-BPEA	Boeing 757-236ER	Caledonian Airways Ltd *Loch of the Clans*	
G-BPEB	Boeing 757-236ER	Caledonian Airways Ltd *Loch Lomond*	
G-BPEC	Boeing 757-236ER	Caledonian Airways Ltd *Loch Katrine*	
G-BPED	Boeing 757-236ER	Caledonian Airways Ltd *Loch Sheil/ Blair Castle*	
G-BPEE	Boeing 757-236ER	Caledonian Airways Ltd *Loch Tay*	
G-BPEF	Boeing 757-236ER	Caledonian Airways Ltd/Gatwick	
G-BPEH	Boeing 757-236ER	Caledonian Airways Ltd/Gatwick	
G-BPEI	Boeing 757-236ER	Caledonian Airways Ltd/Gatwick	
G-BPEJ	—	Caledonian Airways Ltd/Gatwick	
G-BPEK	—	Caledonian Airways Ltd/Gatwick	
G-BPEL	PA-28-151 Warrior	M. E. Benterman	

Notes	Reg.	Type	Owner or Operator
	G-BPEM	Cessna 150K	C. A. Outhwaite
	G-BPEO	Cessna 152	M. E. Benterman
	G-BPER	PA-38-112 Tomahawk	E. Midlands Flying School Ltd
	G-BPES	PA-38-112 Tomahawk	Sherwood Flying Club Ltd/Tollerton
	G-BPEW	Robinson R-22B	Trade Photographic Services Ltd
	G-BPEZ	Colt 77A balloon	A. Stace
	G-BPFA	Knight GK-2 Swallow	G. Knight & D. G. Pridham
	G-BPFB	Colt 77A balloon	S. Ingram
	G-BPFC	Mooney M.20C	Kington Building Supplies Ltd & RV Engineering Ltd
	G-BPFD	Jodel D.112	K. Manley
	G-BPFE	Lightning T.5 (XS452)	Ruanil Investments Ltd/Cranfield
	G-BPFF	Cameron DP-70 airship	Cameron Balloons Ltd
	G-BPFG	SOCATA TB.20 Trinidad	F. T. Arnold
	G-BPFH	PA-28-161 Warrior II	M. H. Kleiser
	G-BPFI	PA-28-181 Archer II	R. N. Dixon-Smith & B. M. Chilvers
	G-BPFJ	Cameron 90 Can SS balloon	The Hot-Air Balloon Co Ltd
	G-BPFK	Bensen B.8M	J. W. Birkett
	G-BPFL	Davis DA-2	C. A. Lightfoot
	G-BPFM	Aeronca 7AC Champion	Foxtrot Mike Group
	G-BPFR	Short SD3-60 Variant 100	Shorts Aircraft Financing Ltd
	G-BPFS	Short SD3-60 Variant 100	Shorts Aircraft Financing Ltd (G-REGN/G-OCIA)
	G-BPFT	Cameron N-77 balloon	Cameron Balloons Ltd
	G-BPFV	Boeing 767-204ER	Britannia Airways Ltd/Luton
	G-BPFX	Colt 21A balloon	The Hot-Air Balloon Co Ltd
	G-BPFY	Consolidated PBY-6A Catalina	D. W. Arnold/Biggin Hill
	G-BPFZ	Cessna 152	J. J. Baumhardt/Southend
	G-BPGA	Mooney M.20J	Medallionair Ltd
	G-BPGB	Cessna 150J	Skegness Air Taxi Service Ltd
	G-BPGC	Air Command 532 Elite	E. C. E. Brown
	G-BPGD	Cameron V-65 balloon	Gone With The Wind Ltd
	G-BPGE	Cessna U.206C	M. V. Owen
	G-BPGF	Thunder Ax7-77 balloon	Dovetail Flying Group
	G-BPGH	EAA Acro Sport 2	Pennine Lightning Film & TV Ltd
	G-BPGI	Colt 69A balloon	Thunder & Colt Ltd
	G-BPGJ	Colt 31A balloon	Thunder & Colt Ltd
	G-BPGK	Aeronca 7AC Chamption	T. M. Williams
	G-BPGL	PA-28 Cherokee 180	C. N. Ellerbrook
	G-BPGM	Cessna 152	Westward Airways (Land's End) Ltd
	G-BPGN	Cameron 90 Tractor SS balloon	Cameron Balloons Ltd
	G-BPGU	PA-28-181 Archer II	G. Underwood
	G-BPGV	Robinson R-22B	Featureford Ltd
	G-BPGX	SOCATA TB.9 Tampico	Air Touring Services Ltd/Biggin Hill
	G-BPGY	Cessna 150H	Three Counties Aero Engineering Ltd/Lasham
	G-BPGZ	Cessna 150G	D. F. & B. L. Sperring
	G-BPHB	PA-28-161 Warrior II	Channel Islands Aero Holdings (Jersey) Ltd
	G-BPHD	Cameron N-42 balloon	P. J. Marshall & M. A. Clarke
	G-BPHE	PA-28-161 Warrior II	Pool Aviation Ltd/Welshpool
	G-BPHF	AB-206A JetRanger	RCR Aviation Ltd/Southampton
	G-BPHG	Robin DR.400/180	K. J. & M. B. White/Redhill
	G-BPHH	Cameron V-77 balloon	C. J. Madigan
	G-BPHJ	Cameron V-77 balloon	C. W. Brown
	G-BPHK	Whittaker MW.7	R. V. Hogg
	G-BPHL	PA-28-161 Warrior II	Teesside Flight Centre Ltd
	G-BPHM	Beech A36 Bonanza	A. P. Vonk
	G-BPHO	Taylorcraft BC-12D	J. Roberts
	G-BPHP	Taylorcraft BC-12-65	A. Liddiard & A. D. Pearce
	G-BPHR	D.H.82A Tiger Moth	N. Parry
	G-BPHS	Cessna 152	Lynair Aviation
	G-BPHT	Cessna 152	A. E. Kedros
	G-BPHU	Thunder Ax7-77 balloon	G. G. Bacon
	G-BPHW	Cessna 140	J. A. Pothecary
	G-BPHX	Cessna 140	Ark Ltd
	G-BPHY	Cameron 110 Cow SS balloon	Cameron Balloons Ltd
	G-BPHZ	M.S.505 Criquet (TA+RC)	The Aircraft Restoration Co/Duxford
	G-BPIC	AB-206B JetRanger 3	Heliwork Services Ltd
	G-BPID	PA-28-161 Warrior II	P. M. Ireland
	G-BPIE	Bell 206B JetRanger	BLS Aviation Ltd/Elstree
	G-BPIF	Bensen-Parsons 2 seat	N. J. Stoneham
	G-BPIH	Rand KR-2	J. R. Rowley
	G-BPII	Denney Aerocraft Kitfox	J. K. Cross

Reg.	Type	Owner or Operator
G-BPIJ	Brantly B.2B	R. B. Paine
G-BPIK	PA-38-112 Tomahawk	Cumbernauld Aviation Ltd
G-BPIL	Cessna 310B	W. A Taylor
G-BPIM	Cameron N-77 balloon	Thermalite Ltd
G-BPIN	Glaser-Dirks DG.400	M. P. Seth-Smith & J. N. Stevenson
G-BPIO	Cessna F.152 II	S. Harcourt
G-BPIP	Slingsby T.31 Motor Cadet III	J. H. Beard
G-BPIR	Scheibe SF.25E Super Falke	Coventry Gliding Club Ltd
G-BPIT	Robinson R-22B	Turnbull Crane Hire Ltd
G-BPIU	PA-28-161 Warrior II	I. R. Jones
G-BPIV	Bristol 149 Bolingbroke Mk IVT	The Aircraft Restoration Co/Duxford
G-BPIX	AA-5A Cheetah	Lowlog Ltd
G-BPIY	Cessna 152	J. J. Baumhardt
G-BPIZ	AA-5B Tiger	D. A. Horsley
G-BPJA	Beech 95-58 Baron	Morse Computers Ltd
G-BPJB	Schweizer 269C	J. F. Britten
G-BPJC	Robinson R-22B	Leicester Helicopters Ltd
G-BPJD	SOCATA Rallye 110ST	J. S. Haslam
G-BPJE	Cameron A-105 balloon	J. S. Eckersley
G-BPJF	PA-38-112 Tomahawk	Air Yorkshire Ltd
G-BPJG	PA-18 Super Cub 150	Trent Valley Aerotowing Ltd
G-BPJH	PA-18 Super Cub 95	P. J. Heron
G-BPJK	Colt 77A balloon	Akal Ltd
G-BPJL	Cessna 152	London Flight Centre (Headcorn) Ltd
G-BPJN	Jodel D.18	J. A. Nugent
G-BPJO	PA-28-161 Cadet	C.S.E. Aviation Ltd/Kidlington
G-BPJP	PA-28-161 Cadet	C.S.E. Aviation Ltd/Kidlington
G-BPJR	PA-28-161 Cadet	C.S.E. Aviation Ltd/Kidlington
G-BPJS	PA-28-161 Cadet	C.S.E. Aviation Ltd/Kidlington
G-BPJT	PA-28-161 Cadet	C.S.E. Aviation Ltd/Kidlington
G-BPJU	PA-28-161 Cadet	C.S.E. Aviation Ltd/Kidlington
G-BPJV	Taylorcraft F-21	J. G. Waller
G-BPJW	Cessna A.150K	Heathgrange Ltd
G-BPJZ	Cameron O-160 balloon	M. L. Gabb
G-BPKA	Boeing 737-4S3	Entrepot Aircraft Ltd
G-BPKB	Boeing 737-4S3	Entrepot Aircraft Ltd
G-BPKC	Boeing 737-4S3	Entrepot Aircraft Ltd
G-BPKD	Boeing 737-4S3	Entrepot Aircraft Ltd
G-BPKE	Boeing 737-4S3	Entrepot Aircraft Ltd
G-BPKF	Grob G.115	Tayside Aviation Ltd/Dundee
G-BPKG	Grob G.115	Tayside Aviation Ltd/Dundee
G-BPKH	Robinson R-22B	Findon Air Services
G-BPKI	EAA Acro Sport 1	J. A. Sykes
G-BPKJ	Colt AS-80 Mk II airship	Thunder & Co Ltd
G-BPKK	Denney Aerocraft Kitfox	T. P. Eglinton & N. E. Whiteman
G-BPKL	Mooney M.20J	Astraflight Ltd
G-BPKM	PA-28-161 Warrior II	M. J. Greasby
G-BPKN	Colt AS-80 Mk II airship	C. Turnbull
G-BPKO	Cessna 140	R. B. Sporik & M. D. Hughes
G-BPKR	PA-28-151 Warrior	R. R. Harris
G-BPKS	Stolp SA.300 Starduster Too	J. A. Hubner
G-BPKT	Piper J-5A Cub Cruiser	W. A. N. Jenkins
G-BPLA	Boeing 737-2K2	Britannia Airways Ltd *Sir Stanley Matthews*/ Luton
G-BPLE	Cameron A-160 balloon	Balloons & Airships International Ltd
G-BPLF	Cameron V-77 balloon	Dalesight Ltd
G-BPLG	Morane-Saulnier M.S.317	F. A. Anderson
G-BPLH	Jodel DR.1051	C. A. Bailey & L. J. Cudd
G-BPLI	Colt 77A balloon	Yanin International Ltd
G-BPLJ	Colt 90A balloon	Thunder & Colt Ltd
G-BPLK	Slingsby T.67C	Slingsby Aviation Ltd/Kirkbymoorside
G-BPLM	AIA Stampe SV-4C	C. J. & K. E. Jenson/Redhill
G-BPLU	Thunder Ax10-160 balloon	Subsearch Ltd
G-BPLV	Cameron V-77 balloon	Jessops (Tailors) Ltd
G-BPLY	Pitts S-2B Special	D. A. Hammant
G-BPLZ	Hughes 369HS	Conguess Aviation Ltd/Conington
G-BPMB	Maule M5-235C Lunar Rocket	A. P. Le Coyte
G-BPMC	Air Command 503 Commander	M. A. Cheshire
G-BPMD	Boeing Stearman A.75L-3 (320)	M. G. Saunders/White Waltham
G-BPME	Cessna 152	London Flight Centre (Headcorn) Ltd
G-BPMF	PA-28-151 Warrior	Logtrip Ltd
G-BPMG	Bensen B.8MR	P. Doherty
G-BPMH	Schempp-Hirth Nimbus 3DM	Southern Sailplanes

Notes	Reg.	Type	Owner or Operator
	G-BPMI	Colt 56A balloon	Thunder & Colt Ltd
	G-BPMJ	Colt 56A balloon	Thunder & Colt Ltd
	G-BPML	Cessna 172M	J. M. Gale & R. D. Andrews
	G-BPMM	Champion 7ECA Citabria	D. M. Griffiths
	G-BPMN	Aerocar Super Coot Model A	P. Napp
	G-BPMO	Cessna 150M	S. L. Mills
	G-BPMP	Douglas C-47A-50-DL (224211)	Wesco 113 Ltd/Cranfield
	G-BPMR	PA-28-161 Warrior II	McIntyre Aviation/Staverton
	G-BPMU	Nord 3202B	John Durkin Technical Services Ltd (G-BIZJ)
	G-BPMV	PA-28-161 Warrior II	J. A. Hilton
	G-BPMW	QAC Quickie Q.2	P. M. Wright (G-OICI/G-OGKN)
	G-BPMX	ARV Super 2	B. Houghton
	G-BPMY	Cameron A-120 balloon	British School of Ballooning
	G-BPNA	Cessna 150L	B. E. Simpson
	G-BPNC	Rotorway Executive	S. J. Hanson
	G-BPND	Boeing 727-2D3	Dan-Air Services Ltd/Gatwick
	G-BPNF	Robinson R-22B	N. S. Madden
	G-BPNG	Bell 206B JetRanger 2	Tindon Ltd (G-ORTC)
	G-BPNI	Robinson R-22B	Arrowbury Ltd
	G-BPNL	QAC Quickie Q.2	J. Catley
	G-BPNM	Cessna 340A	SP Metal UK Ltd
	G-BPNN	Bensen B.8MR	M. E. Vahdat
	G-BPNO	Zlin Z.326 Trener Master	J. A. S. Bailey & S. T. Logan
	G-BPNR	(reserved)	Dan-Air Services Ltd/Gatwick
	G-BPNS	Boeing 727-277	Dan-Air Services Ltd/Gatwick
	G-BPNT	BAe 146-300	Dan-Air Services Ltd/Gatwick
	G-BPNU	Thunder Ax7-77 balloon	J. Fenton
	G-BPNY	Boeing 727-230	Dan-Air Services Ltd/Gatwick
	G-BPNZ	Boeing 737-4Q8	Dan-Air Services Ltd/Gatwick
	G-BPOA	Gloster Meteor T.7 (WF877)	Aces High Ltd/North Weald
	G-BPOB	Sopwith Camel F.1 (replica) (542)	Bianchi Aviation Film Services Ltd/ Booker
	G-BPOD	Stolp SA.300 Starduster Too	A. T. Fines
	G-BPOE	Colt 77A balloon	Albatross Aviation Ltd
	G-BPOF	Robinson R-22B	R. D. Masters
	G-BPOL	Pietenpol Air Camper	G. W. Postance
	G-BPOM	PA-28-161 Warrior II	McIntyre Aviation/Staverton
	G-BPON	PA-34-200T Seneca II	London Flight Centre Air Charter Ltd
	G-BPOO	Montgomerie Bensen B.8MR	M. E. Vahdat
	G-BPOR	Bell 206B JetRanger 2	Thetford Compactors Finance Ltd
	G-BPOS	Cessna 150M	Lanx Engineering Ltd
	G-BPOT	PA-28-181 Archer II	Cumbernauld Aviation Ltd
	G-BPOU	Luscombe 8A Silvaire	E. T. Wicks
	G-BPOV	Cameron 90 Magazine SS balloon	Forbes Europe Inc/France
	G-BPOX	Enstrom 280C Shark	J. Evans
	G-BPOY	Enstrom F-28A	M. & P. Food Products Ltd
	G-BPOZ	Enstrom F-28A	M. & P. Food Products Ltd
	G-BPPA	Cameron O-65 balloon	Rix Petroleum Ltd
	G-BPPB	PA-34-220T Seneca III	A. Smith
	G-BPPC	Robinson R-22 Mariner	Northern Helicopters (Blackpool) Ltd
	G-BPPD	PA-38-112 Tomahawk	AT Aviation Ltd/Cardiff
	G-BPPE	PA-38-112 Tomahawk	Norwich School of Flying
	G-BPPF	PA-38-112 Tomahawk	A. N. Doughty
	G-BPPG	PA-38-112 Tomahawk	AT Aviation Ltd/Cardiff
	G-BPPI	Colt 180A balloon	A. Faulkner
	G-BPPJ	Cameron A-180 Balloon	H. R. Evans
	G-BPPK	PA-28-151 Warrior	Balgold Ltd
	G-BPPL	Enstrom F-28A	M. & P. Food Products Ltd
	G-BPPM	Beech B200 Super King Air	Gama Aviation Ltd/Fairoaks
	G-BPPN	Cessna F.182Q	Hunt Norris Ltd
	G-BPPO	Luscombe 8A Silvaire	M. J. Negus
	G-BPPP	Cameron V-77 balloon	P. F. Smart
	G-BPPR	Air Command 532 Elite	T. D. Inch
	G-BPPS	Mudry CAARP CAP.21	BAC Aviation Ltd/Earls Colne
	G-BPPU	Air Command 532 Elite	J. Hough
	G-BPPW	Schweizer 269C	K. W. Harding
	G-BPPX	Schweizer 269C	Lakeside Helicopters Ltd
	G-BPPY	Hughes 269B	Compass Aviation Ltd
	G-BPPZ	Taylorcraft BC-12D	Zulu Warriors Flying Group
	G-BPRA	Aeronca 11AC Chief	D. F. Micklethwait
	G-BPRC	Cameron Elephant SS balloon	Cameron Balloons Ltd
	G-BPRD	Pitts S-1C Special	S. M. Trickey
	G-BPRI	AS.355F-1 Twin Squirrel	American Aviation Technologies Ltd

Reg.	Type	Owner or Operator	Notes
G-BPRJ	AS.355F-1 Twin Squirrel	G. Greenall	
G-BPRL	AS.355F-1 Twin Squirrel	Wood Hall Helicopters Ltd	
G-BPRM	Cessna F.172L	Nultree Ltd (G-AZKG)	
G-BPRN	PA-28-161 Warrior II	Air Navigation & Trading Co Ltd/Blackpool	
G-BPRO	Cessna A.150K	Armphase Ltd	
G-BPRP	Cessna 150E	P. G. Powter/Shoreham	
G-BPRR	Rand KR-2	M. W. Albery	
G-BPRS	Air Command 532 Elite	B. K. Snoxall	
G-BPRT	Piel CP.328	N. Reddish	
G-BPRV	PA-28-161 Warrior II	AT Aviation Ltd/Cardiff	
G-BPRX	Aeronca 11AC Chief	P. G. Kavanagh/Barton	
G-BPRY	PA-28-161 Warrior II	B. McIntyre	
G-BPRZ	Robinson R-22A	Bristol Rotary Training Ltd	
G-BPSA	Luscombe 8A Silvaire	K. P. Gorman/Staverton	
G-BPSB	Air Command 532 Elite	D. K. Duckworth	
G-BPSE	NA AT-6D Harvard (483009)	Aces High Ltd/North Weald	
G-BPSH	Cameron V-77 balloon	P. G. Hossack	
G-BPSI	Thunder Ax10-160 balloon	Airborne Adventures Ltd	
G-BPSJ	Thunder Ax6-56 balloon	Thunder & Colt Ltd	
G-BPSK	Montgomerie Bensen B.8M	B. Harrison	
G-BPSL	Cessna 177	I. P. Burnett & ptnrs/White Waltham	
G-BPSN	Boeing 757-236	Entrepot Aircraft Ltd	
G-BPSO	Cameron N-90 balloon	L. A. Sadler & K. J. Holt	
G-BPSP	Cameron 90 Ship SS balloon	Forbes Europe Inc	
G-BPSR	Cameron V-77 balloon	K. D. & S. L. Johnson	
G-BPSS	Cameron A-120 balloon	J. P. Clifford	
G-BPSV	Cessna F.406 Caravan II	Bob Crowe Aircraft Sales Ltd	
G-BPSW	Cessna F.406 Caravan II	Directflight Ltd/Norwich	
G-BPSX	Cessna F.406 Caravan II	Directflight Ltd/Norwich	
G-BPSY	Grob G.115	Soaring (Oxford) Ltd	
G-BPSZ	Cameron N-180 balloon	The Balloon Club Ltd	
G-BPTA	Stinson 108-2	D. N. H. Martin/Booker	
G-BPTB	Boeing Stearman A.75N1 (442)	Aero Vintage Ltd	
G-BPTC	Taylorcraft BC-12D	J. R. Surbey	
G-BPTD	Cameron V-77 balloon	J. Lippett	
G-BPTE	PA-28-181 Archer II	London Flight Centre (Stansted) Ltd	
G-BPTF	Cessna 152	London Flight Centre (Stansted) Ltd	
G-BPTG	R. Commander 112TC	A. C. & M. Denny	
G-BPTH	Air Command 532 Elite	R. Wheeler	
G-BPTI	SOCATA TB.20 Trinidad	Lyndon Scaffolding Hire Ltd/Birmingham	
G-BPTJ	PA-34-200T Seneca II	R. B. H. Vetch	
G-BPTL	Cessna 172N	Cleveland Flying School Ltd/Teesside	
G-BPTM	Pitts S-1T Special	RPM Aviation Ltd	
G-BPTO	Zenith CH.200-AA	B. Philips	
G-BPTP	Robinson R-22	Sarahs Lakeland Fudge	
G-BPTR	Robinson R-22	The Helicentre/Blackpool	
G-BPTS	C.A.S.A 1.131E Jungmann	Aerobatic Displays Ltd/Booker	
G-BPTT	Robin DR.400/120	The Cotswold Aero Club Ltd/Staverton	
G-BPTU	Cessna 152	Flyteam Aviation Ltd	
G-BPTV	Bensen B.8	L. Chiappi	
G-BPTW	Cameron A-160 balloon	Newbury Ballooning Co Ltd	
G-BPTX	Cameron O-120 balloon	J. M. Langley	
G-BPTZ	Robinson R-22B	Charmaine Aviation	
G-BPUA	EAA P-2 Biplane	G. H. Cork	
G-BPUB	Cameron V-31 balloon	M. T. Evans	
G-BPUC	QAC Quickie Q.200	R. Wells	
G-BPUD	Ryan PT-22 (I-492)	R. I. Warman	
G-BPUE	Air Command 532 Elite	R. A. Fazackerly	
G-BPUF	Thunder Ax6-56Z balloon	Buf-Puf Balloon Group	
G-BPUG	Air Command 532 Elite	T. A. Holmes	
G-BPUH	Cameron A-180 balloon	Golf Centres Balloons Ltd	
G-BPUI	Air Command 532 Elite	M. A. Turner	
G-BPUJ	Cameron N-90 balloon	Touch Panel Products Ltd	
G-BPUL	PA-18 Super Cub 150	Crissair Ltd	
G-BPUM	Cessna R.182RG	Ray Cochrane Racing Ltd	
G-BPUP	Whittaker MW-7	J. H. Beard	
G-BPUR	Piper J-3L-65 Cub	J3 Group	
G-BPUS	Rans S.9	P. M. Shipman	
G-BPUU	Cessna 140	R. Crossland/Exeter	
G-BPUW	Colt 90A balloon	Huntair Ltd	
G-BPUX	Cessna 150J	H. H. Goodman	
G-BPUY	Cessna 150K	M. Hewison/Luton	
G-BPUZ	Cessna 150M	Premier Plane Leasing Co Ltd	

Notes	Reg.	Type	Owner or Operator
	G-BPVA	Cessna 172F	J. E. Stevens
	G-BPVC	Cameron V-77 balloon	Courtaulds PLC
	G-BPVE	Bleriot 1909 replica	Bianchi Aviation Film Services Ltd/Booker
	G-BPVH	Cub Aircraft J-3C-65 Prospector	D. E. Cooper-Maguire
	G-BPVI	PA-32R-301 Saratoga SP	J. D. Macpherson
	G-BPVJ	Cessna 152	G. C. Winter & T. Richards
	G-BPVK	Varga 2150A Kachina	H. W. Hall
	G-BPVM	Cameron V-77 balloon	Royal Engineers Balloon Club
	G-BPVN	PA-32R-301T Turbo Saratoga SP	Hero Aviation/Stapleford
	G-BPVO	Cassutt Racer IIIM	Lanx Engineering Ltd
	G-BPVP	Aerotek Pitts S-2B Special	N. J. Hunt
	G-BPVT	Thunder Ax7-65 balloon	Anglia Balloon School Ltd
	G-BPVU	Thunder Ax7-77 balloon	J. Burlinson
	G-BPVV	Cameron V-77 balloon	J. L. Seccombe
	G-BPVW	C.A.S.A. 1.131E Jungmann	S. A. W. Becker/Goodwood
	G-BPVX	Cassutt Racer IIIM	A. A. A. White/Barton
	G-BPVY	Cessna 172D	Techspan Aviation Ltd/Booker
	G-BPVZ	Luscombe 8E Silvaire	W. E. Gillham & P. Ryman
	G-BPWA	PA-28-161 Warrior II	Mid America UK Ltd
	G-BPWC	Cameron V-77 balloon	H. B. Roberts
	G-BPWD	Cessna 120	Peregrine Flying Group
	G-BPWE	PA-28-161 Warrior II	AT Aviation Ltd/Cardiff
	G-BPWF	PA-28 Cherokee 140	S. J. Harris
	G-BPWG	Cessna 150M	C. J. Allen
	G-BPWH	Robinson R-22B	R. H. Everett
	G-BPWI	Bell 206B JetRanger 2	Lakeside Helicopters Ltd
	G-BPWK	Sportavia Fournier RF-5B	S. L. Reed
	G-BPWM	Cessna 150L	Lanx Engineering Ltd
	G-BPWN	Cessna 150L	Premier Plane Leasing Co Ltd
	G-BPWO	Cessna 150L	Premier Plane Leasing Co Ltd
	G-BPWP	Rutan LongEz	J. F. O'Hara & A. J. Voyle
	G-BPWR	Cessna R.172K	A. M. Skelton
	G-BPWS	Cessna 172P	Holmes Rentals
	G-BPWT	Cameron DG-19 airship	Airspace Outdoor Advertising Ltd
	G-BPWV	Colt 56A balloon	Cooper Exeter Ltd
	G-BPWW	Piaggio FWP.149D	I. H. Leach-Allen
	G-BPWX	Montgomerie Bensen B.8MR	M. S. Lloyd
	G-BPWY	Isaacs Fury II	R. J. Knights
	G-BPWZ	PA-28-161 Warrior II	Hamilton Compass Aviation Ltd
	G-BPXA	PA-28-181 Archer II	Cherokee Flying Group/Netherthorpe
	G-BPXB	Glaser-Dirks DG.400	Glaser-Dirks UK
	G-BPXE	Enstrom 280C Shark	P. Lancaster
	G-BPXF	Cameron V-65 balloon	D. Pascall
	G-BPXG	Colt 42A balloon	Cooper Group Ltd
	G-BPXH	Colt 17A balloon	Gone With The Wind Ltd
	G-BPXI	PA-23 Aztec 250F	A. R. D. Knott/Elstree
	G-BPXJ	PA-28RT-201T Turbo Arrow IV	Grumman Travel (Surrey) Ltd
	G-BPXP	Thunder Ax10-160 balloon	Wellfarrow Ltd
	G-BPXX	PA-34-200T Seneca II	Hockstar Ltd
	G-BPXY	Aeronca 11AC Chief	S. Hawksworth
	G-BPXZ	Cameron V-77 balloon	M. D. Hammond
	G-BPYA	Rotorway Executive	Orchard Engineering Co Ltd
	G-BPYB	Air Command 532 Elite	P. J. Houtman
	G-BPYC	Cessna 310R	Air Service Training Ltd/Perth
	G-BPYG	Beech C23 Sundowner	K. A. Aubrey
	G-BPYH	Robinson R-22B	PGC Northern (Construction) Ltd
	G-BPYI	Cameron O-77 balloon	Macleod Garage Ltd
	G-BPYJ	Wittman W.8 Tailwind	J. Dixon
	G-BPYK	Thunder Ax7-77 balloon	A. R. Swinnerton
	G-BPYL	Hughes 369D	Aly Aviation Ltd/Henstridge
	G-BPYN	Piper J-3C-65 Cub	The Aquila Group/White Waltham
	G-BPYO	PA-28-181 Archer II	Premier Flight Services Ltd
	G-BPYP	Cameron O-105 balloon	Newbury Ballooning Co Ltd
	G-BPYR	PA-31-310 Turbo Navajo	P. Maxwell-Brown (G-ECMA)
	G-BPYS	Cameron O-77 balloon	D. J. Goldsmith
	G-BPYT	Cameron V-77 balloon	Skylite Aviation Ltd
	G-BPYV	Cameron V-77 balloon	M. E. Weston
	G-BPYW	Air Command 532 Elite	W. V. Tatters
	G-BPYX	Robinson R-22B	Glentworth Scottish Farms Ltd
	G-BPYY	Cameron A-180 balloon	Big Balloon Co
	G-BPYZ	Thunder Ax7-77 balloon	V. J. Baker
	G-BPZA	Luscombe 8A Silvaire	T. P. W. Hyde
	G-BPZB	Cessna 120	C. Grime & J. Cook

Reg.	Type	Owner or Operator	Notes
G-BPZC	Luscombe 8A Silvaire	C. C. & J. M. Lovell	
G-BPZD	SNCAN NC.858S	G. Richards	
G-BPZE	Luscombe 8E Silvaire	S. B. Marsden	
G-BPZF	PA-46-310P Malibu	Jenrick Engineering Services Ltd	
G-BPZG	PA-28R-201T Turbo Arrow III	Salborne Farms Ltd	
G-BPZI	Christen Eagle II	S. D. Quigley	
G-BPZK	Cameron O-120 balloon	D. L. Smith	
G-BPZM	PA-28RT-201 Arrow IV	J. H. Kimber (G-ROYW/G-CRTI)	
G-BPZN	Cessna T.303	R. S. Williams & S. B. Danser (G-RSUL)	
G-BPZO	Cameron N-90 balloon	Seaward PLC	
G-BPZP	Robin DR.400/180R	Booker Gliding Club Ltd	
G-BPZS	Colt 105A balloon	The Balloon Club of GB Ltd	
G-BPZT	Cameron N-90 balloon	Peter Lane Transport Ltd	
G-BPZU	Scheibe SF.25C Falke	G-BPZU Group	
G-BPZV	Cessna T.303	J. F. McGrath	
G-BPZW	SOCATA TB.20 Trinidad	Air Touring Services Ltd/Biggin Hill	
G-BPZX	Cessna 152	Woodward & Co (Sheffield) Ltd	
G-BPZY	Pitts S-1C Special	S. T. A. Albu	
G-BPZZ	Thunder Ax8-105 balloon	Breachwood Motors Ltd	
G-BRAA	Pitts S-1C Special	C. Davidson	
G-BRAB	BAe 146-300	British Aerospace PLC	
G-BRAE	Colt 69A balloon	Jentime Ltd	
G-BRAF	V.S.394 Spitfire FR.XVIII (SM969)	D. W. Arnold/Biggin Hill	
G-BRAJ	Cameron V-77 balloon	H. R. Evans	
G-BRAK	Cessna 172N	J. Lloyd	
G-BRAL	G.159 Gulfstream 1	Ford Motor Co Ltd/Stansted	
G-BRAM	Mikoyan MiG-21PF	Aces High Ltd/North Weald	
G-BRAP	Thermal Aircraft 104	Thermal Aircraft	
G-BRAR	Aeronca 7AC Champion	M. E. Pumford & R. N. Owen	
G-BRAV	PA-23 Aztec 250E	Hartfield Aviation Ltd (G-BBCM)	
G-BRAW	Pitts S-1 Special	P. G. Bond & P. B. Hunter	
G-BRAX	Payne Knight Twister 85B	P. G. Bond & P. B. Hunter	
G-BRAZ	EMB-120RT Brasilia	Air Exel Ltd/Luton	
G-BRBA	PA-28-161 Warrior II	Hendafern Ltd	
G-BRBB	PA-28-161 Warrior II	D. P. Hughes	
G-BRBC	—		
G-BRBD	PA-28-151 Warrior	B. E. Simpson & C. R. Hughes	
G-BRBE	PA-28-161 Warrior II	P. A. Lancaster/Compton Abbas	
G-BRBF	Cessna 152	APB Leasing Ltd/Welshpool	
G-BRBG	PA-28 Cherokee 180	D. C. L. Smith	
G-BRBH	Cessna 150H	P. J. Webb/Elstree	
G-BRBI	Cessna 172N	D. T. Searchfield/Blackbushe	
G-BRBJ	Cessna 172M	L. C. Macknight/Elstree	
G-BRBK	Robin DR.400/180	R. Kemp	
G-BRBL	Robin DR.400/180	Crown Export Services	
G-BRBM	Robin DR.400/180	R. W. Davies/Headcorn	
G-BRBN	Pitts S-1S Special	D. R. Evans	
G-BRBO	Cameron V-77 balloon	Matrix Computers Ltd	
G-BRBP	Cessna 152	Staverton Flying Services Ltd	
G-BRBR	Cameron V-77 balloon	1066 Balloon Group	
G-BRBS	Bensen B.8M	J. Simpson	
G-BRBT	Trotter Ax3-20 balloon	R. M. Trotter	
G-BRBU	Colt 17A balloon	Airship & Balloon Co Ltd	
G-BRBV	Piper J-4A Cub Coupé	J. Schonburg	
G-BRBW	PA-28 Cherokee 140	Cherokee Cruiser Aircraft Group	
G-BRBX	PA-28-181 Archer II	M. J. Ireland	
G-BRBY	Robinson R-22B	Adern Sales Ltd	
G-BRBZ	Beech 400 Beechjet	Bass PLC	
G-BRCA	Jodel D.112	D. I. Walker & W. H. Sherlock	
G-BRCC	Cessna 152	Falcon Flying Services/Biggin Hill	
G-BRCD	Cessna A.152	D. E. Simmons/Shoreham	
G-BRCE	Pitts S-1C Special	R. O. Rogers	
G-BRCF	Montgomerie-Bensen B.8	J. S. Walton	
G-BRCG	Grob G.109	Oxfordshire Sportflying Ltd/Enstone	
G-BRCI	Pitts S-1 Special	R. N. Crosland	
G-BRCJ	Cameron NS-20 balloon	Cameron Balloons Ltd	
G-BRCL	Colt Flying Hat SS balloon	Jentime Ltd	
G-BRCM	Cessna 172L	S. G. E. Plessis & D. C. C. Handley	
G-BRCO	Cameron NS-20 balloon	Flying Pictures Ltd	
G-BRCP	Enstrom F-28F	Southern Air Ltd/Shoreham	
G-BRCR	Cameron V-77 balloon	E. E. Clark	
G-BRCS	Colt 105A balloon	Jentime Ltd	

Notes	Reg.	Type	Owner or Operator
	G-BRCT	Denney Aerocraft Kitfox	Wessex Aviation & Transport Ltd
	G-BRCV	Aeronca 7AC Champion	A. P. Wellings/Sandown
	G-BRCW	Aeronca 11AC Chief	R. B. McComish
	G-BRCX	Colt 105A balloon	Jentime Ltd
	G-BRDB	Zenair CH.701 STOL	D. L. Botwell
	G-BRDC	Thunder Ax7-77 balloon	Purple Rising Balloon Group
	G-BRDD	Avions Mudry CAP.10B	R. D. Dickson/Gamston
	G-BRDE	Thunder Ax7-77 balloon	C. C. Brash
	G-BRDF	PA-28-161 Warrior II	W. London Aero Services Ltd/White Waltham
	G-BRDG	PA-28-161 Warrior II	W. London Aero Services Ltd/White Waltham
	G-BRDJ	Luscombe 8A Silvaire	K. Sheppard & I. R. Green
	G-BRDL	Bell 206B JetRanger	Clyde Helicopters Ltd
	G-BRDM	PA-28-161 Warrior II	W. London Aero Services Ltd/White Waltham
	G-BRDN	M.S.880B Rallye Club	C. R. Owen
	G-BRDO	Cessna 177B	Cardinal Group
	G-BRDP	Colt Jumbo SS balloon	Airship & Balloon Co Ltd
	G-BRDS	Colt Flying Coke Can SS balloon	Thunder & Colt Ltd
	G-BRDT	Cameron DP-70 airship	M. M. Cobbold
	G-BRDU	Cameron DG-14 airship	Cameron Balloons Ltd
	G-BRDV	Viking Wood Products Spitfire Prototype replica (K5054)	C. Du Cros
	G-BRDW	PA-24 Comanche 180	I. P. Gibson/Switzerland
	G-BREA	Bensen B.8M	R. Firth
	G-BREB	Piper J-3C-65 Cub	C. Parr & I. Watts
	G-BREE	Whittaker MW.7	M. J. Hayman
	G-BREH	Cameron V-65 balloon	A. E. & L. C. Rogers
	G-BREK	Piper J-3C-65 Cub	C. Parr & I. Watts
	G-BREL	Cameron O-77 balloon	A. J. Moore & D. J. Green
	G-BREM	Air Command 532 Elite	Modern Air
	G-BREO	Mooney M.20K	Quilon Investments Ltd
	G-BREP	PA-28RT-201 Arrow IV	P. G. McQuaid
	G-BRER	Aeronca 7AC Champion	A. J. O'Shea
	G-BRET	—	—
	G-BREU	Montgomerie-Bensen B.8	M. A. Hayward
	G-BREX	Cameron O-84 balloon	Ovolo Ltd
	G-BREY	Taylorcraft BC-12D	BREY Group
	G-BREZ	Cessna 172M	B. J. Tucker
	G-BRFA	PA-31-350 Navajo Chieftain	Greenclose Aviation Ltd (G-BREW)
	G-BRFB	Rutan LongEz	R. A. Gardiner
	G-BRFC	P.57 Sea Prince T.1 (WP321)	Rural Naval Air Service/Bourn
	G-BRFE	Cameron V-77 balloon	N. J. Appleton
	G-BRFF	Colt 90A balloon	Zycomm Electronics Ltd
	G-BRFH	Colt 90A balloon	Polydron UK Ltd
	G-BRFI	Aeronca 7DC Champion	I. J. Boyd & D. J. McCooke
	G-BRFJ	Aeronca 11AC Chief	Junipa Sales Aviation Ltd
	G-BRFK	Colt Flying Drinks Can SS balloon	Thunder & Colt Ltd
	G-BRFL	PA-38-112 Tomahawk	Technology & Marketing Ltd
	G-BRFM	PA-28-161 Warrior II	GCJ Moffatt & Co Ltd
	G-BRFN	PA-38-112 Tomahawk	Technology & Marketing Ltd
	G-BRFO	Cameron V-77 balloon	Hedge Hoppers Balloon Group
	G-BRFP	Schweizer 269C	Daedalus Aviation Ltd
	G-BRFR	Cameron N-105 balloon	Flying Pictures (Balloons) Ltd
	G-BRFS	Cameron N-90 balloon	Flying Pictures (Balloons) Ltd
	G-BRFU	Fouga CM.170 Magister	P. F. A. Hoar/Cranfield
	G-BRFV	Cessna T.182	Goddard Kay Rogers & Associates Ltd
	G-BRFW	Montgomerie-Bensen B.8 Two Seat	J. M. Montgomerie
	G-BRFX	Pazmany PL.4A	D. E. Hills
	G-BRGD	Cameron O-84 balloon	J. R. H. & M. A. Ashworth
	G-BRGE	Cameron N-90 balloon	Oakfield Farm Products Ltd
	G-BRGF	Luscombe 8E Silvaire	M. H. Wood
	G-BRGG	Luscombe 8A Silvaire	M. P. & V. H. Weatherby
	G-BRGI	PA-28 Cherokee 180	Golf India Aviation Ltd
	G-BRGJ	PA-28-151 Warrior	D. D. Stone
	G-BRGN	BAe Jetstream 3102	British Aerospace PLC (G-BLHC)/ Prestwick
	G-BRGO	Air Command 532 Elite	D. A. Wood
	G-BRGP	Colt Flying Stork SS balloon	Thunder & Colt Ltd
	G-BRGT	PA-32 Cherokee Six 260	G. W. Cartledge
	G-BRGU	Cameron R-60 balloon	Noble Adventures Ltd
	G-BRGX	Rotorway Executive	D. W. J. Lee
	G-BRHA	PA-32RT-300 Lance II	ACG Building Contractors
	G-BRHB	Boeing Stearman B.75N-1	D. Calabritto

Reg.	Type	Owner or Operator	Notes
G-BRHC	Cameron V-77 balloon	G. L. Hicks	
G-BRHE	Piper J-3C-65 Cub	S. M. Kearney	
G-BRHG	Colt 90A balloon	Bath University Students Union	
G-BRHH	Cameron 106 Cow SS balloon	Cameron Ballons Ltd	
G-BRHI	Bell 206B JetRanger 3	Highland Properties Ltd	
G-BRHJ	PA-34-200T Seneca II	Draycott Seneca Group	
G-BRHK	Colt GA-42 airship	Thunder & Colt Ltd	
G-BRHL	Montgomerie-Bensen B.8M	N. D. Marshall	
G-BRHM	Bensen B.8M	D. P. Clout	
G-BRHN	Robinson R-22B	Barhale Surveying Ltd	
G-BRHO	PA-34-200 Seneca	First European (Leasing & Finance) Ltd	
G-BRHP	Aeronca O-58B Grasshopper (31923)	J. G. Townsend	
G-BRHR	PA-38-112 Tomahawk	Hamilton Compass Aviation Ltd	
G-BRHS	PA-38-112 Tomahawk	Hamilton Compass Aviation Ltd	
G-BRHT	PA-38-112 Tomahawk	Hamilton Compass Aviation Ltd	
G-BRHU	Montgomerie-Bensen B.8MR	G. L. & S. R. Moon	
G-BRHV	Colt 180A balloon	Timwing Ltd	
G-BRHW	D.H.82A Tiger Moth	P. J. & A. J. Borsberry	
G-BRHX	Luscombe 8E Silvaire	J. Lakin	
G-BRHY	Luscombe 8E Silvaire	D. Lofts & A. R. W. Taylor	
G-BRHZ	Stephens Akro Astro 235	A. N. Onn & T. R. G. Barnby	
G-BRIA	Cessna 310L	R. C. Pugsley	
G-BRIB	Cameron N-77 balloon	D. Stitt	
G-BRID	Cessna U.206A	Emair Bridlington Ltd	
G-BRIE	Cameron N-77 balloon	Vokins Estates Ltd	
G-BRIF	Boeing 767-204ER	Britannia Airways Ltd/Luton	
G-BRIG	Boeing 767-204ER	Britannia Airways Ltd/Luton	
G-BRIH	Taylorcraft BC-12D	K. E. Ballington	
G-BRII	Zenair CH.600 Zodiac	B. F. Arnall	
G-BRIJ	Taylorcraft F-19	K. E. Ballington	
G-BRIK	T.66 Nipper 3	C. W. R. Piper	
G-BRIL	Piper J-5A Cub Cruiser	M. Stow	
G-BRIM	Cameron O-160 balloon	Chard Balloon Co Ltd	
G-BRIN	SOCATA TB.20 Trinidad	Fletcher Group Holidays Ltd	
G-BRIO	Turner Super T-40A	D. McIntyre	
G-BRIP	Boeing Stearman A.75N1	Rance & ptnrs	
G-BRIR	Cameron V-56 balloon	Century Factors Ltd	
G-BRIS	Steen Skybolt	Cavendish Aviation Ltd	
G-BRIT	Cessna 421C	Coppersmith Ltd	
G-BRIV	SOCATA TB.9 Tampico	CB Group Ltd/Biggin Hill	
G-BRIW	Hughes 269C	Belmont Press Ltd	
G-BRIY	Taylorcraft DF-65 (426183)	J. A. Rollason	
G-BRIZ	D.31 Turbulent	M. C. Hunt	
G-BRJA	Luscombe 8A Silvaire	C. W. Thirtle	
G-BRJB	Zenair CH.600 Zodiac	E. G. Brown	
G-BRJC	Cessna 120	One Twenty Group	
G-BRJE	Boeing 757-236	—	
G-BRJF	Boeing 757-236	—	
G-BRJI	Boeing 757-236	—	
G-BRJK	Luscombe 8A Silvaire	C. J. L. Peat	
G-BRJL	PA-15 Vagabond	D. D. Saint	
G-BRJM	Cameron A-210 balloon	R. S. Hunjan	
G-BRJN	Pitts S-1C Special	G-BRJN Group	
G-BRJR	PA-38-112 Tomahawk	Chester Aviation Ltd	
G-BRJT	Cessna 150H	Technology & Marketing Ltd	
G-BRJU	PA-28-151 Warrior	Newcastle-upon-Tyne Aero Club Ltd	
G-BRJV	PA-28-161 Cadet	Newcastle-upon-Tyne Aero Club Ltd	
G-BRJW	Bellanca 7GCBC Citabria	H. W. Weston/Staverton	
G-BRJX	Rand KR-2	C. Willcocks	
G-BRJY	Rand KR-2	A. H. Franck	
G-BRKA	Luscombe 8F Silvaire	C. H. J. Andrews	
G-BRKB	Cameron N-65 balloon	M. C. Bradley/Hong Kong	
G-BRKC	J/1 Autocrat	J. W. Conlon	
G-BRKD	Piaggio FWP.149D	Operation Ability Ltd	
G-BRKE	Hawker Sea Hurricane XIIA (BW853)	AJD Engineering Ltd	
G-BRKF	Boeing 737-4S3	—	
G-BRKH	PA-28-236 Dakota	P. A. Wright & D. Rawlley	
G-BRKI	Robinson R-22B	Questspan Ltd/Booker	
G-BRKJ	Stoddard-Hamilton Glasair III	R. F. E. Simard	
G-BRKL	Cameron H-34 balloon	Cameron Balloons Ltd	
G-BRKN	Robinson R-22 Mariner	P. M. Webber/Greece	

Notes	Reg.	Type	Owner or Operator
	G-BRKO	Oldfield Baby Great Lakes	C. Wren
	G-BRKP	Colt 31A balloon	Bavarian Balloon Co Ltd
	G-BRKR	Cessna 182R	A. R. D. Brooker
	G-BRKS	Air Command 532 Elite	G. Sandercock
	G-BRKT	PA-28-161 Warrior II	Leisure World (Holdings) Ltd
	G-BRKW	Cameron V-77 balloon	M. W. A. Shemilt
	G-BRKX	Air Command 532 Elite	K. Davis
	G-BRKY	Viking Dragonfly Mk II	G. D. Price
	G-BRKZ	Air Command 532 Elite	S. C. West
	G-BRLB	Air Command 532 Elite	D. Wilson
	G-BRLC	Thunder Ax7-77 balloon	Fuji Photo Film (UK) Ltd
	G-BRLD	Robinson R-22B	Future Music (Chelmsford) Ltd
	G-BRLE	PA-28-181 Archer II	Charles Clowes (Estates) Co Ltd
	G-BRLF	Campbell Cricket	D. Wood
	G-BRLG	PA-28RT-201T Turbo Arrow IV	Specialist Welding & Metallurgical Services Ltd
	G-BRLH	Air Command 532 Elite	Childs Garages (Sherborne) Ltd
	G-BRLI	Piper J-5A Cub Cruiser	A. E. Poulson
	G-BRLJ	Evans VP-2	R. L. Jones
	G-BRLK	Air Command 532 Elite	G. L. Hunt
	G-BRLL	Cameron A-105 balloon	Adventure Flights Ltd
	G-BRLM	BAe 146-100	British Aerospace PLC
	G-BRLN	BAe 146-100	Trident Aviation Leasing Services (Jersey) Ltd
	G-BRLO	PA-38-112 Tomahawk	Scotia Safari Ltd/Prestwick
	G-BRLP	PA-38-112 Tomahawk	Lightstrong Ltd
	G-BRLR	Cessna 150G	D. C. Maxwell
	G-BRLS	Thunder Ax7-77 balloon	M. G. Ferguson & A. J. Nunns
	G-BRLT	Colt 77A balloon	D. Bareford
	G-BRLU	Cameron H-24 balloon	Airspace Outdoor Advertising Ltd
	G-BRLV	CCF Harvard IV (93542)	B. C. Abela
	G-BRLW	Cessna 150M	Cloudfirst Trading Ltd
	G-BRLX	Cameron N-77 balloon	National Power
	G-BRLY	BAe ATP	British Aerospace PLC
	G-BRMA	W.S.51 Dragonfly HR.5 (WG719) ★	International Helicopter Museum/ Weston-s-Mare
	G-BRMB	B.192 Belvedere HC.1 (XG452) ★	International Helicopter Museum/ Weston-s-Mare
	G-BRMC	Stampe et Renard SV-4B	E. K. Coventry
	G-BRMD	Cameron O-160 balloon	Ballooning Endeavours Ltd
	G-BRME	PA-28-181 Archer II	S. Edgar
	G-BRMF	Bell 206B JetRanger 3	Heliwork Services Ltd/Thruxton
	G-BRMG	V.S.384 Seafire XVII (SX336)	P. J. Wood
	G-BRMH	Bell 206B JetRanger 2	RCR Aviation Ltd (G-BBUX)
	G-BRMI	Cameron V-65 balloon	M. Davies
	G-BRMJ	PA-38-112 Tomahawk	P. H. Rogers/Coventry
	G-BRML	PA-38-112 Tomahawk	P. H. Rogers/Coventry
	G-BRMM	Air Command 532 Elite	R. de Serville
	G-BRMN	Thunder Ax7-77 balloon	G. Restell & R. Higham
	G-BRMO	Robinson R-22B	Delta Helicopters Ltd
	G-BRMS	PA-28RT-201 Arrow IV	Fleetbridge Ltd
	G-BRMT	Cameron V-31 Arm Chair SS balloon	R. M. Trotter & K. L. Heron
	G-BRMU	Cameron V-77 balloon	K. J. & G. R. Ibbotson
	G-BRMV	Cameron O-77 balloon	P. D. Griffiths
	G-BRMW	Whittaker MW.7	M. R. Grunwell
	G-BRMY	Short SD3-60	Short Bros PLC/Belfast City
	G-BRNA	Short SD3-60	Short Bros PLC/Belfast City
	G-BRNB	Short SD3-60	Short Bros PLC/Belfast City
	G-BRNC	Cessna 150M	Mercia Aircraft Leasing Ltd
	G-BRND	Cessna 152	Mercia Aircraft Leasing Ltd
	G-BRNE	Cessna 152	Aerohire Ltd/Halfpenny Green
	G-BRNJ	PA-38-112 Tomahawk	S. Eddison
	G-BRNK	Cessna 152	Sheffield Aero Club Ltd/Netherthorpe
	G-BRNL	Cessna 172P	Holmes Rental
	G-BRNM	Chichester-Miles Leopard	Chichester-Miles Consultants Ltd
	G-BRNN	Cessna 152	Sheffield Aero Club Ltd/Netherthorpe
	G-BRNP	Rotorway Executive	C. A. Laycock
	G-BRNR	Schweizer 269C	C.S.E. Aviation Ltd/Kidlington
	G-BRNS	Avid Flyer	Ladel Ltd
	G-BRNT	Robin DR.400/180	M. J. Cowham
	G-BRNU	Robin DR.400/180	Pranconic Ltd
	G-BRNV	PA-28-181 Archer II	Valley Flying Co Ltd

Reg.	Type	Owner or Operator	Notes
G-BRNW	Cameron V-77 balloon	N. Robertson & G. Smith	
G-BRNX	PA-22 Tri-Pacer 150	R. S. Tomlinson & B. Yager	
G-BRNY	Thunder Ax6-56A balloon	P. A. Clent	
G-BRNZ	PA-32 Cherokee Six 300B	Notionfresh Ltd	
G-BROB	Cameron V-77 balloon	R. W. Richardson	
G-BROE	Cameron N-65 balloon	R. H. Sanderson	
G-BROF	Air Command 532 Elite	M. J. Hoskins	
G-BROG	Cameron V-65 balloon	R. Kunert	
G-BROH	Cameron O-90 balloon	A. & W. Derbyshire	
G-BROI	CFM Streak Shadow Srs SA	G. W. Rowbotham	
G-BROJ	Colt 31A balloon	Airship & Balloon Co Ltd	
G-BROL	Colt AS-80 Mk II airship	Wellfarrow Ltd	
G-BROM	ICA IS-282MA	Kent Motor Gliding & Soaring Centre	
G-BROO	Luscombe 8A Silvaire	Bedwell Hey Flying Group	
G-BROP	Van's RV-4	K. E. Armstrong	
G-BROR	Piper J-3C-65 Cub	White Hart Flying Group	
G-BROS	Cameron O-84 balloon	Airship Shop Ltd	
G-BROV	Colt 105A balloon	Thunder & Colt Ltd	
G-BROW	Colt 90A balloon	Thunder & Colt Ltd	
G-BROX	Robinson R-22B	Freshname No 77 Ltd	
G-BROY	Cameron V-77 balloon	Zebedee Balloon Service	
G-BROZ	PA-18 Super Cub 150	P. G. Kynsey	
G-BRPE	Cessna 120	T. W. Greaves	
G-BRPF	Cessna 120	D. Sharp	
G-BRPG	Cessna 120	I. C. Lomax	
G-BRPH	Cessna 120	T. W. Greaves	
G-BRPI	Pitts S-1C Special	J. C. Lister	
G-BRPJ	Cameron N-90 balloon	Paul Johnson Cars Ltd	
G-BRPK	PA-28 Cherokee 140	Gütersloh Flying Club/Germany	
G-BRPL	PA-28 Cherokee 140	Comed Aviation Ltd/Blackpool	
G-BRPM	T.66 Nipper 3	T. C. Horner	
G-BRPN	Enstrom F-28C	Manchester Helicopter Centre/Barton	
G-BRPO	Enstrom 280C	R. Moffett	
G-BRPP	Brookland Hornet	D. E. Cox	
G-BRPR	Aeronca O-58B Grasshopper (43-1952)	G. Underwood	
G-BRPS	Cessna 177B	C. R. Goforth	
G-BRPT	Rans S.10 Sakota	P. A. Aston	
G-BRPU	Beech 76 Duchess	Hamilton Compass Aviation Ltd	
G-BRPV	Cessna 152	Coventry (Civil) Aviation Ltd	
G-BRPX	Taylorcraft BC-12D	M. J. Brett	
G-BRPY	PA-15 Vagabond	J. P. Esson	
G-BRPZ	Luscombe 8A Silvaire	J. D. Rooney/Goodwood	
G-BRRA	V.S.361 Spitfire LF.IX	Historic Aircraft Collection Ltd	
G-BRRB	Luscombe 8E Silvaire	D. J. Willison	
G-BRRD	Scheibe SF.25B Falke	K. E. Ballington	
G-BRRE	Colt 77A balloon	P. Patel	
G-BRRF	Cameron O-77 balloon	Mid-Bucks Farmers Balloon Group	
G-BRRG	Glaser-Dirks DG.500M	A. W. White	
G-BRRH	Ayres S2R-T34 Turbo Thrush	Agricultural Aviation Overseas Ltd	
G-BRRI	Ayres S2R-T34 Turbo Thrush	Agricultural Aviation Overseas Ltd	
G-BRRJ	PA-28RT-201T Turbo Arrow IV	M. & E. Machinery Ltd	
G-BRRK	Cessna 182Q	Clacton Aviation	
G-BRRL	PA-18 Super Cub 95	T. J. McRae	
G-BRRM	PA-28-161 Cadet	R. H. Sellier	
G-BRRN	PA-28-161 Warrior II	C. J. & L. M. Worsley	
G-BRRO	Cameron N-77 balloon	Newbury Building Soc	
G-BRRP	Pitts S-1S Special	J. E. Sweetman/Hong Kong	
G-BRRR	Cameron V-77 balloon	Kent & Sussex Tree Surgeons Ltd	
G-BRRS	Pitts S-1C Special	R. C. Atkinson	
G-BRRT	C.A.S.A. 1-131E Jungmann	R. A. L. Hubbard	
G-BRRU	Colt 90A balloon	Thunder & Colt Ltd	
G-BRRW	Cameron O-77 balloon	D. V. Fowler	
G-BRRX	Hughes 369HS	Valiant Press Ltd	
G-BRRY	Robinson R-22B	Bristow Helicopters Ltd/Redhill	
G-BRRZ	Robinson R-22B	Skylem Ltd	
G-BRSA	Cameron N-56 balloon	Cameron Balloons Ltd	
G-BRSC	Rans S.10 Sakota	R. A.Buckley	
G-BRSD	Cameron V-77 balloon	A. B. Stephens	
G-BRSE	PA-28-161 Warrior II	Air Service Training Ltd/Perth	
G-BRSF	V.S.361 Spitfire F.IX	Sussex Spraying Services Ltd	
G-BRSG	PA-28-161 Cadet	Denham School of Flying Ltd	
G-BRSH	C.A.S.A. 1-131E Jungmann	M. G. Searley	

Notes	Reg.	Type	Owner or Operator
	G-BRSI	PA-28-161 Cadet	Denham School of Flying Ltd
	G-BRSJ	PA-38-112 Tomahawk	Pool Aviation Ltd/Welshpool
	G-BRSK	Boeing Stearman N2S-3 (180)	Great Cloud Designs Ltd
	G-BRSL	Cameron N-56 balloon	S. Budd
	G-BRSN	Rand-Robinson KR-2	K. W. Darby
	G-BRSO	CFM Streak Shadow Srs SA	D. J. Smith
	G-BRSP	Air Command 532 Elite	D. R. G. Griffith
	G-BRSW	Luscombe 8A Silvaire	J. Regan
	G-BRSX	PA-15 Vagabond	C. Milne-Fowler
	G-BRSY	Hatz CB-1	G. A. Barrett & Son
	G-BRSZ	MEM RSZ-05/1 balloon	Zebedee Balloon Service
	G-BRTA	PA-38-112 Tomahawk	R. A. Wakefield
	G-BRTB	Bell 206B JetRanger 2	Harris Technology Ltd
	G-BRTC	Cessna 150G	Thorpe Air Ltd/Goodwood
	G-BRTD	Cessna 152 II	Thorpe Air Ltd/Goodwood
	G-BRTE	Colt 240A balloon	Bavarian Balloon Co Ltd
	G-BRTH	Cameron A-180 balloon	The Ballooning Business Ltd
	G-BRTJ	Cessna 150F	Cubitt Aviation/Fulsham
	G-BRTK	Boeing Stearman E.75	Howard Avis (Aviation) Ltd
	G-BRTL	Hughes 369E	P. C. Shann Management & Research Ltd
	G-BRTM	PA-28-161 Warrior II	Air Service Training Ltd/Perth
	G-BRTN	Beech 95-B58 Baron	Colneway Ltd
	G-BRTO	Cessna 152	Lynair Aviation & Franchi Aviation
	G-BRTP	Cessna 152	Anglia Aviation Ltd
	G-BRTR	Colt GA-42 airship	Thunder & Colt Ltd
	G-BRTS	Bell 206B JetRanger 3	Norwich Aviation Ltd
	G-BRTT	Schweizer 269C	Fairthorpe Ltd/Denham
	G-BRTV	Cameron O-77 balloon	C. Vening
	G-BRTW	Glaser-Dirks DG.400	I. J. Carruthers
	G-BRTX	PA-28-151 Warrior	Compton Abbas Airfield Ltd
	G-BRTZ	Slingsby T.31 Motor Cadet III	M. N. Martin
	G-BRUA	Cessna 152	Compton Abbas Airfield Ltd
	G-BRUB	PA-28-161 Warrior II	Flytrek Ltd/Bournemouth
	G-BRUD	PA-28-181 Archer II	Wilkins & Wilkins Special Auctions Ltd
	G-BRUE	Cameron V-77 balloon	B. J. Newman & P. L. Harrison
	G-BRUG	Luscombe 8E Silvaire	D. G. Lewendon & N. W. Barratt
	G-BRUH	Colt 105A balloon	D. C. Chipping
	G-BRUI	PA-44-180 Seminole	Bath Stone Co Ltd
	G-BRUJ	Boeing Stearman A.75N1	Early Birds Ltd/Staverton
	G-BRUL	Thunder Ax8-105 balloon	H. C. J. Williams
	G-BRUM	Cessna A.152	Aerohire Ltd/Halfpenny Green
	G-BRUN	Cessna 120	O. C. Brun (G-BRDH)
	G-BRUO	Taylor JT.1 Monoplane	P. C. Cardno
	G-BRUR	Grob G.115	Risestat Ltd
	G-BRUS	Cessna 140	M. J. Fogarty
	G-BRUT	Thunder Ax8-90 balloon	Moet & Chandon (London) Ltd
	G-BRUU	EAA Biplane Model P.1	M. J. Fogarty
	G-BRUV	Cameron V-77 balloon	T. W. & R. F. Benbrook
	G-BRUX	PA-44-180 Seminole	Hambrair Ltd/Tollerton
	G-BRUZ	Raven Europe FS-57A balloon	R. H. Etherington
	G-BRVA	Nord 3202B-1	Cavok Ltd (G-BIZL)
	G-BRVB	Stolp SA.300 Starduster Too	R. W. Davies
	G-BRVC	Cameron N-180 balloon	The Apollo Balloon Co Ltd
	G-BRVE	Beech D.17S	Early Birds Ltd/Staverton
	G-BRVF	Colt 77A balloon	Airborne Adventures Ltd
	G-BRVG	North American SNJ-7 Trojan	Early Birds Ltd/Staverton
	G-BRVH	Smyth Model S Sidewinder	I. S. Bellamy
	G-BRVI	Robinson R-22B	Burnell Helicopters Ltd
	G-BRVJ	Slingsby T.31 Motor Cadet III	D. F. Micklethwait & J. R. Paskins
	G-BRVK	Cameron A-210 Balloon	The Balloon Club Ltd
	G-BRVL	Pitts S-1C Special	I. Duncan
	G-BRVN	Thunder Ax7-77 balloon	J. T. Hughes Ltd
	G-BRVO	AS.350B Ecureuil	Radstrong Ltd/Booker
	G-BRVR	Barnett J4B-2	Ilkeston Contractors
	G-BRVS	Barnett J4B-2	Ilkeston Contractors
	G-BRVT	Pitts S-2B Special	C. J. & M. D. Green
	G-BRVU	Colt 77A balloon	H. C. J. Williams
	G-BRVV	Colt 56B balloon	S. J. Hollingsworth
	G-BRVX	Cameron A-210 balloon	Bath Hot Air Balloon Club Ltd
	G-BRVY	Thunder Ax8-90 balloon	G. E. Morris
	G-BRVZ	Jodel D.117	J.G. Patton
	G-BRWA	Aeronca 7AC Champion	D. D. Smith & J. R. Edwards
	G-BRWB	NA T-6G Texan	Aircraft Restorations Ltd/Duxford

Reg.	Type	Owner or Operator	Notes
G-BRWC	Cessna 152	T. Hayselden (Doncaster) Ltd	
G-BRWD	Robinson R22B	J. McW. Henderson	
G-BRWF	Thunder Ax7-77	D. J. Greaves	
G-BRWH	Cameron N-77	D. J. Usher	
G-BRWI	Short SD3-60 Variant 300	Short Bros PLC/Belfast City	
G-BRWJ	Short SD3-60 Variant 300	Short Bros PLC/Belfast City	
G-BRWK	Short SD3-60 Variant 300	Short Bros PLC/Belfast City	
G-BRWL	Short SD3-60 Variant 300	Short Bros PLC/Belfast City	
G-BRWM	Short SD3-60 Variant 300	Short Bros PLC/Belfast City	
G-BRWN	G.159 Gulfstream 1	Aviation Management Consultants Ltd	
G-BRWO	PA-28 Cherokee 140	ML Associates	
G-BRWP	CFM Streak Shadow Srs SA	A. D. Stewart	
G-BRWR	Aeronca 11AC Chief	P. G. Peal	
G-BRWT	Scheibe SF.25C Falke	Brompton Promotions Ltd	
G-BRWU	Luton LA-4A Minor	R. B. Webber & P. K. Pike	
G-BRWV	Brügger MB.2 Colibri	S. J. McCollum	
G-BRWX	Cessna 172P	D. A. Abels	
G-BRWY	Cameron H-34 balloon	Cameron Balloons Ltd	
G-BRWZ	Cameron 90 Macaw SS balloon	Forbes Europe Inc/France	
G-BRXA	Cameron O-120 balloon	A. F. Green	
G-BRXB	Thunder Ax7-77 balloon	H. Peel	
G-BRXC	PA-28-161 Warrior II	Air Service Training Ltd/Perth	
G-BRXD	PA-28-181 Archer II	Gosky Aviation Ltd	
G-BRXE	Taylorcraft BC-12D	V. H. Spencer	
G-BRXF	Aeronca 11AC Chief	G. G. Pugh/Stapleford	
G-BRXG	Aeronca 7AC Champion	X-Ray Golf Flying Group	
G-BRXH	Cessna 120	J. N. Pittock & A. P. Fox	
G-BRXK	Soko P-2 Kraguj	Cavok Ltd	
G-BRXL	Aeronca 11AC Chief (42-78044)	R. L. Jones	
G-BRXN	Montgomerie-Bensen B.8MR	J. C. Aitken	
G-BRXO	PA-34-200T Seneca II	Aviation Services Ltd	
G-BRXP	SNCAN Stampe SV-4C (modified)	P. G. Kavanagh & D. T. Kaberry	
G-BRXS	Howard Special T Minus	H. C. Cox	
G-BRXT	BAe 146-200	British Aerospace PLC	
G-BRXV	Robinson R-22B	E. Wootton	
G-BRXW	PA-24 Comanche 260	R. J. Lane Pharmaceuticals	
G-BRXX	Colt 180A balloon	J. P. Clifford	
G-BRXY	Pietenpol Air Camper	A. E. Morris	
G-BRYA	D.H.C.7-110 Dash Seven	Brymon/Air France *City of Paris*/Plymouth	
G-BRYB	D.H.C.7-110 Dash Seven	Brymon Aviation Ltd *City of Plymouth*/Plymouth	
G-BRYC	D.H.C.7-110 Dash Seven	Brymon/Air France *City of London*/Plymouth	
G-BRYD	D.H.C.7-110 Dash Seven	Brymon Aviation Ltd *City of Exeter*/Plymouth	
G-BRYE	D.H.C.7-102 Dash Seven	Brymon Aviation Ltd *City of Aberdeen*/Plymouth	
G-BRYG	D.H.C.8-102A Dash Eight	Brymon Aviation Ltd *City of Bristol*/Plymouth	
G-BRYH	D.H.C.8-102A Dash Eight	Brymon Aviation Ltd/*City of Edinburgh*/Plymouth	
G-BRYI	D.H.C.8-311 Dash Eight	Brymon Aviation Ltd/*City of Glasgow*/Plymouth	
G-BRYJ	D.H.C.8-311 Dash Eight	Brymon Aviation Ltd/Plymouth	
G-BRYK	—	Brymon Aviation Ltd	
G-BRYM	—	Brymon Aviation Ltd	
G-BRYN	SOCATA TB.20 Trinidad	Jones & Bradbourn (Guernsey) Ltd	
G-BRYO	—	Brymon Aviation Ltd	
G-BRYP	—	Brymon Aviation Ltd	
G-BRZA	Cameron O-77 balloon	L. & R. J. Mold	
G-BRZB	Cameron A-105 balloon	Headland Services Ltd	
G-BRZC	Cameron N-90 balloon	Flying Pictures (Balloons) Ltd	
G-BRZD	Hapi Cygnet SF-2A	L. G. Millen	
G-BRZE	Thunder Ax7-77 balloon	G. V. Beckwith	
G-BRZF	Enstrom 280C	Haversham Helicopters Ltd	
G-BRZG	Enstrom F-28A	Chart Planes Inland Ltd	
G-BRZI	Cameron N-180 balloon	Pegasus Balloon Co Ltd	
G-BRZK	Stinson 108-2	F. H. Wheeler & G. P. A. Elborough	
G-BRZL	Pitts S-1D Special	G. W. Polson-Brown	
G-BRZO	Jodel D.18	J. D. Anson	
G-BRZP	PA-28-161 Warrior II	Air Service Training Ltd/Perth	
G-BRZR	PA-22 Tri-Pacer 150	B. E. Simpson	
G-BRZS	Cessna 172P	YP Flying Group/Blackpool	

Notes	Reg.	Type	Owner or Operator
	G-BRZT	Cameron V-77 balloon	B. Drawbridge
	G-BRZU	Colt Flying Cheese SS balloon	Willow Best Ltd
	G-BRZV	Colt Flying Apple SS balloon	Thrust Drive Ltd
	G-BRZW	Rans S.10 Sakota	D. L. Davies
	G-BRZX	Pitts S-1S Special	G-BRZX Group
	G-BRZZ	CFM Streak Shadow	P. R. Oakes
	G-BSAB	PA-46-350P Malibu Mirage	D. O. Hooper
	G-BSAC	BN-2B-26 Islander	Pilatus BN Ltd/Bembridge
	G-BSAI	Stoddard-Hamilton Glasair III	K. J. & P. J. Whitehead
	G-BSAJ	C.A.S.A. 1-131E Jungmann	P. G. Kynsey/Redhill
	G-BSAK	Colt 21A balloon	Airship & Balloon Co Ltd
	G-BSAO	Steen Skybolt	S. F. Elvins
	G-BSAP	Cameron A-120 balloon	B. J. Petteford
	G-BSAR	Air Command 532 Elite	S. A. Ryder
	G-BSAS	Cameron V-65 balloon	Aire Valley Balloons
	G-BSAT	PA-28-181 Archer II	A1 Aircraft Ltd/Biggin Hill
	G-BSAU	Enstrom F-28F	Southern Air Ltd/Shoreham
	G-BSAV	Thunder Ax7-77 balloon	E. A. Evans & ptnrs
	G-BSAW	PA-28-161 Warrior II	Carill Aviation Ltd/Southampton
	G-BSAX	Piper J-3C-65 Cub	M. B. Proudfoot & ptnrs
	G-BSAY	Cessna 172M	D. B. Zabel
	G-BSAZ	Denney Aerocraft Kitfox	P. E. Hinkley
	G-BSBA	PA-28-161 Warrior II	P. A. Lancaster/White Waltham
	G-BSBB	CCF Harvard IV	J. Woodhouse/Thruxton
	G-BSBC	CCF Harvard IV	J. Woodhouse/Thruxton
	G-BSBD	NA T-6G Texan	J. Woodhouse/Thruxton
	G-BSBE	CCF Harvard IV	Pulsgrove Ltd/Thruxton
	G-BSBF	CCF Harvard IV	Pulsgrove Ltd/Thruxton
	G-BSBG	CCF Harvard IV	Pulsgrove Ltd/Thruxton
	G-BSBH	Short SD3-30★	Ulster Aviation Soc Museum *(stored)*
	G-BSBI	Cameron O-77 balloon	Calibre Motor Co Ltd
	G-BSBK	Colt 105A balloon	Zebra Balloons
	G-BSBM	Cameron N-77 balloon	Nuclear Electric
	G-BSBN	Thunder Ax7-77 balloon	B. Pawson
	G-BSBP	Jodel D.18	R. T. Pratt
	G-BSBR	Cameron V-77 balloon	B. Bromiley
	G-BSBT	Piper J-3C-65 Cub	M. B. & L. J. Proudfoot
	G-BSBU	Firefly 8B	A. R. Peart
	G-BSBV	Rans S.10 Sakota	Sportair UK Ltd
	G-BSBW	Bell 206B JetRanger 3	Cross Lane Aviation Ltd
	G-BSBX	Montgomerie-Bensen B.8MR	B. Ibbott
	G-BSBY	Cessna 150L	D. F. Harrison
	G-BSBZ	Cessna 150M	D. F. Harrison
	G-BSCA	Cameron N-90 balloon	P. J. Marshall & M. A. Clarke
	G-BSCB	Air Command 532 Elite	P. H. Smith
	G-BSCC	Colt 105A balloon	A. F. Selby
	G-BSCD	Hughes 269C	McIntyre Aviation Ltd
	G-BSCE	Robinson R-22B	S. B. Evans & G. F. Burridge
	G-BSCF	Thunder Ax7-77 balloon	V. P. Gardiner
	G-BSCG	Denney Aerocraft Kitfox	A. C. & T. G. Pinkstone
	G-BSCH	Denney Aerocraft Kitfox	Baldoon Leisure Flying Co Ltd
	G-BSCI	Colt 77A balloon	F. W. Farnsworth Ltd
	G-BSCK	Cameron H-34 balloon	Flying Pictures (Balloons) Ltd
	G-BSCL	Robinson R-22B	Ketton Holdings Ltd
	G-BSCM	Denney Aerocraft Kitfox	M. Richardson
	G-BSCN	SOCATA TB.20 Trinidad	T. & G. Engineering Co Ltd & P. W. Huntley
	G-BSCO	Thunder Ax7-77 balloon	F. J. Whalley
	G-BSCP	Cessna 152	Doncaster Aero Club Ltd
	G-BSCR	Cessna 172M	Halsmith (Aircraft Sales) Ltd
	G-BSCS	PA-28-181 Archer II	Wing Task Ltd
	G-BSCU	Colt GA-42 gas airship	Thunder & Colt Ltd
	G-BSCV	PA-28-161 Warrior II	Southwood Flying Group/Southend
	G-BSCW	Taylorcraft BC-65	J. W. Heale
	G-BSCX	Thunder Ax8-105 balloon	Balloon Flights Club Ltd
	G-BSCY	PA-28-151 Warrior	S. G. P. Fowler
	G-BSCZ	Cessna 152	London Flight Centre (Stansted) Ltd
	G-BSDA	Taylorcraft BC-12D	J. F. Morris
	G-BSDB	Pitts S-1C Special	M. K. Whitaker
	G-BSDC	—	—
	G-BSDD	Denney Aerocraft Kitfox	J. Windmill
	G-BSDE	Cameron A-105 balloon	G. V. Beckwith

Reg.	Type	Owner or Operator	Notes
G-BSDF	Cameron N-105 balloon	G. V. Beckwith	
G-BSDG	Robin DR.400/180	B. Hodge	
G-BSDH	Robin DR.400/180	R. L. Brucciani	
G-BSDI	Corben Junior Ace Model E	J. Pearson/Eaglescott	
G-BSDJ	Piper J-4E Cub Coupe	J. Pearson/Eaglescott	
G-BSDK	Piper J-5A Cub Cruiser	B. F. T. Kitt & B. P. Young	
G-BSDL	SOCATA TB.10 Tobago	Consort Aviation Ltd/Sherburn	
G-BSDN	PA-34-200T Seneca II	R. St. Aubin	
G-BSDO	Cessna 152	Bath Stone Co Ltd	
G-BSDP	Cessna 152	Independent Air Services Ltd	
G-BSDS	Boeing Stearman E.75 (118)	E. Hopper	
G-BSDU	Bell 206B JetRanger 3	RJS Aviation Ltd	
G-BSDV	Colt 31A balloon	Airship & Balloon Co Ltd	
G-BSDW	Cessna 182P	Kerygma Trust	
G-BSDX	Cameron V-77 balloon	D. K. Fish	
G-BSDY	Beech 58 Baron	Astra Aviation Ltd	
G-BSEA	Thunder Ax7-77 balloon	R. Titterton	
G-BSED	PA-22 Tri-Pacer 160	Sylmar Aviation & Services Ltd	
G-BSEE	Rans S.9	P. M. Semler	
G-BSEF	PA-28 Cherokee 180	D. J. R. Chapple	
G-BSEG	Ken Brock KB-2	H. A. Bancroft-Wilson	
G-BSEH	Cameron V-77 balloon	G. V. Beckwith	
G-BSEI	Cameron N-90 balloon	Flying Pictures (Balloons) Ltd	
G-BSEJ	Cessna 150M	Hollyclass Ltd	
G-BSEK	Robinson R-22	Skyline Helicopters Ltd	
G-BSEL	Slingsby T.61G Super Falke	RAFGSA/Hullavington	
G-BSEM	Cameron 90 Four-Pack SS balloon	Flying Pictures (Balloons) Ltd	
G-BSEN	Colt 31A balloon	Thunder & Colt Ltd	
G-BSEO	Beech 200 Super King Air	Air Hanson Aircraft Sales Ltd (G-OADT/ G-KBCA)	
G-BSEP	Cessna 172	B. Myers & C. H. Moore/Doncaster	
G-BSER	PA-28 Cherokee 160	Yorkair Ltd/Leeds	
G-BSES	Denney Aerocraft Kitfox	M. Albert-Brecht & J. J. M. Donnelly	
G-BSET	B.206 Srs 1 Basset	Beagle Basset Ltd/Shoreham	
G-BSEU	PA-28-181 Archer II	Euro Aviation 91 Ltd	
G-BSEV	Cameron O-77 balloon	UK Transplant Co-ordinators Assoc	
G-BSEW	Sikorsky S-76A	Bond Helicopters Ltd	
G-BSEX	Cameron A-180 balloon	Heart of England Balloons	
G-BSEY	Beech A36 Bonanza	K. Phillips Ltd	
G-BSEZ	Air Command 532 Elite	D. S. Robinson	
G-BSFA	Aero Designs Pulsar	S. A. Gill	
G-BSFB	C.A.S.A. 1.131E Jungmann 2000	J. A. Sykes	
G-BSFD	Piper J-3C-65 Cub	E. C. English	
G-BSFE	PA-38-112 Tomahawk II	W. S. Robertson	
G-BSFF	Robin DR.400/180R	Lasham Gliding Soc Ltd	
G-BSFJ	Thunder Ax8-105 balloon	Airborne Adventures Ltd	
G-BSFK	PA-28-161 Warrior II	Air Service Training Ltd/Perth	
G-BSFM	Cameron 82 Cheese SS balloon	Gone With The Wind Ltd	
G-BSFN	SE.313B Alouette II	M & P Food Products Ltd	
G-BSFO	Cameron 60 House SS balloon	Clipsal UK Ltd	
G-BSFP	Cessna 152	J. R. Nicholls	
G-BSFR	Cessna 152	Galair Ltd	
G-BSFS	SE.313B Alouette II	M & P Food Products Ltd	
G-BSFT	PA-31 Turbo Navajo	SFT Aviation Ltd (G-AXYC)/Bournemouth	
G-BSFU	SE.313B Alouette II	M & P Food Products Ltd	
G-BSFV	Woods Woody Pusher	C. W. N. Huke	
G-BSFW	PA-15 Vagabond	J. R. Kimberley	
G-BSFX	Denney Aerocraft Kitfox	D. A. McFadyean	
G-BSFY	Denney Aerocraft Kitfox	J. R. Howard	
G-BSGB	Gaertner Ax4 Skyranger balloon	B. Gaertner	
G-BSGC	PA-18 Super Cub 95	G. Churchill	
G-BSGD	PA-28 Cherokee 180	R. J. Cleverley	
G-BSGF	Robinson R-22B	Birchwood Boats Solent Ltd	
G-BSGG	Denney Aerocraft Kitfox	C. G. Richardson	
G-BSGH	Airtour AH-56B balloon	Airtour Balloon Co Ltd	
G-BSGI	BAe 146-300	TNT Express (UK) Ltd	
G-BSGJ	Monnet Sonerai 2	A. N. Burrows	
G-BSGK	PA-34-200T Seneca II	J. A. Burrett & S. W. Frost	
G-BSGL	PA-28-161 Warrior II	Keywest Air Charter Ltd/Liverpool	
G-BSGM	Cameron V-77 balloon	5th Regiment Royal Artillery	
G-BSGN	PA-28-151 Warrior	J. R. Whetlor & M. Gipps/Denham	
G-BSGP	Cameron N-65 balloon	Haywards Heath Building Soc	
G-BSGR	Boeing Stearman E.75	A. G. Dunkerley	

Notes	Reg.	Type	Owner or Operator
	G-BSGS	Rans S.10 Sakota	R. Handley
	G-BSGT	Cessna T.210N	B. J. Sharpe/Booker
	G-BSGV	Rotorway Executive	R. A. Kingston
	G-BSGY	Thunder Ax7-77 balloon	Thunder & Colt Ltd
	G-BSHA	PA-34-200T Seneca II	Warrior Aircraft Sales & Leasing Ltd
	G-BSHB	Colt 69A balloon	Airship & Balloon Co Ltd
	G-BSHC	Colt 69A balloon	Airship & Balloon Co Ltd
	G-BSHD	Colt 69A balloon	Airship & Balloon Co Ltd
	G-BSHE	Cessna 152	J. A. Pothecary/Shoreham
	G-BSHH	Luscombe 8E Silvaire	Golf Centres Balloons Ltd
	G-BSHI	Luscombe 8F Silvaire	W. H. J. Knowles
	G-BSHJ	Luscombe 8E Silvaire	C. R. M. Hart & S. J. Turner
	G-BSHK	Denney Aerocraft Kitfox	A. E. Cree & G. J. Cuzzocrea
	G-BSHM	Slingsby T.31 Motor Cadet III	R. R. Hadley
	G-BSHN	Cessna 152	C. Walsh
	G-BSHO	Cameron V-77 balloon	T. P. Barlass & D. J. Duckworth
	G-BSHP	PA-28-161 Warrior II	Air Service Training Ltd/Perth
	G-BSHR	Cessna F.172N	H. Rothwell (G-BFGE)/Blackpool
	G-BSHS	Colt 105A balloon	Europa Investments (Management) Ltd
	G-BSHT	Cameron V-77 balloon	ECM Construction Ltd
	G-BSHV	PA-18 Super Cub 135	Fen Tigers Flying Group
	G-BSHW	Hawker Tempest II	D. N. H. Martin
	G-BSHX	Enstrom F-28A	Manchester Helicopter Centre/Barton
	G-BSHY	EAA Acro Sport 1	A. W. Hughes & ptnrs
	G-BSHZ	Enstrom F-28F	Heli-Flair Ltd/Goodwood
	G-BSIB	PA-28-161 Warrior II	Bobbington Air Training School Ltd
	G-BSIC	Cameron V-77 balloon	P. D. Worthy
	G-BSIE	Enstrom 280FX	Richard Mullock Homes Ltd
	G-BSIF	Denney Aerocraft Kitfox	R. M. Kimbell & M. H. Wylde
	G-BSIG	Colt 21A balloon	Thunder & Colt Ltd
	G-BSIH	Rutan LongEz	W. S. Allen
	G-BSII	PA-34-200T Seneca II	N. H. N. Gardner
	G-BSIJ	Cameron V-77 balloon	A. S. Jones
	G-BSIK	Denney Aerocraft Kitfox	I. A. Davies & B. Barr
	G-BSIL	Colt 120A balloon	A. Bolger
	G-BSIM	PA-28-181 Archer II	E. Midlands Aircraft Hire Ltd
	G-BSIN	Robinson R-22B	Solent Projects Ltd
	G-BSIO	Cameron 80 Shed SS balloon	Furness Building Soc
	G-BSIP	Cameron V-77 balloon	R. S. Ham
	G-BSIR	Cessna 340	Airmaster Aviation Ltd/Cardiff
	G-BSIT	Robinson R-22B	P. R. Earp
	G-BSIU	Colt 90A balloon	Thunder & Colt Ltd
	G-BSIW	BAe Jetstream 3100	Manx Airlines (Europe) Ltd/Cardiff
	G-BSIY	Schleicher ASK.14	H. F. Lamprey
	G-BSIZ	PA-28-181 Archer II	Firmdale Ltd
	G-BSJA	Cameron N-77 balloon	N. Sanders (G-SPAR)
	G-BSJB	Bensen B.8	J. W. Limbrick
	G-BSJC	Bell 206B JetRanger 3	JETC Helicopters
	G-BSJU	Cessna 150M	Fox Aviation Ltd/E. Midlands
	G-BSJV	Cessna 172N	Fox Aviation Ltd/E. Midlands
	G-BSJW	Everett Srs 2 gyroplane	A. R. Willis
	G-BSJX	PA-28-161 Warrior II	Border Air Training Ltd/Carlisle
	G-BSJY	Murphy Renegade II	J. Hatswell
	G-BSJZ	Cessna 150J	M. Tye
	G-BSKA	Cessna 150M	K. J. Farrance
	G-BSKB	—	—
	G-BSKC	PA-38-112 Tomahawk	Bath Stone Co Ltd
	G-BSKD	Cameron V-77 balloon	P. Thomas
	G-BSKF	Schweizer 269C	J. W. Sandle
	G-BSKG	Maule MXT-7-180	Beeches Auto Services
	G-BSKH	Cessna 421C	Bristol & Mendip Estates Ltd
	G-BSKI	Thunder Ax8-90 balloon	G-BSKI Balloon Group
	G-BSKJ	Mooney M.20J	M. C. Wroe
	G-BSKK	PA-38-112 Tomahawk	Falcon Flying Services/Biggin Hill
	G-BSKL	PA-38-112 Tomahawk	Falcon Flying Services/Biggin Hill
	G-BSKN	Grob G.109B	C. S. Faber
	G-BSKO	Maule MXT-7-180	G. B. Esslemont
	G-BSKP	V.S.379 Spitfire F.XIV	Historic Aircraft Collection Ltd
	G-BSKR	Rand Robinson KR-2	T. D. Saveker
	G-BSKS	Nieuport 28C-1	Historic Aircraft Collection Ltd
	G-BSKT	Maule MXT-7-180	D. D. Smith
	G-BSKU	Cameron O-84 balloon	Alfred Bagnall & Sons (West) Ltd
	G-BSKV	PA-28-181 Archer II	BAe Flying College Ltd/Prestwick

Reg.	Type	Owner or Operator	Notes
G-BSKW	PA-28-181 Archer II	BAe Flying College Ltd/Prestwick	
G-BSKX	PA-28-181 Archer II	BAe Flying College Ltd/Prestwick	
G-BSLA	Robin DR.400/180	A. B. McCoig/Biggin Hill	
G-BSLB	Robinson R-22B	J. H. Turkington & Sons (Contractors) Ltd	
G-BSLC	Robinson R-22B	Modern Air/Fowlmere	
G-BSLD	PA-28RT-201 Arrow IV	Actionwings Ltd	
G-BSLE	PA-28-161 Warrior II	Air Service Training Ltd/Perth	
G-BSLG	Cameron A-180 balloon	Bridges Van Hire Ltd	
G-BSLH	C.A.S.A. 1-131E Jungmann 2000	P. Warden	
G-BSLI	Cameron V-77 balloon	J. D. C. & F. E. Bevan	
G-BSLJ	Denney Aerocraft Kitfox	A. F. Reid	
G-BSLK	PA-28-161 Warrior II	R. A. Rose	
G-BSLL	AS.355F-2 Twin Squirrel	Star Aviation (G-BOGX)	
G-BSLM	PA-28 Cherokee 160	E. Sussex Aviation/Shoreham	
G-BSLN	Thunder Ax10-180 balloon	Albatross Aviation Ltd	
G-BSLO	Cameron A-180 balloon	Adventure Balloon Co Ltd	
G-BSLR	Schweizer 269C	Cuffroy Ltd	
G-BSLT	PA-28-161 Warrior II	Warrior Aircraft Sales & Leasing Ltd	
G-BSLU	PA-28 Cherokee 140	Warrior Aircraft Sales & Leasing Ltd	
G-BSLV	Enstrom 280FX	Kendrick Construction Ltd	
G-BSLW	Bellanca 7ECA Citabria	A. A. & J. A. Killerby/Shoreham	
G-BSLX	WAR Focke-Wulf Fw.190	E. Sussex Aviation/Shoreham	
G-BSLY	Colt AS-80 GD airship	Huntair Ltd	
G-BSLZ	BAe 146-300	TNT Express (UK) Ltd	
G-BSMA	Colt Flying Open Book SS balloon	Jentime Ltd	
G-BSMB	Cessna U.206E	Army Parachute Association/Netheravon	
G-BSMD	Nord 1101 Noralpha	Magnificent Obsessions Ltd	
G-BSME	Bo 208C Junior	D. J. Hampson	
G-BSMF	Avro 652A Anson C.19 (TX183)	G. M. K. Fraser	
G-BSMG	Montgomerie-Bensen B.8M	A. C. Timperley	
G-BSMH	Colt 240A balloon	Formtrack Ltd	
G-BSMI	Schweizer 269C	A. J. Hardy	
G-BSMJ	—	—	
G-BSMK	Cameron O-84 balloon	J. C. Reavley	
G-BSML	Schweizer 269C	Nunkeeling Ltd	
G-BSMM	Colt 31A balloon	D. V. Fowler	
G-BSMN	CFM Streak Shadow	K. Daniels	
G-BSMO	Denney Aerocraft Kitfox	G-BSMO Group	
G-BSMP	PA-34-220T Seneca III	Gabriel Enterprises Ltd	
G-BSMS	Cameron V-77 balloon	C. D. Howes	
G-BSMT	Rans S.10 Sakota	N. Woodworth	
G-BSMU	Rans S.6	W. D. Walker (G-MWJE)	
G-BSMV	PA-17 Vagabond (modified)	R. D. & S. A. Carswell	
G-BSMX	Bensen B.8MR	J. S. E. McGregor	
G-BSMZ	PA-28-161 Warrior II	Air Service Training Ltd/Perth	
G-BSND	Air Command 532 Elite	B. J. Castle	
G-BSNE	Luscombe 8A Silvaire	Aerolite Luscombe Group	
G-BSNF	Piper J-3C-65 Cub	J. A. Hoblyn	
G-BSNG	Cessna 172N	Berry Air/Edinburgh	
G-BSNH	Robinson R-22	Skyline Helicopters Ltd/Booker	
G-BSNI	Bensen B.8V	B. D. Gibbs	
G-BSNJ	Cameron N-90 balloon	D. P. H. Smith	
G-BSNK	—	—	
G-BSNL	Bensen B.8MR	T. R. Grief	
G-BSNN	Rans S.10 Sakota	S. Adams	
G-BSNO	Denney Aerocraft Kitfox	A. G. V. McClintock	
G-BSNP	PA-28-201T Turbo Arrow III	V. Dowd/Stapleford	
G-BSNT	Luscombe 8A Silvaire	B. J. Robe	
G-BSNU	Colt 105A balloon	Sun Life Assurance Soc PLC	
G-BSNV	—	—	
G-BSNW	—	—	
G-BSNX	PA-28-181 Archer II	Lotus Air	
G-BSNY	Bensen B.8M	A. S. Deakin	
G-BSNZ	Cameron O-105 balloon	Aire Valley Balloons	
G-BSOE	Luscombe 8A Silvaire	S. B. Marsden	
G-BSOF	Colt 25A Mk II balloon	Thunder & Colt Ltd	
G-BSOG	Cessna 172M	B. Chapman & A. R. Budden	
G-BSOI	AS.332L Super Puma	Bristow Helicopters Ltd	
G-BSOK	PA-28-161 Warrior II	Hallmark Aviation	
G-BSOM	Glaser-Dirks DG.400	G-BSOM Group	
G-BSON	Green S.25	J. J. Green	
G-BSOO	Cessna 172F	Double Oscar Flying Group	
G-BSOR	CFM Streak Shadow Srs SA	J. P. Sorenson	

Notes	Reg.	Type	Owner or Operator
	G-BSOT	PA-38-112 Tomahawk II	S. Doyle/Glasgow
	G-BSOU	PA-38-112 Tomahawk II	Cormack (Aircraft Services) Ltd/Glasgow
	G-BSOV	PA-38-112 Tomahawk II	Cormack (Aircraft Services) Ltd/Glasgow
	G-BSOW	PA-32R Cherokee Lance 300	Halsmith (Aircraft Sales) Ltd
	G-BSOX	Luscombe 8A Silvaire	D. Gill
	G-BSOY	PA-34-220T Seneca III	BAe Flying College Ltd/Prestwick
	G-BSOZ	PA-28-161 Warrior II	Moray Flying Club Ltd/Kinloss
	G-BSPA	QAC Quickie Q.2	M. Ward
	G-BSPB	Thunder Ax8-84 balloon	Nigs Pertwee Ltd
	G-BSPC	Jodel D.140C	B. E. Cotton/Headcorn
	G-BSPE	Cessna F.172P	P. & M. Jones/Denham
	G-BSPF	Cessna T.303	McDonald Kane Ltd & K. P. Gibbin
	G-BSPG	PA-34-200T Seneca II	Fifo Ltd & C. M. Vlieland-Boddy
	G-BSPI	PA-28-161 Warrior II	Snapfleet Ltd/Wellesbourne
	G-BSPJ	Bensen B.8	P. Soanes
	G-BSPK	Cessna 195A	Walavia
	G-BSPL	CFM Streak Shadow Srs SA	D. G. Cook
	G-BSPM	PA-28-161 Warrior II	W. London Aero Services Ltd/ White Waltham
	G-BSPN	PA-28R-201T Turbo Arrow III	R. G. & W. Allison
	G-BSPR	BN-2B-26 Islander	Pilatus BN Ltd/Bembridge
	G-BSPT	BN-2B-26 Islander	Pilatus BN Ltd/Bembridge
	G-BSPW	Light Aero Avid Flyer C	P. D. Wheatland
	G-BSPX	Lancair 320	C. H. Skelt
	G-BSPY	BN-2A Islander	Glassbrush Ltd (G-AXYM)
	G-BSPZ	PA-28-161 Warrior II	Air Service Training Ltd/Perth
	G-BSRC	Cessna 150M	ASF Aviation Ltd/Bournemouth
	G-BSRD	Cameron N-105 balloon	J. R. Joiner
	G-BSRG	Robinson R-22B	Meridian Helicopters
	G-BSRH	Pitts S-1C Special	J. R. Groom/Biggin Hill
	G-BSRI	Lancair 235	G. Lewis
	G-BSRJ	Colt AA-1050 balloon	Thunder & Colt Ltd
	G-BSRK	ARV Super 2	J. K. Davies
	G-BSRL	Everett Srs 2 gyroplane	R. F. E. Burley
	G-BSRN	SA.365C-1 Dauphin	Nash Group Ltd
	G-BSRP	Rotorway Executive	J. P. Dennison
	G-BSRR	Cessna 182Q	Comet Aviation Ltd
	G-BSRT	Denney Aerocraft Kitfox	L. A. James
	G-BSRU	BAe 146-200	British Aerospace PLC (G-OSKI)
	G-BSRV	BAe 146-200	British Air Ferries Ltd (G-OSUN)/Stansted
	G-BSRX	CFM Streak Shadow	C. Penman
	G-BSRY	Cessna F.406 Caravan II	Field Aircraft Services (Heathrow) Ltd
	G-BSRZ	Air Command 532 Elite 2-seat	A. S. G. Crabb
	G-BSSA	Luscombe 8E Silvaire	Punters Promotions Ltd/Denham
	G-BSSB	Cessna 150L	D. T. A. Rees
	G-BSSC	PA-28-161 Warrior II	Air Service Training Ltd/Perth
	G-BSSD	Cameron O-105 balloon	Gone With The Wind Ltd
	G-BSSE	PA-28 Cherokee 140	Severn Aircraft Co
	G-BSSF	Denney Aerocraft Kitfox	D. M. Orrock
	G-BSSI	Rans S.6 Coyote II	D. A. Farnworth (G-MWJA)
	G-BSSJ	FRED Srs 2	R. F. Jopling
	G-BSSK	QAC Quickie Q.2	D. G. Greatrex
	G-BSSN	Air Command 532 Elite 2-seat	D. S. Robinson
	G-BSSO	Cameron O-90 balloon	J. N. H. Purvis
	G-BSSP	Robin DR.400/180R	Soaring (Oxford) Ltd
	G-BSSR	PA-28-151 Warrior	G. Webster & R. J. Sixsmith
	G-BSST	Concorde 002★	FAA Museum/Yeovilton
	G-BSSV	CFM Streak Shadow	A. M. Green
	G-BSSW	PA-28-161 Warrior II	MJ Leasing/Cardiff
	G-BSSX	PA-28-161 Warrior II	Airpart Supply Ltd/Booker
	G-BSSY	Polikarpov Po-2W	Sussex Spraying Services Ltd
	G-BSSZ	Thunder Ax8-90 balloon	Capital Balloon Club Ltd
	G-BSTC	Aeronca 11AC Chief	B. Bridgman & N. J. Mortimore
	G-BSTD	—	
	G-BSTE	AS.355F-2 Twin Squirrel	McAlpine Helicopters Ltd
	G-BSTG	Bell 206B JetRanger 2	Skyline Helicopters Ltd (G-RIKK)
	G-BSTH	PA-25 Pawnee 235	Scottish Gliding Union Ltd
	G-BSTI	Piper J-3C-65 Cub	I. Fraser & G. L. Nunn
	G-BSTJ	D.H.82A Tiger Moth	R. F. Harvey
	G-BSTK	Thunder Ax8-90 balloon	M. Williams
	G-BSTL	Rand Robinson KR-2	T. M. Scale
	G-BSTM	Cessna 172L	G-BSTM Group/Cambridge
	G-BSTO	Cessna 152	I. Taylor

Reg.	Type	Owner or Operator	Notes
G-BSTP	Cessna 152	FR Aviation Ltd/Bournemouth	
G-BSTR	AA-5 Traveler	James Allan (Aviation & Engineering) Ltd	
G-BSTS	Schleicher ASW.20L	T. I. Gardiner	
G-BSTT	Rans S.6 Coyote II	M. W. Holmes	
G-BSTU	Cessna P.210N	Boomselect Ltd	
G-BSTV	PA-32 Cherokee Six 300	J. V. Hudson	
G-BSTY	Thunder Ax8-90 balloon	J. W. Cato	
G-BSTZ	PA-28 Cherokee 140	H. M. & J. W. Young	
G-BSUA	Rans S.6 Coyote II	P. S. Dopson & A. J. Todd	
G-BSUB	Colt 77A balloon	W. Country Marketing & Licensing Ltd	
G-BSUD	Luscombe 8A Silvaire	J. M. Jeapes	
G-BSUE	Cessna U.206G	R. A. Robinson	
G-BSUF	PA-32RT-300 Lance II	MLP Aviation Ltd/Elstree	
G-BSUH	Cessna 140	J. C. Greenslade	
G-BSUI	Robinson R-22B	C. T. Norman	
G-BSUJ	Brügger MB.2 Colibri	M. A. Farrelly	
G-BSUK	Colt 77A balloon	K. J. Foster	
G-BSUM	Scheibe SF.27MB	M Syndicate	
G-BSUO	Scheibe SF.25C Falke	British Gliding Association Ltd	
G-BSUP	Schweizer 269C	Europe Aviation Ltd	
G-BSUR	Rotorway Executive 90	N. J. Betmell	
G-BSUS	Taylor JT.1 Monoplane	R. Parker	
G-BSUT	Rans S.6 Coyote II	P. J. Clegg	
G-BSUU	Colt 180A balloon	J. P. Clifford	
G-BSUV	Cameron O-77 balloon	R. Moss	
G-BSUW	PA-34-200T Seneca II	Berry Air	
G-BSUX	Carlson Sparrow II	J. Stephenson	
G-BSUZ	Denney Aerocraft Kitfox	E. T. Wicks	
G-BSVA	Christen A.1 Husky	STOL Aviation Ltd	
G-BSVB	PA-28-181 Archer II	Redhill Flying Club	
G-BSVC	Cameron A-120 balloon	First Class Ballooning Ltd	
G-BSVE	Binder CP.301S Smaragd	B. F. Arnall	
G-BSVF	PA-28-161 Warrior II	Airways Aero Associations Ltd/Booker	
G-BSVG	PA-28-161 Warrior II	Airways Aero Associations Ltd/Booker	
G-BSVH	Piper J-3C-65 Cub	A. R. Meakin	
G-BSVI	PA-16 Clipper	Knight Flying Group	
G-BSVJ	—	—	
G-BSVK	Denney Aerocraft Kitfox	K. P. Wordsworth	
G-BSVL	Cessna 560 Citation V	P. & G. S. Thomas/Cardiff	
G-BSVM	PA-28-161 Warrior II	Falcon Flying Services/Biggin Hill	
G-BSVN	Thorp T-18	J. H. Kirkham	
G-BSVO	Sikorsky S-61N	Bristow Helicopters Ltd	
G-BSVP	PA-23 Aztec 250	Time Electronics Ltd/Biggin Hill	
G-BSVR	Schweizer 269C	Nunkeeling Ltd	
G-BSVS	Robin DR.400/100	J. Macdonald	
G-BSVU	Stemme S.10	Sonic Aviation Ltd	
G-BSVV	PA-38-112 Tomahawk	A. J. & C. C. Leicester	
G-BSVW	PA-38-112 Tomahawk	Aeroleasing Ltd/Coventry	
G-BSVX	PA-38-112 Tomahawk	Aeroleasing Ltd/Coventry	
G-BSVY	PA-38-112 Tomahawk	Aeroleasing Ltd/Coventry	
G-BSVZ	Pietenpol Air Camper	A. F. Cashin	
G-BSWA	Luscombe 8A Silvaire	J. W. Street	
G-BSWB	Rans S.10 Sakota	F. A. Hewitt	
G-BSWC	Boeing Stearman E.75	R. J. & N. R. Lancaster	
G-BSWD	Cameron A-180 balloon	Cameron Balloons Ltd	
G-BSWE	PA-18 Super Cub 150	William Mark Holdings Ltd	
G-BSWF	PA-16 Clipper	T. M. Storey	
G-BSWG	PA-17 Vagabond	J. P. Taylor	
G-BSWH	Cessna 152	Airspeed Aviation Ltd/Tatenhill	
G-BSWI	Rans S.10 Sakota	K. E. Sheppard	
G-BSWJ	Cameron O-77 balloon	T. Charlwood	
G-BSWK	Robinson R-22B	Clarity Aviation Ltd	
G-BSWM	Slingsby T.61F	L. J. McKelvie	
G-BSWN	BN-2B-26 Islander	Pilatus BN Ltd/Bembridge	
G-BSWR	BN-2B-26 Islander	Pilatus BN Ltd/Bembridge	
G-BSWS	BN-2B-26 Islander	Pilatus BN Ltd/Bembridge	
G-BSWT	BN-2B-26 Islander	Pilatus BN Ltd/Bembridge	
G-BSWV	Cameron N-77 balloon	Leicester Mercury Ltd	
G-BSWW	Cameron O-105 balloon	R. B. & R. A. Naylor	
G-BSWX	Cameron V-90 balloon	Cameron Balloons Ltd	
G-BSWY	Cameron N-77 balloon	Nottingham Building Soc	
G-BSXA	PA-28-161 Warrior II	Hillvine Ltd	
G-BSXB	PA-28-161 Warrior II	Hillvine Ltd	

Notes	Reg.	Type	Owner or Operator
	G-BSXC	PA-28-161 Warrior II	Hillvine Ltd
	G-BSXD	Soko P-2 Kraguj	C. J. Pearce
	G-BSXE	Bell 206B JetRanger	Sterling Helicopters Ltd
	G-BSXF	Cameron A-180 balloon	Gone With The Wind Ltd
	G-BSXG	Cessna 150K	Midair Aviation Ltd/Bournemouth
	G-BSXH	Pitts S-1 Special	A. Howard
	G-BSXI	Mooney M.20E	Halsmith (Aircraft Sales) Ltd
	G-BSXL	BAe 146-300QT	TNT Express (UK) Ltd
	G-BSXM	Cameron V-77 balloon	C. A. Oxby
	G-BSXN	Robinson R-22B	Solohigh Ltd
	G-BSXP	Air Command 532 Elite	B. J. West
	G-BSXR	Air Command 532 Elite	T. Wing
	G-BSXS	PA-28-181 Archer II	Pipe-Air Ltd
	G-BSXT	Piper J-5A Cub Cruiser	M. G. & K. J. Thompson
	G-BSXW	PA-28-161 Warrior II	MFM Enterprises
	G-BSXX	Whittaker MW.7	H. J. Stanley
	G-BSXY	Oldfield Baby Great Lakes	B. Freeman-Jones
	G-BSYA	Jodel D.18	S. Harrison
	G-BSYB	Cameron N-120 balloon	Cameron Balloons Ltd
	G-BSYC	PA-32R-300 Lance	Arrow Aviation
	G-BSYD	Cameron A-180 balloon	A. A. Brown
	G-BSYE	Cessna 140	P. E. Villiers
	G-BSYF	Luscombe 8A Silvaire	M. K. Whitaker
	G-BSYG	PA-12 Super Cruiser	M. K. Whitaker
	G-BSYH	Luscombe 8A Silvaire	N. R. Osborne
	G-BSYI	AS.355F-1 Twin Squirrel	Lynton Aviation Ltd/Denham
	G-BSYJ	Cameron N-77 balloon	Chub Fire Ltd
	G-BSYK	PA-38-112 Tomahawk	Joyset Ltd
	G-BSYL	PA-38-112 Tomahawk	Joyset Ltd
	G-BSYM	PA-38-112 Tomahawk	Joyset Ltd
	G-BSYO	Piper J-3C-65 Cub	A. Eastelow
	G-BSYP	Bensen B.8M	A. T. Pocklington
	G-BSYS	BAe 146-300	Trident Aviation Leasing Services Ltd
	G-BSYU	Robin DR.400/180	P. A. Desoutter
	G-BSYV	Cessna 150M	Telair Manchester Ltd/Barton
	G-BSYW	Cessna 150M	Telair Manchester Ltd/Barton
	G-BSYX	Cessna 152	Telair Manchester Ltd/Barton
	G-BSYY	PA-28-161 Warrior II	Air Service Training Ltd/Perth
	G-BSYZ	PA-28-161 Warrior II	Air Service Training Ltd/Perth
	G-BSZB	Stolp SA.300 Starduster Too	Cambrian Flying Club/Swansea
	G-BSZC	Beech C-45H	A. A. Hodgson
	G-BSZD	Robin DR.400/180	Trantshore Ltd
	G-BSZF	Jodel DR.250/160	J. B. Randle
	G-BSZG	Stolp SA.100 Starduster	S. W. Watkins
	G-BSZH	Thunder Ax7-77 balloon	M. S. Drinkwater
	G-BSZI	Cessna 152	Eglinton Flying Club Ltd
	G-BSZJ	PA-28-181 Archer II	R. D. Fuller
	G-BSZL	Colt 77A balloon	Airship & Balloon Co Ltd
	G-BSZM	Bensen B.8	J. H. H. Turner
	G-BSZN	Bucker Bu133D-1 Jungmeister	V. Lindsay
	G-BSZO	Cessna 152	Cloudshire Ltd/Wellesbourne
	G-BSZP	Beech 400 Beechjet	Air Hanson Aircraft Sales Ltd/Farnborough
	G-BSZR	PA-28RT-201T Turbo Arrow IV	Venuetime Ltd
	G-BSZS	Robinson R-22B	South West Helicopters Ltd
	G-BSZT	PA-28-161 Warrior II	N. A. Ali
	G-BSZU	Cessna 150F	Midair Aviation Ltd/Bournemouth
	G-BSZV	Cessna 150F	Midair Aviation Ltd/Bournemouth
	G-BSZW	Cessna 152	Midair Aviation Ltd/Bournemouth
	G-BSZX	Cessna 150M	Midair Aviation Ltd/Bournemouth
	G-BSZY	Cameron A-180 balloon	Bryant Group PLC
	G-BTAA	EMB-110P1 Bandeirante	Business Air Ltd (G-BHJY)/Aberdeen
	G-BTAB	BAe 125 Srs 800B	Abbey Investments Co Ltd (G-BOOA)
	G-BTAD	Macair Merlin	A. T. & M. R. Dowie
	G-BTAF	PA-28-181 Archer II	Enpar (North) Ltd
	G-BTAG	Cameron O-77 balloon	H. Phethean & R. A. Shapland
	G-BTAH	Bensen B.8A	T. B. Johnson
	G-BTAJ	PA-34-200T Seneca II	Ravenair Aircraft Engineering Ltd/ Manchester
	G-BTAK	EAA Acro Sport 2	P. G. Harrison
	G-BTAL	Cessna F.152	Thanet Flying Club/Manston
	G-BTAM	PA-28-181 Archer II	RJH Air Services Ltd/Fowlmere
	G-BTAO	Cameron A-180 balloon	R. M. Bishop & D. C. La Beaume

Reg.	Type	Owner or Operator	Notes
G-BTAN	Thunder Ax7-65Z balloon	C. Wilkinson	
G-BTAP	PA-38-112 Tomahawk	I. J. McGarrigle	
G-BTAR	PA-38-112 Tomahawk	Rhodair Maintenance Ltd/Cardiff	
G-BTAS	PA-38-112 Tomahawk	Rhodair Maintenance Ltd/Cardiff	
G-BTAT	Denny Aerocraft Kitfox	Fast Ford Centre Ltd	
G-BTAU	Thunder Ax7-77 balloon	Thunder & Colt Ltd	
G-BTAV	Colt 105A balloon	D. C. Chipping	
G-BTAW	PA-28-161 Warrior II	Enpar (North) Ltd	
G-BTAX	PA-31-350 Navajo Chieftain	Jet West Ltd/Exeter	
G-BTAY	—	—	
G-BTAZ	Evans VP-2	G. S. Poulter	
G-BTBA	Robinson R-22B	Forestdale Hotels Ltd	
G-BTBB	Thunder Ax8-105 balloon	Scotia Balloons Ltd	
G-BTBC	PA-28-161 Warrior II	M. J. L. Macdonald	
G-BTBD	MBB Bo 105D	Bond Helicopters Ltd	
G-BTBE	—	—	
G-BTBF	Super Koala	E. A. Taylor (G-MWOZ)	
G-BTBG	Denny Aerocraft Kitfox	J. Catley	
G-BTBH	Ryan ST3KR	M. H. Pendlebury	
G-BTBI	WAR P-47 Thunderbolt (replica)	J. Berry	
G-BTBJ	Cessna 195B	P. G. Galumbo	
G-BTBK	Cessna 152	Mercia Aircraft Leasing & Sales Ltd	
G-BTBL	Montgomerie-Bensen B.8MR	J. M. Montgomerie	
G-BTBN	Denney Aerocraft Kitfox	Avon Valley Flying Group	
G-BTBO	Cameron N-77 balloon	Cameron Balloons Ltd	
G-BTBP	Cameron N-90 balloon	Cameron Balloons Ltd	
G-BTBR	Cameron DP-80 airship	Cameron Balloons Ltd	
G-BTBS	Cameron N-180 balloon	G. Scaife & B. Smith	
G-BTBT	PA-32R-301 Saratogo SP	B. Taylor	
G-BTBU	PA-18 Super Cub 150	Acebell Aviation Ltd & H. J. Rose	
G-BTBV	Cessna 140	A. Brinkley	
G-BTBW	Cessna 120	A. Brinkley	
G-BTBX	Piper J-3C-65 Cub	A. Brinkley	
G-BTBY	PA-17 Vagabond	M. M. Wallis	
G-BTCA	PA-32R-300 Lance	P. Taylor	
G-BTCB	Air Command 582 Sport	G. Scurrah	
G-BTCC	Grumman F6F-5 Hellcat	Patina Ltd/Duxford	
G-BTCD	P-51D-25-NA Mustang (463221)	Patina Ltd/Duxford	
G-BTCE	Cessna 152	T. Miller	
G-BTCF	CFM Streak Shadow	P. Crossman	
G-BTCH	Luscombe 8E Silvaire	P. D. Sparling	
G-BTCI	PA-17 Vagabond	F. M. Ward	
G-BTCJ	Luscombe 8C Silvaire	C. C. & J. M. Lovell	
G-BTCK	Cameron A-210 balloon	P. J. D. Kerr & A. J. Street	
G-BTCL	Cameron A-210 balloon	P. J. D. Kerr & A. J. Street	
G-BTCM	Cameron N-90 balloon	W. I. Hooker	
G-BTCN	Cameron A-300 balloon	Cameron Balloons Ltd	
G-BTCO	FRED Srs 2	I. P. Manley	
G-BTCR	Rans S.10 Sakota	S. H. Barr	
G-BTCS	Colt 90A balloon	D. N. Belton	
G-BTCT	AS.332L Super Puma	Bristow Helicopters Ltd	
G-BTCU	WSK PZL Antonov An-2T (77)	Wessex Aviation & Transport Ltd	
G-BTCV	Cameron V-90 balloon	Cameron Balloons Ltd	
G-BTCW	Cameron A-180 balloon	Bristol Balloons	
G-BTCX	Hunter F.4	Gray Tuplin Ltd	
G-BTCY	Hunter F.4	Gray Tuplin Ltd	
G-BTCZ	Cameron 84 Chateau SS balloon	Forbes Europe Inc	
G-BTDA	Slingsby T.61G	RAFGSA/Bicester	
G-BTDB	Cameron A-180 balloon	Balloon-A-Drome Ltd	
G-BTDC	Denney Aerocraft Kitfox	D. Collinson	
G-BTDD	CFM Streak Shadow	S. J. Evans	
G-BTDE	Cessna C-165	G. S. Moss	
G-BTDF	Luscombe 8A Silvaire	M. Stow	
G-BTDG	Colt 105A balloon	Thunder & Colt Ltd	
G-BTDH	P.56 Provost T.1	Pulsegrove Ltd/Shoreham	
G-BTDI	Robinson R-22B	A. Palmer	
G-BTDJ	Cessna T.303	European Aviation Services Ltd	
G-BTDK	Cessna 421C	RK Carbon Fibre Ltd/Manchester	
G-BTDN	Denney Aerocraft Kitfox	A. B. Butler	
G-BTDP	TBM-3R Avenger (53319)	A. Haig-Thomas/North Weald	
G-BTDR	Aero Designs Pulsar	R. M. Hughes	
G-BTDS	Colt 77A balloon	C. P. Witter Ltd	
G-BTDT	C.A.S.A. 1-131E Jungmann	T. A. Reed	

Notes	Reg.	Type	Owner or Operator
	G-BTDU	Robin DR.400/180	Aeromarine Ltd/Southampton
	G-BTDV	PA-28-161 Warrior II	Johnston Motors
	G-BTDW	Cessna 152 II	Johnston Motors
	G-BTDX	PA-18 Super Cub 150	Acebell Aviation Ltd/Redhill
	G-BTDY	PA-18 Super Cub 150	Stoneacre Aircraft Ltd
	G-BTDZ	C.A.S.A. 1-131E Jungmann 2000	R. J. Pickin
	G-BTEA	Cameron N-105 balloon	Southern Balloon Group
	G-BTEE	Cameron O-120 balloon	W. H. & J. P. Morgan
	G-BTEF	Pitts S-1 Special	Northwest Aerobatics
	G-BTEG	Taylorcraft BC-65	Aeroship Ltd
	G-BTEH	Colt 77A balloon	Thunder & Colt Ltd
	G-BTEI	Everett Srs 3 gyroplane	J. W. Highton
	G-BTEJ	Boeing 757-208	Britannia Airways Ltd *David Livingstone*/Luton
	G-BTEK	SOCATA TB.20 Trinidad	Air Touring Services Ltd/Biggin Hill
	G-BTEL	CFM Streak Shadow	J. E. Eatwell
	G-BTEN	Thunder Ax7-77 balloon	T. W. Dawson
	G-BTEO	Cameron V-90 balloon	Cameron Balloons Ltd
	G-BTEP	Cameron DP-80 airship	Cameron Balloons Ltd
	G-BETR	Cessna 150J	Universal Air Services Ltd/Sywell
	G-BTES	Cessna 150H	Universal Air Services Ltd/Sywell
	G-BTET	Piper J-3C-65 Cub	W. F. Crozier
	G-BTEU	SA.365N-2 Dauphin	Bond Helicopters Ltd
	G-BTEV	PA-38-112 Tomahawk	T. R. Blockley & J. Mingay/Cardiff
	G-BTEW	Cessna 120	Tindon Ltd/Little Snoring
	G-BTEX	PA-28 Cherokee 140	Tindon Ltd/Little Snoring
	G-BTEZ	Thunder Ax8-90 balloon	G. V. Beckwith
	G-BFTA	Denney Aerocraft Kitfox	K. R. Peek
	G-BTFB	Cameron DG-14 airship	Cameron Balloons Ltd
	G-BTFC	Cessna F.152 II	Tayside Aviation Ltd
	G-BTFD	Colt AS-105 airshiip Mk II	Thunder & Colt Ltd
	G-BTFE	Bensen-Parsons 2-seat gyroplane	I. Brewster
	G-BTFF	Cessna T.310R II	M. C. Searle/Elstree
	G-BTFG	Boeing Stearman A.75N1 (441)	S. J. Ellis
	G-BTFJ	PA-15 Vagabond	Eastbach Aircraft Preservation
	G-BTFK	Taylorcraft BC-12D	J. J. Penney
	G-BTFL	Aeronca 11AC Chief	BTFL Group
	G-BTFM	Cameron O-105 balloon	Edinburgh University Hot Air Balloon Club
	G-BTFN	Beech F33C Bonanza	Robert Hinton Design & Creative Communications Ltd
	G-BTFO	PA-28-161 Warrior II	Flyfar Ltd
	G-BTFP	PA-38-112 Tomahawk	Teesside Flight Centre Ltd
	G-BTFR	Colt AS-105 airship	Heather Flight Ltd
	G-BTFS	Cessna A.150M	Birmingham Airport Flying Group
	G-BTFT	Beech 58 Baron	M. C. Searle/Elstree
	G-BTFU	Cameron N-90 balloon	J. J. Rudoni & A. C. K. Rawson
	G-BTFV	Whittaker MW.7	S. J. Luck
	G-BTFW	Montgomerie-Bensen B.8MR	A. Mansfield
	G-BTFX	Bell 206B JetRanger 2	J. Selwyn Smith (Shepley)/Ltd
	G-BTFY	Bell 206B JetRanger 2	R & M International Helicopters Ltd
	G-BTFZ	Cameron A-120 balloon	A. G. E. Faulkner
	G-BTGA	Boeing Stearman A.751N1	J. C. Lister
	G-BTGB	Robinson R-22B	A. C. Richards
	G-BTGC	PA-38-112 Tomahawk	R. E. Wooldridge & T. Hayselden (Doncaster) Ltd
	G-BTGD	Rand-Robinson KR-2	D. W. Mullin
	G-BTGE	PA-28-181 Archer II	Lotus Air
	G-BTGG	Rans S.10 Sakota	A. R. Cameron
	G-BTGH	Cessna 152	R. S. Trayhurn & P. D. Myson
	G-BTGI	Rearwin 175 Skyranger	T. J. Caddey
	G-BTGJ	Smith DSA-1 Miniplane	G. J. Knowles
	G-BTGK	PA-28-161 Warrior II	S. Dorrington
	G-BTGL	Light Aero Avid Flyer	A. J. Maxwell
	G-BTGM	Aeronca 7AC Champion	Claybourn Garages Ltd
	G-BTGN	Cessna 310R	Air Service Training Ltd/Perth
	G-BTGO	PA-28 Cherokee 140	Hadleyridge Ltd
	G-BTGP	Cessna 150M	A. J. Gomes
	G-BTGR	Cessna 152 II	A. J. Gomes
	G-BTGS	Stolp SA.300 Starduster Too	T. G. Solomon (G-AYMA)/Shoreham
	G-BTGT	CFM Streak Shadow	M. P. Allinson (G-MWPY)
	G-BTGU	PA-34-220T Seneca III	Carill Aviation Ltd
	G-BTGV	PA-34-200T Seneca II	Hollowbrook Flying Group
	G-BTGW	Cessna 152 II	Stapleford Flying Club Ltd

Reg.	Type	Owner or Operator	Notes
G-BTGX	Cessna 152 II	Stapleford Flying Club Ltd	
G-BTGY	PA-28-161 Warrior II	Stapleford Flying Club Ltd	
G-BTGZ	PA-28-181 Archer II	Express Aviation Marketing/Biggin Hill	
G-BTHA	Cessna 182P	N. J. Douglas	
G-BTHB	Bell 212	Autair Helicopters Ltd	
G-BTHC	Bell 212	Autair Helicopters Ltd	
G-BTHD	Yakolev Yak-3U	Patina Ltd/Duxford	
G-BTHE	Cessna 150L	Humberside Police Flying Club	
G-BTHF	Cameron V-90 balloon	N. J. & S. J. Langley	
G-BTHH	Jodel DR.100A	E. J. Horsfall	
G-BTHI	Robinson R-22B	A. M. Green	
G-BTHJ	Evans VP-2	C. J. Moseley	
G-BTHK	Thunder Ax7-77 balloon	Krauss Maffei (UK) Ltd	
G-BTHM	Thunder Ax8-105 balloon	Anglia Balloons	
G-BTHN	Renegade II	Meridian Ultralights Ltd	
G-BTHP	Thorp T.211	Arrow Air Sales/Shipdham	
G-BTHR	SOCATA TB.10 Tobago	Air Touring Services Ltd/Biggin Hill	
G-BTHT	BAe 146-300	British Aerospace PLC	
G-BTHU	Light Aero Avid Flyer	M. Morris	
G-BTHV	MBB Bo 105DBS/4	Bond Helicopters Ltd	
G-BTHW	Beech F33C Bonanza	Robin Lance Aviation Associates Ltd	
G-BTHX	Colt 105A balloon	R. Ollier	
G-BTHY	Bell 206B JetRanger 3	R. & M. International Helicopers Ltd	
G-BTHZ	Cameron V-56 balloon	C. N. Marshall	
G-BTIA	BAe 146-200QC	British Air Ferries Ltd (G-PRIN)/Stansted	
G-BTIB	Dassault Falcon 900B	Glaxo Holdings Ltd	
G-BTIC	PA-22 Tri-Pacer 150	Yorkshire Commercial Properties Ltd	
G-BTID	PA-28-161 Warrior II	Halsmith (Aircraft Sales) Ltd	
G-BTIE	SOCATA TB.10 Tobago	Rotaters Ltd/Machester	
G-BTIF	Denney Aerocraft Kitfox	C. R. Thompson	
G-BTIG	Montgomerie-Bensen B.8MR	D. Beevers	
G-BTIH	PA-28-151 Warrior	B. R. Gaunt	
G-BTII	AA-5B Tiger	B. D. Greenwood	
G-BTIJ	Luscombe 8E Silvaire	C. P. Wadlow	
G-BTIK	Cessna 152	B. R. Pearson/Eaglescott	
G-BTIL	PA-38-112 Tomahawk	B. R. Pearson/Eaglescott	
G-BTIM	PA-28-161 Cadet	London Aviation Ltd/Biggin Hill	
G-BTIN	Cessna 150C	Cormack (Aircraft Services) Ltd	
G-BTIO	SNCAN Stampe SV-4C	L. J. & A. A. Rice	
G-BTIP	Denney Aerocraft Kitfox	P. A. Hardy	
G-BTIR	Denney Aerocraft Kitfox Mk 2	Bluetit Group	
G-BTIS	AS.355F-1 Twin Squirrel	Walsh Aviation (G-TALI)	
G-BTIT	—		
G-BTIU	M.S.892A Rallye Commodore 150	W. H. Cole	
G-BTIV	PA-28-161 Warrior II	Warrior Group/Eaglescott	
G-BTIW	Jodel DR.1050/M1	Circuit Engineering Ltd	
G-BTIX	Cameron V-77 balloon	S. A. Simington	
G-BTIZ	Cameron A-105 balloon	A. Faulkner	
G-BTJA	Luscombe 8E Silvaire	M. W. & L. M. Rudkin	
G-BTJB	Luscombe 8E Silvaire	M. Loxton	
G-BTJC	Luscombe 8F Silvaire	S. C. & M. Goddard	
G-BTJD	Thunder Ax8-90 balloon	T. C. Restell	
G-BTJE	Hiller UH-12E4	T. J. Clark	
G-BTJF	Thunder Ax10-180 balloon	Airborne Adventures Ltd	
G-BTJH	Cameron O-77 balloon	H. Stringer	
G-TBJJ	Beech F33C Bonanza	Neil Brown Engineering Ltd	
G-BTJJ	PA-38-112 Tomahawk	Ravenair Training Ltd/Manchester	
G-BTJK	PA-38-112 Tomahawk	Network Enterprise International Ltd	
G-BTJL	PA-38-112 Tomahawk	Ravenair Training Ltd/Manchester	
G-BTJN	Montgomerie-Bensen B.8MR	A. Hamilton	
G-BTJO	Thunder Ax9-140 balloon	Abbey Plant Co Ltd	
G-BTJS	Montgomerie-Bensen B.8M	J. M. P. Annand & W. M. Coupar	
G-BTJT	BAe 146-300	British Aerospace PLC	
G-BTJU	Cameron V-90 balloon	C. W. Jones (Flooring) Ltd	
G-BTJV	PZL SZD-50-3 Puchacz	Kent Gliding Club Ltd	
G-BTJW	Colt 120A balloon	Picksteed Ltd	
G-BTJX	Rans S.10 Sakota	M. Goacher	
G-BTJY	Bell 212	NK Leasing (Aviation) Ltd	
G-BTJZ	Taylorcraft BC-12D-1	K. E. Ballington	
G-BTKA	Piper J-5A Cub Cruiser	S. J. Rudkin	
G-BTKB	Renegade Spirit 912	G. S. Blundell	
G-BTKD	Denney Aerocraft Kitfox	J. F. White	
G-BTKE	Colt 90A balloon	N. C. Lindsay	

Notes	Reg.	Type	Owner or Operator
	G-BTKF	Thunder Ax7-77 balloon	E. J. Jacobs
	G-BTKG	Light Aero Avid Flyer	P. R. Snowden
	G-BTKH	Colt GA-42 airship	Thunder & Colt Ltd
	G-BTKI	NA T-6G Texan	P. S. & S. M. Warner
	G-BTKJ	G.44 Widgeon	B. J. Snoxall
	G-BTKK	Colt 240A balloon	Heather Flight Ltd
	G-BTKL	MBB Bo 105DB	Veritair Ltd
	G-BTKM	Cameron V-90 balloon	Cameron Balloons Ltd
	G-BTKN	Cameron O-120 balloon	The Ballooning Business Ltd
	G-BTKO	Cameron A-180 balloon	Balloon Flights International Ltd
	G-BTKP	CFM Streak Shadow	K. S. Woodward
	G-BTKR	Cameron O-105 balloon	Cameron Balloons Ltd
	G-BTKS	Rans S.10 Sakota	J. R. I. Rolfe & ptnrs
	G-BTKT	PA-28-161 Warrior II	C. R. Herbert
	G-BTKV	PA-22 Tri-Pacer 160	M. Hanna
	G-BTKW	Cameron O-105 balloon	Decora Manufacturing Ltd
	G-BTKX	PA-28-181 Archer II	Goldhawk Aviation
	G-BTKY	PA-28-181 Archer II	Commanche Travel Ltd/Elstree
	G-BTKZ	Cameron V-77 balloon	S. P. Richards
	G-BTLA	Sikorsky S-76B	RV Aviation Ltd
	G-BTLB	Wassmer WA.52 Europa	M. D. O'Brien/Shoreham
	G-BTLC	SA.365N2 Dauphin 2	Bond Helicopters Ltd
	G-BTLD	BAe 146-300	British Aerospace PLC
	G-BTLE	PA-31-350 Navajo Chieftain	Orient Aviation Ltd
	G-BTLF	Enstrom 280	M. A. Crook
	G-BTLG	PA-28R Cherokee Arrow 200	M. C. Searle/Elstree
	G-BTLH	SOCATA TB.20 Trinidad	Air Touring Services Ltd/Biggin Hill
	G-BTLI	Scheibe SF.25B Falke	S. F. Duerden/Germany
	G-BTLJ	Hughes 369E	Apex Tubulars Ltd
	G-BTLK	Cessna P.210N	Emmi Consultancy
	G-BTLL	Pilatus P3-05	D. L. Masters/Biggin Hill
	G-BTLM	PA-22 Tri-Pacer 160	F & H (Aircraft) Ltd
	G-BTLN	Cessna T.303	Pektron Ltd
	G-BTLO	Colt 120A balloon	Huntair Ltd
	G-BTLP	AA-1C Lynx	Partlease Ltd
	G-BTLR	SA.365N2 Dauphin 2	McAlpine Helicopters Ltd/Hayes
	G-BTLU	BN-2B-26 Islander	Pilatus BN Ltd/Bembridge
	G-BTLV	BN-2B-26 Islander	Pilatus BN Ltd/Bembridge
	G-BTLW	BN-2B-26 Islander	Pilatus BN Ltd/Bembridge
	G-BTLX	BN-2B-26 Islander	Pilatus BN Ltd/Bembridge
	G-BTLY	BN-2B-26 Islander	Pilatus BN Ltd/Bembridge
	G-BTLZ	BN-2B-26 Islander	Pilatus BN Ltd/Bembridge
	G-BTMA	Cessna 172N	Cheshire Air Training School (Merseyside) Ltd
	G-BTMB	Colt 120A balloon	Pickstead Ltd
	G-BTMC	Colt 120A balloon	Pickstead Ltd
	G-BTMD	Colt 120A balloon	Pickstead Ltd
	G-BTME	Cameron O-120 balloon	G. N. & K. A. Conolly
	G-BTMF	Taylorcraft BC-12D	W. R. Savin & B. G. Ell
	G-BTMH	Colt 90A balloon	Douwe Egberts UK Ltd
	G-BTMI	BAe 146-300	Trident Aviation Leasing Services Ltd
	G-BTMJ	Maule MX-7-180	C. M. McGill
	G-BTMK	Cessna R.172K XP	Strand Coachworks
	G-BTML	Cameron 90 Rupert Bear SS balloon	Flying Pictures (Balloons) Ltd
	G-BTMM	Cameron N-105 balloon	M. F. Glue
	G-BTMN	Thunder Ax9-120 S2 balloon	Aerial Display Co Ltd
	G-BTMO	Colt 69A balloon	Thunder & Colt Ltd
	G-BTMP	Everett Srs 2 gyroplane	D. G. Hill
	G-BTMR	Cessna 172M	I. Taylor
	G-BTMS	Light Aero Avid Flyer	M. J. Schyns
	G-BTMT	Denney Aerocraft Kitfox	Skulk Flying Group
	G-BTMU	Thunder Ax8-105 S2 balloon	G. V. Beckwith
	G-BTMV	Everett Srs 2 gyroplane	L. Armes
	G-BTMW	Zenair CH.701 STOL	L. Lewis
	G-BTMX	Denney Aerocraft Kitfox Mk 3	M. E. F. Reynolds
	G-BTMY	Cameron 80 Train SS balloon	Cameron Balloons Ltd
	G-BTMZ	PA-38-112 Tomahawk	Close Oke Ltd
	G-BTNA	Robinson R-22B	MG Group Ltd
	G-BTNB	Robinson R-22B	Davron Aviation
	G-BTNC	AS.365N-2 Dauphin 2	Bond Helicopters Ltd
	G-BTND	PA-38-112 Tomahawk	P. D. Stenning & C. P. Hawker
	G-BTNE	PA-28-161 Warrior II	Cloudshire Ltd

Reg.	Type	Owner or Operator	Notes
G-BTNH	PA-28-161 Warrior II	C. R. Herbert	
G-BTNJ	Cameron V-90 balloon	P. L. Harrison & B. J. Newman	
G-BTNL	Thunder Ax10-180 balloon	Airships Ltd	
G-BTNM	AS.355F-2 Twin Squirrel	McAlpine Helicopters Ltd/Hayes	
G-BTNN	Colt 21A balloon	Thunder & Colt Ltd	
G-BTNO	Aeronca 7AC Champion	O. R. Howe	
G-BTNP	Light Aero Avid Flyer Commuter	N. Evans	
G-BTNR	Denney Aerocraft Kitfox Mk 3	J. W. G. Ellis	
G-BTNS	PZL-104 Wilga 80	R. W. Husband	
G-BTNT	PA-28-151 Warrior	Britannia Airways Ltd/Luton	
G-BTNU	BAe 146-300	Dan-Air Services Ltd (G-BSLS)/Gatwick	
G-BTNV	PA-28-161 Warrior II	J. A. Wilkinson & P. Bolton	
G-BTNW	Rans S.6-ESA Coyote II	A. Barbone	
G-BTNX	Colt 105A balloon	Thunder & Colt Ltd	
G-BTNY	Fairchild M-62A	C. L. H. Parr	
G-BTNZ	AS.332L-1 Super Puma	British International Helicopters Ltd	
G-BTOA	Mong Sport MS-2	J. E. Stevens	
G-BTOB	Colt 160A balloon	Bavarian Balloon Co Ltd	
G-BTOC	Robinson R-22B	T. Kressner	
G-BTOD	PA-38-112 Tomahawk	R. E. Todd	
G-BTOG	D.H.82A Tiger Moth	P. T. Szluha	
G-BTOH	Cameron A-105 balloon	R. E. Jones	
G-BTOI	Cameron N-77 balloon	The Nestle Co Ltd	
G-BTOJ	Mooney M.10 Cadet	D. W. Vernon	
G-BTOK	SOCATA TB.10 Tobago	Air Touring Services Ltd/Biggin Hill	
G-BTOL	Denney Aerocraft Kitfox Mk 3	C. R. Phillips	
G-BTOM	PA-38-112 Tomahawk	R. A. Wakefield	
G-BTON	PA-28 Cherokee 140	W. A. & K. C. Ryan	
G-BTOO	Pitts S-1C Special	F. Sharples/Sandown	
G-BTOP	Cameron V-77 balloon	J. J. Winter	
G-BTOR	Lancair 320	R. W. Fairless	
G-BTOS	Cessna 140	R. E. Todd	
G-BTOT	PA-15 Vagabond	M. Stow	
G-BTOU	Cameron O-120 balloon	Balloon-A-Drome Ltd	
G-BTOV	PZL Mielec Antonov An-2PT	TM Aviation Ltd	
G-BTOW	SOCATA Rallye 180GT	Cambridge University Gliding Trust Ltd	
G-BTOX	Aero Designs Pulsar	J. K. McWhinney	
G-BTOZ	Thunder Ax9-120 S2 balloon	H. G. Davies	
G-BTPA	BAe ATP	British Airways *Strathblane*/Glasgow	
G-BTPB	Cameron N-105 balloon	British Telecom PLC	
G-BTPC	BAe ATP	British Airways *Strathallan*/Glasgow	
G-BTPD	BAe ATP	British Airways *Strathconon*/Glasgow	
G-BTPE	BAe ATP	British Airways *Strathdon*/Glasgow	
G-BTPF	BAe ATP	British Airways *Strathlarn*/Glasgow	
G-BTPG	BAe ATP	British Airways *Strathfillan*/Glasgow	
G-BTPH	BAe ATP	British Airways *Strathnaver*/Glasgow	
G-BTPJ	BAe ATP	British Airways *Strathpeffer*/Glsagow	
G-BTPK	BAe ATP	British Airways *Strathrannoch*/Glasgow	
G-BTPL	BAe ATP	British Airways *Strathspey*/Glasgow	
G-BTPM	BAe ATP	British Airways *Strathory*/Glasgow	
G-BTPN	BAe ATP	British Airways *Strathbrora*/Glasgow	
G-BTPO	BAe ATP	British Airways *Strathclyde*/Glasgow	
G-BTPP	—	—	
G-BTPR	—	—	
G-BTPS	—	—	
G-BTPT	Cameron N-77 balloon	Derbyshire Building Soc	
G-BTPU	Cameron N-105 balloon	G. V. Beckwith	
G-BTPV	Colt 90A balloon	Airship & Balloon Col Ltd	
G-BTPW	Cameron N-105 balloon	Cameron Balloons Ltd	
G-BTPX	Thunder Ax8-90 balloon	J. L. Guy	
G-BTPZ	Isaacs Fury II	P. D. Holt	
G-BTRA	Denney Aerocraft Kitfox Mk 3	T. P. Spurge	
G-BTRB	Colt Mickey Mouse SS balloon	Wellfarrow Ltd	
G-BTRC	Light Aero Avid Speed Wing	A. A. Craig	
G-BTRD	Colt 240A balloon	Bavarian Balloon Co Ltd	
G-BTRE	Cessna F.172H	Hero Aviation/Stapleford	
G-BTRF	Aero Designs Pulsar	C. Smith	
G-BTRG	Aeronca 65C	H. J. Cox	
G-BTRH	Aeronca 7AC Champion	H. J. Cox	
G-BTRI	Aeronca 11CC Super Chief	H. J. Cox	
G-BTRJ	Boeing Stearman B.75N1	G. L. Carpenter	
G-BTRK	PA-28-161 Warrior II	C. R. Herbert	
G-BTRL	Cameron N-105 balloon	J. Lippett	

Notes	Reg.	Type	Owner or Operator
	G-BTRM	Colt 120A balloon	Picksteed Ltd
	G-BTRN	Thunder Ax9-120 S2 balloon	Solar Communications Ltd
	G-BTRO	Thunder Ax8-90 balloon	Capital Balloon Club Ltd
	G-BTRP	Hughes 369E	Southern Air Ltd/Shoreham
	G-BTRR	Thunder Ax7-77 balloon	S. M. Roberts
	G-BTRS	PA-28-161 Warrior II	Actionwings Ltd/Barton
	G-BTRT	PA-28R Cherokee Arrow 200-II	Actionwings Ltd/Barton
	G-BTRU	Robin DR.400/180	R. & M. Engineering Ltd
	G-BTRV	Boeing Stearman B.75N1	J. M. & R. J. Knights
	G-BTRW	Slingsby T.61F Venture T.2	B. Kerby & G. Grainer
	G-BTRX	Cameron V-77 balloon	R. P. Jones & N. P.Hemsley
	G-BTRY	PA-28-161 Warrior II	Air Service Training Ltd/Perth
	G-BTRZ	Jodel D.18	R. M. Johnson & R. Collin
	G-BTSA	Cessna 150K	J. A. Thomas
	G-BTSB	Corben Baby Ace D	W. R. Savin
	G-BTSC	Evans VP-2	B. P. Irish
	G-BTSD	Midget Mustang	R. Fitzpatrick
	G-BTSE	—	—
	G-BTSG	Cessna 414A	T. S. Grimshaw Ltd (G-BTFH)
	G-BTSI	BAe 125-1000	Shell Aircraft Ltd/Heathrow
	G-BTSJ	PA-28-161 Warrior II	Halsmith (Aircraft Sales) Ltd
	G-BTSK	Beech F33C Bonanza	R. N. Goode/White Waltham
	G-BTSL	Cameron Glass SS balloon	M. R. Humphrey & J. R .Clifton
	G-BTSM	Cessna 180A	C. Couston
	G-BTSN	Cessna 150G	H. W. & R. W. Sage
	G-BTSO	Cessna 150M	H. W. & R. W. Sage
	G-BTSP	Piper J-3C-65 Cub	H. W. & R. W. Sage
	G-BTSR	Aeronca IIAC Chief	H. W. & R. W. Sage
	G-BTSS	Colt Flying Shopping Trolley SS balloon	Jentime Ltd
	G-BTST	Bensen B.9	V. Scott
	G-BTSU	Bensen B.8MR	B. T. Goggin
	G-BTSV	Denney Aerocraft Kitfox Mk 3	D. J. Sharland
	G-BTSW	Colt AS-80 Mk II airship	Huntair Ltd
	G-BTSX	Thunder Ax7-77 balloon	C. Moris-Gallimore
	G-BTSY	Lightning F.6	Lightning Association
	G-BTSZ	Cessna 177A	W. B. Pope
	G-BTTA	Hawker Sea Fury FB.10 (WH589)	R. G. Hanna/Duxford
	G-BTTB	Cameron V-90 balloon	Royal Engineers Balloon Club
	G-BTTD	Montgomerie-Bensen B.8M	K. J. Parker
	G-BTTE	Cessna 150L	I. J. Lawson
	G-BTTG	BAe 125-1000A	British Aerospace PLC
	G-BTTH	Beech F33C Bonanza	N. K. Mere/Germany
	G-BTTI	Thunder Ax8-90 balloon	Capital Balloon Club Ltd
	G-BTTJ	Thunder Ax9-120 S2 balloon	G. D. & L. Fitzpatrick
	G-BTTK	Thunder Ax8-105 balloon	Tempowish Ltd
	G-BTTL	Cameron V-90 balloon	A. J. Baird
	G-BTTN	V.S.349 Spitfire Vb	Aerofab Restorations
	G-BTTP	BAe 146-300	British Aerospace PLC
	G-BTTR	Aerotek Pitts S-2A Special	Ebork Ltd
	G-BTTS	Colt 77A balloon	Rutland Balloon Club
	G-BTTT	—	—
	G-BTTU	Cameron V-90 balloon	Heather Flight Ltd
	G-BTTV	Schweizer 269C	C.S.E. Aviation Ltd/Kidlington
	G-BTTW	Thunder Ax7-77 balloon	Thunder & Colt Ltd
	G-BTTX	BAe 125-1000A	British Aerospace PLC
	G-BTTY	Denney Aerocraft Kitfox Mk 2	K. J. Fleming
	G-BTTZ	Slingsby T.61F Venture T.2	I. R. F. Hammond
	G-BTUA	Slingsby T.61F Venture T.2	M. W. Olliver
	G-BTUB	Yakolev C.11	M. G. & J. R. Jefferies
	G-BTUC	EMB-312 Tucano	Short Bros PLC/Belfast City
	G-BTUD	CFM Image	D. G. Cook (G-MWPV)
	G-BTUF	H.S. 125 Srs F403B	British Aerospace PLC
	G-BTUG	SOCATA Rallye 180T	Lasham Gliding Soc
	G-BTUH	Cameron N-65 balloon	B. J. Godding
	G-BTUJ	Thunder Ax9-120 balloon	Thunder & Colt Ltd
	G-BTUK	Aerotek Pitts S-2A Special	Wickenby Aviation Ltd
	G-BTUL	Aerotek Pitts S-2A Special	C. & S. Aviation
	G-BTUM	Piper J-3C-65 Cub	B. G. Ell
	G-BTUN	Colt Flying Drinks Can SS balloon	BIAS UK Ltd
	G-BTUO	Cameron RX-100 balloon	Cameron Balloons Ltd
	G-BTUP	Robinson R-22B	Sloane Helicopters Ltd/Sywell
	G-BTUR	PA-18 Super Cub 95 (modified)	G. Cormack/Glasgow

Reg.	Type	Owner or Operator	Notes
G-BTUS	Whittaker MW.7	J. F. Bakewell	
G-BTUT	PA-34-200T Seneca II	F. B. & G. Holben	
G-BTUU	Cameron O-120 balloon	Henley-on-Thames Air Balloons	
G-BTUV	Aeronca A65TAC Defender	J. T. Ingrouille	
G-BTUW	PA-28-151 Warrior	J. Robinson	
G-BTUX	AS.365N-2 Dauphin 2	Bond Helicopters Ltd/Aberdeen	
G-BTUY	BAe 146-300	British Aerospace PLC	
G-BTUZ	American General AG-5B	The Cabair Group Ltd/Elstree	
G-BTVA	Thunder Ax7-77 balloon	C. E. Wood	
G-BTVB	Everett Srs 3 gyroplane	J. Pumford	
G-BTVC	Denney Aercoraft Kitfox Mk 2	R. Swinden	
G-BTVE	Hawker Demon	Aero Vintage Ltd	
G-BTVF	Rotorway Executive 90	E. P. Sadler	
G-BTVG	Cessna 140	V. C. Gover	
G-BTVH	Colt 77A balloon	D. N. & L. J. Close (G-ZADT/G-ZBCA)	
G-BTVI	BN-2B-26 Islander	Pilatus BN Ltd/Bembridge	
G-BTVJ	BN-2B-26 Islander	Pilatus BN Ltd/Bembridge	
G-BTVK	BN-2B-26 Islander	Pilatus BN Ltd/Bembridge	
G-BTVL	BN-2B-26 Islander	Pilatus BN Ltd/Bembridge	
G-BTVM	BN-2B-26 Islander	Pilatus BN Ltd/Bembridge	
G-BTVN	BN-2B-26 Islander	PIlatus BN Ltd/Bembridge	
G-BTVO	BAe 146-300	British Aerospace PLC	
G-BTVP	Currie Wot	B. V. Mayo & V. Panteli	
G-BTVR	PA-28 Cherokee 140	West of Scotland Flying Club Ltd	
G-BTVS	AS.355F-1 Twin Squirrel	BLS Aviation Ltd (G-STVE/G-TOFF/ G-BKJX)	
G-BTVT	BAe146-200	British Aerospace PLC	
G-BTVU	Robinson R-22B	Sloane Helicopters Ltd/Sywell	
G-BTVV	Cessna F.337G	Taylor Aircraft Services	
G-BTVW	Cessna 152	Cloudshire Ltd	
G-BTVX	Cessna 152	Cloudshire Ltd	
G-BTVY	Cessna 402B	R. K. Spence	
G-BTVZ	Cameron A-140 balloon	Aire Valley Balloons	
G-BTWB	Denney Aerocraft Kifox Mk 3	J. E. Tootell (G-BTTM)	
G-BTWC	Slingsby T.61F Venture T.1	RAFGSA/Bicester	
G-BTWD	Slingsby T.61F Venture T.1	York Gliding Centre	
G-BTWE	Slingsby T.61F Venture T.1	RAFGSA/Bicester	
G-BTWF	D.H.C.1 Chipmunk 22	J. A. & V. G. Sims	
G-BTWG	Thunder Ax10-160 S2 balloon	W. O. T. Holmes & R. J. Barr	
G-BTWH	Thunder Ax7-77 balloon	Jim Barker Motor Factor	
G-BTWI	EAA Acro Sport 1	Detail Offers Ltd	
G-BTWJ	Cameron V-77 balloon	F. W. Barnes	
G-BTWK	Colt 210A balloon	Airship & Balloon Co Ltd	
G-BTWL	WAG-Aero Acro Sport Trainer	D. H. Tonkin	
G-BTWM	Cameron V-77 balloon	D. I. Gray-Fisk	
G-BTWN	Maule MXT-7-180	Aeromarine Ltd	
G-BTWO	—		
G-BTWP	Robinson R-22B	Sloane Helicopters Ltd/Sywell	
G-BTWR	Bell P-63A-7-BE Kingcobra	Patina Ltd/Duxford	
G-BTWS	Thunder Ax7-77 balloon	Bavarian Balloon Co Ltd	
G-BTWU	PA-22 Tri-Pacer 135	G. A. Bentley	
G-BTWV	Cameron O-90 balloon	Bodkin House Hotel	
G-BTWW	AB-206B JetRanger 2	Dollar Air Services Ltd/Coventry	
G-BTWX	SOCATA TB.9 Tampico	Air Touring Services Ltd/Biggin Hill	
G-BTWY	Aero Designs Pulsar	J. J. Pridal & A. K. Pirie	
G-BTWZ	Rans S.10 Sakota	D. G. Hey	
G-BTXB	Colt 77A balloon	Unigas Ltd	
G-BTXC	Team Minimax	M. H. D. Soltau (G-MWFC)	
G-BTXD	Rans S.6-ESA Coyote II	M. Isterling	
G-BTXE	V.S.394 Spitfire F.XVIII	Historic Flying Ltd	
G-BTXF	Cameron V-90 balloon	Gone With The Wind Ltd	
G-BTXG	BAe Jetstream 3100	British Aerospace PLC	
G-BTXH	Colt AS-56 airship	Huntair Ltd	
G-BTXI	Noorduyn AT-16 Harvard IIB	Patina Ltd/Duxford	
G-BTXJ	Robinson R-22B	Sloane Helicopters Ltd/Sywell	
G-BTXK	Thunder Ax7-65 balloon	E. J. Jacobs	
G-BTXM	Colt 21A balloon	Airship & Balloon Co Ltd	
G-BTXN	BAe146-300	Trident Aviation Leasing Ltd	
G-BTXO	BAe146-100	Trident Aviation Leasing Ltd	
G-BTXP	Cameron RX-100 balloon	Cameron Balloons Ltd	
G-BTXR	Cassutt Racer	J. Cull/Popham	
G-BTXS	Cameron O-120 balloon	Southern Balloon Group	
G-BTXT	Maule MXT-7-180	Aeromarine Ltd	

Notes	Reg.	Type	Owner or Operator
	G-BTXU	Cameron A-210 balloon	P. J. D. Kerr & A. J. Street
	G-BTXV	Cameron A-210 balloon	P. J. D. Kerr & A. J. Street
	G-BTXW	Cameron V-77 balloon	K. W. Scott
	G-BTXX	Bellanca 8KCAB Decathlon	R. H. Reeves
	G-BTXY	AS.365N-2 Dauphin 2	Samaero Company Private Ltd
	G-BTXZ	Zenair CH.250	B. F. Arnall
	G-BTYA	Bell 212	Bristow Helicopters Ltd/Redhill
	G-BTYB	Cessna 150L	JJ Aviation
	G-BTYC	Cessna 150L	JJ Aviation
	G-BTYD	Cameron N-90 balloon	S. J. Colin
	G-BTYE	Cameron A-180 balloon	Fight Flight
	G-BTYF	Thunder Ax10-180 S2 balloon	Champagne Flights International Ltd
	G-BTYG	BAe Jetstream 3100	British Aerospace PLC
	G-BTYH	Pottier P.80S	R. Pickett
	G-BTYI	PA-28-181 Archer II	Premier Flight Services Ltd
	G-BTYJ	Schleicher ASH.25	T. I. Gardiner
	G-BTYK	Cessna 310R	Mondiale Aviation Ltd
	G-BTYL	Hunter T.7	Cubitt Aviation Ltd/Foulsham
	G-BTYN	BAe 125-1000A	British Aerospace PLC
	G-BTYO	BAe 125-1000A	British Aerospace PLC
	G-BTYP	BAe 125-1000A	British Aerospace PLC
	G-BTYR	BAe 125-1000A	British Aerospace PLC
	G-BTYS	BAe 125-1000A	British Aerospace PLC
	G-BTYT	Cessna 152	JRB Aviation Ltd/Southend
	G-BTYU	BAe Jetstream 3202	British Aerospace PLC
	G-BTYV	Fokker DR.1 (replica)	A. E. Hutton/North Weald
	G-BTYW	Cessna 120	P. J. Singleton & C. J. Archer
	G-BTYX	Cessna 140	P. J. Singleton & C. J. Archer
	G-BTYY	Curtiss Robin C-2	R. R. L. Windus
	G-BTYZ	Colt 210A balloon	T. M. Donnelly
	G-BTZA	Beech F33A Bonanza	MLP Aviation Ltd/Elstree
	G-BTZB	Yakovlev Yak-50	Patina Ltd/Duxford
	G-BTZC	Colt 90A balloon	P. J. Harlow
	G-BTZD	Yakovlev Yak-1	Historic Aircraft Collection Ltd
	G-BTZE	—	
	G-BTZF	Boeing 737-204ADV	Britannia Airways Ltd *Sir Alliot Verdon Roe* (G-BKHF)/Luton
	G-BTZG	BAe ATP	British Aerospace PLC
	G-BTZH	BAe ATP	British Aerospace PLC
	G-BTZI	BAe ATP	British Aerospace PLC
	G-BTZJ	BAe ATP	British Aerospace PLC
	G-BTZK	BAe ATP	British Aerospace PLC
	G-BTZL	Oldfield Baby Great Lakes	J. M. Roach
	G-BTZM	Boeing Stearman A.75N1	Aerobuild Ltd/Gransden
	G-BTZN	BAe 146-300	Trident Aviation Leasing Services Ltd
	G-BTZO	SOCATA TB.20 Trinidad	C.S.E. Aviation Ltd/Kidlington
	G-BTZP	SOCATA TB.9 Tampico	C.S.E. Aviation Ltd/Kidlington
	G-BTZR	Colt 77B balloon	Thunder & Colt Ltd
	G-BTZS	Colt 77B balloon	Thunder & Colt Ltd
	G-BTZT	BAe Jetstream 3101	British Aerospace PLC
	G-BTZU	Cameron Concept balloon	Cameron Balloons Ltd
	G-BTZV	Cameron V-77 balloon	Cameron Balloons Ltd
	G-BTZW	Piper J-3C-65 Cub	D. A. Woodhams
	G-BTZX	—	
	G-BTZY	Colt 56A balloon	T. M. Donnelly
	G-BTZZ	CFM Streak Shadow	D. R. Stennett
	G-BUAA	Corben Bay Ace D	C. C. & J. M. Lovell
	G-BUAB	Aeronca 11AC Chief	Bailey Aviation Ltd
	G-BUAC	Slingsby T.31 Motor Cadet III	D. A. Wilson
	G-BUAD	Colt AS-105 Mk II airship	Nigs Pertwee Ltd
	G-BUAE	Thunder Ax8-105 S2 balloon	T. Donnelly
	G-BUAF	Cameron N-77 balloon	S. D. Baker
	G-BUAG	Jodel D.18	A. L. Silcox
	G-BUAH	Rotorway Executive 90	I. L. Griffith
	G-BUAI	Everett Srs 3 gyroplane	P. Stanlake
	G-BUAJ	Cameron N-90 balloon	J. R. & S. J. Huggins
	G-BUAK	Thunder Ax8-105 S2 balloon	G. D. & L. Fitzpatrick
	G-BUAL	Colt 105A balloon	H. C. J. Williams
	G-BUAM	Cameron V-77 balloon	Broadland Balloons Ltd
	G-BUAN	Cessna 172N	Bell Aviation
	G-BUAO	Luscombe 8A Silvaire	R. Steel
	G-BUAP	Robin DR.400/180	Aeromarine Ltd
	G-BUAR	V.S.358 Seafire III	Precious Metals Ltd

Reg.	Type	Owner or Operator	Notes
G-BUAS	Thunder Ax10-180 S2 balloon	Scotair Balloons	
G-BUAT	Thunder Ax9-120 balloon	J. Fenton	
G-BUAU	Cameron A-180 balloon	GT Flying Club Ltd	
G-BUAV	Cameron O-105 balloon	K. D. Johnson	
G-BUAW	Pitts S-1C Special	E. J. Hedges	
G-BUAX	Rans S.10 Sakota	J. W. Topham	
G-BUAY	Cameron A-210 balloon	Ballooning World Ltd	
G-BUAZ	Beech F33C Bonanza	MLP Aviation Ltd/Elstree	
G-BUBA	PA-18 Super Cub 150	B. Jackson	
G-BUBL	Thunder Ax8-105 balloon	Moet & Chandon (London) Ltd	
G-BUBU	PA-34-220T Seneca III	Bronor (Holdings) Ltd	
G-BUCA	Cessna A.150K	A. Bucknole	
G-BUCC	C.A.S.A. 1-131E Jungmann 2000	E. J. F. McEntee (G-BUEM)	
G-BUCK	C.A.S.A. 1.131E Jungmann (BU+CK)	Jungmann Flying Group/White Waltham	
G-BUCS	Cessna 150F	A. Bucknole	
G-BUCT	Cessna 150L	A. Bucknole	
G-BUDS	Rand Robinson KR-2	D. W. Munday	
G-BUDY	Colt 17A balloon	Bondbaste Ltd	
G-BUFO	Cameron 70 UFO SS balloon	Airship & Balloon Co·Ltd	
G-BUKK	Bucker Bu133 Jungmeister (U-80)	E. J. F. McEntee/White Waltham	
G-BULL	SA Bulldog 120/128	J. D. Richardson	
G-BUMP	PA-28-181 Archer II	M. Dunlop	
G-BUND	PA-28R-201T Turbo Arrow III	W. S. Stanley	
G-BUNT	AIA Stampe SV-4C	J. F. Graham (G-AYCK)	
G-BUPI	Cameron V-77 balloon	S. A. Masey (G-BOUC)	
G-BURD	Cessna F.172N	RJS Aviation Ltd/Halfpenny Green	
G-BURS	Sikorsky S-76A	Lynton Aviation Ltd (G-OHTL)	
G-BURT	PA-28-161 Warrior II	I. P. Stockwell	
G-BUSB	Airbus A.320-111	British Airways *Isle of Jersey*	
G-BUSC	Airbus A.320-111	British Airways *Isle of Skye*	
G-BUSD	Airbus A.320-111	British Airways *Isle of Mull*	
G-BUSE	Airbus A.320-111	British Airways *Isles of Scilly*	
G-BUSF	Airbus A.320-111	British Airways *Isle of Man*	
G-BUSG	Airbus A.320-211	British Airways *Isle of Wight*	
G-BUSH	Airbus A.320-211	British Airways *Isle of Jura*	
G-BUSI	Airbus A.320-211	British Airways *Isle of Anglesey*	
G-BUSJ	Airbus A.320-211	British Airways *Isle of Sark*	
G-BUSK	Airbus A.320-211	British Airways *Isle of Guernsey*	
G-BUSS	Cameron 90 Bus SS balloon	A. Faulkner	
G-BUSY	Thunder Ax7-77 balloon	M. Drinkwater	
G-BUTE	Anderson EA-1 Kingfisher	T. C. Crawofrd (G-BRCK)	
G-BUTL	PA-24 Comanche 250	D. Buttle (G-ARLB)/Blackbushe	
G-BUTT	Cessna FA.150K	P. L. Borek (G-AXSJ)	
G-BUYI	Thunder Ax7-77 balloon	Chelmsford Management Ltd	
G-BUZI	AS.355F-1 Twin Squirrel	Butane Buzzard Aviation Corp Ltd	
G-BUZZ	AB-206B JetRanger	LTG Aviation Ltd	

Out-of-Sequence Registrations

Notes	Reg.	Type	Owner or Operator
	G-BVAH	Denney Aerocraft Kitfox Mk 3	V. A Hutchinson
	G-BVAN	M.S.892E Rallye 150	C. D. Weiswall
	G-BVAX	Colt 77A balloon	Vax Appliances Ltd
	G-BVER	D.H.C.2 Beaver 1	A. F. Allen (G-BTDM)
	G-BVHM	PA-38-112 Tomahawk	Linkcrest Ltd (G-DCAN)
	G-BVMM	Robin HR.200/100	M. G. Owen
	G-BVMZ	Robin HR.100/210	Chiltern Handbags (London) Ltd
	G-BVPI	Evans VP-1	C. M. Gibson
	G-BVPM	Evans VP-2	P. Marigold
	G-BWAS	PA-31-350 Navajo Chieftain	BWOC Ltd/Bristol
	G-BWAY	Beech A36 Bonanza	Vuewood Ltd
	G-BWBW	Cameron A-180 balloon	Ballooning World Ltd
	G-BWDJ	Jurca MJ.5 Sirocco	A. Burani
	G-BWDT	PA-34-220T Seneca II	Budleigh Estates Ltd (G-BKHS)
	G-BWEC	Cassutt-Colson Variant	N. R. Thomason & M. P. J. Hill
	G-BWFJ	Evans VP-1	G. F. Kennedy
	G-BWHY	Robinson R-22	R. E. Benke
	G-BWJB	Thunder Ax8-105 balloon	Justerini & Brooks Ltd *Whiskey J. & B.*
	G-BWKK	Auster AOP.9 (XP279)	R. W. Fairless & D. R. White
	G-BWMA	Colt 105A balloon	Bristol & West Motor Auction Ltd
	G-BWMB	Jodel D.119	K. Jarman & KM Services Ltd
	G-BWMP	Gulfstream 695A	R. B. Tyler (Plant) Ltd
	G-BWOC	PA-31-350 Navajo Chieftain	BWOC Ltd
	G-BWSI	K&S SA.102.5 Cavalier	B. W. Shaw
	G-BWTX	PA-42-720 Cheyenne III	Broome & Wellington (Aviation) Ltd
	G-BWVE	Bell 206B JetRanger	Willow Vale Electronics Ltd (G-BOSX)
	G-BWWJ	Hughes 269C	Dave Nieman Models Ltd (G-BMYZ)
	G-BWWW	BAe Jetstream 3102	British Aerospace PLC/Dunsfold
	G-BXAX	Cameron N-77 balloon	Flying Pictures Ltd
	G-BXPS	PA-23 Aztec 250	N. H. Bailey (G-AYLY)
	G-BXVI	V.S.361 Spitfire F.XVI (RW386)	D. Arnold
	G-BYAA	Boeing 767-204ER	Britannia Airways Ltd/Luton
	G-BYAB	Boeing 767-204ER	Britannia Airways Ltd/Luton
	G-BYAC	Boeing 767-204ER	Britannia Airways Ltd/Luton
	G-BYAD	Boeing 767-204ER	Britannia Airways Ltd/Luton
	G-BYAE	Boeing 767-204ER	Britannia Airways Ltd/Luton
	G-BYAF	Boeing 767-204ER	Britannia Airways Ltd/Luton
	G-BYEE	Mooney M.20K	Axe & Status Ltd
	G-BYIJ	C.A.S.A. 1-131E Jungmann 2000	K. B. Palmer
	G-BYLL	F.8L Falco	N. J. Langrick/Sherburn
	G-BYLS	Bede BD-4	G. H. Bayliss
	G-BYNG	Cessna T.303	J. M. E. Byng (G-PTWB)
	G-BYOL	Cessna 340A	Jetline Ltd
	G-BYRD	Mooney M.20K	V. J. Holden/Teesside
	G-BYRE	Rans S.10 Sakota	R. J. & M. B. Trickey
	G-BYRN	PA-31-350 Navajo Chieftain	Byrne Group PLC (G-YLAN)
	G-BYSE	AB-206B JetRanger 2	Bewise Ltd (G-BFND)
	G-BYSL	Cameron O-56 balloon	Charles of the Ritz Ltd
	G-BYTE	Robinson R-22B	Datel Electronics Ltd
	G-BZAC	Sikorsky S-76A	British International Helicopters Ltd
	G-BZBH	Thunder Ax6-65 balloon	R. B. & G. Clarke
	G-BZKK	Cameron V-56 balloon	P. J. Green & C. Bosley *Gemini II*
	G-BZZZ	Enstrom F-28C-UK	Chartec Ltd (G-BBBZ)
	G-CAFZ	PA-31-350 Navajo Chieftain	Capital Asset Finance Ltd (G-BPPT)
	G-CALL	PA-23 Aztec 250F	Woodgate Aviation Ltd/Ronaldsway
	G-CALV	PA-39 Twin Comanche 160 C/R	JC Crop Services Ltd (G-AZFO)
	G-CAMM	Hawker Cygnet (replica)	D. M. Cashmore
	G-CAPT	Taylor JT.2 Titch	V. W. B. Davies (G-BTJM)
	G-CAXF	Cameron O-77 balloon	R. D. & S. J. Sarjeant
	G-CAYN	Dornier Do.228-201	Cayenne Ltd (G-MLNR)
	G-CBEA	BAe Jetstream 3102-01	Birmingham European Airways Ltd
	G-CBIL	Cessna 182K	K. A. Clarke/Newcastle
	G-CBJB	Sikorsky S-76A	Bond Helicopters Ltd
	G-CBKT	Cameron O-77 balloon	Caledonian Airways Ltd
	G-CBOR	Cessna F.172N	J. Seville
	G-CCAR	Cameron N-77 balloon	The Colt Car Co Ltd
	G-CCCC	Cessna 172H	K. E. Wilson

Reg.	Type	Owner or Operator	Notes
G-CCCL	Cessna 500 Citation	Tim Leacock Aircraft Sales Ltd (G-BEIZ)	
G-CCDI	Cameron N-77 balloon	Charles Church Developments PLC	
G-CCIX	V.S.361 Spitfire LF.IX	Charles Church Displays Ltd (G-BIXP)	
G-CCON	Beech F33C Bonanza	P. J. Withinshaw	
G-CCOZ	Monnet Sonerai II	P. R. Cozens	
G-CCUB	Piper J-3C-65 Cub	Cormack (Aircraft Services) Ltd	
G-CCVV	V.S.379 Spitfire FR.XIV	Charles Church Displays Ltd	
G-CDBS	MBB Bo 105DBS	Bond Helicopters Ltd/Aberdeen	
G-CDET	Culver LCA Cadet	H. B. Fox/Booker	
G-CDGA	Taylor JT.1 Monoplane	R. M. Larimore	
G-CDGL	Saffery S.330 balloon	C. J. Dodd & G. J. Luckett *Penny*	
G-CDON	PA-28-161 Warrior II	East Midlands Flying Club PLC	
G-CDOS	Beech 95-58 Baron	Astra Aviation Ltd	
G-CDRU	C.A.S.A. 1-131E Jungmann	P. Cunniff/White Waltham	
G-CEAS	HPR-7 Herald 214	Channel Express PLC (G-BEBB)/ Bournemouth	
G-CEGA	PA-34-200T Seneca II	Hendefern Ltd	
G-CEJA	Cameron V-77 balloon	N. L. Jaques (G-BTOF)	
G-CELL	PA-32R-301 Saratoga SP	CEL Electronics Ltd	
G-CERT	Mooney M.20K	Fairline Boats PLC/Conington	
G-CETC	Aeronca 15AC Sedan	J. W. Scale	
G-CEXP	HPR-7 Herald 209	Channel Express PLC (G-BFRJ)/ Bournemouth	
G-CFBI	Colt 56A balloon	G. A. Fisher	
G-CFLT	AS.355F-1 Twin Squirrel	Filemart Ltd (G-BNBI)	
G-CFLY	Cessna 172F	I. Hughes & B. T. Williams	
G-CGHM	PA-28 Cherokee 140	CGH Managements Ltd/Elstree	
G-CGOD	Cameron N-77 balloon	Abbey Plant Co Ltd	
G-CHAA	Cameron O-90 balloon	Cloudhoppers Ltd	
G-CHAL	Robinson R-22B	Chalrey Ltd	
G-CHAR	Grob G.109B	RAFGSA/Bicester	
G-CHAS	PA-28-181 Archer II	C. H. Elliott	
G-CHEM	PA-34-200T Seneca II	B. Butler	
G-CHIK	Cessna F.152	Stapleford Flying Club Ltd (G-BHAZ)	
G-CHIL	Robinson R-22HP	Skyline Helicopters Ltd	
G-CHIP	PA-28-181 Archer II	C. M. Hough/Fairoaks	
G-CHIS	Robinson R-22B	Bradmore Helicopter Leasing	
G-CHLT	Stemme S.10	F. C. Y. Cheung/Hong Kong	
G-CHOK	Cameron V-77 balloon	K. W. Overton	
G-CHOP	Westland-Bell 47G-3B1	P. A. Boitel-Gill	
G-CHRO	Thunder & Colt Flying Book SS balloon	Chronicle Communications Ltd	
G-CHRP	Colt Flying Book SS balloon	Chronicle Communications Ltd	
G-CHRR	Colt Flying Book SS balloon	Chronicle Communications Ltd	
G-CHSR	BAe 146-200	Air UK Ltd/Norwich	
G-CHTA	AA-5A Cheetah	Rapid Spin Ltd (G-BFRC)/Biggin Hill	
G-CHTT	Varga 2150A Kachina	C.H.T. Trace	
G-CHUB	Colt N-51 balloon	Chubb Fire Security Ltd	
G-CHYL	Robinson R-22B	L. M. Dresher	
G-CIAS	BN-2B-21 Islander	Channel Island Air Search Ltd (G-BKJM)	
G-CICI	Cameron R-15 balloon	Ballooning Endeavours Ltd	
G-CIII	Oldfield Baby Great Lakes	G. Cooper	
G-CIPI	AJEP Wittman W.8 Tailwind	G. J. Z. Cipirski (G-AYDU)/Biggin Hill	
G-CITI	Cessna 501 Citation	Messenger Group PLC	
G-CITY	PA-31-350 Navajo Chieftain	Woodgate Aviation Ltd/Ronaldsway	
G-CJBC	PA-28 Cherokee 180	J. B. Cave/Halfpenny Green	
G-CJCI	Pilatus P2-06 (CC+43)	Charles Church Displays Ltd	
G-CJET	Learjet 35A	Interflight (Learjet) Ltd (G-SEBE/G-ZIPS/ G-ZONE)/Gatwick	
G-CJIM	Taylor JT.1 Monoplane	J. Crawford	
G-CJUD	Denney Aerocraft Kitfox	C. W. Judge	
G-CJWS	PA-34-200T Seneca II	C. J. Williams (Electrical) Ltd	
G-CKEN	Wombat autogyro	K. H. Durran	
G-CLAC	PA-28-161 Warrior II	J. D. Moonie	
G-CLEA	PA-28-161 Warrior II	Creative Logistics Enterprises & Aviation Ltd & R. J. Harrison	
G-CLEM	Bo 208A2 Junior	A. W. Webster (G-ASWE)	
G-CLIC	Cameron N-105 balloon	Matrix Computer Maintenance Ltd	
G-CLIK	PA-18 Super Cub 95	N. J. R. Empson/Ipswich	
G-CLIV	PA-28R-201T Turbo Arrow III	C. R. Harrisson	
G-CLOS	PA-34-200 Seneca II	Greenclose Aviation Services Ltd/ Bournemouth	
G-CLRL	Agusta A.109A-II	MDFC Asset Finance Ltd (G-EJCB)	

Notes	Reg.	Type	Owner or Operator
	G-CLUB	Cessna FRA.150M	J. J. Woodhouse
	G-CLUX	Cessna F.172N	J. & K. Aviation/Liverpool
	G-CLYV	Robinson R-22B	C. A. Ecroyd
	G-CMDR	R. Commander 114	J. D. Hallahan & G. C. Bishop
	G-CMGC	PA-25 Pawnee 235	Midland Gliding Club Ltd/Long Mynd
	G-CNIS	Partenavia P.68B	Beechair Ltd (G-BJOF/G-PAUL)
	G-CNMF	BAe 146-200	Air UK Ltd *Vincent Van Gogh*/Norwich
	G-COCO	Cessna F.172M	P. C. Sheard & R. C. Larder
	G-COES	McD Douglas MD-83	Airtours International Aviation Ltd
	G-COIN	Bell 206B JetRanger 2	British Helicopter Service
	G-COKE	Cameron O-65 balloon	M. C. Bradley
	G-COLL	Enstrom 280C-UK-2 Shark	Estate Computer Systems Ltd
	G-COLR	Colt 69A balloon	Graeme Scaife Productions Ltd
	G-COMB	PA-30 Twin Comanche 160B	J. T. Bateson (G-AVBL)/Ronaldsway
	G-COMM	PA-23 Aztec 250C	M. G. Wild (G-AZMG)
	G-COMP	Cameron N-90 balloon	Computacenter Ltd
	G-CONC	Cameron N-90 balloon	British Airways
	G-COOK	Cameron N-77 balloon	IAZ (International) Ltd
	G-COOP	Cameron N-31 balloon	Aire Valley Balloons
	G-COPS	Piper J-3C-65 Cub	R. W. Sproat & C. E. Simpson
	G-COPY	AA-5A Cheetah	Emberden Ltd (G-BIEU)/Biggin Hill
	G-CORC	Bell 206B JetRanger 2	Air Corcoran Ltd (G-CJHI/G-BBFB)
	G-CORD	Slingsby T.66 Nipper 3	B. A. Wright (G-AVTB)
	G-CORK	Air Command 532 Elite	D. N. B. McCorquodale
	G-COTT	Cameron 60 Cottage SS balloon	Nottingham Hot-Air Balloon Club
	G-COWE	Beech C90A King Air	Cowie Aviation Ltd/Newcastle
	G-COWI	Cessna 414A	Milegood Ltd (G-MLCS/G-MHGI/G-BHKK)
	G-COWS	ARV Super 2	T. C. Harrold (G-BONB)
	G-COWZ	Bell 206B JetRanger	Grampian Helicopter Charter Ltd (G-BRDK)
	G-COYS	Colt 42A balloon	Thunder & Colt Ltd
	G-CPCD	CEA DR.221	J. C. Jess & ptnrs
	G-CPFC	Cessna F.152	Falcon Flying Services/Biggin Hill
	G-CPLI	Robinson R-22B	Clifford Packaging Ltd
	G-CPTL	Short SD3-60	Shorts Aircraft Financing Ltd (G-BOFI)
	G-CPTM	PA-28-151 Warrior	T. J. Mackay & C. M. Pollett (G-BTOE)
	G-CPTS	AB-206B JetRanger 2	A. R. B. Aspinall
	G-CRAK	Cameron N-77 balloon	Mobile Windscreens Ltd
	G-CRAN	Robin R.1180T	D. S. Watson
	G-CRAY	Robinson R-22B	Hecray Ltd
	G-CRES	Denney Aerocraft Kitfox	R. J. Cresswell
	G-CRIL	R. Commander 112B	Rockwell Aviation Group/Cardiff
	G-CRIS	Taylor JT.1 Monoplane	C. R. Steer
	G-CRUS	Cessna T.303	B. A. Groves
	G-CRUZ	Cessna T.303	Bank Farm Ltd
	G-CRZY	Thunder Ax8-105 balloon	R. Carr (G-BDLP)/France
	G-CSBM	Cessna F.150M	S. Warwickshire Flying School
	G-CSCS	Cessna F.172N	Conegate Ltd
	G-CSFC	Cessna 150L	Shropshire Aero Club Ltd
	G-CSFT	PA-23 Aztec 250D	Islerealm Ltd (G-AYKU)
	G-CSJH	BAe 146-200	Air UK Ltd/Norwich
	G-CSNA	Cessna 421C	Zulu Airlines Ltd
	G-CSZB	V.807B Viscount	British Air Ferries *Viscount Scotland* (G-AOXU)/Southend
	G-CTCL	SOCATA TB.10 Tobago	Merryfield Leasing Ltd (G-BSIV)
	G-CTIX	V.S.509 Spitfire T.IX (PT462)	Charles Church Displays Ltd
	G-CTKL	CCF Harvard IV (54137)	G. J. & S. P. Keegan
	G-CTOY	Denney Aerocraft Kitfox Mk 3	G. S. Cass
	G-CTRN	Enstrom F-28C-UK	Manchester Helicopter Centre/Barton
	G-CTRX	H.P.137 Jetstream 200	Centrax Ltd (G-BCWW/G-AXUN)/Exeter
	G-CUBB	PA-18 Super Cub 180	G. J. Busby/Booker
	G-CUBI	PA-18 Super Cub 135 (51-15673)	T. Watson
	G-CUBJ	PA-18 Super Cub 150	A. K. Leasing (Jersey) Ltd
	G-CUGA	GA-7 Cougar	Teesside Flight Centre Ltd
	G-CULL	Bell 206B JetRanger	Dollar Air Services Ltd (G-BEWY)/Coventry
	G-CURE	Colt 77A balloon	Flying Pictures (Balloons) Ltd
	G-CWOT	Currie Wot	D. A. Lord
	G-CXCX	Cameron N-90 balloon	Cathay Pacific Airways (London) Ltd
	G-CYLS	Cessna T.303	Gledhill Water Storage Ltd & M. F. Joseph (G-BKXI)/Blackpool
	G-CYMA	GA-7 Cougar	Cyma Petroleum Ltd (G-BKOM)/Elstree
	G-CZAR	Cessna 560 Citation V	Aviation Beauport Ltd/Jersey

Reg.	Type	Owner or Operator	Notes
G-DAAH	PA-28RT-201T Turbo Arrow IV	R. Peplow	
G-DACA	P.57 Sea Prince T.1 ★	P. G. Vallance Ltd/Charlwood	
G-DACC	Cessna 401B	Niglon Ltd (G-AYOU)/Birmingham	
G-DADS	Hughes 369HS	B. Wronski	
G-DAFT	AS.355F-2 Twin Squirrel	Powersense Ltd (G-BNNN)/Hayes	
G-DAJB	Boeing 757-2T7	Monarch Airlines Ltd/Luton	
G-DAKS	Dakota 3 (TS423)	Aces High Ltd/North Weald	
G-DAMI	Robinson R-22B	Aramerco Ltd	
G-DAND	SOCATA TB.10 Tobago	Whitemoor Engineering Co Ltd	
G-DANN	Stampe SV-4B	I. M. White	
G-DARA	PA-34-220T Seneca III	Sunspot Investments Ltd	
G-DARE	PA-34-200T Seneca II	Diamond Airways Ltd (G-WOTS/G-SEVL)	
G-DARL	PA-28 Cherokee 180C	A. R. Liyanage	
G-DASH	R. Commander 112A	Josef D. J. Jons & Co Ltd (G-BDAJ)	
G-DASI	Short SD3-60	Air UK Ltd (G-BKKW)/Norwich	
G-DASU	Cameron V-77 balloon	D. & L. S. Litchfield	
G-DAVE	Jodel D.112	D. A. Porter/Sturgate	
G-DBAF	BAC One-Eleven 201AC	British Air Ferries Ltd (G-ASJG)/Stansted	
G-DBAL	H.S.125 Srs 3B	Osprey Aviation Ltd (G-BSAA)	
G-DBAR	Beech 200 Super King Air	Brown & Root (UK) Ltd	
G-DBII	Cessna 560 Citation V	Artix Ltd	
G-DBMS	Cessna U.206G	BMS Electrical Services Ltd	
G-DCAC	McD Douglas MD-83	Airtours International Aviation Ltd	
G-DCCH	MBB Bo 105D	Devon & Cornwall Police Authority	
G-DCEA	PA-34-200T Seneca II	M. J. Greasby	
G-DCFB	Cessna 425	Foodbrokers Ltd (G-BMSH)	
G-DCIO	Douglas DC-10-30	British Airways *Epping Forest*/Gatwick	
G-DCKK	Cessna F.172N	A. R. Mead/Clacton	
G-DCOX	PA-31-310 Turbo Navajo	Porten Holdings Ltd	
G-DCSW	PA-32R-301 Saratoga SP	Samworth Bros Ltd	
G-DCXL	Jodel D.140C	P. Underhill	
G-DDAY	PA-28R-201T Turbo Arrow III	W. Haynes (G-BPDO)	
G-DDCD	D.H.104 Dove 8	C. Daniel (G-ARUM)/Biggin Hill	
G-DDMV	NA T-6G Texan	E. A. Morgan	
G-DEBB	Beech 35-B33 Debonair	Spitfire Aviation Ltd/Bournemouth	
G-DELB	Robinson R-22B	Osprey Helicopters Ltd	
G-DELI	Thunder Ax7-77 balloon	Heather Flight Ltd	
G-DELL	Robinson R-22B	Delta Helicopters Ltd/Luton	
G-DELS	Robin DR.400/180	W. D. Nightingale	
G-DELT	Robinson R-22B	Mortec Services	
G-DELY	Cessna TU.206G	G. Dommett	
G-DEMH	Cessna F.172M	M. Hammond (G-BFLO)	
G-DEMO	BN-2T Islander	Pilatus BN Ltd (G-BKEA)/Bembridge	
G-DENS	Binder CP.301S Smaragd	W. St G. V. Stoney	
G-DENW	PA-44-180 Seminole	D. A. Woodhams	
G-DERV	Cameron Truck SS balloon	The Hot Air Balloon Co Ltd	
G-DESI	Aero Designs Pulsar XP	D. F. Gaughan	
G-DESS	Mooney M.20J	W. E. Newnes	
G-DEVS	PA-28 Cherokee 180	180 Group (G-BGVJ)	
G-DEXP	ARV Super 2	J. P. Jenkins	
G-DEXY	Beech E90 King Air	Tornado Ltd	
G-DFLT	Cessna F.406 Caravan II	Direct Flight Ltd/Norwich	
G-DFLY	PA-38-112 Tomahawk	I. R. March & N. W. Woodward	
G-DEMH	Cessna F.172M (modified)	M. Hammond (G-BFLO)	
G-DFVA	Cessna R.172K	R. A. Plowright	
G-DGDG	Glaser-Dirks DG.400/17	DG400 Flying Group/Lasham	
G-DGLD	HPR-7 Herald 214	Channel Express Group PLC (G-BAVX) Bournemouth	
G-DGWW	Rand Robinson KR-2	W. Wilson	
G-DHCB	D.H.C.2 Beaver 1	Sealife Ltd (G-BTDL)	
G-DHCI	D.H.C.1 Chipmunk 22	C. J. Crooks (G-BBSE)	
G-DHSW	Boeing 737-3Y0	Monarch Airlines/EuroBerlin	
G-DHTM	D.H.82A Tiger Moth replica	E. G. Waite-Roberts	
G-DHVV	D.H.115 Vampire T.55	Lindsay Wood Promotions Ltd	
G-DHWW	D.H.115 Vampire T.55	Lindsay Wood Promotions Ltd	
G-DHXX	D.H.100 Vampire FB.6	Lindsay Wood Promotions Ltd	
G-DHZZ	D.H.115 Vampire T.55	Lindsay Wood Promotions Ltd	
G-DIAL	Cameron N-90 balloon	Datacentre Ltd	
G-DIAN	Extra EA.230	D. M. Britten	
G-DIAT	PA-28 Cherokee 140	RAF Benevolent Fund's IAT/Bristol & Wessex Aeroplane Club (G-BCGK)/ Lulsgate	
G-DICK	Thunder Ax6-56Z balloon	R. D. Sargeant	

Notes	Reg.	Type	Owner or Operator
	G-DIME	R. Commander 114	Badminton Horse Boxes Ltd
	G-DINA	AA-5B Tiger	J. D. Poole & ptnrs
	G-DING	Colt 77A balloon	G. J. Bell
	G-DINT	B.156 Beaufighter 1F	T. E. Moore
	G-DIPI	Cameron Tub SS balloon	Airship & Balloon Co Ltd
	G-DIPS	Taylor JT.1 Monoplane	B. J. Halls
	G-DIPZ	Colt 17A balloon	Airship & Balloon Co Ltd
	G-DIRE	Robinson R-22B	Direct Self Drive Ltd
	G-DIRK	Glaser-Dirks DG.400	D. M. Chalmers
	G-DIRT	Thunder Ax7-77Z balloon	R. J. Ngbaronye
	G-DISC	Cessna U.206A	I. A. Louttit (G-BGWR)/Exeter
	G-DISK	PA-24 Comanche 250	M. A. McLoughlin (G-APZG)/Booker
	G-DISO	Jodel D.150	P. F. Craven & J. H. Shearer
	G-DIVA	Cessna R.172K XPII	R. A. Plowright & J. A. Kaye/Biggin Hill
	G-DIWY	PA-32 Cherokee Six 300	Industrial Foam Systems Ltd
	G-DIXI	PA-31-350 Navajo Chieftain	Birmingham Aviation Ltd
	G-DIZO	Jodel D.120	D. Aldersea (G-EMKM)
	G-DIZY	PA-28R-201T Turbo Arrow III	Medway Arrow Group
	G-DJEM	AS.350B Ecureuil	Maynard & Harris Plastics Ltd (G-ZBAC/ G-SEBI/G-BMCU)
	G-DJHB	Beech A23-19 Musketeer	M. Wells & J. H. Prankerd (G-AZZE)/Lydd
	G-DJIM	MHCA-I	J. Crawford
	G-DJJA	PA-28-181 Archer II	S. J. Lucas
	G-DJLW	H.S.125 Srs 3B/RA	Lindsay Wood Promotions Ltd (G-AVVB)
	G-DJNH	Denney Aerocraft Kitfox	D. J. N. Hall
	G-DKDP	Grob G.109	Diss Aviation Ltd/Tibenham
	G-DKGF	Viking Dragonfly	K. G. Fathers
	G-DLOM	SOCATA TB.20 Trinidad	J. N. A. Adderley/Guernsey
	G-DLTA	Slingsby T.67M	Sherwood Flying Club Ltd (G-SFTX)
	G-DLTI	Robinson R-22B	Springfield Aviation Ltd
	G-DMCH	Hiller UH-12E	D. McK. Carnegie & ptnrs
	G-DMCS	PA-28R Cherokee Arrow 200-II	D. L. Johns & F. K. Parker (G-CPAC)
	G-DNCS	PA-28R-201T Turbo Arrow III	BRT Arrow Ltd/Barton
	G-DNLD	Cameron 97 Donald SS balloon	The Walt Disney Co Ltd
	G-DNVT	G.1159C Gulfstream IV	Shell Aircraft Ltd/Heathrow
	G-DOCA	Boeing 737-436	British Airways
	G-DOCB	Boeing 737-436	British Airways *River Bush*
	G-DOCC	Boeing 737-436	British Airways
	G-DOCD	Boeing 737-436	British Airways
	G-DOCE	Boeing 737-436	British Airways
	G-DOCF	Boeing 737-436	British Airways
	G-DOCG	Boeing 737-436	British Airways
	G-DOCH	Boeing 737-436	British Airways
	G-DOCI	Boeing 737-436	British Airways
	G-DOCJ	Boeing 737-436	British Airways
	G-DOCK	Boeing 737-436	British Airways
	G-DOCL	Boeing 737-436	British Airways
	G-DOCM	Boeing 737-436	British Airways
	G-DOCN	Boeing 737-436	British Airways
	G-DOCO	Boeing 737-436	British Airways
	G-DOCP	Boeing 737-436	British Airways
	G-DOCR	Boeing 737-436	British Airways
	G-DOCS	Boeing 737	British Airways
	G-DOCT	Boeing 737	British Airways
	G-DOCU	Boeing 737	British Airways
	G-DOCV	Boeing 737	British Airways
	G-DOCW	Boeing 737	British Airways
	G-DOCX	Boeing 737	British Airways
	G-DOCY		British Airways
	G-DOCZ		British Airways
	G-DODD	Cessna F.172P-II	K. Watts/Elstree
	G-DODS	PA-46-310P Malibu	HPM Investments Ltd
	G-DOFY	Bell 206B JetRanger	Cinnamond Ltd
	G-DOGS	Cessna R.182RG	P. Bennett & J. R. Shawe
	G-DOLR	AS.355F-1 Twin Squirrel	Dollar Air Services Ltd (G-BPVB)
	G-DONA	Cessna 152	Franchi Aviation Ltd (G-BIDH)
	G-DONS	PA-28RT-201T Turbo Arrow IV	D. J. Murphy
	G-DOOR	M.S.893E Rallye 180GT	Lynair Flying Group
	G-DOOZ	AS.355F-2 Twin Squirrel	Lynton Aviation Ltd (G-BNSX)
	G-DORB	Bell 206B JetRanger 3	Dorb Crest Homes Ltd
	G-DORK	EMB-110P1 Bandeirante	Aero Services (E. Midlands) Ltd
	G-DOSH	D.H.C.6 Twin Otter 210	Tech Air (Cambridge) Ltd/Southend
	G-DOVE	Cessna 182Q	P. J. Contracting

Reg.	Type	Owner or Operator	Notes
G-DOWN	Colt 31A	M. Williams	
G-DPPA	Bell 206B JetRanger 3	Dyfed-Powys Police Authority	
G-DRAC	Cameron Dracular Skull SS balloon	Shiplake Investments Ltd	
G-DRAG	Cessna 152 (tailwheel)	Roger Clark Mechanical Engineering Ltd (G-BRNF)	
G-DRAI	Robinson R-22B	D. R. Anthony Builders Ltd	
G-DRAW	Colt 77A balloon	Readers Digest Association Ltd	
G-DRAY	Taylor JT.1 Monoplane	L. J. Dray	
G-DRGN	Cameron N-105 balloon	W. I. Hooker & C. Parker	
G-DRJC	Boeing 757-2T7	Monarch Airlines Ltd/Luton	
G-DRNT	Sikorsky S-76A	Bond Helicopters Ltd/Aberdeen	
G-DROP	Cessna U.206C	I. A. Louttit (G-UKNO/G-BAMN)	
G-DRSV	CEA DR.315 (modified)	R. S. Voice	
G-DRYI	Cameron N-77 balloon	J. Barbour & Sons Ltd	
G-DRZF	CEA DR.360	C. A. Parker/Sywell	
G-DSAM	AS.350B Ecureuil	PLM Helicopters Ltd	
G-DSGN	Robinson R-22B	William Towns Ltd	
G-DTOO	PA-38-112 Tomahawk	A. Todd	
G-DUCH	Beech 76 Duchess	Carriage Communications Consultancy Ltd	
G-DUCK	Grumman G.44 Widgeon	L. E. Usher/Ipswich	
G-DUDS	C.A.S.A. 1-131E Jungmann 2000	D. H. Pattison	
G-DUET	Wood Duet	C. Wood	
G-DUGY	Emstrom 280C-UK-2 Shark	Pool Helicopter Services UK Ltd (G-BEEL)	
G-DUNN	Zenair CH.250	A. Dunn	
G-DURX	Thunder 77A balloon	V. Trimble	
G-DUST	Stolp SA.300 Starduster Too	J. V. George	
G-DUVL	Cessna F.172N	A. J. Simpson/Denham	
G-DVON	D.H.104 Devon C.2 (VP955)	C. L. Thatcher	
G-DWHH	Boeing 737-2T7	Monarch Airlines Ltd/Luton	
G-DWMI	Bell 206L-1 LongRanger	Glenwood Helicopters Ltd/Fairoaks	
G-DXRG	Cameron 105 Agfa SS balloon	Cameron Balloons Ltd	
G-DYNE	Cessna 414	Commair Aviation Ltd/E. Midlands	
G-DYOU	PA-38-112 Tomahawk	Airways Aero Associations Ltd/Booker	
G-EAGL	Cessna 421C	Premi-Air Management/Leeds	
G-EBJI	Hawker Cygnet Replica	A. V. Francis	
G-ECAV	Beech 200 Super King Air	GEC Avionics Ltd/Rochester	
G-ECBH	Cessna F.150K	Air Fenland Ltd	
G-ECGC	Cessna F.172N-II	Leicestershire Aero Club Ltd	
G-ECGO	Bo208C Junior	M. F. R. B. Collett	
G-ECHO	Enstrom 280C-UK-2 Shark	ALP Electrical (Maidenhead) Ltd (G-LONS/G-BDIB)/White Waltham	
G-ECJM	PA-28R-201T Turbo Arrow III	Anglosky (G-FESL/G-BNRN)	
G-ECKO	Colt 180A balloon	T. Donnelly	
G-ECOX	Grega GN.1 Air Camper	H. C. Cox	
G-EDDI	Robinson R-22B	Serve Offer Ltd	
G-EDEN	SOCATA TB.10 Tobago	Group Eden/Elstree	
G-EDGE	Jodel D.150	A. D. Edge	
G-EDIT	Beech B95 TravelAir	Warrior Aircraft Sales & Leasing Ltd (G-AXUX)	
G-EDNA	PA-38-112 Tomahawk	MSF Aviation Algarve Ltd	
G-EDOT	Cessna T.337D	A. Brinkley (G-BJIY)	
G-EDRY	Cessna T.303	Pat Eddery Ltd	
G-EEEE	Slingsby T.31 Motor Glider	R. F. Selby	
G-EEGE	Robinson R-22A	The Helicentre (G-BKZK)/Blackpool	
G-EEGL	Christen Eagle II	A. J. Wilson	
G-EENY	GA-7 Cougar	BLS Aviation Ltd/Elstree	
G-EEUP	SNCAN Stampe SV-4C	A. M. Wajih	
G-EEVS	Agusta A.109A Srs II	Wilkes Asset Management Ltd (G-OTSL)	
G-EEZE	Rutan Vari-Eze	A. J. Nurse	
G-EFRY	Rand Robinson KR-2	—	
G-EFTE	Bolkow Bo 207	N. J. Heaton	
G-EGAP	Sequoia F.8L Falco	E. G. A. Prance	
G-EGEE	Cessna 310Q	A. J. Fuller & ptnrs (G-AZVY)	
G-EGEL	Christen Eagle II	MLP Aviation Ltd/Elstree	
G-EGGS	Robin DR.400/180	R. Foot	
G-EGJA	SOCATA TB.20 Trinidad	D. A. Williamson/Alderney	
G-EGLD	PA-28-161 Cadet	J. Appleton	
G-EGLE	Christen Eagle II	R. L. Mitcham & H. Odone/Elstree	
G-EHAP	Sportavia-Pützer RF.7	Old Sarum Fornie Group	
G-EHBJ	C.A.S.A. 1-131E Jungmann 2000	Mangreen Holdings Ltd	
G-EHIL	Westland-Agusta EH.101	Westland Helicopters Ltd/Yeovil	

Notes	Reg.	Type	Owner or Operator
	G-EHMM	Robin DR.400/180R	Booker Gliding Club Ltd
	G-EIIR	Cameron N-77 balloon	Major C. J. T. Davey *Silver Jubilee*
	G-EIST	Robinson R-22B	European Executive Ltd
	G-EITE	Luscombe 8A Silvaire	D. L. Eite
	G-EIWT	Cessna FR.182RG	P. P. D. Howard-Johnston/Edinburgh
	G-EJET	Cessna 550 Citation II	European Jet Ltd (G-DJBE)
	G-EJGO	Z.226HE Trener	N. J. Radford
	G-ELAN	Boeing Stearman B.75N-1 (361)	D. J. Ashley
	G-ELBC	PA-34-200 Seneca II	Stapleford Flying Club Ltd (G-BANS)
	G-ELDG	Douglas DC-9-32	British Midland Airways Ltd *The Orloff Diamond*/E. Midlands
	G-ELDH	Douglas DC-9-32	British Midland Airways Ltd *The Hastings Diamond*/E. Midlands
	G-ELDI	Douglas DC-9-32	British Midland Airways Ltd *The Regent Diamond*/E. Midlands
	G-ELEC	Westland WG.30 Srs 200	Westland Helicopters Ltd (G-BKNV)/Yeovil
	G-ELFI	Robinson R-22B	P. J. Paine
	G-ELIZ	Denney Aerocraft Kitfox	A. J. Ellis
	G-ELOT	Cessna 550 Citation II	Elliotts Brick Ltd
	G-ELRA	BAe 125-1000	British Aerospace PLC
	G-EMAK	PA-28R-201 Arrow III	Arrow Aircraft Group/E. Midlands
	G-EMAZ	PA-28-181 Archer II	Emmair Ltd
	G-EMER	PA-34-200 Seneca II	Clydeside Surveys Ltd/Glasgow
	G-EMMA	Cessna F.182Q	Watkiss Group Aviation
	G-EMMS	PA-38-112 Tomahawk	G. C. J. Moffatt & Co Ltd/Cardiff
	G-EMMY	Rutan Vari-Eze	M. J. Tooze
	G-EMSY	D.H.82A Tiger Moth	B. E. Micklewright (G-ASPZ)
	G-ENAM	Cessna 340A	Freeway Rentals Ltd
	G-ENCE	Partenavia P.68B	P. Davies(G-OROY/G-BFSU)
	G-ENIE	Tipsy T.66 Nipper 3	I. D. Daniels
	G-ENII	Cessna F.172M	J. Howley
	G-ENNA	PA-28-161 Warrior II	A. J. Wood
	G-ENNY	Cameron V-77 balloon	B. G. Jones
	G-ENOA	Cessna F.172F	M. K. Acors (G-ASZW)
	G-ENRY	Cameron N-105 balloon	Numatic International Ltd
	G-ENSI	Beech F33A Bonanza	Special Analysis & Simulation Technology Ltd
	G-ENUS	Cameron N-90 balloon	The Hot-Air Balloon Co Ltd
	G-EOCO	Boeing 707-338C	Anglo Airlines Ltd/Gatwick
	G-EOFF	Taylor JT.2 Titch	G. H. Wylde
	G-EORG	PA-38-112 Tomahawk	Airways Aero Association/Booker
	G-EPDI	Cameron N-77 balloon	R. Moss & Pegasus Aviation Ltd
	G-ERIC	R. Commander 112TC	P. P. Patterson/Newcastle
	G-ERIK	Cameron N-77 balloon	Cultural Resource Management Ltd
	G-ERIX	Boeing Stearman A75N-1	E. E. Rix
	G-ERMO	ARV Super 2	Kenbal Properties Ltd & J. O. Hodgson (G-BMWK)
	G-ERMS	Thunder AS-33 airship	B. R. & M. Boyle
	G-ERNI	PA-28-181 Archer II	E. L. Collins (G-OSSY)
	G-EROS	Cameron H-34 balloon	Evening Standard Co Ltd
	G-ERRY	AA-5B Tiger	P. D. Cullen (G-BFMJ)
	G-ERTY	D.H.82A Tiger Moth	R. F. Tolhurst (G-ANDC)
	G-ESSX	PA-28-161 Warrior II	AT Aviation Ltd (G-BHYY)/Cardiff
	G-ESTE	AA-5A Cheetah	McGeoghan Plant Hire & Excavations Ltd (G-GHNC)
	G-ETBY	PA-32 Cherokee Six 260	Yarnhaven Ltd (G-AWCY)
	G-ETCD	Colt 77A balloon	Philips Electronics Ltd
	G-ETDA	PA-28-161 Warrior II	T. Griffiths
	G-ETDB	PA-38-112 Tomahawk	R. A. Wakefield
	G-ETDC	Cessna 172P	Osprey Air Services Ltd
	G-ETFT	Colt Financial Times SS balloon	Financial Times Ltd (G-BSGZ)
	G-ETIN	Robinson R-22B	E. & I. Whitmore
	G-EURA	Agusta-Bell 47J-2	E. W. Schnedlitz (G-ASNV)
	G-EVAN	Taylor JT.2 Titch	E. Evans
	G-EVER	Robinson R-22B	Everards Brewery Ltd
	G-EWBJ	SOCATA TB.10 Tobago	Longslow Dairy Ltd
	G-EWEL	Sikorsky S-76A	Ratners Group PLC
	G-EWFN	SOCATA TB-20 Trinidad	Trinidad Ltd (G-BRTY)
	G-EWIZ	Pitts S-2E Special	R. H. Jago
	G-EWUD	Cessna F.172F	Parplon Ltd (G-ESSO/G-ATBK)
	G-EXEC	PA-34-200 Seneca	S. J. Green
	G-EXEL	EMB-120RT Brasilia	Air Exel (UK) Ltd/Luton
	G-EXEX	Cessna 404	Atlantic Air Transport Ltd/Coventry

Reg.	Type	Owner or Operator	Notes
G-EXIT	M.S.893E Rallye 180GT	G-Exit Ltd/Rochester	
G-EXLR	BAe 125-1000	British Aerospace PLC	
G-EXOR	Robinson R-22B	Ex-Or Ltd (G-CMCM)	
G-EXPR	Colt 90A balloon	Air Canada Ltd	
G-EYCO	Robin DR.400/180	L. M. Gould	
G-EYES	Cessna 402C	Air Corbiere (G-BLCE)/Coventry	
G-EYRE	Bell 206L-1 LongRanger	Hideroute Ltd (G-STVI)	
G-EZEE	Rutan Vari-Eze	D. & M. Schwier	
G-EZIO	EMB-120RT Brasilia	—	
G-EZOS	Rutan Vari-Eze	O. Smith/Tees-side	
G-FABB	Cameron V-77 balloon	V. P. F. Haines	
G-FABM	Beech 95-B55 Baron	F. B. Miles (G-JOND/G-BMVC)	
G-FAGN	Robinson R-22B	D. L. Weldon	
G-FAIR	SOCATA TB.10 Tobago	Sally Marine Ltd/Guernsey	
G-FALC	Aeromere F.8L Falco	P. W. Hunter (G-AROT)/Elstree	
G-FAMY	Maule M5-180C	Land Reclamation (Southern) Ltd	
G-FANC	Fairchild 24R-46 Argus III	J. I. Hyslop	
G-FANG	AA-5A Cheetah	Church & Co	
G-FANL	Cessna FR.172K XP-II	J. Woodhouse & Co/Staverton	
G-FANN	H.S.125 Srs 600B	Osprey Aviation Ltd (G-BARR)	
G-FARM	SOCATA Rallye 235GT	Bristol Cars Ltd	
G-FARO	Aero Designs Star-Lite SL.1	M. K. Faro	
G-FARR	Jodel D.150	G. H. Farr	
G-FASL	BAe 125 Srs 800B	Fisons PLC/E. Midlands	
G-FAST	Cessna 337G	Seillans Land Investigations Ltd	
G-FAVI	Beech E90 King Air	Flightline Ltd (G-OOAG/G-BAVG)/Southend	
G-FAYE	Cessna F.150M	Cheshire Air Training School Ltd/Liverpool	
G-FBIX	D.H.100 Vampire FB9	D. G. Jones	
G-FBMB	Canadair CL.600-2B16 Challenger	Challenger Aviation Ltd	
G-FBMV	Avro 748 Srs 1	Clewer Aviation Ltd (G-ARMW)	
G-FBWH	PA-28R Cherokee Arrow 180	Servicecentre Systems (Cambs) Ltd	
G-FCHJ	Cessna 340A	P. L. & M. J. E. Builder (G-BJLS)	
G-FCSP	Robin DR.400/180	FCS Photochemicals	
G-FDGM	Beech B60 Duke	Parissi Air Ltd/Perth	
G-FEAD	F.27 Friendship Mk 600	Federal Express/British Air Ferries/*Rick* Southend	
G-FEAE	F.27 Friendship Mk 600	Federal Express/Channel Express (Air Services) Ltd/Bournemouth	
G-FEBE	Cessna 340A	W. P. J. Davison	
G-FEDL	Hughes 369D	Federal Aviation Ltd	
G-FELT	Cameron N-77 balloon	Allan Industries Ltd	
G-FENI	Robinson R-22B	I. Fenwick	
G-FFBR	Thunder Ax8-105 balloon	Fuji Photo Film (UK) Ltd	
G-FFEN	Cessna F.150M	Suffolk Aero Club Ltd/Ipswich	
G-FFLT	H.S.125 Srs 600B	Albion Aviation Management Ltd	
G-FFOR	Cessna 310R	Air Service Training Ltd (G-BMGF)/Perth	
G-FFTI	SOCATA TB.20 Trinidad	Blicqair Ltd	
G-FFTN	Bell 206B JetRanger	Fountain Forestry Ltd	
G-FFWD	Cessna 310R	Keef & Co Ltd (G-TVKE/G-EURO)	
G-FGID	FG-1D Corsair (88297)	Patina Ltd/Duxford	
G-FHAS	Scheibe SF.25E Super Falke	Burn Gliding Club Ltd	
G-FIAT	PA-28 Cherokee 140	RAF Benevolent Fund's IAT/ Bristol & Wessex Aeroplane Club (G-BBYW)/Lulsgate	
G-FIFI	SOCATA TB.20 Trinidad	D. J. & M. Gower (G-BMWS)	
G-FIGA	Cessna 152	G & B Aviation Ltd/Coventry	
G-FIGB	Cessna 152	G & B Aviation Ltd/Coventry	
G-FIJR	L.188C Electra	Air Bridge Carriers Ltd/E Midlands	
G-FIJV	L.188C Electra	Air Bridge Carriers Ltd/E Midlands	
G-FILE	PA-34-200T Seneca	Filemart Ltd	
G-FILO	Robin DR.400/180	F. Friedenberg	
G-FIND	Cessna F.406 Caravan II	Atlantic Air Transport Ltd/Coventry	
G-FINN	Cameron 90 Reindeer SS balloon	Forbes Europe Inc/France	
G-FINS	AB-206B JetRanger 2	R.&M. International Helicopters Ltd (G-FSCL)	
G-FISH	Cessna 310R-II	Bostonair Ltd/Humberside	
G-FISK	Pazmany PL-4A	K. S. Woodard	
G-FISS	Robinson R-22B	B. G. & D. Bushell	
G-FIST	Fieseler Fi.156C Storch	Aero Vintage Ltd	
G-FIZZ	PA-28-161 Warrior II	Arrow Air Centre Ltd/Shipdham	
G-FKKM	PA-28RT-201T Turbo Arrow IV	D. J. Kaye	
G-FLAG	Colt 77A balloon	Thunder & Colt Ltd	

Notes	Reg.	Type	Owner or Operator
	G-FLAK	Beech 95-E55 Baron	S. R. Flack/Elstree
	G-FLCA	Fleet Model 80 Canuck	E. C. Taylor
	G-FLCO	Sequoia F.8L Falco	J. B. Mowforth
	G-FLEA	SOCATA TB.10 Tobago	Fleair Trading Co/Biggin Hill
	G-FLEN	PA-28-161 Warrior II	Winchfield Enterprises Ltd
	G-FLII	GA-7 Cougar	BLS Aviation Ltd (G-GRAC)/Elstree
	G-FLIK	Pitts S.1S Special	R. P. Millinship
	G-FLPI	R. Commander 112A	Tuscany Ltd/Leicester
	G-FLTI	Beech F90 King Air	Flightline Ltd/Southend
	G-FLUG	Gyroflug SC.01B-160 Speed Canard	ITPS Ltd/Cranfield
	G-FLUT	Stitts SA.6B Flut-R-Bug	B. J. Towers
	G-FLYA	Mooney M.20J	Symtec Computer Service Ltd
	G-FLYI	PA-34-200 Seneca	BLS Aviation Ltd (G-BHVO)/Elstree
	G-FLYR	AB-206B JetRanger	Kwik Fit Euro Ltd (G-BAKT)
	G-FLYV	Slingsby T.67M-200	Firefly Aerial Promotions Ltd
	G-FMAL	AB-206A JetRanger	Global Map Ltd (G-RIAN/G-BHSG)
	G-FMAM	PA-28-151 Warrior	Essex Radio PLC (G-BBXV)/Southend
	G-FMUS	Robinson R-22	Cormack (Aircraft Services) Ltd (G-BJBT)/ Glasgow
	G-FNLD	Cessna 172N	Papa Hotel Flying Group
	G-FNLY	Cessna F.172M	London Aviation Ltd (G-WACX/G-BAEX)/ Biggin Hill
	G-FNWY	L.188C Electra	Air Bridge Carriers Ltd/E Midlands
	G-FOEL	PA-31-350 Navajo Chieftain	Oxaero (G-BBXR)/Kidlington
	G-FOGG	Cameron N-90 balloon	J. P. E. Money-Kyrle
	G-FOLY	Aerotek Pitts S-2A Modified	A. A. Laing
	G-FOOD	Beech B200 Super King Air	Specbridge Ltd/Gamston
	G-FORC	SNCAN Stampe SV-4C	G. Pullan
	G-FORD	SNCAN Stampe SV-4B	P. Meeson & R. A. J. Spurrell/ White Waltham
	G-FORE	Bell 47G-4A	London Aviation Ltd/Biggin Hill
	G-FOTO	PA-E23 Aztec 250F	A. Gibson (G-BJDH/G-BDXV)/Elstree
	G-FOWL	Colt 90A balloon	Chesterfield Cold Storage Ltd
	G-FOXA	PA-28-161 Cadet	Leicestershire Aero Club Ltd
	G-FOXC	Denney Aerocraft Kitfox	Junipa Sales (Aviation) Ltd
	G-FOXD	Denney Aerocraft Kitfox	M. Hanley
	G-FOXE	Denney Aerocraft Kitfox	K. M. Pinkard
	G-FOXG	Denney Aerocraft Kitfox	Kitfox Group
	G-FOXI	Denney Aerocraft Kitfox	B. Johns
	G-FOXS	Denney Aerocraft Kitfox	S. P. Watkins & C. C. Rea
	G-FOXX	Denney Aerocraft Kitfox	R. O. F. Harper
	G-FOXZ	Denney Aerocraft Kitfox	M. Smalley & ptnrs
	G-FPCL	GA-7 Cougar	Eurowide Ltd
	G-FPEL	Schweizer 269C	Central Communications Group
	G-FRAA	Dassault Falcon 20F	FR Aviation Ltd/Bournemouth
	G-FRAB	Dassault Falcon 20F	FR Aviation Ltd/Bournemouth
	G-FRAC	Dassault Falcon 20F	FR Aviation Ltd/Bournemouth
	G-FRAD	Dassault Falcon 20E	FR Aviation Ltd (G-BCYF)/Bournemouth
	G-FRAE	Dassault Falcon 20E	FR Aviation Ltd/Bournemouth
	G-FRAF	Dassault Falcon 20E	FR Aviation Ltd/Bournemouth
	G-FRAG	PA-32 Cherokee Six 300E	W. R. Bridges/Southend
	G-FRAH	Dassault Falcon 20DC	FR Aviation Ltd/Bournemouth
	G-FRAI	Dassault Falcon 20E	FR Aviation Ltd/Bournemouth
	G-FRAJ	Dassault Falcon 20E	FR Aviation Ltd/Bournemouth
	G-FRAK	Dassault Falcon 20DC	FR Aviation Ltd/Bournemouth
	G-FRAN	Piper J-3C-90 Cub (480321)	Essex L-4 Group (G-BIXY)
	G-FRAS	Dassault Falcon 20C	FR Aviation Ltd/Bournemouth
	G-FRAT	Dassault Falcon 20C	FR Aviation Ltd/Bournemouth
	G-FRAU	Dassault Falcon 20C	FR Aviation Ltd/Bournemouth
	G-FRAV	Dassault Falcon 20ECM	FR Aviation Ltd/Bournemouth
	G-FRAW	Dassault Falcon 20ECM	FR Aviation Ltd/Bournemouth
	G-FRAX	Cessna 441	FR Aviation Ltd (G-BMTZ)/Bournemouth
	G-FRAY	Cassutt IIIM (modified)	C. I. Fray
	G-FRAZ	Cessna 441	FR Aviation Ltd/Bournemouth
	G-FRCE	H.S. Gnat T.1	Butane Buzzard Aviation Corporation Ltd
	G-FREE	Pitts S-2A Special	Pegasus Flying Group/Fairoaks
	G-FRJB	Britten Sheriff SA-1 ★	Aeropark/E. Midlands
	G-FROZ	Cessna 421C	Air Options Ltd
	G-FRST	PA-44-180T Turbo Seminole	Mondiale Aviation Ltd
	G-FRYS	Christen Eagle II	R. W. J. Foster
	G-FSDC	Enstrom 280C-UK Shark	Southern Air Ltd (G-BKTG)/Shoreham
	G-FSDG	AB-206B JetRanger	Flair (Soft Drinks) Ltd (G-ROOT/G-JETR)

Reg.	Type	Owner or Operator	Notes
G-FSDH	Hughes 269A	Compass Aviation Ltd	
G-FSDT	Hughes 269A	S. G. Oliphant-Hope/Shoreham	
G-FSII	Gregory Free Spirit Mk II	M. J. Gregory & R. P. Hallam	
G-FSPL	PA-32R Cherokee Lance 300	J. D. L. Richardson & Goodridge (UK) Ltd	
G-FTAX	Cessna 421C	Jet West Ltd (G-BFFM)/Exeter	
G-FTFT	Colt Financial Times SS balloon	Financial Times Ltd	
G-FTIL	Robin DR.400/180R	C. C. Blakey	
G-FTIM	Robin DR.400/100	FTI Aviation Ltd/Biggin Hill	
G-FTIN	Robin DR.400/100	FTI Aviation Ltd/Biggin Hill	
G-FTIO	Robin DR.400/100	FTI Aviation Ltd/Biggin Hill	
G-FTWO	AS.355F-2 Twin Squirrel	McAlpine Helicopters Ltd (G-OJOR/ G-BMUS)/Hayes	
G-FUEL	Robin DR.400/180	R. Darch/Compton Abbas	
G-FUGA	Fouga CM.170R Magister	Royalair Services Ltd (G-BSCT)	
G-FUJI	Fuji FA.200-180	R. Gizzi	
G-FULL	PA-28R Cherokee Arrow 200-II	Fuller Aviation (G-HWAY/G-JULI)	
G-FUND	Thunder Ax7-65Z balloon	Soft Sell Ltd	
G-FUZY	Cameron N-77 balloon	Allan Industries Ltd	
G-FUZZ	PA-18 Super Cub 95	G. W. Cline	
G-FWPW	PA-28-236 Dakota	P. A. & F. C. Winters	
G-FWRP	Cessna 421C	Maxfab Ltd	
G-FXII	V.S.366 Spitfire F.XII (EN224)	P. R. Arnold	
G-FXIV	V.S.379 Spitfire FR.XIV (MV370)	R. Lamplough	
G-FZZI	Cameron H-34 balloon	Airship & Balloon Co Ltd	
G-FZZY	Colt 69A balloon	Hot-Air Balloon Co Ltd	
G-FZZZ	Colt 56A balloon	Hot-Air Balloon Co Ltd	
G-GABD	GA-7 Cougar	Scotia Safari Ltd/Prestwick	
G-GACA	P.57 Sea Prince T.1 ★	P. G. Vallance Ltd/Charlwood	
G-GAGA	AA-5B Tiger	Daniels Timetrak Ltd (G-BGPG)/Denham	
G-GAJB	AA-5B Tiger	G. A. J. Bowles (G-BHZN)	
G-GALE	PA-34-200T Seneca II	Gale Construction Co Ltd/Norwich	
G-GAMA	Beech 95-58 Baron	Gama Aviation Ltd (G-BBSD)/Fairoaks	
G-GAME	Cessna T.303	Street Construction (Wigan) Ltd	
G-GANE	Sequoia F.8L Falco	S. J. Gane	
G-GANJ	Fournier RF-6B-100	Soaring Equipment Ltd/Coventry	
G-GARY	Cessna TR.182	G. Hitchen	
G-GASC	Hughes 369HS	Crewhall Ltd (G-WELD/G-FROG)	
G-GASP	PA-28-181 Archer II	G-GASP Flying Group	
G-GASS	Thunder Ax7-77 balloon	Travel Gas (Midlands) Ltd	
G-GAUL	Cessna 550 Citation II	Chauffair Leasing Ltd	
G-GAWA	Cessna 140	R. A. Page (G-BRSM)	
G-GAYL	Learjet 35A	Northern Executive Aviation Ltd (G-ZING)/ Manchester	
G-GAZI	SA.341G Gazelle 1	Stratton Motor Co (Norfolk) Ltd & UCC International Group Ltd (G-BKLU)	
G-GAZZ	SA.341G Gazelle 1	Stratton Motor Co (Norfolk) Ltd & UCC International Group Ltd	
G-GBAO	Robin R.1180TD	J. Kay-Movat	
G-GBLR	Cessna F.150L	Blue Max Flying Group	
G-GBSL	Beech 76 Duchess	R. M. Jones (G-BGVG)	
G-GBUE	Robin DR.400/120A	G. Higgins & ptnrs (G-BPXD)	
G-GCAA	PA-28R Cherokee Arrow 200	Southern Air Ltd/Shoreham	
G-GCAB	PA-30 Twin Comanche 180	Southern Air Ltd/Shoreham	
G-GCAT	PA-28 Cherokee 140B	F. C. Odie (G-BFRH)	
G-GCCL	Beech 76 Duchess	Multirun Ltd	
G-GCJL	BAe Jetstream 4100	British Aerospace PLC/Prestwick	
G-GCKI	Mooney M.20K	G. C. Kent/Tollerton	
G-GCNZ	Cessna 150M	Heathgrange Ltd	
G-GDAM	PA-18 Super Cub 135	G. D. A. Martin	
G-GDAY	Robinson R-22B	Rebelmile Ltd/Blackpool	
G-GDOG	PA-28R Cherokee Arrow 200-II	K. Smith (G-BDXW)	
G-GEAR	Cessna FR.182Q	B. C. J. Lovrey/White Waltham	
G-GEDS	AS.350B Ecureuil	Direct Produce Supplies Ltd (G-HMAN/ G-SKIM/G-BIVP)	
G-GEEE	Hughes 369HS	B. P. Stein (G-BDOY)	
G-GEEP	Robin R.1180T	Organic Concentrates Ltd/Booker	
G-GEES	Cameron N-77 balloon	Mark Jarvis Ltd *Mark Jarvis*	
G-GEEZ	Cameron N-77 balloon	Charnwood Forest Turf Accountants Ltd	
G-GEIL	BAe 125 Srs 800B	Heron Corporation PLC	
G-GEOF	Pereira Osprey 2	G. Crossley	
G-GEUP	Cameron N-77 balloon	D. P. & B. O. Turner	
G-GFAB	Cameron N-105 balloon	The Andrew Brownsword Collection Ltd	

Notes	Reg.	Type	Owner or Operator
	G-GFCA	PA-28-161 Cadet	Swallow Aviation Ltd/Staverton
	G-GFCB	PA-28-161 Cadet	S. F. Tebby & Sons
	G-GFCC	PA-28-161 Cadet	Swallow Aviation Ltd/Staverton
	G-GFCD	PA-34-220T Seneca III	BWOC Ltd (G-KIDS)/Staverton
	G-GFCE	PA-28-161 Warrior II	Swallow Aviation Ltd (G-BNJP)/Staverton
	G-GFCF	PA-28-161 Cadet	Swallow Aviation Ltd (G-RHBH)/Staverton
	G-GFLY	Cessna F.150L	W. Lancashire Aero Club Ltd/Woodvale
	G-GGCC	AB-206B JetRanger 2	Hampton Printing (Bristol) Ltd (G-BEHG)
	G-GGGG	Thunder Ax7-77A balloon	T. A. Gilmour
	G-GGOW	Colt 77A balloon	City of Glasgow District Council
	G-GHIA	Cameron N-120 balloon	Bristol Street Motors (Cheltenham) Ltd
	G-GHIN	Thunder Ax7-77 balloon	G. M. Ghinn
	G-GHRW	PA-28RT-201 Arrow IV	Leavesden Flight Centre Ltd (G-ONAB/ G-BHAK)
	G-GIGI	M.S.893A Rallye Commodore	P. J. C. Phillips (G-AYVX)
	G-GILY	Robinson R-22B	Reynard Racing Cars Ltd
	G-GIRO	Schweizer 269C	D. E. McDowell
	G-GJCB	BAe 125 Srs 800B	J. C. Bamford Excavators Ltd
	G-GJCD	Robinson R-22B	A. G. Forshaw
	G-GLAM	BAe Jetstream 3102-09	Manx Airlines Ltd (G-IBLX)/Ronaldsway
	G-GLAW	Cameron N-90 balloon	George Law Ltd
	G-GLED	Cessna 150M	Firecrest Aviation Ltd/Leavesden
	G-GLOR	Cessna 425	Calmcraft Ltd
	G-GLOS	H.P.137 Jetstream 200	British Aerospace PLC (G-BCGU/ G-AXRI)
	G-GLOW	AS.355-1 Twin Squirrel	Coalite Group PLC (G-PAPA/G-MCAH/ G-CNET)
	G-GLUE	Cameron N-65 balloon	L. J. M. Muir & G. D. Hallett
	G-GMAX	SNCAN Stampe SV-4C	Glidegold Ltd (G-BXNW)
	G-GMJM	McD Douglas MD-83	Airtours International Aviation Ltd
	G-GMSI	SOCATA TB.9 Tampico	ML Associates
	G-GNAT	H.S. Gnat T.1 (XS101)	Ruanil Investments Ltd/Cranfield
	G-GNSY	HPR-7 Herald 209	Channel Express PLC (G-BFRK)/ Bournemouth
	G-GNTA	Saab SF.340A	Business Air Ltd/Aberdeen
	G-GNTB	Saab SF.340A	Business Air Ltd/Aberdeen
	G-GOBP	Bell 206B JetRanger 2	Clyde Helicopters Ltd (G-BOUY)
	G-GOBT	Colt 77A balloon	British Telecom PLC
	G-GOCX	Cameron N-90 balloon	Cathay Pacific Airways Ltd
	G-GOGO	Hughes 369D	A. W. Alloys Ltd
	G-GOLD	Thunder Ax6-56A balloon	Joseph Terry & Sons Ltd
	G-GOLF	SOCATA TB.10 Tobago	E. H. Scamell & ptnrs
	G-GOLO	Robinson R-22B	Croftflight Ltd
	G-GOMM	PA-32R Cherokee Lance 300	A. Kazaz/Leicester
	G-GONE	D.H.112 Venom FB.50	J. E. Davies
	G-GOOS	Cessna F.182Q	S. W. B. Parkinson
	G-GORE	CFM Streak Shadow	D. N. & E. M. Gore
	G-GOSS	Jodel DR.221	D. Folens
	G-GOZO	Cessna R.182	Transmatic Fyllan Ltd (G-BJZO)/Cranfield
	G-GPMW	PA-28RT-201T Turbo Arrow IV	M. Worrall & G. Patterson
	G-GPST	ST.1	P. J. C. Philips
	G-GRAM	PA-31-350 Navajo Chieftain	Superpower Air Services Ltd (G-BRHF)
	G-GRAY	Cessna 172N	Truman Aviation Ltd/Tollerton
	G-GREG	Jodel DR.220 2+2	J. T. Wilson
	G-GREN	Cessna T.310R	Elvedale Holding Ltd
	G-GRID	AS.355F-1 Twin Squirrel	National Grid Co PLC
	G-GRIF	R. Commander 112TCA	M. J. Chilton (G-BHXC)
	G-GROW	Cameron N-77 balloon	Derbyshire Building Society
	G-GSFC	Robinson R-22B	Weller Helicopters Ltd
	G-GSML	Enstrom 280C-UK	Guardwell Security Management Ltd (G-BNNV)
	G-GTAX	PA-31-350 Navajo Chieftain	Jet West Ltd (G-OIAS)/Exeter
	G-GTHM	PA-38-112 Tomahawk	Truman Aviation Ltd/Tollerton
	G-GTPL	Mooney M.20K	W. R. Emberton/Spain
	G-GUNN	Cessna F.172H	J. G. Gunn (G-AWGC)
	G-GUNS	Cameron V-77 balloon	Royal School of Artillery Hot Air Balloon Club
	G-GURL	Cameron A-210 balloon	Hot Airlines Ltd
	G-GUYI	PA-28-181 Archer II	B. Butler
	G-GUYS	PA-34-200T Seneca	H. Jowett & Co Ltd (G-BMWT)
	G-GWEN	Cessna F.172M	R. E. Youngsworth (G-GBLP)
	G-GWHH	AS.355F Twin Squirrel	Wimpey Homes Holdings Ltd (G-BKUL)
	G-GWIL	AS.350B Ecureuil	Talan Ltd
	G-GWIN	Bell 206L-3 LongRanger	Southern Counties Estates Ltd

Reg.	Type	Owner or Operator	Notes
G-GWIT	Cameron O-84 balloon	M. A. Campbell	
G-GWIZ	Colt Clown SS balloon	Oxford Promotions (UK) Ltd	
G-GWYN	Cessna F.172M	Gwyn Aviation	
G-GYAV	Cessna 172N	Southport & Merseyside Aero Club (1979) Ltd	
G-GYMM	PA-28R Cherokee Arrow 200	D. M. Ball (G-AYWW)	
G-GYRO	Bensen B.8	N. A. Pitcher & A. L. Howell	
G-GZDO	Cessna 172N	Cambridge Hall Aviation	
G-HAEC	Commonwealth Mustang 22	R. G. Hanna/Duxford	
G-HAIG	Rutan LongEz	P. N. Haigh	
G-HAJJ	Glaser-Dirks DG.400	P. W. Endean	
G-HALC	PA-28R Cherokee Arrow 200	Halcyon Aviation Ltd	
G-HALL	PA-22 Tri-Pacer 160	F. P. Hall (G-ARAH)	
G-HALP	SOCATA TB.10 Tobago	D. Halpera (G-BITD)/Elstree	
G-HAMA	Beech 200 Super King Air	Gama Aviation Ltd/Fairoaks	
G-HAMP	Bellanca 7ACA Champ	R. J. Grimstead	
G-HANS	Robin DR.400 2+2	Headcorn Flying School Ltd	
G-HAPR	B.171 Sycamore HR.14 (XG547) ★	International Helicopter Museum/Weston-s-Mare	
G-HARE	Cameron N-77 balloon	M. A. Pratt & N. I. Cakebread	
G-HARF	G.1159C Gulfstream 4	Fayair (Jersey) Ltd	
G-HARH	Sikorsky S-76B	Fayair (Jersey) 1984 Ltd	
G-HART	Cessna 152	Atlantic Air Transport Ltd/Coventry	
G-HASL	AA-5A Cheetah	D.B.G. Ltd (G-BGSL)/(stored)	
G-HATZ	Hatz CB-1	J. Pearson	
G-HAUL	Westland WG.30 Srs 300	Westland Helicopters PLC/Yeovil	
G-HAZE	Thunder Ax8-90 balloon	H. A. Ingham	
G-HBAC	AS.355F-1 Twin Squirrel	BAC Ltd (G-HJET)	
G-HBCO	PA-31-325 Navajo C/R	Northern Executive Aviation Ltd/Manchester	
G-HBUG	Cameron N-90 balloon	Datasolve Ltd (G-BRCN)	
G-HCRP	McD Douglas MD-83	Airtours International Aviation Ltd	
G-HCSL	PA-34-220T Seneca III	Hollowbrook Computer Services Ltd	
G-HCTL	PA-31-350 Navajo Chieftain	Field Aircraft Services (Heathrow) Ltd (G-BGOY)	
G-HDBA	H.S.748 Srs 2B	British Aerospace PLC	
G-HDBB	H.S.748 Srs 2B	British Aerospace PLC	
G-HDBD	H.S.748 Srs 2B	British Aerospace PLC	
G-HDEW	PA32R-301 Saratoga SP	Lord Howard de Walden (G-BRGZ)	
G-HEAD	Colt 56 balloon	Colt Balloons Ltd	
G-HELE	Bell 206B JetRanger 3	B. E. E. Smith (G-OJFR)	
G-HELI	Saro Skeeter Mk 12 (XM556) ★	International Helicopter Museum/Weston-s-Mare	
G-HELN	PA-18 Super Cub 95	J. J. Anziani (G-BKDG)/Booker	
G-HELO	Bell 206B JetRanger 2	Surrey Helicopter Hire Ltd (G-BAZN)	
G-HELP	Colt 17A balloon	Airship & Balloon Co Ltd	
G-HELV	D.H.115 Vampire T.55	Hunter Wing Ltd	
G-HELX	Cameron N-31 balloon	Hot-Air Balloon Co Ltd	
G-HELY	Agusta 109A	Candyfleet Ltd	
G-HEMS	SA.365N Dauphin 2	Express Newspapers PLC	
G-HENS	Cameron N-65 balloon	Horrells Dairies Ltd	
G-HENY	Cameron V-77 balloon	R. S. D'Alton	
G-HERA	Robinson R-22B	S. N. H. Boardman-Weston	
G-HERB	PA-28R-201 Arrow III	D. I. Weidner	
G-HERO	PA-32RT-300 Lance II	R. P. Thomas & C. Moore(G-BOGN)	
G-HERS	Jodel D.18	A. Usherwood	
G-HETH	Robinson R-22B	Leach-Lewis Ltd	
G-HEVY	Boeing 707-324C	HeavyLift Cargo Airlines Ltd/Stansted	
G-HEWI	Piper J-3C-90 Cub	Denham Grasshopper Group (G-BLEN)	
G-HEWS	Hughes 369D ★	Spares use/Sywell	
G-HEYY	Cameron 77 Bear SS balloon	Hot-Air Balloon Co Ltd George	
G-HFBM	Curtiss Robin C-2	Colin Crabbe Holdings Ltd	
G-HFCA	Cessna A.150L	Horizon Flying Club Ltd/Ipswich	
G-HFCB	Cessna F.150L	Horizon Flying Club Ltd (G-AZVR)/Ipswich	
G-HFCI	Cessna F.150L	Horizon Flying Club Ltd/Ipswich	
G-HFCL	Cessna F.152	Horizon Flying Club Ltd (G-BGLR)/Ipswich	
G-HFCT	Cessna F.152	Stapleford Flying Club Ltd	
G-HFIX	V.S.361 Spitfire HF.IXe (MJ730)	D. W. Pennell (G-BLAS)	
G-HFLA	Schweizer 269C	Heliflair Ltd	
G-HFLR	Schweizer 269C	Heliflair Ltd	
G-HFTG	PA-23 Aztec 250E	Air Navigation & Training Co Ltd (G-BSOB/G-BCJR)/Blackpool	

Notes	Reg.	Type	Owner or Operator
	G-HGAS	Cameron V-77 balloon	Handygas Ltd
	G-HGPI	SOCATA TB.20 Trinidad	M. J. Jackson/Bournemouth
	G-HHUN	Hunter F.4	Hunter Wing Ltd/Bournemouth
	G-HIEL	Robinson R-22B	Hields Aviation
	G-HIER	Bell 206B JetRanger 3	Rentatruck Self Drive Ltd (G-BRFD)
	G-HIHI	PA-32R-301 Saratoga SP	Aviation Metals Ltd/Cranfield
	G-HILS	Cessna F.172H	R. G. Humphries (G-AWCH)
	G-HILT	SOCATA TB.10 Tobago	P. J. Morrison
	G-HINT	Cameron N-90 balloon	Hinton Garage Bath Ltd
	G-HIRE	GA-7 Cougar	London Aerial Tours Ltd (G-BGSZ)/ Biggin Hill
	G-HIVA	Cessna 337A	High Voltage Applications Ltd (G-BAES)
	G-HIVE	Cessna F.150M	M. P. Lynn (G-BCXT)/Sibson
	G-HLFT	SC.5 Belfast 2	HeavyLift Cargo Airlines Ltd/Stansted
	G-HLIX	Cameron 80 Oil Can balloon	Hot-Air Balloon Co Ltd
	G-HMBB	MBB BK-117B-1C	MBB Helicopter Systems Ltd
	G-HMES	PA-28-161 Warrior II	Cleveland Flying School Ltd/Teesside
	G-HMJB	PA-34-220T Seneca III	M. Gavaghan
	G-HMMM	Cameron N-65 balloon	S. Moss
	G-HMPH	Bell 206B JetRanger2	Mightycraft Ltd (G-BBUY)
	G-HMPT	AB-206B JetRanger	Mightycraft Ltd
	G-HNTR	Hunter T.7 (XL572) ★	Hunter Wing Ltd/Bournemouth
	G-HOCK	PA-28 Cherokee 180	Arabact Ltd (G-AVSH)
	G-HOFM	Cameron N-56 balloon	Hot-Air Balloon Co Ltd
	G-HOHO	Colt Santa Claus SS balloon	Oxford Promotions (UK) Ltd
	G-HOLY	ST.10 Diplomate	Sussex Spraying Services Ltd/Shoreham
	G-HOME	Colt 77A balloon	Anglia Balloon School *Tardis*
	G-HONK	Cameron O-105 balloon	T. F. W. Dixon & Son Ltd
	G-HOOV	Cameron N-56 balloon	H. R. Evans
	G-HOPE	Beech F33A Bonanza	Hurn Aviation Ltd
	G-HOPI	Cameron N-42 balloon	Cameron Balloons Ltd
	G-HOPS	Thunder Ax8-90 balloon	Air Hops Ltd
	G-HORN	Cameron V-77 balloon	Travel Gas (Midlands) Ltd
	G-HOSI	Colt 77A balloon	J. N. Harley (Engineering) Ltd
	G-HOST	Cameron N-77 balloon	D. Grimshaw
	G-HOTI	Colt 77A balloon	R. Ollier
	G-HOTT	Cameron O-120 balloon	D. L. Smith
	G-HOUS	Colt 31A balloon	Anglia Balloons Ltd
	G-HOWE	Thunder Ax7-77 balloon	M. F. Howe
	G-HPAA	BN-2B-26 Islander	Hampshire Police Authority (G-BSWP)
	G-HPLC	Sikorsky S-76B	Air Hanson Ltd/Blackbushe
	G-HPVC	Partenavia P.68 Victor	Airtime (Hampshire) Ltd
	G-HRAY	AB-206B JetRanger 3	Hecray Co Ltd (G-VANG/G-BIZA)
	G-HRHI	B.206 Srs 1 Basset (XS770)	Universal Salvage (Holdings) Ltd
	G-HRIO	Robin HR.100/120	R. L. & G. M. Bagnall
	G-HRIS	Cessna P210N	Birmingham Aviation Ltd
	G-HRLK	Saab 91D/2 Safir	Sylmar Aviation & Services Ltd (G-BRZY)
	G-HRLM	Brügger MB.2 Colibri	R. A. Harris
	G-HROI	R. Commander 112A	H. R. Oldland
	G-HRON	D.H.114 Heron 2	St Helena Airways Ltd (G-AORH)
	G-HRZN	Colt 77A balloon	A. J. Spindler
	G-HSDW	Bell 206B JetRanger	Winfield Shoe Co Ltd
	G-HSHS	Colt 105A balloon	H. & S. Aviation Ltd
	G-HTAX	PA-31-350 Navajo Chieftain	Jet West Ltd/Exeter
	G-HTPS	SA. 341G Gazelle 1	ITPS Ltd (G-BRNI)
	G-HTRF	Robinson R-22B	Hecray Ltd
	G-HUBB	Partenavia P.68B	G-HUBB Ltd
	G-HUCH	Cameron 80 Carrots balloon	Airship & Balloon Co Ltd (G-BYPS)
	G-HUEY	Bell UH-1H	RAF Benevolent Fund/Odiham
	G-HUFF	Cessna 182P	A. E. G. Cousins
	G-HULL	Cessna F.150M	A. D. McLeod
	G-HUMF	Robinson R-22B	J. M. Wicks
	G-HUMT	Bell 206B JetRanger	H. J. Walters
	G-HUNY	Cessna F.150G	T. J. Lynn (G-AVGL)
	G-HURI	CCF Hawker Hurricane IIB (Z7381)	Patina Ltd/Duxford
	G-HURN	Robinson R-22B	Yorkshire Helicopter Centre Ltd
	G-HURR	Hawker Hurricane XII	Autokraft Ltd
	G-HURY	Hawker Hurricane IV (KZ321)	D. W. Arnold/Biggin Hill
	G-HUTT	Denney Aerocraft Kitfox	M. A. J. Hutt
	G-HVDM	V.S.361 Spitfire F.IX	DSG (Guernsey) Ltd
	G-HVRD	PA-31-350 Navajo Chieftain	London Flight Centre Air Charter Ltd (G-BEZU)
	G-HVRS	Robinson R-22B	M. P. & A. L. Wilkinson

Reg.	Type	Owner or Operator	Notes
G-HWBK	Agusta A.109A	Camlet Helicopters Ltd	
G-HWKN	PA-31P Pressurised Navajo	Industrial Marketing Group	
G-HWKR	Colt 90A balloon	Hawker Siddeley Group PLC	
G-HYGA	BAe 125 Srs 800B	Helpfactor Ltd	
G-HYLT	PA-32R-301 Saratoga SP	R. G. Moggridge	
G-HYPO	Colt 180A balloon	The Balloon Club of GB Ltd	
G-IAMP	Cameron H-34 balloon	Air 2 Air Ltd	
G-IBAC	Beech 95-58 Baron	BAC Aviation Ltd/Southend	
G-IBAK	Cessna 421C	MJD Aviation Ltd	
G-IBET	Cameron 70 Can SS balloon	M. R. Humphrey & J. R. Clifton	
G-IBFW	PA-28R-201 Arrow III	Speedway Car & Van Hire Ltd	
G-IBTX	Boeing 737-2M8	GB Airways Ltd (G-BTEB)/Gatwick	
G-IBTY	Boeing 737-2E3	GB Airways (G-BNZT)/Gatwick	
G-IBTZ	Boeing 737-2U4	GB Airways (G-OSLA)/Gatwick	
G-ICED	Cessna 501 Citation	Iceland Frozen Foods PLC/Manchester	
G-ICES	Thunder Ax6-56 balloon	—	
G-IDDI	Cameron N-77 balloon	Allen & Harris Ltd	
G-IDDY	D.H.C.1 Super Chipmunk	A. J. E. Ditheridge (G-BBMS)	
G-IDEA	AA-5A Cheetah	Lowlog Ltd (G-BGNO)	
G-IDJB	Cessna 150L	R. J. Browne	
G-IDWR	Hughes 369HS	Ryburn Air Ltd (G-AXEJ)	
G-IEAA	Boeing 737-33A	Inter European Airways Ltd/Cardiff	
G-IEAB	Boeing 757-23A	Inter European Airways Ltd/Cardiff	
G-IEPF	Robinson R-22B	V. T. Nash	
G-IFIT	PA-31-350 Navajo Chieftain	Cook Aviation Services Ltd (G-NABI/ G-MARG)	
G-IFLI	AA-5A Cheetah	ABC Aviation Ltd	
G-IFLP	PA-34-200T Seneca II	Golf-Sala Ltd	
G-IFOX	Robinson R-22B	Munn & Chapman Ltd	
G-IFTA	PA-31-350 Navajo Chieftain	Interflight (Air Charters) Ltd (G-BAVM) Gatwick	
G-IFTD	Cessna 404	Tristar Cars Ltd (G-BKUN)	
G-IGAR	PA-31-310 Turbo Navajo C	BWOC Ltd	
G-IGHA	PA-34-220T Seneca III	Isle of Gigha Estates Ltd (G-IPUT)	
G-IGLE	Cameron V-90 balloon	A. A. Laing	
G-IHSA	Robinson R-22B	D. P. Fiske	
G-IHSB	Robinson R-22B	Swift Helicopters Ltd	
G-IIAC	Aeronca 11AC Chief	Bailey Aviation Ltd (G-BTPY)	
G-IIAN	Aero Designs Pulsar	I. G. Harrison	
G-IIBD	PA-44-180T Seminole	H. S. Davies	
G-IIIG	Boeing Stearman A.75N1	Early Birds Ltd (G-BSDR)/Staverton	
G-IIII	Aerotek Pitts S-2B Special	B. K. Lecomber	
G-IIIL	Pitts S-1T Special	Skylark Aerobatics	
G-IIIT	Aerotek Pitts S-2A Special	Aerobatic Displays Ltd	
G-IIIX	Pitts S-1S Special	J. E. R. Seeger (G-LBAT/G-UCCI/G-BIYN)	
G-IINA	AS.350B-2 Ecureuil	Endeavour Aviation Ltd	
G-IIRB	Bell 206B JetRanger 3	Robard Consultants Ltd	
G-IJOE	PA-28RT-201T Turbo Arrow IV	Scotlandair Ltd/Glasgow	
G-IJRC	Robinson R-22B	J. R. Clark Ltd (G-BTJP)	
G-IKBP	PA-28-161 Warrior II	Hendafern Ltd/Shoreham	
G-IKIS	Cessna 210M	A. C. Davison	
G-ILES	Cameron O-90 balloon	G. N. Lantos	
G-ILLE	Boeing Stearman A.75L3 (379)	M. H. Pendlebury	
G-ILLS	H.S.125 Srs 3B	S. Gill (G-AVRF)/Luton	
G-ILLY	PA-28-181 Archer II	A. G. & K. M. Spiers	
G-ILSE	Corby CJ-1 Starlet	S. Stride	
G-ILTS	PA-32 Cherokee Six 300	Fadmoor Flying Group (G-CVOK)	
G-ILYS	Robinson R-22B	G. K. Ryatt	
G-IMAG	Colt 77A balloon	Flying Pictures (Balloons) Ltd	
G-IMAX	Cameron O-120 balloon	Air 2 Air Ltd	
G-IMLH	Bell 206A JetRanger 3	Subaru (UK) Ltd	
G-IMLI	Cessna 310Q	Michael Leonard Interiors Ltd (G-AZYK)/ Blackbushe	
G-IMPW	PA-32R-301 Saratoga SP	C. M. Juggins	
G-IMPX	R. Commander 112B	P. A. Day	
G-IMPY	Light Aero Avid Flyer C	T. R. C. Griffin	
G-INAV	Aviation Composites Mercury	Aviation Composites Co Ltd	
G-INCA	Glaser-Dirks DG.400	H. W. Ober	
G-INCH	Montgomerie-Bensen B.8MR	I. H. C. Branson (G-BRES)	
G-INDC	Cessna T.303	Howarth Timber (Aircharters) Ltd	
G-INGB	Robinson R-22B	Filemart Ltd	
G-INMO	PA-31-310 Turbo Navajo	Subaru (UK) Ltd/Coventry	

Notes	Reg.	Type	Owner or Operator
	G-INNY	SE-5A Replica (F5459)	R. M. Ordish/Old Sarum
	G-INOW	Monnet Moni	T. W. Clark
	G-INTC	Robinson R-22B	Intec Project Engineering Ltd
	G-IOOI	Robin DR.400/160	Freshname No 77 Ltd
	G-IOSI	Jodel DR.1051	A. Burbidge & R. Slater
	G-IPEC	SIAI-Marchetti S.205-18F	P. M. Wright (G-AVEG)
	G-IPJC	PA-28R Cherokee Arrow 200	PJC Leasing Ltd
	G-IPRA	Beech A200 Super King Air	Filemart Ltd (G-BGRD)
	G-IPSI	Grob G.109B	G-IPSI Ltd (G-BMLO)
	G-IPSY	Rutan Vari-Eze	R. A. Fairclough/Biggin Hill
	G-IRIS	AA-5B Tiger	E. I. Bett (G-BIXU)
	G-IRLS	Cessna FR.172J	R. C. Chapman
	G-IRLY	Colt 90A balloon	Air Canada Ltd
	G-IRPC	Cessna 182Q	R. P. Carminke (G-BSKM)
	G-ISCA	PA-28RT-201 Arrow IV	D. J. & P. Pay
	G-ISEB	Agusta A.109A II	Walkfine Ltd (G-IADT/G-HBCA)
	G-ISEE	BAe 146-200	British Aerospace PLC
	G-ISEH	Cessna 182R	SEH (Holdings) Ltd (G-BIWS)/Ipswich
	G-ISIS	D.H.82A Tiger Moth	D. R. & M. Wood (G-AODR)
	G-ISLE	Short SD3-60	Manx Airlines Ltd/(G-BLEG) *King Olaf* (1113-1153)
	G-ISMO	Robinson R-22B	Jet Heritage Ltd/Bournemouth
	G-ISPY	Colt GA-42 airship	Airship & Balloon Co Ltd
	G-ISTT	Thunder Ax8-84 balloon	RAF Halton Hot Air Balloon Club
	G-ITDA	PA-32R-301 Saratoga SP	ITD Aviation Ltd
	G-ITPS	Pilatus PC-6/B2-H2 Turbo Porter	ITPS Ltd/Cranfield
	G-ITTU	PA-23 Aztec 250E	D. Byrne & M. Cummings (G-BCSW)
	G-IVAC	Airtour AH-77B balloon	M. G. F. White
	G-IVAN	Shaw TwinEze	I. Shaw
	G-IVAR	Yakovlev Yak-50	R. N. Goode/White Waltham
	G-IVOR	Aeronca 11AC Chief	M. A. Hales/Bourn
	G-IXCC	V.S.361 Spitfire LF.IXe	Charles Church Displays Ltd
	G-IZEL	SA.341G Gazelle 1	Fairview Securities (Investments) Ltd (G-BBHW)
	G-IZMO	Thunder Ax8-90 balloon	Landrell Fabric Engineering Ltd
	G-JACT	Partenavia P.68C	JCT 600 Ltd (G-NVIA)/Leeds
	G-JADE	Beech 95-58 Baron	S. W. B. Parkinson
	G-JAFE	D.H.C.2 Beaver 1	J. M. Jeapes
	G-JAKE	D.H.C.1 Chipmunk 22	J. M. W. Henstock (G-BBMY) Netherthorpe
	G-JAKY	PA-31-325 Turbo Navajo C/R	Ace Aviation Ltd/Glasgow
	G-JANA	PA-28-181 Archer II	Croaker Aviation/Stapleford
	G-JANB	Colt Flying Bottle SS balloon	Justerini & Brooks Ltd
	G-JANE	Cessna 340A	John Hewitson Ltd
	G-JANN	PA-34-220T Seneca III	J. A. Powell
	G-JANS	Cessna FR.172J	I. G. Aizlewood/Luton
	G-JANT	PA-28-181 Archer II	Janair Aviation Ltd
	G-JARA	Robinson R-22B	J. A. R. Allwright
	G-JASE	PA-28-161 Warrior II	J. T. Matthews
	G-JASM	Robinson R-22A	J. L. Lawrence & ptnrs
	G-JASP	PA-23 Turbo Aztec 250E	Landsurcon (Air Survey) Ltd/Staverton
	G-JAZZ	AA-5A Cheetah	Jazz Club
	G-JBDH	Robin DR.400/180	D. Hoolahan/Biggin Hill
	G-JBET	Beech F33A Bonanza	J. Bett/Glasgow
	G-JBJB	Colt 69A balloon	Justerini & Brooks Ltd
	G-JBPR	Wittman W.10 Tailwind	P. A. Rose & J. P. Broadhurst
	G-JBWI	Robinson R-22B	N. J. Wagstaff Leasing
	G-JCAS	PA-28-181 Archer II	C. A. Sprent
	G-JCJC	Colt Flying Jeans SS balloon	J. C. Balloon Co Ltd
	G-JCUB	PA-18 Super Cub 135	Piper Cub Consortium Ltd/Jersey
	G-JDEE	SOCATA TB.20 Trinidad	Melville Associates Ltd (G-BKLA)
	G-JDHI	Enstrom F-28C-UK	B. J. W. Carter (G-BCOT)
	G-JDIX	Mooney M.20B	J. E. Dixon (G-ARTB)
	G-JDTI	Cessna 421C	Eastfield Air Ltd/Sturgate
	G-JEAA	F.27 Friendship Mk 500F	Jersey European Airways Ltd
	G-JEAB	F.27 Friendship Mk 500F	Jersey European Airways Ltd
	G-JEAD	F.27 Friendship Mk 500	Jersey European Airways Ltd
	G-JEAE	F.27 Friendship Mk 500	Jersey European Airways Ltd
	G-JEAF	F.27 Friendship Mk 500	Jersey European Airways Ltd
	G-JEAG	F.27 Friendship Mk 500	Jersey European Airways Ltd
	G-JEAH	F.27 Friendship Mk 500	Jersey European Airways Ltd
	G-JEAI	F.27 Friendship Mk 500	Jersey European Airways Ltd
	G-JEAN	Cessna 500 Citation	Foster Associates Ltd

Reg.	Type	Owner or Operator	Notes
G-JEET	Cessna FA.152	Luton Flight Training (G-BHMF)	
G-JEFF	PA-38-112 Tomahawk	R. J. Alford	
G-JENA	Mooney M.20K	P. Leverkuehn/Biggin Hill	
G-JENI	Cessna R.182	R. A. Bentley	
G-JENN	AA-5B Tiger	Clamair Aviation Ltd	
G-JENS	SOCATA Rallye 100ST	Palmer Pastoral Co Ltd (G-BDEG)	
G-JENY	Baby Great Lakes	J. M. C. Pothecary	
G-JERS	Robinson R-22B	J. E. R. Seeger	
G-JERY	AB-206B JetRanger 2	J. J. Woodhouse (G-BDBR)	
G-JEST	PA-22 Tri-Pacer 160	N. F. Hemming (G-ARGY)	
G-JETA	Cessna 550 Citation II	IDS Aircraft Ltd/Heathrow	
G-JETB	Cessna 550 Citation II	European Jet Ltd	
G-JETC	Cessna 550 Citation II	Colt Car Co Ltd/Staverton	
G-JETE	Cessna 500 Citation	IDS Aircraft Ltd (G-BCKM)/Heathrow	
G-JETH	Hawker Sea Hawk FGA.6 ★	P. G. Vallance Ltd/Charlwood	
G-JETI	BAe 125 Srs 800B	Alkharafi Aviation Ltd	
G-JETK	BAe 125 Srs 800B	Tiger Aviation Ltd (G-GSAM)	
G-JETL	Learjet 35A	Cameron Hall Developments Ltd	
G-JETM	Gloster Meteor T.7 (VZ638) ★	P. G. Vallance Ltd/Charlwood	
G-JETP	P.84 Jet Provost T.52A (T.4)	Hunter Wing Ltd/Bournemouth	
G-JETX	Bell 206B JetRanger	Tripgate Ltd	
G-JFCX	BAe 125 Srs 800B	British Aerospace PLC	
G-JFHL	PA-28-161 Warrior II	C. L. Palmer	
G-JFWI	Cessna F.172N	Staryear Ltd	
G-JGAL	Beech E90 King Air	Vaux (Aviation) Ltd/Newcastle	
G-JGCL	Cessna 414A	M. J. Holt	
G-JGMN	C.A.S.A. 1-131E Jungmann 2000	P. D. Scandrett/Staverton	
G-JHAN	Beech B200 Super King Air	John Hanson Services Ltd	
G-JHAS	Schweizer 269C	Albany Helicopters Ltd	
G-JHEW	Robinson R-22B	Burbage Farms Ltd	
G-JHLN	H.S.748 Srs 2A	Merchant Enterprises Ltd	
G-JILL	R. Commander 112TCA	Hanover Aviation/Elstree	
G-JIMS	Cessna 340A-II	Cox-Johnston Management Services Ltd (G-PETE)/Dundee	
G-JJAN	PA-28-181 Archer II	Redhill Flying Club	
G-JJSG	Learjet 35A	SPL Aviation Ltd	
G-JLEE	AB-206B JetRanger 3	Lee Aviation Ltd (G-JOKE/G-CSKY G-TALY)	
G-JLHS	Beech A36 Bonanza	J. L. Hopkins/Guernsey	
G-JLMW	Cameron V-77 balloon	The Apollo Balloon Co Ltd	
G-JLRW	Beech 76 Duchess	Moorfield Developments Ltd/Elstree	
G-JMDD	Cessna 340A	Thoroughbred Technology Ltd	
G-JMDI	Schweizer 269C	Norvic House Ltd (G-FLAT)	
G-JMHB	Robin DR.400/140	TMA Associates Ltd/Biggin Hill	
G-JMTS	Robin DR.400/180	J. R. Whiting	
G-JMTT	PA-28R-201T Turbo Arrow III	E. W. Passmore (G-BMHM)	
G-JNNB	Colt 90A balloon	Justerini & Brooks Ltd	
G-JODL	Jodel DR.1050/M	M. D. Mold	
G-JODY	Bell 206B JetRanger 3	Maztest Motors Ltd	
G-JOEY	BN-2A Mk III-2 Trislander	Aurigny Air Services (G-BDGG) Guernsey	
G-JOIN	Cameron V-65 balloon	Derbyshire Building Society	
G-JOJO	Cameron A-210 balloon	Worcester Balloons	
G-JOLI	Jodel D.150	K. F. & R. Richardson	
G-JOLY	Cessna 120	J. D. Tarrant/Bristol	
G-JONE	Cessna 172M	A. Pierce	
G-JONI	Cessna FA.152	Luton Flight Training Ltd (G-BFTU)	
G-JONN	Bell 206L-1 LongRanger	Harmeston Holdings Ltd	
G-JONO	Colt 77A balloon	The Sandcliffe Motor Group	
G-JONS	PA-31-350 Navajo Chieftain	Echocliff Properties Ltd	
G-JONZ	Cessna 172P	Jonesco (Preston) Ltd	
G-JOSH	Cameron N-105 balloon	GT Flying Clubs Ltd	
G-JOSY	Enstrom 280FX	S. Oliphant-Hope (G-BSTB)	
G-JOYC	Beech F33A Bonanza	Dunmhor Transport Ltd	
G-JOYT	PA-28-181 Archer II	S. W. Taylor (G-BOVO)/Redhill	
G-JSCL	Rans S.10 Sakota	D. L. Davies	
G-JSMC	McD Douglas MD-83	Airtours International Aviation Ltd	
G-JSSD	SA. Jetstream 3001	British Aerospace (G-AXJZ)/Prestwick	
G-JTCA	PA-23 Aztec 250E	J. D. Tighe (G-BBCU)/Sturgate	
G-JTWO	Piper J-2 Cub	A. T. Hooper & C. C. Silk (G-BPZR)	
G-JTYE	Aeronca 7AC Champion	J. Tye	
G-JUDE	CEA DR.400/180	L. R. Marks	
G-JUDI	AT-6D Harvard III (FX301)	A. A. Hodgson	
G-JUDY	AA-5A Cheetah	Brandon Aviation/Biggin Hill	
G-JUIN	Cessna 303	M. J. Newman/Denham	

Notes	Reg.	Type	Owner or Operator
	G-JUNG	C.A.S.A. 1.131E Jungmann 1000	K. H. Wilson
	G-JURG	R. Commander 114A	Jurgair Ltd
	G-JVAJ	PA-31T1 Cheyenne	Jacques Vert PLC
	G-JVJA	Partenavia P.68C	Twinflite Aviation Ltd (G-BMEI)
	G-JVMR	Partenavia P.68B	Sonardyne Ltd (G-JCTI/G-OJOE) Blackbushe
	G-JWDG	AA-5A Cheetah	JWDG Aviation (G-OCML/G-JAVA)
	G-JWDS	Cessna F.150G	London Aerial Tours Ltd (G-AVNB)
	G-JWFT	Robinson R-22B	Tukair Aircraft Charter
	G-JWIV	Jodel DR.1051	R. A. Bragger
	G-JWSD	Robinson R-22B	J. W. Sparrow Developments Ltd
	G-JXLI	BAe Jetstream 4100	British Aerospace PLC/Prestwick
	G-KAFE	Cameron N-65 balloon	Hot-Air Balloon Co Ltd
	G-KAIR	PA-28-181 Archer II	Academy Lithoplates Ltd/Aldergrove
	G-KARI	Fuji FA.200-160	I. Mansfield & F. M. Fiore (G-BBRE)
	G-KART	PA-28-161 Warrior II	Withercourt Ltd
	G-KARY	Fuji FA.200-180AO	C. J. Zetter (G-BEYP)
	G-KASS	H.S.125 Srs 3B	Eroten Ltd (G-AVPE)
	G-KATE	Westland WG.30 Srs 100	British International Helicopters Ltd Aberdeen
	G-KATH	Cessna P.210N	Wilson-Air Ltd
	G-KATS	PA-28 Cherokee 140	Ipswich School of Flying Ltd (G-BIRC)
	G-KAWA	Denney Aerocraft Kitfox	Oxford Motorcycle Engineers Ltd
	G-KBKB	Thunder Ax8-90 S2 balloon	G. Boulden
	G-KBPI	PA-28-161 Warrior II	Hendafern Ltd (G-BFSZ)/Shoreham
	G-KCAS	Beech 95-B55 Baron	M. J. & J. D. Crymble
	G-KCIG	Sportavia RF-5B	Exeter Sperber Syndicate Ltd
	G-KDET	PA-28-161 Cadet	Rapidspin Ltd/Biggin Hill
	G-KDFF	Scheibe SF.25E Super Falke	M. Lee & K. Dudley
	G-KDIX	Jodel D.9 Bebe	D. J. Wells
	G-KEAA	Beech 65-70 Queen Air	Kent Executive Aviation Ltd (G-REXP G-AYPC)
	G-KEAC	Beech 65-A80 Queen Air	D. Cockburn (G-REXY/G-AVNG)
	G-KEEN	Stolp SA.300 Starduster Too	Holland Aerobatics Ltd
	G-KEMC	Grob G.109	Eye-Fly Ltd
	G-KENB	Air Command 503 Commander	K. Brogden
	G-KENI	Rotorway Executive	J. K. Davies
	G-KENM	Luscombe 8A Silvaire	K. McNaughton
	G-KENN	Robinson R-22B	Cromwell Charter/Southampton
	G-KERC	SNCAN NC.854S	E. H. Gould
	G-KERY	PA-28 Cherokee 180	Kerrytype Ltd (G-ATWO)/Goodwood
	G-KEST	Steen Skybolt	S. Thursfield & K. E. Eld
	G-KEVN	Robinson R-22B	K. P. Gallen (G-BONX)
	G-KEYB	Cameron O-84 balloon	B. P. Key
	G-KEYS	PA-23 Aztec 250F	Wards Aviation Ltd
	G-KEYY	Cameron N-77 balloon	Business Design Group Ltd (G-BORZ)
	G-KFIT	Beech F90 King Air	Kwik Fit Euro Ltd (G-BHUS)/Edinburgh
	G-KFOX	Denney Aerocraft Kitfox	C. H. T. Trace
	G-KFZI	KFZ-1 Tigerfalke	L. R. Williams
	G-KHRE	M.S.893E Rallye 150SV	B. Proctor/Dunkeswell
	G-KIAM	Grob G.109B	D. T. Hulme
	G-KILY	Robinson R-22A	Julians Supermarket Ltd
	G-KIMB	Robin DR.340/140	R. M. Kimbell
	G-KINE	AA-5A Cheetah	BLS Aviation Ltd/Elstree
	G-KING	PA-38-112 Tomahawk	Orkney Flying Club
	G-KINK	Cessna 340	Hulbert of Dudley (Holdings) Ltd (G-PLEV)
	G-KIRK	Piper J-3C-65 Cub	M. J. Kirk
	G-KISS	Rand KR-2	E. A. Rooney
	G-KITE	PA-28-181 Archer II	World Business Publications Ltd/Elstree
	G-KITF	Denney Aerocraft Kitfox	Junipa Sales Aviation Ltd
	G-KITI	Pitts S-2E Special	P. A. Grant
	G-KITY	Denney Aerocraft Kitfox	Kitfox KFM Group
	G-KIWI	Cessna 404 Titan	Aviation Beauport Ltd (G-BHNI)
	G-KJET	Beech B90 King Air	Ashcombe Ltd (G-AXFE)
	G-KKDL	SOCATA TB.20 Trinidad	Kimber Kempster Contractors Ltd (G-BSHU)
	G-KLAY	Enstrom 280C Shark	Percivalls Ltd (G-BGZD)
	G-KLIK	Air Command 532 Elite	Roger Martin (Photography)
	G-KMAC	Bell 206B JetRanger	Specbridge Ltd
	G-KNAP	PA-28-161 Warrior II	R. E. Knapton (G-BIUX)/Finmere
	G-KNDY	Bell 206B JetRanger 3	ASP Helicopter Co Ltd
	G-KNIT	Robinson R-22B	BHM Knitwear Ltd

Reg.	Type	Owner or Operator	Notes
G-KNOW	PA-32 Cherokee Six 300	P. H. Knowland	
G-KODA	Cameron O-77 balloon	United Photofinishers Ltd	
G-KOLI	PZL-110 Koliber 150	T. D. A. George & F. H. Buckland	
G-KOLY	Enstrom F-28C-UK	Oston Air Finance Ltd (G-WWUK/G-BFFN)	
G-KOOL	D.H.104 Devon C.2 ★	E. Surrey Technical College/nr Redhill	
G-KORN	Cameron 70 Brentzen SS balloon	Cameron Balloons Ltd	
G-KOTA	PA-28-236 Dakota	JF Packaging	
G-KRII	Rand KR-2	M. R. Cleveley	
G-KRIS	Maule M5-235C Lunar Rocket	M. G. Pickering	
G-KSVB	PA-24 Comanche 260	C. M. Gill (G-ENIU/G-AVJU)	
G-KTEE	Cameron V-77 balloon	D. C. & N. P. Bull	
G-KUKU	Pfalzkuku (BS676)	A. D. Lawrence	
G-KUTU	Quickie Q2	J. Parkinson & ptnrs	
G-KWAX	Cessna 182E Skylane	A. R. Carrillo & J. E. Brewis	
G-KWIK	Partenavia P.68B	Travelair UK Ltd	
G-KWKI	QAC Quickie Q.200	B. M. Jackson	
G-KYAK	Yakolev C-11 (00)	R. Lamplough/Duxford	
G-KYIN	Cessna 421C	Sulair Services Ltd (G-OAKS)	
G-LACA	PA-28-161 Warrior II	Light Planes (Lancashire) Ltd/Barton	
G-LACB	PA-28-161 Warrior II	Light Planes (Lancashire) Ltd/Barton	
G-LACR	Denney Aerocraft Kitfox	C. M. Rose	
G-LADE	PA-32 Cherokee Six 300E	A. G. & D. Webb	
G-LADN	PA-28-161 Warrior II	E. C. Clark (G-BOLK)/Biggin Hill	
G-LADS	R. Commander 114	D. F. Soul	
G-LAGR	Cameron N-90 balloon	Bass & Tennent Sales Ltd	
G-LAIR	Stoddard-Hamilton Glasair IIS	D. L. Swallow	
G-LAKC	Cessna 404	Lakeside Aviation Ltd (G-BKTW/G-WTVE)/ Aberdeen	
G-LAKD	Cessna 404	Lakeside Aviation Ltd (G-BKWA/G-BELV)/ Aberdeen	
G-LAKE	Lake LA.250	Stanford Ltd	
G-LAKI	Jodel DR.1050	V. Panteli & J. E. Worthy	
G-LAMS	Cessna F.152	J. J. Baumhardt/Southend	
G-LANA	SOCATA TB.10 Tobago	Aero-Go Systems Ltd	
G-LANC	Avro 683 Lancaster X (KB889) ★	Imperial War Museum/Duxford	
G-LAND	Robinson R-22B	Charter Group PLC	
G-LANE	Cessna F.172N	G. C. Bantin	
G-LANG	Denney Aerocraft Kitfox	J. W. Lang	
G-LARA	Robin DR.400/180	Aeromarine Ltd/Southampton	
G-LARE	PA-39 Twin Comanche C/R	J. R. W. Keates/Biggin Hill	
G-LARK	Helton Lark 95	J. Fox	
G-LASR	Stoddard-Hamilton Glasair II	P. Taylor	
G-LASS	Rutan Vari-Eze	G. Lewis/Liverpool	
G-LATC	EMB-110P1 Bandeirante	Business Air Ltd	
G-LAXO	Agusta A.109C	Glaxo Holdings Ltd	
G-LAZR	Cameron O-77 balloon	Laser Civil Engineering Ltd	
G-LBCS	Colt 31A balloon	Airship & Balloon Co Ltd	
G-LBMM	PA-28-161 Warrior II	M. C. Lawton	
G-LBRC	PA-28RT-201 Arrow IV	D. J. V. Morgan & J. C. Lloyd	
G-LCIO	Colt 240A balloon	Star Micronics UK Ltd	
G-LCOK	Colt 69A balloon	Hot-Air Balloon Co Ltd (G-BLWI)	
G-LDYS	Colt 56A balloon	A. Green	
G-LEAM	PA-28-236 Dakota	South Yorkshire Caravans Ltd (G-BHLS)	
G-LEAN	Cessna FR.182	JGH Services Ltd (G-BGAP)/Biggin Hill	
G-LEAP	BN-2T Islander	Army Parachute Association (G-BLND)/ Netheravon	
G-LEAR	Learjet 35A	Northern Executive Aviation Ltd/ Manchester	
G-LEAU	Cameron N-31 balloon	P. L. Mossman	
G-LECA	AS.355F-1 Twin Squirrel	S. W. Electricity Board (G-BNBK)/Bristol	
G-LEDN	Short SD3-30 Variant 100	Janes Aviation Ltd (G-BIOF)/Blackpool	
G-LEED	Denney Aerocraft Kitfox Mk 2	G. T. Leedham	
G-LEES	Glaser-Dirks DG.400	T. B. Sargeant & C. A. Marren	
G-LEGO	Cameron O-77 balloon	C. H. Pearce Construction PLC	
G-LEGS	Short SD3-60	Manx Airlines Ltd (G-BLEF)/*King Magnus Barefoot (1098-1103)*	
G-LEIC	Cessna FA.152	Leicestershire Aero Club Ltd	
G-LEND	Cameron N-77 balloon	Southern Finance Co Ltd	
G-LENN	Cameron V-56 balloon	Anglia Balloon School Ltd	
G-LENS	Thunder Ax7-77Z balloon	Big Yellow Balloon Group	
G-LEON	PA-31-350 Navajo Chieftain	Prospair Aircharter Ltd/Birmingham	
G-LEOS	Robin DR.400/120	J. L. da Costa Sayago & P. A. Milne	

Notes	Reg.	Type	Owner or Operator
	G-LEPF	Fairchild 24R-46A Argus III	J. M. Greenland
	G-LEPI	Colt 160A balloon	Thunder & Colt Ltd
	G-LEVI	Aeronca 7AC Champion	L. Perry & J. P. A. Pumphrey
	G-LEXI	Cameron N-77 balloon	Sedgemoor 500 Balloon Group
	G-LEZE	Rutan LongEz	K. G. M. Loyal & ptnrs
	G-LFIX	V.S.509 Spitfire T.IX (ML407)	Jet Air Ltd/Goodwood
	G-LFSA	PA-38-112 Tomahawk	Liverpool Flying School Ltd (G-BSFC)
	G-LFSI	PA-28 Cherokee 140	Liverpool Flying School Ltd (G-AYKV)
	G-LGIO	Colt 240A balloon	Aerial Display Co
	G-LIAN	Robinson R-22B	Cotwell Air Services
	G-LIBB	Cameron V-77 balloon	B. G. Glibbery
	G-LIBS	Hughes 369HS	Air & General Services Ltd
	G-LICK	Cessna 172N	Dacebow Aviation (G-BNTR)
	G-LIDE	PA-31-350 Navajo Chieftain	Woodgate Executive Air Charter Ltd
	G-LIFE	Thunder Ax6-56Z balloon	M. J. & J. Evans
	G-LIGG	Cessna F.182Q	Navair Ltd (G-THAM)
	G-LIMA	R. Commander 114	Tricolore Ltd/Biggin Hill
	G-LINC	Hughes 369HS	Fairglobe Ltd
	G-LIOA	Lockheed 10A Electra ★ (NC5171N)	Science Museum/Wroughton
	G-LION	PA-18 Super Cub 135 (542457 R-167)	A. W. Kennedy
	G-LIOT	Cameron O-77 balloon	D. Eliot
	G-LIPP	BN-2T Turbine Islander	Rhine Army Parachute Association (G-BKJG)
	G-LISA	Steen Skybolt	T. C. Humphreys
	G-LITE	R. Commander 112A	Rhoburt Ltd/Manchester
	G-LIZA	Cessna 340A	M. D. Joy (G-BMDM)
	G-LIZI	PA-28 Cherokee 160	G. & E. A. Newman (G-ARRP)/Redhill
	G-LIZY	Westland Lysander III (V9300) ★	G. A. Warner/Duxford
	G-LJET	Learjet 35A	Tiger Aviation Ltd/Gatwick
	G-LOAG	Cameron N-77 balloon	Matthew Gloag & Son Ltd
	G-LOAN	Cameron N-77 balloon	Newbury Building Soc
	G-LOCH	Piper J-3C-90 Cub	J. M. Greenland
	G-LOGA	BAe ATP	Loganair Ltd/Glasgow
	G-LOGB	BAe ATP	Loganair Ltd/Glasgow
	G-LOGC	—	—
	G-LOGD	—	—
	G-LOGE	BAe ATP	Loganair Ltd (G-BMYL)/Glasgow
	G-LOGP	BAe Jetstream 3108	Loganair Ltd (G-BPZJ)/Glasgow
	G-LOGR	BAe Jetstream 3102	Loganair Ltd (G-BRGR)/Glasgow
	G-LOGS	Robinson R-22B	M. Chantler & ptnrs
	G-LOGT	BAe Jetstream 3102	Loganair Ltd (G-BSFH)/Glasgow
	G-LOGU	BAe Jetstream 3102	Loganair Ltd (G-BRGL)/Glasgow
	G-LOGV	BAe Jetstream 3102	Loganair Ltd (G-BSZK)/Glasgow
	G-LOND	V.806 Viscount	(withdrawn) (G-AOYI)/Southend
	G-LONG	Bell 206L LongRanger	Walsh Aviation
	G-LOOP	Pitts S-1C Special	B. G. Salter
	G-LOOT	EMB-110P1 Bandeirante	Tech Air (Cambridge) Ltd (G-BNOC)
	G-LORD	PA-34-200T Seneca II	Aerohire Ltd/Halfpenny Green
	G-LORI	H.S.125 Srs 403B	Re-Enforce Trading Co Ltd (G-AYOJ)
	G-LORY	Thunder Ax4-31Z balloon	A. J. Moore
	G-LOSM	Gloster Meteor NF.11 (WM167)	Hunter Wing Ltd/Bournemouth
	G-LOSS	Cameron N-77 balloon	D. K. Fish
	G-LOTI	Bleriot XI (replica)	M. L. Beach
	G-LOUP	Partenavia P.68B	M. H. Wolff (G-OCAL/G-BGMY)
	G-LOVX	Cessna 441 Conquest	Hustlepon Ltd/(G-BLCJ)
	G-LOWA	Colt 77A balloon	The Hot-Air Balloon Co Ltd
	G-LOWE	Monnet Sonerai II	J. L. Kinch
	G-LOYA	Cessna FR.172J	T. R. Scorer (G-BLVT)
	G-LOYD	SA.341G Gazelle 1	Appollo Manufacturing (Derby) Ltd (G-SFTC)
	G-LPGO	Cameron V-77 balloon	J. Walter Thompson Co Ltd
	G-LRBJ	BAe 125-1000	British Aerospace PLC
	G-LRII	Bell 206L LongRanger	Carroll Aircraft Operational Services Ltd
	G-LSFI	AA-5A Cheetah	Norfolk Flight Centre (G-BGSK)/Norwich
	G-LSHI	Colt 77A balloon	Lambert Smith Hampton Ltd
	G-LSLH	Schweizer 269C	Homewood Park (Helicopters) Ltd
	G-LSMI	Cessna F.152	Semloh Aviation Services/Andrewsfield
	G-LTNG	Lightning T.5 (XS451)	Lightning Flying Club
	G-LUAR	SOCATA TB.10 Tobago	CB Air Ltd
	G-LUBE	Cameron N-77 balloon	A. C. K. Rawson
	G-LUCA	Thunder Ax7-77Z balloon	R. De-Leyser
	G-LUCE	Cameron A-210 balloon	Aerial Promotions Ltd

Reg.	Type	Owner or Operator	Notes
G-LUCK	Cessna F.150M	T. J. C. Darby	
G-LUCS	Colt 90A balloon	Bavarian Balloon Co Ltd	
G-LUGG	Colt 21A balloon	The Hot-Air Balloon Co Ltd	
G-LUKE	Rutan LongEz	S. G. Busby	
G-LULU	Grob G.109	Strathtay Flying Group	
G-LUNA	PA-32RT-300T Turbo Lance II	E. Cliffe/Norwich	
G-LUSC	Luscombe 8E Silvaire	M. Fowler	
G-LUSI	Luscombe 8E Silvaire	R. J. Walker & J. Wrayton/O. Sarum	
G-LUST	Luscombe 8E Silvaire	M. Griffiths	
G-LUXE	BAe 146-300	British Aerospace PLC (G-SSSH)/Hatfield	
G-LYDD	PA-31 Turbo Navajo	Janes Aviation Ltd (G-BBDU)/Blackpool	
G-LYNN	PA-32RT-300 Lance II	Crosswind Aviation Ltd (G-BGNV)/Leeds	
G-LYNX	Westland WG.13 Lynx	Westland Helicopters Ltd/Yeovil	
G-LYTE	Thunder Ax7-77 balloon	G. M. Bulmer	
G-MAAC	Advanced Airship Corporation ANR-1	Advanced Airship Corporation Ltd	
G-MABI	Cessna F.150L	Shobdon Aircraft Maintenance (G-BGOJ)	
G-MACH	SIAI-Marchetti SF.260	Cheyne Motors Ltd/Popham	
G-MACK	PA-28R Cherokee Arrow 200	JF Packaging	
G-MAFF	BN-2T Islander	FR Aviation Ltd/(G-BJEO)/Bournemouth	
G-MAFI	Dornier Do.228-200	FR Aviation Ltd/Bournemouth	
G-MAGG	Pitts S-1SE Special	C. A. Boardman	
G-MAGY	AS.350B Ecureuil	Quantel Ltd (G-BIYC)	
G-MAIR	PA-34-200T Seneca II	D. C. Massey	
G-MAJS	Airbus A.300-605R	Monarch Airlines Ltd/Luton	
G-MALA	PA-28-181 Archer II	H. Burtwhistle & Son (G-BIIU)	
G-MALC	AA-5 Traveler	C. B. Drew (G-BCPM)	
G-MALK	Cessna F.172N	K. M. Drewitt & J. G. Jackson/Liverpool	
G-MALS	Mooney M.20K-231	C. J. Davy/Biggin Hill	
G-MALT	Colt Flying Hop balloon	The Hot-Air Balloon Co Ltd	
G-MAMO	Cameron V-77 balloon	The Marble Mosaic Co Ltd	
G-MANN	SA.341G Gazelle 1	Robert Fraser & Partners Ltd (G-BKLW)	
G-MANT	Cessna 210L	CHJW Group (G-MAXY)/Coventry	
G-MANX	FRED Srs 2	T. A. Timms	
G-MARC	AS.350B Ecureuil	Gabriel Enterprises Ltd (G-BKHU)	
G-MARE	Schweizer 269C	The Earl of Caledon	
G-MARR	Cessna 421C	Levenmere Ltd (G-JTIE/G-RBBE)	
G-MARS	Beech 400 Beechjet	Havilland Air Ltd (G-RSRS)	
G-MASA	Air & Space 18A gyroplane	M. A. Schumann (G-MELI)	
G-MASC	Jodel D.150A	K. F. & R. Richardson	
G-MASH	Westland Bell 47G-4A	Defence Products Ltd (G-AXKU)	
G-MASL	Mooney M.20J	Beta Trading Ltd	
G-MATE	Moravan Zlin Z.50LS	V. S. E. Norman	
G-MATI	Stolp SA.300 Starduster Too	M. R. Clark & J. McM. Rosser/Newcastle	
G-MATP	BAe ATP	British Aerospace PLC/Woodford	
G-MATS	Colt GA-42 airship	Flying Pictures (Airships) Ltd	
G-MATT	Robin R.2160	Sierra Flying Group (G-BKRC)/Newcastle	
G-MATZ	PA-28 Cherokee 140	Midland Air Training School (G-BASI)	
G-MAUK	Colt 77A balloon	Airship & Balloon Co Ltd	
G-MAVI	Robinson R-22B	Moorgate Aviation	
G-MAWL	Maule M4-210C Rocket	D. Group	
G-MAXI	PA-34-200T Seneca II	C. W. Middlemass	
G-MAXW	Short SD3-60 Variant 100	Euroworld Airways Ltd (G-BLPY)/Gatwick	
G-MAYO	PA-28-161 Warrior II	Jermyk Engineering/Fairoaks	
G-MCAR	PA-32 Cherokee Six 300D	Miller Aerial Spraying Ltd (G-LADA/ G-AYWK)/Wickenby	
G-MCBP	AIA Stampe SV-4C	Stampe Flying Group (G-BALA)	
G-MCKE	Boeing 757-28A	Monarch Airlines Ltd/Luton	
G-MCOX	Fuji FA.200-180AO	W. Surrey Engineering (Shepperton) Ltd	
G-MCPI	Bell 206B JetRanger 3	D. A. C. Pipe (G-ONTB)	
G-MDAC	PA-28-181 Archer II	B. R. Mckay/Bournemouth	
G-MDAS	PA-31-310 Turbo Navajo C	Universal Data Technology Ltd (G-BCJZ)	
G-MDKD	Robinson R-22B	D. K. Duckworth	
G-MDTV	Cameron N-105 balloon	Ideas Factory	
G-MEAH	PA-28 Cherokee Arrow 200	E. J. Meah (G-BSNM)	
G-MEAN	Agusta A.109A	Castle Air Charters Ltd (G-BRYL/G-ROPE/ G-OAMH)	
G-MEAT	Robinson R-22B	St Merryn Meat Ltd	
G-MEBC	Cessna 310-1	P. H. Johnson (G-ROGA/G-ASVV)	
G-MEDC	Beech 95-58 Baron	D. P. Bennett Ltd	
G-MEGA	PA-28R-201T Turbo Arrow III	Travelworth Ltd	
G-MELD	AA-5A Cheetah	Fletcher Aviation Ltd (G-BHCB)/Blackbushe	

Notes	Reg.	Type	Owner or Operator
	G-MELT	Cessna F.172H	Vectair Aviation Ltd (G-AWTI)
	G-MELV	SOCATA Rallye 235E	Wallis & Sons Ltd (G-BIND)
	G-MEME	PA-28R-201 Arrow III	Henry J. Clare Ltd
	G-MERC	Colt 56A balloon	Castles Northgate Ltd
	G-MERG	Mooney M.20J	Corporate Acquisitions Ltd
	G-MERI	PA-28-181 Archer II	Scotia Safari Ltd/Glasgow
	G-MERL	PA-28RT-201 Arrow IV	M. Giles
	G-MERV	PA-28-161 Warrior II	M. N. Choules
	G-META	Bell 222	The Metropolitan Police/Lippitts Hill
	G-METB	Bell 222	The Metropolitan Police/Lippitts Hill
	G-METC	Bell 222	The Metropolitan Police (G-JAMC)/ Lippitts Hill
	G-METE	Gloster Meteor F.8	Air Support Aviation Systems Ltd
	G-METR	Cessna 414A	Metair Aircraft Ltd
	G-MEUP	Cameron A-120 balloon	N. J. Tovey
	G-MFAL	Gulfstream Commander 690D	Marlborough Fine Art (London) Ltd
	G-MFHL	Robinson R-22B	MFH Ltd
	G-MFLI	Cameron V-90 balloon	J. M. Percival
	G-MFMF	Bell 206B JetRanger 3	S.W. Electricity Board (G-BJNJ)/Bristol
	G-MFMM	Scheibe SF.25C Falke	S. Lancs Falke Syndicate
	G-MHBD	Cameron O-105 balloon	K. Hull
	G-MHCA	Enstrom F-28C-UK	Trimcares Ltd (G-SHWW/G-SMUJ/G-BHTF)
	G-MHCC	Bell 206B JetRanger 2	LRC Helicopters Ltd
	G-MHIH	H.S. 125 Srs 700B	Queens Moat Houses PLC (G-BKAA)
	G-MHSL	MBB Bo 105DBS/4	MBB Helicopter Systems Ltd
	G-MICH	Robinson R-22B	A. P. Codling (G-BNKY)
	G-MICK	Cessna F.172N	S. Grant & ptnrs
	G-MICY	Everett Srs 1 gyroplane	D. M. Hughes
	G-MIDG	Midget Mustang	G. A. Stanley
	G-MIFF	Robin DR.400/180	G. E. Bickerton
	G-MIGI	Colt 105A balloon	MI Group Ltd
	G-MIKE	Brookland Hornet	M. H. J. Goldring
	G-MIKY	Cameron 90 Mickey SS balloon	The Walt Disney Co Ltd
	G-MILE	Cameron N-77 balloon	Miles Air Ltd
	G-MILL	PA-32-301T Turbo Saratoga	S. S. Bernholt
	G-MIMI	SOCATA TB.20 Trinidad	T. J. & P. S. Gower/Biggin Hill
	G-MINI	Currie Wot	D. Collinson
	G-MINT	Pitts S-1S Special	T. G. Sanderson/Tollerton
	G-MINX	Bell 47G-4A	R. F. Warner (G-FOOR)
	G-MISR	Robinson R-22B	Wallis & Son Ltd
	G-MISS	Taylor JT.2 Titch	A. Brennan
	G-MIST	Cessna T.210K	J. Summers (G-AYGM)
	G-MITR	Maule MXT-7-180	A. Mitrega
	G-MITS	Cameron N-77 balloon	Colt Car Co Ltd
	G-MITZ	Cameron N-77 balloon	Colt Car Co Ltd
	G-MKAK	Colt 77A balloon	Airship & Balloon Co Ltd
	G-MKAY	Cessna 172N	Limbros Demolition Ltd
	G-MKIX	V.S.361 Spitfire F.IX (NH238)	D. W. Arnold
	G-MKVB	V.S.349 Spitfire LF.VB (BM597)	T. Routis
	G-MKXI	V.S.365 Spitfire PR.XI (PL965)	C. P. B. Horsley
	G-MLAS	Cessna 182E	*Parachute jump trainer*/St Merryn
	G-MLBU	PA-46-310P Malibu	Northern Scaffold Group Ltd
	G-MLFF	PA-23 Aztec 250E	Brands Hatch Circuit Ltd (G-WEBB/ G-BJBU)
	G-MLGL	Colt 21A balloon	Colt Balloons Ltd
	G-MLUA	PA-28 Cherokee 140	Ian Foster Aviation (G-AYJT)
	G-MLWI	Thunder Ax7-77 balloon	M. L. & L. P. Willoughby
	G-MOAC	Beech F33A Bonanza	Chalkfarm Productions Ltd
	G-MOAK	Schempp-Hirth Nimbus 3DM	P. W. Lever
	G-MOAT	Beech 200 Super King Air	Thurston Aviation (Stansted) Ltd
	G-MOFF	Cameron O-77 balloon	D. M. Moffat
	G-MOGG	Cessna F.172N	I. Grimshaw (G-BHDY)
	G-MOGI	AA-5A Cheetah	T. C. C. Pedley (G-BFMU)
	G-MOGY	Robinson R-22B	Reachmain Ltd
	G-MOHR	Cameron 105 Sarotti balloon	Cameron Balloons Ltd
	G-MOLE	Taylor JT.2 Titch	S. R. Mowle
	G-MOLL	PA-32-301T Turbo Saratoga	K. Morrissey
	G-MOLY	PA-23 Apache 160	R. R. & M. T. Thorogood (G-APFV)/St Just
	G-MONA	M.S.880B Rallye Club	G. L. Thomas
	G-MONB	Boeing 757-2T7ER	Monarch Airlines Ltd/Luton
	G-MONC	Boeing 757-2T7	Monarch Airlines Ltd/Luton
	G-MOND	Boeing 757-2T7	Monarch Airlines Ltd/Luton
	G-MONE	Boeing 757-2T7ER	Monarch Airlines Ltd/Luton

Reg.	Type	Owner or Operator	Notes
G-MONF	Boeing 737-3Y0	Monarch Airlines/EuroBerlin	
G-MONG	Boeing 737-3Y0	Monarch Airlines/Canadian (C-FPWG)	
G-MONH	Boeing 737-3Y0	Monarch Airlines Ltd/EuroBerlin	
G-MONI	Monnet Moni	R. J. Baron	
G-MONJ	Boeing 757-2T7ER	Monarch Airlines Ltd/Luton	
G-MONK	Boeing 757-2T7ER	Monarch Airlines Ltd/Luton	
G-MONM	Boeing 737-3Y0	Monarch Airlines Ltd/EuroBerlin	
G-MONN	Boeing 737-33A	Monarch Airlines Ltd/EuroBerlin	
G-MONP	Boeing 737-33A	Monarch Airlines Ltd/Luton	
G-MONU	Boeing 737-33A	Monarch Airlines Ltd/EuroBerlin	
G-MONV	Boeing 737-33A	Monarch Airlines Ltd/Luton	
G-MOON	Mooney M.20K	M. A. Eccles	
G-MOOR	SOCATA TB.10 Tobago	G. A. Moore (G-MILK)	
G-MOOS	P.56 Provost T.1	T. J. Hanna (G-BGKA)	
G-MORL	Maule MX-7-180	K. Moses	
G-MOTH	D.H.82A Tiger Moth (K2567)	M. C. Russell/Duxford	
G-MOTO	PA-24 Comanche 160	C. C. Letchford & A. J. Redknapp (G-EDHE/ G-ASFH)	
G-MOUL	Maule M6-235	B. C. Abela	
G-MOUR	H.S. Gnat T.1 (XR991)	D. J. Gilmour	
G-MOUS	Cameron 90 Mickey SS balloon	The Walt Disney Co Ltd	
G-MOVE	PA-60 Aerostar 601P	MLP Aviaton Ltd/Elstree	
G-MOVI	PA-32R-301 Saratoga SP	Peter Walker (Heritage) Ltd (G-MARI)	
G-MOZZ	Avions Mudry CAP.10B	Brandzone Ltd	
G-MPBH	Cessna FA.152	Metropolitan Police Flying Club (G-FLIC/ G-BILV)	
G-MPCU	Cessna 402B	Atlantic Air Transport Ltd/Coventry	
G-MPWH	Rotorway Executive	MPW Aviation Ltd	
G-MPWI	Robin HR.100/210	Propwash Investments Ltd/Cardiff	
G-MPWT	PA-34-220T Seneca III	MPW Aviation Ltd	
G-MRPP	PA-34-220T Seneca III	P. E. Pearce	
G-MRSN	Robinson R-22B	P. J. Marson	
G-MRST	PA-28RT-201 Arrow IV	Winchfield Enterprises Ltd	
G-MRTY	Cameron N-77 balloon	R. A. & P. G. Vale	
G-MSDJ	AS.350B-1 Ecureuil	Denis Ferranti Hoverknights Ltd (G-BPOH)	
G-MSFC	PA-38-112 Tomahawk	Sherwood Flying Club Ltd/Tollerton	
G-MSFY	H.S.125 Srs 700B	Mohamed Said Fakhry/Heathrow	
G-MSSA	BN-2T Islander	Pilatus BN Ltd (G-TEMI/G-BJYX)/ Bembridge	
G-MTLE	Cessna 501 Citation	Talan Ltd (G-GENE)	
G-MUFF	AS.355F-1 Twin Squirrel	Lynton Aviation Ltd (G-CORR)	
G-MUIL	Cessna 172M	Torosay Sandpit Ltd	
G-MUIR	Cameron V-65 balloon	L. C. M. Muir	
G-MULL	Douglas DC-10-30	British Airways *New Forest*/Gatwick	
G-MUMS	PA-28-161 Warrior II	A. J. Wood	
G-MUNI	Mooney M.20J	Danyderwen Consultants Co Ltd	
G-MURF	AA-5B Tiger	D. Collins (G-JOAN/G-BFML)	
G-MUSO	Rutan LongEz	M. Moran	
G-MUTE	Colt 31A balloon	Redmalt Ltd	
G-MXVI	V.S.361 Spitfire LF.XVIe (TE184)	Myrick Aviation Services Ltd	
G-NAAS	AS.355F-1 Twin Squirrel	McAlpine Helicopters Ltd (G-BPRG)	
G-NAAT	H.S. Gnat T.1	Hunter Wing Ltd/Bournemouth	
G-NABS	Robinson R-22B	Arian Helicopters Ltd	
G-NACA	Norman NAC.2 Freelance 180	Aeronortec Ltd	
G-NACI	Norman NAC.1 Srs 100	Aeronortec Ltd	
G-NACL	Norman NAC.6 Fieldmaster	Croplease PLC (G-BNEG)	
G-NACM	Norman NAC.6 Fieldmaster	Croplease PLC	
G-NACN	Norman NAC.6 Fieldmaster	Croplease PLC	
G-NACO	Norman NAC.6 Fieldmaster	Croplease PLC	
G-NACP	Norman NAC.6 Fieldmaster	Croplease PLC	
G-NAIL	Cessna 340A	Parelarch Ltd (G-DEXI)	
G-NALI	Cessna 152	N. A. Ali (G-BHVM)	
G-NASA	Lockheed T-33A-5-LO	A. S. Topen (G-TJET)/Cranfield	
G-NASH	AA-5A Cheetah	M. J. Dant/Southampton	
G-NATT	R. Commander 114A	Northgleam Ltd	
G-NATX	Cameron O-65 balloon	A. Faulkner	
G-NATY	H. S. Gnat T.1	F. C. Hackett-Jones	
G-NAVO	PA-31-325 Navajo C/R	Mega Yield Ltd (G-BMPV)	
G-NAZO	PA-31-310 Navajo B	Pathway Holdings Ltd (G-AZIM)	
G-NBDD	Robin DR.400/180	D. Dufton/Sherburn	
G-NBSI	Cameron N-77 balloon	Nottingham Hot-Air Balloon Club	
G-NCUB	Piper J-3C-65 Cub	N. Thomson (G-BGXV)/Norwich	

Notes	Reg.	Type	Owner or Operator
	G-NDGC	Grob G.109	C. H. Appleyard
	G-NDNI	NDN-1 Firecracker	Norman Marsh Aircraft Ltd
	G-NDRW	Colt AS-80 Mk II airship	Huntair Ltd
	G-NEAL	PA-32 Cherokee Six 260	Midland Aircraft Maintenance Ltd (G-BFPY)
	G-NEEL	Rotorway Executive 90	P. N. Haigh
	G-NEEP	Bell 206B JetRanger	Dollar Air Services Ltd/Coventry
	G-NEGS	Thunder Ax7-77 balloon	R. Holden
	G-NEIL	Thunder Ax3 balloon	Islington Motors (Trowbridge) Ltd
	G-NEPB	Cameron N-77 balloon	The Post Office
	G-NEVL	Learjet 35A	Hatfield Executive Aviation Ltd/Cranfield
	G-NEWR	PA-31-350 Navajo Chieftain	Eastern Air Executive Ltd/Sturgate
	G-NEWS	Bell 206B JetRanger 3	Peter Press Ltd
	G-NEWT	Beech 35 Bonanza	D. W. Mickleburgh (G-APVW)
	G-NGBI	AA-5B Tiger	Filemart Ltd (G-JAKK/G-BHWI)/Biggin Hill
	G-NGRM	Spezio DAL.1	P. A. Crawford
	G-NHRH	PA-28 Cherokee 140	H. Dodd
	G-NHVH	Maule M5-235C Lunar Rocket	Commercial Go-Karts Ltd/Exeter
	G-NICH	Robinson R-22B	Panair Ltd
	G-NICK	PA-18 Super Cub 95	J. G. O'Donnell & I. Woolacott
	G-NICO	Robinson R-22B	N. G. Cook
	G-NIFR	Beech 76 Duchess	J. J. Baumhardt
	G-NIGE	Luscombe 8E Silvaire	Pullmerit Ltd (G-BSHG)
	G-NIGS	Thunder Ax7-65 balloon	A. N. F. Pertwee
	G-NIKD	Cameron O-120 balloon	D. S. King
	G-NIKI	Robinson R-22B	N. M. Leatherhead
	G-NIKE	PA-28-181 Archer II	Key Properties Ltd/White Waltham
	G-NIKY	PA-31-350 Navajo Chieftain	Ashcombe Ltd (G-BPAR)
	G-NINA	PA-28-161 Warrior II	Bailey Aviation Ltd (G-BEUC)
	G-NIOS	PA-32R-301 Saratoga SP	Metafin Holdings Ltd
	G-NISR	R. Commander 690A	Z. I. Bilbeisi
	G-NITA	PA-28 Cherokee 180	Universal Air Services Ltd (G-AVVG)
	G-NIUK	Douglas DC-10-30	British Airways *Cairn Edward Forest*/ Gatwick
	G-NJAG	Cessna 207	G. H. Nolan Ltd
	G-NJML	PA-34-220T Seneca III	Oxford Management Ltd
	G-NJSH	Robinson R-22B	T. F. Hawes
	G-NNAC	PA-18 Super Cub 135	P. A. Wilde
	G-NOBI	Spezio Sport HES-1	M. R. Clark
	G-NODE	AA-5B Tiger	Curd & Green Ltd/Elstree
	G-NODY	American General AG-5B	The Cabair Group Ltd/Elstree
	G-NOIR	Bell 222	Arlington Securities Ltd (G-OJLC/G-OSEB/ G-BNDA)
	G-NONI	AA-5 Traveler	E. B. Landsler (G-BBDA)
	G-NORD	SNCAN NC.854	H. J. Taggart
	G-NOTT	Nott ULD-2 balloon	J. R. P. Nott
	G-NOVO	Colt AS-56 airship	Thunder & Colt Ltd
	G-NRDC	NDN-6 Fieldmaster	The Norman Aeroplane Co Ltd/Cardiff
	G-NROA	Boeing 727-217	Dan-Air Services Ltd (G-BKNG)/Gatwick
	G-NSTG	Cessna F.150F	N. S. T. Griffin (G-ATNI)/Blackpool
	G-NTBI	Bell 206B JetRanger 3	E. Midlands Helicopters Ltd
	G-NTOO	SA.365N-2 Dauphin 2	Bond Helicopters Ltd
	G-NTWO	SA.365N-2 Dauphin 2	Bond Helicopters Ltd
	G-NUIG	Beech C90-1 King Air	Norwich Union Fire Insurance Soc (G-BKIP)
	G-NUNK	Hughes 369HS	Nunkeeling Ltd (G-BMSP)
	G-NUTZ	AS.355F-1 Twin Squirrel	Lake & Elliot Helicopters Ltd (G-BLRI)
	G-NWPR	Cameron N-77 balloon	Post Office N.W. Postal Board
	G-NYTE	Cessna F.337G	County Garage Ltd (G-BATH)
	G-NZGL	Cameron O-105 balloon	P. G. & P. M. Vale
	G-NZSS	Boeing Stearman N2S-5 (343251)	Pacific Shelf 331 Ltd
	G-OAAC	Airtour AH-77B balloon	Army Air Corps
	G-OAAL	PA-38-112 Tomahawk	Cumbernauld Aviation Ltd
	G-OAAS	Short SD3-60 Variant 100	Aurigny Air Services Ltd (G-BLIL)/Guernsey
	G-OABC	Colt 69A balloon	Airship & Balloon Co Ltd
	G-OABG	Hughes 369E	A. B. Gee of Ripley
	G-OABI	Cessna 421C	Blue Star Ship Management Ltd
	G-OABY	AB-206 JetRanger 2	Michael A. Lenihan & Associates Ltd (G-BCWM)
	G-OACE	Valentin Taifun 17E	Aero Club Enstone
	G-OADY	Beech 76 Duchess	M. T. Dawson
	G-OAEL	AA-5A Cheetah	Light Aircraft Group
	G-OAFB	Beech 200 Super King Air	A. F. Budge Ltd/Gamston
	G-OAFC	Airtour 56AH balloon	P. J. Donnellan & L. A. Watts

Reg.	Type	Owner or Operator	Notes
G-OAFT	Cessna 152	L. E. Steynor (G-BNKM)	
G-OAFY	SA.341G Gazelle 1	R. J. Best (G-SFTH/G-BLAP)	
G-OAHC	Beech F33C Bonanza	A. H. Clark & Sons (G-BTTF)	
G-OAHF	Boeing 757-27B	Britannia Airways Ltd/Luton	
G-OAJH	AA-5A Cheetah	BLS Aviation (G-KILT/G-BJFA)/Elstree	
G-OAKC	PA-31-350 Navajo Chieftain	Air Kilroe Ltd (G-WSSC)/Manchester	
G-OAKJ	BAe Jetstream 3200	Air Kilroe Ltd (G-BOTJ)/Manchester	
G-OAKL	Beech 200 Super King Air	Air Kilroe Ltd (G-BJZG)/Manchester	
G-OAKM	Beech 200 Super King Air	Air Kilroe Ltd (G-BCUZ)/Manchester	
G-OAKZ	Beech C90A King Air	Barratt Developments Ltd	
G-OALD	SOCATA TB.20 Trinidad	Mike Little Preparations Ltd	
G-OALF	Dornier Do.228-202K	Asterrose Ltd	
G-OAMG	Bell 206B JetRanger 3	Millfields Estate Ltd	
G-OAMY	Cessna 152	Warwickshire Flying Training Centre Ltd/ Birmingham	
G-OANC	PA-28-161 Warrior II	Woodvale Aviation Co Ltd (G-BFAD)	
G-OANI	PA-28-161 Warrior II	J. A. Caliva	
G-OANT	PA-23 Aztec 250	Air Navigation & Trading Ltd (G-TRFM)/ Blackpool	
G-OAPR	Brantly B.2B	Helicopter International Magazine/ Weston-s-Mare	
G-OAPW	Glaser-Dirks DG.400	A. P. Walsh	
G-OARV	ARV Super 2	H. Pound	
G-OASH	Robinson R-22B	A. S. Hawkridge	
G-OATC	PA-31-310 Turbo Navajo C	Roger Clark Mechanical Engineering Ltd (G-OJPW/G-BGCC)	
G-OATP	BAe ATP	Manx Airlines Ltd (G-BZWW)/*King Godred Crovan 1079-1095*/Ronaldsway	
G-OATS	PA-38-112 Tomahawk	Truman Aviation Ltd/Tollerton	
G-OATV	Cameron V-77 balloon	Gone With The Wind Ltd	
G-OAUS	Sikorsky S-76A	Darley Stud Management Co Ltd	
G-OAVX	Beech 200 Super King Air	ATS Aircharter Ltd (G-IBCA/G-BMCA)	
G-OAWY	Cessna 340A	Industrial Alum Ltd	
G-OBAA	Beech B200 Super King Air	BAA PLC	
G-OBAL	Mooney M.20J	Britannia Airways Ltd/Luton	
G-OBAT	Cessna F.152	J. J. Baumhardt	
G-OBBC	Colt 90A balloon	R. A. & M. A. Riley	
G-OBEA	BAe Jetstream 3102-01	Birmingham European Airways Ltd	
G-OBED	PA-34-200T Seneca II	V. J. Holden/Newcastle	
G-OBEL	Cessna 500 Citation	Gator Aviation Ltd (G-BOGA)	
G-OBEY	PA-23 Aztec 250C	Creaton Aircraft Services (G-BAAJ)	
G-OBHD	Short SD3-60 Variant 100	Jersey European Airways Ltd (G-BNDK)	
G-OBHX	Cessna F.172H	Jones Aviation Sales Ltd (G-AWMU)	
G-OBIL	Robinson R-22B	F. C. Noakes & M. R. Tideswell	
G-OBLC	Beech 76 Duchess	Multirun Ltd	
G-OBLK	Short SD3-60 Variant 100	Jersey European Airways Ltd (G-BNDI)	
G-OBMA	Boeing 737-33A	British Midland Airways Ltd/E. Midlands	
G-OBMB	Boeing 737-33A	British Midland Airways Ltd/E. Midlands	
G-OBMC	Boeing 737-33A	British Midland Airways Ltd/E. Midlands	
G-OBMD	Boeing 737-33A	British Midland Airways Ltd/E. Midlands	
G-OBMF	Boeing 737-4Y0	British Midland Airways Ltd/E. Midlands	
G-OBMG	Boeing 737-4Y0	British Midland Airways Ltd/E. Midlands	
G-OBMH	Boeing 737-33A	British Midland Airways Ltd/E. Midlands	
G-OBMJ	Boeing 737-33A	British Midland Airways Ltd/E. Midlands	
G-OBMK	Boeing 737-4Q8	British Midland Airways Ltd/E. Midlands	
G-OBML	Boeing 737-3Q8	British Midland Airways Ltd (G-KKUH)/ E. Midlands	
G-OBMM	Boeing 737-4Y0	British Midland Airways Ltd/E. Midlands	
G-OBMN	Boeing 737-46B	British Midland Airways Ltd (G-BOPJ)/ E. Midlands	
G-OBMO	Boeing 737-4Q8	British Midland Airways Ltd/E. Midlands	
G-OBMP	Boeing 737-3Y0	British Midland Airways Ltd/E. Midlands	
G-OBMS	Cessna F.172N	D. Beverley & W. F. van Schoten	
G-OBMW	AA-5 Traveler	Fretcourt Ltd (G-BDFV)	
G-OBOH	Short SD3-60	Jersey European Airways (G-BNDJ)	
G-OBOZ	Boeing 757-23AF	Anglo Airlines Ltd/Gatwick	
G-OBPG	Brantly B.2B	A. C. Dent (G-AWIO)	
G-OBSF	AA-5A Cheetah	Lowlog Ltd (G-ODSF/G-BEUW)	
G-OBSV	Partenavia P.68B Observer	Porton Holdings Ltd	
G-OBUD	Colt 69A balloon	Hot-Air Balloon Co Ltd	
G-OBUY	Colt 69A balloon	Airship & Balloon Co Ltd	
G-OCAN	Cessna 340A	Ripley Aviation Ltd	
G-OCAR	Colt 77A balloon	M. D. Cookson	

Notes	Reg.	Type	Owner or Operator
	G-OCAT	Eiri PIK-20E	W. A. D. Thorp/Doncaster
	G-OCBA	H.S.125 Srs 3B	Westminster Aviation Ltd (G-MRFB/ G-AZVS)
	G-OCBB	Bell 206B JetRanger 2	CG Group Ltd (G-BASE)
	G-OCBC	Cameron A-120 balloon	Corporate Balloon Co
	G-OCCA	PA-32R-301 Saratoga SP	CC Aviation Ltd (G-BRIX)/Elstree
	G-OCCC	BAe 125 Srs 800B	Consolidated Contractors International
	G-OCCI	BAe 125 Srs 800B	Consolidated Contractors International (UK) Ltd
	G-OCDS	Aviamilano F.8L Falco II	P. G. Greenslade & P. J. Collins (G-VEGL)
	G-OCGJ	Robinson R-22B	Exec-H Flying Centre Ltd/Halfpenny Green
	G-OCHL	Bell 206B JetRanger 3	Brikos Air Ltd
	G-OCJK	Schweizer 269C	M. D. Thorpe
	G-OCJR	SA.341G Gazelle 1	Reeds Motor Co (G-BRGS)
	G-OCND	Cameron O-77 balloon	D. P. H. Smith & Dalby
	G-OCNW	BAC One-Eleven 201AC	British Air Ferries (G-ASJH)/Stansted
	G-OCPC	Cessna FA.152	Westward Airways (Lands End) Ltd/St Just
	G-OCPI	Cessna 500 Citation	Cooling Power Industries Ltd (G-OXEC)
	G-OCPL	AA-5A Cheetah	Walsh Aviation Ltd (G-RCPW/G-BERM)
	G-OCTA	BN-2A Mk III-2 Trislander	Aurigny Air Services Ltd (G-BCXW)
	G-OCTI	PA-32 Cherokee Six 260	J. K. Sharkey (G-BGZX)/Elstree
	G-OCTU	PA-28-161 Cadet	J. P. Alexander
	G-OCUB	Piper J-3C-90 Cub	C. A. Foss & P. A. Brook/Shoreham
	G-OCWC	AA-5A Cheetah	Garrick Aviation (G-WULL)
	G-ODAD	Colt 77A balloon	K. Meehan
	G-ODAH	Aerotek-Pitts S.2A Special	S. E. Marples (G-BDKS)
	G-ODAM	AA-5A Cheetah	D. Hilditch/Elstree
	G-ODAY	Cameron N-56 balloon	C. O. Day (Estate Agents)
	G-ODEL	Falconar F-11-3	G. F. Brummell
	G-ODEN	PA-28-161 Cadet	J. Appleton
	G-ODER	Cameron O-77 balloon	W. H. Morgan
	G-ODHL	Cameron N-77 balloon	DHL International (UK) Ltd
	G-ODIL	Bell 206B JetRanger	Assetglobal Ltd
	G-ODIR	PA-23 Aztec 250D	Metstar Ltd (G-AZGB)
	G-ODIY	Colt 69A balloon	Flying Pictures (Balloons) Ltd
	G-ODJP	Robinson R-22	R. E. Todd
	G-ODLG	D.H.114 Heron 2	D. Liddle-Grainger (G-ARKU)
	G-ODLY	Cessna 310J	R. J. Huband (G-TUBY/G-ASZZ)
	G-ODMC	AS.350B-1 Ecureuil	D. M. Coombs (G-BPVF)
	G-ODMM	PA-31-350 Navajo Chieftain	Birmingham Aviation Ltd
	G-ODNP	Cessna 310R	Bostonair Ltd/Humberside
	G-ODSC	Enstrom 280FX	Heliflair Ltd (G-BSDZ)/Shoreham
	G-OEAC	Mooney M.20J	Trifik Services Ltd
	G-OECH	AA-5A Cheetah	G. W. Plowman & Sons Ltd (G-BKBE)
	G-OEDB	PA-38-112 Tomahawk	Air Delta Bravo Ltd (G-BGGJ)/Elstree
	G-OEDP	Cameron N-77 balloon	M. J. Betts & Eastern Counties Newspapers
	G-OEEC	Short SD3-60 Variant 100	Shorts Aircraft Financing Ltd (G-BPKY)
	G-OEGG	Cameron 65 Egg SS balloon	Airship & Balloon Co Ltd
	G-OESX	PA-23 Aztec 250E	Greenacre Services Ltd (G-BAJX)
	G-OEYE	Rans S.10 Sakota	J. D. Haslam
	G-OFCM	Cessna F172L	F. C. M Aviation Ltd (G-AZUN)/Guernsey
	G-OFBJ	Thunder Ax7-77 balloon	N. D. Hicks
	G-OFER	PA-18 Super Cub 150	M. S. W. Meagher
	G-OFHJ	Cessna 441	Tilling Associates Ltd (G-HSON)
	G-OFIT	SOCATA TB.10 Tobago	G. S.M. Brain (G-BRIU)
	G-OFIZ	Cameron 80 Can SS balloon	Airship & Balloon Co Ltd
	G-OFJS	Robinson R-22B	F. J. Saunders (G-BNXJ)
	G-OFLG	SOCATA TB.10 Tobago	P. Fleming (G-JMWT)
	G-OFLI	Colt 105A balloon	Airship & Balloon Co Ltd
	G-OFLT	EMB-110P1 Bandeirante	Flightline Ltd (G-MOBL)/Southend
	G-OFLY	Cessna 210L	A. P. Mothew/Stapleford
	G-OFOR	Thunder Ax3 balloon	A. Walker
	G-OFOX	Denney Aerocraft Kitfox	P. R. Skeels
	G-OFRB	Everett gyroplane	Roger Savage (Photography)
	G-OFRH	Cessna 421C	Aquarange Ltd (G-NORX)
	G-OFRT	L.188C Electra	Channel Express Group PLC/ Bournemouth
	G-OFTI	PA-28 Cherokee 140	FTI Aviation Ltd (G-BRKU)/Biggin Hill
	G-OFUN	Valentin Taifun 17E	J. A. Sangster/Booker
	G-OGAR	PZL SZD-45A Ogar	N. C. Grayson
	G-OGAS	Westland WG.30 Srs 100	British International Helicopters Ltd (G-BKNW)/Aberdeen
	G-OGCA	PA-28-161 Warrior II	GC Aviation Partnership/Belfast

Reg.	Type	Owner or Operator	Notes
G-OGCI	Short SD3-60 Variant 100	Euroworld Airways Ltd (G-BNBD)/Gatwick	
G-OGEM	PA-28-181 Archer II	GEM Rewinds Ltd	
G-OGET	PA-39 Twin Comanche 160 C/R	P. G. Kitchingman (G-AYXY)	
G-OGGS	Thunder Ax8-84 balloon	G. Gamble & Sons (Quorn) Ltd	
G-OGIL	Short SD3-30 Variant 100	Shorts/Gill Air (G-BITV)/Newcastle	
G-OGJS	Puffer Cozy	G. J. Stamper	
G-OGOA	AS.350B Ecureuil	Lomas Helicopters Ltd (G-PLMD/G-NIAL)	
G-OGOB	Schweizer 269C	Lomas Helicopters (Training) Ltd (G-GLEE/ G-BRUW)	
G-OGOC	Robinson R-22B	M. Horn & Rainbow Wholesale Suppliers Ltd (G-HODG)	
G-OGOS	Everett Autogyro	R. Abercrombie	
G-OGRV	PA-31-350 Navajo Chieftain	A. N. J. & S. L. Palmer (G-BMPX)	
G-OGTS	Air Command 532 Elite	GTS Engineering (Coventry) Ltd	
G-OHCA	SC.5 Belfast (XR363)	HeavyLift Cargo Airlines Ltd/Southend	
G-OHEA	H.S.125 Srs 3B/RA	Rogers Aviation Sales Ltd (G-AVRG)/ Cranfield	
G-OHHL	Robinson R-22B	Hillar Helicopters Ltd	
G-OHMS	AS.355F-1 Twin Squirrel	S.W. Electricity PLC	
G-OHOG	PA-28 Cherokee 140	C. R. Guggenheim (G-AVFY)	
G-OHOT	V.813 Viscount	British Air Ferries Ltd/(G-BMAT/G-AZLT)/ Southend	
G-OIAN	M.S.880B Rallye Club	Ian Richard Transport Services Ltd	
G-OIBM	R. Commander 114	South Coast Computers Ltd (G-BLVZ)	
G-OIBO	PA-28 Cherokee 180	J. D. Skidmore (G-AVAZ)	
G-OICS	Bell 206A JetRanger	Industrial Control Services PLC	
G-OIDW	Cessna F.150GF	I. D. Wakeling	
G-OIEA	PA-31P Pressurised Navajo	Inter European Airways Ltd (G-BBTW)/ Cardiff	
G-OILY	D.H.C-6 Twin Otter 310	BAC Leasing	
G-OIMC	Cessna 152	E. Midlands Flying School Ltd	
G-OING	AA-5A Cheetah ★	Abraxas Aviation Ltd (G-BFPD)/Denham	
G-OINK	Piper J-3C-65 Cub	A. R. Harding (G-BILD/G-KERK)	
G-OIOI	EH Industries EH.101	Westland Helicopters Ltd/Yeovil	
G-OIOW	Hughes 369D	Magnum Helicopters (UK) Ltd	
G-OISF	Fuji FA.200-180	Hamilton Rentals (UK) Ltd (G-BAPT)	
G-OISO	Cessna FRA.150L	Crisptime Ltd (G-BBJW)	
G-OITN	AS.355F-1 Twin Squirrel	Independent Television News Ltd	
G-OJAC	Mooney M.20J	Hornet Engineering Ltd	
G-OJAE	Hughes 269C	Jade Air Engineering Ltd/Shoreham	
G-OJAV	BN-2A Mk III-2 Trislander	Janes Aviation Ltd (G-BDOS)/Blackpool	
G-OJAY	EMB-110PI Bandeirante	J&J Air Charters Ltd/Exeter	
G-OJBA	Beech B200 Super King Air	M1 Machinery Ltd/Luton	
G-OJCB	AB-206B JetRanger 2	G. Day Aviation Ltd	
G-OJCW	PA-32RT-300 Lance II	M. J. Metham/Blackbushe	
G-OJDC	Thunder Ax7-77 balloon	J. Crosby	
G-OJET	BAe 146-100	Manx Airlines Ltd (G-BRJS/G-OBAF/ G-SCHH)/King Harold (1237-1248)	
G-OJGA	Beech 200 Super King Air	RM Aviation Ltd/Leavesden	
G-OJIM	PA-28R-201T Turbo Arrow III	Motomecca Spares Ltd	
G-OJJB	Mooney M.20K	Jeff Brown (Aviation Services)	
G-OJMR	Airbus A.300-605R	Monarch Airlines Ltd/Luton	
G-OJON	Taylor JT.2 Titch	J. H. Fell	
G-OJPI	Robinson R-22B	JPI Group Ltd	
G-OJSY	Short SD3-60	Jersey European/Business Air (G-BKKT)	
G-OJUG	PA-31-350 Navajo Chieftain	Air International (Manchester) Ltd (G-SCOT)	
G-OJVC	J/1N Alpha	M. C. Boddington & P. D. Castle (G-AHCL)/ Sywell	
G-OJVH	Cessna F.150H	Yorkshire Light Aircraft Ltd (G-AWJZ)/ Leeds	
G-OJVI	Robinson R-22B	JV Investments Ltd (G-OJVJ)	
G-OJWS	PA-28-161 Warrior II	Metacomco PLC	
G-OKAG	PA-28R Cherokee Arrow 180	Panorama Design Consultants Ltd	
G-OKAT	AS.350B Ecureuil	Tom Walkinshaw Racing Ltd (G-BGIM)	
G-OKAY	Pitts S-1E Special	Aerial & Aerobatic Service/Booker	
G-OKCC	Cameron N-90 balloon	Kerridge Computer Co Ltd	
G-OKEN	PA-28R-201T Turbo Arrow III	K. Hassall	
G-OKIT	Rotorway Executive	P. T. Waldron	
G-OKSP	Cessna 500 Citation	Chelsea Girl Ltd	
G-OKYA	Cameron V-77 balloon	14/20 Kings Hussars	
G-OKYM	PA-28 Cherokee 140	D. Hotham (G-AVLS)	
G-OLAF	Beech C90 King Air	Westair Flying Services Ltd (G-BFVX)/ Blackpool	

Notes	Reg.	Type	Owner or Operator
	G-OLAH	Short SD3-60 Variant 100	Gill Aviation Ltd (G-BPCO)/G-RMSS/ G-BKKU
	G-OLAU	Robinson R-22B	P. M. Green
	G-OLBA	Short SD3-60 Variant 100	Shorts Aircraft Financing Ltd (G-BOFG)
	G-OLBC	PA-23 Aztec 250	Metronote Business Group Ltd (G-BHCT)/ Denham
	G-OLCA	BAe 146-200	British Aerospace PLC
	G-OLCB	BAe 146-200	British Aerospace PLC
	G-OLCC	BAe ATP	Loganair Ltd/Glasgow
	G-OLCD	BAe ATP	Loganair Ltd/Glasgow
	G-OLDN	Bell 206L LongRanger	A. G. M. Davis (G-TBCA/G-BFAL)
	G-OLDY	Luton LA-5 Major	M. P. & A. P. Sargent
	G-OLEE	Cessna F.152	Aerohire Ltd/Halfpenny Green
	G-OLES	Partenavia P.68C	D. Henrikson (G-JAJV)
	G-OLFC	PA-38-112 Tomahawk	T. F. L. Hayes (G-BGZG)
	G-OLFR	H.S. 125 Srs 403B	Osprey Aviation Ltd (G-BRXR/G-AXYJ)/ Southend
	G-OLFS	M.S.880B Rallye Club	M. A. Kempson (G-AYYZ)/Dunkeswell
	G-OLFT	R. Commander 114	B. C. Richens (G-WJMN)/Redhill
	G-OLGW	Short SD3-60 Variant 100	Sports Products Ltd (G-BOUW)
	G-OLIZ	Robinson R-22B	P & I Data Services Ltd
	G-OLLE	Cameron O-84 balloon	N. A. Robertson
	G-OLLI	Cameron O-31 SS balloon	N. A. Robertson
	G-OLLY	PA-31-350 Navajo Chieftain	Barnes Olsen Aeroleasing Ltd (G-BCES)
	G-OLMA	Partenavia P.68B	C. M. Evans (G-BGBT)
	G-OLRT	Robinson R-22B	Lambourne Racehorse Transport Ltd
	G-OLSC	Cessna 182A	London Skydiving Centre Ltd (G-ATNU)/ Cranfield
	G-OLTN	Short SD3-60 Variant 100	Shorts Aircraft Financing Ltd (G-BOFH)
	G-OLUM	Robinson R-22B	N. J. Hopkinson
	G-OLVR	FRED Srs 2	A. R. Oliver
	G-OMAC	Cessna FR.172E	R. Knox & R. Conway
	G-OMAF	Dornier Do.228-200	FR Aviation Ltd/Bournemouth
	G-OMAR	PA-34-220T Seneca III	Redhill Flying Club
	G-OMAT	PA-28 Cherokee 140	Midland Air Training School (G-JIMY/ G-AYUG)/Coventry
	G-OMAX	Brantly B.2B	P. D. Benmax (G-AVJN)
	G-OMCL	Cessna 550 Citation II	Quantel Ltd/Biggin Hill
	G-OMDH	Hughes 369E	Stilgate Ltd/Booker
	G-OMDS	H.S.748 Srs 2A	Azedcrest Ltd (G-BPFU/G-EDIN)
	G-OMEC	AB-206B JetRanger 3	Star Construction Group Ltd (G-OBLD)
	G-OMED	AA-5B Tiger	Caslon Ltd (G-BERL)/Elstree
	G-OMGA	H.S.125 Srs 600B/2	MAGEC Aviation Ltd (G-BSHL/G-BBMD)/ Luton
	G-OMGB	H.S.125 Srs 600B	MAGEC Aviation Ltd (G-BKBM/G-BCCL)/ Luton
	G-OMGC	H.S.125 Srs 600B	MAGEC Aviation Ltd (G-BKCD/G-BDOA)
	G-OMGE	BAe 125 Srs 800B	GEC Marconi Ltd (G-BTMG)/Luton
	G-OMHC	PA-28RT-201 Arrow IV	M. H. Cundley/Redhill
	G-OMHS	AS.355FD-1 Twin Squirrel	S. W. Electricity PLC
	G-OMIL	Beech 58 Baron	Millhouse Aviation Ltd
	G-OMJB	Bell 206B JetRanger	Martin Brundle (Overseas) Ltd
	G-OMKF	Aero Designs Pulsar	M. K. Faro
	G-OMMC	Mooney M.20J	A. D. Russell/Bourn
	G-OMNI	PA-28R Cherokee Arrow 200D	G. H. Lee
	G-OMOB	Robinson R-22B	Milloak Ltd
	G-OMOG	AA-5A Cheetah	Popham Flight (G-BHWR)
	G-OMPS	PA-28-161 Warrior II	M. & D. Aviation (G-BOHP)
	G-OMRB	Cameron V-77 balloon	M. R. Bayne
	G-OMRG	Hoffmann H.36 Dimona	MRG Systems Ltd (G-BLHG)
	G-ONAF	Naval Aircraft Factory N3N-1	P. M. H. Threadway
	G-ONCL	Colt 77A balloon	N. C. Lindsay
	G-ONEA	Beech 200 Super King Air	Northern Executive Aviation Ltd/ Manchester
	G-ONHH	Forney F-1A Aircoupe	H. Dodd (G-ARHA)
	G-ONKA	Aeronca K	L. D. Chapman
	G-ONOR	Cessna 425	Rockville Investments (Jersey) Ltd (G-BKSA)
	G-ONOW	Bell 206A JetRanger 2	P. D. & S. J. Hughes (G-AYMX)
	G-ONPI	Thunder Ax10-160 balloon	Ballooning World Ltd
	G-ONTA	Hughes 369D	C. Sanders
	G-ONZO	Cameron N-77 balloon	J. A. Kershaw
	G-OODE	SNCAN Stampe SV-4C (G)	The Biplane Co Ltd (G-AZNN)

Reg.	Type	Owner or Operator	Notes
G-OODI	Pitts S-1D Special	R. N. Goode (G-BBBU)/White Waltham	
G-OODW	PA-28-181 Archer II	Goodwood Terrena Ltd	
G-OOFI	Cameron N-77 balloon	I. Fishwick	
G-OOGA	GA-7 Cougar	Autair Ltd	
G-OOJB	Cessna 421C	Ferron Trading Ltd (G-BKSO)	
G-OOLE	Cessna 172M	Bostonair Ltd (G-BOSI)/Humberside	
G-OOLI	Robinson R-22B	Wyatt Air Partnership (G-DMCD)	
G-OONE	Mooney M.20J	N. Skipworth/Booker	
G-OONI	Thunder Ax7-77 balloon	Fivedata Ltd	
G-OONS	AB-206B JetRanger 3	Bellini Aviation Ltd	
G-OONY	PA-28-161 Warrior II	D. A. Field & P. B. Jenkins	
G-OOOA	Boeing 757-28A	Air 2000/Canada 3000 (C-FOOA)	
G-OOOB	Boeing 757-28A	Air 2000/Canada 3000 (C-FOOB)	
G-OOOC	Boeing 757-28A	Air 2000/Canada 3000 (C-FXOC)	
G-OOOD	Boeing 757-28A	Air 2000/Canada 3000 (C-FXOD)	
G-OOOG	Boeing 757-23A	Air 2000 Ltd/Manchester	
G-OOOH	Boeing 757-23A	Air 2000 Ltd/Manchester	
G-OOOI	Boeing 757-23A	Air 2000 Ltd/Manchester	
G-OOOJ	Boeing 757-23A	Air 2000 Ltd/Manchester	
G-OOOM	Boeing 757-225	Air 2000 Ltd/Manchester	
G-OOOO	Mooney M.20J	Michael Jackson Motors Ltd	
G-OOOS	Boeing 757-236	Air 2000 Ltd (G-BRJD)/Manchester	
G-OOOT	Boeing 757-236	Air 2000 Ltd (G-BRJJ)/Manchester	
G-OOOU	Boeing 757-2Y0	Air 2000 Ltd/Manchester	
G-OOOV	Boeing 757-225	Air 2000 Ltd/Manchester	
G-OOOW	Boeing 757-225	Air 2000 Ltd/Manchester	
G-OOSE	Rutan Vari-Eze	J. A. Towers	
G-OOUT	Colt Flying Shuttlecock SS balloon	Shiplake Investments Ltd	
G-OOXP	Pulsar XP	GW Associates Ltd	
G-OPAC	Robinson R-22B	Crest Engineering Ltd	
G-OPAG	PA-34-200 Seneca II	A. H. Lavender (G-BNGB)	
G-OPAL	Robinson R-22B	Service Graphics Ltd	
G-OPAM	Cessna F.152	Stapleford Flying Club Ltd (G-BFZS)	
G-OPAT	Beech 76 Duchess	Ray Holt (Land Drainage) Ltd/(G-BHAO)	
G-OPED	Partenavia P.68B	Pedley Woodwork Ltd/(G-BFKP)	
G-OPFC	BAe 125-1000	British Aerospace PLC	
G-OPIG	ARV Super 2	C. R. Guggenheim (G-BMSJ)	
G-OPIK	Eiri PIK-20E	K. & S. C. A. Dudley	
G-OPIT	CFM Streak Shadow Srs SA	L. W. Opit	
G-OPIX	Cessna 180K	Steve Bicknell Productions Ltd	
G-OPJC	Cessna 152	PJC Leasing Ltd/Stapleford	
G-OPJD	PA-28RT-201T Turbo Arrow IV	North West Aviation Ltd	
G-OPKF	Cameron 90 Bowler SS balloon	Flying Pictures (Balloons) Ltd	
G-OPLC	D.H.104 Dove 8	D. Liddell-Grainger (G-BLRB)	
G-OPOL	H.S.125 Srs F3B/RA	MAGEC Aviation Ltd (G-BXPU/G-IBIS/ G-AXPU)/Luton	
G-OPOP	Enstrom 280C-UK-2 Shark	Crewhall Ltd (G-OFED)	
G-OPPL	AA-5A Cheetah	London School of Flying Ltd (G-BGNN)/ Elstree	
G-OPPP	EMB-110P1 Bandeirante	Streamline Aviation/E. Midlands	
G-OPPS	Mudry CAP.231	Bianchi Aviation Film Services Ltd/Booker	
G-OPRO	MDH Hughes 369E	Prodrive Ltd	
G-OPSF	PA-38-112 Tomahawk	Neric Ltd (G-BGZI)/Pahshanger	
G-OPST	Cessna 182R	Lota Ltd/Shoreham	
G-OPUP	B.121 Pup 2	P. W. Hunter (G-AXEU)	
G-OPWL	Bell 206B JetRanger 3	PWL Records Ltd (G-BPCZ)	
G-OPWS	Mooney M.20K	A. C. Clarke	
G-ORAF	CFM Streak Shadow	G. A. & S. M. Taylor	
G-ORAY	Cessna F.182Q II	S. E. Ward & Sons (Engineers) Ltd (G-BHDN)	
G-ORBY	Sukhoi Su-26MX	R. N. Goode/White Waltham	
G-ORCE	Cessna 550 Citation II	Oracle Corporation UK Ltd (G-MINE)	
G-ORCL	Cessna 421C	Oracle Corporation UK Ltd	
G-ORDN	PA-31R Cherokee Arrow 200-II	M. T. Coppen (G-BAJT)	
G-ORDO	PA-30 Twin Comanche B	A. C. & A. M. Gordon	
G-ORED	BN-2T Islander	The Red Devils (G-BJYW)/Farnborough	
G-OREG	BN-2A Mk III-1 Trislander	Industrial Marketing Group Ltd (G-OAVW/ G-AZLJ)	
G-OREX	Short SD3-60 Variant 100	Euroworld Airways Ltd (G-BMHY)/Gatwick	
G-ORFC	Jurca MJ.5 Sirocco	D. J. Phillips	
G-ORFE	Cameron 76 Golf SS balloon	Balloon-A-Drome Ltd	
G-ORGI	Hawker Hurricane IIB	Charles Church Displays Ltd	
G-ORJS	Bell 206L-3 LongRanger	Carr Aviation	

Notes	Reg.	Type	Owner or Operator
	G-ORJW	Laverda F.8L Falco Srs 4	W. R. M. Sutton
	G-ORMB	Robinson R-22B	R. M. Bailey
	G-ORMP	Cessna 414A	Ascham Aviation (G-KCAV)/Bournemouth
	G-OROB	Robinson R-22B	Corniche Helicopters (G-TBFC)
	G-OROD	PA-18 Super Cub 150	R. J. O. Walker
	G-ORON	Cameron 77A balloon	A. M. Rocliffe
	G-ORPR	Cameron O-77 balloon	Outright PR Ltd
	G-ORSJ	D.H.114 Heron 2	D. Liddle-Grainger (G-ARKW)
	G-ORTM	Glaser-Dirks DG.400	I. M. Stromberg/Barton
	G-ORVB	McCulloch J-2	R. V. Bowles (G-BLGI/G-BKKL)
	G-ORZZ	Robinson R-22B	Heliyorks Flight Training Ltd
	G-OSAB	Enstrom 280FX	Southern Air Ltd/Shoreham
	G-OSAL	Cessna 421C	Cityshare Ltd
	G-OSCC	PA-32 Cherokee Six 300	Plant Aviation Ltd (G-BGFD)/Elstree
	G-OSDI	Beech 95-58 Baron	K. L. Hawes (G-BHFY)
	G-OSEA	BN-2B-26 Islander	W. T. Johnson & Sons (Huddersfield) Ltd (G-BKOL)
	G-OSEE	Robinson R-22B	Aquaprint Ltd
	G-OSFC	Cessna F.152	Stapleford Flying Club Ltd (G-BIVJ)
	G-OSHC	Hughes 269C	Mussett Helicopters Ltd
	G-OSHD	Hughes 269B	Mussett Helicopters Ltd
	G-OSHE	Hughes 269C	Starline Helicopters Ltd/Redhill
	G-OSHL	Robinson R-22B	Sloane Helicopters Ltd
	G-OSIB	Bell 206L-1 LongRanger 2	Cardale Doors Ltd (G-LEIS)
	G-OSIX	PA-32 Cherokee Six 260	Strata Surveys Ltd (G-AZMO)
	G-OSKY	Cessna 172M	G-OSKY (1990)
	G-OSLO	Schwiezer 269C	Metham Aviation Ltd
	G-OSNB	Cessna 550 Citation II	Scottish & Newcastle Breweries PLC (G-JFRS)
	G-OSND	Cessna FRA.150M	Barmoor Aviation (G-BDOU)
	G-OSOO	Hughes 369E	Malcolm Wilson (Motorsport) Ltd
	G-OSPI	Robinson R-22B	B. E. Pond
	G-OSRF	Cessna 421C	Marginslot Ltd/Elstree
	G-OSST	Colt 77A balloon	British Airways PLC
	G-OSTC	AA-5A Cheetah	C. B. Dew
	G-OSUE	Bell 206B JetRanger 3	British Car Auctions (Aviation) Ltd (G-BKBY)
	G-OTAL	ARV Super 2	Cyclone Hovercraft Ltd (G-BNGZ)
	G-OTAM	Cessna 172M	T. W. Woods
	G-OTBY	PA-32 Cherokee Six 300	Brook Shaw Ltd
	G-OTEL	Thunder Ax8-90 balloon	Stakis Hotels & Inns Ltd
	G-OTHE	Enstrom 280C-UK Shark	The Engineering Co Ltd (G-OPJT/G-BKCO)
	G-OTIM	Bensen B.8MV	T. J. Deane
	G-OTMC	Beech 400 Beechjet	Tarmac Aviation Ltd
	G-OTOE	Aeronca 7AC Champion	J. M. Gale (G-BRWW)
	G-OTOW	Cessna 175BX	G-OTOW Flying Group (G-AROC)
	G-OTRG	Cessna TR.182RG	A. Hopper
	G-OTSB	BN-2A Mk III-2 Trislander	Aurigny Air Services Ltd (G-BDTO)
	G-OTSW	Pitts S-1E Special	R. A. Bowes (G-BLHE)
	G-OTUG	PA-18 Super Cub 150	B. Walker & Co (Dursley) Ltd
	G-OTVS	BN-2T Islander	Headcorn Parachute Club Ltd (G-BPBN/G-BCMY)
	G-OTWO	Rutan Defiant	D. G. Foreman
	G-OTYJ	PA-28-161 Cadet	Holmes Rentals (G-OLSF)
	G-OUAE	Cameron 90 Wimmi Airbus SS balloon	Airship & Balloon Co Ltd
	G-OULD	Gould Mk I balloon	C. A. Gould
	G-OUSA	Colt 105A balloon	Continental Airlines Inc
	G-OUVI	Cameron O-105 balloon	Windsor Pharmaceuticals Ltd
	G-OVAA	Colt Jumbo SS balloon	Airship & Balloon Co Ltd
	G-OVAN	SC.7 Skyvan 3 Variant 100	Peterborough Parachute Centre (G-AYZA)/Sibson
	G-OVAX	Colt AS-80 Mk II airship	Vax Appliances Ltd
	G-OVFM	Cessna 120	Industrial Foam Systems Ltd
	G-OVFR	Cessna F.172N	C. & A. Jenkins Ltd
	G-OVID	Light Aero Avid Flyer	M. Stow
	G-OVMC	Cessna F.152 II	Staverton Flying Services Ltd
	G-OVNE	Cessna 401A	M. A. Billings/Ipswich
	G-OVNR	Robinson R-22B	R. A. Kingston & R. Ballard
	G-OWAC	Cessna F.152	Barnes Olson Aeroleasing Ltd (G-BHEB)
	G-OWAK	Cessna F.152	Falcon Flying Services (G-BHEA)
	G-OWAR	PA-28-161 Warrior II	Biblio Graphic Ltd/Denham
	G-OWEL	Colt 105A balloon	Autohaus of Aylesbury Ltd
	G-OWEN	K & S Jungster	R. C. Owen

Reg.	Type	Owner or Operator	Notes
G-OWGC	Slingsby T.61F Venture T.1	Wolds Gliding Club Ltd	
G-OWIN	BN-2A-8 Islander	UK Parachute Services Ltd (G-AYXE)	
G-OWIZ	Luscombe 8A Silvaire	J. Wilson & J. V. George	
G-OWLC	PA-31 Turbo Navajo	D. S. A. Warwick & P. M. Doran (G-AYFZ)	
G-OWNR	Beech 200 Super King Air	Owners Abroad Group PLC/Luton	
G-OWVA	PA-28 Cherokee 140	Woodvale Aviation Co Ltd	
G-OWWF	Colt 2500A balloon	Virgin Atlantic Airways Ltd	
G-OWYN	Aviamilano F.14 Nibbio	J. R. Wynn	
G-OXLI	BAe Jetstream 4100	British Aerospace PLC/Prestwick	
G-OXTC	PA-23 Aztec 250D	Falcon Flying Services (G-AZOD)/ Biggin Hill	
G-OXVI	V.S.361 Spitfire LF.XVIe (TD248)	BAC Aviation Ltd	
G-OYAK	Yakovlev C-11	E. K. Coventry	
G-OZOI	Cessna R.182	Velcourt (East) Ltd (G-ROBK)	
G-OZUP	Colt 77A balloon	Yanin International Ltd	
G-PACE	Robin R.1180T	Millicron Instruments Ltd/Coventry	
G-PACL	Robinson R-22B	R. Richardson	
G-PADI	Cameron V-77 balloon	T. R. Duffell	
G-PALS	Enstrom 280C-UK-2 Shark	Sonus Wholesale Audio Products	
G-PAMI	AS.355F-1 Twin Squirrel	Lynton Aviation Ltd (G-BUSA)	
G-PAMS	PA-60 Aerostar 601P	Avergeln Ltd (G-GAIR)	
G-PAPU	Beech 58PA Baron	ADL Aviation Ltd (G-NIPU)	
G-PARA	Cessna 207	Paraski/Swansea	
G-PARI	Cessna 172RG Cutlass	Applied Signs Ltd	
G-PARR	Cameron 90 Bottle SS balloon	Airship & Balloon Co Ltd	
G-PART	Partenavia P.68B	Phlight Avia Ltd/Coventry	
G-PASA	MBB Bo 105D	Medical Aviation Services Ltd (G-BGWP)/ Shoreham	
G-PASB	MBB Bo 105D	Medical Aviation Services Ltd (G-BDMC)/ Shoreham	
G-PASC	MBB Bo 105DBS/4	Police Aviation Services Ltd (G-BNPS)	
G-PASD	MBB Bo 105DBS/4	Police Aviation Services Ltd (G-BNRS)	
G-PASE	AS.355F-1 Twin Squirrel	Police Aviation Services Ltd	
G-PASF	AS.355F-1 Twin Squirrel	Police Aviation Services Ltd (G-SCHU)	
G-PASX	MBB Bo 105DBS/4	Police Aviation Services Ltd	
G-PASY	BN-2A-26 Islander	Medical Aviation Services Ltd(G-BPCB/ G-BEXA/G-MALI/G-DIVE)/Shoreham	
G-PATY	Colt Flying Sausage balloon	Colt Balloons Ltd	
G-PAWL	PA-28 Cherokee 140	A. M. & D. Fitton (G-AWEU)	
G-PAWS	AA-5A Cheetah	J. Tolhurst	
G-PAXX	PA-20 Pacer 135	D. W. & M. R. Grace	
G-PAZY	Pazmany PL.4A	A. Louth	
G-PBBT	Cameron N-56 balloon	British Telecom PLC	
G-PBHF	Robinson R-22B	Broughton-Hall Security Fencing	
G-PBWH	BAe 125 Srs 800B	Lynton Aviation Ltd	
G-PCUB	PA-18 Super Cub 135	M. J. Wilson/Redhill	
G-PDHJ	Cessna T.182R	P. G. Vallance Ltd	
G-PDOC	PA-44-180 Seminole	Medicare (G-PVAF)	
G-PDON	WMB.2 Windtracker balloon	P. Donnellan	
G-PDSI	Cessna 172N	Don-Air Flying Club/Lasham	
G-PEAL	Aerotek Pitts S-2A	Hallmark Aerobatics Ltd	
G-PEAT	Cessna 421B	Forest City Export Ltd (G-BBIJ)/Manchester	
G-PEEL	BAe ATP	Manx Airlines Ltd/King Somerled (1158-1164)	
G-PEET	Cessna 401A	Air & General Services Ltd	
G-PEGG	Colt 90A balloon	Michael Pegg Partnership Ltd	
G-PEGI	PA-34-200T Seneca II	Tayflite Ltd	
G-PEKT	SOCATA TB.20 Trinidad	Pektron Ltd	
G-PELE	Cameron 80 Pele SS balloon	Cameron Balloons Ltd	
G-PELI	Pelican Club GS	Pelican Aircraft Ltd	
G-PENN	AA-5B Tiger	Compair	
G-PENY	Sopwith LC-1T Triplane (5492)	J. S. Penny	
G-PERL	Robinson R-22B	R. Fawcett	
G-PERR	Cameron 60 bottle balloon	The Balloon Stable Ltd	
G-PERS	Colt Soapbox SS balloon	G. V. Beckwith	
G-PEST	Hawker Tempest II	Autokraft Ltd	
G-PETR	PA-28 Cherokee 140	E. W. Keeble/Ipswich (G-BCJL)	
G-PFAA	EAA Biplane Model P	P. E. Barker	
G-PFAB	Colomban MC.15 Cri-Cri	P. Fabish	
G-PFAC	FRED Srs 2	G. R. Yates	
G-PFAD	Wittman W.8 Tailwind	M. R. Stamp	
G-PFAF	FRED Srs 2	M. S. Perkins	

Notes	Reg.	Type	Owner or Operator
	G-PFAG	Evans VP-1	P. A. Evans
	G-PFAH	Evans VP-1	J. A. Scott
	G-PFAI	Clutton EC.2 Easy Too	G. W. Cartledge
	G-PFAL	FRED Srs 2	J. McD. Robinson
	G-PFAO	Evans VP-1	P. W. Price
	G-PFAP	Currie Wot/SE-5A (C1904)	J. M. Alcock/Syerston
	G-PFAR	Isaacs Fury II (K2059)	C. J. Repik
	G-PFAT	Monnet Sonerai II	H. B. Carter
	G-PFAU	Rand KR-2	D. E. Peace
	G-PFAW	Evans VP-1	R. F. Shingler
	G-PFAY	EAA Biplane	A. K. Lang & A. L. Young
	G-PHIL	Brookland Hornet	A. J. Philpotts
	G-PHON	Cameron Phone SS balloon	Redmalt Ltd (G-BTEY)
	G-PHTG	SOCATA TB.10 Tobago	O. Jerome
	G-PIAF	Thunder Ax7-65 balloon	Ballooning Adventures Ltd
	G-PICS	Cessna 182F	D. A. Cresswell (G-ASHO)
	G-PICT	Colt 180A balloon	Scotia Balloons
	G-PIEL	CP.301A Emeraude	P. R. Thorne (G-BARY)
	G-PIES	Thunder Ax7-77Z balloon	Pork Farms Ltd
	G-PIGS	SOCATA Rallye 150ST	Boonhill Flying Group (G-BDWB)
	G-PIKE	Robinson R-22 Mariner	Mistshine Ltd
	G-PIKK	PA-28 Cherokee 140	L. P. & I. Keegan (G-AVLA)
	G-PINE	Thunder Ax8-90 balloon	J. A. Pine
	G-PINT	Cameron 65 Barrel SS balloon	D. K. Fish
	G-PIPE	Cameron N-56 Pipe SS balloon	Carreras Rothmans Ltd
	G-PIPS	Van's RV-4	C. J. Marsh
	G-PITS	Pitts S-2AE	D. Rolfe
	G-PITZ	Pitts S-2A Special	C. England
	G-PIXS	Cessna 336	Astral Aerial Surveys Ltd
	G-PJCB	Agusta A.109A-II	J. C. Bamford Excavators Ltd
	G-PJMD	Hughes 369D	Dodici Ltd (G-BMJV)
	G-PJRT	BAe Jetstream 4100	British Aerospace PLC/Prestwick
	G-PKBD	Douglas DC-9-32	British Midland Airways Ltd *Jubilee Diamond*/E. Midlands
	G-PKBE	Douglas DC-9-32	British Midland Airways Ltd *Excelsior Diamond*/E. Midlands
	G-PKBM	Douglas DC-9-32	British Midland Airways Ltd *The Tiffany Diamond*/E. Midlands
	G-PLAN	Cessna F.150L	Jones Aviation Ltd/Blackpool
	G-PLAS	GA-7 Cougar	S. J. A. Smith (G-BGHL)/Biggin Hill
	G-PLAX	AS.355F-1 Twin Squirrel	Dollar Air Services Ltd (G-BPMT)
	G-PLAY	Robin R.2100A	Cotswold Aero Club Ltd/Staverton
	G-PLEE	Cessna 182Q	W. J. & M. Barnes
	G-PLIV	Pazmany PL.4	B. P. North
	G-PLMA	AS.350B Ecureuil	PLM Helicopters Ltd (G-BMMA)
	G-PLMB	AS.350B Ecureuil	PLM Helicopters Ltd (G-BMMB)
	G-PLMC	AS.350B Ecureuil	PLM Helicopters Ltd (G-BKUM)
	G-PLME	AS.350B-1 Ecureuil	PLM Helicopters Ltd (G-BONN)
	G-PLOW	Hughes 269B	Sulby Aerial Surveys Ltd (G-AVUM)
	G-PLUG	Colt 105A balloon	Eastern Electricity PLC
	G-PLUS	PA-34-200T Seneca II	C. G. Strasser/Jersey
	G-PLYD	SOCATA TB.20 Trinidad	Crocker Air Services/Biggin Hill
	G-PMAM	Cameron V-65 balloon	P. A. Meecham
	G-PMNL	Extra EA.230	Aerobatic Displays Ltd/Booker
	G-PNAV	PA-31P Pressurised Navajo	Tech Air (Cambridge) Ltd
	G-PNNY	Cessna 500 Citation	Merlin Marine Aviation (Jersey) Ltd
	G-POAV	SA.365N-1 Dauphin 2	The Peninsular & Oriental Steam Navigation Co Ltd (G-BOPI)
	G-POLE	Rutan LongEz	Madison Aviation Ltd
	G-POLO	PA-31-350 Navajo Chieftain	Aircam Technical Services/Teesside
	G-POLY	Cameron N-77 balloon	Empty Wallets Balloon Group
	G-POND	Oldfield Baby Great Lakes	N. Davis
	G-PONY	Colt 31A balloon	Ace Balloons (Bath) Ltd
	G-POOH	Piper J-3C-65 Cub	P. & H. Robinson
	G-POOL	ARV Super 2	Falstaff Finance Ltd (G-BNHA)
	G-POPE	Eiri PIK-20E-1	C. J. Hadley
	G-POPI	SOCATA TB.10 Tobago	Rocol Aviation Ltd (G-BKEN)
	G-POPP	Colt 105A balloon	Flying Pictures (Balloons) Ltd
	G-POPS	PA-34-220T Seneca III	R. Killen
	G-PORK	AA-5B Tiger	Regishire Ltd (G-BFHS)
	G-PORT	Bell 206B JetRanger 3	C. Clark
	G-POSH	Colt 56A balloon	Columna Ltd (G-BMPT)
	G-POSN	BAe 125 Srs 800B	P&O Containers (Assets) Ltd

Reg.	Type	Owner or Operator	Notes
G-POST	EMB-110P1 Bandeirante	David Martin Couriers Ltd	
G-POTS	Cessna FA.150K	L. J. Potts (G-AYUY)	
G-POWL	Cessna 182R	Glasdon Group Ltd/Blackpool	
G-PPLH	Robinson R-22B	Henderson Financial Management Ltd	
G-PPLI	Pazmany PL.1	G. Anderson	
G-PPPE	Colt 77A balloon	Thunder & Colt Ltd	
G-PPPP	Denney Aerocraft Kitfox	P. Eastwood	
G-PRAG	Brügger MB.2 Colibri	R. J. Hodder & ptnrs	
G-PRIM	PA-38-112 Tomahawk	Braddock Ltd	
G-PRIT	Cameron N-90 balloon	J. M. Albury	
G-PROP	AA-5A Cheetah	Blackbushe School of Flying Ltd(G-BHKU)	
G-PROV	P.84 Jet Provost T.52A (T.4)	Hunter Wing Ltd/Bournemouth	
G-PRTT	Cameron N-31 balloon	J. M. Albury	
G-PRUE	Cameron O-84 balloon	Lalondes Residential Ltd	
G-PRXI	V.S.365 Spitfire PR.XI (PL983)	D. W. Arnold/Biggin Hill	
G-PSCI	Bell 206B JetRanger 3	Scammell Properties Ltd (G-BOKD)	
G-PSVS	Beech 95-58 Baron	Stesco Ltd/Guernsey	
G-PTER	Beech C90 King Air	Moseley Group (PSV) Ltd (G-BIEE)	
G-PTRE	SOCATA TB.20 Trinidad	Openmid Ltd (G-BNKU)	
G-PTWO	Pilatus P2-05 (RF+16)	C. M. Lee	
G-PUBS	Colt 56 Glass SS balloon	The Balloonatics	
G-PUDD	Robinson R-22B	Riggarna UK Ltd	
G-PUFF	Thunder Ax7-77A balloon	Intervarsity Balloon Club *Puffin II*	
G-PULS	Aero Designs Pulsar	M. J. McBride	
G-PUMA	AS.332L Super Puma	Bond Helicopters Ltd	
G-PUMB	AS.332L Super Puma	Bond Helicopters Ltd	
G-PUMD	AS.332L Super Puma	Bond Helicopters Ltd	
G-PUME	AS.332L Super Puma	Bond Helicopters Ltd	
G-PUMG	AS.332L Super Puma	Bond Helicopters Ltd	
G-PUMH	AS.332L Super Puma	Bond Helicopters Ltd	
G-PUMI	AS.332L Super Puma	Bond Helicopters Ltd	
G-PUMJ	AS.332L Super Puma	Bond Helicopters Ltd (G-BLZJ)	
G-PUMK	AS.332L Super Puma	Bond Helicopters Ltd	
G-PUML	AS.332L Super Puma	Bond Helicopters Ltd	
G-PUNK	Thunder Ax8-105 balloon	G. E. Harris	
G-PURE	Cameron 70 Can SS balloon	The Hot-Air Balloon Co Ltd	
G-PURR	AA-5A Cheetah	D. T. Smith (G-BJDN)	
G-PURS	Rotorway Executive	J. E. Houseman	
G-PUSI	Cessna T.303	W. R. Swinburn Ltd	
G-PUSS	Cameron N-77 balloon	Bristol Balloons	
G-PYRO	Cameron N-65 balloon	N. A. Mitchell	
G-RAAD	Mooney M.20L	As-Al Ltd	
G-RAAR	BAe 125 Srs 800B	Osprey Executive Aviation Ltd/Southend	
G-RACA	P.57 Sea Prince T.1 ★	Stratford Aircraft Collection/Long Marston	
G-RACH	Robinson R-22B	South West Helicopters Ltd	
G-RACO	PA-28R Cherokee Arrow 200-II	Graco Group Ltd	
G-RAEM	Rutan LongEz	G. F. H. Singleton	
G-RAFA	Grob G.115	RAF College Flying Club Ltd/Cranwell	
G-RAFB	Grob G.115	RAF College Flying Club Ltd/Cranwell	
G-RAFC	Robin R.2112	Noel Penny Turbines Ltd	
G-RAFE	Thunder Ax7-77 balloon	A. J. W. Rose	
G-RAFF	Learjet 35A	Graff Aviation Ltd/Heathrow	
G-RAFG	Slingsby T.67C	S. J. Donkin	
G-RAFT	Rutan LongEz	MAC Communications Ltd	
G-RAFW	Mooney M.20E	S. L. Monksfield (G-ATHW)	
G-RAIL	Colt 105A balloon	Ballooning World Ltd	
G-RAIN	Maule M5-235C Lunar Rocket	D. S. McKay & J. A. Rayment/ Hinton-in-the-Hedges	
G-RALE	SA.341G Gazelle 1	Malcolm Wilson (Motorsport) Ltd (G-SFTG)	
G-RALI	Hughes 369HS	Kallas Ltd (G-BLKO)	
G-RAMI	Bell 206B JetRanger 3	R. & M. International Helicopters Ltd	
G-RAMP	Piper J-3C-65 Cub	K. N. Whittall	
G-RAMS	PA-32R-301 Saratoga SP	Peacock & Archer Ltd/Manchester	
G-RAND	Rand KR-2	R. L. Wharmby	
G-RANS	Rans S.10 Sakota	J. D. Weller	
G-RANY	Cessna 421C	Booth Plant & Equipment Ltd (G-BHLA)	
G-RANZ	Rans S-10 Sakota	B. A. Phillips	
G-RAPE	Colt 300A balloon	Adventure Balloon Co Ltd	
G-RAPH	Cameron O-77 balloon	P. H. Jenkins	
G-RAPP	Cameron H-34 balloon	Cameron Balloons Ltd	
G-RARE	Thunder Ax5-42 SS balloon	International Distillers & Vintners Ltd	
G-RASC	Evans VP-2	R. A. Codling	

Notes	Reg.	Type	Owner or Operator
	G-RASS	Bell 206L-1 LongRanger 1	Arlington Securities Ltd (G-JLBI)
	G-RATE	AA-5A Cheetah	GP Services (G-BIFF)
	G-RAVL	H.P.137 Jetstream Srs 200	Cranfield Institute of Technology (G-AWVK)
	G-RAYS	Zenair CH.250	R. E. Delves
	G-RBIN	Robin DR.400/2+2	Headcorn Flying School Ltd
	G-RBOS	Colt AS-105 airship ★	Science Museum/Wroughton
	G-RBOW	Thunder Ax-7-65 balloon	P. G. & S. D. Viney
	G-RBUT	Hughes 369HS	R. C. Button
	G-RCMF	Cameron V-77 balloon	Mouldform Ltd
	G-RDCI	R. Commander 112A	A. C. Hendriksen (G-BFWG)
	G-RDON	WMB.2 Windtracker balloon	P. J. Donnellan (G-BICH)
	G-READ	Colt 77A balloon	CB Helicopters Ltd
	G-REAP	Pitts S-1S Special	S. Howes
	G-REAT	GA-7 Cougar	Autair Ltd
	G-REBE	Bensen B.8MR	Chartersteps Ltd
	G-REBI	Colt 90A balloon	United Friendly Insurance PLC (G-BOYD)
	G-REBL	Hughes 269B	M. I. Edwards
	G-RECK	PA-28 Cherokee 140B	Phoenix Aviation Services Ltd (G-AXJW)
	G-RECO	Jurca MJ-5L Sirocco	J. D. Tseliki
	G-REEK	AA-5A Cheetah	Velopend Ltd
	G-REEN	Cessna 340	E. & M. Green (G-AZYR)/Guernsey
	G-REES	Jodel D.140C	M. D. S. Hood/Redhill
	G-REFI	Enstrom 280C-UK	Nash & Partners Ltd
	G-REGS	Thunder Ax7-77 balloon	M. E. Gregory
	G-REID	Rotorway Scorpion 133	G. F. Burridge & S. B. Evans
	G-REIS	PA-28R-201T Turbo Arrow III	G. Webster & J. D. Caudwell
	G-RENE	Renegade 912	D. Evans
	G-RENO	SOCATA TB.10 Tobago	Lamond Ltd
	G-RENT	Robinson R-22B	Rentatruck Self Drive Ltd
	G-REPM	PA-38-112 Tomahawk	Nultree Ltd
	G-REST	Beech P35 Bonanza	C. R. Taylor (G-ASFJ)
	G-RETA	C.A.S.A. 1.131 Jungmann	J. S. Allison/Denham
	G-REVS	Bell 206B JetRanger	J. C. Palmer (G-AWOL)
	G-REXS	PA-28-181 Archer II	Channel Islands Aero Holdings (Jersey) Ltd
	G-REZE	Rutan Vari-Eze	S. D. Brown & S. P. Evans
	G-RFAB	Cessna 182R	J. T. Reynolds (G-BIXT)
	G-RFIL	Colt 77A balloon	Regency Films International Ltd
	G-RFSB	Sportavia RF-5B	S. W. Brown
	G-RGII	Cessna 172RG	North West Aviation Ltd
	G-RGUS	Fairchild 24R-46A Argus 3 (44-83184)	R. C. Handcraff/Shoreham
	G-RHCC	PA-31-350 Navajo Chieftain	Monde-Air Aviation Ltd/Leavesden
	G-RHCN	Cessna FR.182RG	R. H. C. Neville
	G-RHHT	PA-32RT-300 Lance II	M. A. Hales
	G-RICC	AS.350B-2 Ecureuil	McAlpine Helicopters Ltd & Gabriel Enterprises Ltd (G-BTXA)
	G-RICH	Cessna F.152	Ford Equipment Hire
	G-RICK	Beech 95-B55 Baron	R. M. S. Holland (G-BAAG)
	G-RIDE	Stephens Akro	R. Mitchell/Coventry
	G-RIDS	Lancair 235	R. Y. Kendal
	G-RIFA	SA.341G Gazelle 1	Air & General Services Ltd (G-ORGE/G-BBHU)
	G-RIFB	Hughes 269C	Air & General Services Ltd
	G-RIFC	SA.341G Gazelle 1	Griffair Ltd (G-SFTD)
	G-RIGB	Thunder Ax7-77 balloon	Antrum & Andrews Ltd
	G-RIGS	PA-60 Aerostar 601P	Rigs Design Services Ltd/Fairoaks
	G-RILL	Cessna 421C	Maxwell Restaurants Ltd (G-BGZM)/Elstree
	G-RILY	Monnet Sonerai II	R. Wheeler
	G-RIND	Cessna 335	ATA Grinding Processes/Leavesden
	G-RINO	Thunder Ax7-77 balloon	D. J. Head
	G-RISE	Cameron V-77 balloon	D. L. Smith
	G-RIST	Cessna 310R-II	Air Service Training Ltd (G-DATS)/Perth
	G-RITA	Cessna 340A	C. Good
	G-RJAH	Boeing Stearman A.75N1	R. J. Horne
	G-RJER	McD Douglas MD-83	Airtours International Aviation Ltd
	G-RJET	BAe146-100	British Aerospace PLC
	G-RJMI	AA-5A Cheetah	Garrick Aviation
	G-RJMS	PA-28R-201 Arrow III	Robin James Ltd
	G-RJWW	Maule M5-235C Lunar Rocket	Paw Flying Services Ltd (G-BRWG)
	G-RLFI	Cessna FA.152	Tayside Aviation Ltd (G-DFTS)/Dundee
	G-RLMC	Cessna 421C	R. D. Lygo
	G-RMGN	AS.355F-1 Twin Squirrel	VIP Marine & Aviation Ltd (G-BMCY)

Reg.	Type	Owner or Operator	Notes
G-RNAS	D.H.104 Sea Devon C.20 (XK896)	D. W. Hermiston-Hooper/Staverton	
G-RNGR	AB-206B JetRanger 3	Unicorn Software Ltd	
G-RNIE	Cameron 70 Ball SS balloon	Airship & Balloon Co Ltd	
G-RNLI	V.S.236 Walrus 1	R. E. Melton	
G-RNRM	Cessna A.185F	RN & R. Marines Sport Parachute Association	
G-RNTV	PA-30 Twin Comanche 160C	J. L. Vaughan (G-AXDL)	
G-ROAR	Cessna 401	H. W. Weston (G-BZFL/G-AWSF)/ Staverton	
G-ROBB	Grob G.109B	A. P. Mayne	
G-ROBI	Grob G.109B	A. W. McGarrigle/Cardiff	
G-ROBN	Robin R.1180T	J. G. Beaumont	
G-ROBO	Robinson R-22B	Cabair Air Taxis Ltd/Elstree	
G-ROBS	Robinson R-22B	Corniche Helicopters (G-BPDH)	
G-ROBY	Colt 17A balloon	Airship & Balloon Co Ltd	
G-ROCH	Cessna T.303	R. S. Bentley	
G-ROCK	Thunder Ax7-77 balloon	The Long Rake Spar Co Ltd	
G-ROCR	Schweizer 269C	KC Holdings	
G-RODD	Cessna 310R II	R. J. Herbert Engineering Ltd (G-TEDD/ G-MADI)	
G-RODI	Isaacs Fury (K3731)	M. R. Baker/Shoreham	
G-RODS	A-Bell 206B JetRanger 2	Crook & Son (G-NOEL/G-BCWN)	
G-RODY	A-Bell 206A JetRanger	Crook & Son (G-ROGR/G-AXMM)	
G-ROGG	Robinson R-22B	Catto Helicopters	
G-ROLA	PA-34-200T Seneca	Highsteeple Ltd	
G-ROLF	PA-32R-301 Saratoga SP	P. F. Larkins	
G-ROLL	Pitts S-2A Special	RPM Aviation Ltd/Guernsey	
G-ROLO	Robinson R-22B	Osprey Helicopters Ltd	
G-ROMA	Hughes 369S	Helicopters (Northern) Ltd (G-ROPI/ G-ONPP)/Blackpool	
G-RONG	PA-28R Cherokee Arrow 200-II	W. R. Griffiths	
G-RONI	Cameron V-77 balloon	R. E. Simpson	
G-RONS	Robin DR.400/180	R. & K. Baker	
G-RONT	Enstrom F-28A	R. Thomas (G-BDAW)	
G-RONW	FRED Srs 2	K. Atkinson	
G-ROOF	Brantly B.2B	S. Lee (G-AXSR)	
G-ROOK	Cessna F.172P	Crop Aviation (UK) Ltd	
G-RORO	Cessna 337B	C. Keane (G-AVIX)	
G-RORY	Piaggio FW P.149D	R. McCarthy (G-TOWN)/Booker	
G-ROSE	Evans VP-1	W. K. Rose	
G-ROSI	Thunder Ax7-77 balloon	Scotia Balloons Ltd	
G-ROTI	Luscombe 8A Silvaire	A. L. Chapman & ptnrs	
G-ROTO	Rotorway Executive 90	S. R. Porter	
G-ROTR	Brantly B.2B	GP Services	
G-ROTS	CFM Streak Shadow Srs SA	H. R. Cayzer	
G-ROUP	Cessna F.172M	Stapleford Flying Club Ltd (G-BDPH)	
G-ROUS	PA-34-200T Seneca II	C.S.E. Aviation Ltd/Kidlington	
G-ROUT	Robinson R-22B	Hooley Bridge Helicopter Services	
G-ROVE	PA-18 Super Cub 135	Cormack (Aircraft Services) Ltd/Glasgow	
G-ROWL	AA-5B Tiger	Aviation Simulation/Biggin Hill	
G-ROWN	Beech 200 Super King Air	Chauffair Ltd (G-BHLC)	
G-ROWS	PA-28-151 Warrior	Mustarrow Ltd	
G-ROYY	Robinson R-22B	Tudor Motorcycles	
G-ROZY	Cameron R.36 balloon	Jacques W. Soukup Ltd	
G-RPEZ	Rutan LongEz	B. A. Fairston & D. Richardson	
G-RRRR	Privateer Motor Glider	R. F. Selby	
G-RRSG	Thunder Ax7-77 balloon	M. T. Stevens	
G-RRTM	Sikorsky S-70C	Rolls-Royce PLC/Filton	
G-RSWW	Robinson R-22B	Woodstock Enterprises	
G-RUBB	AA-5B Tiger	R. Bessant	
G-RUBI	Thunder Ax7-77 balloon	Anglia Balloon School Ltd	
G-RUBY	PA-28RT-201T Turbo Arrow IV	R. S. Stopp (G-BROU)	
G-RUDD	Cameron V-65 balloon	N. A. Apsey	
G-RUDI	QAC Quickie Q.2	R. Brandenberger	
G-RUGB	Cameron 89 Egg SS balloon	The Hot-Air Balloon Co Ltd	
G-RUIA	Cessna F.172M	F. Daly	
G-RUMN	AA-1A Trainer	M. A. Hales/Cranfield	
G-RUMP	Robinson R-22B	I. P. Crane	
G-RUNT	Cassutt Racer IIIM	S. B. Jones	
G-RUSO	Robinson R-22B	Universal Salvage (Holdings) Ltd	
G-RUSS	Cessna 172N	Leisure Lease/Southend	
G-RWIN	Rearwin 175	G. Kay	
G-RWSS	Denney Aerocraft Kitfox	R. W. Somerville	

Notes	Reg.	Type	Owner or Operator
	G-RWWW	W.S.55 Whirlwind HCC.12 (XR486)	R. Windley
	G-RZZB	Robinson R-22B	Heli-Link Ltd
	G-SAAB	R. Commander 112TC	S. Richmen (G-BEFS)
	G-SAAM	Cessna T.182R	Hopstop Ltd (G-TAGL)/Elstree
	G-SABA	PA-28R-201T Turbo Arrow III	G. I. Cooper (G-BFEN)
	G-SABR	F-86A Sabre	Golden Apple Operations Ltd
	G-SACA	Cessna 152 II	LAR Aviation Ltd (G-HOSE)/Shoreham
	G-SACB	Cessna F.152 II	Westward Airways (Land's End) Ltd (G-BFRB)/St Just
	G-SACD	Cessna F.172H	Northbrook College of Design & Technology (G-AVCD)/Shoreham
	G-SACE	Cessna F.150L	C. A. Morris (G-AZLK)
	G-SACF	Cessna 152 II	T. M. & M. L. Jones
	G-SACI	PA-28-161 Warrior II	Southern Aero Club/Shoreham
	G-SACO	PA-28-161 Warrior II	Southern Aero Club/Shoreham
	G-SACR	PA-28-161 Cadet	Sherburn Aero Club Ltd
	G-SACS	PA-28-161 Cadet	Sherburn Aero Club Ltd
	G-SACT	PA-28-161 Cadet	Sherburn Aero Club Ltd
	G-SACU	PA-28-161 Cadet	Sherburn Aero Club Ltd
	G-SACZ	PA-28-161 Warrior II	Southern Aero Club/Shoreham
	G-SADE	Cessna F.150L	Bath Stone Co Ltd (G-AZJW)
	G-SAFE	Cameron N-77 balloon	Nottingham Hot Air Balloon Club
	G-SAGA	Grob G.109B	G-GROB Ltd/Booker
	G-SAGE	Luscombe 8A Silvaire	S. J. Sage (G-AKTL)
	G-SAHI	Trago Mills SAH-1	Lovaux Ltd/Bournemouth
	G-SAIR	Cessna 421C	Air Support Aviation Services Ltd
	G-SALA	PA-32 Cherokee Six 300E	Stonebold Ltd
	G-SALI	Cessna 421C	Rapid 3864 Ltd/Luton
	G-SALL	Cessna F.150L (Tailwheel)	J. A. Millar-Craig & M. R. Shelton
	G-SAMA	PA-31-350 Navajo Chieftain	Asseman Ltd
	G-SAMG	Grob G.109B	RAFGSA/Bicester
	G-SAMM	Cessna 340A	M. R. Cross
	G-SAMS	M.S.880B Rallye Club	K. Lewis
	G-SAMZ	Cessna 150D	N. E. Sames (G-ASSO)
	G-SANB	Beech E90 King Air	ITPS Ltd (G-BGNU)/Cranfield
	G-SAND	Schweizer 269C	Aerocroft Ltd
	G-SARA	PA-28-181 Archer II	R. H. Ford/Elstree
	G-SARH	PA-28-161 Warrior II	Bath Stone Co Ltd
	G-SARO	Saro Skeeter Mk 12	F. F. Chamberlain
	G-SASU	AS.355F-1 Twin Squirrel	Gulf & UK Industrial Consultants Ltd (G-BSSM/G-BMTC/G-BKUK)
	G-SATI	Cameron 105 Sphere balloon	Cameron Balloons Ltd
	G-SATL	Cameron 105 Sphere SS balloon	Cameron Balloons Ltd
	G-SATO	PA-23 Aztec 250E	P. L. Creffield (G-BCXP)/Southend
	G-SAUF	Colt 90A balloon	K. H. Medau
	G-SAVE	PA-31-350 Navajo Chieftain	Merrixair Ltd/Exeter
	G-SBAS	Beech B200 Super King Air	Bond Helicopters Ltd (G-BJJV)/Aberdeen
	G-SBUS	BN-2A-26 Islander	Isles of Scilly Skybus Ltd (G-BMMH)/St Just
	G-SCAH	Cameron V-77 balloon	S. C. A. Howarth
	G-SCAN	Vinten-Wallis WA-116/100	K. H. Wallis
	G-SCAT	Cessna F.150F	Cheshire Air Training School (Merseyside) Ltd (G-ATRN)/Liverpool
	G-SCFO	Cameron O-77 balloon	M. K. Grigson
	G-SCPL	PA-28 Cherokee 140	Hillview Ltd (G-BPVL)/Staverton
	G-SCTT	HPR-7 Herald 210	Channel Express Group PLC (G-ASPJ)/Bournemouth
	G-SCUB	PA-18 Super Cub 135 (542447)	N. D. Needham Farms
	G-SCUH	Boeing 737-3Q8	Dan-Air Services Ltd/Gatwick
	G-SDEV	D.H.104 Sea Devon C.20	P. C. Gill & W. Gentle
	G-SDLW	Cameron O-105 balloon	Somerset Balloon Safaris Ltd
	G-SEAB	Republic RC-3 Seabee	P. C. J. Farries
	G-SEAH	Hawker Sea Hawk FB.3	Jet Heritage Ltd/Bournemouth
	G-SEAS	PA-31-310 Navajo C	Sea Surveillance Ltd
	G-SEAT	Colt 42 balloon	Airship & Balloon Co Ltd
	G-SEED	Piper J-3C-65 Cub	J. H. Seed
	G-SEEK	Cessna T.210N	Melrose Pigs Ltd
	G-SEGO	Robinson R-22B	G. Seago
	G-SEJW	PA-28-161 Warrior II	Truman Aviation Ltd/Tollerton
	G-SELL	Robin DR.400/180	L. S. Thorne
	G-SEND	Colt 90A balloon	Redmalt Ltd
	G-SEPT	Cameron N-105 balloon	Deproco UK Ltd
	G-SERA	Enstrom F-28A-UK	W. R. Pitcher (G-BAHU)

Reg.	Type	Owner or Operator	Notes
G-SETA	AS.355F-1 Twin Squirrel	McAlpine Helicopters Ltd (G-NEAS/ G-CMMM/G-BNBJ)	
G-SEVA	SE-5A replica (F141)	I. D. Gregory	
G-SEVE	Cessna 172N	S. Patterson	
G-SEWL	PA-28-151 Warrior	A. R. Sewell & Sons/Andrewsfield	
G-SEXY	AA-1 Yankee	H. Morris (G-AYLM)	
G-SFHR	PA-23 Aztec 250F	E. L. Becker & J. Harper (G-BHSO)	
G-SFPA	Cessna F.406	Scottish Fisheries Protection Agency	
G-SFPB	Cessna F.406	Scottish Fisheries Protection Agency	
G-SFRY	Thunder Ax7-77 balloon	R. J. Fry	
G-SFTS	NDN-1T Turbo Firecracker	Marinco Ltd	
G-SFTZ	Slingsby T.67M Firefly	Firefly Aerial Promotions Ltd	
G-SGAS	Colt 77A balloon	Avongas Ltd	
G-SHAA	Enstrom 280-UK	Manchester Helicopter Centre/Barton	
G-SHAW	PA-30 Twin Comanche 160B	CCR Holding Co Ltd	
G-SHCC	AB-206B JetRanger 2	St Marys Golf Club Ltd	
G-SHDD	Enstrom F-28C	Durston Air Services Ltd (G-BNBS)	
G-SHED	PA-28-181 Archer II	S. V. Smeeth (G-BRAU)	
G-SHEL	Cameron O-56 balloon	The Shell Company of Hong Kong Ltd	
G-SHFL	Cameron N-77 balloon	M. C. Bradley/Hong Kong	
G-SHGG	Enstrom 280C Shark	Haversham Helicopters Ltd	
G-SHIP	PA-23 Aztec 250F ★	Midland Air Museum/Coventry	
G-SHIV	GA-7 Cougar	Autair Helicopters Ltd/Luton	
G-SHKK	Hughes 269A	Starline Helicopters Ltd	
G-SHNN	Enstrom 280C	Farm Supply Co (Thirsk) Ltd	
G-SHOO	Hughes TH-55A	Starline Helicopters Ltd	
G-SHOT	Cameron V-77 balloon	Bucks Hot-Air Balloon Group	
G-SHOW	M.S.733 Alycon	Vintage Aircraft Team/Cranfield	
G-SHPP	Hughes TH-55A	R. P. Bateman & A. C. Braithwaite	
G-SHRR	AB-206B JetRanger 2	Vamplas Glass Design Ltd (G-FSDA/ G-AWJW)	
G-SHSS	Enstrom 280C-UK Shark	Free Flight Aviation Ltd (G-BENO)	
G-SHST	Colt 180A balloon	G. V. Beckwith	
G-SHUG	PA-28R-201T Turbo Arrow III	N. E. Rennie	
G-SHUU	Enstrom 280C-UK-2 Shark	H. Ingham (G-OMCP/G-KENY/G-BJFG)	
G-SHVV	Bell 206B JetRanger 2	Starline Helicopters Ltd/Booker	
G-SHZZ	Bell 206B JetRanger 3	Starline Helicopters Ltd (G-BNUW)	
G-SIAN	Cameron V-77 balloon	S. M. Jones	
G-SIGN	PA-39 Twin Comanche 160 C/R	Comanche Travel Ltd/Elstree	
G-SING	Beech B60 Duke	Sasha Fashions International Ltd/ Leavesden	
G-SION	PA-38-112 Tomahawk II	Bath Stone Co Ltd	
G-SIPA	SIPA 903	T. J. McRae (G-BGBM)	
G-SITE	AS.355F-1 Twin Squirrel	Charter Group PLC (G-BPHC)	
G-SIXC	Douglas DC-6A	Atlantic Air Transport Ltd/Coventry	
G-SIXX	Colt 77A balloon	G. E. Harris & S. C. Kinsey	
G-SJAB	PA-39 Twin Comanche 160 C/R	Foyle Flyers Ltd	
G-SJGM	Cessna 182R	Crystal Air Ltd	
G-SKAN	Cessna F.172M	Aircraft Rentals Humberside Ltd (G-BFKT)	
G-SKIL	Cameron N-77 balloon	Flying Pictures (Balloons) Ltd	
G-SKIP	Cameron N-77 balloon	Skipton Building Soc	
G-SKKA	PA-31 Turbo Navajo	J. J. Baumhardt (G-FOAL/G-RMAE/ G-BAEG)	
G-SKKB	PA-31 Turbo Navajo	Bulldog Aviation Ltd/(G-BBDS)/Earls Colne	
G-SKKC	Cessan 404	J. J. Baumhardt (G-OHUB)/Southend	
G-SKSA	Airship Industries SKS.500	Airship Industries Ltd/Cardington	
G-SKSC	Airship Industries SKS.600	Interport Marine Agencies Ltd	
G-SKSG	Airship Industries SKS.600/03	Interport Marine Agencies Ltd	
G-SKYE	Cessna TU.206G	RAF Sport Parachute Association	
G-SKYH	Cessna 172N	Elgor Hire Purchase & Credit Ltd/ Southend	
G-SKYI	Air Command 532 Elite	Skyrider Aviation Ltd	
G-SKYM	Cessna F.337E	Bencray Ltd (G-AYHW) (*stored*)/Blackpool	
G-SKYP	Cameron A-120 balloon	PSH Skypower Ltd	
G-SKYS	Cameron O-84 balloon	J. R. Christopher	
G-SLAC	Cameron N-77 balloon	The Scottish Life Assurance Co	
G-SLCI	Thunder Ax8-90 balloon	S. L. Cuhat	
G-SLEA	Mudry/CAARP CAP.10B	P. D. Southerington/Sturgate	
G-SLII	Cameron O-90 balloon	S. L. Cuhat	
G-SLIM	Colt 56A balloon	Hot-Air Balloon Co Ltd	
G-SLOT	Cessna 340A	Bristol Uniforms Ltd	
G-SLUG	Short SD3-30 Variant 100	Tech Air (Cambridge) Ltd (G-METP/G-METO/ G-BKIE)	

Notes	Reg.	Type	Owner or Operator
	G-SLYN	PA-28-161 Warrior II	G. E. Layton
	G-SMAF	Sikorsky S-76A	Fayair (Jersey) 1984 Ltd
	G-SMAX	Cameron O-105 balloon	Cameron Balloons Ltd
	G-SMHK	Cameron D-38 airship	San Miguel Brewery Ltd
	G-SMIG	Cameron O-65 balloon	Hong Kong Balloon & Airship Club
	G-SMJJ	Cessna 414A	Gull Air Ltd/Guernsey
	G-SMTC	Colt Flying Hut SS balloon	Shiplake Investments Ltd
	G-SMTH	PA-28 Cherokee 140	G. N. Smith (G-AYJS)
	G-SNAP	Cameron V-77 balloon	P. A. George
	G-SNAX	Colt 69A balloon	Derwent Valley Foods Ltd
	G-SNDY	Piper J-3C-65 Cub	R. R. K. Mayall
	G-SNOB	Beech A.36 Bonanza	R. I. Craddock (G-BEIK)
	G-SNOW	Cameron V-77 balloon	M. J. Snow
	G-SOAS	PA-60 Aerostar 601P	Kenilgate Ltd
	G-SOFA	Cameron N-65 balloon	GT Flying Club Ltd
	G-SOFI	PA-60 Aerostar 601P (Machen Superstar II)	Allzones Travel Ltd/Biggin Hill
	G-SOFT	Thunder Ax7-77 balloon	Bristol Software Factory Ltd
	G-SOLA	Aero Designs Star-Lite SL.1	P. Clifton & A. Clarke
	G-SOLD	Robinson R-22A	Travel Management Ltd
	G-SOLO	Pitts S-2S Special	Fyat Ltd/Booker
	G-SONA	SOCATA TB.10 Tobago	J. Greenwood (G-BIBI)
	G-SONY	Aero Commander 200D	General Airline Ltd (G-BGPS)
	G-SOOE	Hughes 369E	Arrow Aviation Co Ltd/Manchester
	G-SOOS	Colt 21A balloon	P. J. Stapley
	G-SOOT	PA-28 Cherokee 180	D. J. & K. R. Thomas (G-AVNM)
	G-SOUL	Cessna 310R	Atlantic Air Transport Ltd/Coventry
	G-SPAM	Light Aero Avid Aerobat	C. M. Hicks
	G-SPEY	AB-206B JetRanger 3	Castle Air Charters Ltd (G-BIGO)
	G-SPIN	Pitts S-2A Special	R. N. Goode/White Waltham
	G-SPIT	V.S.379 Spitfire FR.XIV (MV363)	B. J. S. Grey (G-BGHB)/Duxford
	G-SPOL	MBB Bo 105CBS/4	Clyde Helicopters Ltd
	G-SSBS	Colting Ax77 balloon	K. J. & M. E. Gregory
	G-SSFT	PA-28-161 Warrior II	SFT Aviation Ltd (G-BHIL)/Bournemouth
	G-SSJT	Cessna 210L	J. Taylor
	G-SSOZ	Cessna 550 Citation II	Arrows Aviation Co Ltd
	G-SSRS	Cessna 172N	Romair
	G-SSWV	Sportavia Fournier RF-5B	J. L. Collins & J. A. Melville
	G-STAG	Cameron O-65 balloon	Holker Estates Ltd
	G-STAK	Bell 206B JetRanger 2	Tyringham Charter & Group Services Ltd (G-BNIS)
	G-STAN	F.27 Friendship Mk.200	Air UK *Jimmy Saville OBE*/Norwich
	G-STAT	Cessna U.206F	SMK Engineers Ltd
	G-STEF	Hughes 369HS	D. J. L. Wood (G-BKTK)
	G-STEP	Schweizer 269C	M. D. Thorpe
	G-STEV	Jodel DR.221	S. W. Talbot/Long Marston
	G-STMI	Robinson R-22B	South East Helicopters Ltd/Southend
	G-STMP	SNCAN Stampe SV-4A	W. R. Partridge
	G-STOX	Bell 206B JetRanger 2	Tickstop Ltd (G-BNIR)
	G-STOY	Robinson R-22B	Tickstop Ltd
	G-STRK	CFM Streak Shadow Srs SA	M. E. Dodd
	G-STST	Bell 206B JetRanger 3	Petrochemical Supplies Ltd
	G-STUA	Aerotek Pitts S-2A Special (modified)	Aero-Balance Aviation/White Waltham
	G-STVN	HPR-7 Herald 210	Channel Express Group PLC/Bournemouth
	G-STWO	ARV Super 2	Falstaff Finance Ltd
	G-STYL	Pitts S-1S Special	B. MacMillan
	G-SUKI	PA-38-112 Tomahawk	Bath Stone Co Ltd (G-BPNV)
	G-SULL	PA-32R-301 Saratoga SP	B. R. Chaplin
	G-SULY	Monnet Moni	M. J. Sullivan
	G-SUNI	Bell 206B JetRanger 3	Sunley Holdings PLC
	G-SUPA	PA-18 Super Cub 150	Crop Aviation (UK) Ltd
	G-SUPR	BAe Jetstream 3200	British Aerospace PLC/Prestwick
	G-SURG	PA-30 Twin Comanche 160B	A. R. Taylor (G-VIST/G-AVHZ)
	G-SUSI	Cameron V-77 baloon	H. S. & C. J. Dryden
	G-SUSY	P-51D-25-NA Mustang (472773)	P. J. Morgan
	G-SUZI	Beech 95-B55 Baron	Directfield Ltd (G-BAXR)
	G-SUZN	PA-28-161 Warrior II	Bath Stone Co Ltd
	G-SUZY	Taylor JT.1 Monoplane	E. J. Blackoe
	G-SVHA	Partenavia P.68B	David Martin Couriers Ltd
	G-SVIV	SNCAN Stampe SV-4C	A. J. Clarry & S. F. Bancroft
	G-SVJM	AS.355F-1 Twin Squirrel	UB Air Ltd & Jensen & Nicholson Ltd (G-BOPS)

Reg.	Type	Owner or Operator	Notes
G-SWAG	EMB-110P1 Bandeirante	Tech Air (Cambridge) Ltd (G-CLAW)	
G-SWEB	Cameron N-90 balloon	Air 2 Air Ltd	
G-SWFT	Beech 200 Super King Air	Airswift Ltd (G-SIBE/G-MCEO/G-BILY)	
G-SWIF	V.S.541 Swift F.7	Jet Heritage Ltd/Bournemouth	
G-SWIM	Taylor Coot Amphibian (modified)	P. C. J. Farries	
G-SWIS	D.H.100 Vampire F.6	Hunter Wing Ltd/Bournemouth	
G-SWOT	Currie Super Wot	B. Brown	
G-SWPR	Cameron N-56 balloon	A. Brown	
G-SYFW	Focke-Wulf Fw.190 replica (2+1)	M. R. Parr	
G-TACK	Grob G.109B	Oval (275) Ltd/Bristol	
G-TAFF	C.A.S.A. 1.131 Jungmann	Custompac Ltd (G-BFNE)	
G-TAFO	Extra EA.230	A. J. E. Smith (G-PIKN)	
G-TAFY	Piper J-3F-65 Cub	C. P. Goodley	
G-TAGS	PA-28-161 Warrior II	Air Service Training Ltd/Perth	
G-TAIL	Cessna 150J	Routair Aviation Services Ltd/Southend	
G-TAIR	PA-34-200T Seneca II	Wessex Mouldings Ltd	
G-TAMY	Cessna 421B	Malcolm Enamellers (Midlands) Ltd	
G-TAPE	PA-23 Aztec 250D	Merlix Ltd (G-AWVW)	
G-TART	PA-28-236 Dakota	Withercourt Ltd	
G-TATT	GY-20 Minicab	L. Tattershall	
G-TAXI	PA-23 Aztec 250E	Yorkair Ltd/Leeds	
G-TAYI	Grob G.115	Tayside Aviation Ltd (G-DODO)/Dundee	
G-TAYS	Cessna F.152	Tayside Aviation Ltd (G-LFCA)	
G-TBAG	Murphy Renegade II	M. R. Tetley	
G-TBIO	SOCATA TB.10 Tobago	H. M. Fenn & J. E. Hailes	
G-TBIX	MDH Hughes 369E	Weetabix Ltd/Sywell	
G-TBSL	Colt 90A balloon	Tubesales (UK) Ltd	
G-TBXX	SOCATA TB.20 Trinidad	JDM Electrical & Mechanical Services Ltd/ Denham	
G-TBZO	SOCATA TB.20 Trinidad	D. L. Clarke & J. S. Monk	
G-TCAN	Colt 69A balloon	Thunder & Colt Ltd	
G-TCAR	Robin HR.100/210	Gibad Aviation Ltd	
G-TCMP	Robinson R-22B	R. P. Nash	
G-TCTC	PA-28RT-201 Arrow IV	Terry Coleman (UK) Ltd	
G-TCUB	Piper J-3C-65 Cub	N. R. Windley	
G-TDAD	SOCATA TB.20 Trinidad	R. C. Watts	
G-TDFS	IMCO Callair A.9	Dollarhigh Ltd (G-AVZA)	
G-TEAC	AT-6C Harvard IIA (EX280)	E. C. English/Bourn	
G-TECC	Aeronca 7AC Champion	T. E. C. Cushing/Little Snoring	
G-TECH	R. Commander 114	P. A. Reed (G-BEDH)/Denham	
G-TECK	Cameron V-77 balloon	G. M. N. Spencer	
G-TEDF	Cameron N-90 balloon	Fort Vale Engineering Ltd	
G-TEDS	SOCATA TB.10 Tobago	E. W. Lyon (G-BHCO)	
G-TEDY	Evans VP-1	C. J. D. Edwards (G-BHGN)	
G-TEFC	PA-28 Cherokee 140	A. J. Cornish	
G-TEFH	Cessna 500 Citation	Birmingham Aviation Ltd (G-BCII)	
G-TELL	Cessna 421C	Holding & Barnes Ltd	
G-TELY	Agusta A.109A-II	Castle Air Charters Ltd	
G-TEMP	PA-28 Cherokee 180	W. D. Hubble (G-AYBK)	
G-TEMT	Hawker Tempest II	Autokraft Ltd	
G-TENT	J/1N Alpha	R. Callaway-Lewis (G-AKJU)	
G-TERI	Beech F33A Bonanza	T. & D. E. Beanland/Jersey	
G-TERY	PA-28-181 Archer II	T. Barlow (G-BOXZ)/Barton	
G-TESS	Quickie Q.2	D. Evans	
G-TEST	PA-34-200 Seneca	Stapleford Flying Club Ltd (G-BLCD)	
G-TEWS	PA-28 Cherokee 140	M. J. & M. J. Tew (G-KEAN/G-AWTM)	
G-TFCI	Cessna FA.152	Tayside Aviation Ltd/Dundee	
G-TFRB	Air Command 532 Elite	F. R. Blennerhassett	
G-TFOX	Denney Aerocraft Kitfox Mk 2	F. A. Roberts	
G-TFUN	Valentin Taifun 17E	NW Taifun Group	
G-TGAS	Cameron O-160 balloon	R. S. Hunjan	
G-TGER	AA-5B Tiger	A. Wuensche (G-BFZP)	
G-THAN	Cessna F.406 Caravan II	Air Thanet Ltd/Manston	
G-THCL	Cessna 550 Citation II	Tower House Consultants Ltd	
G-THEA	Boeing Stearman E.75	L. M. Walton	
G-THGS	SA.365N-1 Dauphin 2	HeavyLift Cargo Airlines Ltd (G-BPOJ)	
G-THOM	Thunder Ax6-56 balloon	T. H. Wilson	
G-THOR	Thunder Ax8-105 balloon	N. C. Faithful *Turncoat*	
G-THOS	Thunder Ax7-77 balloon	Thos Wood & Son (Builders) Ltd	
G-THSL	PA-28R-201 Arrow III	G. Fearnley/Southend	
G-THUR	Beech 200 Super King Air	Thurston Aviation (Stansted) Ltd	
G-TIBC	Cameron A-180 balloon	Aerial Promotions Ltd	

Notes	Reg.	Type	Owner or Operator
	G-TICK	Cameron V-77 balloon	T. J. Tickler
	G-TIDS	Jodel D.150	J. B. Dovey/Ipswich
	G-TIGA	D.H.82A Tiger Moth	Truman Aviation Ltd (G-AOEG)
	G-TIGB	AS.332L Super Puma	Bristow Helicopters Ltd (G-BJXC)
	G-TIGC	AS.332L Super Puma	Bristow Helicopters Ltd (G-BJYH)
	G-TIGE	AS.332L Super Puma	Bristow Helicopters Ltd (G-BJYJ)
	G-TIGF	AS.332L Super Puma	Bristow Helicopters Ltd
	G-TIGG	AS.332L Super Puma	Bristow Helicopters Ltd
	G-TIGH	AS.332L Super Puma	Bristow Helicopters Ltd
	G-TIGI	AS.332L Super Puma	Bristow Helicopters Ltd
	G-TIGJ	AS.332L Super Puma	Bristow Helicopters Ltd
	G-TIGK	AS.332L Super Puma	Bristow Helicopters Ltd
	G-TIGL	AS.332L Super Puma	Bristow Helicopters Ltd
	G-TIGM	AS.332L Super Puma	Bristow Helicopters Ltd
	G-TIGO	AS.332L Super Puma	Bristow Helicopters Ltd
	G-TIGP	AS.332L Super Puma	Bristow Helicopters Ltd
	G-TIGR	AS.332L Super Puma	Bristow Helicopters Ltd
	G-TIGS	AS.332L Super Puma	Bristow Helicopters Ltd
	G-TIGT	AS.332L Super Puma	Bristow Helicopters Ltd
	G-TIGU	AS.332L Super Puma	Bristow Helicopters Ltd
	G-TIGV	AS.332L Super Puma	Bristow Helicopters Ltd
	G-TIGW	AS.332L Super Puma	Bristow Helicopters Ltd
	G-TIGZ	AS.332L Super Puma	British International Helicopters Ltd
	G-TIII	Aerotek Pitts S-2A	Aerobatic Displays Ltd (G-BGSE)/Booker
	G-TILE	Robinson R-22B	S. Lee
	G-TILL	Robinson R-22B	G. Till
	G-TILT	Bell 206B JetRanger 3	Edington PLC (G-BRJO)
	G-TIMB	Rutan Vari-Eze	T. M. Bailey (G-BKXJ)
	G-TIME	Ted Smith Aerostar 601P	J. J. Donn
	G-TIMJ	Rand KR-2	N. Seaton
	G-TIMK	PA-28-181 Archer II	T. Baker
	G-TIMS	Falconar F-12A	T. Sheridan
	G-TIMW	PA-28 Cherokee 140C	W. H. Sanders (G-AXSH)
	G-TINA	SOCATA TB.10 Tobago	A. Lister
	G-TINS	Cameron N-90 balloon	Bass & Tennent Sales Ltd
	G-TKPZ	Cessna 310R	Auxili-Air Aviation Ltd (G-BRAH)/ Humberside
	G-TKYO	Boeing 747-212B	Virgin Atlantic Airways Ltd *Maiden Japan*
	G-TLOL	Cessna 421C	Littlewoods Organisation Ltd/Liverpool
	G-TLTD	Cessna 182Q	Gray Tuplin Ltd
	G-TMMC	AS.355F-1 Twin Squirrel	The Colt Car Co Ltd (G-JLCO)
	G-TNTA	BAe 146-200QT	TNT Roadfreight (UK) Ltd
	G-TNTB	BAe 146-200QT	TNT Roadfreight (UK) Ltd
	G-TNTD	BAe 146-200QT	TNT Express (UK) Ltd (G-BOMJ)
	G-TNTE	BAe 146-300QT	TNT Express (UK) Ltd (G-BRPW)
	G-TNTG	BAe 146-300QT	TNT Express (UK) Ltd (G-BSUY)
	G-TNTN	Thunder Ax6-56 balloon	D. P. & A. Dickinson
	G-TOAD	Jodel D.140B	Mothballs Ltd
	G-TOAK	SOCATA TB.20 Trinidad	Self Adhesive Fixings Ltd
	G-TOBA	SOCATA TB.10 Tobago	E. Downing
	G-TOBE	PA-28R Cherokee Arrow 200	J. Bradley & Barry Ltd (G-BNRO)
	G-TOBI	Cessna F.172K	G. Hall (G-AYVB)
	G-TODD	ICA IS-28M2A	C. I. Roberts & C. D. King
	G-TOFT	Colt 90A balloon	Norwest Holst Construction Ltd
	G-TOGA	PA-32-301 Saratoga	Toga Flying Four Group
	G-TOMI	H.S.125 Srs 600B	Falcon Jet Centre Ltd(G-BBEP/G-BJOY)/ Heathrow
	G-TOMO	BAC One-Eleven 487GK	Anglo Cargo Airlines Ltd/Manston
	G-TOMS	PA-38-112 Tomahawk	R. J. Alford
	G-TOMY	Mitsubishi Mu.300 Diamond	Lynton Aviation Ltd
	G-TONE	Pazmany PL.4	J. A. Walmsley
	G-TONI	Cessna 421C	M. Scott
	G-TONW	McD Douglas MD-83	Airtours International Aviation Ltd
	G-TOOL	Thunder Ax8-105 balloon	W. J. Honey
	G-TOPS	AS.355F-1 Twin Squirrel	ICS Worldwide Couriers Ltd (G-BPRH)
	G-TORE	P.84 Jet Provost T.3A	Butane Buzzard Aviation Corpn Ltd
	G-TOTO	Cessna F.177RG	C. R. & J. Cox (G-OADE/G-AZKH)
	G-TOTY	Robinson R-22B	Northern Helicopters Ltd
	G-TOUR	Robin R.2112	Barnes Martin Ltd
	G-TOWS	PA-25 Pawnee 260	Blackpool & Fylde Gliding Club Ltd
	G-TOYS	Enstrom 280C-UK-2 Shark	B. Murphy (G-BISE)
	G-TPHK	BAe 125 Srs 800B	Tiphook PLC (G-FDSL)/Biggin Hill
	G-TREE	Bell 206B JetRanger 3	LGH Aviation Ltd

Reg.	Type	Owner or Operator	Notes
G-TREN	Boeing 737-4S3	Dan-Air Services Ltd (G-BRKG)/Gatwick	
G-TRIC	D.H.C.1 Chipmunk 22A	D. M. Barnett (G-AOSZ)	
G-TRIK	Bell 206B JetRanger 2	Annabelle Casion Ltd (G-BMWY)	
G-TRIM	Monnet Moni	J. E. Bennell	
G-TRIN	SOCATA TB.20 Trinidad	South East Aviation Ltd	
G-TRIO	Cessna 172M	Biggin Hill School of Flying (G-BNXY)	
G-TRIP	PA-32R-301 Saratoga SP	C. P. Lockyer (G-HOSK)	
G-TRIX	V.S.509 Spitfire T.IX (PV202)	R. J. F. Parker	
G-TROP	Cessna 310R	R. P. Nash/Norwich	
G-TRUC	Cassutt Speed One	J. A. H. Chadwick	
G-TRUK	Stoddard-Hamilton Glasair RG	Compustar Ltd	
G-TRUX	Colt 77A balloon	Highway Truck Rental Ltd	
G-TSAM	BAe 125 Srs 800B	British Aerospace PLC/Hatfield	
G-TSFT	PA-28-161 Warrior II	SFT Aviation Ltd (G-BLDJ)/Bournemouth	
G-TSGJ	PA-28-181 Archer II	Golf Juliet Flying Club	
G-TSIX	AT-6C Harvard IIA	D. Taylor/E. Midlands	
G-TTAM	Taylor JT.2 Titch	A. J. Manning	
G-TTEL	PA-E23 Aztec 250D	Target Technology Electronics Ltd (G-BBXE)	
G-TTHC	Robinson R-22B	Paul Hopper Entertainments Ltd	
G-TTPT	McD Douglas MD-83	Airtours International Aviation Ltd	
G-TTWO	Colt 56A balloon	P. N. Tilney	
G-TUBS	Beech 65-80 Queen Air	A. H. Bowers (G-ASKM)/Staverton	
G-TUDR	Cameron V-77 balloon	Jacques W. Soukup Ltd	
G-TUGG	PA-18 Super Cub 150	Ulster Gliding Club Ltd	
G-TUKE	Robin DR.400/160	Tukair/Headcorn	
G-TURB	D.31 Turbulent	A. Ryan-Fecitt	
G-TURK	Cameron 80 Sultan SS balloon	Forbes Europe Inc/France	
G-TURN	Steen Skybolt	M. Hammond	
G-TVMM	Cessna 310Q	F. G. Quartermaine (G-CETA/G-BBIM)	
G-TVSI	Campbell Cricket	W. H. Beevers (G-AYHH)	
G-TVTV	Cameron 90 TV SS balloon	Cameron Balloons Ltd	
G-TWEL	PA-28-181 Archer II	Universal Salvage (Holdings) Ltd	
G-TWEY	Colt 69A balloon	British Telecom Thameswey	
G-TWIN	PA-44-180 Seminole	Leavesden Flight Centre Ltd	
G-TWIZ	R. Commander 114	B. C. & P. M. Cox/Biggin Hill	
G-TWOB	BN-2B-26 Islander	Pilatus BN Ltd (G-BKJJ)/Bembridge	
G-TYGA	AA-5B Tiger	Hovemere Ltd (G-BHNZ)/Biggin Hill	
G-TYRE	Cessna F.172M	Staverton Flying Services Ltd	
G-UDAY	Robinson R-22B	Oakover Holdings Ltd	
G-UERN	BN-2B-26 Islander	Air & General Services Ltd/Biggin Hill	
G-UEST	Bell 206B JetRanger 2	Leisure & Retail Consultants Ltd (G-ROYB/G-BLWU)	
G-UFLY	Cessna F.150H	Westair Flying Services Ltd (G-AVVY)/Blackpool	
G-UIDA	Aero Designs Star-Lite SL.1	I. J. Widger (G-BRKK)	
G-UIDE	Jodel D.120	S. T. Gilbert/Popham	
G-UIET	BAe ATP	Manx Airlines Ltd/King Reginald (1187-1229)	
G-UILD	Grob G.109B	Runnymede Consultants Ltd	
G-UKAC	BAe 146-300	Air UK Ltd/Stansted	
G-UKAG	BAe 146-300	Air UK Ltd/Stansted	
G-UKCA	H.S.125 Srs 700B	MAGEC Aviation Ltd/Luton	
G-UKHP	BAe 146-300	Air UK Ltd/Stansted	
G-UKID	BAe 146-300	Air UK Ltd/Stansted	
G-UKJF	BAe 146-100	Air UK Ltd/Stansted	
G-UKLA	Boeing 737-4Y0	Air UK Leisure Ltd St Andrew/Stansted	
G-UKLB	Boeing 737-4Y0	Air UK Leisure Ltd St Bernard/Stansted	
G-UKLC	Boeing 737-42C	Air UK Leisure Ltd St Christopher/Stansted	
G-UKLD	Boeing 737-42C	Air UK Leisure Ltd St David/Stansted	
G-UKLE	Boeing 737-4Y0	Air UK Leisure Ltd St Edmund/Stansted	
G-UKLF	Boeing 737-42C	Air UK Leisure Ltd St Francis/Stansted	
G-UKLG	Boeing 737-42C	Air UK Leisure Ltd St George/Stansted	
G-UKLN	BAe 146-200	Air UK Ltd (G-BNKJ)/Stansted	
G-UKNZ	Colt Flying Harp SS balloon	Flying Pictures Ltd	
G-UKPC	BAe 146-100	Air UK Ltd (G-BKXZ)/Stansted	
G-UKRB	Colt 105A balloon	Airship & Balloon Co Ltd	
G-UKRC	BAe 146-300	Air UK Ltd (G-BSMR)/Stansted	
G-UKRH	BAe 146-200	Air UK Ltd/(G-BRNG)/Stansted	
G-UKSC	BAe 146-300	Air UK Ltd/Stansted	
G-UMBO	Thunder Ax7-77A balloon	Airship & Balloon Co Ltd	
G-UNDY	Cessna 340	Morris Cohen (Underwear) Ltd (G-BBNR)	
G-UNIK	AB-206B JetRanger 2	RCR Aviation Ltd (G-TPPH/G-BCYP)	

Notes	Reg.	Type	Owner or Operator
	G-UNIP	Cameron Oil Container SS balloon	Flying Pictures (Balloons) Ltd
	G-UNST	Beech F33C Bonanza	I. G. Meredith
	G-UPCC	Robinson R-22B	E. C. Cooke (G-MUSS)
	G-UPDN	Cameron V-65 balloon	R. J. O. Evans
	G-UPMW	Robinson R-22B	M. Wood Haulage
	G-UPPP	Colt 77A balloon	M. Williams
	G-UPPY	Cameron DP-80 balloon	Jacques W. Soukup Enterprises LTd
	G-UPUP	Cameron V-77 balloon	M. White
	G-UROP	Beech 95-B55 Baron	Pooler International Ltd
	G-URRR	Air Command 582 Sport	L. Armes
	G-USAM	Cameron Uncle Sam balloon	Jacques W. Soukup Enterprises Ltd
	G-USGB	Colt 105A balloon	Thunder & Colt Ltd
	G-USIL	Thunder Ax7-77 balloon	Solarmoor Ltd
	G-USMC	Cameron 90 Chestie SS balloon	Jacques W. Soukup Enterprises Ltd
	G-USSR	Cameron 90 Doll SS balloon	Jacques W. Soukup Enterprises Ltd
	G-USSY	PA-28-181 Archer II	Thruxton Helicopter & Equipment Sales
	G-USTI	Cameron H-34 balloon	Allen & Harris Ltd
	G-USTV	Messerschmitt Bf.109G-2 (6)	Imperial War Museum/Duxford
	G-USTY	FRED Srs 2	K. Jones
	G-UTSI	Rand KR-2	K. B. Gutridge
	G-UTSY	PA-28R-201 Arrow III	D. G. Perry/Stapleford
	G-UTZY	SA.341G Gazelle 1	Davinci Aviation Ltd (G-BKLV)
	G-UZEL	SA.341G Gazelle 1	Kepak Ltd (G-BRNH)
	G-UZLE	Colt 77A balloon	Flying Pictures (Balloons) Ltd
	G-VAGA	PA-15 Vagabond	E. J. McEntee/White Waltham
	G-VAJT	M.S.894E Rallye 220GT	R. W. B. Rolfe
	G-VARG	Varga 2150A Kachina	J. Hannibal/Halfpenny Green
	G-VAUK	PA-31-350 Navajo Chieftain	John Mowlem & Co PLC (G-GWEA)
	G-VAUN	Cessna 340	F. E. Peacock & Son (Thorney) Ltd
	G-VCJH	Robinson R-22B	Great Northern Helicopters Ltd
	G-VCSI	Rotorway Executive	Qual-Rect Ltd
	G-VDIR	Cessna T.310R	Van Diemen International Racing Ltd
	G-VELA	SIAI-Marchetti S.205-22R	D. P. & P. A. Dawson
	G-VENI	D.H.112 Venom FB.50	Source Premium & Promotional Consultants Ltd
	G-VERT	Bell 222	Arlington Securities PLC (G-JLBZ/G-BNDB)
	G-VGIN	Boeing 747-243B	Virgin Atlantic Airways Ltd *Scarlet Lady*/Gatwick
	G-VHFA	PA-23 Aztec 250	Hartfield Aviation Ltd (G-BZFE/G-AZFE)
	G-VIBA	Cameron DP-80 airship	Jacques W. Soukup Enterprises Ltd
	G-VICK	PA-31 Turbo Navajo	Porten Holdings Ltd (G-AWED)
	G-VICM	Beech F33C Bonanza	Charles W. Michie Ltd
	G-VIDI	D.H.112 Venom FB.50 (WE402)	Source Premium & Promotional Consultants Ltd
	G-VIEW	Vinten-Wallis WA-116/100	K. H. Wallis
	G-VIII	V. S. Spitfire LF.VIII (MT719)	Reynard Racing Cars Ltd/Duxford
	G-VIKE	Bellanca 1730A Viking	Peter Dolan & Co Ltd
	G-VIPS	Learjet 35A	Executive Air Charter Ltd (G-SOVN/G-PJET)/Biggin Hill
	G-VIRG	Boeing 747-287B	Virgin Atlantic Airways Ltd *Maiden Voyager*/Gatwick
	G-VISA	Cessna A.152	K. W. Felton
	G-VITE	Robin R.1180T	G-VITE Flying Group
	G-VIVA	Thunder Ax7-65 balloon	J. S. Spearing
	G-VIXN	D.H.110 Sea Vixen FAW.2 (XS587) ★	P. G. Vallance Ltd/Charlwood
	G-VIZZ	Sportavia RS.180 Sportsman	Executive Air Sport Ltd/Exeter
	G-VJAI	GA-7 Cougar	United Breweries (International) Ltd (G-OCAB/G-BICF)/Elstree
	G-VJAY	H.S.125 Srs F400B	Jensen & Nicholson (S) Pte Ltd (G-AYLG)
	G-VJCB	Agusta A.109A II	J. C. Bamford Excavators Ltd (G-BOUA)
	G-VJCT	Partenavia P.68C	Montrose Leasing Ltd
	G-VJET	Avro 698 Vulcan B.2 (XL426)	R. E. Jacobsen
	G-VJFK	Boeing 747-238B	Virgin Atlantic Airways Ltd/Gatwick
	G-VJIM	Colt 77 Jumbo Jim SS balloon	Airship & Balloon Co Ltd
	G-VLAD	Yakolev Yak-50	R. Goode/Staverton
	G-VLAX	Boeing 747-238B	Virgin Atlantic Airways Ltd *California Girl*/Gatwick
	G-VMAX	Mooney M.20K	Glidegold Ltd
	G-VMDE	Cessna P.210N	Royton Express Deliveries (Welwyn) Ltd
	G-VMIA	Boeing 747-123	Virgin Atlantic Airways Ltd (G-HIHO)/Gatwick

Reg.	Type	Owner or Operator	Notes
G-VNOM	D.H.112 Venom FB.50	A. Topen/Cranfield	
G-VODA	Cameron N-77 balloon	Racal Telecom PLC	
G-VOID	PA-28RT-201 Arrow IV	A. M. Gardner	
G-VOLT	Cameron N-77 balloon	National Power	
G-VOYG	Boeing 747-283B	Virgin Atlantic Airways Ltd (G-BMGS)/ Gatwick	
G-VPII	Evans VP-2	V. D. J. Hitchings (G-EDIF)	
G-VPLC	Beech 200 Super King Air	Vickers Shipbuilding & Engineering Ltd	
G-VRES	Beech A200 Super King Air	Northern Executive Aviation Ltd/ Manchester	
G-VRGN	Boeing 747-212B	Virgin Atlantic Airways Ltd *Maid of Honour*/ Gatwick	
G-VRVI	Cameron O-90 balloon	Cooling Services Ltd	
G-VSEL	Beech 200 Super King Air	Vickers Shipbuilding & Engineering Ltd (G-SONG/G-BKTI)/Barrow	
G-VSOP	Cameron 60 Bottle SS balloon	J. R. Parkington & Co Ltd	
G-VTAX	PA-31-350 Navajo Chieftain	Jet West Ltd/Exeter	
G-VTII	D.H.115 Vampire T.11 (WZ507)	J. Turnbull & ptnrs/Cranfield	
G-VTOL	H.S. Harrier T.52 (ZA250) ★	Brooklands Museum of Aviation/ Weybridge	
G-VULC	Avro 698 Vulcan B.2 (XM655)	R. E. Jacobsen	
G-VVBK	PA-34-200T Seneca II	Computaplane Ltd (G-BSBS/G-BDRI)	
G-WAAC	Cameron N-56 balloon	Newbury Ballooning Co Ltd	
G-WACA	Cessna F.152	Wycombe Air Centre Ltd	
G-WACB	Cessna F.152	Wycombe Air Centre Ltd	
G-WACC	Cessna F.152	Wycombe Air Centre Ltd	
G-WACE	Cessna F.152	Wycombe Air Centre Ltd	
G-WACF	Cessna 152	Wycombe Air Centre Ltd	
G-WACG	Cessna F.152	Wycombe Air Centre Ltd	
G-WACH	Cessna FA.152	Wycombe Air Centre Ltd	
G-WACI	Beech 76 Duchess	Wycombe Air Centre Ltd	
G-WACJ	Beech 76 Duchess	Wycombe Air Centre Ltd	
G-WACK	Short SD3-60 Variant 100	Loganair Ltd (G-BMAJ)/Glasgow	
G-WACL	Cessna F.172N	Wycombe Air Centre Ltd (G-BHGG)	
G-WACO	Waco UPF.7	RGV (Aircraft Services) & Co/Staverton	
G-WACP	PA-28 Cherokee 180	Hartmann Ltd (G-BBPP)/Booker	
G-WACR	PA-28 Cherokee 180	Wycombe Air Centre Ltd (G-BCZF)	
G-WACS	Cessna F.152	Hartmann Ltd/Booker	
G-WACT	Cessna F.152 II	Hartmann Ltd (G-BKFT)/Booker	
G-WACU	Cessna FA.152	Hartmann Ltd (G-BJZU)/Booker	
G-WACV	Cessna 182N	Deeperton Ltd (G-AZEA)/Booker	
G-WACW	Cessna 172P	Wycombe Air Centre Ltd	
G-WACY	Cessna F.172P	Wycombe Air Centre Ltd	
G-WACZ	Cessna F.172M	Wycombe Air Centre Ltd (G-BCUK)	
G-WAGI	Robinson R-22B	J. Wagstaff	
G-WAIR	PA-32-301 Saratoga	Ware Aviation Ltd	
G-WAIT	Cameron V-77 balloon	G. & D. A. Waite	
G-WAKO	Waco UPF-7	North West Aviation Ltd/Liverpool	
G-WALL	Beech 95-58PA Baron	C. D. Weiswall/Elstree	
G-WALS	Cessna A.152	Redhill Flying Club	
G-WALT	Cameron Flying Castle SS balloon	Cameron Balloons Ltd	
G-WARD	Taylor JT.1 Monoplane	G. D. & P. J. Ward	
G-WARE	PA-28-161 Warrior II	W. J. Ware	
G-WARI	PA-28-161 Warrior II	Garrick Aviation	
G-WARK	Schweizer 269C	Warwickshire Constabulary	
G-WARR	PA-28-161 Warrior II	T. J. & G. M. Laundy	
G-WASH	Noble 1250 balloon	Noble Adventures Ltd	
G-WASP	Brantly B.2B	W. C. Evans & M. L. Morris (G-ASXE)	
G-WATH	Colt 77A balloon	Ballooning Adventures Ltd	
G-WATS	PA-34-220T Seneca III	Edington PLC (G-BOVJ)	
G-WATT	Cameron Cooling Tower SS balloon	National Power	
G-WATZ	PA-28-151 Warrior	Air Nova/Liverpool	
G-WBAT	Wombat gyroplane	C. D. Julian (G-BSID)	
G-WBPR	BAe 125 Srs 800B	Trusthouse Forte PLC/Heathrow	
G-WBTS	Falconair F-11	W. C. Brown (G-BDPL)	
G-WCAT	Colt Flying Mitt SS balloon	Interline Develoments Ltd	
G-WCEI	M.S.894E Rallye 220GT	T. W. Pullin (G-BAOC)	
G-WDEB	Thunder Ax-7-77 balloon	W. de Bock	
G-WEEZ	Mooney M.20J	Weyland Ltd	
G-WELI	Cameron N-77 balloon	A. K. F. Violett	
G-WELL	Beech E90 King Air	CEGA Aviation Ltd/Goodwood	

Notes	Reg.	Type	Owner or Operator
	G-WELS	Cameron N-65 balloon	K. J. Vickery
	G-WEND	PA-28RT-201 Arrow IV	Chingford Magnetic Signs
	G-WENT	BAe Jetstream 3102-09	Manx Airlines Ltd (G-IBLW)/Ronaldsway
	G-WERY	SOCATA TB.20 Trinidad	Wery Flying Group/Sherburn
	G-WEST	Agusta A.109A	Westland Helicopters Ltd/Yeovil
	G-WESX	CFM Streak Shadow	Wessex Aviation Ltd
	G-WETI	Cameron N-31 balloon	C. A. Butter & J. J. T. Cooke
	G-WGCS	PA-18 Super Cub 95	T. M. Storey/Shoreham
	G-WGEL	Boeing 737-2U4	Dan-Air Services Ltd (G-ILFC/G-BOSL)/ Gatwick
	G-WGSC	Pilatus PC-6/B2-H4 Turbo Porter	D. M. Penny
	G-WHAT	Colt 77A balloon	Thunder & Colt Ltd
	G-WHIM	Colt 77A balloon	D. L. Morgan
	G-WHIR	Montgomerie Bensen B.8MR	A. P. Barden (G-BROT)
	G-WHIZ	Pitts S-1 Special	K. M. McLeod
	G-WHIZ†	V.701 Viscount ★	Saltwell Park (G-AMOE)/Gateshead
	G-WHOW	Thunder Ax7-65 balloon	Thunder & Colt Ltd
	G-WHRL	Schweizer 269C	Wessex Whirlybirds Ltd
	G-WICK	Partenavia P.68B	Strix Ltd & ptnrs (G-BGFZ)
	G-WIEN	Rans S.10 Sakota	N. P. Rieser
	G-WILD	Pitts S-1T Special	G. H. Wilson
	G-WILI	PA-32R-301 Saratoga SP	Minster Enterprises Ltd
	G-WILK	Beech B200 Super King Air	Tim Leacock Aircraft Sales Ltd
	G-WILY	Rutan LongEz	P. D. Bruce
	G-WIMP	Colt 56A balloon	C. Wolstenholme Wimp
	G-WINE	Thunder Ax7-77Z balloon	R. Brooker
	G-WINK	AA-5B Tiger	D. G. Winks
	G-WINS	PA-32 Cherokee Six 300	First Time Racing Ltd
	G-WIRE	AS.355F-1 Twin Squirrel	National Grid Co PLC (G-CEGB/G-BLJL)
	G-WIRL	Robinson R-22B	T. Goring
	G-WISK	Schweizer 269C	Charter & Transport Services Ltd
	G-WITE	Cessna 414A	Air & General Services Ltd (G-LOVO/ G-KENT)
	G-WIZO	PA-34-220T Seneca III	Extrajet Ltd
	G-WIZZ	AB-206B JetRanger 2	Crest Engineering Ltd
	G-WMCC	BAe Jetstream 3102-01	Birmingham European Airways Ltd (G-TALL)
	G-WMPA	AS.355F-2 Twin Squirrel	W. Midlands Police Authority/Birmingham
	G-WMTM	AA-5B Tiger	T. & W. E. Menham/Biggin Hill
	G-WOLD	Scheibe SF.25E Falke	Wolds Gliding Club Ltd (G-BOVM)/ Pocklington
	G-WOLF	PA-28 Cherokee 140	P. R. Wernham
	G-WOOD	Beech 95-B55A Baron	T. D. Broadhurst (G-AYID)
	G-WOSP	Bell 206B JetRanger 3	Lakeside Helicopters Ltd
	G-WOTG	BN-2T Islander	RAF Sport Parachute Association (G-BJYT)
	G-WOZA	PA-32RT-300 Lance II	K. T. P. Ratcliffe (G-BYBB)
	G-WPLC	Beech 200 Super King Air	Whitbread & Co PLC
	G-WRCF	Beech 200 Super King Air	W. R. C. M. Foyle/Luton
	G-WREN	Pitts S-2A Special	Northamptonshire School of Flying Ltd/ Sywell
	G-WRFM	Enstrom 280C-UK Shark	Trimlook Ltd (G-CTSI/G-BKIO)
	G-WRIT	Thunder Ax7-77A balloon	J. Edge
	G-WRLD	Cameron R-15 balloon	Cameron Balloons Ltd
	G-WRMN	Glaser-Dirks DG.400	W. R. McNair
	G-WROX	PA-31-350 Navajo Chieftain	Levenmere Ltd (G-BNZI)
	G-WSEC	Enstrom F-28C	J. Mills (G-BONF)
	G-WSFT	PA-23 Aztec 250F	SFT Aviation Ltd (G-BTHS)/Bournemouth
	G-WSKY	Enstrom 280C-UK-2 Shark	Footlea Ltd (G-BEEK)
	G-WSSL	PA-31-350 Navajo Chieftain	Compass Aviation Ltd
	G-WTFA	Cessna F.182P	David Martin Couriers Ltd
	G-WULF	WAR Focke-Wulf Fw.190 (08)	P. C. Logsdon
	G-WWII	V.S. 379 Spitfire XIV (SM832)	Patina Ltd/Duxford
	G-WYBC	Partenavia P.68C	Wild Touch Aviazione Ltd (G-SITU/G-NEWU/ G-BHJX)
	G-WYCH	Cameron 90 Witch SS balloon	Jacques W. Soukup Enterprises Ltd
	G-WYLX	Cessna 550 Citation II	Tim Leacock Aircraft Sales Ltd (G-JETD)
	G-WYMP	Cessna F.150J	L. Scattergood & R. Hall (G-BAGW)
	G-WYNN	Rand KR-2	W. Thomas
	G-WYNS	Aero Designs Pulsar XP	G. Griffith
	G-WYNT	Cameron N-56 balloon	Jacques W. Soukup Enterprises Ltd
	G-WYPA	MBB Bo 105DBS/4	W. Yorkshire Police Authority
	G-WYTE	Bell 47G-2A-1	CKS Air Ltd/Southend
	G-WYZZ	Air Command 532 Elite	C. H. Gem (G-BPAK)

Reg.	Type	Owner or Operator	Notes
G-WZZZ	Colt AS-56 airship	Hot-Air Balloon Co Ltd	
G-XALP	Schweizer 269C	R. F. Jones	
G-XCUB	PA-18 Super Cub 150	M. C. Barraclough	
G-XGBE	Cessna 340A	G. B. Express Ltd (G-MAGS)	
G-XIIX	Robinson R-22B	Defence Products Ltd	
G-XPOL	AS.355F-1 Twin Squirrel	Aeromega Ltd (G-BPRF)	
G-XRAY	Rand KR-2	R. S. Smith	
G-XRMC	BAe 125 Srs 800B	RMC Group Services Ltd	
G-XSFT	PA-23 Aztec 250F	SFT Aviation Ltd (G-CPPC/G-BGBH)/ Bournemouth	
G-XSKY	Cameron N-77 balloon	Birds Eye Walls Ltd	
G-XTRA	Extra EA.230	Firebird Aerobatics Ltd/Booker	
G-XVIA	V.S.361 Spitfire LF. XVIe (RW382)	Historic Flying Ltd	
G-XXIV	AB-206B JetRanger 3	Defence Products Ltd	
G-YAWW	PA-28R-201T Turbo Arrow III	Barton Aviation Ltd	
G-YBAA	Cessna FR.172J	J. Blackburn	
G-YEOM	PA-31-350 Navajo Chieftain	Foster Yeoman Ltd/Exeter	
G-YEWS	Rotorway Executive	D. G. Pollard	
G-YIII	Cessna F.150L	Skyviews & General Ltd/Sherburn	
G-YNOT	D.62B Condor	T. Littlefair (G-AYFH)	
G-YOGI	Robin DR.400/140B	R. M. Gosling (G-BDME)	
G-YORK	Cessna F.172M	H. G. Keighley/Sherburn	
G-YOTT	Cessna 425	E. & M. Green (G-NORC)/Guernsey	
G-YPSY	Andreasson BA-4B	H. P. Burrill	
G-YROI	Air Command Commander 532	W. B. Lumb	
G-YROS	Bensen B.80-D	C. Tuxworth	
G-YROY	Montgomerie Bensen B.8MR	R. D. Armishaw	
G-YSFT	PA-23 Aztec 250F	SFT Aviation Ltd (G-BEJT)/Bournemouth	
G-YSKY	PA-31-350 Navajo Chieftain	J. J. Baumhardt/Southend	
G-YTWO	Cessna F.172M	Sherburn Aero Club Ltd	
G-YUCS	PA-32R-301 Saratoga SP	Eastman Securities Ltd (G-BSOL)	
G-YUGO	H.S.125 Srs 1B/R-522	RCR Aviation Ltd (G-ATWH)	
G-YULL	PA-28 Cherokee 180E	Lansdowne Chemical Co (G-BEAJ)/ Kidlington	
G-YUMM	Cameron N-90 balloon	Wunderbar Ltd	
G-YUPI	Cameron N-90 balloon	H. C. Wright	
G-ZAND	Robinson R-22B	Williamson Hotels Ltd	
G-ZAPA	Cessna 404 Titan	Titan Airways Ltd/Stansted	
G-ZAPB	Cessna 404 Titan	Titan Airways Ltd (G-HIGS/G-ODAS)/ Stansted	
G-ZAPC	Short SD3-30 Variant 100	Titan Airways Ltd (G-RNMO/G-BFZW)/ Stansted	
G-ZARA	Nord 3400	D. E. Bain & ptnrs	
G-ZARI	AA-5B Tiger	P. L. Pilch (G-BHVY)/Biggin Hill	
G-ZAZA	PA-18 Super Cub 95	Airbourne Taxi Services Ltd	
G-ZBRA	Thunder Ax10-160 balloon	Zebra Ballooning	
G-ZELL	SA.341G Gazelle 1	D. K. Shead	
G-ZERO	AA-5B Tiger	Snowadem Ltd/Luton	
G-ZFDB	AS.355F-1 Twin Squirrel	Haydon-Baillie Naval & Aircraft Museum (G-BLEV)/Southampton	
G-ZIGG	Robinson R-22B	J. Nivison	
G-ZIGI	Robin DR.400/180	Aeromarine Ltd	
G-ZIPI	Robin DR.400/180	Stahl Engineering Co Ltd/Headcorn	
G-ZIPP	Cessna E.310Q	ZIPP Group (G-BAYU)	
G-ZIPY	Wittman W.8 Tailwind	M. J. Butler	
G-ZLIN	Z.526 Trener Master	R. P. Hallam	
G-ZSFT	PA-23 Aztec 250	SFT Aviation Ltd (G-SALT/G-BGTH)/ Bournemouth	
G-ZSOL	Zlin Z.50L	A. J. E. Ditheridge	
G-ZULU	PA-28-161 Warrior II	Denham School of Flying Ltd	
G-ZUMP	Cameron N-77 balloon	Allen & Harris Ltd	
G-ZUSS	EMB-110P1 Bandeirante	Tech Air (Cambridge) Ltd (G-REGA)	
G-ZZIP	Mooney M.20J	D. A. H. Dixon	

Toy Balloons

Notes	Reg.	Type	Owner or Operator
	G-FYAK	European E.21	J. E. Christopher
	G-FYAN	Williams	M. D. Williams
	G-FYAO	Williams	M. D. Williams
	G-FYAT	Osprey Mk 4D	L. A. Cotgrove
	G-FYAU	Williams MK 2	M. D. Williams
	G-FYAV	Osprey Mk 4E2	C. D. Egan & C. Stiles
	G-FYAZ	Osprey Mk 4D2	M. A. Roblett
	G-FYBA	Portswood Mk XVI	C. R. Rundle
	G-FYBD	Osprey Mk 1E	M. Vincent
	G-FYBE	Osprey Mk 4D	M. Vincent
	G-FYBF	Osprey Mk V	M. Vincent
	G-FYBG	Osprey Mk 4G2	M. Vincent
	G-FYBH	Osprey Mk 4G	M. Vincent
	G-FYBI	Osprey Mk 4H	M. Vincent
	G-FYBP	European E.84PW	D. Eaves
	G-FYBR	Osprey Mk 4G2	A. J. Pugh
	G-FYBU	Portswood Mk XVI	M. A. Roblett
	G-FYBX	Portswood Mk XVI	I. Chadwick
	G-FYCC	Osprey Mk 4G2	A. Russell
	G-FYCL	Osprey Mk 4G	P. J. Rogers
	G-FYCN	Osprey Mk 4D	C. F. Chipping
	G-FYCO	Osprey Mk 4B	C. F. Chipping
	G-FYCP	Osprey Mk 1E	C. F. Chipping
	G-FYCR	Osprey MK 4D	C. F. Chipping
	G-FYCT	Osprey Mk 4D	S. T. Wallbank
	G-FYCU	Osprey Mk 4D	G. M. Smith
	G-FYCV	Osprey Mk 4D	M. Thomson
	G-FYCW	Osprey Mk 4D	M. L. Partridge
	G-FYCZ	Osprey Mk 4D2	P. Middleton
	G-FYDC	European EDH-1	D. Eaves & H. Goddard
	G-FYDD	Osprey Mk 4D	A. C. Mitchell
	G-FYDF	Osprey Mk 4D	K. A. Jones
	G-FYDI	Williams Westwind Two	M. D. Williams
	G-FYDK	Williams Westwind Two	M. D. Williams
	G-FYDM	Williams Westwind Four	M. D. Williams
	G-FYDN	European 8C	P. D. Ridout
	G-FYDO	Osprey Mk 4D	N. L. Scallan
	G-FYDP	Williams Westwind Three	M. D. Williams
	G-FYDS	Osprey Mk 4D	N. L. Scallan
	G-FYDW	Osprey Mk 4B	R. A. Balfre
	G-FYEB	Rango Rega	N. H. Ponsford
	G-FYEG	Osprey Mk 1C	P. E. Prime
	G-FYEI	Portswood Mk XVI	A. Russell
	G-FYEJ	Rango NA.24	N. H. Ponsford
	G-FYEK	Unicorn UE.1C	D. & D. Eaves
	G-FYEL	European E.84Z	D. Eaves
	G-FYEO	Eagle Mk 1	M. E. Scallon
	G-FYEV	Osprey Mk 1C	M. E. Scallen
	G-FYEZ	Firefly Mk 1	M. E. & N. L. Scallan
	G-FYFA	European E.84LD	D. Goddard & D. Eaves
	G-FYFG	European E.84DE	D. Eaves
	G-FYFH	European E.84DS	D. Eaves
	G-FYFI	European E.84DS	M. Stelling
	G-FYFJ	Williams Westland 2	M. D. Williams
	G-FYFK	Williams Westland 2	D. Feasey
	G-FYFN	Osprey Saturn 2	J. & M. Woods
	G-FYFT	Rango NA-32BC	Rango Kite & Balloon Co
	G-FYFV	Saffrey Grand Edinburgh	I. G. & G. M. McIntosh
	G-FYFW	Rango NA-55	Rango Kite & Balloon Co
	G-FYFY	Rango NA-55RC	A. M. Lindsay
	G-FYGA	Rango NA-50RC	Rango Kite & Balloon Co
	G-FYGB	Rango NA-105RC	Rango Kite & Balloon Co
	G-FYGC	Rango NA-42B	L. J. Wardle
	G-FYGG	Buz-B20	D. P. Busby & S. Spink
	G-FYGH	Busby Buz B.20W	D. P. Busby
	G-FYGI	Rango NA-55RC	Advertair Ltd
	G-FYGJ	Airspeed 300	N. Wells
	G-FYGK	Rango NA-42POC	Rango Balloon & Kite Co

Microlights

Reg.	Type	Notes	Reg	Type	Notes
G-MBAA	Hiway Skytrike Mk 2		G-MBEJ	Electraflyer Eagle	
G-MBAB	Hovey Whing-Ding II		G-MBEN	Eipper Quicksilver MX	
G-MBAD	Weedhopper JC-24A		G-MBEP	American Aerolights Eagle	
G-MBAF	R. J. Swift 3		G-MBES	Skyhook Cutlass	
G-MBAJ	Chargus T.250		G-MBET	MEA Mistral Trainer	
G-MBAL	Hiway Demon		G-MBEU	Hiway Demon T.250	
G-MBAM	Skycraft Scout 2		G-MBEV	Chargus Titan 38	
G-MBAN	American Aerolights Eagle		G-MBFA	Hiway Skytrike 250	
G-MBAR	Skycraft Scout		G-MBFE	American Aerolights Eagle	
G-MBAS	Typhoon Tripacer 250		G-MBFF	Southern Aerosports	
G-MBAU	Hiway Skytrike			Scorpion	
G-MBAW	Pterodactyl Ptraveller		G-MBFG	Skyhook Sabre	
G-MBAZ	Rotec Rally 2B		G-MBFJ	Chargus Typhoon T.250	
G-MBBA	Ultraflight Lazair		G-MBFK	Hiway Demon	
G-MBBB	Skycraft Scout 2		G-MBFM	Hiway Hang Glider	
G-MBBG	Weedhopper JC-24B		G-MBFU	Ultrasports Tripacer	
G-MBBH	Flexiform Sealander 160		G-MBFX	Hiway Skytrike 250	
G-MBBI	Ultraflight Mirage		G-MBFY	Mirage II	
G-MBBJ	Hiway Demon Trike		G-MBFZ	M. S. S. Goldwing	
G-MBBM	Eipper Quicksilver MX		G-MBGA	Solar Wings Typhoon	
G-MBBN	Eagle Microlight		G-MBGB	American Aerolights Eagle	
G-MBBT	Ultrasports Tripacer 330		G-MBGF	Twamley Trike	
G-MBBU	Southdown Savage		G-MBGJ	Hiway Skytrike Mk 2	
G-MBBW	Flexiform Hilander		G-MBGK	Electra Flyer Eagle	
G-MBBX	Chargus Skytrike		G-MBGP	Solar Wings Typhoon	
G-MBBY	Flexiform Sealander			Skytrike	
G-MBBZ	Volmer Jensen VJ-24W		G-MBGR	Eurowing Goldwing	
G-MBCA	Chargus Cyclone T.250		G-MBGS	Rotec Rally 2B	
G-MBCD	La Mouette Atlas		G-MBGT	American Aerolights Eagle	
G-MBCE	American Aerolights Eagle		G-MBGV	Skyhook Cutlass	
G-MBCF	Pterodactyl Ptraveler		G-MBGW	Hiway Skytrike	
G-MBCG	Ultrasports Tripacer T.250		G-MBGX	Southdown Lightning	
G-MBCI	Hiway Skytrike		G-MBGY	Hiway Demon Skytrike	
G-MBCJ	Mainair Sports Tri-Flyer		G-MBHA	Trident Trike	
G-MBCK	Eipper Quicksilver MX		G-MBHC	Chargus Lightning T.250	
G-MBCL	Hiway Demon Triflyer		G-MBHD	Hiway Vulcan Trike	
G-MBCM	Hiway Demon 175		G-MBHE	American Aerolights Eagle	
G-MBCN	Hiway Super Scorpion		G-MBHH	Flexiform Sealander	
G-MBCO	Flexiform Sealander			Skytrike	
	Buggy		G-MBHJ	Hornet Skyhook Cutlass	
G-MBCR	Ultraflight Mirage		G-MBHK	Flexiform Skytrike	
G-MBCU	American Aerolights Eagle		G-MBHP	American Aerolights	
G-MBCV	Hiway Skytrike			Eagle II	
G-MBCX	Airwave Nimrod 165		G-MBHT	Chargus T.250	
G-MBCZ	Chargus Skytrike 160		G-MBHW	American Aerolights Eagle	
G-MBDC	Skyhook Cutlass		G-MBHX	Pterodactyl Ptraveller	
G-MBDD	Skyhook Skytrike		G-MBHZ	Pterodactyl Ptraveller	
G-MBDE	Flexiform Skytrike		G-MBIA	Flexiform Sealander	
G-MBDF	Rotec Rally 2B			Skytrike	
G-MBDG	Eurowing Goldwing		G-MBIC	Maxair Hummer	
G-MBDH	Hiway Demon Triflyer		G-MBID	American Aerolights Eagle	
G-MBDI	Flexiform Sealander		G-MBII	Hiway Skytrike	
G-MBDJ	Flexiform Sealander		G-MBIO	American Aerolights Eagle	
	Triflyer			Z Drive	
G-MBDM	Southdown Sigma Trike		G-MBIT	Hiway Demon Skytrike	
G-MBDN	Hornet Atlas		G-MBIU	Hiway Super Scorpion	
G-MBDR	U.A.S. Stormbuggy		G-MBIV	Flexiform Skytrike	
G-MBDU	Chargus Titan 38		G-MBIW	Hiway Demon Tri-Flyer	
G-MBDW	Ultrasports Tripacer			Skytrike	
	Skytrike A		G-MBIY	Ultra Sports	
G-MBDX	Electraflyer Eagle		G-MBIZ	Mainair Tri-Flyer	
G-MBDZ	Eipper Quicksilver MX		G-MBJA	Eurowing Goldwing	
G-MBEA	Hornet Nimrod		G-MBJD	American Aerolights Eagle	
G-MBEB	Hiway Skytrike 250 Mk II		G-MBJE	Airwave Nimrod	
G-MBED	Chargus Titan 38		G-MBJF	Hiway Skytrike Mk II	
G-MBEE	Hiway Super Scorpion		G-MBJG	Airwave Nimrod	
	Skytrike 160		G-MBJI	Southern Aerosports	
G-MBEG	Eipper Quicksilver MX			Scorpion	

Reg.	Type	Notes	Reg	Type	Notes
G-MBJK	American Aerolights Eagle			Canard	
G-MBJL	Airwave Nimrod		G-MBOR	Chotia 460B Weedhopper	
G-MBJM	Striplin Lone Ranger		G-MBOT	Hiway 250 Skytrike	
G-MBJN	Electraflyer Eagle		G-MBOU	Wheeler Scout	
G-MBJO	Birdman Cherokee		G-MBOV	Southdown Lightning Trike	
G-MBJP	Hiway Skytrike		G-MBOX	American Aerolights Eagle	
G-MBJR	American Aerolights Eagle		G-MBPA	Weedhopper Srs 2	
G-MBJS	Mainair Tri-Flyer		G-MBPC	American Aerolights Eagle	
G-MBJT	Hiway Skytrike II		G-MBPD	American Aerolights Eagle	
G-MBJU	American Eagle 215B		G-MBPE	Ultrasports Trike	
G-MBJZ	Eurowing Catto CP.16		G-MBPG	Hunt Skytrike	
G-MBKA	Mistral Trainer		G-MBPJ	Moto-Delta	
G-MBKC	Southdown Lightning		G-MBPL	Hiway Demon	
G-MBKD	Chargus T.250		G-MBPM	Eurowing Goldwing	
G-MBKG	Batchelor-Hunt Skytrike		G-MBPN	American Aerolights Eagle	
G-MBKH	Southdown Skytrike		G-MBPO	Volnik Arrow	
G-MBKS	Hiway Skytrike 160		G-MBPS	Gryphon Willpower	
G-MBKT	Mitchell Wing B.10		G-MBPU	Hiway Demon	
G-MBKU	Hiway Demon Skytrike		G-MBPW	Weedhopper	
G-MBKV	Eurowing Goldwing		G-MBPX	Eurowing Goldwing	
G-MBKW	Pterodactyl Ptraveller		G-MBPY	Ultrasports Tripacer 330	
G-MBKZ	Hiway Skytrike		G-MBPZ	Flexiform Striker	
G-MBLA	Flexiform Skytrike		G-MBRB	Electraflyer Eagle 1	
G-MBLB	Eipper Quicksilver MX		G-MBRD	American Aerolights Eagle	
G-MBLD	Flexiform Striker		G-MBRE	Wheeler Scout	
G-MBLF	Hiway Demon 195 Tri Pacer		G-MBRF	Weedhopper 460C	
			G-MBRH	Ultraflight Mirage Mk II	
G-MBLH	Flexwing Tri-Flyer 330		G-MBRK	Huntair Pathfinder	
G-MBLJ	Eipper Quicksilver MX		G-MBRM	Hiway Demon	
G-MBLK	Southdown Puma		G-MBRO	Hiway Skytrike 160	
G-MBLM	Hiway Skytrike		G-MBRS	American Aerolights Eagle	
G-MBLN	Pterodactyl Ptraveller		G-MBRV	Eurowing Goldwing	
G-MBLO	Sealander Skytrike		G-MBRZ	Hiway Vulcan 250	
G-MBLR	Ultrasports Tripacer		G-MBSA	Ultraflight Mirage II	
G-MBLS	MEA Mistral		G-MBSC	Ultraflight Mirage II	
G-MBLU	Southdown Lightning L.195		G-MBSD	Southdown Puma DS	
G-MBLV	Ultrasports Hybrid		G-MBSF	Ultraflight Mirage II	
G-MBLY	Flexiform Sealander Trike		G-MBSG	Ultraflight Mirage II	
G-MBLZ	Southern Aerosports Scorpion		G-MBSN	American Aerolights Eagle	
			G-MBSR	Southdown Puma DS	
G-MBME	American Aerolights Eagle Z Drive		G-MBSS	Ultrasports Puma 2	
			G-MBST	Mainair Gemini Sprint	
G-MBMG	Rotec Rally 2B		G-MBSW	Ultraflight Mirage II	
G-MBMJ	Mainair Tri-Flyer		G-MBSX	Ultraflight Mirage II	
G-MBMO	Hiway Skytrike 160		G-MBTA	UAS Storm Buggy 5 Mk 2	
G-MBMR	Ultrasports Tripacer Typhoon		G-MBTB	Davies Tri-Flyer S	
G-MBMS	Hornet		G-MBTC	Weedhopper	
G-MBMT	Mainair Tri-Flyer		G-MBTF	Mainair Tri-Flyer Skytrike	
G-MBMU	Eurowing Goldwing		G-MBTG	Mainair Gemini	
G-MBMW	Solar Wings Typhoon		G-MBTH	Whittaker MW.4	
G-MBMZ	Sealander Tripacer		G-MBTI	Hovey Whing Ding	
G-MBNA	American Aerolights Eagle		G-MBTJ	Solar Wings Microlight	
G-MBNF	American Aerolights Eagle		G-MBTO	Mainair Tri-Flyer 250	
G-MBNG	Hiway Demon Skytrike		G-MBTS	Hovey WD-II Whing-Ding	
G-MBNH	Southern Airsports Scorpion		G-MBTW	Raven Vector 600	
			G-MBTZ	Huntair Pathfinder	
G-MBNJ	Eipper Quicksilver MX		G-MBUA	Hiway Demon	
G-MBNK	American Aerolights Eagle		G-MBUB	Horne Sigma Skytrike	
G-MBNN	Southern Microlight Gazelle P.160N		G-MBUC	Huntair Pathfinder	
			G-MBUD	Wheeler Scout Mk III	
G-MBNT	American Aerolights Eagle		G-MBUE	MBA Tiger Cub 440	
G-MBNY	Steer Terror Fledge II		G-MBUH	Hiway Skytrike	
G-MBNZ	Hiway Skytrike Demon		G-MBUI	Wheeler Scout Mk I	
G-MBOA	Flexiform Hilander		G-MBUK	Mainair 330 Tri Pacer	
G-MBOD	American Aerolights Eagle		G-MBUL	American Aerolights Eagle	
G-MBOE	Solar Wing Typhoon Trike		G-MBUO	Southern Aerosports Scorpion	
G-MBOF	Pakes Jackdaw				
G-MBOH	Microlight Engineering Mistral		G-MBUP	Hiway Skytrike	
			G-MBUT	UAS Storm Buggy	
G-MBOK	Dunstable Microlight		G-MBUZ	Wheeler Scout Mk II	
G-MBOM	Hiway Hilander		G-MBVA	Volmer Jensen VJ-23E	
G-MBON	Eurowing Goldwing		G-MBVC	American Aerolights Eagle	
			G-MBVH	Mainair Triflyer Striker	

Reg.	Type	Notes	Reg	Type	Notes
G-MBVJ	Skyhook Trike		G-MBZU	Skyhook Sabre C	
G-MBVK	Ultraflight Mirage II		G-MBZV	American Aerolights Eagle	
G-MBVL	Southern Aerosports Scorpion		G-MBZZ	Southern Aerosports Scorpion	
G-MBVP	Mainair Triflyer 330 Striker		G-MGAG	Aviasud Mistral	
G-MBVR	Rotec Rally 2B		G-MGOM	Medway Hybred 44XLR	
G-MBVS	Hiway Skytrike		G-MGOO	Renegade Spirit UK Ltd	
G-MBVT	American Aerolights Eagle		G-MGUY	CFM Shadow Srs BD	
G-MBVU	Flexiform Sealander Triflyer				
G-MBVV	Hiway Skytrike		G-MJAA	Ultrasports Tripacer	
G-MBVW	Skyhook TR.2		G-MJAB	Ultrasports Skytrike	
G-MBVY	Eipper Quicksilver MX		G-MJAD	Eipper Quicksilver MX	
G-MBWA	American Aerolights Eagle		G-MJAE	American Aerolights Eagle	
G-MBWB	Hiway Skytrike		G-MJAF	Ultrasports Puma 440	
G-MBWD	Rotec Rally 2B		G-MJAG	Skyhook TR1	
G-MBWE	American Aerolights Eagle		G-MJAH	American Aerolights Eagle	
G-MBWF	Mainair Triflyer Striker		G-MJAI	American Aerolights Eagle	
G-MBWG	Huntair Pathfinder		G-MJAJ	Eurowing Goldwing	
G-MBWH	Designability Duet I		G-MJAL	Wheeler Scout 3	
G-MBWL	Huntair Pathfinder		G-MJAM	Eipper Quicksilver MX	
G-MBWO	Hiway Demon Skytrike		G-MJAN	Hiway Skytrike	
G-MBWP	Ultrasports Trike		G-MJAO	Hiway Skytrike	
G-MBWR	Hornet		G-MJAP	Hiway 160	
G-MBWT	Huntair Pathfinder		G-MJAR	Chargus Titan	
G-MBWU	Hiway Demon Skytrike		G-MJAV	Hiway Demon Skytrike 244cc	
G-MBWW	Southern Aerosports Scorpion		G-MJAZ	Aerodyne Vector 610	
G-MBWX	Southern Aerosports Scorpion		G-MJBF	Southdown Puma 330	
			G-MJBH	American Aerolights Eagle	
G-MBWY	American Aerolights Eagle		G-MJBK	Swallow AeroPlane Swallow B	
G-MBXB	Southdown Sailwings Puma		G-MJBL	American Aerolights Eagle	
G-MBXE	Hiway Skytrike		G-MJBN	American Aerolights Eagle	
G-MBXF	Hiway Skytrike		G-MJBS	Ultralight Stormbuggy	
G-MBXI	Hiway Skytrike		G-MJBT	Eipper Quicksilver MX	
G-MBXJ	Hiway Demon Skytrike		G-MJBV	American Aerolights Eagle	
G-MBXK	Ultrasports Puma		G-MJBX	Pterodactyl Ptraveller	
G-MBXO	Sheffield Trident		G-MJBZ	Huntair Pathfinder	
G-MBXP	Hornet Skytrike		G-MJCA	Skyhook Sabre	
G-MBXR	Hiway Skytrike 150		G-MJCB	Hornet 330	
G-MBXT	Eipper Quicksilver MX2		G-MJCC	Ultrasports Puma	
G-MBXW	Hiway Skytrike		G-MJCD	Sigma Tetley Skytrike	
G-MBXX	Ultraflight Mirage II		G-MJCE	Ultrasports Tripacer	
G-MBYD	American Aerolights Eagle		G-MJCF	Maxair Hummer	
G-MBYF	Skyhook TR2		G-MJCG	S.M.C. Flyer Mk 1	
G-MBYH	Maxair Hummer		G-MJCH	Ultraflight Mirage II	
G-MBYI	Ultraflight Lazair		G-MJCI	Kruchek Firefly 440	
G-MBYJ	Hiway Super Scorpion IIC		G-MJCJ	Hiway Spectrum	
G-MBYK	Huntair Pathfinder Mk 1		G-MJCK	Southern Aerosports Scorpion	
G-MBYL	Huntair Pathfinder 330		G-MJCL	Eipper Quicksilver MX	
G-MBYM	Eipper Quicksilver MX		G-MJCN	S.M.C. Flyer Mk 1	
G-MBYO	American Aerolights Eagle		G-MJCP	Huntair Pathfinder	
G-MBYR	American Aerolights Eagle		G-MJCU	Tarjani	
G-MBYS	Ultraflight Mirage II		G-MJCW	Hiway Super Scorpion	
G-MBYT	Ultraflight Mirage II		G-MJCY	Eurowing Goldwing	
G-MBYU	American Aerolights Eagle		G-MJCZ	Southern Aerosports Scorpion 2	
G-MBYX	American Aerolights Eagle				
G-MBYY	Southern Aerosports Scorpion		G-MJDA	Hornet Trike Executive	
			G-MJDB	Birdman Cherokee	
G-MBZA	Ultrasports Tripacer 330		G-MJDE	Huntair Pathfinder	
G-MBZB	Hiway Skytrike		G-MJDG	Hornet Supertrike	
G-MBZF	American Aerolights Eagle		G-MJDH	Huntair Pathfinder	
G-MBZG	Twinflight Scorpion 2 seat		G-MJDI	Southern Flyer Mk 1	
G-MBZH	Eurowing Goldwing		G-MJDJ	Hiway Skytrike Demon	
G-MBZI	Eurowing Goldwing		G-MJDK	American Aerolights Eagle	
G-MBZK	Ultrasports Tripacer 250		G-MJDO	Southdown Puma 440	
G-MBZL	Weedhopper		G-MJDP	Eurowing Goldwing	
G-MBZM	UAS Storm Buggy		G-MJDR	Hiway Demon Skytrike	
G-MBZN	Ultrasports Puma		G-MJDU	Eipper Quicksilver MX2	
G-MBZO	Mainair Triflyer 330		G-MJDW	Eipper Quicksilver MX	
G-MBZP	Skyhook TR2		G-MJDX	Moyes Mega II	
G-MBZT	Solarwings Skytrike		G-MJDY	Ultrasports Solarwings	

Reg.	Type	Notes	Reg	Type	Notes
G-MJEC	Ultrasports Puma		G-MJIS	American Aerolights Eagle	
G-MJEE	Mainair Triflyer Trike		G-MJIU	Eipper Quicksilver MX	
G-MJEF	Gryphon 180		G-MJIV	Pterodactyl Ptraveller	
G-MJEG	Eurowing Goldwing		G-MJIY	Flexiform Voyage	
G-MJEH	Rotec Rally 2B		G-MJIZ	Southdown Lightning	
G-MJEJ	American Aerolights Eagle		G-MJJA	Huntair Pathfinder	
G-MJEK	Hiway Demon 330		G-MJJB	Eipper Quicksilver MX	
	Skytrike		G-MJJD	Birdman Cherokee	
G-MJEL	GMD-01 Trike		G-MJJF	Sealey	
G-MJEO	American Aerolights Eagle		G-MJJJ	Moyes Knight	
G-MJEP	Pterodactyl Ptraveller		G-MJJK	Eipper Quicksilver MX2	
G-MJER	Flexiform Striker		G-MJJL	Solar Wings Storm	
G-MJET	Stratos Prototype 3 Axis 1		G-MJJM	Birdman Cherokee Mk 1	
G-MJEX	Eipper Quicksilver MX		G-MJJN	Ultrasports Puma	
G-MJEY	Southdown Lightning		G-MJJO	Flexiform Skytrike Dual	
G-MJFB	Flexiform Striker		G-MJJS	Swallow AeroPlane	
G-MJFD	Ultrasports Tripacer			Swallow B	
G-MJFF	Huntair Pathfinder		G-MJJU	Hiway Demon	
G-MJFH	Eipper Quicksilver MX		G-MJJV	Wheeler Scout	
G-MJFI	Flexiform Striker		G-MJJX	Hiway Skytrike	
G-MJFJ	Hiway Skytrike 250		G-MJJY	Tirith Firefly	
G-MJFK	Flexiform Skytrike Dual		G-MJJZ	Hiway Demon 175	
G-MJFL	Mainair Tri-Flyer 440			Skytrike	
G-MJFM	Huntair Pathfinder		G-MJKA	Skyhook Sabre Trike	
G-MJFO	Eipper Quicksilver MX		G-MJKB	Striplin Skyranger	
G-MJFP	American Aerolights Eagle		G-MJKC	Mainair Triflyer 330 Striker	
G-MJFS	American Aerolights Eagle		G-MJKE	Mainair Triflyer 330	
G-MJFV	Ultrasports Tripacer		G-MJKF	Hiway Demon	
G-MJFX	Skyhook TR-1		G-MJKG	John Ivor Skytrike	
G-MJGC	Hornet		G-MJKH	Eipper Quicksilver MX II	
G-MJGD	Huntair Pathfinder		G-MJKI	Eipper Quicksilver MX	
G-MJGE	Eipper Quicksilver MX		G-MJKJ	Eipper Quicksilver MX	
G-MJGG	Skyhook TR-1		G-MJKO	Goldmarque 250 Skytrike	
G-MJGI	Eipper Quicksilver MX		G-MJKP	Hiway Super Scorpion	
G-MJGL	Chargus Titan 38		G-MJKR	Rotec Rally 2B	
G-MJGM	Hiway Demon 195 Skytrike		G-MJKS	Mainair Triflyer	
G-MJGN	Greenslade Monotrike		G-MJKU	Hiway Demon 175	
G-MJGO	Barnes Avon Skytrike		G-MJKV	Hornet	
G-MJGT	Skyhook Cutlass Trike		G-MJKX	Ultralight Skyrider	
G-MJGV	Eipper Quicksilver MX2			Phantom	
G-MJGW	Solar Wings Trike		G-MJKY	Hiway Skytrike	
G-MJGX	Ultrasports Puma 250		G-MJLA	Ultrasports Puma 2	
G-MJHA	Hiway Skytrike 250 Mk II		G-MJLB	Ultrasports Puma 2	
G-MJHC	Ultrasports Tripacer 330		G-MJLD	Wheeler Scout Mk III	
G-MJHE	Hiway Demon Skytrike		G-MJLF	Southern Microlight Trike	
G-MJHF	Skyhook Sailwing Trike		G-MJLH	American Aerolights	
G-MJHK	Hiway Demon 195			Eagle 2	
G-MJHM	Ultrasports Trike		G-MJLI	Hiway Demon Skytrike	
G-MJHN	American Aerolights Eagle		G-MJLJ	Flexiform Sealander	
G-MJHO	Shilling Bumble Bee Srs 1		G-MJLL	Hiway Demon Skytrike	
G-MJHP	American Aerolights Eagle		G-MJLM	Mainair Triflyer 250	
G-MJHR	Southdown Lightning		G-MJLO	Goldmarque Skytrike	
G-MJHU	Eipper Quicksilver MX		G-MJLR	Skyhook SK-1	
G-MJHV	Hiway Demon 250		G-MJLS	Rotec Rally 2B	
G-MJHW	Ultrasports Puma 1		G-MJLT	American Aerolights Eagle	
G-MJHX	Eipper Quicksilver MX		G-MJLU	Skyhook	
G-MJHZ	Southdown Sailwings		G-MJLY	American Aerolights Eagle	
G-MJIA	Flexiform Striker		G-MJMA	Hiway Demon	
G-MJIB	Hornet 250		G-MJMB	Weedhopper	
G-MJIC	Ultrasports Puma 330		G-MJME	Ultrasports Tripacer Mega II	
G-MJID	Southdown Sailwings		G-MJMM	Chargus Vortex	
	Puma DS		G-MJMP	Eipper Quicksilver MX	
G-MJIE	Hornet 330		G-MJMR	Solar Wings Typhoon	
G-MJIF	Mainair Triflyer		G-MJMS	Hiway Skytrike	
G-MJIG	Hiway Demon Skytrike		G-MJMT	Hiway Demon Skytrike	
G-MJIH	Ultrasports Tripacer		G-MJMW	Eipper Quicksilver MX2	
G-MJIJ	Ultrasports Tripacer 250		G-MJMX	Ultrasports Tripacer	
G-MJIK	Southdown Sailwings		G-MJNB	Hiway Skytrike	
	Lightning		G-MJNE	Hornet Supreme Dual	
G-MJIL	Bremner Mitchell B.10			Trike	
G-MJIN	Hiway Skytrike		G-MJNH	Skyhook Cutlass Trike	
G-MJIO	American Aerolights Eagle		G-MJNK	Hiway Skytrike	
G-MJIR	Eipper Quicksilver MX		G-MJNL	American Aerolights Eagle	

Reg.	Type	Notes	Reg	Type	Notes
G-MJNM	American Aerolights Double Eagle		G-MJTE	Skyrider Airsports Phantom	
G-MJNN	Ultraflight Mirage II		G-MJTF	Gryphon Wing	
G-MJNO	American Aerolights Double Eagle		G-MJTH	S.M.D. Gazelle	
			G-MJTI	Huntair Pathfinder II	
G-MJNP	American Aerolights Eagle		G-MJTL	Aerostructure Pipistrelle 2B	
G-MJNR	Ultralight Solar Buggy		G-MJTM	Aerostructure Pipistrelle 2B	
G-MJNS	Swallow AeroPlane Swallow B		G-MJTN	Eipper Quicksilver MX	
			G-MJTO	Jordan Duet Srs 1	
G-MJNT	Hiway Skytrike		G-MJTP	Flexiform Striker	
G-MJNU	Skyhook Cutlass		G-MJTR	Southdown Puma DS Mk 1	
G-MJNV	Eipper Quicksilver MX		G-MJTU	Skyhook Cutlass 185	
G-MJNY	Skyhook Sabre Trike		G-MJTW	Eurowing Trike	
G-MJOA	Chargus T.250 Vortex		G-MJTX	Skyrider Phantom	
G-MJOC	Huntair Pathfinder		G-MJTY	Huntair Pathfinder	
G-MJOD	Rotec Rally 2B		G-MJTZ	Skyrider Airsports Phantom	
G-MJOE	Eurowing Goldwing		G-MJUB	MBA Tiger Cub 440	
G-MJOG	American Aerolights Eagle		G-MJUC	MBA Tiger Cub 440	
G-MJOI	Hiway Demon		G-MJUE	Southdown Lightning II	
G-MJOJ	Flexiform Skytrike		G-MJUH	MBA Tiger Cub 440	
G-MJOK	Mainair Triflyer 250		G-MJUI	Flexiform Striker	
G-MJOL	Skyhook Cutlass		G-MJUJ	Eipper Quicksilver Mk II	
G-MJOM	Southdown Puma 40F		G-MJUK	Eipper Quicksilver MX II	
G-MJOO	Southdown Puma 40F		G-MJUL	Southdown Puma Sprint	
G-MJOR	Solair Phoenix		G-MJUM	Flexiform Striker	
G-MJOS	Southdown Lightning 170		G-MJUO	Eipper Quicksilver MX II	
G-MJOU	Hiway Demon 175		G-MJUP	Weedhopper B	
G-MJOV	Solar Wings Typhoon		G-MJUR	Skyrider Airsports Phantom	
G-MJOW	Eipper Quicksilver MX		G-MJUS	MBA Tiger Cub 440	
G-MJPA	Rotec Rally 2B		G-MJUT	Eurowing Goldwing	
G-MJPC	American Aerolights Double Eagle		G-MJUU	Eurowing Goldwing	
			G-MJUW	MBA Tiger Cub 440	
G-MJPD	Hiway Demon Skytrike		G-MJUX	Skyrider Airsports Phantom	
G-MJPE	Hiway Demon Skytrike		G-MJUY	Eurowing Goldwing	
G-MJPG	American Aerolights Eagle 430R		G-MJUZ	Dragon Srs 150	
			G-MJVA	Skyrider Airsports Phantom	
G-MJPI	Flexiform Striker		G-MJVC	Hiway Skytrike	
G-MJPJ	Flexiform Dual Trike 440		G-MJVE	Hybred Skytrike	
G-MJPK	Hiway Vulcan		G-MJVF	CFM Shadow	
G-MJPO	Eurowing Goldwing		G-MJVG	Hiway Skytrike	
G-MJPS	American Aerolights Eagle 430R		G-MJVJ	Flexiform Striker Dual	
			G-MJVL	Flexiform Striker	
G-MJPT	Dragon		G-MJVM	Dragon 150	
G-MJPU	Solar Wings Typhoon		G-MJVN	Ultrasports Puma 440	
G-MJPV	Eipper Quicksilver MX		G-MJVP	Eipper Quicksilver MX II	
G-MJRA	Hiway Demon		G-MJVR	Flexiforn Striker	
G-MJRE	Hiway Demon		G-MJVT	Eipper Quicksilver MX	
G-MJRG	Ultrasports Puma		G-MJVU	Eipper Quicksilver MX II	
G-MJRH	Hiway Skytrike		G-MJVV	Hornet Supreme Dual	
G-MJRI	American Aerolights Eagle		G-MJVW	Airwave Nimrod	
G-MJRK	Flexiform Striker		G-MJVX	Skyrider Phantom	
G-MJRL	Eurowing Goldwing		G-MJVY	Dragon Srs 150	
G-MJRN	Flexiform Striker		G-MJVZ	Hiway Demon Tripacer	
G-MJRO	Eurowing Goldwing		G-MJWB	Eurowing Goldwing	
G-MJRP	Mainair Triflyer 330		G-MJWD	Solar Wings Typhoon XL	
G-MJRR	Striplin Skyranger Srs 1		G-MJWE	Hiway Demon	
G-MJRS	Eurowing Goldwing		G-MJWG	MBA Tiger Cub	
G-MJRT	Southdown Lightning DS		G-MJWI	Flexiform Striker	
G-MJRU	MBA Tiger Cub 440		G-MJWJ	MBA Tiger Cub 440	
G-MJRX	Ultrasports Puma II		G-MJWK	Huntair Pathfinder	
G-MJSA	Mainair 2-Seat Trike		G-MJWN	Flexiform Striker	
G-MJSE	Skyrider Airsports Phantom		G-MJWO	Hiway Skytrike	
G-MJSF	Skyrider Airsports Phantom		G-MJWR	MBA Tiger Cub 440	
G-MJSL	Dragon 200		G-MJWS	Eurowing Goldwing	
G-MJSO	Hiway Skytrike		G-MJWU	Maxair Hummer TX	
G-MJSP	MBA Super Tiger Cub 440		G-MJWV	Southdown Puma MS	
G-MJSS	American Aerolights Eagle		G-MJWW	MBA Super Tiger Cub 440	
G-MJST	Pterodactyl Ptraveler		G-MJWX	Flexiform Striker	
G-MJSU	MBA Tiger Cub		G-MJWY	Flexiform Striker	
G-MJSV	MBA Tiger Cub		G-MJWZ	Ultrasports Panther XL	
G-MJSY	Eurowing Goldwing		G-MJXA	Flexiform Striker	
G-MJTC	Solar Wings Typhoon		G-MJXB	Eurowing Goldwing	
G-MJTD	Gardner T-M Scout		G-MJXD	MBA Tiger Cub 440	

Reg.	Type	Notes	Reg	Type	Notes
G-MJXE	Hiway Demon		G-MMBC	Hiway Super Scorpion	
G-MJXF	MBA Tiger Cub 440		G-MMBD	Spectrum 330	
G-MJXJ	MBA Tiger Cub 440		G-MMBE	MBA Tiger Cub 440	
G-MJXM	Hiway Skytrike		G-MMBF	American Aerolights Eagle	
G-MJXR	Huntair Pathfinder II		G-MMBH	MBA Super Tiger Cub 440	
G-MJXS	Huntair Pathfinder II		G-MMBJ	Solar Wings Typhoon	
G-MJXT	Phoenix Falcon 1		G-MMBK	American Aerolights Eagle	
G-MJXV	Flexiform Striker		G-MMBL	Southdown Puma	
G-MJXX	Flexiform Striker Dual		G-MMBN	Eurowing Goldwing	
G-MJXY	Hiway Demon Skytrike		G-MMBS	Flexiform Striker	
G-MJXZ	Hiway Demon		G-MMBT	MBA Tiger Cub 440	
G-MJYA	Huntair Pathfinder		G-MMBU	Eipper Quicksilver MX II	
G-MJYC	Ultrasports Panther XL Dual 440		G-MMBV	Huntair Pathfinder	
			G-MMBW	MBA Tiger Cub 440	
G-MJYD	MBA Tiger Cub 440		G-MMBX	MBA Tiger Cub 440	
G-MJYF	Mainair Gemini Flash		G-MMBY	Solar Wings Panther	
G-MJYG	Skyhook Orion Canard		G-MMBZ	Solar Wings Typhoon P	
G-MJYI	Mainair Triflyer		G-MMCD	Southdown Lightning DS	
G-MJYJ	MBA Tiger Cub 440		G-MMCE	MBA Tiger Cub 440	
G-MJYL	Airwave Nimrod		G-MMCF	Solar Wings Panther 330	
G-MJYM	Southdown Puma Sprint		G-MMCG	Eipper Quicksilver MX I	
G-MJYP	Mainair Triflyer 440		G-MMCI	Southdown Puma Sprint	
G-MJYR	Catto CP.16		G-MMCJ	Flexiform Striker	
G-MJYS	Southdown Puma Sprint		G-MMCM	Southdown Puma Sprint	
G-MJYT	Southdown Puma Sprint		G-MMCN	Solar Wings Storm	
G-MJYV	Mainair Triflyer 2 Seat		G-MMCO	Southdown Sprint	
G-MJYW	Wasp Gryphon III		G-MMCR	Eipper Quicksilver MX	
G-MJYX	Mainair Triflyer		G-MMCS	Southdown Puma Sprint	
G-MJYY	Hiway Demon		G-MMCV	Solar Wings Typhoon III	
G-MJYZ	Flexiform Striker		G-MMCX	MBA Super Tiger Cub 440	
G-MJZA	MBA Tiger Cub		G-MMCY	Flexiform Striker	
G-MJZB	Flexiform Striker Dual		G-MMCZ	Flexiform Striker	
G-MJZC	MBA Tiger Cub 440		G-MMDB	La Mouette Atlas	
G-MJZD	Mainair Gemini Flash		G-MMDC	Eipper Quicksilver MXII	
G-MJZE	MBA Tiger Cub 440		G-MMDD	Huntair Pathfinder	
G-MJZF	La Mouette Atlas 16		G-MMDE	Solar Wings Typhoon	
G-MJZG	Mainair Triflyer 440		G-MMDF	Southdown Lightning Phase II	
G-MJZH	Southdown Lightning 195				
G-MJZI	Eurowing Goldwing		G-MMDG	Eurowing Goldwing	
G-MJZJ	Hiway Cutlass Skytrike		G-MMDH	Manta Fledge 2B	
G-MJZK	Southdown Puma Sprint 440		G-MMDI	Hiway Super Scorpion	
			G-MMDJ	Solar Wings Typhoon	
G-MJZL	Eipper Quicksilver MX II		G-MMDK	Flexiform Striker	
G-MJZO	Flexiform Striker		G-MMDN	Flexiform Striker	
G-MJZP	MBA Tiger Cub 440		G-MMDO	Southdown Sprint	
G-MJZT	Flexiform Striker		G-MMDP	Southdown Sprint	
G-MJZU	Flexiform Striker		G-MMDR	Huntair Pathfinder II	
G-MJZW	Eipper Quicksilver MX II		G-MMDS	Ultrasports Panther XLS	
G-MJZX	Maxair Hummer TX		G-MMDT	Flexiform Striker	
G-MJZZ	Skyhook Cutlass		G-MMDU	MBA Tiger Cub 440	
G-MMAC	Dragon Srs 150		G-MMDV	Ultrasports Panther	
G-MMAE	Dragon Srs 150		G-MMDW	Pterodactyl Pfledgling	
G-MMAG	MBA Tiger Cub 440		G-MMDX	Solar Wings Typhoon	
G-MMAH	Eipper Quicksilver MX II		G-MMDY	Southdown Puma Sprint	
G-MMAI	Dragon Srs 150		G-MMDZ	Flexiform Dual Strike	
G-MMAJ	Mainair Tri-Flyer 440		G-MMEB	Hiway Super Scorpion	
G-MMAK	MBA Tiger Cub 440		G-MMEE	American Aerolights Eagle	
G-MMAL	Flexiform Striker Dual		G-MMEF	Hiway Super Scorpion	
G-MMAM	MBA Tiger Cub 440		G-MMEG	Eipper Quicksilver MX	
G-MMAN	Flexiform Striker		G-MMEI	Hiway Demon	
G-MMAO	Southdown Puma Sprint		G-MMEJ	Flexiform Striker	
G-MMAP	Hummer TX		G-MMEK	Solar Wings Typhoon XL2	
G-MMAR	Southdown Puma Sprint MS		G-MMEL	Solar Wings Typhoon XL2	
			G-MMEM	Solar Wings Typhoon XL2	
G-MMAS	Southdown Sprint		G-MMEN	Solar Wings Typhoon XL2	
G-MMAT	Southdown Puma Sprint MS		G-MMEP	MBA Tiger Cub 440	
			G-MMES	Southdown Puma Sprint	
G-MMAU	Flexiform Rapier		G-MMET	Skyhook Sabre TR-1 Mk II	
G-MMAW	Mainair Rapier		G-MMEU	MBS Tiger Cub 440	
G-MMAX	Flexiform Striker		G-MMEW	MBA Tiger Cub 440	
G-MMAZ	Southdown Puma Sprint		G-MMEX	Solar Wings Sprint	
G-MMBA	Hiway Super Scorpion		G-MMEY	MBA Tiger Cub 440	
G-MMBB	American Aerolights Eagle		G-MMEZ	Southdown Puma Sprint	

Reg.	Type	Notes	Reg.	Type	Notes
G-MMFB	Flexiform Striker		G-MMJC	Southdown Sprint	
G-MMFC	Flexiform Striker		G-MMJD	Southdown Puma Sprint	
G-MMFD	Flexiform Striker		G-MMJE	Southdown Puma Sprint	
G-MMFE	Flexiform Striker		G-MMJF	Ultrasports Panther Dual 440	
G-MMFG	Flexiform Striker				
G-MMFI	Flexiform Striker		G-MMJG	Mainair Tri-Flyer 440	
G-MMFJ	Flexiform Striker		G-MMJH	Southdown Puma Sprint	
G-MMFK	Flexiform Striker		G-MMJJ	Solar Wings Typhoon	
G-MMFL	Flexiform Striker		G-MMJK	Hiway Demon	
G-MMFM	Piranha Srs 200		G-MMJL	Flexiform 1+1 Sealander	
G-MMFN	MBA Tiger Cub 440		G-MMJM	Southdown Puma Sprint	
G-MMFS	MBA Tiger Cub 440		G-MMJN	Eipper Quicksilver MX II	
G-MMFT	MBA Tiger Cub 440		G-MMJO	MBA Tiger Cub 440	
G-MMFW	Skyhook Cutlass		G-MMJS	MBA Tiger Cub	
G-MMFX	MBA Tiger Cub 440		G-MMJT	Southdown Puma Sprint MS	
G-MMFY	Flexiform Dual Striker				
G-MMFZ	AES Sky Ranger		G-MMJU	Hiway Demon	
G-MMGA	Bass Gosling		G-MMJV	MBA Tiger Cub 440	
G-MMGB	Southdown Puma Sprint		G-MMJW	Southdown Puma Sprint	
G-MMGC	Southdown Puma Sprint		G-MMJX	Teman Mono-Fly	
G-MMGD	Southdown Puma Sprint		G-MMJY	MBA Tiger Cub 440	
G-MMGE	Hiway Super Scorpion		G-MMJZ	Skyhook Pixie	
G-MMGF	MBA Tiger Cub 440		G-MMKA	Ultrasports Panther Dual	
G-MMGL	MBA Tiger Cub 440		G-MMKB	Ultralight Flight Mirage II	
G-MMGN	Southdown Puma Sprint		G-MMKC	Southdown Puma Sprint MS	
G-MMGO	MBA Tiger Cub 440				
G-MMGP	Southdown Puma Sprint		G-MMKD	Southdown Puma Sprint	
G-MMGR	Flexiform Dual Striker		G-MMKE	Birdman Chinook WT-11	
G-MMGS	Solar Wings Panther Dual		G-MMKF	Ultrasports Panther Dual 440	
G-MMGT	Solar Wings Typhoon				
G-MMGU	Flexiform Sealander		G-MMKG	Solar Wings Typhoon XL	
G-MMGV	Whittaker MW.5 Sorcerer Srs A		G-MMKH	Solar Wings Typhoon XL	
			G-MMKI	Ultrasports Panther 330	
G-MMGX	Southdown Puma		G-MMKJ	Ultrasports Panther 330	
G-MMGY	Dean Piranha 1000		G-MMKK	Mainair Flash	
G-MMHA	Skyhook TR-1 Pixie		G-MMKL	Mainair Flash	
G-MMHB	Skyhook TR-1 Pixie		G-MMKM	Flexiform Dual Striker	
G-MMHD	Hiway Demon 175		G-MMKO	Southdown Puma Sprint	
G-MMHE	Southdown Puma Sprint MS		G-MMKP	MBA Tiger Cub 440	
			G-MMKR	Southdown Lightning DS	
G-MMHF	Southdown Puma Sprint		G-MMKS	Southdown Lightning 195	
G-MMHG	Solar Wings Storm		G-MMKT	MBA Tiger Cub 440	
G-MMHJ	Flexiform Hilander		G-MMKU	Southdown Puma Sprint MS	
G-MMHK	Hiway Super Scorpion				
G-MMHL	Hiway Super Scorpion		G-MMKV	Southdown Puma Sprint	
G-MMHM	Goldmarque Gyr		G-MMKW	Solar Wings Storm	
G-MMHP	Hiway Demon		G-MMKY	Jordan Duet	
G-MMHR	Southdown Puma Sprint DS		G-MMKZ	Ultrasports Puma 440	
			G-MMLB	MBA Tiger Cub 440	
G-MMHS	SMD Viper		G-MMLD	Solar Wings Typhoon S	
G-MMHT	Flexiform Viper		G-MMLE	Eurowing Goldwing SP	
G-MMHX	Hornet Invader 440		G-MMLF	MBA Tiger Cub 440	
G-MMHY	Hornet Invader 440		G-MMLG	Solar Wings Typhoon S4 XL	
G-MMHZ	Solar Wings Typhoon XL				
G-MMIB	MEA Mistral		G-MMLH	Hiway Demon	
G-MMIC	Luscombe Vitality		G-MMLI	Solar Wings Typhoon S	
G-MMID	Flexiform Dual Striker		G-MMLJ	—	
G-MMIE	MBA Tiger Cub 440		G-MMLK	MBA Tiger Cub 440	
G-MMIF	Wasp Gryphon		G-MMLL	Midland Ultralights Sirocco	
G-MMIH	MBA Tiger Cub 440		G-MMLN	MBA Tiger Cub 440	
G-MMII	Southdown Puma Sprint 440		G-MMLN	Skyhook Pixie	
			G-MMLO	Skyhook Pixie	
G-MMIJ	Ultrasports Tripacer		G-MMLP	Southdown Sprint	
G-MMIL	Eipper Quicksilver MX II		G-MMLU	—	
G-MMIM	MBA Tiger Cub 440		G-MMLV	Southdown Puma 330	
G-MMIO	Huntair Pathfinder II		G-MMLW	—	
G-MMIR	Mainair Tri-Flyer 440		G-MMLX	Ultrasports Panther	
G-MMIS	Hiway Demon		G-MMLY	—	
G-MMIV	Southdown Puma Sprint		G-MMLZ	Mainair Tri-Flyer	
G-MMIW	Southdown Puma Sprint		G-MMMB	Mainair Tri-Flyer	
G-MMIX	MBA Tiger Cub 440		G-MMMD	Flexiform Dual Striker	
G-MMIY	Eurowing Goldwing		G-MMMG	Eipper Quicksilver MXL	
G-MMIZ	Southdown Lightning II		G-MMMH	Hadland Willow	

Reg.	Type	Notes	Reg	Type	Notes
G-MMMI	Southdown Lightning		G-MMRU	Tirith Firebird FB-2	
G-MMMJ	Southdown Sprint		G-MMRV	MBA Tiger Cub 440	
G-MMMK	Hornet Invader		G-MMRW	Flexiform Dual Striker	
G-MMML	Dragon 150		G-MMRX	Willmot J.W.1	
G-MMMN	Ultrasports Panther Dual 440		G-MMRY	Chargus T.250	
G-MMMP	Flexiform Dual Striker		G-MMRZ	Ultrasports Panther Dual 440	
G-MMMR	Flexiform Striker		G-MMSA	Ultrasports Panther XL	
G-MMMS	MBA Tiger Cub 440		G-MMSC	Mainair Gemini	
G-MMMT	Hornet Sigma		G-MMSE	Eipper Quicksilver MX	
G-MMMU	Skyhook Cutlass CD		G-MMSF	—	
G-MMMV	Skyhook Cutlass Dual		G-MMSG	Solar Wings Panther XL	
G-MMMW	Flexiform Striker		G-MMSH	Solar Wings Panther XL	
G-MMMX	Hornet Nimrod		G-MMSM	Mainair Gemini Flash	
G-MMNA	Eipper Quicksilver MX II		G-MMSN	Mainair Gemini	
G-MMNB	Eipper Quicksilver MX		G-MMSO	Mainair Tri-Flyer 440	
G-MMNC	Eipper Quicksilver MX		G-MMSP	Mainair Gemini Flash	
G-MMND	Eipper Quicksilver MX II-Q2		G-MMSR	MBA Tiger Cub 440	
G-MMNE	Eipper Quicksilver MX II		G-MMSS	Solar Wings Panther 330	
G-MMNF	Hornet		G-MMST	Southdown Puma Sprint	
G-MMNG	Solar Wings Typhoon XL Buzzard		G-MMSU	American Aerolights Eagle B	
G-MMNN					
G-MMNP	Ultrasports Panther 250		G-MMSV	Southdown Puma Sprint	
G-MMNS	Mitchell U-2 Super Wing		G-MMSW	MBA Tiger Cub 440	
G-MMNT	Flexiform Striker		G-MMSZ	Medway Half Pint	
G-MMNU	Ultrasports Panther		G-MMTA	Ultrasports Panther XL	
G-MMNW	Mainair Tri-Flyer 330		G-MMTC	Ultrasports Panther Dual	
G-MMNX	Solar Wings Panther XL		G-MMTD	Mainair Tri-Flyer 330	
G-MMNZ	—		G-MMTE	Mainair Gemini	
G-MMOA	—		G-MMTF	Southdown Puma Sprint	
G-MMOB	Southdown Sprint		G-MMTG	Mainair Gemini	
G-MMOD	MBA Tiger Cub 440		G-MMTH	Southdown Puma Sprint	
G-MMOF	MBA Tiger Cub 440		G-MMTI	Southdown Puma Sprint	
G-MMOG	Huntair Pathfinder		G-MMTJ	Southdown Puma Sprint	
G-MMOH	Solar Wings Typhoon XL		G-MMTK	Medway Hybred	
G-MMOI	MBA Tiger Cub 440		G-MMTL	Mainair Gemini	
G-MMOJ	—		G-MMTM	Mainair Tri-Flyer 440	
G-MMOK	Solar Wings Panther XL		G-MMTO	Mainair Tri-Flyer	
G-MMOL	Skycraft Scout R3		G-MMTR	Ultrasports Panther	
G-MMOO	Southdown Storm		G-MMTS	Solar Wings Panther XL	
G-MMOW	Mainair Gemini Flash		G-MMTT	Solar Wings Panther XL	
G-MMOX	Mainair Gemini Flash		G-MMTV	American Aerolights Eagle	
G-MMOY	Mainair Gemini Sprint		G-MMTX	Mainair Gemini 440	
G-MMPD	Mainair Tri-Flyer		G-MMTY	Fisher FP.202U	
G-MMPE	Eurowing Goldwing		G-MMTZ	Eurowing Goldwing	
G-MMPG	Southdown Puma		G-MMUA	Southdown Puma Sprint	
G-MMPH	Southdown Puma Sprint		G-MMUB	Ultrasports Tripacer 250	
G-MMPI	Pterodactyl Ptraveller		G-MMUC	Mainair Gemini 440	
G-MMPJ	Mainair Tri-Flyer 440		G-MMUE	Mainair Gemini Flash	
G-MMPL	Flexiform Dual Striker		G-MMUF	Mainair Gemini	
G-MMPN	Chargus T250		G-MMUG	Mainair Tri-Flyer	
G-MMPO	Mainair Gemini Flash		G-MMUH	Mainair Tri-Flyer	
G-MMPR	Dragon 150		G-MMUJ	Southdown Puma Sprint 440	
G-MMPT	SMD Gazelle				
G-MMPU	Ultrasports Tripacer 250		G-MMUK	Mainair Tri-Flyer	
G-MMPW	Airwave Nimrod		G-MMUL	Ward Elf E.47	
G-MMPX	Ultrasports Panther Dual 440		G-MMUM	MBA Tiger Cub 440	
			G-MMUN	Ultrasports Panther Dual XL	
G-MMPZ	Teman Mono-Fly		G-MMUO	Mainair Gemini Flash	
G-MMRA	Mainair Tri-Flyer 250		G-MMUP	Airwave Nimrod 140	
G-MMRC	Southdown Lightning		G-MMUS	Mainair Gemini	
G-MMRD	Skyhook Cutlass CD		G-MMUU	ParaPlane PM-1	
G-MMRF	MBA Tiger Cub 440		G-MMUV	Southdown Puma Sprint	
G-MMRH	Hiway Demon		G-MMUW	Mainair Gemini Flash	
G-MMRI	Skyhook Sabre		G-MMUX	Mainair Gemini	
G-MMRJ	Solar Wings Panther XL		G-MMVA	Southdown Puma Sprint	
G-MMRK	Ultrasports Panther XL		G-MMVC	Ultrasports Panther XL	
G-MMRL	Solar Wings Panther XL		G-MMVG	MBA Tiger Cub 440	
G-MMRM	—		G-MMVH	Southdown Raven	
G-MMRN	Southdown Puma Sprint		G-MMVI	Southdown Puma Sprint	
G-MMRO	Mainair Gemini 440		G-MMVJ	Southdown Puma Sprint	
G-MMRP	Mainair Gemini		G-MMVL	Ultrasports Panther XL-S	
G-MMRT	Southdown Puma Sprint		G-MMVM	Whiteley Orion 1	

Reg.	Type	Notes	Reg	Type	Notes
G-MMVN	Solar Wings Typhoon		G-MMYZ	Southdown Puma Sprint	
G-MMVO	Southdown Puma Sprint		G-MMZA	Mainair Gemini Flash	
G-MMVP	Mainair Gemini Flash		G-MMZB	Mainair Gemini Flash	
G-MMVR	Hiway Skytrike 1		G-MMZC	Mainair Gemini Flash	
G-MMVS	Skyhook Pixie		G-MMZE	Mainair Gemini Flash	
G-MMVT	Mainair Gemini Flash		G-MMZF	Mainair Gemini Flash	
G-MMVW	Skyhook Pixie		G-MMZG	Ultrasports Panther XL-S	
G-MMVX	Southdown Puma Sprint		G-MMZH	Ultrasports Tripacer	
G-MMVY	American Aerolights Eagle		G-MMZI	Medway 130SX	
G-MMVZ	Southdown Puma Sprint		G-MMZJ	Mainair Gemini Flash	
G-MMWA	Mainair Gemini Flash		G-MMZK	Mainair Gemini Flash	
G-MMWC	Eipper Quicksilver MXII		G-MMZL	Mainair Gemini Flash	
G-MMWF	Hiway Skytrike 250		G-MMZM	Mainair Gemini Flash	
G-MMWG	Greenslade Mono-Trike		G-MMZN	Mainair Gemini Flash	
G-MMWH	Southdown Puma Sprint 440		G-MMZO	Microflight Spectrum	
			G-MMZP	Ultrasports Panther XL	
G-MMWI	Southdown Lightning		G-MMZR	Southdown Puea Sprint	
G-MMWJ	Pterodactyl Ptraveler		G-MMZS	Eipper Quicksilver MX1	
G-MMWK	Hiway Demon		G-MMZU	Southdown Puma DS	
G-MMWL	Eurowing Goldwing		G-MMZV	Mainair Gemini Flash	
G-MMWM	—		G-MMZW	Southdown Puma Sprint	
G-MMWN	Ultrasports Tripacer		G-MMZX	Southdown Puma Sprint	
G-MMWO	Ultrasports Panther XL		G-MMZY	Ultrasports Tripacer 330	
G-MMWP	American Aerolights Eagle		G-MMZZ	Maxair Hummer	
G-MMWR	—		G-MNAA	Striplin Sky Ranger	
G-MMWS	Mainair Tri-Flyer		G-MNAC	Mainair Gemini Flash	
G-MMWT	CFM Shadow		G-MNAD	Mainair Gemini Flash	
G-MMWX	Southdown Puma Sprint		G-MNAE	Mainair Gemini Flash	
G-MMWY	Skyhook Pixie		G-MNAF	Solar Wings Panther XL	
G-MMWZ	Southdown Puma Sprint		G-MNAG	Hiway Skytrike 1	
G-MMXB	—		G-MNAH	Solar Wings Panther XL	
G-MMXC	Mainair Gemini Flash		G-MNAI	Ultrasports Panther XL-S	
G-MMXD	Mainair Gemini Flash		G-MNAJ	Solar Wings Panther XL-S	
G-MMXE	Mainair Gemini Flash		G-MNAK	Solar Wings Panther XL-S	
G-MMXG	Mainair Gemini Flash		G-MNAL	MBA Tiger Cub 440	
G-MMXH	Mainair Gemini Flash		G-MNAM	Solar Wings Panther XL-S	
G-MMXI	Horizon Prototype		G-MNAN	Solar Wings Panther XL-S	
G-MMXJ	Mainair Gemini Flash		G-MNAO	Solar Wings Panther XL-S	
G-MMXK	Mainair Gemini Flash		G-MNAP	—	
G-MMXL	Mainair Gemini Flash		G-MNAR	Solar Wings Panther XL-S	
G-MMXM	Mainair Gemini Flash		G-MNAT	Solar Wings Pegasus XL-R	
G-MMXN	Southdown Puma Sprint		G-MNAU	Solar Wings Pegasus XL-R	
G-MMXO	Southdown Puma Sprint		G-MNAV	Southdown Puma Sprint	
G-MMXP	Southdown Puma Sprint		G-MNAW	Solar Wings Pegasus XL-R	
G-MMXR	Southdown Puma DS		G-MNAX	Solar Wings Pegasus XL-R	
G-MMXT	Mainair Gemini Flash		G-MNAY	Ultrasports Panther XL-S	
G-MMXU	Mainair Gemini Flash		G-MNAZ	Solar Wings Pegasus XL-R	
G-MMXV	Mainair Gemini Flash		G-MNBA	Solar Wings Pegasus XL-R	
G-MMXW	Mainair Gemini		G-MNBB	Solar Wings Pegasus XL-R	
G-MMXX	Mainair Gemini		G-MNBC	Solar Wings Pegasus XL-R	
G-MMXY	—		G-MNBD	Mainair Gemini Flash	
G-MMXZ	Eipper Quicksilver MXII		G-MNBE	Southdown Puma Sprint	
G-MMYA	Solar Wings Pegasus XL		G-MNBF	Mainair Gemini Flash	
G-MMYB	Solar Wings Pegasus XL		G-MNBG	Mainair Gemini Flash	
G-MMYD	CFM Shadow Srs B		G-MNBH	Southdown Puma Sprint	
G-MMYE	—		G-MNBI	Ultrasports Panther XL	
G-MMYF	Southdown Puma Sprint		G-MNBJ	Skyhook Pixie	
G-MMYG	—		G-MNBK	Hiway Skytrike	
G-MMYH	—		G-MNBL	American Aerolights Z Eagle	
G-MMYI	Southdown Puma Sprint				
G-MMYJ	Southdown Puma Sprint		G-MNBM	Southdown Puma Sprint	
G-MMYK	Southdown Puma Sprint		G-MNBN	Mainair Gemini Flash	
G-MMYL	Cyclone 70		G-MNBP	Mainair Gemini Flash	
G-MMYM	—		G-MNBR	Mainair Gemini Flash	
G-MMYN	Ultrasports Panther XL		G-MNBS	Mainair Gemini Flash	
G-MMYO	Southdown Puma Sprint		G-MNBT	Mainair Gemini Flash	
G-MMYP	—		G-MNBU	Mainair Gemini Flash	
G-MMYR	Eipper Quicksilver MXII		G-MNBV	Mainair Gemini Flash	
G-MMYS	Southdown Puma Sprint		G-MNBW	Mainair Gemini	
G-MMYT	Southdown Puma Sprint		G-MNBY	Mainair Gemini	
G-MMYU	Southdown Puma Sprint		G-MNCA	Hiway Demon 175	
G-MMYV	Webb Trike		G-MNCB	Mainair Gemini Flash	
G-MMYY	Southdown Puma Sprint		G-MNCD	Harmsworth Trike	

Reg.	Type	Notes	Reg	Type	Notes
G-MNCF	Mainair Gemini Flash		G-MNFZ	Southdown Puma Sprint	
G-MNCG	Mainair Gemini Flash		G-MNGA	Aerial Arts Chaser 110SX	
G-MNCH	Lancashire Micro Trike 330		G-MNGB	Mainair Gemini Flash	
G-MNCI	Southdown Puma Sprint		G-MNGD	Quest Air Services	
G-MNCJ	Mainair Gemini Flash		G-MNGF	Solar Wings Pegasus	
G-MNCK	Southdown Puma Sprint		G-MNGG	Solar Wings Pegasus XL-R	
G-MNCL	Southdown Puma Sprint		G-MNGH	Skyhook Pixie	
G-MNCM	CFM Shadow Srs B		G-MNGJ	Skyhook Zipper	
G-MNCO	Eipper Quicksilver MXII		G-MNGK	Mainair Gemini Flash	
G-MNCP	Southdown Puma Sprint		G-MNGL	Mainair Gemini Flash	
G-MNCR	Flexiform Striker		G-MNGM	Mainair Gemini Flash	
G-MNCS	Skyrider Airsports Phantom		G-MNGN	Mainair Gemini Flash	
G-MNCU	Medway Hybred		G-MNGO	Solar Wings Storm	
G-MNCV	Medway Typhoon XL		G-MNGR	Southdown Puma Sprint	
G-MNCW	Hornet Dual Trainer		G-MNGS	Southdown Puma 330	
G-MNCX	Mainair Gemini Flash		G-MNGT	Mainair Gemini Flash	
G-MNCZ	Solar Wings Pegasus XL		G-MNGU	Mainair Gemini Flash	
G-MNDA	Thruster TST		G-MNGW	Mainair Gemini Flash	
G-MNDB	Southdown Puma Sprint		G-MNGX	Southdown Puma Sprint	
G-MNDC	Mainair Gemini Flash		G-MNGY	Hiway Skytrike 160	
G-MNDD	Mainair Scorcher Solo		G-MNGZ	Mainair Gemini Flash	
G-MNDE	Medway Half Pint		G-MNHB	Solar Wings Pegasus XL-R	
G-MNDF	Mainair Gemini Flash		G-MNHC	Solar Wings Pegasus XL-R	
G-MNDG	Southdown Puma Sprint		G-MNHD	Solar Wings Pegasus XL-R	
G-MNDH	Hiway Skytrike		G-MNHE	Solar Wings Pegasus XL-R	
G-MNDI	MBA Tiger Cub 440		G-MNHF	Solar Wings Pegasus XL-R	
G-MNDM	Mainair Gemini Flash		G-MNHG	Solar Wings Pegasus XL-R	
G-MNDO	Mainair Flash		G-MNHH	Solar Wings Panther XL-S	
G-MNDP	Southdown Puma Sprint		G-MNHI	Solar Wings Pegasus XL-R	
G-MNDU	Midland Sirocco 377GB		G-MNHJ	Solar Wings Pegasus XL-R	
G-MNDV	Midland Sirocco 377GB		G-MNHK	Solar Wings Pegasus XL-R	
G-MNDW	Midland Sirocco 377GB		G-MNHL	Solar Wings Pegasus XL-R	
G-MNDY	Southdown Puma Sprint		G-MNHM	Solar Wings Pegasus XL-R	
G-MNDZ	Southdown Puma Sprint		G-MNHN	Solar Wings Pegasus XL-R	
G-MNEF	Mainair Gemini Flash		G-MNHP	Solar Wings Pegasus XL-R	
G-MNEG	Mainair Gemini Flash		G-MNHR	Solar Wings Pegasus XL-R	
G-MNEH	Mainair Gemini Flash		G-MNHS	Solar Wings Pegasus XL-R	
G-MNEI	Medway Hybred 440		G-MNHT	Solar Wings Pegasus XL-R	
G-MNEK	Medway Half Pint		G-MNHU	Solar Wings Pegasus XL-R	
G-MNEL	Medway Half Pint		G-MNHV	Solar Wings Pegasus XL-R	
G-MNEM	Solar Wings Pegasus Dual		G-MNHW	Medway Half Pint	
G-MNEN	Southdown Puma Sprint		G-MNHX	Solar Wings Typhoon S4	
G-MNEO	Southdown Raven		G-MNHZ	Mainair Gemini Flash	
G-MNEP	Aerostructure Pipstrelle P.2B		G-MNIA	Mainair Gemini Flash	
			G-MNIB	American Aerolights Eagle 215B	
G-MNER	CFM Shadow Srs B				
G-MNET	Mainair Gemini Flash		G-MNID	Mainair Gemini Flash	
G-MNEV	Mainair Gemini Flash		G-MNIE	Mainair Gemini Flash	
G-MNEW	Mainair Tri-Flyer		G-MNIF	Mainair Gemini Flash	
G-MNEX	Mainair Gemini Flash		G-MNIG	Mainair Gemini Flash	
G-MNEY	Mainair Gemini Flash		G-MNIH	Mainair Gemini Flash	
G-MNEZ	Skyhook TR1 Mk 2		G-MNII	Mainair Gemini Flash	
G-MNFA	Solar Wings Typhoon		G-MNIL	Southdown Puma Sprint	
G-MNFB	Southdown Puma Sprint		G-MNIM	Maxair Hummer	
G-MNFC	Midland Ultralights Sirocco 377GB		G-MNIN	Designability Duet	
			G-MNIO	Mainair Gemini Flash	
G-MNFE	Mainair Gemini Flash		G-MNIP	Mainair Gemini Flash	
G-MNFF	Mainair Gemini Flash		G-MNIR	Skyhook Pixie 130	
G-MNFG	Southdown Puma Sprint		G-MNIS	CFM Shadow Srs B	
G-MNFH	Mainair Gemini Flash		G-MNIT	Aerial Arts 130SX	
G-MNFI	Medway Half Pint		G-MNIU	Solar Wings Pegasus Photon	
G-MNFJ	Mainair Gemini Flash				
G-MNFK	Mainair Gemini Flash		G-MNIV	Solar Wings Typhoon	
G-MNFL	AMF Chevron		G-MNIW	Airwave Nimrod 165	
G-MNFM	Mainair Gemini Flash		G-MNIX	Mainair Gemini Flash	
G-MNFN	Mainair Gemini Flash		G-MNIY	Skyhook Pixie Zipper	
G-MNFP	Mainair Gemini Flash		G-MNIZ	Mainair Gemini Flash	
G-MNFR	Wright Tri-Flyer		G-MNJA	Southdown Lightning Skytrike	
G-MNFT	Mainair Gemini Flash				
G-MNFV	Ultrasports Trike		G-MNJB	Southdown Raven	
G-MNFW	Medway Hybred 44XL		G-MNJC	MBA Tiger Cub 440	
G-MNFX	Southdown Puma Sprint		G-MNJD	Southdown Puma Sprint	
G-MNFY	Hornet 250		G-MNJE	Southdown Puma Sprint	

Reg.	Type	Notes	Reg	Type	Notes
G-MNJF	Dragon 150		G-MNMC	Southdown Puma MS	
G-MNJG	Mainair Tri-Flyer		G-MNMD	Southdown Raven	
G-MNJH	Solar Wings Pegasus Flash		G-MNME	Hiway Skytrike	
G-MNJI	Solar Wings Pegasus Flash		G-MNMF	Maxair Hummer TX	
G-MNJJ	Solar Wings Pegasus Flash		G-MNMG	Mainair Gemini Flash	
G-MNJK	Solar Wings Pegasus Flash		G-MNMH	Mainair Gemini Flash	
G-MNJL	Solar Wings Pegasus Flash		G-MNMI	Mainair Gemini Flash	
G-MNJM	Solar Wings Pegasus Flash		G-MNMJ	Mainair Gemini Flash	
G-MNJN	Solar Wings Pegasus Flash		G-MNMK	Solar Wings Pegasus XL-R	
G-MNJO	Solar Wings Pegasus Flash		G-MNML	Southdown Puma Sprint	
G-MNJP	Solar Wings Pegasus Flash		G-MNMM	Aerotech MW.5 Sorcerer	
G-MNJR	Solar Wings Pegasus Flash		G-MNMN	Medway Microlights Hybred 44	
G-MNJS	Southdown Puma Sprint				
G-MNJT	Southdown Raven		G-MNMO	Mainair Gemini Flash	
G-MNJU	Mainair Gemini Flash		G-MNMR	Solar Wings Typhoon 180	
G-MNJV	Medway Half Pint		G-MNMS	Wheeler Scout	
G-MNJW	Mitchell Wing B10		G-MNMT	Southdown Raven	
G-MNJX	Medway Hybred 44XL		G-MNMU	Southdown Raven	
G-MNJY	Medway Half Pint		G-MNMV	Mainair Gemini Flash	
G-MNJZ	Aerial Arts Alpha 130SX		G-MNMW	Aerotech MW.6 Merlin	
G-MNKA	Solar Wings Pegasus Photon		G-MNMY	Cyclone 70	
			G-MNNA	Southdown Raven	
G-MNKB	Solar Wings Pegasus Photon		G-MNNB	Southdown Raven	
			G-MNNC	Southdown Raven	
G-MNKC	Solar Wings Pegasus Photon		G-MNND	Solar Wings Pegasus Flash	
			G-MNNE	Mainair Gemini Flash	
G-MNKD	Solar Wings Pegasus Photon		G-MNNF	Mainair Gemini Flash	
			G-MNNG	Solar Wings Photon	
G-MNKG	Solar Wings Pegasus Photon		G-MNNI	Mainair Gemini Flash	
			G-MNNJ	Mainair Gemini Flash	
G-MNKH	Solar Wings Pegasus Photon		G-MNNK	Mainair Gemini Flash	
			G-MNNL	Mainair Gemini Flash	
G-MNKI	Solar Wings Pegasus Photon		G-MNNM	Mainair Scorcher Solo	
			G-MNNN	Southdown Raven	
G-MNKJ	Solar Wings Pegasus Photon		G-MNNO	Southdown Raven	
			G-MNNP	Mainair Gemini Flash	
G-MNKK	Solar Wings Pegasus Photon		G-MNNR	Mainair Gemini Flash	
			G-MNNS	Eurowing Goldwing	
G-MNKL	Mainair Gemini Flash		G-MNNT	Medway Microlights Hybred	
G-MNKM	MBA Tiger Cub 440		G-MNNU	Mainair Gemini Flash	
G-MNKN	Skycraft Scout Mk III		G-MNNV	Mainair Gemini Flash	
G-MNKO	Solar Wings Pegasus Flash		G-MNNY	Solar Wings Pegasus Flash	
G-MNKP	Solar Wings Pegasus Flash		G-MNNZ	Solar Wings Pegasus Flash	
G-MNKR	Solar Wings Pegasus Flash		G-MNPA	Solar Wings Pegasus Flash	
G-MNKS	Solar Wings Pegasus Flash		G-MNPB	Solar Wings Pegasus Flash	
G-MNKT	Solar Wings Typhoon S4		G-MNPC	Mainair Gemini Flash	
G-MNKU	Southdown Puma Sprint		G-MNPD	Midland Ultralights 130SX	
G-MNKV	Solar Wings Pegasus Flash		G-MNPF	Mainair Gemini Flash	
G-MNKW	Solar Wings Pegasus Flash		G-MNPG	Mainair Gemini Flash	
G-MNKX	Solar Wings Pegasus Flash		G-MNPH	Flexiform Dual Striker	
G-MNKY	Southdown Raven		G-MNPI	Southdown Pipistrelle 2C	
G-MNKZ	Southdown Raven		G-MNPL	Ultrasports Panther 330	
G-MNLB	Southdown Raven X		G-MNPP	Romain Cobra Biplane	
G-MNLC	Southdown Raven		G-MNPR	Hiway Demon 175	
G-MNLE	Southdown Raven X		G-MNPV	Mainair Scorcher Solo	
G-MNLH	Romain Cobra Biplane		G-MNPW	AMF Chevron	
G-MNLI	Mainair Gemini Flash		G-MNPX	Mainair Gemini Flash	
G-MNLK	Southdown Raven		G-MNPY	Mainair Scorcher Solo	
G-MNLL	Southdown Raven		G-MNPZ	Mainair Scorcher Solo	
G-MNLM	Southdown Raven		G-MNRA	CFM Shadow Srs B	
G-MNLN	Southdown Raven		G-MNRD	Ultraflight Lazair	
G-MNLO	Southdown Raven		G-MNRE	Mainair Scorcher Solo	
G-MNLP	Southdown Raven		G-MNRF	Mainair Scorcher Solo	
G-MNLS	Southdown Raven		G-MNRG	Mainair Scorcher Solo	
G-MNLT	Southdown Raven		G-MNRI	Hornet Dual Trainer	
G-MNLU	Southdown Raven		G-MNRJ	Hornet Dual Trainer	
G-MNLV	Southdown Raven		G-MNRK	Hornet Dual Trainer	
G-MNLW	Medway Halt Pint		G-MNRL	Hornet Dual Trainer	
G-MNLX	Mainair Gemini Flash		G-MNRM	Hornet Dual Trainer	
G-MNLY	Mainair Gemini Flash		G-MNRN	Hornet Dual Trainer	
G-MNLZ	Southdown Raven		G-MNRP	Southdown Raven	
G-MNMA	Solar Wings Pegasus Flash		G-MNRR	Southdown Raven X	
G-MNMB	Solar Wings Pegasus Flash		G-MNRS	Southdown Raven	

Reg.	Type	Notes	Reg	Type	Notes
G-MNRT	Midland Ultralights Sirocco		G-MNUR	Mainair Gemini Flash II	
G-MNRU	Midland Ultralights Sirocco		G-MNUS	Mainair Gemini Flash II	
G-MNRW	Mainair Gemini Flash II		G-MNUT	Southdown Raven X	
G-MNRX	Mainair Gemini Flash II		G-MNUU	Southdown Raven X	
G-MNRY	Mainair Gemini Flash		G-MNUV	Southdown Raven X	
G-MNRZ	Mainair Scorcher Solo		G-MNUW	Southdown Raven X	
G-MNSA	Mainair Gemini Flash		G-MNUX	Solar Wings Pegasus XL-R	
G-MNSB	Southdown Puma Sprint		G-MNUY	Mainair Gemini Flash II	
G-MNSD	Solar Wings Typhoon		G-MNUZ	Mainair Gemini Flash II	
G-MNSE	Mainair Gemini Flash		G-MNVA	Solar Wings Pegasus XL-R	
G-MNSF	Hornet Dual Trainer		G-MNVB	Solar Wings Pegasus XL-R	
G-MNSH	Solar Wings Pegasus Flash II		G-MNVC	Solar Wings Pegasus XL-R	
			G-MNVE	Solar Wings Pegasus XL-R	
G-MNSI	Mainair Gemini Flash		G-MNVF	Solar Wings Pegasus Flash II	
G-MNSJ	Mainair Gemini Flash				
G-MNSK	Hiway Skytrike		G-MNVG	Solar Wings Pegasus Flash II	
G-MNSL	Southdown Raven X				
G-MNSM	Hornet Demon		G-MNVH	Solar Wings Pegasus Flash II	
G-MNSN	Solar Wings Pegasus Flash II				
			G-MNVI	CFM Shadow Srs B	
G-MNSO	Solar Wings Pegasus Flash II		G-MNVJ	CFM Shadow Srs B	
			G-MNVK	CFM Shadow Srs B	
G-MNSP	Aerial Arts 130SX		G-MNVL	Medway Half Pint	
G-MNSR	Mainair Gemini Flash		G-MNVM	Southdown Raven X	
G-MNSS	American Aerolights Eagle		G-MNVN	Southdown Raven X	
G-MNST	Vector 600		G-MNVO	Hovey Whing-Ding II	
G-MNSV	CFM Shadown Srs B		G-MNVP	Southdown Raven X	
G-MNSW	Southdown Raven X		G-MNVR	Mainair Gemini Flash II	
G-MNSX	Southdown Raven X		G-MNVS	Mainair Gemini Flash II	
G-MNSY	Southdown Raven X		G-MNVT	Mainair Gemini Flash II	
G-MNSZ	Noble Hardman Snowbird		G-MNVU	Mainair Gemini Flash II	
G-MNTB	Solar Wings Typhoon S4		G-MNVV	Mainair Gemini Flash II	
G-MNTC	Southdown Raven X		G-MNVW	Mainair Gemini Flash II	
G-MNTD	Aerial Arts Chaser 110SX		G-MNVY	Solar Wings Pegasus Photon	
G-MNTE	Southdown Raven X				
G-MNTF	Southdown Raven X		G-MNVZ	Solar Wings Pegasus Photon	
G-MNTG	Southdown Raven X				
G-MNTH	Mainair Gemini Flash		G-MNWA	Southdown Raven X	
G-MNTI	Mainair Gemini Flash		G-MNWB	Thruster TST	
G-MNTK	CFM Shadow Srs B		G-MNWC	Mainair Gemini Flash II	
G-MNTL	Arbee Wasp Gryphon		G-MNWD	Mainair Gemini Flash	
G-MNTM	Southdown Raven X		G-MNWF	Southdown Raven X	
G-MNTN	Southdown Raven X		G-MNWG	Southdown Raven X	
G-MNTO	Southdown Raven X		G-MNWH	Aerial Arts 130SX	
G-MNTP	CFM Shadow Srs B		G-MNWI	Mainair Gemini Flash II	
G-MNTS	Mainair Gemini Flash II		G-MNWJ	Mainair Gemini Flash II	
G-MNTT	Medway Half Pint		G-MNWK	CFM Shadow Srs B	
G-MNTU	Mainair Gemini Flash II		G-MNWL	Aerial Arts 130SX	
G-MNTV	Mainair Gemini Flash II		G-MNWM	CFM Shadow Srs B	
G-MNTW	Mainair Gemini Flash II		G-MNWN	Mainair Gemini Flash II	
G-MNTX	Mainair Gemini Flash II		G-MNWO	Mainair Gemini Flash II	
G-MNTY	Southdown Raven X		G-MNWP	Solar Wings Pegasus Flash II	
G-MNTZ	Mainair Gemini Flash II				
G-MNUA	Mainair Gemini Flash II		G-MNWR	Medway Hybred 44LR	
G-MNUB	Mainair Gemini Flash II		G-MNWT	Southdown Raven	
G-MNUC	Solar Wings Pegasus Flash II		G-MNWU	Solar Wings Pegasus Flash II	
G-MNUD	Solar Wings Pegasus Flash II		G-MNWV	Solar Wings Pegasus Flash II	
G-MNUE	Solar Wings Pegasus Flash II		G-MNWW	Solar Wings Pegasus XL-R	
			G-MNWX	Solar Wings Pegasus XL-R	
G-MNUF	Mainair Gemini Flash II		G-MNWY	CFM Shadown Srs B	
G-MNUG	Mainair Gemini Flash II		G-MNWZ	Mainair Gemini Flash II	
G-MNUH	Southdown Raven X		G-MNXA	Southdown Raven X	
G-MNUI	Skyhook Cutlass Dual		G-MNXB	Solar Wings Photon	
G-MNUJ	Solar Wings Pegasus Photon		G-MNXC	Aerial Arts 110SX	
			G-MNXD	Southdown Raven	
G-MNUK	Midland Ultralights SX130		G-MNXE	Southdown Raven X	
G-MNUL	Midland Ultralights SX130		G-MNXF	Southdown Raven	
G-MNUM	Southdown Puma Sprint MS		G-MNXG	Southdown Raven X	
			G-MNXI	Southdown Raven X	
G-MNUO	Mainair Gemini Flash II		G-MNXJ	Medway Half Pint	
G-MNUP	Mainair Gemini Flash II		G-MNXK	Medway Half Pint	

Reg.	Type	Notes	Reg	Type	Notes
G-MNXM	Medway Hybred 44XLR		G-MTAH	Mainair Gemini Flash II	
G-MNXN	Medway Hybred 44XLR		G-MTAI	Solar Wings Pegasus XL-R	
G-MNXO	Medway Hybred 44XLR		G-MTAJ	Solar Wings Pegasus XL-R	
G-MNXP	Solar Wings Pegasus Flash II		G-MTAK	Solar Wings Pegasus XL-R	
			G-MTAL	Solar Wings Photon	
G-MNXR	Mainair Gemini Flash II		G-MTAM	Solar Wings Pegasus Flash	
G-MNXS	Mainair Gemini Flash II				
G-MNXT	Mainair Gemini Flash II		G-MTAO	Solar Wings Pegasus XL-R	
G-MNXU	Mainair Gemini Flash II		G-MTAP	Southdown Raven X	
G-MNXW	Mainair Gemini Flash II		G-MTAR	Mainair Gemini Flash II	
G-MNXX	CFM Shadow Srs BD		G-MTAS	Whittaker MW.5 Sorcerer	
G-MNXY	Whittaker MW.5 Sorcerer		G-MTAT	Solar Wings Pegasus XL-R	
G-MNXZ	Whittaker MW.5 Sorcerer		G-MTAU	Solar Wings Pegasus XL-R	
G-MNYA	Solar Wings Pegasus Flash II		G-MTAV	Solar Wings Pegasus XL-R	
			G-MTAW	Solar Wings Pegasus XL-R	
G-MNYB	Solar Wings Pegasus XL-R		G-MTAX	Solar Wings Pegasus XL-R	
G-MNYC	Solar Wings Pegasus XL-R		G-MTAY	Solar Wings Pegasus XL-R	
G-MNYD	Aerial Arts 110SX Chaser		G-MTAZ	Solar Wings Pegasus XL-R	
G-MNYE	Aerial Arts 110SX Chaser		G-MTBA	Solar Wings Pegasus XL-R	
G-MNYF	Aerial Arts 110SX Chaser		G-MTBB	Southdown Raven X	
G-MNYG	Southdown Raven		G-MTBC	Mainair Gemini Flash II	
G-MNYH	Southdown Puma Sprint		G-MTBD	Mainair Gemini Flash II	
G-MNYI	Southdown Raven X		G-MTBE	CFM Shadow Srs BD	
G-MNYJ	Mainair Gemini Flash II		G-MTBF	Mirage Mk II	
G-MNYK	Mainair Gemini Flash II		G-MTBG	Mainair Gemini Flash II	
G-MNYL	Southdown Raven X		G-MTBH	Mainair Gemini Flash II	
G-MNYM	Southdown Raven X		G-MTBI	Mainair Dual Trainer	
G-MNYO	Southdown Raven X		G-MTBJ	Mainair Gemini Flash II	
G-MNYP	Southdown Raven X		G-MTBK	Southdown Raven X	
G-MNYS	Southdown Raven X		G-MTBL	Solar Wings Pegasus XL-R	
G-MNYT	Solar Wings Pegasus XL-R		G-MTBM	Airwave Nimrod	
G-MNYU	Solar Wings Pegasus XL-R		G-MTBN	Southdown Raven X	
G-MNYV	Solar Wings Pegasus XL-R		G-MTBO	Southdown Raven X	
G-MNYW	Solar Wings Pegasus XL-R		G-MTBP	Aerotech MW.5 Sorcerer	
G-MNYX	Solar Wings Pegasus XL-R		G-MTBR	Aerotech MW.5 Sorcerer	
G-MNYY	Solar Wings Pegasus Flash II		G-MTBS	Aerotech MW.5 Sorcerer	
			G-MTBT	Aerotech MW.5 Sorcerer	
G-MNYZ	Solar Wings Pegasus Flash		G-MTBU	Solar Wings Pegasus XL-R	
			G-MTBV	Solar Wings Pegasus XL-R	
G-MNZA	Solar Wings Pegasus Flash II		G-MTBW	Mainair Gemini Flash II	
			G-MTBX	Mainair Gemini Flash II	
G-MNZB	Mainair Gemini Flash II		G-MTBY	Mainair Gemini Flash II	
G-MNZC	Mainair Gemini Flash II		G-MTBZ	Southdown Raven X	
G-MNZD	Mainair Gemini Flash II		G-MTCA	CFM Shadow Srs B	
G-MNZE	Mainair Gemini Flash II		G-MTCB	Snowbird Mk III	
G-MNZF	Mainair Gemini Flash II		G-MTCC	Mainair Gemini Flash II	
G-MNZG	Aerial Arts 110SX		G-MTCD	Southdown Raven X	
G-MNZH	AMF Chevron 2-32		G-MTCE	Mainair Gemini Flash II	
G-MNZI	Prone Power Typhoon 2		G-MTCG	Solar Wings Pegasus XL-R	
G-MNZJ	CFM Shadow Srs BD		G-MTCH	Solar Wings Pegasus XL-R	
G-MNZK	Solar Wings Pegasus XL-R		G-MTCJ	Aerial Arts Avenger	
G-MNZL	Solar Wings Pegasus XL-R		G-MTCK	Solar Wings Pegasus Flash	
G-MNZM	Solar Wings Pegasus XL-R				
G-MNZN	Solar Wings Pegasus Flash II		G-MTCL	Southdown Raven X	
			G-MTCM	Southdown Raven X	
G-MNZO	Solar Wings Pegasus Flash II		G-MTCN	Solar Wings Pegasus XL-R	
			G-MTCO	Solar Wings Pegasus XL-R	
G-MNZP	CFM Shadow Srs B		G-MTCP	Aerial Arts Chaser 110SX	
G-MNZR	CFM Shadown Srs BD		G-MTCR	Solar Wings Pegasus XL-R	
G-MNZS	Aerial Arts 130SX		G-MTCT	CFM Shadow Srs BD	
G-MNZU	Eurowing Goldwing		G-MTCU	Mainair Gemini Flash II	
G-MNZV	Southdown Raven X		G-MTCV	Microflight Spectrum	
G-MNZW	Southdown Raven X		G-MTCW	Mainair Gemini Flash	
G-MNZX	Southdown Raven X		G-MTCX	Solar Wings Pegasus XL-R	
G-MNZY	Striker Tri-Flyer 330		G-MTCY	Southdown Raven X	
G-MNZZ	CFM Shadow Srs B		G-MTCZ	Ultrasports Tripacer 250	
G-MTAA	Solar Wings Pegasus XL-R		G-MTDA	Hornet Dual Trainer	
G-MTAB	Mainair Gemini Flash II		G-MTDB	Owen Pola Mk 1	
G-MTAC	Mainair Gemini Flash II		G-MTDC	Owen Pola Mk 1	
G-MTAD	Mainair Gemini Skyflash		G-MTDD	Aerial Arts Chaser 110SX	
G-MTAE	Mainair Gemini Flash II		G-MTDE	American Aerolights 110SX	
G-MTAF	Mainair Gemini Flash II				
G-MTAG	Mainair Gemini Flash II				

Reg.	Type	Notes	Reg	Type	Notes
G-MTDF	Mainair Gemini Flash II		G-MTGJ	Solar Wings Pegasus XL-R	
G-MTDG	Solar Wings Pegasus XL-R		G-MTGK	Solar Wings Pegasus XL-R	
G-MTDH	Solar Wings Pegasus XL-R		G-MTGL	Solar Wings Pegasus XL-R	
G-MTDI	Solar Wings Pegasus XL-R		G-MTGM	Solar Wings Pegasus XL-R	
G-MTDJ	Medway Hybred 44XL		G-MTGO	Mainair Gemini Flash	
G-MTDK	Aerotech MW.5 Sorcerer		G-MTGP	Thruster TST Mk 1	
G-MTDL	Solar Wings Pegasus XL-R		G-MTGR	Thruster TST Mk 1	
G-MTDM	Mainair Gemini Flash II		G-MTGS	Thruster TST Mk 1	
G-MTDN	Ultraflight Lazair IIIE		G-MTGT	Thruster TST Mk 1	
G-MTDO	Eipper Quicksilver MXII		G-MTGU	Thruster TST Mk 1	
G-MTDP	Solar Wings Pegasus XL-R		G-MTGV	CFM Shadow Srs BD	
G-MTDR	Mainair Gemini Flash II		G-MTGX	Hornet Dual Trainer	
G-MTDS	Solar Wings Photon		G-MTGY	Southdown Lightning	
G-MTDT	Solar Wings Pegasus XL-R		G-MTHB	Aerotech MW.5B Sorcerer	
G-MTDU	CFM Shadow Srs BD		G-MTHC	Raven X	
G-MTDV	Solar Wings Pegasus XL-R		G-MTHD	Hiway Demon 195	
G-MTDW	Mainair Gemini Flash II		G-MTHF	Solar Wings Pegasus XL-R	
G-MTDX	CFM Shadow Srs BD		G-MTHG	Solar Wings Pegasus XL-R	
G-MTDY	Mainair Gemini Flash II		G-MTHH	Solar Wings Pegasus XL-R	
G-MTDZ	Eipper Quicksilver MXII		G-MTHI	Solar Wings Pegasus XL-R	
G-MTEA	Solar Wings Pegasus XL-R		G-MTHJ	Solar Wings Pegasus XL-R	
G-MTEB	Solar Wings Pegasus XL-R		G-MTHK	Solar Wings Pegasus XL-R	
G-MTEC	Solar Wings Pegasus XL-R		G-MTHL	Solar Wings Pegasus XL-R	
G-MTED	Solar Wings Pegasus XL-R		G-MTHM	Solar Wings Pegasus XL-R	
G-MTEE	Solar Wings Pegasus XL-R		G-MTHN	Solar Wings Pegasus XL-R	
G-MTEF	Solar Wings Pegasus XL-R		G-MTHO	Solar Wings Pegasus XL-R	
G-MTEG	Mainair Gemini Flash II		G-MTHP	Solar Wings Pegasus XL-R	
G-MTEH	Mainair Gemini Flash II		G-MTHS	CFM Shadow Srs BD	
G-MTEJ	Mainair Gemini Flash II		G-MTHT	CFM Shadow Srs BD	
G-MTEK	Mainair Gemini Flash II		G-MTHU	Hornet Dual Trainer	
G-MTEL	Mainair Gemini Flash II		G-MTHV	CFM Shadow Srs BD	
G-MTEM	Mainair Gemini Flash II		G-MTHW	Mainair Gemini Flash II	
G-MTEN	Mainair Gemini Flash II		G-MTHX	Mainair Gemini Flash IIA	
G-MTEO	Midland Ultralight Sirocco 337		G-MTHY	Mainair Gemini Flash IIA	
			G-MTHZ	Mainair Gemini Flash IIA	
G-MTER	Solar Wings Pegasus XL-R		G-MTIA	Mainair Gemini Flash IIA	
G-MTES	Solar Wings Pegasus XL-R		G-MTIB	Mainair Gemini Flash IIA	
G-MTET	Solar Wings Pegasus XL-R		G-MTIC	Mainair Gemini Flash IIA	
G-MTEU	Solar Wings Pegasus XL-R		G-MTID	Southdown Raven X	
G-MTEV	Solar Wings Pegasus XL-R		G-MTIE	Solar Wings Pegasus XL-R	
G-MTEW	Solar Wings Pegasus XL-R		G-MTIF	Solar Wings Pegasus XL-R	
G-MTEX	Solar Wings Pegasus XL-R		G-MTIG	Solar Wings Pegasus XL-R	
G-MTEY	Mainair Gemini Flash II		G-MTIH	Solar Wings Pegasus XL-R	
G-MTEZ	Ultraflight Lazair IIIE		G-MTII	Solar Wings Pegasus XL-R	
G-MTFA	Solar Wings Pegasus XL-R		G-MTIJ	Solar Wings Pegasus XL-R	
G-MTFB	Solar Wings Pegasus XL-R		G-MTIK	Southdown Raven X	
G-MTFC	Medway Hybred 44XLR		G-MTIL	Mainair Gemini Flash IIA	
G-MTFE	Solar Wings Pegasus XL-R		G-MTIM	Mainair Gemini Flash IIA	
G-MTFF	Mainair Gemini Flash II		G-MTIN	Mainair Gemini Flash IIA	
G-MTFG	AMF Chevvron 232		G-MTIO	Solar Wings Pegasus XL-R	
G-MTFH	Aerotech MW.5B Sorcerer		G-MTIP	Solar Wings Pegasus XL-R	
G-MTFI	Mainair Gemini Flash II		G-MTIR	Solar Wings Pegasus XL-R	
G-MTFJ	Mainair Gemini Flash II		G-MTIS	Solar Wings Pegasus XL-R	
G-MTFL	AMF Lazair IIIE		G-MTIT	Solar Wings Pegasus XL-R	
G-MTFM	Solar Wings Pegasus XL-R		G-MTIU	Solar Wings Pegasus XL-R	
G-MTFN	Aerotech MW.5 Sorcerer		G-MTIV	Solar Wings Pegasus XL-R	
G-MTFO	Solar Wings Pegasus XL-R		G-MTIW	Solar Wings Pegasus XL-R	
G-MTFP	Solar Wings Pegasus XL-R		G-MTIX	Solar Wings Pegasus XL-R	
G-MTFR	Solar Wings Pegasus XL-R		G-MTIY	Solar Wings Pegasus XL-R	
G-MTFS	Solar Wings Pegasus XL-R		G-MTIZ	Solar Wings Pegasus XL-R	
G-MTFT	Solar Wings Pegasus XL-R		G-MTJA	Mainair Gemini Flash IIA	
G-MTFU	CFM Shadow Series BD		G-MTJB	Mainair Gemini Flash IIA	
G-MTFX	Mainair Gemini Flash		G-MTJC	Mainair Gemini Flash IIA	
G-MTFY	CFM Shadow Srs BD		G-MTJD	Mainair Gemini Flash IIA	
G-MTFZ	CFM Shadow Srs BD		G-MTJE	Mainair Gemini Flash IIA	
G-MTGA	Mainair Gemini Flash		G-MTJF	Mainair Gemini Flash IIA	
G-MTGB	Thruster TST Mk 1		G-MTJG	Medway Hybred 44XLR	
G-MTGC	Thruster TST Mk 1		G-MTJH	Solar Wings Pegasus Flash	
G-MTGD	Thruster TST Mk 1				
G-MTGE	Thruster TST Mk 1		G-MTJI	Raven X	
G-MTGF	Thruster TST Mk 1		G-MTJK	Mainair Gemini Flash IIA	
G-MTGH	Mainair Gemini Flash IIA		G-MTJL	Mainair Gemini Flash IIA	
G-MTGI	Solar Wings Pegasus XL-R		G-MTJM	Mainair Gemini Flash IIA	

Reg.	Type	Notes	Reg	Type	Notes
G-MTJN	Midland Ultralights Sirocco 377GB		G-MTMT	Mainair Gemini Flash IIA	
			G-MTMU	Mainair Gemini Flash IIA	
G-MTJP	Medway Hybred 44XLR		G-MTMV	Mainair Gemini Flash IIA	
G-MTJR	Solar Wings Pegasus XL-R		G-MTMW	Mainair Gemini Flash IIA	
G-MTJS	Solar Wings Pegasus XL-Q		G-MTMX	CFM Shadow Srs BD	
G-MTJT	Mainair Gemini Flash IIA		G-MTMY	CFM Shadow Srs BD	
G-MTJV	Mainair Gemini Flash IIA		G-MTMZ	CFM Shadow Srs BD	
G-MTJW	Mainair Gemini Flash IIA		G-MTNB	Raven X	
G-MTJX	Hornet Dual Trainer		G-MTNC	Mainair Gemini Flash IIA	
G-MTJY	Mainair Gemini Flash IIA		G-MTND	Medway Hybred 44XLR	
G-MTJZ	Mainair Gemini Flash IIA		G-MTNE	Medway Hybred 44XLR	
G-MTKA	Thruster TST Mk 1		G-MTNF	Medway Hybred 44XLR	
G-MTKB	Thruster TST Mk 1		G-MTNG	Mainair Gemini Flash IIA	
G-MTKD	Thruster TST Mk 1		G-MTNH	Mainair Gemini Flash IIA	
G-MTKE	Thruster TST Mk 1		G-MTNI	Mainair Gemini Flash IIA	
G-MTKG	Solar Wings Pegasus XL-R		G-MTNJ	Mainair Gemini Flash IIA	
G-MTKH	Solar Wings Pegasus XL-R		G-MTNK	Weedhopper JC-24B	
G-MTKI	Solar Wings Pegasus XL-R		G-MTNL	Mainair Gemini Flash IIA	
G-MTKJ	Solar Wings Pegasus XL-R		G-MTNM	Mainair Gemini Flash IIA	
G-MTKK	Solar Wings Pegasus XL-R		G-MTNN	Mainair Gemini Flash IIA	
G-MTKL	—		G-MTNO	Solar Wings Pegasus XL-Q	
G-MTKM	Gardner T-M Scout S.2		G-MTNP	Solar Wings Pegasus XL-Q	
G-MTKN	Mainair Gemini Flash IIA		G-MTNR	Thruster TST Mk 1	
G-MTKO	Mainair Gemini Flash IIA		G-MTNS	Thruster TST Mk 1	
G-MTKP	Solar Wings Pegasus XL-R		G-MTNT	Thruster TST Mk 1	
G-MTKR	CFM Shadow Srs BD		G-MTNU	Thruster TST Mk 1	
G-MTKS	CFM Shadow Srs BD		G-MTNV	Thruster TST Mk 1	
G-MTKU	CFM Shadow Srs BD		G-MTNW	Thruster TST Mk 1	
G-MTKV	Mainair Gemini Flash		G-MTNX	Mainair Gemini Flash II	
G-MTKW	Mainair Gemini Flash IIA		G-MTNY	Mainair Gemini Flash IIA	
G-MTKX	Mainair Gemini Flash IIA		G-MTNZ	Solar Wings Pegasus XL-Q	
G-MTKY	Mainair Gemini Flash IIA		G-MTOA	Solar Wings Pegasus XL-R	
G-MTKZ	Mainair Gemini Flash IIA		G-MTOB	Solar Wings Pegasus XL-R	
G-MTLA	Mainair Gemini Flash IIA		G-MTOC	Solar Wings Pegasus XL-R	
G-MTLB	Mainair Gemini Flash IIA		G-MTOD	Solar Wings Pegasus XL-R	
G-MTLC	Mainair Gemini Flash IIA		G-MTOE	Solar Wings Pegasus XL-R	
G-MTLD	Mainair Gemini Flash IIA		G-MTOF	Solar Wings Pegasus XL-R	
G-MTLE	See main Register		G-MTOG	Solar Wings Pegasus XL-R	
G-MTLG	Solar Wings Pegasus XL-R		G-MTOH	Solar Wings Pegasus XL-R	
G-MTLH	Solar Wings Pegasus XL-R		G-MTOI	Solar Wings Pegasus XL-R	
G-MTLI	Solar Wings Pegasus XL-R		G-MTOJ	Solar Wings Pegasus XL-R	
G-MTLJ	Solar Wings Pegasus XL-R		G-MTOK	Solar Wings Pegasus XL-R	
G-MTLK	Raven X		G-MTOL	Solar Wings Pegasus XL-R	
G-MTLL	Mainair Gemini Flash IIA		G-MTOM	Solar Wings Pegasus XL-R	
G-MTLM	Thruster TST Mk 1		G-MTON	Solar Wings Pegasus XL-R	
G-MTLN	Thruster TST Mk 1		G-MTOO	Solar Wings Pegasus XL-R	
G-MTLO	Thruster TST Mk 1		G-MTOP	Solar Wings Pegasus XL-R	
G-MTLP	Thruster TST Mk 1		G-MTOR	Solar Wings Pegasus XL-R	
G-MTLR	Thruster TST Mk 1		G-MTOS	Solar Wings Pegasus XL-R	
G-MTLS	Solar Wings Pegasus XL-R		G-MTOT	Solar Wings Pegasus XL-R	
G-MTLT	Solar Wings Pegasus XL-R		G-MTOU	Solar Wings Pegasus XL-R	
G-MTLU	Solar Wings Pegasus XL-R		G-MTOV	Solar Wings Pegasus XL-R	
G-MTLV	Solar Wings Pegasus XL-R		G-MTOW	Solar Wings Pegasus XL-R	
G-MTLW	Solar Wings Pegasus XL-R		G-MTOX	Solar Wings Pegasus XL-R	
G-MTLX	Medway Hybred 44XLR		G-MTOY	Solar Wings Pegasus XL-R	
G-MTLY	Solar Wings Pegasus XL-R		G-MTOZ	Solar Wings Pegasus XL-R	
G-MTLZ	Whittaker MW.5 Sorceror		G-MTPA	Mainair Gemini Flash IIA	
G-MTMA	Mainair Gemini Flash IIA		G-MTPB	Mainair Gemini Flash IIA	
G-MTMB	Mainair Gemini Flash IIA		G-MTPC	Raven X	
G-MTMC	Mainair Gemini Flash IIA		G-MTPE	Solar Wings Pegasus XL-R	
G-MTMD	Whittaker MW.6 Merlin		G-MTPF	Solar Wings Pegasus XL-R	
G-MTME	Solar Wings Pegasus XL-R		G-MTPG	Solar Wings Pegasus XL-R	
G-MTMF	Solar Wings Pegasus XL-R		G-MTPH	Solar Wings Pegasus XL-R	
G-MTMG	Solar Wings Pegasus XL-R		G-MTPI	Solar Wings Pegasus XL-R	
G-MTMH	Solar Wings Pegasus XL-R		G-MTPJ	Solar Wings Pegasus XL-R	
G-MTMI	Solar Wings Pegasus XL-R		G-MTPK	Solar Wings Pegasus XL-R	
G-MTMJ	Maxair Hummer		G-MTPL	Solar Wings Pegasus XL-R	
G-MTMK	Raven X		G-MTPM	Solar Wings Pegasus XL-R	
G-MTML	Mainair Gemini Flash IIA		G-MTPN	Solar Wings Pegasus XL-Q	
G-MTMM	CFM Shadow Srs BD		G-MTPO	Solar Wings Pegasus XL-Q	
G-MTMO	Raven X		G-MTPP	Solar Wings Pegasus XL-R	
G-MTMP	Hornet Dual Trainer/Raven		G-MTPR	Solar Wings Pegasus XL-R	
G-MTMR	Hornet Dual Trainer/Raven		G-MTPS	Solar Wings Pegasus XL-Q	

Reg.	Type	Notes	Reg	Type	Notes
G-MTPT	Thruster TST Mk Mk 1		G-MTTS	Mainair Gemini Flash IIA	
G-MTPU	Thruster TST Mk 1		G-MTTU	Solar Wings Pegasus XL-R	
G-MTPV	Thruster TST Mk 1		G-MTTW	Mainair Gemini Flash IIA	
G-MTPW	Thruster TST Mk 1		G-MTTX	Solar Wings Pegasus XL-Q	
G-MTPX	Thruster TST Mk 1		G-MTTY	Solar Wings Pegasus XL-Q	
G-MTPY	Thruster TST Mk 1		G-MTTZ	Solar Wings Pegasus XL-Q	
G-MTPZ	Solar Wings Pegasus XL-R		G-MTUA	Solar Wings Pegasus XL-R	
G-MTRA	Mainair Gemini Flash IIA		G-MTUB	Thruster TST Mk 1	
G-MTRB	Mainair Gemini Flash IIA		G-MTUC	Thruster TST Mk 1	
G-MTRC	Midlands Ultralights Sirocco 377GB		G-MTUD	Thruster TST Mk 1	
			G-MTUE	Thruster TST Mk 1	
G-MTRD	Midlands Ultralights Sirocco 377GB		G-MTUF	Thruster TST Mk 1	
			G-MTUG	Thruster TST Mk 1	
G-MTRE	Whittaker MW.6 Merlin		G-MTUH	Solar Wings Pegasus XL-R	
G-MTRF	Mainair Gemini Flash IIA		G-MTUI	Solar Wings Pegasus XL-R	
G-MTRG	Mainair Gemini Flash IIA		G-MTUJ	Solar Wings Pegasus XL-R	
G-MTRH	Hiway Demon		G-MTUK	Solar Wings Pegasus XL-R	
G-MTRJ	AMF Chevvron 232		G-MTUL	Solar Wings Pegasus XL-R	
G-MTRK	Hornet Dual Trainer		G-MTUN	Solar Wings Pegasus XL-Q	
G-MTRL	Hornet Dual Trainer		G-MTUO	Solar Wings Pegasus XL-Q	
G-MTRM	Solar Wings Pegasus XL-R		G-MTUP	Solar Wings Pegasus XL-Q	
G-MTRN	Solar Wings Pegasus XL-R		G-MTUR	Solar Wings Pegasus XL-Q	
G-MTRO	Solar Wings Pegasus XL-R		G-MTUS	Solar Wings Pegasus XL-Q	
G-MTRP	Solar Wings Pegasus XL-R		G-MTUT	Solar Wings Pegasus XL-Q	
G-MTRR	Solar Wings Pegasus XL-R		G-MTUU	Mainair Gemini Flash IIA	
G-MTRS	Solar Wings Pegasus XL-R		G-MTUV	Mainair Gemini Flash IIA	
G-MTRT	Raven X		G-MTUX	Medway Hybred 44XLR	
G-MTRU	Solar Wings Pegasus XL-Q		G-MTUY	Solar Wings Pegasus XL-Q	
G-MTRV	Solar Wings Pegasus XL-Q		G-MTUZ	Hornet Dual Trainer	
G-MTRW	Raven X		G-MTVA	Solar Wings Pegasus XL-R	
G-MTRX	Whittaker MW.5 Sorceror		G-MTVB	Solar Wings Pegasus XL-R	
G-MTRY	Noble Hardman Snowbird IV		G-MTVC	Solar Wings Pegasus XL-R	
G-MTRZ	Mainair Gemini Flash IIA		G-MTVE	Solar Wings Pegasus XL-R	
G-MTSA	Mainair Gemini Flash IIA		G-MTVF	Solar Wings Pegasus XL-R	
G-MTSB	Mainair Gemini Flash IIA		G-MTVG	Mainair Gemini Flash IIA	
G-MTSC	Mainair Gemini Flash IIA		G-MTVH	Mainair Gemini Flash IIA	
G-MTSD	Raven X		G-MTVI	Mainair Gemini Flash IIA	
G-MTSE	Flexiform Striker		G-MTVJ	Mainair Gemini Flash IIA	
G-MTSF	Aerial Arts Chaser 110SX		G-MTVK	Solar Wings Pegasus XL-R	
G-MTSG	CFM Shadow Srs BD		G-MTVL	Solar Wings Pegasus XL-R	
G-MTSH	Thruster TST Mk 1		G-MTVM	Solar Wings Pegasus XL-R	
G-MTSI	Thruster TST Mk 1		G-MTVN	Solar Wings Pegasus XL-R	
G-MTSJ	Thruster TST Mk 1		G-MTVO	Solar Wings Pegasus XL-R	
G-MTSK	Thruster TST Mk 1		G-MTVP	Thruster TST Mk 1	
G-MTSL	Thruster TST Mk 1		G-MTVR	Thruster TST Mk 1	
G-MTSM	Thruster TST Mk 1		G-MTVS	Thruster TST Mk 1	
G-MTSN	Solar Wings Pegasus XL-R		G-MTVT	Thruster TST Mk 1	
G-MTSO	Solar Wings Pegasus XL-R		G-MTVU	Thruster TST Mk 1	
G-MTSP	Solar Wings Pegasus XL-R		G-MTVV	Thruster TST Mk 1	
G-MTSR	Solar Wings Pegasus XL-R		G-MTVX	Solar Wings Pegasus XL-Q	
G-MTSS	Solar Wings Pegasus XL-R		G-MTVY	Solar Wings Pegasus XL-Q	
G-MTST	Thruster TST Mk 1		G-MTVZ	Powerchute Raider	
G-MTSU	Solar Wings Pegasus XL-R		G-MTWA	Solar Wings Pegasus XL-R	
G-MTSV	Solar Wings Pegasus XL-R		G-MTWB	Solar Wings Pegasus XL-R	
G-MTSX	Solar Wings Pegasus XL-R		G-MTWC	Solar Wings Pegasus XL-R	
G-MTSY	Solar Wings Pegasus XL-R		G-MTWD	Solar Wings Pegasus XL-R	
G-MTSZ	Solar Wings Pegasus XL-R		G-MTWE	Solar Wings Pegasus XL-R	
G-MTTA	Solar Wings Pegasus XL-R		G-MTWF	Mainair Gemini Flash IIA	
G-MTTB	Solar Wings Pegasus XL-R		G-MTWG	Mainair Gemini Flash IIA	
G-MTTC	Solar Wings Pegasus XL-R		G-MTWH	CFM Shadow Srs BD	
G-MTTD	Solar Wings Pegasus XL-R		G-MTWK	CFM Shadow Srs Bd	
G-MTTE	Solar Wings Pegasus XL-R		G-MTWL	CFM Shadow Srs BD	
G-MTTF	Aerotech MW.6 Merlin		G-MTWM	CFM Shadow Srs BD	
G-MTTG	Excalibur TriPacer 250		G-MTWN	CFM Shadow Srs BD	
G-MTTH	CFM Shadow Srs BD		G-MTWO	Weedhopper JC-24B	
G-MTTI	Mainair Gemini Flash IIA		G-MTWP	CFM Shadow Srs BD	
G-MTTK	Southdown Lightning DS		G-MTWR	Mainair Gemini Flash IIA	
G-MTTL	Hiway Sky-Trike		G-MTWS	Mainair Gemini Flash IIA	
G-MTTM	Mainair Gemini Flash IIA		G-MTWW	Solar Wings Typhoon	
G-MTTN	Ultralight Flight Phantom		G-MTWX	Mainair Gemini Flash IIA	
G-MTTO	Mainair Gemini Flash IIA		G-MTWY	Thruster TST Mk 1	
G-MTTP	Mainair Gemini Flash IIA		G-MTWZ	Thruster TST Mk 1	
G-MTTR	Mainair Gemini Flash IIA		G-MTXA	Thruster TST Mk 1	

Reg.	Type	Notes	Reg	Type	Notes
G-MTXB	Thruster TST Mk 1		G-MVAB	Mainair Gemini Flash IIA	
G-MTXC	Thruster TST Mk 1		G-MVAC	CFM Shadow Srs BD	
G-MTXD	Thruster TST Mk 1		G-MVAD	Mainair Gemini Flash IIA	
G-MTXE	Hornet Dual Trainer		G-MVAF	Southdown Puma Sprint	
G-MTXG	Solar Wings Pegasus XL-Q		G-MVAG	Thruster TST Mk 1	
G-MTXH	Solar Wings Pegasus XL-Q		G-MVAH	Thruster TST Mk 1	
G-MTXI	Solar Wings Pegasus XL-Q		G-MVAI	Thruster TST Mk 1	
G-MTXJ	Solar Wings Pegasus XL-Q		G-MVAJ	Thruster TST Mk 1	
G-MTXK	Solar Wings Pegasus XL-Q		G-MVAK	Thruster TST Mk 1	
G-MTXL	Noble Hardman Snowbird Mk IV		G-MVAL	Thruster TST Mk 1	
G-MTXM	Mainair Gemini Flash IIA		G-MVAM	CFM Shadow Srs BD	
G-MTXO	Whittaker MW.6		G-MVAN	CFM Shadow Srs BD	
G-MTXP	Mainair Gemini Flash IIA		G-MVAO	Mainair Gemini Flash IIA	
G-MTXR	CFM Shadow Srs BD		G-MVAP	Mainair Gemini Flash IIA	
G-MTXS	Mainair Gemini Flash IIA		G-MVAR	Solar Wings Pegasus XL-R	
G-MTXT	MBA Tiger Cub 440		G-MVAS	Solar Wings Pegasus XL-R	
G-MTXU	Noble Hardman Snowbird Mk IV		G-MVAT	Solar Wings Pegasus XL-R	
			G-MVAU	Solar Wings Pegasus XL-R	
G-MTXV	Noble Hardman Snowbird Mk IV		G-MVAV	Solar Wings Pegasus XL-R	
			G-MVAW	Solar Wings Pegasus XL-Q	
G-MTXW	Noble Hardman Snowbird Mk IV		G-MVAX	Solar Wings Pegasus XL-Q	
			G-MVAY	Solar Wings Pegasus XL-Q	
G-MTXY	Hornet Dual Trainer		G-MVAZ	Solar Wings Pegasus XL-Q	
G-MTXZ	Mainair Gemini Flash IIA		G-MVBA	Solar Wings Pegasus XL-Q	
G-MTYA	Solar Wings Pegasus XL-Q		G-MVBB	CFM Shadow Srs BD	
G-MTYC	Solar Wings Pegasus XL-Q		G-MVBC	Aerial Arts Tri-Flyer 130SX	
G-MTYD	Solar Wings Pegasus XL-Q		G-MVBD	Mainair Gemini Flash IIA	
G-MTYE	Solar Wings Pegasus XL-Q		G-MVBE	Mainair Scorcher	
G-MTYF	Solar Wings Pegasus XL-Q		G-MVBF	Mainair Gemini Flash IIA	
G-MTYG	Solar Wings Pegasus XL-Q		G-MVBG	Mainair Gemini Flash IIA	
G-MTYH	Solar Wings Pegasus XL-Q		G-MVBH	Mainair Gemini Flash IIA	
G-MTYI	Solar Wings Pegasus XL-Q		G-MVBI	Mainair Gemini Flash IIA	
G-MTYK	Solar Wings Pegasus XL-Q		G-MVBJ	Solar Wings Pegasus XL-R	
G-MTYL	Solar Wings Pegasus XL-Q		G-MVBK	Mainair Gemini Flash IIA	
G-MTYM	Solar Wings Pegasus XL-Q		G-MVBL	Mainair Gemini Flash IIA	
G-MTYN	Solar Wings Pegasus XL-Q		G-MVBM	Mainair Gemini Flash IIA	
G-MTYO	Solar Wings Pegasus XL-Q		G-MVBN	Mainair Gemini Flash IIA	
G-MTYP	Solar Wings Pegasus XL-Q		G-MVBO	Mainair Gemini Flash IIA	
G-MTYR	Solar Wings Pegasus XL-Q		G-MVBP	Thruster TST Mk 1	
G-MTYS	Solar Wings Pegasus XL-Q		G-MVBR	Thruster TST Mk 1	
G-MTYT	Solar Wings Pegasus XL-Q		G-MVBS	Thruster TST Mk 1	
G-MTYU	Solar Wings Pegasus XL-Q		G-MVBT	Thruster TST Mk 1	
G-MTYV	Raven X		G-MVBY	Solar Wings Pegasus XL-R	
G-MTYW	Raven X		G-MVBZ	Solar Wings Pegasus XL-R	
G-MTYX	Raven X		G-MVCA	Solar Wings Pegasus XL-R	
G-MTYY	Solar Wings Pegasus XL-R		G-MVCB	Solar Wings Pegasus XL-R	
G-MTZA	Thruster TST Mk 1		G-MVCC	CFM Shadow Srs BD	
G-MTZB	Thruster TST Mk 1		G-MVCD	Medway Hybred 44XLR	
G-MTZC	Thruster TST Mk 1		G-MVCE	Mainair Gemini Flash IIA	
G-MTZD	Thruster TST Mk 1		G-MVCF	Mainair Gemini Flash IIA	
G-MTZE	Thruster TST Mk 1		G-MVCH	Noble Hardman Snowbird Mk IV	
G-MTZF	Thruster TST Mk 1				
G-MTZG	Mainair Gemini Flash IIA		G-MVCI	Noble Hardman Snowbird Mk IV	
G-MTZH	Mainair Gemini Flash IIA				
G-MTZI	Solar Wings Pegasus XL-R		G-MVCJ	Noble Hardman Snowbird Mk IV	
G-MTZJ	Solar Wings Pegasus XL-R				
G-MTZK	Solar Wings Pegasus XL-R		G-MVCL	Solar Wings Pegasus XL-Q	
G-MTZL	Mainair Gemini Flash IIA		G-MVCM	Solar Wings Pegasus XL-Q	
G-MTZM	Mainair Gemini Flash IIA		G-MVCN	Solar Wings Pegasus XL-Q	
G-MTZN	Mainair Gemini Flash IIA		G-MVCO	Solar Wings Pegasus XL-Q	
G-MTZO	Mainair Gemini Flash IIA		G-MVCP	Solar Wings Pegasus XL-Q	
G-MTZP	Solar Wings Pegasus XL-Q		G-MVCR	Solar Wings Pegasus XL-Q	
G-MTZR	Solar Wings Pegasus XL-Q		G-MVCS	Solar Wings Pegasus XL-Q	
G-MTZS	Solar Wings Pegasus XL-Q		G-MVCT	Solar Wings Pegasus XL-Q	
G-MTZT	Solar Wings Pegasus XL-Q		G-MVCU	Solar Wings Pegasus XL-Q	
G-MTZU	Solar Wings Pegasus XL-Q		G-MVCV	Solar Wings Pegasus XL-Q	
G-MTZV	Mainair Gemini Flash IIA		G-MVCW	CFM Shadow Srs BD	
G-MTZW	Mainair Gemini Flash IIA		G-MVCY	Mainair Gemini Flash IIA	
G-MTZX	Mainair Gemini Flash IIA		G-MVCZ	Mainair Gemini Flash IIA	
G-MTZY	Mainair Gemini Flash IIA		G-MVDA	Mainair Gemini Flash IIA	
G-MTZZ	Mainair Gemini Flash IIA		G-MVDB	Medway Hybred 44XLR	
G-MVAA	Mainair Gemini Flash IIA		G-MVDC	Medway Hybred 44XLR	
			G-MVDD	Thruster TST Mk 1	

Reg.	Type	Notes	Reg	Type	Notes
G-MVDE	Thruster TST Mk 1		G-MVGF	Aerial Arts Chaser S	
G-MVDF	Thruster TST Mk 1		G-MVGG	Aerial Arts Chaser S	
G-MVDG	Thruster TST Mk 1		G-MVGH	Aerial Arts Chaser S	
G-MVDH	Thruster TST Mk 1		G-MVGI	Aerial Arts Chaser S	
G-MVDI	Thruster TST Mk 1		G-MVGJ	Aerial Arts Chaser S	
G-MVDJ	Medway Hybred 44XLR		G-MVGK	Aerial Arts Chaser S	
G-MVDK	Aerial Arts Chaser S		G-MVGL	Medway Hybred 44XLR	
G-MVDL	Aerial Arts Chaser S		G-MVGM	Mainair Gemini Flash IIA	
G-MVDM	Aerial Arts Chaser S		G-MVGN	Solar Wings Pegasus XL-R	
G-MVDN	Aerial Arts Chaser S		G-MVGO	Solar Wings Pegasus XL-R	
G-MVDO	Aerial Arts Chaser S		G-MVGR	Solar Wings Pegasus XL-R	
G-MVDP	Aerial Arts Chaser S		G-MVGS	Solar Wings Pegasus XL-R	
G-MVDR	Aerial Arts Chaser S		G-MVGT	Solar Wings Pegasus XL-Q	
G-MVDS	Hiway Skytrike		G-MVGU	Solar Wings Pegasus XL-Q	
G-MVDT	Mainair Gemini Flash IIA		G-MVGV	Solar Wings Pegasus XL-Q	
G-MVDU	Solar Wings Pegasus XL-R		G-MVGW	Solar Wings Pegasus XL-Q	
G-MVDV	Solar Wings Pegasus XL-R		G-MVGX	Solar Wings Pegasus XL-Q	
G-MVDW	Solar Wings Pegasus XL-R		G-MVGY	Medway Hybred 44XL	
G-MVDX	Solar Wings Pegasus XL-R		G-MVGZ	Ultraflight Lazair IIIE	
G-MVDY	Solar Wings Pegasus XL-R		G-MVHA	Aerial Arts Chaser S	
G-MVDZ	Solar Wings Pegasus XL-R		G-MVHB	Powerchute Raider	
G-MVEA	Solar Wings Pegasus XL-R		G-MVHC	Powerchute Raider	
G-MVEB	Solar Wings Pegasus XL-R		G-MVHD	CFM Shadow Srs BD	
G-MVEC	Solar Wings Pegasus XL-R		G-MVHE	Mainair Gemini Flash IIA	
G-MVED	Solar Wings Pegasus XL-R		G-MVHF	Mainair Gemini Flash IIA	
G-MVEE	Medway Hybred 44XLR		G-MVHG	Mainair Gemini Flash IIA	
G-MVEF	Solar Wings Pegasus XL-R		G-MVHH	Mainair Gemini Flash IIA	
G-MVEG	Solar Wings Pegasus XL-R		G-MVHI	Thruster TST Mk 1	
G-MVEH	Mainair Gemini Flash IIA		G-MVHJ	Thruster TST Mk 1	
G-MVEI	CFM Shadow Srs BD		G-MVHK	Thruster TST Mk 1	
G-MVEJ	Mainair Gemini Flash IIA		G-MVHL	Thruster TST Mk 1	
G-MVEK	Mainair Gemini Flash IIA		G-MVHM	Whittaker MW.5 Sorcerer	
G-MVEL	Mainair Gemini Flash IIA		G-MVHN	Aerial Arts Chaser S	
G-MVEN	CFM Shadow Srs BD		G-MVHO	Solar Wings Pegasus XL-Q	
G-MVEO	Mainair Gemini Flash IIA		G-MVHP	Solar Wings Pegasus XL-Q	
G-MVEP	Mainair Gemini Flash IIA		G-MVHR	Solar Wings Pegasus XL-Q	
G-MVER	Mainair Gemini Flash IIA		G-MVHS	Solar Wings Pegasus XL-Q	
G-MVES	Mainair Gemini Flash IIA		G-MVHT	Solar Wings Pegasus XL-Q	
G-MVET	Mainir Gemini Flash IIA		G-MVHU	Solar Wings Pegasus XL-Q	
G-MVEV	Mainair Gemini Flash IIA		G-MVHV	Solar Wings Pegasus XL-Q	
G-MVEW	Mainair Gemini Flash IIA		G-MVHW	Solar Wings Pegasus XL-Q	
G-MVEX	Solar Wings Pegasus XL-Q		G-MVHX	Solar Wings Pegasus XL-Q	
G-MVEY	Solar Wings Pegasus XL-Q		G-MVHY	Solar Wings Pegasus XL-Q	
G-MVEZ	Solar Wings Pegasus XL-Q		G-MVHZ	Hornet Dual Trainer	
G-MVFA	Solar Wings Pegasus XL-Q		G-MVIA	Solar Wings Pegasus XL-R	
G-MVFB	Solar Wings Pegasus XL-Q		G-MVIB	Mainair Gemini Flash IIA	
G-MVFC	Solar Wings Pegasus XL-Q		G-MVIC	Mainair Gemini Flash IIA	
G-MVFD	Solar Wings Pegasus XL-Q		G-MVID	Aerial Arts Chaser S	
G-MVFE	Solar Wings Pegasus XL-Q		G-MVIE	Aerial Arts Chaser S	
G-MVFF	Solar Wings Pegasus XL-Q		G-MVIF	Medway Hybred 44XLR	
G-MVFG	Solar Wings Pegasus XL-Q		G-MVIG	CFM Shadow Srs B	
G-MVFH	CFM Shadow Srs BD		G-MVIH	Mainair Gemini Flash IIA	
G-MVFJ	Thruster TST Mk 1		G-MVIL	Noble Hardman Snowbird Mk IV	
G-MVFK	Thruster TST Mk 1				
G-MVFL	Thruster TST Mk 1		G-MVIM	Noble Hardman Snowbird Mk IV	
G-MVFM	Thruster TST Mk 1				
G-MVFN	Thruster TST Mk 1		G-MVIN	Noble Hardman Snowbird Mk IV	
G-MVFO	Thruster TST Mk 1				
G-MVFP	Solar Wings Pegasus XL-R		G-MVIO	Noble Hardman Snowbird Mk IV	
G-MVFR	Solar Wings Pegasus XL-R				
G-MVFS	Solar Wings Pegasus XL-R		G-MVIP	AMF Chevvron 232	
G-MVFT	Solar Wings Pegasus XL-R		G-MVIR	Thruster TST Mk 1	
G-MVFU	Solar Wings Pegasus XL-R		G-MVIS	Thruster TST Mk 1	
G-MVFV	Solar Wings Pegasus XL-R		G-MVIU	Thruster TST Mk 1	
G-MVFW	Solar Wings Pegasus XL-R		G-MVIV	Thruster TST Mk 1	
G-MVFX	Solar Wings Pegasus XL-R		G-MVIW	Thruster TST Mk 1	
G-MVFY	Solar Wings Pegasus XL-R		G-MVIX	Mainair Gemini Flash IIA	
G-MVFZ	Solar Wings Pegasus XL-R		G-MVIY	Mainair Gemini Flash IIA	
G-MVGA	Aerial Arts Chaser S		G-MVIZ	Mainair Gemini Flash IIA	
G-MVGB	Medway Hybred 44XLR		G-MVJA	Mainair Gemini Flash IIA	
G-MVGC	AMF Chevvron 232		G-MVJB	Mainair Gemini Flash IIA	
G-MVGD	AMF Chevvron 232		G-MVJC	Mainair Gemini Flash IIA	
G-MVGE	AMF Chevvron 232		G-MVJD	Solar Wings Pegasus XL-R	

Reg.	Type	Notes	Reg	Type	Notes
G-MVJE	Mainair Gemini Flash IIA		G-MVMK	Medway Hybred 44XLR	
G-MVJF	Aerial Arts Chaser S		G-MVML	Aerial Arts Chaser S	
G-MVJG	Aerial Arts Chaser S		G-MVMM	Aerial Arts Chaser S	
G-MVJH	Aerial Arts Chaser S		G-MVMN	Mainair Gemini Flash IIA	
G-MVJI	Aerial Arts Chaser S		G-MVMO	Mainair Gemini Flash IIA	
G-MVJJ	Aerial Arts Chaser S		G-MVMP	Eipper Quicksilver MXII	
G-MVJK	Aerial Arts Chaser S		G-MVMR	Mainair Gemini Flash IIA	
G-MVJL	Mainair Gemini Flash IIA		G-MVMT	Mainair Gemini Flash IIA	
G-MVJM	Microflight Spectrum		G-MVMU	Mainair Gemini Flash IIA	
G-MVJN	Solar Wings Pegasus XL-Q		G-MVMV	Aerotech MW.5 (K)	
G-MVJO	Solar Wings Pegasus XL-Q			Sorcerer	
G-MVJP	Solar Wings Pegasus XL-Q		G-MVMW	Mainair Gemini Flash IIA	
G-MVJR	Solar Wings Pegasus XL-Q		G-MVMX	Mainair Gemini Flash IIA	
G-MVJS	Solar Wings Pegasus XL-Q		G-MVMY	Mainair Gemini Flash IIA	
G-MVJT	Solar Wings Pegasus XL-Q		G-MVMZ	Mainair Gemini Flash IIA	
G-MVJU	Solar Wings Pegasus XL-Q		G-MVNA	Powerchute Raider	
G-MVJV	Solar Wings Pegasus XL-Q		G-MVNB	Powerchute Raider	
G-MVJW	Solar Wings Pegasus XL-Q		G-MVNC	Powerchute Raider	
G-MVJX	Solar Wings Pegasus XL-Q		G-MVND	Powerchute Raider	
G-MVJZ	Birdman Cherokee		G-MVNE	Powerchute Raider	
G-MVKA	Medway Hybred 44XLR		G-MVNF	Powerchute Raider	
G-MVKB	Medway Hybred 44XLR		G-MVNG	Powerchute Raider	
G-MVKC	Mainair Gemini Flash IIA		G-MVNI	Powerchute Raider	
G-MVKE	Solar Wings Pegasus XL-R		G-MVNJ	Powerchute Raider	
G-MVKF	Solar Wings Pegasus XL-R		G-MVNK	Powerchute Raider	
G-MVKG	Solar Wings Pegasus XL-R		G-MVNL	Powerchute Raider	
G-MVKH	Solar Wings Pegasus XL-R		G-MVNM	Mainair Gemini Flash IIA	
G-MVKI	Solar Wings Pegasus XL-R		G-MVNN	Whittaker MW.5 (K)	
G-MVKJ	Solar Wings Pegasus XL-R			Sorcerer	
G-MVKK	Solar Wings Pegasus XL-R		G-MVNO	Aerotech MW.5 (K)	
G-MVKL	Solar Wings Pegasus XL-R			Sorcerer	
G-MVKM	Solar Wings Pegasus XL-R		G-MVNP	Aerotech MW.5 (K)	
G-MVKN	Solar Wings Pegasus XL-Q			Sorcerer	
G-MVKO	Solar Wings Pegasus XL-Q		G-MVNR	Aerotech MW.5 (K)	
G-MVKP	Solar Wings Pegasus XL-Q			Sorcerer	
G-MVKR	Solar Wings Pegasus XL-Q		G-MVNS	Aerotech MW.5 (K)	
G-MVKS	Solar Wings Pegasus XL-Q			Sorcerer	
G-MVKT	Solar Wings Pegasus XL-Q		G-MVNT	Whittaker MW.5 (K)	
G-MVKU	Solar Wings Pegasus XL-Q			Sorcerer	
G-MVKV	Solar Wings Pegasus XL-Q		G-MVNU	Aerotech MW.5 Sorcerer	
G-MVKW	Solar Wings Pegasus XL-Q		G-MVNV	Aerotech MW.5 Sorcerer	
G-MVKX	Solar Wings Pegasus XL-Q		G-MVNW	Mainair Gemini Flash IIA	
G-MVKY	Aerial Arts Chaser S		G-MVNX	Mainair Gemini Flash IIA	
G-MVKZ	Aerial Arts Chaser S		G-MVNY	Mainair Gemini Flash IIA	
G-MVLA	Aerial Arts Chaser S		G-MVNZ	Mainair Gemini Flash IIA	
G-MVLB	Aerial Arts Chaser S		G-MVOA	Aerial Arts Alligator	
G-MVLC	Aerial Arts Chaser S		G-MVOB	Mainair Gemini Flash IIA	
G-MVLD	Aerial Arts Chaser S		G-MVOD	Aerial Arts Chaser 110SX	
G-MVLE	Aerial Arts Chaser S		G-MVOE	Solar Wings Pegasus XL-R	
G-MVLF	Aerial Arts Chaser S		G-MVOF	Mainair Gemini Flash IIA	
G-MVLG	Aerial Arts Chaser S		G-MVOG	Huntair Pathfinder Mk 1	
G-MVLH	Aerial Arts Chaser S		G-MVOH	CFM Shadow Srs B	
G-MVLJ	CFM Shadow Srs B		G-MVOI	Noble Hardman Snowbird	
G-MVLL	Mainair Gemini Flash IIA			Mk IV	
G-MVLM	Solar Wings Pegasus		G-MVOJ	Noble Hardman Snowbird	
	Bandit			Mk IV	
G-MVLP	CFM Shadow Srs BD		G-MVOK	Noble Hardman Snowbird	
G-MVLR	Mainair Gemini Flash IIA			Mk IV	
G-MVLS	Aerial Arts Chaser S		G-MVOL	Noble Hardman Snowbird	
G-MVLT	Aerial Arts Chaser S			Mk IV	
G-MVLU	Aerial Arts Chaser S		G-MVOM	Medway Hybred 44XLR	
G-MVLW	Aerial Arts Chaser S		G-MVON	Mainair Gemini Flash IIA	
G-MVLX	Solar Wings Pegasus XL-Q		G-MVOO	AMF Chevvron 232	
G-MVLY	Solar Wings Pegasus XL-Q		G-MVOP	Aerial Arts Chaser S	
G-MVLZ	Solar Wings Pegasus XL-Q		G-MVOS	Southdown Raven	
G-MVMA	Solar Wings Pegasus XL-Q		G-MVOT	Thruster TST Mk 1	
G-MVMB	Solar Wings Pegasus XL-Q		G-MVOU	Thruster TST Mk 1	
G-MVMC	Solar Wings Pegasus XL-Q		G-MVOV	Thruster TST Mk 1	
G-MVMD	Powerchute Raider		G-MVOW	Thruster TST Mk 1	
G-MVME	Thruster TST Mk 1		G-MVOX	Thruster TST Mk 1	
G-MVMG	Thruster TST Mk 1		G-MVOY	Thruster TST Mk 1	
G-MVMI	Thruster TST Mk 1		G-MVPA	Mainair Gemini Flash IIA	
G-MVMJ	Thruster TST Mk 1		G-MVPB	Mainair Gemini Flash IIA	

Reg.	Type	Notes	Reg	Type	Notes
G-MVPC	Mainair Gemini Flash IIA		G-MVTF	Aerial Arts Chaser S	
G-MVPD	Mainair Gemini Flash IIA		G-MVTG	Solar Wings Pegasus XL-Q	
G-MVPE	Mainair Gemini Flash IIA		G-MVTI	Solar Wings Pegasus XL-Q	
G-MVPF	Medway Hybred 44XLR		G-MVTJ	Solar Wings Pegasus XL-Q	
G-MVPG	Medway Hybred 44XLR		G-MVTK	Solar Wings Pegasus XL-Q	
G-MVPH	Whittaker MW.6 Merlin		G-MVTL	Aerial Arts Chaser S	
G-MVPI	Mainair Gemini Flash IIA		G-MVTM	Aerial Arts Chaser S	
G-MVPJ	Rans S.5		G-MVUA	Mainair Gemini Flash IIA	
G-MVPK	CFM Shadow Srs B		G-MVUB	Thruster T.300	
G-MVPL	Medway Hybred 44XLR		G-MVUC	Medway Hybred 44XLR	
G-MVPM	Whittaker MW.6 Merlin		G-MVUD	Medway Hybred 44XLR	
G-MVPN	Whittaker MW.6 Merlin		G-MVUE	Solar Wings Pegasus XL-Q	
G-MVPO	Mainair Gemini Flash IIA		G-MVUF	Solar Wings Pegasus XL-Q	
G-MVPR	Solar Wings Pegasus XL-Q		G-MVUG	Solar Wings Pegasus XL-Q	
G-MVPS	Solar Wings Pegasus XL-Q		G-MVUH	Solar Wings Pegasus XL-Q	
G-MVPT	Solar Wings Pegasus XL-Q		G-MVUI	Solar Wings Pegasus XL-Q	
G-MVPU	Solar Wings Pegasus XL-Q		G-MVUJ	Solar Wings Pegasus XL-Q	
G-MVPV	Solar Wings Pegasus XL-Q		G-MVUK	Solar Wings Pegasus XL-Q	
G-MVPW	Solar Wings Pegasus XL-R		G-MVUL	Solar Wings Pegasus XL-Q	
G-MVPX	Solar Wings Pegasus XL-Q		G-MVUM	Solar Wings Pegasus XL-Q	
G-MVPY	Solar Wings Pegasus XL-Q		G-MVUN	Solar Wings Pegasus XL-Q	
G-MVPZ	Rans S.5		G-MVUO	AMF Chevvron 232	
G-MVRA	Mainair Gemini Flash IIA		G-MVUP	Aviasud Mistral	
G-MVRB	Mainair Gemini Flash IIA		G-MVUR	Hornet ZA	
G-MVRC	Mainair Gemini Flash IIA		G-MVUS	Aerial Arts Chaser S	
G-MVRD	Mainair Gemini Flash IIA		G-MVUT	Aerial Arts Chaser S	
G-MVRE	CFM Shadow Srs BD		G-MVUU	Hornet R-ZA	
G-MVRF	Rotec Rally 2B		G-MVVF	Medway Hybred 44XLR	
G-MVRG	Aerial Arts Chaser S		G-MVVG	Medway Hybred 44XLR	
G-MVRH	Solar Wings Pegasus XL-Q		G-MVVH	Medway Hybred 44XLR	
G-MVRI	Solar Wings Pegasus XL-Q		G-MVVI	Medway Hybred 44XLR	
G-MVRJ	Solar Wings Pegasus XL-Q		G-MVVJ	Medway Hybred 44XLR	
G-MVRK	Solar Wings Pegasus XL-Q		G-MVVK	Solar Wings Pegasus XL-R	
G-MVRL	Aerial Arts Chaser S		G-MVVM	Solar Wings Pegasus XL-R	
G-MVRM	Mainair Gemini Flash IIA		G-MVVN	Solar Wings Pegasus XL-Q	
G-MVRN	Rans S.4 Coyote		G-MVVP	Solar Wings Pegasus XL-Q	
G-MVRO	CFM Shadow Srs BD		G-MVVR	Medway Hybred 44XLR	
G-MVRP	CFM Shadow Srs BD		G-MVVS	Southdown Puma Sprint	
G-MVRR	CFM Shadow Srs BD		G-MVVT	CFM Shadow Srs BD	
G-MVRT	CFM Shadow Srs BD		G-MVVU	Aerial Arts Chaser S	
G-MVRU	Solar Wings Pegasus XL-Q		G-MVVW	Aerial Arts Chaser S	
G-MVRV	Powerchute Kestrel		G-MVVX	Powerchute Raider	
G-MVRW	Solar Wings Pegasus XL-Q		G-MVVY	Powerchute Raider	
G-MVRX	Solar Wings Pegasus XL-Q		G-MVVZ	Powerchute Raider	
G-MVRY	Medway Hybred 44XLR		G-MVWA	Powerchute Raider	
G-MVRZ	Medway Hybred 44XLR		G-MVWB	Powerchute Raider	
G-MVSA	Solar Wings Pegasus XL-Q		G-MVWD	Powerchute Raider	
G-MVSB	Solar Wings Pegasus XL-Q		G-MVWE	Powerchute Raider	
G-MVSC	Solar Wings Pegasus XL-Q		G-MVWF	Powerchute Raider	
G-MVSD	Solar Wings Pegasus XL-Q		G-MVWG	Powerchute Raider	
G-MVSE	Solar Wings Pegasus XL-Q		G-MVWH	Powerchute Raider	
G-MVSG	Aerial Arts Chaser S		G-MVWI	Powerchute Raider	
G-MVSI	Medway Hybred 44XLR		G-MVWJ	Powerchute Raider	
G-MVSJ	Aviasud Mistral 532		G-MVWK	Powerchute Raider	
G-MVSK	Aerial Arts Chaser S		G-MVWL	Powerchute Raider	
G-MVSL	Aerial Arts Chaser S		G-MVWM	Powerchute Raider	
G-MVSM	Midland Ultralights Sirocco		G-MVWN	Thruster T.300	
G-MVSN	Mainair Gemini Flash IIA		G-MVWO	Thruster T.300	
G-MVSO	Mainair Gemini Flash IIA		G-MVWP	Thruster T.300	
G-MVSP	Mainair Gemini Flash IIA		G-MVWR	Thruster T.300	
G-MVSR	Medway Hybred 44XLR		G-MVWS	Thruster T.300	
G-MVSS	Hornet RS-ZA		G-MVWU	Medway Hybred 44XLR	
G-MVST	Mainair Gemini Flash IIA		G-MVWV	Medway Hybred 44XLR	
G-MVSU	Microflight Spectrum		G-MVWW	Aviasud Mistral 532	
G-MVSV	Mainair Gemini Flash IIA		G-MVWX	Microflight Spectrum	
G-MVSW	Solar Wings Pegasus XL-Q		G-MVWZ	Aviasud Mistral	
G-MVSX	Solar Wings Pegasus XL-Q		G-MVXA	Whittaker MW.6 Merlin	
G-MVSY	Solar Wings Pegasus XL-Q		G-MVXB	Mainair Gemini Flash IIA	
G-MVSZ	Solar Wings Pegasus XL-Q		G-MVXC	Mainair Gemini Flash IIA	
G-MVTA	Solar Wings Pegasus XL-Q		G-MVXD	Medway Hybred 44XLR	
G-MVTC	Mainair Gemini Flash IIA		G-MVXE	Medway Hybred 44XLR	
G-MVTD	Whittaker MW.6 Merlin		G-MVXF	Weedhopper JC-31A	
G-MVTE	Whittaker MW.6 Merlin		G-MVXG	Aerial Arts Chaser S	

Reg.	Type	Notes	Reg	Type	Notes
G-MVXH	Microflight Spectrum		G-MWAC	Solar Wings Pegasus XL-Q	
G-MVXI	Medway Hybred 44XLR		G-MWAD	Solar Wings Pegasus XL-Q	
G-MVXJ	Medway Hybred 44XLR		G-MWAE	CFM Shadow Srs BD	
G-MVXK	Medway Hybred 44XLR		G-MWAF	Solar Wings Pegasus XL-R	
G-MVXL	Thruster TST Mk 1		G-MWAG	Solar Wings Pegasus XL-R	
G-MVXM	Medway Hybred 44XLR		G-MWAH	Hornet RS-ZA	
G-MVXN	Aviasud Mistral		G-MWAI	Solar Wings Pegasus XL-R	
G-MVXO	Aerial Arts Chaser S		G-MWAJ	Renegade Spirit UK	
G-MVXP	Aerial Arts Chaser S		G-MWAK	Solar Wings Pegasus XL-Q	
G-MVXR	Mainair Gemini Flash IIA		G-MWAL	Solar Wings Pegasus XL-Q	
G-MVXS	Mainair Gemini Flash IIA		G-MWAM	Thruster T.300	
G-MVXT	Mainair Gemini Flash IIA		G-MWAN	Thruster T.300	
G-MVXU	Aviasud Mistral		G-MWAO	Thruster T.300	
G-MVXV	Aviasud Mistral		G-MWAP	Thruster T.300	
G-MVXW	Rans S.4 Coyote		G-MWAR	Thruster T.300	
G-MVXX	AMF Chevvron 232		G-MWAS	Thruster T.300	
G-MVXY	AMF Paracat 1-24		G-MWAT	Solar Wings Pegasus XL-Q	
G-MVXZ	Minimax		G-MWAU	Mainair Gemini Flash IIA	
G-MVYA	Aerial Arts Chaser S		G-MWAV	Solar Wings Pegasus XL-R	
G-MVYB	Solar Wings Pegasus XL-Q		G-MWAW	Whittaker MW.6 Merlin	
G-MVYC	Solar Wings Pegasus XL-Q		G-MWBH	Hornet RS-ZA	
G-MVYD	Solar Wings Pegasus XL-Q		G-MWBI	Medway Hybred 44XLR	
G-MVYE	Thruster TST Mk 1		G-MWBJ	Medway Sprint	
G-MVYG	Hornet R-ZA		G-MWBK	Solar Wings Pegasus XL-Q	
G-MVYH	Hornet R-ZA		G-MWBL	Solar Wings Pegasus XL-Q	
G-MVYI	Hornet R-ZA		G-MWBM	Hornet RS-ZA	
G-MVYJ	Hornet R-ZA		G-MWBN	Hornet RS-ZA	
G-MVYK	Hornet R-ZA		G-MWBO	Rans S.4	
G-MVYM	Hornet R-ZA		G-MWBP	Hornet RS-ZA	
G-MVYN	Hornet R-ZA		G-MWBR	Hornet RS-ZA	
G-MVYO	Hornet R-ZA		G-MWBU	Hornet RS-ZA	
G-MVYP	Medway Hybred 44XLR		G-MWBV	Hornet RS-ZA	
G-MVYR	Medway Hybred 44XLR		G-MWBW	Hornet RS-ZA	
G-MVYS	Mainair Gemini Flash IIA		G-MWBX	Hornet RS-ZA	
G-MVYT	Noble Hardman Snowbird Mk IV		G-MWBY	Hornet RS-ZA	
G-MVYU	Noble Hardman Snowbird Mk IV		G-MWBZ	Hornet RS-ZA	
G-MVYV	Noble Hardman Snowbird Mk IV		G-MWCA	Hornet RS-ZA	
			G-MWCB	Solar Wings Pegasus XL-Q	
G-MVYW	Noble Hardman Snowbird Mk IV		G-MWCC	Solar Wings Pegasus XL-R	
			G-MWCE	Mainair Gemini Flash IIA	
G-MVYX	Noble Hardman Snowbird Mk IV		G-MWCF	Solar Wings Pegasus XL-R	
			G-MWCG	Microflight Spectrum	
G-MVYY	Aerial Arts Chaser S508		G-MWCH	Rans S.6	
G-MVYZ	CFM Shadow Srs BD		G-MWCI	Powerchute Kestrel	
G-MVZA	Thruster T.300		G-MWCJ	Powerchute Kestrel	
G-MVZB	Thruster T.300		G-MWCK	Powerchute Kestrel	
G-MVZC	Thruster T.300		G-MWCL	Powerchute Kestrel	
G-MVZD	Thruster T.300		G-MWCM	Powerchute Kestrel	
G-MVZE	Thruster T.300		G-MWCN	Powerchute Kestrel	
G-MVZF	Thruster T.300		G-MWCO	Powerchute Kestrel	
G-MVZG	Thruster T.300		G-MWCP	Powerchute Kestrel	
G-MVZH	Thruster T.300		G-MWCR	Southdown Puma Sprint	
G-MVZI	Thruster T.300		G-MWCS	Powerchute Kestrel	
G-MVZJ	Solar Wings Pegasus XL-Q		G-MMCT	Powerchute Kestrel	
G-MVZK	Challenger II		G-MWCU	Solar Wings Pegasus XL-R	
G-MVZL	Solar Wings Pegasus XL-Q		G-MWCV	Solar Wings Pegasus XL-Q	
G-MVZM	Aerial Arts Chaser S		G-MWCW	Mainair Gemini Flash IIA	
G-MVZN	Aerial Arts Chaser S		G-MWCX	Medway Hybred 44XLR	
G-MVZO	Medway Hybred 44XLR		G-MWCY	Medway Hybred 44XLR	
G-MVZP	Renegade Spirit UK		G-MWCZ	Medway Hybred 44XLR	
G-MVZR	Aviasud Mistral		G-MWDA	Jakeway Powered Parachute	
G-MVZS	Mainair Gemini Flash IIA				
G-MVZT	Solar Wings Pegasus XL-Q		G-MWDB	CFM Shadow Srs BD	
G-MVZU	Solar Wings Pegasus XL-Q		G-MWDC	Solar Wings Pegasus XL-R	
G-MVZV	Solar Wings Pegasus XL-Q		G-MWDD	Solar Wings Pegasus XL-Q	
G-MVZW	Hornet R-ZA		G-MWDE	Hornet RS-ZA	
G-MVZX	Renegade Spirit UK		G-MWDF	Hornet RS-ZA	
G-MVZY	Aerial Arts Chaser S		G-MWDG	Hornet RS-ZA	
G-MVZZ	AMF Chevvron 232		G-MWDH	Hornet RS-ZA	
G-MWAA	Medway Hybred 44XLR		G-MWDI	Hornet RS-ZA	
G-MWAB	Mainair Gemini Flash IIA		G-MWDJ	Mainair Gemini Flash IIA	
			G-MWDK	Solar Wings Pegasus XL-R	
			G-MWDL	Solar Wings Pegasus XL-R	

Reg.	Type	Notes	Reg	Type	Notes
G-MWDM	Renegade Spirit UK		G-MWGU	Powerchute Kestrel	
G-MWDN	CFM Shadow Srs BD		G-MWGV	Powerchute Kestrel	
G-MWDO	Spencer Cub		G-MWGW	Powerchute Kestrel	
G-MWDP	Thruster TST Mk 1		G-MWGY	Powerchute Kestrel	
G-MWDS	Thruster T.300		G-MWHC	Solar Wings Pegasus XL-Q	
G-MWDZ	Eipper Quicksilver MXL II		G-MWHD	Microflight Spectrum	
G-MWEA	Mosler Motors N.3 Pup		G-MWHE	Microflight Spectrum	
G-MWEE	Solar Wings Pegasus XL-Q		G-MWHF	Solar Wings Pegasus XL-Q	
G-MWEF	Solar Wings Pegasus XL-Q		G-MWHG	Solar Wings Pegasus XL-Q	
G-MWEG	Solar Wings Pegasus XL-Q		G-MWHH	Team Minimax	
G-MWEH	Solar Wings Pegasus XL-Q		G-MWHI	Mainair Gemini Flash IIA	
G-MWEI	Mainair Gemini Flash IIA		G-MWHJ	Solar Wings Pegasus XL-Q	
G-MWEK	Whittaker MW.5 Sorcerer		G-MWHK	Renegade Spirit UK	
G-MWEL	Mainair Gemini Flash IIA		G-MWHL	Solar Wings Pegasus XL-Q	
G-MWEM	Medway Hybred 44XLR		G-MWHM	Whittaker MW.6 Merlin	
G-MWEN	CFM Shadow Srs BD		G-MWHO	Mainair Gemini Flash IIA	
G-MWEO	Whittaker MW.5 Sorcerer		G-MWHP	Rans S.6	
G-MWEP	Rans S.4		G-MWHR	Mainair Gemini Flash IIA	
G-MWER	Solar Wings Pegasus XL-Q		G-MWHS	AMF Chevvron 232	
G-MWES	Rans S.4		G-MWHT	Solar Wings Pegasus Quasar	
G-MWET	Hornet RS-ZA				
G-MWEU	Hornet RS-ZA		G-MWHU	Solar Wings Pegasus Quasar	
G-MWEV	Hornet RS-ZA				
G-MWEY	Hornet RS-ZA		G-MWHV	Solar Wings Pegasus Quasar	
G-MWEZ	CFM Shadow Srs CD				
G-MWFA	Solar Wings Pegasus XL-R		G-MWHW	Solar Wings Pegasus XL-Q	
G-MWFB	CFM Shadow Srs BD		G-MWHX	Solar Wings Pegasus XL-Q	
G-MWFD	Team Minimax		G-MWHY	Mainair Gemini Flash IIA	
G-MWFE	Robin 330/Lightning 195		G-MWHZ	Trion J-1	
G-MWFF	Rans S.4		G-MWIA	Mainair Gemini Flash IIA	
G-MWFG	Powerchute Kestrel		G-MWIB	Aviasud Mistral	
G-MWFH	Powerchute Kestrel		G-MWIC	Whittaker MW.5 Sorcerer	
G-MWFI	Powerchute Kestrel		G-MWID	Solar Wings Pegasus XL-Q	
G-MWFJ	Powerchute Kestrel		G-MWIE	Rans S.6	
G-MWFK	Powerchute Kestrel		G-MWIG	Mainair Gemini Flash IIA	
G-MWFL	Powerchute Kestrel		G-MWIH	Mainair Gemini Flash IIA	
G-MWFN	Powerchute Kestrel		G-MWII	Medway Hybred 44XLR	
G-MWFO	Solar Wings Pegasus XL-R		G-MWIJ	Medway Hybred 44XLR	
G-MWFP	Solar Wings Pegasus XL-R		G-MWIK	Medway Hybred 44XLR	
G-MWFS	Solar Wings Pegasus XL-Q		G-MWIL	Medway Hybred 44XLR	
G-MWFT	MBA Tiger Cub 440		G-MWIM	Solar Wings Pegasus Quasar	
G-MWFU	Quad City Challenger II UK				
			G-MWIN	Mainair Gemini Flash IIA	
G-MWFV	Quad City Challenger II UK		G-MWIO	Rans S.4	
G-MWFW	Rans S.4		G-MWIP	Whittaker MW.6 Merlin	
G-MWFX	Quad City Challenger II UK		G-MWIR	Solar Wings Pegasus XL-Q	
			G-MWIS	Solar Wings Pegasus XL-Q	
G-MWFY	Quad City Challenger II UK		G-MWIT	Solar Wings Pegasus XL-Q	
			G-MWIU	Solar Wings Pegasus XL-Q	
G-MWFZ	Quad City Challenger II UK		G-MWIV	Mainair Gemini Flash IIA	
			G-MWIW	Solar Wings Pegasus Quasar	
G-MWGA	Rans S.5				
G-MWGB	Medway Hybred 44XLR		G-MWIX	Solar Wings Pegasus Quasar	
G-MWGC	Medway Hybred 44XLR				
G-MWGD	Medway Hybred 44XLR		G-MWIY	Solar Wings Pegasus Quasar	
G-MWGE	Medway Hybred 44XLR				
G-MWGF	Renegade Spirit UK		G-MWIZ	CFM Shadow Srs BD	
G-MWGG	Mainair Gemini Flash IIA		G-MWJB	—	
G-MWGH	—		G-MWJC	Solar Wings Pegasus Quasar	
G-MWGI	Whittaker MW.5 (K) Sorcerer		G-MWJD	Solar Wings Pegasus Quasar	
G-MWGJ	Whittaker MW.5 (K) Sorcerer		G-MWJF	CFM Shadow Srs BD	
G-MWGK	Whittaker MW.5 (K) Sorcerer		G-MWJG	Solar Wings Pegasus XL-R	
			G-MWJH	Solar Wings Pegasus Quasar	
G-MWGL	Solar Wings Pegasus XL-Q				
G-MWGM	Solar Wings Pegasus XL-Q		G-MWJI	Solar Wings Pegasus Quasar	
G-MWGN	Rans S.4				
G-MWGO	Aerial Arts Chaser 110SX		G-MWJJ	Solar Wings Pegasus Quasar	
G-MWGP	Renegade Spirit UK				
G-MWGR	Solar Wings Pegasus XL-Q		G-MWJK	Solar Wings Pegasus Quasar	
G-MWGT	Powerchute Kestrel				

Reg.	Type	Notes	Reg	Type	Notes
G-MWJL	AMF Chevvron 232		G-MWMP	Solar Wings Pegasus XL-Q	
G-MWJM	AMF Chevvron 232		G-MWMR	Solar Wings Pegasus XL-R	
G-MWJN	Solar Wings Pegasus XL-Q		G-MWMS	Mainair Gemini Flash	
G-MWJO	Solar Wings Pegasus XL-Q		G-MWMT	Mainair Gemini Flash IIA	
G-MWJP	Medway Hybred 44XLR		G-MWMU	CFM Shadow Srs CD	
G-MWJR	Medway Hybred 44XLR		G-MWMV	Solar Wings Pegasus XL-R	
G-MWJS	Solar Wings Pegasus Quasar		G-MWMW	Renegade Spirit UK	
			G-MWMX	Mainair Gemini Flash IIA	
G-MWJT	Solar Wings Pegasus Quasar		G-MWMY	Mainair Gemini Flash IIA	
			G-MWMZ	Solar Wings Pegasus XL-Q	
G-MWJU	Solar Wings Pegasus Quasar		G-MWNA	Solar Wings Pegasus XL-Q	
			G-MWNB	Solar Wings Pegasus XL-Q	
G-MWJV	Solar Wings Pegasus Quasar		G-MWNC	Solar Wings Pegasus XL-Q	
			G-MWND	Tiger Cub Developments RL.5A	
G-MWJW	Whittaker MW.5 Sorcerer				
G-MWJX	Medway Puma Sprint		G-MWNE	Mainair Gemini Flash IIA	
G-MWJY	Mainair Gemini Flash IIA		G-MWNF	Renegade Spirit UK	
G-MWJZ	CFM Shadow Srs CD		G-MWNG	Solar Wings Pegasus XL-Q	
G-MWKA	Renegade Spirit UK		G-MWNH	Powerchute Mk III	
G-MWKE	Hornet R-ZA		G-MWNI	—	
G-MWKO	Solar Wings Pegasus XL-Q		G-MWNJ	—	
G-MWKP	Solar Wings Pegasus XL-Q		G-MWNK	Solar Wings Pegasus Quasar	
G-MWKW	Microflight Spectrum				
G-MWKX	Microflight Spectrum		G-MWNL	Solar Wings Pegasus Quasar	
G-MWKY	Solar Wings Pegasus XL-Q				
G-MWKZ	Solar Wings Pegasus XL-Q		G-MWNM	Solar Wings Pegasus Quasar	
G-MWLA	Rans S.4				
G-MWLB	Medway Hybred 44XLR		G-MWNN	Solar Wings Pegasus Quasar	
G-MWLC	Medway Hybred 44XLR				
G-MWLD	CFM Shadow Srs BD		G-MWNO	AMF Chevvron 232	
G-MWLE	Solar Wings Pegasus XL-R		G-MWNP	AMF Chevvron 232	
G-MWLF	Solar Wings Pegasus XL-R		G-MWNR	Renegade Spirit UK	
G-MWLG	Solar Wings Pegasus XL-R		G-MWNS	Mainair Gemini Flash IIA	
G-MWLH	Solar Wings Pegasus XL-R		G-MWNT	Mainair Gemini Flash IIA	
G-MWLI	Solar Wings Pegasus Quasar		G-MWNU	Mainair Gemini Flash IIA	
			G-MWNV	Powerchute Kestrel	
G-MWLJ	Solar Wings Pegasus Quasar		G-MWNW	Powerchute Kestrel	
			G-MWNX	Powerchute Kestrel	
G-MWLK	Solar Wings Pegasus Quasar		G-MWNY	Powerchute Kestrel	
			G-MWNZ	Powerchute Kestrel	
G-MWLL	Solar Wings Pegasus XL-Q		G-MWOA	Powerchute Kestrel	
G-MWLM	Solar Wings Pegasus XL-Q		G-MWOB	Powerchute Kestrel	
G-MWLN	Whittaker MW.6-S Fatboy Flyer		G-MWOC	Powerchute Kestrel	
			G-MWOD	Powerchute Kestrel	
G-MWLO	Whittaker MW.6 Merlin		G-MWOE	Powerchute Kestrel	
G-MWLP	Mainair Gemini Flash IIA		G-MWOF	Microflight Spectrum	
G-MWLR	Mainair Gemini Flash IIA		G-MWOG	—	
G-MWLS	Medway Hybred 44XLR		G-MWOH	Solar Wings Pegasus XL-R	
G-MWLT	Mainair Gemini Flash IIA		G-MWOI	Solar Wings Pegasus XL-R	
G-MWLU	Solar Wings Pegasus XL-R		G-MWOJ	Mainair Gemini Flash IIA	
G-MWLW	Team Minimax		G-MWOK	Mainair Gemini Flash IIA	
G-MWLX	Mainair Gemini Flash IIA		G-MWOL	Mainair Gemini Flash IIA	
G-MWLY	Rans S.4		G-MWOM	Solar Wings Pegasus Qasar TC	
G-MWLZ	Rans S.4				
G-MWMA	Powerchute Kestrel		G-MWON	CFM Shadow Srs CD	
G-MWMB	Powerchute Kestrel		G-MWOO	Renegade Spirit UK	
G-MWMC	Powerchute Kestrel		G-MWOP	Solar Wings Pegasus Quasar	
G-MWMD	Powerchute Kestrel				
G-MWME	Powerchute Kestrel		G-MWOR	Solar Wings Pegasus XL-Q	
G-MWMF	Powerchute Kestrel		G-MWOS	Cosmos Chronos	
G-MWMG	Powerchute Kestrel		G-MWOT	Icarus Covert Insertion & Recovery Vehicle	
G-MWMH	Powerchute Kestrel				
G-MWMI	Solar Wings Pegasus Quasar		G-MWOU	Medway Hybred 44XLR	
			G-MWOV	Whittaker MW.6 Merlin	
G-MWMJ	Solar Wings Pegasus Quasar		G-MWOW	CFM Shadow Srs B	
			G-MWOX	Solar Wings Pegasus XL-Q	
G-MWMK	Solar Wings Pegasus Quasar		G-MWOY	Solar Wings Pegasus XL-Q	
			G-MWPA	Mainair Gemini Flash IIA	
G-MWML	Solar Wings Pegasus Quasar		G-MWPB	Mainair Gemini Flash IIA	
			G-MWPC	Mainair Gemini Flash IIA	
G-MWMM	Mainair Gemini Flash IIA		G-MWPD	Mainair Gemini Flash IIA	
G-MWMN	Solar Wings Pegasus XL-Q		G-MWPE	Solar Wings Pegasus XL-Q	
G-MWMO	Solar Wings Pegasus XL-Q		G-MWPF	Mainair Gemini Flash IIA	

Reg.	Type	Notes	Reg	Type	Notes
G-MWPG	Microflight Spectrum		G-MWTB	Solar Wings Pegasus XL-Q	
G-MWPH	Microflight Spectrum		G-MWTC	Solar Wings Pegasus XL-Q	
G-MWPI	Microflight Spectrum		G-MWTD	Spectrum	
G-MWPJ	Solar Wings Pegasus XL-Q		G-MWTE	Spectrum	
G-MWPK	Solar Wings Pegasus XL-Q		G-MWTF	Mainair Gemini	
G-MWPL	MBA Tiger Cub 440		G-MWTG	Mainair Gemini Flash IIA	
G-MWPM	Medway Flaven		G-MWTH	Mainair Gemini Flash IIA	
G-MWPN	CFM Shadow Srs CD		G-MWTI	Solar Wings Pegasus XL-Q	
G-MWPO	Mainair Gemini Flash IIA		G-MWTJ	CFM Shadow Srs CD	
G-MWPP	CFM Streak Shadow (G-BTEM)		G-MWTK	Solar Wings Pegasus XL-R	
			G-MWTL	Solar Wings Pegasus XL-R	
G-MWPR	Whittaker MW6 Merlin		G-MWTM	Solar Wings Pegasus XL-R	
G-MWPS	Renegade Spirit UK		G-MWTN	CFM Shadow Srs CD	
G-MWPT	Hunt Avon Trike		G-MWTO	Mainair Gemini Flash IIA	
G-MWPU	Solar Wings Pegasus Quasar TC		G-MWTP	CFM Shadow Srs CD	
			G-MWTR	Mainair Gemini Flash IIA	
G-MWPX	Solar Wings Pegasus XL-R		G-MWTS	Whittaker MW.6-S Fatboy Flyer	
G-MWPZ	Renegade Spirit UK				
G-MWRA	Mainair Gemini Flash IIA		G-MWTT	Rans S.6-ESD Coyote II	
G-MWRB	Mainair Gemini Flash IIA		G-MWTU	Solar Wings Pegasus XL-R	
G-MWRC	Mainair Gemini Flash IIA		G-MWTV	Solar Wings Pegasus XL-R	
G-MWRD	Mainair Gemini Flash IIA		G-MWTW	Whittaker MW.6 Merlin	
G-MWRE	Mainair Gemini Flash IIA		G-MWTX	Medway Hybred 44XLR	
G-MWRF	Mainair Gemini Flash IIA		G-MWTY	Mainair Gemini Flash IIA	
G-MWRG	Mainair Gemini Flash IIA		G-MWTZ	Mainair Gemini Flash IIA	
G-MWRH	Mainair Gemini Flash IIA		G-MWUA	CFM Shadow Srs CD	
G-MWRI	Mainair Gemini Flash IIA		G-MWUB	Solar Wings Pegasus XL-R	
G-MWRJ	Mainair Gemini Flash IIA		G-MWUC	Solar Wings Pegasus XL-R	
G-MWRK	Rans S.6		G-MWUD	Solar Wings Pegasus XL-R	
G-MWRL	CFM Shadow Srs CD		G-MWUE	Solar Wings Pegasus XL-R	
G-MWRM	Medway Hybred 44XLR		G-MWUF	Solar Wings Pegasus XL-R	
G-MWRN	Solar Wings Pegasus XL-R		G-MWUG	Solar Wings Pegasus XL-R	
G-MWRO	Solar Wings Pegasus XL-R		G-MWUH	Renegade Spirit UK	
G-MWRP	Solar Wings Pegasus XL-R		G-MWUI	AMF Chevvron 232C	
G-MWRR	Mainair Gemini Flash IIA		G-MMUJ	Medway Hybred 44XLR	
G-MWRS	Ultravia Super Pelican		G-MWUK	Rans S.6-ESD Coyote II	
G-MWRT	Solar Wings Pegasus XL-R		G-MWUL	Rans S.6-ESD Coyote II	
G-MWRU	Solar Wings Pegasus XL-R		G-MWUM	Rans S.6-ESD Coyote II	
G-MWRV	Solar Wings Pegasus XL-R		G-MWUN	Rans S.6-ESD Coyote II	
G-MWRW	Solar Wings Pegasus XL-Q		G-MWVO	Solar Wings Pegasus XL-Q	
G-MWRX	Solar Wings Pegasus XL-Q		G-MWUP	Solar Wings Pegasus XL-R	
G-MWRY	CFM Shadow Srs CD		G-MWUR	Solar Wings Pegasus XL-R	
G-MWRZ	AMF Chevvron 232		G-MWUS	Solar Wings Pegasus XL-R	
G-MWSA	Team Minimax		G-MWUT	Solar Wings Pegasus XL-R	
G-MWSB	Mainair Gemini Flash IIA		G-MWUU	Solar Wings Pegasus XL-R	
G-MWSC	Rans S.6-ESD Coyote II		G-MWUV	Solar Wings Pegasus XL-R	
G-MWSD	Solar Wings Pegasus XL-Q		G-MWUW	Solar Wings Pegasus XL-Q	
G-MWSE	Solar Wings Pegasus XL-R		G-MWUX	Solar Wings Pegasus XL-Q	
G-MWSF	Solar Wings Pegasus XL-R		G-MWUY	Solar Wings Pegasus XL-Q	
G-MWSG	Solar Wings Pegasus XL-R		G-MWUZ	Solar Wings Pegasus XL-Q	
G-MWSH	Solar Wings Pegasus Quasar TC		G-MWVA	Solar Wings Pegasus XL-Q	
			G-MWVB	Solar Wings Pegasus XL-R	
G-MWSI	Solar Wings Pegasus Quasar TC		G-MWVC	Solar Wings Pegasus XL-R	
			G-MWVE	Solar Wings Pegasus XL-R	
G-MWSJ	Solar Wings Pegasus XL-Q		G-MWVF	Solar Wings Pegasus XL-R	
G-MWSK	Solar Wings Pegasus XL-Q		G-MWVG	CFM Shadow Srs CD	
G-MWSL	Mainair Gemini Flash IIA		G-MWVH	CFM Shadow Srs CD	
G-MWSM	Mainair Gemini Flash IIA		G-MWVI	Whittaker MW.6 Merlin	
G-MWSN	Solar Wings Pegasus Quasar TC		G-MWVJ	Mainair Mercury	
			G-MWVK	Mainair Mercury	
G-MWSO	Solar Wings Pegasus XL-R		G-MWVL	Rans S.6-ESD Coyote II	
G-MWSP	Solar Wings Pegasus XL-R		G-MWVM	Solar Wings Pegasus Quasar II	
G-MWSR	Solar Wings Pegasus XL-R				
G-MWSS	Medway Hybred 44XLR		G-MWVN	Mainair Gemini Flash IIA	
G-MWST	Medway Hybred 44XLR		G-MWVO	Mainair Gemini Flash IIA	
G-MWSU	Medway Hybred 44XLR		G-MWVP	Renegade Spirit UK	
G-MWSV	Solar Wings Pegasus Quasar TC		G-MWVR	Mainair Gemini Flash IIA	
			G-MWVS	Mainair Gemini Flash IIA	
G-MWSW	Whittaker MW.6 Merlin		G-MWVT	Mainair Gemini Flash IIA	
G-MWSX	Whittaker MW.5 Sorcerer		G-MWVU	Medway Hybred 44XLR	
G-MWSY	Whittaker MW.5 Sorcerer		G-MWVV	Solar Wings Pegasus XL-Q	
G-MWSZ	CFM Shadow Srs CD		G-MWVW	Mainair Gemini Flash IIA	
G-MWTA	Solar Wings Pegasus XL-Q		G-MWVX	Quad City Challenger II UK	

Reg.	Type	Notes	Reg	Type	Notes
G-MWVY	Mainair Gemini Flash IIA		G-MWYO	CGS Hawk II Arrow	
G-MWVZ	Mainair Gemini Flash IIA		G-MWYP	CGS Hawk I Arrow	
G-MWWA	Solar Wings Pegasus Quasar II		G-MWYR	CGS Hawk AG Arrow	
			G-MWYS	—	
G-MWWB	Mainair Gemini Flash IIA		G-MWYT	—	
G-MWWC	Mainair Gemini Flash IIA		G-MWYU	Solar Wings Pegasus XL-Q	
G-MWWD	Mainair Gemini Flash IIA		G-MWYZ	Solar Wings Pegasus XL-Q	
G-MWWE	Team Minimax				
G-MWWF	Kolb Twinstar Mk 3		G-MYAA	CFM Shadow Srs CD	
G-MWWG	Solar Wings Pegasus XL-Q		G-MYCC	Renegade Spirit UK	
G-MWWH	Solar Wings Pegasus XL-Q		G-MYCD	CFM Shadow Srs CD	
G-MWWI	Mainair Gemini Flash IIA		G-MYDS	Quad City Challenger II UK	
G-MWWJ	Mainair Gemini Flash IIA		G-MYGS	Whittaker MW.5 (K) Sorcerer	
G-MWWK	Mainair Gemini Flash IIA				
G-MWWL	Rans S.6-ESD Coyote II		G-MYJE	CFM Shadow Srs CD	
G-MWWM	Kolb Twinstar Mk 2		G-MYJP	Renegade Spirit UK	
G-MWWN	Mainair Gemini Flash IIA		G-MYKE	CFM Shadow Srs BD	
G-MWWO	Solar Wings Pegasus XL-R		G-MYNA	CFM Shadow Srs BD	
G-MWWP	Rans S.4		G-MYND	Mainair Gemini Flash IIA	
G-MWWR	Spectrum		G-MYPG	Solar Wings Pegasus XL-Q	
G-MWWS	Thruster T.300		G-MYRK	Renegade Spirit UK	
G-MWWT	Thruster Super T.300		G-MYST	Aviasud Mistral	
G-MWWU	Air Creation Fun 18 GTBI		G-MYTH	CFM Shadow Srs BD	
G-MWWV	Solar Wings Pegasus XL-Q		G-MZDP	AMF Chevvron 232	
G-MWWW	Whittaker MW.6-S Fatboy Flyer		G-MZIP	Renegade Spirit UK	
			G-MZOO	Renegade Spirit UK	
G-MWWX	Spectrum		G-MZRS	CFM Shadow Srs CD	
G-MWWY	Spectrum		G-MZZZ	Whitaker MW.6-S Fatboy Flyer	
G-MWWZ	Cyclone Chaser S				
G-MWXA	Mainair Gemini Flash IIA				
G-MWXB	Mainair Gemini Flash IIA				
G-MWXC	Mainair Gemini Flash IIA				
G-MWXD	Mainair Gemini Flash IIA				
G-MWXE	Flexiform Skytrike				
G-MWXF	Mainair Mercury				
G-MWXG	Solar Wings Pegasus Quasar IITC				
G-MWXH	Solar Wings Pegasus Quasar IITC				
G-MWXI	Solar Wings Pegasus Quasar IITC				
G-MWXJ	Mainair Mercury				
G-MWXK	Mainair Mercury				
G-MWXL	Mainair Gemini Flash IIA				
G-MWXM	Solar Wings Pegasus XL-R				
G-MWXN	Mainair Gemini Flash IIA				
G-MWXO	Mainair Gemini Flash IIA				
G-MWXP	Solar Wings Pegasus XL-Q				
G-MWXR	Solar Wings Pegasus XL-Q				
G-MWXS	Mainair Gemini Flash IIA				
G-MWXT	AMF Chevvron 232C				
G-MWXU	Mainair Gemini Flash IIA				
G-MWXV	Mainair Gemini Flash IIA				
G-MWXW	Cyclone Chaser S				
G-MWXX	Cyclone Chaser S 447				
G-MWXY	Cyclone Chaser S 447				
G-MWXZ	Cyclone Chaser S 508				
G-MWYA	Mainair Gemini Flash IIA				
G-MWYB	Solar Wings Pegasus XL-Q				
G-MWYC	Solar Wings Pegasus XL-Q				
G-MWYD	CFM Shadow Srs C				
G-MWYE	Rans S.6-ESD Coyote II				
G-MWYF	Rans S.6				
G-MWYG	Mainair Gemini Flash IIA				
G-MWYH	Mainair Gemini Flash IIA				
G-MWYI	Solar Wings Pegasus Quasar II				
G-MWYJ	Solar Wings Pegasus Quasar IITC				
G-MWYK	Mainair Gemini Flash IIA				
G-MWYL	Mainair Gemini Flash IIA				
G-MWYM	Cyclone Chaser S 1000				
G-MWYN	Rans S.6-ESD Coyote II				

Military to Civil Cross-Reference

Serial carried	Civil identity	Serial carried	Civil identity
2+1 (Luftwaffe)	G-SYFW	236800 (A-44 USAAF)	G-BHPK
8 (Luftwaffe)	G-WULF	314887 (USAAF)	G-AJPI
23 (USAAC)	N49272	315509 (USAAF)	G-BHUB
26 (US)	G-BAVO	329417 (USAAF)	G-BDHK
45 (Aeronavale)	G-BHFG	329471 (F-44 USAAF)	G-BGXA
75	G-AFDX	329601 (D-44 USAAF)	G-AXHR
77	G-BTCU	329854 (R-44 USAAF)	G-BMKC
118 (USAAC)	G-BSDS	329934 (B-72 USAAF)	G-BCPH
120 (Fr AF)	G-AZGC	330485 (C-44 USAAF)	G-AJES
152/17	G-ATJM	343251 (USAAC)	G-NZSS
157 (Fr AF)	G-AVEB	413048 (E-39 USAAF)	G-BCXJ
168	G-BFDE	414151 (HO-M USAAF)	NL314BG
177 (Irish AC)	G-BLIW	426183 (IY USAAC)	G-BRIY
180 (USN)	G-BRSK	430823	N1042B
192 (Fr AF)	G-BKPT	43-1952 (USAAC)	G-BRPR
208 (USN)	N75664	454467 (J-44 USAAF)	G-BILI
320 (USAAC)	G-BPMD	454537 (J-04 USAAF)	G-BFDL
361 (USN)	G-ELAN	461748	G-BHDK
379 (USAAC)	G-ILLE	463221 (G4-5 USAAF)	G-BTCD
385 (RCAF)	G-BGPB	472216 (HO-L USAAF)	G-BIXL
422-15	G-AVJO	472773 (AJ-C USAF)	G-SUSY
425/17	G-BEFR	479766 (D-63 USAAF)	G-BKHG
441 (USN)	G-BTFG	474004 (VF-R USAF)	N51RR
442 (USN)	G-BPTB	480015 (USAAF)	G-AKIB
542	G-BPOB	480133 (B-44 USAAF)	G-BDCD
671 (RCAF)	G-BNZC	480321 (H-44 USAAF)	G-FRAN
855 (USAAC)	N56421	480480 (E-44 USAAF)	G-BECN
897 (USN)	G-BJEV	483009 (USAF)	G-BPSE
1164 (USAAC)	G-BKGL	41-33275 (USAAC CE)	G-BICE
1420 (Polish AF)	G-BMZF	42-78044 (USAAC)	G-BRXL
2009	G-BEFR	44-30861	N9089Z
2345	G-ATVP	44-79609 (PR USAAF)	G-BHXY
2807 (VE-103 USN)	G-BHTH	44-80594 (USAAF)	G-BEDJ
3066	G-AETA	44-83184	G-RGUS
3398 (FrAF)	G-BFYO	45-49192	N47DD
3460	G-BMFG	511371 (USAAF VF-S)	NL1051S
4253/18	G-BFPL	542447	G-SCUB
5492	G-PENY	542457	G-LION
5894	G-BFVH	542474 (R-184)	G-PCUB
7198/18	G-AANJ	51-15227 (USN)	G-BKRA
7797 (USAAF)	G-BFAF	51-15673 (USAAF)	G-CUBI
8449M	G-ASWJ	54-21261 (USAF)	N33VC
14863 (USAAF)	G-BGOR	607327 (09-L USAAF)	G-ARAO
16693 (693 RCAF)	G-BLPG	A16-199 (SF-R RAAF)	G-BEOX
18393 (C.A.F.)	G-BCYK	A8226	G-BIDW
20385 (385 RCAF)	G-BGPB	B1807	G-EAVX
24485 (DF-A USAAF)	G-BEDF	B4863	G-BLXT
31923 (USAAC)	G-BRHP	B6291	G-ASOP
34037 (USAAF)	N9115Z	B6401	G-AWYY
53319 (USN)	G-BTDP	B7270	G-BFCZ
54137 (USN 69)	G-CTKL	C1904 (Z)	G-PFAP
56321 (U-AB RNorAF)	G-BKPY	C4994	G-BLWM
88297	G-FGID	D5397/17	G-BFXL
88349 (USN)	N55JP	D7889	G-AANM
93542 (LTA-542 USAF)	G-BRLV	D8096 (D)	G-AEPH
115042 (TA-042 USAF)	G-BGHU	E-15 (RNethAF)	G-BIYU
115302 (TP USAAF)	G-BJTP	E3B-369 (781-32 Span AF)	G-BPDM
151632 (USAAF)	NL9494Z	E449	G-EBJE
18-2001 (USAAF)	G-BIZV	EM-01 (Spanish AF)	G-AAOR
121714	NX700HL	F141 (G)	G-SEVA
133722	NX1337A	F235 (B)	G-BMDB
224211 (M2-Z USAF)	G-BPMP	F904	G-EBIA
226671 (MX-X USAAF)	NX47DD	F938	G-EBIC
231983 (USAAF)	F-BDRS	F939 (6)	G-EBIB

Serial carried	Civil identity	Serial carried	Civil identity
F943	G-BIHF	T9707	G-AKKR
F4516	G-ACAA	T9738	G-AKAT
F5447 (N)	G-BKER	U-80 (Swiss AF)	G-BUKK
F5459 (Y)	G-INNY	U-0247 (Class B identity)	G-AGOY
F8010	G-BDWJ	U-142 (Swiss AF)	G-BONE
F8614	G-AWAU	V1075	G-AKPF
G-48-1 (Class B)	G-ALSX	V3388	G-AHTW
H2311	G-ABAA	V9281 (RU-M)	G-BCWL
H5199	G-ADEV	V9300	G-LIZY
— (I-492 USAAC)	G-BPUD	V9441 (AR-A)	G-AZWT
J-1605 (Swiss AF)	G-BLID	W5856	G-BMGC
J-1758 (Swiss AF)	G-BLSD	Z2033	G-ASTL
J9941 (57)	G-ABMR	Z7015	G-BKTH
— (K-33 USAAF)	G-BJLH	Z7197	G-AKZN
K1786	G-AFTA	Z7381 (XR-T)	G-HURI
K2050	G-ASCM	AP507 (KX-P)	G-ACWP
K2059	G-PFAR	AR213 (PR-D)	G-AIST
K2567	G-MOTH	AR501 (NN-D)	G-AWII
K2568	G-APMM	BB807	G-ADWO
K2572	G-AOZH	BM597 (PR-O)	G-MKVB
K3215	G-AHSA	BS676 (K-U)	G-KUKU
K3731	G-RODI	BW853	G-BRKE
K4235	G-AHMJ	DE208	G-AGYU
K5054	G-BRDV	DE363	G-ANFC
K5414 (XV)	G-AENP	DE623	G-ANFI
L2301	G-AIZG	DE992	G-AXXV
N1854	G-AIBE	DF128 (RCO-U)	G-AOJJ
N2308 (HP-B)	G-AMRK	DF155	G-ANFV
N4877 (VX-F)	G-AMDA	DF198	G-BBRB
N5180	G-EBKY	DG590	G-ADMW
N5182	G-APUP	DR613	G-AFJB
N5195	G-ABOX	EM720	G-AXAN
N6290	G-BOCK	EM903	G-APBI
N6452	G-BIAU	EN224	G-FXII
N6466	G-ANKZ	EX280	G-TEAC
N6532	G-ANTS	EZ259	G-BMJW
N6847	G-APAL	FE992	G-BDAM
N6848	G-BALX	FH153	G-BBHK
N6965	G-AJTW	FR870	NL1009N
N6985	G-AHMN	FS728	G-BAFM
N9191	G-ALND	FT239	G-BIWX
N9238	G-ANEL	FT391	G-AZBN
N9389	G-ANJA	FX301 (FD-NQ)	G-JUDI
N9510	G-AOEL	HB275	N5063N
P5865 (LE-W)	G-BKCK	HB751	G-BCBL
P6382	G-AJRS	HM580	G-ACUU
R-163 (RNethAF)	G-BIRH	JV928 (Y)	G-BLSC
R-167 (RNethAF)	G-LION	KB889	G-LANC
R1914	G-AHUJ	KB976 (LQ-K)	G-BCOH
R4907	G-ANCS	KG874 (YS-L)	G-DAKS
R4959	G-ARAZ	KL161	N88972
R5086	G-APIH	KZ321	G-HURY
S1287	G-BEYB	LB294	G-AHWJ
S1579	G-BBVO	LB312	G-AHXE
T5424	G-AJOA	LB375	G-AHGW
T5493	G-ANEF	LF858	G-BLUZ
T5672	G-ALRI	LZ766	G-ALCK
T5854	G-ANKK	MD497	G-ANLW
T5879	G-AXBW	MH434	G-ASJV
T6099	G-AOGR	MJ627	G-BMSB
T6313	G-AHVU	MJ730 (GN-F)	G-HFIX
T6645	G-AIIZ	ML407 (OU-V)	G-LFIX
T6818	G-ANKT	ML417 (2I-T)	G-BJSG
T6991	G-ANOR	MP425	G-AITB
T7281	G-ARTL	MT438	G-AREI
T7404	G-ANMV	MT719 (YB-J)	G-VIII
T7909	G-ANON	MV154	G-BKMI
T7997	G-AOBH	MV363	G-SPIT

Serial carried	Civil identity	Serial carried	Civil identity
MV370 (AV-L)	G-FXIV	WB531	G-BLRN
NF875 (603/CH)	G-AGTM	WB585 (RCU-X)	G-AOSY
NH238 (D-A)	G-MKIX	WB588 (D)	G-AOTD
NJ695	G-AJXV	WB660	G-ARMB
NJ703	G-AKPI	WB702	G-AOFE
NJ719	G-ANFU	WB703	G-ARMC
NM181	G-AZGZ	WB763	G-BBMR
NP181	G-AOAR	WD286 (J)	G-BBND
NP184	G-ANYP	WD292	G-BCRX
NP303	G-ANZJ	WD305	G-ARGG
NX611	G-ASXX	WD363 (5)	G-BCIH
NZ5628	N240CA	WD379 (K)	G-APLO
PL965	G-MKVI	WD388	G-BDIC
PL983	G-PRXI	WD413	G-BFIR
PT462	G-CTIX	WE402	G-VIDI
PV202 (VZ-M)	G-TRIX	WE569	G-ASAJ
RG333	G-AIEK	WF877	G-BPOA
RG333	G-AKEZ	WG307	G-BCYJ
RH377	G-ALAH	WG316	G-BCAH
RL962	G-AHED	WG348	G-BBMV
RM221	G-ANXR	WG350	G-BPAL
RM689 (MN-E)	G-ALGT	WG422 (16)	G-BFAX
RN218 (N)	G-BBJI	WG472	G-AOTY
RR299 (HT-E)	G-ASKH	WG719	G-BRMA
RT486	G-AJGJ	WH589 (115)	G-BTTA
RT520	G-ALYB	WJ237 (113/O)	G-BLTG
RW382 (NG-C)	G-XVIA	WJ358	G-ARYD
RW386	G-BXVI	WJ945	G-BEDV
SM832	G-WWII	WK522	G-BCOU
SM969	G-BRAF	WK611	G-ARWB
SX336	G-BRMG	WK622	G-BCZH
TA634 (8K-K)	G-AWJV	WK628	G-BBMW
TA719	G-ASKC	WL626	G-BHDD
TD248	G-OXVI	WM167	G-LOSM
TE184	G-MXVI	WP321 (750/CU)	G-BRFC
TE566 (DU-A)	G-BLCK	WP788	G-BCHL
TJ569	G-AKOW	WP790	G-BBNC
TJ672	G-ANIJ	WP800 (2)	G-BCXN
TS423	G-DAKS	WP808	G-BDEU
TS798	G-AGNV	WP835	G-BDCB
TW384	G-ANHZ	WP843	G-BDBP
TW439	G-ANRP	WP857 (24)	G-BDRJ
TW467 (ROD-F)	G-ANIE	WP903	G-BCGC
TW511	G-APAF	WP971	G-ATHD
TW517	G-BDFX	WP977	G-BHRD
TW536 (TS-V)	G-BNGE	WR410 (N)	G-BLKA
TW591	G-ARIH	WT933	G-ALSW
TW641	G-ATDN	WV198	G-BJWY
TX183	G-BSMF	WV493	G-BDYG
VF516	G-ASMZ	WV686	G-BLFT
VF526	G-ARXU	WV740	G-BNPH
VF548	G-ASEG	WV783	G-ALSP
VL348	G-AVVO	WW397 (N-E)	G-BKHP
VL349	G-AWSA	WZ507	G-VTII
VM360	G-APHV	WZ662	G-BKVK
VP955	G-DVON	WZ711	G-AVHT
VR192	G-APIT	WZ868 (H)	G-BCIW
VR249	G-APIY	WZ876	G-BBWN
VR259	G-APJB	XB733	G-ATBF
VS356	G-AOLU	XF597 (AH)	G-BKFW
VS610	G-AOKL	XF690	G-MOOS
VS623	G-AOKZ	XF785	G-ALBN
VX118	G-ASNB	XF836 (J-G)	G-AWRY
VX926	G-ASKJ	XF877 (JX)	G-AWVF
VZ638	G-JETM	XG452	G-BRMB
VZ728	G-AGOS	XG547	G-HAPR
WA576	G-ALSS	XJ389	G-AJJP
WA577	G-ALST	XJ763	G-BKHA

MILITARY/CIVIL CROSS REFERENCE

Serial carried	Civil identity	Serial carried	Civil identity
XK417	G-AVXY	XR944	G-ATTB
XK482	G-BJWC	XR991	G-MOUR
XK896	G-RNAS	XS101	G-GNAT
XK940	G-AYXT	XS451	G-LTNG
XL426	G-VJET	XS452 (BT)	G-BPFE
XL502	G-BMYP	XS587	G-VIXN
XL572	G-HNTR	XS770	G-HRHI
XL717	G-AOXG	XT788 (442)	G-BMIR
XL809	G-BLIX	XW635	G-AWSW
XL929	G-BNPU	XW784	G-BBRN
XM553	G-AWSV	ZA250	G-VTOL
XM556	G-HELI	6+ (Luftwaffe)	G-USTV
XM575	G-BLMC	14+ (Luftwaffe)	G-BJAX
XM655	G-VULC	F+IS (Luftwaffe)	G-BIRW
XM685	G-AYZJ	BU+CK (Luftwaffe)	G-BUCK
XN351	G-BKSC	CC+43 (Luftwaffe)	G-CJCI
XN435	G-BGBU	LG+01 (Luftwaffe)	G-AYSJ
XN437	G-AXWA	NJ+C11 (Luftwaffe)	G-ATBG
XN441	G-BGKT	RF+16 (Luftwaffe)	G-PTWO
XN637	G-BKOU	TA+RC (Luftwaffe)	G-BPHZ
XP279	G-BWKK	VK+AZ (Luftwaffe)	G-BFHG
XP282	G-BGTC	ZA+WN (Luftwaffe)	G-AZMH
XP328	G-BKHC	6J+PR	G-AWHB
XP355	G-BEBC	97+04 (Luftwaffe)	G-APVF
XR240	G-BDFH	∞ (Russian AF)	G-KYAK
XR241	G-AXRR	— (Luftwaffe)	G-BOML
XR267	G-BJXR	146-11042 (7)	G-BMZX
XR363	G-OHCA	146-11083 (5)	G-BNAI
XR486	G-RWWW		

G-BKRL Chichester-Miles Leopard.   AJW

218

G-BMWE ARV Super 2. *AJW*

© BRYS Boeing 767-204 of Britannia Airways, G-BNYS

G-BRYG D.H.C. 8-120A Dash Eight of Brymon Airways.   AJW

221

G-OAAS Short SD3-60 Variant 100 of Aurigny Air Services. *A.W.*

G-OPLC D.H.104 Dove 8.   AJW

223

СССР-86104 Ilyushin Il-86 of Aeroflot/Greenair. *(W.*

EI-CCU BAC One-Eleven 531FS of Ryanair.   AJW

N751AT Boeing 757-212ER of American Trans Air. *AJW*

OO-EEE Beech 99A of European Expedite.   AJW

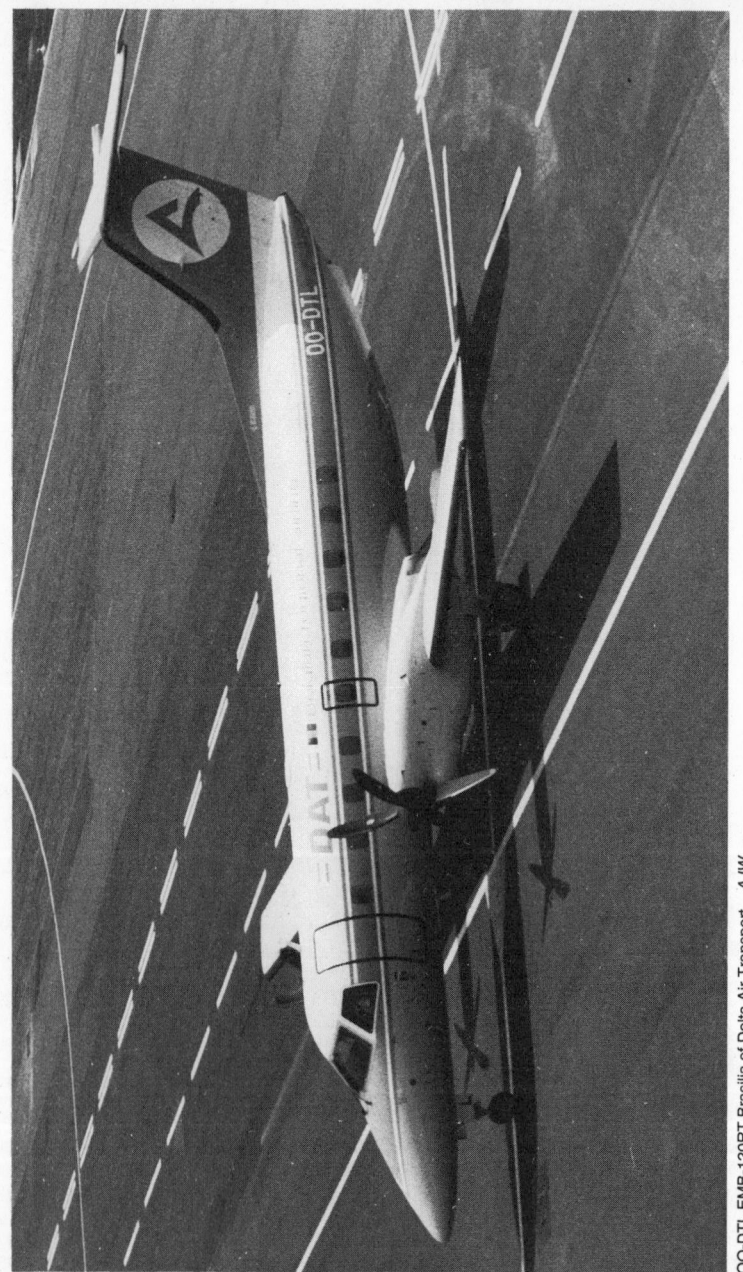

OO-DTL EMB-120RT Brasilia of Delta Air Transport. *AJW*

Overseas Airliner Registrations

(Aircraft included in this section are those most likely to be seen at UK and major European airports on scheduled or charter services.)

A6 (United Arab Emirates)

Reg.	Type	Owner or Operator
A6-EKA	Airbus A.310-304	Emirate Airlines
A6-EKB	Airbus A.310-304	Emirate Airlines
A6-EKC	Airbus A.300-605R	Emirate Airlines
A6-EKD	Airbus A.300-605R	Emirate Airlines
A6-EKE	Airbus A.300-605R	Emirate Airlines
A6-EKF	Airbus A.300-605R	Emirate Airlines
A6-	Airbus A.310-304	Emirate Airlines
A6-	Airbus A.310-304	Emirate Airlines
A6-	Airbus A.310-304	Emirate Airlines
A6-KUA	Airbus A.310-304	Kuwait Airways
A6-KUB	Airbus A.310-304	Kuwait Airways
A6-KUC	Airbus A.310-304	Kuwait Airways
A6-KUD	Airbus A.310-304	Kuwait Airways
A6-KUE	Airbus A.310-304	Kuwait Airways

A40 (Oman)

A40-GF	Boeing 767-3P6ER (601)	Gulf Air
A40-GG	Boeing 767-3P6ER (602)	Gulf Air
A40-GH	Boeing 767-3P6ER (603)	Gulf Air
A40-GI	Boeing 767-3P6ER (604)	Gulf Air
A40-GJ	Boeing 767-3P6ER (605)	Gulf Air
A40-GK	Boeing 767-3P6ER (606)	Gulf Air
A40-GL	Boeing 767-3P6ER (607)	Gulf Air
A40-GM	Boeing 767-3P6ER (608)	Gulf Air
A40-GN	Boeing 767-3P6ER (609)	Gulf Air
A40-GO	Boeing 767-3P6ER	Gulf Air
A40-GP	Boeing 767-3P6ER	Gulf Air
A40-GR	Boeing 767-3P6ER	Gulf Air
A40-GS	Boeing 767-3P6ER	Gulf Air
A40-GT	Boeing 767-3P6ER	Gulf Air
A40-GU	Boeing 767-3P6ER	Gulf Air
A40-GV	Boeing 767-3P6ER	Gulf Air
A40-TA	L-1011-385 TriStar 200 (105)	Gulf Air
A40-TB	L-1011-385 TriStar 200 (106)	Gulf Air
A40-TT	L-1011-385 TriStar 200 (107)	Gulf Air
A40-TV	L-1011-385 TriStar 200 (108)	Gulf Air
A40-TW	L-1011-385 TriStar 200 (101)	Gulf Air
A40-TX	L-1011-385 TriStar 200 (102)	Gulf Air
A40-TY	L-1011-385 TriStar 200 (103)	Gulf Air
A40-TZ	L-1011-385 TriStar 200 (104)	Gulf Air

AP (Pakistan)

AP-AXA	Boeing 707-340C	Pakistan International Airlines
AP-AXG	Boeing 707-340C	Pakistan International Airlines
AP-AYV	Boeing 747-282B	Pakistan International Airlines
AP-AYW	Boeing 747-282B	Pakistan International Airlines
AP-AZW	Boeing 707-351B	Pakistan International Airlines
AP-BAK	Boeing 747-240B (SCD)	Pakistan International Airlines
AP-BAT	Boeing 747-240B (SCD)	Pakistan International Airlines
AP-BBK	Boeing 707-323C	Pakistan International Airlines
AP-BCL	Boeing 747-217B	Pakistan International Airlines
AP-BCM	Boeing 747-217B	Pakistan International Airlines
AP-BCN	Boeing 747-217B	Pakistan International Airlines
AP-BCO	Boeing 747-217B	Pakistan International Airlines

B (China/Taiwan)

B-160	Boeing 747-209F	China Airlines
B-161	Boeing 747-409	China Airlines
B-162	Boeing 747-409	China Airlines
B-163	Boeing 747-409	China Airlines

Notes	Reg.	Type	Owner or Operator
	B-164	Boeing 747-409	China Airlines
	B-165	Boeing 747-409	China Airlines
	B-1862	Boeing 747SP-09	China Airlines
	B-1864	Boeing 747-209B (SCD)	China Airlines
	B-1866	Boeing 747-209B	China Airlines
	B-1880	Boeing 747SP-09	China Airlines
	B-1886	Boeing 747-209B	China Airlines
	B-1888	Boeing 747-209B	China Airlines
	B-1894	Boeing 747-209F (SCD)	China Airlines
	B-2404	Boeing 707-3J6B	CAAC/Air China
	B-2406	Boeing 707-3J6B	CAAC/Air China
	B-2414	Boeing 707-3J6C	CAAC/Air China
	B-2416	Boeing 707-3J6C	CAAC/Air China
	B-2420	Boeing 707-3J6C	CAAC/Air China
	B-2442	Boeing 747SP-J6	CAAC/Air China
	B-2444	Boeing 747SP-J6	CAAC/Air China
	B-2446	Boeing 747-2J6B (SCD)	CAAC/Air China
	B-2448	Boeing 747-2J6B (SCD)	CAAC/Air China
	B-2450	Boeing 747-2J6B (SCD)	CAAC/Air China
	B-2452	Boeing 747SP-J6	CAAC/Air China
	B-2454	Boeing 747SP-27	CAAC/Air China
	B-2456	Boeing 747-4J6 (SCD)	CAAC/Air China
	B-2458	Boeing 747-4J6 (SCD)	CAAC/Air China
	B-2460	Boeing 747-4J6 (SCD)	CAAC/Air China
	B-2462	Boeing 747-2J6F (SCD)	CAAC/Air China

Note: China Airlines also operates N4508H and N4522V, both Boeing 747SP-09s.

C5 (Gambia)

Note: Air Gambia operates Boeing 707s on lease.

C9 (Mozambique)

C9-BAE	Ilyushin IL-62M	Linhas Aéreas de Mocambique (LAM) *Mozambique*

Note: LAM also operates DC-10-30 F-GDJK on lease from UTA.

C-F and C-G (Canada)

C-FBCA	Boeing 747-475 (884)	Canadian Airlines International
C-FBEF	Boeing 767-233ER (617)	Air Canada
C-FBEG	Boeing 767-233ER (618)	Air Canada
C-FBEM	Boeing 767-233ER (619)	Air Canada
C-FCAB	Boeing 767-375ER (631)	Canadian Airlines International
C-FCAE	Boeing 767-375ER (632)	Canadian Airlines International
C-FCAF	Boeing 767-375ER (633)	Canadian Airlines International
C-FCAG	Boeing 767-375ER (634)	Canadian Airlines International
C-FCAJ	Boeing 767-375ER (635)	Canadian Airlines International
C-FCAU	Boeing 767-375ER (636)	Canadian Airlines International
C-FCRA	Boeing 747-475 (882)	Canadian Airlines International
C-FCWW	Douglas DC-8-55F	ACS of Canada
C-FDJC	Boeing 747-1D1 (411)	Nationair
C-FDWW	Douglas DC-8-55F	ACS of Canada *Gilles Roudeau*
C-FFUN	Boeing 737-1D1 (412)	Nationair
C-FIWW	Douglas DC-8-55F	ACS of Canada
C-FOCA	Boeing 767-375ER (640)	Canadian Airlines International
C-FOOA	Boeing 757-28A	Canada 3000/Air 2000 (G-OOOA)
C-FOOB	Boeing 757-28A	Canada 3000/Air 2000 (G-OOOB)
C-FOOE	Boeing 757-28A	Canada 3000 Airlines
C-FPCA	Boeing 767-375ER (637)	Canadian Airlines International
C-FTCA	Boeing 767-375ER (638)	Canadian Airlines International
C-FTIK	Douglas DC-8-73AF (867)	Air Canada
C-FTIO	Douglas DC-8-73AF (871)	Air Canada
C-FTIQ	Douglas DC-8-73AF (873)	Air Canada
C-FTIR	Douglas DC-8-73AF (874)	Air Canada
C-FTIS	Douglas DC-8-73AF (875)	Air Canada
C-FTNA	L.1011-385 TriStar 150 (501)	Air Transat
C-FTNB	L.1011-385 TriStar 150 (549)	Air Transat
C-FTNC	L.1011-385 TriStar 150 (503)	Air Transat
C-FTOC	Boeing 747-133 (303)	Air Canada
C-FTOD	Boeing 747-133 (304)	Air Canada

Reg.	Type	Owner or Operator	Notes
C-FTOE	Boeing 747-133 (305)	Air Canada	
C-FXCA	Boeing 767-375ER (639)	Canadian Airlines International	
C-FXOC	Boeing 757-28AER	Canada 3000/Air 2000 (G-OOOC)	
C-FXOD	Boeing 757-28A	Canada 3000/Air 2000 (G-OOOD)	
C-FXOF	Boeing 757-28A	Canada 3000 Airlines	
C-FXOK	Boeing 757-23A	Canada 3000 Airlines	
C-GAGA	Boeing 747-233B (SCD) (306)	Air Canada	
C-GAGB	Boeing 747-233B (SCD) (307)	Air Canada	
C-GAGC	Boeing 747-238B (SCD) (308)	Air Canada	
C-GAUY	Boeing 767-233 (609)	Air Canada	
C-GAVA	Boeing 767-233 (610)	Air Canada	
C-GAVC	Boeing 767-233ER (611)	Air Canada	
C-GAVF	Boeing 767-233ER (612)	Air Canada	
C-GCAW	Boeing 767-375ER	Canadian Airlines International	
C-GCPC	Douglas DC-10-30 (901)	Canadian Airlines International Empress of Amsterdam	
C-GCPD	Douglas DC-10-30 (902)	Canadian Airlines International Empress of British Colombia	
C-GCPE	Douglas DC-10-30ER (903)	Canadian Airlines International Empress of Buenos Aires	
C-GCPF	Douglas DC-10-30ER (904)	Canadian Airlines International Empress of Santiago	
C-GCPG	Douglas DC-10-30ER (905)	Canadian Airlines International Empress of Fiji	
C-GCPH	Douglas DC-10-30ER (906)	Canadian Airlines International Empress of Lima	
C-GCPI	Douglas DC-10-30ER (907)	Canadian Airlines International Empress of Auckland	
C-GCPJ	Douglas DC-10-30 (908)	Canadian Airlines International Empress of Rome	
C-GDSP	Boeing 767-233ER (613)	Air Canada	
C-GDSS	Boeing 767-233ER (614)	Air Canada	
C-GDSU	Boeing 767-233ER (615)	Air Canada	
C-GDSY	Boeing 767-233ER (616)	Air Canada	
C-GLCA	Boeing 767-375ER (641)	Canadian Airlines International	
C-GMWW	Boeing 747-475 (881)	Canadian Airlines International Maxwell W. Ward	
C-	Boeing 767-375ER	Canadian Airlines International	
C-	Boeing 767-375ER	Canadian Airlines International	
C-GMXB	Douglas DC-8-61 (811)	Nationair	
C-GMXL	Douglas DC-8-61 (813)	Nationair	
C-GMXY	Douglas DC-8-62 (822)	Nationair	
C-GNXC	Boeing 757-28A (521)	Nationair	
C-GNXH	Boeing 747-129 (SCD) (413)	Nationair	
C-GNXI	Boeing 757-28A (522)	Nationair	
C-GQBA	Douglas DC-8-63 (806)	Nationair	
C-GQBF	Douglas DC-8-63 (807)	Nationair	
C-GSCA	Boeing 767-375ER (642)	Canadian Airlines International	
C-GTSZ	L.1011-385 TriStar 150 (548)	Air Transat	
C-GXCA	Boeing 767-375ER	Canadian Airlines Interantional	

Note: Airline fleet number carried on aircraft is shown in parenthesis.

CCCP (ex-Soviet Union)

All aircraft listed are operated by Aeroflot unless shown otherwise. The registrations are prefixed by CCCP in each case. The airline is likely to be split between the various independent States, possibly with new country codes and registration system.

Reg.	Type	Notes	Reg.	Type	Notes
65014	Tu-134A		65050	Tu-134A	
65020	Tu-134A		65051	Tu-134A	
65024	Tu-134A		65054	Tu-134A	
65027	Tu-134A		65064	Tu-134A	
65028	Tu-134A		65072	Tu-134A	
65035	Tu-134A		65073	Tu-134A	
65036	Tu-134A		65076	Tu-134A	
65038	Tu-134A		65077	Tu-134A	
65040	Tu-134A		65079	Tu-134A	
65042	Tu-134A		65087	Tu-134A	
65044	Tu-134A		65089	Tu-134A	
65048	Tu-134A		65107	Tu-134A	
65049	Tu-134A		65119	Tu-134A	

Notes	Reg.	Type	Notes	Reg	Type
	65134	Tu-134A		65714	Tu-134A
	65135	Tu-134A		65717	Tu-134A-3
	65139	Tu-134A		65730	Tu-134A
	65141	Tu-134A		65739	Tu-134A
	65145	Tu-134A		65750	Tu-134A
	65550	Tu-134A		65757	Tu-134A
	65551	Tu-134A		65758	Tu-134A
	65552	Tu-134A-3		65765	Tu-134A
	65553	Tu-134A-3		65769	Tu-134A-3
	65554	Tu-134A-3		65770	Tu-134A-3
	65555	Tu-134A		65772	Tu-134A
	65557	Tu-134A-3		65777	Tu-134A-3
	65601	Tu-134		65780	Tu-134A
	65602	Tu-134		65781	Tu-134A-3
	65603	Tu-134		65782	Tu-134A
	65604	Tu-134		65783	Tu-134A-3
	65608	Tu-134		65784	Tu-134A-3
	65609	Tu-134		65785	Tu-134A-3
	65610	Tu-134		65786	Tu-134A-3
	65611	Tu-134		65790	Tu-134A-3
	65612	Tu-134		65791	Tu-134A
	65613	Tu-134		65794	Tu-134A
	65614	Tu-134		65801	Tu-134A
	65615	Tu-134		65802	Tu-134A
	65616	Tu-134		65815	Tu-134A
	65617	Tu-134		65835	Tu-134A
	65618	Tu-134		65837	Tu-134A
	65619	Tu-134		65851	Tu-134A
	65620	Tu-134		65854	Tu-134A
	65621	Tu-134		65862	Tu-134A
	65622	Tu-134A		65863	Tu-134A
	65625	Tu-134		65864	Tu-134A
	65627	Tu-134		65872	Tu-134A
	65628	Tu-134		65888	Tu-134A
	65629	Tu-134		65891	Tu-134A
	65630	Tu-134		65892	Tu-134A
	65631	Tu-134		65893	Tu-134A
	65632	Tu-134		65894	Tu-134A
	65633	Tu-134		65904	Tu-134A
	65634	Tu-134		65905	Tu-134A-3
	65635	Tu-134		65911	Tu-134A-3
	65636	Tu-134		65912	Tu-134A-3
	65637	Tu-134		65916	Tu-134A
	65639	Tu-134		65919	Tu-134A
	65644	Tu-134		65921	Tu-134A-3
	65645	Tu-134A		65923	Tu-134A
	65646	Tu-134A		65926	Tu-134A
	65647	Tu-134A		65935	Tu-134A
	65648	Tu-134A		65939	Tu-134A
	65649	Tu-134A		65951	Tu-134A
	65650	Tu-134A		65953	Tu-134A
	65651	Tu-134A		65954	Tu-134A
	65652	Tu-134A		65955	Tu-134A
	65653	Tu-134A		65956	Tu-134A
	65654	Tu-134A		65965	Tu-134A
	65655	Tu-134A		65967	Tu-134A-3
	65656	Tu-134A		65971	Tu-134A
	65657	Tu-134A		65972	Tu-134A
	65658	Tu-134A		65973	Tu-134A
	65659	Tu-134A		65974	Tu-134A
	65660	Tu-134A		65976	Tu-134A
	65661	Tu-134A		65977	Tu-134A-3
	65662	Tu-134A		65978	Tu-134A-3
	65663	Tu-134A		76466	IL-76TD
	65664	Tu-134A		76467	IL-76TD
	65665	Tu-134A		76468	IL-76TD
	65666	Tu-134A		76469	IL-76TD
	65667	Tu-134A		76470	IL-76TD
	65669	Tu-134A		76471	IL-76TD
	65680	Tu-134A-3		76472	IL-76TD
	65681	Tu-134A		76473	IL-76TD
	65697	Tu-134A		76474	IL-76TD
	65703	Tu-134A		76475	IL-76TD

Reg.	Type	Notes	Reg	Type	Notes
76476	IL-76TD		85031	Tu-154	
76477	IL-76TD		85034	Tu-154	
76478	IL-76TD		85035	Tu-154	
76479	IL-76TD		85037	Tu-154	
76482	IL-76TD		85038	Tu-154	
76484	IL-76TD		85039	Tu-154	
76485	IL-76TD		85040	Tu-154	
76487	IL-76TD		85041	Tu-154	
76488	IL-76TD		85042	Tu-154	
76489	IL-76TD		85043	Tu-154	
76491	IL-76TD		85044	Tu-154	
76493	IL-76TD		85049	Tu-154	
76494	IL-76TD		85050	Tu-154	
76495	IL-76TD		85051	Tu-154	
76496	IL-76TD		85052	Tu-154	
76497	IL-76TD		85055	Tu-154	
76498	IL-76TD		85056	Tu-154	
76499	IL-76TD		85057	Tu-154	
76750	IL-76TD		85059	Tu-154A	
76752	IL-76TD		85060	Tu-154A	
76754	IL-76TD		85061	Tu-154A	
76755	IL-76TD		85062	Tu-154C	
76757	IL-76TD		85063	Tu-154C	
76758	IL-76TD		85064	Tu-154A	
76761	IL-76TD		85065	Tu-154A	
76764	IL-76TD		85066	Tu-154A	
76777	IL-76TD		85067	Tu-154C	
76780	IL-76TD		85068	Tu-154B	
76781	IL-76TD		85069	Tu-154A	
76784	IL-76TD		85070	Tu-154A	
76785	IL-76TD		85071	Tu-154A	
76786	IL-76TD		85072	Tu-154A	
76787	IL-76TD		85074	Tu-154A	
76788	IL-76TD		85075	Tu-154B	
76789	IL-76TD		85076	Tu-154A	
76792	IL-76TD		85078	Tu-154A	
76794	IL-76TD		85079	Tu-154A	
76795	IL-76TD		85080	Tu-154A	
76800	IL-76TD		85081	Tu-154C	
76801	IL-76TD		85082	Tu-154A	
			85083	Tu-154A	
82008	An-124 Air Foyle		85084	Tu-154A	
82009	An-124		85085	Tu-154A	
82027	An-124 Air Foyle		85086	Tu-154A	
82033	An-124		85087	Tu-154A	
82042	An-124 Heavy Lift/		85088	Tu-154A	
	Volga Dnepr		85089	Tu-154A	
82043	An-124 Heavy Lift/		85090	Tu-154A	
	Volga Dnepr		85091	Tu-154A	
85001	Tu-154		85092	Tu-154B-1	
85002	Tu-154		85093	Tu-154A	
85003	Tu-154		85094	Tu-154A	
85004	Tu-154		85096	Tu-154B-2	
85005	Tu-154		85098	Tu-154A	
85006	Tu-154		85099	Tu-154A	
85007	Tu-154		85100	Tu-154A	
85008	Tu-154		85101	Tu-154A	
85009	Tu-154		85103	Tu-154A	
85010	Tu-154		85104	Tu-154A	
85011	Tu-154		85105	Tu-154A	
85012	Tu-154		85106	Tu-154B-2	
85013	Tu-154		85107	Tu-154A	
85014	Tu-154		85108	Tu-154A	
85015	Tu-154		85109	Tu-154B-1	
85016	Tu-154		85110	Tu-154A	
85017	Tu-154		85111	Tu-154A	
85018	Tu-154		85112	Tu-154A	
85020	Tu-154		85113	Tu-154A	
85021	Tu-154		85114	Tu-154A	
85022	Tu-154		85115	Tu-154A	
85024	Tu-154		85116	Tu-154A	
85029	Tu-154		85117	Tu-154A	
85030	Tu-154		85118	Tu-154B	

Notes	Reg.	Type	Notes	Reg	Type
	85119	Tu-154A		85199	Tu-154B
	85120	Tu-154B		85200	Tu-154B
	85121	Tu-154B		85201	Tu-154B
	85122	Tu-154B		85202	Tu-154B
	85123	Tu-154B		85203	Tu-154B
	85124	Tu-154B		85204	Tu-154B
	85125	Tu-154B		85205	Tu-154B
	85129	Tu-154B		85206	Tu-154B
	85130	Tu-154B		85207	Tu-154B
	85131	Tu-154B		85210	Tu-154B
	85132	Tu-154B		85211	Tu-154B
	85133	Tu-154B		85212	Tu-154B
	85134	Tu-154B		85213	Tu-154B
	85135	Tu-154B		85214	Tu-154B
	85136	Tu-154B		85215	Tu-154B
	85137	Tu-154B		85216	Tu-154B
	85138	Tu-154B		85217	Tu-154B
	85139	Tu-154B		85218	Tu-154B
	85140	Tu-154B		85219	Tu-154B
	85141	Tu-154B		85220	Tu-154B
	85142	Tu-154B		85221	Tu-154B
	85143	Tu-154B		85222	Tu-154B
	85145	Tu-154B		85223	Tu-154B
	85146	Tu-154B		85226	Tu-154B
	85147	Tu-154B		85227	Tu-154B
	85148	Tu-154B		85228	Tu-154B
	85149	Tu-154B		85229	Tu-154B-1
	85150	Tu-154B		85230	Tu-154B-1
	85151	Tu-154B		85231	Tu-154B-1
	85152	Tu-154B		85232	Tu-154B-1
	85153	Tu-154B		85233	Tu-154B-1
	85154	Tu-154B		85234	Tu-154B-1
	85155	Tu-154B		85235	Tu-154B-1
	85156	Tu-154B		85236	Tu-154B-1
	85157	Tu-154B		85237	Tu-154B-1
	85158	Tu-154B		85238	Tu-154B-1
	85160	Tu-154B		85240	Tu-154B-1
	85162	Tu-154B		85241	Tu-154B-1
	85163	Tu-154B		85242	Tu-154B-1
	85164	Tu-154B		85243	Tu-154B-1
	85165	Tu-154B		85244	Tu-154B-1
	85166	Tu-154B		85245	Tu-154B-1
	85167	Tu-154B		85246	Tu-154B-1
	85168	Tu-154B		85247	Tu-154B-1
	85169	Tu-154B		85248	Tu-154B-1
	85170	Tu-154B		85249	Tu-154B-1
	85171	Tu-154B		85250	Tu-154B-1
	85172	Tu-154B		85251	Tu-154B-1
	85173	Tu-154B		85252	Tu-154B-1
	85174	Tu-154B		85253	Tu-154B-1
	85176	Tu-154B		85255	Tu-154B-1
	85177	Tu-154B		85256	Tu-154B-1
	85178	Tu-154B		85257	Tu-154B-1
	85179	Tu-154B		85259	Tu-154B-1
	85180	Tu-154B		85260	Tu-154B-1
	85181	Tu-154B		85261	Tu-154B-1
	85182	Tu-154B		85263	Tu-154B-1
	85183	Tu-154B		85264	Tu-154B-1
	85184	Tu-154B		85265	Tu-154B-1
	85185	Tu-154B		85266	Tu-154B-1
	85186	Tu-154B		85267	Tu-154B-1
	85187	Tu-154B		85268	Tu-154B-1
	85188	Tu-154B		85269	Tu-154B-1
	85189	Tu-154B		85270	Tu-154B-1
	85190	Tu-154B		85271	Tu-154B-1
	85191	Tu-154B		85272	Tu-154B-1
	85192	Tu-154B		85273	Tu-154B-1
	85193	Tu-154B		85274	Tu-154B-1
	85194	Tu-154B		85275	Tu-154B-1
	85195	Tu-154B		85276	Tu-154B-1
	85196	Tu-154B		85277	Tu-154B-1
	85197	Tu-154B		85279	Tu-154B-1
	85198	Tu-154B		85280	Tu-154B-1

Reg.	Type	Notes	Reg	Type	Notes
85281	Tu-154B-1		85358	Tu-154B-2	
85282	Tu-154B-1		85359	Tu-154B-2	
85283	Tu-154B-1		85360	Tu-154B-2	
85284	Tu-154B-1		85361	Tu-154B-2	
85285	Tu-154B-1		85362	Tu-154B-2	
85286	Tu-154B-1		85363	Tu-154B-2	
85287	Tu-154B-1		85364	Tu-154B-2	
85288	Tu-154B-1		85365	Tu-154B-2	
85289	Tu-154B-1		85366	Tu-154B-2	
85290	Tu-154B-1		85367	Tu-154B-2	
85291	Tu-154B-1		85368	Tu-154B-2	
85292	Tu-154B-2		85369	Tu-154B-2	
85293	Tu-154B-1		85370	Tu-154B-2	
85294	Tu-154B-1		85371	Tu-154B-2	
85295	Tu-154B-1		85372	Tu-154B-2	
85296	Tu-154B-1		85373	Tu-154B-2	
85297	Tu-154B-1		85374	Tu-154B-2	
85298	Tu-154B-1		85375	Tu-154B-2	
85299	Tu-154B-1		85376	Tu-154B-2	
85300	Tu-154B-2		85377	Tu-154B-2	
85301	Tu-154B-2		85378	Tu-154B-2	
85302	Tu-154B-2		85379	Tu-154B-2	
85303	Tu-154B-2		85380	Tu-154B-2	
85304	Tu-154B-2		85381	Tu-154B-2	
85305	Tu-154B-2		85382	Tu-154B-2	
85306	Tu-154B-2		85383	Tu-154B-2	
85307	Tu-154B-2		85384	Tu-154B-2	
85308	Tu-154B-2		85385	Tu-154B-2	
85309	Tu-154B-2		85386	Tu-154B-2	
85310	Tu-154B-2		85387	Tu-154B-2	
85311	Tu-154B-2		85388	Tu-154B-2	
85312	Tu-154B-2		85389	Tu-154B-2	
85313	Tu-154B-2		85390	Tu-154B-2	
85314	Tu-154B-2		85391	Tu-154B-2	
85315	Tu-154B-2		85392	Tu-154B-2	
85316	Tu-154B-2		85393	Tu-154B-2	
85317	Tu-154M		85394	Tu-154B-2	
85318	Tu-154B-2		85395	Tu-154B-2	
85319	Tu-154B-2		85396	Tu-154B-2	
85321	Tu-154B-2		85397	Tu-154B-2	
85322	Tu-154B-2		85398	Tu-154B-2	
85323	Tu-154B-2		85399	Tu-154B-2	
85324	Tu-154B-2		85400	Tu-154B-2	
85327	Tu-154B-2		85401	Tu-154B-2	
85328	Tu-154B-2		85402	Tu-154B-2	
85329	Tu-154B-2		85403	Tu-154B-2	
85330	Tu-154B-2		85404	Tu-154B-2	
85331	Tu-154B-2		85405	Tu-154B-2	
85332	Tu-154B-2		85406	Tu-154B-2	
85333	Tu-154B-2		85407	Tu-154B-2	
85334	Tu-154B-2		85409	Tu-154B-2	
85335	Tu-154B-2		85410	Tu-154B-2	
85336	Tu-154B-2		85411	Tu-154B-2	
85337	Tu-154B-2		85412	Tu-154B-2	
85338	Tu-154B-2		85414	Tu-154B-2	
85339	Tu-154B-2		85416	Tu-154B-2	
85340	Tu-154B-2		85417	Tu-154B-2	
85341	Tu-154B-2		85418	Tu-154B-2	
85343	Tu-154B-2		85419	Tu-154B-2	
85344	Tu-154B-2		85421	Tu-154B-2	
85345	Tu-154B-2		85423	Tu-154B-2	
85346	Tu-154B-2		85424	Tu-154B-2	
85347	Tu-154B-2		85425	Tu-154B-2	
85348	Tu-154B-2		85426	Tu-154B-2	
85349	Tu-154B-2		85427	Tu-154B-2	
85350	Tu-154B-2		85429	Tu-154B-2	
85351	Tu-154B-2		85430	Tu-154B-2	
85352	Tu-154B-2		85431	Tu-154B-2	
85353	Tu-154B-2		85432	Tu-154B-2	
85354	Tu-154B-2		85433	Tu-154B-2	
85355	Tu-154B-2		85434	Tu-154B-2	
85356	Tu-154B-2		85435	Tu-154B-2	
85357	Tu-154B-2		85436	Tu-154B-2	

Notes	Reg.	Type	Notes	Reg	Type
	85437	Tu-154B-2		85519	Tu-154B-2
	85438	Tu-154B-2		85520	Tu-154B-2
	85439	Tu-154B-2		85521	Tu-154B-2
	85440	Tu-154B-2		85522	Tu-154B-2
	85441	Tu-154B-2		85523	Tu-154B-2
	85442	Tu-154B-2		85524	Tu-154B-2
	85443	Tu-154B-2		85525	Tu-154C-2
	85444	Tu-154B-2		85526	Tu-154B-2
	85445	Tu-154B-2		85527	Tu-154B-2
	85446	Tu-154B-2		85528	Tu-154B-2
	85448	Tu-154B-2		85529	Tu-154B-2
	85449	Tu-154B-2		85530	Tu-154B-2
	85450	Tu-154B-2		85532	Tu-154B-2
	85451	Tu-154B-2		85533	Tu-154B-2
	85452	Tu-154B-2		85534	Tu-154B-2
	85453	Tu-154B-2		85535	Tu-154B-2
	85454	Tu-154B-2		85536	Tu-154B-2
	85455	Tu-154B-2		85537	Tu-154B-2
	85456	Tu-154B-2		85538	Tu-154B-2
	85457	Tu-154B-2		85539	Tu-154B-2
	85458	Tu-154B-2		85540	Tu-154B-2
	85459	Tu-154B-2		85542	Tu-154B-2
	85460	Tu-154B-2		85545	Tu-154B-2
	85461	Tu-154B-2		85546	Tu-154B-2
	85462	Tu-154B-2		85547	Tu-154B-2
	85463	Tu-154B-2		85548	Tu-154B-2
	85464	Tu-154B-2		85549	Tu-154B-2
	85465	Tu-154B-2		85550	Tu-154B-2
	85466	Tu-154B-2		85551	Tu-154B-2
	85467	Tu-154B-2		85552	Tu-154B-2
	85468	Tu-154B-2		85553	Tu-154B-2
	85469	Tu-154B-2		85554	Tu-154B-2
	85470	Tu-154B-2		85555	Tu-154B-2
	85471	Tu-154B-2		85556	Tu-154B-2
	85472	Tu-154B-2		85557	Tu-154B-2
	85475	Tu-154B-2		85558	Tu-154B-2
	85476	Tu-154B-2		85559	Tu-154B-2
	85477	Tu-154B-2		85560	Tu-154B-2
	85478	Tu-154B-2		85561	Tu-154B-2
	85479	Tu-154B-2		85562	Tu-154B-2
	85480	Tu-154B-2		85563	Tu-154B-2
	85481	Tu-154B-2		85564	Tu-154B-2
	85482	Tu-154B-2		85565	Tu-154B-2
	85485	Tu-154B-2		85566	Tu-154B-2
	85486	Tu-154B-2		85567	Tu-154B-2
	85487	Tu-154B-2		85568	Tu-154B-2
	85489	Tu-154B-2		85570	Tu-154B-2
	85490	Tu-154B-2		85571	Tu-154B-2
	85491	Tu-154B-2		85572	Tu-154B-2
	85492	Tu-154B-2		85573	Tu-154B-2
	85494	Tu-154B-2		85574	Tu-154B-2
	85495	Tu-154B-2		85575	Tu-154B-2
	85496	Tu-154B-2		85577	Tu-154B-2
	85497	Tu-154B-2		85578	Tu-154B-2
	85498	Tu-154B-2		85579	Tu-154B-2
	85499	Tu-154B-2		85580	Tu-154B-2
	85500	Tu-154B-2		85581	Tu-154B-2
	85501	Tu-154B-2		85582	Tu-154B-2
	85502	Tu-154B-2		85583	Tu-154B-2
	85503	Tu-154B-2		85584	Tu-154B-2
	85504	Tu-154B-2		85585	Tu-154B-2
	85505	Tu-154B-2		85586	Tu-154B-2
	85506	Tu-154B-2		85587	Tu-154B-2
	85507	Tu-154B-2		85588	Tu-154B-2
	85508	Tu-154B-2		85589	Tu-154B-2
	85509	Tu-154B-2		85590	Tu-154B-2
	85510	Tu-154B-2		85591	Tu-154B-2
	85511	Tu-154B-2		85592	Tu-154B-2
	85512	Tu-154B-2		85593	Tu-154B-2
	85513	Tu-154B-2		85594	Tu-154B-2
	85514	Tu-154B-2		85595	Tu-154B-2
	85515	Tu-154B-2		85596	Tu-154B-2
	85516	Tu-154B-2		85597	Tu-154B-2
	85518	Tu-154B-2		85598	Tu-154B-2

Reg.	Type	Notes	Reg	Type	Notes
85600	Tu-154B-2		85677	Tu-154M	
85601	Tu-154B-2		85678	Tu-154M	
85602	Tu-154B-2		85679	Tu-154M	
85603	Tu-154B-2		85680	Tu-154M	
85604	Tu-154B-2		85681	Tu-154M	
85605	Tu-154B-2		85682	Tu-154M	
85606	Tu-154B-2		85683	Tu-154M	
85607	Tu-154B-2		85684	Tu-154M	
85608	Tu-154B-2		85685	Tu-154M	
85609	Tu-154M		85686	Tu-154M	
85610	Tu-154M		85687	Tu-154M	
85611	Tu-154M		85688	Tu-154M	
85612	Tu-154M		85689	Tu-154M	
85613	Tu-154M		85690	Tu-154M	
85614	Tu-154M		85691	Tu-154M	
85615	Tu-154M		85692	Tu-154M	
85616	Tu-154M		85693	Tu-154M	
85617	Tu-154M		85694	Tu-154M	
85618	Tu-154M		85695	Tu-154M	
85619	Tu-154M		85696	Tu-154M	
85621	Tu-154M		85697	Tu-154M	
85622	Tu-154M		85698	Tu-154M	
85623	Tu-154M		85699	Tu-154M	
85624	Tu-154M				
85625	Tu-154M		86000	IL-86	
85626	Tu-154M		86002	IL-86	
85627	Tu-154M		86003	IL-86	
85628	Tu-154M		86004	IL-86	
85629	Tu-154M		86005	IL-86	
85630	Tu-154M		86006	IL-86	
85631	Tu-154M		86007	IL-86	
85632	Tu-154M		86008	IL-86	
85633	Tu-154M		86009	IL-86	
85634	Tu-154M		86010	IL-86	
85635	Tu-154M		86011	IL-86	
85636	Tu-154M		86012	IL-86	
85637	Tu-154M		86013	IL-86	
85638	Tu-154M		86014	IL-86	
85639	Tu-154M		86015	IL-86	
85640	Tu-154M		86016	IL-86	
85641	Tu-154M		86017	IL-86	
85642	Tu-154M		86018	IL-86	
85643	Tu-154M		86050	IL-86	
85644	Tu-154M		86051	IL-86	
85645	Tu-154M		86052	IL-86	
85646	Tu-154M		86053	IL-86	
85647	Tu-154M		86054	IL-86	
85648	Tu-154M		86055	IL-86	
85649	Tu-154M		86056	IL-86	
85650	Tu-154M		86057	IL-86	
85651	Tu-154M		86058	IL-86	
85652	Tu-154M		86059	IL-86	
85653	Tu-154M		86060	IL-86	
85654	Tu-154M		86061	IL-86	
85655	Tu-154M		86062	IL-86	
85656	Tu-154M		86063	IL-86	
85657	Tu-154M		86064	IL-86	
85658	Tu-154M		86065	IL-86	
85659	Tu-154M		86066	IL-86	
85660	Tu-154M		86067	IL-86	
85661	Tu-154M		86068	IL-86	
85662	Tu-154M		86069	IL-86	
85663	Tu-154M		86070	IL-86	
85665	Tu-154M		86071	IL-86	
85666	Tu-154M		86072	IL-86	
85667	Tu-154M		86073	IL-86	
85668	Tu-154M		86074	IL-86	
85669	Tu-154M		86075	IL-86	
85670	Tu-154M		86076	IL-86	
85671	Tu-154M		86077	IL-86	
85672	Tu-154M		86078	IL-86	
85674	Tu-154M		86079	IL-86	
85675	Tu-154M		86080	IL-86	
85676	Tu-154M		86081	IL-86	

Notes	Reg.	Type	Notes	Reg	Type
	86082	IL-86		86485	IL-62M
	86083	IL-86		86486	IL-62M
	86084	IL-86		86487	IL-62M
	86085	IL-86		86488	IL-62M
	86086	IL-86		86489	IL-62M
	86087	IL-86		86490	IL-62M
	86088	IL-86		86491	IL-62M
	86089	IL-86		86492	IL-62M
	86090	IL-86		86493	IL-62M
	86091	IL-86		86494	IL-62M
	86092	IL-86		86495	IL-62M
	86093	IL-86		86496	IL-62M
	86094	IL-86		86497	IL-62M
	86095	IL-86		86498	IL-62M
	86096	IL-86		86499	IL-62M
	86097	IL-86		86500	IL-62M
	86098	IL-86		86501	IL-62M
	86099	IL-86		86502	IL-62M
	86100	IL-86		86503	IL-62M
	86101	IL-86		86504	IL-62M
	86102	IL-86		86505	IL-62M
	86103	IL-86		86506	IL-62M
	86104	IL-86		86507	IL-62M
	86105	IL-86		86508	IL-62M
	86106	IL-86		86509	IL-62M
	86107	IL-86		86510	IL-62M
	86108	IL-86		86511	IL-62M
	86109	IL-86		86512	IL-62M
	86110	IL-86		86513	IL-62M
	86111	IL-86		86514	IL-62M
	86112	IL-86		86515	IL-62M
	86113	IL-86		86516	IL-62M
	86114	IL-86		86517	IL-62MK
	86115	IL-86		86518	IL-62M
	86116	IL-86		86519	IL-62M
	86117	IL-86		86520	IL-62MK
	86118	IL-86		86521	IL-62M
	86119	IL-86		86522	IL-62M
	86120	IL-86		86523	IL-62M
				86524	IL-62M
	86450	IL-62		86527	IL-62MK
	86451	IL-62		86528	IL-62MK
	86452	IL-62M		86529	IL-62MK
	86453	IL-62M		86530	IL-62MK
	86454	IL-62M		86531	IL-62M
	86455	IL-62M		86532	IL-62MK
	86456	IL-62M		86533	IL-62M
	86457	IL-62M		86534	IL-62MK
	86458	IL-62M		86535	IL-62M
	86459	IL-62M		86536	IL-62M
	86460	IL-62		86537	IL-62M
	86461	IL-62		86538	IL-62M
	86462	IL-62M		86539	IL-62MK
	86463	IL-62M		86540	IL-62M
	86464	IL-62M		86555	IL-62M
	86465	IL-62M		86558	IL-62M
	86466	IL-62MK		86573	IL-62M
	86467	IL-62MK		86574	IL-62M
	86468	IL-62MK		86575	IL-62M
	86469	IL-62M		86576	IL-62M
	86471	IL-62M		86577	IL-62M
	86472	IL-62M		86578	IL-62M
	86473	IL-62M		86579	IL-62M
	86474	IL-62M		86605	IL-62
	86475	IL-62M		86606	IL-62
	86476	IL-62M		86607	IL-62M
	86477	IL-62M		86608	IL-62
	86478	IL-62M		86609	IL-62
	86479	IL-62M		86610	IL-62
	86480	IL-62M		86611	IL-62
	86481	IL-62M		86612	IL-62
	86482	IL-62M		86613	IL-62
	86483	IL-62M		86614	IL-62
	86484	IL-62M		86615	IL-62

Reg.	Type	Notes	Reg	Type	Notes
86616	IL-62		86677	IL-62	
86617	IL-62		86678	IL-62	
86618	IL-62		86679	IL-62	
86619	IL-62M		86680	IL-62	
86620	IL-62M		86681	IL-62	
86621	IL-62M		86682	IL-62	
86622	IL-62M		86683	IL-62	
86623	IL-62M		86684	IL-62	
86624	IL-62M		86685	IL-62	
86648	IL-62		86686	IL-62	
86649	IL-62		86687	IL-62	
86650	IL-62		86688	IL-62	
86652	IL-62		86689	IL-62	
86653	IL-62		86690	IL-62	
86654	IL-62		86691	IL-62	
86655	IL-62		86692	IL-62M	
86656	IL-62M		86693	IL-62M	
86657	IL-62		86694	IL-62	
86658	IL-62M		86695	IL-62	
86659	IL-62M		86696	IL-62	
86661	IL-62		86697	IL-62	
86662	IL-62		86698	IL-62	
86663	IL-62		86699	IL-62	
86664	IL-62		86700	IL-62M	
86665	IL-62		86701	IL-62M	
86666	IL-62		86702	IL-62M	
86667	IL-62		86703	IL-62M	
86668	IL-62		86704	IL-62M	
86669	IL-62		86705	IL-62M	
86670	IL-62		86706	IL-62M	
86672	IL-62		86708	IL-62MK	
86673	IL-62M		86709	IL-62MK	
86674	IL-62		86710	IL-62MK	
86675	IL-62		86711	IL-62M	
86676	IL-62		86712	IL-62M	

CN (Morocco)

Reg.	Type	Notes
CN-CCF	Boeing 727-2B6	Royal Air Maroc *Fez*
CN-CCG	Boeing 727-2B6	Royal Air Maroc *L'Oiseau de la Providence*
CN-CCH	Boeing 727-2B6	Royal Air Maroc *Marrakech*
CN-CCW	Boeing 727-2B6	Royal Air Maroc *Agadir*
CN-RMB	Boeing 707-351C	Royal Air Maroc *Tangier*
CN-RMC	Boeing 707-351C	Royal Air Maroc *Casablanca*
CN-RME	Boeing 747-2B6B (SCD)	Royal Air Maroc
CN-RMF	Boeing 737-4B6	Royal Air Maroc
CN-RMG	Boeing 737-4B6	Royal Air Maroc
CN-RMH	Boeing 737-2T5	Royal Air Maroc
CN-RMI	Boeing 737-2B6	Royal Air Maroc *El Ayounne*
CN-RMJ	Boeing 737-2B6	Royal Air Maroc *Oujda*
CN-RMK	Boeing 737-2B6	Royal Air Maroc *Smara*
CN-RML	Boeing 737-2B6	Royal Air Maroc
CN-RMM	Boeing 737-2B6C	Royal Air Maroc
CN-RMN	Boeing 737-2B6C	Royal Air Maroc
CN-RMO	Boeing 727-2B6	Royal Air Maroc
CN-RMP	Boeing 727-2B6	Royal Air Maroc
CN-RMQ	Boeing 727-2B6	Royal Air Maroc
CN-RMR	Boeing 727-2B6	Royal Air Maroc
CN-RMS	Boeing 747SP-44	Royal Air Maroc
CN-RMT	Boeing 757-2B6	Royal Air Maroc
CN-RMU	Boeing 737-53A	Royal Air Maroc
CN-RMV	Boeing 737-5B6	Royal Air Maroc
CN-RMW	Boeing 737-5B6	Royal Air Maroc
CN-RMX	Boeing 737-4B6	Royal Air Maroc
CN-RMY	Boeing 737-5B6	Royal Air Maroc
CN-RMZ	Boeing 757-2B6	Royal Air Maroc

CS (Portugal)

Reg.	Type	Notes
CS-TEA	L.1011-385 TriStar 500	TAP — Air Portugal *Luis de Camoes*
CS-TEB	L.1011-385 TriStar 500	TAP — Air Portugal *Infante D. Henrique*
CS-TEC	L.1011-385 TriStar 500	TAP — Air Portugal *Gago Coutinho*
CS-TED	L.1011-385 TriStar 500	TAP — Air Portugal *Bartolomeu de Gusmao*

Notes	Reg.	Type	Owner or Operator
	CS-TEE	L.1011-385 TriStar 500	TAP — Air Portugal *St Antonio de Lisboa*
	CS-TEF	L.1011-385 TriStar 500	TAP — Air Portugal *Fernando Pessoa*
	CS-TEG	L.1011-385 TriStar 500	TAP — Air Portugal *Eca de Queiroz*
	CS-TEH	Airbus A.310-304	TAP — Air Portugal *Bartolomeu Dias*
	CS-TEI	Airbus A.310-304	TAP — Air Portugal *Fernao de Magalhaes*
	CS-TEJ	Airbus A.310-304	TAP — Air Portugal *Pedro Nunes*
	CS-TEK	Boeing 737-282	TAP — Air Portugal *Ponta Delgada*
	CS-TEL	Boeing 737-282	TAP — Air Portugal *Funchal*
	CS-TEM	Boeing 737-282	TAP — Air Portugal *Setubal*
	CS-TEN	Boeing 737-282	TAP — Air Portugal *Braga*
	CS-TEO	Boeing 737-282	TAP — Air Portugal *Evora*
	CS-TEP	Boeing 737-282	TAP — Air Portugal *Porto*
	CS-TEQ	Boeing 737-282C	TAP — Air Portugal *Vila Real*
	CS-TER	Boeing 737-230	TAP — Air Portugal *Aveiro*
	CS-TES	Boeing 737-230	TAP — Air Portugal *Viana do Castelo*
	CS-TET	Boeing 737-2K9	Air Atlantis *Viseu*
	CS-TEU	Boeing 737-2K9	Air Atlantis *Porto Santo*
	CS-TEV	Boeing 737-230	Air Atlantis
	CS-TEW	Airbus A.310-304	TAP — Air Portugal *Vasco da Gama*
	CS-TEX	Airbus A.310-304	TAP — Air Portugal *Joao XXI*
	CS-TEY	Airbus A.310-304	TAP — Air Portugal *Pedro Alvares Cabral*
	CS-TIA	Boeing 737-382	TAP — Air Portugal *Madeira*
	CS-TIB	Boeing 737-382	TAP — Air Portugal *Acores*
	CS-TIC	Boeing 737-382	TAP — Air Portugal *Algarve*
	CS-TID	Boeing 737-382	TAP — Air Portugal
	CS-TIE	Boeing 737-382	TAP — Air Portugal
	CS-TIF	Boeing 737-3K9	Air Atlantis
	CS-TIG	Boeing 737-3K9	Air Atlantis
	CS-TIH	Boeing 737-3K9	Air Atlantis
	CS-TII	Boeing 737-382	Air Atlantis
	CS-TIJ	Boeing 737-382	Air Atlantis
	CS-TIK	Boeing 737-382	Air Atlantis
	CS-TIL	Boeing 737-382	Air Atlantis
	CS-TIR	Boeing 737-3K2	Air Atlantis
	CS-TKA	Boeing 727-2J4RE	Air Columbus *Cristovao Colombo*
	CS-TKB	Boeing 727-2J4RE	Air Columbus
	CS-TMB	Boeing 737-291	Air Sul
	CS-TMC	Boeing 737-291	Air Sul
	CS-TMD	Boeing 737-2K5	Air Sul
	CS-TME	Boeing 737-2K5	Air Sul
	CS-TPA	Fokker 100	Portugalia *Albatroz*
	CS-TPB	Fokker 100	Portugalia *Pelicano*
	CS-TPC	Fokker 100	Portugalia

CU (Cuba)

CU-T1208	Ilyushin IL-62M	Cubana *Capt Wifredo Perez*
CU-T1209	Ilyushin IL-62M	Cubana
CU-T1215	Ilyushin IL-62M	Cubana
CU-T1216	Ilyushin IL-62M	Cubana
CU-T1217	Ilyushin IL-62M	Cubana
CU-T1218	Ilyushin IL-62M	Cubana
CU-T1225	Ilyushin IL-62M	Cubana
CU-T1226	Ilyushin IL-62M	Cubana
CU-T1252	Ilyushin IL-62M	Cubana
CU-T1259	Ilyushin IL-62M	Cubana
CU-T1280	Ilyushin IL-62M	Cubana
CU-T1282	Ilyushin IL-62M	Cubana

D (Germany)

D-AAST	S.E.210 Caravelle 10R	Aero Lloyd (*stored*)
D-ABAK	S.E.210 Caravelle 10R	Aero Lloyd (*stored*)
D-ABEA	Boeing 737-330	Lufthansa *Saarbrücken*
D-ABEB	Boeing 737-330	Lufthansa *Xanten*
D-ABEC	Boeing 737-330	Lufthansa
D-ABED	Boeing 737-330	Lufthansa
D-ABEE	Boeing 737-330	Lufthansa
D-ABEF	Boeing 737-330	Lufthansa
D-ABEH	Boeing 737-330	Lufthansa
D-ABEI	Boeing 737-330	Lufthansa
D-ABEK	Boeing 737-330	Lufthansa

Reg.	Type	Owner or Operator	Notes
D-ABEL	Boeing 737-330	Lufthansa	
D-ABEM	Boeing 737-330	Lufthansa	
D-ABEN	Boeing 737-330	Lufthansa	
D-ABEO	Boeing 737-330	Lufthansa	
D-ABEP	Boeing 737-330	Lufthansa	
D-ABER	Boeing 737-330	Lufthansa	
D-ABES	Boeing 737-330	Lufthansa	
D-ABFB	Boeing 737-230	Lufthansa *Flensburg*	
D-ABFP	Boeing 737-230	Lufthansa *Offenbach*	
D-ABFR	Boeing 737-230	Lufthansa *Solingen*	
D-ABFS	Boeing 737-230	Lufthansa *Oldenburg*	
D-ABFU	Boeing 737-230	Lufthansa *Mülheim a.d.Ruhr*	
D-ABFW	Boeing 737-230	Lufthansa *Wolfsburg*	
D-ABFX	Boeing 737-230	Lufthansa *Tübingen*	
D-ABFY	Boeing 737-230	Lufthansa *Göttingen*	
D-ABFZ	Boeing 737-230	Lufthansa *Wilhelmshaven*	
D-ABGE	Boeing 737-230F	German Cargo	
D-ABHA	Boeing 737-230	Lufthansa *Koblenz*	
D-ABHB	Boeing 737-230	Lufthansa *Goslar*	
D-ABHC	Boeing 737-230	Lufthansa *Friedrichshafen*	
D-ABHE	Boeing 737-230F	German Cargo	
D-ABHF	Boeing 737-230	Lufthansa *Heilbronn*	
D-ABHH	Boeing 737-230	Lufthansa *Marburg*	
D-ABHK	Boeing 737-230	Lufthansa *Bayreuth*	
D-ABHL	Boeing 737-230	Lufthansa *Worms*	
D-ABHM	Boeing 737-230	Lufthansa *Landshut*	
D-ABHN	Boeing 737-230	Lufthansa *Trier*	
D-ABHP	Boeing 737-230	Lufthansa *Erlangen*	
D-ABHR	Boeing 737-230	Lufthansa *Darmstadt*	
D-ABHS	Boeing 737-230	Lufthansa *Remscheid*	
D-ABHU	Boeing 737-230	Lufthansa *Konstanz*	
D-ABHW	Boeing 737-230	Lufthansa *Baden Baden*	
D-ABIA	Boeing 737-530	Lufthansa *Regensburg*	
D-ABIB	Boeing 737-530	Lufthansa *Wuppertal*	
D-ABIC	Boeing 737-530	Lufthansa *Coburg*	
D-ABID	Boeing 737-530	Lufthansa *Osnabrück*	
D-ABIE	Boeing 737-530	Lufthansa *Hildesheim*	
D-ABIF	Boeing 737-530	Lufthansa *Landau*	
D-ABIH	Boeing 737-530	Lufthansa *Völklingen*	
D-ABII	Boeing 737-530	Lufthansa *Lörrach*	
D-ABIK	Boeing 737-530	Lufthansa *Rastatt*	
D-ABIL	Boeing 737-530	Lufthansa *Memmingen*	
D-ABIM	Boeing 737-530	Lufthansa *Salzgitter*	
D-ABIN	Boeing 737-530	Lufthansa *Langenhangen*	
D-ABIO	Boeing 737-530	Lufthansa *Wesel*	
D-ABIP	Boeing 737-530	Lufthansa	
D-ABIR	Boeing 737-530	Lufthansa	
D-ABIS	Boeing 737-530	Lufthansa	
D-ABIT	Boeing 737-530	Lufthansa	
D-ABIU	Boeing 737-530	Lufthansa	
D-ABIW	Boeing 737-530	Lufthansa	
D-ABIX	Boeing 737-530	Lufthansa *Bamberg*	
D-ABIY	Boeing 737-530	Lufthansa *Wuerzburg*	
D-ABIZ	Boeing 737-530	Lufthansa *Gelsenkirchen*	
D-ABJA	Boeing 737-530	Lufthansa *Pforzheim*	
D-ABJB	Boeing 737-530	Lufthansa	
D-ABJC	Boeing 737-530	Lufthansa	
D-ABJD	Boeing 737-530	Lufthansa	
D-ABJE	Boeing 737-530	Lufthansa	
D-ABJF	Boeing 737-530	Lufthansa	
D-ABJH	Boeing 737-530	Lufthansa	
D-ABJI	Boeing 737-530	Lufthansa	
D-ABJK	Boeing 737-530	Lufthansa	
D-ABJL	Boeing 737-530	Lufthansa	
D-ABJM	Boeing 737-530	Lufthansa	
D-ABJN	Boeing 737-530	Lufthansa	
D-ABJP	Boeing 737-530	Lufthansa	
D-ABJR	Boeing 737-530	Lufthansa	
D-ABKA	Boeing 737-430	Lufthansa	
D-ABKB	Boeing 737-430	Lufthansa	
D-ABKC	Boeing 737-430	Lufthansa	
D-ABKD	Boeing 737-430	Lufthansa	
D-ABKF	Boeing 737-430	Lufthansa	

Notes	Reg.	Type	Owner or Operator
	D-ABKH	Boeing 737-430	Lufthansa
	D-ABKK	Boeing 737-430	Lufthansa
	D-ABKN	Boeing 727-230	Lufthansa
	D-ABMA	Boeing 737-230	Lufthansa *Idar-Oberstein*
	D-ABMB	Boeing 737-230	Lufthansa *Ingolstadt*
	D-ABMC	Boeing 737-230	Lufthansa *Norderstedt*
	D-ABMD	Boeing 737-230	Lufthansa *Paderborn*
	D-ABME	Boeing 737-230	Lufthansa *Schweinfurt*
	D-ABMF	Boeing 737-230	Lufthansa *Verden*
	D-ABNA	Boeing 757-230	Condor Flugdienst/Sudflug
	D-ABNB	Boeing 757-230	Condor Flugdienst/Sudflug
	D-ABNC	Boeing 757-230	Condor Flugdienst/Sudflug
	D-ABND	Boeing 757-230	Condor Flugdienst/Sudflug
	D-ABNE	Boeing 757-230	Condor Flugdienst/Sudflug
	D-ABNF	Boeing 757-230	Condor Flugdienst/Sudflug
	D-ABNH	Boeing 757-230	Condor Flugdienst/Sudflug
	D-ABNI	Boeing 757-230	Condor Flugdienst/Sudflug
	D-ABNK	Boeing 757-230	Condor Flugdienst/Sudflug
	D-ABNL	Boeing 757-230	Condor Flugdienst/Sudflug
	D-ABNM	Boeing 757-230	Condor Flugdienst/Sudflug
	D-ABNN	Boeing 757-230	Condor Flugdienst/Sudflug
	D-ABNO	Boeing 757-230	Condor Flugdienst/Sudflug
	D-ABTA	Boeing 747-430 (SCD)	Lufthansa *Sachsen*
	D-ABTB	Boeing 747-430 (SCD)	Lufthansa
	D-ABTC	Boeing 747-430 (SCD)	Lufthansa *Brandenburg*
	D-ABTD	Boeing 747-430 (SCD)	Lufthansa *Hamburg*
	D-ABTE	Boeing 747-430 (SCD)	Lufthansa *Sachsen-Anhalt*
	D-ABTF	Boeing 747-430 (SCD)	Lufthansa *Thüeringen*
	D-ABTH	Boeing 747-430 (SCD)	Lufthansa
	D-ABUA	Boeing 767-330ER	Condor Flugdienst
	D-ABUB	Boeing 767-330ER	Condor Flugdienst
	D-ABUC	Boeing 767-330ER	Condor Flugdienst
	D-ABUD	Boeing 767-330ER	Condor Flugdienst
	D-ABUX	Boeing 767-330ER	Condor Flugdienst/Sudflug
	D-ABUY	Boeing 767-330ER	Condor Flugdienst/Sudflug
	D-ABUZ	Boeing 767-330ER	Condor Flugdienst/Sudflug
	D-ABVA	Boeing 747-430	Lufthansa *Berlin*
	D-ABVB	Boeing 747-430	Lufthansa *Bonn*
	D-ABVC	Boeing 747-430	Lufthansa *Baden-Württemberg*
	D-ABVD	Boeing 747-430	Lufthansa/Condor Flugdienst
	D-ABVE	Boeing 747-430	Lufthansa *Potsdam*
	D-ABVF	Boeing 747-430	Lufthansa/Condor Flugdienst
	D-ABVH	Boeing 747-430	Lufthansa
	D-ABVK	Boeing 747-430	Lufthansa
	D-ABVL	Boeing 747-430	Lufthansa
	D-ABVM	Boeing 747-430	Lufthansa
	D-ABVN	Boeing 747-430	Lufthansa
	D-ABWA	Boeing 737-330	Condor Flugdienst *Claus Gillmann*
	D-ABWB	Boeing 737-330	Condor Flugdienst
	D-ABWC	Boeing 737-330	Condor Flugdienst
	D-ABWD	Boeing 737-330	Condor Flugdienst
	D-ABWE	Boeing 737-330	Condor Flugdienst
	D-ABWF	Boeing 737-330	Condor Flugdienst
	D-ABWH	Boeing 737-330	Condor Flugdienst
	D-ABXA	Boeing 737-330	Lufthansa *Giessen*
	D-ABXB	Boeing 737-330	Lufthansa *Passau*
	D-ABXC	Boeing 737-330	Lufthansa *Delmenhorst*
	D-ABXD	Boeing 737-330	Lufthansa *Siegen*
	D-ABXE	Boeing 737-330	Lufthansa *Hamm*
	D-ABXF	Boeing 737-330	Lufthansa *Minden*
	D-ABXH	Boeing 737-330	Lufthansa *Cuxhaven*
	D-ABXI	Boeing 737-330	Lufthansa *Berchtesgaden*
	D-ABXK	Boeing 737-330	Lufthansa *Ludwigsburg*
	D-ABXL	Boeing 737-330	Lufthansa *Neuss*
	D-ABXM	Boeing 737-330	Lufthansa *Herford*
	D-ABXN	Boeing 737-330	Lufthansa *Böblingen*
	D-ABXO	Boeing 737-330	Lufthansa *Schwäbisch-Gmünd*
	D-ABXP	Boeing 737-330	Lufthansa *Fulda*
	D-ABXR	Boeing 737-330	Lufthansa *Celle*
	D-ABXS	Boeing 737-330	Lufthansa *Sindelfingen*
	D-ABXT	Boeing 737-330	Lufthansa *Reutlingen*
	D-ABXU	Boeing 737-330	Lufthansa *Seeheim-Jugenheim*
	D-ABXW	Boeing 737-330	Lufthansa *Hanau*

Reg.	Type	Owner or Operator	Notes
D-ABXX	Boeing 737-330	Lufthansa *Bad Homberg v.d. Höhe*	
D-ABXY	Boeing 737-330	Lufthansa *Hof*	
D-ABXZ	Boeing 737-330	Lufthansa *Bad Mergentheim*	
D-ABYJ	Boeing 747-230B (SCD)	Lufthansa *Hessen*	
D-ABYK	Boeing 747-230B (SCD)	Lufthansa *Rheinland-Pfalz*	
D-ABYL	Boeing 747-230B (SCD)	Lufthansa *Saarland*	
D-ABYM	Boeing 747-230B (SCD)	Lufthansa *Schleswig-Holstein*	
D-ABYO	Boeing 747-230F (SCD)	Lufthansa *America*	
D-ABYP	Boeing 747-230B	Lufthansa *Niedersachen*	
D-ABYQ	Boeing 747-230B	Lufthansa *Bremen*	
D-ABYR	Boeing 747-230B (SCD)	Lufthansa *Nordrhein-Westfalen*	
D-ABYS	Boeing 747-230B (SCD)	Lufthansa *Bayern*	
D-ABYT	Boeing 747-230F (SCD)	German Cargo	
D-ABYU	Boeing 747-230F (SCD)	Lufthansa *Asia*	
D-ABYW	Boeing 747-230F (SCD)	German Cargo	
D-ABYX	Boeing 747-230B (SCD)	Lufthansa *Köln*	
D-ABYY	Boeing 747-230F (SCD)	German Cargo	
D-ABYZ	Boeing 747-230B (SCD)	Lufthansa *Frankfurt*	
D-ABZA	Boeing 747-230B (SCD)	Lufthansa *Düsseldorf*	
D-ABZB	Boeing 747-230F (SCD)	Lufthansa *Europa*	
D-ABZC	Boeing 747-230B (SCD)	Lufthansa *Hannover*	
D-ABZD	Boeing 747-230B	Lufthansa *Kiel*	
D-ABZE	Boeing 747-230B (SCD)	Lufthansa *Stuttgart*	
D-ABZF	Boeing 747-230F (SCD)	Lufthansa *Africa*	
D-ABZH	Boeing 747-230B	Lufthansa *Bonn*	
D-ABZI	Boeing 747-230F (SCD)	Lufthansa *Australia*	
D-ACBA	Boeing 737-505	Lufthansa	
D-ACBB	Boeing 737-505	Lufthansa	
D-ACBC	Boeing 737-505	Lufthansa	
D-ACVK	S.E.210 Caravelle 10R	Aero Lloyd *Otto Trump* (stored)	
D-ADBO	Douglas DC-10-30	Lufthansa	
D-ADCO	Douglas DC-10-30	Lufthansa	
D-ADDO	Douglas DC-10-30	Lufthansa *Duisburg*	
D-ADEP	F.27 Friendship Mk 600	Ratioflug	
D-ADFO	Douglas DC-10-30	Lufthansa	
D-ADGO	Douglas DC-10-30	Lufthansa	
D-ADHO	Douglas DC-10-30	Lufthansa	
D-ADJO	Douglas DC-10-30	Lufthansa *Essen*	
D-ADKO	Douglas DC-10-30	Lufthansa	
D-ADLO	Douglas DC-10-30	Lufthansa *Nurnberg*	
D-ADMO	Douglas DC-10-30	Lufthansa *Dortmund*	
D-ADPO	Douglas DC-10-30	Condor Flugdienst	
D-ADQO	Douglas DC-10-30	Condor Flugdienst	
D-ADSO	Douglas DC-10-30	Condor Flugdienst	
D-ADUA	Douglas DC-8-73AF	German Cargo	
D-ADUC	Douglas DC-8-73AF	German Cargo	
D-ADUE	Douglas DC-8-73AF	German Cargo	
D-ADUI	Douglas DC-8-73AF	German Cargo	
D-ADUO	Douglas DC-8-73AF	German Cargo	
D-AELC	F.27 Friendship Mk 600	WDL	
D-AELD	F.27 Friendship Mk 600	WDL	
D-AELE	F.27 Friendship Mk 600	WDL	
D-AERB	McD Douglas MD-11	LTU	
D-AERE	L.1011-385 TriStar 1	LTU	
D-AERL	L.1011-385 TriStar 500	LTU	
D-AERM	L.1011-385 TriStar 1	LTU	
D-AERN	L.1011-385 TriStar 200	LTU	
D-AERP	L.1011-385 TriStar 1	LTU	
D-AERT	L.1011-385 TriStar 500	LTU	
D-AERU	L.1011-385 TriStar 100	LTU	
D-AERV	L.1011-385 TriStar 500	LTU	
D-AERW	McD Douglas MD-11	LTU	
D-AERX	McD Douglas MD-11	LTU	
D-AERY	L.1011-385 TriStar 1	LTU	
D-AERZ	McD Douglas MD-11	LTU	
D-AFEH	F.27 Friendship Mk 600	Ratioflug/Federal Express	
D-AFKA	Fokker 50	Lufthansa CityLine	
D-AFKB	Fokker 50	Lufthansa CityLine	
D-AFKC	Fokker 50	Lufthansa CityLine	
D-AFKD	Fokker 50	Lufthansa CityLine	
D-AFKE	Fokker 50	Lufthansa CityLine	
D-AFKF	Fokker 50	Lufthansa CityLine	
D-AFKG	Fokker 50	Lufthansa CityLine	

Notes	Reg.	Type	Owner or Operator
	D-AFKH	Fokker 50	Lufthansa CityLine
	D-AFKI	Fokker 50	Lufthansa CityLine
	D-AFKJ	Fokker 50	Lufthansa CityLine
	D-AFKK	Fokker 50	Lufthansa CityLine
	D-AFKL	Fokker 50	Lufthansa CityLine
	D-AFKM	Fokker 50	Lufthansa CityLine
	D-AFKN	Fokker 50	Lufthansa CityLine
	D-AFKO	Fokker 50	Lufthansa CityLine
	D-AFKP	Fokker 50	Lufthansa CityLine
	D-AFKR	Fokker 50	Lufthansa CityLine
	D-AFKU	Fokker 50	Lufthansa CityLine
	D-AFKV	Fokker 50	Lufthansa CityLine
	D-AFKX	Fokker 50	Lufthansa CityLine
	D-AFKY	Fokker 50	Lufthansa CityLine
	D-AFKZ	Fokker 50	Lufthansa CityLine
	D-AGEA	Boeing 737-35B	Germania
	D-AGEB	Boeing 737-35B	Germania
	D-AGEC	Boeing 737-35B	Germania/Condor Flugdienst
	D-AGED	Boeing 737-35B	Germania/Condor Flugdienst
	D-AGEE	Boeing 737-35B	Germania
	D-AGEG	Boeing 737-35B	Germania
	D-AGEH	Boeing 737-3L9	Germania
	D-AG	Boeing 737-3L9	Germania
	D-AG	Boeing 737-3L9	Germania
	D-AGWC	McD Douglas MD-83	Aero Lloyd
	D-AGWD	McD Douglas MD-83	Aero Lloyd
	D-AHLA	Airbus A.310-304	Hapag-Lloyd
	D-AHLB	Airbus A.310-304	Hapag-Lloyd
	D-AHLC	—	—
	D-AHLD	Boeing 737-5K5	Hapag-Lloyd
	D-AHLE	Boeing 737-5K5	Hapag-Lloyd
	D-AHLF	Boeing 737-5K5	Hapag-Lloyd
	D-AHLI	Boeing 737-5K5	Hapag-Lloyd
	D-AHLJ	Boeing 737-4K5	Hapag-Lloyd
	D-AHLK	Boeing 737-4K5	Hapag-Lloyd
	D-AHLL	Boeing 737-4K5	Hapag-Lloyd
	D-AHLN	Boeing 737-5K5	Hapag-Lloyd
	D-AHLO	Boeing 737-4K5	Hapag-Lloyd
	D-AHLP	Boeing 737-4K5	Hapag-Lloyd
	D-AHLQ	Boeing 737-4K5	Hapag-Lloyd
	D-AHLR	Boeing 737-4K5	Hapag-Lloyd
	D-AHLV	Airbus A.310-204	Hapag-Lloyd
	D-AHLW	Airbus A.310-204	Hapag-Lloyd
	D-AHLX	Airbus A.310-204	Hapag-Lloyd
	D-AHLZ	Airbus A.310-204	Hapag-Lloyd
	D-AIAH	Airbus A.300-603	Lufthansa *Lindau/Bodenzee*
	D-AIAI	Airbus A.300-603	Lufthansa *Erbach/Odenwald*
	D-AIAK	Airbus A.300-603	Lufthansa *Kronberg/Taunus*
	D-AIAL	Airbus A.300-603	Lufthansa *Stade*
	D-AIAM	Airbus A.300-603	Lufthansa *Rosenheim*
	D-AIAN	Airbus A.300-603	Lufthansa *Nördlingen*
	D-AIAP	Airbus A.300-603	Lufthansa *Donauwörth*
	D-AIAR	Airbus A.300-603	Lufthansa *Bingen am Rhein*
	D-AIAS	Airbus A.300-603	Lufthansa *Moenchengladbach*
	D-AIAT	Airbus A.300-603	Lufthansa
	D-AIAU	Airbus A.300-603	Lufthansa
	D-AIBA	Airbus A.340-211	Lufthansa
	D-AIBB	Airbus A.340-211	Lufthansa
	D-AIBC	Airbus A.340-211	Lufthansa
	D-AIBD	Airbus A.340-211	Lufthansa
	D-AIBE	Airbus A.340-211	Lufthansa
	D-AIBF	Airbus A.340-211	Lufthansa
	D-AIBG	Airbus A.340-211	Lufthansa
	D-AIBH	Airbus A.340-211	Lufthansa
	D-AICA	Airbus A.310-203	Lufthansa *Neustadt an der Weinstrausse*
	D-AICB	Airbus A.310-203	Lufthansa *Garmisch-Partenkirchern*
	D-AICC	Airbus A.310-203	Lufthansa *Kaiserslautern*
	D-AICD	Airbus A.310-203	Lufthansa *Detmold*
	D-AICF	Airbus A.310-203	Lufthansa *Rüdesheim am Rhein*
	D-AICH	Airbus A.310-203	Lufthansa *Lüneburg*
	D-AICK	Airbus A.310-203	Lufthansa *Westerland-Sylt*
	D-AICL	Airbus A.310-203	Lufthansa *Rothenburg ob der Tauber*
	D-AICM	Airbus A.310-203	Lufthansa
	D-AICN	Airbus A.310-203	Lufthansa *Lubeck*

Reg.	Type	Owner or Operator	Notes
D-AICP	Airbus A.310-203	Lufthansa *Bremerhaven*	
D-AICR	Airbus A.310-203	Lufthansa *Freudenstadt*	
D-AICS	Airbus A.310-203	Lufthansa *Recklinghausen*	
D-AIDA	Airbus A.310-304	Condor Flugdienst/Lufthansa	
D-AIDB	Airbus A.310-304	Lufthansa *Fürth*	
D-AIDC	Airbus A.310-304	Condor Flugdienst/Lufthansa	
D-AIDD	Airbus A.310-304	Lufthansa *Emden*	
D-AIDE	Airbus A.310-304	Lufthansa *Speyer*	
D-AIDF	Airbus A.310-304	Lufthansa *Aschaffenburg*	
D-AIDH	Airbus A.310-304	Lufthansa *Wetzlar*	
D-AIDI	Airbus A.310-304	Lufthansa *Fellbach*	
D-AIDK	Airbus A.310-304	Lufthansa *Donaueschingen*	
D-AIDL	Airbus A.310-304	Lufthansa *Obersdorf*	
D-AIDM	Airbus A.310-304	Lufthansa	
D-AIDN	Airbus A.310-304	Lufthansa	
D-AIPA	Airbus A.320-211	Lufthansa *Buxtehude*	
D-AIPB	Airbus A.320-211	Lufthansa *Heidelberg*	
D-AIPC	Airbus A.320-211	Lufthansa *Braunschweig*	
D-AIPD	Airbus A.320-211	Lufthansa *Freiburg*	
D-AIPE	Airbus A.320-211	Lufthansa *Kassel*	
D-AIPF	Airbus A.320-211	Lufthansa *Leipzig*	
D-AIPH	Airbus A.320-211	Lufthansa *Munster*	
D-AIPK	Airbus A.320-211	Lufthansa *Wiesbaden*	
D-AIPL	Airbus A.320-211	Lufthansa *Ludwigshafen*	
D-AIPM	Airbus A.320-211	Lufthansa *Troisdorf*	
D-AIPN	Airbus A.320-211	Lufthansa *Kulmbach*	
D-AIPP	Airbus A.320-211	Lufthansa *Starnberg*	
D-AIPR	Airbus A.320-211	Lufthansa *Kaufbeuren*	
D-AIPS	Airbus A.320-211	Lufthansa *Augsburg*	
D-AIPT	Airbus A.320-211	Lufthansa *Cottbus*	
D-AIPU	Airbus A.320-211	Lufthansa *Dresden*	
D-AIPW	Airbus A.320-211	Lufthansa *Schwerin*	
D-AIPX	Airbus A.320-211	Lufthansa *Mannheim*	
D-AIPY	Airbus A.320-211	Lufthansa *Magdeburg*	
D-AIPZ	Airbus A.320-211	Lufthansa *Erfurt*	
D-AIQA	Airbus A.320-211	Lufthansa	
D-AIQB	Airbus A.320-211	Lufthansa *Bielefeld*	
D-AIQC	Airbus A.320-211	Lufthansa	
D-AIQD	Airbus A.320-211	Lufthansa	
D-AIQE	Airbus A.320-211	Lufthansa	
D-AIQF	Airbus A.320-211	Lufthansa	
D-AIQH	Airbus A.320-211	Lufthansa	
D-AIQK	Airbus A.320-211	Lufthansa	
D-AIQL	Airbus A.320-211	Lufthansa	
D-AIQM	Airbus A.320-211	Lufthansa	
D-AIQN	Airbus A.320-211	Lufthansa	
D-AIQP	Airbus A.320-211	Lufthansa	
D-AISY	F.27 Friendship Mk 600	Ratioflug/Federal Express	
D-AJET	BAe 146-200	EPC-Contiflug	
D-ALLA	Douglas DC-9-32	Aero Lloyd	
D-ALLB	Douglas DC-9-32	Aero Lloyd	
D-ALLC	Douglas DC-9-32	Aero Lloyd	
D-ALLD	McD Douglas MD-83	Aero Lloyd	
D-ALLE	McD Douglas MD-83	Aero Lloyd	
D-ALLF	McD Douglas MD-83	Aero Lloyd	
D-ALLG	McD Douglas MD-87	Aero Lloyd	
D-ALLH	McD Douglas MD-87	Aero Lloyd	
D-ALLI	McD Douglas MD-87	Aero Lloyd	
D-ALLJ	McD Douglas MD-87	Aero Lloyd	
D-ALLK	McD Douglas MD-83	Aero Lloyd	
D-ALLL	McD Douglas MD-83	Aero Lloyd	
D-ALLM	McD Douglas MD-83	Aero Lloyd	
D-ALLN	McD Douglas MD-83	Aero Lloyd	
D-ALLO	McD Douglas MD-83	Aero Lloyd	
D-ALLP	McD Douglas MD-83	Aero Lloyd	
D-ALLQ	McD Douglas MD-83	Aero Lloyd	
D-ALLR	McD Douglas MD-83	Aero Lloyd	
D-AL	McD Douglas MD-83	Aero Lloyd	
D-AL	McD Douglas MD-83	Aero Lloyd	
D-AMUM	Boeing 757-2G5	LTU-Sud	
D-AMUN	Boeing 767-3G5ER	LTU-Sud	
D-AMUR	Boeing 767-3G5ER	LTU-Sud	
D-AMUS	Boeing 767-3G5ER	LTU-Sud	
D-AMUU	Boeing 757-225	LTU-Sud	

Notes	Reg.	Type	Owner or Operator
	D-AMUV	Boeing 757-2G5ER	LTU-Sud
	D-AMUW	Boeing 757-2G5ER	LTU-Sud
	D-AMUX	Boeing 757-2G5ER	LTU-Sud
	D-AMUY	Boeing 757-2G5ER	LTU-Sud
	D-AMUZ	Boeing 757-2G5	LTU-Sud
	D-ANFA	Aerospatiale ATR-72-202	Nürnberger Flugdienst (NFD)
	D-ANFB	Aerospatiale ATR-72-202	Nürnberger Flugdienst (NFD)
	D-ANFC	Aerospatiale ATR-72-202	Nürnberger Flugdienst (NFD)
	D-ANFD	Aerospatiale ATR-72-202	Nürnberger Flugdienst (NFD)
	D-AN	Aerospatiale ATR-72-202	Nürnberger Flugdienst (NFD)
	D-AN	Aerospatiale ATR-72-202	Nürnberger Flugdienst (NFD)
	D-ANTJ	BAe 146-200QT	NFD/TNT Express Europe
	D-BAAA	Aerospatiale ATR-42-300	Nürnberger Flugdienst (NFD)
	D-BAKA	F.27 Friendship Mk 100	WDL
	D-BAKI	F.27 Friendship Mk 100	WDL
	D-BAKO	F.27 Friendship Mk 100	WDL
	D-BAKU	F.27 Friendship Mk 100	WDL
	D-BBBB	Aerospatiale ATR-42-300	Nürnberger Flugdienst (NFD)
	D-BCCC	Aerospatiale ATR-42-300	Nürnberger Flugdienst (NFD)
	D-BCRM	Aerospatiale ATR-42-300	R.F.G.
	D-BCRN	Aerospatiale ATR-42-300	R.F.G.
	D-BCRO	Aerospatiale ATR-42-300QC	R.F.G.
	D-BCRP	Aerospatiale ATR-42-300QC	R.F.G.
	D-BCRQ	Aerospatiale ATR-42-300	R.F.G.
	D-BCRR	Aerospatiale ATR-42-300	R.F.G.
	D-BDDD	Aerospatiale ATR-42-300	Nürnberger Flugdienst (NFD)
	D-BEAT	D.H.C. 8-311 Dash Eight	Contactair/D.L.T.
	D-BEEE	Aerospatiale ATR-42-300	Nürnberger Flugdienst (NFD)
	D-BELT	D.H.C.8-311 Dash Eight	Contactair/D.L.T.
	D-BERT	D.H.C.8-103 Dash Eight	Contactair/D.L.T.
	D-BEST	D.H.C.8-103 Dash Eight	Contactair/D.L.T.
	D-BEYT	D.H.C.8-311 Dash Eight	Contactair/D.L.T.
	D-BFFF	Aerospatiale ATR-42-300	Nürnberger Flugdienst (NFD)
	D-BGGG	Aerospatiale ATR-42-300	Nürnberger Flugdienst (NFD)
	D-BHHH	Aerospatiale ATR-42-300	Nürnberger Flugdienst (NFD)
	D-BIII	Aerospatiale ATR-42-300	Nürnberger Flugdienst (NFD)
	D-BIRT	D.H.C.8-103 Dash Eight	Interot Airways
	D-BJJJ	Aerospatiale ATR-42-300	Nürnberger Flugdienst (NFD)
	D-BOBA	D.H.C.8-311 Dash Eight	Hamburg Airlines
	D-BOBL	D.H.C.8-102 Dash Eight	Hamburg Airlines
	D-BOBO	D.H.C.8-102 Dash Eight	Hamburg Airlines
	D-BOBU	D.H.C.8-311 Dash Eight	Hamburg Airlines
	D-BOBY	D.H.C.8-102 Dash Eight	Hamburg Airlines
	D-CABE	Swearingen SA227AC Metro III	Nürnberger Flugdienst (NFD)
	D-CABI	Swearingen SA227AC Metro III	Nürnberger Flugdienst (NFD)
	D-CCCC	Douglas DC-3	Classic Wings
	D-CDIA	Saab SF.340A	Delta Air
	D-CDIB	Saab SF.340A	Delta Air
	D-CDIC	Saab SF.340A	Delta Air
	D-CDID	Saab SF.340A	Delta Air
	D-CDIE	Saab SF.340A	Delta Air
	D-CDIF	Saab SF.340A	Delta Air
	D-CDIG	Saab SF.340A	Delta Air
	D-CDIH	Saab SF.340A	Delta Air
	D-CDIZ	Dornier Do.228-201	Delta Air
	D-CHOF	Dornier Do.228-201	Nürnberger Flugdienst (NFD)
	D-CIRB	Beech 1900C-1	Interot Airways
	D-CISA	Beech 1900C	Interot Airways
	D-CKVW	Swearingen SA227AC Metro III	Nürnberger Flugdienst (NFD)
	D-CMIC	Dornier Do.228-202K	Ratioflug
	D-CONA	BAe Jetstream 3102	Contactair
	D-CONU	BAe Jetstream 3102	Contactair
	D-ICRJ	Swearingen SA226TC Metro II	R.F.G.
	D-ICRK	Swearingen SA226TC Metro II	R.F.G.
	D-ICRL	Swearingen SA226TC Metro II	R.F.G.
	D-IHCW	Swearingen SA226TC Metro II	R.F.G.

EC (Spain)

	EC-BIG	Douglas DC-9-32	Iberia *Villa de Madrid*
	EC-BIH	Douglas DC-9-32	Aviaco *Ciudad de Barcelona*
	EC-BIJ	Douglas DC-9-32	Iberia *Santa Cruz de Tenerife*
	EC-BIK	Douglas DC-9-32	Aviaco *Castillo de Guanapa*

Reg.	Type	Owner or Operator	Notes
EC-BIL	Douglas DC-9-32	Viva Air	
EC-BIM	Douglas DC-9-32	Iberia *Ciudad de Santander*	
EC-BIN	Douglas DC-9-32	Iberia *Ciudad de Palma de Mallorca*	
EC-BIO	Douglas DC-9-32	Iberia *Villa de Bilbao*	
EC-BIP	Douglas DC-9-32	Aviaco *Castillo de Monteagudo*	
EC-BIR	Douglas DC-9-32	Iberia *Ciudad de Valencia*	
EC-BIS	Douglas DC-9-32	Iberia *Ciudad de Alicante*	
EC-BIT	Douglas DC-9-32	Iberia *Ciudad de San Sebastian*	
EC-BIU	Douglas DC-9-32	Viva Air	
EC-BPF	Douglas DC-9-32	Viva Air	
EC-BPG	Douglas DC-9-32	Iberia *Ciudad de Vigo*	
EC-BPH	Douglas DC-9-32	Iberia *Ciudad de Gerona*	
EC-BQT	Douglas DC-9-32	Iberia *Ciudad de Murcia*	
EC-BQU	Douglas DC-9-32	Iberia *Ciudad de La Coruna*	
EC-BQV	Douglas DC-9-32	Iberia *Ciudad de Ibiza*	
EC-BQX	Douglas DC-9-32	Iberia *Ciudad de Valladolid*	
EC-BQY	Douglas DC-9-32	Aviaco	
EC-BQZ	Douglas DC-9-32	Iberia *Sta. Cruz de Palma*	
EC-BRQ	Boeing 747-256B	Iberia *Calderon de la Barca*	
EC-BYD	Douglas DC-9-32	Aviaco *Ciudad de Arrecife de Lanzarote*	
EC-BYE	Douglas DC-9-32	Aviaco *Ciudad de Mahon*	
EC-BYF	Douglas DC-9-32	Aviaco	
EC-BYG	Douglas DC-9-32	Aviaco *Ciudad de Pamplona*	
EC-BYH	Douglas DC-9-32	Aviaco *Castillo de Butron*	
EC-BYI	Douglas DC-9-32	Aviaco *Francisco de Pizarro*	
EC-BYJ	Douglas DC-9-32	Aviaco	
EC-CAI	Boeing 727-256	Iberia *Castilla la Nueva*	
EC-CAJ	Boeing 727-256	Iberia *Cataluna*	
EC-CAK	Boeing 727-256	Iberia *Aragon*	
EC-CBA	Boeing 727-256	Iberia *Vascongadas*	
EC-CBB	Boeing 727-256	Iberia *Valencia*	
EC-CBC	Boeing 727-256	Iberia *Navarra*	
EC-CBD	Boeing 727-256	Iberia *Murcia*	
EC-CBE	Boeing 727-256	Iberia *Leon*	
EC-CBF	Boeing 727-256	Iberia *Gran Canaria*	
EC-CBG	Boeing 727-256	Iberia *Extremadura*	
EC-CBH	Boeing 727-256	Iberia *Galicia*	
EC-CBI	Boeing 727-256	Iberia *Asturias*	
EC-CBJ	Boeing 727-256	Iberia *Andalucia*	
EC-CBK	Boeing 727-256	Iberia *Baleares*	
EC-CBL	Boeing 727-256	Iberia *Tenerife*	
EC-CBM	Boeing 727-256	Iberia *Castilla La Vieja*	
EC-CBO	Douglas DC-10-30	Iberia *Costa del Sol*	
EC-CBP	Douglas DC-10-30	Iberia *Costa Dorada*	
EC-CEZ	Douglas DC-10-30	Iberia *Costa del Azahar*	
EC-CFA	Boeing 727-256	Iberia *Jerez Xeres Sherry*	
EC-CFB	Boeing 727-256	Iberia *Rioja*	
EC-CFC	Boeing 727-256	Iberia *Tarragona*	
EC-CFD	Boeing 727-256	Iberia *Montilla-Moriles*	
EC-CFE	Boeing 727-256	Iberia *Penedes*	
EC-CFF	Boeing 727-256	Iberia *Valdepenas*	
EC-CFG	Boeing 727-256	Iberia *La Mancha*	
EC-CFH	Boeing 727-256	Iberia *Priorato*	
EC-CFI	Boeing 727-256	Iberia *Carinena*	
EC-CFK	Boeing 727-256	Iberia *Ribeiro*	
EC-CGN	Douglas DC-9-32	Aviaco *Martin Alonso Pinzon*	
EC-CGO	Douglas DC-9-32	Aviaco *Pedro Alonso Nino*	
EC-CGP	Douglas DC-9-32	Aviaco *Juan Sebastian Elcano*	
EC-CGQ	Douglas DC-9-32	Aviaco *Alonso de Ojeda*	
EC-CGR	Douglas DC-9-32	Aviaco *Francisco de Orellana*	
EC-CID	Boeing 727-256	Iberia *Malaga*	
EC-CIE	Boeing 727-256	Iberia *Esparragosa*	
EC-CLB	Douglas DC-10-30	Iberia *Costa Blanca*	
EC-CLD	Douglas DC-9-32	Aviaco *Hernando de Soto*	
EC-CLE	Douglas DC-9-32	Aviaco *Juan Ponce de Leon*	
EC-CSJ	Douglas DC-10-30	Iberia *Costa de la Luz*	
EC-CSK	Douglas DC-10-30	Iberia *Cornisa Cantabrica*	
EC-CTR	Douglas DC-9-34CF	Cargosur	
EC-CTS	Douglas DC-9-34CF	Cargosur	
EC-CTT	Douglas DC-9-34CF	Cargosur	
EC-CTU	Douglas DC-9-34CF	Cargosur	
EC-DCC	Boeing 727-256	Iberia *Albarino*	
EC-DCD	Boeing 727-256	Iberia *Chacoli-Txakoli*	

Notes	Reg.	Type	Owner or Operator
	EC-DCE	Boeing 727-256	Iberia *Mentrida*
	EC-DDV	Boeing 727-256	Iberia *Acueducto de Segovia*
	EC-DDX	Boeing 727-256	Iberia *Monasterio de Poblet*
	EC-DDY	Boeing 727-256	Iberia *Cuevas de Altamira*
	EC-DDZ	Boeing 727-256	Iberia *Murallas de Avila*
	EC-DEA	Douglas DC-10-30	Iberia *Rias Gallegas*
	EC-DGB	Douglas DC-9-34	Iberia
	EC-DGC	Douglas DC-9-34	Aviaco *Castillo de Sotomayor*
	EC-DGD	Douglas DC-9-34	Aviaco *Castillo de Arcos*
	EC-DGE	Douglas DC-9-34	Aviaco *Castillo de Bellver*
	EC-DHZ	Douglas DC-10-30	Iberia *Costas Canarias*
	EC-DIA	Boeing 747-256B	Iberia *Tirso de Molina*
	EC-DIB	Boeing 747-256B	Iberia *Cervantes*
	EC-DLC	Boeing 747-256B (SCD)	Iberia *Francisco de Quevedo*
	EC-DLD	Boeing 747-256B (SCD)	Iberia *Lupe de Vega*
	EC-DLE	Airbus A.300B4-120	Iberia *Donana*
	EC-DLF	Airbus A.300B4-120	Iberia *Teide*
	EC-DLG	Airbus A.300B4-120	Iberia *Las Tablas de Daimiel*
	EC-DLH	Airbus A.300B4-120	Iberia *Aigues Tortes*
	EC-DNP	Boeing 747-256B	Iberia *Juan Ramon Jimenez*
	EC-DNQ	Airbus A.300B4-120	Iberia *Islas Cies*
	EC-DNR	Airbus A.300B4-120	Iberia *Ordesa*
	EC-ECR	Boeing 737-3Y0	Air Europa
	EC-ECS	Boeing 737-375	Air Europa
	EC-EEK	Boeing 747-256B (SCD)	Iberia *Garcia Lorca*
	EC-EFU	McD Douglas MD-83	Meridiana Air *Isla de Lanzarote*
	EC-EFX	Boeing 757-2G5	LTE International Airways *Bluebird I*
	EC-EGH	Boeing 757-2G5	LTE International Airways *Bluebird II*
	EC-EHA	Boeing 737-3L9	Air Europa
	EC-EHT	McD Douglas MD-83	Spanair *Sunrise*
	EC-EID	Boeing 737-3T0	Meridiana Air
	EC-EIG	McD Douglas MD-83	Spanair *Sunlight*
	EC-EIK	McD Douglas MD-83	Aviaco
	EC-EJQ	McD Douglas MD-83	Spanair *Sunshine*
	EC-EJU	McD Douglas MD-83	Spanair *Sunbird*
	EC-EJZ	McD Douglas MD-83	Meridiana Air
	EC-EKM	McD Douglas MD-83	Meridiana Air
	EC-ELJ	Boeing 737-3QB	Viva Air
	EC-ELM	Douglas DC-8-62F	Cargosur
	EC-ELT	BAe 146-200QT	Pan Air Lineas Aéreas/TNT
	EC-ELY	Boeing 737-3K9	Viva Air
	EC-EMD	Douglas DC-8-62F	Cargosur
	EC-EMG	McD Douglas MD-83	Meridiana Air
	EC-EMI	Boeing 737-4Y0	Nortjet *Alava*
	EC-EMT	McD Douglas MD-83	Aviaco *Puerta de Alcala*
	EC-EMX	Douglas DC-8-62F	Cargosur
	EC-EMY	Boeing 737-4Y0	Nortjet *Guipuzcoa*
	EC-ENQ	Boeing 757-2G5	LTE International Airways *Bluebird III*
	EC-EOL	Boeing 757-236	Air Europa
	EC-EOM	McD Douglas MD-83	Oasis International Airlines
	EC-EON	Airbus A.300B4	Iberia *Penalara*
	EC-EOO	Airbus A.300B4	Iberia
	EC-EOZ	McD Douglas MD-83	Spanair *Sunbeam*
	EC-EPA	BAe 146-200QT	Pan Air Lineas Aéreas/TNT
	EC-EPL	McD Douglas MD-83	Spanair *Sunseeker*
	EC-EPM	McD Douglas MD-83	Oasis International Airlines
	EC-EPN	Boeing 737-4Y0	Nortjet *Vizcaya*
	EC-EQI	Douglas DC-8-62F	Cargosur
	EC-ESC	Boeing 757-236ER	Air Europa
	EC-ESJ	McD Douglas MD-83	Spanair *Sunflower*
	EC-EST	Boeing 737-3L9	Air Europa
	EC-ETB	Boeing 737-4Y0	Futura International Airways
	EC-ETZ	Boeing 757-225	LTE International Airways *Bluebird IV*
	EC-EUC	McD Douglas MD-87	Iberia *Ciudad de Burgos*
	EC-EUD	McD Douglas MD-87	Iberia *Ciudad de Toledo*
	EC-EUE	McD Douglas MD-87	Iberia *Ciudad de Sevilla*
	EC-EUG	McD Douglas MD-87	Iberia
	EC-EUL	McD Douglas MD-87	Iberia *Ciudad de Cadiz*
	EC-EUZ	McD Douglas MD-83	Aviaco *Ria de Vigo*
	EC-EVB	McD Douglas MD-87	Iberia *Arrecife de Lanzarote*
	EC-EVC	Boeing 757-236	Air Europa
	EC-EVE	Boeing 737-4YO	Futura International Airways
	EC-EVU	McD Douglas MD-83	Aviaco *Covadonga*

Reg.	Type	Owner or Operator	Notes
EC-EXF	McD Douglas MD-87	Iberia *Ciudad de Pamplona*	
EC-EXG	McD Douglas MD-87	Iberia *Ciudad de Almeria*	
EC-EXH	Boeing 757-2ER	Air Europa	
EC-EXM	McD Douglas MD-87	Iberia *Ciudad de Zaragoza*	
EC-EXN	McD Douglas MD-87	Iberia *Ciudad de Badajoz*	
EC-EXR	McD Douglas MD-87	Iberia *Ciudad de Oviedo*	
EC-EXT	McD Douglas MD-87	Iberia *Ciudad de Albacete*	
EC-EXX	McD Douglas MD-83	Oasis International Airlines	
EC-EXY	Boeing 737-4Y0	Futura International Airways	
EC-EYB	McD Douglas MD-87	Iberia *Ciudad de Onis*	
EC-	Boeing 767-300ER	Spanair	
EC-EYS	Douglas DC-9-15MC	Air Sur	
EC-EYX	McD Douglas MD-87	Iberia *Ciudad de Caceres*	
EC-EYY	McD Douglas MD-87	Iberia *Ciudad de Barcelona*	
EC-EYZ	McD Douglas MD-87	Iberia *Ciudad de Las Palmas*	
EC-EZA	McD Douglas MD-87	Iberia *Ciudad de Segovia*	
EC-EZR	McD Douglas MD-83	Meridiana Air	
EC-EZS	McD Douglas MD-87	Iberia *Cuidad de Mahon*	
EC-EZU	McD Douglas MD-83	Oasis International Airlines	
EC-FAS	Airbus A.320-211	Iberia *Sierra de Cazoria*	
EC-FBP	Boeing 737-4YO	Futura International Airways	
EC-FBQ	Airbus A.320-211	Iberia	
EC-FBR	Airbus A.320-211	Iberia *Segura*	
EC-FBS	Airbus A.320-211	Iberia *Timanfaya*	
EC-FCU	Boeing 767-3YOER	Spanair *Baleares*	
EC-FDA	Airbus A.320-211	Iberia *Lagunas de Ruidera*	
EC-FDB	Airbus A.320-211	Iberia *Lago de Sanabria*	
EC-FEB	McD Douglas MD-83	Oasis International Airlines	
EC-FEE	Boeing 757-236	Air Europa	
EC-FEF	Boeing 757-236	Air Europa	
EC-FEO	Airbus A.320-211	Iberia *Delta del Ebro*	
EC-FEP	McDouglas MD-83	Oasis International Airways	
EC-FER	Boeing 737-3Q8	Viva Air	
EC-FET	Boeing 737-3Q8	Viva Air	
EC-FEY	McD Douglas MD-87	Iberia *Ciudad de Jaen*	
EC-FEZ	McD Douglas MD-87	Iberia	
EC-FFA	McD Douglas MD-87	Iberia *Ciudad de Avila*	
EC-FFB	Boeing 737-3A4	Viva Air (EC-EHX)	
EC-FFC	Boeing 737-3Q8	Viva Air (EC-EII)	
EC-FFH	McD Douglas MD-87	Iberia *Ciudad de Logrono*	
EC-FFI	McD Douglas MD-87	Iberia	
EC-FFK	Boeing 757-236	Air Europa	
EC-FFN	Boeing 737-36E	Viva Air	
EC-FFY	BAe 146-300	—	
EC-FGG	Boeing 737-3S3	Air Europa	
EC-FGH	Airbus A.320-211	Iberia *Caldera du Taburiente*	
EC-FGM	McD Douglas MD-88	Aviaco	
EC-FGQ	McD Douglas MD-81	Oasis International Airways	
EC-FGR	Airbus A.320-211	Iberia *Dehesa de Moncaya*	
EC-FGU	Airbus A.320-211	Iberia *Sierra Espuna*	
EC-FGV	Airbus A.320-211	Iberia *Monfrague*	
EC-FHD	McD Douglas MD-87	Iberia	
EC-FHK	McD Douglas MD-87	Iberia *Ciudad de Tarragona*	
EC-FHR	Boeing 737-36E	Viva Air	
EC-FIC	Airbus A.320-211	Iberia *Sierra de Grazalema*	

EI (Republic of Ireland)

Including complete current Irish Civil Register

EI-ABI	D.H.84 Dragon	Aer Lingus *Iolar* (EI-AFK)
EI-ADV	PA-12 Super Cruiser	R. E. Levis
EI-AFF	B.A. Swallow 2 ★	J. McCarthy
EI-AFN	B.A. Swallow 2 ★	J. McCarthy
EI-AGB	Miles M.38 Messenger 4 ★	J. McLoughlin
EI-AGD	Taylorcraft Plus D ★	H. Wolf
EI-AGJ	J/1 Autocrat	W. G. Rafter
EI-AHA	D.H.82A Tiger Moth ★	J. H. Maher
EI-AHR	D.H.C.1 Chipmunk 22 ★	C. Lane
EI-AKM	Piper J-3C-65 Cub	Setanta Flying Group
EI-ALH	Taylorcraft Plus D	N. Reilly
EI-ALP	Avro 643 Cadet	J. C. O'Loughlin
EI-ALU	Avro 631 Cadet	M. P. Cahill (*stored*)

Notes	Reg.	Type	Owner or Operator
	EI-AMK	J/1 Autocrat	Irish Aero Club
	EI-AND	Cessna 175A	M. A. Cooke
	EI-ANT	Champion 7ECA Citabria	S. Donohoe
	EI-ANY	PA-18 Super Cub 95	Bogavia Group
	EI-AOB	PA-28 Cherokee 140	J. Surdival & ptnrs
	EI-AOK	Cessna F.172G	R. J. Cloughley & N. J. Simpson
	EI-AOP	D.H.82A Tiger Moth ★	Institute of Technology/Dublin
	EI-AOS	Cessna 310B	Joyce Aviation Ltd
	EI-APF	Cessna F.150F	L. O. Kennedy
	EI-APS	Schleicher ASK.14	SLG Group
	EI-ARH	Currie Wot/S.E.5 Replica	L. Garrison
	EI-ARM	Currie Wot/S.E.5 Replica	L. Garrison
	EI-ARW	Jodel D.R.1050	P. Walsh & P. Ryan
	EI-ASD	Boeing 737-248C	Aer Lingus *St Ide*
	EI-ASE	Boeing 737-248C	Aer Lingus *St Fachtna*
	EI-ASG	Boeing 737-248 ★	*Instructional airframe*/Dublin
	EI-ASH	Boeing 737-248	Aer Lingus *St Eugene*
	EI-ASI	Boeing 747-148	Aer Lingus *St Patrick*
	EI-ASJ	Boeing 747-148	Aer Lingus *St Colmcille*
	EI-ASL	Boeing 737-248C	Aer Lingus *St Killian*
	EI-AST	Cessna F.150H	Liberty Flying Group
	EI-ATC	Cessna 310G	Iona National Airways Ltd
	EI-ATJ	B.121 Pup 1	Wexford Aero Club
	EI-ATK	PA-28 Cherokee 140	Mayo Flying Club Ltd
	EI-ATS	M.S.880B Rallye Club	ATS Group
	EI-AUC	Cessna FA.150K Aerobat	Kestrel Flying Group
	EI-AUE	M.S.880B Rallye Club	Kilkenny Flying Club Ltd
	EI-AUG	M.S.894 Rallye Minerva 220	K. O'Leary
	EI-AUJ	M.S.880B Rallye Club	P. Mulhall
	EI-AUM	J/1 Autocrat	J. G. Rafter
	EI-AUO	Cessna FA.150K Aerobat	Kerry Aero Club
	EI-AUS	J/5F Aiglet Trainer	T. Stephens & T. Lennon
	EI-AUT	Forney F-1A Aircoupe	Joyce Aviation Ltd
	EI-AUV	PA-23 Aztec 250C	Shannon Executive Aviation
	EI-AUY	Morane-Saulnier M.S.502	G. Warner/Duxford
	EI-AVB	Aeronca 7AC Champion	P. Ryan
	EI-AVC	Cessna F.337F	337 Flying Group
	EI-AVM	Cessna F.150L	P. Kearney
	EI-AVN	Hughes 369HM	Helicopter Maintenance Ltd
	EI-AWE	Cessna F.150M	Third Flight Group
	EI-AWH	Cessna 210J	Cork Flying Club Ltd
	EI-AWP	D.H.82A Tiger Moth	A. Lyons
	EI-AWR	Malmo MFI-9 Junior	M. R. Nesbitt & S. Duignan
	EI-AWU	M.S.880B Rallye Club	Longford Aviation Ltd
	EI-AWW	Cessna 414	Shannon Executive Aviation Ltd
	EI-AYA	M.S.880B Rallye Club	D. Bothwell & ptnrs
	EI-AYB	GY-80 Horizon 180	Westwing Flying Group
	EI-AYD	AA-5 Traveler	P. Howick & ptnrs
	EI-AYF	Cessna FRA.150L	Garda Flying Club
	EI-AYI	M.S.880B Rallye Club	J. McNamara
	EI-AYK	Cessna F.172M	S. T. Scully
	EI-AYL	A.109 Airedale	J. Ronan
	EI-AYN	BN-2A Islander	Aer Arran
	EI-AYO	Douglas DC-3A ★	Science Museum, Wroughton
	EI-AYR	Schleicher ASK-16	Kilkenny Airport Ltd
	EI-AYS	PA-22 Colt 108	M. Skelly & R. Hall
	EI-AYV	M.S.892A Rallye Commodore 150	P. Murtagh
	EI-AYW	PA-23 Aztec 250	Chutehall International Ltd
	EI-AYY	Evans VP-1	M. Donoghue
	EI-BAF	Thunder Ax6-56 balloon	W. G. Woollett
	EI-BAJ	SNCAN Stampe SV-4C	Dublin Tiger Group
	EI-BAO	Cessna F.172G	Garda Flying Group
	EI-BAR	Thunder Ax8-105 balloon	J. Burke & V. Hourihane
	EI-BAS	Cessna F.172M	Falcon Aviation Ltd
	EI-BAT	Cessna F.150M	J. Barrow
	EI-BAV	PA-22 Colt 108	J. Davy
	EI-BAY	Cameron V-77 balloon	F. N. Lewis
	EI-BBC	PA-28 Cherokee 180C	B. Healy
	EI-BBD	Evans VP-1	Volksplane Group
	EI-BBE	Champion 7FC Tri-Traveler (tailwheel)	P. Forde & D. Connaire
	EI-BBG	M.S.880B Rallye Club	Weston Ltd

Reg.	Type	Owner or Operator	Notes
EI-BBI	M.S.892 Rallye Commodore	Kilkenny Airport Ltd	
EI-BBJ	M.S.880B Rallye Club	Weston Ltd	
EI-BBK	A.109 Airedale	H. S. Igoe	
EI-BBM	Cameron O-65 balloon	Dublin Ballooning Club	
EI-BBN	Cessna F.150M	Sligo N.W. Aero Club	
EI-BBO	M.S.893E Rallye 180GT	J. G. Lacey & ptnrs	
EI-BBV	Piper J-3C-65 Cub	F. Cronin	
EI-BCE	BN-2A-26 Islander	Aer Arann	
EI-BCF	Bensen B.8M	T. A. Brennan	
EI-BCH	M.S.892A Rallye Commodore 150	The Condor Group	
EI-BCJ	F.8L Falco 1 Srs 3	D. Kelly	
EI-BCK	Cessna F.172K	H. Caulfield	
EI-BCL	Cessna 182P	Iona National Airways	
EI-BCM	Piper J-3C-65 Cub	Kilmoon Flying Group	
EI-BCN	Piper J-3C-65 Cub	Snowflake Flying Group	
EI-BCO	Piper J-3C-65 Cub	J. Molloy	
EI-BCP	D.628 Condor	A. Delaney	
EI-BCR	Boeing 737-281	Aer Lingus St Oliver Plunkett	
EI-BCS	M.S.880B Rallye Club	J. Murphy	
EI-BCT	Cessna 411A	Avmark (Ireland) Ltd	
EI-BCU	M.S.880B Rallye Club	Weston Ltd	
EI-BCW	M.S.880B Rallye Club	Kilkenny Flying Club	
EI-BCY	Beech 200 Super King Air (232)	Minister of Defence	
EI-BDH	M.S.880B Rallye Club	Munster Wings Ltd	
EI-BDK	M.S.880B Rallye Club	Limerick Flying Club Ltd	
EI-BDL	Evans VP-2	J. Duggan	
EI-BDM	PA-23 Aztec 250D ★	Industrial Training School	
EI-BDP	Cessna 182P	S. Bruton	
EI-BDR	PA-28 Cherokee 180	K. Bickerdyke	
EI-BDY	Boeing 737-2E1	Aer Lingus Teo St Brigid	
EI-BEA	M.S.880B Rallye 100ST	Weston Ltd	
EI-BEB	Boeing 737-248	Aer Lingus Teo St Eunan	
EI-BEC	Boeing 737-248	Aer Lingus Teo St Fiacre	
EI-BED	Boeing 747-130	Aer Linte Eireann Teo St Kieran	
EI-BEE	Boeing 737-281	Aer Lingus Teo St Cronan	
EI-BEI	—	Aer Lingus Teo	
EI-BEJ	—	Aer Lingus Teo	
EI-BEN	Piper J-3C-65 Cub	J. J. Sullivan	
EI-BEO	Cessna 310Q	Iona National Airways	
EI-BEP	M.S.892A Rallye Commodore 150	H. Lynch & J. O'Leary	
EI-BEY	Naval N3N-3 ★	Huntley & Huntley Ltd	
EI-BFF	Beech A.23 Musketeer	E. Hopkins	
EI-BFH	Bell 212	Irish Helicopters Ltd	
EI-BFI	M.S.880B Rallye 100ST	J. O'Neill	
EI-BFJ	Beech A.200 Super King Air (234)	Minister of Defence	
EI-BFM	M.S.893E Rallye 235GT	J. K. Group	
EI-BFO	Piper J-3C-90 Cub	M. Slattery	
EI-BFP	M.S.800B Rallye 100ST	Weston Ltd	
EI-BFR	M.S.880B Rallye 100ST	G. P. Moorhead	
EI-BFV	M.S.880B Rallye 100T	Ormond Flying Club	
EI-BGA	SOCATA Rallye 100ST	J. J. Frew	
EI-BGB	M.S.880B Rallye Club	Limerick Flying Club	
EI-BGD	M.S.880B Rallye Club	N. Kavanagh	
EI-BGG	M.S.892E Rallye 150GT	M. J. Hanlon	
EI-BGH	Cessna F.172N	Iona National Airways	
EI-BGJ	Cessna F.152	Hibernian Flying Club	
EI-BGO	Canadair CL-44D-4J ★	Irish Airports Authority/Dublin	
EI-BGP	Cessna 414A	Iona National Airways	
EI-BGS	M.S.893E Rallye 180GT	M. Farrelly	
EI-BGT	Colt 77A balloon	K. Haugh	
EI-BGU	M.S.880B Rallye Club	M. F. Neary	
EI-BHB	M.S.887 Rallye 125	Hotel Bravo Flying Club	
EI-BHC	Cessna F.177RG	P. V. Maguire	
EI-BHD	Sikorsky S-61N	Irish Helicopters Ltd	
EI-BHF	M.S.892A Rallye Commodore 150	B. Mullen	
EI-BHI	Bell 206B JetRanger 2	J. Mansfield	
EI-BHK	M.S.880B Rallye Club	J. Lawlor & B. Lyons	
EI-BHL	Beech E90 King Air	Stewart Singlam Fabrics Ltd	
EI-BHM	Cessna 337E	The Ross Flying Group	
EI-BHN	M.S.893A Rallye Commodore 180	K. O'Driscoll & ptnrs	
EI-BHP	M.S.893A Rallye Commodore 180	Spanish Point Flying Club	
EI-BHT	Beech 77 Skipper	Waterford Aero Club	
EI-BHV	Champion 7EC Traveler	Condor Group	

Notes	Reg.	Type	Owner or Operator
	EI-BHW	Cessna F.150F	R. Sharpe
	EI-BHY	SOCATA Rallye 150ST	D. Killian
	EI-BIB	Cessna F.152	Galway Flying Club
	EI-BIC	Cessna F.172N	Oriel Flying Group Ltd
	EI-BID	PA-18 Super Cub 95	D. MacCarthy
	EI-BIF	SOCATA Rallye 235E	Empire Enterprises Ltd
	EI-BIG	Zlin 526	P. von Lonkhuyzen
	EI-BIJ	AB-206B JetRanger 2	Celtic Helicopters Ltd
	EI-BIK	PA-18 Super Cub 180	Dublin Gliding Club
	EI-BIM	M.S.880B Rallye Club	D. Millar
	EI-BIO	Piper J-3C-65 Cub	Monasterevin Flying Club
	EI-BIR	Cessna F.172M	B. Harrison & ptnrs
	EI-BIS	Robin R.1180TD	Robin Aiglon Group
	EI-BIT	M.S.887 Rallye 125	Spanish Point Flying Club
	EI-BIU	Robin R.2112A	Wicklow Flying Group
	EI-BIV	Bellanca 8KCAB Citabria	Aerocrats Flying Group
	EI-BIW	M.S.880B Rallye Club	E. J. Barr
	EI-BJA	Cessna FRA.150L	Blackwater Flying Group
	EI-BJC	Aeronca 7AC Champion	R. J. Bentley
	EI-BJG	Robin R.1180	N. Hanley
	EI-BJJ	Aeronca 15AC Sedan	A. A. Alderdice & S. H. Boyd
	EI-BJK	M.S.880B Rallye 110ST	Jordan Larkin Flying Group
	EI-BJL	Cessna 550 Citation II	Helicopter Maintenance Ltd
	EI-BJM	Cessna A.152	Leinster Aero Club
	EI-BJO	Cessna R.172K	P. Hogan & G. Ryder
	EI-BJS	AA-5B Tiger	P. Morrisey
	EI-BJW	D.H.104 Dove 6 ★	Waterford Museum
	EI-BKC	Aeronca 115AC Sedan	J. Lynch
	EI-BKD	Mooney M.20J	Limerick Warehousing Ltd
	EI-BKF	Cessna F.172H	M. & M. C. Veale
	EI-BKK	Taylor JT.1 Monoplane	Waterford Aero Club
	EI-BKM	Zenith CH.200	D. van de Braam
	EI-BKN	M.S.880B Rallye 100ST	Weston Ltd
	EI-BKS	Eipper Quicksilver	Irish Microlight Ltd
	EI-BKT	AB-206B JetRanger 3	Irish Helicopters Ltd
	EI-BKU	M.S.892A Rallye Commodore 150	Limerick Flying Club
	EI-BLB	SNCAN Stampe SV-4C	J. E. Hutchinson & R. A. Stafford
	EI-BLD	Bolkow Bo 105C	Irish Helicopters Ltd
	EI-BLE	Eipper Microlight	R. P. St George-Smith
	EI-BLG	AB-206B JetRanger 3	Monarch Property Services Ltd
	EI-BLN	Eipper Quicksilver MX	O. J. Conway & B. Daffy
	EI-BLO	Catto CP.16	R. W. Hall
	EI-BLR	PA-34-200T Seneca II	R. Paris
	EI-BLU	Evans VP-1	S. Pallister
	EI-BLY	Sikorsky S-61N	Irish Helicopters Ltd
	EI-BMA	M.S.880B Rallye Club	W. Rankin & M. Kelleher
	EI-BMB	M.S.880B Rallye 100T	Clyde Court Development Ltd
	EI-BMC	Hiway Demon Skytrike	S. Pallister
	EI-BMF	Laverda F.8L Falco	M. Slazenger & H. McCann
	EI-BMH	M.S.880B Rallye Club	N. J. Bracken
	EI-BMI	SOCATA TB.9 Tampico	Weston Ltd
	EI-BMJ	M.S.880B Rallye 100T	Weston Ltd
	EI-BMK	Cessna 310Q	Iona National Airways Ltd
	EI-BML	PA-23 Aztec 250	Bruton Aircraft Engineering Ltd
	EI-BMM	Cessna F.152 II	Iona National Airways Ltd
	EI-BMN	Cessna F.152 II	Iona National Airways Ltd
	EI-BMO	Robin R.2160	L. Gavin & ptnrs
	EI-BMS	Cessna F.177RG	A. M. Smyth
	EI-BMU	Monnet Sonerai II	P. Forde & D. Connaire
	EI-BMV	AA-5 Traveler	E. Tierney & K. Harold
	EI-BMW	Vulcan Air Trike	L. Maddock
	EI-BNA	Douglas DC-8-63CF	Aer Turas Teo
	EI-BNB	Lake LA-4-200 Buccaneer	L. McNamara & M. Ledwith
	EI-BNC	Cessna F.152	Iona National Airlines
	EI-BND	Conroy CL-44-0	HeavyLift Cargo Airlines Ltd/Stansted
	EI-BNF	Goldwing Canard	T. Morelli
	EI-BNG	M.S.892A Rallye Commodore 150	Shannon Executive Aviation
	EI-BNH	Hiway Skytrike	M. Martin
	EI-BNJ	Evans VP-2	G. A. Cashman
	EI-BNK	Cessna U.206F	Irish Parachute Club Ltd
	EI-BNL	Rand KR-2	K. Hayes
	EI-BNP	Rotorway 133	R. L. Renfroe
	EI-BNT	Cvjetkovic CA-65	B. Tobin & P. G. Ryan

Reg.	Type	Owner or Operator	Notes
EI-BNU	M.S.880B Rallye Club	P. A. Doyle	
EI-BOA	Pterodactyl Ptraveller	A. Murphy	
EI-BOE	SOCATA TB.10 Tobago	P. Byron & ptnrs	
EI-BOH	Eipper Quicksilver	J. Leech	
EI-BOK	PA-23 Aztec 250E	K. A. O'Connor	
EI-BOM	Boeing 737-2T4	Air Tara Ltd (*leased to Delta A/L*)	
EI-BON	Boeing 737-2T4	Air Tara Ltd (*leased to Delta A/L*)	
EI-BOO	PA-23 Aztec 250C	K. A. O'Connor	
EI-BOR	Bell 222	Westair Ltd	
EI-BOV	Rand KR-2	G. O'Hara & G. Callan	
EI-BOX	Duet	K. Riccius	
EI-BPB	PA-28R Cherokee Arrow 200	Rathcoole Flying Club	
EI-BPE	Viking Dragonfly	G. Bracken	
EI-BPI	EMB-110P1 Bandeirante	Iona National Airways Ltd	
EI-BPJ	Cessna 182A	J. Matthews & V. McCarthy	
EI-BPL	Cessna F.172K	Phoenix Flying	
EI-BPM	AS.350B Ecureuil	Helicopter Maintenance Ltd	
EI-BPO	Puma Skytrike	A. Morelli	
EI-BPP	Quicksilver MX	J. A. Smith	
EI-BPS	PA-30 Twin Comanche 160	Group Air	
EI-BPT	Skyhook Sabre	T. McGrath	
EI-BPU	Hiway Demon	A. Channing	
EI-BRH	Mainair Gemini Flash	F. Warren & T. McGrath	
EI-BRK	Flexiform Trike	L. Maddock	
EI-BRM	Cessna 172Q	Iona National Airways	
EI-BRO	Cessna F.152	Iona National Airways	
EI-BRP	Canadair CL-44J	HeavyLift (*stored*)/Southend	
EI-BRS	Cessna P.172D	D. & M. Hillery	
EI-BRT	Flexwing M17727	M. J. McCrystal	
EI-BRU	Evans VP-1	R. Smith & T. Coughlan	
EI-BRV	Hiway Demon	M. Garvey & C. Tully	
EI-BRW	Ultralight Deltabird	A. & E. Aerosports	
EI-BRX	Cessna FRA.150L	P. O'Donnell	
EI-BSB	Jodel D.112	W. Kennedy	
EI-BSC	Cessna F.172N	S. Phelan	
EI-BSD	Enstrom F-28A	Clark Aviation	
EI-BSF	H.S.748 Srs 1 ★	S.E. Aviation Museum/Waterford	
EI-BSG	Bensen B.80	J. Todd	
EI-BSK	SOCATA TB.9 Tampico	Weston Ltd	
EI-BSL	PA-34-220T Seneca	E. L. Symons	
EI-BSN	Cameron O-65 balloon	W. Woollett	
EI-BSO	PA-28 Cherokee 140B	D. Rooney	
EI-BSQ	Thundercolt Ax6-56Z balloon	D. Hooper	
EI-BSR	Lake LA.4-200 Buccaneer	Derg Developments Ltd	
EI-BST	Bell 206B JetRanger	Celtic Helicopters Ltd	
EI-BSU	Champion 7KCAB	R. Bentley	
EI-BSV	SOCATA TB.20 Trinidad	J. Condron	
EI-BSW	Solar Wings Pegasus XL-R	E. Fitzgerald	
EI-BSX	Piper J-3C-65 Cub	J. & T. O'Dwyer	
EI-BTC	McD Douglas MD-82	Irish Aerospace Ltd (*leased in US*)	
EI-BTD	McD Douglas MD-82	Irish Aerospace Ltd (*leased in US*)	
EI-BTF	Boeing 737-3Y0	Air Tara Ltd (*leased to Corse Air*)	
EI-BTN	L.1101-385 TriStar 1	Air Tara Ltd (*leased to Air America*)	
EI-BTS	Boeing 747-283B	Air Tara Ltd (*leased to Philippine A/L*)	
EI-BTT	Boeing 737-3Y0	Air Tara Ltd (*leased to Corse Air*)	
EI-BTX	McD Douglas MD-82	Air Tara Ltd (*leased to AeroMexico*)	
EI-BTY	McD Douglas MD-82	Air Tara Ltd	
EI-BUA	Cessna 172M	Skyhawks Flying Club	
EI-BUC	Jodel D.9 Bebe	L. Maddock	
EI-BUD	Boeing 737-348	Aer Lingus *St Lawrence O'Toole*	
EI-BUE	Boeing 737-348	Aer Lingus *St Ciara*	
EI-BUF	Cessna 210N	210 Group	
EI-BUG	SOCATA ST.10 Diplomate	J. Cooke	
EI-BUH	Lake LA.4-200 Buccaneer	Derg Aviation (Group) Ltd	
EI-BUJ	M.S.892A Rallye Commodore 150	T. Cunniffe	
EI-BUL	MW-5 Sorcerer	J. Conlon	
EI-BUM	Cessna 404	Iona National Airways Ltd	
EI-BUN	Beech 76 Duchess	S. Ryle	
EI-BUO	Lavery Sea Hawker	C. Lavery & C. Donaldson	
EI-BUQ	—	Ryanair Ltd	
EI-BUR	PA-38-112 Tomahawk	Leoni Aviation Ltd	
EI-BUS	PA-38-112 Tomahawk	Leoni Aviation Ltd	
EI-BUT	M.S.893A Commodore 180	T. Keating	

Notes	Reg.	Type	Owner or Operator
	EI-BUU	Solar Wings Pegasus XL-R	R. L. T. Hudson
	EI-BUV	Cessna 172RG	J. J. Spollen
	EI-BUW	Noble Hardman Snowbird IIIA	T.I.F.C. & I.S. Ltd
	EI-BUX	Agusta A.109A	Orring Ltd
	EI-BUY	Cessna 551 Citation 2	Tool & Mould Steel (Ireland) Ltd
	EI-BUZ	Robinson R-22	Leoni Aviation Ltd
	EI-BVA	Cessna 404 Titan	Iona National Airways Ltd
	EI-BVB	Whittaker MW.6 Merlin	R. England
	EI-BVC	Cameron N-65 balloon	E. Shepherd
	EI-BVE	Jodel D.9 Bebe	J. Greene
	EI-BVF	Cessna F.172N	First Phantom Group
	EI-BVH	RomBac One-Eleven 561RC	Ryanair Ltd *The Spirit of Tara*
	EI-BVI	BAC One-Eleven 525FT	Ryanair Ltd
	EI-BVJ	AMF Chevvron 232	W. T. King & S. G. Dunne
	EI-BVK	PA-38 Tomahawk	Shannon Executive Aviation
	EI-BVN	Bell 206B Jet Ranger 3	Helicopter Hire (Ireland) Ltd
	EI-BVP	Cessna T.303	Iona National Airways Ltd
	EI-BVQ	Cameron Can SS balloon	T. McCormack
	EI-BVS	Cessna 172RG	P. Bruno
	EI-BVT	Evans VP-2	J. J. Sullivan
	EI-BVU	Cessna 152	Iona National Airways Ltd
	EI-BVW	Cessna 152	Iona National Airways Ltd
	EI-BVX	EMB-110P1 Bandeirante	Iona National Airways Ltd
	EI-BVY	Zenith 200AA-RW	J. Matthews & ptnrs
	EI-BVZ	Scheibe SF.25B Falke	D. Lamb & ptnrs
	EI-BWD	McD Douglas MD-83	Air Tara Ltd *(leased to BWIA)*
	EI-BWF	Boeing 747-283B	Air Tara Ltd *(leased to Argentina)*
	EI-BWT	BAC One-Eleven 414ED	Air Tara Ltd
	EI-BXA	Boeing 737-448	Aer Lingus Teo *St Conleth*
	EI-BXB	Boeing 737-448	Aer Lingus Teo *St Gall*
	EI-BXC	Boeing 737-448	Aer Lingus Teo *St Brendan*
	EI-BXD	Boeing 737-448	Aer Lingus Teo *St Colman*
	EI-BXI	Boeing 737-448	Aer Lingus Teo *St Finnian*
	EI-BXK	Boeing 737-448	Aer Lingus Teo *St Caimin*
	EI-BXL	—	Aer Lingus Teo
	EI-BXM	—	Aer Lingus Teo
	EI-BXN	Microlight	C. O'Donaghue
	EI-BXO	Fouga CM.170 Magister	G. W. Connolly
	EI-BXP	PA-23 Aztec 250E	Aer Arran
	EI-BXR	Aerospatiale ATR-42-300	Ryanair Ltd
	EI-BXS	Aerospatiale ATR-42-300	Ryanair Ltd
	EI-BXT	D.62B Condor	J. Sweeney
	EI-BXU	PA-28-161 Warrior II	W. T. King
	EI-BXX	AB-206B JetRanger	Leoni Aviation Ltd
	EI-BXY	Boeing 737-2S3	Aer Lingus Teo *St Canice*
	EI-BXZ	Flexiwing	R. England
	EI-BYA	Thruster TST Mk 1	E. Fagan
	EI-BYB	Robinson R-22B	R. McGrogan
	EI-BYC	Bensen B.8MR	C. Kirwan
	EI-BYD	Cessna 150J	Kestrel Flying Group
	EI-BYE	PA-31-350 Navajo Chieftain	EI-Air Exports Ltd
	EI-BYF	Cessna 150M	Twentieth Air Training Group
	EI-BYG	SOCATA TB.9 Tampico	Weston Ltd
	EI-BYH	Cessna 340A	Claddagh Air Carriers
	EI-BYJ	Bell 206B JetRanger	Celtic Helicopters Ltd
	EI-BYK	PA-23 Aztec 250E	M. F. Hilary
	EI-BYL	Zenith CH.250	A. Corcoran & J. Martin
	EI-BYN	Cessna 550 Citation II	Stickbury Enterprises Ltd
	EI-BYO	Aerospatiale ATR-42-300	Ryanair Ltd
	EI-BYP	Aerospatiale ATR-42-300	Ryanair Ltd *(reservation)*
	EI-BYQ	Aerospatiale ATR-42-300	Ryanair Ltd *(reservation)*
	EI-BYS	Robinson R-22B	G. V. Maloney
	EI-BYT	AS.350B Ecureuil	Helicopter Hire
	EI-BYV	Hughes 369D	Irish Helicopters Ltd
	EI-BYW	Thruster 3 Axis	S. P. McCaffrey
	EI-BYX	Champion 7GCAA	J. Keane & P. Gallagher
	EI-BYY	Piper J-3C-85 Cub	A. J. Haines
	EI-BYZ	PA-44-180 Seminole	European College of Aeronautics
	EI-BZA	Boeing 747-283B	Air Tara Ltd *(leased to Philippine A/L)*
	EI-BZB	Airbus A.300C4	GPA Finance *(leased to Philippine A/L)*
	EI-BZD	Douglas DC-10-30	GPA Finance Ltd *(leased to Garuda)*
	EI-BZE	Boeing 737-3Y0	GPA Group Ltd *(leased to Philippine A/L)*
	EI-BZF	Boeing 737-3Y0	GPA Group Ltd *(leased to Philippine A/L)*

Reg.	Type	Owner or Operator	Notes
EI-BZH	Boeing 737-3Y0	GPA Group Ltd (leased to Philippine A/L)	
EI-BZI	Boeing 737-3Y0	GPA Group Ltd (leased to Philippine A/L)	
EI-BZJ	Boeing 737-3Y0	GPA Group Ltd (leased to Philippine A/L)	
EI-BZK	Boeing 737-3Y0	GPA Group Ltd (leased to Philippine A/L)	
EI-BZL	Boeing 737-3Y0	GPA Group Ltd (leased to Philippine A/L)	
EI-BZM	Boeing 737-3Y0	GPA Group Ltd (leased to Philippine A/L)	
EI-BZN	Boeing 737-3Y0	GPA Group Ltd (leased to Philippine A/L)	
EI-BZU	Douglas DC-8-71	GPA Group Ltd (leased to Kenya Airways)	
EI-BZZ	Douglas DC-9-15	GPA Finance Ltd (stored)	
EI-CAA	Cessna Fr.172J	K. O'Connor	
EI-CAB	Grob G.115	European College of Aeronautics	
EI-CAC	Grob G.115	European College of Aeronautics	
EI-CAD	Grob G.115	European College of Aeronautics	
EI-CAE	Grob B.115	European College of Aeronautics	
EI-CAF	Bell 206B JetRanger 2	Irish Helicopters Ltd	
EI-CAG	PA-31 Navajo	Leoni Aviation Ltd	
EI-CAH	G.1159C Gulfstream 4	Ardesis Ltd	
EI-CAJ	O'Leary Biplane	J. O. Leary	
EI-CAK	Douglas DC-8-63AF	Aer Turas Teo	
EI-CAN	Aerotech MW.5 Sorcerer	J. Conlon	
EI-CAO	Cameron O-84 balloon	K. Haugh	
EI-CAP	Cessna R.182RG	P. Byrne	
EI-CAR	Schweizer 269C	Island Helicopters Ltd	
EI-CAT	Cessna 421C	S. E. Ryle Ltd	
EI-CAU	AMF Chevvron 232	H. Sydner	
EI-CAW	Bell 206B JetRanger	Celtic Helicopters Ltd	
EI-CAX	Cessna P.210N	N. Dunne	
EI-CAY	Mooney M.20C	Ranger Flights Ltd	
EI-CAZ	FH.227D Friendship	Iona National Airways	
EI-CBB	Douglas DC-9-15	GPA Finance Ltd (stored)	
EI-CBC	Aerospatiale ATR-72	Air Tara Ltd	
EI-CBD	Aerospatiale ATR-72	Air Tara Ltd	
EI-CBF	Aerospatiale ATR-42-300	Air Tara Ltd (leased to Trans World Express)	
EI-CBG	Douglas DC-9-51	GPA Finance Ltd (leased to Hawaiian)	
EI-CBH	Douglas DC-9-51	GPA Finance Ltd (leased to Hawaiian)	
EI-CBI	Douglas DC-9-51	Air Tara Ltd (leased to Hawaiian)	
EI-CBJ	D.H.C. 8-102 Dash Eight	GPA Group Ltd (leaesd in Alaska)	
EI-CBK	Aerospatiale ATR-42-300	Air Tara Ltd	
EI-CBN	McD Douglas MD-83	Air Tara Ltd	
EI-CBO	McD Douglas MD-83	Air Tara Ltd	
EI-CBP	Boeing 737-3YO	Air Tara Ltd (leased to LAM)	
EI-CBQ	Boeing 737-3YO	Air Tara Ltd (leased to LAM)	
EI-CBR	McD Douglas MD-83	Irish Aerospace	
EI-CBS	McD Douglas MD-83	Irish Aerospace	
EI-CBU	—	Air Tara Ltd	
EI-CBV	D.H.C.8-102 Dash Eight	Air Tara Ltd	
EI-CBW	Airbus A.300B4-203	Air Tara Ltd	
EI-CBX	McD Douglas MD-83	Air Tara Ltd	
EI-CBY	McD Douglas MD-83	Air Tara Ltd	
EI-CBZ	McD Douglas MD-83	Air Tara Ltd	
EI-CCA	Beech 19A Musketeer	J. Donoher	
EI-CCB	PA-44-180 Seminole	European College of Aeronautics	
EI-CCC	McD Douglas MD-83	Irish Aerospace Ltd	
EI-CCD	Grob G.115A	European College of Aeronautics	
EI-CCE	McD Douglas MD-83	Irish Aerospace Ltd	
EI-CCF	Aeronca 11AC Chief	O. Bruton	
EI-CCG	Robinson R-22B	Leoni Aviation Ltd	
EI-CCH	Piper J-3C-65 Cub	M. Slattery	
EI-CCJ	Cessna 152	Irish Aero Club	
EI-CCK	Cessna 152	Irish Aero Club	
EI-CCL	Cessna 152	Irish Aero Club	
EI-CCM	Cessna 152	Irish Aero Club	
EI-CCN	Grob G.115A	European College of Aeronautics	
EI-CCO	PA-44-180 Seminole	European College of Aeronautics	
EI-CCP	Cessna 152 II	Hiberian Flying Club	
EI-CCQ	Slingsby T.31F Motor Cadet	Kerry Aero Club Ltd	
EI-CCR	Gulfstream 690D	Earl of Granard	
EI-CCS	Enstrom 280C-UK	Orring Ltd	
EI-CCT	Robinson R-22B	Air Investments Ltd	
EI-CCU	BAC One-Eleven 531FS	Ryanair Ltd	
EI-CCV	Cessna R.172K-XP	Kerry Aero Club	
EI-CCW	BAC One-Eleven 509EW	Ryanair Ltd	
EI-CCX	BAC One-Eleven 531FS	Ryanair Ltd	

Notes	Reg.	Type	Owner or Operator
	EI-CCY	AA-1B Trainer	N. & C. Whisler
	EI-CCZ	Cessna F.150L	Comprehensive Enterprises Ltd
	EI-CDA	Boeing 737-548	Aer Lingus Teo *St Columba*
	EI-CDB	Boeing 737-548	Aer Lingus Teo *St Albert*
	EI-CDC	Boeing 737-548	Aer Lingus Teo *St Munchen*
	EI-CDD	Boeing 737-548	Aer Lingus Teo *St Macartan*
	EI-CDE	Boeing 737-548	Aer Lingus Teo *St Jarlath*
	EI-CDF	Boeing 737-548	Aer Lingus Teo
	EI-CDG	Boeing 737-548	Aer Lingus Teo
	EI-CDH	Boeing 737-548	Aer Lingus Teo
	EI-CDI	McD Douglas MD-11	GPA Group (*leased to Garuda*)
	EI-CDJ	McD Douglas MD-11	GPA Group (*leased to Garuda*)
	EI-CDK	McD Douglas MD-11	GPA Group (*leased to Garuda*)
	EI-CDL	McD Douglas MD-11	GPA Group (*leased to Garuda*)
	EI-CDM	McD Douglas MD-11	GPA Group (*leased to Garuda*)
	EI-CDN	McD Douglas MD-11	GPA Group (*leased to Garuda*)
	EI-CDO	BAC One-Eleven 518FG	Ryanair Ltd
	EI-CDP	Cessna 182L	O. Bruton
	EI-CDQ	SA.300 Starduster Too	J. Keane
	EI-CDR	—	—
	EI-CDS	—	—
	EI-CDT	—	—
	EI-CDU	—	—
	EI-CDV	Cessna 150F	Blue Heron Aircraft
	EI-CDW	Robinson R-22B	J. Martyn
	EI-CDX	Cessna 210K	Falcon Aviation Ltd
	EI-CDY	McD Douglas MD-83	Irish Aerospace Ltd
	EI-CDZ	Luscombe 8A Silvaire	S. Bruton
	EI-CEA	—	—
	EI-CEB	Airbus A.300B4	GPA Finance Ltd
	EI-CEC	PA-31-350 Navajo Chieftain	M. Knopek
	EI-CED	D.H.C.8-311 Dash Eight	GPA Finance Ltd
	EI-CEF	Robinson R-22HP	Santail Ltd
	EI-CEG	M.S.893A Rallye 180GT	M. Farrelly
	EI-CEH	McD Douglas MD-83	Irish Aerospace Ltd
	EI-CEI	—	—
	EI-CEJ	Robinson R-22B	R. McGrogan
	EI-CFA	Saab SF.340B	Aer Lingus Commuter *St Eithne*
	EI-CFB	Saab SF.340B	Aer Lingus Commuter *St Aoife*
	EI-CFC	Saab SF.340B	Aer Lingus Commuter *St Finbarr*
	EI-CFD	Saab SF.340B	Aer Lingus Commuter *St Senan*
	EI-CFE	Robinson R-22B	Windsor Motors Ltd
	EI-CFF	PA-12 Super Cruiser	J. O'Dwyer & J. Molloy
	EI-CFG	CP.301B Emeraude	Southlink Ltd
	EI-CFH	PA-12 Super Cruiser	G. Treacy
	EI-CFI	PA-34-200T Seneca II	—
	EI-CFJ	—	—
	EI-CFK	Varga 2150A Kachina	W. M. Patterson
	EI-CFL	—	—
	EI-CFM	—	—
	EI-CFN	—	—
	EI-CFO	—	—
	EI-CFP	Cessna 172P	S. Bruton
	EI-CFQ	—	—
	EI-CFR	—	—
	EI-CFS	—	—
	EI-CFT	—	—
	EI-CGO	Douglas DC-8-63AF	Aer Turas Teo
	EI-CHL	Bell 206B JetRanger 3	Celtic Helicopters Ltd
	EI-CUB	Piper J-3C-65 Cub	Galway Flying Club
	EI-EDR	PA-28R Cherokee Arrow 200	Victor Mike Flying Group Ltd
	EI-FDX	Cessna 208	Iona National Airways (FedEx)
	EI-FEA	F.27 Friendship Mk 600	Iona National Airways/Federal Express
	EI-FKA	Fokker 50	Aer Lingus Commuter *St Fionnan*
	EI-FKB	Fokker 50	Aer Lingus Commuter *St Fergal*
	EI-FKC	Fokker 50	Aer Lingus Commuter *St Fidelma*
	EI-FKD	Fokker 50	Aer Lingus Commuter *St Flannan*
	EI-FKE	Fokker 50	Aer Lingus Commuter *St Pappin*
	EI-FKF	Fokker 50	Aer Lingus Commuter *St Ultan*
	EI-FKG	—	Aer Lingus Commuter
	EI-FKH	—	Aer Lingus Commuter
	EI-FKI	—	Aer Lingus Commuter
	EI-FKJ	—	Aer Lingus Commuter

Reg.	Type	Owner or Operator	Notes
EI-KOC	Bellanca 7KCAB Citabria	K. O'Connor	
EI-LJG	Canadair CL.601-3A Challenger	Irish Beef Processors Ltd	
EI-LMG	Bell 206L-3 LongRanger	Ven Air	
EI-SNN	Cessna 650 Citation III	Westair Aviation Ltd	
EI-TCK	Cessna 421C	T. C. Killeen	
EI-XMC	Robinson R-22B	McAuliffe Photographic Laboratories	
EI-XMA	Robinson R-22B	Leoni Aviation Ltd	

EL (Liberia)

EL-AJC	Boeing 707-430 ★	Airport Fire Services/Bournemouth	
EL-AJO	Douglas DC-8-55F	Liberia World Airways	
EL-AJQ	Douglas DC-8-54F	Liberia World Airways	
EL-AJT	Boeing 707-344B	Liberia World Airways	
EL-AKA	Boeing 707-123B	Omega Air	
EL-AKB	Boeing 707	Air Gambia	
EL-AKC	Boeing 707-323B	Air Gambia	
EL-JNS	Boeing 707-323C	Transway Air Services	
EL-ZGS	Boeing 707-309C	Jet Cargo Liberia	

EP (Iran)

EP-IAA	Boeing 747SP-86	Iran Air *Fars*	
EP-IAB	Boeing 747SP-86	Iran Air *Kurdistan*	
EP-IAC	Boeing 747SP-86	Iran Air *Khuzestan*	
EP-IAD	Boeing 747SP-86	Iran Air *Rushdie*	
EP-IAG	Boeing 747-286B (SCD)	Iran Air *Azarabadegan*	
EP-IAH	Boeing 747-286B (SCD)	Iran Air *Khorasan*	
EP-IAM	Boeing 747-186B	Iran Air	

ET (Ethiopia)

ET-AIE	Boeing 767-260ER	Ethiopian Airlines	
ET-AIF	Boeing 767-260ER	Ethiopian Airlines	
ET-AIV	Boeing 707-327C	Ethiopian Airlines	
ET-AIZ	Boeing 767-260ER	Ethiopian Airlines/Air Tanzania	
ET-AJS	Boeing 757-260PF	Ethiopian Airlines	
ET-AJX	Boeing 757-260ER	Ethiopian Airlines	
ET-AJY	Boeing 757-260ER	Ethiopian Airlines	
ET-AKC	Boeing 757-260ER	Ethiopian Airlines	
ET-A	Boeing 757-260ER	Ethiopian Airlines	
ET-A	Boeing 757-260ER	Ethiopian Airlines	

F (France)

F-BGNR	V.708 Viscount ★	Air Service Training Ltd/Perth	
F-BIUK	F.27 Friendship Mk 100	—	
F-BJEN	S.E.210 Caravelle 10B	Air Charter	
F-BLHX	Nord 262A	Compagnie Air Littoral	
F-BMKS	S.E.210 Caravelle 10B	Jet Europe	
F-BOJD	Boeing 727-228	Air France	
F-BPJK	Boeing 727-228	Air France	
F-BPJL	Boeing 727-228	Air France	
F-BPJO	Boeing 727-228	Air France	
F-BPJP	Boeing 727-228	Air France	
F-BPJQ	Boeing 727-228	Air France	
F-BPJR	Boeing 727-228	Air Charter	
F-BPJS	Boeing 727-228	Air France/Air Charter	
F-BPJT	Boeing 727-228	Air France/Air Charter	
F-BPJU	Boeing 727-214	Air Charter	
F-BPJV	Boeing 727-214	Air Charter	
F-BPPA	Aero Spacelines Super Guppy-201	Airbus Industrie *Airbus Skylink 2*	
F-BPUA	F.27 Friendship Mk 500	Air France	
F-BPUB	F.27 Friendship Mk 500	Air France	
F-BPUC	F.27 Friendship Mk 500	Air France	
F-BPUD	F.27 Friendship Mk 500	Air France	
F-BPUE	F.27 Friendship Mk 500	Air France	
F-BPUF	F.27 Friendship Mk 500	Air France	
F-BPUG	F.27 Friendship Mk 500	Air France	
F-BPUH	F.27 Friendship Mk 500	Air France	

Notes	Reg.	Type	Owner or Operator
	F-BPUI	F.27 Friendship Mk 500	Air France
	F-BPUJ	F.27 Friendship Mk 500	Air France
	F-BPUK	F.27 Friendship Mk 500	Air France
	F-BPUL	F.27 Friendship Mk 500	Air France
	F-BPVA	Boeing 747-128	Air France
	F-BPVB	Boeing 747-128	Air France
	F-BPVD	Boeing 747-128	Air France
	F-BPVE	Boeing 747-128	Air France
	F-BPVF	Boeing 747-128	Air France
	F-BPVG	Boeing 747-128	Air France
	F-BPVH	Boeing 747-128	Air France
	F-BPVJ	Boeing 747-128	Air France
	F-BPVK	Boeing 747-128	Air France
	F-BPVL	Boeing 747-128	Air France
	F-BPVM	Boeing 747-128	Air France
	F-BPVN	Boeing 747-128	Air France
	F-BPVP	Boeing 747-128	Air France
	F-BPVR	Boeing 747-228F (SCD)	Air France
	F-BPVS	Boeing 747-228B (SCD)	Air France
	F-BPVT	Boeing 747-228B (SCD)	Air France
	F-BPVU	Boeing 747-228B (SCD)	Air France
	F-BPVV	Boeing 747-228F (SCD)	Air France
	F-BPVX	Boeing 747-228B (SCD)	Air France
	F-BPVY	Boeing 747-228B	Air France
	F-BPVZ	Boeing 747-228F (SCD)	Air France
	F-BRUN	Beech 99	T.A.T.
	F-BSUM	F.27 Friendship Mk 500	Air France
	F-BSUN	F.27 Friendship Mk 500	Air France
	F-BSUO	F.27 Friendship Mk 500	Air France
	F-BTDB	Douglas DC-10-30	Union de Transports Aériens (UTA)
	F-BTDC	Douglas DC-10-30	Union de Transports Aériens (UTA)
	F-BTDD	Douglas DC-10-30	Union de Transports Aériens (UTA)
	F-BTDE	Douglas DC-10-30	Union de Transports Aériens (UTA)
	F-BTDG	Boeing 747-3B3 (SCD)	Union de Transports Aériens (UTA)
	F-BTDH	Boeing 747-3B3 (SCD)	Union de Transports Aériens (UTA)
	F-BTGV	Aero Spacelines Super Guppy-201	Airbus Industrie *Airbus Skylink 1*
	F-BTMJ	Beech 99A	T.A.T.
	F-BTMK	Beech 99A	T.A.T.
	F-BTOA	S.E.210 Caravelle 12	Air Inter (*stored*)
	F-BTOC	S.E.210 Caravelle 12	Air Inter (*stored*)
	F-BTOE	S.E.210 Caravelle 12	Air Inter (*stored*)
	F-BTSC	Concorde 101	Air France
	F-BTSD	Concorde 101	Air France
	F-BTTA	Mercure 100	Air Inter
	F-BTTB	Mercure 100	Air Inter
	F-BTTD	Mercure 100	Air Inter
	F-BTTE	Mercure 100	Air Inter
	F-BTTF	Mercure 100	Air Inter
	F-BTTG	Mercure 100	Air Inter
	F-BTTH	Mercure 100	Air Inter
	F-BTTI	Mercure 100	Air Inter
	F-BTTJ	Mercure 100	Air Inter
	F-BUAE	Airbus A.300B2	Air Inter
	F-BUAF	Airbus A.300B2	Air Inter
	F-BUAG	Airbus A.300B2	Air Inter
	F-BUAH	Airbus A.300B2	Air Inter
	F-BUAI	Airbus A.300B2	Air Inter
	F-BUAJ	Airbus A.300B2	Air Inter
	F-BUAK	Airbus A.300B2	Air Inter
	F-BUAL	Airbus A.300B4	Air Inter
	F-BUAM	Airbus A.300B2	Air Inter
	F-BUAN	Airbus A.300B2	Air Inter
	F-BUAO	Airbus A.300B2	Air Inter
	F-BUAP	Airbus A.300B2	Air Inter
	F-BUAQ	Airbus A.300B4	Air Inter
	F-BUAR	Airbus A.300B4	Air Inter
	F-BUTI	F.28 Fellowship 1000	T.A.T.
	F-BVFA	Concorde 101	Air France
	F-BVFB	Concorde 101	Air France
	F-BVFC	Concorde 101	Air France
	F-BVFD	Concorde 101	Air France
	F-BVFF	Concorde 101	Air France
	F-BVFJ	Nord 262A	T.A.T.

Reg.	Type	Owner or Operator	Notes
F-BVGA	Airbus A.300B2	Air France	
F-BVGB	Airbus A.300B2	Air France	
F-BVGC	Airbus A.300B2	Air France	
F-BVGD	Airbus A.300B2	Air Inter	
F-BVGE	Airbus A.300B2	Air Inter	
F-BVGF	Airbus A.300B2	Air Inter	
F-BVGG	Airbus A.300B4	Air France	
F-BVGH	Airbus A.300B4	Air France	
F-BVGI	Airbus A.300B4	Air Charter	
F-BVGJ	Airbus A.300B4	Air France	
F-BVGL	Airbus A.300B4	Air France	
F-BVGM	Airbus A.300B4	Air France	
F-BVGN	Airbus A.300B4	Air France	
F-BVGO	Airbus A.300B4	Air France	
F-BVGP	Airbus A.300B4	Air France	
F-BVGQ	Airbus A.300B4	Air France	
F-BVGR	Airbus A.300B4	Air France	
F-BVGS	Airbus A.300B4	Air France	
F-BVGT	Airbus A.300B4	Air Charter	
F-BVJL	Beech 99A	T.A.T.	
F-BYAB	F.27 Friendship Mk 600	Air Jet	
F-GATS	EMB-110P2 Bandeirante	Compagnie Air Littoral *Hérault*	
F-GBBR	F.28 Fellowship 1000	T.A.T./Air France	
F-GBBS	F.28 Fellowship 1000	T.A.T./Air France	
F-GBBT	F.28 Fellowship 1000	T.A.T./Air France	
F-GBBX	F.28 Fellowship 1000	T.A.T./Air France	
F-GBEA	Airbus A.300B2	Air Inter	
F-GBEB	Airbus A.300B2	Air Inter	
F-GBEC	Airbus A.300B2	Air France	
F-GBEJ	Nord 262B	Compagnie Air Littoral	
F-GBEK	Nord 262A	Compagnie Air Littoral	
F-GBGA	EMB-110P2 Bandeirante	Brit Air	
F-GBLE	EMB-110P2 Bandeirante	Air Atlantique	
F-GBME	EMB-110P2 Bandeirante	Air Atlantique	
F-GBMF	EMB-110P2 Bandeirante	Compagnie Air Littoral	
F-GBMG	EMB-110P2 Bandeirante	Brit Air	
F-GBOX	Boeing 747-2B3F (SCD)	Air France	
F-GBRM	EMB-110P2 Bandeirante	Air Atlantique	
F-GBRQ	FH.227B Friendship	T.A.T.	
F-GBRU	F.27J Friendship	T.A.T.	
F-GBRV	F.27J Friendship	T.A.T./ACE Transvalair	
F-GBYA	Boeing 737-228	Air France	
F-GBYB	Boeing 737-228	Air France/Air Charter	
F-GBYC	Boeing 737-228	Air France	
F-GBYD	Boeing 737-228	Air France	
F-GBYE	Boeing 737-228	Air France	
F-GBYF	Boeing 737-228	Air France	
F-GBYG	Boeing 737-228	Air France	
F-GBYH	Boeing 737-228	Air France	
F-GBYI	Boeing 737-228	Air France	
F-GBYJ	Boeing 737-228	Air France	
F-GBYK	Boeing 737-228	Air France	
F-GBYL	Boeing 737-228	Air France	
F-GBYM	Boeing 737-228	Air France	
F-GBYN	Boeing 737-228	Air France	
F-GBYO	Boeing 737-228	Air France	
F-GBYP	Boeing 737-228	Air France	
F-GBYQ	Boeing 737-228	Air France	
F-GCBA	Boeing 747-228B	Air France	
F-GCBB	Boeing 747-228B (SCD)	Air France	
F-GCBD	Boeing 747-228B (SCD)	Air France	
F-GCBE	Boeing 747-228F (SCD)	Air France	
F-GCBF	Boeing 474-228B (SCD)	Air France	
F-GCBG	Boeing 747-228B (SCD)	Air France	
F-GCBH	Boeing 747-228B (SCD)	Air France	
F-GCBI	Boeing 747-228B (SCD)	Air France	
F-GCBJ	Boeing 747-228B (SCD)	Air France	
F-GCBK	Boeing 747-228F (SCD)	Air France	
F-GCBL	Boeing 747-228F (SCD)	Air France	
F-GCBM	Boeing 747-228F	Air France	
F-GCDA	Boeing 727-228	Air France	
F-GCDB	Boeing 727-228	Air France/Air Charter	

Notes	Reg.	Type	Owner or Operator
	F-GCDC	Boeing 727-228	Air France
	F-GCDD	Boeing 727-228	Air France
	F-GCDE	Boeing 727-228	Air France
	F-GCDF	Boeing 727-228	Air France
	F-GCDG	Boeing 727-228	Air France
	F-GCDH	Boeing 727-228	Air France
	F-GCDI	Boeing 727-228	Air France
	F-GCFC	FH.227B Friendship	T.A.T.
	F-GCGH	FH.227B Friendship	T.A.T.
	F-GCGQ	Boeing 727-227	—
	F-GCJL	Boeing 737-222	Euralair/Air Charter
	F-GCJO	FH.227B Friendship	ACE Transvalair
	F-GCJV	F.27 Friendship Mk 400	Air Jet
	F-GCLA	EMB-110P1 Bandeirante	Aigle Azur
	F-GCLL	Boeing 737-222	Euralair/Air Charter
	F-GCLM	FH.227B Friendship	ACE Transvalair
	F-GCLO	FH.227B Friendship	T.A.T./ACE Transvalair
	F-GCLQ	FH.227B Friendship	T.A.T.
	F-GCMV	Boeing 727-2X3	Air Charter
	F-GCMX	Boeing 727-2X3	Air Charter
	F-GCPT	FH.227B Friendship	T.A.T.
	F-GCPU	FH.227B Friendship	T.A.T.
	F-GCPX	FH.227B Friendship	T.A.T.
	F-GCPY	FH.227B Friendship	T.A.T.
	F-GCSL	Boeing 737-222	Euralair/Air Charter
	F-GCVJ	S.E.210 Caravelle 12	Air Inter (*stored*)
	F-GCVK	S.E.210 Caravelle 12	Air Inter (*stored*)
	F-GCVL	S.E.210 Caravelle 12	Air Provence
	F-GCVM	S.E.210 Caravelle 12	Air Provence
	F-GDAQ	L.100-30 Hercules	Jet Fret
	F-GDFC	F.28 Fellowship 4000	T.A.T./Air France
	F-GDFD	F.28 Fellowship 4000	T.A.T./Air France
	F-GDFY	S.E.210 Caravelle 10B	—
	F-GDFZ	S.E.210 Caravelle 10B	—
	F-GDJK	Douglas DC-10-30	Lineas Aereas de Mocambique (LAM)
	F-GDJM	Douglas DC-8-62CF	Minerve
	F-GDJU	S.E.210 Caravelle 10B	Air Toulouse
	F-GDMR	Swearingen SA.226TC Metro II	Compagnie Air Littoral
	F-GDRM	Douglas DC-8-73	Minerve
	F-GDSG	UTA Super Guppy	Airbus Industrie *Airbus Skylink 3*
	F-GDSK	F.28 Fellowship 4000	T.A.T./Air France
	F-GDUS	F.28 Fellowship 2000	T.A.T.
	F-GDUT	F.28 Fellowship 2000	T.A.T./Air France
	F-GDUU	F.28 Fellowship 2000	T.A.T.
	F-GDUV	F.28 Fellowship 2000	T.A.T.
	F-GDUY	F.28 Fellowship 4000	T.A.T.
	F-GDUZ	F.28 Fellowship 4000	T.A.T./Air France
	F-GDXL	Aerospatiale ATR-42-300	Brit Air
	F-GDXT	F.27J Friendship	Stellair
	F-GEAI	UTA Super Guppy	Airbus Industrie *Airbus Skylink 4*
	F-GEBU	Swearingen SA.226TC Metro II	Compagnie Air Littoral
	F-GECK	F.28 Fellowship 1000	T.A.T./Air France
	F-GEDR	EMB-110 P1 Bandeirante	Stellair
	F-GEGD	Aerospatiale ATR-42-300	Compagnie Air Littoral/Air France
	F-GEGE	Aerospatiale ATR-42-300	Compagnie Air Littoral
	F-GEGF	Aerospatiale ATR-42-300	Compagnie Air Littoral/Air France
	F-GELG	Saab SF.340A	Brit Air/Air France
	F-GELP	S.E.210 Caravelle	Air Charter
	F-GEMA	Airbus A.310-203	Air France
	F-GEMB	Airbus A.310-203	Air France
	F-GEMC	Airbus A.310-203	Air France
	F-GEMD	Airbus A.310-203	Air France
	F-GEME	Airbus A.310-203	Air France
	F-GEMF	Airbus A.310-203	Air France
	F-GEMG	Airbus A.310-203	Air France
	F-GEMN	Airbus A.310-304	Air France
	F-GEMO	Airbus A.310-304	Air France
	F-GEMP	Airbus A.310-304	Air France
	F-GEMQ	Airbus A.310-304	Air France
	F-GEOM	Douglas DC-3C	—
	F-GEPC	S.E. 210 Caravelle 10B3	Aero France International
	F-GEQJ	Aerospatiale ATR-42-300	T.A.T.
	F-GESB	EMB-110P1 Bandeirante	Stellair

Reg.	Type	Owner or Operator	Notes
F-GESM	Douglas DC-8-73CF	Minerve	
F-GETA	Boeing 747-3B3 (SCD)	Air France	
F-GETB	Boeing 747-3B3 (SCD)	Air France	
F-GEXA	Boeing 747-4B3	Union de Transports Aeriens (UTA)	
F-GEXB	Boeing 747-4B3	Union de Transports Aeriens (UTA)	
F-GEXI	Boeing 737-2L9	Air Charter/Europe Aero Service	
F-GEXJ	Boeing 737-2Q8	Air Charter/Europe Aero Service	
F-GEXX	F.28 Fellowship 1000	T.A.T.	
F-GEXZ	F.27J Friendship	Stellair	
F-GFAE	D.H.C.6 Twin Otter 310	T.A.T.	
F-GFAF	D.H.C.6 Twin Otter 310	T.A.T.	
F-GFAG	D.H.C.6 Twin Otter 310	T.A.T.	
F-GFBA	S.E.210 Caravelle 10B	—	
F-GFBZ	Saab SF.340A	Brit Air	
F-GFEN	EMB-120 Brasilia	Compagnie Air Littoral/Air France	
F-GFEO	EMB-120 Brasilia	Compagnie Air Littoral/Air France	
F-GFEP	EMB-120 Brasilia	Compagnie Air Littoral/Air France	
F-GFEQ	EMB-120 Brasilia	Compagnie Air Littoral/Air France	
F-GFER	EMB-120 Brasilia	Compagnie Air Littoral/Air France	
F-GFES	Aerospatiale ATR-42-300	Compagnie Air Littoral/Air France	
F-GFIJ	Swearingen SA226TC Metro II	Compagnie Air Littoral	
F-GFIK	Swearingen SA226TC Metro II	Compagnie Air Littoral	
F-GFIN	EMB-120 Brasilia	Compagnie Air Littoral/Air France	
F-GFJH	Aerospatiale ATR-42-300	Brit Air/Air France	
F-GFJP	Aerospatiale ATR-42-300	Brit Air/Air France	
F-GFJS	F.27 Friendship Mk 600	Air Jet	
F-GFJV	Swearingen SA226TC Metro II	T.A.T.	
F-GFJX	Swearingen SA226TC Metro II	T.A.T.	
F-GFKA	Airbus A.320-111	Air France Ville de Paris	
F-GFKB	Airbus A.320-111	Air France Ville de Rome	
F-GFKD	Airbus A.320-111	Air France Ville de Londres	
F-GFKE	Airbus A.320-111	Air France Ville de Bonn	
F-GFKF	Airbus A.320-111	Air France Ville de Madrid	
F-GFKG	Airbus A.320-111	Air France Ville d'Amsterdam	
F-GFKH	Airbus A.320-211	Air France Ville de Bruxelles	
F-GFKI	Airbus A.320-211	Air France Ville de Lisbonne	
F-GFKJ	Airbus A.320-211	Air France Ville de Copenhagen	
F-GFKK	Airbus A.320-211	Air France Ville d'Athenes	
F-GFKL	Airbus A.320-211	Air France Ville de Dublin	
F-GFKM	Airbus A.320-211	Air France Ville de Luxembourg	
F-GFKN	Airbus A.320-211	Air France	
F-GFKO	Airbus A.320-211	Air France	
F-GFKP	Airbus A.320-211	Air France Ville de Nice	
F-GFKQ	Airbus A.320-111	Air France	
F-GFKR	Airbus A.320-211	Air France Ville de Berlin	
F-GFKS	Airbus A.320-211	Air France	
F-GFKT	Airbus A.320-211	Air France	
F-GFKU	Airbus A.320-211	Air France	
F-GFKV	Airbus A.320-211	Air France	
F-GFKX	Airbus A.320-211	Air France	
F-GFKY	Airbus A.320-211	Air France	
F-GFKZ	Airbus A.320-211	Air France	
F-GFLV	Boeing 737-2K5	Air Charter/Air France	
F-GFLX	Boeing 737-2K5	Air Charter/Air France	
F-GFTB	EMB-120RT Brasilia	Air Exel	
F-GFUA	Boeing 737-33A	Air Charter/Air France	
F-GFUB	Boeing 737-33A	Air Charter	
F-GFUC	Boeing 737-33A	Air Charter	
F-GFUD	Boeing 737-33A	Air Charter	
F-GFUE	Boeing 737-3B3	Air Charter	
F-GFUF	Boeing 737-3B3	Air Charter	
F-GFUG	Boeing 737-4B3	Air Charter	
F-GFUH	Boeing 737-4B3	Air Charter	
F-GFUJ	Boeing 737-33A	Air Charter	
F-GFUK	Boeing 747-2D3B	Air France	
F-GFYL	Boeing 737-2A9C	Euralair/Air Charter	
F-GFYN	Aerospatiale ATR-42-300	Compagnie Air Littoral/Air France	
F-GFZB	McD Douglas MD-83	Air Liberte	
F-GGBV	Saab SF.340A	Aigle Azur	
F-GGEA	Airbus A.320-111	Air Inter	
F-GGEB	Airbus A.320-111	Air Inter	
F-GGEC	Airbus A.320-111	Air Inter	
F-GGEE	Airbus A.320-111	Air Inter	

Notes	Reg.	Type	Owner or Operator
	F-GGEF	Airbus A.320-111	Air Inter
	F-GGEG	Airbus A.320-111	Air Inter
	F-GGFI	Boeing 737-210C	T.A.T.
	F-GGFJ	Boeing 737-248C	T.A.T.
	F-GGGR	Boeing 727-2H3	—
	F-GGKD	S.E.210 Caravelle 10B	Air Service Nantes
	F-GGLK	Aerospatiale ATR-42-300	T.A.T.
	F-GGLR	Aerospatiale ATR-42-300	Brit Air
	F-GGMA	McD Douglas MD-83	Airmust
	F-GGMB	McD Douglas MD-83	Airmust
	F-GGMC	McD Douglas MD-83	Airmust
	F-GGMD	McD Douglas MD-83	Jet Alsace
	F-GGME	McD Douglas MD-83	Jet Alsace
	F-GG	McD Douglas MD-83	Airmust
	F-GGML	Boeing 737-53A	Euralair International/Air France
	F-GGMZ	Douglas DC-10-30	Airmust
	F-GGPA	Boeing 737-242C	T.A.T.
	F-GGPB	Boeing 737-204C	T.A.T.
	F-GGPC	Boeing 737-204C	T.A.T.
	F-GGPN	FH.227B Friendship	—
	F-GGSV	Swearingen SA226TC Metro II	Air Vendee
	F-GGTD	EMB-120RT Brasilia	Air Exel *Nord-Pas de Calais*
	F-GGTE	EMB-120RT Brasilia	Air Exel
	F-GGTF	EMB-120RT Brasilia	Air Exel
	F-GGTG	EMB-120RT Brasilia	Air Exel
	F-GGTH	EMB-120RT Brasilia	Air Exel
	F-GGTI	EMB-120RT Brasilia	Air Exel
	F-GHBM	Boeing 747-283B	—
	F-GHDB	Saab SF.340A	Brit Air/Air France
	F-GHEB	McD Douglas MD-83	Air Liberte
	F-GHEC	McD Douglas MD-83	Air Liberte
	F-GHED	McD Douglas MD-83	Air Liberte
	F-GHEF	Airbus A.300-622R	Air Liberte
	F-GHEG	Airbus A.300-622R	Air Liberte
	F-GHEI	McD Douglas MD-83	Air Liberte
	F-GHEJ	Airbus A.310-304	Air Liberte
	F-GHEK	McD Douglas MD-83	Air Liberte
	F-GHEX	EMB-120RT Brasilia	Alsavia/T.A.T.
	F-GHEY	EMB-120RT Brasilia	Alsavia/T.A.T.
	F-GHGD	Boeing 767-27EER	Air France
	F-GHGE	Boeing 767-27EER	Air France
	F-GHGF	Boeing 767-3Q8ER	Air France
	F-GHGG	Boeing 767-3Q8ER	Air France
	F-GHGH	Boeing 767-37EER	Air France
	F-GHGM	Airbus A.310-304	—
	F-GHGO	McD Douglas MD-83	Air Liberte
	F-GHGP	McD Douglas MD-83	Air Liberte
	F-GHIA	EMB-120RT Brasilia	Compagnie Air Littoral
	F-GHIB	EMB-120RT Brasilia	Compagnie Air Littoral
	F-GHJE	Aerospatiale ATR-42-300	Brit Air
	F-GHKN	S.E.210 Caravelle 10B	Air Toulouse
	F-GHKO	S.E.210 Caravelle 10B	Air Toulouse
	F-GHME	Aerospatiale ATR-42-300	Brit Air
	F-GHMI	Saab SF.340A	Brit Air/Air France
	F-GHMJ	Saab SF.340A	Brit Air
	F-GHMK	Saab SF.340A	Brit Air
	F-GHOI	Douglas DC-10-30	Union de Transports Aériens (UTA)
	F-GHOL	Boeing 737-53C	Euralair International/Air France
	F-GHPI	Aerospatiale ATR-42-300	Brit Air
	F-GHPK	Aerospatiale ATR-42-300	Brit Air
	F-GHPU	Aerospatiale ATR-72-201	Brit Air
	F-GHPV	Aerospatiale ATR-72-201	Brit Air
	F-GHPX	Aerospatiale ATR-72-201	Brit Air
	F-GHPY	Aerospatiale ATR-72-201	Brit Air
	F-GHPZ	Aerospatiale ATR-42-300	Brit Air
	F-GHQA	Airbus A.320-211	Air Inter
	F-GHQB	Airbus A.320-211	Air Inter
	F-GHQC	Airbus A.320-211	Air Inter
	F-GHQD	Airbus A.320-211	Air Inter
	F-GHQE	Airbus A.320-211	Air Inter
	F-GHQF	Airbus A.320-211	Air Inter
	F-GHQF	Airbus A.320-211	Air Inter
	F-GHQG	Airbus A.320-211	Air Inter

Reg.	Type	Owner or Operator	Notes
F-GHQH	Airbus A.320-211	Air Inter	
F-GHQI	Airbus A.320-211	Air Inter	
F-GHQJ	Airbus A.320-211	Air Inter	
F-GHQK	Airbus A.320-211	Air Inter	
F-GHQL	Airbus A.320-211	Air Inter	
F-GHQM	Airbus A.320-211	Air Inter	
F-GHQN	Airbus A.320-211	Air Inter	
F-GHQO	Airbus A.320-211	Air Inter	
F-GHQP	Airbus A.320-211	Air Inter	
F-GHQR	Airbus A.320-211	Air Inter	
F-GHUL	Boeing 737-53C	Euralair/Air Charter	
F-GHVA	Swearingen SA227AC Metro III	Air Vendee	
F-GHVC	Swearingen SA227AC Metro III	Air Vendee	
F-GHVD	Swearingen SA227AC Metro III	Air Vendee	
F-GHVE	Swearingen SA227AC Metro III	Air Vendee	
F-GHVF	Swearingen SA227AT Merlin IV	Air Vendee	
F-GHVG	Swearingen SA227AC Metro III	Air Vendee	
F-GHVL	Boeing 737-53C	Euralair International/Air France	
F-GHVS	Saab SF.340B	Air Vendee	
F-GHVT	Saab SF.340B	Air Vendee	
F-GHVU	Saab SF.340B	Air Vendee	
F-GHXB	F.27J Friendship	Air Service Nantes	
F-GHXK	Boeing 737-2A1	—	
F-GHXL	Boeing 737-2S3	—/Air Charter	
F-GHXM	Boeing 737-53A	—/Air Charter	
F-GHXN	Boeing 737-53A	—	
F-GIAH	F.28 Fellowship 1000	T.A.T./Air France Caribbean	
F-GIAI	F.28 Fellowship 1000	T.A.T.	
F-GIAJ	F.28 Fellowship 1000	T.A.T.	
F-GIAK	F.28 Fellowship 1000	T.A.T.	
F-GIDM	Fokker 100	Compagnie Air Littoral	
F-GIDN	Fokker 100	Compagnie Air Littoral	
F-GIDO	Fokker 100	Compagnie Air Littoral	
F-GIDP	Fokker 100	Compagnie Air Littoral	
F-GIDQ	Fokker 100	Compagnie Air Littoral	
F-GIDT	Fokker 100	Compagnie Air Littoral	
F-GIHR	F.27J Friendship	—	
F-GIJS	Airbus A.300B4	Air Inter	
F-GIJT	Airbus A.300B4	Air Inter	
F-GIJU	Airbus A.300B4	Air Inter	
F-GIMH	F.28 Fellowship 1000	T.A.T.	
F-GINL	Boeing 737-53C	Euralair International	
F-GIOA	Fokker 100	T.A.T.	
F-GIOB	Fokker 100	T.A.T.	
F-GIOC	Fokker 100	T.A.T.	
F-GIOD	Fokker 100	T.A.T.	
F-GIOE	Fokker 100	T.A.T.	
F-GIOF	Fokker 100	T.A.T.	
F-GIOG	Fokker 100	T.A.T.	
F-GIOH	Fokker 100	T.A.T.	
F-GIOV	Fokker 100	T.A.T.	
F-GIPD	F.27A Friendship	Uni-Air	
F-GIRC	Aerospatiale ATR-42-300	—	
F-GISA	Boeing 747-428 (SCD)	Air France	
F-GISB	Boeing 747-428 (SCD)	Air France	
F-GISC	Boeing 747-428 (SCD)	Air France	
F-GISD	Boeing 747-428 (SCD)	Air France	
F-GISE	Boeing 747-428 (SCD)	Air France	
F-GISF	Boeing 747-428 (SCD)	Air France	
F-GISG	Boeing 747-428 (SCD)	Air France	
F-GITA	Boeing 747-428	Air France	
F-GITB	Boeing 747-428	Air France	
F-GITC	Boeing 747-428	Air France	
F-GITD	Boeing 747-428	Air France	
F-GITE	Boeing 747-428	Air France	
F-GJAK	EMB-120RT Brasilia	Compagnie Air Littoral	
F-GJDL	Boeing 737-210C	Air Charter/Euralair	
F-GJDM	S.E.210 Caravelle 10B	STAIR	
F-GJNA	Boeing 737-528	Air France	
F-GJNB	Boeing 737-528	Air France	
F-GJNC	Boeing 737-528	Air France	
F-GJND	Boeing 737-528	Air France	
F-GJNE	Boeing 737-528	Air France	

Notes	Reg.	Type	Owner or Operator
	F-GJNF	Boeing 737-528	Air France
	F-GJNG	Boeing 737-528	Air France
	F-GJNH	Boeing 737-528	Air France
	F-GJNI	Boeing 737-528	Air France
	F-GJNJ	Boeing 737-528	Air France
	F-GJNK	Boeing 737-528	Air France
	F-GJNL	Boeing 737-528	Air France
	F-GJTP	Beech 1900C	T.A.T./Flandre Air
	F-GJVA	Airbus A.320-211	Air Inter
	F-GJVB	Airbus A.320-211	Air Inter
	F-GJVC	Airbus A.320-211	Air Inter
	F-GJVD	Airbus A.320-211	Air Inter
	F-GJVE	Airbus A.320-211	Air Inter
	F-GJVF	Airbus A.320-211	Air Inter
	F-GKCS	Boeing 707-369C	Pan Europe Air
	F-GKCT	Boeing 707-369C	Pan Europe Air
	F-GKJC	F.27 Friendship Mk 600	Air Jet
	F-GKLA	Boeing 747-121	Corse Air
	F-GKMP	Douglas DC-10-30	Airmust
	F-GKNA	Aerospatiale ATR-42-300	T.A.T.
	F-GKNB	Aerospatiale ATR-42-300	T.A.T.
	F-GKNC	Aerospatiale ATR-42-300	T.A.T.
	F-GKND	Aerospatiale ATR-42-300	T.A.T.
	F-GKOA	Aerospatiale ATR-72-202	T.A.T.
	F-GKOB	Aerospatiale ATR-72-202	T.A.T.
	F-GKOC	Aerospatiale ATR-72-202	T.A.T.
	F-GKOD	Aerospatiale ATR-72-202	T.A.T.
	F-GKOE	Aerospatiale ATR-72-202	T.A.T.
	F-GKOF	Aerospatiale ATR-72-202	T.A.T.
	F-GKOG	Aerospatiale ATR-72-202	T.A.T.
	F-GKOH	Aerospatiale ATR-72-202	T.A.T.
	F-GKOI	Aerospatiale ATR-72-202	T.A.T.
	F-GKOJ	Aerospatiale ATR-72-202	T.A.T.
	F-GKOK	Aerospatiale ATR-72-202	T.A.T.
	F-GKOL	Aerospatiale ATR-72-202	T.A.T.
	F-GKOM	Aerospatiale ATR-72-202	T.A.T.
	F-GKON	Aerospatiale ATR-72-202	T.A.T.
	F-GKST	Beech 1990-1	Proteus Air System
	F-GKXA	Airbus A.320-211	Air France
	F-GLMX	Douglas DC-10-30	Airmust
	F-GLNI	BAe 146-200	Air Jet
	F-GPAN	Boeing 747-2B3F (SCD)	Air France
	F-GTNT	BAe 146-200QT	Euralair/TNT
	F-GTNU	BAe 146-200QT	Euralair/TNT
	F-ODJG	Boeing 747-2Q2B	Air Gabon
	F-ODLX	Douglas DC-10-30	Airmust *Diamant*
	F-ODLY	Douglas DC-10-30	Airmust *Turquoise*
	F-ODLZ	Douglas DC-10-30	Airmust *Saphir*
	F-ODSV	Airbus A.310-304	Somali Airlines (*to become 6O-SHH*)
	F-ODVD	Airbus A.310-304	Royal Jordanian *Prince Hashem*
	F-ODVE	Airbus A.310-304	Royal Jordanian *Princess Iman*
	F-ODVF	Airbus A.310-304	Royal Jordanian *Princess Raiyah*
	F-ODVG	Airbus A.310-304	Royal Jordanian *Prince Faisal*
	F-ODVH	Airbus A.310-304	Royal Jordanian *Prince Hamazeh*
	F-ODVI	Airbus A.310-304	Royal Jordanian *Princess Haya*

Note: UTA also operates one DC-10-30 registered N54649.

HA (Hungary)

	HA-LBI	Tupolev Tu-134A-3	Malev
	HA-LBK	Tupolev Tu-134A-3	Malev
	HA-LBN	Tupolev Tu-134A-3	Malev
	HA-LBO	Tupolev Tu-134A-3	Malev
	HA-LBP	Tupolev Tu-134A-3	Malev
	HA-LBR	Tupolev Tu-134A-3	Malev
	HA-LCA	Tupolev Tu-154B-2	Malev
	HA-LCB	Tupolev Tu-154B-2	Malev
	HA-LCE	Tupolev Tu-154B-2	Malev
	HA-LCG	Tupolev Tu-154B-2	Malev
	HA-LCH	Tupolev Tu-154B-2	Malev
	HA-LCM	Tupolev Tu-154B-2	Malev

Reg.	Type	Owner or Operator	Notes
HA-LCN	Tupolev Tu-154B-2	Malev	
HA-LCO	Tupolev Tu-154B-2	Malev	
HA-LCP	Tupolev Tu-154B-2	Malev	
HA-LCR	Tupolev Tu-154B-2	Malev	
HA-LCU	Tupolev Tu-154B-2	Malev	
HA-LCV	Tupolev Tu-154B-2	Malev	
HA-LEA	Boeing 737-2QB	Malev	
HA-LEB	Boeing 737-2M8	Malev	
HA-LEC	Boeing 737-2T5	Malev	
HA-LED	Boeing 737-3Y0	Malev	
HA-LEF	Boeing 737-3Y0	Malev	
HA-LEG	Boeing 737-3Y0	Malev	
HA-L	Boeing 767-200	Malev	
HA-L	Boeing 767-200	Malev	
HA-TAB	BAe 146-200QT	TNT/Malev	

HB (Switzerland)

Reg.	Type	Owner or Operator	Notes
HB-AHB	Saab SF.340A	Crossair	
HB-AHC	Saab SF.340A	Crossair	
HB-AHD	Saab SF.340A	Crossair	
HB-AHM	Saab SF.340A	Crossair	
HB-AHO	Saab SF.340A	Crossair	
HB-AHR	Saab SF.340A	Crossair	
HB-AHS	Saab SF.340A	Crossair	
HB-AHT	Saab SF.340A	Crossair	
HB-AKA	Saab SF.340B	Crossair	
HB-AKB	Saab SF.340B	Crossair	
HB-AKC	Saab SF.340B	Crossair	
HB-AKD	Saab SF.340B	Crossair	
HB-AKE	Saab SF.340B	Crossair	
HB-AKF	Saab SF.340B	Crossair	
HB-AKG	Saab SF.340B	Crossair	
HB-AKH	Saab SF.340B	Crossair	
HB-AKI	Saab SF.340B	Crossair	
HB-AKK	Saab SF.340B	Crossair	
HB-AKL	Saab SF.340B	Crossair	
HB-AKM	Saab SF.340B	Crossair	
HB-AKN	Saab SF.340B	Crossair	
HB-AKO	Saab SF.340B	Crossair	
HB-AKP	Saab SF.340B	Crossair	
HB-IAN	Fokker 50	Crossair	
HB-IAO	Fokker 50	Crossair	
HB-IAP	Fokker 50	Crossair	
HB-IAR	Fokker 50	Crossair	
HB-IAS	Fokker 50	Crossair	
HB-IBF	Douglas DC-8-63	ASA Air Starline	
HB-IGC	Boeing 747-357 (SCD)	Swissair Bern	
HB-IGD	Boeing 747-357 (SCD)	Swissair Basel	
HB-IGG	Boeing 747-357 (SCD)	Swissair Ticino	
HB-IHK	Douglas DC-10-30	Balair	
HB-IHM	Douglas DC-10-30ER	Swissair Valais-Wallis	
HB-IHN	Douglas DC-10-30ER	Swissair St Gallen	
HB-IHO	Douglas DC-10-30ER	Swissair Uri	
HB-	Douglas DC-10-30CF	Balair	
HB-IIA	Boeing 737-3M8	TEA Basle	
HB-IIB	Boeing 737-3M8	TEA Basle	
HB-IKK	McD Douglas MD-82	Alisarda (Italy)	
HB-IKL	McD Douglas MD-82	Alisarda (Italy)	
HB-INA	McD Douglas MD-82	Swissair Höri	
HB-INB	McD Douglas MD-82	Balair	
HB-INC	McD Douglas MD-81	Swissair Lugano	
HB-IND	McD Douglas MD-81	Swissair Bachenbülach	
HB-INE	McD Douglas MD-81	Swissair Rümlang	
HB-INF	McD Douglas MD-81	Swissair Appenzell a.Rh.	
HB-ING	McD Douglas MD-81	Swissair Winkel	
HB-INH	McD Douglas MD-81	Swissair Winterthur	
HB-INI	McD Douglas MD-81	Swissair Kloten	
HB-INK	McD Douglas MD-81	Swissair Opfikon	
HB-INL	McD Douglas MD-81	Swissair Jura	
HB-INM	McD Douglas MD-81	Swissair Lausanne	
HB-INN	McD Douglas MD-81	Swissair Bülach	

Notes	Reg.	Type	Owner or Operator
	HB-INO	McD Douglas MD-81	Swissair *Bellinzona*
	HB-INP	McD Douglas MD-81	Swissair *Oberglatt*
	HB-INR	McD Douglas MD-82	Balair
	HB-INS	McD Douglas MD-81	Swissair *Meyrin*
	HB-INT	McD Douglas MD-81	Swissair *Grand-Saconnex*
	HB-INU	McD Douglas MD-81	Swissair *Vernier*
	HB-INV	McD Douglas MD-81	Swissair *Dubendorf*
	HB-INW	McD Douglas MD-82	Balair
	HB-INX	McD Douglas MD-81	Swissair *Wallisellen*
	HB-INY	McD Douglas MD-81	Swissair *Bassersdorf*
	HB-INZ	McD Douglas MD-81	Swissair *Regensdorf*
	HB-IPA	Airbus A.310-221	Swissair *Aargau*
	HB-IPB	Airbus A.310-221	Swissair *Neuchatel*
	HB-IPC	Airbus A.310-221	Swissair *Schwyz*
	HB-IPD	Airbus A.310-221	Swissair *Solothurn*
	HB-IPE	Airbus A.310-221	Swissair *Basel-Land*
	HB-IPF	Airbus A.310-322	Swissair *Glarus*
	HB-IPG	Airbus A.310-322	Swissair *Zug*
	HB-IPH	Airbus A.310-322	Swissair *Appenzell i. Rh*
	HB-IPI	Airbus A.310-322	Swissair *Luzern*
	HB-IPK	Airbus A.310-322	Balair
	HB-IPL	Airbus A.310-325	Balair
	HB-IPM	Airbus A.310-325	Balair
	HB-IPN	Airbus A.310-325	Balair
	HB-ISB	Douglas DC-3C	Classic Air
	HB-ISC	Douglas DC-3C	Classic Air
	HB-ISG	F.27 Friendship Mk 200	Sunshine Aviation
	HB-ISH	F.27 Friendship Mk 200	Sunshine Aviation *Locarno*
	HB-ISX	McD Douglas MD-81	Swissair *Binningen*
	HB-ISZ	McD Douglas MD-83	Balair
	HB-IUA	McD Douglas MD-87	CTA
	HB-IUB	McD Douglas MD-87	CTA
	HB-IUC	McD Douglas MD-87	CTA
	HB-IUD	McD Douglas MD-87	CTA
	HB-IUG	McD Douglas MD-81	Swissair *Illnau-Effretikon*
	HB-IUH	McD Douglas MD-81	Swissair *Wangen-Brüttisellen*
	HB-IVA	Fokker 100	Swissair *Aarau*
	HB-IVB	Fokker 100	Swissair *Biel/Bienne*
	HB-IVC	Fokker 100	Swissair *Chur*
	HB-IVD	Fokker 100	Swissair *Dietlikon*
	HB-IVE	Fokker 100	Swissair *Baden*
	HB-IVF	Fokker 100	Swissair *Sion*
	HB-IVG	Fokker 100	Swissair *Genthod*
	HB-IVH	Fokker 100	Swissair *Stadel*
	HB-IVI	Fokker 100	Swissair
	HB-IVK	Fokker 100	Swissair
	HB-IWA	McD Douglas MD-11	Swissair *Obwalden*
	HB-IWB	McD Douglas MD-11	Swissair *Graubünden*
	HB-IWC	McD Douglas MD-11	Swissair *Vaud*
	HB-IWD	McD Douglas MD-11	Swissair *Thurgau*
	HB-IWE	McD Douglas MD-11	Swissair *Nidwalden*
	HB-IWF	McD Douglas MD-11	Swissair *Schafthausen*
	HB-IWG	McD Douglas MD-11	Swissair *Valais/Wallis*
	HB-IWH	McD Douglas MD-11	Swissair *St Gallen*
	HB-IWI	McD Douglas MD-11	Swissair *Uri*
	HB-IWK	McD Douglas MD-11	Swissair *Fribourg*
	HB-IWL	McD Douglas MD-11	Swissair *Appenzell a.Rh*
	HB-IWM	McD Douglas MD-11	Swissair *Jura*
	HB-IXB	BAe 146-200A	Crossair
	HB-IXC	BAe 146-200A	Crossair
	HB-IXD	BAe 146-200A	Crossair
	HB-IXF	BAe 146-200	Crossair
	HB-IXG	BAe 146-200	Crossair
	HB-IXH	BAe 146-200	Crossair
	HB-IXK	BAe 146-200	Crossair
	HB-IXZ	BAe 146-300	Crossair

Note: Swissair also operates two Boeing 747-357s which retain their US registrations N221GE and N221GF and are named *Genéve* and *Zurich* respectively.

HK (Colombia)

HK-2980X	Boeing 747-259B (SCD)	Avianca *Cartagena de Indias*

HL (Korea)

HL7315	Douglas DC-10-30	Korean Air
HL7316	Douglas DC-10-30	Korean Air
HL7317	Douglas DC-10-30	Korean Air
HL7441	Boeing 747-230F	Korean Air
HL7443	Boeing 747-2B5B	Korean Air
HL7447	Boeing 747-230B	Korean Air
HL7451	Boeing 747-2B5F (SCD)	Korean Air
HL7452	Boeing 747-2B5F (SCD)	Korean Air
HL7453	Boeing 747-212B	Korean Air
HL7454	Boeing 747-2B5B (SCD)	Korean Air Cargo
HL7458	Boeing 747-2B5B	Korean Air
HL7459	Boeing 747-2B5F (SCD)	Korean Air
HL7463	Boeing 747-2B5B	Korean Air
HL7464	Boeing 747-2B5B	Korean Air
HL7468	Boeing 747-3B5	Korean Air
HL7469	Boeing 747-3B5	Korean Air
HL7470	Boeing 747-3B5 (SCD)	Korean Air
HL7471	Boeing 747-273C	Korean Air
HL7474	Boeing 747-2S4F (SCD)	Korean Air
HL7475	Boeing 747-2B5F (SCD)	Korean Air
HL7476	Boeing 747-2B5F (SCD)	Korean Air
HL7477	Boeing 747-4B5	Korean Air
HL7478	Boeing 747-4B5	Korean Air
HL7479	Boeing 747-4B5	Korean Air
HL7480	Boeing 747-4B5 (SCD)	Korean Air
HL7481	Boeing 747-4B5	Korean Air
HL7482	Boeing 747-4B5 (SCD)	Korean Air
HL7483	Boeing 747-4B5	Korean Air
HL7484	Boeing 747-4B5	Korean Air
HL7485	Boeing 747-4B5	Korean Air

HS (Thailand)

HS-TGA	Boeing 747-2D7B	Thai Airways International *Visuthakasatriya*
HS-TGB	Boeing 747-2D7B	Thai Airways International *Sirisobhakya*
HS-TGC	Boeing 747-2D7B	Thai Airways International *Dararasmi*
HS-TGD	Boeing 747-3D7	Thai Airways International *Suchada*
HS-TGE	Boeing 747-3D7	Thai Airways International *Chutamat*
HS-TGF	Boeing 747-2D7B	Thai Airways International *Phimara*
HS-TGG	Boeing 747-2D7B	Thai Airways International *Sriwanna*
HS-TGH	Boeing 747-4D7	Thai Airways International
HS-TGJ	Boeing 747-4D7	Thai Airways International
HS-TGK	Boeing 747-4D7	Thai Airways International
HS-T	Boeing 747-4D7	Thai Airways International
HS-T	Boeing 747-4D7	Thai Airways International
HS-T	Boeing 747-4D7	Thai Airways International
HS-TGS	Boeing 747-2D7B	Thai Airways International *Chainarai*
HS-TMA	Douglas DC-10-30ER	Thai Airways International *Kwanmuang*
HS-TMB	Douglas DC-10-30ER	Thai Airways International *Thepalai*
HS-TMC	Douglas DC-10-30ER	Thai Airways International *Sri Ubon*

HZ (Saudi Arabia)

HZ-AHA	L.1011-385 TriStar 200	Saudia — Saudi Arabian Airlines
HZ-AHB	L.1011-385 TriStar 200	Saudia — Saudi Arabian Airlines
HZ-AHC	L.1011-385 TriStar 200	Saudia — Saudi Arabian Airlines
HZ-AHD	L.1011-385 TriStar 200	Saudia — Saudi Arabian Airlines
HZ-AHE	L.1011-385 TriStar 200	Saudia — Saudi Arabian Airlines
HZ-AHF	L.1011-385 TriStar 200	Saudia — Saudi Arabian Airlines
HZ-AHG	L.1011-385 TriStar 200	Saudia — Saudi Arabian Airlines
HZ-AHH	L.1011-385 TriStar 200	Saudia — Saudi Arabian Airlines
HZ-AHI	L.1011-385 TriStar 200	Saudia — Saudi Arabian Airlines
HZ-AHJ	L.1011-385 TriStar 200	Saudia — Saudi Arabian Airlines
HZ-AHL	L.1011-385 TriStar 200	Saudia — Saudi Arabian Airlines
HZ-AHM	L.1011-385 TriStar 200	Saudia — Saudi Arabian Airlines
HZ-AHN	L.1011-385 TriStar 200	Saudia — Saudi Arabian Airlines
HZ-AHO	L.1011-385 TriStar 200	Saudia — Saudi Arabian Airlines
HZ-AHP	L.1011-385 TriStar 200	Saudia — Saudi Arabian Airlines
HZ-AHQ	L.1011-385 TriStar 200	Saudia — Saudi Arabian Airlines

Notes	Reg.	Type	Owner or Operator
	HZ-AHR	L.1011-385 TriStar 200	Saudia — Saudi Arabian Airlines
	HZ-AIA	Boeing 747-168B	Saudia — Saudi Arabian Airlines
	HZ-AIB	Boeing 747-168B	Saudia — Saudi Arabian Airlines
	HZ-AIC	Boeing 747-168B	Saudia — Saudi Arabian Airlines
	HZ-AID	Boeing 747-168B	Saudia — Saudi Arabian Airlines
	HZ-AIE	Boeing 747-168B	Saudia — Saudi Arabian Airlines
	HZ-AIF	Boeing 747SP-68	Saudia — Saudi Arabian Airlines
	HZ-AIG	Boeing 747-168B	Saudia — Saudi Arabian Airlines
	HZ-AIH	Boeing 747-168B	Saudia — Saudi Arabian Airlines
	HZ-AII	Boeing 747-168B	Saudia — Saudi Arabian Airlines
	HZ-AIJ	Boeing 747SP-68	Saudia — Saudi Arabian Airlines
	HZ-AIK	Boeing 747-368	Saudia — Saudi Arabian Airlines
	HZ-AIL	Boeing 747-368	Saudia — Saudi Arabian Airlines
	HZ-AIM	Boeing 747-368	Saudia — Saudi Arabian Airlines
	HZ-AIN	Boeing 747-368	Saudia — Saudi Arabian Airlines
	HZ-AIO	Boeing 747-368	Saudia — Saudi Arabian Airlines
	HZ-AIP	Boeing 747-368	Saudia — Saudi Arabian Airlines
	HZ-AIQ	Boeing 747-368	Saudia — Saudi Arabian Airlines
	HZ-AIR	Boeing 747-368	Saudia — Saudi Arabian Airlines
	HZ-AIS	Boeing 747-368	Saudia — Saudi Arabian Airlines
	HZ-AIT	Boeing 747-368	Saudia — Saudi Arabian Airlines
	HZ-AIU	Boeing 747-268F	Saudia — Saudi Arabian Airlines
	HZ-AJA	Airbus A.300-620	Saudia — Saudi Arabian Airlines
	HZ-AJB	Airbus A.300-620	Saudia — Saudi Arabian Airlines
	HZ-AJC	Airbus A.300-620	Saudia — Saudi Arabian Airlines
	HZ-AJD	Airbus A.300-620	Saudia — Saudi Arabian Airlines
	HZ-AJE	Airbus A.300-620	Saudia — Saudi Arabian Airlines
	HZ-AJF	Airbus A.300-620	Saudia — Saudi Arabian Airlines
	HZ-AJG	Airbus A.300-620	Saudia — Saudi Arabian Airlines
	HZ-AJH	Airbus A.300-620	Saudia — Saudi Arabian Airlines
	HZ-AJI	Airbus A.300-620	Saudia — Saudi Arabian Airlines
	HZ-AJJ	Airbus A.300-620	Saudia — Saudi Arabian Airlines
	HZ-AJK	Airbus A.300-620	Saudia — Saudi Arabian Airlines

Note: Saudia also operates other aircraft on lease.

I (Italy)

Notes	Reg.	Type	Owner or Operator
	I-AEJB	Boeing 767-283ER	Air Europe SpA
	I-AEJC	Boeing 767-283ER	Air Europe SpA
	I-BUSB	Airbus A.300B4	Alitalia *Tiziano*
	I-BUSC	Airbus A.300B4	Alitalia *Botticelli*
	I-BUSD	Airbus A.300B4	Alitalia *Caravaggio*
	I-BUSF	Airbus A.300B4	Alitalia *Tintoretto*
	I-BUSG	Airbus A.300B4	Alitalia *Canaletto*
	I-BUSH	Airbus A.300B4	Alitalia *Mantegna*
	I-BUSJ	Airbus A.300B4	Alitalia *Tiepolo*
	I-BUSL	Airbus A.300B4	Alitalia *Pinturicchia*
	I-BUSM	Airbus A.300B2	Alitalia *Raffaello*
	I-BUSN	Airbus A.300B2	Alitalia
	I-BUSP	Airbus A.300B4	Alitalia
	I-BUSQ	Airbus A.300B4	Alitalia *Michelangelo*
	I-BUSR	Airbus A.300B4	Alitalia
	I-BUST	Airbus A.300B4	Alitalia *Piero della Francesca*
	I-DACM	McD Douglas MD-82	Aero Trasporti Italiani (ATI) *La Spezia*
	I-DACN	McD Douglas MD-82	Aero Trasporti Italiani (ATI) *Rieti*
	I-DACP	McD Douglas MD-82	Aero Trasporti Italiani (ATI) *Padova*
	I-DACQ	McD Douglas MD-82	Alitalia *Taranto*
	I-DACR	McD Douglas MD-82	Alitalia *Carrara*
	I-DACS	McD Douglas MD-82	Alitalia *Valtellina*
	I-DACT	McD Douglas MD-82	Alitalia *Maratea*
	I-DACU	McD Douglas MD-82	Aero Trasporti Italiani (ATI) *Fabriano*
	I-DACV	McD Douglas MD-82	Aero Trasporti Italiani (ATI) *Riccione*
	I-DACW	McD Douglas MD-82	Alitalia *Vieste*
	I-DACX	McD Douglas MD-82	Aero Trasporti Italiani (ATI) *Piacenza*
	I-DACY	McD Douglas MD-82	Alitalia *Novara*
	I-DACZ	McD Douglas MD-82	Aero Trasporti Italiani (ATI) *Castelfidardo*
	I-DAND	McD Douglas MD-82	Alitalia *Bolzano*
	I-DANF	McD Douglas MD-82	Aero Trasporti Italiani (ATI *Vicenza*
	I-DANG	McD Douglas MD-82	Alitalia
	I-DANH	McD Douglas MD-82	Alitalia
	I-DANL	McD Douglas MD-82	Alitalia

Reg.	Type	Owner or Operator	Notes
I-DANM	McD Douglas MD-82	Alitalia	
I-DANP	McD Douglas MD-82	Alitalia	
I-DANQ	McD Douglas MD-82	Alitalia	
I-DANR	McD Douglas MD-82	Alitalia	
I-DANU	McD Douglas MD-82	Alitalia	
I-DANV	McD Douglas MD-82	Alitalia	
I-DANW	McD Douglas MD-82	Alitalia	
I-DAVA	McD Douglas MD-82	Aero Trasporti Italiani (ATI) *Cuneo*	
I-DAVB	McD Douglas MD-82	Aero Trasporti Italiani (ATI) *Ferrara*	
I-DAVC	McD Douglas MD-82	Aero Trasporti Italiani (ATI) *Lucca*	
I-DAVD	McD Douglas MD-82	Aero Trasporti Italiani (ATI) *Mantova*	
I-DAVF	McD Douglas MD-82	Aero Trasporti Italiani (ATI) *Oristano*	
I-DAVG	McD Douglas MD-82	Aero Trasporti Italiani (ATI) *Pesaro*	
I-DAVH	McD Douglas MD-82	Aero Trasporti Italiani (ATI) *Salerno*	
I-DAVI	McD Douglas MD-82	Alitalia *Assisi*	
I-DAVJ	McD Douglas MD-82	Alitalia *Parma*	
I-DAVK	McD Douglas MD-82	Alitalia *Pompei*	
I-DAVL	McD Douglas MD-82	Aero Trasporti Italiani (ATI) *Reggio Calabria*	
I-DAVM	McD Douglas MD-82	Alitalia *Caserta*	
I-DAVN	McD Douglas MD-82	Aero Trasporti Italiani (ATI) *Volterra*	
I-DAVP	McD Douglas MD-82	Aero Trasporti Italiani (ATI) *Gorizia*	
I-DAVR	McD Douglas MD-82	Aero Trasporti Italiani (ATI)	
I-DAVS	McD Douglas MD-82	Aero Trasporti Italiani (ATI)	
I-DAVT	McD Douglas MD-82	Aero Trasporti Italiani (ATI)	
I-DAVU	McD Douglas MD-82	Aero Trasporti Italiani (ATI)	
I-DAVV	McD Douglas MD-82	Aero Trasporti Italiani (ATI)	
I-DAVW	McD Douglas MD-82	Aero Trasporti Italiani (ATI) *Camerino*	
I-DAVX	McD Douglas MD-82	Aero Trasporti Italiani (ATI) *Asti*	
I-DAVZ	McD Douglas MD-82	Aero Trasporti Italiani (ATI) *Brescia*	
I-DAWA	McD Douglas MD-82	Alitalia *Roma*	
I-DAWB	McD Douglas MD-82	Alitalia *Cagliari*	
I-DAWC	McD Douglas MD-82	Alitalia *Campobasso*	
I-DAWD	McD Douglas MD-82	Alitalia *Catanzaro*	
I-DAWE	McD Douglas MD-82	Alitalia *Milano*	
I-DAWF	McD Douglas MD-82	Alitalia *Firenze*	
I-DAWG	McD Douglas MD-82	Alitalia *L'Aquila*	
I-DAWH	McD Douglas MD-82	Alitalia *Palermo*	
I-DAWI	McD Douglas MD-82	Alitalia *Ancona*	
I-DAWJ	McD Douglas MD-82	Alitalia *Genova*	
I-DAWL	McD Douglas MD-82	Alitalia *Perugia*	
I-DAWM	McD Douglas MD-82	Alitalia *Potenza*	
I-DAWO	McD Douglas MD-82	Alitalia *Bari*	
I-DAWP	McD Douglas MD-82	Alitalia *Torino*	
I-DAWQ	McD Douglas MD-82	Alitalia *Trieste*	
I-DAWR	McD Douglas MD-82	Alitalia *Venezia*	
I-DAWS	McD Douglas MD-82	Alitalia *Aosta*	
I-DAWT	McD Douglas MD-82	Aero Trasporti Italiani (ATI) *Napoli*	
I-DAWU	McD Douglas MD-82	Alitalia *Bologna*	
I-DAWV	McD Douglas MD-82	Aero Trasporti Italiani (ATI) *Trento*	
I-DAWW	McD Douglas MD-82	Aero Trasporti Italiani (ATI) *Riace*	
I-DAWY	McD Douglas MD-82	Aero Trasporti Italiani (ATI) *Agrigento*	
I-DAWZ	McD Douglas MD-82	Aero Trasporti Italiani (ATI) *Avellino*	
I-DEMC	Boeing 747-243B (SCD)	Alitalia *Taormina*	
I-DEMD	Boeing 747-243B (SCD)	Alitalia *Cortina d'Ampezzo*	
I-DEMF	Boeing 747-243B (SCD)	Alitalia *Portofino*	
I-DEMG	Boeing 747-243B	Alitalia *Cervinia*	
I-DEML	Boeing 747-243B	Alitalia *Sorrento*	
I-DEMN	Boeing 747-243B	Alitalia *Portocervo*	
I-DEMP	Boeing 747-243B	Alitalia *Capri*	
I-DEMR	Boeing 747-243F (SCD)	Alitalia *Stresa*	
I-DEMS	Boeing 747-243B	Alitalia *Monte Argentario*	
I-DEMT	Boeing 747-243B (SCD)	Alitalia *Monte Catini*	
I-DEMV	Boeing 747-243B	Alitalia *Sestriere*	
I-DEMW	Boeing 747-243B (SCD)	Alitalia *Spoleto*	
I-DEMY	Boeing 747-230B	Alitalia *Asolo*	
I-DIBR	Douglas DC-9-32	Alitalia *Isola di Capri*	
I-DIBS	Douglas DC-9-32	Alitalia *Isola d'Elba*	
I-DIBT	Douglas DC-9-32	Alitalia *Isola di Murano*	
I-DIBU	Douglas DC-9-32	Alitalia *Isola di Pantellaria*	
I-DIBV	Douglas DC-9-32	Alitalia *Isola d'Ischia*	
I-DIBW	Douglas DC-9-32	Alitalia *Isola del Giglio*	
I-DIBX	Douglas DC-9-32	Alitalia *Isola di Giannutri*	
I-DIBY	Douglas DC-9-32	Alitalia *Isola di Panarea*	
I-DIBZ	Douglas DC-9-32	Alitalia *Isola di Lipari*	

Notes	Reg.	Type	Owner or Operator
	I-DIKM	Douglas DC-9-32	Alitalia *Isola di Positano*
	I-DIKP	Douglas DC-9-32	Alitalia *Isola di Marettimo*
	I-DIKR	Douglas DC-9-32	Alitalia *Piemonte*
	I-DIZE	Douglas DC-9-32	Alitalia *Isola della Meloria*
	I-DUPA	McD Douglas MD-11C	Alitalia *Teatro alla Scala*
	I-DUPB	McD Douglas MD-11C	Alitalia *Valli dei Templi*
	I-DUPE	McD Douglas MD-11C	Alitalia *Arena di Verona*
	I-DUPI	McD Douglas MD-11C	Alitalia *Fontona di Trevi*
	I-DUPO	McD Douglas MD-11C	Alitalia *Canal Grande*
	I-DUPU	McD Douglas MD-11C	Alitalia *Ponte Vecchio*
	I-FLRV	BAe 146-200	Meridiana
	I-FLRW	BAe 146-200	Meridiana
	I-FLRX	BAe 146-200	Meridiana
	I-FLRZ	BAe 146-200	Meridiana
	I-JETA	Boeing 737-229	Ital Jet
	I-RIBC	Douglas DC-9-32	Alitalia *Isola di Lampedusa*
	I-RIBD	Douglas DC-9-32	Alitalia *Isola di Montecristo*
	I-RIBJ	Douglas DC-9-32	Alitalia *Isola della Capraia*
	I-RIBN	Douglas DC-9-32	Alitalia *Isola della Palmaria*
	I-RIBQ	Douglas DC-9-32	Alitalia *Isola di Pianosa*
	I-RIKS	Douglas DC-9-32	Aero Trasporti Italiani (ATI) *Basilicata*
	I-RIKT	Douglas DC-9-32	Aero Trasporti Italiani (ATI) *Trento Alto Adige*
	I-RIKV	Douglas DC-9-32	Alitalia *Isola di Vulcano*
	I-RIKZ	Douglas DC-9-32	Alitalia *Isola di Linosa*
	I-RIZA	Douglas DC-9-32	Alitalia *Isola di Palmorola*
	I-RIZB	Douglas DC-9-32	Alitalia *Abruzzo*
	I-RIZC	Douglas DC-9-32	Alitalia *Molise*
	I-RIZF	Douglas DC-9-32	Alitalia *Isola di Spargi*
	I-RIZG	Douglas DC-9-32	Alitalia *Isola di Nisida*
	I-RIZH	Douglas DC-9-32	Alitalia *Isola di Ponza*
	I-RIZJ	Douglas DC-9-32	Alitalia *Umbria*
	I-RIZK	Douglas DC-9-32	Alitalia *Toscana*
	I-RIZL	Douglas DC-9-32	Alitalia *Romagna*
	I-RIZN	Douglas DC-9-32	Aero Transporti Italiani (ATI) *Calabria*
	I-RIZP	Douglas DC-9-32	Alitalia *Veneto*
	I-RIZQ	Douglas DC-9-32	Alitalia *Erice*
	I-RIZR	Douglas DC-9-32	Aero Trasporti Italiani (ATI) *Marche*
	I-RIZS	Douglas DC-9-32	Aero Trasporti Italiani (ATI) *Compania*
	I-RIZT	Douglas DC-9-32	Aero Trasporti Italiani (ATI) *Friuli Venezia Giulia*
	I-RIZU	Douglas DC-9-32	Aero Trasporti Italiani (ATI) *Valle d'Aosta*
	I-RIZV	Douglas DC-9-32	Aero Trasporti Italiani (ATI) *Lazio*
	I-RIZW	Douglas DC-9-32	Aero Transporti Italiani (ATI) *Lombardia*
	I-RIZX	Douglas DC-9-32	Alitalia *Isola di Procida*
	I-RIZY	Douglas DC-9-32	Alitalia *Isola di Alicudi*
	I-SMEA	Douglas DC-9-51	Meridiana
	I-SMEE	Douglas DC-9-51	Meridiana
	I-SMEI	Douglas DC-9-51	Meridiana
	I-SMEJ	Douglas DC-9-51	Meridiana
	I-SMEO	Douglas DC-9-51	Meridiana
	I-SMEP	McD Douglas MD-82	Meridiana
	I-SMER	McD Douglas MD-82	Meridiana
	I-SMET	McD Douglas MD-82	Meridiana
	I-SMEU	Douglas DC-9-51	Meridiana
	I-SMEV	McD Douglas MD-82	Meridiana
	I-	McD Douglas MD-82	Meridiana
	I-	McD Douglas MD-82	Meridiana
	I-	McD Douglas MD-82	Meridiana
	I-TNTC	BAe146-200QT	Mistral Air/TNT

Note: Meridiana also uses two DC-9-82s which retain their Swiss registrations HB-IKK and HB-IKL.

JA (Japan)

	JA8071	Boeing 747-446	Japan Airlines
	JA8072	Boeing 747-446	Japan Airlines
	JA8073	Boeing 747-446	Japan Airlines
	JA8074	Boeing 747-446	Japan Airlines

Reg.	Type	Owner or Operator	Notes
JA8075	Boeing 747-446	Japan Airlines	
JA8076	Boeing 747-446	Japan Airlines	
JA8077	Boeing 747-446	Japan Airlines	
JA8078	Boeing 747-446	Japan Airlines	
JA8079	Boeing 747-446	Japan Airlines	
JA8080	Boeing 747-446	Japan Airlines	
JA8081	Boeing 747-446	Japan Airlines	
JA8082	Boeing 747-446	Japan Airlines	
JA8083	Boeing 747-446	Japan Airlines	
JA8084	Boeing 747-446	Japan Airlines	
JA8085	Boeing 747-446	Japan Airlines	
JA8086	Boeing 747-446	Japan Airlines	
JA8087	Boeing 747-446	Japan Airlines	
JA8088	Boeing 747-446	Japan Airlines	
JA8089	Boeing 747-446	Japan Airlines	
JA8090	Boeing 747-446	Japan Airlines	
JA8104	Boeing 747-246B	Japan Airlines	
JA8105	Boeing 747-246B	Japan Airlines	
JA8106	Boeing 747-246B	Japan Airlines	
JA8107	Boeing 747-146F (SCD)	Japan Airlines	
JA8108	Boeing 747-246B	Japan Airlines	
JA8110	Boeing 747-246B	Japan Airlines	
JA8111	Boeing 747-246B	Japan Airlines	
JA8112	Boeing 747-146A	Japan Airlines	
JA8113	Boeing 747-246B	Japan Airlines	
JA8114	Boeing 747-246B	Japan Airlines	
JA8115	Boeing 747-146A	Japan Airlines	
JA8116	Boeing 747-146A	Japan Airlines	
JA8122	Boeing 747-246B	Japan Airlines	
JA8123	Boeing 747-246F (SCD)	Japan Airlines	
JA8125	Boeing 747-246B	Japan Airlines	
JA8130	Boeing 747-246B	Japan Airlines	
JA8131	Boeing 747-246B	Japan Airlines	
JA8132	Boeing 747-246F	Japan Airlines	
JA8140	Boeing 747-246B	Japan Airlines	
JA8141	Boeing 747-246B	Japan Airlines	
JA8144	Boeing 747-246F (SCD)	Japan Airlines	
JA8149	Boeing 747-246B	Japan Airlines	
JA8150	Boeing 747-246B	Japan Airlines	
JA8151	Boeing 747-246F (SCD)	Japan Airlines	
JA8154	Boeing 747-246B	Japan Airlines	
JA8155	Boeing 747-246B	Japan Airlines	
JA8160	Boeing 747-221F (SCD)	JUST	
JA8161	Boeing 747-246B	Japan Airlines	
JA8162	Boeing 747-246B	Japan Airlines	
JA8163	Boeing 747-346	Japan Airlines	
JA8165	Boeing 747-221F (SCD)	Japan Airlines	
JA8166	Boeing 747-346	Japan Airlines	
JA8169	Boeing 747-246B	Japan Airlines	
JA8171	Boeing 747-246F (SCD)	Japan Airlines	
JA8173	Boeing 747-346	Japan Airlines	
JA8174	Boeing 747-281B	All Nippon Airways	
JA8175	Boeing 747-281B	All Nippon Airways	
JA8177	Boeing 747-346	Japan Airlines	
JA8178	Boeing 747-346	Japan Airlines	
JA8179	Boeing 747-346	Japan Airlines	
JA8180	Boeing 747-246F (SCD)	Japan Airlines	
JA8181	Boeing 747-281B	All Nippon Airways	
JA8182	Boeing 747-281B	All Nippon Airways	
JA8185	Boeing 747-346	Japan Airlines	
JA8190	Boeing 747-281B	All Nippon Airways	
JA8192	Boeing 747-2D3B	All Nippon Airways	
JA8193	Boeing 747-212B (SCD)	Japan Airlines	
JA8535	Douglas DC-10-40	Japan Airlines	
JA8538	Douglas DC-10-40	Japan Airlines	
JA8541	Douglas DC-10-40	Japan Airlines	
JA8542	Douglas DC-10-40	Japan Airlines	
JA8543	Douglas DC-10-40	Japan Airlines	
JA8545	Douglas DC-10-40	Japan Airlines	
JA8547	Douglas DC-10-40	Japan Airlines	

Note: Japan Airlines also operates a Boeing 747-246F which retains its US registration N211JL and two 747-346s N212JL and N213JL.

JY (Jordan)

JY-ADP	Boeing 707-3D3C	Royal Jordanian *Mafreq*
JY-AEC	Boeing 707-384C	Royal Jordanian *Um Qais*
JY-AGA	L.1011-385 TriStar 500	Royal Jordanian *Amman*
JY-AGB	L.1011-385 TriStar 500	Royal Jordanian *Princess Alia*
JY-AGC	L.1011-385 TriStar 500	Royal Jordanian *Princes Zein*
JY-AGD	L.1011-385 TriStar 500	Royal Jordanian *Prince Ali*
JY-AGE	L.1011-385 TriStar 500	Royal Jordanian *Princess Aysha*
JY-AJK	Boeing 707-384C	Royal Jordanian *City of Jerash*
JY-HKJ	L.1011-385 TriStar 500	Jordan Government

Note: Royal Jordanian also operates six A.310-304s registered F-ODVD, F-ODVE, F-ODVF, F-ODVG, F-ODVH and F-ODVI. The marks JY-CAD, JY-CAE, JY-CAF, JY-CAG, JY-CAH and JY-CAI respectively have been reserved for them.

LN (Norway)

LN-AKA	F.27 Friendship Mk 200	Busy Bee
LN-AKB	F.27 Friendship Mk 200	Busy Bee
LN-AKC	F.27 Friendship Mk 200	Busy Bee
LN-AKD	F.27 Friendship Mk 200	Busy Bee
LN-BBA	Fokker 50	Busy Bee
LN-BBB	Fokker 50	Busy Bee
LN-BBC	Fokker 50	Busy Bee
LN-BBD	Fokker 50	Busy Bee
LN-BBE	Fokker 50	Busy Bee
LN-BRA	Boeing 737-405	Braathens SAFE *Eirik Blodoeks*
LN-BRB	Boeing 737-405	Braathens SAFE *Inge Bardson*
LN-BRC	Boeing 737-505	Braathens SAFE
LN-BRD	Boeing 737-505	Braathens SAFE
LN-BRE	Boeing 737-405	Braathens SAFE
LN-BRG	Boeing 737-505	Braathens SAFE
LN-BRI	Boeing 737-405	Braathens SAFE
LN-BRK	Boeing 737-505	Braathens SAFE
LN-BRL	Boeing 737-296	Braathens SAFE *Sigurd Munn*
LN-BRM	Boeing 737-505	Braathens SAFE
LN-BRN	Boeing 737-505	Braathens SAFE
LN-BRO	Boeing 737-505	Braathens SAFE
LN-BRP	Boeing 737-405	Braathens SAFE
LN-BRQ	Boeing 737-405	Braathens SAFE
LN-BRT	Boeing 737-505	Braathens SAFE
LN-BRU	Boeing 737-505	Braathens SAFE
LN-BRV	Boeing 737-505	Braathens SAFE
LN-BRW	Boeing 737-505	Braathens SAFE
LN-FOG	L-188AF Electra	Fred Olsen Airtransport/DHL
LN-FOH	L-188AF Electra	Fred Olsen Airtransport/DHL
LN-FOI	L-188CF Electra	Fred Olsen Airtransport/DHL
LN-FOL	L-188AF Electra	Fred Olsen Airtransport/EMS
LN-KLK	Convair 440	Norsk Metropolitan Fly Klubb
LN-KOC	EMB-120RT Brasilia	Norsk Air
LN-KOD	EMB-120RT Brasilia	Norsk Air
LN-KOE	EMB-120RT Brasilia	Norsk Air
LN-MOB	Beech 200 Super King Air	Morefly
LN-NOR	Boeing 737-33A	Norway Airlines *City of Stavanger*
LN-NOS	Boeing 737-33A	Norway Airlines *City of Trondheim*
LN-NPD	F.27 Friendship Mk 100	Busy Bee
LN-NPI	F.27 Friendship Mk 100	Busy Bee
LN-NPM	F.27 Friendship Mk 100	Busy Bee
LN-RCC	Boeing 767-283ER	S.A.S. *Freydis Viking*
LN-RCD	Boeing 767-383ER	S.A.S. *Gyda Viking*
LN-RCE	Boeing 767-383ER	S.A.S. *Aase Viking*
LN-RLA	Douglas DC-9-41	S.A.S. *Are Viking*
LN-RLB	Douglas DC-9-41	S.A.S. *Arne Viking*
LN-RLE	McD Douglas MD-81	S.A.S. *Trygve Viking*
LN-RLF	McD Douglas MD-82	S.A.S. *Finn Viking*
LN-RLG	McD Douglas MD-82	S.A.S. *Trond Viking*
LN-RLH	Douglas DC-9-41	S.A.S. *Einar Viking*
LN-RLN	Douglas DC-9-41	S.A.S. *Halldor Viking*
LN-RLP	Douglas DC-9-41	S.A.S. *Froste Viking*
LN-RLR	McD Douglas MD-82	S.A.S. *Kettil Viking*

Reg.	Type	Owner or Operator	Notes
LN-RLS	Douglas DC-9-41	S.A.S. *Asmund Viking*	
LN-RLT	Douglas DC-9-41	S.A.S. *Audun Viking*	
LN-RLU	Douglas DC-9-41	S.A.S. *Eivind Viking*	
LN-RLX	Douglas DC-9-41	S.A.S. *Sote Viking*	
LN-RLZ	Douglas DC-9-41	S.A.S. *Bodvar Viking*	
LN-RMA	McD Douglas MD-81	S.A.S. *Hasting Viking*	
LN-RMB	McD Douglas MD-83	Scanair	
LN-RMD	McD Douglas MD-82	Scanair	
LN-RMF	McD Douglas MD-83	S.A.S. *Torgny Viking*	
LN-RMG	McD Douglas MD-87	S.A.S. *Snorre Viking*	
LN-RMH	McD Douglas MD-87	S.A.S. *Solmund Viking*	
LN-RMJ	McD Douglas MD-81	S.A.S. *Rand Viking*	
LN-RMK	McD Douglas MD-87	S.A.S. *Ragnhild Viking*	
LN-RML	McD Douglas MD-81	S.A.S. *Aud Viking*	
LN-RMM	McD Douglas MD-81	S.A.S. *Blenda Viking*	
LN-RMN	McD Douglas MD-82	S.A.S.	
LN-RMO	McD Douglas MD-81	S.A.S.	
LN-RMP	McD Douglas MD-87	S.A.S.	
LN-RMR	McD Douglas MD-81	S.A.S.	
LN-RMS	McD Douglas MD-81	S.A.S.	
LN-RMT	McD Douglas MD-81	S.A.S.	
LN-RNB	Fokker 50	S.A.S. Commuter *Bardufoss*	
LN-RNC	Fokker 50	S.A.S. Commuter *Evenes*	
LN-RND	Fokker 50	S.A.S. Commuter *Lakselv*	
LN-RNE	Fokker 50	S.A.S. Commuter *Alta*	
LN-RNF	Fokker 50	S.A.S. Commuter *Kirkenes*	
LN-RNG	Fokker 50	S.A.S. Commuter *Bodö*	
LN-RNH	Fokker 50	S.A.S. Commuter *Trondheim*	
LN-SUA	Boeing 737-205	Braathens SAFE *Halvdan Svarte*	
LN-SUE	F.27 Friendship Mk 100	Busy Bee	
LN-SUF	F.27 Friendship Mk 100	Busy Bee	
LN-SUL	F.27 Friendship Mk 100	Busy Bee	
LN-WND	Douglas DC-3C	Dakota Norway	

Note: Braathens also operates the Boeing 737-205s N73FS, N73TH, N197QQ, N890FS, N891FS, N7031A and N7031F (ex-LN-SUB, -SUK, -SUI, -SUQ, -SUJ, -SUH and -SUM respectively) plus N197AL.

LV (Argentina)

LV-MLO	Boeing 747-287B	Aerolineas Argentinas	
LV-MLP	Boeing 747-287B	Aerolineas Argentinas	
LV-MLR	Boeing 747-287B	Aerolineas Argentinas	
LV-OEP	Boeing 747-287B	Aerolineas Argentinas	
LV-OHV	Boeing 747SP-27	Aerolineas Argentinas	
LV-OOZ	Boeing 747-287B	Aerolineas Argentinas	
LV-OPA	Boeing 747-287B	Aerolineas Argentinas	

Note: Aerolineas Argentinas also operates a Boeing 747-283B as EI-BWF.

LX (Luxembourg)

LX-ACV	Boeing 747-271C (SCD)	Cargolux *City of Esch/Alzette*	
LX-BCV	Boeing 747-271C (SCD)	Cargolux	
LX-DCV	Boeing 747-228F	Cargolux	
LX-ECV	Boeing 747-271C (SCD)	Cargolux *City of Luxembourg*	
LX-LGA	Fokker 50	Luxair	
LX-LGB	Fokker 50	Luxair	
LX-LGC	Fokker 50	Luxair *Prince Guillaume*	
LX-LGD	Fokker 50	Luxair *Prince Felix*	
LX-LGE	Fokker 50	Luxair	
LX-LGF	Boeing 737-4C9	Luxair	
LX-LGG	Boeing 737-4C9	Luxair	
LX-LGH	Boeing 737-2C9	Luxair *Prince Guillaume*	
LX-LGI	Boeing 737-2C9	Luxair *Princesse Marie-Astrid*	
LX-LGL	EMB-120RT Brasilia	Luxair	
LX-LG	EMB-120RT Brasilia	Luxair	
LX-LGN	Boeing 737-229	Luxair	
LX-LG	Boeing 737-4C9	Luxair	
LX-LG	Boeing 737-4C9	Luxair	
LX-LGX	Boeing 747SP-44	Luxair	
LX-ZCV	Boeing 747-2D3B	Cargolux	

Notes	Reg.	Type	Owner or Operator

LZ (Bulgaria)

LZ-BAC	Antonov AN-12	Balkan Bulgarian Airlines
LZ-BAE	Antonov AN-12	Balkan Bulgarian Airlines
LZ-BAF	Antonov AN-12	Balkan Bulgarian Airlines
LZ-BEA	Ilyushin IL-18D	Balkan Bulgarian Airlines
LZ-BEH	Ilyushin IL-18V	Balkan Bulgarian Airlines
LZ-BEI	Ilyushin IL-18V	Balkan Bulgarian Airlines
LZ-BEU	Ilyushin IL-18V	Balkan Bulgarian Airlines
LZ-BOA	Boeing 737-53A	Balkan Bulgarian Airlines
LZ-BOB	Boeing 737-53A	Balkan Bulgarian Airlines
LZ-BOC	Boeing 737-53A	Balkan Bulgarian Airlines
LZ-	Boeing 767-300ER	Balkan Bulgarian Airlines
LZ-	Boeing 767-300ER	Balkan Bulgarian Airlines
LZ-BTA	Tupolev Tu-154B	Balkan Bulgarian Airlines
LZ-BTC	Tupolev Tu-154B	Balkan Bulgarian Airlines
LZ-BTD	Tupolev Tu-154B	Balkan Bulgarian Airlines
LZ-BTE	Tupolev Tu-154B	Balkan Bulgarian Airlines
LZ-BTF	Tupolev Tu-154B	Balkan Bulgarian Airlines
LZ-BTG	Tupolev Tu-154B	Balkan Bulgarian Airlines
LZ-BTH	Tupolev Tu-154M	Balkan Bulgarian Airlines
LZ-BTI	Tupolev Tu-154M	Balkan Bulgarian Airlines
LZ-BTJ	Tupolev Tu-154B-1	Palair Macedonian
LZ-BTK	Tupolev Tu-154B	Balkan Bulgarian Airlines
LZ-BTL	Tupolev Tu-154B	Balkan Bulgarian Airlines
LZ-BTM	Tupolev Tu-154B	Balkan Bulgarian Airlines
LZ-BTN	Tupolev Tu-154M	Balkan Bulgarian Airlines
LZ-BTO	Tupolev Tu-154B-1	Balkan Bulgarian Airlines
LZ-BTP	Tupolev Tu-154B-1	Balkan Bulgarian Airlines
LZ-BTQ	Tupolev Tu-154M	Balkan Bulgarian Airlines
LZ-BTR	Tupolev Tu-154B-2	Balkan Bulgarian Airlines
LZ-BTS	Tupolev Tu-154B-2	Balkan Bulgarian Airlines
LZ-BTT	Tupolev Tu-154B-2	Balkan Bulgarian Airlines
LZ-BTU	Tupolev Tu-154B-2	Balkan Bulgarian Airlines
LZ-BTV	Tupolev Tu-154B-2	Balkan Bulgarian Airlines
LZ-BTW	Tupolev Tu-154M	Balkan Bulgarian Airlines
LZ-BTX	Tupolev Tu-154M	Balkan Bulgarian Airlines
LZ-BTY	Tupolev Tu-154M	Balkan Bulgarian Airlines
LZ-BTZ	Tupolev Tu-154M	Balkan Bulgarian Airlines
LZ-JXA	Airbus A.310-324	Jes Air
LZ-JXB	Airbus A.310-222	Jes Air
LZ-MIG	Tupolev Tu-154M	Varna International Airways (VIA)
LZ-MIK	Tupolev Tu-154M	Varna International Airways (VIA)
LZ-MIL	Tupolev Tu-154M	Varna International Airways (VIA)
LZ-MIR	Tupolev Tu-154M	Varna International Airways (VIA)
LZ-MIS	Tupolev Tu-154M	Varna International Airways (VIA)
LZ-TUG	Tupolev Tu-134A-3	Balkan Bulgarian Airlines
LZ-TUK	Tupolev Tu-134A	Balkan Bulgarian Airlines
LZ-TUM	Tupolev Tu-134A-3	Balkan Bulgarian Airlines
LZ-TUP	Tupolev Tu-134A	Balkan Bulgarian Airlines
LZ-TUS	Tupolev Tu-134A	Balkan Bulgarian Airlines
LZ-TUT	Tupulev Tu-134A-3	Balkan Bulgarian Airlines
LZ-TUU	Tupolev Tu-134A-3	Balkan Bulgarian Airlines
LZ-TUV	Tupolev Tu-134A-3	Balkan Bulgarian Airlines
LZ-TUZ	Tupolev Tu-134A-3	Balkan Bulgarian Airlines

N (USA)

N11AB	Boeing 737-4K5	Air Berlin
N14AZ	Boeing 707-336C	Seagreen Air Transport
N18AZ	Boeing 707-351C	Seagreen Air Transport
N20UA	Douglas DC-8-61	American International Airlines
N22UA	Douglas DC-8-61	United Aviation Services
N23UA	Douglas DC-8-61F	American International Airways
N25AB	Boeing 737-4YO	Air Berlin
N26UA	Douglas DC-8-61	United Aviation Services
N27UA	Douglas DC-8-61	United Aviation Services
N29UA	Douglas DC-8-61	United Aviation Services
N30UA	Douglas DC-8-61	United Aviation Services
N47UA	Douglas DC-8-61	United Aviation Services
N48UA	Douglas DC-8-61	United Aviation Services

Reg.	Type	Owner or Operator	Notes
N67AB	Boeing 737-3Y0	Air Berlin	
N73FS	Boeing 737-205	Braathens SAFE *Magnus den Gode*	
N73TH	Boeing 737-205	Braathens SAFE *Magnus Erlingsson*	
N105WA	Douglas DC-10-30CF	World Airways	
N106WA	Douglas DC-10-30CF	World Airways	
N107WA	Douglas DC-10-30CF	World Airways	
N108WA	Douglas DC-10-30CF	World Airways	
N112WA	Douglas DC-10-30CF	World Airways	
N116KB	Boeing 747-312	Singapore Airlines	
N117AA	Douglas DC-10-10ER	American Airlines	
N117KC	Boeing 747-312	Singapore Airlines	
N119KE	Boeing 747-312	Singapore Airlines	
N120KF	Boeing 747-312	Singapore Airlines	
N121KG	Boeing 747-312	Singapore Airlines	
N122KH	Boeing 747-312	Singapore Airlines	
N123KJ	Boeing 747-312	Singapore Airlines	
N124KK	Boeing 747-312	Singapore Airlines	
N125AA	Douglas DC-10-10ER	American Airlines	
N125KL	Boeing 747-312	Singapore Airlines	
N133JC	Douglas DC-10-40	Northwest Airlines	
N133TW	Boeing 747-156	Trans World Airlines	
N134TW	Boeing 747-156	Trans World Airlines	
N137AA	Douglas DC-10-30	American Airlines	
N138AA	Douglas DC-10-30	American Airlines	
N139AA	Douglas DC-10-30	American Airlines	
N140AA	Douglas DC-10-30	American Airlines	
N140UA	Boeing 747SP-21	United Airlines	
N141AA	Douglas DC-10-30	American Airlines	
N141UA	Boeing 747SP-21	United Airlines	
N141US	Douglas DC-10-40	Northwest Airlines	
N142AA	Douglas DC-10-30	American Airlines	
N142UA	Boeing 747SP-21	United Airlines	
N143AA	Douglas DC-10-30	American Airlines	
N143UA	Boeing 747SP-21	United Airlines	
N144AA	Douglas DC-10-30	American Airlines	
N144JC	Douglas DC-10-40	Northwest Airlines	
N144UA	Boeing 747SP-21	United Airlines	
N145UA	Boeing 747SP-21	United Airlines	
N145US	Douglas DC-10-40	Northwest Airlines	
N146UA	Boeing 747SP-21	United Airlines	
N146US	Douglas DC-10-40	Northwest Airlines	
N147UA	Boeing 747SP-21	United Airlines	
N147US	Douglas DC-10-40	Northwest Airlines	
N148UA	Boeing 747SP-21	United Airlines	
N148US	Douglas DC-10-40	Northwest Airlines	
N149UA	Boeing 747SP-21	United Airlines	
N149US	Douglas DC-10-40	Northwest Airlines	
N150UA	Boeing 747SP-21	United Airlines	
N150US	Douglas DC-10-40	Northwest Airlines	
N151UA	Boeing 747-222B	United Airlines	
N151US	Douglas DC-10-40	Northwest Airlines	
N152UA	Boeing 747-222B	United Airlines	
N152US	Douglas DC-10-40	Northwest Airlines	
N153UA	Boeing 747-123	United Airlines	
N153US	Douglas DC-10-40	Northwest Airlines	
N154UA	Boeing 747-123	United Airlines	
N154US	Douglas DC-10-40	Northwest Airlines	
N155UA	Boeing 747-123	United Airlines	
N155US	Douglas DC-10-40	Northwest Airlines	
N156UA	Boeing 747-123	United Airlines	
N156US	Douglas DC-10-40	Northwest Airlines	
N157UA	Boeing 747-123	United Airlines	
N157US	Douglas DC-10-40	Northwest Airlines	
N158UA	Boeing 747-238B	United Airlines	
N158US	Douglas DC-10-40	Northwest Airlines	
N159UA	Boeing 747-238B	United Airlines	
N159US	Douglas DC-10-40	Northwest Airlines	
N160UA	Boeing 747-238B	United Airlines	
N160US	Douglas DC-10-40	Northwest Airlines	
N161UA	Boeing 747-238B	United Airlines	
N161US	Douglas DC-10-40	Northwest Airlines	
N162US	Douglas DC-10-40	Northwest Airlines	
N163AA	Douglas DC-10-30	American Airlines	

OVERSEAS AIRLINERS

Notes	Reg.	Type	Owner or Operator
	N163UA	Boeing 747-238B	United Airlines
	N164AA	Douglas DC-10-30	American Airlines
	N164UA	Boeing 747-238B	United Airlines
	N165UA	Boeing 747-238B	United Airlines
	N166AA	Douglas DC-10-10ER	American Airlines
	N171DN	Boeing 767-332ER	Delta Air Lines
	N171UA	Boeing 747-422	United Airlines *Spirit of Seattle II*
	N172DN	Boeing 767-332ER	Delta Air Lines
	N172UA	Boeing 747-422	United Airlines
	N173DN	Boeing 767-332ER	Delta Air Lines
	N173UA	Boeing 747-422	United Airlines
	N174DN	Boeing 767-332ER	Delta Air Lines
	N174UA	Boeing 747-422	United Airlines
	N175DN	Boeing 767-332ER	Delta Air Lines
	N175UA	Boeing 747-422	United Airlines
	N176DN	Boeing 767-332ER	Delta Air Lines
	N176UA	Boeing 747-422	United Airlines
	N177DN	Boeing 767-332ER	Delta Air Lines
	N177UA	Boeing 747-422	United Airlines
	N178DN	Boeing 767-332ER	Delta Air Lines
	N178UA	Boeing 747-422	United Airlines
	N179DN	Boeing 767-332ER	Delta Air Lines
	N179UA	Boeing 747-422	United Airlines
	N180DN	Boeing 767-332ER	Delta Air Lines
	N180UA	Boeing 747-422	United Airlines
	N181DN	Boeing 767-332ER	Delta Air Lines
	N181UA	Boeing 747-422	United Airlines
	N182DN	Boeing 767-332ER	Delta Air Lines
	N182UA	Boeing 747-422	United Airlines
	N183UA	Boeing 747-422	United Airlines
	N184UA	Boeing 747-422	United Airlines
	N185AT	L-1011 TriStar 50	American Trans Air
	N185UA	Boeing 747-422	United Airlines
	N186AT	L.1011 TriStar 50	American Trans Air
	N187AT	L.1011 TriStar 50	American Trans Air
	N188AT	L.1011 TriStar 50	American Trans Air
	N189AT	L.1011 TriStar 50	American Trans Air
	N190AT	L.1011 TriStar 50	American Trans Air
	N191AT	L.1011 TriStar 50	American Trans Air
	N192AT	L.1011 TriStar 50	American Trans Air
	N193AT	L.1011 TriStar 50	American Trans Air
	N195AT	L.1011 TriStar 150	American Trans Air
	N197AL	Boeing 737-2E1	Braathens SAFE
	N197QQ	Boeing 737-205	Braathens SAFE *Haakon den Gode*
	N202AE	Boeing 747-2B4B (SCD)	Middle East Airlines
	N203AE	Boeing 747-2B4B (SCD)	Middle East Airlines
	N204AE	Boeing 747-2B4B	Middle East Airlines
	N211JL	Boeing 747-221F	Japan Air Lines
	N211NW	Douglas DC-10-30	Northwest Airlines
	N212JL	Boeing 747-346	Japan Air Lines
	N213JL	Boeing 747-346	Japan Air Lines
	N220NW	Douglas DC-10-30	Northwest Airlines
	N221GE	Boeing 747-357	Swissair *Genéve*
	N221GF	Boeing 747-357	Swissair *Zurich*
	N221NW	Douglas DC-10-30	Northwest Airlines
	N223NW	Douglas DC-10-30	Northwest Airlines
	N224NW	Douglas DC-10-30	Northwest Airlines
	N225NW	Douglas DC-10-30	Northwest Airlines
	N226NW	Douglas DC-10-30	Northwest Airlines
	N227NW	Douglas DC-10-30	Northwest Airlines
	N301FE	Douglas DC-10-30AF	Federal Express
	N301TW	Boeing 747-282B	Trans World Airlines
	N302FE	Douglas DC-10-30AF	Federal Express
	N302TW	Boeing 747-282B	Trans World Airlines
	N303FE	Douglas DC-10-30AF	Federal Express
	N303TW	Boeing 747-257B	Nationair
	N304FE	Douglas DC-10-30AF	Federal Express
	N304TW	Boeing 747-257B	—
	N305FE	Douglas DC-10-30AF	Federal Express *John David*
	N305TW	Boeing 747-284B	Trans World Airlines
	N306FE	Douglas DC-10-30AF	Federal Express *John Peter Jr*
	N307FE	Douglas DC-10-30AF	Federal Express *Erin Lee*
	N308FE	Douglas DC-10-30AF	Federal Express *Ann*

Reg.	Type	Owner or Operator	Notes
N309FE	Douglas DC-10-30AF	Federal Express *Stacey*	
N310FE	Douglas DC-10-30AF	Federal Express *John Shelby*	
N311FE	Douglas DC-10-30AF	Federal Express *Abe*	
N312AA	Boeing 767-223ER	American Airlines	
N312FE	Douglas DC-10-30AF	Federal Express *Angela*	
N313AA	Boeing 767-223ER	American Airlines	
N313FE	Douglas DC-10-30AF	Federal Express *Brandon Parks*	
N314FE	Douglas DC-10-30AF	Federal Express *Caitlin-Ann*	
N315AA	Boeing 767-223ER	American Airlines	
N315FE	Douglas DC-10-30AF	Federal Express *Kevin*	
N316AA	Boeing 767-223ER	American Airlines	
N316FE	Douglas DC-10-30AF	Federal Express *Brandon*	
N317AA	Boeing 767-223ER	American Airlines	
N319AA	Boeing 767-223ER	American Airlines	
N320AA	Boeing 767-223ER	American Airlines	
N321AA	Boeing 767-223ER	American Airlines	
N322AA	Boeing 767-223ER	American Airlines	
N323AA	Boeing 767-223ER	American Airlines	
N324AA	Boeing 767-223ER	American Airlines	
N325AA	Boeing 767-223ER	American Airlines	
N327AA	Boeing 767-223ER	American Airlines	
N328AA	Boeing 767-223ER	American Airlines	
N329AA	Boeing 767-223ER	American Airlines	
N330AA	Boeing 767-223ER	American Airlines	
N332AA	Boeing 767-223ER	American Airlines	
N334AA	Boeing 767-223ER	American Airlines	
N335AA	Boeing 767-223ER	American Airlines	
N336AA	Boeing 767-223ER	American Airlines	
N338AA	Boeing 767-223ER	American Airlines	
N339AA	Boeing 767-223ER	American Airlines	
N341HA	L.188C Electra	Channel Express Group PLC/Bournemouth	
N345HC	Douglas DC-10-30ER	Finnair	
N351AA	Boeing 767-323ER	American Airlines	
N352AA	Boeing 767-323ER	American Airlines	
N353AA	Boeing 767-323ER	American Airlines	
N354AA	Boeing 767-323ER	American Airlines	
N355AA	Boeing 767-323ER	American Airlines	
N356WS	Douglas DC-8-54F	TPI International Airways	
N357AA	Boeing 767-323ER	American Airlines	
N358AA	Boeing 767-323ER	American Airlines	
N359AA	Boeing 767-323ER	American Airlines	
N360AA	Boeing 767-323ER	American Airlines	
N361AA	Boeing 767-323ER	American Airlines	
N362AA	Boeing 767-323ER	American Airlines	
N363AA	Boeing 767-323ER	American Airlines	
N366AA	Boeing 767-323ER	American Airlines	
N368AA	Boeing 767-323ER	American Airlines	
N369AA	Boeing 767-323ER	American Airlines	
N370AA	Boeing 767-323ER	American Airlines	
N371AA	Boeing 767-323ER	American Airlines	
N372AA	Boeing 767-323ER	American Airlines	
N373AA	Boeing 767-323ER	American Airlines	
N374AA	Boeing 767-323ER	American Airlines	
N376AM	Boeing 767-323ER	American Airlines	
N377AN	Boeing 767-323ER	American Airlines	
N378AN	Boeing 767-323ER	American Airlines	
N379AA	Boeing 767-323ER	American Airlines	
N380AN	Boeing 767-323ER	American Airlines	
N381AA	Boeing 767-323ER	American Airlines	
N382AA	Boeing 767-323ER	American Airlines	
N383AA	Boeing 767-323ER	American Airlines	
N384AA	Boeing 767-323ER	American Airlines	
N385AA	Boeing 767-323ER	American Airlines	
N386AA	Boeing 767-323ER	American Airlines	
N417DG	Douglas DC-10-30	Aeromexico *Ciudad de Mexico*	
N470EV	Boeing 747-273C	Evergreen International Airlines	
N471EV	Boeing 747-273C	Evergreen International Airlines	
N472EV	Boeing 747-131	Evergreen International Airlines	
N473EV	Boeing 747-121F (SCD)	Evergreen International Airlines	
N474EV	Boeing 747-121	Evergreen International Airlines	
N475EV	Boeing 747-121F (SCD)	Evergreen International Airlines	
N477EV	Boeing 747SR-46 (SCD)	Evergreen International Airlines	
N478EV	Boeing 747SR-46 (SCD)	Evergreen International Airlines	

Notes	Reg.	Type	Owner or Operator
	N479EV	Boeing 747-132 (SCD)	Evergreen International Airlines
	N480EV	Boeing 747-121 (SCD)	Evergreen International Airlines
	N481EV	Boeing 747-132	Evergreen International Airlines
	N482EV	Boeing 747-212B (SCD)	Evergreen International Airlines
	N483EV	Boeing 747-121	Evergreen International Airlines
	N484EV	Boeing 747-121	Evergreen International Airlines
	N485EV	Boeing 747-212B (SCD)	Evergreen International Airlines
	N522SJ	L-100-20 Hercules	Southern Air Transport
	N601AA	Boeing 747SP-31	American Airlines
	N601FE	McD Douglas MD-11F	Federal Express
	N601FF	Boeing 747-127 (SCD)	Tower Air *Sam*
	N601TW	Boeing 767-231ER	Trans World Airlines
	N601UA	Boeing 767-222ER	United Airlines
	N601US	Boeing 747-151	Northwest Airlines
	N602AA	Boeing 747SP-31	American Airlines
	N602FE	McDouglas MD-11F	Federal Express
	N602FF	Boeing 747-124	Tower Air
	N602TW	Boeing 767-231ER	Trans World Airlines
	N602UA	Boeing 767-222ER	United Airlines
	N602US	Boeing 747-151	Northwest Airlines
	N603FE	McD Douglas MD-11F	Federal Express
	N603FF	Boeing 747-130	Tower Air *Suzie*
	N603TW	Boeing 767-231ER	Trans World Airlines
	N603UA	Boeing 767-222ER	United Airlines
	N603US	Boeing 747-151	Northwest Airlines
	N604FE	McD Douglas MD-11F	Federal Express
	N604FF	Boeing 747-121	Tower Air
	N604UA	Boeing 767-222ER	United Airlines
	N604US	Boeing 747-151	Northwest Airlines
	N605FE	McD Douglas MD-11F	Federal Express
	N605FF	Boeing 747-136	Tower Air
	N605PE	Boeing 747-243B (021)	Continental Airlines *(to become N33021)*
	N605UA	Boeing 767-222ER	United Airlines
	N605US	Boeing 747-151	Northwest Airlines
	N606FE	McD Douglas MD-11F	Federal Express
	N606FF	Boeing 747-136	Tower Air
	N606UA	Boeing 767-222ER	United Airlines
	N606US	Boeing 747-151	Northwest Airlines
	N607FE	McD Douglas MD-11F	Federal Express
	N607PE	Boeing 747-238B (022)	Continental Airlines *(to become N50022)*
	N607UA	Boeing 767-222ER	United Airlines
	N607US	Boeing 747-151	Northwest Airlines
	N608FE	McD Douglas MD-11F	Federal Express
	N608UA	Boeing 767-222ER	United Airlines
	N608US	Boeing 747-151	Northwest Airlines
	N609UA	Boeing 767-222ER	United Airlines
	N609US	Boeing 747-151	Northwest Airlines
	N610UA	Boeing 767-222ER	United Airlines
	N610US	Boeing 747-151	Northwest Airlines
	N611UA	Boeing 767-222ER	United Airlines
	N611US	Boeing 747-251B	Northwest Airlines
	N612US	Boeing 747-251B	Northwest Airlines
	N613US	Boeing 747-251B	Northwest Airlines
	N614US	Boeing 747-251B	Northwest Airlines
	N615US	Boeing 747-251B	Northwest Airlines
	N616US	Boeing 747-251F (SCD)	Northwest Airlines
	N617US	Boeing 747-251F (SCD)	Northwest Airlines
	N618US	Boeing 747-251F (SCD)	Northwest Airlines
	N619US	Boeing 747-251F (SCD)	Northwest Airlines
	N620FE	Boeing 747-133	Federal Express
	N620US	Boeing 747-135	Northwest Airlines
	N621FE	Boeing 747-133	Federal Express
	N621US	Boeing 747-135	Northwest Airlines
	N622US	Boeing 747-251B	Northwest Airlines
	N623US	Boeing 747-251B	Northwest Airlines
	N624US	Boeing 747-251B	Northwest Airlines
	N625FE	Boeing 747-132F (SCD)	Federal Express
	N625US	Boeing 747-251B	Northwest Airlines
	N626US	Boeing 747-251B	Northwest Airlines
	N627FE	Boeing 747-121F (SCD)	Federal Express
	N627US	Boeing 747-251B	Northwest Airlines
	N628US	Boeing 747-251B	Northwest Airlines
	N629US	Boeing 747-251F (SCD)	Northwest Airlines

Reg.	Type	Owner or Operator	Notes
N630FE	Boeing 747-124F	Federal Express	
N630US	Boeing 747-2J9F	Northwest Airlines	
N631FE	Boeing 747-249F (SCD)	Federal Express	
N631US	Boeing 747-251B	Northwest Airlines	
N632FE	Boeing 747-249F (SCD)	Federal Express	
N632US	Boeing 747-251B	Northwest Airlines	
N633FE	Boeing 747-249F	Federal Express	
N633US	Boeing 747-227B	Northwest Airlines	
N634FE	Boeing 747-245F (SCD)	Federal Express	
N634US	Boeing 747-227B	Northwest Airlines	
N635FE	Boeing 747-245F (SCD)	Federal Express	
N635US	Boeing 747-227B	Northwest Airlines	
N636FE	Boeing 747-245F (SCD)	Federal Express	
N636US	Boeing 747-251B	Northwest Airlines	
N637US	Boeing 747-251B	Northwest Airlines	
N638FE	Boeing 747-245F (SCD)	Federal Express	
N638US	Boeing 747-251B	Northwest Airlines	
N639FE	Boeing 747-2R7F (SCD)	Federal Express	
N639US	Boeing 747-251F (SCD)	Northwest Airlines	
N640FE	Boeing 747-245F (SCD)	Federal Express	
N640US	Boeing 747-251F (SCD)	Northwest Airlines	
N641FE	Boeing 747-245F (SCD)	Federal Express	
N641UA	Boeing 767-322ER	United Airlines	
N642UA	Boeing 767-322ER	United Airlines	
N643UA	Boeing 767-322ER	United Airlines	
N644UA	Boeing 767-322ER	United Airlines	
N645UA	Boeing 767-322ER	United Airlines	
N645US	Boeing 767-201ER	USAir *Pride of Piedmont*	
N646UA	Boeing 767-322ER	United Airlines	
N646US	Boeing 767-201ER	USAir *City of London*	
N647US	Boeing 767-201ER	USAir *City of Charlotte*	
N648US	Boeing 767-201ER	USAir *City of Tampa*	
N649US	Boeing 767-201ER	USAir *City of Los Angeles*	
N650TW	Boeing 767-205ER	Trans World Airlines	
N650US	Boeing 767-201ER	USAir *Pride of Baltimore*	
N651US	Boeing 767-2B7ER	USAir	
N652US	Boeing 767-2B7ER	USAir	
N653US	Boeing 767-2B7ER	USAir	
N654US	Boeing 767-2B7ER	USAir	
N655US	Boeing 767-2B7ER	USAir *Edwin L. Colodny*	
N661AV	Douglas DC-8-63AF	Arrow Air	
N661US	Boeing 747-451	Northwest Airlines	
N662US	Boeing 747-451	Northwest Airlines	
N663US	Boeing 747-451	Northwest Airlines	
N664US	Boeing 747-451	Northwest Airlines	
N665US	Boeing 747-451	Northwest Airlines	
N666US	Boeing 747-451	Northwest Airlines	
N667US	Boeing 747-451	Northwest Airlines	
N668US	Boeing 747-451	Northwest Airlines	
N669US	Boeing 747-451	Northwest Airlines	
N670US	Boeing 747-451	Northwest Airlines	
N671UP	Boeing 747-123F (SCD)	United Parcel Service	
N672UP	Boeing 747-123F (SCD)	United Parcel Service	
N673UP	Boeing 747-123F (SCD)	United Parcel Service	
N674UP	Boeing 747-123F (SCD)	United Parcel Service	
N675UP	Boeing 747-123F (SCD)	United Parcel Service	
N676UP	Boeing 747-123F (SCD)	United Parcel Service	
N677UP	Boeing 747-123F (SCD)	United Parcel Service	
N681UP	Boeing 747-123F (SCD)	United Parcel Service	
N682UP	Boeing 747-121F (SCD)	United Parcel Service	
N724DA	L.1011-385 TriStar 200	Delta Air Lines	
N736DY	L.1011-385 TriStar 250	Delta Air Lines	
N737D	L.1011-385 TriStar 250	Delta Air Lines	
N740DA	L.1011-385 TriStar 250	Delta Air Lines	
N741DA	L.1011-385 TriStar 250	Delta Air Lines	
N741PR	Boeing 747-2F6B	Philippine Airlines	
N742PR	Boeing 747-2F6B	Philippine Airlines	
N743PR	Boeing 747-2F6B	Philippine Airlines	
N744PR	Boeing 747-2F6B	Philippine Airlines	
N750AT	Boeing 757-212ER	American Trans Air	
N751AT	Boeing 757-212ER	American Trans Air	
N751DA	L-1011-385 TriStar 500	Delta Air Lines	
N752AT	Boeing 757-212ER	American Trans Air	

Notes	Reg.	Type	Owner or Operator
	N752DA	L-1011-385 TriStar 500	Delta Air Lines
	N753DA	L-1011-385 TriStar 500	Delta Air Lines
	N754DL	L.1011-385 TriStar 500	Delta Air Lines
	N755DL	L.1011-385 TriStar 500	Delta Air Lines
	N756DR	L.1011-385 TriStar 500	Delta Air Lines
	N757AT	Boeing 757-212ER	American Trans Air
	N	Boeing 757-2Q8ER	American Trans Air
	N	Boeing 757-2Q8ER	American Trans Air
	N759DA	L.1011-385 TriStar 500	Delta Air Lines
	N760DH	L.1011-385 TriStar 500	Delta Air Lines
	N761DA	L.1011-385 TriStar 500	Delta Air Lines
	N762BE	L.1011-385 TriStar 50	Hawaiian Air *Waikiki*
	N762DA	L.1011-385 TriStar 500	Delta Air Lines
	N763DL	L.1011-385 TriStar 500	Delta Air Lines
	N764BE	L.1011-385 TriStar 50	Hawaiian Air *Wahwaii*
	N764DA	L.1011-385 TriStar 500	Delta Air Lines
	N765BE	L.1011-385 TriStar 50	Hawaiian Air *Kauai*
	N765DA	L.1011-385 TriStar 500	Delta Air Lines
	N766BE	L.1011-385 TriStar 50	Hawaiian Air *Oahu*
	N	L.1011-385 TriStar 500	Delta Air Lines
	N	L.1011-385 TriStar 500	Delta Air Lines
	N	L.1011-385 TriStar 500	Delta Air Lines
	N	L.1011-385 TriStar 500	Delta Air Lines
	N772CA	Douglas DC-8-62	Rich International Airways
	N791AL	Douglas DC-8-62AF	Arrow Air
	N791FT	Douglas DC-8-73AF	Emery Worldwide
	N792FT	Douglas DC-8-73AF	Emery Worldwide
	N793AL	Douglas DC-8-63AF	Arrow Air
	N794AL	Douglas DC-8-63AF	Burlington Express
	N795FT	Douglas DC-8-73AF	Emery Worldwide
	N796AL	Douglas DC-8-63AF	Emery Worldwide
	N796FT	Douglas DC-8-73AF	Emery Worldwide
	N797AL	Douglas DC-8-63AF	Emery Worldwide
	N798AL	Douglas DC-8-62CF	Arrow Air
	N801CK	Douglas DC-8-55F	American International Airways
	N801DE	McD Douglas MD-11	Delta Air Lines
	N801DL	Airbus A.310-222	Delta Air Lines
	N801UP	Douglas DC-8-73AF	United Parcel Service
	N802BN	Douglas DC-8-62AF	Arrow Air
	N802DE	McD Douglas MD-11	Delta Air Lines
	N802DL	Airbus A.310-222	Delta Air Lines
	N802UP	Douglas DC-8-73AF	United Parcel Service
	N803CK	Douglas DC-8-54F	American International Airways
	N803DE	McD Douglas MD-11	Delta Air Lines
	N803DL	Airbus A.310-222	Delta Air Lines
	N803UP	Douglas DC-8-63AF	United Parcel Service
	N804CK	Douglas DC-8-73AF	American International Airways
	N804DE	McD Douglas MD-11	Delta Air Lines
	N804DL	Airbus A.310-222	Delta Air Lines
	N804UP	Douglas DC-8-73AF	United Parcel Service
	N805CK	Douglas DC-8-51F	American International Airways
	N805DE	McD Douglas MD-11	Delta Air Lines
	N805DL	Airbus A.310-222	Delta Air Lines
	N805UP	Douglas DC-8-73CF	United Parcel Service
	N806DE	McD Douglas MD-11	Delta Air Lines
	N806DL	Airbus A.310-222	Delta Air Lines
	N806UP	Douglas DC-8-73AF	United Parcel Service
	N807CK	Douglas DC-8-55F	American International Airways
	N807DE	McD Douglas MD-11	Delta Air Lines
	N807DL	Airbus A.310-222	Delta Air Lines
	N807UP	Douglas DC-8-73AF	United Parcel Service
	N808CK	Douglas DC-8-55F	American International Airways
	N808DE	McD Douglas MD-11	Delta Air Lines
	N808UP	Douglas DC-8-73AF	United Parcel Service
	N809CK	Douglas DC-8-73AF	American International Airways
	N809DE	McD Douglas MD-11	Delta Air Lines
	N809UP	Douglas DC-8-73AF	United Parcel Service
	N810CK	Douglas DC-8-52F	American International Airways
	N810UP	Douglas DC-8-71AF	United Parcel Service
	N811CK	Douglas DC-8-63AF	American International Airways
	N811DL	Airbus A.310-324	Delta Air Lines
	N811UP	Douglas DC-8-73AF	United Parcel Service
	N812DL	Airbus A.310-324	Delta Air Lines

Reg.	Type	Owner or Operator	Notes
N812UP	Douglas DC-8-73AF	United Parcel Service	
N813DL	Airbus A.310-324	Delta Air Lines	
N813UP	Douglas DC-8-73AF	United Parcel Service	
N814DL	Airbus A.310-324	Delta Air Lines	
N814UP	Douglas DC-8-73AF	United Parcel Service	
N815EV	Douglas DC-8-73CF	Evergreen International Airlines	
N815DL	Airbus A.310-324	Delta Air Lines	
N816EV	Douglas DC-8-73CF	Evergreen International Airlines	
N816DL	Airbus A.310-324	Delta Air Lines	
N817E	Douglas DC-8-51F	American International Airways	
N817EV	Douglas DC-8-62AF	Evergreen International Airlines	
N817DL	Airbus A.310-324	Delta Air Lines	
N818DL	Airbus A.310-324	Delta Air Lines	
N818UP	Douglas DC-8-73AF	United Parcel Service	
N819DL	Airbus A.310-324	Delta Air Lines	
N819UP	Douglas DC-8-73AF	United Parcel Service	
N820DL	Airbus A.310-324	Delta Air Lines	
N821DL	Airbus A.310-324	Delta Air Lines	
N822DL	Airbus A.310-324	Delta Air Lines	
N823DL	Airbus A.310-324	Delta Air Lines	
N824DL	Airbus A.310-324	Delta Air Lines	
N836UP	Douglas DC-8-73AF	United Parcel Service	
N840UP	Douglas DC-8-73AF	United Parcel Service	
N851UP	Douglas DC-8-73AF	United Parcel Service	
N852UP	Douglas DC-8-73AF	United Parcel Service	
N865F	Douglas DC-8-63AF	Emery Worldwide	
N866UP	Douglas DC-8-73AF	United Parcel Service	
N867BX	Douglas DC-8-63AF	Burlington Express	
N867UP	Douglas DC-8-73AF	United Parcel Service	
N868BX	Douglas DC-8-63AF	Burlington Express	
N868UP	Douglas DC-8-73AF	United Parcel Service	
N869BX	Doulgas DC-8-63AF	Burlington Express	
N870BX	Doulgas DC-8-63AF	Burlington Express	
N870SJ	Douglas DC-8-71AF	Southern Air Transport	
N870TV	Douglas DC-8-73AF	Emery Worldwide	
N871SJ	Douglas DC-8-71AF	Southern Air Transport	
N872SJ	Douglas DC-8-71AF	Southern Air Transport	
N873SJ	Douglas DC-8-71AF	Southern Air Transport	
N874SJ	Douglas DC-8-71AF	Southern Air Transport	
N874UP	Douglas DC-8-73AF	United Parcel Service	
N875SJ	Douglas DC-8-71AF	Southern Air Transport	
N880UP	Douglas DC-8-73AF	United Parcel Service	
N889TW	Boeing 727-31	Trans World Airlines	
N890FS	Boeing 737-205	Braathens SAFE *Hakon Sverresson*	
N891FS	Boeing 737-205	Braathens SAFE *Magnus Barfot*	
N894UP	Douglas DC-8-73AF	United Parcel Service	
N901SJ	L.100-30 Hercules	Southern Air Transport	
N902SJ	L.100-30 Hercules	Southern Air Transport	
N903SJ	L.100-30 Hercules	Southern Air Transport	
N904SJ	L.100-30 Hercules	Southern Air Transport	
N906R	Douglas DC-8-63AF	Emery Worldwide	
N907SJ	L.100-30 Hercules	Southern Air Transport	
N908SJ	L.100-30 Hercules	Southern Air Transport	
N909SJ	L.100-30 Hercules	Southern Air Transport	
N910SJ	L.100-30 Hercules	Southern Air Transport	
N912SJ	L.100-30 Hercules	Southern Air Transport	
N916SJ	L.100-30 Hercules	Southern Air Transport	
N918SJ	L.100-30 Hercules	Southern Air Transport	
N919SJ	L.100-30 Hercules	Southern Air Transport	
N920SJ	L.100-30 Hercules	Southern Air Transport	
N921R	Douglas DC-8-63AF	Emery Worldwide	
N921SJ	L.100-30 Hercules	Southern Air Transport	
N923SJ	L.100-30 Hercules	Southern Air Transport	
N929R	Douglas DC-8-63AF	Emery Worldwide	
N950R	Douglas DC-8-63AF	Emery Worldwide	
N951R	Douglas DC-8-63AF	Emery Worldwide	
N952R	Douglas DC-8-63AF	Emery Worldwide	
N957R	Douglas DC-8-63AF	Emery Worldwide	
N959R	Douglas DC-8-63AF	Emery Worldwide	
N961R	Douglas DC-8-73AF	Emery Worldwide	
N964R	Douglas DC-8-63AF	Emery Worldwide	
N990CF	Douglas DC-8-62AF	Emery Worldwide	
N993CF	Douglas DC-8-62AF	Emery Worldwide	

Notes	Reg.	Type	Owner or Operator
	N994CF	Douglas DC-8-62AF	Emery Worldwide
	N995CF	Douglas DC-8-62AF	Emery Worldwide
	N996CF	Douglas DC-8-62AF	Emery Worldwide
	N997CF	Douglas DC-8-62AF	Emery Worldwide
	N998CF	Douglas DC-8-62AF	Emery Worldwide
	N1309E	Boeing 747-306	K.L.M. *Admiral Richard E. Byrd*
	N1738D	L.1011-385 TriStar 250	Delta Air Lines
	N1739D	L.1011-385 TriStar 250	Delta Air Lines
	N1750B	McD Douglas MD-11	American Airlines
	N1751A	McD Douglas MD-11	American Airlines
	N1752K	McD Douglas MD-11	American Airlines
	N1753	McD Douglas MD-11	American Airlines
	N1754	McD Douglas MD-11	American Airlines
	N1755	McD Douglas MD-11	American Airlines
	N1756	McD Douglas MD-11	American Airlines
	N1757A	McD Douglas MD-11	American Airlines
	N1758B	McD Douglas MD-11	American Airlines
	N1759	McD Douglas MD-11	American Airlines
	N1760A	McD Douglas MD-11	American Airlines
	N1761R	McD Douglas MD-11	American Airlines
	N1762B	McD Douglas MD-11	American Airlines
	N1763	McD Douglas MD-11	American Airlines
	N1764B	McD Douglas MD-11	American Airlines
	N1804	Douglas DC-8-62F	Arrow Air
	N1805	Douglas DC-8-62	Rich International Airways
	N2674U	Douglas DC-8-73AF	Emery Worldwide
	N3016Z	Douglas DC-10-30	Zambia Airways *Nkwazi*
	N3024W	Douglas DC-10-30	Nigeria Airways
	N3140D	L.1011-385 TriStar 500 (598)	B.W.I.A.
	N4508H	Boeing 747SP-09	China Airlines
	N4522V	Boeing 747SP-09	China Airlines
	N4703U	Boeing 747-122 (SCD)	Pan Am *Clipper Nautilus*
	N4704U	Boeing 747-122	Pan Am *Clipper Belle of the Sea*
	N4710U	Boeing 747-122	Pan Am *Clipper Sea Lark*
	N4711U	Boeing 747-122 (SCD)	Pan Am *Clipper Witch of the Waves*
	N4712U	Boeing 747-122 (SCD)	Pan Am *Clipper Tradewind*
	N4714U	Boeing 747-122	United Airlines
	N4716U	Boeing 747-122	United Airlines
	N4717U	Boeing 747-122	United Airlines
	N4718U	Boeing 747-122	United Airlines
	N4719U	Boeing 747-122	United Airlines
	N4720U	Boeing 747-122	United Airlines
	N4723U	Boeing 747-122	United Airlines
	N4724U	Boeing 747-122	United Airlines
	N4727U	Boeing 747-122	United Airlines
	N4728U	Boeing 747-122	United Airlines
	N4729U	Boeing 747-122	United Airlines
	N4732U	Boeing 747-122	United Airlines
	N4735U	Boeing 747-122	United Airlines
	N5535	L.188 Electra	Channel Express Group PLC/Bournemouth
	N5539	L.188 Electra	Channel Express Group PLC/Bournemouth
	N7031A	Boeing 737-205	Braathens SAFE *Sigurd Jorsalfar*
	N7031F	Boeing 737-205	Braathens SAFE *Magnus Lagaboter*
	N7035T	L.1011-385 TriStar 100	Trans World Airlines
	N7036T	L.1011-385 TriStar 100	Trans World Airlines
	N7043U	Douglas DC-8-63AF	Arrow Air
	N7375A	Boeing 767-323ER	American Airlines
	N7622U	Boeing 727-222	United Airlines
	N7638U	Boeing 727-222	United Airlines
	N7642U	Boeing 727-222	United Airlines
	N7643U	Boeing 727-222	United Airlines
	N7644U	Boeing 727-222	United Airlines
	N7645U	Boeing 727-222	United Airlines
	N7646U	Boeing 727-222	United Airlines
	N7647U	Boeing 727-222	United Airlines
	N8034T	L.1011-385 TriStar 100	Trans World Airlines
	N8228P	Douglas DC-10-30	Aeromexico *Castillo de Chapultepec*
	N8968U	Douglas DC-8-62AF	Arrow Air
	N8974U	Douglas DC-8-62	Rich International Airways
	N9670	Boeing 747-123 (SCD)	Pan Am *Clipper Empress of the Skies*
	N9674	Boeing 747-123	Pan Am *Clipper Beacon Light*
	N10024	Boeing 747-238B	Continental Airlines
	N12060	Boeing 747-243B	Continental Airlines

Reg.	Type	Owner or Operator	Notes
N12061	Douglas DC-10-30	Continental Airlines *Richard M. Adams*	
N12064	Douglas DC-10-30	Continental Airlines	
N13066	Douglas DC-10-30	Continental Airlines	
N14062	Douglas DC-10-30	Continental Airlines	
N14063	Douglas DC-10-30	Continental Airlines	
N16020	Boeing 747-243B	Continental Airlines	
N17010	Boeing 747-143	Continental Airlines	
N17011	Boeing 747-143	Continental Airlines	
N17025	Boeing 747-238B	Continental Airlines	
N19072	Douglas DC-10-30	Continental Airlines	
N31018	L.1011-385 TriStar 50	Trans World Airlines	
N31019	L.1011-385 TriStar 50	Trans World Airlines	
N31021	L.1011-385 TriStar 50	Trans World Airlines	
N31022	L.1011-385 TriStar 50	American Trans Air	
N31023	L.1011-385 TriStar 50	Trans World Airlines	
N31024	L.1011-385 TriStar 50	Trans World Airlines	
N31029	L.1011-385 TriStar 100	Trans World Airlines	
N31030	L.1011-385 TriStar 100	Trans World Airlines	
N31031	L.1011-385 TriStar 100	Trans World Airlines	
N31032	L.1011-385 TriStar 100	Trans World Airlines	
N31033	L.1011-385 TriStar 100	Trans World Airlines	
N33021	Boeing 747-243B	Continental Airlines	
N39356	Boeing 767-323ER	American Airlines	
N39364	Boeing 767-323ER	American Airlines	
N39365	Boeing 767-323ER	American Airlines	
N39367	Boeing 767-323ER	American Airlines	
N41020	L.1011-385 TriStar 50	Trans World Airlines	
N41068	Douglas DC-10-30	Continental Airlines	
N50022	Boeing 747-238B	Continental Airlines	
N53110	Boeing 747-131	Trans World Airlines	
N53116	Boeing 747-131	Trans World Airlines	
N54649	Douglas DC-10-30	U.T.A.	
N68060	Douglas DC-10-30	Continental Airlines *Robert F. Six*	
N68065	Douglas DC-10-30	Continental Airlines *Robert P. Gallaway*	
N78019	Boeing 747-230B	Continental Airlines	
N78020	Boeing 747-243B	Continental Airlines	
N81025	L.1011-385 TriStar 100	Trans World Airlines	
N81026	L.1011-385 TriStar 100	Trans World Airlines	
N81027	L.1011-385 TriStar 50	Trans World Airlines	
N81028	L.1011-385 TriStar 100	Trans World Airlines	
N93104	Boeing 747-131	Trans World Airlines	
N93105	Boeing 747-131	Trans World Airlines	
N93106	Boeing 747-131	Trans World Airlines	
N93107	Boeing 747-131	Trans World Airlines	
N93108	Boeing 747-131	Trans World Airlines	
N93109	Boeing 747-131	Trans World Airlines	
N93117	Boeing 747-131	Trans World Airlines	
N93119	Boeing 747-131	Trans World Airlines	

OD (Lebanon)

OD-AFD	Boeing 707-3B4C	Middle East Airlines	
OD-AFE	Boeing 707-3B4C	Middle East Airlines	
OD-AFM	Boeing 720-023B	Middle East Airlines	
OD-AFY	Boeing 720-023B	Trans Mediterranean Airways	
OD-AGB	Boeing 720-023B	Middle East Airlines	
OD-AGD	Boeing 707-323C	Trans Mediterranean Airways	
OD-AGF	Boeing 720-047B	Middle East Airlines	
OD-AGO	Boeing 707-321C	Trans Mediterranean Airways	
OD-AGP	Boeing 707-321C	Trans Mediterranean Airways	
OD-AGS	Boeing 707-331C	Trans Mediterranean Airways	
OD-AGU	Boeing 707-347C	Middle East Airlines	
OD-AGV	Boeing 707-347C	Middle East Airlines	
OD-AGX	Boeing 707-327C	Trans Mediterranean Airways	
OD-AGY	Boeing 707-327C	Trans Mediterranean Airways	
OD-AHC	Boeing 707-323C	Middle East Airlines	
OD-AHD	Boeing 707-323C	Middle East Airlines	
OD-AHE	Boeing 707-323C	Middle East Airlines	
OD-AHF	Boeing 707-323B	Middle East Airlines	

Note: MEA also uses the 747s N202AE, N203AE and N204AE when not on lease.

Notes	Reg.	Type	Owner or Operator

OE (Austria)

Reg.	Type	Owner or Operator
OE-ILF	Boeing 737-3Z9	Lauda Air *Bob Marley*
OE-ILG	Boeing 737-3Z9	Lauda Air *John Lennon*
OE-LAA	Airbus A.310-324	Austrian Airlines *New York*
OE-LAB	Airbus A.310-324	Austrian Airlines *Tokyo*
OE-LAC	Airbus A.310-324	Austrian Airlines *Paris*
OE-LAD	Airbus A.310-324	Austrian Airlines
OE-LAU	Boeing 767-3Z9ER	Lauda Air *Johann Strauss*
OE-	Boeing 767-3Z9ER	Lauda Air
OE-LDP	McD Douglas MD-81	Austrian Airlines *Niederösterreich*
OE-LDR	McD Douglas MD-81	Austrian Airlines *Wien*
OE-LDS	McD Douglas MD-81	Austrian Airlines *Burgenland*
OE-LDT	McD Douglas MD-81	Austrian Airlines *Kärnten*
OE-LDU	McD Douglas MD-81	Austrian Airlines *Steiermark*
OE-LDV	McD Douglas MD-81	Austrian Airlines *Oberösterreich*
OE-LDW	McD Douglas MD-81	Austrian Airlines *Salzburg*
OE-LDX	McD Douglas MD-82	Austrian Airlines *Tirol*
OE-LDY	McD Douglas MD-82	Austrian Airlines *Vorarlberg*
OE-LDZ	McD Douglas MD-82	Austrian Airlines *Graz*
OE-LLH	D.H.C.8-103 Dash Eight	Tyrolean Airways
OE-LLI	D.H.C.8-103 Dash Eight	Tyrolean Airways
OE-LLK	D.H.C.8-103 Dash Eight	Tyrolean Airways *Stadt Salzburg*
OE-LLL	D.H.C.8-103 Dash Eight	Tyrolean Airways *Stadt Graz*
OE-LLM	D.H.C.8-103 Dash Eight	Tyrolean Airways *Stadt Klagenfurt*
OE-LLN	D.H.C.8-103 Dash Eight	Tyrolean Airways *Stadt Linz*
OE-LLP	D.H.C.8-103 Dash Eight	Tyrolean Airways
OE-LLS	D.H.C.7-102 Dash Seven	Tyrolean Airways *Stadt Innsbruck*
OE-LLU	D.H.C.7-102 Dash Seven	Tyrolean Airways *Stadt Wien*
OE-LLV	D.H.C.8-311 Dash Eight	Tyrolean Airways *Land Tirol*
OE-LMA	McD Douglas MD-82	Austrian Airlines *Linz*
OE-LMB	McD Douglas MD-82	Austrian Airlines *Eisenstadt*
OE-LMC	McD Douglas MD-82	Austrian Airlines *Baden*
OE-LMD	McD Douglas MD-83	Austrian Airlines *Villach*
OE-LMK	McD Douglas MD-87	Austrian Airlines *St Pölten*
OE-LML	McD Douglas MD-87	Austrian Airlines *Salzburg*
OE-LMM	McD Douglas MD-87	Austrian Airlines *Innsbruck*
OE-LMN	McD Douglas MD-87	Austrian Airlines *Klagenfurt*
OE-LMO	McD Douglas MD-87	Austrian Airlines *Bregenz*
OE-LNH	Boeing 737-4Z9	Lauda Air
OE-	Boeing 737-4Z9	Lauda Air

OH (Finland)

Reg.	Type	Owner or Operator
OH-LAA	Airbus A.300B4-203	Kar-Air
OH-LAB	Airbus A.300B4-203	Kar-Air
OH-LGA	McD Douglas MD-11	Finnair
OH-LGB	McD Douglas MD-11	Finnair
OH-LGC	McD Douglas MD-11	Finnair
OH-LGD	McD Douglas MD-11	Finnair
OH-LHA	Douglas DC-10-30ER	Finnair *Iso Antti*
OH-LHB	Douglas DC-10-30ER	Finnair
OH-LHD	Douglas DC-10-30ER	Finnair
OH-LHE	Douglas DC-10-30ER	Finnair
OH-LMA	McD Douglas MD-87	Finnair
OH-LMB	McD Douglas MD-87	Finnair
OH-LMC	McD Douglas MD-87	Finnair
OH-LMG	McD Douglas MD-83	Finnair
OH-LMH	McD Douglas MD-82	Finnair
OH-LMN	McD Douglas MD-82	Finnair
OH-LMO	McD Douglas MD-82	Finnair
OH-LMP	McD Douglas MD-82	Finnair
OH-LMR	McD Douglas MD-83	Finnair
OH-LMS	McD Douglas MD-83	Finnair
OH-LMT	McD Douglas MD-83	Finnair
OH-LMU	McD Douglas MD-83	Finnair
OH-LMV	McD Douglas MD-83	Finnair
OH-LMW	McD Douglas MD-82	Finnair
OH-LMX	McD Douglas MD-82	Finnair
OH-LMY	McD Douglas MD-82	Finnair
OH-LMZ	McD Douglas MD-82	Finnair

Reg.	Type	Owner or Operator	Notes
OH-LNB	Douglas DC-9-41	Finnair	
OH-LNC	Douglas DC-9-41	Finnair	
OH-LND	Douglas DC-9-41	Finnair	
OH-LNE	Douglas DC-9-41	Finnair	
OH-LNF	Douglas DC-9-41	Finnair	
OH-LYN	Douglas DC-9-51	Finnair	
OH-LYO	Douglas DC-9-51	Finnair	
OH-LYP	Douglas DC-9-51	Finnair	
OH-LYR	Douglas DC-9-51	Finnair	
OH-LYS	Douglas DC-9-51	Finnair	
OH-LYT	Douglas DC-9-51	Finnair	
OH-LYU	Douglas DC-9-51	Finnair	
OH-LYV	Douglas DC-9-51	Finnair	
OH-LYW	Douglas DC-9-51	Finnair	
OH-LYX	Douglas DC-9-51	Finnair	
OH-LYY	Douglas DC-9-51	Finnair	
OH-LYZ	Douglas DC-9-51	Finnair	

Note: Finnair also operates a DC-10-30ER which retains its US registration N345HC.

OK (Czechoslovakia)

OK-CFH	Tupolev Tu-134A	Ceskoslovenske Aerolinie (CSA)	
OK-DFI	Tupolev Tu-134A	CSA	
OK-EFJ	Tupolev Tu-134A	CSA	
OK-EFK	Tupolev Tu-134A	CSA	
OK-FBF	Ilyushin IL-62	CSA	
OK-GBH	Ilyushin IL-62	CSA *Usti Nad Labem*	
OK-HFL	Tupolev Tu-134A	CSA	
OK-HFM	Tupolev Tu-134A	CSA	
OK-IFN	Tupolev Tu-134A	CSA	
OK-JBI	Ilyushin IL-62M	CSA *Plzen*	
OK-JBJ	Ilyushin IL-62M	CSA *Hradec Kralové*	
OK-KBK	Ilyushin IL-62M	CSA *Ceske Budejovice*	
OK-KBN	Ilyushin IL-62M	CSA	
OK-OBL	Ilyushin IL-62M	CSA *Ostrava*	
OK-PBM	Ilyushin IL-62M	CSA	
OK-SCA	Tupolev Tu-154M	CSA *Mesto Piestany*	
OK-TCB	Tupolev Tu-154M	CSA *Karlovy Vary*	
OK-TCC	Tupolev Tu-154M	CSA *Teplice*	
OK-TCD	Tupolev Tu-154M	CSA *Trencianské Teplic*	
OK-UCE	Tupolev Tu-154M	CSA *Marianské Laze*	
OK-UCF	Tupolev Tu-154M	CSA *Smokovec*	
OK-VCG	Tupolev Tu-154M	CSA *Luhacovice*	
OK-WAA	Airbus A.310-304	CSA *Praha*	
OK-WAB	Airbus A.310-304	CSA *Bratislava*	

OO (Belgium)

OO-CDE	Boeing 707-365C	AMI Cargo	
OO-DHB	Convair Cv.580	European Air Transport (DHL)	
OO-DHC	Convair Cv.580	European Air Transport (DHL)	
OO-DHD	Convair Cv.580	European Air Transport (DHL)	
OO-DHE	Convair Cv.580	European Air Transport (DHL)	
OO-DHF	Convair Cv.580	European Air Transport (DHL)	
OO-DHG	Convair Cv.580	European Air Transport (DHL)	
OO-DHH	Convair Cv.580	European Air Transport (DHL)	
OO-DHI	Convair Cv.580	European Air Transport (DHL)	
OO-DHJ	Convair Cv.580	European Air Transport (DHL)	
OO-DHL	Convair Cv.580	European Air Transport (DHL)	
OO-DHM	Boeing 727-31C	European Air Transport (DHL)	
OO-DHN	Boeing 727-31C	European Air Transport (DHL)	
OO-DHO	Boeing 727-31C	European Air Transport (DHL)	
OO-DJA	F.28 Fellowship 3000	Delta Air Transport	
OO-DJB	F.28 Fellowship 4000	Delta Air Transport	
OO-DJE	BAe 146-200	Delta Air Transport	
OO-DJF	BAe 146-200	Delta Air Transport	
OO-DJG	BAe 146-200	Delta Air Transport	
OO-DJH	BAe 146-200	Delta Air Transport	
OO-DJI	BAe 146-200	Delta Air Transport	
OO-DJJ	BAe 146-200	Delta Air Transport	
OO-DTF	EMB-120RT Brasilia	Delta Air Transport	

Notes	Reg.	Type	Owner or Operator
	OO-DTG	EMB-120RT Brasilia	Delta Air Transport
	OO-DTH	EMB-120RT Brasilia	Delta Air Transport
	OO-DTI	EMB-120RT Brasilia	Delta Air Transport
	OO-DTJ	EMB-120RT Brasilia	Delta Air Transport
	OO-DTK	EMB-120RT Brasilia	Delta Air Transport
	OO-DTL	EMB-120RT Brasilia	Delta Air Transport
	OO-DTN	EMB-120RT Brasilia	Delta Air Transport
	OO-D	EMB-120RT Brasilia	Delta Air Transport
	OO-D	EMB-120RT Brasilia	Delta Air Transport
	OO-EEE	Beech 99A	European Expedite
	OO-FEF	F.27 Friendship Mk 600	Flanders Airlines/Federal Express
	OO-FEG	F.27 Friendship Mk 600	Eurojet International/Federal Express
	OO-FFF	Swearingen SA227AC Metro III	—
	OO-GGG	Swearingen SA227AC Metro III	—
	OO-HUB	Convair Cv.580	European Air Transport (DHL)
	OO-ILH	Boeing 737-4Q8	Air Belgium
	OO-ILI	Boeing 757-23A	Air Belgium
	OO-ILJ	Boeing 737-46B	Air Belgium
	OO-JPA	Swearingen SA226AT Merlin IVA	European Air Transport
	OO-JPI	Swearingen SA226TC Metro II	European Air Transport
	OO-JPN	Swearingen SA226AT Merlin IVA	European Air Transport
	OO-MJD	EMB-120RT Brasilia	DAT Air Meuse
	OO-MJE	Boeing 146-200	DAT Air Meuse
	OO-PHC	Boeing 737-248	Skyjet
	OO-PHE	Boeing 737-248	Skyjet
	OO-RXL	Saab SF.340B	—
	OO-RXM	Saab SF.340B	—
	OO-SBJ	Boeing 737-46B	Sobelair *Juliette*
	OO-SBM	Boeing 737-429	Sobelair
	OO-SBQ	Boeing 737-229	Sobelair
	OO-SBT	Boeing 737-229	Sobelair
	OO-SBZ	Boeing 737-329	Sobelair
	OO-SCA	Airbus A.310-222	Sabena
	OO-SCB	Airbus A.310-222	Sabena
	OO-SCC	Airbus A.310-322	Sabena
	OO-SDD	Boeing 737-229	Sabena
	OO-SDE	Boeing 737-229	Sabena
	OO-SDF	Boeing 737-229	Sabena
	OO-SDG	Boeing 737-229	Sabena
	OO-SDJ	Boeing 737-229C	Sabena
	OO-SDK	Boeing 737-229C	Sabena
	OO-SDL	Boeing 737-229	Sabena
	OO-SDM	Boeing 737-229	Sabena
	OO-SDN	Boeing 737-229	Sabena
	OO-SDO	Boeing 737-229	Sabena
	OO-SDP	Boeing 737-229C	Sabena
	OO-SDR	Boeing 737-229C	Sabena
	OO-SDV	Boeing 737-329	Sabena
	OO-SDW	Boeing 737-329	Sabena
	OO-SDX	Boeing 737-329	Sabena
	OO-SDY	Boeing 737-329	Sabena
	OO-SGA	Boeing 747-129A (SCD)	Sabena
	OO-SGC	Boeing 747-329 (SCD)	Sabena
	OO-SGD	Boeing 747-329 (SCD)	Sabena
	OO-SLA	Douglas DC-10-30CF	Sabena
	OO-SLB	Douglas DC-10-30CF	Sabena
	OO-SLE	Douglas DC-10-30CF	Sabena *(For Federal Express)*
	OO-SVL	F.27 Friendship Mk 100	Flanders Airlines
	OO-SVM	F.27 Friendship Mk 100 (SCD)	Flanders Airlines
	OO-SVN	F.27 Friendship Mk 100	Flanders Airlines
	OO-SYA	Boeing 737-329	Sabena
	OO-SYB	Boeing 737-329	Sabena
	OO-SYC	Boeing 737-429	Sabena
	OO-SYD	Boeing 737-429	Sabena
	OO-SYE	Boeing 737-529	Sabena
	OO-SYF	Boeing 737-429	Sabena
	OO-SYG	Boeing 737-529	Sabena
	OO-SYH	Boeing 737-529	Sabena
	OO-SYI	Boeing 737-529	Sabena
	OO-SYJ	Boeing 737-529	Sabena
	OO-SYK	Boeing 737-529	Sabena
	OO-SYL	Boeing 737-529	Sabena
	OO-SYM	Boeing 737-529	Sabena

Reg.	Type	Owner or Operator	Notes
OO-SYN	Boeing 737-529	Sabena	
OO-SYO	Boeing 737-529	Sabena	
OO-SYP	Boeing 737-529	Sabena	
OO-	Boeing 737-529	Sabena	
OO-TEF	Airbus A.300B1	*stored*/Brussels	
OO-VGC	Swearingen SA226AT Merlin IV	Flanders Airlines	
OO-VGD	Swearingen SA226AT Merlin IV	Flanders Airlines	

OY (Denmark)

Reg.	Type	Owner or Operator
OY-APF	F.27 Friendship Mk 500	Business Flight
OY-AZW	Swearingen SA226TC Metro II	Newair
OY-BDD	Nord 262A-21	Cimber Air
OY-BHT	EMB-110P2 Bandeirante	Muk Air
OY-BNM	EMB-110P2 Bandeirante	Muk Air
OY-BVF	F.27 Friendship Mk 600	Business Flight
OY-BVG	Beech 1900C-1	Business Flight
OY-BVH	F.27 Friendship Mk 200	Business Flight
OY-BVI	Beech 1900C-1	Business Flight
OY-BYN	Swearingen SA226TC Metro II	Muk Air
OY-CCH	Beech 1900C-1	Alkair/Emery Worldwide
OY-CCL	F.27 Friendship Mk.600	Alkair
OY-CCN	F.27 Friendship Mk 600	Alkair
OY-CIB	Aerospatiale ATR-42-300	Cimber Air
OY-CIC	Aerospatiale ATR-42-300	Cimber Air
OY-CID	Aerospatiale ATR-42-300	Cimber Air/Lufthansa CityLine
OY-CIE	Aerospatiale ATR-42-300	Cimber Air/Lufthansa CityLine
OY-CIF	Aerospatiale ATR-42-300	Cimber Air/Lufthansa CityLine
OY-CIG	Aerospatiale ATR-42-300	Cimber Air/Lufthansa CityLine
OY-CIH	Aerospatiale ATR-42-300	Cimber Air
OY-CNA	Airbus A.300B4	Conair/ZAS Airline of Egypt
OY-CND	Airbus A.320-231	Conair
OY-CNE	Airbus A.320-231	Conair
OY-CNF	Airbus A.320-231	Conair
OY-CNG	Airbus A.320-231	Conair
OY-CNH	Airbus A.320-231	Conair
OY-CNI	Airbus A.320-231	Conair
OY-CNK	Airbus A.300B4	Conair/ZAS Airline of Egypt
OY-CNL	Airbus A.300B4	Conair/ZAS Airline of Egypt
OY-CPG	EMB-110P1 Bandeirante	Sun-Air International
OY-CRR	H.P. 137 Jetstream 1	Newair
OY-CRS	H.P. 137 Jetstream 1	Newair
OY-CRT	H.P. 137 Jetstream 1	Newair
OY-DDA	Douglas DC-3	Danish Air Lines
OY-FEG	F.27 Friendship Mk 600	Starair/Federal Express
OY-KAE	Fokker 50	S.A.S. Commuter *Hans*
OY-KAF	Fokker 50	S.A.S. Commuter *Sigvat*
OY-KAG	Fokker 50	S.A.S. Commuter *Odensis*
OY-KAH	Fokker 50	S.A.S. Commuter *Bjorn*
OY-KAI	Fokker 50	S.A.S. Commuter *Skjold*
OY-KAK	Fokker 50	S.A.S. Commuter *Turid*
OY-KDL	Boeing 767-383ER	S.A.S. *Tjodhild Viking*
OY-KDM	Boeing 767-383ER	S.A.S.
OY-KDN	Boeing 767-383ER	S.A.S. *Ulf Viking*
OY-KDO	Boeing 767-383ER	S.A.S. *Svea Viking*
OY-KGD	Douglas DC-9-21	S.A.S. *Ubbe Viking*
OY-KGE	Douglas DC-9-21	S.A.S. *Orvar Viking*
OY-KGF	Douglas DC-9-21	S.A.S. *Rolf Viking*
OY-KGI	Douglas DC-9-41	S.A.S. *Bent Viking*
OY-KGL	Douglas DC-9-41	S.A.S. *Angantyr Viking*
OY-KGM	Douglas DC-9-41	S.A.S. *Arnfinn Viking*
OY-KGO	Douglas DC-9-41	S.A.S. *Holte Viking*
OY-KGP	Douglas DC-9-41	S.A.S. *Torbern Viking*
OY-KGR	Douglas DC-9-41	S.A.S. *Holger Viking*
OY-KGS	Douglas DC-9-41	S.A.S. *Hall Viking*
OY-KGT	McD Douglas MD-81	S.A.S. *Hake Viking*
OY-KGY	McD Douglas MD-81	S.A.S. *Rollo Viking*
OY-KGZ	McD Douglas MD-81	S.A.S. *Hagbard Viking*
OY-KHC	McD Douglas MD-81	S.A.S. *Faste Viking*
OY-KHE	McD Douglas MD-82	S.A.S. *Saxo Viking*
OY-KHF	McD Douglas MD-87	S.A.S. *Ragnar Viking*
OY-KHG	McD Douglas MD-81	S.A.S. *Alle Viking*

Notes	Reg.	Type	Owner or Operator
	OY-KHI	McD Douglas MD-87	S.A.S. *Torkel Viking*
	OY-KHK	McD Douglas MD-81	S.A.S. *Roald Viking*
	OY-KHL	McD Douglas MD-81	S.A.S. *Knud Viking*
	OY-KHM	McD Douglas MD-81	S.A.S. *Mette Viking*
	OY-KHN	McD Douglas MD-81	S.A.S. *Dan Viking*
	OY-KHO	McD Douglas MD-81	S.A.S. *Dana Viking*
	OY-KHP	McD Douglas MD-81	S.A.S. *Arild Viking*
	OY-KHR	McD Douglas MD-81	S.A.S.
	OY-KHS	McD Douglas MD-81	S.A.S. *Jarl Viking*
	OY-KHT	McD Douglas MD-82	S.A.S.
	OY-KHU	McD Douglas MD-87	S.A.S.
	OY-KHW	McD Douglas MD-87	S.A.S.
	OY-KHY	McD Douglas MD-82	S.A.S.
	OY-KHZ	McD Douglas MD-82	S.A.S.
	OY-KIA	Douglas DC-9-21	S.A.S. *Guttorm Viking*
	OY-KIB	Douglas DC-9-21	S.A.S. *Gunder Viking*
	OY-KID	Douglas DC-9-21	S.A.S. *Rane Viking*
	OY-KIE	Douglas DC-9-21	S.A.S. *Skate Viking*
	OY-KIF	Douglas DC-9-21	S.A.S. *Svipdag Viking*
	OY-MAA	Boeing 737-5L9	Maersk Air
	OY-MAB	Boeing 737-5L9	Maersk Air
	OY-MAC	Boeing 737-5L9	Maersk Air
	OY-MAD	Boeing 737-5L9	Maersk Air
	OY-MAE	Boeing 737-5L9	Maersk Air
	OY-MMD	Boeing 737-3L9	Maersk Air *Vaermland*
	OY-MMF	Boeing 737-3L9	Maersk Air
	OY-MMG	Fokker 50	Maersk Air
	OY-MMH	Fokker 50	Maersk Air
	OY-MMI	Fokker 50	Maersk Air
	OY-MMJ	Fokker 50	Maersk Air
	OY-MMS	Fokker 50	Maersk Air
	OY-MMT	Fokker 50	Maersk Air
	OY-MMU	Fokker 50	Maersk Air
	OY-MMV	Fokker 50	Maersk Air
	OY-MUA	EMB-110P1 Bandeirante	Muk Air
	OY-MUB	Short SD3-30	Muk Air
	OY-SAT	Boeing 727-2J4	Sterling Airways
	OY-SBE	Boeing 727-2J4	Sterling Airways
	OY-SBF	Boeing 727-2J4	Sterling Airways
	OY-SBG	Boeing 727-2J4	Sterling Airways
	OY-SBH	Boeing 727-2B7	Sterling Airways
	OY-SBI	Boeing 727-270	Sterling Airways
	OY-SBN	Boeing 727-2B7	Sterling Airways
	OY-SBO	Boeing 727-2K3	Sterling Airways
	OY-SHA	Boeing 757-2J4	Sterling Airways
	OY-SHB	Boeing 757-2J4	Sterling Airways
	OY-SRA	F.27 Friendship Mk 600	Starair
	OY-SRB	F.27 Friendship Mk 600	Alkair
	OY-SRC	F.27 Friendship Mk 600	Starair
	OY-SRR	F.27 Friendship Mk 600	Starair
	OY-SRZ	F.27 Friendship Mk 600	Starair
	OY-STH	S.E.210 Caravelle 10B	Sterling Airways
	OY-STI	S.E.210 Caravelle 10B	Sterling Airways
	OY-STM	S.E.210 Caravelle 10B	Sterling Airways
	OY-SUJ	Cessna 500 Citation	Sun Air
	OY-SVF	BAe Jetstream 3100	Sun Air
	OY-SVL	Cessna 500 Citation	Sun Air
	OY-TOV	Nord 262A-30	Cimber Air

PH (Netherlands)

	PH-AGA	Airbus A.310-203	K.L.M. *Rembrandt*
	PH-AGB	Airbus A.310-203	K.L.M. *Jeroen Bosch*
	PH-AGC	Airbus A.310-203	K.L.M. *Albert Cuyp*
	PH-AGD	Airbus A.310-203	K.L.M. *Marinus Ruppert*
	PH-AGE	Airbus A.310-203	K.L.M. *Jan Steen*
	PH-AGF	Airbus A.310-203	K.L.M. *Frans Hals*
	PH-AGG	Airbus A.310-203	K.L.M. *Vincent van Gogh*
	PH-AGH	Airbus A.310-203	K.L.M. *Peiter de Hoogh*
	PH-AGI	Airbus A.310-203	K.L.M. *Jan Toorop*
	PH-AGK	Airbus A.310-203	K.L.M. *Johannes Vermeer*
	PH-BDA	Boeing 737-306	K.L.M. *Willem Barentz*

Reg.	Type	Owner or Operator	Notes
PH-BDB	Boeing 737-306	K.L.M. *Olivier van Noort*	
PH-BDC	Boeing 737-306	K.L.M. *Cornelis De Houteman*	
PH-BDD	Boeing 737-306	K.L.M. *Anthony van Diemen*	
PH-BDE	Boeing 737-306	K.L.M. *Abel J. Tasman*	
PH-BDG	Boeing 737-306	K.L.M. *Michiel A. D. Ruyter*	
PH-BDH	Boeing 737-306	K.L.M. *Petrus Plancius*	
PH-BDI	Boeing 737-306	K.L.M. *Maarten H. Tromp*	
PH-BDK	Boeing 737-306	K.L.M. *Jan H. van Linschoten*	
PH-BDL	Boeing 737-306	K.L.M. *Piet Heyn*	
PH-BDN	Boeing 737-306	K.L.M. *Willem van Ruysbroeck*	
PH-BDO	Boeing 737-306	K.L.M. *Jacob van Heemskerck*	
PH-BDP	Boeing 737-306	K.L.M. *Jacob Rogeveen*	
PH-BDR	Boeing 737-406	K.L.M. *Willem C. Schouten*	
PH-BDS	Boeing 737-406	K.L.M. *Jorris van Spilbergen*	
PH-BDT	Boeing 737-406	K.L.M. *Gerrit de Veer*	
PH-BDU	Boeing 737-406	K.L.M. *Marco Polo*	
PH-BDW	Boeing 737-406	K.L.M. *Leifur Eirksson*	
PH-BDY	Boeing 737-406	K.L.M. *Vasco da Gama*	
PH-BDZ	Boeing 737-406	K.L.M. *Christophorus Columbus*	
PH-BFA	Boeing 747-406	K.L.M. *City of Atlanta*	
PH-BFB	Boeing 747-406	K.L.M. *City of Bangkok*	
PH-BFC	Boeing 747-406 (SCD)	K.L.M. *City of Calgary*	
PH-BFD	Boeing 747-406 (SCD)	K.L.M. *City of Dubai*	
PH-BFE	Boeing 747-406 (SCD)	K.L.M. *City of Melbourne*	
PH-BFF	Boeing 747-406 (SCD)	K.L.M. *City of Freetown*	
PH-BFG	Boeing 747-406	K.L.M. *City of Guayaquil*	
PH-BFH	Boeing 747-406 (SCD)	K.L.M. *City of Hong Kong*	
PH-BFI	Boeing 747-406 (SCD)	K.L.M. *City of Jakarta*	
PH-BFK	Boeing 747-406 (SCD)	K.L.M. *City of Karachi*	
PH-BFL	Boeing 747-406	K.L.M. *City of Lima*	
PH-BFM	Boeing 747-406 (SCD)	K.L.M. *City of Mexico*	
PH-BFN	Boeing 747-406	K.L.M. *City of Nairobi*	
PH-BFO	Boeing 747-406	K.L.M. *City of Ottawa*	
PH-BFP	Boeing 747-406	K.L.M.	
PH-BTA	Boeing 737-406	K.L.M. *Fernao de Magelhaes*	
PH-BTB	Boeing 737-406	K.L.M. *Henry Hudson*	
PH-BTC	Boeing 737-406	K.L.M. *David Livingstone*	
PH-BTD	Boeing 737-406	K.L.M. *James Cook*	
PH-BTE	Boeing 737-406	K.L.M. *Roald Amundsen*	
PH-BTF	Boeing 737-406	K.L.M. *Alexander von Humboldt*	
PH-BUH	Boeing 747-306 (SCD)	K.L.M. *Dr Albert Plesman*	
PH-BUI	Boeing 747-306 (SCD)	K.L.M. *Wilbur Wright*	
PH-BUK	Boeing 747-306 (SCD)	K.L.M. *Louis Blériot*	
PH-BUL	Boeing 747-306 (SCD)	K.L.M. *Charles A. Lindbergh*	
PH-BUM	Boeing 747-306 (SCD)	K.L.M. *Sir Charles E. Kingsford-Smith*	
PH-BUN	Boeing 747-306 (SCD)	K.L.M. *Anthony H. G. Fokker*	
PH-BUO	Boeing 747-306	K.L.M. *Missouri*	
PH-BUP	Boeing 747-306	K.L.M. *The Ganges*	
PH-BUR	Boeing 747-306	K.L.M. *The Indus*	
PH-BUU	Boeing 747-306 (SCD)	K.L.M. *Sir Frank Whittle*	
PH-BUV	Boeing 747-306 (SCD)	K.L.M. *Sir Geoffrey de Havilland*	
PH-BUW	Boeing 747-306 (SCD)	K.L.M. *Leonardo da Vinci*	
PH-CHB	F.28 Fellowship 4000	K.L.M. CityHopper *Birmingham*	
PH-CHD	F.28 Fellowship 4000	K.L.M. CityHopper *Maastricht*	
PH-CHF	F.28 Fellowship 4000	K.L.M. CityHopper *Guernsey*	
PH-CHN	F.28 Fellowship 4000	K.L.M. CityHopper	
PH-DDA	Douglas DC-3	Dutch Dakota Association	
PH-DTA	Douglas DC-10-30	K.L.M. *Johann Sebastian Bach*	
PH-DTB	Douglas DC-10-30	K.L.M. *Ludwig van Beethoven*	
PH-DTC	Douglas DC-10-30	K.L.M. *Frédéric François Chopin*	
PH-DTD	Douglas DC-10-30	K.L.M. *Maurice Ravel*	
PH-FKT	F-27 Friendship Mk 600	Schreiner Airways	
PH-FWS	EMB-110P1 Bandeirante	Freeway Air	
PH-FWT	EMB-110P1 Bandeirante	Freeway Air	
PH-FXA	Dornier Do.228-202K	Flexair	
PH-HVG	Boeing 737-3K2	Transavia *Wubbo Ockels*	
PH-HVJ	Boeing 737-3K2	Transavia *Nelli Cooman*	
PH-HVK	Boeing 737-3K2	Transavia *Evert van Benthem*	
PH-HVM	Boeing 737-3K2	Transavia	
PH-HVN	Boeing 737-3K2	Transavia	
PH-HVT	Boeing 737-3K2	Transavia	
PH-HVV	Boeing 737-3K2	Transavia	
PH-HVW	Boeing 737-3K2	Transavia	

Notes	Reg.	Type	Owner or Operator
	PH-KFD	F.27 Friendship Mk 200	K.L.M. CityHopper *(stored)*
	PH-KFE	F.27 Friendship Mk 600	K.L.M. CityHopper *(stored)*
	PH-KFG	F.27 Friendship Mk 200	K.L.M. CityHopper *(stored)*
	PH-KJA	BAe Jetstream 3108	BASE Business Airlines
	PH-KJB	BAe Jetstream 3108	BASE Business Airlines
	PH-KSA	Saab SF.340B	K.L.M. CityHopper
	PH-KSB	Saab SF.340B	K.L.M. CityHopper
	PH-KSC	Saab SF.340B	K.L.M. CityHopper
	PH-KSD	Saab SF.340B	K.L.M. CityHopper
	PH-KSE	Saab SF.340B	K.L.M. CityHopper
	PH-KSF	Saab SF.340B	K.L.M. CityHopper
	PH-KSG	Saab SF.340B	K.L.M. CityHopper
	PH-KSH	Saab SF.340B	K.L.M. CityHopper
	PH-KSI	Saab SF.340B	K.L.M. CityHopper
	PH-KSK	Saab SF.340B	K.L.M. CityHopper
	PH-KSL	Saab SF.340B	K.L.M. CityHopper
	PH-KSM	Saab SF.340B	K.L.M. CityHopper
	PH-KVA	Fokker 50	K.L.M. CityHopper
	PH-KVB	Fokker 50	K.L.M. CityHopper
	PH-KVC	Fokker 50	K.L.M. CityHopper
	PH-KVD	Fokker 50	K.L.M. CityHopper
	PH-KVE	Fokker 50	K.L.M. CityHopper
	PH-KVF	Fokker 50	K.L.M. CityHopper
	PH-KVG	Fokker 50	K.L.M. CityHopper
	PH-KVH	Fokker 50	K.L.M. CityHopper
	PH-KVI	Fokker 50	K.L.M. CityHopper
	PH-KVK	Fokker 50	K.L.M. CityHopper
	PH-MBN	Douglas DC-10-30CF	Martinair *Anthony Ruys*
	PH-MBP	Douglas DC-10-30CF	Martinair *Hong Kong*
	PH-MBT	Douglas DC-10-30CF	K.L.M. *George Gershwin*
	PH-MBZ	Douglas DC-9-82	Martinair *Prinses Juiliana*
	PH-MCA	Airbus A.310-203	Martinair *Prins Bernhard*
	PH-MCB	Airbus A.310-203CF	Martinair *Prins Maurits*
	PH-MCE	Boeing 747-21AC (SCD)	Martinair *Prins van Oranje*
	PH-MCF	Boeing 747-21AC (SCD)	Martinair *Prins Claus*
	PH-MCG	Boeing 767-31AER	Martinair *Prins Johan Friso*
	PH-MCH	Boeing 767-31AER	Martinair *Prins Constantijn*
	PH-MCI	Boeing 767-31AER	Martinair
	PH-MCK	Boeing 767-31AER	Martinair
	PH-MCL	Boeing 767-31A	Martinair
	PH-MCM	Boeing 767-31A	Martinair
	PH-MCN	Boeing 747-228F	Martinair
	PH-SAD	F.27 Friendship Mk 200	K.L.M. CityHopper *(stored)*
	PH-SDH	D.H.C.8-102 Dash Eight	Schreiner Airways
	PH-SDI	D.H.C.8-301A Dash Eight	Schreiner Airways/Sabena
	PH-SDJ	D.H.C.8-301A Dash Eight	Schreiner Airways/Sabena
	PH-SFA	F.27 Friendship Mk 400	Schreiner Airways
	PH-SFE	F.27 Friendship Mk 300	Schreiner Airways
	PH-SFI	F.27 Friendship Mk 500	Schreiner Airways
	PH-TKA	Boeing 757-2K2	Transavia
	PH-TKB	Boeing 757-2K2	Transavia
	PH-TVH	Boeing 737-222	Transavia *Neil Armstrong*
	PH-TVP	Boeing 737-2K2	Transavia
	PH-TVR	Boeing 737-2K2	Transavia
	PH-TVS	Boeing 737-2K2	Transavia
	PH-TVX	Boeing 737-2K2	Transavia/K.L.M.

Note: K.L.M. also operates Boeing 747-306, N1309E.

PK (Indonesia)

	PK-GIA	Douglas DC-10-30	Garuda Indonesian Airways
	PK-GIB	Douglas DC-10-30	Garuda Indonesian Airways
	PK-GIC	Douglas DC-10-30	Garuda Indonesian Airways
	PK-GID	Douglas DC-10-30	Garuda Indonesian Airways
	PK-GIE	Douglas DC-10-30	Garuda Indonesian Airways
	PK-GIF	Douglas DC-10-30	Garuda Indonesian Airways
	PK-GSA	Boeing 747-2U3B	Garuda Indonesian Airways
	PK-GSB	Boeing 747-2U3B	Garuda Indonesian Airways
	PK-GSC	Boeing 747-2U3B	Garuda Indonesian Airways
	PK-GSD	Boeing 747-2U3B	Garuda Indonesian Airways
	PK-GSE	Boeing 747-2U3B	Garuda Indonesian Airways
	PK-GSF	Boeing 747-2U3B	Garuda Indonesian Airways

Reg.	Type	Owner or Operator	Notes
PK-PLR	L.100-30 Hercules	HeavyLift Cargo Airlines	
PK-PLU	L.100-30 Hercules	HeavyLift Cargo Airlines	
PK-PLV	L.100-30 Hercules	HeavyLift Cargo Airlines	
PK-PLW	L.100-30 Hercules	HeavyLift Cargo Airlines	

Note: The DC-10-30 EI-BZD is also operated by Garuda.

PP (Brazil)

PP-VMA	Douglas DC-10-30	VARIG	
PP-VMB	Douglas DC-10-30	VARIG	
PP-VMD	Douglas DC-10-30	VARIG	
PP-VMQ	Douglas DC-10-30	VARIG	
PP-VMS	Douglas DC-10-30	VARIG	
PP-VMT	Douglas DC-10-30F	VARIG Cargo	
PP-VMU	Douglas DC-10-30F	VARIG Cargo	
PP-VMV	Douglas DC-10-30	VARIG	
PP-VMW	Douglas DC-10-30	VARIG	
PP-VMX	Douglas DC-10-30	VARIG	
PP-VMY	Douglas DC-10-30	VARIG	
PP-VMZ	Douglas DC-10-30	VARIG	
PP-VNA	Boeing 747-2L5B (SCD)	VARIG	
PP-VNB	Boeing 747-2L5B (SCD)	VARIG	
PP-VNC	Boeing 747-2L5B (SCD)	VARIG	
PP-VNH	Boeing 747-341 (SCD)	VARIG	
PP-VNI	Boeing 747-341 (SCD)	VARIG	
PP-VOA	Boeing 747-341	VARIG	
PP-VOB	Boeing 747-341	VARIG	
PP-VOC	Boeing 747-341	VARIG	
PP-VPI	Boeing 747-475	VARIG	

RP (Philippines)

Note: Philippine Airlines operates four Boeing 747-2F6Bs which retain their U.S.
identities N741PR, N742PR, N743PR and N744PR, two 747-283Bs registered
EI-BTS and EI-BZA and two 747-211Bs registered N207AE and N208AE.

S2 (Bangladesh)

S2-ACO	Douglas DC-10-30	Bangladesh Biman City of Hazrat-Shar Makhdoom (R.A.)	
S2-ACP	Douglas DC-10-30	Bangladesh Biman City of Dhaka	
S2-ACQ	Douglas DC-10-30	Bangladesh Biman City of Hz Shah Jalal (R.A.)	
S2-ACR	Douglas DC-10-30	Bangladesh Biman The New Era	

S7 (Seychelles)

S7-AAS	Boeing 767-2Q8ER	Air Seychelles Aldabra	

SE (Sweden)

SE-CFP	Douglas DC-3	Flygande Veteraner Fridtjof Viking	
SE-DAK	Douglas DC-9-41	S.A.S. Ragnvald Viking	
SE-DAM	Douglas DC-9-41	S.A.S. Starkad Viking	
SE-DAN	Douglas DC-9-41	S.A.S. Alf Viking	
SE-DAP	Douglas DC-9-41	S.A.S. Torgils Viking	
SE-DAR	Douglas DC-9-41	S.A.S. Agnar Viking	
SE-DAS	Douglas DC-9-41	S.A.S. Garder Viking	
SE-DAU	Douglas DC-9-41	S.A.S. Hadding Viking	
SE-DAW	Douglas DC-9-41	S.A.S. Gotrik Viking	
SE-DAX	Douglas DC-9-41	S.A.S. Helsing Viking	
SE-DBM	Douglas DC-9-41	S.A.S. Ossur Viking	
SE-DBO	Douglas DC-9-21	Nordic East	
SE-DDP	Douglas DC-9-41	S.A.S. Brun Viking	
SE-DDR	Douglas DC-9-41	S.A.S. Atle Viking	
SE-DDS	Douglas DC-9-41	S.A.S. Alrik Viking	
SE-DDT	Douglas DC-9-41	S.A.S. Amund Viking	
SE-DEI	BAe 146-200QT	Malmö Aviation/TNT	
SE-DFR	McD Douglas MD-81	S.A.S. Ingjald Viking	
SE-DFS	McD Douglas MD-82	S.A.S. Gaut Viking	

Notes	Reg.	Type	Owner or Operator
	SE-DFT	McD Douglas MD-82	S.A.S. *Assur Viking*
	SE-DFU	McD Douglas MD-82	S.A.S. *Isulv Viking*
	SE-DFX	McD Douglas MD-82	S.A.S. *Ring Viking*
	SE-DFY	McD Douglas MD-81	S.A.S. *Ottar Viking*
	SE-DGE	F.28 Fellowship 4000	Linjeflyg
	SE-DGF	F.28 Fellowship 4000	Linjeflyg
	SE-DGG	F.28 Fellowship 4000	Linjeflyg
	SE-DGH	F.28 Fellowship 4000	Linjeflyg
	SE-DGI	F.28 Fellowship 4000	Linjeflyg
	SE-DGK	F.28 Fellowship 4000	Linjeflyg
	SE-DGL	F.28 Fellowship 4000	Linjeflyg
	SE-DGM	F.28 Fellowship 4000	Linjeflyg
	SE-DGN	F.28 Fellowship 4000	Linjeflyg
	SE-DGO	F.28 Fellowship 4000	Linjeflyg
	SE-DGP	F.28 Fellowship 4000	Linjeflyg
	SE-DGR	F.28 Fellowship 4000	Linjeflyg
	SE-DGS	F.28 Fellowship 4000	Linjeflyg *Svea*
	SE-DGT	F.28 Fellowship 4000	Linjeflyg *Tora*
	SE-DGU	F.28 Fellowship 4000	Linjeflyg *Ulla*
	SE-DGX	F.28 Fellowship 4000	Linjeflyg *Kryss*
	SE-DHA	S.E.210 Caravelle 10B3	Transwede
	SE-DHB	McD Douglas MD-83	Transwede
	SE-DHC	McD Douglas MD-83	Transwede
	SE-DHD	McD Douglas MD-83	Transwede
	SE-DHG	McD Douglas MD-87	Transwede
	SE-DHI	McD Douglas MD-87	Transwede
	SE-DHN	McD Douglas MD-83	Transwede
	SE-DHS	Douglas DC-10-10	Scanair *Baloo*
	SE-DHT	Douglas DC-10-10	Scanair *Dumbo*
	SE-DHU	Douglas DC-10-10	Scanair *Bamse*
	SE-DHX	Douglas DC-10-10	(leased to Sun Country)
	SE-DHY	Douglas DC-10-10	Scanair *Snoopy*
	SE-DHZ	Douglas DC-10-10	Scanair *Moby Dick*
	SE-DIA	McD Douglas MD-81	S.A.S. *Ulvrik Viking*
	SE-DIB	McD Douglas MD-87	S.A.S. *Varin Viking*
	SE-DIC	McD Douglas MD-87	S.A.S. *Grane Viking*
	SE-DID	McD Douglas MD-82	S.A.S. *Spjute Viking*
	SE-DIF	McD Douglas MD-87	S.A.S. *Hjorulv Viking*
	SE-DIH	McD Douglas MD-87	S.A.S. *Slagfinn Viking*
	SE-DII	McD Douglas MD-81	S.A.S. *Sigtrugg Viking*
	SE-DIK	McD Douglas MD-82	S.A.S. *Stenkil Viking*
	SE-DIL	McD Douglas MD-81	S.A.S. *Tord Viking*
	SE-DIM	BAe 146-300QT	Malmö Aviation /TNT
	SE-DIN	McD Douglas MD-81	S.A.S. *Eskil Viking*
	SE-DIP	McD Douglas MD-87	S.A.S. *Jarl Viking*
	SE-DIR	McD Douglas MD-81	S.A.S. *Nora Viking*
	SE-DIS	McD Douglas MD-81	S.A.S. *Sigmund Viking*
	SE-DIT	BAe 146-300QT	Malmö Aviation/TNT
	SE-DIU	McD Douglas MD-87	S.A.S.
	SE-DIX	McD Douglas MD-81	S.A.S. *Anund Viking*
	SE-DIY	McD Douglas MD-81	S.A.S.
	SE-DIZ	McD Douglas MD-82	S.A.S.
	SE-DKO	Boeing 767-383ER	S.A.S. *Ingegerd Viking*
	SE-DKP	Boeing 767-283ER	S.A.S. *Sigrid Viking*
	SE-DKU	Boeing 767-383ER	S.A.S. *Tor Viking*
	SE-DKX	Boeing 767-383ER	S.A.S.
	SE-DLC	Douglas DC-9-41	S.A.S. *Eiliv Viking*
	SE-DLD	Boeing 737-205	Time Air Sweden
	SE-DLG	Boeing 737-3Q8	Time Air Sweden
	SE-DLN	Boeing 737-3Y0	—
	SE-DLO	Boeing 737-3Y0	—
	SE-DLP	Boeing 737-205	Time Air Sweden/Sultan Air
	SE-DLS	McD Douglas MD-83	Transwede
	SE-DLU	McD Douglas MD-83	Transwede
	SE-	McD Douglas MD-83	Transwede
	SE-	McD Douglas MD-83	Transwede
	SE-DMA	McD Douglas MD-87	S.A.S.
	SE-DMB	McD Douglas MD-81	S.A.S.
	SE-DMC	McD Douglas MD-87	S.A.S.
	SE-DMD	McD Douglas MD-81	S.A.S.
	SE-DME	McD Douglas MD-81	S.A.S.
	SE-DMF	McD Douglas MD-81	S.A.S.
	SE-DMG	McD Douglas MD-81	S.A.S.

Reg.	Type	Owner or Operator	Notes
SE-DMH	McD Douglas MD-82	S.A.S.	
SE-DMI	McD Douglas MD-82	S.A.S.	
SE-DNA	Boeing 737-59D	Linjeflyg *Medelpad*	
SE-DNB	Boeing 737-59D	Linjeflyg *Jaemtland*	
SE-DNC	Boeing 737-53A	Linjeflyg *Skane*	
SE-DND	Boeing 737-59D	Linjeflyg *Vaesterbotten*	
SE-DNE	Boeing 737-59D	Linjeflyg *Smaland*	
SE-DNF	Boeing 737-5Q8	Linjeflyg *Vaermland*	
SE-DNG	Boeing 737-5Q8	Linjeflyg *Gotland*	
SE-DNH	Boeing 737-5Q8	Linjeflyg	
SE-	Boeing 737-5Q8	Linjeflyg	
SE-	Boeing 737-5Q8	Linjeflyg	
SE-DOA	Boeing 767-383ER	S.A.S. *Yrsa Viking*	
SE-DOB	Boeing 767-383ER	S.A.S. *Helga Viking*	
SE-DPA	Boeing 737-33A	Falcon Cargo/Linjeflyg	
SE-DPB	Boeing 737-33A	Falcon Cargo	
SE-DPC	Boeing 737-33A	Falcon Cargo	
SE-DPH	McD Douglas MD-83	Scanair	
SE-IVR	L-188CF Electra	Falcon Cargo	
SE-IVS	L-188CF Electra	Falcon Cargo	
SE-IVT	L-188CF Electra	Falcon Cargo	
SE-IVY	V.815 Viscount	(stored)	
SE-IZU	L-188CF Electra	Falcon Cargo	
SE-KBP	FH.227E Friendship	Malmö Aviation	
SE-KGA	FH.227B Friendship	Malmö Aviation	
SE-KGB	FH.227B Friendship	Malmö Aviation	
SE-KGC	F.27 Friendship Mk 600	Malmö Aviation/TNT	
SE-LFA	Fokker 50	S.A.S. Commuter *Jorund*	
SE-LFB	Fokker 50	S.A.S. Commuter *Sture*	
SE-LFC	Fokker 50	S.A.S. Commuter *Ylva*	
SE-LFK	Fokker 50	S.A.S. Commuter *Alvar*	
SE-LFN	Fokker 50	S.A.S. Commuter *Edmund*	
SE-LFO	Fokker 50	S.A.S. Commuter *Folke*	
SE-LFP	Fokker 50	S.A.S. Commuter *Ingemar*	
SE-LFR	Fokker 50	S.A.S. Commuter *Vagn*	
SE-LFS	Fokker 50	S.A.S. Commuter *Vigge*	

SP (Poland)

SP-LBA	Ilyushin IL-62M	Polskie Linie Lotnicze (LOT) *Juliusz Sowacki*	
SP-LBB	Ilyushin IL-62M	LOT *Jgnacy Paderewski*	
SP-LBC	Ilyushin IL-62M	LOT *Joseph Conrad-Korzeniowski*	
SP-LBD	Ilyushin IL-62M	LOT *General Wladystaw Sikorski*	
SP-LBE	Ilyushin IL-62M	LOT *Stanislaw Moniuszho*	
SP-LBF	Ilyushin IL-62M	LOT *Fryderyk Chopin*	
SP-LBH	Ilyushin IL-62M	LOT	
SP-LCA	Tupolev Tu-154M	LOT	
SP-LCB	Tupolev Tu-154M	LOT	
SP-LCC	Tupolev Tu-154M	LOT	
SP-LCD	Tupolev Tu-154M	LOT	
SP-LCE	Tupolev Tu-154M	LOT	
SP-LCF	Tupolev Tu-154M	LOT	
SP-LCG	Tupolev Tu-154M	LOT	
SP-LCH	Tupolev Tu-154M	LOT	
SP-LCI	Tupolev Tu-154M	LOT	
SP-LCK	Tupolev Tu-154M	LOT	
SP-LCL	Tupolev Tu-154M	LOT	
SP-LCM	Tupolev Tu-154M	LOT	
SP-LCN	Tupolev Tu-154M	LOT	
SP-LHA	Tupolev Tu-134A	LOT	
SP-LHB	Tupolev Tu-134A	LOT	
SP-LHC	Tupolev Tu-134A	LOT	
SP-LHD	Tupolev Tu-134A	LOT	
SP-LHE	Tupolev Tu-134A	LOT	
SP-LHF	Tupolev Tu-134A	LOT	
SP-LHG	Tupolev Tu-134A	LOT	
SP-LOA	Boeing 767-25DER	LOT *Gneizao*	
SP-LOB	Boeing 767-25DER	LOT *Kracow*	
SP-LPA	Boeing 767-35DER	LOT *Warszawa*	
SP-LSF	Ilyushin IL-18E	LOT	
SP-LSI	Ilyushin IL-18D	LOT	

Notes	Reg.	Type	Owner or Operator

ST (Sudan)

	Reg.	Type	Owner or Operator
	ST-AFA	Boeing 707-3J8C	Sudan Airways
	ST-AFB	Boeing 707-3J8C	Sudan Airways
	ST-AIX	Boeing 707-369C	Sudan Airways
	ST-AKW	Boeing 707-330C	Sudan Airways
	ST-ALP	Boeing 707-338C	Trans Arabian Air Transport
	ST-DRS	Boeing 707-368C	Sudan Airways
	ST-NSR	Boeing 707-330B	Sudan Airways

SU (Egypt)

	Reg.	Type	Owner or Operator
	SU-AOU	Boeing 707-366C	EgyptAir *Khopho*
	SU-APD	Boeing 707-366C	EgyptAir *Khafrah*
	SU-AVX	Boeing 707-366C	EgyptAir *Tutankhamun*
	SU-AVY	Boeing 707-366C	EgyptAir *Akhenaton*
	SU-AVZ	Boeing 707-366C	EgyptAir *Mena*
	SU-AXK	Boeing 707-366C	EgyptAir *Seti I*
	SU-BCB	Airbus A.300B4	EgyptAir *Osiris*
	SU-BCC	Airbus A.300B4	EgyptAir *Nout*
	SU-BDF	Airbus A.300B4	EgyptAir *Hathor*
	SU-BDG	Airbus A.300B4	EgyptAir *Aton*
	SU-DAA	Boeing 707-351C	ZAS Airline of Egypt
	SU-DAC	Boeing 707-336C	ZAS Airline of Egypt
	SU-GAH	Boeing 767-266ER	EgyptAir *Nefertiti*
	SU-GAI	Boeing 767-266ER	EgyptAir *Nefertari*
	SU-GAJ	Boeing 767-266ER	EgyptAir *Tiye*
	SU-GAL	Boeing 747-366 (SCD)	EgyptAir *Hatshepsut*
	SU-GAM	Boeing 747-366 (SCD)	EgyptAir *Cleopatra*
	SU-GAO	Boeing 767-366ER	EgyptAir *Ramses II*
	SU-GAP	Boeing 767-366ER	EgyptAir *Thutmosis III*
	SU-GAR	Airbus A.300-622R	EgyptAir *Zoser*
	SU-GAS	Airbus A.300-622R	EgyptAir *Cheops*
	SU-GAT	Airbus A.300-622R	EgyptAir *Chephren*
	SU-GAU	Airbus A.300-622R	EgyptAir *Mycerinus*
	SU-GAV	Airbus A.300-622R	EgyptAir *Menes*
	SU-GAW	Airbus A.300-622R	EgyptAir *Ahmuse*
	SU-GAX	Airbus A.300-622R	EgyptAir *Tut-Ankh-Amun*
	SU-GAY	Airbus A.300-622R	EgyptAir *Seti I*
	SU-GAZ	Airbus A.300-622R	EgyptAir

Note: ZAS also operates the A.300s OY-CNA, OY-CNK and OY-CNL on lease from Conair.

SX (Greece)

	Reg.	Type	Owner or Operator
	SX-BCA	Boeing 737-284	Olympic Airways *Apollo*
	SX-BCB	Boeing 737-284	Olympic Airways *Hermes*
	SX-BCC	Boeing 737-284	Olympic Airways *Hercules*
	SX-BCD	Boeing 737-284	Olympic Airways *Hephaestus*
	SX-BCE	Boeing 737-284	Olympic Airways *Dionysus*
	SX-BCF	Boeing 737-284	Olympic Airways *Poseidon*
	SX-BCG	Boeing 737-284	Olympic Airways *Phoebus*
	SX-BCH	Boeing 737-284	Olympic Airways *Triton*
	SX-BCI	Boeing 737-284	Olympic Airways *Proteus*
	SX-BCK	Boeing 737-284	Olympic Airways *Nereus*
	SX-BCL	Boeing 737-284	Olympic Airways *Isle of Thassos*
	SX-BEB	Airbus A.300B4	Olympic Airways *Odysseus*
	SX-BEC	Airbus A.300B4	Olympic Airways *Achilleus*
	SX-BED	Airbus A.300B4	Olympic Airways *Telemachus*
	SX-BEE	Airbus A.300B4	Olympic Airways *Nestor*
	SX-BEF	Airbus A.300B4	Olympic Airways *Ajax*
	SX-BEG	Airbus A.300B4	Olympic Airways *Diomedes*
	SX-BEH	Airbus A.300B4	Olympic Airways *Peleus*
	SX-BEI	Airbus A.300B4	Olympic Airways *Neoptolemos*
	SX-BKA	Boeing 737-484	Olympic Airways *Vergina*
	SX-BKB	Boeing 737-484	Olympic Airways *Olynthos*
	SX-BKC	Boeing 737-484	Olympic Airways *Philipoli*
	SX-BKD	Boeing 737-484	Olympic Airways *Amphipoli*
	SX-BKE	Boeing 737-484	Olympic Airways *Stagira*
	SX-BKF	Boeing 737-484	Olympic Airways *Dion*

Reg.	Type	Owner or Operator	Notes
SX-CBA	Boeing 727-284	Olympic Airways *Mount Olympus*	
SX-CBB	Boeing 727-284	Olympic Airways *Mount Pindos*	
SX-CBC	Boeing 727-284	Olympic Airways *Mount Parnassus*	
SX-CBD	Boeing 727-284	Olympic Airways *Mount Helicon*	
SX-CBE	Boeing 727-284	Olympic Airways *Mount Athos*	
SX-CBF	Boeing 727-284	Olympic Airways *Mount Taygetus*	
SX-CBG	Boeing 727-230	Olympic Airways *Mount Menalon*	
SX-CBH	Boeing 727-230	Olympic Airways *Mount Vermio*	
SX-CBI	Boeing 727-230	Olympic Airways *Mount Dirfis*	
SX-	McD Douglas MD-83	Appollonian Airways	
SX-	McD Douglas MD-83	Appollonian Airways	
SX-OAB	Boeing 747-284B	Olympic Airways *Olympic Eagle*	
SX-OAC	Boeing 747-212B	Olympic Airways *Olympic Spirit*	
SX-OAD	Boeing 747-212B	Olympic Airways *Olympic Flame*	
SX-OAE	Boeing 747-212B	Olympic Airways *Olympic Peace*	

TC (Turkey)

Reg.	Type	Owner or Operator	Notes
TC-ABA	S.E.210 Caravelle 10B1R	Istanbul Airlines *Mine*	
TC-ADA	Boeing 737-4Y0	Istanbul Airlines	
TC-	Boeing 737-4Y0	Istanbul Airlines	
TC-AFB	Boeing 727-228	Noble Air *Vatan*	
TC-AFC	Boeing 727-228	Noble Air *Ulus*	
TC-AFD	Boeing 727-230	Noble Air *Girne*	
TC-AFE	Boeing 727-230	Noble Air *Yesilada*	
TC-AFG	Boeing 727-231	Noble Air	
TC-AFK	Boeing 737-4Y0	Pegasus Airlines	
TC-AFL	Boeing 737-4Y0	Pegasus Airlines	
TC-AGA	Boeing 737-4Y0	Istanbul Airlines	
TC-AKA	S.E.210 Caravelle 10B1R	Istanbul Airlines *Gül*	
TC-ALA	S.E.210 Caravelle 10B1R	Istanbul Airlines *Orkide*	
TC-ASA	S.E.210 Caravelle 10B1R	Istanbul Airlines *Nergis*	
TC-ATA	Boeing 737-4Y0	Istanbul Airlines	
TC-GRA	Tupolev Tu-154M	Greenair *Cappadocia*	
TC-GRB	Tupolev Tu-154M	Greenair *Perestroika*	
TC-GRC	Tupolev Tu-154M	Greenair *Fenerbahce*	
TC-GRD	Tupolev Tu-134A-3	Greenair *Besiktas*	
TC-GRE	Tupolev Tu-134A-3	Greenair *Galatasary*	
TC-JAB	Douglas DC-9-32	Türk Hava Yollari (THY) *Bogazici*	
TC-JAD	Douglas DC-9-32	Türk Hava Yollari (THY) *Anadolu*	
TC-JAE	Douglas DC-9-32	Türk Hava Yollari (THY) *Trakya*	
TC-JAF	Douglas DC-9-32	Türk Hava Yollari (THY) *Ege*	
TC-JAG	Douglas DC-9-32	Türk Hava Yollari (THY) *Akdeniz*	
TC-JAK	Douglas DC-9-32	Türk Hava Yollari (THY) *Karadeniz*	
TC-JAL	Douglas DC-9-32	Türk Hava Yollari (THY) *Halic*	
TC-JBF	Boeing 727-2F2	Türk Hava Yollari (THY) *Adana*	
TC-JBG	Boeing 727-2F2	Cyprus Turkish Airlines	
TC-JBJ	Boeing 727-2F2	Türk Hava Yollari (THY) *Diyarbakir*	
TC-JBK	Douglas DC-9-32	Türk Hava Yollari (THY) *Aydin*	
TC-JBL	Douglas DC-9-32	Türk Hava Yollari (THY) *Gediz*	
TC-JBM	Boeing 727-2F2	Türk Hava Yollari (THY) *Menderes*	
TC-JCA	Boeing 727-2F2	Türk Hava Yollari (THY) *Edirne*	
TC-JCB	Boeing 727-2F2	Türk Hava Yollari (THY) *Kars*	
TC-JCD	Boeing 727-2F2	Türk Hava Yollari (THY) *Sinop*	
TC-JCE	Boeing 727-2F2	Türk Hava Yollari (THY) *Hatay*	
TC-JCK	Boeing 727-243	Türk Hava Yollari (THY) *Erciyes*	
TC-JCL	Airbus A.310-203	Türk Hava Yollari (THY) *Seyhan*	
TC-JCM	Airbus A.310-203	Türk Hava Yollari (THY) *Ceyhan*	
TC-JCN	Airbus A.310-203	Türk Hava Yollari (THY) *Dicle*	
TC-JCO	Airbus A.310-203	Türk Hava Yollari (THY) *Firat*	
TC-JCR	Airbus A.310-203	Türk Hava Yollari (THY) *Kizilirmak*	
TC-JCS	Airbus A.310-203	Türk Hava Yollari (THY) *Yesilirmak*	
TC-JCU	Airbus A.310-203	Türk Hava Yollari (THY) *Sakarya*	
TC-JCV	Airbus A.310-304	Türk Hava Yollari (THY) *Aras*	
TC-JCY	Airbus A.310-304	Türk Hava Yollari (THY) *Coruh*	
TC-JCZ	Airbus A.310-304	Türk Hava Yollari (THY) *Ergene*	
TC-JDA	Airbus A.310-304	Türk Hava Yollari (THY) *Aksu*	
TC-JDB	Airbus A.310-304	Türk Hava Yollari (THY) *Goksu*	
TC-JDC	Airbus A.310-304	Türk Hava Yollari (THY) *Meric*	
TC-JDD	Airbus A.310-304	Türk Hava Yollari (THY)	
TC-JDE	Boeing 737-4Y0	Türk Hava Yollari (THY)	
TC-JDF	Boeing 737-4Y0	Türk Hava Yollari (THY)	

Notes	Reg.	Type	Owner or Operator
	TC-JDG	Boeing 737-4Y0	Türk Hava Yollari (THY)
	TC-JDH	Boeing 737-4Y0	Türk Hava Yollari (THY)
	TC-	Boeing 737-4Q8	Türk Hava Yollari (THY)
	TC-	Boeing 737-4Q8	Türk Hava Yollari (THY)
	TC-	Boeing 737-4Q8	Türk Hava Yollari (THY)
	TC-	Boeing 737-4Q8	Türk Hava Yollari (THY)
	TC-	Boeing 737-4Q8	Türk Hava Yollari (THY)
	TC-	Boeing 737-4Q8	Türk Hava Yollari (THY)
	TC-JFA	Boeing 727-264	Türk Hava Yollari (THY) *Ortaköy*
	TC-JFB	Boeing 727-264	Türk Hava Yollari (THY) *Vaniköy*
	TC-	Boeing 747-212B	Türk Hava Yollari (THY)
	TC-JUP	Boeing 737-205	Sultan Air
	TC-JUR	Boeing 737-205	Sultan Air
	TC-JUS	Boeing 737-2Q8	Sultan Air
	TC-JUU	Boeing 737-2K9	Sultan Air
	TC-MAB	Douglas DC-8-61	Birgenair
	TC-RUT	Boeing 727-230	TUR European Airways
	TC-SUN	Boeing 737-3Y0	Sun Express
	TC-SUP	Boeing 737-3Y0	Sun Express
	TC-SUR	Boeing 737-3Y0	Sun Express
	TC-TUR	Boeing 727-230	TUR European Airways
	TC-VAB	Boeing 737-248	VIP Air

TF (Iceland)

	TF-ABJ	Boeing 737-201C	Atlanta Icelandic/Finnair Cargo
	TF-ABT	Boeing 737-205C	Atlanta Icelandic *Spirit of Nome 1924 Alaska*
	TF-ABG	L-1011-385 TriStar	Atlanta Icelandic
	TF-AIA	Boeing 727-276	Atlantic Island Air
	TF-FIA	Boeing 737-408	Icelandair *Aldis*
	TF-FIB	Boeing 737-408	Icelandair *Eydis*
	TF-FIC	Boeing 737-408	Icelandair *Vedis*
	TF-FID	Boeing 737-4Q8	Icelandair
	TF-FIH	Boeing 757-208ER	Icelandair *Haldis*
	TF-FII	Boeing 757-208ER	Icelandair *Fanndis*
	TF-FLM	F.27 Friendship Mk 200	Icelandair
	TF-FLN	F.27 Friendship Mk 200	Icelandair
	TF-FLO	F.27 Friendship Mk 200	Icelandair
	TF-FLP	F.27 Friendship Mk 200	Icelandair
	TF-FLS	F.27 Friendship Mk 200	Icelandair
	TF-	Fokker 50	Icelandair
	TF-	Fokker 50	Icelandair
	TF-	Fokker 50	Icelandair
	TF-	Fokker 50	Icelandair
	TF-RMR	Boeing 727-225	Atlantic Island Air

TJ (Cameroon)

	TJ-CAB	Boeing 747-2H7B (SCD)	Cameroon Airlines *Mont Cameroun*

TR (Gabon)

	TR-LBV	L-100-30 Hercules	Air Gabon Cargo

Note: Air Gabon operates Boeing 747-2Q2B F-ODJG on lease which will become TR-LXK.

TS (Tunisia)

	TS-IMA	Airbus A.300B4	Tunis-Air *Amilcar*
	TS-IMB	Airbus A.320-211	Tunis-Air *Fahrat Hached*
	TS-IMC	Airbus A.320-211	Tunis-Air *7 Novembre*
	TS-IMD	Airbus A.320-211	Tunis-Air *Khereddine*
	TS-	Airbus A.320-211	Tunis-Air
	TS-IOC	Boeing 737-2H3	Tunis-Air *Salammbo*
	TS-IOD	Boeing 737-2H3C	Tunis-Air *Bulla Regia*
	TS-IOE	Boeing 737-2H3	Tunis-Air *Zarzis*
	TS-IOF	Boeing 737-2H3	Tunis-Air *Sousse*
	TS-	Boeing 737-5H3	Tunis-Air
	TS-	Boeing 737-5H3	Tunis-Air
	TS-JHN	Boeing 727-2H3	Tunis-Air *Carthago*
	TS-JHQ	Boeing 727-2H3	Tunis-Air *Tozeur-Nefta*
	TS-JHR	Boeing 727-2H3	Tunis-Air *Bizerte*

Reg.	Type	Owner or Operator	Notes
TS-JHS	Boeing 727-2H3	Tunis-Air *Kairouan*	
TS-JHT	Boeing 727-2H3	Tunis-Air *Sidi Bousaid*	
TS-JHU	Boeing 727-2H3	Tunis-Air *Hannibal*	
TS-JHV	Boeing 727-2H3	Tunis-Air *Jugurtha*	
TS-JHW	Boeing 727-2H3	Tunis-Air *Ibn Khaldoun*	

TU (Ivory Coast)

TU-TAC	Airbus A.310-304	Air Afrique	
TU-TAL	Douglas DC-10-30	Air Afrique *Libreville*	
TU-TAM	Douglas DC-10-30	Air Afrique	
TU-TAN	Douglas DC-10-30	Air Afrique *Niamey*	
TU-TAO	Airbus A.300B4-203	Air Afrique *Nouackchott*	
TU-TAS	Airbus A.300B4-203	Air Afrique *Bangui*	
TU-TAT	Airbus A.300B4-203	Air Afrique	
TU-TCF	Douglas DC-8-63CF	Air Afrique *Ndjamena*	

V2 (Antigua)

Note: Seagreen Air Transport operates two Boeing 707s registered N14AZ and N18AZ.

V5 (Namibia)

V5-SPF	Boeing 747SP-44	Air Namibia	

V8 (Brunei)

V8-RBA	Boeing 757-2M6ER	Royal Brunei Airlines	
V8-RBB	Boeing 757-2M6ER	Royal Brunei Airlines	
V8-RBC	Boeing 757-2M6ER	Royal Brunei Airlines	
V8-RBD	Boeing 767-284ER	Royal Brunei Airlines	
V8-RBE	Boeing 767-33AER	Royal Brunei Airlines	

VH (Australia)

VH-EBA	Boeing 747-238B	Qantas Airways *City of Ipswich*	
VH-EBB	Boeing 747-238B	Qantas Airways *City of Newcastle*	
VH-EBP	Boeing 747-238B	Qantas Airways *City of Adelaide*	
VH-EBQ	Boeing 747-238B	Qantas Airways *City of Bunbury*	
VH-EBR	Boeing 747-238B	Qantas Airways *City of Hobart*	
VH-EBS	Boeing 747-238B	Qantas Airways *City of Longreach*	
VH-EBT	Boeing 747-338	Qantas Airways *City of Wagga Wagga*	
VH-EBU	Boeing 747-338	Qantas Airways *City of Warrnambool*	
VH-EBV	Boeing 747-338	Qantas Airways *Geraldton*	
VH-EBW	Boeing 747-338	Qantas Airways *City of Tamworth*	
VH-EBX	Boeing 747-338	Qantas Airways *City of Wodonga*	
VH-EBY	Boeing 747-338	Qantas Airways *City of Mildura*	
VH-OJA	Boeing 747-438	Qantas Airways *City of Canberra*	
VH-OJB	Boeing 747-438	Qantas Airways *City of Sydney*	
VH-OJC	Boeing 747-438	Qantas Airways *City of Melbourne*	
VH-OJD	Boeing 747-438	Qantas Airways *City of Brisbane*	
VH-OJE	Boeing 747-438	Qantas Airways *City of Adelaide*	
VH-OJF	Boeing 747-438	Qantas Airways *City of Perth*	
VH-OJG	Boeing 747-438	Qantas Airways *City of Hobart*	
VH-OJH	Boeing 747-438	Qantas Airways *City of Darwin*	
VH-OJI	Boeing 747-438	Qantas Airways *Longreach*	
VH-OJJ	Boeing 747-438	Qantas Airways *Winton*	
VH-OJK	Boeing 747-438	Qantas Airways *City of Sale*	
VH-OJL	Boeing 747-438	Qantas Airways *City of Gosford*	
VH-OJM	Boeing 747-438	Qantas Airways *City of Ballaret*	
VH-OJN	Boeing 747-438	Qantas Airways *City of Dubbo*	
VH-OJO	Boeing 747-438	Qantas Airways	
VH-OJP	Boeing 747-438	Qantas Airways	

VR-H (Hong Kong)

VR-HIA	Boeing 747-267B	Cathay Pacific Airways	
VR-HIB	Boeing 747-267B	Cathay Pacific Airways	
VR-HIC	Boeing 747-267B	Cathay Pacific Airways	
VR-HID	Boeing 747-267B	Cathay Pacific Airways	

Notes	Reg.	Type	Owner or Operator
	VR-HIE	Boeing 747-267B	Cathay Pacific Airways
	VR-HIF	Boeing 747-267B	Cathay Pacific Airways
	VR-HIH	Boeing 747-267B	Cathay Pacific Airways
	VR-HII	Boeing 747-367	Cathay Pacific Airways
	VR-HIJ	Boeing 747-367	Cathay Pacific Airways
	VR-HIK	Boeing 747-367	Cathay Pacific Airways
	VR-HKG	Boeing 747-267B	Cathay Pacific Airways
	VR-HKK	Boeing 707-336C	Air Hong Kong
	VR-HKL	Boeing 707-321C	Air Hong Kong
	VR-HKM	Boeing 747-132F	Air Hong Kong
	VR-HKN	Boeing 747-132F	Air Hong Kong
	VR-HOL	Boeing 747-367	Cathay Pacific Airways
	VR-HOM	Boeing 747-367	Cathay Pacific Airways
	VR-HON	Boeing 747-367	Cathay Pacific Airways
	VR-HOO	Boeing 747-467	Cathay Pacific Airways
	VR-HOP	Boeing 747-467	Cathay Pacific Airways
	VR-HOR	Boeing 747-467	Cathay Pacific Airways
	VR-HOS	Boeing 747-467	Cathay Pacific Airways
	VR-HOT	Boeing 747-467	Cathay Pacific Airways
	VR-HOU	Boeing 747-467	Cathay Pacific Airways
	VR-HOV	Boeing 747-467	Cathay Pacific Airways
	VR-HOW	Boeing 747-467	Cathay Pacific Airways
	VR-HOX	Boeing 747-467	Cathay Pacific Airways
	VR-HOY	Boeing 747-467	Cathay Pacific Airways
	VR-HOZ	Boeing 747-467	Cathay Pacific Airways
	VR-	Boeing 747-467	Cathay Pacific Airways
	VR-	Boeing 747-467	Cathay Pacific Airways
	VR-HVX	Boeing 747-267F (SCD)	Cathay Pacific Airways
	VR-HVY	Boeing 747-236F (SCD)	Cathay Pacific Airways *Hong Kong Jumbo*
	VR-HVZ	Boeing 747-267F (SCD)	Cathay Pacific Airways

VT (India)

VT-EBE	Boeing 747-237B	Air-India *Emperor Shahjehan*
VT-EBN	Boeing 747-237B	Air-India *Emperor Rajendra Chola*
VT-EBO	Boeing 747-237B	Air-India *Emperor Vikramaditya*
VT-EDU	Boeing 747-237B	Air-India *Emperor Akbar*
VT-EFJ	Boeing 747-237B	Air-India *Emperor Chandragupta*
VT-EFU	Boeing 747-237B	Air-India *Emperor Krishna Deva Royal*
VT-EGA	Boeing 747-237B	Air-India *Emperor Samudra Gupta*
VT-EGB	Boeing 747-237B	Air-India *Emperor Mahendra Varman*
VT-EGC	Boeing 747-237B	Air-India *Emperor Harsha Vardhana*
VT-EJG	Airbus A.310-304	Air-India *Vamuna*
VT-EJH	Airbus A.310-304	Air-India *Tista*
VT-EJI	Airbus A.310-304	Air-India *Saraswati*
VT-EJJ	Airbus A.310-304	Air-India *Beas*
VT-EJK	Airbus A.310-304	Air-India *Gomti*
VT-EJL	Airbus A.310-304	Air-India *Sabarmati*
VT-ENQ	Boeing 747-212B	Air-India *Himalaya*
VT-EPW	Boeing 747-337 (SCD)	Air-India *Shivaji*
VT-EPX	Boeing 747-337 (SCD)	Air-India *Narasimha Varman*
VT-EQS	Airbus A.310-304	Air-India *Krishna*
VT-EQT	Airbus A.310-304	Air-India *Narmada*

Note: Air-India Cargo operates Douglas DC-8s and Boeing 747s on lease from various airlines.

XA (Mexico)

XA-AMR	Douglas DC-10-30	Aeromexico
XA-RIY	Douglas DC-10-30	Aeromexico *Jose Marie Morelos*

Note: Aeromexico also operates DC-10-30s N8228P *Castillo de Chapultepec* and N417DG *Ciudad de Mexico*.

XT (Burkina Faso)

XT-ABX	Boeing 707-336C	Naganagani

YI (Iraq)

YI-AGE	Boeing 707-370C	Iraqi Airways
YI-AGF	Boeing 707-370C	Iraqi Airways
YI-AGG	Boeing 707-370C	Iraqi Airways
YI-AGK	Boeing 727-270	Iraqi Airways *Ninevah*

Reg.	Type	Owner or Operator	Notes
YI-AGL	Boeing 727-270	Iraqi Airways *Basrah*	
YI-AGM	Boeing 727-270	Iraqi Airways	
YI-AGN	Boeing 747-270C (SCD)	Iraqi Airways *Tigris*	
YI-AGO	Boeing 747-270C (SCD)	Iraqi Airways *Euphrates*	
YI-AGP	Boeing 747-270C (SCD)	Iraqi Airways *Shat-al-Arab*	
YI-AGQ	Boeing 727-270	Iraqi Airways *Ataameem*	
YI-AGR	Boeing 727-270	Iraqi Airways *Babylon*	
YI-AGS	Boeing 727-270	Iraqi Airways	
YI-AKO	Ilyushin IL-76M	Iraqi Airways	
YI-AKP	Ilyushin IL-76M	Iraqi Airways	
YI-AKQ	Ilyushin IL-76M	Iraqi Airways	
YI-AKS	Ilyushin IL-76M	Iraqi Airways	
YI-AKT	Ilyushin IL-76M	Iraqi Airways	
YI-AKU	Ilyushin IL-76M	Iraqi Airways	
YI-AKV	Ilyushin IL-76M	Iraqi Airways	
YI-AKW	Ilyushin IL-76M	Iraqi Airways	
YI-AKX	Ilyushin IL-76M	Iraqi Airways	
YI-ALL	Ilyushin IL-76M	Iraqi Airways	
YI-ALP	Ilyushin IL-76M	Iraqi Airways	
YI-ALQ	Ilyushin IL-76MD	Iraqi Airways	
YI-ALR	Ilyushin IL-76MD	Iraqi Airways	
YI-ALS	Ilyushin IL-76MD	Iraqi Airways	
YI-ALT	Ilyushin IL-76MD	Iraqi Airways	
YI-ALU	Ilyushin IL-76MD	Iraqi Airways	
YI-ALV	Ilyushin IL-76MD	Iraqi Airways	
YI-ALW	Ilyushin IL-76MD	Iraqi Airways	
YI-ALX	Ilyushin IL-76MD	Iraqi Airways	
YI-ANA	Ilyushin IL-76MD	Iraqi Airways	
YI-ANB	Ilyushin IL-76MD	Iraqi Airways	
YI-ANC	Ilyushin IL-76MD	Iraqi Airways	
YI-AND	Ilyushin IL-76MD	Iraqi Airways	
YI-ANE	Ilyushin IL-76MD	Iraqi Airways	
YI-ANF	Ilyushin IL-76MD	Iraqi Airways	
YI-ANG	Ilyushin IL-76MD	Iraqi Airways	
YI-ANH	Ilyushin IL-76MD	Iraqi Airways	
YI-ANI	Ilyushin IL-76MD	Iraqi Airways	

YK (Syria)

Reg.	Type	Owner or Operator	Notes
YK-AGA	Boeing 727-294	Syrian Arab Airlines *October 6*	
YK-AGB	Boeing 727-294	Syrian Arab Airlines *Damascus*	
YK-AGC	Boeing 727-294	Syrian Arab Airlines *Palmyra*	
YK-AHA	Boeing 747SP-94	Syrian Arab Airlines *16 Novembre*	
YK-AHB	Boeing 747SP-94	Syrian Arab Airlines *Arab Solidarity*	
YK-AIA	Tupolev Tu-154M	Syrian Arab Airlines	
YK-AIB	Tupolev Tu-154M	Syrian Arab Airlines	
YK-AIC	Tupolev Tu-154M	Syrian Arab Airlines	
YK-ATA	Ilyushin IL-76M	Syrian Arab Airlines	
YK-ATB	Ilyushin IL-76M	Syrian Arab Airlines	
YK-ATC	Ilyushin IL-76M	Syrian Arab Airlines	
YK-ATD	Ilyushin IL-76M	Syrian Arab Airlines	

YR (Romania)

Reg.	Type	Owner or Operator	Notes
YR-ABA	Boeing 707-3K1C	Tarom	
YR-ABC	Boeing 707-3K1C	Tarom	
YR-ABM	Boeing 707-321C	Tarom	
YR-ABN	Boeing 707-321C	Tarom	
YR-ADA	Antonov 26	Tarom	
YR-ADB	Antonov 26	Tarom	
YR-ADC	Antonov 26	Tarom	
YR-ADE	Antonov 26	Tarom	
YR-ADG	Antonov 26	Tarom	
YR-ADH	Antonov 26	Tarom	
YR-ADJ	Antonov 26	Tarom	
YR-ADK	Antonov 26	Tarom	
YR-ADL	Antonov 26	Tarom	
YR-ADM	Antonov 26	Tarom	
YR-ADN	Antonov 26	Tarom	
YR-	Airbus A.310-325	Tarom	
YR-	Airbus A.310-325	Tarom	
YR-	Airbus A.310-325	Tarom	
YR-BCG	BAC One-Eleven 401AK	Tarom	

Notes	Reg.	Type	Owner or Operator
	YR-BCH	BAC One-Eleven 402AP	Tarom
	YR-BCI	BAC One-Eleven 525FT	Tarom
	YR-BCJ	BAC One-Eleven 525FT	Tarom
	YR-BCK	BAC One-Eleven 525FT	Tarom
	YR-BCL	BAC One-Eleven 525FT	Tarom
	YR-BCN	BAC One-Eleven 525FT	Tarom
	YR-BCO	BAC One Eleven 525FT	Tarom
	YR-BRA	RomBac One-Eleven 561RC	Tarom
	YR-BRB	RomBac One-Eleven 561RC	Tarom
	YR-BRC	RomBac One-Eleven 561RC	Tarom
	YR-BRD	RomBac One-Eleven 561RC	Tarom
	YR-BRE	RomBac One-Eleven 561RC	Tarom
	YR-BRF	RomBac One-Eleven 561RC	Tarom
	YR-BRH	RomBac One-Eleven 561RC	Tarom
	YR-IMA	Ilyushin IL-18D	Tarom
	YR-IMD	Ilyushin IL-18V	Tarom
	YR-IME	Ilyushin IL-18V	Tarom
	YR-IMF	Ilyushin IL-18V	Tarom
	YR-IMG	Ilyushin IL-18V	Tarom
	YR-IMJ	Ilyushin IL-18D	Tarom
	YR-IML	Ilyushin IL-18D	Tarom
	YR-IRA	Ilyushin IL-62	Tarom
	YR-IRB	Ilyushin IL-62	Tarom
	YR-IRC	Ilyushin IL-62	Tarom
	YR-IRD	Ilyushin IL-62M	Tarom
	YR-IRE	Ilyushin IL-62M	Tarom
	YR-TPA	Tupolev Tu-154B	Tarom
	YR-TPB	Tupolev Tu-154B	Tarom
	YR-TPC	Tupolev Tu-154B	Tarom
	YR-TPD	Tupolev Tu-154B	Tarom
	YR-TPE	Tupolev Tu-154B-1	Tarom
	YR-TPF	Tupolev Tu-154B-1	Tarom
	YR-TPG	Tupolev Tu-154B-1	Tarom
	YR-TPI	Tupolev Tu-154B-2	Tarom
	YR-TPK	Tupolev Tu-154B-2	Tarom
	YR-TPL	Tupolev Tu-154B-2	Tarom

YU (Yugoslavia)

Notes	Reg.	Type	Owner or Operator
	YU-AGE	Boeing 707-340C	Jugoslovenski Aerotransport
	YU-AGG	Boeing 707-340C	Jugoslovenski Aerotransport
	YU-AHJ	Douglas DC-9-32	Adria Airways
	YU-AHN	Douglas DC-9-32	Jugoslovenski Aerotransport
	YU-AHU	Douglas DC-9-32	Jugoslovenski Aerotransport
	YU-AHV	Douglas DC-9-32	Jugoslovenski Aerotransport
	YU-AHW	Douglas DC-9-33RC	Adria Airways
	YU-AJF	Douglas DC-9-32	Adria Airways
	YU-AJH	Douglas DC-9-32	Jugoslovenski Aerotransport
	YU-AJI	Douglas DC-9-32	Jugoslovenski Aerotransport
	YU-AJJ	Douglas DC-9-32	Jugoslovenski Aerotransport .
	YU-AJK	Douglas DC-9-32	Jugoslovenski Aerotransport
	YU-AJL	Douglas DC-9-32	Jugoslovenski Aerotransport
	YU-AJM	Douglas DC-9-32	Jugoslovenski Aerotransport
	YU-AJZ	McD Douglas MD-81	Adria Airways
	YU-AKB	Boeing 727-2H9	Jugoslovenski Aerotransport
	YU-AKD	Boeing 727-2L8	Aviogenex *Split*
	YU-AKE	Boeing 727-2H9	Jugoslovenski Aerotransport
	YU-AKF	Boeing 727-2H9	Jugoslovenski Aerotransport
	YU-AKG	Boeing 727-2H9	Jugoslovenski Aerotransport
	YU-AKH	Boeing 727-2L8	Aviogenex *Dubrovnik*
	YU-AKI	Boeing 727-2H9	Jugoslovenski Aerotransport
	YU-AKJ	Boeing 727-2H9	Jugoslovenski Aerotransport
	YU-AKK	Boeing 727-2H9	Jugoslovenski Aerotransport
	YU-AKL	Boeing 727-2H9	Jugoslovenski Aerotransport
	YU-AKM	Boeing 727-243	Aviogenex *Pula*
	YU-AKO	Boeing 727-276	Aviogenex
	YU-AMA	Douglas DC-10-30	Jugoslovenski Aerotransport *Nikola Tesla*
	YU-AMB	Douglas DC-10-30	Jugoslovenski Aerotransport *Edvard Rusijan*
	YU-AMC	Douglas DC-10-30	Jugoslovenski Aerotransport
	YU-AMD	Douglas DC-10-30	Jugoslovenski Aerotransport
	YU-AME	McD Douglas MD-11	Jugoslovenski Aerotransport
	YU-AMF	McD Douglas MD-11	Jugoslovenski Aerotransport
	YU-AMG	McD Douglas MD-11	Jugoslovenski Aerotransport

Reg.	Type	Owner or Operator	Notes
YU-ANB	McD Douglas MD-82	Adria Airways	
YU-ANC	McD Douglas MD-82	Adria Airways	
YU-AND	Boeing 737-3H9	Jugoslovenski Aerotransport	
YU-ANF	Boeing 737-3H9	Jugoslovenski Aerotransport	
YU-ANG	McD Douglas MD-82	Adria Airways	
YU-ANH	Boeing 737-3H9	Jugoslovenski Aerotransport	
YU-ANI	Boeing 737-3H9	Jugoslovenski Aerotransport	
YU-ANJ	Boeing 737-3H9	Jugoslovenski Aerotransport	
YU-ANK	Boeing 737-3H9	Jugoslovenski Aerotransport	
YU-ANL	Boeing 737-3H9	Jugoslovenski Aerotransport	
YU-ANO	McD Douglas MD-82	Adria Airways	
YU-ANP	Boeing 737-2K3	Aviogenex *Zadar*	
YU-ANU	Boeing 737-2K3	Aviogenex *Tivat*	
YU-ANV	Boeing 737-3H9	Jugoslovenski Aerotransport	
YU-ANW	Boeing 737-3H9	Jugoslovenski Aerotransport	
YU-AOA	Airbus A.320-231	Adria Airways	
YU-AOD	Airbus A.320-231	Adria Airways	
YU-AOE	Airbus A.320-231	Adria Airways	
YU-AOF	Boeing 737-2K5	Aviogenex	
YU-AOG	Boeing 737-2K5	Aviogenex	

YV (Venezuela)

YV-134C	Douglas DC-10-30	Viasa	
YV-135C	Douglas DC-10-30	Viasa	
YV-136C	Douglas DC-10-30	Viasa	
YV-137C	Douglas DC-10-30	Viasa	
YV-138C	Douglas DC-10-30	Viasa	
YV-139C	Douglas DC-10-30	Viasa	

Z (Zimbabwe)

Z-WKS	Boeing 707-330B	Air Zimbabwe	
Z-WKU	Boeing 707-330B	Air Zimbabwe	
Z-WMJ	Douglas DC-8-55F	Affretair *Captain Jack Malloch*	
Z-WPE	Boeing 767-2N0ER	Air Zimbabwe *Victoria Falls*	
Z-WPF	Boeing 767-2N0ER	Air Zimbabwe	
Z-WSB	Douglas DC-8-55F	Affretair	

ZK (New Zealand)

ZK-NBS	Boeing 747-419	Air New Zealand *Mataatua*	
ZK-NBT	Boeing 747-419	Air New Zealand	
ZK-N	Boeing 747-419	Air New Zealand	
ZK-NZV	Boeing 747-219B	Air New Zealand *Aotea*	
ZK-NZW	Boeing 747-219B	Air New Zealand *Tainui*	
ZK-NZX	Boeing 747-219B	Air New Zealand *Takitimu*	
ZK-NZY	Boeing 747-219B	Air New Zealand *Te Arawa*	
ZK-NZZ	Boeing 747-219B	Air New Zealand *Tokomaru*	

ZP (Paraguay)

ZP-CCE	Boeing 707-321B	Lineas Aéreas Paraguayas	
ZP-CCF	Boeing 707-321B	Lineas Aéreas Paraguayas	
ZP-CCG	Boeing 707-321B	Lineas Aéreas Paraguayas	
ZP-CCH	Douglas DC-8-63	Lineas Aéreas Paraguayas	

ZS (South Africa)

ZS-SAL	Boeing 747-244B	South African Airways *Tafelberg*	
ZS-SAM	Boeing 747-244B	South African Airways *Drakensberg*	
ZS-SAN	Boeing 747-244B	South African Airways *Lebombo*	
ZS-SAO	Boeing 747-244B	South African Airways *Magaliesberg*	
ZS-SAP	Boeing 747-244B	South African Airways *Swartberg*	
ZS-SAR	Boeing 747-244B (SCD)	South African Airways *Waterberg*	
ZS-SAT	Boeing 747-344	South African Airways *Johannesburg*	
ZS-SAU	Boeing 747-344	South African Airways *Cape Town*	
ZS-SAV	Boeing 747-444	South African Airways *Durban*	
ZS-SAW	Boeing 747-444	South African Airways *Bloemfontein*	

Notes	Reg.	Type	Owner or Operator

3B (Mauritius)

	3B-NAG	Boeing 747SP-44	Air Mauritius *Chateau du Reduit*
	3B-NAJ	Boeing 747SP-44	Air Mauritius *Chateau Mon Plaisir*
	3B-NAK	Boeing 767-23BER	Air Mauritius *City of Curepipe*
	3B-NAL	Boeing 767-23BER	Air Mauritius *City of Port Louis*
	3B-NAQ	Boeing 747SP-27	Air Mauritius *Chateau Benares*
	3B-NAR	Boeing 747SP-44	Air Mauritius

3D (Swaziland)

	3D-ASB	Boeing 707-323C	Air Swazi Cargo

4R (Sri Lanka)

	4R-ULA	L.1011-385 TriStar 500	Air Lanka
	4R-ULB	L.1011-385 TriStar 500	Air Lanka
	4R-ULC	L.1011-385 TriStar 100	Air Lanka *City of Jayawardanapura*
	4R-ULE	L.1011-385 TriStar 50	Air Lanka *City of Ratnapura*
	4R-ULM	L.1011-385 TriStar 200	Air Lanka
	4R-ULN	L.1011-385 TriStar 200	Air Lanka

4X (Israel)

	4X-ABN	Boeing 737-258	El Al/Arkia
	4X-ABO	Boeing 737-258	El Al/Arkia
	4X-ATG	Boeing 707-323B	Arkia
	4X-ATX	Boeing 707-358C	El Al/Arkia
	4X-AXA	Boeing 747-258B	El Al
	4X-AXB	Boeing 747-258B	El Al
	4X-AXC	Boeing 747-258B	El Al
	4X-AXD	Boeing 747-258C	El Al
	4X-AXF	Boeing 747-258C	El Al
	4X-AXG	Boeing 747-258F (SCD)	El Al
	4X-AXH	Boeing 747-258B	El Al
	4X-AXQ	Boeing 747-238B	El Al
	4X-AXZ	Boeing 747-124F (SCD)	El Al
	4X-EAA	Boeing 767-258	El Al
	4X-EAB	Boeing 767-258	El Al
	4X-EAC	Boeing 767-258ER	El Al
	4X-EAD	Boeing 767-258ER	El Al
	4X-EBL	Boeing 757-258	El Al
	4X-EBM	Boeing 757-258	El Al
	4X-EBR	Boeing 757-258	El Al
	4X-EBS	Boeing 757-258ER	El Al
	4X-EBT	Boeing 757-258ER	El Al
	4X-ELA	Boeing 757-458	El Al
	4X-ELB	Boeing 757-458	El Al

5A (Libya)

	5A-DAI	Boeing 727-224	Libyan Arab Airlines
	5A-DAK	Boeing 707-3L5C	Libyan Arab Airlines
	5A-DIA	Boeing 727-2L5	Libyan Arab Airlines
	5A-DIB	Boeing 727-2L5	Libyan Arab Airlines
	5A-DIC	Boeing 727-2L5	Libyan Arab Airlines
	5A-DID	Boeing 727-2L5	Libyan Arab Airlines
	5A-DIE	Boeing 727-2L5	Libyan Arab Airlines
	5A-DIF	Boeing 727-2L5	Libyan Arab Airlines
	5A-DIG	Boeing 727-2L5	Libyan Arab Airlines
	5A-DIH	Boeing 727-2L5	Libyan Arab Airlines
	5A-DII	Boeing 727-2L5	Libyan Arab Airlines
	5A-DIX	Boeing 707-348C	Libyan Arab Airlines
	5A-DIY	Boeing 707-348C	Libyan Arab Airlines
	5A-DJM	Boeing 707-321B	Libyan Arab Airlines
	5A-DJU	Boeing 707-351C	Libyan Arab Airlines
	5A-	Tupolev Tu-154M	Libyan Arab Airlines

Note: Services to the UK suspended.

Reg.	Type	Owner or Operator	Notes

5B (Cyprus)

5B-DAG	BAC One Eleven 537GF	Cyprus Airways	
5B-DAH	BAC One Eleven 537GF	Cyprus Airways	
5B-DAJ	BAC One Eleven 537GF	Cyprus Airways	
5B-DAQ	Airbus A.310-203	Cyprus Airways *Soli*	
5B-DAR	Airbus A.310-203	Cyprus Airways	
5B-DAS	Airbus A.310-203	Cyprus Airways *Salamis*	
5B-DAT	Airbus A.320-231	Cyprus Airways *Praxandros*	
5B-DAU	Airbus A.320-231	Cyprus Airways	
5B-DAV	Airbus A.320-231	Cyprus Airways *Kinyras*	
5B-DAW	Airbus A.320-231	Cyprus Airways *Agapinor*	
5B-DAX	Airbus A.310-204	Cyprus Airways *Engomi*	
5B-DAY	Boeing 707-338C	Avistar	
5B-	Airbus A.320-231	Cyprus Airways	
5B-DBA	Airbus A.320-231	Cyprus Airways	
5B-DBB	Airbus A.320-231	Eurocypria Airways	
5B-DBC	Airbus A.320-231	Eurocypria Airways	

5H (Tanzania)

Note: Air Tanzania operates a Boeing 767-260ER ET-AIZ on lease from Ethiopean Airlines.

5N (Nigeria)

5N-ABK	Boeing 707-3F9C	Nigeria Airways	
5N-ANN	Douglas DC-10-30	Nigeria Airways *Yunkari*	
5N-AOK	BAC One-Eleven 320AZ	Okada Air	
5N-AOM	BAC One-Eleven 420EL	Okada Air	
5N-AOP	BAC One-Eleven 320AZ	Okada Air	
5N-AOQ	Boeing 707-355C	Okada Air	
5N-AOS	BAC One-Eleven 420EL	Okada Air	
5N-AOZ	BAC One-Eleven 320AZ	Okada Air	
5N-ARQ	Boeing 707-338C	DAS Air Cargo	
5N-ASY	Boeing 707-351C	EAS Cargo	
5N-ATY	Douglas DC-8-55F	Flash Airlines	
5N-ATZ	Douglas DC-8-55F	Flash Airlines	
5N-AUE	Airbus A.310-222	Nigeria Airways *River Yobe*	
5N-AUF	Airbus A.310-222	Nigeria Airways	
5N-AUH	Airbus A.310-222	Nigeria Airways *Rima River*	
5N-AVX	BAC One-Eleven 424EU	G.A.S. Air	
5N-AWE	Douglas DC-8-55F	Kabo Air	
5N-AWO	Boeing 707-321C	G.A.S. Air	
5N-AXQ	BAC One-Eleven 432FD	Okada Air	
5N-AXT	BAC One-Eleven 432FD	Okada Air	
5N-AYR	BAC One-Eleven 409AY	Okada Air	
5N-AYS	BAC One-Eleven 416EK	Okada Air	
5N-AYT	BAC One-Eleven 416EK	Okada Air	
5N-AYU	BAC One-Eleven 401AK	Okada Air	
5N-AYV	BAC One-Eleven 408EF	Okada Air	
5N-AYW	BAC One-Eleven 416EK	Okada Air	
5N-BIN	BAC One-Eleven 539GL	Okada Air	
5N-EHI	BAC One-Eleven 401AK	Okada Air	
5N-KBM	BAC One-Eleven 215AU	Kabo Air	
5N-KBT	BAC One-Eleven 204AF	Kabo Air	
5N-OMO	BAC One-Eleven 301AG	Okada Air	
5N-ORO	BAC One-Eleven 539GL	Okada Air	
5N-TOM	BAC One-Eleven 217EA	Okada Air	

Note: Nigeria Airways operates a DC-10-30 which retains its US identity N3024W (5N-AUI reserved)

5R (Madagascar)

5R-MFT	Boeing 747-2B2B (SCD)	Air Madagascar *Tolom Piavotana*	

5X (Uganda)

5X-ARQ	Boeing 707-338C	DAS Air Cargo	
5X-DAR	Boeing 707-321C	DAS Air Cargo	
5X-UCF	L-100-30 Hercules	Uganda Air Cargo *The Silver Lady*	
5X-UCM	Boeing 707-324C	Uganda Airlines	

Notes	Reg.	Type	Owner or Operator

5Y (Kenya)

5Y-AXG	Boeing 707-321C	RACE Cargo Airlines
5Y-BEL	Airbus A.310-304	Kenya Airways *Nyayo Star*
5Y-BEN	Airbus A.310-304	Kenya Airways *Harambee Star*
5Y-BFT	Airbus A310-304	Kenya Airways *Uhuru Star*
5Y-BGI	Boeing 757-23A	Kenya Airways *Jamhuri Star*
5Y-BHG	Boeing 757-23A	Kenya Airways *Umoja Star*
5Y-ZEB	Douglas DC-8-63	African Safari Airways

Note: African Safari also operates DC-8-63 which carries the registration HB-IBF.

6O (Somalia)

6O-SBT	Boeing 707-330B	Somali Airlines
6O-SHH	Airbus A.310-304	Somali Airlines

Note: The A.310 may retain its French identity F-ODSV

6Y (Jamaica)

Note: Air Jamaica operates its UK services jointly with British Airways.

7O (Yemen)

7O-ACT	Tupolev Tu-154M	Alyemda
7O-ACV	Boeing 727-2N8	Yemenia (ex 4W-ACF)
7O-ACW	Boeing 727-2N8	Yemenia (ex 4W-ACG)
7O-ACX	Boeing 727-2N8	Yemenia (ex 4W-ACH)
7O-ACY	Boeing 727-2N8	Yemenia (ex 4W-ACI)
7O-ACZ	Boeing 727-2N8	Yemenia (ex 4W-ACJ)

7T (Algeria)

7T-VEA	Boeing 727-2D6	Air Algerie *Tassili*
7T-VEB	Boeing 727-2D6	Air Algerie *Hoggar*
7T-VED	Boeing 737-2D6C	Air Algerie *Atlas Saharien*
7T-VEE	Boeing 737-2D6C	Air Algerie *Oasis*
7T-VEF	Boeing 737-2D6	Air Algerie *Saoura*
7T-VEG	Boeing 737-2D6	Air Algerie *Monts des Ouleds Neils*
7T-VEH	Boeing 737-2D6	Air Algerie *Lalla Khadidja*
7T-VEI	Boeing 727-2D6	Air Algerie *Djebel Amour*
7T-VEJ	Boeing 737-2D6	Air Algerie *Chrea*
7T-VEK	Boeing 737-2D6	Air Algerie *Edough*
7T-VEL	Boeing 737-2D6	Air Algerie *Akfadou*
7T-VEM	Boeing 737-2D6	Air Algerie *Mont du Ksall*
7T-VEN	Boeing 737-2D6	Air Algerie *La Soummam*
7T-VEO	Boeing 737-2D6	Air Algerie *La Titteri*
7T-VEP	Boeing 727-2D6	Air Algerie *Mont du Tessala*
7T-VEQ	Boeing 727-2D6	Air Algerie *Le Zaccar*
7T-VER	Boeing 737-2D6	Air Algerie *Le Souf*
7T-VES	Boeing 737-2D6C	Air Algerie *Le Tadmaït*
7T-VET	Boeing 727-2D6	Air Algerie *Georges du Rhumel*
7T-VEU	Boeing 727-2D6	Air Algerie *Djurdjura*
7T-VEV	Boeing 727-2D6	Air Algerie
7T-VEW	Boeing 727-2D6	Air Algerie
7T-VEX	Boeing 727-2D6	Air Algerie *Djemila*
7T-VEY	Boeing 737-2D6	Air Algerie *Rhoufi*
7T-VEZ	Boeing 737-2T4	Air Algerie *Monts du Daia*
7T-VJA	Boeing 737-2T4	Air Algerie *Monts des Babors*
7T-VJB	Boeing 737-2T4	Air Algerie *Monts des Bibons*
7T-VJC	Airbus A.310-203	Air Algerie
7T-VJD	Airbus A.310-203	Air Algerie
7T-VJE	Airbus A.310-203	Air Algerie/Libyan Arab
7T-VJF	Airbus A.310-203	Air Algerie
7T-VJG	Boeing 767-3D6	Air Algerie
7T-VJH	Boeing 767-3D6	Air Algerie
7T-VJI	Boeing 767-3D6	Air Algerie

9G (Ghana)

9G-ANA	Douglas DC-10-30	Ghana Airways
9G-MKA	Douglas DC-8-55F	MK Air Cargo
9G-OLF	Boeing 707-379C	RACE Cargo Airlines

Note: RACE Cargo Airlines also operates a 707 registered 5Y-AXG.

Reg.	Type	Owner or Operator	Notes

9H (Malta)

9H-ABA	Boeing 737-2Y5	Air Malta *Manuel de Vilhena*	
9H-ABB	Boeing 737-2Y5	Air Malta *Phillipe Villiers de L'isle Adam*	
9H-ABC	Boeing 737-2Y5	Air Malta *Claude de la Sengle*	
9H-ABE	Boeing 737-2Y5	Air Malta *Alof de Wignacourt*	
9H-ABF	Boeing 737-2Y5	Air Malta *Manuel Pinto*	
9H-ABG	Boeing 737-2Y5	Air Malta *Jean de Lavalette*	
9H-ABP	Airbus A.320-211	Air Malta *Nicholas de Cottoner*	
9H-ABQ	Airbus A.320-211	Air Malta	

Note: Air Malta also operates other aircraft on lease during the summer.

9J (Zambia)

9J-AFL	Douglas DC-8-71	Zambia Airways	
9J-AFO	Boeing 757-23APF	Zambia Airways	

Note: Zambia Airways operates DC-10-30 N3016Z *Nkwazi* on lease.

9K (Kuwait)

9K-ADA	Boeing 747-269B (SCD)	Kuwait Airways *Al Sabahiya*	
9K-ADB	Boeing 747-269B (SCD)	Kuwait Airways *Al Jaberiya*	
9K-ADC	Boeing 747-269B (SCD)	Kuwait Airways *Al Murbarakiya*	
9K-ADD	Boeing 747-269B (SCD)	Kuwait Airways *Al Salmiya*	
9K-AHA	Airbus A.310-222	Kuwait Airways *Al-Jahra*	
9K-AHB	Airbus A.310-222	Kuwait Airways *Gharnada*	
9K-AHC	Airbus A.310-222	Kuwait Airways *Kadhma*	
9K-AHD	Airbus A.310-222	Kuwait Airways *Failaka*	
9K-AHE	Airbus A.310-222	Kuwait Airways *Burghan*	
9K-AHI	Airbus A.300-620C	Kuwait Airways *Ali-Rawdhatain*	
9K-AIA	Boeing 767-269ER	Kuwait Airways *Alriggah*	
9K-AIC	Boeing 767-269ER	Kuwait Airways *Garouh*	

Note: Many of Kuwait's fleet were seized by Iraq in August 1990. Five A.310s registered
A6-KUA, A6-KUB, A6-KUC, A6-KUD and A6-KUE are also operated.

9M (Malaysia)

9M-MHI	Boeing 747-236B	Malaysian Airline System	
9M-MHJ	Boeing 747-236B	Malaysian Airline System	
9M-MHK	Boeing 747-3H6 (SCD)	Malaysian Airline System	
9M-MHL	Boeing 747-4H6 (SCD)	Malaysian Airline System	
9M-MHM	Boeing 747-4H6 (SCD)	Malaysian Airline System	
9M-MHN	Boeing 747-4H6 (SCD)	Malaysian Airline System	
9M-MHO	Boeing 747-4H6	Malaysian Airline System	
9M-MPA	Boeing 747-4H6	Malaysian Airline System	
9M-MPB	Boeing 747-4H6	Malaysian Airline System	

9N (Nepal)

9N-ACA	Boeing 757-2F8	Royal Nepal Airlines	
9N-ACB	Boeing 757-2F8C	Royal Nepal Airlines	

9Q (Zaire)

9Q-CBW	Boeing 707-329C	Scibe Airlift Zaire	
9Q-CGO	Boeing 707-321C	Zairean Airlines	
9Q-CLG	Douglas DC-8-63CF	Air Zaire *Domaine de la Nsélé*	
9Q-CLI	Douglas DC-10-30	Air Zaire *Mont Ngaliema*	
9Q-CSB	Boeing 707-373C	Sicotra Aviation	
9Q-CTK	Boeing 707-436	Zairean Airlines	
9Q-CVH	Douglas DC-8-55F	Katale Aero Transport	

9V (Singapore)

9V-SKA	Boeing 747-312	Singapore Airlines	
9V-SKD	Boeing 747-312	Singapore Airlines	
9V-SKM	Boeing 747-312 (SCD)	Singapore Airlines	
9V-SKN	Boeing 747-312 (SCD)	Singapore Airlines	
9V-SKP	Boeing 747-312 (SCD)	Singapore Airlines	

Notes	Reg.	Type	Owner or Operator
	9V-SKQ	Boeing 747-212F (SCD)	Singapore Airlines
	9V-SMA	Boeing 747-412	Singapore Airlines
	9V-SMB	Boeing 747-412	Singapore Airlines
	9V-SMC	Boeing 747-412	Singapore Airlines
	9V-SMD	Boeing 747-412	Singapore Airlines
	9V-SME	Boeing 747-412	Singapore Airlines
	9V-SMF	Boeing 747-412	Singapore Airlines
	9V-SMG	Boeing 747-412	Singapore Airlines
	9V-SMH	Boeing 747-412	Singapore Airlines
	9V-SMI	Boeing 747-412	Singapore Airlines
	9V-SMJ	Boeing 747-412	Singapore Airlines
	9V-SMK	Boeing 747-412	Singapore Airlines
	9V-SML	Boeing 747-412	Singapore Airlines
	9V-SMM	Boeing 747-412	Singapore Airlines
	9V-SMN	Boeing 747-412	Singapore Airlines
	9V-SMO	Boeing 747-412	Singapore Airlines
	9V-SMP	Boeing 747-412	Singapore Airlines
	9V-SQP	Boeing 747-212B	Singapore Airlines
	9V-SQQ	Boeing 747-212B	Singapore Airlines
	9V-SQR	Boeing 747-212B	Singapore Airlines
	9V-SQS	Boeing 747-212B	Singapore Airlines

Note: Singapore Airlines also operates Boeing 747-312 N116KB, N117KC, N119KE, N120KF, N121KG, N122KH, N123KJ, N124KK and N125KL.

9XR (Rwanda)

9XR-JA	Boeing 707-328C		Air Rwanda

9Y (Trinidad and Tobago)

9Y-TGJ	L.1011 TriStar 500		B.W.I.A. *Flamingo*
9Y-TGN	L.1011 TriStar 500		B.W.I.A.
9Y-THA	L.1011 TriStar 500 (597)		B.W.I.A.

Note: B.W.I.A. also operates a TriStar 500 which retains its US registration N3140D.

Overseas Registrations

Aircraft included in this section are those based in the UK but which retain their non-British identities.

Reg.	Type	Owner or Operator	Notes
A40-AB	V.1103 VC10 ★	Brooklands Museum (G-ASIX)	
CF-EQS	Boeing-Stearman PT-17 ★	Imperial War Museum/Duxford	
CF-KCG	Grumman TBM-3E Avenger AS.3★	Imperial War Museum/Duxford	
D-HMQV	Bolkow Bo 102 ★	International Helicopter Museum/ Weston-s-Mare	
D-IFSB	D.H.104 Dove 6★	Mosquito Aircraft Museum	
F-BDRS	Boeing B-17G (231983) ★	Imperial War Museum/Duxford	
F-BMCY	Potez 840*	Sumburgh Fire Service	
N1MF	Cessna 421B	Pelmont Aviation Inc/Cranfield	
N2FU	Learjet 35A	Motor Racing Developments Inc	
N14KH	Christen Eagle II	R. Frohmayer	
N15AW	Cessna 500 Citation	A. W. Alloys Ltd	
N15SC	Learjet 35A	Sea Containers Associates/Luton	
N18E	Boeing 247D ★	Science Museum/Wroughton	
N18V	Beech D.17S Traveler (PB1)	R. Lamplough	
N33VC	Lockheed T-33A (54-21261)	Old Flying Machine Co/Duxford	
N34AB	Beech T-34 Mentor	Warbirds of GB Ltd	
N47DD	Republic P-47D Thunderbolt (45-49192)★	Imperial War Museum/Duxford	
N49UR	Canadair CL.601 Challenger	Kingson Corporation	
N51JJ	P-51 Mustang (463221)	B. J. S. Grey/Duxford	
N51RR	P-51D Mustang (474008)	D. Gilmour/North Weald	
N59NA	Douglas C-47A	Aces High Ltd (G-AKNB)/North Weald	
N71AF	R. Commander 680W	Metropolitan Aviation	
N153JS	Nieuport 24 (replica)	A. E. Hutton/North Weald	
N154JS	Airco D.H.5 (replica)	A. E. Hutton/North Weald	
N158C	S.24 Sandringham (VH-BRC) ★	Southampton Hall of Aviation	
N167F	P-51D Mustang (473877)	RLS 51 Ltd/Duxford	
N179NP	Vought F4U-7 Corsair	D. W. Arnold/Biggin Hill	
N232J	Hawker Sea Fury FB.11	R. Lamplough/North Weald	
N240CA	F-4U-4B Corsair (NZ5628)	R. Hanna/Duxford	
N260QB	Pitts S-2S Special	D. Baker	
N365F	Hawker Sea Fury FB10	J. Bradshaw	
N416FS	F-100F Super Sabre	Flight Refuelling Ltd/Bournemouth	
N417FS	F-100F Super Sabre	Flight Refuelling Ltd/Bournemouth	
N418FS	F-100F Super Sabre	Flight Refuelling Ltd/Bournemouth	
N425EE	Cessna 425	J. W. MacDonald	
N444M	Grumman G.44 Widgeon (1411)	M. Dunkerley/Biggin Hill	
N490CC	Cessna 551 Citation II	A. W. Alloys Ltd	
N500LN	Howard 500	D. Baker	
N535SM	R. Commander 680	J. E. Tuberty	
N707TJ	Boeing Stearman A.75N1	V. S. E. Norman (Crunchie)	
N750M	Grumman G.44 Widgeon★	L. E. Usher	
N902FR	Dassault Falcon 20DC	Flight Refuelling Ltd/Bournemouth	
N903FR	Dassault Falcon 20DC	Flight Refuelling Ltd/Bournemouth	
N904FR	Dassault Falcon 20DC	Flight Refuelling Ltd/Bournemouth	
N906FR	Dassault Falcon 20DC	Flight Refuelling Ltd/Bournemouth	
N907FR	Dassault Falcon 20DC	Flight Refuelling Ltd/Bournemouth	
N908FR	Dassault Falcon 20DC	Flight Refuelling Ltd/Bournemouth	
N909FR	Dassault Falcon 20DC	Flight Refuelling Ltd/Bournemouth	
N909WJ	FM-2 Wildcat	D. W. Arnold/Biggin Hill	
N999PJ	M.S.760 Paris 2	Aces High Ltd/North Weald	
N1042B	B-25J Mitchell (430823)	Aces High Ltd/North Weald	
N1344	Ryan PT-22	H. Mitchell	
N1447Q	Cessna 150L	US Embassy Flying Club	
N1755C	Cessna 180	Alconbury Aero Club	
N2700	Fairchild C-119G	Aces High Ltd (G-BLSW)/North Weald	
N2929W	PA-28-151 Warrior	R. Lobell	
N3600X	Dassault Falcon 10	Xerox Corporation/Heathrow	
N3851Q	Cessna 172K	Bentwaters Aero Club/Woodbridge	
N3983N	Agusta A.109A	NSM Aviation	
N4151D	TF-51D Mustang	Warbirds of GB Ltd	
N4306Z	PA-28 -161 Warrior II	USAF Aero Club/Upper Heyford	
N4565L	Douglas DC.3	Hibernian Dakota Flight Ltd/Ipswich	
N4596N	Boeing Stearman PT-13D	N. Mason & D. Gilmour/North Weald	
N4712V	Boeing Stearman PT-13D	Wessex Aviation & Transport Ltd	
N4727V	Spad S.VII (S4523)	Imperial War Museum/Duxford	
N4806E	Douglas A-26C Invader ★	R. & R. Cadman/Southend	
N5063V	Beech D.18S (HB275)	Harvard Formation Team (G-BKGM)	
N5237V	Boeing B-17G (483868) ★	RAF Bomber Command Museum/Hendon	

Notes	Reg.	Type	Owner or Operator
	N5824H	PA-38 Tomahawk	Lakenheath Aero Club
	N6178C	F7F-3 Tigercat	Planesailing Air Displays/Duxford
	N6268	Travel Air Model 2000	Personal Plane Services Ltd
	N6526D	P-51D Mustang ★	RAF Museum/Henlow
	N6827C	TBM-3E Avenger (X-2)	R. Hanna/Duxford
	N7614C	B-25J Mitchell	Imperial War Museum/Duxford
	N7777G	L.749A Constellation ★	Science Museum (G-CONI)/Wroughton
	N8155E	Mooney M.20A	D. Skans
	N9089Z	TB-25J Mitchell (44-30861) ★	Aces High Ltd (G-BKXW)/North Weald
	N9115Z	TB-25N Mitchell (34037) ★	RAF Bomber Command Museum/Hendon
	N9606H	Fairchild M.62A Cornell ★	Rebel Air Museum/Earls Colne
	N9950	P-40N Kittyhawk	D. W. Arnold/Biggin Hill
	N15798	CCF Harvard IV (Zero)	Old Flying Machine Co/Duxford
	N26178	Cessna 550 Citation II	A. W. Alloys Ltd
	N26634	PA-24 Comanche 250	P. Biggs (G-BFKR)
	N30228	Piper J-3C-65 Cub	C. Morris
	N33600	Cessna L-19A Bird Dog (111989) ★	Museum of Army Flying/Middle Wallop
	N43069	PA-28-161 Warrior II	Lakenheath Aero Club
	N43401	PA-28-161 Warrior II	Cabair/Elstree
	N49272	Ryan PT-23 (23)	H. Mitchell
	N50993	Ryan PT-22	V. S. E. Norman
	N53127	Boeing Stearman A.75N1	—
	N54558	Cessna F.152	J. J. Baumhardt
	N54922	Boeing Stearman N25-4	V. S. E. Norman (Crunchie)
	N56028	Ryan PT-22	V. S. E. Norman
	N56421	Ryan PT-22 (855)	PT Flight/Cosford
	N58566	BT-13 Valiant	PT Flight/Cosford
	N70290	B.121 Pup	Lakenheath Aero Club
	N75664	Boeing Stearman E.75N1	—
	N88972	B-25D-30-ND Mitchell (KL161)	Fighter Collection/Duxford
	N90005	G.1159A Gulfstream 3	Siebe PLC
	N91342	PA-38-112 Tomahawk	Lakenheath Aero Club
	N91437	PA-38-112 Tomahawk	Lakenheath Aero Club
	N91457	PA-38-112 Tomahawk	Lakenheath Aero Club
	N91590	PA-38-112 Tomahawk	Lakenheath Aero Club
	N91764	Cessna 152 II (tailwheel)	Wessex Aviation & Transport Ltd
	N96240	Beech D.18S	J. Hawke (G-AYAH)
	N99153	T-28C Trojan ★	Norfolk & Suffolk Aviation Museum/Flixton
	NC88ZK	Boeing-Stearman PT-17	R. Hanna/Duxford
	NC5171N	Lockheed 10A Electra ★	Science Museum (G-LIOA)/Wroughton
	NC15214	Waco UKC-S	P. H. McConnell/White Waltham
	NC16403	Cessna C.34 Airmaster	Kennet Aircraft Ltd (G-BSEB)
	NL314BG	P-51D Mustang (414151)	D. W. Arnold/Biggin Hill
	NL1009N	P-40N Kittyhawk (FR870)	B. J. S. Grey/Duxford
	NL1051S	P-51D-25-NA Mustang (511371)	Myrick Aviation/Southend
	NL9494Z	TB-25N Mitchell (151632)	Visionair Ltd
	NX11SN	Yakolev C-11	Old Flying Machine Co/Duxford
	NX47DD	Republic P-47D Thunderbolt (226671)	The Fighter Collection/Duxford
	NX55JP	FG-1D Corsair	Old Flying Machine Co/Duxford
	NX100TF	F6F-5K Hellcat	The Fighter Collection/Duxford
	NX700HL	F8F-2B Bearcat (121714)	B. J. S. Grey/Duxford
	NX800H	F8F-2 Bearcat	D. W. Arnold/Biggin Hill
	NX1337A	F4U-7 Corsair (133722)	L. M. Walton/Duxford
	NX49092	F4U-4 Corsair	D. W. Arnold/Biggin Hill
	VH-BRC	See N158C	
	VH-SNB	D.H.84 Dragon ★	Museum of Flight/E. Fortune
	VH-UTH	GAL Monospar ST-12 ★	Newark Air Museum (stored)
	VR-BEP	WS.55 Whirlwind 3 ★	East Midlands Aeropark (G-BAMH)
	VR-BET	WS.55 Whirlwind 3 ★	International Helicopter Museum (G-ANJV)/Weston-s-Mare
	VR-BEU	WS.55 Whirlwind 3 ★	International Helicopter Museum (G-ATKV)/Weston-s-Mare
	VR-BHN	Boeing 727-30	Jade Air Leasing
	VR-BJI	Lockheed Jetstar	Denis Vanguard International Ltd
	VR-BKC	Boeing 727-1H2	USAL Inc
	VR-BKY	H.S.125 Srs F.3B	Corporate Jet Services
	VR-BKZ	H.S.125 Srs 700A	Dennis Vanguard International
	VR-BLA	Canadair CL.600.2A12 Challenger	Granaway Ltd
	VR-BLP	BAe 125 Srs 800A	BP Flight Operations Ltd
	VR-BLQ	BAe 125 Srs 800A	BP Flight Operations Ltd
	VR-BLR	G.1159C Gulfstream IV	BP Flight Operations Ltd
	VR-BLX	F.27 Friendship Mk 400	BP Flight Operations Ltd
	VR-BLY	F.27 Friendship Mk 400	BP Flight Operations Ltd
	VR-BLZ	F.27 Friendship Mk 400	BP Flight Operations Ltd
	VR-CBE	Boeing 727-46	Resebury Corporation
	5N-ABW	Westland Widgeon 2 ★	International Helicopter Museum (G-AOZE)/Weston-s-Mare

Radio Frequencies

The frequencies used by the larger airfields/airports are listed below. Abbreviations used: TWR — Tower, APP — Approach, A/G — Air-ground advisory. It is possible for changes to be made from time to time with the frequencies allocated which are all quoted in Megahertz (MHz).

Airfield	TWR	APP	A/G	Airfield	TWR	APP	A/G
Aberdeen	118.1	120.4		Ingoldmells			130.45
Aldergrove	118.3	120.0		Inverness	122.6		
Alderney	125.35			Ipswich	118.325		
Andrewsfield			130.55	Jersey	119.45	120.3	
Barton			122.7	Kidlington	118.875	130.3	
Barrow			123.2	Land's End	130.7		
Belfast City	130.75	130.85		Leavesden	122.15		
Bembridge			123.25	Leeds	120.3	123.75	
Biggin Hill	134.8	129.4		Leicester			122.25
Birmingham	118.3	131.325		Liverpool	118.1	119.85	
Blackbushe			122.3	London City	118.075	128.05	
Blackpool	118.4	135.95		Long Marston			130.1
Bodmin			122.7	Luton	120.2	128.75	
Booker			126.55	Lydd	120.7	131.3	
Bourn			129.8	Manchester	118.625	119.4	
Bournemouth	125.6	119.625		Manston	128.775	126.35	
Bristol	133.85	132.4		Netherthorpe			123.5
Cambridge	122.2	123.6		Newcastle	119.7	126.35	
Cardiff	125.0	125.85		North Denes			120.45
Carlisle			123.6	Norwich	118.9	119.35	
Compton Abbas			122.7	Panshanger			120.25
Conington			129.725	Perth	119.8	122.3	
Coventry	119.25	122.0		Plymouth	122.6	133.55	
Cranfield	123.2	122.85		Popham			129.8
Denham			130.72	Prestwick	118.15	120.55	
Doncaster			122.9	Redhill			123.275
Dundee	122.9			Rochester			122.25
Dunkeswell			123.47	Ronaldsway	118.9	120.85	
Dunsfold	124.32	119.825		Sandown			123.5
Duxford			123.5	Seething			122.6
East Midlands	124.0	120.125		Sherburn			122.6
Edinburgh	118.7	121.2		Shipdham			123.05
Elstree			122.4	Shobdon			123.5
Exeter	119.8	128.15		Shoreham	125.4	123.15	
Fairoaks			123.42	Sibson			122.3
Felthorpe			123.5	Sleap			122.45
Fenland			122.925	Southampton	118.2	120.225	
Filton	124.95	122.725		Southend	127.725	128.95	
Gamston			130.47	Stansted	118.15	125.55	
Gatwick	134.225	128.575		Stapleford			122.8
Glasgow	118.8	119.1		Staverton	125.65	122.9	
Goodwood	120.65	122.45		Sumburgh	118.25	123.15	
Guernsey	119.95	128.65		Swansea	119.7	119.7	
Halfpenny Green			123.0	Swanton Morley			123.5
Hatfield	130.8	123.35		Sywell			122.7
Haverfordwest			122.2	Teesside	119.8	118.85	
Hawarden	124.95	123.35		Thruxton			130.45
Hayes Heliport			123.65	Tollerton			122.8
Headcorn			122.0	Wellesbourne			130.45
Heathrow	118.7	119.2		White Waltham			122.6
	118.5	119.5		Wick	119.7		
Hethel			122.35	Wickenby			122.45
Hucknall			130.8	Woodford	126.925	130.05	
Humberside	118.55	123.15		Yeovil	125.4	130.8	

Three-letter flight codes are now in general use. Those listed below identify both UK and overseas carriers appearing in the book.

Code	Airline	
AAF	Aigle Azur	F
AAG	Air Atlantique	G
AAL	American A/L	N
AAN	Oasis	EC
AAW	Aberdeen A/W	G
ABB	Air Belgium	OO
ABR	Air Bridge	G
ACA	Air Canada	C
ACF	Air Charter Intl	F
ADR	Adria A/W	YU
AEA	Air Europa	EC
AEF	Aero Lloyd	D
AFL	Aeroflot	CCCP
AFM	Affretair	Z
AFR	Air France	F
AGX	Aviogenex	YU
AHK	Air Hong Kong	VR-H
AIA	Air Atlantis	CS
AIC	Air-India	VT
AIH	Airtours	G
ALK	Air Lanka	4R
AMC	Air Malta	9H
AMM	Air 2000	G
AMT	American Trans Air	N
ANA	All Nippon A/W	JA
ANC	Anglo Cargo	G
ANZ	Air New Zealand	ZK
APW	Arrow Air	N
ARG	Argentine A/W	LV
ATI	ATI	I
ATT	Aer Turas	EI
AUA	Austrian A/L	OE
AUR	Aurigny A/S	G
AVA	Avianca	HK
AVD	Air Vendee	F
AWC	Titan A/W	G
AYC	Aviaco	EC
AZA	Alitalia	I
AZI	Air Zimbabwe	Z
AZR	Air Zaire	9Q
BAC	BAC Charter	G
BAF	British Air Ferries	G
BAL	Britannia A/L	G
BAW	British Airways	G
BBB	Balair	HB
BBC	Bangladesh Biman	S2
BCS	European A/T	OO
BEA	Birmingham European	G
BEE	Busy Bee	LN
BER	Air Berlin	N
BIH	British Intl Heli	G
BKT	Caledonian	G
BMA	British Midland	G
BRA	Braathens	LN
BRY	Brymon A/W	G
BWA	BWIA	9Y
BZH	Brit Air	F
CCA	CAAC	B
CDN	Canadian A/L Intl	C
CFG	Condor	D
CIC	Celtic Air	G
CLX	Cargolux	LX
CMM	Canada 3000 A/L	C
CNB	Air Columbus	CS
COA	Continental A/L	N
CPA	Cathay Pacific	VR-H
CRL	Corse Air	F
CRX	Crossair	HB
CSA	Czech A/L	OK
CTA	CTA	HB
CYP	Cyprus A/W	5B
DAH	Air Algerie	7T
DAL	Delta A/L	N
DAN	Dan-Air	G
DAT	Delta Air Transport	OO
DLH	Lufthansa	D
DLT	DLT	D
DMA	Maersk Air	OY
DQI	Cimber Air	OY
DYA	Alyemda	7O
EGY	Egypt Air	SU
EIA	Evergreen Intl	N
EIN	Aer Lingus	EI
ELY	El Al	4X
ENJ	Nortjet	EC
ETH	Ethiopian A/L	ET
EUI	Euralair	F
EWW	Emery	N
EXS	Channel Express	G
EXX	Air Exel UK	G
FDE	Federal Express	N
FGT	Fairflight	G
FIN	Finnair	OH
FOB	Ford	G
FOF	Fred Olsen	LN
FUA	Futura	EC
FXY	Flexair	PH
GBL	GB Airways	G
GEC	German Cargo	D
GFA	Gulf Air	A40
GFG	Germania	D
GHA	Ghana A/W	9G
GIA	Garuda	PK
GIL	Gill Air	G
GNT	Business Air	G
GRN	Greenair	TC
HAL	Hawaiian A/L	N
HAS	Hamburg A/L	D
HLA	HeavyLift	G
HLF	Hapag-Lloyd	D
IAW	Iraqi A/W	YI
IBE	Iberia	EC
ICE	Icelandair	TF
IEA	Inter European	G
INS	Instone A/L	G
IRA	Iran Air	EP
ISL	Eagle Air	TF
IST	Istanbul A/L	TC
ITF	Air Inter	F
JAL	Japan A/L	JA
JAT	JAT	YU
JAV	Janes Aviation	G
JEA	Jersey European A/W	G
KAC	Kuwait A/W	9K
KAL	Korean Air	HL
KAR	Kar-Air	OH
KIS	Contactair	D
KLM	KLM	PH
KQA	Kenya A/W	5Y
LAA	Libyan Arab A/L	5A
LAZ	Bulgarian A/L	LZ
LDA	Lauda Air	OE
LGL	Luxair	LX
LIB	Air Liberte	F
LIN	Linjeflyg	SE
LIT	Air Littoral	F
LKA	Alkair	OY
LOG	Loganair	G
LOT	Polish A/L (LOT)	SP
LTE	LTE	EC
LTS	LTU Sud.	D
LTU	LTU	D
MAH	Malev	HA
MAS	Malaysian A/L	9M
MAU	Air Mauritius	3B
MDN	Meridiana	EC
MEA	Middle East A/L	OD
MIN	Minerve	F
MNX	Manx A/L	G
MON	Monarch A/L	G
MOR	Morefly	LN
MPH	Martinair	PH
NAD	Nobleair	TC
NAW	Newair	OY
NCR	Air Sur	EC
NEX	Northern Executive	G
NFD	NFD	D
NGA	Nigeria A/W	5N
NSA	Nile Safaris	ST
NWA	Northwest A/L	N
NXA	Nationair	C
OAL	Olympic A/L	SX
OYC	Conair	OY
PAL	Philippine A/L	RP
PGA	Portugalia	CS
PGT	Pegasus	TC
PIA	Pakistan Intl	AP
QFA	Qantas	VH
QSC	African Safaris	5Y
RAM	Royal Air Maroc	CN
RBA	Royal Brunei	V8
RFG	RFG	D
RIA	Rich Intl	N
RJA	Royal Jordanian	JY
RNA	Royal Nepal A/L	9N
ROT	Tarom	YR
RWD	Air Rwanda	9XR
RYR	Ryanair	EI
SAA	South African A/W	ZS
SAB	Sabena	OO
SAS	SAS	SE OY LN
SAW	Sterling A/W	OY
SAY	Suckling A/W	G
SDI	Saudi	HZ
SEY	Air Seychelles	S7
SIA	Singapore A/L	9V
SJM	Southern AT	N
SLA	Sobelair	OO
SPP	Spanair	EC
STR	Stellair	F
SUD	Sudan A/W	ST
SWE	Swedair	SE
SWR	Swissair	HB
SXS	Sun Express	TC
SYR	Syrian Arab	YK
TAP	Air Portugal	CS
TAR	Tunis Air	TS
TAT	TAT	F
TCT	TUR European	TC
THA	Thai A/W Intl	HS
THG	Thurston	G

THY	Turkish A/L	TC	UAE	Emirates A/L	A6	VIA	Viasa		YV
TLE	Air Toulouse	F	UAL	United A/L	N	VIR	Virgin Atlantic		G
TMA	Trans Mediterranean	OD	UGA	Uganda A/L	5X	VIV	Viva Air		EC
TOW	Tower Air	N	UKA	Air UK	G	VKG	Scanair	SE OY	LN
TRA	Transavia	PH	UKL	Air UK Leisure	G	VRG	Varig		PP
TSC	Air Transat	C	UPA	Air Foyle	G	WDL	WDL		D
TSW	TEA Basle	HB	UPS	United Parcels	N	WOA	World A/W		N
TWA	TWA	N	USA	USAir	N	ZAC	Zambia A/W		9J
TWE	Transwede	SE	UTA	UTA	F	ZAS	ZAS A/L of Egypt		SU
TYR	Tyrolean	OE	UYC	Cameroon A/L	TJ				

PH-FXA Dornier Do.228-202K of Flexair. *AJW*

PH-KSB Saab SF.340B of KLM CityHopper. *AJW*

British Aircraft Preservation Council Register

The British Aircraft Preservation Council was formed in 1967 to co-ordinate the works of all bodies involved in the preservation, restoration and display of historical aircraft. Membership covers the whole spectrum of national, Service, commercial and voluntary groups, and meetings are held regularly at the bases of member organisations. The Council is able to provide a means of communication, helping to resolve any misunderstandings or duplication of effort. Every effort is taken to encourage the raising of standards of both organisation and technical capacity amongst the member groups to the benfit of everyone interested in aviation. To assist historians, the B.A.P.C. register has been set up and provides an identity for those aircraft which do not qualify for a Service serial or inclusion in the UK Civil Register.

Aircraft on the current B.A.P.C. Register are as follows:

Notes	Reg.	Type	Owner or Operator
	6	Roe Triplane Type IV (replica)	Greater Manchester Museum of Science & Technology
	7	Southampton University MPA	Southampton Hall of Aviation
	8	Dixon ornithopter	The Shuttleworth Trust
	9	Humber Monoplane (replica)	Airport Terminal/Birmingham
	10	Hafner R.II Revoplane	Museum of Army Flying/Middle Wallop
	12	Mignet HM.14	Museum of Flight/E. Fortune
	13	Mignet HM.14	Brimpex Metal Treatments
	14	Addyman standard training glider	N. H. Ponsford
	15	Addyman standard training glider	The Aeroplane Collection Ltd
	16	Addyman ultra-light aircraft	N. H. Ponsford
	17	Woodhams Sprite	The Aeroplane Collection Ltd
	18	Killick MP Gyroplane	N. H. Ponsford
	19	Bristol F.2b	Brussels Air Museum
	20	Lee-Richards annular biplane (replica)	Newark Air Musem
	21	Thruxton Jackaroo	M. J. Brett
	22	Mignet HM.14 (G-AEOF)	Aviodome/Schiphol, Holland
	25	Nyborg TGN-III glider	Midland Air Museum
	27	Mignet HM.14	M. J. Abbey
	28	Wright Flyer (replica)	Bygone Times Antique Warehouse/ Eccleston
	29	Mignet HM.14 (replica) (G-ADRY)	Brooklands Museum of Aviation/ Weybridge
	32	Crossley Tom Thumb	Midland Air Museum
	33	DFS.108-49 Grunau Baby IIb	Russavia Collection
	34	DFS.108-49 Grunau Baby IIb	D. Elsdon
	35	EoN primary glider	Russavia Collection
	36	Fieseler Fi.103 (V-1) (replica)	Kent Battle of Britain Museum/Hawkinge
	37	Blake Bluetit	The Shuttleworth Trust
	38	Bristol Scout replica (A1742)	Historical Aircraft Museum/RAF St Athan
	40	Bristol Boxkite (replica)	Bristol City Museum
	41	B.E.2C (replica) (6232)	Historical Aircraft Museum/RAF St Athan
	42	Avro 504 (replica) (H1968)	Historical Aircraft Museum/RAF St Athan
	43	Mignet HM.14	Lincolnshire Aviation Museum
	44	Miles Magister (L6906)	Berkshire Aviation Group (G-AKKY)/ Woodley
	45	Pilcher Hawk (replica)	Stanford Hall Museum
	46	Mignet HM.14	Alan McKechnie Racing Ltd
	47	Watkins Monoplane	Historical Aircraft Museum/RAF St Athan
	48	Pilcher Hawk (replica)	Glasgow Museum of Transport
	49	Pilcher Hawk	Royal Scottish Museum/Edinburgh
	50	Roe Triplane Type 1	Science Museum/S. Kensington
	51	Vickers Vimy IV	Science Museum/S. Kensington
	52	Lilienthal glider	Science Museum Store/Hayes
	53	Wright Flyer (replica)	Science Museum/S. Kensington
	54	JAP-Harding monoplane	Science Museum/S. Kensington
	55	Levavasseur Antoinette VII	Science Museum/S. Kensington
	56	Fokker E.III (210/16)	Science Museum/S. Kensington
	57	Pilcher Hawk (replica)	Science Museum/S. Kensington
	58	Yokosuka MXY-7 Ohka II (15-1585)	FAA Museum/Yeovilton
	59	Sopwith Camel (replica) (D3419)	Historical Aircraft Museum/RAF St Athan
	60	Murray M.1 helicopter	The Aeroplane Collection Ltd
	61	Stewart man-powered ornithopter	Lincolnshire Aviation Museum
	62	Cody Biplane (304)	Science Museum/S. Kensington
	63	Hurricane (replica) (L1592)	Torbay Aircraft Museum
	64	Hurricane (replica) (P3059)	Kent Battle of Britain Museum/Hawkinge

Reg.	Type	Owner or Operator	Notes
65	Spitfire (replica) (QV-K)	Kent Battle of Britain Museum/Hawkinge	
66	Bf'109 (replica) (1480)	Kent Battle of Britain Museum/Hawkinge	
67	Bf 109 (replica) (14)	Midland Air Museum	
68	Hurricane (replica) (H3426)	Midland Air Museum	
69	Spitfire (replica) (QV-K)	Torbay Aircraft Museum	
70	Auster AOP.5 (TJ398)	Aircraft Preservation Soc of Scotland	
71	Spitfire (replica) (P9390)	Norfolk & Suffolk Aviation Museum	
72	Hurricane (replica) (V7767)	N. Weald Aircraft Restoration Flight	
73	Hurricane (replica)	Queens Head/Bishops Stortford	
74	Bf 109 (replica) (6)	Torbay Aircraft Museum	
75	Mignet HM.14 (G-AEFG)	Nigel Ponsford	
76	Mignet HM.14 (G-AFFI)	Yorkshire Air Museum/Elvington	
77	Mignet HM.14 (replica) (G-ADRG)	Cotswold Aircraft Restoration Group	
79	Fiat G.46-4 (MM53211)	British Air Reserve/Lympne	
80	Airspeed Horsa (TL659)	Museum of Army Flying	
81	Hawkridge Dagling	Russavia Collection	
82	Hawker Hind (Afghan)	RAF Museum/Hendon	
83	Kawasaki Ki-100-1b	Aerospace Museum/Cosford	
84	Nakajima Ki-46 (Dinah III)	Historical Aircraft Museum/RAF St Athan	
85	Weir W-2 autogyro	Museum of Flight/E. Fortune	
86	de Havilland Tiger Moth (replica)	Yorkshire Aircraft Preservation Soc	
87	Bristol Babe (replica) (G-EASQ)	Bomber County Museum/Hemswell	
88	Fokker Dr 1 (replica) (102/18)	Fleet Air Arm Museum	
89	Cayley glider (replica)	Greater Manchester Museum of Science & Technology	
90	Colditz Cock (replica)	Torbay Aircraft Museum	
91	Fieseler Fi 103 (V.1)	Lashenden Air Warfare Museum	
92	Fieseler Fi 103 (V.1)	Historical Aircraft Museum/RAF St Athan	
93	Fieseler Fi 103 (V.1)	Imperial War Museum/Duxford	
94	Fieseler Fi 103 (V.1)	Aerospace Museum/Cosford	
95	Gizmer autogyro	F. Fewsdale	
96	Brown helicopter	NE Aircraft Museum	
97	Luton L.A.4A Minor	NE Aircraft Museum	
98	Yokosuka MXY-7 Ohka II	Greater Manchester Museum of Science & Technology	
99	Yokosuka MXY-7 Ohka II	Aerospace Museum/Cosford	
100	Clarke glider	RAF Museum/Hendon	
101	Mignet HM.14	Lincolnshire Aviation Museum	
103	Pilcher glider (replica)	Personal Plane Services Ltd	
105	Blériot XI (replica)	Aviodome/Schiphol, Holland	
106	Blériot XI (164)	RAF Museum/Hendon	
107	Blériot XXVII (433)	RAF Museum/Hendon	
108	Fairey Swordfish IV (HS503)	RAF Museum/Henlow store	
109	Slingsby Kirby Cadet TX.1	RAF Museum/Henlow store	
110	Fokker D.VII replica (static) (5125)	—	
111	Sopwith Triplane replica (static) (N5492)	FAA Museum/Yeovilton	
112	D.H.2 replica (static) (5964)	Museum of Army Flying/Middle Wallop	
113	S.E.5A replica (static) (B4863)	—	
114	Vickers Type 60 Viking (static)	Brooklands Museum of Aviation/Weybridge	
115	Mignet HM.14	Essex Aviation Group/Andrewsfield	
116	Santos-Dumont Demoiselle (replica)	Cornwall Aero Park/Helston	
117	B.E.2C (replica)	N. Weald Aircraft Restoration Flight	
118	Albatros D.V. (replica)	N. Weald Aircraft Restoration Flight	
119	Bensen B.7	N.E. Aircraft Museum	
120	Mignet HM.14 (G-AEJZ)	Bomber County Museum/Hemswell	
121	Mignet HM.14 (G-AEKR)	S. Yorks Aviation Soc	
122	Avro 504 (replica)	British Broadcasting Corp	
123	Vickers FB.5 Gunbus (replica)	A. Topen (*stored*)/Cranfield	
124	Lilienthal Glider Type XI (replica)	Science Museum/S. Kensington	
125	Clay Cherub (G-BDGP)	B. R. Clay	
126	D.31 Turbulent (static)	Midland Air Museum store	
127	Halton Jupiter MPA	Shuttleworth Trust	
128	Watkinson Cyclogyroplane Mk IV	International Helicopter Museum/Weston-s-Mare	
129	Blackburn 1911 Monoplane (replica)	Cornwall Aero Park/Helston store	
130	Blackburn 1912 Monoplane (replica)	Cornwall Aero Park/Helston store	
131	Pilcher Hawk (replica)	C. Paton	
132	Blériot XI (G-BLXI)	EMK Aeroplane Co Ltd	

Notes	Reg.	Type	Owner or Operator
	133	Fokker Dr 1 (replica) (425/17)	Torbay Aircraft Museum
	134	Pitts S-2A static (G-RKSF)	Torbay Aircraft Museum
	135	Bristol M.1C (C4912)	Leisure Sport Ltd/Thorpe Park
	136	Deperdussin Seaplane (replica)	Leisure Sport Ltd/Thorpe Park
	137	Sopwith Baby Floatplane (replica)	(8151) Leisure Sport Ltd/Thorpe Park
	138	Hansa Brandenburg W.29 Floatplane (replica) (2292)	Leisure Sport Ltd/Thorpe Park
	139	Fokker Dr 1 (replica) 150/17	Leisure Sport Ltd/Thorpe Park
	140	Curtiss R3C-2 Floatplane (replica)	Leisure Sport Ltd/Thorpe Park
	141	Macchi M.39 Floatplane (replica)	Planes of Fame Museum/Chino, US
	142	SE-5A (replica) (F5459)	Cornwall Aero Park/Helston
	143	Paxton MPA	R. A. Paxton/Staverton
	144	Weybridge Mercury MPA	Cranwell Gliding Club
	145	Oliver MPA	D. Oliver (*stored*)/Warton
	146	Pedal Aeronauts Toucan MPA	Shuttleworth Trust
	147	Bensen B.7	Norfolk & Suffolk Aviation Museum
	148	Hawker Fury II (replica) (K7271)	Aerospace Museum/Cosford
	149	Short S.27 (replica)	FAA Museum (*stored*)/Yeovilton
	150	SEPECAT Jaguar GR.1 (replica)	(XX724) RAF Exhibition Flight
	151	SEPECAT Jaguar GR.1 (replica)	(XZ363) RAF Exhibition Flight
	152	BAe Hawk T.1 (replica) (XX163)	RAF Exhibition Flight
	153	Westland WG.33	International Helicopter Museum/ Weston-s-Mare
	154	D.31 Turbulent	Lincolnshire Aviation Museum
	155	Panavia Tornado GR.1 (replica) (ZA600)	RAF Exhibition Flight
	156	Supermarine S-6B (replica) (S1595)	Leisure Sport Ltd
	157	Waco CG-4A	Pennine Aviation Museum
	158	Fieseler Fi 103 (V.1)	Joint Bomb Disposal School/Chattenden
	159	Yokosuka MXY-7 Ohka II	Joint Bomb Disposal School/Chattenden
	160	Chargus 108 hang glider	Museum of Flight/E. Fortune
	161	Stewart Ornithopter Coppelia	Bomber County Museum
	162	Goodhart Newbury Manflier MPA	Science Museum/Wroughton
	163	AFEE 10/42 Rotabuggy (replica)	Museum of Army Flying/Middle Wallop
	164	Wight Quadruplane Type 1 (replica)	Wessex Aviation Soc/Wimborne
	165	Bristol F.2b (E2466)	RAF Museum/Hendon
	167	S.E.5A replica	Newark Air Museum
	168	D.H.60G Moth static replica (G-AAAH)	Hilton Hotel/Gatwick
	169	SEPECAT Jaguar GR.1 (static replica) (XX110)	No 1 S. of T.T. RAF Halton
	170	Pilcher Hawk (replica)	A. Gourlay/Strathallan
	171	BAe Hawk T.1 (replica) (XX297)	RAF Exhibition Flight/Abingdon
	172	Chargus Midas Super 8 hang glider	Science Museum/Wroughton
	173	Birdman Promotions Grasshopper	Science Museum/Wroughton
	174	Bensen B.7	Science Museum/Wroughton
	175	Volmer VJ-23 Swingwing	Greater Manchester Museum of Science & Technology
	176	SE-5A (replica) (A4850)	S. Yorkshire Aircraft Preservation Soc
	177	Avro 504K (replica) (G1381)	Brooklands Museum of Aviation/ Weybridge
	178	Avro 504K (replica) (E373)	Bygone Times Antique Warehouse/ Eccleston
	179	Sopwith Camel (replica)	N. Weald Aircraft Restoration Flight
	180	McCurdy Silver Dart (replica)	RAF Museum/Cardington
	181	RAF B.E.2b (replica)	RAF Museum/Cardington
	182	Wood Ornithopter	Greater Manchester Museum of Science & Technology
	183	Zurowski ZP.1	Newark Air Museum
	184	Spitfire IX (replica) (EN398)	Aces High Ltd/North Weald
	185	Waco CG-4A (243809)	Museum of Army Flying/Middle Wallop
	186	D.H.82B Queen Bee (K3584)	Mosquito Aircraft Museum
	187	Roe Type 1 biplane (replica)	Brooklands Museum of Aviation/ Weybridge
	188	McBroom Cobra 88	Science Museum/Wroughton
	189	Bleriot XI (replica)	—
	190	Spitfire (replica)	Biggin Hill Museum
	191	BAe Harrier GR.5 (replica) (ZD472)	RAF Exhibition Flight
	192	Weedhopper JC-24	The Aeroplane Collection
	193	Hovey WD-11 Whing Ding	The Aeroplane Collection
	194	Santos Dumont Demoiselle	Brooklands Museum of Aviation/

Reg.	Type	Owner or Operator	Notes
	(replica)	Weybridge	
195	Moonraker 77 hang glider	Museum of Flight/E. Fortune	
196	Sigma 2M hang glider	Museum of Flight/E. Fortune	
197	Cirrus III hang glider	Museum of Flight/E. Fortune	
198	Fieseler Fi.103 (V-1)	Imperial War Museum/Lambeth	
199	Fieseler Fi.103 (V-1)	Science Museum/S. Kensington	
200	Benson B.7	K. Fern Collection/Stoke	
204	McBroom Hang Glider	The Aeroplane Collection	
208	SE-5A (replica)	Prince's Mead Shopping Precinct/ Farnborough	

Note: Registrations/Serials carried are mostly false identities. MPA = Man Powered Aircraft.

G-BKGD Westland WG.30 of British International Helicopters.   *AJW*

9H-ABP Airbus A.320-211 of Air Malta.   *AJW*

Future Allocations Log (In-Sequence)

The grid provides the facility to record future in-sequence registrations as they are issued or seen. To trace a particular code, refer to the left hand column which contains the three letters following the G pre-fix. The final letter can be found by reading across the columns headed A to Z. For example, the box for G-BUFD is located five rows down (BUF) and then four across to the D column.

G-	A	B	C	D	E	F	G	H	I	J	K	L	M	N	O	P	R	S	T	U	V	W	X	Y	Z
BUB																									
BUC																									
BUD																									
BUE																									
BUF																									
BUG																									
BUH																									
BUI																									
BUJ																									
BUK																									
BUL																									
BUM																									
BUN																									
BUO																									
BUP						'																			
BUR																									
BUS																									
BUT																			.						
BUU																									
BUV																									
BUW																									
BUX																									
BUY																									
BUZ																									
BVA																									
BVB																									
BVC																									
BVD																									
BVE																	.								
BVF																									
BVG																									
BVH																									
BVI																									
BVJ																									
BVK	A	B	C	D	E	F	G	H	I	J	K	L	M	N	O	P	R	S	T	U	V	W	X	Y	Z

Future Allocations Log
(Out-of-Sequence)

This grid can be used to record out-of-sequence registrations as they are issued or seen. The first column is provided for the ranges prefixed with G-B, ie from G-BUxx to G-Bxx. The remaining columns cover the sequences from G-Cxxx to G-Zxxx and in this case it is necessary to insert the last three letters in the appropriate section.

G-B	G-C	G-E	G-G	G-J	G-L	G-N	G-O	G-P	G-S	G-U
										G-V
	G-D	G-F	G-H		G-M	G-O				
				G-K						
										G-W
								G-R		
									G-T	
										G-X
G-C	G-E	G-G	G-I	G-L	G-N					
										G-Y
										G-Z

Overseas Airliners Registration Log

This grid may be used to record airliner registrations not included in the main section

Reg	Type	Operator

Addenda

New or restored British registrations

Reg.	Type	Owner or Operator	Notes
G-AOSF	D.H.C. 1 Chipmunk 22	D. Mercer	
G-ARRW	Avro 748 Srs 1	Clewer Aviation Ltd	
G-AYAN	Slingsby T.31 Motor Cadet III	A. Nelson	
G-CCAT	AA-5A Cheetah	BLS Aviation Ltd (G-OAJH/G-KILT/ G-BJFA)/Elstree	
G-DAPH	Cessna 180K	M. R. L. Astor	
G-DLDL	Robinson R-22B	D. A. Lawson	
G-GIII	G.1159A Gulfstream 3	Aravco Ltd (G-BSAN)/Heathrow	
G-HAMI	Fuji FA.200-180	Hamilton Rentals (UK) Ltd (G-OISF/ G-BAPT)	
G-IEYE	Robin DR.400/180	Aeromarine Ltd	
G-LEEZ	Bell 206L-1 LongRanger	WAL Holdings Ltd (G-BPCT)	
G-LIPE	Robinson R-22B	Sloane Helicopters Ltd & Westleigh Construction Ltd (G-BTXJ)	
G-MONR	Airbus A.300-605R	Monarch Airlines Ltd/Luton	
G-MONS	Airbus A.300-605R	Monarch Airlines Ltd/Luton	
G-NSGI	Cessna 421C	Northern Scaffold Group PLC	
G-OKEY	Robinson R-22B	Key Properties Ltd	
G-OXRG	Colt Film Can SS balloon	Flying Pictures (Balloons) Ltd	
G-RAVI	Colt 300A balloon	R. S. Hunjan	
G-ROSY	Robinson F-22B	Aquaprint Ltd	
G-STEN	Stemme S.10	W. A. H. Kahn	
G-TJHI	Cessna 500 Citation	Tim Leacock Aircraft Sales Ltd (G-CCCL/G-BEIZ)	
G-TNTK	BAe 146-300QT	TNT Express (UK) Ltd (G-BSXL)	
G-XLXL	Robin DR.400/160	Reinsurance Flying Group (G-BAUD)	

Cancellations

G-BAIY, G-BAUD, G-BDSO, G-BEFP, G-BETF, G-BKAN, G-BKTT, G-GNHN, G-BNMM, G-BNXN, G-BOTC, G-BPCT, G-BRAZ, G-BRGU, G-BRXT, G-BSEO, G-BSLL, G-BSXL, G-BTEG, G-BTKR, G-BTUP, G-BTXJ, G-BTYU, G-CCCL, G-OAJH, G-OISF, G-DWMI, G-OMDS, G-ORGI, G-PERR, G-RASS, G-SATO, G-VSEL.

New overseas registrations

Notes	Reg.	Type	Owner or Operator
	D-AFKT	Fokker 50	Lufthansa CityLine
	D-AFKW	Fokker 50	Lufthansa CityLine
	EC-FGT	BAe 146-300	Meridiana
	EC-FHA	Boeing 767-3Y0ER	Spanair Canarias
	EC-FHU	BAe 146-300	Meridiana
	EC-FIA	Airbus A.320-211	Iberia
	EI-FEX	Cessna 208	Iona National Airways (FedEx)
	EI-TLA	Douglas DC-8-71	TransLift Airways
	EI-TLB	Douglas DC-8-71	TransLift Airways
	HL7486	Boeing 747-4B5	Korean Air
	HL7487	Boeing 747-4B5	Korean Air
	HS-TGL	Boeing 747-4D7	Thai Airways International
	I-FLYY	Douglas DC-9-51	Eurofly
	I-ELYZ	Douglas DC-9-51	Eurofly
	LX-LGM	EMB-120RT Brasilia	Luxair
	LZ-ABA	Airbus A.320-231	Balkan Bulgarian Airlines
	OE-LAT	Boeing 767-31AER	Lauda Air
	OO-LTE	Boeing 737-3M8	European Airlines
	OO-LTJ	Boeing 737-3M8	EuroBelgium Airways
	OO-LTM	Boeing 737-3M8	EuroBelgium Airways
	PH-XLA	EMB-120RT Brasilia	Air Exel Netherlands (G-BRAZ)
	SE-DNI	Boeing 737-59D	Linjeflyg Norrbotten
	SL-AAA	Airbus A.320-231	Adria Airways (YU-AOA)
	SL-AAB	Airbus A.310-231	Adria Airways (YU-AOD)
	SL-AAC	Airbus A.310-231	Adria Airways (YU-AOE)
	SL-ABA	McD Douglas MD-82	Adria Airways (YU-ANB)
	SL-ABB	McD Douglas MD-82	Adria Airways (YU-ANC)
	SL-ABC	McD Douglas MD-82	Adria Airways (YU-ANG)
	SL-ABD	McD Douglas MD-82	Adria Airways (YU-ANO)
	SL-ABE	McD Douglas MD-81	Adria Airways (YU-AJZ)
	SL-ABF	Douglas DC-9-32	Adria Airways (YU-AHJ)
	SL-ABG	Douglas DC-9-32RC	Adria Airways (YU-AHW)
	SL-ABH	Douglas DC-9-32	Adria Airways (YU-AJF)
	VH-OJQ	Boeing 747-438	Qantas Airways
	VH-OJR	Boeing 747-438	Qantas Airways
	ZK-NBU	Boeing 747-419	Air New Zealand

Country code SL has been issued to the independent State of Slovenia hence the above reregistrations.

Cancellations
D-ABKN, D-CCCC, F-BPJK, F-BPJL, F-BPJT, F-BVGS, OY-KHO, PH-MBZ, PH-MCK.